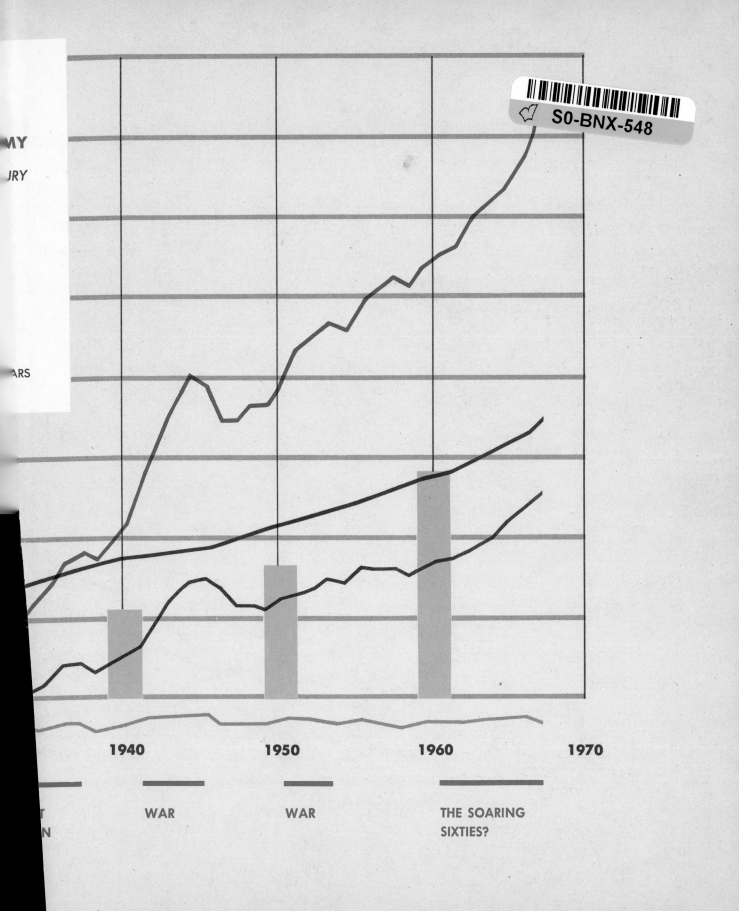

MY

URY

ARS

1940 1950 1960 1970

WAR WAR THE SOARING
SIXTIES?

ECONOMICS   An Introduction to Analysis and Policy

ECON

AN INTRODUCTION TO

SIXTH EDITION

OMICS

ANALYSIS AND POLICY

GEORGE LELAND BACH

*Frank E. Buck Professor
of Economics and Public Policy,
Stanford University*

PRENTICE-HALL, INC.

Englewood Cliffs, New Jersey

ECONOMICS

An Introduction to Analysis and Policy

SIXTH EDITION

George Leland Bach

Current printing (last digit):

10   9   8   7   6   5   4   3

PRENTICE-HALL INTERNATIONAL, INC., *London*

PRENTICE-HALL OF AUSTRALIA, PTY., LTD., *Sydney*

PRENTICE-HALL OF CANADA, LTD., *Toronto*

PRENTICE-HALL OF INDIA, PVT., LTD., *New Delhi*

PRENTICE-HALL OF JAPAN, INC., *Tokyo*

PREFACE

This is, frankly and enthusiastically, a book on political economy. It is a book on economic theory, but equally a book on how to use economic theory in thinking about complex problems for yourself. It is a book designed for either a full-year or a one-semester course, for instructors who wish to put either micro- or macro-economics first.

The focus throughout is on what the *student* does. The evidence is overwhelming that students retain little of what they learn in college economics courses unless they become interested enough to continue to use it as they read the newspaper and vote, after they leave the classroom. If we do not manage to kindle a real interest in economics, we have lost the battle at the outset. If we don't give students concepts and methods which they can use *for themselves* after graduation, little will last.

This edition not only looks new; it is new, with the following innovations.

- It builds on new developments in learning theory and research.

    Student motivation—big and little current problems to involve students.

    Clear focus on objectives—what the student should learn *and* keep.

    Learning retention—through repeated, explicit *use* of concepts and principles.

- It stresses economics as a modern empirical science.

- It has a new, different approach to macro theory, stressing interaction of aggregate supply and demand forces.

v

- It offers in-depth analyses of macro stabilization and growth policy—domestic and international.

    Student motivation and reinforced learning through the repeated *use* of theory.

- It expands the analysis of the Public Sector.

- It has modern, tested supplements to help students and teachers.

    Experience-tested "programmed" materials covering micro and macro theory (*Macroeconomics* and *Microeconomics*, two programmed supplementary texts prepared jointly with Professors Richard Attiyeh and Keith Lumsden).

    New color transparencies for large classes, stressing analytical development.

    Experience-tested supplementary readings and workbook (*Economic Analysis and Policy* and *Workbook*, prepared with Professors Myron Joseph and Norton Seeber).

Over successive editions, my indebtedness to colleagues and friends in the profession has snowballed to the point where it is impossible to list all those who deserve credit. For this sixth edition, however, I must thank especially my present and former colleagues, Professors Richard Attiyeh (University of California, La Jolla), Trenery Dolbear (The Brookings Institution), Myron Joseph (Carnegie-Mellon University), Keith Lumsden (Stanford University), Phillip Saunders (Carnegie-Mellon University), and Norton Seeber (Oakland University). Professor Michael Lovell of Carnegie-Mellon University continues to share authorship of the new mathematical appendixes. Professors Keith Evans of San Fernando Valley State College, Bert Hickman of Stanford University, Stewart Lee of Geneva College, and Carey Thompson of the University of Texas have been especially helpful on particular sections. The usual warning that only I am responsible for the final outcome needs to be added, however, for I have accepted only some of the suggestions advanced. Lastly, I want to add my appreciation to Ronald Nelson and Harry Rinehart of Prentice-Hall for their patient help in making the book more readable and attractive throughout; to Lynette Sweet for many hours of typing on the manuscript; and to Frank Jones for his valuable assistance on the index.

CONTENTS

PART ONE   THE FOUNDATIONS OF ECONOMIC ANALYSIS, 1

  ONE   ECONOMICS IN THE MODERN WORLD, 2

  TWO   PRIVATE ENTERPRISE, PROFITS,
AND THE PRICE SYSTEM: AN OVERVIEW, 12

  THREE   ECONOMICS AS AN EMPIRICAL SCIENCE, 24

PART TWO   NATIONAL INCOME, EMPLOYMENT, AND ECONOMIC GROWTH, 37

  A.   THEORY

  FOUR   NATIONAL INCOME, PRODUCTION, AND PRICES, 38

  FIVE   AGGREGATE SUPPLY AND AGGREGATE DEMAND, 55

  SIX   THE MODERN THEORY OF INCOME,
EMPLOYMENT, AND PRICES, 61

SEVEN   THE DETERMINANTS OF CONSUMPTION
AND PRIVATE INVESTMENT, 74

EIGHT   MONEY, AGGREGATE DEMAND,
AND THE PRICE LEVEL, 85

NINE   ECONOMIC FLUCTUATIONS AND FORECASTING, 99

B. POLICY

TEN   STABILIZATION POLICIES: GOALS AND COSTS, 118

ELEVEN   MONEY, FINANCIAL INSTITUTIONS,
AND THE FEDERAL RESERVE, 132

TWELVE   MONETARY POLICY, 155

THIRTEEN   FISCAL POLICY, 171

FOURTEEN   THE PRACTICAL PROBLEMS
OF STABILIZATION POLICY, 184

C. ECONOMIC GROWTH

FIFTEEN   THE THEORY OF ECONOMIC GROWTH, 197

SIXTEEN   ECONOMIC GROWTH IN THE UNITED STATES, 209

SEVENTEEN   GROWTH POLICY IN THE UNITED STATES, 221

EIGHTEEN   GROWTH IN THE UNDERDEVELOPED COUNTRIES, 231

Appendix to Part Two: CURRENT RESEARCH, 255

PART THREE   MARKETS, THE PRICE SYSTEM, AND THE ALLOCATION OF RESOURCES, 257

NINETEEN   BUSINESS ENTERPRISE IN THE
               MODERN ECONOMY, 259

TWENTY   THE CONSUMER AND MARKET DEMAND, 273

TWENTY-ONE   DEMAND, SUPPLY, AND MARKET PRICES, 286

TWENTY-TWO   THE BUSINESS FIRM AND ITS COSTS, 298

TWENTY-THREE   THE BUSINESS FIRM: COMPETITIVE OUTPUT
               AND PRICE IN THE SHORT RUN, 312

TWENTY-FOUR   LONG-RUN COMPETITIVE EQUILIBRIUM
AND ECONOMIC EFFICIENCY, 321

TWENTY-FIVE   MONOPOLY, 336

TWENTY-SIX   MONOPOLISTIC COMPETITION, 347

TWENTY-SEVEN   OLIGOPOLY, COLLUSION,
AND THE MIXED ECONOMY, 359

TWENTY-EIGHT   GOVERNMENT AND BUSINESS, 373

Appendix to Part Three: CURRENT RESEARCH, 390

PART FOUR   THE DISTRIBUTION OF INCOME, 391

TWENTY-NINE   HOW INCOME IS DISTRIBUTED:
THE PRICING OF PRODUCTIVE SERVICES, 392

THIRTY   WAGES AND SALARIES: APPLYING THE THEORY, 403

THIRTY-ONE   UNIONS, COLLECTIVE BARGAINING,
               AND PUBLIC POLICY, 415

THIRTY-TWO   THE PROBLEMS OF POVERTY AND INSECURITY, 431

THIRTY-THREE   PROPERTY INCOMES:
               RENT, INTEREST, AND CAPITAL, 446

THIRTY-FOUR   PROFITS, 456

               Appendix to Part Four: CURRENT RESEARCH, 462

PART FIVE   THE PUBLIC SECTOR, 463

THIRTY-FIVE   THE PUBLIC SECTOR:
               FUNCTIONS AND EXPENDITURES, 464

THIRTY-SIX   THE PUBLIC SECTOR: TAXES, 478

               Appendix to Part Five: CURRENT RESEARCH, 496

PART SIX   THE INTERNATIONAL ECONOMY, 497

THIRTY-SEVEN   INTERNATIONAL TRADE AND LENDING, 498

THIRTY-EIGHT   INTERNATIONAL ADJUSTMENTS
AND THE BALANCE OF PAYMENTS, 512

THIRTY-NINE   TARIFFS AND FREE TRADE, 519

FORTY   GOLD AND CURRENT
BALANCE-OF-PAYMENTS PROBLEMS, 528

Appendix to Part Six: CURRENT RESEARCH, 544

PART SEVEN   PERSPECTIVES ON ECONOMIC CHANGE, 545

FORTY-ONE   THE ECONOMICS OF CHANGE, 546

FORTY-TWO   COMPARATIVE ECONOMIC SYSTEMS: U.S.A.,
U.S.S.R., AND THE MIXED ECONOMIES, 559

Appendix to Part Seven: CURRENT RESEARCH, 581

MATHEMATICAL APPENDIXES, 582

INDEX, 589

SUGGESTED OUTLINES FOR ALTERNATIVE COURSE PLANS

COURSE A **EMPHASIZING MACRO-ECONOMICS**
(About 330 pages)

The Foundations of Economic Analysis

Chapter
1. Economics in the Modern World
2. Private Enterprise, Profits, and the Price System: An Overview
3. Economics as an Empirical Science

Supply, Demand, and the Allocation of Resources (Optional, for instructors who want a brief foundation in micro-economics).

20. The Consumer and Market Demand
21. Demand, Supply, and Market Prices
24. Long Run Competitive Equilibrium and Economic Efficiency
37. The Public Sector: Functions and Expenditures

National Income, Employment, and Economic Growth

A. Theory
4. National Income, Production, and Prices
5. Aggregate Supply and Aggregate Demand
6. The Modern Theory of Income, Employment, and Prices
7. The Determinants of Consumption and Private Investment
8. Money, Aggregate Demand, and the Price Level
9. Economic Fluctuations and Forecasting

B. Policy
10. Stabilization Policies: Goals and Costs
11. Money, Financial Institutions, and the Federal Reserve
12. Monetary Policy
13. Fiscal Policy
14. The Practical Problems of Stabilization Policy

C. Economic Growth
15. The Theory of Economic Growth
16. Economic Growth in the United States
17. Growth Policy in the United States
18. Growth in the Underdeveloped Countries

An Integrative Overview
42. Comparative Economic Systems: U.S.A., U.S.S.R., and the Mixed Economies

COURSE B EMPHASIZING MICRO-ECONOMICS
(About 275 pages)

The Foundations of Economic Analysis

Chapter
1. Economics in the Modern World
2. Private Enterprise, Profits, and the Price System: An Overview
3. Economics as an Empirical Science

Markets, the Price System, and the Allocation of Resources

19. Business Enterprise in the Modern Economy
20. The Consumer and Market Demand
21. Demand, Supply, and Market Prices
22. The Business Firm and Its Costs
23. The Business Firm: Competitive Output and Price in the Short Run
24. Long-Run Competitive Equilibrium and Economic Efficiency
25. Monopoly
26. Monopolistic Competition
27. Oligopoly, Collusion, and the Mixed Economy
28. Government and Business

The Distribution of Income

29. How Income is Distributed: The Pricing of Productive Services
30. Wages and Salaries: Applying the Theory
31. Unions, Collective Bargaining, and Public Policy
32. The Problems of Poverty and Insecurity
33. Property Incomes: Rent, Interest and Capital
34. Profits

The Public Sector

35. The Public Sector: Functions and Expenditures
36. The Public Sector: Taxes

Concluding Overview

41. The Economics of Change
42. Comparative Economic Systems: U.S.A., U.S.S.R., and the Mixed Economies

(Optional units for those who want to include additional material in the course)

National Income and Fiscal Policy (About 60 pages)

4. National Income, Production, and Prices
5. Aggregate Supply and Aggregate Demand
6. The Modern Theory of Income, Employment and Prices
13. Fiscal Policy
14. The Practical Problems of Stabilization Policy

The International Economy (About 50 pages)

37. International Trade and Lending
38. International Adjustments and the Balance of Payments
39. Tariffs and Free Trade
40. Gold and Current Balance-of-Payments Problems

COURSE C SUGGESTED DIVISION OF TEXT FOR YEAR-LONG (TWO-SEMESTER) COURSE

First Semester (About 290 pages)

Part One
The Foundations of Economic Analysis
Part Two
National Income, Employment, and Economic Growth
Part Five
The Public Sector

Second Semester (About 290 pages)

Part Three
Markets, the Price System, and the Allocation of Resources
Part Four
The Distribution of Income
Part Six
The International Economy
Part Seven
Perspectives on Economic Change

THE FOUNDATIONS
OF
ECONOMIC ANALYSIS

ONE

ECONOMICS
IN THE MODERN WORLD

International Living Standards.

Incomes in the United States.

Changing Job Patterns in the U.S.

Government and the Economy.

Big Business in the Economy.

Unemployment and Inflation.

Economic Growth—the Future.

A Sampler of Smaller Problems.

Economics in a Democracy.

Objectives of the Book.

Some Suggestions on How To Use the Book.

Economics is the study of how the goods and services we want get produced, and how they are distributed among us. This part we call economic analysis. Economics is also the study of how we can make the system of production and distribution work better. This part we call economic policy. Economic analysis is the necessary foundation for sound economic policy. This is a book about both economic analysis and policy. It is a book about the big economic problems of our time.

Without concrete examples, such a definition conveys little meaning. Consider the following examples, chosen to give you some impression of the range of problems with which economics deals. Then we shall turn in later chapters to how economists analyze such problems, large and small, through the use of theory and its application.

INTERNATIONAL
LIVING STANDARDS

Over the face of the earth, three billion human beings live in widely varying economic circumstances. Look at Table 1-1 for a summary picture.

The figures in the table are obtained by adding together the money value of all the goods and services produced in each country in 1966 (clothes, food, buildings, machinery, automobiles, defense products), and dividing each total by the number of people in that country. The figures shown are rough, but, with the possible exception of the so-called underdeveloped, or less developed, countries they are usable approximations. For the major

2

Western countries, we know they are reasonably accurate.

Compare the United States per capita output of $3,770 with the figures for Communist China, India, and Ethiopia, all under $100. The United States has been called an affluent society; no word other than poverty can descibe the living standards of the hundreds of millions in the underdeveloped nations. We are the "haves," they are the "have-nots." Although most of the industrialized Western world falls in the $1,000-and-up per capita output group, nearly two-thirds of the world's population—nearly two billion human beings—live in countries with per capita incomes of $150 per year or less.

TABLE 1-1			
WORLD PER CAPITA OUTPUT, 1966 *			
Country	Dollars	Country	Dollars
United States	$3,770	Italy	$1,200
Sweden	2,930	Japan	1,010
Canada	2,630	Brazil	300
West Germany	2,050	Peru	200
France	1,850	Thailand	120
Netherlands	1,730	India	78
United Kingdom	1,640	Communist China	76 **
U.S.S.R.	1,450	Ethiopia	55

* Author's estimates based on United Nations and O.E.E.C. data except for China and Russia: Converted to U.S. dollars in 1966 prices. For more complete data and an explanation of what is included and excluded, see Table 18-1.

** Extremely rough estimate.

The figures in Table 1-1 to some extent compare incomparables. The Indian or Chinese peasant, living in a rough hut in a tiny village, with no clothes except what he wears, with a monotonous diet of fish or rice, a man who lives out his years never going more than 25 miles from his birthplace, has so little in common with the American or West European that the figures may have little real meaning. The same is true for the African tribesman. But the figures do say unmistakably that we are extremely rich by comparison with the billions who live in the underdeveloped countries, and that they are bitterly poor.

Why is this so? And why has the United States, a relatively new nation, raced ahead of the other major industrial nations of the Western world, most of whom were there long before us? Casual observation suggests that all the high-income countries in Table 1-1 are predominantly "capitalist" or "free enterprise." Not until we reach the U.S.S.R., about halfway down the list, do we come to a "communist" country, while the very poor nations shown are either communist or have placed much less reliance on private enterprise institutions than we. Is this the answer? Or is there another reason?

Why nations, and individuals in those nations, receive the incomes they do is one of the big questions economists try to answer. It will be a major question for us throughout this book.

INCOMES IN THE UNITED STATES

The United States is the richest nation in the world. In 1967, for example, we produced some $785 billion worth of goods and services. Over $175 billion of this total went for national defense and other government services like highways and education. Another $110 billion consisted of "producers' goods"—factories, machinery, new buildings, and other equipment for producing more and better consumer goods in the future. The biggest chunk, two-thirds of the total, was made up of consumer goods and services—autos, beef steak, clothing, medical services, and the like.

Against this background, consider Fig. 1-1, which shows the incomes received by American families in 1966. The median family income was $7,400 for a statistically average family of about three and one-half individuals; half of all families received more than this and half less. At the top, nearly 10 per cent of all families received incomes over $15,000, and the five million families in this group received over $150 billion, more than 20 per cent of the national income. At the very top, 1.7 per cent received over $25,000. Another 20 per cent of all families received between $10,000 and $15,000, so that nearly 30 per cent of all families had incomes above $10,000. At the bottom, even with America's affluence, 8 per cent of all families received incomes under $2,000, and those families received only a little over 1 per cent of the total income.

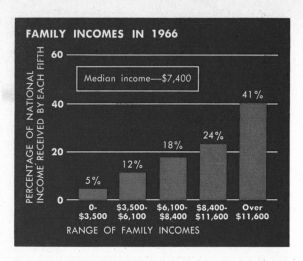

FIG. 1-1 The United States has a wide range of family incomes. Each bar shows one-fifth of all families. Three-fifths of all families received between $3,500 and $11,600 in 1966, but the fifth receiving more than $11,600 had 41 per cent of all the income. Half of all families got more than $7,400, and half less. (Source: U.S. Department of Commerce.)

Why? Why does our society exhibit these great differentials in family incomes? Why do the top 10 per cent receive nearly a quarter of all income, while the bottom 10 per cent receive only 2 per cent.

FIG. 1-2 The past century has seen a dramatic change in the way Americans earn their livings. Today 60 per cent of all jobs are in service industries, only 40 per cent in industries which produce physical goods. Note the drastic decline in agriculture. (Source: National Resources Committee and U.S. Department of Commerce.)

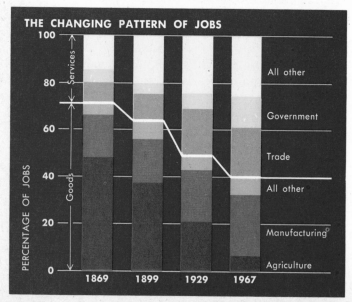

A related question: Why is poverty still a massive social problem in our prosperous economy? In 1966, about seven million families had money incomes of less than $3,000; their median income was only $1,800, and over one million of the families were raising four or more children on that income. About five million people living alone had incomes below $1,500. Together these two groups included nearly 30 million Americans, nearly one-sixth of the population. Many social observers have written that the world of poverty is a world of desolation, of hopelessness, of bitterness and resentment, of slums, of discrimination. It is a world of Negroes and Puerto Ricans living in the great slums; of old men and women living alone in rented rooms; of poor southern farmers living in ramshackle huts without plumbing; of fatherless families whose mothers struggle to support their children; of failures and rejects for a dozen other reasons.

Economists ask: Why these income differentials? Why are the poor, poor, and the rich, rich? They also ask: If we don't like it, what can we do about it? These are two themes that will recur over and over in the chapters to come—why are things the way they are (economic analysis), and what can we do to improve them (economic policy)?

CHANGING JOB PATTERNS IN THE U.S.

Figure 1-2 shows the jobs Americans work at today, and the great changes in our job patterns that have occurred over the past century. A hundred years ago, nearly 75 per cent of all jobs involved the production of goods (coal, steel, food, clothing, etc.), only one-quarter the production of services (doctors, lawyers, amusements, transportation, etc.). Today, the picture is reversed. Only 40 per cent of all jobs are devoted to producing physical goods, 60 per cent to producing services. And the trend toward more services continues.

Figure 1-3 shows even more vividly how job patterns have been changing since 1929. Why have they changed? What will job patterns look like in 1975? What determines the jobs at which

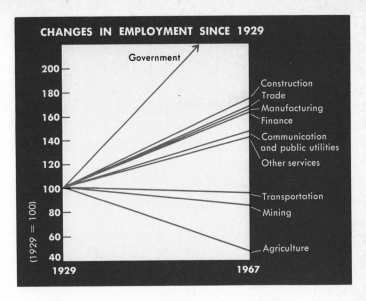

FIG. 1-3 The pattern of employment has continued to change rapidly over recent decades. American economic growth has been characterized by a high degree of mobility. (Source: U.S. Department of Labor.)

we work and make our livings? And, looking back to the preceding section, which will be the high-paid, and which the low-paid jobs? Economics is about these issues.

GOVERNMENT AND THE ECONOMY

Most people in the U.S.—about five-sixths of the total—work for themselves or for private employers. But looked at another way, one person out of six is on a government payroll (if we include the armed services)—over 14 million people.

In 1967, governments (federal, state, and local) bought about one-fifth of all the goods and services produced in the economy. Government spending included not only salaries of government jobholders, but primarily payments for missiles, highways, schools, and other things bought for the benefit of the citizens. In addition, governments made nearly $70 billion of "transfer payments"—payments like old-age pensions, unemployment benefits and interest on the national debt, for which the recipient renders no direct service. To get the money for these expenditures, governments took a huge chunk of our incomes and taxes—about $240 billion in 1967. Figure 1-4 shows the picture for that year.

In addition, governments make and enforce a maze of regulations over what we may and may not do in our economic activities. They regulate our banks and financial institutions. Federal law sets the minimum wage employers must pay, and prescribes that business must deal with workers and unions when they so choose. In their contracts with businesses, governments set elaborate standards of performance and specify that businesses cannot discriminate against employees on the basis of race, creed, or color. Government says businesses cannot agree to fix prices and cannot merge together to form bigger businesses if this would substantially reduce competition.

How big should government be? How much should it intervene in the economic processes of our basically private market economy? These are questions that will recur over and over through the chapters to come. They are questions that raise some of the most difficult issues of public policy, at federal, state, and local levels.

FIG. 1-4 Of $243 billion of federal, state, and local government spending in 1967, national defense and international aid took about a third, with social security and education the other biggest single items. (Sources: U.S. Budget and U.S. Department of Commerce.)

GOVERNMENT SPENDING, 1967

Total: $243 billion (slices in billions of dollars

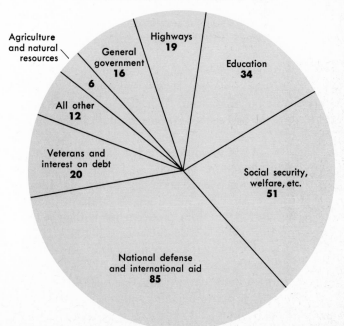

BIG BUSINESS IN THE ECONOMY

Ours has been called a business economy. Most of us earn our livings by working for businesses. We buy most of our products from businesses. Many of us own parts of businesses, directly or through ownership of stock.

In total, there are some ten million business firms in the United States. About nine million of these are relatively small businesses run by individual owners, three million of them in agriculture and most of the others as small-scale retail outlets, cleaning establishments, service stations, the professions, and the like. About one million are business "corporations." These business corporations, generally owned jointly by many people, do the bulk of the nation's business, employ over 60 per cent of its workers, and account for about two-thirds of all privately produced output. The biggest modern corporations are true Goliaths. In 1967, for example, the assets of the American Telephone & Telegraph Company (the world's largest business) exceeded $30 billion, and General Motors' sales of over $20 billion were larger than the entire national output of most of the world's economies.

Why has big business thrived so mightily in some parts of our economy (especially manufacturing), while little businesses continue to dominate other sectors like retailing, beauty shops, and personal services? Should the American consumer and the American worker welcome huge businesses or fear them? Which sorts of businesses give the best services to the consumer at the lowest cost?

In some industries a few large firms dominate the entire market. Figure 1-5 shows the dominant market position held by the four largest firms in six major industries. By contrast, in agriculture no one firm produces more than a tiny fraction of the total national output, and in most areas of retailing there are many firms seeking the consumer's business. In between these extremes are many industries which have a moderately large number of firms, but far from the huge number of small firms that characterize agriculture.

What are the results of market concentra-

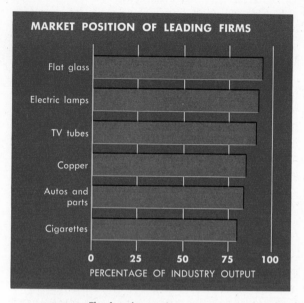

FIG. 1-5 The four largest firms dominate the market in many leading American industries. (Source: Federal Trade Commission. Data are for 1963.)

tions like those pictured in Fig. 1-5? Is such concentration a danger to the consumer? What kinds of firms and market arrangements are most efficient in producing the goods and services we as consumers want? Again, these are questions on which economic analysis focuses.

UNEMPLOYMENT AND INFLATION

Over the past two centuries, the American economy has been the greatest economic success story in the history of mankind. The evidence is vividly presented in Table 1-1. But American history also tells a story of intermittent booms and depressions.

Figures 1-6 and 1-7 picture two sides of this problem. In a private enterprise economy we have never completely eliminated unemployment, and intermittently the percentage of our labor force out of work has risen to 5, 10, and even, in the Great Depression of the 1930's, to nearly 25 per cent. Depression and massive unemployment bring immeasurable hardship and waste. Idle men and idle machines mean hunger and desolation, famine and want in the midst of potential plenty, the erosion of human dignity.

On the other hand, there have been intermittent "booms," with sharply rising prices—inflation. When prices rise, the amount of goods and services you can buy with a dollar falls correspondingly, though incomes rise so most people have more dollars to spend. Figure 1-7 shows the intermittent erosion over the past century in the purchasing power of a dollar as prices have, on the average, risen much more than they have fallen. A close look at the chart suggests that the big inflations (that is, the big drops in the purchasing power of a dollar) have come during and soon after major wars—in the early 1920's and again in the 1940's and 1950's; but remember that these have also been periods of booming prosperity, which has also often been associated with inflation. Clearly, inflation is a more complex issue than merely looking at how much less one dollar will buy when prices rise.

Why does our economy intermittently generate periods of unemployment and depression, and then periods of prosperity and inflation? Must a private enterprise economy accept such economic instability or have we now learned how to eliminate unemployment and inflation through the use of government monetary and tax-expenditure policies? Dare we risk increasing the national debt to increase government spending aimed to fight unemployment? These questions have loomed large in economics since the 1930's. They pose again interacting questions of economic analysis and economic policy.

ECONOMIC GROWTH—THE FUTURE

The American standard of living today is the world's highest. We have achieved this position of eminence in only two short centuries. Will our economy continue to grow at the rate of the past two centuries? Will other nations catch us and overtake us, or will we widen the gap? What will be the future of the economic race between the U.S. and the U.S.S.R., between capitalism and communism?

Table 1-2 provides some interesting data. The first column shows, for a number of leading nations, the annual percentage increase in output per capita over the past century. The second

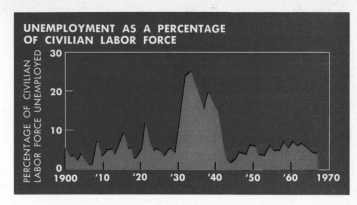

FIG. 1-6 Unemployment soars in depressions, and even in recessions. What is a reasonable minimum level of unemployment for us to shoot at? (Source: U.S. Department of Labor.)

FIG. 1-7 Inflation has repeatedly eroded the value of the dollar, with the biggest price increases coming during and after major wars. (Source: U.S. Department of Labor.)

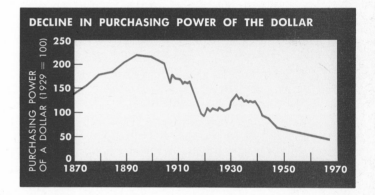

column shows the same data, but only for the period since 1950. Will the recent higher growth rates persist with their rapid improvement in living standards? What accounts for some of the fascinating differences among the nations shown

TABLE 1-2		
GROWTH IN PER CAPITA PRODUCTION *		
Country	1865–1965	1950–1965
Japan	3.0	8.8
Sweden	2.2	3.3
United States	2.1	2.8
Russia (U.S.S.R.)	2.0	5.0
France	1.6	3.9
Germany	1.6	5.9
United Kingdom	1.2	2.4
Italy	1.2	4.9

* First column based on data for approximately 100 years. For sources, see Chapter 15.

7

—for example, the remarkable surge of Japan during the past century and, especially, during the period since World War II?

Table 1-2 does not include the underdeveloped countries which hold over two-thirds of the world's people. India and Communist China alone contain about one out of every three human beings alive. Yet there is little evidence that the average standard of living of the Indian or Chinese peasant—that is, Indian or Chinese output per capita—is significantly higher now than it was a thousand years ago. The gap in living standards between the underdeveloped nations and the Western world is widening dramatically, not closing!

Is there an answer in the experience of the Western industrialized world for the poverty-stricken masses of the underdeveloped nations? What can those nations do to help themselves, or what can we do to help them to get started on the path towards self-sustaining economic growth? What are the key factors in rapid economic growth? Perhaps no questions in economics are more important than these, for it is only through growth in output per capita that the living standards of the people of the world can rise over the long run.

A SAMPLER OF SMALLER PROBLEMS

All the preceding examples have been big problems, at the national or international level. But economics is equally concerned with "little" problems, close to home in everyday life. You work summers as a resort waitress; why is your hourly wage what it is? You are studying to be an accountant; will electronic computers replace people in many middle-management jobs, and what will they do to accountants' salaries?

Most big cities require licenses to operate taxicabs. For example, in New York City there is a fixed supply of some 25,000 such licenses, which can be bought and sold by taxi operators. Is the public better served by such a system of limited licenses than by one of open entry for anyone who will obey city-specified rules on rates and service? Many cities regulate the rates parking lot operators can charge, to prohibit their "gouging" the public on special occasions such as big ball-game days; others have rent ceilings for apartments in low-income areas. What are the real effects of such regulations? Whom do they help and whom do they hurt? Your city has to raise more tax revenues to finance its spending on education and general services; what are the relative advantages and disadvantages of a city sales tax, a wage tax, and higher property taxes? Economic issues are everywhere in everyday life.

ECONOMICS IN A DEMOCRACY

These are the problems of economics. They, and many others like them—big and little, national and local, public and personal—are the problems of this book. Some are difficult and complex, some are simple. All are problems of the real world around us every day. To understand them, it is necessary both to understand some basic economic concepts and principles and to understand how to use those concepts and principles in analyzing different problems. In order to reach intelligent conclusions on government policy and private policy, economic analysis is the essential foundation. For without such analysis, debates may be lively, but they are likely to generate more heat than light—to be primarily an airing of hunches and emotions, rather than rational analysis of issues involved.

Throughout your life, economics will play a major role in determining what you do and how happy you are doing it. If there are depressions or inflations, you will not be able to escape them. Your income will depend largely on how effectively you participate in the economic process. Thus, from a purely selfish point of view, it will pay you to understand how your economic system works.

But the main reason citizens in a democracy need to understand the economic system is that they are voters as well as active participants in the economy. Not long ago governments didn't interfere much in economic life, but that time has passed. Today, almost everybody agrees that the government should provide national defense, highways, education, and a score of other services not forthcoming through the private enterprise economy; that it should regulate the supply of money; that it should protect consumers against the excesses of monopoly; that it should prohibit exploitation of child labor; that it should help avoid depressions and inflations. Fill out the list for yourself. Many people believe the government should do many more things—provide old-age and medical protection for the poor, support the prices of farm products, legislate minimum wages, even guarantee full employment.

This is a book on "political economy." It is concerned with using economic analysis to find answers to the problems above and to many more. The goal is to understand how our economy works *and* how we may hope to make it work better. The political economist doesn't sit on the sidelines. He is interested in what to do about the big and little problems we face, as well as in understanding how the economy works just for the sake of understanding it.

But if you expect to find the answers in this book to what you or the government should and should not do, you're in for a disappointment. *The job of a course in economic analysis is to give you the tools and the background for making up your own mind on the important economic issues of the day, and to teach you how to use the tools —not to tell you what to think.* Better understanding of how the system works will go a long way toward making you a more intelligent citizen. But you should recognize from the outset that even with a thorough understanding of economics, not everybody will come out with the same answers on the problems of public policy. This is because we have different ideas on where the nation ought to be headed. Some people, for example, think that avoiding inflation is the most important thing. Others believe that assuring everyone a reasonable minimum income should have first priority. Any respectable economist will advise the government to do different things, depending on which of these objectives is placed first. Such conflicts among the goals of different individuals and groups are an important part of the modern American democracy in action.

OBJECTIVES OF THE BOOK

If you're going to spend several months or a year studying a book, you deserve to know what the author thinks he is trying to accomplish. A good deal of the flavor of this book has been given in the preceding pages. It's a mixture of analysis and policy. But specifically, the book is aimed at these objectives:

1. *To provide an overview of the way our individualistic, largely private-enterprise economic system works.*

2. *To focus attention on the big problems faced by our economic system, and to arouse an interest in economic problems that will last after you leave college.* If your use of the concepts in this book ends with the final exam, the book will have failed. Its real goal is to help you read the newspaper, argue understandingly with your neighbor, and vote intelligently on economic issues over the years ahead.

3. *To provide a few fundamental analytical economic concepts and principles that will stick with you and help you in thinking about economic problems for yourself.* You need an economic toolkit.

4. *To help develop an orderly, systematic way of sizing up and thinking through economic problems—of applying the concepts and theories in your economic toolkit.* There's nothing unique about straight thinking in economics. But heated emotions, prejudices, and gossip are especially likely to get in the way of objectivity in discussing labor relations, the national debt, and other such subjects. In economics as elsewhere you have to know what the problem is before you can solve it. You need to marshal your analytical tools and use them carefully and systematically, instead of rushing blindly ahead on the first tack that comes to your mind. You need to check your conclusions against other evidence and against other conclusions on the same question. And, if you want to understand more in the future than you do now, you need to stop frequently and ask yourself: What have I learned by thinking through each problem?

The habit of orderly, careful thinking is something you can't learn in any one course alone. But a major purpose of this book is to repeat the process over and over in economics, in the hope that it will stick both here and in other fields. Chapter 3 has a good deal more to say on this important subject.

5. *To provide enough descriptive material on*

the present economic system to give you a foundation for understanding what the problems are. Without understanding a problem in its whole setting, there's little chance of solving it effectively. And knowing the facts is a first step. But the book makes no pretense of supplying an encyclopedic description of the modern economy. It takes the position that your main job is to learn how to think straight for yourself, not to cram your head full of facts. A mind cluttered with transient details seldom sees the major issues. And few things will be deader 20 years from now than many of today's facts. In any case, the evidence is clear that we don't remember most of the facts we memorize anyway. So learn the main outlines of the economic system and the facts you need to understand each problem that you study. But don't make a fetish of facts.

Throughout the book, whenever policy issues are posed, you will find a recurring theme: *Decide for yourself what you think should be done!* This is not because economists have no ideas on what should be done, or because economic analysis does not suggest strongly what ought to be done. We do have ideas, often strong ones, on public policy issues, and on many of these issues economic analysis points a clear path. *But the main goal of the book is to give you the tools you will need, and experience in using those tools to reach your own conclusions.*

SOME SUGGESTIONS ON HOW TO USE THE BOOK

The most important suggestions on how to use this book are contained in the preceding sections. But there are some tricks in using a book like this that may help you do a better job than just plowing through the assignment each day.

1. Know where you're going before you start reading. Before you start a chapter, go back and look at its place in the table of contents. Then *skim* through the chapter itself. Every chapter is organized so that the major headings mark off the main parts. These headings are designed to give a summary picture of what is covered, and to provide an outline of the chapter to help you keep the main points in focus. With this framework in mind, then study the chapter thoroughly.

2. As you read, keep asking yourself, "What is the main point of this paragraph and of this section?" Try to put the ideas in your own words. Some sections are largely descriptive. Some are full of tightly reasoned analysis, usually supplemented by an example of how the analysis might apply. It's important to remember that the analysis is the main point; don't let the example become the center of your attention except as an example. The old-fashioned devices of underscoring main points in the text and making notations in the margins can help in studying and reviewing throughout the book.

3. Much of economics is cumulative. So if you don't understand a paragraph or a section the first time you read it, don't kid yourself. Be sure you understand as you go along. Otherwise, as the course goes on, things are likely to get progressively foggier, not clearer.

4. When you've finished reading, review to see what you've really learned. A tough but very useful test is to shut the book, put aside any notes you have taken, and then write down in a few sentences the fundamental points of the chapter. If you can do this, you've read the right way— concentrating on the fundamentals and using the rest of the chapter as a setting for understanding them. If it takes you more than a page, you may have read the chapter well, but you had better recheck to be sure you have the central points clearly in mind.

For Analysis and Discussion

Throughout the text, these end-of-chapter questions are designed as a basis for class and out-of-class analysis and discussion. They are "think" questions. Drill and self-test questions, to test whether you understand the mechanics of the theory presented and its use, are available in M. Joseph and N. Seeber, *Workbook in Economics*, 4th edition (Englewood Cliffs, N. J.: Prentice-Hall, Inc., 1968), designed specifically for use with this text.

1. What factors seem to you most important in explaining why our standard of living is so high compared with India's? With England's? Can you explain the order of the countries in Table 1-1?
2. Why has employment in agriculture declined so steadily over the past century relative to that in other major sectors of the economy like manufacturing and services?
3. What do you think are the main reasons why many Americans are so poor, as indicated by Fig. 1-1, while a relatively few others receive such high incomes?
4. Is the government spending shown in Fig. 1-4 too large? How do you decide whether it is too large compared to the private sector of the economy?
5. If another major depression like that of the 1930's occurs, how seriously do you think it will affect you and your family? What if a rapid inflation occurs, in which prices double over the next few years? From your own point of view, which is the more serious problem for the economy to avoid? Why?
6. Suppose you are visiting abroad and are alarmed to find a large amount of anti-American sentiment, on the ground that America is extremely wealthy and could well afford to give more aid to less wealthy peoples, rather than selfishly clinging to most of the goods we produce. How would you go about explaining to the local residents why the present distribution of real income among the nations is a fair and proper one?

TWO

PRIVATE ENTERPRISE, PROFITS, AND THE PRICE SYSTEM: AN OVERVIEW

The Foundations of Economic Progress.

Limited Resources Mean We Must "Economize."

Choosing among Alternatives.

Cooperation and Competition
in a Private-Enterprise Economy.

How a Private-Enterprise System Solves
the Basic Economic Problems.

The Circular Flow of Spending and Production.

Individual Freedom and the Role of Government.

The Mixed Economy.

Capitalism Today.

How is it that we in America are, by and large, well-fed, well-clothed, and well-housed, while most of the world is dismally poor? What explains the incomes we receive—$125,000 for Willie Mays, $20,000 for a master plumber, $2,000 for a bracero fruit-picker? What has brought about rapid changes in job patterns over the years in the United States? Why has big business boomed in some sectors of the economy, while in others it has made little headway against small concerns?

There are no simple answers to these questions. Indeed, most of the book is aimed at answering them and others like them. As an introduction to the more detailed analysis that follows, this chapter sketches out briefly the foundations upon which our economic welfare rests and provides a simple overview of the way our modern American economy operates.

THE FOUNDATIONS OF ECONOMIC PROGRESS

Our ability to produce the goods and services we want depends on the resources at our disposal and our knowledge of how to use them. The United States is rich in natural resources; it is rich in produced resources, such as factories, houses, and machinery; and it is rich in human resources, the most important of all. The American worker on the production line is the best educated, the best fed, and the most productive in the world. American engineering and mass production know-how have produced Detroit's fabulous auto plants, Pittsburgh's steel mills, Oak Ridge's atomic energy installation. Vast research expenditures generate a steady stream of new products and new methods. And the American businessman manages somehow to keep the whole combination going in a way that excites the mixed envy, dismay, and sometimes disdain of his less aggressive counterparts in the rest of the world. These resources and this technology are the real foundations of the American standard of living—of our sweeping growth over the centuries.

In addition, we have developed a high degree of economic specialization and a complex exchange system. How many people do you depend on to get your everyday economic wants satisfied? You may say, not many. But think a minute. Who built the house you live in, and who provided all the materials to build it? How about the car that you drove to school, or the shoes if you came afoot? Where did your breakfast come from—the eggs, bread, butter, milk, and so on? How many people contributed to the production of your clothes, and of the textbooks you read? Suppose you take in a movie tonight, or watch TV. How many people have had a hand in making this possible?

To produce all the things we want takes many people, each specializing on what he can do best. Charlie Chaplin immortalized the forlorn worker on the assembly line, day after day screwing his single bolt onto the cars as they went by. But specialization goes far deeper than this. The engineer who designs the plant is a specialist. So is the lawyer who sees that the title to the land is clear. So is the banker who lends part of the money for the construction. So are the accountant who keeps the records and the secretary who does the typing. Only by dividing up tasks and developing highly specialized human skills and equipment can the economy obtain the benefits of "mass production."

But specialization and division of labor would be fruitless without a system for exchanging the goods and services produced by the specialists. The lawyer, the banker, the truck driver, the engineer—all would starve if the intricate system of exchange we take for granted didn't enable them to buy the food they need with the incomes they earn. Even the farmer who might eat his own carrots and potatoes would be in desperate straits if he were really cast on his own—without electricity, new clothing, gas and repairs for his car, mail delivery, and the thousand things he gets from other specialists. Every minute of our daily lives we depend on the specialization and exchange all of us take for granted. None of us would dare specialize if we couldn't count on being able to exchange our services and products for the wide range of things we want.

(1) *Productive resources*, (2) *technology*, (3) *specialization*, and (4) *exchange. These are the four foundation stones of the productive power of the American economy—and of every other highly developed modern economy, communist or capitalist.* These four basic factors make the difference between poverty and plenty. Many of the commonest economic fallacies are rooted in the neglect of these simple truths.

LIMITED RESOURCES MEAN WE MUST "ECONOMIZE"

Limited resources—which force us to choose among alternative uses of them—are the basic economic problem in every economy. There is not enough of everything so that everyone can have all he wants. If nature somehow provided bountifully all the things we want, there would be no need to work, no need to arrange for economic production, no need to choose among alternatives. We could have all we want of everything free, without working. But very few things are so plentiful. Human wants are vast, perhaps infinite. Resources to fulfill these wants are limited. They are "scarce."

For most of the world, economic scarcity is painfully evident. Even we in the United States are far from rich enough to escape the ever-present need to "economize"—that is, to choose between alternatives when we would like to have both. At the individual level, few of us have all the money we want. If you have a vacation trip to Florida this year, you can't afford a new suit. If you buy a new car, you can't afford a new hi-fi too. Time is a scarce resource too. It would be nice this afternoon to play golf, to go to the movies, to study, and to pick up some spare cash by working. But you can't do them all at the same time.

Scarcity, and the problem of choice it raises, is as ever-present at the group and national level as in our individual lives. If we use land for a shopping center, we can't use it for a school. If we use steel for autos, we can't use it for refrigerators. If we use engineers to design missiles and intercontinental rockets, they can't work on airplanes and factories.

For the nation, the heavy hand of war points up vividly this fundamental dilemma of scarcity. Modern war is fantastically expensive, in money and, more fundamentally, in man and materials. In 1967 we spent over $70 billion—over 10 per cent of our national income—directly on war and preparation for war. If the government had merely left this money in the hands of the taxpapers, on the average every American family would have had nearly $1,500 more to spend on clothes, housing, and the like. Behind the diversion of money to military spending is the diversion of productive resources—men, machines, and materials. In a fully employed economy, we must choose between guns and butter, between missiles and margarine. If we use a big chunk of our productive resources for national defense, our standard of living in civilian goods is going to be correspondingly lower. There is enough electronic equipment in one space missile to provide a telephone system for a small city.

The Need To Economize

Because resources are scarce relative to what we want to do with them, we must "economize" them. That is, we must choose among alternative ways of using our resources so as to satisfy the largest possible share of human wants with them. We need to economize time, money, and productive resources, anything that is scarce. So far in history, no economy has been rich enough to escape this problem of economizing—of choosing between alternative uses of resources that are too limited to satisfy all human wants. Probably no society ever will be. This is the central problem of economics—though it takes a strange twist in depressions, as we shall see presently.

It is easy to see that we must choose among the products we would like to have produced with our limited resources. But it may be less obvious that how fast the economy grows—that is, how fast we increase our total output—also depends on where we allocate our limited resources. To grow, an economy must use part of its productive resources to build up future productive capacity, rather than using them all to satisfy today's wants. If we use steel to make autos and refrigerators for today, we cannot use it to build factories that will increase production in future years. If our engineers build TV sets, they cannot spend their time on basic research to raise our future standard of living. Thus, one of the choices every economy must make is between present and future. To grow fast means foregoing consumption today. Shall we live less well today so we and our children can live better tomorrow?

Unemployment and Depression: An Exception?

Few deny the basic fact of economic scarcity in the world today. Yet in America the newspaper headlines sometimes tell of millions unemployed, of factories idle because the public doesn't buy enough cars, of massive waste of men and machines because there isn't enough demand to buy the goods and services that could be produced with everyone at work. How can this be reconciled with the proposition that limited resources and scarcity are the basic economic problem?

Widespread unemployment of men and factories reflects a breakdown in our economic machinery. Resources are still limited relative to the vast unsatisfied human wants they might help to fulfill. People still desire better houses, more food, more autos, more of almost everything—if only they had the incomes to buy them. The unemployed want jobs. Businessmen want to increase production and give them jobs—if only they could sell the products. A million men involuntarily unemployed for a year mean between $5 billion and $10 billion worth of potential output lost forever.

The problem of depression and unemployment, which generally reflects insufficient total demand to induce profit-seeking businesses to keep our resources fully employed, has been a central one for America. In depression, we mistakenly and involuntarily allocate part of our scarce productive resources into unemployment and waste.

CHOOSING AMONG ALTERNATIVES

When resources are limited relative to wants, we must choose among alternative ways of using the resources—among alternative products we might use the resources to produce. We face the need to economize.

Economists are fond of illustrating this problem with a simple example—an economy that must choose between guns and butter, between missiles and margarine. Guns and butter symbolize any two competing groups of commodities for which we might use our resources.

The Production-Possibilities Curve

Assume that our economy has a fixed stock of productive resources (land, labor, machines, and the like) and of technological knowledge about how to use these resources in producing the things we want. With these resources and this technological know-how, we can produce guns or butter—military or civilian goods—or some combination of the two. To simplify, assume that only these two commodities (or groups) can be produced.

Table 2-1 shows the range of possibilities open to us. If we use all our resources to produce butter, we can have 10 million pounds a year. Or if we use all our resources to produce guns, we can have 50,000 guns. In between various combinations are possible—for example, 8 million pounds of butter and 15,000 guns, or 6 million pounds of butter and 25,000 guns, and so on.

The point of this table is to show the many production possibilities open to us, even when we

assume a very simple economy producing only two products. Of course, guns and butter are merely arbitrary examples. We might have used highways (a public good) and refrigerators (a private good), or any other pair of products to illustrate the same point. The important thing to see is that there is a trade-off between the two commodities. With limited resources we can get more of one only by giving up some of the other. We face the problem of economizing.

It is convenient for many purposes to put the production-possibilities table in the form of a curve, or graph. This is done in Fig. 2-1.

Economists use graphs a great deal, so it is important to understand how to read them. In Fig. 2-1, we show millions of pounds of butter along the horizontal axis, and thousands of guns along the vertical axis. Each heavy dot plots one of the production possibility combinations from Table 2-1. For example, the top dot shows that we may produce no guns and ten million pounds of butter. The next dot shows we may produce eight million pounds of butter and 15,000 guns, and so on for the other dots. The figure is merely a graphical representation of the table.

It is generally convenient to join the dots

TABLE 2-1		
PRODUCTION POSSIBILITIES FOR GUNS AND BUTTER		
Alternatives	Butter (millions of pounds)	Guns (thousands)
1	10	0
2	8	15
3	6	25
4	4	40
5	2	45
6	0	50

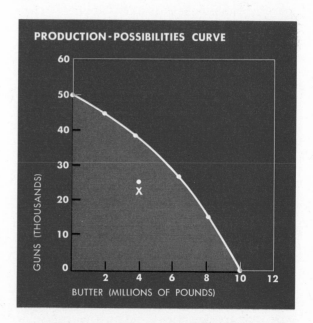

PRODUCTION-POSSIBILITIES CURVE

FIG. 2-1 The curve shows how much butter, how many guns, or what combination of guns and butter we can produce with our limited stock of resources.

together with a line, or curve, to show approximately what the situation would have been if we had plotted all the dozens of possible intermediate combinations, instead of merely the six shown in the table. As the table indicates, the more guns we make, the less butter we can have, and vice versa. The production-possibilities curve we have plotted shows the alternatives open to us, given our limited stock of resources.

Some Applications

The production-possibilities curve can help illuminate a variety of economic problems. Suppose that, possibly because of a depression, the economy only produces 25,000 guns and four million pounds of butter, as shown by the dot labeled "x" to the left of the production-possibilities curve. This dot shows that the economy is not fully utilizing its productive capacity, as in fact happens during depressions. To operate at point "x" is clearly to waste productive resources. We could have had an additional two million pounds of butter and the same number of guns, or an additional 15,000 guns and the same amount of butter, if we had employed all our resources.

Economists sometimes say that when an economy operates at point "x" it is operating inside the production-possibilities "frontier." That is, the production-possibilities curve shows the largest amounts of production that we can have with our limited resources. We are inside the frontier when for some reason we don't fully utilize our productive capacity.

Now suppose that the population increases so that we have more workers than before, or that scientists improve technology so that we can obtain more output from the same amount of resources. Thus, in year two there will be a new production-possibilities curve to the right of the year-one curve. This can be illustrated as in Fig. 2-2. The curve labeled "year one" is the same as in Fig. 2-1. The curve for "year two" is further out, to the right. It shows that the production possibilities are larger than before; the production frontier has moved out. This new curve for year two shows economic growth. The economy can now produce a larger total output—more missiles with the same amount of margarine, or vice versa, or a combination involving more of both.

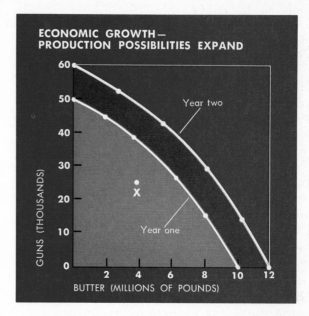

FIG. 2-2   If a nation's resources expand or its technology improves, its production-possibilities curve moves out, to the right. This expansion of productive capacity is the essence of economic growth.

An economy producing only two goods may seem extremely over-simplified. Yet many times throughout the chapters ahead, a production-possibilities curve will prove a useful simplification—to illustrate the possibilities of moving the production frontier out, the results of operating inside the production frontier, or the ever-present need to choose among alternative uses of resources in a fully employed economy. Unless we can move the production-possibilities curve out, we can have more of one product only at the cost of accepting less of another.

COOPERATION AND COMPETITION IN A PRIVATE-ENTERPRISE ECONOMY

Let us move on now to the complex real economy, to consider how we do decide among alternative uses of resources and how the economy's total production frontier may move out.

Man lives by cooperating with his fellow men. In all economics there is no more basic truth. And in the modern American economy this cooperation is indescribably broad and complex.

To satisfy our simplest wants, we rely upon the efforts of innumerable people in all parts of the world, and on the labors of generations past. Yet this vast cooperative system, as a system, has not been consciously designed by man. No human director tells the 80 million workers in the United States where to work, what to do, or how to do it. Somehow the system seems to organize itself, with a minimum of central planning or directing.

Man can organize, and indeed he has organized much. Tens of thousands of workers are employed in some large industrial plants. Often many of these huge plants are joined together in a single organization. The American Telephone and Telegraph Company, for example, spreads over the entire United States, with over half a million employees and assets of over $30 billion. But in spite of the immense power of such huge aggregations, each business concern plays a tiny part in the total picture of organizing economic resources to satisfy human wants. And in spite of the great expansion of government controls, the private-enterprise economy still does the bulk of the job in its long-established unplanned way—in contrast to the central plans that control our biggest rival, the Soviet economy.

The Incredible American Economy

It's easy to find things the matter with a basically private-enterprise, "unplanned" economy, like ours. But thoughtful observers have long been impressed by its remarkable efficiency in producing the infinite variety of goods and services consumers want.

Consider New York City, teeming with eight million people crowded into a few square miles. As Bastiat, a famous economist, remarked about the Paris of a hundred years ago, here are millions of human beings who would all starve in a short time without a constant flow of provisions into the metropolis. Hardly one could support himself for more than a few days without help from the far corners of the nation. "Imagination is baffled," Bastiat wrote, "when it tries to appreciate the vast multiplicity of commodities which must enter tomorrow in order to preserve the inhabitants from falling prey to the convulsions of famine, rebellion, and pillage. Yet all sleep, and their slumbers are not disturbed for a single minute by the prospect of such a frightful catastrophe."

Every day, New York City gets hundreds of tons of meat, huge amounts of fresh vegetables, coal, oil, furniture. Every year, it gets millions of shirts, automobiles, rugs, hairnets, movie films, and more other goods and services than you can think of. Yet no individual, business, or government agency plans it that way. The same is true, on a smaller scale, of every city and village throughout the country.

Who sees to it that all these millions of products are where they're needed when they're needed? What organizes this indescribably complex economy?

Suppose for a moment that you have just been made complete economic dictator, and that for some unfortunate reason you have no idea how much of everything is now being produced. You have to tell every one of 80 million workers just what to do, decide just how much of each commodity and service shall be produced, and determine who shall get how much of what is made—all this so that the amount of everything produced will be equal to the amount wanted, and so that no productive resources will be wasted through involuntary unemployment!

How, for example, would you decide whether Joe Smith ought to spend his time grinding fine edges on a machine tool later to be used in manufacturing tractors later to be used in producing corn later to be fed to hogs later to be eaten as pork; or whether he ought to spend his time making TV cabinets, or running a locomotive, or operating a corner grocery store? What would you do about the minor problem of how many sheep to raise, when each sheep yields both wool and mutton, the demands for which are almost completely independent? Wool is used for clothing, blankets, rugs; mutton is used for dinner. How are you going to make them come out even, even if you have somehow decided on the total number of sheep to be raised? How would you decide who is to have the tractors and corn and cabinets and mutton and wool once they are produced? Or, to take an apparently simple problem, how would you decide how many raincoats to make next year? This is the merest suggestion of the problems faced—and it matters not whether the economic system is capitalist, communist, fascist, or what not. Somehow these decisions have to be made. We must discover what our production possibilities are, must make full use of them, and must do so in a way that will go as far as possible toward satisfying the mixture of wants of some 200 million people.

The Organizers: Self-Interest and Competition

In a basically private-enterprise economy like ours, we rely chiefly on private initiative, in search of wages and profits, to get the job done. If we as a group want something badly enough, we are willing to pay for it. If we want shoes, there will be a profit to be made in producing shoes. Businessmen, recognizing this potential profit, begin producing more shoes. People go to work where businesses will pay the best wages, in general where consumer demands are strongest. As output increases, a point is reached when just as many shoes are being produced as consumers are willing to pay for at a price that is just high enough to cover the full production costs. If businessmen compete actively, prices will be held down to a level that just covers the costs of production.

The same general pattern of production in search of profits goes on for thousands of other products simultaneously. Consumer spending guides profit-seekers to where the potential profits are largest. Where profit prospects look brightest, they offer jobs and bid raw materials and capital in to increase production. Millions of workers work where they will, generally where wages are best but taking into account working conditions and the like. Consumer demands through the market process determine where on the production-possibilities curve we operate.

This is the mechanism by which the "private-enterprise, free-price system" does this indescribably complex job. It decides what's to be produced, how to get it produced, and how to distribute it to 200 million consumers. As Adam Smith pointed out in his famous *Wealth of Nations* back in 1776, the desire for personal profit within the framework of a *competitive* economic system works almost like an "invisible hand" to guide the system toward the greatest possible welfare of all.

Perhaps Adam Smith was overenthusiastic in relying so heavily on individual self-interest and competition as a beneficent invisible hand. But the first big lesson to learn about a private-enterprise economy is that it gets its vast job done for the most part automatically and impersonally, through the profit and price system. Nobody decides any more than his own affairs. Yet everyone deciding in his own self-interest seems to do the trick. In a private-enterprise economy, absence of planning and control does not mean chaos. Rather, it means order in an economy so complex that no mind could comprehend it and bring order without the price system or something like it to do the job.

But this is a lesson that must not be overlearned. We can understand and admire the way the private-enterprise, free-price system ticks on year after year, impersonally solving its millions of intertwined problems, and still not shut our eyes to its failings. And failings there are—drastic ones, some people think. The public has looked increasingly to government intervention to assure competition among businessmen; to set minimum standards for wages and working conditions; to regulate industries (like broadcasting and telephone service) where the public interest is paramount and free competition is not feasible; and to provide a wide range of services (like education, highways, national defense, and police protection) that can't reasonably be obtained on a private-profit basis for the bulk of the public. In fact, government is now so involved in the economy that many people call ours a "mixed" rather than a "private-enterprise" economy. For the moment, however, leave the government out, while we get a slightly more complete overview of how a private-enterprise economy solves the basic economic problems. It all comes back to the central economic problem—how to use our limited resources to satisfy the public's vast human wants as fully as possible.

HOW A PRIVATE-ENTERPRISE SYSTEM SOLVES THE BASIC ECONOMIC PROBLEMS

Consider now how a private-enterprise system allocates resources to solve four basic economic problems.

How the Market System Decides
What To Produce

Under a private-enterprise, free-price system, consumers control what is produced. Consumers register their preferences through the amount of money they spend on various goods and services. The more you want something, the more money you will spend on it and the higher price you will be willing to pay for it. This is how the price system decides which are the most important goods and services to produce.

But one point is vital. In order to count, consumers' demands have to be backed up with dollars. No matter how badly you want a Buick and a fine house, your desires become effective in the market only to the extent they are backed up by the ability to pay. The price mechanism is hard-boiled, impersonal. It produces Cadillacs for millionaires when poor youngsters have no toys. Prices reflect not how much consumers "need" goods and services, but how much they are willing and able to pay for them.

How the Market System
Gets the Goods Produced

Businessmen are out to make profits, and they find profits where selling prices are higher than costs. Thus, businessmen move to those industries where consumers bid prices up, and where their own ingenuity and other factors such as plentiful labor and materials can bring costs down. Workers and owners of other productive resources generally move toward higher-pay, away from lower-pay jobs, though their decisions are also influenced by their preferences on location, working conditions, and the like. This combination of consumers' demands, workers' job preferences, and businessmen's desire for profits gets the goods produced that consumers want most, at the lowest possible cost.

Thus, the businessman is essentially a link between consumers and productive resources. His social function is to organize productive activity in the most efficient (lowest-cost) way possible, and to channel productive resources toward industries where consumer demand is strongest. Profits are the mainspring of the system—the carrot in front of the profit-seeker. In seeking profits, the businessman performs a vital social function.

How the Market System
Distributes Products

Who gets the goods that are produced? The price system allocates them to those who have the desire and the income to buy them. There are two steps in this process.

The first is the distribution of money incomes. We earn our incomes primarily by working for businessmen, helping to produce the goods and services consumers want. The prices we get for our services depend on how much we are worth to the businesses we work for. Competition forces the businessman to pay each of us about what we contribute to the sale value of what he is producing. The incomes we receive in this way largely determine what we can afford to buy.

The second step is the distribution of goods and services among those with money income to pay for them. The price of each commodity is bid up until the buyers least able and willing to pay for it are eliminated. This does not necessarily mean that low-income buyers are eliminated completely. Often it means that they can afford only a few units at the price established, while higher-income groups can afford more. Poor people buy steaks, but not many. In other cases, such as mink coats and country estates, the poor are eliminated from the market.

How the Market System Decides
Between Present and Future: Economic Growth

As was indicated above, we can use our productive resources either for current consumption or for capital accumulation (that is, machinery, buildings, and so on) to help increase future production. That is, by building new factories and other productive facilities, we can shift the economy's production possibilities curve out. Here again, the private-enterprise system depends largely on the free decisions of consumers and profit-seekers to allocate resources between present and future.

Looking at the growth process in money terms, we must save some of our incomes and invest in building new factories and the like, rather than spending everything on consumption. In our individualistic economy, each person and each businessman decides how much of his income he wants to save. If these savings are a large proportion of our total income, investment can be large relative to current consumption and the economy will grow rapidly. If we save only a small portion of our total income and investment is correspondingly small, the growth in productive capacity will be slow.

But here the private-enterprise system may have trouble. Sometimes when people save, businessmen don't see enough potential gain in making new investments in capital goods to match, or use up, the savings. Then the savings "lie idle" instead of being spent. This means unemployment and depression. The economy wastefully operates inside the production-possibilities frontier. Other times, businessmen grow unduly enthusiastic over future prospects and invest far beyond the rates at which people plan to save. This speeds up capital accumulation and economic growth. But it also may bring overinvestment and inflation. Excess productive capacity develops; factories can't sell their output; investment is cut back; workers are laid off. Thus, miscalculations and overbuilding can mean uneven growth, with inflationary booms and ensuing depressions.

Solving All the Problems Simultaneously

These four major decisions are not made separately. Rather, they are all interdependent. The economic system is a huge, interconnected set of markets, each with many buyers and sellers. All four big decisions are simultaneously the out-come of millions of free, individual choices by people largely concerned with their own private welfare. Since most buyers buy in many different markets, what they buy of one good affects what they will buy of another. Most sellers must compete with many other sellers for the labor they hire, the raw materials they use, the dollars they borrow to build their plants. The process of production both provides goods to meet consumer demands and generates incomes for workers who are in turn consumers. And each consumer constantly chooses between saving or buying something now with his income.

The private-enterprise, free-price system, then, makes all four of its major decisions simultaneously, each composed of millions of concurrent self-interest subdecisions by consumers, workers, businessmen, bankers, and other participants in the economic process. How all these complex decisions are simultaneously and continuously made and how they interact in our economic system is the core of the study of economics.[1] (Remember that we're temporarily omitting a big group of desired goods and services—those produced by governments—where demand is reflected through different channels.)

THE CIRCULAR FLOW OF SPENDING AND PRODUCTION

It is important to see that income in a private-enterprise economy flows around a circle. Businesses pay wages, interest, and other income to the public. The public, as consumers, spends this income back to businesses in payment for finished goods and services. This demand, in turn, leads businessmen to hire workers to produce more goods and services for consumers.

Figure 2-3 shows this circular flow of income. The inner line shows consumers spending to businesses (top half) and businesses spending back to the public through paying wages and interest (bottom half). The outer line shows the

FIG. 2-3 The circular flow of economic activity.

THE CIRCULAR FLOW OF ECONOMIC ACTIVITY

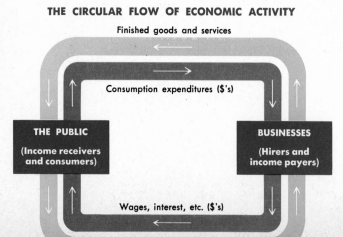

Finished goods and services

Consumption expenditures ($'s)

THE PUBLIC
(Income receivers and consumers)

BUSINESSES
(Hirers and income payers)

Wages, interest, etc. ($'s)

[1] In mathematical terms, it may be helpful to think of all these interdependent markets and decisions as a large system of simultaneous equations. In fact, one of the first clear perceptions of the entire process was by Leon Walras, one of the first mathematical economists, who saw it just that way about a century ago.

corresponding reverse flow of productive services and final products. On the bottom half, labor and other productive services are being hired by business from the public. On the top half, finished goods are moving from businesses to consumers.

Which comes first, business spending or consumer spending? This is a chicken-and-egg question. The main point is that neither can go on for long without the other. Consumers without jobs and incomes make for very poor business. And a business with products that no one buys is a good bet for bankruptcy. Economic activity in a private-enterprise system is a continuous flow of productive services and finished products, facilitated by a matching counterflow of money spending, and guided by the price system into thousands of different product channels within the main streams shown in the diagram.

You can readily see that this picture is oversimplified. The government has been left out. And there's no place for savings and production of capital goods that aren't sold to consumers. But the simple picture points up the central role of the circular-flow process. Unless there is a continuous flow of money-spending by businesses to the public and by the public to businesses, we're in trouble. If something dams up the flow of spending, depression and unemployment result, and the economy wastefully operates inside its production frontier.

INDIVIDUAL FREEDOM
AND THE ROLE OF GOVERNMENT

The French and American revolutions that gave us political democracy provided the ideological framework for economic individualism. Political democracy and modern private-enterprise economics arose in the same historical setting, part of the same broad sweep of history.

Individual freedom and self-interest were at the core of this revolution of the eighteenth and nineteenth centuries. In politics, every man should be free to vote as he pleased—to look out for his own interests at the ballot box. In economic life, every man should be free to seek his own self-interest—to work where he wished, and to spend his money on whatever he wanted most. Self-interest and individual initiative were the

driving forces for the common good. The ballot box in politics and the market in economics were the ultimate, impartial arbiters of differences of opinion.

This philosophy assigned to government only a small role. The less that government interfered with individual freedom, the better. This was the "laissez-faire" philosophy of the nineteenth century. To be sure, individualism never went so far as to exclude government intervention altogether. True freedom necessarily involves some restrictions on freedom. A society that gave you freedom to murder your neighbor whenever you felt like it would be anarchy.

So it was in the economic sphere. Clearly the government needed to establish and enforce a few "rules of the game" for the free-enterprise system. One basic rule was the guarantee that no one should be deprived of life, liberty, or property without due process of law. Another was the long-standing rule against fraud and against default on contracts. But the rules should be simple, and government should have no business in economic life outside these rules.

As time passed, the public's outlook changed. More and more questions were raised about the ability of an automatic, uncontrolled price system to make vital economic decisions acceptably. Mass production and the modern corporation swept away the possibility of an economy of tiny, highly competitive firms. Powerful unions replaced the individual worker in bargaining with big business. Throughout the economy, concentration of economic power and reliance on group activity spread steadily.

Moreover, with a wealthier, more complex society, people wanted more things that couldn't be readily provided through private profit-incentive in the market place—schools, highways, national defense, parks, and the like. Besides setting the rules of the private-enterprise game, governments were called on to do more and more things directly. Today federal, state, and local governments buy one-fifth of all the goods and services produced in the economy.

At the same time, common concern grew for the individual who couldn't take care of himself. Willingness to abide by the impersonal income allocations of the market steadily diminished. Desire to "do something" about booms and depressions became widespread. A subtle shift in the meaning attached to the words "individual freedom" marked the changing tenor of the times. The rules of the game have grown into an intricate mass of law and administrative controls. The government has become a major participant in the economic game, as well as the umpire.

THE MIXED ECONOMY

Today, ours is a mixed economy—still basically private-enterprise but with large areas of government control and direct participation. It's up to you to decide whether you like what's been going on—whether you want to move back toward the traditional private-enterprise system, or on toward a more administered, planned economy, or in some other direction.

This is no ivory-tower, academic issue, dreamed up for college classrooms. It is a basic issue of public economic policy today. Should we try to shore up the free-price system and its individualistic implications? Or should we accept the new power groupings and set up government procedures to work with them toward a more administered economy? Clearly the government must step in to provide national defense and highways, but how about slum-clearance and public housing? Nearly everyone agrees the government should provide free schooling for all children, but how about assuring minimum health standards and old-age security? Everyone agrees that we need to level off booms and depressions. Can the government take on this job and still perform in a manner consistent with the basic philosophy of private-enterprise nonintervention? Individual freedom is no longer a simple concept.

At the end of this book, we shall step back and compare our private-enterprise system with the communist approach, which is a powerful economic, social, and political force in the world of today. Some people feel that the American economy is already far down the primrose path to socialism. But compared with most of the rest of the world, private enterprise is still rampant in America. As a college student and as a citizen, you need to do a lot of careful, unemotional thinking about where the American economy really is, and which way you want it to go.

CAPITALISM TODAY

"Capitalism" is a term often used but seldom defined. Words so used often generate more heat than light, and "capitalism" has over the years become a fighting word for many who advocate and oppose it. Recourse to the dictionaries and to the learned treatises of economists and historians unfortunately does not resolve the dilemma of just what we should mean when we say capitalism, for these authorities are far from agreement.

So, instead of talking about capitalism, this book uses such less colorful but more descriptive terms as the "private-enterprise, free-price system" and "market system" in referring to the big private sector of the modern American economy. But, though we shall generally eschew the emotionally colored term, a brief note on "capitalism" may be useful. Many writers agree that a "capitalist" economy is marked by at least three major characteristics:

1. Private ownership of property prevails.
2. Property has been accumulated by individuals and businesses, and this accumulated "capital" provides incomes to its owners.
3. Individuals and businesses are free to seek their own economic gain; the profit motive plays a central role in economic life.
4. Some writers add to this list a highly developed banking and credit system.

This list gives the basic flavor of such a system. But once we look at the points in detail, the trouble begins. How free must individuals be to own and use property if a system is to be termed "capitalism"? Is an income tax that takes away part of your income each year, depending on how much you earn, consistent with capitalism? Does a federal law that limits the monopoly power you can attain violate the essential freedoms of capitalism? Is government operation of the postal system enough to make the system "noncapitalist"? Many people may accept substantially the above definition of capitalism, yet disagree widely among themselves about how "capitalist" the American economy actually is.

We shall be concerned with all these questions and others like them. But there is little to be gained by debating just which measures are and which are not consistent with "capitalism" when there is so little agreement on what the term means. Instead, we will concentrate on trying to decide whether proposed policy measures are good or bad on their merits, taking into full account the different social goals held by different groups in America today. In talking about a "basically private-enterprise, free-price system" throughout most of the book, we will be talking about the system many writers call "modern capitalism." If you like the term, use it. But don't let your emotional attachment or antagonism toward it get in the way of thinking objectively about the issues.

REVIEW

Concepts To Remember

This chapter has introduced some important concepts that will be reused many times throughout the book. Better recheck the following especially to be sure you have them firmly in mind:

productive resources
technology
specialization
exchange
economizing
production-possibilities curve

production-possibilities frontier
private-enterprise, free-price economy
economic growth
circular flow
laissez-faire
"capitalism"

For Analysis and Discussion

1. "Man lives by cooperating with his fellow men. In all economics there is no more fundamental truth than this." "The core of the competitive, free-market system is the driving urge of most men to get ahead in the world, to rise above their fellow men."

Are these two statements about the American economic system consistent or contradictory? If they are consistent, how do you reconcile their apparent contradiction?

2. The price system allocates resources where consumers spend their dollars. Thus the rich man has far more influence than the poor man. Is this compatible with the democratic presumption that every man is equal?

3. The federal government and most state governments levy heavy taxes on liquor. This increases the price of liquor and tends to discourage drinking. Should Congress influence how you spend your money this way? How about your state legislature?

4. Look back at Figs. 1-2 and 1-3. Can you explain better now why the big changes in employment shown there have occurred?

5. Does the present level of government spending tend to raise or lower our standard of living? Use a production-possibilities curve in explaining your answer.

6. Suppose American college students were to develop a craze for pork chop sandwiches, instead of hamburgers. Trace through as carefully as you can the impact of this craze on the allocation of the economy's productive resources. Would such a shift be good or bad?

7. Leading movie stars receive annual salaries up in the hundreds of thousands of dollars. Some baseball players receive $50,000 to $100,000 for the eight-month season. Yet an intelligent, skilled, hard-working nurse or farmer will ordinarily earn not more than $6,000 or so per year.

   a. Are such differences predictable results of the free-market system, or do they reflect breakdowns in the functioning of the system?

   b. Do you approve of such inequalities in the distribution of income? Why or why not?

THREE

ECONOMICS AS AN EMPIRICAL SCIENCE

The Tax Cut of 1964—An Example.

Economics as an Empirical Science.

Economic Analysis and Public Policy.

The Problem of Economic Goals: A Digression.

Appendix: Some Common Fallacies.

Straight thinking is hard work. Few of us have acquired the careful, orderly mental habits and disciplines demanded by straight thinking.

For many people, straight thinking in economics is especially difficult. Not that economics is inherently more difficult or more complex than many other fields. It isn't. But economics is so mixed up with our everyday lives that, without realizing it, we've accumulated a mass of opinions, ideas, hearsay, and half-truths that subtly dominate our minds when economic questions arise.

When we want to build a bridge, it never occurs to us to start without calling in expert engineers to design it. If we want expert advice on physics, we ask the physicists. Few people consider themselves experts on bridgebuilding just because they drive across a bridge every day going to work, or on physics just because they live in the physical world. Yet many people, especially if they've "met a payroll," somehow feel that they're experts on economics simply because they successfully earn a living in the economic world.

It's not surprising that most people have views on the big economic issues outlined in Chapter 1. They're in the newspapers every day, in every election campaign. And the tendency for every man to be his own economist is strengthened by the fact that economics is close to the pocketbook. It is especially hard to be objective about things that affect us intimately. But merely living in the economic world or meeting a payroll doesn't make us experts on how the economy operates, any more than having teeth makes us experts on dental health and how to fill cavities. Economics is concerned with the way the whole economy operates, not with how to run a better grocery or bank. And these are quite different things.

The purpose of this chapter is to provide a broad-brush picture of the way economics can help you to do your own intelligent thinking about economic issues. It's about the way economists analyze these problems, and about the way you can learn to analyze them for yourself.

THE TAX CUT OF 1964—AN EXAMPLE

Let's begin with an example—a highly simplified analysis (since this is merely an introductory overview) of the way economics helped us to understand a major economic issue and to predict the consequences of an important tax change. After this introduction, we will look more systematically at modern economics as an empirical science, and at the problem of doing your own straight thinking in economics.

In the early 1960's, the economy was performing reasonably well. Most people had jobs with good pay, profits were substantial. Yet there was substantial unemployment—the economy was operating well inside its production possibilities frontier. Over 5 per cent of the labor force was unemployed. If this figure could have been reduced to 3 or 4 per cent, the nation could have had perhaps $30 to $40 billion worth of additional goods and services. We had the productive capacity in men and machines, but it was wasted because total demand for goods and services was not large enough to make it profitable for businessmen to hire workers and produce this extra output.

To remedy this situation, Presidents Kennedy and Johnson, following the advice of many economists, recommended a major cut in income taxes on individuals and businesses, without a corresponding reduction in federal spending. They reasoned that if consumers had more money left to spend after paying their tax bills (that is, if their "disposable incomes" were larger because of lower tax bills), total spending on goods and services would increase and businesses would hire more workers and increase output to meet this demand.

They proposed a tax cut of about $10 billion. They argued that, in fact, aggregate spending and

hence incomes received by workers and others in the society would actually rise by more than $10 billion—possibly by $20 or $25 billion as a result of this tax cut. This would occur because the new consumer expenditures would be received by others who would in turn spend more, hire more workers and buy more goods. This spending would in turn increase the incomes of others, who would in their turn have more to spend. This respending effect, called the "multiplier" effect by economists, would thus help substantially to raise incomes and reduce unemployment.

Consider the essential steps in the reasoning. In essence, these economists had a "model," or "theory," of how the economy functions, and of how the effects of the tax cut would work their way through this economy. Their first assumption was that if consumers received an increase in disposable incomes (because their tax bills were reduced), *other things equal* they would spend a large portion (probably over 90 per cent) of this increased disposable income on consumer goods and services, rather than use it to pay off debts or just hold on to it. Second, the economists had a model of typical business firms which indicated that in response to increased consumer spending these firms would hire more workers and furnish more goods, in the process paying out more incomes to those whom they hired and to suppliers from whom they bought raw materials. Third, in the economists' model, the government would borrow funds to maintain government spending unchanged after the tax cut, and this borrowing would not produce an offsetting reduction in private spending by drawing away spendable funds from private consumers or businesses. If the borrowing should correspondingly reduce private spending, obviously the desired increase in total spending on goods and services would not result. Fourth, to provide the specific estimate that total national income would rise by about $25 billion as a result of the $10 billion tax cut, their model had to include estimates showing how much consumer spending would rise per dollar of additional disposable income (perhaps 95 cents), how many new workers would be hired per dollar of additional consumer spending, and the like.

Many people were skeptical of the argument for the tax cut. For example, they argued that consumers would in fact not increase their spending on goods and services by anything like 95 cents for each dollar of new disposable income, but would in effect hoard the additional income they received or use it to pay off debts. Skeptics raised other objections as well, but let us focus attention for now on this particular counterargument.

Most economists firmly rejected the counterargument. Why? Because economists have made elaborate empirical (factual) investigations of the relationship between consumers' disposable income and their spending. These studies have consistently showed that, *other things equal*, for high-employment periods of moderately stable growth such as we had during the 1960's consumers spend a remarkably stable proportion of additional disposable incomes—generally around 94–96 per cent, given some months to adjust to larger incomes. Sophisticated economists know that this figure is only a first approximation, and that it reflects a complex interplay of forces behind the scenes. But as a rough approximation it was a safe assumption that, barring other special forces at work, consumers would spend the largest portion of their new disposable income on goods and services within, say, six months to a year.

Who was right? After the tax cut was passed by Congress in early 1964, the effects on the economy were very close to the predictions of the economists who advocated the cut. Although it is difficult to measure precisely the results of any action in a complex economy, consumers did behave almost exactly as the model predicted, and the national income did rise by almost exactly the $25 billion predicted. The tax cut was widely acclaimed a great success.

What is the point of this example? It is both (1) to show you, in a very simplified way, how economists use models of major economic relationships to predict what will happen under different circumstances, and (2) to emphasize that such models must rest on careful empirical research about the behavior patterns assumed if they are to be reliable. Without such a model of consumer and business behavior and of the interactions between them, the impact of the tax cut would have been pure guesswork.

The results in 1964 were impressive. But a warning! We have only seen that employment and national income in 1964 following the tax cut turned out about the way many economists predicted they would. This result lends credibility to the economic analysis used and to the claim that the good results were caused by the tax cut. But this is not *necessarily* so. The cause may have been something else. In fact, some economists argue that the happy results came about primarily because another part of the government, the Federal Reserve System, rapidly increased the supply of money available to consumers and businesses through the banking system, and that the increased spending and employment reflected mainly this increase in the stock of money. These other economists have a different model (which we shall spell out later), and the results were also consistent with their model. Thus, it is not clear from this evidence which of the two big causes (the tax cut or increased money in the economy) deserved the most credit.

In our complex world it is never possible to be absolutely sure about the consequences of major public actions when several things are going on at once. But the stakes are large, and we must make decisions on economic policy issues, like those aimed at eliminating undesirable unemployment. In the 1964 case above, our models give us a strong presumption that both causes were important, as we shall see later on. The better our models are, the more fully validated they are by empirical evidence on the major interactions among the variables, the more confident we can be of our ability to predict the consequences of alternative economic policies.

ECONOMICS AS AN EMPIRICAL SCIENCE

Against the backdrop of this oversimplified example, turn now to a more systematic look at how modern economics operates as an empirical science, and how it can help you towards straight thinking on economic issues.

Use of Simplified Models: Theory

The most apparent fact about economic reality is its complexity. There are millions of businesses, 200 million consumers, hundreds of thousands of different products, multiple stages in the production of nearly every product. Faced with this overwhelming complexity, we obviously have to find some way of simplifying things down to manageable proportions. The first job is to simplify.

In order to do so, the economist, like other scientists, begins by developing an analytical framework, or model, of the reality he wants to analyze. This model focuses on the main elements and main relationships in the complex real economic world he is studying. For example, in the tax case above the main elements of the model were consumer behavior, business behavior in response to increased demand, and the respending cycle in response to the original increase in disposable incomes.

Such simplified models are often called "theories." They make no pretense of being accurate descriptions of any part of the economy. If they were completely accurate they would defeat their own purpose by getting back to all the detail. Instead, they are intended as highly simplified abstractions of the main elements of the reality to which they apply.

The notion of a model, or theory, may be illustrated by a noneconomic example. Suppose you want to understand how a bicycle works—a theory of its operation. You could study every detail of a single bicycle, or a large number of them, examining the tires, the handlebars, the sprocket, the paint, and so on. But if you could instead get a simple diagram, or a stripped-down working model of a bicycle, you'd get to the essentials quicker. This diagram wouldn't be concerned with all the details of paint, style, quality of steel, and so on. Instead, it would show the fundamental parts of the bicycle—wheels, frame, sprockets, driving chain, brake—and the basic relationships among these parts. The diagram would show how foot pressure applied to the pedals turns the sprocket wheel; how the chain connects this large sprocket to a smaller one at the center of the back wheel of the bicycle; and how, because of the difference in the size of the sprocket wheels, pressure on the foot pedal exerts a multiplied pressure in turning the back wheel. The diagram should also indicate the important numerical relationships, for example, between the sizes of the large and small

sprockets of the pedal and the back wheel.[1] People have used such a model of a bicycle many times, and its predictions have been thoroughly validated by empirical evidence. The theory, or model, is thus a good one in that it helps us to understand the way a bicycle works and to predict the consequences of changing the main variables—for example, the sizes of the two sprocket wheels. The theory "works."

So it is in economics. A model is a simplified diagram indicating the main elements in any situation, and the main interactions among these elements. The more firmly validated these relationships are by empirical observation of many cases, the safer we feel in using them in our model. Some models are very sketchy, merely identifying the main elements and loosely stating their interrelationships. Others specify precisely the relationships connecting the main variables, as when specific physical principles are used in explaining the operation of a bicycle. Unless we are reasonably precise as to the main economic forces at work and their interactions, with empirically validated quantitative statements of these relationships, we cannot safely predict how the economy will react to particular events or policy measures like the tax cut.

An economic model may be stated as a diagram, and many graphs are used in the pages ahead. It may be stated in words, as in the bicycle case; this will be done many times. Or it may be stated in mathematical terms, but except for a little simple algebra and geometry used in the diagrams, we shall use little mathematics.[2] Most economic models can be stated in any of these three ways.

Last, it is important to emphasize that the economist doesn't apologize for the fact that his theories don't describe the real world precisely and in detail. On the contrary, like any other scientist,

[1] In terms of basic physics, it might help to have explanatory notes on the diagram indicating that the principles of mechanical advantage are used, with the pedal being a second-class lever and the relative sizes of the gear wheels being crucial in determining the speed and power resulting from any given foot pressure on the pedals.

[2] However, there is a set of special Mathematical Appendixes at the end of the book for students familiar with calculus. References are indicated in the chapters to which these Appendixes apply.

he says that any theory is a skeleton, or a framework, to help simplify and understand the intricate complexity he is attempting to understand and predict.

"Other Things Equal" and "Equilibrium"

The real world is far too complex for us to analyze everything at once. Thus, in common with many other scientists, economists use the concept of holding "other things equal," or "constant."

In the chemistry laboratory, we hold "other things equal" through controlled experiments. We put two elements (say hydrogen and oxygen) together in a test tube *under controlled conditions*, and get water if the proportions are two to one. In the bicycle example above, we hold friction, gravity, air pressure, and various other factors constant (or assume them away altogether) in analyzing the way the bicycle works. So it is in economics. To understand, say, what happens when consumers receive larger disposable incomes because of a tax cut, we may want to assume that many other things are "constant"—for example, the stock of money in the economy, political conditions, and the like—in order to simplify the job of analyzing the result of the tax cut. If at the same time that taxes are cut, war should break out, obviously consumers might use their additional disposable income differently than under peacetime conditions. In the real world, "other factors" may not stay constant; but by assuming temporarily that they will do so, we can isolate the impact of the increased after-tax income in which we are interested.

This idea is closely related to the concept of "equilibrium," which is also widely used by scientists. In chemistry, for instance, after we've combined hydrogen and oxygen to form water, this equilibrium state is maintained until something disturbs it. In the same way, economists generally think of the economic system as tending to move toward equilibrium when some disturbing change occurs; and in analyzing the movement of any sector of the economy toward equilibrium after it is disturbed, they commonly hold many "other things equal" in order to isolate the effects of the change being studied.

Consider a simple example related to the tax cut above. We may say a household (or a consumer) is in equilibrium when it spends just that proportion of its income on all different products which bring it the greatest total satisfaction, and saves the rest. Say the household is receiving $100 per week and spending $95 on a variety of goods and services while saving $5 per week. Now its disposable income rises to $110 weekly because of the tax cut. It is now obviously out of equilibrium because, unless it increases its spending on consumer goods and services, it will be saving $15 per week, a large increase in the percentage saved. This saving increase may well occur temporarily, because it takes time to adjust to changes in our economic affairs. But the household will presumably want to adjust toward a new equilibrium pattern of spending with its larger income. At the new higher level of income, it may decide to save a larger proportion of its disposable income, or it may decide that 5 per cent is still about right. Either way, once it has adjusted its spending to the desired allocation of its income among all possible uses, it is again "in equilibrium." *We mean by equilibrium a situation in which everybody is satisfied to keep on doing what he is doing. In economic equilibrium, there's nothing at work to change the economic behavior under consideration.*

To repeat, "equilibrium" and "other things equal" are purely analytical concepts. No one believes that in the real world "other things" do always stay equal when we are trying to analyze the behavior of the economy, or that economic units are always in equilibrium. Use of these concepts simply helps us to trace through what *would* happen *if* all "other things" in the economic system remained unchanged until the new factor under consideration (such as the tax cut) had fully worked itself out. But don't think that this makes economic analysis just an intellectual game. Such analysis can give us powerful conclusions as to the *direction* the economy, or parts of it, will move in response to different individual actions or government policies, even if it can't tell us just what the end result will be some time hence in a world of many simultaneous crosscurrents.

Empirical Foundations
for Economic Analysis

The social scientist, unfortunately, seldom can run controlled experiments. We can't get everything else in the economy to stand still while we lower income taxes 10 per cent to see just what would happen. Nor can we get at the results by putting a few people off in a closed room and lowering their income tax 10 per cent. So the social scientist is never as sure and precise as the physical and natural scientist can be.

But it's easy to overstate the differences, too. Economics is increasingly an empirical science, which is building up a vast body of quantitative knowledge about the behavior of economic units and the interactions among them.

How, for example, can we be *sure* about what proportion of their new disposable income consumers will spend in the event of a tax cut? The answer is, there is no way to be *sure*. But through intensive empirical analysis of consumer behavior in the past, we can greatly increase our confidence in the prediction we may make. And modern statistical techniques make it increasingly possible for us to use past information as a basis for predicting the future.

Suppose we speculate ("hypothesize") that the amount people spend on goods and services in any year will depend on the disposable income they have in that year. We hypothesize that consumer spending is a "function of" disposable income. That is, we hypothesize that consumer spending depends on, or is predictably related to, the disposable income they receive. Economists might write the functional relationship:

$$C = f(DI)$$

where C stands for consumption, f for "a function of" (perhaps with a value of .95 in this case), and DI for disposable income.

Suppose now that we get records showing the disposable incomes and consumption spending of a large number of families over the past ten years. Looking at these records, we find that many families have spent about .95 of their disposable incomes on consumption in most years, but there are lots of exceptions. For example,

young families seem consistently to spend more than .95, families in their 50's spend less, and retired families spend more. (These differences make sense if you think about it; young families are just starting up, buying new durable goods, raising babies, and the like, so they are able to save little; older families, once their homes are established and the children raised, find it easier to save out of their incomes; while retired families have reduced incomes and spend down past savings.) We also find that in years when incomes have risen rapidly, the percentage spent on consumption falls below .95. (Again, this seems reasonable, because it takes time for people to adjust their spending to new higher incomes.) And so we might examine many other special forces at work. But over all, for the average of all families in periods of reasonably stable, prosperous times, consumption hovers around .94 to .96 of disposable income.

In addition, we might observe a sample of families this year to see how they behave. Looking at them one at a time, we find wide diversity. But again, on the average, they seem to come out at about the .95 level for this year.

What could we infer from this statistical analysis? We should have to be careful, because we have seen exceptions to our general presumption. Certainly we could not safely predict the behavior of any particular family without knowing a lot about that family. But on the imaginary evidence cited just above, we would be increasingly comfortable in saying that, *other things equal*, in reasonably stable, prosperous periods consumers as a group will spend about .95 of any new disposable income on goods and services, given a reasonable amount of time to adjust to the new income.

This is an oversimplified example, but it suggests the way in which we must go about building up reliable quantitative information on economic behavior. Actually, as we shall see in Part Two, consumer behavior is a good deal more complex than this, and we need a more elaborate theory to explain and predict it satisfactorily. So it is with most other parts of economic life. Economics, like any other empirical science, must continually develop new theories, test them out against the world, and reformulate them in the light of empirical evidence.

Prediction with Economic Theories

Thus far we have been talking mainly about a simple economic relationship—how much families will spend on consumption out of an additional dollar of disposable income. If we return now to the more complex issue of the total economic results of a tax cut like the one in 1964, the problem is more complex. Here we need a theory with several subparts and a complex set of interactions among them. The more convinced we are about the reliability of our understanding of the subparts of the system, the stronger our faith can be in our predictions about the consequences of the tax cut on employment and income.

How can we test how good a *total* theory is? There are two ways. One is to examine the assumptions on which the theory rests and the internal logic that it builds on those assumptions. The other is to make a pragmatic test of how well it actually predicts in the real world the variables in which we are interested (here employment and income). Both are valuable.

In the first approach, we ask two questions: (1) Do the assumptions of the theory correspond to the reality to which it is being applied? (2) Is the internal reasoning of the theory logically correct? If both these conditions are met, the theory should be useful for explanation and prediction. But there are problems. Most important, the world is so complex that it's hard to be sure that our assumptions are correct and that they are the only relevant ones for our problem. Remember that in the tax-cut example above, some economists suggested that leaving the money stock out of the analytical model left out the really important causal factor.

As a practical matter, therefore, many economists now rely more on the second test—how well does the theory actually predict? Economists thus try a model out to see what it predicts, and then check the prediction against the real world they are trying to explain. If the prediction is poor, they distrust the model, no matter how beautiful its logic. If a model based on dubious assumptions gives good predictions, they are inclined to use it, but only tentatively. For then they are uncertain about whether it predicts well because it is sound, or merely by chance. Alas, we can never be absolutely sure a model is "correct," even if it has predicted correctly in a number of past situations. It is always·possible that the result may be the consequence of some other set of factors that we haven't thought about and don't have in our model. But the more frequently a model predicts correctly, the more confident of it we have a right to be.

Lastly, we can never be sure of our predictions for another reason—we can never know that the future will be like the past. Even though consumer spending of disposable income has been extremely consistent in the past, it may change tomorrow. It may change because consumers simply decide to behave differently. Or, more likely, it may change because of a change in other circumstances which affect consumer behavior. For example, international tensions may grow, and in such an uncertain world consumers might decide to save more than in the past.

All these warnings are important. There are many uncertainties about our understanding of the economic world. But much of economic theory has met both the tests discussed above. And there is no uncertainty about the path to better understanding. It is the path of economics as an empirical science, which involves an interacting pattern of basic empirical research, the development of better analytical models, and continuing checks on the predictive power of the new models. Happily, modern economics is making rapid progress as an empirical science, and much of this progress underlies the chapters to come.

One last introductory comment concerning theory and practice. You often hear someone say, "That's good theory, but it doesn't work in practice." What the speaker must mean, if he is talking sense, is either that it is not good theory because it doesn't help explain the real world, or that it is good theory but it is being inexpertly used. A theory (the use of an abstract model) is good only when it *does* work in practice—that is, when it is useful in helping to understand the problem to which it is being applied.

ECONOMIC ANALYSIS
AND PUBLIC POLICY

This book focuses on both analysis and its use in helping you think through the public-policy issues America faces. There is no one best way of thinking straight about policy problems—for instance, what should be done to check an inflation or avoid unemployment. But most experts agree that an orderly, systematic job of thinking through a "decision" problem of this sort (be it in economics or any other field) must include the following broad interacting steps:

1. *First, define the problem.* In economic policy issues, defining the problem usually has two parts: (a) understanding the situation in which the problem exists, and (b) clarifying the objectives you want to achieve. In simple words, you need to clarify where you are and where you want to go. In 1964, for instance, what was the basic economic situation, and what specific goals did we want to accomplish with the proposed tax cut? Unless you're straight on these two questions, you're likely to behave like a headless horseman, rushing this way and that, trying one tack after another, but getting more exercise than results. Unless we know where we are and where we want to go, our chances of getting there are poor.

2. *Second, map out the main alternative ways of achieving the desired goals—the alternative paths from where we are to where we want to be.* In the 1964 unemployment case, for example, there might have been three major approaches: increase the public's spending power through cutting taxes, increase the money supply, or raise government spending. No one can see in advance what all the fruitful alternatives may be, but a plan that covers systematically the major alternatives suggested by preliminary analysis will usually save time and help keep the main issues uppermost.

3. *Third, analyze carefully the alternative policies outlined in step 2.* "To analyze" means to trace through carefully the effects of the different policies. Here the analytical models you've learned

will come in handy. Economic theory should help you make a tentative choice on the best steps to take. Perhaps in the analysis of your three main alternatives you'll hit on a fourth one you hadn't thought of at first. Although it's important to systematize your thinking, it's equally important to remain flexible and alert for new solutions.

4. When you finally have a tentative solution to the problem (for example, pass a law that puts ceilings on all prices and wages), don't stop! *The fourth step is: Check your solution*—both against flaws in your own analysis resulting from fallacies or blind spots, and against past experience. The world has had recessions and unemployment before, and governments have tried to eliminate them before. If your preferred alternative has failed before, why? It's no fun to have to throw out a solution after you've gone through a lot of analysis to get it. But if your checking suggests that something is wrong, take another look.

THE PROBLEM OF ECONOMIC GOALS:
A DIGRESSION

Clearly defined goals are necessary as a basis for making an intelligent choice among alternative courses of action. In a free society, every person has the right, and the duty, to make up his own mind on economic policy issues.

Does our present economic system do a good job? Nobody can honestly answer this question until he has thought through what he wants the system to accomplish. In the same way, you can't judge whether a piece of furniture is doing a good job until you specify what you want—color, design, comfort, durability, strength, and so on. If you put major weight on how a chair looks and your roommate on how it feels, you may end up arguing about whether or not it's a good buy. And someone else who says that durability is all-important may come up with a still different answer. And so it is with the economic system.

Some Tentative Goals

Consider the following list of objectives for the American economic system:

1. Progress: A rising average standard of living.
2. Individual freedom and opportunity.
3. Economic security.
4. Production in accordance with consumer demands.
5. An equitable distribution of income.

Would a system that produced these five things look good to you? If you're a typical American, it might, since this list is an attempt to mirror widely expressed goals. But make up your own set. The main purpose in presenting the list above is to give us something to work with, not to suggest that you ought to agree with it.

If you think about the list a minute, you'll see that there are two main problems. First, some of the words are ambiguous: What does "individual freedom" mean? You and your neighbor may have quite different ideas. Second, the objectives may conflict with one another. How compatible are individual freedom to do as you please and security against the risks of economic life? What if the lure of big incomes is the only way to get maximum progress, but we also want to attain a more equal distribution of incomes?

There are no easy answers to such questions. Different people do have different "value judgments" about what is most important in the world, and most of us have conflicting value judgments even within our own minds. It's your job as an individual to straighten out your own thinking by clarifying what ends you think are most impor-

tant, and by weighing them when you have to give up some of one to get more of another. It's the job of an individualistic, democratic system to compromise the differing judgments of different individuals in order to reflect the wishes of the majority while respecting minority views. Over and over, we shall see that we face a "trade-off" among economic goals; we can get more of one thing only by taking less of another.

To provide a common basis for analysis, throughout this book we will use these five *tentative* criteria for judging how well our system works. So stop here to ask yourself what these goals mean to you, and whether you'd substitute some others. Then see how well your list and your interpretations check with your friends'. For example, as you see it now, is individual economic freedom consistent with government imposition of taxes on you when you don't personally benefit from the government expenditure? Is individual freedom consistent with a law requiring all workers in a plant to join a union if they benefit from the wages it negotiates? What does economic security mean? Does this goal conflict with getting maximum output to raise our standard of living?

Conflicts among goals, and the need to resolve them, will reappear time after time in the pages ahead. So, whatever you decide your own social goals are, keep them clearly in mind in the following chapters as your basis for judging particular proposals and evaluating how well our economic system works.

REVIEW

Concepts To Remember

Be especially sure you understand the following concepts introduced in this chapter:

model	function
theory	hypothesis
"equilibrium"	statistical generalization
"other things equal"	

For Analysis and Discussion

1. Why should we assume "other things equal" in economics when we know they aren't that way in the real world?
2. We suspect that 10-year-olds' demand for ice cream cones depends on the temperature, their allowances, and the price of ice cream cones. Can

you write an equation showing the demand for cones (D_c) as a function of these three explanatory variables? How might we go about determining the relative importance of the explanatory variables for 10-year-olds in a particular community?

3. According to the "laws" of probability, if you toss an unbiased penny 100 times, it will come down heads and tails about 50 times each. How does this compare with an economic "law"—for example, that with people's wants for a commodity unchanged, an increase in the amount produced will, in competitive markets, lead to a lower price?

4. "Theory is all right for college professors, but not for me. I'm a practical man. Give me the facts and they'll speak for themselves." Do you agree or disagree with this sentiment? Why? How do facts speak for themselves?

5. Do you agree with the broad economic goals listed on pp. 31–32? How would you rank them in importance?

6. Should wealthy citizens of New York be taxed to provide schooling and food for poor sharecroppers in Alabama? To provide better housing for slum-dwellers in New York? Can you justify your position against someone who differs with you?

7. (*Based on the Appendix*) Analyze the validity of the following statements. In each case, explain carefully why you accept or reject the statement.

   a. What goes up must come down. (True about prices?)

   b. Sales taxes burden the poor, so they are inequitable taxes.

   c. In the past, booms have always been followed by depressions, so we can look forward to a real depression in the next few years.

   d. Millions are hungry in Asia, but government-owned wheat rots in storage bins. The administration's farm policy couldn't be more nonsensical.

   e. American industry is owned by the man in the street. A recent study by the New York Stock Exchange shows that 20 million Americans own stock in corporations.

Appendix

SOME COMMON FALLACIES

The preceding sections have outlined the positive job of straight thinking in economics. But the buzzing, booming, confusing world of economics seems to produce controversy everywhere. This appendix is intended to point up some of the common fallacies lying in wait for the unwary. As with the previous material, they show up everywhere you go, not merely in economics.

Wishing It Were So. One of the commonest of human frailties is to believe the things we want to believe. The boss believes his employee-education program is opening the worker's eyes to the necessity of large profits for continued prosperity—and he may be a surprised man the next time the wage contract comes up for renewal if he's just been wishing it were so.

This is one of the most insidious fallacies. We tend to talk to people who agree with us, to read the newspaper that reports things the way we like, and to run away from information and conclusions that are painful to us. Confronted with two interpretations of an event, one favorable and the other unfavorable, most of us will choose the favorable one. The union members believe the company could pay lots higher wages if only it would. Top management believes that all right-thinking people see that management is right and labor wrong in most wage disputes. Just wishing it were so?

Post Hoc, Propter Hoc. Suppose there's a bad depression. The government pays out large sums on public works projects. Six months later we're on the way up. Was the government spending the cause of the recovery?

Many people would say "yes." The government

spent, and recovery came. What could be clearer? But maybe the recovery was on its way anyhow, and the government spending did no good at all. The observed evidence tells us that government spending *may* have caused the recovery. But the mere fact that one event precedes another doesn't necessarily mean the first caused the second. To assume that causation can be determined so simply is the fallacy of *post hoc, propter hoc*—"after this, therefore because of it." Keep your ears open and notice how often people rely on this sort of reasoning, especially in discussing economic problems.

The Fallacy of Composition. Next, perhaps the most dangerous fallacy of all in economics—the fallacy of composition. Suppose one rancher increases his cattle production. He can reasonably expect that the increase will bring him more money when marketing time comes round. But suppose that all ranchers decide to raise more beef cattle this year. Will they get more money for the cattle in total? Quite possibly not. More cattle coming to market will, other things equal, push down the price of cattle. If prices fall a long way because of the increased production, the total revenue to all cattle farmers may be less for the larger output of cattle. Clearly what is true for one rancher alone is not necessarily true for all ranchers taken together.

Consider another example. Saving is obviously a sensible procedure for most families. But suppose that in a depression everyone decides to increase his savings. What this will mean, other things equal, is that everyone cuts down on his consumption expenditures. Unless someone else spends more, merchants' sales will fall off. People may lose their jobs. Incomes fall, and with lower incomes people may actually find they are able to save *less* than before. How can a decision that is so obviously sound as an individual matter have such unintended, perverse results in the aggregate?

There are examples elsewhere too. Suppose you're in a crowded hall and can't see the stage very well. So you stand on your chair, and can see beautifully. But now suppose everyone else stands on his chair too. As a result, no one is better off. You can't conclude that what worked for you will work for the whole crowd.

To assume that what is true of one part will necessarily be true of the whole is the fallacy of composition. It may not seem reasonable that when we aggregate everybody together, everything may go topsy-turvy from the way it looked when we considered one person alone. But it does in economics, in a surprising number of cases. It's easy but fallacious

to assume that what you know about the individual family or business is necessarily true for the whole economy.

Reasoning by Analogy. One of the most effective ways to explain something is to use an analogy. For example, in trying to explain the effect of continued repression on human behavior you may say, "Not letting someone express his feelings is like building up steam in a boiler." This conveys a vivid impression; if those feelings aren't let out, the person is going to burst like an overheated boiler.

Is the analogy a fallacy, or a very useful means of communication? It may be either, depending on how closely a human being with repressions actually corresponds to a steam boiler. It would be difficult to communicate without using analogies, but don't let the analogies lead you farther than can be justified by careful analysis. Analogies are everywhere. For example, is a monopolist in economic life a robber baron?

The Dog and the Bone. Consider the following syllogism, as this particular form of reasoning is called:

Major premise: All dogs like bones.
Minor premise: Roger likes bones.
Therefore: Roger is a dog.

How about it? Is Roger a dog? You should see in a minute that the conclusion doesn't follow from the premises at all. Roger may be a man, or a woodchuck, or anything else that likes bones. Maybe he's a dog, but this reasoning doesn't give you any basis for believing it.

Now try this syllogism:

Major premise: All dogs like bones.
Minor premise: Roger is a dog.
Therefore: Roger likes bones.

Here the logic is airtight. If the first and second statements (the premises) are true, it necessarily follows that the conclusion is true: Roger likes bones. Why? Because the major premise states that *all* dogs like bones; and the minor premise states that Roger is a dog and hence included in the group covered by the major premise. If Roger is included in the group described by the major premise, anything that is true of all the major-premise group must be true of Roger.

The fallacy in the first syllogism is called the fallacy of the "undistributed middle." The minor premise doesn't get Roger included under the major premise. Hence, we don't know whether statements about the major-premise group are also true of Roger.

This may seem to have very little to do with economics, but in fact syllogistic reasoning crops up constantly in our daily conversations. Consider this example: "Necessities shouldn't be taxed, so potatoes should be exempted from sales taxes." If you look at it, this is nothing but a syllogism with a missing minor premise:

Major premise: Necessities shouldn't be taxed.
Minor premise: Potatoes should be exempted
Therefore: from taxation.

Set up this way, it is obvious that the minor premise has to be, "Potatoes are a necessity," to make the reasoning sound. If in fact potatoes aren't a necessity, the conclusion won't necessarily follow. It may be desirable to avoid taxing potatoes, but the conclusion cannot be demonstrated from the major premise alone.

This example is a very simple one. Most syllogisms are not quite so easy to detect and clear up; often the conclusion is stated first, with the premises following "Because" or some other similar word. For example, "Potatoes shouldn't be taxed because we shouldn't tax necessities." Keeping your eye out for fallacious logic is an effective way to ferret out crooked thinking.

Facts That Aren't Facts. The second syllogism above looks airtight, but can we really be sure that Roger likes bones? The answer is, yes—if . . . only if the statements in the major and minor premises are in fact true. Do all dogs really like bones, and is Roger really a dog? [3]

When is a fact a fact? In the economic world, there are very few facts like the major premise above: "All things are this way," or "this is *always* thus and so." Such statements are called universal propositions. It is important to recognize that a universal proposition can never be completely validated by evidence. We can never examine all the cases to find out whether it was always true in the past, but even more important we can never be sure that it will always be true in the future even if it has always been true in the past.

[3] Note that these are the same two warnings stressed a few pages back in evaluating theoretical models: Be sure the basic assumptions are sound, and that the reasoning is logically correct.

An accurate statement is much more likely to be :"Most dogs like bones," or "The best evidence is that about 80 per cent of all dogs like bones," or "Nearly all collies chew on bones when they are hungry." This fallacy of accepting a general assertion as a fact when it isn't necessarily always so is closely related to the discussion above on statistical verification or rejection of theories. For most economic statements, we need to specify carefully the conditions under which they are said to be true, and to look hard at the empirical evidence on how true they have been in the similar situations in the past. We need to be especially careful about extending the "facts" of the past into the future, unless we are confident that the circumstances that produced the facts in the past will be reproduced in the future.

These warnings immediately play havoc with airtight syllogistic logic, but unfortunately that's the way the world is. Don't throw your knowledge about syllogisms out the window, however. You can still use it just as before, except that your statements generally need to be *probabilistic* rather than absolute. If 80 per cent of all dogs like bones (assumed to be an established proposition) and if Roger is a dog, we have *a priori* a four-out-of-five chance that Roger will like bones. This is a pretty high likelihood, but you still have to be cautious about the fifth chance.

It is impossible here to go into statistics and the rules of statistical inference that tell just what it's safe to conclude from combinations of probabilistic statements. But you should get used to the fact that facts are seldom absolute—that they are usually "almost always" true, or maybe only 60 per cent true. Often they're true under some circumstances and false under others. This kind of world makes flatly "right" or "wrong" conclusions less common than many people like to think.

Generalizing from Small Samples. Another warning related to the same problem of using empirical evidence. "Red-headed people are hot-tempered. I know! I have two red-haired friends and they're both hot-tempered." Or, to go back to the dog-and-bone case: "I know that dogs like bones, because I have a dog and he likes bones!" Such statements are a favorite way of backing up your position that you "know for a fact."

To generalize about all red-headed people or about all dogs on a sample of one or two is extremely dangerous, unless you have some convincing reason to suppose that this tiny sample is representative of the whole universe of red-haired people or dogs. There is probably no commoner fallacy than that of generalizing unthinkingly from small samples. We are continually learning from what we see and do; this is the commonest way of extending our knowledge. Thus, we inevitably build up tentative generalizations about the world from our everyday experience. But your own limited experience may or may not be typical. The safest generalizations have been established by careful, systematic observation of a large number of cases. The same question again: When is a fact a fact?

Black, or White, or Gray? There is another related fallacy. If one is not wary, he can go astray by (explicitly or implicitly) assuming that there is no middle ground between two extremes. On a foggy day, someone asks, "Is it raining?" You reply, "No." "Then," he may retort, "you mean it is sunny." But of course it may just be foggy. Often there is a perfectly logical middle ground between what appear at first glance to be two mutually exclusive alternatives; the alternatives stated may not exhaust the possible situations. The wise observer of the economic scene is the one who sees the grays in their proper shadings—not the one who sees everything as black or white, true or false.

NATIONAL INCOME, EMPLOYMENT, AND ECONOMIC GROWTH

FOUR

NATIONAL INCOME, PRODUCTION, AND PRICES[1]

Measures of National Production and Income.

Changing Price Levels and Price Indexes.

Growth in the American Economy.

Gross National Product as a Measure of Economic Well-Being.

Appendix: Data for National Income Accounts.

The economic history of the United States is a great success story. In less than 200 years, our country has grown from a few struggling colonies into the world's richest nation. In the present century alone, our total national output (adjusted to eliminate the effect of price inflation) has risen sixfold.

But it has been a bumpy ride up. There was a major financial crisis in 1907; a big inflation after World War I; a terrible depression from 1929 to 1939; and another big inflation during and after World War II. We can be proud of our success, but we must face the fact too that our rapid economic growth has been marred by inflationary booms and by depressions.

Economists once took it for granted that our private-enterprise system would automatically restore itself to full-employment prosperity whenever it got far off the track. But no more! Today we have grave doubts that the system is self-stabilizing, and since the 1930's *the* biggest economic issue has been how to devise government policies that will eliminate both depressions and inflations.

Part Two analyzes the determinants of the over-all levels of production, income, and employment in our economy. In nontechnical terms, the big problems are: what makes us grow rapidly or slowly, why do we have booms and depressions, and how can we make the economy perform better? The purpose of this first chapter is to provide some of the major analytical concepts we need to

[1] Some instructors may prefer to use Parts Three and Four on microeconomics and the distribution of income before Part Two on macroeconomics. These Parts are written to be equally usable in either order.

38

understand these problems—basically, the concepts of the national income accounts.

MEASURES OF NATIONAL PRODUCTION AND INCOME

Modern economics is an empirical science. To understand and regulate the behavior of an enormously complex economy, we need measures of its performance. We need a measure of its total output of goods and services, and a measure of the total income received by all its people. We also need more detailed measures—of how much people have left to spend after paying their taxes, of corporate profits, of family and business saving, and so on.

The "national income accounts" provide these measures. We'll start with the "gross national product," the measure of the economy's total production of goods and services, and work down to some of the more detailed measures. The primary goal is to lay a foundation for explaining why people and businesses receive the incomes they do, and why they spend their incomes as they do. For the combined spending of individuals, businesses, and governments goes far, in our market-oriented economy, to explain why sometimes there's inflation and sometimes unemployment.

To begin, a basic question: What do economists mean by "production"?

Economic Production Defined

To the economist, production is the creation of any good or service that people are willing to pay for. Raising wheat is production, and so is making the wheat into flour and the flour into bread. It is also production for the local grocer to have the bread on his shelf when you want it, or to deliver the bread to your door. The agricultural, manufacturing, and marketing services all satisfy human wants, and people are willing to pay for them.

In fact, over half the people employed in the United States today are engaged in rendering services rather than in manufacturing or raising anything. Half of what you pay goes for middlemen's services—the retailer, the wholesaler, the banker, the trucker, and many others. Lots of people object violently to this situation. "There are too many middlemen!" they say. Maybe there are. But if you stop to think about it you'll run head-on into this question: Are there too many manufacturers, or too many farmers? The real economic test for all producers of goods or services is whether they satisfy a consumer demand—not how many pounds of physical stuff they produce.

There is nothing moral or ethical about production as the economist defines it. Making and selling cigarettes is production, just like raising and selling food. And getting food from the farmer to you is just as much production as raising the crops. The test of the private-enterprise economy is the test of the market. If an act helps satisfy a want that someone is willing to pay for, that act is production.

Gross National Product

Gross national product is the nation's total production of goods and services (usually for a year), valued in terms of the market prices of the goods and services produced. This concept goes directly back to the definition of production above: Production is whatever people will pay for, and what they pay is an economic valuation of the worth of the product or service. Gross national product (abbreviated "g.n.p.") includes all the economic production in the country in any given time period.

Gross national product is stated in money terms, since this is the only meaningful way of adding together the output of such diverse goods and services as carrots, machine tools, maid service, air travel, and Fords. Strictly, then, g.n.p. is the money value of total national production for any time period.

Gross national product is also the nation's total expenditures on goods and services produced during the year. Each unit produced is matched by an expenditure on the unit. Most goods and services produced are bought outright. But how about the ones produced but not sold? Economists regard these as having been bought by the producers who hold them, as inventories. Then it is clear that the production and expenditure totals are identical.

G.n.p. is also the total income received by all sellers of goods and services. What someone spends on current output, someone else receives as income. This is g.n.p. seen from the receipts side.

Thus, it doesn't matter whether we look at gross national product as (1) the value of all goods and services produced, (2) the sum of all expenditures on those goods and services, or (3) the (gross) incomes received for producing the goods and services. They are all the same thing, and we get the same total each way.

There are two ways to calculate g.n.p., each designed to avoid the danger of double counting in a complex economy. One way is to sum up all expenditures on *final* products sold to consumers or to businesses for final use as producers' goods— all spending on potatoes, factories, autos, missiles, legal services, and so on. Note the word "final." Miners dig iron ore out of the ground and sell it to Bethlehem Steel. Bethlehem makes the ore into steel and sells the steel to Westinghouse. Westinghouse makes the steel into refrigerators and sells them to you and me. We don't count the value of the iron ore, plus the value of the steel, plus the value of the refrigerator. That would involve counting the iron ore three times. Instead, everything that is used in another product during the year shows up and is counted only in the *final* product (in this case, refrigerators), since the value of the final product will reflect the value of all the raw materials, labor, and other productive services included in it.

Producers' goods, like machinery, which are bought by businesses, pose an obvious problem here, since they are not directly incorporated into the final consumers' goods the way raw materials are. We count machinery and other producers' goods once, when they reach *their* final buyer— for example, when Ford buys a new punch press. Remember that goods in process at the end of the time period are counted as inventories (purchased by the owner) in the latest stage they have reached. This process of summing up all final purchases is called the "final-products approach" to estimating g.n.p.

Gross national product can also be estimated in another (equivalent) way: by the "value-added" method. Here the estimators establish the value added to each product by each producer, then sum up all these values. For example, in converting the iron ore to steel above, Bethelehem adds something to the value of the product it passes along. This added value is the difference between what Bethelehem pays for the ore, coal, and other products that it uses and the price at which it sells the steel to Westinghouse; roughly, it is the wages, interest, and rents paid by Bethlehem, plus the profit it earns. Similarly, we can compute the value added by Westinghouse. And so on for each productive unit in the economy. By summing up all the values added, we come out with the gross national product, again avoiding double counting.

Table 4-1 shows who buys the goods and services in the g.n.p., a useful breakdown in a market-directed economy where production is mainly in response to market demand. Purchasers are divided into three big groups: consumers, businesses (buying "investment," or "producers'," goods), and governments. To provide historical perspective, Fig. 4-1 then presents the same data from 1929 to 1967. Take a look at the three major segments.

TABLE 4-1
U.S. GROSS NATIONAL PRODUCT, 1966 *

Components	In Billions
Consumer purchases	$465
Business investment expenditures (including foreign)	122
Government purchases	153
Total	$740

* Data from U.S. Department of Commerce.

1. The biggest part of total production has consistently been goods and services for consumers—electric fans, stoves, dresses, movies, medical services, hats, and all the other things that consumers buy.

2. The next group is private investment in "producers'" or "capital" goods. These are buildings, machinery, equipment, and other capital goods used in the production of further goods or services. Such producers' goods are purchased primarily by businesses. But houses are also included in the investment-goods category, on the

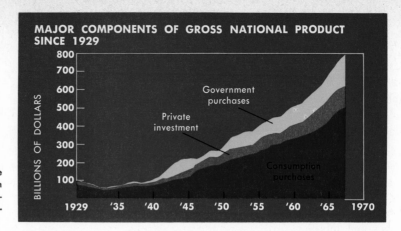

MAJOR COMPONENTS OF GROSS NATIONAL PRODUCT SINCE 1929

Government purchases

Private investment

Consumption purchases

BILLIONS OF DOLLARS

800 700 600 500 400 300 200 100

1929 '35 '40 '45 '50 '55 '60 '65 1970

FIG. 4-1 Consumers buy most of the g.n.p. The other third is divided between private investment and government purchases. (Source: U.S. Department of Commerce.)

grounds that they are so durable that in effect they represent investment goods rendering consumer services, even though they are often owned directly by consumers.[2] Business investment also includes—as inventories—any increase in unsold goods in process or final form.

Three important warnings about the private-investment category.

First, "investment" means the purchase of investment goods (buildings, machinery, and so on) *produced during the year*. For example, if someone buys a ten-year-old factory, this is not investment; the factory was included in the gross national product ten years ago, when it was built.

Second, investment does *not* include mere financial transfers, such as the purchase of stocks and bonds. For example, if you buy a share of General Motors stock from me, this is not investment for purposes of the national income accounts, since it does not pay for any new production.

Third, note that investment includes *gross* purchases of investment goods. It includes production that merely replaces depreciating buildings, machinery, and equipment, as well as production that represents a net increase in society's stock of capital goods. We come to the *net* increase in the nation's capital goods in the section on "net national product" below.

3. Government purchases of goods and services include both consumption and investment goods. Federal, state, and local governments buy food, police services, and other current consump-

tion items, as well as investment goods such as roads, buildings, and parks. But notice that government purchases of goods and services do not include all government expenditures. Governments also spend large sums on "transfer payments" (such as unemployment insurance and social security payments) that are not payments for currently produced goods and services and are hence not included in gross national product.

4. We have included "foreign investment," or "net exports," in private investment here, although often it is shown as a separate item. In 1966, for example, the U.S. exported $5 billion more than it imported, and to be complete we must include this net production in g.n.p. We will pull it out for special attention in Part Six, on "The International Economy."

To summarize, g.n.p. is made up of: (1) consumer goods and services bought by individuals and households, (2) investment goods bought mainly by businesses, and (3) both consumer and investment goods and services bought by federal, state, and local governments. *In all three categories, remember that only goods and services produced during the current year count; transfers of existing assets are excluded.*

Net National Product

Gross national product is by far the most widely used measure of the total production of final goods and services in the economy. But it includes some producers' goods that just replace already-existing producers' goods that are "depreciating," or wearing out. If a truck lasts ten years, we might say that one-tenth of it is used up every year, and the oil company that owns it would con-

---

[2] Although it is reasonable to treat new private housing as investment, note that houses differ only in degree from such durable consumer goods as autos, refrigerators, and vacuum cleaners, which are treated as consumption goods.

sider this tenth as an annual cost that year.[3] So it is with all other producers' goods; they wear out. Thus, before a firm or the economy as a whole adds anything *net* to its stock of producers' goods, part of the new trucks, buildings, and machines each year must go to replacing the ones wearing out.

Net national product (n.n.p.) is the net production of goods and services. It is gross national product, less those goods that merely replace depreciating buildings and machines. In 1966, for example, gross national product was $740 billion. Depreciation (sometimes called "capital consumption allowances") was estimated at $63 billion. Thus, *net* national product was $677 billion, about 10 percent less than gross national product. In other words, about 10 percent of our total output went to replace depreciating producers' goods and houses. Net national product measures the total production of goods and services available for current consumption and for adding to our stock of producers' equipment, including housing.

National Income

National income is the total of all income earned by the "factors of production"—land, labor, capital, and management. The national income is basically the net national product viewed from the income side. National income is always less than the net national product, however. The factors of production (laborers, managers, machinery, and so forth) do not actually receive as income the full value of their output, because businesses that hire them must pay indirect taxes (sales taxes, excises, and property taxes) to the government, which cut down on the income left to pay to the factors of production. If we subtract indirect business taxes from n.n.p., we have left the national income that goes to all factors of production. In 1966, the indirect tax deduction was $66 billion. Deducting this from net national product of $677 billion, we get a national income of $610 billion.[4]

---

[3] Accountants have more complicated depreciation plans, which recognize the fact that buildings and machines do not necessarily wear out at constant rates.

[4] This omits some minor items with which we needn't be concerned.

Table 4-2 shows the share of the national income earned by each major factor of production. Note the large share of salaries and wages—70 per cent in 1966. This percentage hasn't varied far from two-thirds of the total national income over several decades, though there seems to have been a gradual upward trend. The other main sources of income fluctuate more widely over business cycles.

TABLE 4-2
U.S. NATIONAL INCOME, 1966 *

Source of Income	In Billions
Total	$610
Wages and salaries	433
Net income of unincorporated business **	58
Corporation profits ***	80
Interest	20
Rental income	19

  * Data from U.S. Department of Commerce.
  ** Mainly farmers and professional men in business for themselves.
  *** Of which $34 billion was paid out in income taxes and $26 billion was plowed back as reinvested earnings. Dividends paid out to stockholders were $20 billion.

Personal Income
and Disposable Personal Income

"Personal income" is the total income received by all individuals in the country—what individuals actually have to spend, save, or pay taxes with. Personal income is less than the national income, mainly because national income includes total corporation profits whereas individuals receive only part of these profits in dividends. As the last footnote to Table 4-2 indicates, nearly half of corporation profits go to Uncle Sam as corporation income taxes, and part of what's left is plowed back into businesses rather than paid out to stockholders. We must subtract these amounts from national income to get income actually paid out to individuals; in 1966 their dividends were only $21 billion out of total profits of $80 billion. On the other hand, individuals receive large net "transfer payments" (social security, interest on the national debt, and so forth), which are personal income to them although they are not part

of the national income (since they don't reflect any current production). We must add these transfer payments in ro get total personal income. (Details are shown in Table 4-4 below.)

In 1966, total personal income was $580 billion. Table 4-3 shows what people did with this income: First, they paid their personal taxes. What they had left we call "disposable personal income." Most of this they spent on consumption and the rest they saved. *The concept of "disposable personal income" (what people have left after they pay their taxes) will be very important later on in our analysis of consumer spending and saving behavior.*

TABLE 4-3
U.S. PERSONAL INCOME

		In Billions
Total personal income		$580
Less: Personal income taxes	$75	
Equals: Disposable personal income		505
Of which:		
Consumer outlays		478
Personal saving		27

* Data from U.S. Department of Commerce. Consumer outlays include $12 billion of consumer interest payments which are excluded from the "consumer purchases" shown in Table 4-1. The Department of Commerce defines "consumer expenditures" to include only consumer payments for goods and services.

The Integrated
National Income Accounts [5]

If you have the concepts of gross national product and personal income well in hand, you're prepared to cope with a good many problems. For example, most newspaper stories and business magazines focus on these measures. But for clear thinking in some of the following analysis, you

[5] Within the last few years, a new set of social accounts has been released by the Federal Reserve System. These are called the "flow of funds accounts." They include all financial transactions in the economy, including payments in the stock market, for other financial transfers, for existing assets, and for a variety of other purposes not included in the national income accounts. These new money-flows accounts are being integrated with the present established national income accounts, and now provide a complete picture of money payments throughout the economy.

TABLE 4-4
THE NATIONAL INCOME ACCOUNTS FOR 1966 *

		In Billions
Gross National Product		$740
Deduct: Capital consumption allowances (mainly business depreciation allowances)	$63	
Net National Product		677
Deduct: Indirect business taxes	66	
National Income		610
Deduct: Corporation profits taxes	34	
Corporate savings (undistributed profits)	26	
Social security taxes	37	
Add: Transfer and interest payments	66	
Personal Income		580
Deduct: Personal taxes	75	
Disposable Personal Income		505
Of which: Consumer Outlays **		478
Personal Saving		27

* A few minor items are omitted, which explain the apparent discrepancies in the table.

** Includes $12 billion of interest paid by consumers not considered an expenditure on goods and services.

need to have a more detailed grasp of the relationships between the various parts of the total income and product accounts. Table 4-4 summarizes the complete set of interconnections for 1966, beginning with the gross national product total. Figure 4-2 shows the same set of interconnections as a flow diagram, tracing the entire income-and-payments flow. This figure ties the circular flow of gross national product back to the simple, fundamental circular flow diagram in Fig. 2-3.

In Fig. 4-2, begin with gross national product of $740, as in Table 4-4. Then $63 billion of capital consumption (depreciation) allowances drains off as a form of private saving, leaving $677 billion of net national product. From n.n.p., another $66 billion drains off to the government through indirect business taxes, leaving national income of $610 billion. From this, corporate income taxes, social security taxes, and corporate saving (undistributed profits) are drained off; while interest on the government debt and other transfer payments are added back into the income stream, to make up $580 billion of personal income. The resulting personal income total is

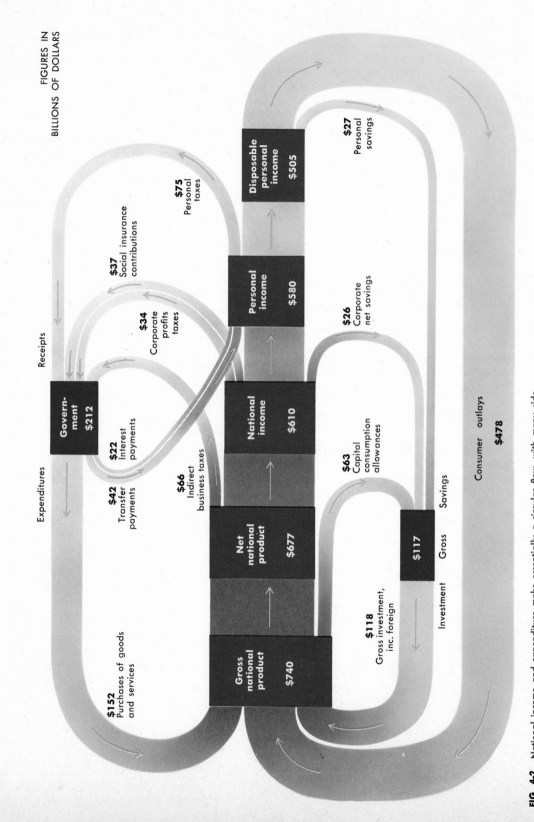

FIGURES IN BILLIONS OF DOLLARS

FIG. 4-2 National income and expenditure make essentially a circular flow, with many side loops. This is a more complete version of the simple circular money flow introduced in Fig. 2-3. Some minor items are omitted; "consumer outlays" include $12 billion consumer interest payments generally excluded from "consumer expenditures" and g.n.p. Figures shown are for 1966.

reduced to personal disposable income by the payment of personal income taxes, and then part of disposable income goes into personal savings while the bulk flows on into consumption expenditures. These consumption expenditures in turn become part of gross national product.

Now add back in the private investment and government spending flows—the private savings that flow into investment expenditures and the government tax receipts that flow into government spending on goods and services. Together these three types of spending make up gross national product, the three big components of aggregate demand for currently produced goods and services—consumption, investment, and government spending. Remember them, for they provide the core of the analysis of Chapters 6, 7 and 8.

CHANGING PRICE LEVELS AND PRICE INDEXES

When prices change, g.n.p. expressed in terms of dollars is no longer an adequate measure of the real goods and services produced. A 100 per cent increase in real national output would mean a great rise in the national standard of living. But doubling g.n.p. merely through doubling prices is no real economic gain at all. In order to separate "real" from merely "dollar" changes in individual and national incomes, we have to make an adjustment for price-level changes.

Figure 4-3 indicates the big fluctuations in prices in the United States over the last two centuries. The problem of price-level changes is no minor one.

What Is a Price Index?

In 1929, a family income of $1,300 would have bought a group of goods and services called a "subsistence standard of living." In 1933, you could have bought the same collection of goods and services for about $900. By 1967, you would have needed about $2,500.

If all prices changed in the same proportion in the same direction at the same time, measuring price-level changes would be simple. But the world

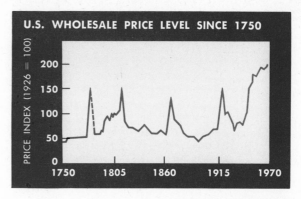

FIG. 4-3 Prices have fluctuated sharply throughout our history. The big peaks have come during or after major wars. So far, there has been no price slump since World War II. (Source: U.S. Department of Labor.)

of real prices is not simple and orderly. Even in the big price rises shown in Fig. 4-3, some prices declined and others rose at very different rates. Yet, even though not all prices rose, we say that the "price level" rose because the average of all prices rose. The price of the same market basket of goods was higher than before.

Table 4-5 shows how to calculate a simple "price index" for a "market basket" of four commodities, to show whether their price level went up or down between 1958 and 1968. A price index is a measure of price-level changes.

With 1958 as the "base year," the price of each item in that year is 100 per cent of itself. This is what people mean when they say, "Take 1958 as 100." Then we compute what percentage each 1968 price is of the 1958 price. For example, eggs at 6 cents each are 120 per cent of the 1958 price. This 120 per cent is the 1968 "price relative" for eggs, since it shows the 1968 price relative to that in 1958. To find the change in the price level (the average of all four prices), we simply take the average of the four 1968 price relatives, which gives us 108 per cent for the 1968 price level. (The percentage sign is usually omitted for convenience.) Of course, most price indexes include more commodities, but they are made in a generally similar way.[6]

[6] The final index numbers merely indicate the relation of average prices in the two years. We could just as well have taken 1968 as 100, in which case the 1958 index would have been 93. Although the actual index numbers would have been different, either set shows equally well the relative price levels in the two years: 93/100 = 100/108. Thus the year chosen as 100 has little significance.

45

TABLE 4-5		
PRICE INDEX FOR 1968 WITH 1958 AS BASE YEAR		
Product	1958	1968
Eggs, each	5¢ = 100%	6¢ = 120% ⎡of the 1958 price⎤
Hamburger, per lb	40¢ = 100%	50¢ = 125% ⎢ " ⎥
Turnips, per lb	9¢ = 100%	6¢ = 67% ⎢ " ⎥
Apples, per lb	10¢ = 100%	12¢ = 120% ⎣ " ⎦
	4) 400%	4) 432%
	100% = price level in 1958	108% = price level in 1968

This simple method of calculating price-level changes may give misleading results, however. It tacitly assumes that eggs, hamburger, turnips, and apples are equally important. A 10 per cent change in the price of hamburger influences the index exactly as much as a 10 per cent change in the price of turnips. Actually, hamburger is more important than turnips in most budgets, and it seems logical that the price of hamburger should affect the index more.

Thus, in most price indexes, each price is "weighted" according to its importance. For example, the U.S. Bureau of Labor Statistics weights the prices in its widely-used consumers' price ("cost-of-living") index as follows. The statisticians take a "market basket" of the goods and services bought during the early 1960's by typical urban wage earners' families. Choosing some 400 of the most important prices, they weight each roughly in accordance with the proportion of the family's total expenditure for that commodity. If the family bought lots of potatoes, potatoes make up a sizeable part of the weekly market basket; rent is a big item in the basket. In effect, the market-basket approach weights the price of each commodity according to the amount spent on that commodity weekly.

Having decided on the contents of the hypothetical market basket, the B.L.S. gets its price index by comparing the cost of the basket from one week to the next. The index now uses 1957–59 as a base period (100). So a weekly index reading of 120 means that the cost of the market basket is up 20 per cent from the 1957–59 price level for those goods and services.

Price Indexes for Different Price Levels

Since a price level is merely an average of some group of prices, we can speak of many different price levels. One may reflect the prices paid by a group of consumers (their cost of living); another, the prices paid by wholesalers; another, the level of wages in manufacturing.

Figure 4-4 shows the movements of four important price indexes from 1929 through 1966. What price level is most significant depends on what you are talking about. If you want to measure changes in the cost of living for a particular group, the logical choice is an index of the prices of the goods and services the group buys. Given the wide diversity of price movements, it is hard to devise a single price index that will be a significant measure for the whole economy. The closest approach is an index developed by the Department of Commerce to eliminate the effects of price-level movements from the gross national product. This adjustment is spoken of as "deflating" the g.n.p. In it, first special indexes are computed for the different major sectors of g.n.p., and then these are combined to obtain a "g.n.p. deflator." The result is a price index for all goods and services in the gross national product.

Figure 4-5 compares g.n.p. since 1870 in the actual (current) prices that prevailed each year with g.n.p. in constant (1964) prices.[7] We often

[7] Remember from above that we could have chosen some year other than 1964 as the "base" year for calculating constant-price g.n.p. over the years. Another base year would give different absolutue levels for the constant-price g.n.p. but would not change the relative movements in the two curves.

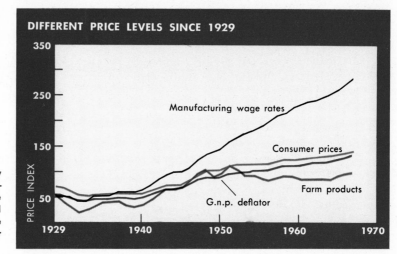

DIFFERENT PRICE LEVELS SINCE 1929

Manufacturing wage rates

Consumer prices

G.n.p. deflator

Farm products

PRICE INDEX

350

250

150

50

1929   1940   1950   1960   1970

FIG. 4-4 Different prices move diversely in the American economy. The g.n.p.-deflator series comes closest to showing the price changes for all currently-produced goods and services. Note the wage-rate index. (Sources: U.S. Departments of Labor and Commerce.)

speak of the constant-price g.n.p. as "real" g.n.p., since with the elimination of price-level changes the g.n.p. index measures real changes in output of goods and services. In periods of rapidly changing prices, like World War II, the money g.n.p. figures clearly give a misleading picture of how rapidly real g.n.p. is rising.

How Good Are the Price Indexes?

How accurately do the well-known price indexes mirror the price changes they are intended to summarize? The most widely used indexes are prepared by the government—the consumers' price index, the wholesale price index, and the g.n.p. deflator. These are the product of years of hard work and millions of dollars, and they're as good as the experts can make them. Many privately made indexes fall short of these standards of excellence, even though they may serve useful purposes. Others are extremely accurate, though they measure only a few prices—for example, the well-known Dow Jones index of a small group of leading stock prices.

How good the price indexes are is no mere academic question. Millions of workers' wages are adjusted periodically under their union contracts for changes in the "cost-of-living," which are usually measured by the B.L.S. consumers' price index. Other indexes are used daily in business and government decision-making. In 1959 President Eisenhower appointed a group of the country's leading economists and statisticians to restudy the B.L.S. consumers' price index. Their report gave the index high marks, but pointed to a number of

tough statistical problems yet to be solved. For example, they found that the index probably doesn't recognize quality improvements as effectively as it should. For example, suppose Ford ups the horsepower in next year's models and adds a new type carburetor, but doesn't change the price. Should the index show the price of Fords unchanged, or lower (because you get more car for your money)? If lower, how much? Many economists believe the B.L.S. consumers' price index shows prices rising perhaps one per cent a year too fast because of the difficulty of reflecting promptly such changes due to new products and quality improvements, but this is a highly debatable issue. If in fact the index overstates price increases by one per cent a year, most of the apparent "infla-

FIG. 4-5 G.n.p. has grown rapidly, but in spurts, over the past century. The solid line shows g.n.p. in current dollars, while the dashed line shows g.n.p. in dollars of constant (1964) purchasing power. The dashed line thus shows the growth in real output over the century. (Sources: National Bureau of Economic Research and U.S. Department of Commerce.)

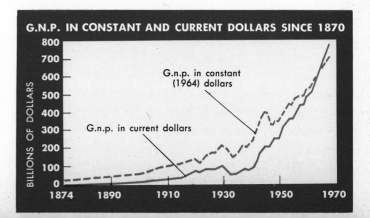

G.N.P. IN CONSTANT AND CURRENT DOLLARS SINCE 1870

G.n.p. in constant (1964) dollars

G.n.p. in current dollars

BILLIONS OF DOLLARS

800
700
600
500
400
300
200
100
0

1874   1890   1910   1930   1950   1970

tion" (rise in the c.p.i.) between 1957 and 1964 was illusory, and we instead had substantially stable consumer prices.

Price Levels
and the Value of Money

The value of money varies inversely with the general price level. Suppose that all prices (retail, wholesale, wages, rents, securities, and so forth) exactly doubled. There would be no question about the purchasing power, or value, of a dollar. It would be cut exactly in half. And if all prices were to fall by 50 per cent, the purchasing power of a dollar would double. The value of money, like the value of other things, is measured by what we can get in exchange for it. A rise in the average level of all prices *is* a fall in the value of money. The two are simply different ways of saying the same thing.

But to measure changes in the value of money in the real world is much harder than this example suggests. Money represents generalized purchasing power over all goods and services. To measure changes in the value of money itself, therefore, we ideally need an index that summarizes the movement in all prices, and no such index exists. Remember that prices of all existing assets, as well as g.n.p. items, would have to be covered. But we can construct indexes accurate enough to show that the value of money has fluctuated sharply. The rough data on wholesale prices back to 1750 shown in Figure 4-3 demonstrate vividly that the dollar has not been a stable standard of value. On the contrary! It is as if our yardstick had intermittently contracted to eighteen inches and then stretched to six feet.

GROWTH IN THE AMERICAN ECONOMY

America's economic success story can be told in two simple statements:

1. Total real g.n.p. has grown rapidly and vigorously, far more so than in any other country over the past two centuries.
2. Real g.n.p. has grown far more rapidly than the number of people at work—that is, output per person has also risen rapidly.

But a black mark has to be chalked up too:

3. Growth has been spasmodic and uneven, interrupted by depressions and recessions with wasteful unemployment of men and productive capacity.

Growth in Total Output

Figure 4-5 shows the growth in gross national product over the past century. The graph tells the story. Gross national product in actual prices rose from $7 billion to nearly $800 billion. If you take out the price inflation, the growth is less, but it's still phenomenal—from about $25 billion to over $700 billion in constant (1964) dollars. This is a nearly 30-fold increase. On an annual basis, g.n.p. grew between 3 and 3½ per cent. This rate doesn't sound like much in a single year, but it compounds fast as the decades go by, in a geometric progression. Take $1 to start and do the arithmetic to see what it amounts to in 100 years. An annual growth rate of 3½ per cent will more than double g.n.p. every two decades.

Growth Rates—A Digression

Figure 4-6, which takes an even longer look at American economic history, emphasizes the importance of thinking about annual growth *rates*—i.e., about the percentage increase per year. The left-hand portion shows real national income —in constant prices—from 1800 to 1966. This chart makes it look as if the growth rate had speeded up enormously in the last half-century. The line goes almost straight up, with an increase of $400 billion in the last 50 years.

But take a look at the right-hand portion. This shows exactly the same data (national income since 1800, in constant prices) on a "ratio," or "logarithmic," scale. In contrast to regular charts, which give equal vertical distance to equal *absolute* increases, this ratio scale on the vertical axis gives equal distance to equal *percentage* increases. Thus, on the ratio scale an increase from five to ten takes about a third of an inch vertically, and an increase from 100 to 200, or from 500 to 1,000, takes exactly the same distance.

A ratio scale permits easy comparison of annual growth rates over the long period. A constant *percentage* increase—say 3 per cent per year

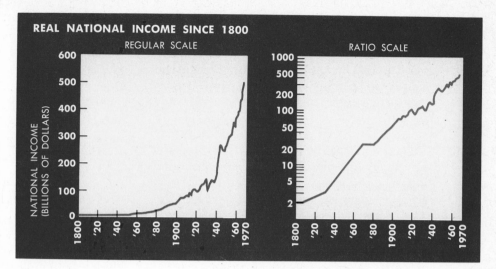

REAL NATIONAL INCOME SINCE 1800

FIG. 4-6 Both halves of the chart show the same data—national income in constant dollars since 1800. But the ratio scale shows that the annual growth rate has been quite stable over the past century, not rising sharply as the regular scale suggests. (Sources: National Industrial Conference Board and U.S. Department of Commerce.)

—will show as an equal vertical increase each year—a steadily rising straight line. If the growth rate is 4 per cent, the line will be steeper. If it is only 2 per cent, the line will be flatter.

Thus when we look at the right-hand section of Fig. 4-6, we see the past in different perspective. What looks on the regular interval scale like a big increase in the recent growth rate turns out when seen on the ratio scale to be just about the same annual growth rate as over most of our history.

Growth in Output per Worker and per Capita

This growth in national output reflects in part the steady increase in the number of people working. But over the past century, only somewhat over 1 per cent of the roughly 3 per cent annual growth in real output has come from more workers. The other 2 per cent a year represents increased output per worker, which in turn reflects more capital, improving technology, and better management, as well as improved worker skills and education.

Look at the chart just inside the front cover of this book. The top line shows real gross national product soaring upward. But right under it is output per man-hour, climbing steadily too. A worker today turns out over three times as much per hour as he did in 1900, and six times as much as a century ago. Who deserves the credit for this extraordinary advance? By the end of the book you should be able to answer.

Figure 4-7 shows the growth in real income

(or output) per capita since 1800. As in the other charts, data before the present century are rough, and are plotted only once each decade to give a picture of major trends. Note the big increase in recent decades—but remember that this is a regular-interval, not a ratio, scale.

Booms and Depressions

Figures 4-5, 4-6, and 4-7 also illustrate how spasmodic our economic growth has been. Connect the peaks of the real g.n.p. curve in Fig. 4-5 since 1929, and you'll have roughly the growth in full-employment capacity of the economy. The area between your line and actual g.n.p. roughly measures the potential output lost because the economy operated below potential. It may not look like much, but it has been estimated that we lost at least $200 billion worth of output (in

FIG. 4-7 Per capita real income has grown rapidly but erratically over the past century, apparently less rapidly during the early 1800's. Note the big World War II spurt, but remember that this is not a ratio scale. (Data from Fig. 4-6 divided by population.)

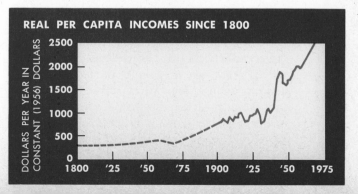

REAL PER CAPITA INCOMES SINCE 1800

today's prices) in the 1930's alone through unemployment. This was equal to three full years of actual output during the ten depression years. Recent estimates show a waste of $30–50 billion a year over the 1958–64 period because the economy fell short of full-capacity output, even in those reasonably prosperous years. The enormous waste of unemployment is vividly portrayed by the very curves that show our persistent and rapid growth. (The booms and depressions don't show before the 1920's, since the earlier data are plotted only once each decade.)

G.N.P. AS A MEASURE
OF ECONOMIC WELL-BEING

Growth in real g.n.p. provides one good measure of the rise in the nation's economic well-being. This is the figure you see most often in the newspapers and the news magazines, and we will use it too. But some warnings are in order:

1. For many purposes, gross national product is more useful on a *per capita* or *per family* basis. Ultimately, g.n.p. has economic usefulness to the individuals in a nation. A big nation like China is poor with a large g.n.p.; a small one like Switzerland is well off with a small g.n.p. Total g.n.p. figures alone can be seriously misleading.

2. As we have seen, wide price-level fluctuations have been common. To get a meaningful measure of actual growth in output, we must use data valued in constant prices—i.e., *real* g.n.p.

3. Gross national product places no value on leisure. Over the past century, the average work-week has been cut nearly in half—from 75 hours to about 40—and vacations have lengthened greatly. No accurate monetary value can be placed on this gain, but to disregard it would be a gross error indeed.

4. G.n.p. data cover for the most part only goods and services that pass through money transactions. They take no account of such important items as nonpaid housewives' services. If Mrs. A. and Mrs. B. both do their own housework, neither's services show up in gross national product. If they simply exchanged housework and paid each other $3,000 a year, neither would be better

off; yet gross national product would be $6,000 higher. For the economy as a whole this would amount to billions of dollars. In only a few cases, such as the estimated value of services from owner-occupied homes, has it proved practicable to include real production that is not sold for money.

5. Durable consumer goods (for example, autos and refrigerators) are included in gross national product when they are produced. Yet many of them are used over several years. The statistics imply that all consumers' durables are used up and represent income only in the year in which they are produced. Thus, the real income (services) actually received by using durables is greater in depression years than is shown by the g.n.p., since few new durables are produced but many old ones are in use. Conversely, it is lower than reported by g.n.p. in booms when consumers' durables are produced faster than they are used.

6. Gross national product says nothing about *what* goods and services get produced. Most economists presume that goods produced through the private economy reflect roughly the desires of the buying public, weighted by the size of their pocketbooks. But there are some questions about this, especially when government enters. Is a dollar spent on national defense or highways, financed through taxes, more or less important to our economic well-beings than a dollar spent privately on food or clothing? For example, real g.n.p. in 1944 was about twice the 1929 peak level. About half the total 1944 output was munitions, services of troops, and other activities directly associated with winning the war. Was the country twice as well off economically? Should schools and highways be included dollar for dollar with beefsteak and Buicks? The g.n.p. accounts say yes.

A comparable problem arises as our economy increases in complexity. Now we build complex subway, elevated, and street transport systems in our cities. They provide incomes to thousands and serve millions daily, contributing billions to the annual gross national product. Do these billions reflect increased well-being for our city-dwellers, or instead do they reflect a huge amount of resources devoted to the painful necessity of getting around in crowded cities? How does our economy compare with that of a rural nation that has a lower g.n.p. partly because it has (and needs) no elaborate city transport systems? Is the rural nation as much worse off economically as the g.n.p. figures suggest?

7. Money income figures do not necessarily measure the satisfaction associated with earning and spending incomes. Sometimes this is termed "psychic" income. For example, a research scientist receives a regular salary (money income), with which he obtains goods and services (real income). But many researchers also derive special satisfaction from the type of work they do. They like the continued search for knowledge, the contact with other scientists, and the comparative freedom to allocate their time the way they want. Other workers may hate their jobs. Presumably it's the ultimate psychic income we get from working and consuming that matters most, and g.n.p. is only a crude measure of this.

It is important to remember all these problems in using g.n.p. as a measure of national well-being. But with all their failings, per capita real gross national product data are a very useful first approximation for this difficult job of measurement.

REVIEW

Concepts To Remember

This chapter introduces some of the most important concepts in economics. The following checklist is to help you make sure that you have them firmly in mind:

production	gross private investment
gross national product	producers', or capital, goods
"real" gross national product	personal consumption
"value added"	net national product
"final-products approach"	capital consumption allowance
depreciation allowance	ratio, or logarithmic, scale
national income	per capita income and output
personal income	price level
disposable personal income	price index
personal savings	value of money

For Analysis and Discussion

1. Which of the following is production, as defined by the economist?
    a. Delivering milk.
    b. Making steel.
    c. Selling cigarettes to minors.
    d. Collecting funds for the United Fund.
    e. Winning a beauty contest.
2. In the national income accounts, production is measured by what people pay for it. Is it therefore true that a dollar spent on liquor, on missiles for defense, and on bread are all equally important?
3. Using Fig. 4-2, explain each diversion from the main circular flow of income, and trace through the way in which it returns to the main stream. Did government add to or deduct from the flow of spending in 1966?
4. A recent congressional investigation found that over half the consumer price of many food products went to middlemen at different levels—retailers, wholesalers, and so on. In some cases, as little as 20 per cent of the final price represented payments to the farmer who originally produced the food. Farm and consumer groups testifying before the committee urged action to rectify this situation.

a. Do you agree that Congress should take some action? Why or why not?

b. If Congress should act, what should it do?

5. Is gross national product, net national product, or disposable personal income after taxes a better measure of the overall performance of the economy? Why?

6. The steady growth in service workers is a sign of weakness in our economy, because they produce no *real* goods output comparable to farm output of food and raw materials. (True or false? Why?)

7. From the data below on disposable personal income and the consumer price index, compute disposable personal income for the years shown in constant (1947–49) dollars. Did "real" disposable income fluctuate more or less than money disposable income?

	Current Disposable Personal Income	Consumer Price Index (1947–49 = 100)	Disposable Personal Income in 1947–49 Dollars
1929	$ 83 billion	73	———
1933	46 "	55	———
1939	70 "	60	———
1959	337 "	126	———
1967	545 "	144	———

8. Suppose that prices for certain products in 1957 and 1967 were as follows:

	1957	1967
Round steak (per pound)	$ .70	$ 1.00
Butter (per pound)	.90	.75
Men's suits (each)	40.00	60.00
Ford sedans (each)	1,600.00	2,800.00
Student notebooks (each)	1.00	1.00

a. Construct a price index showing the change in the price level of these commodities from 1957 to 1967. If you feel you need further data, explain why, make a reasonable assumption on the data, and then construct the index.

b. Does this index give a reasonably good picture of the change in the cost of living between 1957 and 1967? Why or why not?

c. Would the index reflect reasonably the change in your own (individual) cost of living? If not, what changes would need to be made to have the index reflect accurately changes in your own cost of living?

Appendix

DATA FOR NATIONAL INCOME ACCOUNTS

This Appendix presents some background information on the g.n.p. accounts, and the actual data over most of the past century.

Table 4-6 presents some of the major national income accounts since 1869, the first year for which reasonably reliable g.n.p. estimates are available. Data for the related series not shown in the table may be found in *Historical Statistics of the United States*

TABLE 4-6

UNITED STATES NATIONAL PRODUCT, INCOME, AND EMPLOYMENT

Year or Yearly Average	Gross National Product * (In Billions of 1964 Dollars)	Gross National Product †	National Income †	Disposable Personal Income †	Consumer Expenditures †	Total Employment ** (In Millions)
			(In Billions of Current Dollars)			
1869–78		7	7			19
1879–88		11	10			23
1889–98		15	13			27
1899–1908	90	22	20			32
1909–18	121	40	36			39
1919–28	162	85	70			44
1929	218	104	87	83	79	48
1931	184	76	59	63	61	42
1933	153	56	40	45	46	39
1935	183	72	57	58	56	42
1937	219	90	74	71	67	46
1939	227	90	73	70	67	46
1941	287	125	104	92	82	51
1943	374	193	168	132	102	55
1945	393	214	182	150	123	53
1947	337	234	198	170	166	58
1949	352	258	218	190	181	59
1951	412	329	279	228	210	61
1952	429	347	292	239	220	61
1953	449	365	306	253	233	62
1954	440	363	302	257	238	61
1955	473	398	330	274	257	63
1956	484	419	351	293	270	65
1957	493	442	367	309	285	65
1958	486	445	367	318	293	64
1959	518	483	400	337	314	66
1960	531	504	415	352	329	67
1961	542	520	427	365	339	66
1962	579	560	458	385	355	67
1963	595	590	481	404	374	68
1964	631	631	517	437	401	69
1965	677	681	559	469	436	71
1966	731	740	610	505	465	73

* Data before 1929 based on John Kendrick, in *Studies in Income and Wealth*, Vol. 16 (National Bureau of Economic Research); thereafter from U.S. Departments of Commerce and Labor.

† Data before 1919 from National Bureau of Economic Research, and National Industrial Conference Board; thereafter from U.S. Department of Commerce.

** Total civilian employment. Data prior to 1914 from NICB; thereafter from Bureau of Labor Statistics.

(Washington, D.C., U.S. Government Printing Office, 1960); in the annual Economic Report of the President; and in the monthly *Economic Indicators* (Joint Economic Committee of Congress) for recent years. *Economic Indicators* provides the best simple, up-to-date summary of most important national economic series.

How accurate are the data that make up the national income accounts? Nobody knows exactly.

The Department of Commerce and private research workers have spent years improving techniques for estimating the magnitudes involved. Most of the components are estimated directly from sample information. For example, the business inventory estimates rest on current samples of businesses maintained by the Department of Commerce and the Securities and Exchange Commission. Wages and salaries are estimated from samples of different sectors of the economy. Tax payments are taken directly from current government tax receipts. Personal savings are estimated by the Department of Commerce and the Securities and Exchange Commission, with checks from Federal Reserve Board estimates. All these estimates are cross-checked as thoroughly as possible, both by employing two methods of estimating and by using different sources. After a year or so, more complete data for checking is available from individual and business federal income-tax returns.

But the series are only estimates, and sometimes estimates based on skimpy samples. Perhaps large chunks·of income are omitted entirely (though this seems unlikely). The absolute level of the aggregates is hard to check, because only during na-

tional censuses do we get complete coverage of the population, and census information only partially meets the needs of the national income calculators. Income-tax returns fill in a mass of data, but they miss part of the population—and there is always a question about how much income goes unreported. Probably the year-to-year changes in the national income data are more accurate than the absolute levels, since any classes of income missed probably stay missed. Certainly, the farther back the figures go beyond the last quarter-century, the less reliable they become. But whatever their failings, these national income accounts are the best we have, and they are probably superior to those available anywhere else in the world.

FIVE

AGGREGATE SUPPLY
AND
AGGREGATE DEMAND

A Simple Model.

Aggregate Supply.

Aggregate Demand, Unemployment and Inflation.

Growth in Productive Capacity.

Why do we have booms, depressions, inflations and unemployment? What determines how fast an economy grows? For over a century economists have examined these problems. Today, we have a reasonably good understanding, though enough unanswered questions remain that they get more attention in current economic research than does any other area.

The next five chapters present the basic theory of income, employment, and prices—the general analytical model that has proved most useful in understanding what determines the overall level of income, employment, and prices in the American economy. No section of the book is more important for you to understand thoroughly. Chapters 10–14 then turn to the question of stabilization policy—how to avoid unemployment and inflation in our economy, using the basic analysis to evaluate alternative government stabilization policies. Last, Chapters 15–18 focus on long-run economic growth; what determines the rate at which different economies grow over the long run, both here and in the underdeveloped world—and what we can do to speed economic growth, on which a rising standard of living for the world's billions ultimately depends.

A SIMPLE MODEL

To understand the complex real economic world, it is useful to begin with a very simple model. You will recall from Chapter 3 that the essence of a model is that it focuses on a few critical variables and the relationships among

55

them, abstracting from many details in order to highlight these essentials.

We want to understand the determinants of real g.n.p., of aggregate employment, and of the price level. Let us begin by focusing on two major variables—aggregate demand and aggregate supply. Aggregate demand is simply the combined expenditures of consumers, businesses, and governments that make up g.n.p., though at first we shall simplify even further by leaving the government out of the picture. Thus, aggregate demand is simply the sum of consumption and investment expenditure on currently produced goods and services.

Aggregate supply is the total amount of goods and services that will be produced (supplied) in response to different levels of aggregate demand. In our private-enterprise economy (leaving government aside for the moment), goods and services are produced only when they can be sold at a profitable price. If there is no market demand, businesses will soon stop producing. Thus, we think of supply as a schedule of different amounts that will be produced in response to different levels of aggregate demand.

Obviously, as we look back on any time period, aggregate demand and the amount produced (supplied) will be the same. What is produced (measured in dollars) is identical with what is spent on it. This is simply g.n.p. looked at from the production and expenditure sides. But whether the two sides are equal at a high or low level of g.n.p.—whether at full employment and prosperity or at unemployment and depression—will depend in this simple model entirely on the level of aggregate demand. The amount produced (aggregate supply) responds solely to aggregate demand.

Now let us spell out the model in a little more detail.

AGGREGATE SUPPLY

What determines the economy's aggregate supply schedule? *The "real" productive capacity of any economic system sets the upper limit to its real g.n.p. at any time.* This productive capacity—the economy's production possibilities curve for total

output from Chapter 2—depends on its underlying real productive resources, its technology, and its economic organization.[1] But an economy need not achieve this full production potential. History shows that nations often fall short of obtaining the maximum production possible from their economies, for example in the Great Depression of the 1930's. This failure reflects a shortage of aggregate demand. There is not enough total spending by consumers and businesses to buy all the goods that could be produced at full employment.

Conversely, aggregate spending may exceed the productive capacity of the economy at existing prices. If that occurs, prices are bid up and there is inflation.

The Short-Run Supply Schedule and Supply Curve

At any given time, the production-possibilities curve for an economy is given. The economy may produce less than the maximum indicated by its production-possibilities frontier, but it cannot produce more. Given this fact, let us make up an aggregate-supply schedule for the economy, assuming that the full-employment production limit is $400 billion. Column 1 in Table 5-1 simply shows different assumed levels of aggregate demand; column 2 shows the amount that will be produced in response to each level of demand. As long as the economy is below its capacity limit, rising demand calls forth more output, dollar for dollar. But after full capacity is reached, more demand cannot increase output further. The result will be inflation, but this doesn't show in Table 5-1, because the aggregate supply schedule there is in real (constant price) terms. Above $400 billion of aggregate demand, total *real* output is unchanged at $400 billion, although money g.n.p. rises with inflation.

It is useful to represent this aggregate supply schedule graphically as an aggregate "supply curve" for the economy. This curve will show how

[1] Over time, some economies have been able to increase their productive capacity rapidly, while others seem to get nowhere. But for the moment we take the nation's production-possibilities curve as given. This is reasonable since we want to begin by analyzing the behavior of the economy at a given point in time.

much will be produced (supplied) in response to different levels of aggregate demand.[2]

In Fig. 5-1, we show on the horizontal axis the amount supplied—that is, real g.n.p. (in initial prices). On the vertical axis we show *aggregate demand—total spending by all those who buy goods and services in the economy in this period.* (We investigate in detail the forces determining aggregate demand in Chapters 6 and 7.) Equal distances show equal amounts on both axes.

At one extreme, if there is no demand, nothing will be produced in our profit-motivated economy. At the other extreme, OQ_3 shows the maximum real output possible for the economy in this period. Output OQ_3 corresponds to $400 billion in Table 5-1. More generally, it corresponds to a point on the nation's production-possibilities frontier, since OQ_3 is the maximum output feasible for the economy this year. No matter how much people spend and try to buy, more than this cannot be produced. Below OQ_3, as people spend more or less, businesses will increase or decrease output in response to this demand.

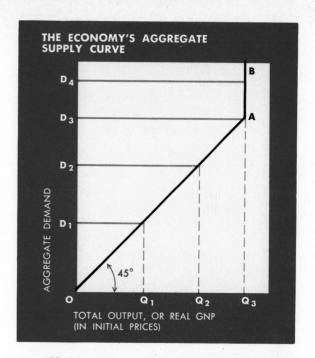

THE ECONOMY'S AGGREGATE SUPPLY CURVE

FIG. 5-1 Curve OA suggests that as aggregate demand rises, output will be increased proportionately without any price increase (inflation) up to full-employment output OQ_3. If demand increases further, however, the result will be purely rising prices since output cannot be expanded further in the short run.

TABLE 5-1	
AGGREGATE DEMAND AND AGGREGATE SUPPLY	
Aggregate Demand	Aggregate Supply (in Real Terms)
$100 billion	$100 billion
200 "	200 "
300 "	300 "
400 "	400 "
500 "	400 "
600 "	400 "

For example, if aggregate demand is zero, output will be zero. If aggregate demand is OD_1, businessmen will produce real g.n.p. OQ_1. At OQ_1, the economy would be operating far inside its production-possibilities frontier. If aggregate de-

[2] We shall see the terms "supply schedule" and supply curve" are used somewhat differently here from Parts Three and Four, where they apply to individual business firms and markets. Here, the supply schedule shows the aggregate amounts that will be produced in response to different levels of *aggregate demand.* Later, supply schedules for individual firms will show the amounts produced in response to different *prices* for the product concerned.

mand rises to OD_2, output will rise to OQ_2. Thus, if we can imagine the output levels called forth by all possible levels of aggregate demand from zero to OD_3, we would have the line OA, rising at a 45-degree angle from the zero point in Fig. 5-1. It rises at a 45-degree angle because for each level of OD, real output on the horizontal axis is an identical amount. *We call this line OA the economy's aggregate supply curve; it shows how much the economy would produce at each different level of aggregate demand.*

But once the economy reaches its full employment g.n.p. (here OQ_3), it cannot increase output further, no matter how high aggregate demand rises. Thus, the aggregate supply curve OA becomes perpendicular at that point; Fig. 5-1 extends it up to become OAB. Further increases in demand, say aggregate demand of OD_4, will simply bid up prices rather than calling forth more output. Intuitively, it is easy to see that if aggregate demand rises into this range, inflation will be the result. Figure 5-1 suggests that the total *money* g.n.p. will now be OD_4, of which OD_3 is real output corresponding to OQ_3, while the rest is simply higher prices. Actually, we shall see later that demand OD_4 might generate a cumulative rise in prices rather than an equilibrium g.n.p. of OD_4, but we postpone this problem temporarily.

It is important to recognize that by the same reasoning as above, we are assuming that if aggregate demand falls, the results are just the reverse of those that occur when demand rises. Given the aggregate supply curve OAB, when aggregate demand falls from OD_4 to OD_3 the result is purely lower prices. But when demand falls from OD_3 to OD_2 or to OD_1, the result is purely reduced real g.n.p., not falling prices. *That is, we assume temporarily that below full-employment output, rising or falling aggregate demand will alter only real g.n.p., while after full-employment has been reached changes in demand will affect only the price level.* We shall see later that this is not strictly true, but it is a useful temporary assumption.

Thus, at any given time, in this simplest model the level of aggregate demand determines the aggregate output of this economy. Given supply curve OAB, if demand is less than OD_3, real g.n.p. is less than potential full-employment g.n.p., and productive resources are wasted. If aggregate demand is more than OD_3, there will be full employment but there will be inflation in addition. Only if aggregate demand is just OD_3 will the economy operate precisely at full employment without inflation.

Aggregate demand and aggregate supply are key concepts to remember through all of economics. Much of the next eight chapters center around the determinants of these big, key variables. Changes in their relationship to each other provide the framework for analyzing booms and depressions, inflation and unemployment, economic growth and stagnation. Remember them, and the simple little model we have just developed. For it underlies all the more complex, detailed analysis that follows.

AGGREGATE DEMAND, UNEMPLOYMENT AND INFLATION

Our model is of course a highly oversimplified representation of the real world. Let us now make it a little more complex, to show how

to analyze more fully when rising demand will call forth additional output, when inflation, and when a mixture of both.

In the real world, it is not true that rising aggregate demand will always call forth solely dollar for dollar increases in real g.n.p. up to full employment, and pure inflation thereafter. Actually, we would expect some prices to begin to rise before full employment is reached, because increases in demand might cause production bottlenecks and shortages in some sectors of the economy before full employment occurred in others. Demand would normally rise faster for some products than for others.

To show this situation, Fig. 5-2 reproduces the aggregate supply curve from Fig. 5-1, as solid line OAB. But it adds a dashed segment which rounds off the corner where solid OAB has a sharp kink at A. *If this dashed segment is correct, it shows that prices will begin to rise before we reach full employment. Put otherwise, it shows that we can reach full employment output OQ_3 only with*

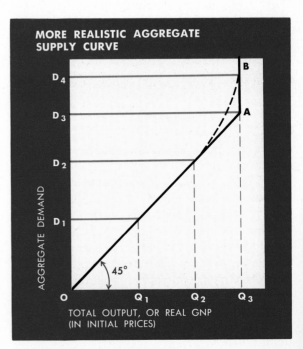

MORE REALISTIC AGGREGATE SUPPLY CURVE

FIG. 5-2 As the dashed section of OB shows, when an economy approaches full employment prices ordinarily begin to rise before full capacity output is reached. Here full-employment output OQ_3 can be achieved only with aggregate demand OD_4, which would imply substantial inflation.

aggregate demand OD₄ and the considerable inflation that implies.

Try using Fig. 5-2 to predict the consequences of different levels of demand. If demand rises from OD_1 to OD_2 the result is still purely rising output and employment as before; note that real g.n.p. of OQ_1 implies massive unemployment with the economy operating at less than half its capacity. But suppose demand moves on up to OD_3. Now, with the new dashed supply curve, some of the growth in aggregate demand will still induce more output but some will go into higher prices. To push the economy all the way to its full-employment output of OQ_3, we must now have aggregate demand of OD_4, and with it a lot of inflation. Demand OD_3 won't do the job any more.

This situation can pose a difficult dilemma for economic policy-makers. As we approach OQ_3, is it desirable to expand aggregate demand further in order to reduce unemployment to a bare minimum, even though this brings on some inflation? Or is it better to keep aggregate demand. at a lower level, accepting some unemployment but also avoiding inflation? This is a problem which will be very much in the picture when we come to stabilization policy problems in Chapters 10–14.

A second modification of our Fig. 5-1 model is in order if we want to use it in analyzing the impact of rising demand on unemployment and prices. In the real world, full-employment g.n.p. is never the precise amount implied by the vertical section of the aggregate supply curve in Figs. 5-1 and 5-2. As wages and prices rise, housewives, students, and older people enter the labor force. Workers put in longer hours. Industrial engineers find ways of increasing output per man-hour. Production managers push plants beyond their quoted capacities for months, even years. With enough pressure, there are many ways of getting a little more output. As demand rises, the full-employment ceiling on output is a mushy one, rather than a precise production possibilities frontier. To reflect this accurately, the vertical segment of OAB should bend over a little to the right. Eventually it must become vertical for any given time period, but the full-employment ceiling is less definite than it appears at first glance.

GROWTH IN PRODUCTIVE CAPACITY

The aggregate supply curves in Figs. 5-1 and 5-2 are for a given time period—say a year. They are what economists often call short-run supply curves. Over longer periods, of course, the productive capacity of an economy can grow—for example, through investment in new factories, increases in the labor force, and technological progress. In that event, full-employment output each year is larger than the year before—the production possibilities frontier moves out. It is important to note that if productive capacity grows this way, what is full-employment aggregate demand for one year will be inadequate to call forth full-employment output the next year.

We can show this readily in Fig. 5-3. It reproduces supply curve OAB from Fig. 5-1, and adds on extended segments ACC and ADD to

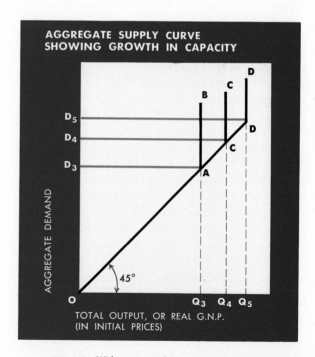

FIG. 5-3 With more productive resources and improved technology, an economy's productive capacity increases. With increased capacity, more aggregate demand is required to call forth full-employment output. In years two and three, here full-employment capacity has risen to OQ_4 and OQ_5, respectively.

show how potential real g.n.p. moves out year after year with new investment, more labor, and advancing technology. By the same token Fig. 5-3 shows that larger aggregate demand will be needed each year to call forth full capacity g.n.p.

Thus, the aggregate supply curve for year 2 is OCC. Potential real g.n.p. has moved out to OQ_4, and demand OD_4 is required to assure full-employment. In year 3 the aggregate supply curve becomes ODD. Potential real g.n.p. has now moved out to OQ_5, and the necessary aggregate demand up to OD_5.

Chapters 6 to 14 are primarily concerned with the short-run behavior of the economy. They generally take the productive capacity of the economy as substantially fixed, although you can see that this short-run fixed supply curve model is not quite accurate. Then, in Chapters 15 through 18 we will turn specifically to the question of long-term economic growth, and the expansion of capacity will be the center of attention. It is important both to utilize our existing capacity fully in the short run and to expand this productive capacity over the long run.

REVIEW

Concepts To Remember

This chapter introduces two basic concepts that will be used over and over. Be sure you understand *aggregate demand* and *aggregate supply.*

For Analysis and Discussion

1. Explain the relationship between an economy's production-possibilities curve and its aggregate supply curve.
2. Does the aggregate supply curve in Fig. 5-1 or that in Fig. 5-2 make it easier for the economy to achieve full employment without inflation? Explain.
3. In a private-enterprise, profit-motivated economy, why is it reasonable to say that aggregate production will depend on the level of aggregate demand?
4. After an economy reaches full employment, raising aggregate expenditure must always cause inflation. (True or false? Does the time period involved influence your answer?)

SIX

THE MODERN THEORY OF INCOME, EMPLOYMENT, AND PRICES[1]

Simple Static G.N.P. Model.

Changing Investment—the Multiplier.

Induced Investment and Dynamic Processes.

Government Taxes and Expenditures (Fiscal Policy).

The Multiplier in the Real World.

Appendix: Econometric Models.

In the short run, whether we have depression, prosperity or inflation depends largely on the level of aggregate demand. What determines the level of aggregate demand, is thus an extremely important question. In Chapter 5 we simply assumed different levels of aggregate demand. Now we must add an explanation of demand to combine with the aggregate supply curve developed there.

To answer this question, most modern economists use an "income-expenditures" model, which stresses that one big part of aggregate demand—what people spend on consumption—depends primarily on the incomes they receive. What businesses and governments spend is determined mainly by other forces. This analysis focuses attention on the three big components of gross national product from Chapter 4—on private consumption spending, private investment spending, and government spending, on their determinants, and on their interrelationships. (We shall continue temporarily to ignore international considerations, postponing them to Part Six.) [2]

[1] Section I of the Mathematical Appendix, at the end of this text, presents the central argument of this chapter in mathematical terms. Students who know calculus and find mathematical formulations helpful may find the Appendix a useful aid, but it is recommended for use only *after* the following text sections have been read.

[2] This general approach was first popularized by a noted economist, John Maynard Keynes, during the depression of the 1930's. Keynes achieved wide fame because he was one of the earliest outspoken advocates of fighting depressions with deficit spending. Whatever you think about that issue—it's a central issue in Chapter 13—you should understand that the present chapter deals only with neutral analytic tools that can help you understand the determinants of aggregate demand; but they don't tell you what we should do about the problem of depressions and inflations.

SIMPLE STATIC G.N.P. MODEL

To simplify, first assume temporarily that there is no government spending or taxation. Thus, aggregate demand is the sum of consumption (C) plus private investment spending (I). Since aggregate demand is also equal to gross national product, we can also say that g.n.p. equals $C + I$. (Economists typically use Y to represent national income or g.n.p., and so will we.)

Second, *assume (what many economists consider a reasonable first approximation to reality) that consumption spending depends entirely on the incomes that people receive, and not on any other factor. Moreover, the portion of their income households don't spend on consumption, they save. Since saving is simply that amount of income received which is not spent on consumption, savings also depend on the amount of income people receive.*

Third, assume temporarily that business investment spending is *autonomously* determined. That is, businessmen decide how much to invest on the basis of considerations other than consumer spending and saving. What this means as a practical matter is that we simply take business investment spending as given for any time period at this stage of the analysis.

Thus, given these assumptions, in this simple income-expenditures model aggregate demand in each year will be the sum of two parts: business investment spending (a given amount determined autonomously), and consumption spending (which is dependent on the incomes that households receive). But income, which determines consumption, is in turn partially made up of consumption spending. Thus it should be clear that g.n.p., consumption, and investment are all interacting in what we may call a simultaneously determined system. Given these assumptions, we can readily show how consumption and investment spending interact to produce an equilibrium level of aggregate demand (and hence g.n.p.) each year. The reasoning can be presented verbally, graphically, or algebraically. It's done all three ways below, because different people find different approaches most helpful. Note therefore that the following sections repeat the *same* analysis in these different forms.

Algebraic Presentation

We have defined aggregate demand as being equal to g.n.p., which is equal to consumption plus investment spending. Let Y stand for aggregate demand and g.n.p. Then:

$$Y = C + I$$

Now assume that consumption spending is always just .75 of income (that is, people spend three-fourths of their incomes on consumption and save one-fourth), so that:

$$C = .75 \cdot Y$$

Saving (S) is the portion of their income that households don't spend on consumption. Thus, $S = .25Y$. Remember that investment (I) is *autonomous*; it is independently determined. That is, business investment spending depends on expected profits, on new inventions, or some other forces, *but not on consumption spending or saving.* Suppose, now, that business investment spending is 100 this year, so:

$$I = 100$$

Now, substitute the values for C and I in our original equation, $Y = C + I$. We get:

$$Y = .75 \cdot Y + 100$$

Using the rules of elementary algebra, move the .75Y to the left side of the equation. This changes the sign from plus to minus, and we have:

$$Y - .75Y = 100, \text{ or}$$
$$.25Y = 100, \text{ or}$$
$$Y = \frac{100}{.25}, \text{ and}$$
$$Y = 400$$

Equilibrium aggregate demand, or g.n.p., will be 400 if investment is 100 and people spend three-fourths of all the income they receive on consumption.

This is the "equilibrium" level of g.n.p., given our assumptions. That is, it is the level to which aggregate demand and g.n.p. will move, and the level at which they will stay once they get there, unless something new comes along to change them. It is this equilibrium level of g.n.p. (aggregate demand) we are trying to explain in this chapter.

Verbal Presentation

Put the reasoning in words. Given our assumptions about consumption and investment decisions, g.n.p. couldn't stay lower than 400. To see why not, suppose g.n.p. were 300. Then people would be spending 225 on consumption (.75 of 300) and saving 75 (.25 of 300). But business investment spending of 100 added to consumption spending of 225 would give a g.n.p. of 325. This g.n.p. is inconsistent with our assumption of a g.n.p. of 300; 300 could not be an equilibrium level given our assumptions. Now try g.n.p. at 325; it is also too low to be consistent with our assumptions, by the the same reasoning. So is any other level below 400. At any g.n.p. below 400, the savings being withdrawn from current income would be less than the 100 of investment spending being spent into g.n.p., and thus larger investment spending would push g.n.p. up toward 400. This statement puts the reasoning in terms of the lower loop of Fig. 4-2, and lets you see the economic reasoning rather than just stating the logical requirements for an equilibrium g.n.p.

Conversely, try any level of g.n.p. higher than 400—say, 500. Then consumption plus investment spending would not be enough to be consistent with that assumed level. Consumption would be 375 (.75 of 500) and investment 100, totaling only 475. At a 500 level of g.n.p., people would want to save 125, more than is being invested. Hence g.n.p. would fall, toward 400. Only at 400 will the sum of investment (100) plus consumption (three fourths of g.n.p.) just equal the current g.n.p. of 400, so g.n.p. will remain unchanged. *To put it another way, equilibrium is reached only when the amount being withdrawn from the income stream through saving each period just offsets the amount being inserted through investment.*

We can look at this adjustment mechanism another (equivalent) way. Assume again that g.n.p. is 500. This means that businesses are producing 500. But on the demand side buyers would purchase only 475, i.e., 375 of consumption goods

(three-fourths of 500) plus 100 of investment goods. Unsold inventories would pile up, and businesses would reduce production (g.n.p.). And so it would be for any other g.n.p. above 400. Conversely, if we assume a g.n.p. less than 400, then demand $(C + I)$ would be larger than production. For example, if g.n.p. (production) were 300, demand would be 325—100 of investment plus the 225 people would consume if their incomes were 300. Inventories would be used up and businesses would increase production (g.n.p.) to meet the larger demand. G.n.p. would thus rise toward 400.

Work out as many examples as you like and you'll always get one and only one equilibrium value of aggregate demand and g.n.p. Equilibrium requires that the public decide to save just the amount businesses have decided to invest. Of course, the particular numbers in our example are arbitrary. If business investment is higher, say 150, the equilibrium g.n.p. is higher. If consumers spend 80 per cent of their income on consumption, equilibrium g.n.p. will be higher. Try it and see. But the reasoning—the underlying economic adjustment process—is unchanged.

Graphic Presentation

The same reasoning can be presented in graphical terms. Note that this presentation adds nothing to the reasoning above. It's just another way of presenting the same analysis. But in doing so, let us change the numbers and let us make the model more realistic by introducing a more realistic "consumption function," which is what economists call the relation between people's income and their consumption spending. The only difference from the example above is a new assumption, that people consume a lower percentage of their incomes at high than at low incomes, instead of always just three-fourths. This shift will, of course, change the equilibrium level of g.n.p. Again, consumption and saving depend entirely on g.n.p. and investment is fixed at 100.

The Consumption and Saving Schedules

Figure 6-1 shows these new consumption and saving functions. On the left-hand chart, line CC plots consumption spending against g.n.p.

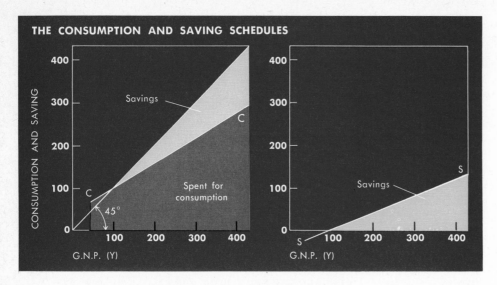

THE CONSUMPTION AND SAVING SCHEDULES

CONSUMPTION AND SAVING

Savings

C

Spent for consumption

45°

C

G.N.P. (Y)

Savings

S

S

G.N.P. (Y)

FIG. 6-1 The left-hand portion of this figure shows that people will spend a smaller proportion of their income on consumption as income rises, and save a larger proportion. The right-hand portion shows the same saving behavior by itself.

at different levels of g.n.p. In addition, the chart has a 45° line, every point on which is equidistant from the two axes. Thus, at any point on it, total consumption would just equal total g.n.p. If line CC coincided with the 45° line, there would be no saving. Whenever the consumption curve (CC) is below the 45° line, part of g.n.p. is being saved. For example, at a g.n.p. of 200, the economy would spend 160 on consumption and save 40. However, if g.n.p. were as low as 50, people would spend more than their full incomes on consumption; they would "dissave" by borrowing or drawing on past savings.[3]

The right-hand part of Fig. 6-1 shows the corresponding saving schedule (SS). This is drawn simply by taking the amount saved at each level of g.n.p. from the left-hand portion. Saving will be negative at low income levels when CC

[3] For readers who know mathematics, the equation of this consumption function is: $C = a + b(Y)$, where a and b are constants with $a = 40$ and $b = .6$. Therefore, $C = 40 + .6Y$. That is, consumption is always 40 plus .6 of the amount of income received. The basic $Y = C + I$ equation can be solved just as before by making the new substitution for C. Thus:

$$Y = (40 + .6Y) + 100, \text{ or}$$
$$Y - .6Y = 40 + 100$$
$$.4Y = 140, \text{ so}$$
$$Y = 350$$

The Mathematical Appendix at the end of the book and the appendix to this chapter on "Econometric Models" show more fully how simple mathematical systems can be used to determine equilibrium g.n.p. levels under more complicated conditions.

exceeds total g.n.p., and will be positive at higher income levels. The SS curve will, of course, cross the zero line at the same income level as the CC curve cuts the 45° line, where all g.n.p. is spent on consumption—at 100 in this case.

Now add investment. We continue to assume that it is 100—determined "autonomously" by forces independent of the level of consumption and income. On Fig. 6-2 we plot investment in line II. This line is horizontal because investment is 100 whatever the level of g.n.p. II intersects the SS curve at a g.n.p. of 350, and this is the equilibrium level. That is, given our assumptions on consumption and investment behavior, aggregate demand and g.n.p. will move to 350 if it is at any

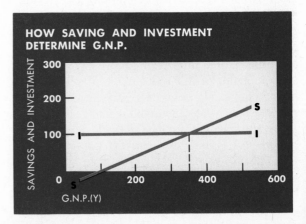

HOW SAVING AND INVESTMENT DETERMINE G.N.P.

SAVINGS AND INVESTMENT

S

I

I

S

G.N.P.(Y)

FIG. 6-2 Equilibrium g.n.p. is established where the public wishes to save just enough to match the amount being invested.

other level. No other g.n.p. can persist, under our assumptions. (Note that equilibrium g.n.p. here is different from the preceding example, because we have assumed a different consumption function. People no longer spend just 75 per cent of their incomes on consumption.)

Again, why is 350 the equilibrium level? The reasoning is the same as before: because at this level of g.n.p. the amount businessmen invest is exactly offset by the amount people want to save. Thus, the circular flow of income will be complete and stable. Consumers will receive 350 each year, and (reading from the left-hand portion of Fig. 6-2) they will spend 250 on consumption and save 100. *Each year*, businesses will invest 100, just equal to the amount people save; and so on for each succeeding time period. Equilibrium will be achieved only at the income level where consumers want to save just enough to match business investment spending.

Now a second way *of showing the same results* graphically. Figure 6-3 shows the consumption and investment functions on the same graph.

It adds to consumption spending (the *CC* curve of Fig. 6-1) 100 of investment spending at each income level each year. Thus, $C + I$ is the amount that households and businesses will spend on consumption plus investment at each level of g.n.p. Now, since consumption and investment spending are on the vertical axis, and total g.n.p. is on the horizontal axis, the 45° line shows all the points where aggregate demand ($C + I$) will just equal total production (g.n.p.).

In Fig. 6-3 aggregate demand ($C + I$) just equals g.n.p. (cuts the 45° line) at 350. At 350 and only at 350 does the sum of consumption and investment spending just equal g.n.p. (production).

Test the result. As before, assume any g.n.p. lower than 350 (say 300), and you will see that it can't last. At a g.n.p. of 300, consumption plus investment spending, shown by $C + I$, would be above the 45° line. Thus, business sales would exceed production, and businesses would increase production. G.n.p. would rise toward 350. The opposite is true if we assume g.n.p. is anything higher than 350, say 400. At a g.n.p. of 400, $C + I$ would be less than 400; people would not buy all the goods being produced; unsold inventories would pile up; and g.n.p. would fall toward 350.

A crucial reminder: *All the above analysis assumes that consumption and saving are functions solely of income received. If consumption spending changes for any other reason, the equilibrium level of income will be changed.* In the model, such a change would be shown as a shift in the consumption function (on the chart, a shift of the *CC* line to the right or left).

Equilibrium Not Necessarily Full Employment

It is important to recognize that an equilibrium g.n.p. does not necessarily imply that there is full employment. Look back at the aggregate supply curve in Fig. 5-1. If our equilibrium g.n.p. level is less than OD_3 and OQ_3, there will be unemployment and the economy will be operating inside its production possibilities frontier. If equilibrium g.n.p. is above OD_3, the result will be inflation. "Equilibrium" g.n.p. as we have defined it is thus a neutral analytical concept. It does not imply anything, either good or bad, about

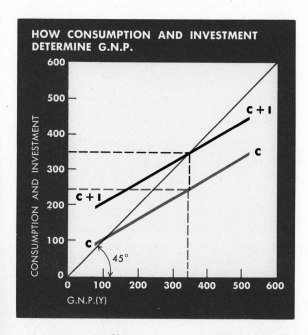

FIG. 6-3 Equilibrium g.n.p. is established where the sum of consumption- and investment-spending (on the vertical axis) just equals g.n.p. (on the horizontal axis). This gives the same equilibrium level as Fig. 6-2.

the level of employment or how well the economic system is performing.

CHANGING INVESTMENT— THE MULTIPLIER

Suppose now that businessmen decide to increase their spending on investment, perhaps because of a new invention. This decision will raise the *II* curve in Fig. 6-2 and the *C + I* curve in Fig. 6-3. The result, common sense tells you, will be a higher equilibrium level of g.n.p. after the increase in investment. Conversely, a decrease in investment spending will lead to a lower equilibrium level.

These results are obvious enough, but one additional fact may not be: *Each dollar of increase in autonomous investment will increase aggregate demand and g.n.p. by a larger, or multiplied, amount.* This is because as each new dollar of investment is spent, it becomes income to a consumer who saves part but respends the rest on consumption. This respending constitutes income to someone else, who in turn saves part but respends the rest. And so on. The number of times the final increase in income (g.n.p.) exceeds the new investment is called the "multiplier." For example, if one additional dollar of investment spending generates four additional dollars of g.n.p., the multiplier is four.

Marginal Propensity
To Consume

To explore this process more fully, we now need to be more precise about the consumption function, and to distinguish between the "average propensity to consume" and the "marginal propensity to consume." Suppose that total income (g.n.p.) is 100 and people are spending 75 on consumption and saving 25 each period. Then the *average* propensity to consume is .75; people are spending .75 of their incomes on consumption. However, it does not necessarily follow that if they receive additional income they would maintain this same consumption-income ratio. Suppose their incomes now rise to 110 but they only spend .5 of this additional 10 of income. Then the *marginal* propensity to consume is .5. The

marginal propensity to consume is simply the proportion of additional, or marginal, income which is spent on consumption. It is the marginal propensity on which we need to focus our attention when we are analyzing *changes* in the level of g.n.p., since it is the marginal propensity to consume that tells us what percentage of additional income people spend on consumption.

The Multiplier

Begin with an equilibrium g.n.p. level of 350 and assume that the *marginal* propensity to consume is .75. Suppose now that businessmen decide to increase their investment spending by 10. When the 10 is spent on new investment (say, plant construction), it becomes income to the recipients, who then spend 7.5 on consumption and save 2.5. The 7.5 of consumption spending becomes income to someone else who in turn respends 75 per cent (5.6) on consumption and saves 25 per cent (1.9). The 5.6 becomes income to someone else, and so the process goes. Remember that savings are withdrawn from the income stream and are *not* respent in this model; nor do they stimulate more business investment spending. We get a table like the following.[4]

	New Income	New Consumption	New Saving
Initiating New Investment	10	7.5	2.5
On Round 2	7.5	5.6	1.9
On Round 3	5.6	4.2	1.4
On Round 4	4.2	3.2	1.0
	.	.	.
	.	.	.
	40	30	10

The table shows only the first four rounds, but it gives the general picture. The 10 of new investment generates a chain of respending on consumption—called the "multiplier" effect—that leads to new income of much more than 10. Each round makes a smaller net addition to income than its predecessor, because part of the new in-

---

[4] Assume for this example that the businesses get the funds for the extra 10 of investment by borrowing newly created funds from the banks, rather than by saving out of their own current incomes.

come is drained off into saving by each recipient, and by assumption these savings are *not* respent nor do they stimulate additional business investment. If you carry the arithmetic to its conclusion, you will find that the total new g.n.p. generated is 40 (including the 10 of new investment). Of this total, 30 is spent on consumption and 10 is saved, in accordance with our marginal propensity to consume of .75. The new equilibrium g.n.p. is 40 higher, total consumption 30 higher, and total savings and investment each 10 higher than before. The expansion process has continued until the amount people want to save of their higher income just matches the 10 of new investment. Adding these increments to the original equilibrium values, we get a new equilibrium total g.n.p. level of 390. The multiplier is four, since income has risen by 40 in response to 10 of new business investment.

This result is shown graphically in Fig. 6-4. The CC and C + I curves before the increase in investment are shown as solid lines, reproduced directly from Fig. 6-3. Now we add 10 more of investment at each level of income. In other words $C' + I'$ (the black line) now represents

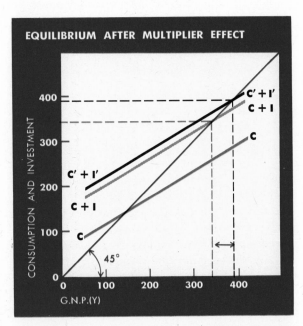

EQUILIBRIUM AFTER MULTIPLIER EFFECT

FIG. 6-4 An additional 10 of investment raises the C + I curve to C' + I', and brings the new equilibrium level of g.n.p. of 390, up 40 from the previous equilibrium. The investment multiplier is 4.

consumption plus 110, instead of plus 100, at each level of realized g.n.p. The CC line is unchanged because it was originally drawn to show what households would spend on consumption at each level of g.n.p. But the new equilibrium level of g.n.p. is 390, up 40. This is where the new $C' + I'$ curve cuts the 45° line, even though investment has increased only 10.

If this looks like graphical trickery, consider the economic common sense of this multiplier effect of new investment on consumption and g.n.p. Under what conditions is the effect powerful, and when is it weak? Just how does it work? There are four important points:

1. The multiplier effect hinges on the fact that people respend on consumption part of each increment of income they receive. If at any point they save all their new income, the respending spiral stops short.

2. The larger the proportion of its additional income that the public respends each round, the larger will be the multiplier effect. Conversely, the larger the proportion saved each round, the smaller will be the multiplier effect.

3. The size of the multiplier is given precisely by the formula:

$$M = \frac{1}{1 - \text{Marginal propensity to consume}}$$

Thus, if the marginal propensity to consume is .75, the multiplier will be

$$M = \frac{1}{1 - .75} = \frac{1}{.25} = 4.$$

Hence, an increase of $1 in investment would mean an increase of $4 in g.n.p. If the economy's marginal propensity to consume out of g.n.p. were .90, the multiplier would be 10. (Work out the .90 case in the equation, and check yourself by working out a table like the one in the preceding section. You will find that the formula merely summarizes the arithmetic.) An easy way to look at it is this: The multiplier is the reciprocal of the marginal propensity to save, *still using our simple assumptions.* Thus, if consumers save one-fourth of their new income, the multiplier is 4. If one-tenth, the multiplier is 10. And so on.

4. Last, review again the economic reason-

ing behind this formula. For example, with a marginal propensity to consume of .75, why is the new *equilibrium* level of g.n.p. higher by just four times the level of additional investment spending? Because at any assumed g.n.p. level below equilibrium, people would want to save less than the new level of investment, and the responding rounds would continue to raise g.n.p. *Equilibrium is achieved only when the public's income is such that it wants to save just enough to offset the amount being invested. Only if these two just match will the circular flow of income be continuous and stable.*

This is the basic multiplier process. But a warning is needed. In the real world, with government taxes and spending and with business as well as consumer saving, the picture becomes more complex. To calculate real-world multipliers, wait for the section, "The Multiplier in the Real World," a few pages later on.

The Paradox of Thrift

This reasoning suggests a curious paradox. If consumers decide to save a larger percentage of their incomes, this increased propensity to save may in fact lead to a lower multiplier, lower consumption, a lower g.n.p., a decrease in induced investment, and a *lower* level of aggregate saving in the new (temporary or permanent) equilibrium. Here is an example of the fallacy of composition. More saving may be a very good thing for the individual household, but a simultaneous attempt by many households to save more out of their incomes *may* throw the economy into a recession which makes us all worse off. This is the paradox of thrift.

But note that an increase in the economy's propensity to save *need* not throw us into a recession. If the increased thriftiness comes in a period of inflation, it can have the happy result of pulling aggregate demand down toward maximum potential real g.n.p. and reducing inflationary pressure. And even in noninflationary periods, the drop in consumption *may* be offset by increased private investment or government spending—which leads us on to the next section. But the paradox of thrift may pose a real problem when the economy is on the verge of unemployment or in a recession.

INDUCED INVESTMENT AND DYNAMIC PROCESSES

Thus far we have assumed that investment decisions are autonomous—that is, determined independently of the level of consumption. But actually, the level of sales and the resulting business profits are surely an important determinant of business investment plans. If we say that business investment is dependent on consumer spending in the proceding period, we get what economists call "dynamic" analysis. In that case, the new equilibrium level in Fig. 6-4 would not be a lasting equilibrium, since the higher consumer spending would in turn induce more business investment. The new induced investment in turn would lead to a further multiplier effect on consumption and g.n.p. Intuitively, you might expect such a process to spiral upward indefinitely—and under some conditions it would. But under others, we can explain why the spiral would die out, or even reverse itself and start downward.

This study of dynamic processes is the essence of the study of booms and depressions (business cycles). But it is better to postpone such dynamic analysis until we have equilibrium analysis clearly in hand. We shall return to dynamic processes in detail in Chapter 9.

GOVERNMENT TAXES AND EXPENDITURES (FISCAL POLICY)

Now let us put government taxes and spending into our model, to bring it into closer correspondence with the real world. Government taxes take away part of the spendable income of households and businesses, and governments spend on current output. Thus, we need to add government on both the spending and saving sides of the picture.

Up to this point we have said that the equilibrium condition is:

$$GNP = C + I = C + S$$

If consumer plans to save differ from business plans to invest in the private economy, the level of g.n.p. will move up or down until people want to save just enough to offset business investment. Now add government to this equation.

We can treat government tax collections as being similar to private savings; they constitute a leakage out of the respending stream. Similarly, we can treat government spending on goods and services as being similar to private• investment spending; government spending constitutes effective demand for goods and services. At least to a first approximation, government spending may be considered as autonomous spending; that is, it can be viewed as determined by forces other than the current level of g.n.p.

We now have a slightly more complex model in which both private investment and government spending are autonomous expenditures while consumption spending is an induced expenditure; and on the other side both private savings and government tax receipts are withdrawals from the income stream. Thus the new equilibrium condition is:

$$C + I + GE = C + S + GR$$

where GE is government expenditure and GR is government tax receipts. That is, if the sum of private investment plus government expenditures (autonomous spending) exceeds the "leakages" from the spending stream through private savings and tax receipts, g.n.p. will rise. Conversely, g.n.p. will fall if investment plus government spending is less than the leakages through saving and tax receipts.

This reasoning can also be readily presented in graphic form. Look back at Fig. 6-3. To get the new $(C + I + GE)$ aggregate demand curve, merely reduce the $(C + I)$ curve there by the amount taxes reduce private spending, and add government spending to the new $(C + I)$ curve so obtained. This new $(C + I + GE)$ curve may fall directly on the previous $(C + I)$ curve, or above or below it, depending on whether government spending is more or less than the amount by which taxes reduce private spending.[5] Where

[5] Actually, the problem is a little more complicated. Since in the real world, consumption is a function, as we shall see, of disposable personal income rather than of g.n.p., a change in taxes may affect the ratio of consumption to g.n.p. But this complication may be temporarily postponed.

the new total $(C + I + GE)$ curve cuts the 45° line will be the equilibrium level of g.n.p., for exactly the same reasons as explained the previous equilibrium level for an entirely private economy. The equilibrium condition is: *Gross national product must be such that private savings plus government tax collections just match autonomous expenditure (private investment plus government spending).*

Obviously, this statement suggests that higher government spending without offsetting tax increases may be used to raise aggregate demand and real g.n.p., because of the help given by the multiplier effect. Look ahead to Fig. 13-1. There we have added 10 of government spending from new money, *which therefore does not reduce private spending through tax collections.* With a marginal propensity to consume of .75, the multiplier is 4, and total income is increased by 40, to a new equilibrium level of 390. Increasing government spending by 10 has raised g.n.p. by 40, just as 10 of increased private investment would do. To repeat, the equilibrium condition with the government in the picture is $C + I + GE = C + S + GR$. Government taxes have the same leakage effect as private saving, and government spending has the same effect as private investment. If government spending and private investment continue at their new levels, g.n.p. will stay at 390. If government spending drops back to its original level, equilibrium g.n.p. will fall back to 350.

Surpluses and Deficits—
Public and Private

There is no reason, of course, why government taxes and spending must exactly balance in each time period. Neither, once we introduce government into our model, is there any reason why private saving and private investment must exactly balance in each time period. Thus, the private part of the economy may be investing more than it saves at equilibrium g.n.p., while the government is collecting more taxes than it spends. In that case the private economy would be running a "deficit" and the government a "surplus." Conversely, the private economy might be running a surplus by saving more than it invests while the government is running a deficit by spending more than it collects in taxes. Governments were spending more than they collected in taxes while the private sector was saving more than it invested.

It should be clear, then, that it is the *combined* $(I + GE)$ which is the base for our multiplier effect, once we put the government in. This fact provides the base for modern "fiscal policy." As Fig. 13-1 suggests, if government spending rises without an offsetting reduction in private investment spending, the resultant multiplier effect will raise g.n.p. by more than the amount of the government spending. More on this in Chapter 13.

THE MULTIPLIER IN THE REAL WORLD

Once we introduce government spending as a base for multiplier effects, we must also introduce government taxes as a leakage from the income stream comparable to private saving, as was pointed out above. And there is another leakage from the spending stream we have also thus far neglected—the fact that business firms, as well as households, may save. If we want to estimate the multiplier effect of any increment of private

or government spending in the real world, therefore, we must, in effect, calculate the marginal propensity to consume *out of total g.n.p.* This ratio will always be lower than households' marginal propensity to consume out of disposable personal income. This is because consumption spending is being compared with disposable personal income in the latter case, while in the former it is being compared with total g.n.p. (i.e., disposable personal income plus taxes plus depreciation allowances).

For example, if consumption spending is $400 billion, disposable personal income is $450 billion, and g.n.p. is $600 billion, then the average propensity to consume out of disposable income is approximately .9, but only .67 out of g.n.p. The relevant multiplier for estimating the impact of new investment on g.n.p. *if* we assume the marginal propensity is the same as the average, would be 3. To use a multiplier of 10 (based on households' .9 propensity to consume out of disposable personal income) would be wrong, because it would neglect all the leakages from the circular spending flow except household saving. Specifically, it would neglect business savings and all government tax collections.

REVIEW

Concepts To Remember

This is a major chapter. Its analytical concepts and models are used through all the rest of the book. Be sure you understand the basic reasoning in the chapter, and the following new concepts:

income-expenditure approach	equilibrium g.n.p.
consumption function	underemployment equilibrium
average propensity to consume	the multiplier
marginal propensity to consume	autonomous investment
saving function	induced investment
average and marginal propensities to save	paradox of thrift

For Analysis and Discussion

1. Assume that gross national product is $600 billion. Investment is $100 billion. Consumption expenditures are $500 billion. Assume no government participation in the income stream:
   a. If investment rises to $125 billion, with the marginal propensity to consume = .8, what will be the new equilibrium level of gross national product?
   b. Explain why this will be an equilibrium level—i.e., the level that will be established and maintained unless other unspecified factors intervene.

2. Would you expect that decisions to save for the year ahead in the economy would ordinarily be about the same as decisions to invest? Why or why not?

3. Changes in investment cause changes in saving for the economy as a whole, rather than vice versa. (True or false? Why?)

4. What is the "paradox of thrift"? Explain why its strange result occurs.

5. Suppose that in a hypothetical economy g.n.p. is running at an annual rate of $600 billion. Other major items in the national income accounts are as follows:

Consumption	$400	billion
Investment	70	"
Savings	100	"
Government expenditures	130	"
Taxes	100	"

The marginal propensity to consume is three-fourths. (For purposes of this problem, take the three-fourths marginal propensity to consume against income before taxes.)

Suppose that the government now balances its budget through a reduction in government expenditures while maintaining taxes at the level of $100 billion. What will be the effect on the levels of income, consumption, and savings? Explain.

6. Assume the following conditions in an economy that includes a government sector.

Government spending	$44	billion
Government tax receipts (obtained from a tax which is independent of the level of g.n.p.)	44	"
Consumption expenditure = $30 billion plus 8/9 of the g.n.p. remaining after payment of taxes		
Investment expenditure	24	"
G.n.p. = C + I + G		

a. Calculate the equilibrium levels of g.n.p., consumption, and savings.

b. Investment increases to an annual rate of $29 billion and remains constant at that level. Calculate the new equilibrium levels of g.n.p., consumption, and savings.

c. Under the conditions first described, government spending increases to an annual rate of $80 billion and annual tax receipts are raised to $80 billion. Both figures then remain constant. Calculate new equilibrium levels of g.n.p., consumption, and savings.

7. Explain why if the private sector runs a "deficit" (i.e., invests more than it saves) the public sector must run an exactly offsetting "surplus" (i.e., collect more in taxes than it spends).

Appendix

ECONOMETRIC MODELS

Modern economics, like other sciences, has come increasingly to use precisely stated analytical models which are often most conveniently put in mathematical form. Modern economics also has become increasingly empirical—that is, concerned with measuring its variables in the real world, as distinguished from merely theorizing about them. Thus, "econometrics" has become an increasingly important branch of economics.

Econometrics deals with the science of economic measurement, as is obvious from its components, "econo" and "metrics." Broadly, econometrics involves setting up precise models of economic phenomena in mathematical form; then measuring in the real world the variables and relationships included in the model; and then solving the model to see how closely it conforms to or can predict actual economic behavior.

Simple Income-Determination Models.[6]   The simple model back on page 62 provides an example. We specify a model:

$$Y = C + I, \text{ and}$$
$$C = f(Y), \text{ where } f \text{ stands for "function."}$$

So this equation says that C is a function of (or depends on) Y. The model is obviously too simple to represent the real world precisely, but assume for the moment that it does. Next we have to measure in the real world the crucial variables and relationships specified by the model. Suppose we find that I is always 100 and is independent of Y and C; and estimate that C is always just .75 of Y. Then we can insert these values in $Y = C + I$, as on page 62, and get our final equation: $400 = 300 + 100$.

But note that our model, if it is a true model of the real world, can tell us other things. If I rises to 125, we can predict that, other things remaining unchanged, g.n.p. will rise to 500; this follows directly by inserting the new value for I in the model—since C is always .75 of Y, I must always be .25 of Y. So an econometric model is in effect a forecasting device, which says that *if* we know the values of some of the crucial variables and relationships, *then* we can predict others—in this model, g.n.p. and consumption.

More Complex Simultaneous-Equation Models.[7] More complex econometric models involve precisely the same basic steps: specification of the model, measurement of the relationships and variables, and solution of the model (system of equations). Some years ago, *Business Week*, while poking a little fun at econometricians, summed up the method of econometrics effectively in the sketch on page 73.

Note that the basic model is stated in the system of multiple equations in #3. Equations 1, 2, and 3 are "behavioral" equations; that is, they describe the behavior of units in the economy. Equations 4 and 5 are "identities"; that is, they merely state what we have defined as being identical. For example, we define g.n.p. as the sum of consumption plus investment plus government spending. Obviously, equations 1 through 3 are the critical ones. The solution of the model (that is, the value of g.n.p.) depends on solving the set of five equations simultaneously, just as in the real world all the

factors are interacting simultaneously to determine g.n.p.

This is a more complex model than was used in Chapter 6, though it is still too simple to represent the real world effectively. The government is added, and investment is made a function of profits in the preceding time period. (P_{-1} means profits in the preceding time period; most econometricians label all their variables with time subscripts since time is so important in most economic relationships.) This model will predict this year's national income and consumption *if* we know last year's profits (to predict I in equation #2) and government expenditures. These two—last year's profits, and government spending—turn out to be the crucial "independent variables" which control the predicted level of national income, given the relationships specified in the model. In fact, if we want to predict more than one year ahead we need a more complex model, since profits this year will obviously depend partly on the levels of C, I, and G this year (as well as on other variables). Thus, a more complete model would need a behavioral equation to integrate the determinants of profits into the system. Then, only government spending would remain a truly independent variable; and even that might turn out to depend on some of the other variables, such as tax receipts of the government. If so, the model would then require another behavioral equation to specify government spending.

All this may begin to sound complex, and it is. There are now several econometric models of the economy involving 20 to 70 equations. Moreover, a nationwide group of economists has recently completed, in preliminary form, a massive econometric model of the economy which involves over 200 equations. How well it "works" remains to be seen; it was developed by building up a large number of submodels of particular sectors of the economy and then putting them together in the over-all model.[8]

Problems of Statistical Estimation.   Building an econometric model requires an underlying theory. But equally it requires careful statistical estimation of the variables and relationships in the equations. A good econometrician is thus as much a statistician as an economist. Statistical estimation of complex economic relationships is a difficult job indeed, as was suggested in Chapter 3 and is pointed out in

[6] These are technically called "single-equation" models, since, although they begin with more than one equation, they reduce to one equation for statistical fitting to the real-world situation they represent.

[7] These are called "simultaneous equation" models, since several equations must be fitted statistically on a simultaneous basis.

[8] For a reasonably complete, yet reasonably simple, explanation of econometric models—what they are, how they are constructed, and how they work—see W. Butler and R. Kavesh, eds., *How Business Economists Forecast* (Prentice-Hall, 1966), Chapter 1.

more detail in Chapter 7. Interactions among important variables in our economy—for example, among personal consumption, disposable income, the money stock, holdings of liquid assets, and the like—are complex and sometimes shifting.

Modern statisticians are gradually developing methods to handle such complex interrelationships and forecasting problems. They are too intricate to belong here. But remember that progress in understanding what determines what in the economy depends heavily on this kind of behind-the-scenes interacting theoretical and empirical work.

The Junior Econometrician's Work Kit.

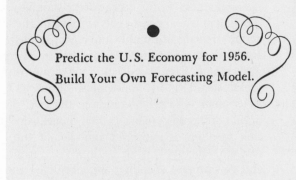

Predict the U. S. Economy for 1956.
Build Your Own Forecasting Model.

DIRECTIONS:

1. Make up a theory. You might theorize, for instance, that (1) next year's consumption will depend on next year's national income; (2) next year's investment will depend on this year's profits; (3) tax receipts will depend on future Gross National Product. (4) GNP is the sum of consumption, investment, and government expenditures. (5) National income equals GNP minus taxes.

2. Use symbols for words. Call consumption, C; national income, Y; investment, I; preceding year's profits, P_{-1}; tax receipts, T; Gross National Product, G; government expenditures, E.

3. Translate your theories into mathematical equations:

(1) $C = aY + b$ (4) $G = C + I + E$
(2) $I = cP_{-1} + d$ (5) $Y = G - T$
(3) $T = eG$

This is your forecasting model. The small letters, a, b, c, d, e, are the constants that make things come out even. For instance, if horses (H) have four legs (L), then $L = aH$; or $L = 4H$. This can be important in the blacksmith business.

4. Calculate the constants. Look up past years' statistics on consumption, income, and so on. From these find values for a, b, c, d, and e that make your equation come out fairly correct.

5. Now you're ready to forecast. Start by forecasting investment from this year's profits. Look up the current rate of corporate profits — it's around $42-billion. The model won't tell what federal, state, and local governments will spend next year — that's politics. But we can estimate it from present budget information — it looks like around $75-billion.

6. Put all available figures into your model. (We've put in the constants for you.)

(1) $C = .7Y + 40$ (4) $G = C + I + 75$
(2) $I = .9 \times 42 + 20$ (5) $Y = G - T$
(3) $T = .2G$

7. Solve the equations. You want values of C, I, T, G, Y. Hints: Do them in this order — (2), (1), (4), (3), (5). In solving (1), remember that I and E are both part of G, $Y = G - T$, and $T = .2G$.

8. Results. (See if yours are the same.) For 1956, consumption will be $260.0-billion; investment, $57.8-billion; GNP, $392.8-billion; tax receipts, $78.6-billion; national income, $314.2-billion. These results are guaranteed — provided that the theories on which they're based are valid.

Reprinted with permission from *Business Week*, September 24, 1955

SEVEN

THE DETERMINANTS
OF CONSUMPTION
AND PRIVATE
INVESTMENT

Consumption Expenditures.

Private Investment Expenditures.

Completing the G.N.P. Model.

Chapters 5 and 6 provided a simple model showing how real g.n.p. is determined by the interaction of aggregate supply and aggregate demand. In the short run, since the aggregate supply curve is essentially fixed, the level of aggregate demand (total spending by households, businesses, and governments) largely determines the level of real output and employment. In that model, consumption spending is entirely a function of the level of g.n.p. (income), while both private investment and government spending are considered autonomous—that is, unaffected by the level of g.n.p. Thus, the simple multiplier effects in Chapter 6 depend on the partially unreal assumptions that private investment and government spending are autonomously determined, and that consumption spending is passively dependent on income received.

Obviously that model is oversimplified. You may reasonably suspect that consumption spending is affected by factors other than income. Moreover, Chapter 6 did not look into the actual determinants of private investment spending, which you may safely suspect are complex. It is the purpose of this chapter to examine in more detail the determinants of consumption and private investment spending.

CONSUMPTION EXPENDITURES

The Relation
of Consumption to Income

It seems intuitively reasonable to suppose that consumption expenditures depend heavily on the incomes that people receive. Careful studies have been made of what happens to aggregate consumption expenditures when aggregate disposable personal income rises and falls. As far back as our data go, they show aggregate consumption rising and falling with aggregate disposable personal income; and, of course, they show that, on the average, this same relationship holds for individual families. However, if we look at individual families one by one, we find widely varying behavior masked by the average figures.

Consider first the aggregate relationships. Figure 7-1 plots the relationship between total disposable personal income and total consumption expenditures in the economy in each year from 1922 through 1966. For example, in 1960, d.p.i. (read off the bottom scale) was about $352 billion and personal consumption expenditures (read off the vertical scale) were $329 billion. For 1933, the lowest year, d.p.i. was only $45 billion while personal consumption expenditures were $46 billion, actually more than disposable personal income. People used accumulated savings and went into debt to keep themselves fed, clothed, and housed when incomes plummeted in the depression.

The line running from southwest to northeast on the chart is drawn to "fit" the dots plotted. The fact that most years fall about on the straight line shows that the relationship between disposable income and consumption spending has been a rather stable one. But the fact that some years are substantially off the line shows equally that the stable relationship has not always held. During World War II, for example, consumption spending fell far below what would normally have been expected for the high incomes received during those years.

Put in common-sense language, this evidence says that the percentage of d.p.i. spent on consumption rises as incomes fall in a depression (since people try hard not to cut back their living standards as much as their incomes fall). Con-

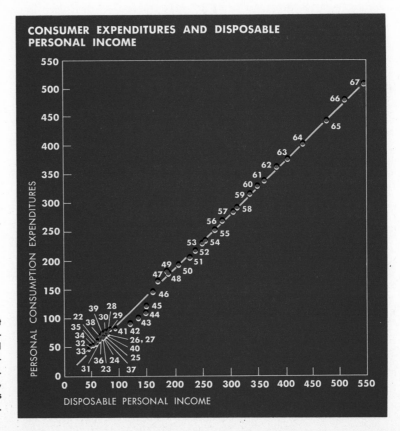

FIG. 7-1 In the depression people spent nearly all their disposable income on consumption. During World War II they saved a large proportion. Since then their spending-saving behavior has been quite stable. Note that the trend line leans over a little, showing how much consumption spending is less than disposable income. (Source: U.S. Department of Commerce.)

versely, when incomes rise sharply in a boom, the percentage spent on consumption falls (to around 94–96 per cent in the generally prosperous years since 1950). And under special circumstances like World War II, when many goods were unavailable and the government urged everyone to save more to avoid inflation, the consumption percentage may fall much further—down to about 75 per cent in 1943 and 1944. The fact that the "fitted" line leans over toward the right shows that the percentage relationship is not a constant one, like $C = .9$ (d.p.i.). Such an equation would give us a line which shows zero consumption at zero d.p.i. But we see that households in fact raised their consumption to over 100 per cent of d.p.i. in 1932, when income was well above zero.[1]

Such analysis of historical relationships is an example of the research that provides sound empirical foundations for the models used in economic analysis, as in Chapter 6. However, we shall see in the following sections that the consumption-income relationships are in fact more complex than those shown in Fig. 7-1, and to get useful predicting relationships we need to take more factors into account.

The Saving Function

By definition, consumers save that portion of their disposable income which they do not spend on consumption. The relationship between con-

[1] For readers who know mathematics, the equation that approximately fits the solid line is $C = a + b(Y)$, where a and b are constants which show the relationship between consumption (C) and disposable income (Y). This is the consumption function used on page 64 above.

sumer saving and disposable personal income is shown in Fig. 7-2, which gives the percentage of d.p.i. *saved* each year. The underlying data are the same as those for Figure 7-1. The percentage saved is of course one minus the percentage consumed for each year.

Figure 7-2 indicates vividly the high percentage of d.p.i. saved in the war years, and the negative savings in 1932–33 at the bottom of the Great Depression. But more significantly it stresses the nearly constant percentage saved (about 4–6 per cent) during the entire period of reasonably stable, prosperous times since 1950.

What Determines Consumption Expenditures?

The preceding data reinforce our intuitive presumption that consumption spending depends mainly on disposable personal income. But the data also warn us that other forces may shift the propensity to consume, slightly or dramatically. We need now to take a more detailed look at the forces which have influenced consumption spending over the past half century.

Income—Present, Past, and Future. Empirical studies show a close relationship between present income and current consumer spending. But sophisticated statistical work over the past decade has suggested that adding in past income and income expectations gives a better explanation of consumer spending than does present income alone.

The influence of past income is persistent. Once families have become used to any real con-

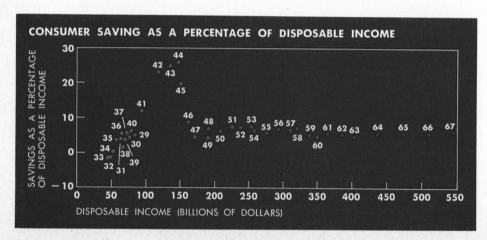

CONSUMER SAVING AS A PERCENTAGE OF DISPOSABLE INCOME

FIG. 7-2 Personal saving has been a stable percentage of disposable personal income in peacetime prosperity, but has fluctuated sharply in depressions and wars. (Source: U.S. Department of Commerce.)

sumption level, they are reluctant to slide back down to a lower level, even if their income drops. Rather than reduce their standard of living as income falls, they will (at least temporarily) reduce their saving levels to well below the amount they would have saved at that income on the way up.

Similarly, when incomes rise sharply, consumption spending rises more slowly. That is, with rising incomes the marginal propensity to consume is lower in the short run than in the long run. For example, following the big federal income tax cut in 1964 which directly increased disposable personal incomes, the percentage of d.p.i. saved rose temporarily, and then gradually shifted back to its earlier level, as previous studies of consumption indicated it would do. Consumption spending takes time to adjust.

Recently, some research workers have advanced a more sophisticated hypothesis. They suggest that consumption spending is a substantially constant and similar proportion of disposable income for average families at *all* income levels —*if* we exclude major disruptions like war and mass depression, *if* we include consumer durables (especially houses, autos, and household furnishings) with saving (investment), *and if we consider their "permanent" or "life-span" incomes rather than the particular income of any given year, which may be distorted by special factors.* It is the last clause which is the crucial one.

One version of this approach says that families, consciously or subconsciously, estimate their long-range income over the years ahead (over their entire life cycle), and adjust their current consumption spending and saving to their rough expectations for the entire period. As a college professor, I have a pretty good idea how my salary will rise over the years ahead to retirement, barring major calamities and other such special factors. The same is true for many other families. Thus, during their early married years most couples spend most of their income and even go into debt to start families and set up households. A little later, as income rises and these special expenses have passed, they begin to save more, for retirement, to send their children to college, and so on. After their houses are well furnished and their children are educated, they commonly save at a

much higher rate. Late in life, after they retire, the saving ratio drops again and often becomes negative. Looking over this life span, the average ratio of consumption to income is, if the investigations of this group stand up under further scrutiny, surprisingly similar for typical families at different income levels. By the same token, consumption is a quite stable function of income for the population as a whole.

The "permanent income" hypothesis is the other way of putting the analysis. It says that families base their consumption on what they expect their "permanent" income to be. Temporary deviations in income up or down from this permanent expectation will generally not greatly affect consumption spending. Rather, if income falls temporarily, the family will cut back its savings, use up its liquid assets, or go into debt to maintain consumption. If income bulges temporarily, the bulge is likely to go mainly into saving (including consumer durables). Just how families actually decide what their "permanent," or life-span, income is, is not clear; past incomes presumably provide the best indicator.

What is the evidence on the life-span and permanent-income models? Good statistical evidence is hard to get, and interpretation of the data in relation to these models is a tricky problem. Most economists believe that the evidence to date generally supports the models, but with enough contradictory data to require a suspended judgment so far as practical use of the model is concerned.

Money, Liquid Assets, and Other Wealth. If a family has an unusually large accumulation of money and other liquid assets (currency, bank deposits, government bonds, and so on), it probably feels freer to spend out of current income than it would otherwise. If its liquid assets are unusually low, the reverse will be true. This seems an intuitively reasonable hypothesis.

And there is some empirical support for it. During World War II, government borrowing placed nearly $250 billion of new liquid assets (money and government securities) in the hands of the public. After the war, this huge accumulation began to burn a hole in the public's pocket. Between 1945 and 1947, consumption spending rose from 81 to 98 per cent of d.p.i. Then, as incomes and prices caught up to a more normal relationship to liquid assets, the consumption-income relationship eased back down to previous high-employment peacetime levels.

The facts are clear. But just how much weight should be given to money and other liquid assets is debatable. Skeptics point out that other factors (especially the pent-up demand for consumer durables unavailable during the war) may also help explain the postwar spending burst. Current research suggests that households' money holdings (of deposits and currency) may exert an important casual influence directly on consumer spending, through channels to be explained in Chapter 8. But this analysis attributes little causal power to other liquid assets. Best evidence to date is that when money balances (and possibly other liquid assets) get far larger relative to current income (or to consumers' total wealth) than the public is used to, they exert a strong pressure toward higher spending. But it's less clear that small variations in money or liquid assets play an important causal role. Reserve judgment until Chapter 8, which integrates money and other liquid assets into our basic aggregate demand model.

More broadly, it is clear that, other things equal, a family with large wealth (ownership of economic assets such as money, stocks, bonds, houses and consumer durables) will spend more on consumption than will a low-wealth family with the same income. For example, suppose a family receives an annual income of $10,000 and has accumulated wealth of $25,000. Imagine now that a wealthy relative dies and leaves family another $25,000. We would expect its level of consumption to rise even if the father's salary stayed at $10,000. Note, incidentally, that this effect is closely related to the "permanent" income hypothesis above. With more wealth, the family's permanent, or life-time average, income has increased, since the family's income now includes the interest, dividends, or other yield on the additional $25,000 of wealth.

Summary: Economists agree that wealth exerts an important effect on the level of consumption, though we must be careful not to double-count the wealth by also counting its effect on permanent income. Some, but not all, econometric evidence suggests that money, as one special form of wealth, exerts a special effect on consumption spending, beyond the impact of the *total* wealth owned by households.

Consumer Credit. One way of getting around the limitation of income is to borrow money or buy on credit. A net increase in consumer credit correspondingly increases consumer spending power, beyond that provided by current income. Until the last couple of decades, consumers did little credit buying except in purchasing homes. But since World War II a huge volume of houses and consumer durables (especially automobiles) has been bought on credit. By 1967, families were nearly $100 billion in debt on consumer goods, compared to $6 billion in 1929 and in 1946. This growth thus represented a net addition of over $90 billion to total consumer spending power over the period. Mortgage debt on houses approached $250 billion in 1967, up over $200 billion since 1946. In total, such new credit to households thus increased family buying power by nearly $300 billion over the 1946–67 period.

But there is a counterforce at work here too. The deeper consumers are in debt, the less they can count on increasing this supplement to current income in future periods, and the greater is the potential inroad on current consumption spending from required payments on the debt. If you are in debt, interest and debt repayments must be met before current income can be devoted to consumption expenditures. By 1967, the proportion of current disposable income committed in this way had crept up to 15 per cent, which correspondingly restricted consumers' power to spend disposable income on goods and services.

Availability of Goods. During World War II, you just couldn't buy lots of "hard goods" like refrigerators and automobiles, because their production was cut back or eliminated by the war. Reflecting this and other factors, the economy's consumption ratio dropped to below 75 per cent of d.p.i. in 1943 and 1944. By 1946, consumers had accumulated an enormous backlog of demand for such consumer durables, which undoubtedly helps explain the big postwar buying surge. Such shortages of goods are rare, but they may exert a powerful force on the consumption function when they occur.

Consumer Stocks of Durable Goods. The converse effect occurs when consumers have built up unusually large stocks of durable goods. Consumer spending on nondurables (food, clothing, and so on) and on services (housing, utilities, etc.) is relatively stable, but spending on durables (automobiles, refrigerators, TV sets, etc.) fluctuates sharply with fluctuations in income. Since such durables last, their purchase can be postponed far more readily than the purchase of food or services. Thus, after consumers have engaged in a big buying spree on durables (for example, 8 million autos in 1955), they are likely to slack off their buying until the new durables are at least a few years old, even though consumer income holds up. Note that this example applies to only one sector of consumer spending, not necessarily to total consumption expenditures.

Price Expectations. If you expect prices to rise, the time to buy is now, before things go up. If you expect deflation, you had better hold off postponable purchases until prices go down. Changing expectations of future prices can thus bring violent shifts in the consumption-income relationship. Immediately after the outbreak of the Korean War in 1950, for example, current consumer saving dropped almost to zero as consumers rushed to stock up before prices skyrocketed and goods vanished from the market. Such drastic shifts in price expectations are rare, but when they do occur, they can dominate the more stable consumption-income relationships that generally prevail.

Long-run Stability and Short-run Instability. Where do all these considerations leave us on the determinants of consumer spending? Some modern statistical efforts to answer this question are presented in the following section. But at the risk of over-simplification, we can say that over the long pull the ratio of consumption to disposable personal income has been quite stable. At high-employment levels, it has seldom varied from the 94–96 per cent range, moving outside that range for long only in response to strong, identifiable special forces, such as war. In spite of short-run

fluctuations, consumers as a whole appear to adjust their consumption habits to rising incomes over the long run so as to maintain about the same average ratio of consumption to disposable income as in past prosperity periods. Will this tendency persist over the years ahead? Nobody knows. But the historical relationship has prevailed long enough to make it a reasonably good bet.

The Consumption Function— Modern Statistical Evidence

While the above generalizations give us some guides to consumption behavior, they are too rough to be satisfactory for national forecasting purposes—for example, when we want to predict the probable effects of a tax cut or tax increase. Thus, modern econometricians (economists who are interested in both economic theory and the statistical testing of their theories) have devoted a great deal of attention to analyzing precisely the empirical relationship between the various causes listed above and consumption spending in the past.

A number of modern studies agree that we can generally get a good approximation of the likely change in consumption for the quarter or year ahead if we can predict changes in disposable income *and* changes in wealth (or perhaps money) held by consumers. As is suggested above, this prediction seems to improve if we substitute for current disposable income a somewhat more sophisticated measure of "permanent" or "life-cycle" income. Rough approximations of these concepts have been made by assuming that people will take an average of their income over the past several years as a predictor of their permanent or life-cycle income, once adjustments are made for their age, family status, and the like.

Another approach is to break down consumer spending into a number of major components—spending on services, on nondurable goods, on automobiles, on other durable goods, and the like. One well-known econometric model, for example, relates changes in spending on nondurable goods to disposable income, the level of spending on nondurables in the preceding period, and holdings of liquid assets in the preceding period, plus a "catch-all" factor for other variables. Note that the inclusion of spending on nondurables in the preceding period reflects the importance of previous consumption levels; this reflects the fact that consumers' current consumption spending is considerably influenced by what they spent last quarter or in other recent quarters. They are reluctant to cut back their spending drastically, even if their income level falls.

Econometricians write this relationship in the following way. Actual numbers are inserted for the relationship from one well-known study:

$$\triangle ND = .224 \triangle Y + .205 \triangle ND_{-1} + .143 \triangle L_{-1} - .149 \,[2]$$

In this equation, $\triangle$ means change from the last quarter to this one; ND means spending on non-durables; Y means disposable personal income; L means liquid asset holdings; $_{-1}$ means in the quarter preceding this one; and no subscript means in the present quarter, or the one being predicted. Similar, but separate, equations have been worked out in this model for consumer spending on automobiles, other durables, services, and housing.[3]

We cannot yet confidently forecast closely what consumer spending will be as a result of changes in the other major variables, even when we abstract from such special forces as war. But careful econometric work is rapidly building up our knowledge and increasing our ability to predict the consequences of changes in tax rates or other actions which influence consumer spending.

PRIVATE INVESTMENT EXPENDITURE

So far we have assumed that investment spending is *autonomous*. Thus we have been able to consider private investment spending (together with government spending) as an independent driving force, to which (through the multiplier effect) total g.n.p. and consumer spending adjust. Now we must look at the determinants of private investment expenditure in more detail. We shall see that while private investment expenditure is partly autonomous, it is also related closely to the level of consumer spending. That is, rising consumption may induce more investment, as well as the other way around. Thus, a more thorough look at the system will require us to complete the circle: Investment spending → more consumption → more private investment → more consumption . . . etc.

Investment spending is largely business spending—on plant, equipment, machinery, and inventories. Only one component of private investment is made directly by households—new single-family housing—and this seldom accounts for over a quarter of the total. Private investment spending reflects primarily the decisions made by businessmen—presidents, finance committees, boards of directors, and others, all the way down to the corner grocer.[4]

Private investment spending has been the most dynamic and unstable major component of the gross national product. Most economists think it plays a central role in explaining both economic growth and fluctuations. Figure 7-3 shows the fluctuation in private investment spending since 1929. The top line is gross, or total, investment. The lower line is net investment, which subtracts the allowance to replace capital goods worn out (depreciated) during that year. Only the lower line represents the net addition to our capital stock each year.

What Determines Private Investment Spending?

What determines private business investment spending? As with consumer expenditure, the answer is gradually being clarified through both theoretical and empirical work. Begin again with a simplified model. Later we shall look at some of the modern empirical evidence.

Fundamentally, expected profits determine how much a business will spend on investment in

[2] This —.149 reflects the effects of all other factors not included in the three explanatory variables listed. But see also the following footnote.

[3] See D. B. Suits, "Forecasting with an Econometric Model," *American Economic Review*, March, 1962. For students who know mathematics, all of this article may be interesting. It includes comparable forecasting equations for all major sectors of the economy and for many of the subsectors in those major groupings. See especially the last section of the article, which lists all the forecasting equations.

[4] If consumer durables are included in investment, the proportion determined directly by households is higher, but still only about one-half.

any given year. When a businessman thinks he can invest in a new machine and get back over the life of the machine what it costs, plus running expenses, plus interest on the money invested, plus some extra return (profit), he will probably make the investment. *He will invest when the expected rate of return on his invested capital exceeds the going rate of interest (cost of capital) he must pay for funds to make the investment.*

The Marginal Efficiency
of Investment

Economists call the expected rate of return on investment the "marginal efficiency of investment" (m.e.i.). Suppose, for example, a businessman is thinking of buying a new milling machine for his plant. He knows the machine will cost $10,000 and his engineers estimate that it will increase the annual output of the plant by about $2,000, with unchanged costs for labor and materials. To maintain the machine, however, will cost about $500 a year. (To make the example easy, assume the machine lasts indefinitely.) Thus, the expected annual net return on the $10,-000 investment in the machine will be $1,500. The marginal efficiency of investment would thus be 15 per cent (that is, $15 return annually on every $100 invested). If he could borrow money at, say, 5 per cent to buy the machine, it looks like a good investment.[5]

What factors determine the marginal efficiency of investment in typical cases? Some of the major ones are:

Expected Product Demand. The dominant consideration is the expected demand for the firm's product. Note that it is *expected* net return on investment that matters. Thus, whenever a businessman *expects* the demand for his product to rise, this anticipation increases the *expected* rate of return he can get by investing in new plant and equipment that will increase his output or improve the quality of his product. The fact that expectations govern the marginal efficiency of investment makes it subject to wide fluctuations, depending on how things look to the businessman.

[5] For a more complete and precise analysis of how to compute the net rate of return on investments and how businessmen sometimes look at the investment problem, see Chapter 33.

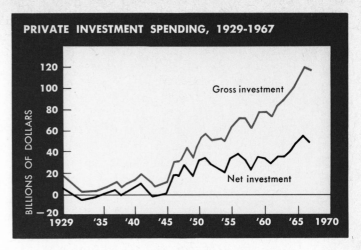

PRIVATE INVESTMENT SPENDING, 1929-1967

BILLIONS OF DOLLARS

Gross investment

Net investment

FIG. 7-3 Private investment spending fluctuates sharply. It is now higher than ever before, but gross investment is roughly the same percentage of g.n.p. as in other prosperous periods.

If the world looks black, down goes the marginal efficiency of investment. *Note here the tie back to consumer spending. One of the big forces influencing the expected return on new investment is consumer spending—more broadly, the total demand for business' products.*

Technology and Innovation. Research and development push the marginal efficiency of investment up. If a new machine promises to lower costs or improve product quality, this promise will be reflected in a larger expected net return on the investment. Some investment is justified just to replace old machinery with duplicate equipment, but technological advance is the foundation of most present-day investment in plant and equipment.

Taxes. With modern corporation income tax rates, businessmen are primarily concerned with the expected rate of return on investment *after taxes.* In 1967, all corporations except the smallest paid income taxes of about 50 per cent on their profits. (If we take this factor into account, the milling-machine investment above loses a lot of its glamour.) An increase in corporation tax rates, other things equal, will lower the marginal efficiency of investment; a decrease will raise it.

General Outlook. A businessman can never estimate precisely all the factors involved over the life of a major investment. Will demand for the final product really be what he expects? Will tax rates stay the same? Will the government step in and regulate his business? Will a new machine come along that will make this one obsolete? With all this uncertainty, the general outlook of the businessman often plays a big role in his final decision on whether or not to invest.

Interest Rates— "The Cost of Money"

The other side of the picture is the interest rate—the cost of the money needed to make the investment under consideration. If the businessman has to borrow the funds needed, we can get a direct figure for the cost of money—maybe it's 5 per cent. But even if he has the money already, possibly in retained earnings from previous profits, he must still figure "implicit" interest on the funds used, since when he ties them up here he will be foregoing interest he could earn by investing them elsewhere. Then the proper interest rate to charge is harder to estimate, but he must settle on some figure for his calculation. We'll look at the details presently.

The Investment Schedule and Investment Decisions

At any time, many alternative investment opportunities are open to any business, some promising high rates of return, some low. We can graph these investment opportunities as in Fig. 7-4. Curve II is the investment schedule. It shows how much investment will be made at different rates of interest which businessmen must pay for the money to finance the investment.

Suppose we list all the possible investment opportunities which one business firm foresees for next year. A few projects will promise a high rate of return; more will promise at least a medium rate; many will be available that promise at least a very low rate. Plot these in curve II. A few investments (about $140,000) promise 5 per cent or more; about $300,000 promise 4 per cent or more; and so on. Note that the $300,000 includes all that promise 4 per cent *or higher*; it includes the $140,000 that promise 5 per cent.

Now we easily see how much a rational, profit-seeking businessman will invest. Suppose the interest rate he must pay or charge himself is 4 per cent. Then any investment opportunity on his investment schedule that will yield above 4 per cent is profitable. Figure 7-4 shows that this business should invest about $300,000 if the interest cost is 4 per cent, taking on all the projects promising to yield 4 per cent or higher. If the interest cost is 5 per cent, it will only pay to invest about $140,000 this year—only in those projects above where the 5 per cent line intersects II. Each point on II shows how much will be invested at that interest rate. It shows investment as a function of the interest rate ($I = f(i)$).

A Modification. This analysis is straightforward enough, and the logic is impeccable. In the business world, however, most businessmen seem to insist on introducing a big "safety factor," or they may call it something else. Company after company requires an expected return of 15 or 20 per cent on new investment before taking action, even though it can go to banks or the open market and borrow at 5 or 6 per cent. What is the answer to this paradox?

Taxes are part of the story. They take about half of most business profits. Another answer is the safety factor suggested above. Businessmen say they never know whether things will turn out as well as expected. Another answer is the reluctance of many businessmen to go into debt, even when it is directly profitable to do so. A fourth possibility is that businessmen calculate the effective cost of money to themselves as much higher than current market interest rates, especially if

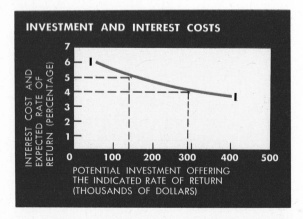

FIG. 7-4 The curve, *II*, shows the amount of investment it will pay to undertake at each level of the interest rate.

they must issue new stock to get funds. But these questions get further into business finance than we can go at this point. All we can do is note the real-world fact that most businesses want an expected rate of return well above the market rate of interest before they will invest. This fact does not change the general principle indicated above, but it does reduce the number of investment opportunities that many businessmen will consider attractive at any given time.

To summarize: Business investment spending in any given time period is determined by the marginal efficiency of investment in relation to the interest rate (cost of capital). Many business firms consciously go through the type of analysis outlined above for each major investment considered. Others make their calculations much more roughly. Some operate by hunch and intuition. For present purposes, assume that our model gives a rough approximation for the economy as a whole.

Business Investment in Inventories. The above analysis of business investment applies basically to business investment in plant and equipment—buildings, machinery, and the like. Business investment in inventories (raw materials, goods in process, and finished goods still on hand) raises other special problems which become especially important when we consider booms and depressions—short-run economic fluctuations. For the moment, only a warning that inventory investment is a special problem, one we will examine in more detail in Chapter 9 on business fluctuations. This warning does not change the general principle stated in the preceding sections.

Business Saving:

A Digression

Thus far we have assumed that all savings are made by households. What people don't spend on consumption they save. But of course businesses also save. And business savings constitute a leakage from the income stream, just as do household savings. Business savings reduce the size of the multiplier effect of any autonomous spending in the economy.

Business savings come from two sources: profits not paid out to owners ("undistributed profits") and depreciation reserves (to replace wearing-out capital equipment). Since World War II, such business savings have made up well over half of the economy's total gross saving. In 1966, for example, business gross saving totaled about $90 billion, compared to about $27 billion of personal saving. But business net saving was only about $28 billion through its retention of undistributed profits; the other $62 billion was depreciation allowances.

Although business savings constitute a leakage from the income stream, most of them are reinvested directly by the business firms themselves, as indicated above. Businesses generally prefer to use their own savings before going out to borrow from others. Eastman Kodak and du Pont are examples of companies that have grown almost entirely through reinvestment of retained earnings. But in the g.n.p. accounts and for multiplier analysis in our model, business saving must be added to personal saving as a leakage that reduces the economy's marginal propensity to consume out of g.n.p. This is parallel to the way we include gross business investment in g.n.p., even when it is financed by internally generated savings.[6]

COMPLETING
THE G.N.P. MODEL

Now that we recognize that the interest rate, expected profits, and other factors must be considered to explain business investment spending, clearly we need to complicate the simple model of Chapters 5 and 6 to introduce these additional relationships. This is done in the two following chapters.

Chapter 8 introduces money into the model, since money both influences the interest rate and otherwise influences household and business expenditure. Chapter 9 moves on to the complex problem of economic fluctuations (booms and depressions) and the short-run economic "dy-

---

[6] Net foreign investment, one of the categories in the g.n.p. accounts, is neglected throughout this chapter, even though it may have a multiplier effect on g.n.p. similar to that of domestic private investment. Net foreign investment has been relatively small since World War II, and it is more convenient to leave it for consideration in Part Six on "The International Economy."

namics" involved in these fluctuations. Here we will recognize the fact that investment influences consumption and income through the multiplier, and that consumption and income in turn influence investment, so there may be an upward spiral where more investment → more consumption → more investment → more consumption. . . . But, intriguingly, the spiral doesn't go on indefinitely, once it's started either upward or downward. Chapter 9 analyzes why.

REVIEW

Concepts To Remember

Be sure you understand the following new analytical concepts introduced in this chapter.

marginal efficiency of investment	"cost of capital"
interest rate	investment schedule
implicit interest	business saving

For Analysis and Discussion

1. What are the main factors which determine your personal consumption expenditure? What forces would you expect to shift your consumption function over the next ten years?
2. How would you expect the marginal propensity to consume to compare for families at the same income level (say $8,000 per year) at the following ages for the head of the family: 25, 40, 60, 75? Explain your answer.
3. During much of 1967, consumption outlays totaled only about 93 per cent of disposable personal income. How would you have gone about determining whether this unusually high savings ratio was likely to be permanent or temporary?
4. Investment spending has often fluctuated sharply during booms and depressions. Using the model of business investment decision-making in the chapter, can you explain why this is likely?
5. Explain how you would decide whether to invest in a new set of store furnishings if you were the owner of an ice cream parlor.
6. Would you expect higher interest rates to stimulate or retard business investment? Explain why, using a graph like Fig. 7-4.

EIGHT

MONEY, AGGREGATE DEMAND, AND THE PRICE LEVEL[1]

The Facts.

Money in the Income-Expenditures Model.

The Quantity Theory—The Classical Economists.

Money, Velocity, and Aggregate Demand.

Why Do People Hold Money?

The Modern Synthesis.

How Important Is Money After All?

Appendix: Simultaneous Equilibrium in Goods and Money Markets.

Chapters 6 and 7 explained aggregate demand with little mention of money. There, spending depended largely on incomes received. But we receive our incomes in the form of money, and somehow it seems that money must be too important to leave out. This chapter puts money into the model.

Since spending does appear to depend largely on incomes received, we need to ask how more or less money will raise or lower incomes.[2] Some economists say the relationship is simple—just create more money and it will almost automatically circulate through the system, creating more income and aggregate demand as it is spent. If either consumers or businesses get more money, they'll spend more. But it's not clear that the answer is so simple.

This chapter has five main sections. The first summarizes the major facts about money and its relationship to g.n.p. and prices during this century. The second explains the minor role which money plays in the "Keynesian" income-expenditures model developed in Chapters 6 and 7. The third and fourth sections go back into intellectual history to look at the analysis of the "classical" economists who accorded money a *central* role in explaining aggregate demand and prices. The fifth pulls both Keynesian and classical models together in a "modern synthesis," which recognizes that both have important elements of truth.

[1] Teachers who want their students to understand monetary mechanics (the operations of the banking system) before considering money in relation to aggregate demand, should assign Chapter 11 before Chapter 8.

[2] Money is defined as checking, or demand, deposits and currency. Details in Chapter 11.

THE FACTS

What are the facts about money in relation to gross national product and the price level? Figure 8-1 summarizes these relationships since 1900.

The bottom line shows the growth in the stock of money, averaging 5¼ per cent per annum since 1900. The next two lines show that "real" gross national product (that is, g.n.p. in constant prices) rose at about 3½ per cent per annum over the same period, while money g.n.p. rose at about 5¾ per cent annually. The top line shows that the price level rose by an average of about 2¼ per cent annually, the difference between money gross national product and real gross national product.

It is clear that the increase in the money stock on the average paralleled closely the growth in *money* g.n.p.; and that about two-thirds of the growth in money g.n.p. was growth in real output while about one-third was inflation.

Deviations from these average (trend) growth lines are as interesting as the trends themselves. The big inflation of World War I is clearly visible. The money stock shot up from 1915 to 1920 as new money was created to finance the war, and prices soared roughly apace. About 1927, the money stock began to fall below the economy's 3+ per cent real long-term growth rate, and the long depression of the 1930's began two years later. The great collapse (in both output and prices) came between 1929 and 1933, when the money supply was contracting severely.

World War II was different from World War I. Again, much of the war was financed by

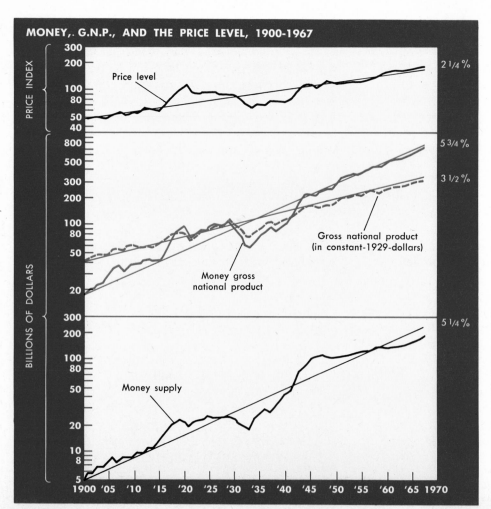

MONEY, G.N.P., AND THE PRICE LEVEL, 1900-1967

FIG. 8-1 The money stock has risen about 5¼ per cent annually, and money g.n.p. a little faster. G.n.p. in constant dollars has grown only about 3½ per cent annually, however, and a price rise of about 2¼ per cent per annum accounts for the difference. Has the excess of money supply over the growth in real g.n.p. caused the inflation? (Sources: Federal Reserve Board, U.S. Department of Commerce, and National Bureau of Economic Research.)

newly created money. But widespread price and wage controls held inflation to a creep during the war, and it was not until their removal after 1946 that prices rose rapidly. Thus, the inflationary pressure generated by new money was more spread out than during World War I. Strikingly, the growth in the money supply leveled off around the mid-1950's; it rose only about 1 per cent a year over the next several years. This period included the "weak" recoveries of 1956–57, 1959–60 and 1961–62, and the recessions of 1958 and 1960–61. The money supply began to grow more rapidly again in 1963, and so did g.n.p.

Some economists infer from these facts that the money supply exercises a powerful effect on the level of real output and prices. They argue that when the money supply rises much faster than the growth in the economy's real output potential, inflation results. Growth in the money supply parallel to growth in potential real g.n.p. (about 3+ per cent per annum over the past half century) would go far to ensure stable economic growth. But others say that this is too simple an analysis of a highly complex problem, and that it overstates the role of money.

MONEY IN THE INCOME-EXPENDITURES MODEL

Let us look first at the role of money in the income-expenditures model presented in Chapters 6 and 7. J. M. Keynes, the father of the income-expenditures approach back in the 1930's, said that money matters, but not very much. Money generally plays only an indirect part in determining aggregate demand. In the Keynes model, consumers' spending depends primarily on households' disposable income, not on the stock of money they have. Investment spending, however, depends on the relationship between the marginal efficiency of capital and the interest rate, and the interest rate in turn is set partially by the stock of money. Since the interest rate is the price people pay to borrow money, more money will lower the interest rate, other things equal, by increasing the supply side of the supply and demand equation. Thus, he recognized that putting more money into the system could lower the rate of interest,

and thus indirectly could stimulate investment. Conversely, less money would (other things equal) raise the interest rate and thereby restrict investment.

The way money fits into the income-expenditures model can be easily seen from the following causal chain. If the government adds more money to the system, it affects g.n.p. as follows:

$$+ M \rightarrow - i \rightarrow + I \rightarrow + \text{g.n.p.}$$

where M stands for money, i stands for interest rate, I stands for investment, and g.n.p. is aggregate spending. Note that in this approach more money does not directly stimulate consumption spending; its only effect is through lowering the interest rate and thereby stimulating investment.

Moreover, Keynes argued, variations in interest rates are generally smaller than variations in the marginal efficiency of investment. The marginal efficiency depends on *expectations* of profits and other factors in the future, which may shift widely. Thus, moderate changes in the stock of money, bringing about only moderate changes in interest rates, generally have a relatively unimportant influence on total investment spending. Keynes argued that investment spending is thus relatively insensitive to changes in interest rates. But this degree of sensitivity is a factual issue, on which the evidence is mixed. Some of the relevant information is presented later in this chapter.

If we accept this analysis of the place of money in the determination of aggregate spending, then government-induced changes in the stock of money may influence aggregate spending somewhat, but only indirectly.

THE QUANTITY THEORY— THE CLASSICAL ECONOMISTS

By contrast, the classical economists—the long tradition from Adam Smith through David Ricardo and Alfred Marshall, up to the decade of the 1920's—gave money a central role in explaining aggregate spending. They had two main points. First, the amount of money will determine aggregate money spending; and second, variations in aggregate money spending will affect the price level but not real g.n.p. except for temporary aberrations.

First, if people have more or less money, they will spend more or less. People don't hold money for its own sake, but for what it will buy. In general, the rate at which they spend the money they get will be stable, or change only gradually. Thus, changes in the amount of money will generally lead to proportional changes in total spending.

Second, these variations in total spending will mainly just bid the price level up or down, without changing the level of real output and employment. The classical economists argued that a free-market economic system would ordinarily tend to be self-equilibrating at approximately full employment. They reasoned that whenever resources are unemployed or unsold, their market price will move down until it falls low enough so that everything offered is hired or sold. There may be temporary deviations from full employment and, indeed, these deviations may involve booms and depressions. But they will be aberrations, explained largely by special external factors such as wars or famines; by cumulative, herd-like sweeps of expectations that lead to gluts of over-production or to depressions; and especially by the erratic behavior of the monetary system. Over the long pull, the economic system will always tend toward full employment. More or less money will change spending proportionately, and more or less spending will lead to a correspondingly higher or lower price level, not to a change in real output.

In terms of our earlier diagrams, this classical position can be put as follows. The economy will always tend to operate on its production-possibilities frontier—i.e., at full employment. Thus, in Fig. 5-1 the economy's short-run aggregate supply curve is, as a practical matter, not OAB, but instead a vertical line rising from the horizontal axis at OQ_3. This is because the economy will tend to operate at full employment whatever the level of aggregate demand is. If aggregate demand falls, prices will fall but output and employment (real g.n.p.) will be unchanged; if aggregate demand rises, prices will rise but real g.n.p. will remain unchanged. Money-induced fluctuations in aggregate spending would lead primarily to fluctuations in the general price level. This was

called the "quantity theory of money," because in it the quantity of money roughly determined the price level.[3]

To be sure, the classical economists didn't think that money affected only the price level. They knew that price inflation and deflation are often interrelated with the over-all level of economic activity, that financial crisis means unemployment and bad business as well, and that inflation often means price speculation and a disruption of productive relationships. Increasingly, they came to see that if, in fact, prices did not move *flexibly* up or down in relation to changing aggregate demand, such changes in demand would have a direct impact on the level of real g.n.p. and employment. Thus, economists gradually came to see that changes in price levels, production, and employment were all interrelated parts of the same process. We turn now to look in more detail at how the classical (monetary) economists explained the role of money.

MONEY, VELOCITY, AND AGGREGATE DEMAND

First, how did the classical economists link up changes in money with changes in aggregate demand (money g.n.p.)? They asked, (1) how much money do people have, and (2) how fast do they spend it? A simple "equation of exchange" (proposed by Professor Irving Fisher a half-century ago) points up the relationships involved in this approach. The equation is:

$$MV = PT = GNP$$

M stands for the amount of money in the hands of the public; V for the average "velocity of circulation," or the number of times each dollar is spent per time period; P for the price level, or average price per unit sold; and T for the number of units sold during each time period, i.e., for the "real" volume of transactions carried out at average price P. If we think of T as the real goods and services produced in any year, it becomes the real g.n.p. of the economy; and P can be thought of as

---

[3] These remarks do less than justice to the classical economists, but the purpose here is merely to give some background on their view of money's role, not to paint a complete picture of what different economists thought.

the "g.n.p. deflator" from Chapter 4. Then V is called "income velocity" because it shows the average number of times each year a dollar is spent on income-creating transactions in the g.n.p. accounts.[4]

For example, in a very simple hypothetical economy, suppose M is $1,000. Suppose further that during some year 2,000 units of physical goods are sold, and that their average price is $2. The T (real g.n.p.) in our equation would then be 2,000, and the P would be $2; PT equals $4,000, the total amount paid for the goods sold. This leaves the V, the average number of times per year each dollar is spent. Here the V is obviously 4, since total expenditures on the goods sold were $4,000 (P times T) so each of the one thousand dollars must have been spent four times during the year on the average to account for the $4,000 of expenditures. The whole equation is then

$$MV = PT, \text{ or}$$
$$\$1,000 \times 4 = \$2 \times 2,000$$

If you think a minute about this equation, you will see that the two sides are defined so that they will always be equal. MV is simply the total amount *spent* on goods and services during the time period—the total number of dollars multiplied by the average number of times each dollar is spent in the period. PT is the total amount *received* for goods and services during the period—the number of units sold multiplied by the average price per unit. The two are identical; what someone spends, someone else receives. If we now add another $1,000 of money in our example, and keep V and T unchanged, clearly P will have to be $4 to make the equation balance at $8,000. In

economic terms, prices would be twice as high on the average because expenditures doubled but only the same physical volume of goods was sold.

The equation of exchange is obviously a truism. It just says that every dollar spent by someone is received by someone else. Why, then, is it a significant analytical tool? The answer is, because it sets out four important variables on which attention may usefully be centered in analyzing booms and depressions, inflations and deflations. And it sets forth these variables in a way that points up some of their broad relationships— for example, it is the amount of money people have, multiplied by the average number of times each dollar is spent, that gives the total annual amount of spending. The equation certainly doesn't provide any answers, but it is a simple framework for looking at the complex real world. It skips over the whole detailed analysis of consumer and business spending decisions in Chapters 6-7. But it suggests that behind the scenes, the quantity of money may be a basic factor controlling the level of spending.

M, V, and Total Spending

The equation of exchange focuses attention on M and V as determinants of the level of aggregate demand. Think of the receipts (PT) side as being by and large passive, as the classical economists did. Then the equation says that an increase in the amount of money will lead to a higher volume of expenditures, unless it is offset by a decrease in the velocity at which the money is spent.

World War II provides an historical example. The money stock increased from about $36 billion to $110 billion, largely because we financed the war in considerable part by creating new money. The equation of exchange suggests that with such a big increase in the money supply, g.n.p. should have risen in the same proportion unless income velocity increased or decreased during the war.

What did happen? V declined substantially over the war period, and total spending rose much less than in proportion to the money supply. On the average, people held their dollars longer before spending them. This was partly because many goods were unavailable, partly because there was a lot of patriotic pressure against spending, and partly because interest rates were so low that hold-

[4] Obviously we could include in T *all* transactions during the period, adding in purchases of stocks and bonds, of existing houses, of second-hand automobiles, and so on. Then MV and PT would not be equal to money g.n.p., but to a larger total which would include sales of existing assets as well. This would greatly increase the dollar figures on each side of the equation, since there is a huge volume of transactions each year that do not represent expenditures on current output. In 1966, g.n.p. was about $740 billion, whereas total expenditures on all transactions were estimated roughly at $6 to $7 trillion—perhaps ten times g.n.p. If we use this broader approach, V reflects spending on all transactions, and is called "transactions velocity." We would have to use this approach, for example, if we were interested in a general price level which includes prices of existing assets as well as of currently produced goods and services.

ing securities was a relatively unattractive alternative to holding money. As a result, money g.n.p. (MV) rose only from $91 billion to $211 billion, as indicated in the lines for 1939 and 1946 in the table below:

1929: M ($ 26 billion) × V (4.0) = g.n.p. ($104 billion)
1939: M ($ 36 billion) × V (2.5) = g.n.p. ($ 91 billion)
1946: M ($110 billion) × V (1.9) = g.n.p. ($211 billion)
1966: M ($170 billion) × V (4.3) = g.n.p. ($740 billion)

The 1929 and 1966 lines of the table provide some historical perspective. Back at the peak of the boom in the 1920's, V was high. People were spending their money fast, holding their idle money balances to a minimum. Then came the big drop of the depression and war years, as billions were piled up in temporarily idle balances. After World War II, people began to spend down their accumulated balances, and V rose persistently. Higher interest rates provided an inducement to put idle money into securities and other assets, and as money became "tighter" both businesses and individuals were again forced to "economize" their cash balances, cutting them back to the minimum consistent with their needs.

If V were stable, changes in M would be a good predictor of g.n.p. Indeed, by controlling M we could control g.n.p. Professor Fisher argued that by and large his V (which was a little different from ours) was relatively stable over long periods, so that changes in M could be expected to have roughly proportionate effects on PT.[5] This expectation simplified the job to predicting M, and M is something (as we shall see in Chapter 11) the government can control reasonably well. He emphasized, however, that over short periods V might fluctuate sharply, largely because people's expectations about future prices and business conditions might shift in response to temporary conditions. Still, these shifts would be temporary, and the stabler long-term V was fundamental.

Has the evidence borne Fisher out? Yes and no. The table above makes V look highly unstable. But over the long pull, V has been reasonably stable. Figure 8-2 provides the data since 1900. If we eliminate the Great Depression and the World War II period, V has generally stayed in the 3–4 range. But that's a fairly wide range, and nothing more than a long-term relationship is clear. In general, both M and V have dropped sharply in depressions and have increased in booms. The World War II experience cited above provides an instructive example of how far astray an assumption that V is stable can lead you if you use it as an automatic predictor.[6]

$MV = PT$ needs to be used with care. Certainly the crude quantity theory of money (that prices always change in proportion to the stock of money) to which the equation is sometimes tied is not acceptable; nor does the quantity theory necessarily follow from the equation. But simple as it is, $MV = PT$ provides a useful framework for thinking about money in relation to prices and output, especially over the long run and when big changes in the money supply occur.

WHY DO PEOPLE HOLD MONEY?

We understand reasonably well what controls the supply of money (M). But the classical economists were never very satisfactory in explain-

FIG. 8-2 Income velocity has been relatively stable over the long run, with a gradual updrift. However, it rises and falls in booms and depressions, and sometimes falls dramatically for special reasons—note the World War II period. (Calculated by dividing money stock into money g.n.p. for each year.)

[5] In fact, Fisher went further and argued that changes in M would generally lead to corresponding changes in P, since T as well as V would be roughly stable—a simple version of the "quantity theory of money."

[6] Much evidence now suggests that short-term fluctuations in V can be largely explained by variations in interest rates. When interest rates are high, people and businesses keep their idle money balances to a minium and V is high. When interest rates are low, the reverse is true. More on this effect later.

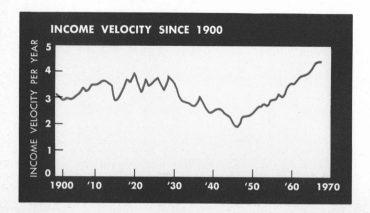

INCOME VELOCITY SINCE 1900

INCOME VELOCITY PER YEAR
5
4
3
2
1
0
1900 '10 '20 '30 '40 '50 '60 1970

ing changes in V. Households and businesses don't generally decide to spend their money faster or slower. We need something that corresponds better to our knowledge of the way people make their spending decisions, if we are to have an acceptable theory of money in relation to spending.

Thinking along this line led another group of classical economists to the "cash-balances" approach, which emphasized the demand for money (then called "cash") balances. Nobody wants to hold money for its own sake—you can't eat it, drink it, or use it directly for anything. Money yields no return unless it is invested. People will spend the money they get unless there is some special reason for holding on to it. The crucial question therefore is: How big are the money balances that people feel they need to hold? Why do people hold this no-yield asset, money, instead of exchanging it for something of more direct use?

The big answer is, people hold money because of the buying power it gives them over goods and services, now and in the future. If John Doe decides he doesn't need to hold as much money as he has on hand, he will spend it. But if he feels that he needs a larger money balance, he will hold down his expenditures relative to his income to build up his money balance. Conversely, if people want to reduce their cash balances, they increase their expenditures. Thus, changes in the desired level of money balances will have a direct impact on current spending. They don't change the amount of money there is to hold, but they do change V and hence the level of aggregate demand. Obviously, this approach is closely related to the money-velocity approach.

Recent analyses of why people decide to hold more or less money have generally stressed three motives for holding money: the "transactions" motive (having enough money for day-to-day individual and business purposes); the "precautionary" motive (having money on hand to be prepared for unforeseen contingencies); and the "speculative" motive (holding money because you think the prices of things you want to buy are coming down). When these motives grow stronger, total expenditures by individuals and businesses drop, given any fixed amount of money for the public to hold, because people will hold on to more of their money rather than spend it.

Conversely, when the motives for holding money are weakening, you can look for increased spending. These motives provide a framework for analyzing the money balances that people will try to hold. If you combine them with an analysis of what determines the amount of M there is to hold, you have the core of the "cash-balances" approach.

Increasingly, modern economists have tried to simplify and clarify the public's demand for money balances. Recent empirical studies suggest that the demand for money is basically a function of (that is, is dependent on) two variables: the level of income and the interest rate on close money substitutes like bonds. Thus, they write the demand for money balances as follows:

$$M^d = f(Y, i),$$

where M^d is the demand for money to hold, Y is income, and i is the interest rate. Higher income (Y) means a higher demand for money to hold, for transactions and possibly for precautionary purposes.[7] Conversely, a higher interest rate on money substitutes induces people to hold *less* money, i.e., to shift from money to interest-yielding assets. This equation appears to fit past experience well, and hence, presumably, can provide a reasonable forecast of how much of any additional M people will choose to hold and how much to spend at any time. But the research results are not conclusive, and more econometric work is needed before we can be sure of the results.

Equilibrium and the Demand for "Real Balances." Suppose that we all decide to build up our money balances by decreasing our expenditures relative to our incomes; as a group we want to hold more purchasing power in the form of money balances. We want to increase our "real money balances," sometimes just called "real balances."

Will the result be higher money balances all around? If your inclination is to say yes, stop

---

[7] If we take Y to stand for "permanent," or average life-long, income, the accuracy of the equation improves substantially, since people's demand for money apparently does not vary with all short-run fluctuations in incomes received.

and think again. With any given supply of money, there can be no change in the *total* amount of money balances held, because there isn't any more money for the public to hold. Thus, the result of a general attempt to build up money balances is a *decrease* in total expenditures as V decreases, *not* an increase in total balances, as long as the total amount of money is unchanged. (Remember the fallacy of composition.)

Will this concerted attempt to accumulate purchasing power be completely thwarted? The answer is no. By pulling down total expenditures, the public's desire to build up its money balances will ultimately decrease prices (and probably production and employment as well). As prices fall, the existing amount of money will command more real goods and services. Thus, even though the total stock of money remains unchanged, the public will succeed in increasing its "real balances." People don't plan it that way, but they increase the real value of their money balances by bringing on deflation, and possibly depression with it. When prices have fallen enough to give existing money balances the desired amount of real purchasing power in relation to incomes and other assets, the public's demand for money balances will again be in equilibrium. People (households, businesses, and others) will again be satisfied to hold just the amount of money that exists.[8]

THE MODERN SYNTHESIS

Both the income-expenditures model of Chapters 6 and 7 and the money-balances model of this chapter provide plausible explanations of how aggregate demand is determined. Both have something to contribute; the problem now is to merge them.

The income-expenditures model says that equilibrium can be attained *only* when households are spending in relation to their incomes at the rate

they prefer, and *only* when businessmen are investing at the rate they judge will maximize their profits. This is an analysis in terms of income flows—through consumption and investment expenditures.

The monetary (money-balances) model says that the system will be in equilibrium *only* when households and businesses are content to hold just the existing stock of money. This equilibrium will occur when each economic unit has allocated its total wealth (assets) among money, other liquid assets (bonds, savings accounts, etc.), and real assets (houses, durable goods, etc.) so that the marginal return from the last dollar invested in each kind of asset is the same. If this were not so, it would pay to shift out of the low yield assets into higher-yield assets. For example, if a family had too much money, it would use this "excess" money to acquire other assets, such as an auto, clothes, or bonds. It would spend down its money balance until the marginal satisfaction obtained from the last dollar held in money just balances that received from the last dollar invested in bonds, housing, and any other asset the family wants. Then its asset portfolio would be in equilibrium. If *MU* is the marginal utility, or satisfaction, obtained from the last dollar invested, then equilibrium is obtained when:

$$MU \text{ (money)} = MU \text{ (bonds)} =$$
$$MU \text{ (clothing)} = MU \text{ (autos)} \ldots \text{etc.}$$

for all assets held.

Thus, for equilibrium to be obtained in the economy, both the "flows" of the income-expenditures model and the "stocks" of the money-balances model must be in equilibrium. Unless all economic units are in equilibrium on both accounts—that is, unless they are content to keep on doing what they are doing—they will change their behavior and bring about a movement in the economic system toward the desired equilibrium state.

Let us now examine in more detail the over-all "portfolio-balancing" mechanism through which, according to the monetary approach, money will have its impact on aggregate demand. This is just an extension of the money-balances reasoning from the preceding section. Every asset held yields some return, or satisfaction. Money

---

[8] It is important to note that if prices are flexible downward as spending falls, the attempt to increase real balances will succeed without any decrease in real output and employment. But if prices and costs are "sticky" downward, the result is likely to be a big decline in output and employment before prices fall far enough to satisfy the increased demand for real balances.

provides generalized, riskless, immediately available purchasing power but no interest return. Securities provide interest or dividends and possibly the expectation of capital gains, although they also involve some risk. Capital goods (like machinery) provide a direct contribution to business profits. Consumers' durable goods provide current services to their users. Each individual will maximize his satisfaction (or yield)—that is, his portfolio of all his assets will be "balanced"—when he obtains equal satisfaction from the last dollar allotted to each kind of asset. When he achieves this position, he is in equilibrium, since he cannot increase his total satisfaction by changing the mix of assets he holds. Then, MU (money) $= MU$ (autos) $= MU$ (bonds) . . . etc.

Note that this portfolio-balancing may lead households or businesses to spend either more or less. Suppose that an individual can obtain more satisfaction by spending a dollar on consumer durables than from holding that dollar as money. Then, if he is rational, he will spend the dollar. He can increase his total satisfaction (yield) by doing so. The same proposition is true about business asset portfolios—they are "balanced" only when the marginal return per dollar obtained on all types of assets held is equal. If, therefore, individuals or businesses find that the marginal returns on different assets are different, they will always move toward equilibrium by shifting out of assets with lower marginal yields into higher-yielding ones. And this will lead them to spend more or less on different assets.

It is important to note also that this increased spending may or may not directly increase g.n.p. If you reduce your money balance by buying General Motors stock, U.S. bonds, or an existing house, this is merely an exchange of existing assets. Your expenditure does not directly increase g.n.p. But if you buy a new coat, or have your car repaired, your money expenditure does directly increase g.n.p. Similarly, a business may shift out of money into new plant and equipment, thus directly increasing the investment component of g.n.p. *It is this portfolio-balancing that provides the linkage between money stocks on the one hand and the flows of consumption and investment spending in the g.n.p. accounts, on the other.*

M Increases Aggregate Demand: An Example

Since the portfolio-balancing process and its connection with changes in g.n.p. are complex, it may be helpful to trace through a simple example. Suppose the government simply prints up some new money and gives it to the public, say in the form of unemployment relief. This increases the total assets (wealth) of the public and simultaneously increases disposable personal income. Let us trace through the effects of this increase in M.

The public now has more money than previously. If it was previously satisfied with its money holdings (i.e., its asset portfolios were balanced), it now has too much money compared to other assets, such as consumers' goods or securities. The marginal satisfaction from holding money has fallen relative to that on other assets, since the public has more money but no more of other things. It therefore will spend some of the new money for other assets. This will bid up prices of other things and thus gradually decrease the satisfaction obtainable by spending an additional dollar on them. The public will continue to spend its new money balances until rising prices restore an equilibrium in the rates of return provided by a marginal dollar held in money and in all other assets. Thus, *on the asset side*, more M leads to more spending, as people act to rebalance their portfolios.[9]

On the income-flows side, the increase in disposable income will lead to more consumption, and through the multiplier to a higher g.n.p. Equilibrium is re-established when g.n.p. reaches a new level where consumers are at their desired consumption-income ratios and businesses are at their

[9] To see why a rise in the price of a security or other asset is the same thing as a decline in the yield on it, consider the following. Suppose the security is a $100 government bond paying 3 per cent (that is, $3 a year), and is due in ten years. If the price is bid up to $110 the annual real yield falls to about 2 percent. This is because, offset against the annual interest payment of $3, the bond buyer must consider the $10 he will lose when he gets back in ten years only $100 instead of the $110 he paid. Spreading this "capital loss" evenly over the ten years takes away $1 return per year, lowering the effective annual yield to $2, which is an effective interest rate of 2 per cent. (Actually, it is a little less than 2 per cent, since you get $2 per year on an investment of $110.) This same type of effect holds for other assets which provide a given yield.

desired investment levels relative to their receipts and profit expectations.

Thus, households and businesses throughout the economy adjust *both* their asset portfolios *and* their current spending patterns until they are content with new equilibria attained on both fronts. Both adjustments go on simultaneously.[10]

Money and Income Flows
as a Basis for Government Policy

Nearly everyone agrees that both money and the income-flow factors of Chapters 6 and 7 are important determinants of aggregate demand, and that we must take both into account. But which is more powerful, and which relationship is more stable so we can rely upon it in predicting the future behavior of the system? Suppose, for example, there is unemployment and we want to raise aggregate demand by $10 billion. One approach: We might print up $2.5 billion of new money and give it out in the form of relief payments, on the reasoning that income velocity in 1967 was about 4, so the new money would raise g.n.p. by about $10 billion. Another approach: We might not change M at all but instead reduce personal income taxes by $4–5 billion without correspondingly reducing government expenditures. This increase in d.p.i. would increase consumer spending by nearly as much, and the multiplier on autonomous spending appears to be 2–2½. Thus, the result should be an increase of about $10 billion in g.n.p. Which approach is better? Is the figure for income velocity (4 in this example) more reliable than the figure for the multiplier (2–2½ in this example) in predicting the new g.n.p.?

The answer from econometric studies is mixed. Neither income velocity nor the multiplier is as predictably stable as their advocates would like. As a practical matter, if we want an increase of $10 billion in aggregate demand, to use either increased M or decreased taxes alone risks partial success. For example, the tax reduction may increase g.n.p., but if M stays constant the growing

transactions demand for money will raise interest rates which will partially check the upswing by reducing businesses' incentive to invest. To increase M alone (say, by buying up outstanding bonds with new money) does not increase anyone's disposable income or profits, and the income-expenditures advocates question whether the policy will accomplish more than slightly reducing the interest yield on bonds. Depending on the particular circumstances, either the tax or the monetary approach may be the more appropriate one if we must choose. *But most experts agree that it is safer to use them both simultaneously if this is feasible.*

In the meantime, more research is needed to clarify the quantitative importance of the income and money factors in household and business behavior. The simple income-expenditures model of Chapters 6 and 7 (before money was introduced) implicitly implied that V (i.e., the demand for money) would passively adjust to permit the equilibrium level of g.n.p. predicted by the model, whatever the level of M. If, for example, we cut taxes by $1 billion but did not change the money stock, the multiplier described by the Chapter 5 model would provide an increase of $4 billion in g.n.p. But if there is no more M, this rise in g.n.p. would imply that V automatically rises to permit the $4 billion increase in g.n.p. Conversely, the monetary approach implicitly implies a passive adjustment in m.p.c. to permit g.n.p. to follow changes in M. Suppose, for example, we increase the money stock by $1 billion but make no change in taxes, government expenditures, or the other income-flow variables. The monetary approach tells us that, if V is stable at, say, 4, g.n.p. will rise by $4 billion. But this increase implies a facilitating upward adjustment in consumers' marginal propensity to consume. To decide whether tax or monetary policy is a more powerful device to regulate aggregate demand, we need to know more about the relative stabilities of the demand for money and the economy's propensity to spend out of disposable income.[11]

[10] A harder example: Suppose the government issues the new M by buying up bonds from the public. Now the public has more M, but no increase in total wealth, since it has exchanged bonds for money. Try tracing through the effect of more M here on aggregate demand. Hint: The income-expenditures model will predict a very small effect.

[11] Modern econometricians are working to determine the relative influence on g.n.p. of changes in M and in autonomous expenditure (often roughly defined as private investment plus most government spending). For example, to oversimplify, they say: Suppose we statistically relate changes in g.n.p. to changes in M, and then separately re-

Whatever the exact empirical values of V, m.p.c., and m.e.i. in any particular case, the modern synthesis reminds us that the economic system simultaneously responds to two aspects of the public's behavior. (1) The public receives incomes, and it spends, saves, and invests out of these incomes (an analysis in terms of income "flows"). (2) The public has a portfolio of assets (money, securities, capital goods, and consumer goods), and it balances the assets in its portfolio to achieve the most desirable "mix" at all times (an analysis in terms of asset "stocks"). Whenever the public is not satisfied with its position on either assets or income-expenditure relationships, it will readjust accordingly, buying or selling assets and spending or saving more or less. It is important to recognize that these two aspects of economic behavior proceed simultaneously and interact continuously. The system will move toward a

new equilibrium whenever the public is out of equilibrium on either set of accounts.

HOW IMPORTANT IS MONEY AFTER ALL?

So how important is money? Some of the older classical economists surely erred in focusing solely on money as the central force determining the level of aggregate demand and prices. But the logic of portfolio balancing is persuasive, and the relatively stable long-run relationship between M and money g.n.p., when changing interest rates are allowed for, is hard to brush off. Surely money has always played a critical role in the big inflations. Runaway increases in the money stock have invariably been associated with soaring prices, usually in a dog-chasing-his-own-tail upward spiral where more money leads to higher prices, which leads the government to print more money to pay its bills, which leads to still higher prices, and so on. In such spirals, the money-balances analysis is highly relevant. The speculative motive takes over; people want to get rid of their money as fast as they can convert it into goods if they expect prices to rise further. The expected yield on M becomes negative, because people expect inflation to erode its value. People hold only the minimum of M needed for current transactions.

Lastly, one other fact about the importance of money stands out: Real g.n.p. has grown stably in this country only when the money supply was growing at least *roughly* at the same rate as the productive capacity of the economy. Nearly everyone agrees that a growing money supply is a *necessary* condition for a growing real g.n.p. Some believe that it is a *sufficient* condition to induce stable growth in our economy. The implications of the two conclusions for long-run monetary policy are, happily, similar. But until we have clearer evidence, few economists are prepared to rely solely on stable growth in M to provide stable growth in aggregate demand. These analytical chapters suggest that we need to remember both the income-expenditures and monetary approaches as a foundation for sound fiscal and monetary policy aimed at stabilizing the growth of the American economy.

---

late changes in g.n.p. to changes in A (autonomous expenditure). The results look like this, for the 10-year period ending with 1966. (In the equations, t stands for time period, so t is this quarter, $t-1$ is one quarter back, etc.; and Δ stands for "change in.")

(1) $\Delta GNP_t = 5.61b. + 3.94\ (\Delta M)_{t-3}$ $r^2 = .553$
(2) $\Delta GNP_t = 4.94b. + 1.08\ (\Delta A)_{t-1}$ $r^2 = .400$

Equation (1) says that the quarterly change in g.n.p. equalled $5.61 billion plus $3.94 for each $1 increase in M three quarters previously. Put otherwise, a $1 increase in M was associated with a $3.94 increase in g.n.p. three quarters later. Equation (2) says that a $1 increase in A was associated with a $1.08 increase in g.n.p. one quarter later. The r^2 in each case is called the "coefficient of determination." It shows how much of the total actual change in g.n.p. each quarter is explained by the M or A, respectively. Thus, ΔM in this simple test explained a little more of Δg.n.p. than did ΔA.

But actually, of course, both M and A exert influence on g.n.p. simultaneously. If we put both variables in the same equation, we get:

(3) $\Delta GNP = 4.00b. + 2.52\ (\Delta M)_{t-3} + .670\ (\Delta A)_{t-1}$
   $r^2 = .658$

This equation shows that ΔM and ΔA together explain appreciably more (65.8 per cent) of Δg.n.p. than does either alone. Quarterly changes in g.n.p. (annual rates) over the 10 years were $4 billion plus $2.52 for each $1 increase in M and 67 cents for each $1 increase in A, with the time lags shown.

This example suggests how econometricians go about using historical evidence to judge how much different factors influence g.n.p. But the example is greatly oversimplified, and it is important to remember that the figures shown do not provide a satisfactory answer on the relative importance of M and A for real-world use.

REVIEW

Concepts To Remember

The following new concepts in this chapter are worth careful review:

equation of exchange	demand for money
velocity of circulation	transactions motive
income velocity	speculative motive
transactions velocity	precautionary motive
money balances	quantity theory of money
"real" balances	portfolio-balancing

For Analysis and Discussion

1. By and large, would you expect prices to rise in proportion to any major increase in the supply of money? Why or why not?
2. Suppose the government holds the stock of money roughly constant over the next decade. Would you expect constant, rising, or falling price and income levels? Explain.
3. Is your own spending rate primarily a function of your recent income, of your cash balance, or of other factors? Which of the approaches described in this chapter is most helpful in explaining your own spending behavior?
4. Suppose the 1975 full-employment potential g.n.p. is $1 trillion. How big a money supply do you estimate will be needed to finance this g.n.p.?
5. Suppose the public's demand for money balances increases because of fear and uncertainty at the beginning of a recession. If the government wants to keep prices and employment stable, what should it do about the stock of money?
6. "In depression an increase in the money supply leads to more jobs; in prosperity to inflation." Is this quotation correct? Does the equation of exchange help in analyzing it?
7. Explain why an equilibrium level of g.n.p. requires equilibrium in *both* the "flow" decisions which consumers and businesses make about their spending *and* the "stock" decisions as to the form in which consumers and businesses hold their assets.

Appendix

SIMULTANEOUS EQUILIBRIUM IN GOODS AND MONEY MARKETS

The latter sections of Chapter 8 emphasize that both money and income flows are important in understanding the level of g.n.p. Equilibrium requires (a) that households and firms be satisfied to hold just the amount of money that is in existence, and also (b) that they be spending and saving the amounts that they prefer in relation to their incomes. That is, there must be equilibrium in the money market (the demand for and supply of money) and in the goods market (the demand for and supply of real g.n.p.).

This dual equilibrium condition can be illustrated by a relatively simple diagram. Suppose there is some given stock of money (M_s = constant) and the public has a fixed demand function for real money balances ($M_d = f_1 (i, Y)$). In Fig. 8-3, then, curve LM shows the combination of interest rates and levels of g.n.p. that are consistent with this given stock of money and the given demand of the public to hold real money balances. For example, if the interest rate is 2 per cent, the LM curve shows that this will be consistent with a g.n.p. of $150 billion.

If the interest rate is 4 per cent, it will be consistent with a g.n.p. of $250 billion. At each point on the *LM* curve the amount of *M* demanded by the public just equals the amount in existence, i.e., $M_d = M_s$.

Why does *LM* slope upward—that is, why are higher levels of g.n.p. consistent with higher interest rates? The reason is that higher interest rates will lead the public to economize on money; at high interest rates, it will want to hold a smaller stock of money for speculative and precautionary purposes than it would at lower interest rates. This will release more of the total money stock for transactions purposes, raising the level of g.n.p. consistent with the given money stock. To translate this into traditional monetary terms, the income velocity of circulation of any given money stock will be higher, the higher is the interest rate which can be obtained on substitutes for money.

Now consider the *IS* curve. This shows all the different levels of investment-saving equilibria that will be consistent with different interest rates and different levels of g.n.p. Here again, there are two underlying assumptions: The consumption function $(C = f_2(Y))$, and the investment function $(I = f_3(i))$ are both fixed. Then at an interest rate of 4 per cent, the equilibrium level of g.n.p., where *I* equals *S*, will be 150. If the interest rate is 2 per cent, the equilibrium level of g.n.p., where *I* equals *S*, will be 250.

The *IS* curve thus shows the possible equilibrium levels in the goods market (real g.n.p.) for different levels of the interest rate; at each point on *IS*, $I = S = Y - C$. The *IS* curve slopes downward because the higher the interest rate, the lower will be the amount of investment and hence the lower the equilibrium level of g.n.p. at which saving is equal to investment.

For the economy to be in equilibrium, both the money and goods markets must be in equilibrium. Thus, we have four basic assumptions, or basic relationships, in the economy, two of which govern the money market and two govern the goods (real g.n.p.) market. Equations (1) to (3) picture the money market, equations (4) to (6) the goods market.

(1) $M_s = $ constant
(2) $M_d = f_1(Y, i)$
(3) $M_s = M_d$ (equilibrium condition)
(4) $C = f_2(Y)$
(5) $I = f_3(i)$
(6) $I = S = Y - C$ (equilibrium condition)

If the basic functions are as pictured by the *IS* and *LM* curves in Fig. 8-3, then equilibrium g.n.p.

must be $200 billion and the equilibrium interest rate must be 3 per cent. Only at these levels of g.n.p. and the interest rate will *both* the money market and the goods simultaneously be in equilibrium.

To see why this must be so, suppose the interest rate were 4 per cent. Then the goods market (g.n.p.) would be in equilibrium only at an output of 150. But with a 4 per cent interest rate the money market would be in equilibrium only with g.n.p. at 250. Clearly 4 per cent is not a sustainable level for the interest rate. At that rate, the public would attempt to reduce its money balances and the rate would fall toward 3 per cent. As the interest rate falls, investment rises and g.n.p. increases from 150 toward 200. That is, both the interest rate and real output will move toward the equilibrium position indicated by the intersection of the curves.

Or suppose the level of g.n.p. is 250. This is also clearly an unsustainable level. In the goods market this would imply an interest rate of about 2 per cent for equilibrium. But if the interest rate were 2 per cent, the *LM* curve says there would be insufficient money spending to sustain the 250 billion g.n.p. The public's demand for money would force the interest rate up, and the higher interest rate would produce a lower level of real g.n.p. To repeat, only at an interest rate of 3 per cent and a gross national product of $200 billion would there be simultaneous equilibrium in both the goods and the money markets.

This *IS-LM* diagram can help in predicting the effects of policy changes—for example, an increase

FIG. 8-3 Intersection of *IS* and *LM* curves shows the level of g.n.p. and the interest rate which simultaneously equate supply and demand in the markets for both money and goods.

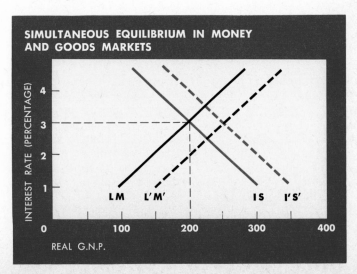

SIMULTANEOUS EQUILIBRIUM IN MONEY AND GOODS MARKETS

in the money stock or in the public's marginal propensity to consume. Suppose, for example, that the government increases the money stock, the demand for money balances remaining unchanged. This will move the entire LM curve to the right, to L^1M^1. The new L^1M^1 curve shows a higher level of g.n.p. consistent with each interest rate, since there is more money. With the LM curve shifted to the right, the new equilibrium g.n.p. for the economy (where L^1M^1 and IS intersect) will be higher than before, and the new interest rate lower than before.

Or suppose the public's marginal propensity to consume rises. This will shift the IS curve to the right (to I^1S^1), because now a higher equilibrium level of g.n.p. will be associated with each level of investment and hence with each interest rate. The new equilibrium for the economy will be at the new intersection between I^1S^1 and LM, with both g.n.p. and the interest rate higher than before. If both LM and IS shift as indicated above, check for yourself to see the effect on the interest rate and g.n.p.

It is important to note that the quantitative effects of such changes will depend on the slopes of the IS and LM curves. Try drawing a flatter IM and steeper IS curve, and trace out the effects of the same changes in M and in m.p.c. analyzed in the preceding two paragraphs. How different are the resulting equilibrium g.n.p. and interest rate levels?

NINE

ECONOMIC
FLUCTUATIONS
AND FORECASTING [1]

Growth and Fluctuations in America.

The Cumulative Upswing.

Upper Turning Point:
Why Doesn't Prosperity Continue Forever?

The Downswing.

Some Special Factors.

Growth and Fluctuations Again.

Appendix A: Economic Forecasting.

Appendix B: A Formal Multiplier-Accelerator Model.

The long pull of American economic growth is impressive. But that growth has come spasmodically, in spurts separated by recessions and sometimes major depressions. Prosperity, with heavy investment spending, means rapid economic growth. Unemployment and recession mean lagging economic growth.

In perspective, the booms and depressions of American history are thus fluctuations around a long-term growth trend. And this is the right way to look at them. For seldom has the trough of a recession been lower than the peak of the boom before last. Growth has been more dominant in our history than fluctuations. But this doesn't mean that repeated booms and depressions have been unimportant. Far from it! Some economists believe we have conquered the business cycle, and that wise use of monetary and fiscal policy can now produce stable economic growth. But even if this belief happily turns out to be true, we need to understand the forces producing economic fluctuations to be able to counteract them effectively. And the theory of the preceding chapters gives us the basis for this understanding.

GROWTH AND FLUCTUATIONS
IN AMERICA

The long sweep of growth in America, interrupted by repeated recessions, is shown by Fig. 16-1 and by the top line of the graph inside the

[1] Some instructors may prefer to assign Chapter 15 on growth theory at this point. It is written to be usable in either order.

front cover. Figure 9-1 points up both these characteristics another way. The fluctuations of real g.n.p. around its persistent growth rate of about 3–4 per cent per year are bounded on the top and bottom by two trend lines, roughly connecting the peaks of the booms and the troughs of the depressions. Thus, growth can be seen as the basic process, with the economy pushing up toward the bounds of productive capacity in boom periods and slumping down toward an (ill-defined) floor in depressions and milder recessions. The vertical shaded areas are recession or depression periods. Note that the light (upswing) periods are substantially longer than the shaded (recession) areas. This emphasizes that growth is the basic process which dominates our economic history, and that growth occurs in the recovery-prosperity periods.[2]

Business-cycle experts have dissected the upward sweep of g.n.p. into its component parts. Most believe they can discern fairly regular fluctuations in g.n.p. and employment, usually every 3 to 5 years, but sometimes with shorter or longer

[2] The top of the World War II boom (1942–45) is shown above the dashed line because the economy was then clearly operating beyond its normal capacity level. Housewives, old people, and children were temporarily pulled into the labor force, and workers were called on for vast amounts of overtime to meet wartime production goals.

duration. These are what are commonly called "business cycles," a misnomer if the term connotes a truly regular "cycle" of fluctuations. Beyond these fluctuations, the experts also find "long swings," especially in construction and investment activity, averaging from 10 to 20 years in duration. These surges in investment activity appear to have been occurring at least since the early 1800's, but they are less clear and well-defined than the shorter fluctuations. And they don't show up well in Fig. 9-1 because they are obscured by the sharper shorter fluctuations. Nevertheless, some experts argue that when we are in the upward phase of the long swings, growth is strong and rapid; in the down phase of long swings recoveries tend to be anemic and the growth rate slows down.

One way of studying economic fluctuations is to separate the fluctuations from the long-term upward trend, or growth. Figure 9-2 does this for industrial production, a major sector of the modern American economy. This sector is also one that fluctuates widely in booms and depressions. To construct Fig. 9-2, we first draw a "trend" line through the actual monthly data for industrial production (per capita) over the period, a rapidly, irregularly rising series. A trend line is a line drawn roughly through the middle of the fluctuating series—so the readings on the industrial produc-

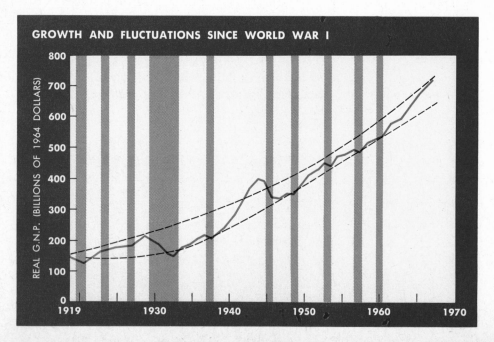

GROWTH AND FLUCTUATIONS SINCE WORLD WAR I

FIG. 9-1 The shaded areas show the recessions and depressions since 1919. Recessions since World War II have been mild, hardly more than a flattening out of the growth in real g.n.p., though quarterly data would show sharper fluctuations. (Source: U.S. Department of Commerce and National Bureau of Economic Research.)

tion curve above the trend line about equal those below it.[3] If, then, we lay the trend line out flat, it becomes the zero line in Fig. 9-2. Thus, periods when industrial production was above the trend line are shown above zero, and conversely for those below.

All the data are shown as percentage deviations from trend. Thus, the prosperity of 1961–64 runs about 10–15 per cent above "normal," as does that of 1905–07. In absolute terms, of course, industrial production for 1961–64, and its expansion from the preceding low, were many times what they were for 1905–07. The vast area below normal in the 1930's and those above normal since the 1940's on the chart are thus far smaller in comparison with earlier cycles than they would be plotted in terms of absolute, rather than percentage, deviation.

The huge depression of the 1930's and the great output expansion during World War II stand out. But most recessions and prosperities have involved smaller percentage deviations from the long-run growth trend.

The Anatomy
of Economic Fluctuations

The big booms and depressions in America have all involved major swings in real g.n.p., employment, and money income. The great de-

[3] Any elementary statistics book will provide information on the precise statistical techniques used in "fitting" trend lines to data. There are several techniques, which may be considered substantially equivalent for our purposes.

pressions, like the 1930's, have meant massive unemployment, vast grey idle factories, financial disaster for millions, endless days of increasingly desperate job-hunting, hunger, and malnutrition. Most college students today cannot remember a great depression, for you have never seen one. Perhaps there will never be another, but we cannot be sure.[4] The big booms have been the opposite—more jobs than workers, soaring wages and prices, big profits, speculation on the stock market, good times for everybody, but uncertainty about how long it will all last.

In the big booms and depressions, nearly everything goes up or down together. But underneath the surface, different parts of the economy expand and contract at different rates, and indeed in many fluctuations some sectors of the economy are actually contracting while others are expanding.

Figure 9-3 shows employment and three major components of real g.n.p. in the United States over the past 35 years. Their roughly synchronous behavior is obvious. It is equally obvious that production of durable goods fluctuates far more violently than nondurables, services, or employment. In fact, fluctuations in total production

[4] Some "feel" of the great depression is provided by "Black Depression" from Frederick L. Allen's *Only Yesterday* (New York: Harper and Row, 1939) and the dreary, desperate saga "Job Hunters" from E. W. Bakke's *The Unemployed Worker* (New Haven: Yale University Press, 1940), both reprinted in M. L. Joseph, N. Seeber, and G. L. Bach's *Economic Analysis and Policy: Background Readings for Current Issues* (Englewood Cliffs, N.J.: Prentice-Hall, 1966).

FIG. 9-2 The curve shows percentage deviations from the long-term upward trend of U.S. industrial production. Areas above the zero line are above trend, and similarly for readings below. (Source: Cleveland Trust Company.)

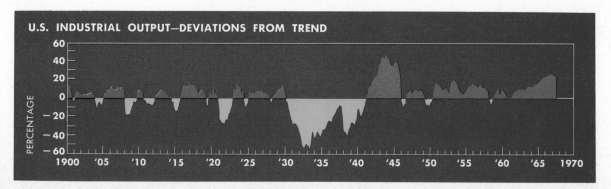

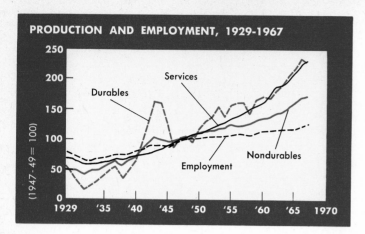

FIG. 9-3 The major components of production and employment fluctuate roughly together, but with very different amplitudes. All curves except "Employment" show actual production, with 1947–49 = 100. Note the big fluctuations in output of durables. (Source: U.S. Department of Commerce.)

and employment occur largely in the capital-goods and durable consumer-goods industries—steel, electrical machinery, locomotives, automobiles, refrigerators. Fluctuations are much milder in shoes, clothing, foods, and other relatively non-durable consumer goods. And the stability of spending on services is remarkable; the growth curve hardly wobbles since the 1930's, in spite of repeated recessions. This does not mean that services and nondurable consumer-goods industries are unaffected by cyclical fluctuations, but the heart of the problem lies in the capital and durable consumer-goods industries.

If this were a more advanced text on economic fluctuations, we would need to look at hundreds of series rather than only a few major ones. The National Bureau of Economic Research, the leading private research organization on business cycles, has plotted hundreds of economic series and found that there is a wide spectrum of movements up and down. Some series normally lead the economy in both directions, some lag far behind, and others are spread out in between. Thus, orders for new machinery may turn down, the average work week in factories may be just flattening off, national income may be rising strongly, and the unemployment rate may be falling gradually, all at the same time as a recovery moves upward. Since hundreds of different components of total economic activity are important and since their movements vary so widely, the Bureau defines a recession as a period

in which over half the important components are falling, and recovery when over half are rising. Most economists prefer to focus on a few big, critical measures, like real g.n.p., employment, industrial production, investment, and the like, but it is important never to forget the great complexity of movement in the real world.

Are There Business Cycles? Are there business cycles—regularly recurring booms and recessions? By now the answer should be clear. It is "no," if you stress the "regularly." Some upswings are long and strong, others short and weak. Some recessions are mild, others become massive depressions. But the answer is "yes," if you mean only that there are intermittent periods of prosperity, followed by recessions. Given these facts, many economists have dropped the words "business cycles" in favor of the term "fluctuations," which doesn't connote such regularity. A few argue that there is no business cycle at all, only a series of responses to more-or-less random disturbances like wars, crop failures, and political changes.

Business-Cycle Theory

Ever since booms and depressions began, people have been trying to figure out why they occur. Professional economists have worked out a variety of theories. Businessmen, financiers, labor leaders, and the man in the street have their business-cycle theories too. The man who says, "The bigger the boom, the bigger the bust!" has an implicit theory about how booms and busts are related. The man who says, "What goes up must come down!" also has at least a partial theory about the relation of booms and depressions.

Different writers have emphasized everything from sun spots to Wall Street as the primary cause of booms and depressions. A theory that seems to explain all business cycles simply and neatly is heady stuff. But alas, no one has come up with one simple theory that does in fact explain all our fluctuations. However, there is widespread agreement on a central analytical framework for looking at the dynamically interacting variables.

This framework is provided by Chapters 5 to 8. It suggests that we should focus on changes in aggregate demand relative to the economy's growing productive capacity. Aggregate demand is made up of consumption and investment spending (if we temporarily ignore government spending), and these in turn are influenced by the supply of money and interest rates. Booms are *dynamic*, cumulative, interacting processes in which increased investment stimulates more consumption, which in turn raises business sales and profits, and stimulates more investment. Similarly, recessions are cumulating downward processes in which the dynamic interaction between contracting consumption and contracting investment is the core of the contraction. In both, expansions and contractions of the money stock may play an important role.

We shall, therefore, focus on these three major variables (consumption, investment, and money) and on their dynamic interactions—both because this approach provides a relatively simple framework and because it is the way most economists themselves go about explaining complex real-world economic fluctuations. In essence, we shall use a simple theoretical model with three main relationships, temporarily omitting government.

1. The level of g.n.p. at any time is primarily determined by the level of private investment and a multiplier whose size depends on the total leakages (saving) in the system.

2. Investment in any period is partly a function of income and consumption in the preceding period; thus there is a "feedback" effect of consumption on investment as well as a causal link from investment to income and consumption.

3. Changes in the supply of and demand for money also affect the equilibrium toward which the system moves at any time.

It is the dynamic interaction among these three, sometimes strongly affected by random shocks such as wars, that is the essence of "business cycles."

THE CUMULATIVE UPSWING

Let us begin with an economy recovering from a recession. Assume that something happens to start an upswing. Then we shall trace through

its progress. This stimulus leads to prosperity, and then to a downturn, which in turn is followed by a recession, possibly by a full-fledged depression. In examining the upswing, note how each expansive factor gradually develops self-limiting tendencies, which increasingly act to put a ceiling on the prosperity and to turn the economy down into recession.

Rising Consumption

Rising Consumption Through the Multiplier. To begin, assume that for some reason investment spending increases, perhaps because a new product or machine is invented. This new investment spending will generate a multiplied amount of income and consumer spending, through the multiplier. Just how much consumption rises for each dollar of new investment depends, of course, on the "leakages" through saving in each round of spending. Apparently a multiplier of 2 to 3 is approximately accurate for the American economy; remember, it's the relation of consumption spending to g.n.p., not to disposable personal income, that provides the relevant multiplier for explaining g.n.p. (see page 70).

The consumption/disposable-income ratio tends to be high in bad times. At the bottom of a depression, consumption may be nearly 100 per cent of disposable income; if the *marginal* propensity to consume is similarly high, the multiplier will be large. As incomes rise into prosperity, though, the marginal propensity to save typically rises, reducing the multiplier on each additional investment dollar. Whatever the exact marginal propensity to consume, *it is rising incomes that are the main foundation for rising consumption spending in the upswing. Consumption spending rises primarily because incomes rise; consumption plays a relatively passive role in the upswing.*

Other Inducements to Rising Consumption. As the economy comes out of a depression, more spendable income is the only thing likely to give a major boost to consumption spending. But if the revival takes hold, there are three additional special factors that may increase the marginal propensity to consume, pushing towards a larger multiplier.

First, consumers may have a backlog demand for consumer durables—refrigerators, stoves, autos, and radios—piled up from the depression. You can use the same refrigerator a long time if you're good at minor repairs and don't mind foregoing the latest improvements, but you're not likely to be very happy about it. And try as you will to avoid it, the day will come when you have to buy another refrigerator or have the food spoil in hot weather. The postponement of purchases of durable goods is one reason depressions last. Catching up on these postponed purchases is one of the big lifts in revival.

Second, as revival moves along and prices begin to rise, consumers may begin to expect still higher prices ahead. Expectations of rising prices generally speed consumer buying, but this is a boost we can't count on with any confidence until the upswing is well under way.

Third, as times improve consumer credit may become more readily available to marginal borrowers. Such credit permits consumers to spend more in relation to current income than they otherwise might.

These three special boosts may come into play simultaneously, separately, or not at all in the upswing. The first is likely to be strongest early in revival and then gradually weaken as revival sweeps upward. The second is unpredictable, but it is most likely after the boom is in full swing and rising prices are widespeard. The third depends on the behavior of lenders, and ultimately of the monetary authorities. Easy loans to consumers are most likely to come with improving expectations and rosy hopes.

But remember: Rising consumption in the upswing depends largely on rising incomes, and thus indirectly on rising investment.

Rising Investment

The "Accelerator." Rising consumer spending means rising sales for businesses. This will deplete inventories and push firms toward capacity limits in factories and stores. Thus, rising sales sooner or later will stimulate more investment. This effect of more consumption spending in inducing more investment we call the "accelerator," or the "acceleration effect." *It provides the link to complete the cumulative interaction in the up-*

swing: more investment → more income → more consumption → more investment, and so on. In summary, the upswing is a cumulative multiplier-accelerator process.[5]

Unless the original burst of investment and its multiplied effect on consumption in turn induce more investment, there will be no cumulative upswing—only a hump on the floor of the depression. But if the rise in consumer spending *does* produce a substantial accelerator effect, then the revival is on. The further induced investment in turn produces its multiplier effect, which in its turn may induce further investment. How big and how repetitive the acceleration effect is, are crucial questions in determining whether the revival grows or withers. If both the multiplier and the accelerator are large, any revival that gets started will be an explosive one, with consumption and investment interacting vigorously. If either is zero, that's the end of the upswing.

How strong will the accelerator in fact be? The answer is, different at different times. Rising incomes and sales will induce new investment whenever they make the *desired* amount of plant and equipment larger than the *actual* amount on hand. Thus, if sales rise and the producer has no excess productive capacity, his desired stock of plant and equipment will clearly exceed his present stock, since without more capacity he can't meet the expanding demand. But if he begins with excess capacity, he has more plant and equipment than he currently needs, so even increased sales won't necessarily raise his desired stock above what he has.

Pragmatically, when the economy is just emerging from a serious recession, the outlook for a larger accelerator effect from rising sales is bad, for two reasons:

1. Idle capacity is widespead during depression, and moderate increases in demand can often be met by using existing idle equipment.

2. Businessmen, whatever the capacity situation is, may cautiously wait to see whether the

[5] Appendix B to this chapter presents a formal model of the cumulative multiplier-accelerator process which shows that under certain (not unrealistic) conditions, the combination of accelerator and multiplier effects can induce cyclical fluctuations in national income even when the original stimulus of investment does not fluctuate.

increased demand is permanent. If they do, no acceleration effect will ocur. Their desired stock of capital depends on the permanence they attach to the increased demand.

But if revival progresses and idle capacity vanishes, further increases in consumer spending are more and more likely to stimulate new investment. History and theory both suggest that the acceleration effect can be powerful.

In some cases, an increase in consumer demand may stimulate a much more than proportional increase in investment spending on plant and equipment, providing a large accelerator. Suppose, for example, that the shoe industry produces 100 million pairs of shoes per year; that it has 1,000 shoe machines, each producing 100,000 pairs per year; and that the average life of shoe machines is 10 years. This means that 100 machines wear out and have to be replaced each year.

Now suppose that consumer demand rises by 10 per cent next year, to 110 million pairs. To meet this demand, if they have no excess capacity or extra inventories, shoe manufacturers will have not only to replace the regular 100 machines wearing out but also to buy 100 new machines to produce the additional 10 million pairs demanded. In this case, a 10 percent increase in final product demand leads to a 100 per cent increase in the demand for plant and equipment.

But the acceleration effect is not a stable booster for the upswing. Suppose consumer demand stays at 110 million in the third year. Now manufacturers will have the productive capacity needed to meet this demand if they replace only the regular 100 worn-out machines. (None of the extra new machines need replacement yet, of course.) Thus, the demand for new machines drops back to the original level of 100 per year, a drop of 50 per cent, even though consumer demand stays unchanged at the new higher level.

Worse, assume that in the fourth year consumer demand for shoes drops below the original level, to 90 million pairs annually. Then manufacturers don't have to buy any new shoe machines at all. They don't even have to replace the ones that wear out that year. The demand for new machines drops to zero as a result of a relatively small drop in the demand for shoes.

This shoe illustration, though purely hypothetical, does indicate how modest shifts in consumer demand can, through the acceleration effect, give rise to sharp spurts of induced investment or to correspondingly steep slumps, even though neither is likely to be permanent.

The accelerator is likely to be especially large for durable goods. For example, if houses ordinarily last 50 years, each year about $\frac{1}{50}$ of all houses may be replaced (say, 1 million houses annually). Assume that as the result of higher incomes in a recovery, 1 million young couples who had been living with relatives decide they want new homes. This increase of $\frac{1}{50}$, or 2 per cent, in the total stock of homes demanded will result in a 100 per cent increase in the demand for new homes. Here again, note that the induced new investment in houses is a temporary lump that will vanish the next year unless there is a further increase in the number of young people setting up their own houses.[6]

The acceleration effect can account for a big part of the observed changes in investment as consumption rises. But not for all of them. Some other determinants of the cyclical behavior of investment may be at least as important.

Shifting Cost-Price Relationships. Back in Chapter 7, we said that decisions to invest depend basically on the relationship between the marginal efficiency of investment and the interest rate (cost of money). Rising consumer demand will increase the marginal efficiency of investment and the desired stock of capital, other things equal. But common sense says that the marginal efficiency of capital also depends on the cost-price relationships involved in making the product concerned. If costs rise faster than selling prices, rising consumer demand won't stimulate much new investment, except possibly in cost-saving equipment.

When a revival is just beginning, businessmen can increase output and build new plants without incurring higher construction or unit operating costs—because there are still much unemployed plant capacity and manpower in the

---

[6] Examples like these two are tricky and are to be viewed only as illustrations of possible results. Slight changes in the assumed conditions can give drastically different results.

economy. Costs stay low as demand and prices rise in the upswing; unemployment tends to hold wage rates down, and higher plant operating rates tend to reduce costs per unit of output in existing plants. Profit margins widen, increasing the marginal efficiency of capital and providing more funds to finance new investment.

But as the boom sweeps upward, excess capacity and unemployment are eliminated. Increasingly, *both* operating costs (e.g., wages and materials) *and* the cost of money (interest rates) rise as demands for funds increase. Thus, the return on investment is often squeezed by rising costs as the recovery turns into a boom. Businessmen complain about the "profit squeeze," and about the shortage of profits to finance new plant and equipment. Shifting cost-price relationships are an important factor in investment decisions over the cycle, and a profit squeeze per unit of output typically develops with full prosperity, thus helping to check the upswing.

Innovation and the Development of New Industries. Historically, most big booms have centered around the development of a few important new industries. For example, during the 1800's railroad-building, with the resultant demand for iron and steel products, was especially important. The boom of the 1920's centered around the auto and electrical industries. Actually, the inventions underlying these industries had been made years before. It was the utilization of these inventions on a large scale through developmental investment that produced the booms they dominated. And when the investment opportunities surrounding these new industries were temporarily exploited, the central thrust of the boom was gone.

Was the development of new industries at those particular times induced by the revivals then beginning, or were the revivals created by new industries? The effect ran both ways. Whether such innovations actually set off a revival or not, they play a major role in most major booms. Once a few entrepreneurs have successfully braved the uncertain paths of profit by introducing new products and new methods, others are eager to follow. With big new industries, booms are long and lusty. Without them, the chances for lusty prosperities are weaker and growth slows down.

Some economists believe that major new innovations are the key to the "long swings" noted above.

Inventory Investment and the "Inventory Cycle." Investment in business inventories plays a special role in business fluctuations. Fluctuations in inventory investment constitute one of the most regular subcycles in economic activity. Many "business cycles" are predominantly inventory cycles. When inventories become scarce relative to rising sales, businessmen try to build inventories back up to desired levels. Businesses tend to overbuy in building them up, and thus overshoot what they consider desirable inventories. Trying to unload these excess inventories, they generally overshoot again, plummeting themselves into a position where inventories are short—and they're all ready to start up again. This is too simple a picture, but it is reasonably accurate.

Figure 9-4 shows the persistence and vigor of these inventory fluctuations. Note that the chart shows changes in *net* inventory investment; this is in accordance with the national income accounts, which count as inventory investment the net increase or decrease in the total stock of inventories held by business. Thus, any figure above the zero line shows inventories building up; any figure below zero shows inventories being depleted. If you compare Fig. 9-4 with the earlier data on total investment and g.n.p., you'll see that plummeting net inventory investment accounted for much of the recession drops of 1949, 1954, 1958, and 1960, and of the upswings in 1950, 1955, 1958, and 1961. If, as some argue, we are beginning to get major cyclical fluctuations under control, the inventory cycle may be our stickiest remaining cyclical problem.

In essence, the inventory cycle amounts to this: When businesses are accumulating inventories, production is running ahead of consumption. Obviously this can go on only for so long; the day of reckoning must come. Conversely, when business inventories are declining, consumption is running ahead of production. Obviously this too can go on for only so long. In 1967, business inventories in the whole economy (at all levels—manufacturers, wholesales, and retailers) totaled about $135 billion. Over the long pull this total

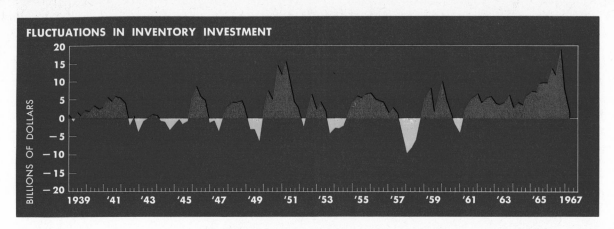

FIG. 9-4 The inventory cycle shows sharp, large fluctuations in inventory investment, which are a major factor in many of the smaller swings in aggregate economic activity.

can be expected to rise roughly with the growth in total sales—perhaps 4 per cent a year assuming no inflation. But you can be sure that any inventory accumulation much faster than that won't last for long. And you can be equally sure that if inventory falls far short of that rate, there's going to be an upswing in inventory investment.

Construction as a Special Factor. Investment in business and residential construction has bulked large in most booms. Construction activity reaches back into almost every corner of the economy. Semi-independent construction cycles averaging around 15–20 years have been evident for the past century; these may play a big role in the economy's "long swings." Thus, construction booms have strengthened some general upswings and weak construction has retarded others. This semi-independent construction cycle is particularly evident in residential housing; plant construction shows a closer affinity to general business activity.

The reasons for this construction pattern are far from clear. They are apparently linked with the average durability of buildings and with the cycle in general business activity. After a vast construction boom, like that of the 1920's, construction needs are satiated. Not only were millions of houses erected, but a tremendous volume of office and industrial construction was completed in the space of a few years. Under the impetus of inflated expectations, speculative building activity spread like wildfire. Enough skyscrapers were erected in three years to serve the country's needs for five times that long. With this supply of residential and business housing, little need for new construc-

tion had developed by 1933–37, when the next revival in business activity occurred. The building market was still satiated, and construction contributed little to the revival.

But by the end of World War II, expanding population and the long period of low-level construction activity had created a strong demand for new housing and office buildings. Rising incomes in the boom supported housing demands, and booming home construction contributed strongly to the upswings of the early postwar period. The construction cycle is far from independent of general business fluctuations, whatever the exact causal relationships between the two.

Money in the Upswing

The cumulative upswing in production, employment, and income may be financed by the existing money supply for a while, as businesses and consumers draw on "idle" balances and V rises. But before long, new money is needed to finance the growing volume of business. Businesses need more working capital to expand operations and longer-term funds to finance new investment in plant and equipment. With higher incomes consumers want to hold larger money balances. On all sides, the demand for money rises.

Will the rising demand for money be met by more M, or will it result in higher interest rates and a growing drag on the upswing process? The commercial banks, and behind them the government (through the Federal Reserve), are the only source of new money for the system as a whole, as we shall see in Chapter 11. Every major upswing has been marked by a substantial increase in the volume of bank credit and money.

Early in the upswing, as customers' demand for loans increases and as better times lessen the apparent risks in lending, bankers are glad to expand loans. But as revival progresses, loans expand and the public draws more currency from the banks. As banks' excess reserves are used up, interest rates rise and bankers begin to "ration" their remaining credit to preferred borrowers. Unless the Federal Reserve provides more money for the system, credit stringency will gradually impose a ceiling on the upswing as businesses cannot borrow the money they need to expand.

The ceiling is not a firm one. As money tightens and interest rates rise, businesses and families increasingly economize on the money balances they hold. When working capital is scarce, corporate treasurers squeeze their idle cash down to the lowest possible levels. Households put their unneeded money to work in securities or other ways when interest rates offered on such investments rise. Thus V rises and partially offsets the credit ceiling imposed by a shortage of money. But there are limits on how small cash balances can be and still meet the needs of expanding businesses. The rising V can slow the impact of the credit ceiling, but not eliminate it. Only the provision of more money by the Federal Reserve can do that (more details on the process in Chapter 11). More money is necessary for a lusty upswing.

UPPER TURNING POINT: WHY DOESN'T PROSPERITY CONTINUE FOREVER?

Prosperity is wonderful. Why can't it go on forever? Maybe it can, and there are good reasons for believing our chances now are a lot better than ever before. But history warns us to expect a downswing sooner or later. Some reasons have been suggested on the preceding pages.

The cumulative upswing is many-sided and interacting. Early in the rise, everything seems to work together toward prosperity. But as the boom continues, the economic system becomes increasingly "vulnerable" to shocks that may precipitate a downturn, especially if the upswing is a rapid one. Inflationary booms in particular typically produce distorted patterns of activity that are difficult to maintain indefinitely.

What actually turns economic activity downward? Sometimes there is a spectacular financial crisis, as in 1907 and 1929. But economic change is complex, and often some phases of economic activity turn down while others are still moving lustily upward. Sometimes it is hard to say whether the economy is still moving up or has turned down; it depends on where you look.

So the experts have become increasingly wary of predicting just what particular factor is likely to spark the downturn. Rather, a series of developments gradually set the stage for a downswing, and in such a setting it becomes increasingly likely that something will give the push that sets the economy unmistakably downward, even though we may not recognize it until months later.

The main limiting "environmental" factors appear to be:

1. Piling up of business inventories.
2. Accumulation of large stocks of new durables in consumer's hands.
3. Consumer resistance to rising prices.
4. End of the upward "acceleration" effect, and resulting decline in investment spending.[7]
5. Rising costs.
6. Accumulation of vast amounts of new productive capacity.
7. Utilization of available new technological developments, and growing scarcity of promising large-scale investment outlets.
8. Exhaustion of excess bank reserves.
9. Weakening of confidence and expectations.

Sometimes a boom keeps going until it faces all these hurdles simultaneously. Sometimes the downturn comes when only two or three seem to present serious problems. Basically, the boom ends when the entire conjuncture gradually shifts over from favorable to unfavorable—when the driving forces of the upswing (especially spending

---

[7] In the multiplier-accelerator model in Appendix B, the accelerator alone is sufficient to generate upper and lower turning points in g.n.p.

on investment and consumer durables) give way to disappointed expectations in the face of increasingly saturated markets.

All this has left the government out of the picture. Yet increasingly, government action is a critical consideration in turning points. Government spending and tax policies and Federal Reserve monetary policy may be used to avoid the downturn and recession. Such government action is the focus of attention in the next five chapters. If we are to achieve stable economic growth at high employment without inflation, it's clear we need positive government assistance to turn the trick.

THE DOWNSWING

A recession looks pretty much like a boom in reverse. But the multiplier and the acceleration effects work downward instead of upward. Decreasing investment pulls out the support for a multiplied amount of income. Falling incomes mean falling consumption expenditures, which in turn reduce the incentive to invest. The cumulative upward spiral that made hearts glad seems diabolically designed as it races downward into depression.

Once a downswing gets under way, the path toward depression may be direct and cumulative. Businessmen, somewhat disappointed in sales and profits as prosperity levels off, are uneasy. Under such conditions, it takes only a downturn in expectations to undermine investment and production plans. Attempts to unload inventories and to obtain cash lead to the very price declines that sellers are trying to "beat" and to still worse expectations for the future.

On the other hand, not all downturns turn into major depressions, just as not all recoveries soar into full-fledged booms. Since World War II, sustained consumer spending on nondurables and services has proved a massive block against a downward spiral. Business investment in plant and equipment has been more resistant to panic cutbacks than in earlier decades. Perhaps most important, government spending provides a big stable block of demand, and government tax and expenditure systems now automatically lead to quick

tax-liability reductions when incomes fall and to increased unemployment compensation transfer payments which help to maintain personal incomes. And private unemployment insurance plans supplement this support.

The behavior of the banking system is especially important in major downswings. Traditionally, recessions led to "runs" on the banks, as people lost confidence in their safety and withdrew their deposits. With deteriorating expectations, bankers called for repayments of loans, both to obtain funds to meet withdrawals and because they feared borrowers might become unable to repay. But at such times borrowers were in no position to pay. Bank pressure forced them to liquidate inventories and securities to obtain funds, just when the demand for both was sagging. This induced further declines in prices, employment, and incomes, speeding the downward spiral.

Since the monetary reforms of the 1930's, there is strong reason to hope that recession-period banking pressures that previously forced mass liquidation have been eliminated. Federal deposit insurance has substantially eliminated the likelihood of widespread runs on banks. And the Federal Reserve authorities now have both the power and the stated intention of providing to member banks the funds needed to avoid massive credit liquidation at such times. With the terrific downward monetary pressures of past depressions hopefully eliminated, our chances of avoiding major depressions have been greatly improved.

Upturn or Stagnation?

If a depression occurs, will business activity turn up again, or will the system bump along the bottom indefinitely?

Take the list of hurdles facing a boom as it reaches its peak, reverse them, and you have a picture of the potentially favorable forces that make an upturn increasingly likely as the downswing continues. The gradual buildup of potential demand for consumers' and producers' durables as old stocks wear out is one of the surest and most powerful forces. But many economists lack confidence that the economic system will turn itself up without a prolonged depression if it is again permitted to reach the depths of the 1930's.

Positive government action to check the downswing and turn the system back up has become a dominant part of any consideration of lower turning-points.

SOME SPECIAL FACTORS

The Role of the Stock Market

In spite of its prominent position in the public eye, the stock market generally plays a minor role in business cycles. Rising security prices do help to speed the upswing, and a collapse of prices on the stock market may help set off or intensify a downswing. But usually these events bring more newspaper headlines than they justify on the basis of their importance in determining real output and employment.

The stock market has four main channels of impact. First, the biggest effect is probably psychological—a symbol of better or worse times for businessmen and the general public. How important all the talk is varies from time to time, with only big changes in the market probably having identifiable effects on investment and consumption spending. Second, rising stock prices mean paper profits for stockholders. With more wealth, at least on paper, stockholders probably are inclined to spend more out of their incomes or out of capital gains. Third, from the point of view of corporations, higher stock prices mean a lower cost of capital for expansion. If a firm needs long-term funds, it can sell new stock at a higher price; that is, it can obtain new funds at a lower cost for the money obtained. Fourth, if rising stock prices have been heavily financed by borrowed money, a downturn in the market may precipitate a major collapse in stock prices, as lenders call for cash. A high market based on credit is thus far more vulnerable than a "cash" market, and hence more likely to be a cyclically destabilizing force.

Stock prices have usually preceded cyclical movements in general business, though by no definite lead. As boom psychology spreads, speculative activity increases on the stock exchange. This was most spectacular in the boom of 1928–29, when speculative activity reached heights completely out of touch with the actual profit possibilities or the general level of business activity. Such a speculative boom carried within itself the seeds of its own destruction.

Once the bubble was pricked in late 1929, security prices nose-dived, pushed downward by calls of the New York bankers for repayment of loans that had financed most of the purchases. The result was a mass destruction of paper profits such as the world had never seen before. The break in the market provided the psychological turning point of the boom—people found their airy dreams ruined, their financial security vanished, their certainty of permanent prosperity and an easy future turned to utter uncertainty. Financial crisis has often characterized the upper turning point of the cycle. But with reforms in our financial system since the crash of 1929, financial crises seem likely to play a less prominent role in the future.[8]

International Aspects of Business Fluctuations

One component of gross investment omitted above is investment abroad ("net foreign investment"). Such investment need not be formal investment abroad in plant and equipment; a current excess of exports over imports represents a net demand for U.S. output and is considered investment abroad in the national income accounts. The excess of exports over imports represents goods produced in this country which do not move into current U.S. consumption, just as inventories accumulated by domestic business are not currently consumed. Such a net export balance provides employment and incomes in the United States, just as does domestic investment; its multiplier effect is similar. The main difference is that with foreign investment the goods produced go abroad rather than being used domestically.

How important is the foreign-trade multiplier? Not very, most of the time. The United States net export surplus has seldom exceeded $5 billion. Our foreign trade has seldom exceeded 5 per cent of total g.n.p. But this is a far from trivial amount, and foreign trade is far more important for most other nations. In Brazil, for

---

[8] For a lively, popular account of the crash of 1929, see J. K. Galbraith, *The Great Crash* (Boston: Houghton, Mifflin, 1955).

example, domestic income, employment, and prices depend heavily on the international demand for coffee, lumber, and a few other main exports, and on the prices Brazil has to pay for her imports. We shall return to the whole problem of international interactions in detail in Part 6.

GROWTH AND FLUCTUATIONS AGAIN

Can we have rapid, stable growth without booms and depressions in our basically private-enterprise, profit-motivated economy? Look back at Fig. 9-1. History warns against overoptimism, unless we've learned how to turn the trick through governmental monetary and fiscal policy. Some economists think we have.

In principle, there's no reason investment has to come in surges which overbuild. But as long as we rely on the private profit motive to induce investments, the likelihood is high that investments will cumulate when times are good, and slump when times are bad—even though the long-term trend is strongly and persistently upward as a foundation for a growing economy. Increasingly, therefore we have turned to government monetary and fiscal policy for help in offsetting big swings in private aggregate demand $(C + I)$ so as to smooth out the inflationary booms and depressions that have plagued us in the past. If government stabilization policy can actually produce stable economic growth without depressions, unemployment, or inflation, the gain to mankind will be measured in hundreds of billions of dollars. Chapters 10 to 14 look in detail at the prospects and at the problems we face.

REVIEW

Concepts To Remember

This chapter re-uses most of the important concepts introduced in Chapters 4 to 8. In addition to those, be sure you have a firm understanding of the following:

business cycle	inventory cycle
boom	innovation
recession and depression	cycle turning points
deviations from trend	foreign-trade multiplier
accelerator	

For Analysis and Discussion

1. Why can't a boom go on forever? Or can it? If your answer is "yes," what change promises to make the future different from the past?
2. One group of business-cycle analysts argues that booms and depressions are caused by expansions and contractions in the quantity of money. Can you see any important weaknesses in this argument? If so, what are they?
3. "The bigger the boom, the bigger the bust." Is this often-heard statement true or false? Support your answer by a careful analysis of reasons why or why not.
4. The following factors are generally agreed to play important roles in cyclical upswings. Analyze how the force of each changes as national income rises from depression levels to prosperity, and how each gradually helps set the stage for the upper turning-point:
   a. The banking system.
   b. The public's propensity to consume.
   c. Consumer and business price expectations.
   d. Induced investment (the acceleration effect).
   e. Cost-price relationships as they affect investment.
   f. Inventory levels.
   g. Consumer and business "psychology."

5. How many factors can you list that might reasonably be expected to provide a strong impetus to an upswing from a long, deep depression? Evaluate the likely force of each.
6. (*Based on the Appendix*) Forecast the g.n.p. over the year ahead, using the analytical framework provided by this chapter and by Chapters 5–8.

Appendix A

ECONOMIC FORECASTING

All economic policy, public or private, involves making forecasts about the future. If the government is to help stabilize the economy, it must know whether next year promises unemployment or a boom in order to make its counter-cyclical stabilization decisions wisely. The businessman must forecast his sales for months ahead to plan purchases of materials, inventory levels, sales quotas for his marketing department, and the like. He must forecast years ahead if he is to make his long-range plans soundly—when to expand plant and equipment, when the firm will need to obtain additional capital funds, what his needs will be for managers, engineers, and the like. And in most cases, the company's outlook is closely tied to the general level of business conditions.

Thus, both the government and the businessman have to make economic forecasts, like it or not. If they fail to make explicit forecasts, they are making implicit forecasts, perhaps without realizing it—that tomorrow will be about like today, that present trends will continue, that the outlook story in yesterday's *Wall Street Journal* was probably about right. Increasingly, both government and business officials have begun to face up consciously to the need for the best possible economic forecasts as a basis for their forward planning.

How Well Can We Forecast?   How well can we forecast, using the models of the preceding chapters or other approaches as a foundation? First, no one can forecast *precisely* very far into the future, no matter how glibly he talks or how much he charges for his services. Second, real experts, using the latest tools and the mass of statistical data now available, can do a reasonably reliable job for perhaps six months to a year ahead for over-all activity (say, g.n.p.), but the reliability goes down rapidly as the distance into the future increases. Third, especially for longer-range forecasts, it is realistic to recognize that ranges (say, a g.n.p. between $80 and $100 billion higher for two years hence) are more

reliable forecasts than those which pick a particular figure. Unfortunately, there is no way of making reliable "point" forecasts far ahead in the complex real world; but happily, for many purposes more feasible "range" forecasts often provide much of the information we really need for making today's action decisions.

Short-range Forecasting.   Suppose you are a congressman, voting on a proposal to cut taxes. Or suppose you are a businessman, manufacturing sewing machines and now facing production decisions on machines to be sold in the autumn-winter sales season which comes six months hence; you know that in the past your sales have fluctuated closely with disposable personal income. In each case, you'd face a similar forecasting problem. How could you go about it?

Maybe you'd want to spend your time reading and thinking about the predictions of others—government economists, professional forecasting services, business magazines, academicians. But even if you rely on these, you need to have some criteria for judging among the conflicting predictions you're likely to find.

First, your economics should tell you that economic fluctuations are complex, ever-changing phenomena, and that there is no fool-proof way of predicting aggregate business activity, even six months ahead. Beware of the man who has the sure-fire answer!

Inertia Models. Economics also suggests that there is a large amount of inertia in such a huge, diverse economy as ours. Disposable personal income (or any other of the major aggregates) is unlikely to be enormously different next autumn from this spring, unless some big special development is in the offing. Partly this is just because the economy is so large, with so many different factors influencing disposable personal income, that only in major expansions or contractions will most of them be moving strongly in the same direction over a short period. Employment in autos may be rising, but construction is easing off and the stock market is soft. Government spending moves up, but international developments have oils and chemicals in the doldrums. And so it goes. Moreover, "built-in countercyclical flexibility" in government taxes and expenditures, as we shall see presently, helps to offset short-term tendencies up or down in the economy.

So one simple type of short-run forecast, which has a higher batting average than many, is just to assume the next half-year will be about like the past one, unless there is a *strong* reason to modify this prediction. A more sophisticated "inertia" approach is to extend the rate of change of the present six months out a half year; this assumes that the present direction will continue at about the same rate. This one will do better than straight inertia in strong expansion or contraction periods, but it will miss more widely around the turning points. Still another inertia approach, preferred by many economists, is merely to extrapolate, say, a 3–4 per cent per annum growth for the next half-year unless there's strong evidence to the contrary, since real disposable personal income has shown a long, persistent growth at about that rate over the past two decades. None of these is very elegant, and obviously they give only rough approximations. But each recognizes the basic fact of inertia for short-run forecasting, and they don't miss because of mistaken judgments of forecasters based on hunches, waves of hearsay, and the like, which are common in the newspapers and magazines.

G.N.P. Models. If you want a more careful, thorough forecast, most leading economists (in industry, government, and the universities) now use the gross national product accounts as a framework, and try to estimate each major component separately. Then they fit the parts together to see whether they are consistent, and check for likely interactions that may have been missed in studying the individual parts. Chapter 4 provides the breakdown commonly used (though many forecasters look in considerably more detail); and Chapters 5 to 8 indicate most of the interrelationships among the major variables that forecasters typically work with.

For example, nearly everyone forecasts separately private investment, consumer expenditures, and government expenditures to get gross national product. Then they need separate estimates on government taxes and depreciation accounts to get to national income, and estimates of transfer payments and personal income taxes to get to disposable personal income.

How, for example, can we estimate that volatile item, business investment? For plant and equipment spending, we now have businessmen's own forecasts of their investment spending a year ahead, collected and published regularly by the U.S. Department of Commerce. These figures give a pretty good short-run benchmark. We can check them to see whether projected spending is way out of line with historical relationships to, say, consumer buying of final goods. The more extreme the estimates look, the more we may want to modify them. We know that investment seldom booms when there is substantial unused capacity. And we know that businessmen typically underestimate their reactions to upturns or downturns in aggregate demand.

For investment in inventories, we also have the published plans of businessmen from time to time. But these forecasts have proved less reliable. We need to look at the ratio of inventories to sales in relation to historical standards, and to whether purchasers are facing full-capacity production conditions that may force them to wait for deliveries. We need to look at how fast businesses have been accumulating or using up inventories over the past year or two. The "inventory cycle" (see Figure 9-4) is one of the more regular phenomena in business fluctuations; businesses seldom accumulate or reduce inventories on a large scale for more than two years or so at a stretch except during really major booms or depressions. If inventories have been accumulating at, say, a $10 billion annual rate for the past year or so, you can be pretty sure a drop-off in this rate isn't far away. Over the long pull, businesses won't continue to produce large inventories they don't sell. Nor will they be willing to deplete their inventories below what they consider sound business levels. On the average, we can expect that total inventories will grow at somewhere near the same rate as total sales in the economy—say, 3–4 per cent per annum in the absence of inflation.

To finish estimating private investment, we'd need a separate analysis of home construction, of foreign investment, and so on in detail for all investment categories.

Similarly, we can estimate consumer spending from different sides, and thus cross-check. The University of Michigan's Survey Research Center examines consumer buying attitudes and intentions quarterly, and publishes the results. These will give some clues. But consumer spending depends mainly on the disposable income consumers receive, so we need to rely heavily here on the forecasts of private and business investment plus transfer payments, adjusted by all the special factors that may affect the propensity to consume in the short run (consumer credit, the current stock of consumer durables, the rate of family formation, and so on—see Chapter 6).

Then we need to look at the government—at tax and expenditure rates, at monetary policy expectations, at special government activities in any field that might affect economic activity. The federal budget calls for careful attention, since federal spending and tax receipts exercise such a big effect on the economy. Happily, the government publishes detailed estimates semiannually.

Put this analysis of the individual categories together in the national income accounts, cross-check to see whether the individual estimates appear consistent with one another, and you should have a substantial improvement on the simpler inertia type of forecast we began with.

Econometric Models. The fastest growing modern forecasting method evolves out of the preceding one. It is the use of formal econometric models. It uses the same variables and relationships as those in the preceding paragraphs, but bases their relationships on statistical studies of past experience, and then obtains final estimates of the end variables (say, g.n.p.) by solving the set of equations in the econometric model, which, in essence, assumes that the statistically validated relationships of the past will hold in the future.

This approach is for the experts, even more than the preceding one. But the essentials are presented nontechnically in the Appendix to Chapter 6 on econometric models.

As the Chapter 6 Appendix indicates, even the best econometric models are still only reasonably good forecasting devices, and much more research is needed to pin down the critical statistical relationships and to establish their stability. Nonetheless, forecasting through econometric models is the most "scientific" method we have, based on the hard facts of history, and it promises to grow steadily as the basic approach among the experts.

"Leading Indicators." A last approach emphasizes leads and lags. The National Bureau of Economic Research has studied the behavior of hundreds of economic series in business fluctuations since the middle 1800's, and has found that some economic series usually lead others. Typically leading series include construction contracts, new orders for producers' durables, new business incorporations, length of the work week in manufacturing, common stock prices, and business failures (inverted). No one alone is reliable, but if most or all of the so-called leading indicators are moving up or down together, this suggests that other parts of the economy will follow. Since most of the leading series exhibit irregular jags from month to month, it's often hard to separate out the false signals from the real ones they may be giving about turning points. For very short-range forecasts the leading indicators now provide valuable forecasting evidence, especially when interpreted by the experts. But don't be misled by the newspaper accounts; the leading indicators fall far short of providing a layman's guide to the future.[9]

It should be clear by now that short-run economic forecasting is a tough job. But substantial progress has been made in the last quarter-century, both through improved methods and vastly more data. How close do the experts come? The President's Council of Economic Advisers produces the most widely used regular forecasts, at the beginning of each year. They are sophisticated experts, with the full statistical resources of the government to draw on, and they use a combination of methods, cross-checking each against the other. By and large in recent years they have done well, only once missing by more than 2 per cent for the year ahead. Their forecasts for 1964 and 1966 tell the story. In January 1964 they forecast a 1964 g.n.p. of $624 billion, and the final figure was, almost too good to be true, $628 billion. But their forecast for 1966, using substantially the same methods, undershot the mark by $14 billion, when the war in Vietnam and booming private expenditures produced a g.n.p. of $740 billion, compared to their forecast of $726 billion. They were about 2 per cent short of the actual g.n.p.

A miss of only $14 billion in a $700 billion economy seems good to many observers. And it is. But $14 billion may mean the difference between satisfactory employment and economic slack, and the Council is dissatisfied unless it comes closer. Some private forecasters do about as well, sometimes better, often worse.[10]

Long-range Forecasting   Long-range economic forecasts pose different problems. This is the prob-

[9] The leading, coincident, and lagging series are now published monthly by the U.S. Department of Commerce in *Business Cycle Developments*, together with a substantial amount of related information.

[10] The bookstores are full of books on forecasting, especially on forecasting the stock market. Measured scientifically by tests of what their success would have been had they they been used in the past, many of them, alas, aren't much good. A good recent basic text, with stress on modern quantitative and econometric approaches, is W. Butler and R. Kavesh, eds., *How Business Economists Forecast* (Prentice-Hall, 1966); see especially Part I.

lem of forecasting the growth rate of the economy, the topic of Chapters 15–18. Generally, a reasonably wide range of likely figures for five or ten years ahead will serve the government's or company's planning purposes about as well as a specific figure, since what is usually needed is an order-of-magnitude picture of the situation several years ahead. Many businessmen insist on having a specific figure for such long-range estimates, but this is pure wishful thinking. No economist, statistician, businessman, government official, or anyone else can be sure of his forecast for the g.n.p. or any other major economic variable 5 or 10 years ahead within 5 per cent (which would allow an error margin of some $40 billion on an $800 billion g.n.p.).

A good economist *can* lay out the major factors determining the economy's long-term growth rate. He can point out the importance and likely effects of alternative government policies aimed at providing purchasing power sufficient to assure high employment. He can provide careful forecasts of the major variables involved, and of their interaction.

A concluding note if you're headed for business. These warnings need not be discouraging to the thoughtful manager. For long-range forecasts *can* be made that will provide reasonably reliable order-of-magnitude estimates for the total economy, estimates that are close enough to provide a rough basis for business long-range planning. In any case, individual industry forecasts (say, of sewing machine sales) are the critical requirements for the business firm. What the total-economy forecasts can do is only provide the general setting for the individual market studies required. The bare statement that g.n.p. in 1970–72 will probably at least approach $1 trillion, and may be higher, is enough alone to pose the growth problem squarely to any firm that expects to hold or increase its share of the market.

Appendix B

A FORMAL MULTIPLIER-ACCELERATOR MODEL

This Appendix presents a simple formal model to illustrate the types of dynamic interaction that may occur between the multiplier and the accelerator. It will be most interesting to those who like precise, theoretical reasoning, and especially to those who know mathematics.

Suppose, in Table 9-1, that we begin with national income at 1,000. Now (say because there is a temporary war scare), businesses increase their investment rate by 100 in periods 1 and 2. The war scare then vanishes, and businessmen are prepared to drop their investment spending back to the original level. What will be the impact of this temporary surge of new investment?

Assume, for this example, that the marginal propensity to consume is .8 out of the income of the *preceding* period (perhaps a more reasonable assumption than that consumption is related to *current* income). Assume also that businessmen are led to make new investments (say in inventories, plant, and equipment) when sales improve, and that such new induced, accelerator-type investment is just equal to the rise in consumption (that is, business sales to consumers) during the immediately preceding period.

On the basis of these *illustrative* assumptions, now trace through the dynamic results of this orig-inal surge of assumed autonomous business investment.

In Table 9-1, the 100 of new autonomous investment in period 1 becomes income to its recipients in that period, raising the period 1 total-income level to 1,100. This rise in income increases consumption in period 2 by 80, which is .8 of the new income in period 1. The burst of autonomous business investment continues in period 2, by assumption. Adding together the new investment and new consumption in period 2, we get 180 of new income over the original level; this gives a total income of 1,180 for period 2. The higher income in period 2 in turn raises consumption in period 3; in addition, the preceding rise in consumption induces 80 of new business investment, raising total income to 1,224. And so the process goes.

This cumulative upward expansion arises out of the interacting multiplier and accelerator effects. Common sense tells us that if we increase the strength of either the multiplier or accelerator we will get a more rapid income expansion. If we weaken either, the rise in income will be slower. And these results can readily be checked by substituting a different propensity to consume or a different accelerator in the table.

This dynamic model provides a simple frame-

TABLE 9-1
DYNAMIC INCOME-EXPENDITURE MODEL

	Total Income (1)	Change from Original Level in:		
		Investment (2)	Consumption (3)	Income (4)
Original level	1,000			
Period 1	1,100	+100		+100
Period 2	1,180	+100	+ 80	+180
Period 3	1,224	+ 80	+144	+224
Period 4	1,243	+ 64	+179	+243
Period 5	1,229	+ 35	+194	+229
Period 6	1,198	+ 15	+183	+198
Period 7	1,147	− 11	+158	+147

Assume: Original autonomous investment of 100 in periods 1 and 2 (in Col. 2).

Thereafter: To obtain change from original level: Consumption equals .8 of income during preceding period.

Investment equals the increase (+ or −) in consumption (i.e., business sales) in preceding period over the next preceding period. For example, investment in period 3 is +80, because consumption was 80 higher in period 2 than in period 1.

Thus: Col. 1 equals 1,000 (original income) plus Col. 4 (change in income).

Col. 2 equals 100 in periods 1 and 2 (new assumed investment), and changes in Col. 3 in preceding period for all succeeding periods (since induced investment equals the preceding change in consumption).

Col. 3 equals .8 of Col. 4 during preceding period (since consumption is always .8 of the national income of the preceding period).

Col. 4 equals Col. 2 plus Col. 3 (since national income equals investment plus consumption).

The same model in equations (as explained in Appendix to Chapter 6, on "Econometric Models"):

$$C_t = .8Y_{t-1}$$
$$I_t = C_{t-1} - C_{t-2}$$
$$Y_t = C_t + I_t$$

where C = consumption, I = investment, Y = income, and the subscript shows the time period. Thus t is any time period, $t-1$ the preceding period, and so on.

work that may help you understand the cumulative upswing of the boom and the downswing of depression. But, once it's started, why does national income ever stop going up or down? Notice that income rises ever more slowly from period 1 through period 4. Since induced investment depends on the *change* in consumption, induced investment gradually falls and the acceleration effect gradually weakens, in spite of the continued upward multiplier effect of whatever new investment there is. By period 5, new investment has dropped off substantially, and the drop in investment is enough to more than offset the continued rise in consumption. Thus, total income falls slightly in period 5, and the

expansion has passed its upper turning point. Moreover, once consumption begins to fall, investment becomes a negative figure (by our accelerator assumption). This sets off a negative multiplier effect, and the downswing is under way. The block of autonomous investment has set off an upswing, which has eventually checked itself and has become a downswing. And the accelerator has given us an upper turning point unaided by other factors. Moreover, if you trace the process further, you'll see that it also reverses the downswing a few periods later.

If you think easily in mathematical terms, putting the model in the simple system of equations shown under Table 9-1 may be helpful. These are "difference equations," and the solution of the system mathematically gives the pattern of changes in income worked out arithmetically in Table 9-1.

This dynamic model gives some idea of the possible results of interacting multiplier and acceleration effects. But don't be too impressed with it. Changing the values of the accelerator and multiplier can substantially change the pattern you get for national income over a series of time periods. If you increase both—the multiplier to a very high marginal propensity to consume, and the accelerator to 3 or 4—you will find that national income "explodes" upward once anything starts it up. If you trace out the model given in Table 9-1 for about 15 periods, you will find that income "damps" back down toward the original income level of 1,000. If you use lower values for the multiplier and accelerator, national income will return to the 1,000 level faster. Moreover, if you make induced investment a function of the *level* of national income in the preceding period, rather than of the *change* in national income, you will get a still different pattern of interaction.[11]

Thus, the purpose of this simple dynamic model is not to show how business fluctuations really work. Rather, it is to focus attention on the importance of the propensity to consume and on induced investment, on the factors that influence these key variables, and on some possible interactions among the critical factors.

[11] For *constant* values of the multiplier and accelerator, an autonomous rise in investment to a new higher level will induce (a) an explosive, continued rise in income when both the multiplier and accelerator are large, (b) no cumulative upward process when either the multiplier or accelerator is zero, and (c) cyclical fluctuations around the new income level if one is weak and the other strong. In some cases under (c), the fluctuations will be damped—that is, they will gradually die out. In others, they may be constant or expanding in amplitude. For a precise statement of these cases, given different constant values for the multiplier and accelerator, see P. A. Samuelson, "Interactions Between the Multiplier Analysis and the Principle of Acceleration," in *Readings in Business Cycle Theory* (Philadelphia: Blakiston Press, 1944).

TEN

STABILIZATION POLICIES: GOALS AND COSTS

Economic Analysis as the Basis for Policy.

The Goals of Stabilization Policy.

The Costs of Unemployment.

The Costs of Inflation.

The Trade-Off Between High Employment and Stable Prices.

Can we maintain high-level employment without inflation? Almost everyone agrees on this as a major goal. Depression and mass unemployment bring waste and human misery. Inflation erodes the value of savings and may lead to disruptive speculation. But there is less agreement on how to achieve this combined goal. And if we must give up one goal to achieve the other, how shall we decide which should give way?

On such complex problems, we don't know all the answers. But economics as an empirical science has made great headway in recent decades, both in building better analytical models of the economy and in checking out these models through extensive empirical investigations. Fortunately, by now there is substantial agreement (far more than the general public often realizes) on some broad lines of monetary and fiscal policy to help achieve stable growth. We may not know exactly what leads people to venture over their depth in swimming, but we can agree that it's good policy to have a competent lifeguard on duty. In the same way, there remain disagreements about the causes of unemployment and inflation, but the disputants still agree on some major policies to minimize these problems.

This chapter looks in detail at some of the major goals of economic policy and at the issues involved in choosing among them. It tries to clarify the goals, and to present modern empirical evidence on the advantages and costs of each of the major goals. Then the next four chapters consider specific governmental monetary and fiscal policies to help achieve the goals—mainly to stabilize the economy at high employment without inflation.

ECONOMIC ANALYSIS
AS THE BASIS FOR POLICY

Economic policy is concerned with how we can make the economy serve us better. Economic analysis (that is, economic theory) is the necessary foundation for sound economic policy. Chapters 5 to 9 have been devoted largely to economic analysis—to developing theoretical models that help to explain the levels of aggregate demand, real output, employment and prices in our basically private-enterprise economy. Now comes the chance to use the theory that you have learned. For this is the theory that should provide a foundation for deciding what governmental policies are most likely to help us achieve our economic goals.

Chapter 3 stressed that there are four big steps to follow in thinking through most policy problems.

1. *First, define the problem.* This usually involves two parts: (a) understanding the existing situation, and (b) clarifying the objectives you want to achieve through policy action. You need to get a clear picture of where you are and where you want to go.

2. *Second, map out the main alternative ways of achieving the stated objectives—the main alternative paths from where you are to where you want to be.*

3. *Third, analyze carefully the alternative policies outlined broadly in step 2, and make a judgment as to which promises to help most in achieving the goals specified in the first step.*

4. *Fourth, check your solution, both for flaws in your own analysis and against past experience.* History has a way of throwing light on flaws in even the most careful analysis of contemporary problems.

THE GOALS
OF STABILIZATION POLICY

There is widespread agreement on two overriding goals for domestic macro-economic policy.

1. High-level employment of men and machines, avoiding the wastes of large-scale involuntary unemployment.
2. A reasonably stable price level.

Many, though by no means all, would add two others:

3. More rapid economic growth.
4. Maintenance of "equilibrium" in our international balance of payments.

Virtually everyone agrees, moreover, that policies to achieve these goals must be consistent with a high level of freedom for individuals and businesses in our economic life. Our basic presumption in favor of extensive economic freedom establishes a framework within which generally acceptable governmental policies must fit, except for periods of war or other national crisis.

The basic analyses of economic growth and of international economic relations come later, in Chapters 15 to 18 and 37 to 40, respectively. Thus, this chapter and the immediately following ones are focused on the central problems of maintaining high employment and a stable price level in the domestic economy.

The Trade-Off Problem—
Conflicting Goals

High-level employment and a stable price level are both desirable. Hopefully, we can achieve both. But, alas, these goals may sometimes conflict—we can have one only at the cost of giving up the other.

Look back at Fig. 5-2, at the dotted line that cuts across the corner at A. This shows that when aggregate demand rises, some inflation begins before we reach full employment. When there is widespread unemployment (e.g., with g.n.p. at OQ_1) obviously increased aggregate demand will lead mainly to more output and employment, not to higher prices. But as unemployment is reduced, more demand is increasingly likely to lead to higher prices. Wages are bid up as labor becomes scarce. Unions demand higher pay and costs rise. Rising aggregate demand leads to full employment in some industries before unemployment and excess capacity are eliminated in others.

Then further increases in aggregate demand bid up prices in the "bottleneck" industries before unemployment of men and machines is eliminated elsewhere.

What then? How shall we trade off the employment of 500,000 more men against a 1 per cent increase in the consumer price index? This is no imaginary problem. It has been a major dilemma of macro-economic policy over the past decade. For between 1953 and 1965 the economy persistently had more unemployment than in previous boom periods. Unemployment rose to 6 or 7 per cent of the labor force during recession periods and seldom was reduced below 5 per cent during upswings. But over the same period prices crept upward, not rapidly, but fast enough to warn that more aggregate demand might produce substantial inflation. Expansionary monetary-fiscal policy to eliminate unemployment thus was continually restrained by the danger that too much aggregate demand could restart the substantial inflation that followed World War II.

If we face the problem of conflicting goals, one path is to search for solutions that will eliminate this dilemma. But if we cannot find such a solution, so that in fact we face a trade-off between the two goals, an intelligent decision about policy requires a careful weighing of the relative advantages of achieving each of the goals. And it is important to see that as a practical matter, the choice is not all-or-none, not, is full employment or price stability more important? Instead, typically it is: Shall we seek a little more employment at the cost of a little more inflation? The real problems are marginal problems—a little more aggregate demand to cut employment a little more as against the disadvantages of a little more inflation.

THE COSTS OF UNEMPLOYMENT

The case for high-level employment of men and machines is clear. Involuntary unemployment means waste of productive capacity. It means less clothing, fewer refrigerators, highways, and factories than we could otherwise have. It means human misery, resentment, shame, decay of skills, degrading deprivation for the unemployed and their families. It means a lower average standard of living for the nation, and slower economic growth for our children and grandchildren.

How much has this waste cost? Figure 10-1 gives a rough measure of this cost since 1953. The straight line is a rough measure of high-employment capacity output for the economy; it is drawn by joining together the peaks of output during prosperous peacetime periods of high employment. It gives a rough measure of the economy's growing capacity if unemployment stays at about 4 per cent. The fluctuating line below shows actual g.n.p. during the same period (in constant purchasing power dollars). Thus the colored area between the two lines is a rough measure of how far actual g.n.p. fell short of reasonably obtainable g.n.p. over the years shown.

These estimates suggest that the economy may have wasted as much as $50 billion per year through unemployment in the post-World War II recession years, such as 1958 and 1961. Over the 1955–65 decade we wasted some $300–$500 billion in potential real output (at current prices)—or in terms of wasted manpower, the equivalent of some 20–30 million man-years of work.

Back in the Great Depression of the 1930's, the waste was a far greater proportion of our potential production. In 1933, for example, actual g.n.p. was less than two-thirds of potential, and many estimates indicate that as much as $200

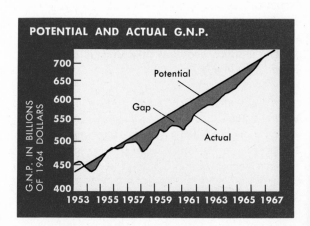

FIG. 10-1 Actual g.n.p. has seldom matched our productive potential, even when potential is defined (as here) as involving only 96 per cent of full employment. (Source: Council of Economic Advisers.)

billion of potential output was wasted through unemployment during the decade of the 1930's, compared to a total actual g.n.p. of less than $800 billion during the decade. Unemployment in 1932 and 1933 was between 20 and 30 per cent of the total labor force, and many of the employed held only part-time jobs.

How Low Can Unemployment Be?

Figure 10-1 sets "high-level employment" output as that attainable with 4 per cent unemployment. But whether 2, 3, 4, or 5 per cent unemployment represents a reasonable goal is a hotly debated issue. Our aspiration levels vary with our achievements. During the early 1950's, when average unemployment fell to 3 per cent or less, about 3 per cent seemed a reasonable goal for stabilization policy to shoot at. With the discouraging results of the late 1950's and early 1960's, many people lowered their aspirations to 4 per cent, or even to 5 per cent, unemployment.

The fear that inflation may result from larger aggregate demand to fight unemployment bulks large in modern controversy. Some observers argue that most of the unemployed below 4 or 5 per cent are unemployables, ne'er-do-wells, and the structurally unemployed who could be drawn into other jobs through rising aggregate demand only at the cost of substantial inflation. But their opponents point to earlier prosperities when unemployment fell to 3 per cent or even less, both during the decade after World War II and during the 1920's. They argue that this shows that such unemployment rates are indeed feasible in a prosperous, free economy like ours if aggregate demand is adequate.

Clearly there is some unavoidable minimum of unemployment. In a large, free economy like ours, hundreds of thousands of people are always on the move. In 1966, for example, some 10 million people changed jobs. It takes time for people to move from one job to another. In seasonal industries such as agriculture and construction, there is sure to be some unemployment in the slack season. Such unemployment is often called "frictional" unemployment. Moreover, there are always some essentially "unemployable" people looking for jobs—individuals with very poor health, with very low mental capacities, with no

training, and the like. Still others are potentially employable, but their skills and locations are badly out of line with job openings or their wage demands are unrealistically high for what they can offer; these are the "structurally" unemployed. There is some level of aggregate demand that will put all such individuals to work in short order, but it is very high indeed, and it would surely generate widespread inflation before it provided jobs for all.

How large is the unavoidable minimum unemployment? There is no precise answer, because clearly with enough pressure of aggregate demand (as in World War II) unemployment can be reduced to almost zero, and indeed millions of new workers can be drawn into the labor force by high wages. But such policies clearly involve massive inflationary pressures. Careful empirical studies suggest that perhaps 2–3 per cent of the labor force may be taken as a reasonable approximation of frictional unemployment plus job seekers who are, for practical purposes, unemployable under normal conditions.[1]

Other nations set us a goal to shoot at. In all of western Europe, since World War II unemployment rates have been much lower than we have achieved, in most cases varying between 1 and 2 per cent of the labor force over the past decade. But these results have generally been achieved at the cost of somewhat higher inflation than in the United States.

One last general observation on the problem of unemployment rates. If actual unemployment is 6 per cent and the frictional minimum is estimated at 3 per cent, can we conclude that the economy is operating at 3 per cent below capacity? No. More probably, output is 6–8 per cent below the system's capacity. The reason is partly that with substantial unemployment many workers are on a part-time basis. As demand rises and unemployment falls, these people shift to a full-employment basis so the number of man-hours of work rises more rapidly than the number of employed. More important, with widespread unemployment many persons drop out of the labor force because they become too discouraged to

[1] See, e.g. *The Extent and Nature of Frictional Unemployment*, published by the Joint Economic Committee of Congress in 1959.

continue looking for jobs. When aggregate demand and employment opportunities rise, many, especially women and "marginal" workers, return to the labor force. Thus, in unemployment periods there is always a reservoir of potential labor force entrants and of "hidden unemployment," made up of workers who are not reported as unemployed in the statistics because they are not actually seeking work. We have no accurate figures on the extent of this invisible labor supply, but recent research suggests it may be substantial compared to reported unemployment.

The Human Costs of Unemployment

Fewer than 15 per cent of today's 200 million people were adults in 1930 at the onset of the Great Depression of the 1930's. Thus, most of today's Americans have no memory of that period and its devastating impact on human morale and well-being, as well as on the aggregate production of the economy.

Figure 10-2 presents the cold statistics. Unemployment reached a peak of approximately 25 per cent of the labor force in 1933, and it averaged between 15 and 20 per cent for the entire decade of the 30's. Moreover, it must be remembered that many of the people employed were on a part-time basis at drastically reduced rates of pay, and there were millions of "hidden unemployed" barely eking out an existence in agriculture. At the bottom of the depression surely not more than two-thirds of the total labor force had regular full-time jobs, and some estimates put the figure nearer one-half.

FIG. 10-2 Unemployment soars in depressions, and even in recessions. What is a reasonable minimum level of unemployment for us to shoot at? (Source: U.S. Department of Labor.)

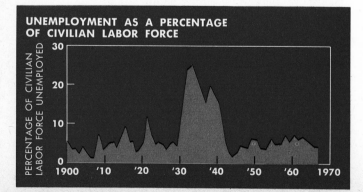

UNEMPLOYMENT AS A PERCENTAGE OF CIVILIAN LABOR FORCE

PERCENTAGE OF CIVILIAN LABOR FORCE UNEMPLOYED

30

20

10

0

1900   '10   '20   '30   '40   '50   '60   1970

But statistics are bloodless things. Listen to the testimony given by an economist before a Senate subcommittee investigating unemployment in 1932: [2]

Mr. deSchweinitz: When I appeared before the subcommittee last December, I stated that there were 233,000 persons out of work in Philadelphia. . . . There are now 298,000 persons out of work. . . . In December I told you that 43,000 families were receiving relief, today 55,000 families are receiving relief.

In December, our per family grant was $4.39 per week per family. It is now $4.23 per family. Of this $4.23 per family, about $3.93 is an allowance for food. . . .

I want to tell you about an experience we had here in Philadelphia when our private funds were exhausted and before public funds became available. . . . There was a period of about 11 days when many families received nothing from us. We have received reports from workers as to how these families managed. The material I am about to give you is typical, although it is based on a small sample.

One woman said she borrowed 50¢ from a friend and bought stale bread for 3½¢ per loaf, and that is all they had for 11 days except for one or two meals.

One woman went along the docks and picked up vegetables that fell from the wagons. Sometimes the fish vendors gave her fish at the end of the day. On two different occasions this family was without food for a day and a half.

The gas company was careful not to turn off gas in a great many of these families, so in some instances food could be cooked.

Another family did not have food for two days. Then the husband went out and gathered dandelions and the family lived on them.

I should also like to say that when we talk to people to ask about unemployment, they say, "Well, people manage to get along somehow or other, don't they? You do not have very many people who really drop dead of starvation." That is true. Actually, death from starvation is not a frequent occurrence. . . . They live on inadequacies, and because they live on inadequacies the thing does not become dramatic, and we do not hear about it. Yet the cost in

[2] *Federal Cooperation in Unemployment Relief*, Hearings before Senate Committee on Manufactures, 72nd Congress, 1st Session (1932), pp. 20–26. This testimony and that which follows is reproduced more completely in D. A. Shannon, *The Great Depression* (Englewood Cliffs, N. J.: Prentice-Hall, 1960).

human suffering is just as great as if they starved to death overnight.

Now listen to the testimony of another witness, given before a House subcommittee at about the same time.[3]

Mr. Ameringer: The last thing I saw on the night I left Seattle was numbers of women searching for scraps of food in the refuse piles of the principal markets of that city. A number of Montana citizens told me of thousands of bushels of wheat left in the field uncut on account of its low price that hardlly paid for the harvesting. In Oregon I saw thousands of bushels of apples rotting in the orchards. Only absolutely flawless apples were still salable, at from 40–50¢ a box containing 200 apples. At the same time, there are millions of children who, on account of the poverty of their parents, will not eat one apple this winter.

While I was in Oregon, the *Portland Oregonian* bemoaned the fact that thousands of ewes were killed by the sheep raisers because they did not bring enough in the market to pay the freight on them. And while Oregon sheep raisers fed mutton to the buzzards, I saw men picking meat scraps in the garbage cans in the cities of New York and Chicago. I talked to one man in a restaurant in Chicago. He told me of his experience in raising sheep. He said that he had killed 3,000 sheep this fall and thrown them down the canyon because it cost $1.10 to ship a sheep, and then he would get less than a dollar for it. He said he could not afford to feed the sheep, and he would not let them starve, so he just cut their throats and threw them down the canyon.

The roads of the west and southwest teem with hungry hitchhikers. The campfires of homeless are seen along every railroad track. . . . Between Clarksville and Russellville, Arkansas, I picked up a family. The woman was hugging a dead chicken under a ragged coat. When I asked her where she had procured the fowl, first she told me she had found it dead in the road, and then added in grim humor, "They promised me a chicken in the pot, and now I got mine."

Most American families were not in such desperate straits. But fear was everywhere. In every American city, hordes of families were evicted from their apartments, often moving in

[3] *Unemployment in the United States*, Hearings before House Committee on Labor, 72nd Congress, 1st Session (1932), pp. 98–99.

with other families until ten or twelve people would be sharing three or four rooms, often shivering through the winter in heatless houses because they could afford little or no coal. Many fought to maintain respectability. Clerks put pieces of cardboard inside their shoes before setting out on endless job-hunting rounds; previously well-to-do families wiped out in the stock-market crash struggled back to get poorer jobs and to use part of their drastically reduced incomes to pay on their debts. But for many, long-continued failure wiped out self-respect and the will to try. Parks were sprinkled with desolate men in shabby clothes, merely sitting. Many more of them remained home.

John Steinbeck pictured the plight of thousands of migrant workers in his *The Grapes of Wrath*, a story of the bitter despair as families, pushed off their land by poverty and the great dust storms of the 1930's, wandered through the Southwest, looking for work anywhere, scraping by on almost nothing in their battered jalopies, homeless and often pursued by the police and "respectable" citizens in communities that did not want them.

These are the costs of massive unemployment and depression. Such conditions are hard to imagine today. Perhaps another great depression will never come; let us hope not.

Is such evidence on the human cost of unemployment relevant today? Today, unemployment is far more modest even at the depths of our postwar recessions. Nationwide unemployment insurance provides temporary financial support for regular workers laid off. Government relief payments help others. Many unions have obtained private unemployment compensation plans to supplement government benefits. But at best, these provide only a fraction of regular wage incomes, and all have time limits, often as short as 13 weeks. Moreover, to receive unemployment insurance benefits, one must have held a regular job, and hundreds of thousands of unemployed persons fail to qualify on this test. The impact of modern unemployment is far less devastating now than during the desperate days of the 1930's. But in the depressed areas—for example in the soft coal fields of the Appalachians—many workers have been out of jobs for years. Discouragement,

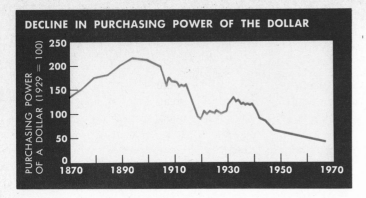

FIG. 10-3 Inflation has repeatedly eroded the value of the dollar, with the biggest price increases coming during and after major wars. (Source: U.S. Department of Labor.)

and then despair, take over when no job is available week after week and month after month.

Moderate unemployment in the postwar recessions has weighed very unevenly on the population. Most mature, skilled workers have retained their jobs, or found others quickly if they are laid off. The unskilled, the uneducated, the nonwhites, and young people without experience have borne the brunt of unemployment. In 1964, a typical year when total unemployment was less than 6 per cent for the nation, the unemployment rate among nonwhites was 11 per cent; among job-seekers under age 20 it was 16 per cent. In Chicago at mid-1964, Negroes accounted for 13 per cent of the total labor force, but for over 40 per cent of the unemployed. Moreover, in 1964, a reasonably prosperous year, there were over 2 million workers unemployed so long that they had exhausted all their unemployment compensation benefits, and the figure was growing by over 40,-000 a week. The human costs of unemployment are real. It is of little solace to the unemployed worker that aggregate unemployment totals only 5 per cent of the labor force if he has no job and little hope of finding one to support his family.

THE COSTS OF INFLATION

Nearly everyone agrees that substantial inflation or deflation is a bad thing. The case for stable prices is less obvious and clear-cut than that for high employment of human and other resources. To evaluate a stable price level as a national goal, to be set alongside high employment of men and machines, we need to look at the costs of inflation and deflation in case we do

not maintain a reasonably stable price level. And our price level has been far from stable. Figure 10-3 presents the evidence.

What Is Inflation?

Inflation is often discussed with more heat than light. One reason is the wide range of definitions that people have in mind when they talk about it. When you use the word inflation to mean a rise in the price level and your neighbor uses it to mean more money printed by those irresponsible fellows in Washington, it's no wonder you don't succeed in talking much sense about it—especially if neither of you bothers to make clear how you are defining inflation. Socrates said, "If you want to argue with me, first define your terms." And he was right. There are several common definitions of inflation, so we have to be clear about which we are using.

"Inflation," in this book, means a rise in the price level of all currently produced goods and services—that is, a rise in the average price of all goods and services in the gross national product. This definition is used because it is simple and direct, because we have a readily available index to measure it (the g.n.p. deflator), and because it is close to what the man in the street means when he talks about inflation.

But it is important to recognize what is *not* included in this definition. Higher prices in the stock market aren't included. Neither are higher wages. Neither is more money and credit. All these things are usually found when inflation, as we define it, occurs; but when we say inflation we shall mean the rise in g.n.p. prices per se.[4]

Using this definition, who gains and who loses when price levels move up (or down)? Does inflation ruin everybody except a few sly profiteers? Is deflation a fine thing for creditors, who can then collect dollars that have stepped-up buying power? Broadly speaking, the economic impact of inflation can be analyzed by asking two questions: (1) Does inflation increase or decrease the total real g.n.p. of the economy? (2) How

[4] Some people prefer more complex definitions—for example, one that says inflation is an overextension of credit. Such definitions often raise serious problems of measurement and clear analytical use; what is "overextension"? But the main point is to decide just what definition one is using, and then stick to it.

TABLE 10-1

HALF-LIFE OF A DOLLAR WITH INFLATION

Annual Rate of Inflation	Years To Lose Half of Purchasing Power
1 per cent	70
2 " "	35
3 " "	23
4 " "	18
5 " "	14

on) and calculate the loss in their purchasing power due to inflation between 1939 and 1966, the loss is well over half a trillion dollars. Of course this huge loss of purchasing power did not represent a loss of real wealth to society as a whole, since real income and wealth were not reduced correspondingly. However, it did reflect a massive shift of buying power over society's current output and accumulated assets from net monetary creditors to others whose buying power rose with the inflation.

If everyone could anticipate inflation accurately, most people could adjust their asset holdings to avoid this redistribution of wealth. For example, lenders would charge high enough interest rates to take into account the expected loss of purchasing power per dollar over the life of the loan. But in fact, many inflations are partially or completely unanticipated. And many people, especially the poor and uneducated, don't understand the process well enough to protect themselves even if they do think inflation is coming. The uneducated laborer can hardly take his life savings of $500 and go into the stock market instead of holding money or government bonds. If he is heavily in debt to buy a house, actually inflation may help him rather than harm him; but this is largely an incidental effect, not one he plans as an inflation hedge.

How Bad Is Inflation?

How bad is inflation, putting all the above effects together? Try the following exercise to test how well you understand the central principles. Evaluate this statement by a well-known senator: "Inflation reduces the buying power of every dollar, and impoverishes the American people. It is a national disaster!"

There is no doubt about the first half of the first sentence. It is true by definition—by our definition, at least. We defined inflation as rising prices, and higher prices do reduce the purchasing power of any dollar. But the second half of the sentence needs a closer look, in spite of its apparent plausibility. Does it follow from the acceptable first portion that inflation impoverishes the American people? A reasonable first step is to look at history.

Consider 1950 to 1960 as an example. Over the decade there was considerable inflation. The B.L.S. consumer price index rose from 100 to 124, using 1950 as the base year. In 1950, national income was $242 billion; in 1960, it was $417 billion. If we adjust the 1960 national income figure downward to eliminate the effect of inflation, we get a 1960 real income of $336 billion in 1950 prices. This was an increase of $94 billion (almost 35 per cent) over the 1950 income. Even allowing for possible error in the B.L.S. price index, it is hard to see how this inflation impoverished the American people as a whole. Although one dollar would buy less in 1960 than in 1950, the increase in money incomes received far outdistanced the loss caused by rising prices; real output and income rose. History clearly shows that inflation does not necessarily impoverish the American people.

To return to a first principle, it is the goods and services produced in an economy that basically determine the national standard of living. Higher prices mean that the purchasing power of any *given* national money income is less than when prices are low. But what happens to *real* output produced and consumed is the fundamental test.

But this historical evidence doesn't prove that inflation did no harm. Real output might have risen even more with a stable price level. Certainly the historical evidence doesn't prove that inflation *caused* the increase in output, so we are not justified in giving inflation credit for the extra goods and services produced. Moreover, even though the public as a whole (and per capita) clearly had more real income in 1960 than in 1950, many people were harmed by the inflation—people whose money incomes were relatively fixed and who were net monetary creditors.

Inflation, as always, altered the distribution of the national output and wealth, so that even with a larger pie to divide some pieces were smaller in 1960 then in 1950.

Putting the whole picture together, was the senator right—is inflation a national disaster? It hardly looks that way for the 1950's. In summary, in analyzing any inflation, first look at the impact on real output per capita as the best single guide to what happened to national economic well-being. Second, ask what happened to the distribution of real income, and decide whether the redistribution was good or bad. Third, ask what happened to the distribution of wealth— the differential impact on net monetary debtors and creditors, and the position of savers as against spenders. Last, look to the future, to see whether the inflationary developments have set the stage for an economic downturn or have slowed the rate of economic growth.[7]

[7] This analysis has omitted the effects of inflation on our competitive position in international markets. These international effects, which may be very important, are analyzed in Part 6.

THE TRADE-OFF BETWEEN HIGH EMPLOYMENT AND STABLE PRICES

High employment and a reasonably stable price level are both desirable social goals. Put the other way, the costs of both unemployment and inflation are real and substantial. But which goal should take precedence *if* we must choose—avoiding unemployment or avoiding inflation?

The economic cost of unemployment of men and machines is real and evident—potential output wasted. The economic cost of moderate inflation is less clear. Thus many economists argue that our first goal should be to avoid unemployment, even if it involves accepting some inflation. But others disagree. Make up your own mind on the trade-off you think is appropriate between avoiding unemployment and avoiding inflation. For we turn next to government fiscal and monetary policies, and you can't judge meaningfully what is the best policy to adopt unless you know what you're trying to accomplish.

REVIEW

Concepts To Remember

This chapter adds some important new analytical concepts to those developed in earlier chapters. Be sure that you understand especially the following:

unemployment	inflation
frictional unemployment	hyperinflation
structural unemployment	trade-off between policy goals
bottlenecks	

For Analysis and Discussion

1. If we face a choice between reducing unemployment further or avoiding inflation, which goal should have top priority? Why?
2. "The cost of unemployment is wasted resources, that of inflation merely a redistribution of income and wealth." Is this quotation correct? Is it a convincing argument for generally preferring high employment over stable prices in case of a conflict?
3. "So long as unemployment stays at moderate levels (say under 5 per cent), it does not justify strong aggregate demand measures that risk inflation since most of the unemployed are either loafers or temporarily unemployable because they need specific retraining to fit the jobs that more aggregate demand would open up. Thus, the case for more demand to fight unemployment is a weak one." Analyze this argument.
4. "The American public as a whole is economically worse off today than

in 1939 in spite of the apparent huge rise in national income, because inflation has eaten away more than the nominal increase in total income." (True or false? Check the facts for yourself, using *Economic Indicators,* or the *Economic Report of the President.*)

5. Suppose three classes of individuals constitute the total population of an economy: (1) Wealthy, high-income individuals who live entirely on income from their bond coupons; (2) low-income wage and salary earners; and (3) businessmen who employ the workers and live on the profits they make. Analyze the likely effects of an inflation on the three income groups in this economy. Who, if anybody, is hurt by the inflation? Who, if anybody, is helped by it? State clearly any assumptions you make in your analysis.

6. Who is really hurt by inflation, and who gains from it—when inflation is only a few per cent a year? What is the effect on you?

ELEVEN

MONEY, FINANCIAL INSTITUTIONS, AND THE FEDERAL RESERVE

Part A: Private Financial Institutions and the Money Supply.

The Supply of Currency (Government-Issued Money).

The Supply of Bank Money: Checking Deposits.

Potential Creation of Credit by an Individual Bank.

Limits to Credit Creation by an Individual Bank.

Credit Creation and Contraction by the Banking System.

Money and the Creation of Near-Monies.

Part B: The Federal Reserve System and the Money Supply.

The Federal Reserve System.

The Federal Reserve, Interest Rates, and the Supply of Money.

Conclusion.

Appendix: The Individual Bank and the Banking System.

Without money, our complex exchange economy would grind to a halt. Without financial intermediaries like banks, insurance companies, and savings and loan associations to link savers and investors, the circular flow of income would stagnate. Thus, regulation of the supply of money and of the financial intermediaries provides a major channel for government control of aggregate demand. This chapter explains how our monetary and banking system works. Chapter 12 focuses on monetary policy—on how the monetary authorities can help us achieve stable economic growth without unemployment or inflation.

Money and Near-Monies

Think for a minute about what life would be like under a barter economy. Suppose you have a pig. But what you really want is a spool of thread, two new shirts, a movie, and a newspaper. You hear that B down the road has made some shirts. But unless B happens to want some pork chops, you're still out of luck. Your neighbor, C, wants a pig, but he has only lumber to trade. If you're lucky, you may be able to get lumber from C and swap that to B for shirts. But it's going to take some fancy haggling to work out a fair trade with such indivisible products, even if you all have a basic desire to swap. But with money as a medium of exchange and as a standard unit for quoting exchange prices, it's easy to avoid this kind of difficulty. Money is a universally accepted unit of purchasing power, freely spendable and easy to store if you want to postpone spending your income.

When you hear the word money, you think of coins and paper bills. But for hundreds of years cattle served as money in the ancient world. In the Late Roman Empire, small, square pieces of leather were used. Two hundred years ago, hides and wampum beads served as money in North America. Only recently has the world widely adopted the coins and paper notes that we now use; and today we are moving away from them to bank checks except for small transactions. Money cannot be defined merely in terms of the substances that we use for it at any time.

A useful definition of money must be based on what money *does*, not on what it *looks like*. *Actually, around 80 per cent of all payments in the United States today are made by bank checks, only about 20 per cent by currency (i.e., coins and paper money).* We have become so accustomed to using bank checks as money that for practical purposes payment by check is the equivalent of payment by currency, even though the check is a "credit" instrument that is good only if the bank will pay the sum indicated.

Money, therefore, is defined here as the total of currency and bank checking deposits, since these two constitute the nation's generally acceptable media of payment. The top part of Table 11-1 shows the amount of these two major types of money in existence in 1967. *It is very important to note that the bulk of our money is bank checking deposits, not currency, and that the great bulk of our payments are made by bank checks.*

Only a thin line separates actual money from a variety of "near-monies," shown in the bottom half of the table, that are readily convertible into currency or checking deposits. Bank savings deposits, savings and loan shares, short-term U.S. government securities, U.S. savings bonds redeemable on the owner's demand, and

TABLE 11-1 MONEY AND NEAR-MONIES IN THE UNITED STATES *		In Billions
Money		$175
Currency	$ 38	
Checking deposits	137	
Important Near-Monies		542
Saving deposits	213	
Savings and loan shares	114	
Liquid U.S. government securities	120	
Insurance policies (cash value)	95	

* As of Jan. 1, 1967. Currency shown is that held by the public outside banks. Only government securities redeemable on demand or due within one year are included. Data from *Federal Reserve Bulletin* and *Life Insurance Fact Book*.

the cash surrender value of insurance policies are probably the most important of these near-monies. But there are many more that are only a little less easily convertible, including the great mass of longer-term government bonds.

Any of these near-monies serves one function of money reasonably well—that of a store of value. In one way, they are better than money, for the holder receives interest on most near-monies and none on money itself. Balanced against this, the near-money must be converted into actual money before it can be spent. This always involves some inconvenience or delay, and sometimes a risk that the near-money can be converted only at a loss—for example, when government securities must be sold before maturity. The factors that induce people and businesses to shift back and forth between money and near-monies often play an important role in determining how well the economic system works.

Part A: Private Financial Institutions and the Money Supply

Many kinds of private financial institutions have developed over the years to meet people's changing needs. Some of these, such as savings and loan associations and insurance companies, receive long-term savings and channel them on into real investment in buildings, equipment, and the like. Others, such as the ordinary ("commer-cial") banks, serve as depositories for both currently used funds and longer-term savings.

Banks

There are now about 13,000 "commercial" banks in the United States, which accept both "savings" (or time) accounts and "checking" (or demand) accounts. The presumption is that savings accounts represent funds put in the bank for relatively long periods of time, while checking deposits are funds that you may want to use promptly. Thus banks generally feel freer to make long-term loans when their savings deposits go up than when their checking accounts increase. Technically, banks can require depositors to give 30 or 60 days' notice before withdrawing savings deposits, but they almost never do. Actually, the dividing line between savings and checking deposits is not very sharp once the funds have been deposited in the bank. But there *is* one fundamental difference: Checking deposits are spendable money, since depositors can write checks on them. Depositors cannot write checks on savings deposits. A savings deposit can be spent only by withdrawing it in the form of hand-to-hand currency or by transferring it to a checking account.

Harking back to the circular income flow diagram in Figure 4-2, it's obvious that saved funds have to be matched by equal investment or government spending if money income is to continue to flow smoothly through the economy. Do the financial "intermediaries" succeed in connecting up savers with borrowers who will spend the savings back into the income stream? Sometimes they do, and sometimes they don't. Often the commercial banks actually increase or decrease the nation's money supply by their own actions, as we shall see below.

Other
Financial Intermediaries

Financial middlemen have grown up to accommodate about every imaginable type of saver and borrower. Savings and loan associations are much like the savings departments of commercial banks; they draw mainly the savings of lower- and middle-income individuals, make mainly real-estate loans, and have grown enormously since World War II. Life-insurance companies are huge financial intermediaries. Total premiums paid on life-insurance policies and annuities in 1967 were nearly $20 billion, of which almost half represented savings—that is, accumulation of reserves by the insurance companies against future policyholder claims. Insurance companies use these

funds in many ways—for government bonds, real-estate and business loans, and direct real-estate and business investments. "Consumer finance," or "sales finance," companies get most of their funds secondhand from the banks and insurance companies, and then lend these funds directly to consumers at higher rates.

Federal, state, and local governments, though they're out of place in this section on private institutions, have become important financial middlemen between savers and investors. Whenever governments borrow from private savers to finance their expenditures, they're behaving much as private financial middlemen do, though the resulting forms of real investment are different— roads, schools, and space missiles, instead of factories and houses.

Direct Conversion of Savings

Often no financial intermediary is involved in the investment of savings. Every year, businesses re-invest billions of dollars of their own earnings in buildings, equipment, and other investment goods. Individuals buy new houses, which are considered a form of investment in the national income accounts. Individual savers also invest directly in new stocks and bonds, leading on toward real investment.

Financial Investment
and Real Investment

In everyday conversation, the term "investment" is used in several different ways. Often it means *financial* investment—that is, the process of taking funds and "investing" them in stocks, bonds, or the like. Sometimes it also means "investing" in real assets, like houses, as when you buy a new or used house. Each usage is justified by the dictionary, but it is important to remember that in economics, harking back to Chapter 4, the term investment is defined specifically to mean *real* investment in *currently produced* capital goods—factories, machinery, housing, and the like. Thus, if you buy a government bond, this is often considered investment in the newspapers and everyday conversation, but it is not investment as the economist defines the term. In economics, if I use my savings to build a new house, that's real investment. But if I buy General Motors stock, that's only a financial transfer, which passes my savings on to the man who sells me the stock, or to General Motors if it's new stock issue. The question then is: What does that man, or General Motors, do with the funds? Only if the funds go on into real investment in newly produced capital goods or housing is there investment in the economic sense of the term.

THE SUPPLY OF CURRENCY
(GOVERNMENT-ISSUED MONEY)

Most financial intermediaries take savers' funds and channel them on toward investment without increasing or decreasing the stock of spendable money. But the commercial banks, unlike others, may actually increase or decrease the stock of money as they make and collect on loans and investments. In fact, the supply of money in our society depends largely on the lending activities of the commercial banks. Most of the rest of Part A of this chapter, therefore, is devoted to an analysis of the way commercial banks operate, and the way they may increase the nation's money stock through their lending activities.

But first, a brief section on the forces governing the supply of *currency*—government-issued coins and paper money. Currency makes up only about one-fifth of our money supply, and it is used primarily to finance small transactions. As a practical matter, whenever you have a bank deposit account, you can readily get currency, merely by writing a check on your account. Indeed, this is the way currency is placed in the hands of the public. Although it is formally issued by the government (mainly the Federal Reserve Banks, to be explained presently), new currency is made available to the general public through providing it to the banks, which in turn pay it out to depositors on demand. In essence, the Federal Reserve always stands ready to print up enough currency to permit the public to get currency in exchange for any deposits it has.

Table 11-2 shows the kinds of currency now held by the public. Note that "Federal Reserve notes," which constitute most of the paper money you see, make up 90 per cent of all currency. "Other paper money" is mainly silver certificates, which are gradually being replaced by Federal Reserve notes, so that soon our currency system will be made up entirely of F.R. notes and coins.

TABLE 11-2	
CURRENCY IN CIRCULATION *	
	In Billions
Federal Reserve notes	$39
Other paper money	1
Coins	4
Total	$44

* As of January 1, 1967. Includes $5 billion of currency held in bank vaults which was excluded from Table 11-1.

What Determines the Amount of Currency in Circulation?

What determines the amount of currency outstanding? The answer is, to repeat, the Federal Reserve always prints up enough money to give bank depositors all they want in exchange for their deposits. Thus, it is the stock of bank deposits that basically determines the size of the nation's money stock. Once the public has deposits, it can obtain more currency at will. If for some reason the public has more currency than it wants to hold, it simply puts the currency back in the bank and receives a deposit in exchange.

Thus, basically, it is the public's demand for currency that determines how many coins are minted and how much paper money is printed. Remember, though, that although most people probably think of currency as the main form of money, in fact it plays a minor role in our monetary system. People ordinarily keep about one-fifth of their total money holdings in the form of currency, and about four-fifths in demand deposits. Although this ratio varies from time to time, as a general rule the monetary authorities can predict that if households and businesses receive $100 of additional deposits, they will withdraw about $20 of it in the form of new currency.

THE SUPPLY OF BANK MONEY: CHECKING DEPOSITS

Commercial Banks
and the "Creation" of Deposits

Currency is government money issued directly by the Treasury and the Federal Reserve. But the great bulk of our money is not issued by the government at all. Rather, it is provided by the commercial banks in their day-to-day business of making loans and "investments."[1] *The distinguishing feature of modern commercial banking is its ability, through making loans and investments, to "monetize" the debts of others, and thereby in effect to create demand deposits (checking accounts) which serve as money.*

Thus, the commercial banks (that is, the banks we all know and deal with) in good times generally lend out more than we have deposited in them. In bad times, they may insist on repayment of the same loans, wiping out the deposits created when the loans were made. Far from being a passive link in the savings-investment process, commercial banks may drastically affect the flow of funds from savers into real investment.

To understand this rather startling statement that commercial banks "create" checking deposits, you need to know something about how a commercial bank works. The easiest way to get this picture is to look at a simplified balance sheet

[1] When banks make "investments," these are financial investments in government bonds or other securities. Banks do not make *real* investments in the economic sense except to a very minor extent.

of a bank, and then to trace through a few transactions. This will give you an understanding of the nature of deposits and how they get created.

The Bank's Balance Sheet

Banks, like other business institutions, keep a running financial record of what they own and what they owe to other people. What they own and what is owed to them are their "assets." What they owe to other people are their "liabilities." The difference between the two is the "net worth" of the business to its owners, the stockholders. When these three main categories are put together in one statement, they are called a "balance sheet."

A typical bank balance sheet looks like the one below, except we have omitted a lot of minor items to make the essential categories stand out.

What this balance sheet says is that on June 30, 1968, the bank owned cash of $400,000, bonds valued at $800,000, and a building and fixtures valued at $50,000. In addition, it had loaned out $400,000 to customers, who owed the money back to the bank. These are its *assets*.

Offsetting these assets, the bank had deposits of $1,500,000, partly demand and partly time deposits. These deposits are *liabilities*, because they are sums the bank promises to pay to the depositors on demand or on due notice.

The difference between the assets and liabilities is $150,000, which is the estimated *net worth* of the bank. Part of this net worth was originally paid in by the stockholders as "capital" when they bought stock to start the bank. The rest is "surplus and undivided profits," which are mainly the profits made by the bank and not paid

Report of Condition
VICTORY BANK AND TRUST COMPANY
Victory, U.S.A.
June 30, 1968

Assets		Liabilities and Net Worth	
Cash	$ 400,000	Demand deposits	$ 900,000
Bonds	800,000	Savings deposits	600,000
Loans outstanding	400,000	Net worth	150,000
Building and fixtures	50,000		
	$1,650,000		$1,650,000

out to the owners. This breakdown of net worth is not shown on our simplified balance sheet.

POTENTIAL CREATION OF CREDIT BY AN INDIVIDUAL BANK

If we make some highly simplified assumptions, the basic operations of the Victory Bank are laid bare. Assume for the moment that: (1) the bank is on an isolated island where there are no other banks and no communication with other countries; (2) all payments on the island are made by bank check, and no currency is used by the public (the "Cash" item on the balance sheet may, for example, be gold); and (3) there are no laws to control the volume of loans the bank can make.

Suppose now that you, a substantial businessman on the island, go to the banker and ask to borrow $1,000. Your credit is good, and he agrees to make the loan. What happens to the bank's balance sheet?

On the assets side "Loans Outstanding" go up $1,000, and on the liabilities side "Demand Deposits" go up the same amount. Remember that all payments are made by check, so you will simply take your loan as an addition to your checking deposit at the bank. Instead of giving you currency, the banker gives you a checking account. The balance sheet still balances, as it always must. *But now there is $1,000 more spendable money (checking deposits) in existence merely as a result of the bank's making a loan to you. There is no change at all in the amount of "cash" in existence. The bank has taken your promise to pay (which could not serve as money) and has given you its promise to pay on the order of your check (which is widely acceptable money). It has "monetized" your debt.*[2]

This result is shown readily by a simplified bank balance sheet (sometimes called a

[2] Banks ordinarily deduct interest on loans in advance. Thus the bank would give you perhaps $970 and keep the other $30 for interest; you would repay the full $1,000. This process of deducting interest in advance is called "discount" rather than charging "interest." Suppose for simplicity, however, that the bank gives you the full $1,000.

T-account), listing only the *changes* that take place in this transaction. It shows that loans have increased $1,000 on the assets side and that deposits have increased $1,000 on the liabilities side of the balance sheet.

Assets		Liabilities	
Loans	+$1,000	Deposits	+$1,000

Chances are you've borrowed the money because you want to spend it. What happens when you do spend it? Say you buy some machinery from John Jones, and write him a check for $1,000. When Jones presents the check at the bank for payment, $1,000 is taken out of your account and put in his. Since all payments are made by check, he will not want any currency to take home; he merely wants the $1,000 in his checking account so he can spend it when he likes. The new $1,000 of checking deposits has been spent once and is now available for Jones to spend again.

A few days later, Jones buys a new roof for his house, and pays for it with the $1,000. Then the $1,000 is transferred again, from Jones' account to the roofer's account. Now the $1,000 has financed $2,000 of transactions, and the money is as ready for spending again as if the bank had printed up a thousand one-dollar bills and lent them to you. Obviously the new deposit can be spent over and over as long as it is in existence.

In the meantime, what has been happening on the bank's balance sheet? Nothing. The $1,000 checking deposit has been moving from one account to another, but the over-all totals on the balance sheet have remained unchanged since your loan was first entered on the books. The additional deposit was created by the loan. It remains outstanding until the loan is paid off, and may be spent (transferred) any number of times in the meantime.

Some day your loan will come due. If you're a sound businessman, you will have built up your own checking account in preparation for the day by holding on to receipts you get from your customers. On the due date, you go in to see the banker and write him a check for $1,000 on your own account. He returns your promissory note to you, and the loan is paid off. But look at what this does to the bank's balance sheet.

Loans are down by $1,000, since the loan to you is paid off. And deposits are down by $1,000, since you have written a $1,000 check against your account payable to the bank, and this check is not transferred to any other depositor. Repayment of the loan just reverses the original entries that were made when you borrowed the money. The loan was made by giving you a deposit account to write checks on. Repayment of the loan wipes out that checking account, and at the same time wipes out your debt to the bank. The whole transaction has been perfectly businesslike. It has thousands of counterparts every day in the United States. Yet, in effect, the bank has acted like a little mint, creating the checking deposit it lends you and wiping it out when you repay the loan.

Look at the T-account now. It still shows the +$1,000 in loans and deposits from the initial loan. But now we add a —$1,000 for both deposits and loans. The balance sheet is back to its original position, but the economy had an extra $1,000 of money while the loan was outstanding.

	Assets		Liabilities	
Loans	+$1,000		Deposits	+$1,000
	— 1,000			— 1,000

How many other loans can the banker make simultaneously? Obviously, there is no reason why he has to stop with you. Since the public does all its business by check, and since there is no other bank on the island, he need not worry about currency withdrawals or loss of deposits to another bank. It is hard to see what will put a ceiling on the volume of loans the banker can extend. And he could just as well extend credit by buying bonds. Suppose that instead of lending $1,000 to you he buys a new $1,000 bond issued by the island government. The bank enters a $1,000 checking account for the government, which the government can spend when it pleases. The checking deposit is created in exactly the same way, and it stays in existence (however often it is spent) until the bank is repaid for the bond. Since the bank collects interest on every loan or investment made, this looks like a very good thing indeed for the banker and his stockholders.

But it all sounds a little like never-never land. You probably suspect there's a catch in it some place. If people could draw out currency, you say, the banker couldn't go around creating money like that just by writing down entries on his books. And you'd be right—partly right. We need to explore what happens when people can withdraw currency. But before you throw out our whole simplified example, remember one fact from a few pages back: About 80 per cent of all transactions in the United States today are made by bank check. The simple example is not far off on that score after all.

LIMITS TO CREDIT CREATION BY AN INDIVIDUAL BANK

Why don't banks keep on expanding their loans and earning more interest indefinitely, if all they have to do is create new checking accounts by making entries on their books? Now remove the simplifying assumptions of our island economy, one by one, to get a real-world situation like the one that exists in the United States today. But there is still no Federal Reserve to regulate the banks and to provide more currency; the amount is fixed.

Currency Withdrawals

Keep the other assumptions unchanged but assume now that the island's money-using habits are like those in the United States today. The people want to hold about a fifth of their total money supply in the form of currency. Suppose that the bank's "cash" account consists of currency—gold coins or paper currency originally printed by the government.

Now the banker has to be more careful. His balance sheet shows $400,000 of cash. If he is reasonably sure that the 4-to-1 ratio between deposits and currency wanted by the public will continue, he can calculate roughly how far he can safely go in extending new credit. Every time he adds $5 to his deposits the public will withdraw $1 of it in currency. Thus, he might be safe in expanding his deposits nearly $2,000,000, of which he would expect to lose about $400,000 in currency, if he didn't mind seeing his cash account go down to almost zero.

Actually, the banker wouldn't want to run anywhere near that close on his currency lest the bank be unable to meet unexpected depositors' demands and "go broke." Bankers are traditionally conservative people who try to be very sure that they have plenty of currency to meet their obligations. Nevertheless, the basic relationship of currency to potential credit expansion is clear. Whenever there is a chance of a currency withdrawal, the bank must be sure it has enough currency to meet the requests of depositors. This public demand is typically small relative to the total volume of deposits, but the *potential* currency demand imposes a real restriction on the bank. After a banker has been in business a while, he develops a pretty good feel for how heavy currency drains will be at different times of the year and under different circumstances, and governs himself accordingly as a normal part of his business operations. But he also usually keeps a good margin of safety.

There is one other question we should answer before going on to remove the next assumption. What if people lose confidence in the bank and all want their money in currency right now? The answer is painfully clear. The depositors who demand the first $400,000 can be paid off, but the rest are out of luck. In a fractional-reserve banking system—that is, one where the total cash reserves are only a fraction of the system's deposits—the banks cannot pay off all their depositors in currency, for the simple reason that they don't have that much currency. This fact was faced with painful regularity during past financial crises and depressions in the United States. The worst was in 1932–33, when a spreading panic of bank "runs" by people wanting to withdraw their deposits in currency forced the government to close all the banks in the country temporarily to protect them all from bankruptcy. At the end of the "bank holiday," public confidence had been restored enough to permit banks to reopen on a gradual basis.

This situation re-emphasizes the basic fact: Bank deposits largely represent credit extended through banks' making loans and investments, not the deposit of currency in banks. This is obviously

true in the Victory Bank, since it has only $400,000 in cash but deposits of $1,500,000. It is equally true in the United States today, where the total "cash" reserves of all commercial banks are about $60 billion and total deposits (demand plus savings) are nearly $400 billion.

Legal Reserve Requirements

Suppose now that the islanders get to worrying about whether their bank is sound (or maybe they hear about the way things are done in the United States), and pass a law requiring the bank to hold cash reserves equal to at least 20 per cent of its deposits. (Before reading further, ask yourself whether you would favor this law, and why you would or would not.)

This legal requirement puts a real crimp in the bank's expansion possibilities. With $400,000 of cash, the bank can have only $2,000,000 of deposits. It already has $1,500,000, so the limit of its new deposits (credit extension) is $500,000. The actual working limit is less, because the banker needs to worry about likely currency withdrawals as well as about the legal reserve requirement. *Thus, a legal cash-reserve requirement against deposits puts an upper limit on the amount of credit the bank can extend, since new loans or investments mean new deposits.*

How many deposits can be supported on any given reserve depends on the level of the reserve requirement. With a 20 per cent reserve requirement, the bank legally can have five times as many deposits as it has reserves. If the reserve requirement is 50 per cent of deposits, then the bank can only have twice as many deposits as it has reserves. If the reserve requirement is 10 per cent, deposits can be ten times reserves. In fact, the legal reserve requirement now averages about 13 per cent for banks in the United States.

The real function of bank reserve requirements is, thus, to limit the total volume of bank credit that can be extended. Although bank reserve requirements do serve the purpose of protecting the security of customers' deposits to some extent, it should be clear by now that nothing short of 100 per cent reserves would guarantee the continuous availability of cash for all depositors. With much smaller cash reserves, the thing that really keeps the banking system solvent is the confidence of the public in each other's checks. So long as nobody wants much more currency than usual, the banks get along fine. But if everyone tried to get currency for his deposits at the same time, the legal reserve requirement would be of only minor help in paying off the depositors. The basic purpose of reserve requirements is to limit the amount of credit the banks can extend, and hence to limit the amount of deposits they can create.

A few institutional details about legal reserve requirements in the United States are worth attention, although they don't change the basic principles stated above.

1. Only "cash" is counted in computing banks' legal reserves. Government securities and other assets may be nearly as liquid as cash, but they are *not* part of a bank's legal reserve. They become reserves in the eyes of the law only when they are converted into cash.[3]

2. When a bank has more cash reserves than the law requires it to have, the excess is termed *"excess reserves."* Whenever a bank has excess reserves, it feels some pressure to expand its loans and investments. Idle reserves earn no interest. Thus, the banker generally tries to keep excess reserves at the lowest level consistent with his liquidity needs and the availability of safe loans and investments.

3. There are different reserve requirements for different banks and for different types of deposits. Banks that are members of the Federal Reserve System (see Part B of this chapter) have their reserve requirements set by that federal authority. "Nonmember" banks have their requirements set by state laws or state authorities. In either case, reserve requirements are generally higher on demand deposits than on time deposits,

and on large city banks than on small country banks.

Adverse Clearing Balances

Now drop the last special assumption—that there is only one bank doing business—and return the Victory Bank to the U.S.A. Here there are lots of other banks in operation, and the Victory Bank needs to take this fact into account. If the Victory Bank makes loans to its customers, there is a good chance that they will write checks to people who do business elsewhere. And when this happens, the Victory Bank has to pay cash to the other bank. This is a most important change in the bank's position.

In a many-bank system, the most important limitation on the power of an individual bank to expand credit to the legal limit permitted by its reserves is the fear it will lose reserves to other banks. If Bank A has to pay cash to Bank B when they settle up the checks written back and forth between their customers, we say that Bank A has an "adverse clearing balance." *And to Bank A an adverse clearing balance is just like a currency drain—it takes away cash reserves.*

Ordinarily, the checks written against any bank and the checks it has to collect against other banks roughly balance off. You send $500 to Philadelphia to pay a bill, and your neighbor gets a payment from Philadelphia. But if the Victory Bank expands its credit more rapidly than other banks do, it's likely to lose reserves on balance. Recognizing this likelihood, few bankers would make new loans and investments amounting to anything like $5,000 on $1,000 of excess reserves (assuming a 20 per cent reserve requirement) unless they had some special reason to suppose that they would not lose reserves through adverse clearing balances. Indeed, bankers ordinarily hesitate to extend new credit much beyond their *excess* reserves.

To summarize what we have said so far about banks and the supply of money: (1) One function of financial institutions is to channel savings to borrowers. This activity has no direct effect on the volume of money. (2) Commercial banks are distinguished from other savings institutions in that, as a group, they do not simply lend

[3] In the United States, a bank's legal reserves are usually less than the "cash" shown in its balance sheet. Cash on the balance sheet includes currency in the bank's vault and deposits at other private banks and in the Federal Reserve Banks. For Federal Reserve member banks, only deposits with the Federal Reserve Bank and "vault cash" are considered legal reserves. Since this detail is unimportant for many purposes, we will consider all cash shown to be reserves. But this assumption won't work if you try to use actual published banking statistics.

out the money that people have deposited, but actually "create" money by giving borrowers current spending power in exchange for future promises to repay the bank. (3) The power of an individual commercial bank to expand credit on its reserves is limited by (a) legal reserve requirements, and by the dangers of (b) currency withdrawals by customers and (c) adverse clearing balances.

CREDIT CREATION
AND CONTRACTION
BY THE BANKING SYSTEM

Any one bank that expands loans when other banks are not expanding is checked by adverse clearing balances. *But when we view the banking system as a whole, the limitation imposed by adverse clearing balances disappears. This is because the reserves one bank loses another gains. Since the banking system as a whole loses no reserves through adverse clearing balances, it can create deposits through lending up to the multiple permitted by the legal reserve requirement ratio, just as could the island bank above.* If, for example, the legal reserve requirement against deposits is 20 per cent, the banking system can expand deposits up to five times its reserves.

Of course, the banking system faces limitations from the withdrawal of currency by deposits and from increases in reserve banks, just as did the Victory Bank above. For currency withdrawals reduce the volume of total reserves in the banking system, and higher legal reserve requirements reduce the multiple by which deposits can exceed reserves. But the apparent check of adverse clearing balances vanishes when we consider all banks together.[4]

It is easy to see that adverse clearing balances don't limit the expansion power of the banking system. But since individual banks normally must be careful not to lend much beyond their excess reserves, normally the banking system only gradually expands deposits to the legal limit on new reserves.[5]

Sometimes, however, the banking system expands credit very rapidly. For example, during World War II the banking system created $100 billion of new deposits (money) by purchasing new government securities from the U.S. Treasury. During each "War Loan Drive" the commercial banks bought billions of dollars of new government bonds, and paid for them by giving the government demand deposits to spend. In a War Loan Drive, for example, the banks would buy $10 billion of new government bonds and a corresponding $10 billion of new deposits would be created in a single day. The banks would enter $10 billion of deposits for the U.S. government on their books, with a matching asset of $10 billion of new bonds they had acquired. The government could then spend the money, and the new deposits became part of the money supply for spending and respending. Never before had this country seen such mass creation of deposits, and never before had the process of bank-credit creation been demonstrated with such simplicity.

The money creation process works in reverse too. If one dollar of reserves is the basis for five dollars of outstanding bank deposits created by loans and investments, the loss of each dollar of reserves may force contraction of five dollars in deposits. Indeed, if banks are fully "loaned up" to their legal required reserve limit, loss of reserves must cause a contraction of deposits, and hence of loans and investments.

Such a contraction is brought about when banks reduce their loans or investments; remember the $1,000 reduction in deposits when the Victory Bank loan was paid off above. If the banks run short of reserves and cannot obtain more, they reduce their deposits by calling in loans as they come due or by selling bonds. As in the Victory Bank case, the borrower accumulates a $1,000 deposit to pay off his loan when it comes due; he writes a check to the bank on the due

---

[4] Since the Federal Reserve imposes higher legal reserve requirements against demand deposits than against savings deposits, the power of the banking system to expand credit depends to some extent on whether the public chooses to hold its deposits in demand or saving accounts.

[5] For doubters, the Appendix to this chapter explains in detail how the banking system can expand deposits fivefold on new reserves, assuming a 20 per cent reserve requirement, even though no individual bank ever lends out more than its excess reserves.

day; and the bank's deposits and loans are both reduced by $1,000. The transaction is the exact reverse of that which created the deposits when the loan was originally made. The process would be the same if the government paid off some of its debt which the banks had bought and were holding in the form of bonds.

Sometimes, as with credit expansion, credit contraction snowballs in a massive way. In the Great Depression of the early 1930's, for example, nearly one-third of the nation's money supply (mainly demand deposits) was wiped out through the contraction of bank loans and investments. Banks lost reserves rapidly as the public withdrew currency in a scare wave, and this forced them to call for payment of loans and sell off their government bonds. Bank deposits plus currency fell from $46 billion to $30 billion between 1929 and 1933. Remember that each dollar of currency withdrawn removes the reserve base for several dollars of deposits and loans and investments.[6]

MONEY AND THE CREATION
OF NEAR-MONIES

Only commercial banks can "create" money, because by law only they can hold demand (checking) deposits. But savings deposits, savings and loan shares, and other near-monies are close substitutes for money as a store of purchasing power. And other financial institutions can "create" near-monies, as banks "create" demand deposits. Moreover, by shifting their savings between checking deposits and time deposits at

[6] In view of the important part bank-credit expansion and contraction play in business cycles, some economists advocate requiring 100 per cent reserves behind all bank deposits. They argue that this step would do much to lessen the severity of business fluctuations. They point out that businessmen and others who wish to borrow could continue to do so, through "savings and loan organizations." These organizations would receive savings from the public, but could lend only as much as savers deposited, rather than being able to create money as the banks do at present. The present banks might be split into two parts. One part would act as a storehouse for funds that savers simply wanted to keep idle for checking or other purposes (on which depositors would probably have to pay service charges). The other part would act as a savings and loan organization to receive savings (paying interest on them) and to lend these savings to borrowers at a higher rate of interest.

banks and savings and loan associations, the public can change the amount of checking deposits (money) in existence.

Suppose John Doe, seeing an ad promising 5 per cent at a savings and loan association, saves part of his paycheck and buys a $100 savings and loan share, which is much the same thing as putting a $100 savings deposit in the savings and loan association. Or he may just withdraw $100 from his own checking account and transfer it to the S. and L. Either way, he transfers $100 from a commercial bank demand deposit to the savings and loan association. Demand deposits are down, S. and L. time deposits are up correspondingly. But the S. and L. association will probably soon redeposit the $100 in its own checking account at a commercial bank, so that it can spend or lend the money itself.

Look now at the results: First, commercial bank reserves and demand deposits are unchanged in total. But second, John has a fine $100 money substitute in his savings and loan share; this will presumably decrease the amount of actual money (currency and checking deposits) he needs to hold at any given time to carry on his transactions and have an adequate margin of liquidity. It thus frees a bigger share of demand deposits for "active" use in making payments for goods and services. Third, the savings and loan association has $100, most of which it will now feel free to lend out to new borrowers. John's decision to substitute a near-money for actual money in his own financial position has *both* increased the nation's total supply of money plus near-monies, *and* increased the total lending power of all financial institutions, since the commercial banks have lost no reserves and the savings and loan association has gained $100 in additional lending power (less whatever part of the total it feels it must hold as a ready cash reserve).

Thus, we must add to the money-creating powers of the commercial banks a similar power of other financial intermediaries (for example, mutual savings banks and insurance companies) to "create" near-monies, as individuals and businesses transfer money holdings into near-monies. In total, therefore, the power of the financial system to generate money plus near-monies far exceeds its power to create money alone.

It is important to note that shifts of deposits between commercial banks and other financial intermediaries can thus influence the size of the money stock and the amount of total deposits supportable on any volume of bank reserves. If the public decides to shift its bank deposits from demand to savings accounts, this directly reduces the total stock of money, since savings deposits are not spendable money. But it also increases the total volume of deposits (demand plus savings) supportable on any given level of reserve, since reserve requirements are lower against time than against demand deposits. *The money stock is, therefore, not entirely under the control of the government which controls the volume of bank reserves, although it is clear that by regulating the volume of reserves the government can generally control the volume of deposits which banks create.*

Part B: The Federal Reserve System and the Money Supply

The Constitution gives to Congress the power to "coin money and regulate the value thereof." Congress has since delegated most of this power to the Federal Reserve System, which was established in 1914 after years of painful experience with repeated financial crises. The following pages first describe the Federal Reserve System and indicate briefly how it carries out its day-to-day activities. Then we analyze more fully how the Federal Reserve influences interest rates and the supply of money, the "Fed's" main channels for regulating the level of aggregate demand.

THE FEDERAL RESERVE SYSTEM

The Federal Reserve is the major agency established by Congress to provide currency for the nation; to furnish a wide variety of financial services to the government and to the economy; and, most important, to regulate the total amount of money and to maintain "monetary and credit conditions favorable to sound business activity in all fields—agricultural, industrial, commercial." [7]

Organization

The Federal Reserve System is made up of the following:

1. The Board of Governors.
2. The 12 Federal Reserve Banks.

[7] *The Federal Reserve System: Its Purposes and Functions* (Board of Governors of the Federal Reserve System), p. 23. This little booklet provides a simple, authoritative statement of the aims and operations of the Federal Reserve System.

3. The Federal Open Market Committee.
4. The member banks.

1. The Board of Governors is composed of seven members, appointed by the President and confirmed by the Senate. Members are appointed for 14 years. One term expires every two years, an effort to safeguard the Board as far as possible from political pressure groups. In most matters, the Board of Governors is ultimately responsible for the major policies of the 12 Federal Reserve Banks; and, since the Federal Reserve Banks in turn supervise and regulate the member banks, ultimate responsibility for the entire system is largely centralized in the Board of Governors.

2. Each of the 12 Federal Reserve Banks serves a certain district in the United States. The banks are located in Boston, New York, Philadelphia, Cleveland, Richmond, Atlanta, Chicago, St. Louis, Minneapolis, Kansas City, Dallas, and San Francisco. Each Federal Reserve Bank was founded by the sale of stock to member banks, which are required to buy stock. Though technically they are thus privately owned, the Federal Reserve Banks are operated in the public interest, not for profit.

3. The Federal Open Market Committee consists of the seven members of the Board of Governors, plus five of the presidents of the Federal Reserve Banks. This 12-member committee determines the system's policy on open-market operations—that is, the purchase and sale of government securities in the open market. These operations, explained below, are the primary means by which the Federal Reserve authorities

attempt to control the volume of bank credit. Although the Board of Governors does not determine open-market policy independently, its seven members constitute a majority of the Open Market Committee.

4. The member banks include all national banks (chartered by the federal government) in the United States and those state banks that agree to conform to the requirements set up for member banks. In 1967, about 6,000 of the 13,000 commercial banks in the United States were member banks, but the nonmember banks were almost all small ones, representing only about 10 per cent of the total deposits of the banking system.

Service Functions of the Federal Reserve

Before we turn to the major policy functions of the Fed, its important, though routine, service functions deserve a brief survey.

Holding Member-Bank Reserves. Each member bank must by law keep its legally required reserves on deposit at its Federal Reserve Bank.[8] These reserve balances at the Reserve Banks are essentially checking accounts that the member banks maintain with the Federal Reserve, just as an individual has a checking account with a commercial bank. A member bank must always keep the reserve required by law, but beyond this requirement it is free to draw on, or add to, its reserve account as it wishes. If it needs currency to pay out to its customers, it simply draws the needed amount from its excess reserve balance at the Federal Reserve Bank. Member banks receive no interest on their reserve balances.[9]

Furnishing Currency for Circulation. All currency in the United States is issued either by the Federal Treasury or by the Federal Reserve Banks. Treasury currency—mainly coins—makes up about 10 per cent of the total. It is issued by the Treasury but is placed in circulation largely through the Reserve Banks and the commercial banks. The Reserve Banks themselves issue Federal Reserve notes, which make up nearly all our paper money. Federal Reserve notes are liabilities of the issuing Federal Reserve Bank, and also of the federal government. Each Federal Reserve note must be backed fully by collateral held by the issuing Bank. At least 25 per cent must be gold; the other 75 per cent may be gold, government bonds, or other designated acceptable security.[10]

Furnishing currency for circulation is a continuing operation. New currency is constantly being put into circulation to replace old, worn currency. Currency in circulation grows gradually as the economy grows, and increases temporarily at certain periods of the year, such as Christmas and the Fourth of July, when people and businesses want more hand-to-hand money. Currency is put into circulation very simply. The banks get currency by drawing on their reserve accounts at the Reserve Banks and pay out the currency to customers who make withdrawals from their deposit accounts. The Reserve Banks always keep large supplies of paper money and coin on hand to meet the needs of member banks. If the public has more currency than it wants, it simply redeposits the currency in commercial banks, which in turn redeposit the excess in their reserve accounts at the Federal Reserve Banks. The Federal Reserve thus stands ready to furnish currency for circulation whenever the member banks need it.

Clearing and Collecting Checks. Most payments in the United States are made by means of bank checks. And most bank checks drawn on out-of-town banks are "cleared" through the Federal Reserve System to avoid shipping currency. Suppose Jones in Chicago sells a $100 bill of goods to Smith in Detroit, and Smith pays by a check on his Detroit bank. Jones deposits the check at his bank in Chicago. The Chicago bank sends the check to the Chicago Federal Reserve Bank, which increases the reserves of the Chicago bank by $100 and decreases the reserves of the Detroit bank by $100. The check is then sent to the Detroit bank,

---

[8] Except for the "vault cash" (currency) which it keeps in its own vaults.

[9] The use of the word "reserve" in banking is quite different from that in ordinary business accounting, as we shall see in the Appendix to Chapter 19.

[10] Actually, the gold is stored mainly in Treasury vaults; the Federal Reserve holds instead paper "gold certificates." As this was written, serious consideration was being given to the possibility of eliminating this 25 per cent gold requirement.

which decreases Smith's account by $100. Jones in Chicago has his $100; Smith in Detroit has $100 less. And since both banks keep their reserves with the Chicago Federal Reserve Bank, the check is cleared simply by increasing the reserve account of the Chicago bank and decreasing the account of the Detroit bank. No currency has to be shipped around the country.

When Jones and Smith are in different Federal Reserve districts (say Chicago and New York), the process is identical except that the New York and Chicago Federal Reserve Banks must settle their accounts. They offset the checks due to each other through an "Interdistrict Settlement Fund."

To give some idea of the magnitude of this clearing function, in 1966 the Federal Reserve System handled nearly 6 billion checks, with a total value of nearly $2 trillion. This total included many checks on nonmember banks, which are permitted to use the Federal Reserve check-clearing facilities.

Supervising Member Banks. Banks in this country are supervised by several authorities. The Federal Reserve supervises all member banks. Other federal and state authorities also supervise banks. The same bank may be subject to supervision by as many as three authorities. Generally these authorities cooperate, but not always.

Each Federal Reserve Bank examines the member banks in its own district. The examiners make detailed reports to the Federal Reserve Bank on the management, the loans and investments, and the general condition of each member bank. If any member bank refuses to conform to the standards of sound banking practice specified by the Federal Reserve, the Board of Governors may remove its officers and directors or take away its right to make use of Federal Reserve credit facilities. These punitive powers seldom need to be exercised.

Fiscal Agent for the Federal Government. The Federal Reserve Banks are bankers for the federal government. They carry most of the government's checking accounts; they handle the issue and redemption of government securities; and they act as fiscal agent for the government in numerous other ways. The government is contin-

uously receiving tax funds, borrowing, paying out funds for salaries, planes, and so on. It issues and redeems huge volumes of securities. These activities keep many of the Federal Reserve personnel busy.

THE FEDERAL RESERVE, INTEREST RATES, AND THE SUPPLY OF MONEY

In the United States, the Federal Reserve is the "central bank." Its major job is to maintain sound monetary conditions which will help achieve a stably growing, prosperous economy.

Federal Reserve control over the supply of money and interest rates is exercised largely by controlling the volume and use of member-bank reserves. Without excess reserves, commercial banks cannot extend more credit. Excess reserves make possible (but do not assure) expansion of bank earning assets and deposits. Thus, Federal Reserve powers are designed largely to provide or withdraw excess reserves.

The Fundamental Nature of Central Banking

A Federal Reserve Bank is a central bank— a banker's bank. Member-bank reserves *are* member-bank deposits at the Reserve Banks. Thus, Federal Reserve control over the volume of member-bank reserves is, in fact, control over the volume of its own deposits. And the Fed can create or destroy the reserves which provide commercial banks' powers to lend and invest.

Before the establishment of the Federal Reserve as a central bank in 1914, the nation's commercial banks faced periodic crises. Mass currency withdrawals by depositors in times of panic exhausted reserves and forced widespread bank failures, because there was no way to convert good but nonliquid loans into currency on short notice. The Federal Reserve was established largely to remedy this situation. Member-bank reserves were to be held by the Reserve Banks, and the Reserve authorities were given power to provide new reserves for member banks in times of need.

The ability to create new bank reserves and to provide liquidity to commercial-bank assets is the distinguishing feature of a true central bank. The Federal Reserve can create new reserves (member-bank deposits) by buying bonds or making loans to member banks, just as member banks create deposits by buying bonds or making loans to businesses and individuals. It does this the same way as commercial banks extend credit—by giving deposits in exchange for borrowers' promises to repay at a later date. If a member bank wants more reserves (i.e., deposits at the Fed), it can borrow at the Fed, giving its own promise to repay. Or it can sell some of its government bonds to the Fed, receiving reserves (deposits at the Fed) in payment. In either case, the Fed "creates" the new reserves, by giving the member bank a new deposit (reserve) in exchange for the new assets it receives from the member bank.

Main Federal Reserve Powers

The Fed attempts to control the volume and direction of commercial bank lending and investing, and hence the volume of bank deposits, through the following seven major channels. The first three (open-market operations, reserve requirements, and the rediscount rate) are aimed largely at controlling the total supply, or "quantity," of credit, through regulating the commercial banks' excess reserves. The others are aimed more at controlling the flow of credit to particular uses, such as speculation. These latter are thus called "selective," or "qualitative," credit controls. In regulating the supply of credit, the Fed also influences interest rates—the "cost" of money.

Open-Market Operations

Purchase and sale of U.S. government securities in the open market is the major device used by the Fed to control the volume of member-bank reserves. By buying "Governments," the Fed increases member-bank reserves; by selling Governments, it reduces member-bank reserves. To understand how this works, consider first the combined balance sheet of the Federal Reserve Banks, shown at the bottom of this page.

This shows the two big assets of the F.R. Banks, gold and government securities. The offsetting major liabilities are member bank deposits and F.R. notes. *It is essential to remember that the "cash reserves" shown on commercial-bank statements are mainly not actual currency but are instead deposits held at the Federal Reserve Banks.*

1. *The Federal Reserve can create new reserves for the commercial banks by buying government bonds in the open market—thereby stimulating the commercial banks to make new loans and investments.* If the Federal Reserve wants to encourage more bank loans, it goes into the open market and buys $1,000 worth of U.S. government bonds, say from a commercial bank.[11] To pay for these bonds, it simply gives the bank a $1,000 deposit credit (new reserve balance) at the Federal Reserve. The commercial bank has $1,000 of new reserves, and they are all excess reserves since its deposits have not been changed by the transaction. The Federal Reserve has created a $1,000 member-bank deposit (reserve account) against the government bond. Since the

[11] Remember that the Fed, while part of the government, is quite separate from the U.S. Treasury. The Fed does not issue any bonds itself, but merely buys and sells government bonds that have been issued previously by the Treasury.

FEDERAL RESERVE BANKS
Jan. 1, 1967
(In Billions of Dollars)

Gold	$13		Member-bank deposits	$19
U.S. securities	44		F.R. notes	40
	$57 *			$59 *

* Does not balance because minor items are omitted.

commercial banks have $1,000 of new excess reserves, they are in a position to expand their loans by four or five times that amount, depending on legal reserve requirements.[12]

Consider the T-accounts for the commercial and the Federal Reserve Banks. They show the $1,000 addition to excess reserves on the books of both the Fed and the commercial bank.

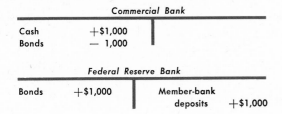

Does all this seem a little like black magic—new commercial-bank reserves created out of nowhere by the Federal Reserve Banks, reserves which in turn can provide the basis for a much larger amount of commercial-bank deposits, also created out of nowhere? In a sense, it is. But each dollar of new member-bank reserves at the Fed is matched by a newly acquired government bond, and each new deposit at the commercial bank will be matched by a borrower's promise to repay. There is no magic. But through this process the Fed is able to "create" new member-bank reserves, which are often called "high-powered money" since they can in turn serve as the reserves behind a larger volume of newly-created deposits at commercial banks.

Is there a limitation on how many new reserves the Federal Reserve can create in this way? No direct limit. Until 1965 the Fed was required to have a 25 per cent gold reserve against member-bank deposits, but now there is no such requirement. Indirectly, gold may limit the Fed's expansionary power. It must still hold 25 cents in gold against each dollar of Federal Reserve notes issued. Since currency expands roughly in proportion to bank deposits, bank credit expansion will indirectly require more gold to back the expanding

currency held by the public.[13] But the gold drag here is a small one, since currency makes up only about one-fifth of the total money stock and each dollar of currency requires only 25 cents of gold. Thus, *very roughly* each dollar of money expansion will require only about 5 cents of gold (i.e., $\frac{1}{5}$ of $\frac{1}{4} = \frac{1}{20}$ of the new money).

How effective is the Federal Reserve in lowering interest rates and stimulating new commercial-bank loans when it provides new reserves? More reserves push a banker to extend new credit, for no banker likes to lose the interest he might earn on idle reserves. In those rare cases where excess reserves are already large because bankers don't see any "sound" borrowers looking for loans, still more excess reserves may not help much. But don't forget that banks can also buy government bonds. If their excess reserves are increased when no desirable loans are available, they may increase the volume of deposits by buying up government bonds. History suggests that with rare exceptions commercial bankers have increased their loans and investments about as far as their excess reserves permit. The big exception was the depression of the 1930's, when the commercial banks held billions of dollars of excess reserves for nearly a decade.

Note that the Fed's open market purchases also directly push down interest rates on bonds. Fed purchases will tend to bid up the prices of bonds which is equivalent to forcing down the interest yield on the bonds. (See the footnote on page 93 if you don't remember why.) Since lower interest rates also help to stimulate the economy, open market purchases are a two-pronged weapon against recession.

2. *When the Open Market Committee wants to decrease member-bank reserves, it sells government securities in the open market to whoever bids for them—individuals, businesses, or banks. This reduces commercial-bank reserves*

---

[12] There is substantially, but not quite, the same effect if the Fed buys the bond from a business or individual. Trace through the effect for yourself. Section (2) below will suggest the analysis if you need help.

[13] On rare occasions the Federal Reserve has faced the danger of running out of gold. For what happens in such cases, see Chapter 12. By 1967, there was widespread support for elimination of the remaining 25 per cent gold set-aside against Federal Reserve notes, in order to free all our gold for international uses if needed.

when the Federal Reserve is paid for the bonds. Consider how.

If a member bank buys the bond, it pays by giving $1,000 of its reserves to the Federal Reserve; on the bank's balance sheet, "cash" goes down and "bonds" go up by $1,000. Thus, the bank loses a full $1,000 of excess reserves, since its deposits remain unchanged. If a business or individual buys the bond from the Reserve, the effect is almost the same. He pays by a check on his bank. His bank's reserves are reduced by $1,000 when the Federal Reserve presents the check for collection. The member bank's deposits also drop by the $1,000 transferred from the bond buyer's account to the Federal Reserve. Since the bank loses $1,000 in both deposits and reserves, its required reserves are $200 lower but its excess reserves drop by $800. Excess reserves contract a little less than in the bank-purchase case, but the general effect is similar.

If the bank buys the bonds, the T-account entries at the commercial bank are as shown above the dotted line. If an individual buys it, the entries are as shown below the dotted line.[14]

Cash	−$1,000
Bonds	+ 1,000
....	....
Cash	− 1,000

Deposits	−$1,000

Federal Reserve open-market sales can limit bank credit expansion when they reduce excess reserves to low levels. The Federal Reserve might face a problem if banks had large excess reserves on hand, for the banks could then lose reserves and still have an adequate base for new loans and investments. But in recent decades excess reserves have been small, and the Fed has had plenty of government bonds to absorb all the excess reserves of the banking system if it wants to.

Rediscount Rate Changes

When a member bank runs short of reserves, it may borrow from its Federal Reserve Bank, just as you and I borrow at a commercial bank. In such a case the member bank could "rediscount" notes. The member bank has made loans to customers against customers' promises to repay, called "notes," or "commercial paper." It can "rediscount" these notes with its Federal Reserve Bank—that is, it can use the note as collateral to borrow additional reserves. The rate of interest, or discount, charged by the Federal Reserve to member banks is called the "rediscount rate." Or member banks may borrow using government securities as collateral. In rediscounting, the initiative is in the hands of the commercial banker to increase his reserves, while open-market operations are at the discretion of the Fed.

The Fed raises the rediscount rate to discourage member-bank borrowing and lowers the rate to encourage it. But few bankers like to borrow, and most borrow only when they badly need to in order to get additional reserves. Moreover, the Fed discourages member bank borrowing except on a temporary basis. Thus, the rediscount rate is of relatively minor direct importance. But changes in the rediscount rate have an important psychological effect on the banking and business communities because they are viewed as evidence of the Fed's general position on monetary expansion or restraint.[15]

Changes in Member-Bank Reserve Requirements

In 1933, a drastic new power was given to the Board of Governors—the power to raise and lower legal reserve requirements for member banks. Reserve requirements against demand deposits can be varied between 10 and 22 per cent for city banks and 7 and 14 per cent for country banks, and against time deposits between 3 and 6 per cent for all banks.

By raising reserve requirements, the Board wipes out member banks' excess reserves and directly restricts credit expansion. Suppose a member bank has $1,000,000 deposits and $200,000 reserves, and the required legal reserve ratio is 16 per cent. It has a comfortable $40,000 of excess

[14] If the buyer pays in currency, he reduces the amount of currency in circulation, also a reduction in the money stock. But payment in currency is very unusual.

[15] Sometimes you see the term "free reserves." These are excess reserves *less* commercial-bank borrowing from the Fed. Since each commercial bank must repay its borrowing promptly, many experts believe that free reserves are better than excess reserves as an indication of commercial banks' ability to extend new credit. When free reserves are negative, they are called "net borrowed reserves."

reserves. If the Board raises the legal requirement to 20 per cent, the reserve required jumps to $200,000 and the bank's excess reserve is wiped out. Conversely, lowering legal reserve requirements increases excess reserves.

Changing reserve requirements is a relatively heavy, blunt tool of credit control, compared with the gradual, flexible way open-market operations can be used. Thus, the Reserve authorities change reserve requirements only infrequently, depending instead primarily on open-market operations.

"Selective" Credit Controls

The preceding general controls over bank reserves are often called "indirect" controls, since they only control the total volume of bank lending, the level of interest rates, and the stock of money. They leave the private banker free to allocate his funds as he wishes among different borrowers. In addition, the Fed has smaller "direct," or "selective," controls over particular bank loans and uses to which bank credit is put. These selective controls permit the Fed to influence directly the uses of bank credit. Many economists question the effectiveness of such controls, because money, once created, flows freely from one sector of the economy to the other, and it is very difficult to control any one sector by limiting lending directly to it. But such selective controls may have important temporary effects.

Maximum Interest Rates on the Deposits. The Fed has the power to set maximum interest rates on different classes of deposits, and other regulatory agencies have similar powers over other financial intermediaries, such as the savings and loan associations. By raising or lowering these interest rates differently at different institutions, the bank supervisors can significantly influence the competitive positions of the different financial institutions for savers' funds, and thus indirectly influence where savers' funds go.

For example, in the 1960's, the S. & L.'s bid many deposits away from the commercial banks, and channeled these funds into mortgages to finance home building, especially in the West. Originally, there were no governmental ceilings on the rates which S. & L.'s could pay their depositors, but commercial banks had maximum rates on their savings deposits. In the mid-1960's, the Fed raised the maximum rates which commercial banks might pay, and thus permitted them to bid deposits back away from the S. & L.'s. This channeled funds away from the housing industry toward the broader uses made by commercial banks of their lending power.

Once detailed direct controls are instituted which influence the competitive position of different financial institutions, difficult questions of equity arise, and there is an unfortunate tendency for such direct controls to proliferate.

Control of Stock-market Credit: Margin Requirements. Often customers buy stocks and bonds "on margin." That is, they pay the broker a cash "margin" (down payment) and borrow the rest of the purchase price from the broker, leaving the newly purchased securities as collateral for the loan. The broker, in turn, typically borrows from commercial banks what the security buyer does not put up as margin (cash). The smaller the margin required, the more the buyer can borrow of the purchase price. If margin requirements are raised, therefore, the use of bank credit for purchasing securities is restricted. If margin requirements are lowered, it becomes easier to buy securities on credit.

The Fed has power to set minimum margin requirements for dealings on the major securities exchanges, ranging up to 100 per cent cash payments. In the wild stock market speculation of the late 1920's, most stock was bought on margins of 10 per cent or less, so speculators found it easy to bid up prices on borrowed money. Now, with margin requirements much higher, most stock is bought with full cash payment, or with relatively little borrowing. Most economists believe that Federal Reserve margin requirements exercise a healthy restraint on speculative stock purchases under boom conditions.

"Direct Pressure" or "Moral Suasion." When the Fed wants to discourage bank lending, it may use "direct pressure," or "moral suasion," on the bankers. Bank examiners may be instructed to tighten up their requirements for "good" loans and investments. Reserve officials may send letters

to offending member banks, pointing out the dangers of "speculative" loans and investments. Reserve officials may frown when member banks come to the discount window for temporary loans. The Reserve officials may also make public statements warning against inflation and overexpansion of credit. In extreme cases, the Reserve Banks may simply refuse to lend to offending member banks that need additional reserves for expansion. There is not much evidence that such moral suasion is very effective. There is even less hope that it can do anything to persuade bankers to make more loans in hard times.

Consumer Credit Controls. During World War II and in the Korean War, the Fed was temporarily given power to regulate consumer credit (on installment purchases and charge accounts) and real-estate credit. On both housing and consumer credit, the Fed imposed minimum down payments and maximum repayment periods. Raising down payments made it hard to buy without cash in hand; shortening the total payment period increased the monthly payment required. For many buyers, these steps appeared to restrain purchases more than would a rise in the prices of durables or houses.

The wartime goal was partly to restrain inflationary consumer demand, partly to divert demand away from the durables that competed directly with war production. But many people objected, especially the lower-income groups who couldn't afford to pay cash for everything. Why, they asked, should the few cars and refrigerators go exclusively to the rich? In wartime, shouldn't rationing or some other equitable system of distributing scarce goods be adopted, rather than merely shutting out the poor by imposing drastic controls on borrowing? Such consumer-credit controls lasted through the war and as long afterward as inflationary pressures continued strong. But in 1952, Congress eliminated them, and repeatedly has refused to restore them in spite of requests from both the Board and the President for reinstatement at least on a "stand-by" basis.

CONCLUSION

In perspective, the Fed has enormous powers to check any credit expansion—indeed, to force mass contraction—if it chooses to use them. By dumping all its $45 billion of government securities on the market and by raising reserve requirements to their legal limits, the Fed could bring on a massive deflation sure to send the entire economic system into chaos. Of course, the Federal Reserve officials would never consider such a foolish action. But this points up the great power inherent in the Federal Reserve's restrictive measures. The main problem is to use the existing controls effectively, not to seek more powerful weapons.

The Fed's ability to stimulate bank lending is also great and it has substantially unlimited power to create new reserves through open-market operations. Only the 25 per cent gold requirement against Federal Reserve notes might inhibit this power. But success on the expansion side is a little less sure. Banks need not necessarily make new loans in recession merely because they receive new excess reserves. By flooding the banking system with excess reserves, the Fed can almost surely expand the nation's money stock, since the banks will buy government securities even if they won't lend to business concerns and consumers. But if direct loans to business and consumers are needed to stimulate investment and consumption, the problem may be a tough one. And, as Chapter 8 indicated, even if deposits are expanded through purchase of government bonds, the public may choose to convert its new demand deposits into money substitutes like savings deposits, rather than spending new funds on goods and services.

But even with these limitations, the Fed's powers are great. The real issue is how to use these powers most effectively to achieve a stably growing, high-employment economy without inflation. This is the task of monetary policy, to which we now turn in Chapter 12.

REVIEW

Concepts and Institutions To Remember

This chapter has introduced several important concepts and institutions. Be especially sure you understand the following:

money	credit contraction
currency	Board of Governors
demand (checking) deposits	Open Market Committee
savings and time deposits	Federal Reserve Banks
near-monies	member banks
bank credit	gold reserves
commercial bank	"creation" of bank reserves
financial intermediary	open-market operations
credit creation	rediscount rate
bank reserves	selective credit controls
excess reserves	margin requirements
reserve requirements	consumer credit
adverse clearing balance	

For Analysis and Discussion

1. Why is currency worth more than its value as paper and ink?
2. Get a copy of a recent balance sheet from one of your local banks. What main types of credit does this bank extend? Which of these types of credit would you expect to be most liquid (most readily convertible into cash) in case of a serious recession in over-all business activity?
3. If banks hold "reserves" equal to only a small fraction of their deposits, are you safe in depositing your money in a bank? Explain why or why not.
4. If you were a banker, would you hold excess reserves? Why or why not?
5. In a small, isolated economy (i.e., no foreign trade) with money-using habits comparable to those of the United States, there are five identical banks. Each bank's balance sheet is as shown below. The law prescribes that banks must hold a 25 per cent cash reserve against deposits. There is no central bank.

Cash	$ 6,000,000	Deposits	$23,000,000
Loans	12,000,000	Capital and Surplus	5,000,000
Government Securities ...	10,000,000		
	$28,000,000		$28,000,000

    a. A customer of Bank A mines $1 million of gold (considered as cash for reserve purposes) and deposits it in his bank. Trace through any *likely* expansion of the money supply by Bank A and by the entire banking system. What would be the *maximum* expansion possible? Specify clearly any assumptions that you make and state your reasoning carefully and precisely.

    b. Is the banking system in a more or less *sound* position as a result of the gold deposit and the consequences you have predicted above? Explain why or why not.

6. Explain how the transfer of your $100 deposit from a commercial bank to a savings and loan association can increase society's stock of liquid assets (money plus near-monies).
7. In what ways are the objectives of a central bank (like the Federal Reserve) different from those of a commercial bank?

8. Explain the main weapons the Fed has to check an inflationary boom.
9. The powers of the Federal Reserve to restrict credit expansion in booms are greater than those to stimulate credit expansion in a depressed period. (True or false? Why?)
10. Suppose the Federal Reserve takes the following actions. In each case, explain what will be the likely effect on the total money supply:
    a. It sells $1 billion of government securities to the banks.
    b. It lowers reserve requirements to 10 per cent for all member banks.
    c. It buys $1 billion of government securities from individuals and business concerns.
    d. It buys direct from the United States Treasury $1 billion of newly issued government securities.
    e. It lowers rediscount rates by 1 per cent.
11. Suppose the economy is in a serious depression. The commercial banks have substantial excess reserves. What steps would you advocate that the Federal Reserve take to help stimulate lending and recovery? Why?

Appendix

THE INDIVIDUAL BANK
AND THE BANKING SYSTEM

If no individual bank lends more than its excess reserves, how can the banking *system* expand credit five-fold on its excess reserves (assuming a 20 per cent reserve requirement)? An example can show how it works.

Assume, to begin with, that the Victory Bank has $1,000 excess reserves, and that all other banks are loaded up to their legal limits. As the Victory Bank makes new loans and investments, its reserves are gradually drawn away to other banks, and its credit expansion possibilities are limited. But the reserves the Victory Bank loses, some other bank gains.

Suppose Victory makes a new loan of $1,000, just the amount of its excess reserves. The T-account then looks like this, including the original $1,000 of excess reserves but excluding the rest of the original balance sheet. Consider first only the entries above the dotted line.

Victory Bank—Stage 1			
Excess reserve	$1,000		
Loans	+ 1,000	Deposits	+$1,000
Cash	− 1,000	Deposits	− 1,000

Soon the borrower writes a check for the entire $1,000, and the check is deposited in Bank B. This action transfers both the $1,000 deposit and the matching $1,000 cash reserve from the Victory Bank to B. On the Victory Bank T-account, deduct $1,000 from cash and from deposits, as shown below the dotted line, to see the Bank's new position. Victory is left with $1,000 of increased loans, on which it happily earns interest.

Bank B now has $1,000 of new reserves and $1,000 of new deposits. We can set up a T-account for Bank B, showing (Stage 2) + $1,000 for both the new cash and deposits, above the first dotted line. Of the new reserves, only $200 is required to back the new $1,000 deposit, so $800 is excess. Obviously, B is now safe in extending at least $800 of new loans, since it has that much excess reserves.

Bank B—Stage 2			
Cash	+$1,000	Deposits	+$1,000
Loans	+ 800	"	+ 800
Cash	− 800	"	− 800

So B makes a new $800 loan, creating $800 of additional deposits. This is shown on B's T-account, below the first dotted line.

Now the borrower spends the money to a customer of Bank C. Bank B loses the $800 in deposits and in reserves to Bank C. The loss is shown below the second dotted line on B's accounts. Note that, on the liability side B still has the $1,000 original deposit created by Victory Bank; on the asset side, it still has a matching $200 of new reserves from Victory, plus $800 of its own new loans. It is earning interest on its new $800 loan.

But C now has $800 of new deposits and the $800 of new reserves from B (Stage 3). This is shown in a new T-account, set up for C; the items are shown above the dotted line.

Bank C—Stage 3

Cash	+$800	Deposits	+$800
Loans	+ 640	"	+ 640

The total of new deposits has now risen to $1,800 ($1,000 in B and $800 in C), matched by $1,800 of new loans, even though no bank has lent a penny beyond its available excess reserves. Bank C, moreover, now has $640 of excess reserves ($800 new reserves, of which only $160 is required to back its $800 of new deposits). On these excess reserves it can safely make at least $640 of new loans, shown below the dotted line on its T-account. This will raise the total of new deposits to $2,440 against the original $1,000 of excess reserves. (The $2,440 total includes $1,000 in Bank B and $1,440 in Bank C at this stage.) And the expansion process can obviously continue. Trace it another stage for yourself, assuming that C's borrower spends his deposit to someone who banks with D; or the effect is the same if the reserves go back to the Victory Bank, or to any other. The expansion can continue until total deposits have

risen to $5,000 against the $1,000 of excess reserves. Each individual bank rightly hesitates to lend out more than its excess reserves, but the reserves it loses go to some other bank.

This process of cumulative deposit expansion is diagrammed in Figure 11-1. Assume that Bank A receives $1,000 of new reserves, say because $1,000 of newly mined gold is deposited. This $1,000 deposit requires only $200 of new reserves, so Bank A is entirely safe in expanding its loans and investments by $800, as shown in the dark-colored bar for Bank A. (Note that the bank names don't match those in the preceding example.)

Now Bank A's new borrower writes a check to a customer of Bank B, and the $800 is transferred to Bank B. Bank B now has $800 of new deposits and $800 of new reserves, which means that it has excess reserves of $640 since required reserves increase by only $160. It is perfectly safe in lending out an additional $640, and does so, as shown in the diagram. This $640 may now be transferred to a customer of some other bank (C), which then has new deposits and excess reserves on which to expand its loans. At each stage, the deposits created by previous transactions are piled on top, in the dotted sections, to show the cumulative increase.

As the diagram shows, this process can continue, piling up new deposits that arise from new loans, until a total of $5,000 of new deposits is reached (the tall unshaded bar at the right), including the original $1,000 deposit produced by the gold

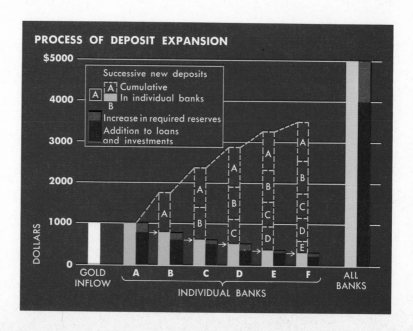

FIG. 11-1 One thousand dollars of new reserves (gold) ultimately serves as the foundation for $5,000 of new deposits, as banks make new loans and investments— even though no bank ever lends out more than its own excess reserves.

deposit. This is just what we would expect: $1,000 of new reserves has been able to support $5,000 of new deposits, given a 20 per cent legal reserve requirement against deposits. The tall shaded bar at the right shows the $4,000 of new loans and the $1,000 of new required reserves, just using up the original $1,000 of new gold reserves, so the growth must now stop. Moreover, this expansion has taken place even though no individual bank has ever lent out more than the excess reserves it actually has on hand. So when your banker tells you that he would never

lend out more money than he has in excess reserves, he may be quite correct. Yet the banking system as a whole creates deposits equal to many times its cash reserves.

The critical point is that the banking system is not limited by adverse clearing balances. The reserves one bank loses, another gains. For the banking system as a whole, the only over-all drain on reserves comes from currency withdrawals, from international gold flows, or from Federal Reserve or Treasury policies.

TWELVE

MONETARY POLICY

The Theory of Monetary Policy.

Policies To Restrain Aggregate Demand.

Policies To Stimulate Aggregate Demand.

Stable Growth in the Money Stock?

The Lessons of Monetary Experience.

Gold and Monetary Policy.

Can we maintain high-level employment and reasonably stable prices in a growing economy? The stakes are high, and the costs of failure are large.

To achieve these dual goals, aggregate demand must grow stably, just fast enough to take a growing high-employment output off the market at stable prices. Chapters 5–9 suggest that there is little reason to suppose the private economy on its own will generate just this amount of aggregate demand. Thus, we must turn to government for help in achieving the needed level of total spending.

Monetary policy (control over the money supply and interest rates) and fiscal policy (government spending and taxing) are the two main tools the government has to help keep aggregate demand growing stably. Monetary policy is the subject of this chapter, fiscal policy the subject of the next.

THE THEORY
OF MONETARY POLICY

Under the "gold standard" which prevailed in the western world during the century preceding World War II, the stock of money was largely controlled by an impersonal mechanism. The money supply increased and decreased when gold flowed in or out of a nation. But even in those days, many argued against leaving the supply of money solely to this mechanism. Instead, they argued, a "central bank" should be responsible for controlling the money stock in order to minimize inflations and depressions. The Bank of England

155

is generally considered the forerunner of other central banks, and the "Old Lady of Threadneedle Street" (as the Bank is often called) has played a significant part in influencing British monetary conditions for three centuries. The United States was one of the last major nations to establish a central bank. Our Federal Reserve was set up in 1914.[1] But over the decades since, we have come to rely on Federal Reserve policy as one of our two big guns in the war against unemployment and inflation.

Monetary Policy, Interest Rates, and the Money Stock

Chapters 5 to 9 provided the analytical foundation for monetary policy. If we want to increase or decrease aggregate demand, the central bank should increase or decrease M. Remember the main channels of effect.

The neo-Keynesian model suggests that more M may act only by increasing investment spending through reducing the rate of interest. Then the chain of effects runs like this:

$$+ M \rightarrow - r \rightarrow + I \rightarrow + \text{G.N.P.}$$

That is, an increase in M leads to a lower interest rate, which in turn leads to more investment, which in turn leads to a higher g.n.p. directly and through the multiplier. Or we could show the effects on a 45 degree diagram, like those in Chapter 6. Using Fig. 6-4 on page 67, the increased M and resulting lower interest rate would raise the level of investment, thus raising the $C + I$ curve and increasing the equilibrium level of income.

Or more money may have a broader and more direct effect, as is argued by the portfolio-balancers. More M may lead not only to more investment through lower interest rates but also directly to more investment and consumption spending. This occurs because an increase in M will lower the marginal return on money relative to other assets, and will lead consumers and businesses to spend down their money balances, acquiring other assets (including both investment and consumer goods) instead.

[1] Two earlier government-sponsored banks (the First and Second Banks of the United States) had only brief lives and did not act as full-fledged central banks.

What Is the Right Amount of Money?

If total spending were a constant multiple of the stock of money (that is, if V were constant), then the task of monetary policy would be relatively simple. Determine the desired level of money g.n.p., and then move the stock of money up or down to obtain that desired level. But we know that the public's demand for money balances varies, and that the V in $MV = PT$ varies. Thus, to determine the right M to produce any desired level of aggregate money spending, we must take into account changes in the public's demand for money balances. Figure 8-2 pictured the fluctuations in income velocity since 1900.

In a growing economy, the amount of money needed will gradually rise. *Prima facie*, we might expect the need for more money to grow apace with the growth in real output potential—say about 4 per cent a year. But just how fast M needs to grow in a growing economy will depend on how fast the public's demand for money balances rises at full-employment levels.

The public's demand for money balances depends on its level of income (or wealth) and on interest rates on money substitutes. The higher the income (or wealth) of the public, the larger, other things equal, will be the money balances it wishes to hold. The higher the interest rate on money substitutes, the lower will be the money balances it wishes to hold, because higher interest rates will lead people to shift their assets out of money (which yields no interest) into securities or other assets that do yield interest. Thus, for any level of aggregate demand we want to achieve, the right amount of M is that amount which the public desires to hold at that desired level of g.n.p. and at existing interest rates. More M than this amount will lead to higher spending than we want; less M will lead to lower spending.

The presumption that we need more M if we want a growing g.n.p. generally holds in the short run as well. The reasoning is familiar by now. But it may be useful to test it out by looking at an example which shows the interaction between M and government fiscal policy. Suppose that we want to raise aggregate demand to eliminate unemployment, and that to provide the stimulus we increase government spending without raising taxes. The rise in government spending will set off a multiplier effect on g.n.p., as desired. But the rising g.n.p. will also increase the public's demand for money balances, and hence raise the interest rate unless M is increased so there will be more money to meet the growing demand. This higher interest rate will partially check the rising investment and g.n.p. Thus, *if there is no increase in M*, the expansionary fiscal policy will generate a higher interest rate which will *partially* offset, or limit, the expansionary multiplier effect of government spending on g.n.p.[2] But if M is increased at the same time, this potential monetary drag can be avoided.[3]

Summary: The right amount of money depends both on the desired level of aggregate demand (g.n.p.) and on the public's demand to hold money balances at that level of g.n.p. and of interest rates. A rising g.n.p. without an increase in M will tend to raise interest rates and thus limit the growth in g.n.p. Thus, it is important that M grow gradually over the long pull and that monetary and fiscal policy be coordinated when we are trying to increase or decrease aggregate demand.

POLICIES TO RESTRAIN
AGGREGATE DEMAND

If the Fed wants to restrain aggregate demand, it can sell bonds in the open market or raise required reserves to reduce excess reserves. Since the commercial banks typically operate with small excess reserves (because they earn no interest on such idle funds), either action can have a

---

[2] For logicians: If you want to trace the logic out completely, note that in the case of a constant M, the higher interest rate not only reduces the growth in I but also slightly reduces the public's demand for M to hold. Thus there is a second-order effect that *partly* offsets the drag effect, since the lessened demand for M to hold will somewhat increase velocity.

[3] As a practical matter, looking ahead to the use of fiscal policy, this suggests always financing part or all of anti-recession deficits by selling bonds to the banks so as to increase M at least enough to avoid increases in interest rates. If this is done, you can readily see that it becomes very hard to separate how much of the total expansionary effect on g.n.p. is caused by the increased government spending (fiscal policy) and how much by the increased M (monetary policy).

direct and powerful restrictive effect on the extension of bank credit. The Fed can also raise the rediscount rate, which makes it more expensive for commercial banks to borrow additional reserves when they run tight. This is a less powerful restraint, since banks are still able to borrow additional reserves if they are willing to pay the higher rate. But the rediscount rate is widely viewed as an indicator of the Fed's general attitude on credit conditions, and thus has an important symbolic, psychological impact. The Fed has plenty of powers to restrain aggregate demand if it wants to use them.

The Impact
of Monetary Restriction

When the economy is expanding, a growing money stock is needed. Businesses need more for "working capital" to finance larger inventories, to meet higher payrolls, to buy more materials. They need more to finance fixed investment in machinery, equipment, and buildings. Although expanding sales provide some of the funds needed, typically businesses must turn to banks for additional funds to expand. Consumers too need more money to finance the higher volume of transactions. These facts can be summed up in the demand-for-money function indicated above; the public desires to hold more money as the level of income and wealth rises. And the basic source of more money for the system is bank lending, which in turn rests on the availability of more reserves provided by the Fed. Note, therefore, that in a growing economy, if the Fed merely does nothing to provide additional reserves, this policy of inaction implies a gradual tightening of the money markets and a rise in interest rates, since demand for M rises but supply does not.

What do the banks do when their excess reserves are squeezed? They often raise their interest rates—the prices they charge on credit. Alternatively, banks often "ration" credit to their customers before they raise interest rates. Instead of using higher rates to eliminate the customers least willing to pay more for money, they allocate their scarce credit to their oldest and best customers. They consider this sound long-run policy, just as many businesses don't try to squeeze the last penny out of good customers in periods of temporary shortages. Either way, tight money tends to check the upswing.

Bankers hate to impose credit rationing on good customers. Instead, they often sell off part of their government securities and use the funds to meet customers' loan demands. But such switches from government securities to loans are limited by the volume of securities the banks already have and by falling government bond prices if many banks try to sell simultaneously. Bankers may also get new reserves by borrowing at the Fed. But the Fed can close this loophole by raising the rediscount rate and frowning on rediscounting. Thus, banks may partially escape Federal Reserve pressure, but the possibilities are limited as long as the Fed keeps the pressure on.

When credit becomes tighter and interest rates rise, businesses and consumers try to avoid the pinch by economizing on money balances—that is, by reducing their money balances to the barest minimum needed to carry on their transactions and meet precautionary needs. The same amount of money thus does more work; V is speeded up, and the restraint of tighter money is partially avoided. The higher interest rates are forced by the credit squeeze, the greater is the inducement to convert "idle" money balances into interest-yielding securities and savings deposits. These shifts make previously idle money available for active use.

Figure 12-1 shows this effect clearly. The dot for each year shows the average interest rate on "prime" short-term loans and the average turn-over (or velocity) of demand deposits at some 400 city banks outside New York City (which is eliminated to avoid the huge volume of stock-market transactions there). Velocity varies directly with interest rates. For example, note the low interest rates and velocity during the depression years. These velocity figures include many transactions not contained in the g.n.p. accounts, and thus are only a very imperfect approximation to changes in income velocity. But in some respects they are more interesting, since they show what happens to the total use of demand deposits when interest rates rise or fall. If we plot income velocity against interest rates for the same years, the same general relationship is revealed.

But there are limits on how far working cash balances can be reduced. The public and the banks can avoid the pressure of Federal Reserve restraint temporarily, but only temporarily if the authorities make money tighter and tighter. The rise in V introduces a buffer against the impact of tighter money. It should be clear, however, that the Fed can ultimately have as strong an impact as it wishes, by raising reserve requirements sharply and by selling a large enough volume of government securities.

Don't jump from this fact to the conclusion that the job of the Federal Reserve is easy. Its power to check economic expansion is enormous, but overly drastic action may throw the baby out with the bathwater. The Fed's job is to check the inflation and level off the boom, not to plunge the economy into depression. Tightening up

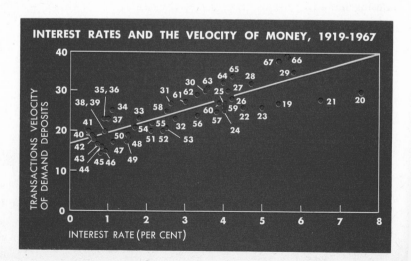

FIG. 12-1 As interest rates rise, the turn-over of demand deposits goes up. It pays people to economize on the use of money and to reduce their idle balances. (Source: Federal Reserve Board.)

credit just enough to level off consumption and investment, or to keep their growth at just the right rate, is a difficult and delicate task.

The Differential Effects of Tight Money

When money tightens, some borrowers are squeezed more than others. Banks naturally tend to allocate their scarce funds to old, established customers. Conversely, new small firms and individuals tend to be squeezed out, especially when their credit rating is not high. Tight money squeezes home construction especially, because high interest rates bulk large in total monthly mortgage payments and because many banks rank such loans below those to businesses that they see as long-run customers.

The differential effects of tight money are too complex for examination here. But it is important to see that bitter claims of inequity may be expected from potential borrowers who are shut out when interest rates rise and there aren't enough loans to go around. There is no way to restrict aggregate demand without turning away somebody, and the big, grade-A borrowers aren't likely to be the ones turned away.

A further complication arises when the monetary authorities use direct controls (ceiling interest rates) to regulate the flow of savings to different financial institutions. S. and L.'s, for example, lend almost entirely to builders and home buyers. Thus, if they are permitted to pay high rates to the depositors while commercial banks are limited to lower rates, both S. and L.'s and the housing industry are favored relative to commercial banks and industries which borrow from the banks. Use of such direct controls involves open government action to favor some sectors over others. But even general monetary restraint must shut out someone from credit if it is to do its job. There is no way monetary policy can avoid restraining some potential borrowers more than others.

The Problem of Timing and Lags

Consider now another Federal Reserve problem in deciding what to do at any given time. The problem breaks down into two big questions:

First, what is the state of the economy now, and where is it going in the absence of further monetary policy action? Second, what shall we do to mold this pattern into one of stable economic growth without inflation? Look at Fig. 12-2, which provides a very rough picture of a business cycle, and put yourself in the position of a member of the Federal Reserve Board.

First, you have to decide where you are now. At A, B, C, or D? You don't know for sure, and neither does anybody else. Suppose you think we're probably well along in a strong business upswing—say at about B. Then the problem is, how near the top? And how long will the inflation and prosperity continue if you do nothing? Is the boom weakening, with a downturn just around the corner? Or does the upswing have months or years of healthy prosperity left in it, so that it would be a shame to damp it? Or is the economy overheating so fast that inflation and speculation will generate a collapse unless the pace is slowed? If only you knew! [4]

Second, given your best decision as to where we are and where we're headed, you have to decide what the Fed should do now. Suppose that you suspect we're at B, and that inflation poses a serious problem. Should you raise reserve requirements? Sell bonds in the open market to tighten

[4] For a discussion of how government and other economists forecast economic conditions, see the Appendix to Chapter 9.

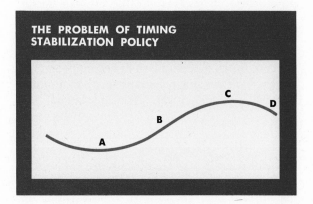

THE PROBLEM OF TIMING STABILIZATION POLICY

FIG. 12-2 The Federal Reserve authorities seldom know where we are in the cycle, or just how long it will take their actions to exercise their full effects. What is the right monetary policy if you think we're probably at B, but there's a good chance it may be C instead?

reserves? Or is the safe thing just to wait till we're clearly at D if that comes, and then fight the recession, on the ground that it's better not to risk killing off prosperity?

Note that here you face two subproblems. One is, *how much* effect will any Federal Reserve action have on the course of business activity? If you sell $1 billion of government bonds, will this drastically check bank lending, or only slow it slightly? How about raising reserve requirements 10 per cent? The second question is, even if you know what the effect will be, *how long* will it take for the full impact of tighter money to be felt? If you sell bonds tomorrow, this may only gradually shut off lending and that in turn may reduce C and I still later. Thus, the full effects of your action will be spread over months, perhaps over a year or two. By that time the boom may have turned down. Then the (lagged) effect of tight money would be to speed the downturn into recession.

The lags and uncertainties between Federal Reserve actions and their final impact on total spending are substantial. How long will it take the banks to react to tighten reserves? Will they try to sell off government securities and thus temporarily evade the desired restriction on business borrowing? How fast will businesses react to tighter credit and higher interest rates? Will the Fed's action have a strong psychological effect that reduces business investment? Some economists estimate the total lag between Federal Reserve action on reserves and the ultimate major effect on g.n.p. as long as 12–18 months, and suggest that the lag varies depending on prevailing conditions. Most agree that the major effect of Federal Reserve action is felt beginning immediately and spreading over some six to 12 months. But the Fed doesn't know for sure. And it has to act, or let things go their way without control.

Federal Reserve officials have sometimes described their policy as "leaning against the wind." By this they mean that when the economy is moving up they tend gradually to impose a drag on the upswing; and when it is moving down they tend gradually to increase the monetary ease in the system to check the downswing. Question:

Suppose the average lag of the effect of monetary policy is six months. Is a policy of leaning against the wind a sound one at all times?

POLICIES TO STIMULATE AGGREGATE DEMAND

Suppose aggregate demand is inadequate and the Fed wants to help expand it. Its first act is to be sure the banks have plenty of reserves. It can lower reserve requirements and buy government securities in the open market, providing new bank reserves in paying for its purchases. In addition, it can offer to rediscount commercial paper the commercial banks may bring, thus guaranteeing liquidity to the banking system and eliminating the possibility of another 1929–33 debacle, when mass liquidation of bank loans forced the downward spiral ever deeper.

If the Fed provides generous excess reserves, what will the bankers do? With growing excess reserves, they will want to lend, since idle reserves earn no interest. If times are reasonably good, history suggests that the banks will indeed increase their loans promptly. But if the economic horizon is dark in depression, acceptable borrowers are scarce. Businesses need to borrow when they are expanding, not when they are contracting. With adequate reserves, banks will tend to lower their interest rates and make credit readily available to desirable borrowers. But that may or may not produce more loans.

Even in this case, however, bankers can put their reserves to work by buying government securities on the open market. These are always substantially safe, and they pay interest. And buying government securities increases the money stock, just as does making new loans. So flooding the banks with reserves will almost certainly lead to increasing M, bidding up the price of bonds, and (what is the same thing) bidding down the interest rate (the effective yield on bonds).

History presents one big counter-example. After 1933, in the Great Depression, the inflow of gold plus Federal Reserve policy built up large excess reserves at the commercial banks. While bank credit in fact expanded rapidly as reserves built up, it did not expand nearly as rapidly as reserves grew. Thus, for the first time in history, the banking system held a huge volume of excess reserves over a period of years. Some economists suggest that this indicates a "liquidity trap" which we can expect to face again if we get into another serious depression. They argue that monetary policy is thus a very weak stimulant to expansion under such conditions. But others point out that the large excess reserves of the 1930's were the exception to the general rule. Moreover, they stress that pumping reserves into the banking system did in fact increase M rapidly, and that in turn money g.n.p. rose rapidly, once the great monetary contraction of 1929–33 was reversed.

Everyone agrees that easy money is a good thing in recessions, even though there is disagreement over its precise effects. The evidence suggests that lower interest rates are more likely to stimulate long- than short-term investment. On a long loan, like a 30-year mortgage, a small reduction in the interest rate makes a big difference in the monthly payment. Thus, lower interest rates may be a substantial stimulus to long-term private and public projects like houses, public utilities, factories, highways, schools, and the like. Low short-term interest rates are less likely to stimulate investment. Cheaper money lowers the cost of borrowing for working-capital purposes—to meet payrolls, carry inventories, and so on. But here interest is a tiny part of the relevant costs. And the marginal efficiency of investment in inventories, machinery and equipment depends heavily on volatile customer demand and profit expectations.

Since everyone agrees that easy money may help some to expand aggregate demand, why not just flood the banks with reserves to get whatever stimulus more M can produce? The answer is that here, as in fighting inflation, there may be danger of too much as well as too little. If the Fed pours excessive M into the economy, given the lags of policy it may be very hard to check the ensuing inflationary boom without very strong restrictive measures if "overheating" of the economy results. The timing problems faced in fighting recession are roughly comparable to those in

fighting an inflationary boom. Just right is what's needed, not too much or too little!

The Practical Problems of Policy, 1965–1967

The years 1965–1967 provide a lively recent example of the practical problems of applying monetary policy effectively to help stabilize the economy. By mid-1965 the long upswing in economic activity had continued four years, and was picking up speed. Private investment was high relative to g.n.p. and sensitive prices were beginning to rise after a long period of price stability. But unemployment was still about 5 per cent of the labor force. Interest rates had risen a little from 1961 levels, but were still below the levels of the late 1950's. The money stock was growing at about 4 per cent per annum.

What should the Fed do? Slow the rate of money expansion and push up interest rates to check the incipient inflation and investment boom, or keep money easy to help reduce unemployment? Up to December their answer was the latter. They provided enough new reserves to the banks to support a 6 per cent annual growth rate in the money stock, though booming demand for credit began to push up interest rates nevertheless. At last, in December, the Fed raised the discount rate by ½ per cent, against vigorous criticism of President Johnson and other high administrative officials who argued that no more restraint was needed.

But the discount increase was only a mild restrictive move. The Fed continued to provide new reserves to the banks as the demand for credit soared with the boom. Reflecting this situation, interest rates rose steadily in spite of a continued rapid 6 per cent annual growth rate in the money stock. By early 1966, prices were rising substantially and the unemployment rate began to fall rapidly. Business investment rose nearly 20 per cent over the preceding year, which in turn had been a peak. Still, the Johnson Administration did not propose a general tax increase, arguing that the growth was still sustainable and that unemployment was still too high.

What should the Fed do now? Finally, about May 1966, it shut off the growth in bank reserves. As business and consumer demand for credit continued to grow, interest rates shot up. By late summer they had reached 40-year peaks, the money supply had ceased to grow, and the cries of disappointed borrowers were loud and anguished. At the same time the Administration put through a small tax increase on corporations, although still refusing to recommend a general tax increase. Price increases spread, and the unemployment rate fell to 3.7 per cent through the autumn of 1966.

By late 1966, the bloom was off the boom. Housing construction fell sharply as credit tightened and S. & L.'s lost funds to other financial institutions. Although prices continued to rise, reflecting general increases in costs, and unemployment stayed low, business investment plans were scaled back and consumer spending in real terms flattened off. Industrial production turned down. There was no growth in real g.n.p. during the first quarter of 1967. But with some inflation still evident, the unions demanded big wage increases in their 1967 bargains, and unemployment stayed at only 3.7 per cent. What would you do now?

Reacting to the danger of a general downturn, the Fed began again to supply reserves more freely. Interest rates fell, and by March the money stock was growing again at 6–8 per cent per annum, well above the long-term growth rate of the economy. But now, as the danger of a major downturn appeared to ebb, critics began to warn that the Fed was easing too far—that inflation was still the basic problem, and that by late 1967 the lagged effects of easier money would come home to roost in a renewed inflationary boom. On the other hand, many economists, businessmen, and workers warned loudly that the economy was still sliding toward recession.

Fine-tuning the economy through monetary policy is not easy! It's not easy to know where the economy is, much less where it's going. And since monetary policy exerts a lagged effect on the real economy, the problem is even worse. But difficult or not, the Fed has to face the problem and act as best it can to encourage stable economic growth with stable prices. Congress and the people have given it this responsibility—and have kept for themselves the right to criticize!

STABLE GROWTH IN THE MONEY STOCK?

Some economists have suggested a simple rule for the guidance of monetary policy. Just increase the money stock about 4 per cent a year through thick and thin. (The 4 per cent is based on the assumption that this is about the rate of growth in the full-employment capacity of the economy; if the growth rate of the economy is more or less, the growth rate of the money stock could be adjusted accordingly.) These economists argue that, even with the best intentions in the world, the Fed cannot forecast business conditions effectively. Moreover, the lag in effect of monetary policy is uncertain. Thus, Federal Reserve discretionary action is likely to be wrong about as often as it is right, and in fact it has been destabilizing on many occasions in the past. A major example is the collapse of 1929–33, when the Fed permitted the money stock to shrink by nearly one-third.

Suppose we automatically increase M at about the full-employment growth rate of the economy, eschewing all attempts to forecast and to offset every real or imagined fluctuation. To be sure, this might not keep the economy exactly on a stable growth path. There might be small recessions and small booms, which might temporarily involve some unemployment and some inflation. But the policy would avoid big booms and big depressions. Whenever the economy began to fall into serious recession, continued increase in the money stock at the annual 4 per cent rate would provide a massive support against collapse. Conversely, if inflation began, limitation of the growth in M to 4 per cent annually would be a powerful restraint on the inflationary pressures. A constant-growth-in-M rule is not a counsel of perfection; it is advanced as a sensible precept of action which would give by-and-large good results and would avoid the danger of serious errors due to fallible monetary authorities.[5]

[5] For a lively exposition of this proposal, see E. S. Shaw, "Money Supply and Stable Economic Growth," in M. L. Joseph, N. C. Seeber, and G. L. Bach, *Economic Analysis and Policy* (Englewood Cliffs. N. J.: Prentice-Hall, 1966).

Few economists or laymen take seriously the possibility of abolishing the Federal Reserve and substituting a completely inflexible rule of a stably growing money stock. Most observers object that this would tie our hands against unforeseen contingencies, and believe that in a changing world human judgment by conscientious experts will by and large do better than any fixed rule. But many economists who have studied the evidence believe that the reasoning behind the rule has much to offer the Federal Reserve authorities. Whenever M is growing much faster or slower than the full-employment growth rate of the economy, that's a warning flag, and there ought to be a good reason for the divergence.

THE LESSONS
OF MONETARY EXPERIENCE

What has history taught about the effectiveness of monetary policy in the United States, and about the problems of using it? It may be useful to take a brief look at the past, in addition to the 1965–67 example above.

The 1920's—Boom and Bust

World War I was followed by a sharp inflationary boom and then by a short sharp inventory liquidation that drove prices spiraling down. By 1922, the economy had begun a long upward pull —almost a decade of good times and substantially full employment. In 1924 and again in 1927, prosperity was broken by slight hesitations. And increasingly as the boom continued, observers questioned whether times were not a little too good. Real-estate prices climbed as construction activity reached peaks never before dreamed of. After 1926, construction turned down. But the stock market soared as the public proclaimed permanent prosperity. The man in the street, the businessman, and the financier, became speculators "in the market." As stock prices spiraled upward, easy profits were available for the taking, especially since stocks could be bought on margin for only a tiny fraction of their sale price.

In the midst of this speculative fever, some questioned whether such a speculative boom could last. Industrial production leveled off in 1928 and construction activity slumped substantially. The general price level was stable. Federal Reserve authorities were divided among themselves on what was the best policy. Finally, in 1929 they took mild deflationary action, in spite of widespread criticism, raising rediscount rates and speaking out against the excessive use of bank credit for speculative purposes. In late 1929 came the stock-market crash, triggering the worst deflation and depression of America's history.

Lesson: When times are good it's hard to know what's the right policy vis-à-vis speculation and minor fluctuations—what would you have done? And when the boom gets roaring, steps to check it are generally unpopular. The life of a central banker is not easy!

The 1930's—
Crash and Stagnation

As the economy spiraled downward, it was far from clear whether this was a major depression, a temporary stock-market setback, or merely a regular cyclical readjustment, after a long period of rapid economic growth. The Fed reduced discount rates to ease credit in the deflation. By early 1931, there was considerable evidence that the worst was over and that a new footing had been reached for recovery.

But European financial crises in mid-1931 set off world-wide hoarding of gold. Facing this gold loss, the Reserve authorities adopted a tight-money, high-interest policy to keep gold from flowing abroad. This made money hard to get at home in spite of widespread unemployment and the still uncertain recovery. Faced with a conflict of domestic and international goals, the Fed chose the latter. Within a few weeks, business turned down sharply again and the spiral of financial liquidation resumed. A quick return to easier money did not stem the tide. Unemployment soared. Runs on banks developed everywhere. On his inauguration day, Franklin Roosevelt's first major act was to declare a nation-wide "bank holiday," closing all banks until the panic could be calmed and arrangements could be made to keep the financial system from complete collapse.

Following 1933, with Roosevelt's new appointees running the system, the Federal Reserve adopted easy money and low interest rates to fight the depression. Excess reserves were pushed up to $3 billion by late 1935, and then, as recovery seemed on the way, pulled back down to $1 billion in 1937. Soon after, the boomlet of 1936–37 crashed precipitously back to mass unemployment in early 1938. Again there was widespread criticism of the preceding Federal Reserve increases in reserve requirements to restrain rising prices in spite of continued heavy unemployment.

From then on, the banks were flooded with reserves. Excess reserves exceeded $5 billion by the outbreak of war in 1939, in comparison to an average level of under $500 million through the 1920's. Total bank credit and the money stock rose in response to these added reserves. But by 1939, g.n.p. was still only back up to the level of 1929; 8 or 9 million people were unemployed; net private investment for the entire decade was a negative figure.

Lessons: (1) When mass deflation sets in, don't hesitate to flood the economy with liquidity. Hindsight makes it clear that the Reserve authorities made a fatal error in moving so slowly to eliminate the pressure of financial liquidation that swept the whole economy downward. (2) When times are bad, it's still hard to know what is the best policy vis-à-vis minor fluctuations. (3) In a major depression, flooding the economy with liquidity at least checks further financial liquidation and helps to stimulate total spending; but bankers may pile up excess reserves rather than correspondingly expanding loans and deposits. The life of a central banker is not easy!

World War II—War Finance, Gold, and the Congress

During the ten years before World War II, our gold reserves increased from $4 billion to $23 billion, as gold flowed in from abroad for investment and safekeeping during the troubled 1930's. The gold entering the United States was sold to the government through the Federal Reserve Banks. Each dollar of gold increased the reserves of the commercial banks by $1, as the seller of the gold deposited the check paid to him by the government. It also increased the Fed's supply of gold by $1 as the member banks turned the gold over to it. By 1941 the commercial banks had huge excess reserves, and the Federal Reserve also had

gold reserves far beyond the legal requirements against currency outstanding and member-bank reserves.

With soaring war expenditures, Congress raised taxes, but only enough to cover about a third of the war's costs. The Treasury began to borrow to cover the difference. About half the government bonds were sold to the public, exchanging bonds for already-existing money. The other half were sold to the commercial banks, which created new deposits to be spent by the government. This deposit expansion rapidly ate into the excess reserves of the commercial banks; withdrawal of currency into hand-to-hand circulation drained away reserves even faster (currency alone increased by over $20 billion during the war period).

By 1942, the commercial banks' excess reserves were nearly gone. The war blazed on and Treasury borrowing needs skyrocketed. What would you have done? You'd have found some way to permit the Treasury to sell more bonds to the banks in order to get money to finance the war, and that's just what the Federal Reserve authorities did. They could have lowered the reserve-requirement ratio to provide more excess reserves. But the currency drain was so rapid that it alone would have withdrawn all existing bank reserves in about two years. So the Reserve Banks began to buy government securities in the open market, to create *new* bank reserves on which the commercial banks could then buy five times as many newly issued government bonds from the Treasury.

This was money-creation with a vengeance. Preceding a typical "war loan drive," for example, the Federal Reserve bought enough bonds in the open market to build up commercial banks' excess reserves. The banks could then buy all the bonds the Treasury could not sell to the nonbanking public. On a set day during the "drive," bank subscriptions for new bonds from the Treasury would be opened and the bonds allocated. Suppose the Treasury allocated $5 billion to the banks. Then the next day, the banks' balance sheets throughout the country would show *$5 billion* of new deposits for the Treasury, offset by $5 billon of new government bonds held by the banks. If you didn't quite believe that banks created deposits back in

Chapter 11, World War II provided a vivid and irrefutable demonstration on a grand scale.

Between 1941 and 1945, the Federal Reserve created $23 billion of new member-bank reserves through open-market purchases. With these additional reserves, the commercial banks bought $70 billion of government securities and paid out $20 billion of new currency. As was to be expected, each dollar of new reserves served to support about four dollars of new money.

But each new Federal Reserve note took 40 per cent gold reserves, and new member-bank reserves took 35 per cent gold reserves.[6] By 1944, therefore, the Federal Reserve itself began to run short of gold. It still had about the same amount of physical gold, but this gold was "used up" by legal requirements. Without more gold, its power to provide more currency and more bank reserves to help finance the war was threatened.

What would you have done? The Reserve and Treasury authorities went to Congress with the problem, and a suggested solution. There was little dissent. Congress simply lowered the gold-reserve requirement to 25 per cent against both Federal Reserve notes and deposits. The Fed again had excess gold reserves, though there was no more actual gold. The needs of war finance had triumphed over the tradition of gold and financial orthodoxy.

Lessons: (1) The Federal Reserve plus modern fractional reserve banking provides an easy way to manufacture money in almost any amount desired. (2) In wartime, it's hard to keep the dangers of excess money-issue and inflation from being lost sight of in the press of winning the war. (3) Gold provided an ultimate limitation on the money-creating powers of the Fed under the law. But Congress makes the law and Congress can change it, even on gold.

Monetary Policy
and the National Debt, 1946–1951

At the end of World War II, over $275 billion of government debt was outstanding, nearly $100 billion of it held by the banking system. Between $50 and $75 billion of this debt

[6] At that time, the Fed was required to hold gold reserves against both Federal Reserve notes and the deposits (reserves) of member banks.

came due for refunding each year. The Federal Reserve faced a dilemma. (1) If it tightened bank reserves and raised interest rates to check the postwar inflation, the squeeze would induce banks to dump their low-yield government securities on the market to get new reserves in order to make higher-yield business loans. This would force down the price of government bonds, with cries of anguish from the Treasury and the public. (2) On the other hand, if the Fed did nothing to check bank loans to private borrowers, it could ease the Treasury's job in refinancing the national debt by keeping bond prices up and interest rates down; but then it would be lying down on its job as the nation's monetary spearhead against inflation.

Until 1951, the Fed chose the latter path. It stood ready to buy all government bonds from the commercial banks at par, maintaining their price against decline. This action made it cheap and easy for the Treasury to refund the maturing debt. But it also meant that the banks' huge holdings of government securities were as good as excess reserves, since they could be converted into money at no risk at any time. Bank loans to private borrowers soared, as business boomed and prices climbed following the war.

The Treasury, anxious to maintain confidence in the government's credit, liked this policy. A huge volume of short-term securities was outstanding, and the holders might demand cash at maturity if government securities didn't remain attractive. Banks and nonbank holders might also lose confidence and try to sell their longer-term securities, drastically reducing prices. Treasury refunding would then have to be done at sharply increased interest rates, and the future market for government securities might be seriously weakened. Political repercussions from government bond holders could be very unpleasant for the administration in power if bond prices slumped.

Many economists argued, however, that higher interest costs and sagging bond prices were a proper price to pay for the restoration of effective monetary restraint against inflation. The Fed increasingly took this view. If monetary policy was to check inflation, it argued, the Fed must tighten the over-all credit supply, including a rise in interest rates to the federal government itself.

Thus, the Federal Reserve authorities tried gradually to tighten up the money market. Finally, in 1951, in an open break with the Treasury, Federal Reserve support of the price of government bonds was substantially withdrawn. Bond prices fell below par, but bank credit was tightened and interest rates rose. Federal Reserve control over the money supply was partially restored.

But even then, the Federal Reserve officials made it clear they would continue to work closely with the Treasury. Why? In spite of their "non-political" status, Federal Reserve Board members are appointed by the President and are responsible to Congress. They recognize fully their primary role as part of the government. Their job is to work with other government agencies to produce a stably growing economy. Were they actively to combat the government's financial policy, or even fail to cooperate satisfactorily, the President might object strenuously and Congress could at any time alter the semi-independent status of the Federal Reserve. With the major portion of the nation's money supply outstanding against Treasury bonds, it is clear that Federal Reserve monetary policy and Treasury policy in handling the federal debt must be made cooperatively.

Lesson: There are many considerations that must be weighed in forming wise monetary policy. One of the most difficult problems is the weight to be given to Treasury financing needs when they conflict with other stabilization objectives. The life of a central banker is not easy!

The Dilemma of Inflation or Unemployment—The 1950's

Basically, the decade of the 1950's was a period of good times. But 1954 and 1958 brought short recessions reminiscent of 1924 and 1927. After 1954, unemployment hovered around 3 million, until the recession of 1958 shot the figure up to 5 million, the highest since the peak in the post-World War II conversion period. Recovery in 1959–60 failed to restore high-level employment. Technological progress and greater managerial efficiency substantially reduced the number of workers needed to turn out any given output. In the meantime, the U.S.S.R. grew at 7–10 per cent annually compared to our 3–4 per cent for the decade, and consistently outpaced us in the space race. Yet, over the decade in America prices crept up nearly every year, and after 1958 we began to lose gold to foreign nations.

Was tight money—to avoid inflation and to keep up interest rates in order to check the gold outflow—holding down the rate of economic growth and causing unemployment? The Fed generally saw inflation and the gold drain as the major dangers, though it reiterated its goal of fighting both recession and inflation. From 1955 on, it permitted the money supply to grow only slowly, although it quickly eased credit in the recession of 1958. Increasingly, unions and Democratic politicians attacked the Fed as a barrier to a healthy, growing economy. They believed that tight money was short-sighted, for it put the "fetish" of a stable price level over the productivity and human happiness of full employment. Others, including the Reserve authorities, saw the problem differently. Only stable money could provide the foundation for continuing saving and prosperity, and we could not disregard the continuing gold outflow.

Lesson: Even prosperity has its problems. The hardest choices of all are between widely accepted goals which appear to be conflicting. The central banker who places price stability above booming prosperity and rapid economic growth reaps many harsh words. The old refrain: The life . . .

The Sagging or Soaring '60's?

The next in this little series of historical vignettes is the 1960's, first sagging, then soaring. We're still too near the events to form a reliable historical judgment. During the early '60's the basic unemployment-inflation dilemma of the '50's persisted. And the problem was made more serious by our increasing concern over the loss of our gold stock to other nations. Beginning about 1963, however, the Fed, though moving cautiously, provided bank reserves so the money stock would rise at a faster rate, as prices remained relatively stable and the international position of the dollar improved gradually. Whether as effect or coincidentally, the growth rate in g.n.p. stepped up; and by the mid-1960's the U.S. economy was booming. Indeed, by 1965 it was not only booming but private investment was soaring beyond sustainable levels, government spending on the Vietnam war soared, and the price level began to move up substantially. With these signs of a traditional "boom" and clear inflation, the Fed reversed its policy. In 1966, it dragged the growth in bank reserves and the money stock to a halt, and maintained this tight money position through most of the year. By the end of 1966, the bloom was clearly off the boom. The rapid growth in g.n.p. slowed, inventories piled up, consumer demand flattened. And the Fed again shifted policy toward putting more reserves in the banks and encouraging renewed credit expansion.

How successful was this attempt to fine-tune the economy through monetary policy? Expert opinions differ. Some argue that the Fed did well, and helped significantly to keep the economy near a stable growth path. Others saw the Fed as always too late, and then too heavy handed in its attempts to reverse inflationary or deflationary tendencies. Since the government was also attempting to fine-tune the economy through fiscal policy, it's hard to allocate credit or blame as between monetary and fiscal measures. By the time you read this, more evidence will be in on how well these combined efforts succeeded.[7]

GOLD AND MONETARY POLICY

The preceding pages say little about the fact that the United States lives in an increasingly interdependent economic world. During some periods, for example the quarter-century following the mid-1930's, Federal Reserve policy needed to pay little attention to our economic relations with other nations. We had a lion's share of the world's gold reserves, and monetary policy could be focused almost entirely on domestic goals.

But over most of our history it has not been

[7] Every time the Fed tightens money to restrain economic expansion, the critics complain that the Fed is too "independent" and that it should be made directly subservient to the President. For both sides of this controversy see the statements by Representative Wright Patman and G. L. Bach in *Economic Analysis and Policy* (M. Joseph, N. Seeber and G. L. Bach, eds.), pp. 80–86.

thus. And since the late 1950's our concern over gold and the international balance of payments has again played a major role in constraining our domestic monetary policy actions. Although you can only understand the importance of gold and the balance of payments through a detailed look at the international economic relations (in Part Six), it is important in concluding this chapter on monetary policy to recognize briefly the role gold has come again to play.

What Was the "Gold Standard"?

The "gold standard" prevailed in the United States and most major European nations over a good share of the century preceding the 1930's. Although it varied from country to country and period to period, it had two major characteristics. First, changes in the total amount of money in each country were roughly proportional to changes in its gold holdings. Gold itself was not the only kind of money. But as new gold was received by a country, it would serve as the basis for additional money issued in the form of currency or deposits. On $1 worth of new gold, $2, $10, or some other number of dollars of new money might be issued. Similarly, an outflow of gold would reduce the nation's money supply.

Second, each unit of money was "worth" (freely convertible into) a certain number of grains of gold. Until 1934, for example, each United States dollar "contained" 23.22 grains of fine gold; that is, the price of gold was fixed so that 23.22 grains of gold could always be obtained at the Treasury for $1, and vice versa.

Thus, the gold standard in its pure form was essentially an automatic regulator of the supply of money. M was largely dependent on the stock of gold in any nation. Actually, the gold standard was never as automatic in operation as in theory. But it did provide a strong constraining framework for almost all monetary-policy thinking and action over a long period of years.

The Gold Standard
as a Safeguard against Inflation

The main argument for the gold standard in most people's minds is that it will safeguard the economy against overissue of money and inflation.

Since the government must have gold to back each dollar, gold sets a limit to how much money can be created and provides value for the money issued.

But United States history shows clearly that as a practical matter the gold standard is no guarantee against sharp price-level changes. Figure 10-3 shows the big inflation that took place during and following World War I, the precipitious drop following that inflation, and the sharp drop from 1929 to 1933, all while we were on the gold standard. The quantity of money (M) fluctuated widely. This was partly because of swings in our gold stock. But also, as was noted above, as a practical matter the banking system could expand and contract the money supply over a wide range for any given amount of gold reserves, and in addition our monetary authorities often partially offset or augmented the effects of gold flows (not quite kosher for the pure gold standard).

On the other hand, it *is* true that adherence to the gold standard would insure against any such runaway inflation as occurred in Germany after World War I, *if* sticking to the gold standard were politically and economically possible under such circumstances. Then the limited stock of gold would prevent a vast overissue of money. However, under such drastic circumstances it is hard to imagine that any country could remain on a gold standard. Remember from the discussion of hyperinflations in Chapter 10 the enormous political and economic pressures on the German government to pay its bills by creating new money. The drastic monetary disturbances of that period were as much a symptom as a cause of the difficulties of the German economy.

The gold standard has one major advantage in the eyes of those who fear excessive reliance on governmental discretionary authorities. It takes monetary management out of the hands of individuals (in whom we may have limited faith) and puts it on a more-or-less automatic basis (according to gold flows). But most economists today deny that gold flows provide the best guide to how much money the economy needs. If we want to remove power from the hands of government authorities lest they unwisely bring on inflation, there may be better automatic guides—for example, a constant annual growth in M. Perhaps most

important, rigid adherence to a gold standard would tie the monetary authorities' hands against monetary action to combat unemployment and depression.

The Abandonment
of the Gold Standard

It was the desire to "do something" about the depression that largely explains the world-wide abandonment of the gold standard in the 1930's. Countries were increasingly loath to accept deflation as they lost gold. Getting men back to work became the major national goal. European countries faced huge gold drains into private hoards and to the United States. In 1931, England, long the financial center of the world, went off the gold standard. Remaining on gold meant intensified deflation as gold was withdrawn. Off gold, England could expand her money supply to check the depression and falling price level, regardless of gold flows.

England's abandonment of the gold standard was a terrific blow to the confidence of the financial world in those troubled times. The next major country to be hit by gold hoarding was the United States. Within a few months, our monetary authorities felt they must choose between staying on the gold standard (raising interest rates to keep capital from flowing out of the U.S.) or giving up the gold standard to be able to expand the money supply in the face of a falling gold stock.

They accepted the discipline of gold flows and raised interest rates; and national income plummeted again. But finally, in 1934, as part of Roosevelt's emergency program to check the wave of bank failures, all gold was called out of monetary circulation into the Treasury. The United States officially went off the gold standard. Most of the countries of Europe had already taken this step. Some, like France, clung to gold longer, but today no major country retains the prewar gold standard.

The International
Gold Reserve Standard

Today the U.S. and most other major western nations are on what might be called the "international gold reserve standard." Domestic monetary policy retains substantial freedom to counteract booms and depressions, regardless of international gold flows. The stock of money is not tied directly to gold reserves. But gold is used widely as a means of international payment, and provides a basic international reserve for most nations to meet their commitments to other nations arising out of international trade and financial transactions. For many nations, American dollars have also come to be considered part of this international reserve, since dollars are widely acceptable in the payment of international obligations.

Since gold is one major means of international payment, gold tends to move from country to country when one owes more payments to another than vice versa. If a nation consistently spends more abroad (including capital investment and gifts) than it collects from abroad, it has a "deficit" in its international balance of payments,

and tends to lose gold. The converse is true when it receives more payments than it makes. Thus, unless a nation has large gold reserves, there are limits to how long it can run a substantial deficit in its balance of payments, because of the danger that its gold reserves will be exhausted and that it will be unable to meet its international obligations.

Since the late 1950's, the danger that we would lose too much gold has provided a major constraint on the Federal Reserve authorities. If interest rates were lowered here to fight unemployment, capital would flow abroad to seek higher rates there. Although domestic needs often called for easier money to reduce unemployment and speed growth, the Fed felt that it dared not risk the gold loss. This constraint added heavily to the dilemmas facing the Fed. But a more thorough look at this problem must wait for Part Six, "The International Economy."

REVIEW

Concepts To Remember

Be sure you have a firm understanding of the following major new concepts and institutions. They supplement the list at the end of Chapter 11, most of which are essential also for this chapter.

"tight" and "easy" money   gold standard
credit rationing   international gold reserve standard
liquidity trap   gold flows

For Analysis and Discussion

1. Would you say that the Federal Reserve's chances of preventing a severe depression are better now than they were in 1929? Why or why not?
2. Suppose that prices are rising slightly, 5 per cent of the labor force is unemployed, and a recovery in process seems to be running out of steam but you can't be sure. As a member of the Federal Reserve Board, what would you do?
3. Suppose you were a banker with a balance sheet roughly like that of the Victory Bank in Chapter 11. Now the Federal Reserve raises reserve requirements to tighten credit just when the demand for loans from your long-standing business customers is rising. What would you do?
4. When inflation and unemployment coincide, sensible Federal Reserve action would be to raise reserve requirements while buying bonds in the open market. True or false? Explain.
5. If the Treasury must finance a federal budget deficit designed to stimulate the economy, what should the Federal Reserve do? Suppose it holds the stock of bank reserves constant; what would you expect to happen to interest rates and credit conditions?
6. If the Fed wishes to encourage stable growth in real g.n.p. and employ-

ment, what general rules should it follow in determining its policies? Can you see any serious objections to merely increasing the money stock about 4 per cent per year?

7. Since the Federal Reserve Board is in effect part of the federal government, why should there be any formal gold requirements against its notes (i.e., the nation's currency)?

8.   a. On the basis of your analysis of the functioning of the United States monetary system, how would you describe and evaluate the role of gold in the system?

     b. Does the United States have too much, too little, or about the right amount of gold now? What are the criteria you use in deciding how much gold we need?

THIRTEEN

FISCAL POLICY[1]

The Theory of Fiscal Policy.

Increased Spending Versus Tax Cuts.

Discretion Versus Built-In Flexibility.

Does Fiscal Policy Work?

The Balanced-Budget Tradition.

The Mix of Monetary and Fiscal Policy.

Appendix: Different Budget Concepts.

Back in the pre-1930 days, government expenditures and taxes were only about 10 per cent of the national income. But in World War II this figure soared to 50 per cent, and during the 1950's it fell back only to around 25 per cent. Federal, state, and local government spending of over $250 billion annually today exerts an enormous influence on the level and direction of the nation's economic activity. And there is little reason to expect a return to the 1920's.

Before the 1930's, almost no one questioned the wisdom of balancing the federal budget every year. Sometimes the government didn't manage to do it, but everyone was apologetic about the failure. But as the depression deepened in the 1930's, the federal government just couldn't balance the budget, try as both Mr. Hoover and Mr. Roosevelt would. We had federal deficit financing because we couldn't help it. But an increasing number of people, led by the now-famous economist John Maynard Keynes, began to argue that the government's excess spending was actually a good thing in depression. The argument went something like this.

The government should "prime the pump" of private spending. Everyone can agree that it would be foolish to try to have government receipts just equal expenditures every week or every month. Why, then, should the budget be balanced every year, instead of every two, or five, or ten years? Wouldn't the sensible thing be to balance the budget roughly over the length of the business cycle? Government deficit spending in

[1] Some instructors may prefer to assign Chapter 34 on "The Public Sector" before Chapter 13, to provide further background for the discussion of fiscal policy.

depression would help increase total spending and prime the private pump. Later, excess government taxes to pay off the debt in prosperity would help damp down the boom. The deficit would be a temporary expedient.

But as the long black years of the 1930's dragged on, faith in both monetary policy and government pump-priming waned. Talk of a stagnant economy and a chronic deficiency in private investment spread. Emphasis shifted to continuing "compensatory" government spending, aimed at filling in the deficiency of private investment. According to the compensatory spenders, the private economy couldn't carry itself forward to prosperity even when primed by doses of government investment. Government deficit spending should be continued as long and as heavily as necessary to attain and maintain full employment.

THE THEORY OF FISCAL POLICY

Fiscal policy is the use of government spending, taxing, and borrowing to increase or decrease aggregate demand. Aggregate demand is the sum of private spending on consumption and investment *and* government spending (g.n.p. = $C + I + GE$). The government can increase total expenditures by spending more than it currently takes away from private spending in taxes. Conversely, when total private spending is too high, the government can reduce g.n.p. by taxing away more than it spends. Either way, the net change in autonomous spending triggers a multiplier effect.

Look back at the circular flow diagram of Fig. 4-2. The government may spend back more into the income stream than it currently withdraws from it, thus swelling the total. Or it may spend back less, thus reducing the flow of total spending. Obviously the net result depends on the expansionary effect of government spending offset against the depressive effect of tax collections.

An increase in government expenditures raises g.n.p. The increase per dollar of government spending is determined by the multiplier. Each additional dollar of government spending on goods and services adds directly to g.n.p. and becomes income to an individual or a business. Part of this new income will be respent, in the familiar

multiplier-responding process of Chapter 6. If the multiplier for the economy is 2, for example, each dollar of additional government spending will generate an increase of $2 in g.n.p.

An increase in tax collections reduces g.n.p. The decrease per dollar of tax collections again depends on the multiplier. When individuals or businesses pay taxes out of their incomes, they reduce their spending on goods and services. This reduction has a negative multiplier effect, the reverse of the positive multiplier associated with government expenditures. The size of this negative multiplier will depend on much the same factors as those determining the positive multiplier on government spending, as was explained in Chapter 6.

The net multiplier effect of the government budget on the economy depends on the net result of these plus and minus multipliers. The larger the excess of government expenditures over tax receipts (i.e., the larger the deficit), the stronger will be the expansionary effect of governmental fiscal policy, other things equal. Conversely, the larger the excess of tax receipts over expenditures (i.e., the larger the government surplus), the more deflationary government fiscal policy will be. These propositions will need to be qualified somewhat presently, but they provide a powerful first approximation. When we want the government to exert strong expansionary pressure on g.n.p., a substantial government deficit is desirable.

Figure 13-1 presents the analysis graphically. Let the CC and $C + I$ lines be identical with the lines in Fig. 6-4, back on page 67. Equilibrium income would then be 350, where $C + I$ cuts the 45° line. Now suppose the government enters the picture and begins to spend 10 each year without collecting any taxes (perhaps borrowing at the banks). We can thus draw a new government spending layer (GE) on top of the $C + I$ curve. This new $C + I + GE$ curve is 10 higher at every point. As indicated above, the new government spending becomes income to the private economy and has a multiplier effect just like private investment. If the marginal propensity to consume is .75, the new equilibrium level of g.n.p. in Fig. 13-1 will be 390, as the multiplier raises total income by four times the original government spending. Note that this new equilibrium income is identical to that in Fig. 6-4, where the additional autonomous

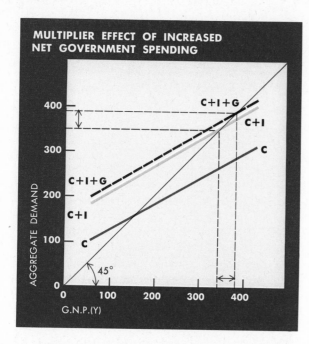

MULTIPLIER EFFECT OF INCREASED NET GOVERNMENT SPENDING

FIG. 13-1 Net new government spending of 10 adds 10 of "investment" and, with a multiplier of 4, raises total income by 40—up to a new equilibrium of 390. This is identical with the multiplier effect of 10 of new private investment in Fig. 6-4.

spending of 10 was private rather than government.

The Balanced-Budget Multiplier

It may appear intuitively that a balanced government budget (i.e., tax collections just equal to government spending) will always be neutral in its effect on g.n.p. But this is not quite correct. An increase in government spending matched by an identical increase in tax collections provides some net expansionary multiplier effect, and a decrease in government expenditures exactly matched by tax reduction has a net deflationary multiplier effect. This is called the "balanced-budget multiplier." It works this way.

Assume that the government increases its spending by $10 million, and that the public's marginal propensity to consume is .5. Disregard any accelerator effects. The $10 million of new government spending immediately constitutes $10 million of new g.n.p., to which the multiplier adds another $10 million through respending. This gives a total increase in g.n.p. of $20 million in the new equilibrium level of g.n.p.

Now trace through the deflationary impact of the $10 million of new taxes to finance the expenditures. With a marginal propensity to consume of .5, private spending will fall by $5 million in the first round, $2.5 million in the second, $1.25 million in the third, and so on as in the preceding example. The total sequence of respending rounds ($5 million plus $2.5 million plus $1.25 million plus. . . .) adds up to a *total* negative multiplied effect of $10 million for the tax increase.

Note that this negative tax multiplier is just $10 million less than the positive expenditure multiplier, just the amount of the budget increase. The respending effects after the first impact of the new government spending and of the new government taxes are the same, but the $10 million increase in government purchases of goods and services became a direct part of g.n.p. whereas the tax payment by the private economy to the government was simply a transfer of purchasing power which is not part of g.n.p. The "balanced-budget multiplier" is thus just 1 in this example; g.n.p. rises by precisely the amount of the increase in government spending financed by an identical increase in government tax receipts. The $20 million addition to g.n.p. exceeds the $10 million reduction by just the amount of the new government spending.

Most economists agree that a balanced-budget multiplier effect of this sort occurs. But it need not be precisely 1. This precise result depends on two assumptions: that the propensities to consume of taxpayers and of those who receive income from government spending are identical; and that the government spending is on goods and services rather than on transfer payments. These assumptions may not be met. Moreover, the balanced-budget multiplier is, at best, only 1. Most economists believe that deficit-financed government spending is a far surer road to a higher g.n.p.

INCREASED SPENDING VERSUS TAX CUTS

If there is unemployment and the government wants to raise g.n.p. through active fiscal policy, should it increase expenditures, or cut tax rates? The answer will depend partly on the relative flexibility of the two approaches, and partly on your socio-economic preferences for "private enterprise" as against "public spending." Consider some of the issues.

Public-Investment Expenditures

"Regular" government expenditures in normal times include extensive investment in highways, education, parks, and so on. These public projects are presumably undertaken because they fill a greater social need than do alternative private uses of the resources. Citizens' dollars are diverted through taxation from private to government spending.

Public-investment projects in depression should be considered in the light of these "regular" needs. Such "net-social-gain" public-investment projects should be the ones undertaken first in depression periods unless there are strong counter-arguments. Next, public projects that were marginal in periods of full employment may be worthwhile when expansionary public spending is needed. For example, a new highway that could not quite be justified on its own merits may become clearly desirable when it can double in brass as a recovery stimulant. But how effective is such spending against unemployment and underspending in the private sector? [2]

1. Outlays on public works directly stimulate the durable-goods and construction industries, where unemployment is often centered. Public expenditures "bunched" on public works can provide a big stimulus to demand in such industries (e.g., construction and steel).

2. Public works, unlike unemployment or relief payments, give us "something to show for our money." Modern schools, parks, and highways are valuable in their own right, beyond the help they provide in raising aggregate demand.

3. By providing jobs for otherwise unemployed workers, public-works projects help maintain the morale, self-respect, and skill of workers. Even with a dole or unemployment compensation to avoid starvation, worker morale may suffer severely from unemployment; self-respect is lost; idleness becomes habitual; skills become rusty or

[2] A more complete analysis of public expenditures will be found in Part Five.

vanish. Such social losses are a major cost of unemployment.

On the other hand, public-investment projects have serious limitations:

1. Most important, flexibility in timing is hard to attain. Public-works projects are generally slow to get started and hard to stop once the need for them is past, because of both their physical nature and their political setting. Every locality and political group demands its share. It takes a long time to draw plans and let contracts for major construction projects. Moreover, it is not practical to cut them off short of completion, once they are begun. A bridge halfway across a river or a partly built schoolhouse must be completed to avoid flagrant waste even if depression has turned to inflation.

2. Public-works projects may perpetuate undesirable relative price-cost maladjustments in the industries where public-works spending is centered. Especially in the construction industry, wages and prices rise rapidly in boom times and stay up when demand slackens. Large government construction projects help keep these costs high.

3. Some types of public works may compete with private investment. This objection is advanced most strongly against government construction of low-cost housing and such combined power, reclamation, and flood-control projects as the Tennessee Valley Authority. Whatever the answer is on these public-works projects, a wide range of available outlets, such as education, highways, parks, and resource conservation, is clearly noncompetitive.

Some observers argue that in our now-affluent society we tend to starve the public sector of the economy. We desperately need better education, cleaner streets, slum clearance, and the like. Instead, we "waste" billions annually creating obsolescence through inessential style changes on cars and refrigerators, on vast attempts to create demand for "unneeded" products. These observers argue that there is a presumption in favor of higher government expenditures on increased "public services" at all times, and that at a minimum we can obtain a balanced-budget multiplier effect by raising both expenditures and tax receipts. When we need to stimulate g.n.p., raising government expenditures is the better way. But others strongly oppose more government activities, and favor leaving to individuals the choice of how they spend the dollars they earn. They say cut taxes rather than increasing government spending. Your preference will obviously depend heavily on your basic attitude about how far the government should go in allocating resources in our economy.

Unemployment Payments

The government may also spend through transfer payments, especially direct relief or "unemployment insurance" payments to the unemployed. This is the cheapest and most direct way to get funds to the needy and to assure that they will be promptly spent. Few unemployed recipients will hold idle the funds they receive. And such payments, if authorized in advance, can begin automatically when unemployment occurs. Indeed, we have built up a nationwide compulsory unemployment insurance plan, financed largely by payroll taxes collected while men are employed, that provides just such an automatic spending program.[3] Transfer payments don't directly raise g.n.p. (give jobs), but their multiplier effects do. And their superior flexibility is a telling plus.

Tax Cuts

Tax cuts are the alternative to increased spending when the government wants to expand aggregate demand. The multiplier effect of any tax cut, as was indicated above, is less than that of the same dollar increase in expenditures. This is because the expenditure counts directly as part of g.n.p., while the tax cut merely increases disposable income. Moreover, cuts in different taxes may have different responding effects. For example, a cut in personal income tax rates is guaranteed to increase disposable personal income accordingly, and the result is highly predictable. Household consumption expenditures will rise roughly in accordance with the long-prevailing

propensity to consume, though there may be a lag as people take time to adjust their consumption spending to higher disposable incomes.[4] The effect of a cut in corporation income taxes is more difficult to predict; but there is widespread agreement that a cut in corporate income taxes is likely to stimulate investment spending.

Many economists favor tax cuts over increases in government spending, on grounds of greater flexibility. Taxes usually can be cut faster than expenditures can be increased, and they can be more readily reversed, at least in principle. A tax cut immediately increases disposable income, and stimulates aggregate demand promptly. Moreover, tax cuts leave households and businesses free to spend their disposable income as they wish, in contrast to the government control over resource-allocation involved in increased government spending on goods and services.

Which is the better way to increase g.n.p., increased expenditures or tax cuts? To summarize, the first big issue is your basic preference for private spending against governmental provision of "public services." The second is the relative flexibility of the two plans. Suppose that some time soon you were faced with the need to spur total spending to fight unemployment because a recovery was topping off too soon, leaving 6 or 7 per cent of the total labor force unemployed. The economy needs a $20 billion increase in aggregate demand. Would you ask Congress to cut taxes or to increase government spending? Try justifying your recommendation to an opposition senator who thinks you are wrong.

DISCRETION
VERSUS BUILT-IN FLEXIBILITY

Flexibility is crucial to the success of fiscal policy. For discretionary fiscal policy to work well, the Administration must recognize promptly what fiscal policy is needed. Then Congress must act promptly to change expenditures or tax rates,

---

[3] For details, see Chapter 32. Actually, unemployment insurance receipts and payments are not included in the regular government budget, though they have much the same effect as regular government taxes and expenditures. Indeed, some economists like to think of unemployment benefits as negative taxes.

[4] If consumers believe the tax cut is a temporary one, and if the "permanent consumption" hypothesis explained in Chapter 7 is correct, then they will increase their consumption spending less than for a permanent tax cut, since consumption under that hypothesis is a roughly stable proportion of *permanent* income.

whichever it chooses. Although there have been some cases of successful, prompt action (for example, the excise tax cut of 1965), these have been the exception rather than the rule. It took Presidents Kennedy and Johnson nearly three years to get the widely-applauded big tax cut of 1964 through Congress. Tax increases are often even more difficult to obtain. Variations in government expenditures to combat economic fluctuations have lagged notoriously behind the apparent need for them.

One way to reduce these lags would be for Congress to delegate limited power to the President to cut or raise tax rates temporarily (in some pattern previously specified by Congress) in case of rising unemployment or inflation. In 1962 President Kennedy asked Congress for this power, to be exercised for a six-month period, subject to Congressional veto at any time. But Congress shows little sign of giving away its exclusive power to vary tax rates.

Another approach is "built-in flexibility" in taxes and government expenditures. Consider the tax side first. Suppose that the budget is balanced and that income and sales tax rates remain unchanged. If, now, a recession occurs and g.n.p. falls, tax collections will automatically fall. Thus, if government expenditures remain constant, the declining tax collections will automatically generate a deficit to help halt the decline in g.n.p. Conversely, if g.n.p. rises and government expen-

ditures stay constant, fixed tax rates will automatically generate a government surplus which will help to halt the rising aggregate expenditures. Since this built-in federal flexibility apparently absorbs about a quarter of changes in g.n.p., it is a powerful automatic stabilizer for the economy. Economists dispute about the exact magnitude of the built-in stabilization effect, but all agree that, with the large size of the government budget in the modern economy, it is a powerful effect.

On the expenditure side, as was indicated above, unemployment insurance provides a comparable automatic countercyclical variation. As with the built-in flexibility of tax collections, no one needs to forecast coming booms or depressions to obtain the stabilizing effect, nor does Congress or any official have to act to set it in motion. The countercyclical effect of unemployment insurance is much smaller in size than that for total tax collections, but Fig. 13-2 illustrates its strong stabilizing effect.[5]

Built-in flexibility of taxes and expenditures provides a very useful countercyclical fiscal effect. Against minor recessions and booms it may be enough to keep the economy near an even keel. But few economists believe that we can count on built-in flexibility to protect us against big booms and depressions, if strong pressures toward either should develop. In such instances, discretionary policy is clearly required to supplement built-in flexibility.

FIG. 13-2 Unemployment insurance provides a strong, automatic counter-cyclical force. While payroll tax collections are fairly stable, benefit payments build up rapidly in recessions and fall rapidly as recovery develops. Data plotted quarterly. (Source: U.S. Department of Labor.)

DOES FISCAL POLICY WORK?

Some critics of modern fiscal policy argue that, however logical it all may sound, it just doesn't work. They cite the evidence of the 1930's, when there were large government deficits but massive unemployment continued. They cite also most of the last decade, when the government ran deficits but unemployment stayed above acceptable levels. Advocates of modern fiscal policy counter these accusations, and further point with

[5] Unemployment insurance has some special weaknesses. For example, if unemployment rises through new additions to the labor force there is no automatic countercyclical effect because the new entrants have built up no claims for unemployment insurance payments.

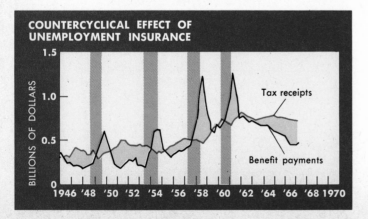

COUNTERCYCLICAL EFFECT OF UNEMPLOYMENT INSURANCE

BILLIONS OF DOLLARS

1.5

1.0

0.5

0

Tax receipts

Benefit payments

1946 '48 '50 '52 '54 '56 '58 '60 '62 '64 '66 '68 1970

pride to the big tax cut of 1964, when the predicted stimulus to the economy worked out exactly according to plan. Who is right?

First, briefly note the evidence. During the 1930's, unemployment rose to a peak of about 13 million people by 1933, over 25 per cent of the total labor force. Moreover, over the following years unemployment averaged over 18 per cent of the total work force (nearly 10 million people) for the decade. The federal government ran a deficit in each year from 1931 to 1940, averaging about $3 billion annually—although the government clearly tried to avoid deficits until the last three or four years of the decade. The unemployment rate fell rapidly after 1939, as aggregate demand (and government deficits) rose with the onset of World War II.

During the 1954–64 decade, the picture was much less dramatic, but in some respects similar. The federal budget showed a deficit in seven of the ten years, while the unemployment rate varied between 4.2 per cent (in 1956) and 6.7 per cent (in 1961). Unemployment never fell as low as the 3 per cent level of 1952–53 and of earlier prosperities.

Soon after 1960, President Kennedy's advisers began to urge a large tax cut to raise aggregate demand, since the economy persistently fell short of full employment. They urged this tax cut in spite of the already substantial federal deficit, even though the tax cut would mean, at least temporarily, an even larger deficit. In 1962 President Kennedy proposed such a tax cut, but the Congress refused to enact it until 1964. The economists' predictions were that the $10 billion tax cut would raise g.n.p. by $20–25 billion, through a combined multiplier-accelerator effect. And in fact almost exactly the predicted result occurred following the tax cut.

How shall we assess this evidence? Defenders of fiscal policy contend that the 1930's were not a fair test of their proposals. First, what deficits did occur were the result of haphazard, unplanned actions. Indeed, government expenditures were *cut* and tax rates *increased* during the first three years of the decade when the depression was spiraling downward. Moreover, state and local governments were actually running surpluses big enough to offset the complete federal deficits un-

til the mid-1930's. Even during the latter part of the decade, when President Roosevelt and the New Dealers finally became convinced that deficit financing was a sensible thing, deficits were still small, only 2 or 3 per cent of g.n.p. With such small deficits in relation to the massive unemployment problem, they understandably didn't eliminate unemployment.

Again in the 1950's and early 1960's, government deficits were not part of a planned attack on unemployment. Rather, they came about haltingly, as the result of haphazard governmental fiscal measures on both tax and expenditure sides.

The Full-Employment Budget

But the main answer of the defenders of fiscal policy is this—that in fact government fiscal policy was *repressive* in spite of the deficits. They argue that the deficits during these periods reflected mainly low income and employment in the economy rather than positive government action to stimulate aggregate demand. Thus to look at the actual government deficits during such a period is to look at the wrong measure of government fiscal policy.

Instead, they say that the proper measure of the stimulative or repressive effect of government fiscal policy is what the federal budget would be at full employment—the "full-employment budget." And in both the 1930's and 1950's, the government persistently ran large full-employment surpluses, not deficits. Thus, the deficits reflected a depressed economy, and the government budget was repressive, not expansionary during these periods. Therefore it is not surprising that unemployment was not eliminated.

In essence, this argument is that the persistent deficits of the 1930's and 1950's–1960's reflected mainly the *involuntary* results of a depressed g.n.p. which pulled tax receipts below government spending levels. Tax rates were too *high*. Each time g.n.p. rose, rising tax receipts would have swung the budget to a surplus long before full employment was reached, given those tax rates. Deficits were "passive," the unintended results of weak aggregate demand—not "active," intended measures against unemployment.

In 1962, for example, the realized government deficit was $6 billion. Yet then-existing tax rates would have produced a federal budget *surplus* of $6 billion had the economy been at full-employment. That is, existing tax rates put a heavy "fiscal drag" on the upswing long before it reached full-employment levels. And so it was for every year from 1954 up to the large tax cut of 1964. *Although actual federal deficits occurred in most of these years, in all of them there was a large "full-employment surplus," exerting a heavy fiscal drag on the economy before it could reach full-employment levels.*

Figure 13-3 shows this effect. The dark bars show the actual recorded federal deficits and surpluses over the last decade, deficits for most years. The light bars show what the budget situation would have been had the economy been at full-employment each year. In every year the federal budget would have shown a substantial surplus at full-employment, and in some years (for example 1960) there would have been a huge government surplus. If, therefore, we look at the true effect of the federal budget over these years, it was consistently repressive. The federal budget's fiscal drag hit every upswing on the head before it could get well started.

How about the tax cut of 1964? Although taxes were cut by about $11 billion at the 1964 level of g.n.p., the actual deficit for 1965 was only $3 billion, compared to $8 billion in 1964, although federal expenditures rose. This reflected the rapid rise in g.n.p. following the tax cut, just in line with the predictions of the tax cut advocates. It is possible that the big upsurge of g.np. and consumption just happened to come right after the tax cut, but it looks to fiscal policy

advocates like a major confirmation of their theory.

Who is right, the critics or the defenders of modern fiscal policy? Have the defenders explained away the apparent failure of budget deficits in the past? Most economists believe that the proponents of modern fiscal policy have the better of the argument. Merely looking at realized deficits is seriously misleading. The full-employment budget provides a useful way of evaluating the impact of government fiscal policy. Perhaps most important, whatever the existing state of the budget (surplus or deficit), moving it toward deficit will stimulate the economy, while moving it toward surplus will repress the economy.

"Fiscal Drag" and Economic Growth

Critics and advocates of modern fiscal policy alike agree on one major point. With our rapidly growing economy, given any level of government spending and any set of tax rates, the federal budget will rapidly move from deficits toward surpluses as g.n.p. increases. With a 3 or 4 per cent annual increase in g.n.p., federal tax receipts rise by $6–8 billion annually. Thus, a budget in balance one year will show a $6–8 billion surplus only a year later with stable federal spending. To avoid this "fiscal drag" resulting merely from the growth of the economy, we must cut federal tax rates by $6–8 billion annually, increase federal expenditures by this amount, or some combination of the two. Looked at another way, holding federal tax rates stable over the next decade would generate a surplus of about $50 billion by 1975, assuming the economy stayed at 4 per cent un-

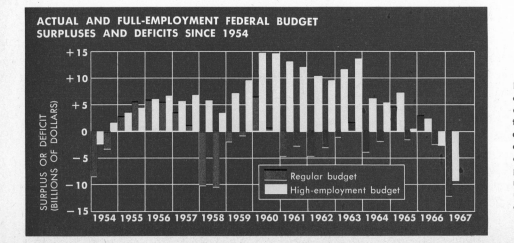

ACTUAL AND FULL-EMPLOYMENT FEDERAL BUDGET SURPLUSES AND DEFICITS SINCE 1954

SURPLUS OR DEFICIT (BILLIONS OF DOLLARS)

Regular budget
High-employment budget

1954 1955 1956 1957 1958 1959 1960 1961 1962 1963 1964 1965 1966 1967

FIG. 13-3 The "full-employment" and actual federal budget give very different pictures of the impact of the budget on the economy, especially during the last decade. Most economists believe the former gives a better indication of the net fiscal push or drag on the economy. The national income accounts budget is used in both cases. (Source: Council of Economic Advisers.)

employment. This potential surplus could finance a vast increase in federal spending on education, urban renewal, health, and the like. Alternatively it would permit large tax cuts if we maintain an unchanged level of federal spending. Perhaps most important, it warns us that we will build up massive deflationary pressure over the decade if we neither cut tax rates nor increase federal spending. The fiscal drag in that case would surely prevent rapid economic growth with full employment.

THE BALANCED-BUDGET TRADITION

This reasoning suggests that government deficits and surpluses are powerful tools in fighting unemployment and inflation. Yet until the 1930's scarcely anyone questioned the proposition that the government's budget should be balanced every year. And today many people still believe a balanced budget is the best thing. We need to take a more detailed look at the consequences of this traditional policy.

Annual Budget Balance

A balanced-budget policy is, in one sense, a "neutral" government policy. The government feeds back into the income stream just what it withdraws—no more and no less. Thus, a balanced budget seems appropriate when we are satisfied with the existing level of total expenditures—roughly, in periods of full employment without inflation.

But suppose recession appears. What does the annually balanced-budget policy call for? With falling g.n.p. and unchanged tax rates, the government's tax receipts will fall. A deficit will be created automatically unless corrective steps are taken. To avoid the deficit, the annual budget-balancers say raise tax rates to get more money or reduce spending to match reduced tax receipts. If you believe that the government ought to be trying to *expand* total spending in order to check the recession, the balanced-budget prescription is clearly wrong. To *reduce* tax rates and *increase* government spending would help raise the level of total spending, but the balanced-budget policy calls for exactly the opposite actions under recession conditions.

Similarly, inflation would generate a budget surplus, calling for tax *reductions* and *increased* spending to avoid a budget surplus, under an annually balanced-budget policy. Again, this seems clearly the wrong prescription for stabilization purposes. It would speed the inflation, rather than check it.

The experience of 1964 provides a vivid example. In mid-1964, unemployment was 5.5 per cent and, at existing tax rates, the predicted federal budget deficit for the year ahead was $8 billion. The balanced budget rule said: Raise taxes sharply and cut government spending, placing a strong deflationary pressure on aggregate demand, even with wide-spread unemployment.

If an annually-balanced-budget fiscal policy is likely to give the wrong answer so often, why did it take so long to discover its weaknesses? There are probably three answers: (1) a faith that by and large the private economy will itself correct deviations from full employment without government intervention; (2) a belief that budget deficits always lead to inflation; and (3) an analogy that if private individuals should balance their own budgets, the government should do likewise. You should be able to form your own judgment on (1) by now. On (2), government deficits certainly tend to raise aggregate demand or keep it from falling, but whether this leads to inflation of course depends heavily on whether the economy is already near full employment. On (3), we shall have more to say in analyzing the effects of a large public debt in the next chapter. For the moment, keep an open mind.

A Cyclically Balanced Budget

The obvious difficulties of annual budget-balancing led, during the 1930's, to the proposal that the budget should be balanced not annually, but over the length of the business cycle. There seemed no great virtue in one year as an arbitrary accounting period. A cyclically balanced budget would permit government fiscal policy to play a positive stabilizing role, running a deficit in depression and a counterbalancing surplus in the following boom—and at the same time maintain the basic character of a balanced budget.

How about this sensible-sounding policy? History suggests one major problem. What if the government runs a big deficit fighting a long, severe depression, and then the following boom turns out to be a weak affair that never gets up to full employment? Should the government then try to collect a large surplus to offset the preceding deficit, even though to do so would depress the economy again? The advocate of a cyclically-balanced-budget policy would presumably say "yes," but common sense rebels at the idea of a big government surplus when the problem is to get out of a recession.

If inflationary booms just offset depressions, a cyclically-balanced-budget could work out precisely right. But if the two needs for fiscal policy turn out not to balance at all, the cyclically-balanced-budget philosophy exposes us to the same false prescriptions as annual budget-balancing.

"Functional Finance"

"Functional finance" is the logical outcome of the new fiscal economics. The "functional finance" advocates say, forget about balancing the budget as a separate goal. Use the government budget as needed to help provide full employment without inflation. If the private economy stagnates, more federal deficits than surpluses are appropriate; a rising government debt is a small price to pay for the avoidance of mass unemployment. If the private economy is too buoyant, continued government surpluses are fine. The major goal is stable economic growth, and we shouldn't become so preoccupied with our tools that we lose sight of our basic objectives. This approach is called "functional finance" because it views the federal budget functionally, as a means toward the goal of stable economic growth.

This policy is the logical conclusion of looking at government fiscal policy as a means of compensating under- or over-spending in the private sector of the economy. This theory says it's the right thing to cut tax rates even though we already face a big deficit *if* aggregate demand at present tax rates is too small to provide prosperity. To paraphrase Admiral Farragut, "Damn the deficits, full speed ahead!"

High-Employment Budget Balance Plus Built-in Flexibility

One last middle-of-the-road budget proposal is worth attention. It proposes that we should first determine federal spending (on nonstabilization grounds); then set tax rates to cover those expenditures at roughly full employment; and then, foregoing discretionary countercyclical fiscal policy, rely on built-in flexibility to keep the economy from swinging to either unemployment or inflation.

For example, suppose federal spending is set at $100 billion because that's the volume of public services we want the government to provide on the assumption we must pay for them through taxes. Then tax rates would be set to yield $100 billion when g.n.p. was at roughly full-employment. With stable tax rates, tax yields would vary directly with any fluctuations in g.n.p.

Assume that we can begin with a full-employment situation. Then, if g.n.p. falls because of recession, tax collections would automatically fall below $100 billion. Government expenditures would be maintained, however, so that a deficit would automatically be created to check falling income and employment. If g.n.p. soars above the full-employment level, tax receipts would rise about $100 billion and an automatic budget surplus would result, tending to check the inflationary boom. Expenditures would be held at $100 billion in either case, except for unemployment benefits and other such automatically countercyclical expenditures. The plan would thus combine "built-in budgetary flexibility" with the basic virtue of making Congress face up to the need to balance expenditures with taxes—at full employment.

Proponents of this plan claim that they are facing political and economic realities that other approaches gloss over. The built-in flexibility plan would require no action on the part of Congress or the Administration in forecasting business developments and in changing tax and expenditure policies to counter changing economic conditions. There would be no need to delegate congressional power over tax rates or spending to get quick action. Congress would need only to establish the basic level of government spending and set tax rates to cover those expenditures at high-level employment. The rest would be automatic; just don't try to change tax rates or expenditures to stabilize the economy, since, as a practical matter, you'll probably do as much harm as good.

But this plan has weaknesses too. First, there's no guarantee the automatically created deficits and surpluses would be big enough to keep small swings from developing into big booms or depressions. Second, if the private economy is basically stagnant or overbuoyant, a federal full-employment budget balance won't compensate for this private under- or over-spending. In those cases, the economy needs positive federal stimulus or response, not the federal neutrality of full-employment budget balance. Full-employment budget balance isn't necessarily a policy that will produce full employment.

THE MIX OF MONETARY AND FISCAL POLICY

Fiscal and monetary policy must be effectively coordinated for optimum results. Unless they are, one may offset the other.

Suppose, for example, the government reduces tax rates to expand aggregate demand. Unless the money stock is simultaneously increased, interest rates will rise and the expansionary force of the tax cut will be partially offset. Why? Because government borrowing will tend to bid up interest rates, and as income rises the public's demand for money balances will also rise, further increasing interest rates. But if the Fed simultaneously provides more money for the system, interest rates can be held down and this offsetting effect can be avoided.

The 1964 experience shows the importance of cooperative monetary and fiscal policy. The big tax cut led to rising incomes, to rising demands for money balances as transaction needs increased, and to upward pressures on interest rates from direct federal borrowing to finance the deficit. But simultaneously the Fed provided new bank reserves which permitted the money stock to grow about 5 per cent during the year, which kept interest rates roughly stable.

This experience also indicates how difficult it is to decide whether monetary policy or fiscal policy deserves most of the credit for the 1964 success. While many economists argue that the tax cut was the big stimulant to the economy, others argue that the expansion in the money stock deserves major credit for stimulating the economy. Our present statistical techniques don't permit us to settle the argument for sure. Happily, we don't have to know just how much credit to give to each. The main lesson is that they need to be used cooperatively.

The need to mesh international and domestic considerations raises different problems of determining the right policy mix. Recently, our international position has called for high interest rates to keep funds invested here instead of abroad, while at home unemployment has called for increased aggregate demand. Under these circumstances, many economists have argued for a tighter monetary policy to raise interest rates in order to solve the international problem, combined with an expansionary fiscal policy to stimulate the domestic economy.

When we come to the problem of long-term economic growth, still another policy mix problem will arise. Suppose, for example, we want to stimulate faster growth when we already have high-level employment and stable prices. We can do so by an easy money policy, producing lower interest rates to stimulate investment. But under these circumstances, this policy will produce excess aggregate demand and inflation. However, if we simultaneously raise taxes to generate a budget surplus, we can restrain demand and counteract the undesired inflationary pressure. Thus, an easy-money policy of low interest rates combined with a budget surplus could help stimulate growth while maintaining high-level employment without inflation. But this low-interest-rate policy, alas, is just the opposite of what we may need for international purposes.

History shows that the world has an unpleasant way of throwing up new problems, every time we think we have the old ones well under control. Prudent economic policy will certainly require flexibility in the way we use monetary and fiscal policy, and a changing mix of these policies to cope with new situations as they arise.

For Analysis and Discussion

1. You are asked to speak before a local businessman's group on whether federal taxes should be increased, lowered, or left unchanged for the next year. Outline the talk you would give, indicating briefly how you would develop each of your major points.

2. If gross national product is $50 billion short of a full-employment level, the public's marginal propensity to consume is .9, and private investment is constant, about how much additional government investment, financed by bank borrowing, would be necessary to raise gross national product to a full-employment level? Explain why, indicating clearly any assumptions you make.

3. Suppose the situation is as in the preceding question, but the level of private investment is not held constant. Would you then expect the amount of government investment required to be larger or smaller? Why?

4. "Since government officials can't forecast accurately what fiscal policy will be needed when, we are better off to rely entirely on built-in fiscal stabilizers." Do you agree? How could we increase the strength of our built-in stabilizers?

5. Does the "full-employment budget surplus" analysis convince you that federal fiscal policy can work effectively, in spite of the co-existence of large deficits and unemployment in the past?

6. State carefully all the advantages and disadvantages you can think of in balancing the federal budget (a) weekly; (b) annually; (c) over the cycle; (d) over a 50-year period; (e) only when business conditions are at the desired level, regardless of how often this occurs. Which alternative is best on the basis of your analysis?

7. Assume that international tensions require a $50 billion increase in military expenditures over the next two years. Would you recommend that the federal government raise the $50 billion by borrowing, or by increasing tax rates? Why? Does the balanced-budget multiplier affect your answer?

8. Suppose you believe that a growth rate of 5 per cent per annum is essential for the American economy. What federal fiscal measures would you advocate to achieve that growth rate?

9. As an economist for the President's Council of Economic Advisers, you are asked to prepare a set of recommendations for action in case a recession develops in the near future. Outline the recommendations, explaining your reasons for supporting these measures.

10. (*Based on the Appendix*) If you are interested mainly in analyzing the effect of government fiscal actions on the level of employment, which of the three major budget concepts is the most useful? Why?

Appendix

DIFFERENT BUDGET CONCEPTS

Each year the President presents a budget to Congress. It proposes expenditures on a wide variety of activities, and estimates the tax receipts that will be obtained under existing tax legislation. Sometimes it proposes new tax legislation. If the proposed expenditures exceed expected tax receipts, the budget proposes a deficit; if expenditures are less than expected tax receipts, it proposes a surplus.

In fact, the federal budget can be viewed in at least four different ways, each of which gives different totals for expenditures and receipts, and hence for the surplus or deficit.

The "Administrative" Budget.   The "administrative" budget is the one that you most frequently encounter in the newspapers. It is the set of expenditures proposed by the President in his regular budget message, for which he asks Congressional approval each year. It represents the focal point for Congressional decision-making with respect to individual government activities, such as spending on national defense.

But the administrative budget does not fully reflect the government's impact on the economy. First, it excludes important activities of the government, notably the entire social security system which is technically operated as a "trust fund" apart from the regular government budget. Other large trust funds are also excluded. Second, the administrative budget makes no distinction between government purchases of goods and services, transfer payments, and government lending operations, all of which are treated equally as government expenditures. The economic effects of these different transactions, however, may be quite different.

The "Cash" Budget.   A second federal budget includes all cash collections and cash payments by the federal government, including those of government trust funds. This budget, which is some $30–40 billion larger than the "administrative" budget, thus provides a better picture of the government's total impact on the economy. It too, however, has failings as an indicator of the impact of the government budget on aggregate demand and current g.n.p.

The National Income Accounts Budget.   A third federal budget includes all the federal expenditures and tax collections which directly affect the national income and product accounts—that is, which directly affect g.n.p. This budget is similar to the cash budget in that it includes the activities of the trust funds. But it differs in that it excludes lending operations and counts tax liabilities as they accrue rather than only as they are actually received by the federal treasury. This income accounts budget provides the most direct measure of the impact of the federal budget on current g.n.p. But it too has its failings, because for some purposes we may want to know how much the federal government is spending, lending or borrowing through the trust funds or other special activities. Thus each of the budgets has its own special purposes.

The "Full-Employment" Budget.   "Full-employment" budget estimates can be made using any of the three budget concepts above. Economists usually use the national-income-accounts concept in making such estimates because they are primarily concerned with the impact of the federal budget on the current operations of the economy—on current output and jobs. However, "full-employment" budget estimates for the cash and administrative budget are also sometimes made.

Statistical Comparison of Budget Concepts.   The following table shows the three main budget concepts for the fiscal year 1968, as estimated by President Johnson in his budget message for that year.[6]

TABLE 13-1

FEDERAL BUDGET CONCEPTS, FISCAL 1968 *

	Expenditures	Receipts	Deficit
	(All Figures in Billions)		
Administrative budget	$137	$119	$19
Cash budget	176	159	17
National Income Accounts budget	171	161	10
Unified budget	176	156	20

* Estimates are from the *Budget in Brief, Fiscal 1969* (U.S. Government Printing Office), page 72. Since the economy was at about 4 per cent unemployment, the "full-employment" budget deficits were about equal to those shown in the "Deficit" column.

[6] In 1968, after the above was written, the Federal government announced that it will shift to a new budget concept in most of its official documents—to "a unified budget." This new budget concept in essence combines all the items previously included in the first three budget concepts, but includes them so that any of the three can be broken out separately by those who want to use them. Table 1 has been revised to show all four budget concepts. A detailed description of the new unified budget and its relation to the older accounts is given in the *Federal Budget in Brief, Fiscal 1969*, U.S. Government Printing Office, pages 63–64.

FOURTEEN
THE PRACTICAL PROBLEMS
OF STABILIZATION
POLICY

Can We Have High Employment Without Inflation?

The Problem of Forecasting and Flexibility.

The Problem of Expanding Government Control.

The Problem of the Public Debt.

Are Depressions Obsolete?

In principle, monetary-fiscal policy to smooth out booms and depressions and to keep aggregate demand on a stable growth path is simple. But will it really work?

The first thing to note is that there isn't much evidence yet. We have had only about three decades of experience with conscious fiscal policy. Congressional and public opinion have only gradually accepted the idea of counter-cyclical budget policy, and advocates of an annually balanced budget are still powerful. Thus fiscal policy has been controversial, halting, and spotty—far from the orderly plan laid out by the functional-finance programers. Even monetary policy has been used in a modern vein only recently.

The results thus far have been mixed. Chalk up the 1930's as poor, but hardly a reasonable test of combined monetary-fiscal policy; the 1940's and '50's as so-so; and the 1960's as definitely promising. Three decades is a very short period, and it would be surprising if our new stabilization tools had proved fully successful in their trial run, especially with such an unsystematic trial period. The World War II experience did demonstrate unmistakably the enormous expansionary power of large-scale deficit spending financed by bank credit. And since 1940 there has been no major recession—the longest generally prosperous period in our history. But we have had some inflation and nagging unemployment during much of the last decade.

This chapter looks at four important practical problems we face in trying to stabilize the growth rate of the economy through monetary and fiscal policy.

CAN WE HAVE HIGH EMPLOYMENT WITHOUT INFLATION?

At the end of World War II, Congress passed the Employment Act of 1946. This announced that it is the policy of the federal government to help achieve the "maximum production, employment and purchasing power" consistent with maintaining a free, private-enterprise economy. Although the language is general, it has been generally interpreted to establish twin goals of high-level employment and reasonably stable prices. More recently, many have added two other goals—more rapid long-run growth and a strong international position for the dollar.

Is There a Conflict Between High Employment and Price Stability?

Either unemployment or inflation alone can be attacked readily by monetary and fiscal policy. The former calls for easy money and an expansionary budget, the latter for the reverse action. But when unemployment and inflation occur together, there is trouble.

Until the 1950's, economists generally assumed that prices would not rise much until reasonably full employment prevailed. But now there are many doubts. A pioneering study by A. W. Phillips of the London School of Economics showed that in England over the past century, whenever unemployment fell below about 5 per cent, wage rates tended to rise faster than was consistent with stable prices. Some American economists believe they see the same general relationship in our economy; others doubt that any such simple relationship holds or that 5 per cent is a critical level. But everyone agrees that as we approach full employment and labor markets become tighter, it is increasingly likely that wage rates will be bid up by employers or pushed up by unions. And everyone agrees that higher wage costs and prices will surely appear in many sectors before the economy as a whole reaches "full" employment (even if full employment is defined to allow for 2 or 3 per cent frictional unemployment).

The B.L.S. consumer price index did creep upward at 1½ per cent annually from 1957 to the mid-1960's while unemployment averaged about 5 per cent. These facts suggest that the high-employment-or-inflation dilemma may be a real one. If we had expanded aggregate demand faster in order to get unemployment down to 3 or 4 per cent, surely the rate of consumer price inflation would have been higher. Alternatively, restricting aggregate demand enough to hold the consumer price index stable would have generated more unemployment than in fact occurred. There was no obviously "right" amount of aggregate demand to solve this problem. Looking back at Fig. 5-2, we seem to be in the area of the dashed line.

Whether or not there is a predictable trade-off between rising prices and falling unemployment is a complex and unsettled issue. Clearly, *in the short run*, rapid increases in demand when the economy is near full employment will generate rising prices before full employment is reached, and we can have lower unemployment only by accepting some inflation. But it is far less clear that *in the long run* the equilibrium level of unemployment can be reduced by inflation. Much evidence suggests that the unemployment-reducing results of inflation are transient.

The Wage-Price Guideposts

In 1962 President Kennedy's Council of Economic Advisers suggested a set of wage-price "guideposts" for unions and businessmen.[1] The Council suggested that if unions and businesses would adhere to these guideposts, aggregate-demand policy by the government could bring full employment and prosperity without inflation. The Council didn't suggest government action to force unions and businesses to adhere to the guideposts, but it did urge them as useful guides to private behavior.

In essence, the guideposts suggest that annual wage increases in all industries should roughly equal the average increase in output per man hour in the economy.[2] With such wage increases, prices

[1] See *Economic Report of the President*, Jan. 1962, Chap. 4.
[2] Three details may help spell out the implications of the guideposts:
1. Wages in particular industries *should not* be directly related to productivity changes in that industry. Thus, if productivity in the automobile industry increases 5 per cent

of final products should be kept stable. Bigger wage increases would be inflationary, while smaller ones would give an undue share of the benefits of increasing productivity to profits. The guideposts were based on the general position that wage rates should behave about as they would in a highly competitive market where supply and demand would tend to produce wage increases equal to increases in "productivity."

Consider a simple example. Assume a stable population and an economy where all income goes to wages and profits. Total output is $300, of which wages are ⅔ and profits ⅓. Now suppose the total output increases by 3 per cent (that is, $9), and that wages are increased by 3 per cent, as suggested by the productivity guidepost. Wages will now rise by $6 (that is, 3 per cent of $200), leaving $3 for increased profits (that is, 3 per cent of $100). Thus, the average-productivity-increase guide would increase both wages and profits by the same percentage, maintaining whatever distribution of income prevailed before. It is important to see that increasing wage rates in proportion to productivity increase does not mean that all of the increase goes to labor, although this is a commonly held misconception.

Since 1962 the guideposts have been the source of violent disagreement. The critics make three main points.

First, if you don't think the present income distribution between wages and profits is fair, preserving it won't be very attractive. Many union members believe that profits are already ex-

orbitant. Many businessmen believe profits are already too low. And at any time individual wage rates in particular firms or industries may be unfairly out of line, too high or too low.

Second, fixed-income people—the pensioners and old people—would like to see prices *decline* with advancing productivity, since unless prices fall they don't share in the fruits of progress.

Third, and most important, both unions and businessmen told the government to keep its nose out. They wanted no government control, and rebelled at the idea that they shouldn't take full advantage of their competitive positions, though some were reluctant to say so publicly. If productivity rises 5 per cent annually in the auto industry, the auto workers are understandably reluctant to settle for only a 3 per cent wage increase, just because productivity elsewhere has increased less than theirs. If you were head of the auto union, would you agree to take a 3 per cent increase when by hard bargaining you could get 5? If you were president of General Motors, would you reduce prices just because the guideposts say that this is desirable when you believe you'll make bigger profits by keeping them up? Would you take a costly strike to hold wages down to help the nation fight inflation, when there's plenty of demand to support higher prices for autos?

Guideposts that ask unions and businesses to forego private gain for the national good, without any government enforcement mechanism, obviously face serious problems. And few Americans want the government to have power to set individual wages and prices. Some guidepost advocates urge government intervention in pattern-setting wage bargains, and pitiless government publicity on inflationary wage and price behavior. But often such informal pressure hasn't been very effective, and the step from it to actual governmental dictation of key wage and price settlements is a short one. Nearly everyone agrees that the guidepost results are sensible, but how to achieve them is another story.

---

per year, but only 3 per cent for the economy as a whole, this does not justify a 5 per cent wage increase in the auto industry. Rather, it calls for a decline in the price of automobiles.

2. Prices should remain approximately stable in industries which have an average rate of productivity increase. Where productivity increases faster than the national average (that is, where per unit costs fall faster than the average), selling prices should decline. Prices should rise where productivity increases more slowly than the average.

3. Some exceptions are justified. Wages should rise less than the national average in industries where unemployment persists, to discourage additional workers from entering the industry and to encourage employers to use more labor in that industry. Wages should rise faster than the average where labor is especially scarce. (Again, these are the results to be expected from highly competitive markets.) Moreover, individual wages could rise more or less than the national average where deviation is needed to correct major inequities.

Structural Unemployment, Aggregate Demand, and Inflation

Recently another doubt has been expressed about the efficacy of expansionary monetary-fiscal policy to reduce unemployment without causing inflation. This is the fear that we have a growing amount of "structural unemployment" which is relatively insensitive to expanding aggregate demand. Structural unemployment is a serious mismatch between the jobs that open up with rising demand and the skills and locations of unemployed workers.

The post-World War II expansions have left substantial amounts of unemployment. While unemployment fell to 2 or 3 per cent in some earlier prosperities, the boom of 1955–57 only reduced it to 4 per cent, that of 1959–60 to only 5 per cent, and that of 1960–67 to just under 4 per cent. Some observers argue that this persistent unemployment reflected not inadequate aggregate demand but instead a more rigid and less mobile economy in which the unemployed workers just don't fit the jobs that open up.

"Structural unemployment" is hard to define precisely. It results from the failure of unemployed workers to move reasonably promptly into other jobs because of lack of information on job openings, inadequate skills for the new jobs available, financial inability to move to other areas, low I.Q.'s, laziness, and the like—in contrast to unemployment caused by inadequate total demand. There are jobs available in the economy, but the structurally unemployed can't find or fill them. With an increased rate of "automation," many feel that structural problems have increased substantially—old skills rapidly become obsolete and major retraining is necessary if the unemployed are to find new jobs.

An example is the middle-aged West Virginia coal miner, thrown out of work a decade ago by mechanization of the mines, uneducated, unskilled except in coal mining, and abjectly poor, living on his little garden patch and perhaps a small government relief check. Even though there are plenty of jobs open elsewhere for college graduates, for skilled machine tool operators, for computer programers, these have little relevance to him. And expanding aggregate demand further isn't going to make much difference to him. It will just bid up the wages of the skilled workers who fit the expanding job categories.

In a rapidly changing economy there are always many thousands, even millions, out of work between jobs as consumer demands shift and technology changes. In 1966, for example, 10

million workers changed jobs sometime during the year. For most workers, such frictional unemployment is brief, although months between jobs is not uncommon. There is some level of aggregate demand (for example, during World War II) that will draw almost everybody into some job promptly. If consumer demand is strong enough, businessmen somehow find the workers needed and train them on the job if there is no other way. The profit incentive is a powerful weapon against structural unemployment. But that much aggregate demand may generate inflationary pressure long before all marginal workers are employed.

There is certainly some structural unemployment in our economy. The West Virginia coal miner above is an example. But the evidence is strong that more aggregate demand effectively pulls most of the unemployed back into jobs, even when they appear to be structurally unemployed. While structural unemployment is always a problem for some, there's little evidence that it's worse now than before.

The recent experience of Pittsburgh, a major steel center, is a good example. In early 1962 the unemployment rate in Pittsburgh was over 11 per cent, compared to a national average of about 6 per cent. Pittsburgh was a major "labor surplus" area. Employment in the steel mills had been declining persistently since World War II. The steel companies could produce one-third more steel than 10 years previously, with fewer men. Pittsburgh was cited as a classic case of structural unemployment—unemployed steelworkers whose jobs were gone forever and who were ill-equipped to take on other jobs and unwilling or unable to move to other areas.

But after the strong economic expansion of 1964, Pittsburgh unemployment at year-end was only 3.7 per cent, compared to over 5 per cent for the nation. Rapidly growing aggregate demand boomed needs for steel in the economy. Mills called displaced workers back to their jobs. But more important, over the years 1960–1964 more than 100,000 people emigrated from the Pittsburgh industrial area as more jobs opened up elsewhere in the United States. Areas like Pittsburgh, specializing in production of durable goods, are especially susceptible to swings in aggregate demand. But the Pittsburgh experience emphasizes that what appears to be long-run structural unemployment may be eaten away rapidly by growing aggregate spending. There is certainly some "hard core" of unemployed workers who will find it very hard to locate and qualify for new jobs. But the hard core is of ice, not of iron. We can melt much of it away under the sun of strong aggregate demand.

Still, steps to improve the mobility of workers between jobs represent a net gain to society. Improving labor mobility and the efficiency of the labor market through government job-information exchanges, retraining programs, moving allowances, and the like, are appropriate to the structural-unemployment problem however big it is. European experiences suggest that far more can be done than we have yet tried. In any event, it is important to see that strong aggregate demand and improved market efficiency are *complementary*, not competitive, policies to help achieve high employment without inflation.

THE PROBLEM OF FORECASTING AND FLEXIBILITY

Fine-tuning the economy for stable economic growth depends on accurate timing of monetary and fiscal policies: knowing when to do what, and then doing it at the right time. This problem has come up repeatedly before.

Any honest economist will admit a lot of uncertainty about just what policy measure should be adopted when. First, economic forecasting is still a long way short of reliability.[3] It's hard to know even where we are in the cycle, much less tell where we'll be six months hence. Second, even when we know what lies ahead we're not sure of the exact impact of different combinations of taxes, government spending, and monetary policy. Is an $8 billion surplus gentle restraint or a sledge-hammer against inflation in a $800 billion economy? Lastly, there's uncertainty about the lag before either monetary or fiscal policy has its full impact on real g.n.p. and employment.

[3] For a fuller discussion of forecasting methods, see the Appendix to Chapter 9.

On monetary policy, the Fed can act promptly once the need is diagnosed. All the authorities need to do is buy or sell bonds in the open market, a matter of hours after the decision is made. So the "inside" lag between need and action can be short. But the "outside" lag between Federal Reserve action and its final impact on output and employment is unfortunately longer, and worse, is uncertain in length. Most economists put the outside lag at from three to nine months on the average; some of the effect on g.n.p. and employment comes immediately but the rest spreads out over many months. If they're right, using monetary policy effectively against minor business fluctuations is tough. Before easy money stimulates more spending, the recession may be over; instead, its impact may come just in time to reinforce the next inflationary boom.

On fiscal policy, it's the "inside" lag that causes most of the trouble. Both the administration and Congress have to be convinced of the need to change taxes and spending to fight the boom or recession, and then they must act. It's a slow total process, especially if the need is to damp an overheating boom. Prosperity is nice. And the prospect of being blamed for a depression strikes horror to the heart of any elected official.

But don't put the blame too readily on "those politicians." Ask yourself what you'd do if you were President or a senator, when it looked like inflation ahead though there was a 25 per cent chance that the real problem would turn out to be recession within six months. To make your answer easier, assume that you don't even plan to run for re-election, and that all you care about are the best interests of the people as a whole. What would you do?

The "outside" lag is shorter for fiscal then for monetary policy. With widespread tax withholding by employers, a change in personal income tax rates is reflected immediately in after-tax take-home pay (disposable personal income). Government spending, once it is begun, directly affects aggregate demand and employment.

Several proposals to improve the administrative-legislative flexibility of stabilization policy have already been noted. One would delegate more tax and spending powers to the President.

Another would adopt a simple, rigid rule, such as an annual 4 per cent increase in the money stock, which would completely avoid administrative discretion. Another would increase the amount of built-in fiscal flexibility in the system. No one has a completely satisfactory answer, but we are gradually improving our ability to focus stabilization policy effectively on the economy.

THE PROBLEM OF EXPANDING GOVERNMENT CONTROL

If the economy persistently tends toward underemployment, compensatory fiscal policy might mean steadily rising government expenditures. Many Americans don't like this picture of larger government spending, because they feel that it would mean expanding government control over private economic affairs.

Views differ violently on whether increased government spending involves undesirable interference with the affairs of private individuals and businesses. One school points out that the government is directly responsible to the people, and we can always vote the rascals out if we don't like what they're doing to us. The other argues that increased government spending is the primrose path to socialism—step by step the government takes over direction of our economic lives. Make up your own mind. Economics gives no clear-cut answer.

But don't forget that when expansionary government fiscal policy is needed, tax reductions can do the job too. So fear of growing government spending need not block active fiscal policy.

One thing is clear on the record to date. The big expansions in government spending have come with war and preparations for war, not with attempts to stabilize the economy. Even the New Deal of the 1930's channeled only a small fraction of the national income through the government in this worst of all depressions, compared to the massive government spending of World War II and the Vietnam conflict. Still, there is little doubt that it is much harder for the government to stop spending than to start. The antirecession projects of today can easily turn into the regular government expenditures of tomorrow

—the farm price-support programs of the 1930's are prominent examples.

THE PROBLEM OF THE PUBLIC DEBT

Much of the controversy over fiscal policy arises because people fear the rising public debt that comes with deficit financing. Since the 1920's, the public debt has increased by over a quarter trillion dollars, to its present level of over $300 billion. Should we view the public debt with alarm? The answer is, not with as much alarm as most people have, but with some. The first step toward an objective assessment of the problem is to look at the facts.

The Facts about the Public Debt

Figure 14-1 shows the public debt (the heavy black line), and the debt as a percentage of the g.n.p. (dashed red line), since 1920. It is clear that our present $340 billion federal debt came largely from World War II. It's also clear that as a percentage of g.n.p. the federal debt has steadily drifted downhill from a peak of about 130 per cent at the end of World War II to below 50 per cent now.

Another useful way of looking at the federal debt is in terms of the interest charges it involves. Figure 14-2 shows annual interest payments on the federal debt since 1920, and again

FIG. 14-1 The federal debt has spurted upward in war periods, but has declined steadily relative to g.n.p. since World War II. (Source: U.S. Treasury and Commerce Departments.)

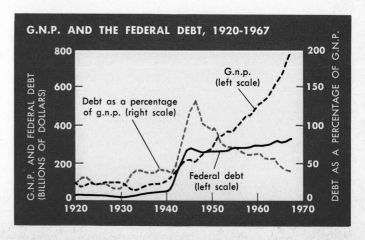

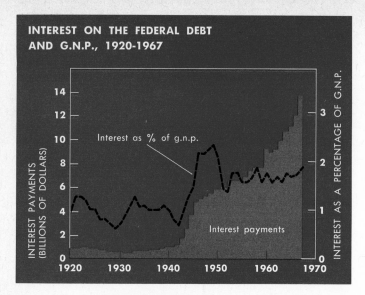

INTEREST ON THE FEDERAL DEBT
AND G.N.P., 1920-1967

Interest as % of g.n.p.

INTEREST PAYMENTS
(BILLIONS OF DOLLARS)

Interest payments

INTEREST AS A PERCENTAGE OF G.N.P.

FIG. 14-2 Annual interest on the federal debt now exceeds $14 billion, but it is less than 2 per cent of g.n.p., and only a slightly higher percentage than during the 1920's. (Source: U.S. Treasury Department; data for fiscal years.)

those payments as a percentage of g.n.p. Since interest rates have risen persistently since World War II, the annual interest payments on the debt have grown to $14 billion, even with a slowly rising debt. This growth has roughly matched the steadily growing g.n.p., so that interest payments have run about 1.5 per cent of g.n.p. over most of the last decade.

It is also interesting to compare public and private debt. Figure 14-3 shows dramatically that private (corporate, household, and farm) debt

FIG. 14-3 Net public and private debt combined now total about $1.5 trillion, but private debt accounts for three-fourths of the total and nearly all the huge increase since World War II. (Sources: U.S. Department of Commerce.)

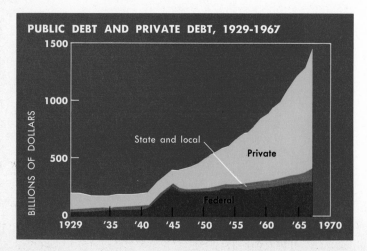

PUBLIC DEBT AND PRIVATE DEBT, 1929-1967

BILLIONS OF DOLLARS

State and local

Private

Federal

accounts for most of the massive growth in total debt since 1929. Of the private debt increase, about half is corporate debt and the other half is debt of individuals and unincorporated businesses. The biggest single item is real estate mortgages, which now exceed the federal debt, having grown from about $30 billion in 1946 to nearly $400 billion in 1968. There's far more private, than public, debt to worry about.

Against these facts consider seven common objections to a large federal debt.

The Danger of Bankruptcy and Economic Collapse

May a big government debt bankrupt the government and lead to economic collapse? "Bankruptcy," as the word is generally used, means inability to pay one's debts when they are due. In this formal sense, the federal government need never go bankrupt, because it always has the power to tax, and the economic capacity of the entire economy to produce provides fundamental ability to pay taxes. Beyond this, the federal government has the power to create money to service or repay the debt. It never needs to default.

But can a big public debt bankrupt "the economy"? Extremely unlikely, is the answer. Payment of interest and principal involves essentially a redistribution of income and assets within the economy, *so long as the debt is domestically held*.[4] It is conceivable, of course, that the government debt might be so large as to lower drastically the credit standing of the government among investors. But United States government bonds are still the world's ultimate gilt-edge investment. Even with its huge debt, the government obtains funds in competitive markets at the lowest interest rates of any borrower. And whatever interest rate the government must pay to borrow, there is nothing involved that will "bankrupt the economy," whatever this vague term actually means.

In looking at the problems raised by a large government debt, most economists emphasize the need to look at the debt *relative to current g.n.p.* As the preceding section indicates, on this score

[4] If the debt is held by foreigners, then payments on interest and principal involve actual costs to the domestic economy rather than merely a redistribution.

the burden of the debt has steadily declined since World War II, while interest payments have remained a roughly constant percentage of g.n.p. If g.n.p. grows at only 3 per cent annually over the years ahead, the increase will be around $20–30 billion annually. Thus the public debt could increase $10 billion or more a year, or over $100 billion in only ten years, and still merely maintain the present ratio of the debt to g.n.p.

Surely the dire predictions of economic collapse because of the public debt are overdone. But there are six more worries to consider.

"A Big Public Debt Must Cause Inflation"

Closely related to the economic collapse argument is the assertion that a big public debt must necessarily cause inflation, sooner or later.

A government deficit, other things equal, surely has an expansionary effect on aggregate demand, because government spending adds more to the income stream than taxes substract. But the result may or may not be inflation, depending largely on how near the economy is to full employment and how many bottlenecks expanding aggregate demand encounters. In any case, it is important to recognize that any inflationary effect arises from the current expansion of total spending generated by the government's deficit spending, not from the existence of public debt per se.

But the "public-debt-causes-inflation" claimants often argue that the larger debt will cause inflation sometime in the future, even if it doesn't now. This argument too is a dubious one. The expansionary pressure of the deficit occurs when the government spending occurs, as was indicated above. The mere existence of the resulting debt a decade later has little or no expansionary effect of total spending. Indeed, the transfer burden involved in interest charges may well be somewhat deflationary, since the transfer is generally from lower- to higher-income groups.

Is there no validity to the inflation-in-the-future fear? Two more arguments are advanced. The first is that when the public holds the new public debt among its assets, its propensity to spend out of current income will be increased. This may be true, but this could hardly generate major inflationary pressure without a huge increase in the public debt outstanding; current

consumption is relatively insensitive to changes in holdings of liquid assets. The second is that the government, saddled with the public debt, will someday create new money to pay it off, and the newly created money will then create inflationary pressures. Obviously this second argument is difficult to rebut or support. How much weight you give it will depend heavily on your faith in governmental processes to produce responsible fiscal behavior. Certainly history shows that there *need* not be repudiation of a large debt through inflation, though some government debts have been eliminated this way.

"It Just Passes the Burden on to Future Generations"

Many people say that borrowing to pay our government bills just passes the cost on to future generations. But this concern is largely fallacious, as a little careful reasoning will show.

Suppose we are fighting a war. The *real* economic cost of war is the resources used up. If we use steel to produce jet engines and missiles, we can't use it for autos and refrigerators. A further real economic cost is the wartime disruption and destruction. However the war is financed—by taxation, by borrowing, or by just printing new money—these real costs are substantially the same. They are borne by the war generation. They cannot be passed on to future generations except insofar as wartime destruction may improverish future generations because we pass on less real capital to them. The dollar cost of the war may be higher if new money or debt financing generates inflation, but the real cost in resources used up by the war is unaffected. If the new debt is accumulated through antidepression deficits that succeed in putting unemployed resources to work, there is little real burden of any sort on the generation involved.

But may not borrowing impose a special burden on future generations,[5] even if it cannot remove the basic burden from the present generation? The answer is that payment of interest

[5] To simplify matters, a "future generation" is assumed to be one that does not overlap with the present generation. The basic reasoning is similar if the generations overlap, but the results are more complicated because then we need to consider the relative positions of working and retired people in the two generations.

and principal by any future generation is just a transfer or redistribution of income within that generation. If the debt is paid off, the future generation is taxing itself to pay itself. If the debt is refunded, the result again is a redistributional one, and indirect transfer effects are minimized. Although the redistributional effects may be important, the crucial factors determining the economic well-being of the future generation are its accumulated real capital and its current real output. Having a money debt from earlier generations does not reduce either, and hence imposes no aggregate real burden on the future generation.[6]

There is one way that borrowing instead of taxing *can* pass a real burden on to future generations, even with an internal debt. This is on the assumption that people who buy bonds consider them as wealth, and base their *lifetime* consumption levels on the higher wealth they now hold. Thus, holding bonds from the war financing, after the war the present generation would consume more than if it had been taxed, and would accumulate correspondingly less capital to be passed on to following generations. In this way, borrowing rather than taxing might burden future generations and lessen the real consumption given up by the present generation because of the war. Some economists believe this is the way people behave; many others are doubtful. In any event, the *main* real costs of government spending and use of resources are as indicated above.

The Transfer Burden
of Interest Payments

Large annual interest costs on a big public debt may impose a real burden, even though these are only transfer payments within the economy— from one of our pockets to the other, considering the nation as a whole. The taxpayer and the interest receiver may be different people. To the individual taxpayer, higher taxes to finance interest payments on the debt seem a very real cost.

Heavy taxation tends to distort people's

---

[6] If the war generation borrows outside the United States, and the future generation has to pay foreign bondholders, then it may be justifiable to speak of a burden of payment being placed on the future generation in the United States.

behavior. If the government takes a big chunk of each additional dollar earned, your incentive to work may diminish. Taxes on particular items raise their cost relative to other items and shift demand away from the taxed goods. Nobody knows just how important such distortions are, but they look substantial. And they surely increase as the tax share of the national income goes up.

Lastly, given our present tax system, taxing to pay interest on the debt tends to shift income from active earners to rentiers, and (to a smaller extent) from the poor to the rich. Soaking the workers and the poor to pay bondholders sounds unjust to many people.

Psychological Deterrents
to Private Investment

Many writers have alleged that concern over the government debt may deter private investment. Direct facts on the issue are hard to come by, but most evidence suggests that the danger is easy to overstress. Business investment depends far more on consumer demand relative to productive capacity and on expected profits, than on the size of the public debt.

The business community and the general public adjust surprisingly quickly to changes in the economic environment. One of the writer's first memories of economics is the bitter controversy that raged during the 1930's over whether a public debt as huge as $50 billion could conceivably be borne without utterly destroying organized economic activity. No one seriously dreamed the debt would ever go so high—the argument concerned a hypothetical ultimate upper limit. By 1936 or so, the $50 billion had been upped to $100 billion, as New Deal borrowing burgeoned. Fifty billion dollars no longer seemed to mean certain disaster. By 1941, the debt of $50 billion was forgotten in the mad scramble for materials, labor, sales, and profits as government and private spending soared with the war. Soon the question, no longer an issue of burning interest, was, what about a $200 billion debt, then $300 billion?

With the present national debt near $350 billion, real per capita income at new highs each year, and the economy growing persistently, public concern over the debt is much weaker than it was a generation ago. The need to reduce the debt is still widely voiced in conservative financial circles, and increases are strongly resisted by many. But there is little reason to believe that if a further increase in debt were required we would not adjust "psychologically" to it as we have to previous increases. The businessman who foregoes otherwise profitable investments because of the debt item on the Treasury daily statement is hard to find.

Debt Management and Monetary Policy

A big federal debt may increase the difficulty of using monetary policy effectively. Billions of dollars of government bonds held by the commercial banks provide a facile base for inflationary credit expansion if the Federal Reserve supports government bond prices. Even if it does not, bank bond holdings represent a huge stock of semiliquid assets. The Governments held by the public also create a vast backlog of spending power for inflationary spending sprees, making control through monetary-fiscal policy more difficult.

If stagnation lies ahead, this liquidity may be helpful. But when inflation looms on the horizon and with continued Treasury refunding and new borrowing ahead, Federal Reserve officials can hardly help feeling hampered by the present big debt. When the Treasury needs to refund $100 billion of federal debt annually, in addition to any new borrowing, it hopes to have security prices high and interest rates low. But these are precisely the conditions that encourage inflation and increase the liquidity of the outstanding public debt. The Federal Reserve can only fight inflation by making the Treasury's job harder. Remember the monetary policy vignette following World War II.

Encouragement of Government Waste

As a matter of practical politics, too easy reliance on borrowing invites easy spending. Experience has shown that when Congress doesn't feel obliged to make expenditures conform to government tax receipts, waste and inefficiency are likely results. This is a homely but important argument against too easy reliance on continued deficit financing.

How Big Should the Public Debt Be?

How big should the public debt be? There is no simple answer to this question, or to the related question—how big can the public debt be? Government debt per se has certain disadvantages. These are not overwhelming. But they create a general presumption against increases in the public debt and for decreases. *Probably the most important principle, however, is that changes in the level of public debt—either increases or decreases —ordinarily exercise a much more direct and forceful effect on the level of current g.n.p. than does any given level of existing debt.*

Current fiscal policy (which may increase or decrease the public debt) is thus generally more crucial than is the level of existing debt. If the major aim is to maintain high-level output, the level of public debt in itself becomes a residual effect of stabilizing fiscal policy. Paying off the debt, viewed in this fundamental fashion, is a secondary reason for running a budget surplus. Whether a budget deficit or surplus is desirable depends predominantly on whether a deflationary or expansionary effect on current g.n.p. is needed. Once we have the public debt, its major effect has been felt. Similarly, the effect of paying off the debt will be largely through the impact of the current budget surplus.

Government Debt as an Offset to Saving

In a high-income economy, individuals and businesses save large amounts annually. These savings must be channeled back into the circular income flow if they are not to exert a deflationary effect. Savers may return the funds themselves by direct investments. But most do not, and instead put their savings into banks, buy bonds or stocks, or acquire other liquid assets. If financial intermediaries like insurance companies receive the savings, then they must channel the funds on into real investments.

To have a smoothly functioning economy, therefore, we must have liquid assets (bonds, stocks, and the like) available for savers and financial intermediaries to buy as part of the machinery for channeling savings on into real investment. Private businesses and individuals want to borrow a lot of savings. But if their demand for savings to make real investments falls short of the savings being made at high-income levels, g.n.p. will contract. New government debt (resulting from a government deficit) is one way of filling this shortage of liquid assets for savers to buy, with the government rather than private borrowers then making the real investment expenditure.

Savers also want to hold money (deposits and currency) as one form of liquid asset. Again, growth in private borrowing at the banks *may* generate just the amount of money the public wants to hold at the desired high-g.n.p. level. But private borrowing may be too large or small to generate this amount of money. If this is the case, increases or decreases in the public debt provide a device for helping the Federal Reserve to provide just the amount of money the public wants to hold at the high-employment g.n.p. level. Remember that of our present money stock of about $170 billion, $100 billion represents money created against new government debt during World War II. As an interesting exercise, ask yourself what would happen if the government paid off this debt.[7]

ARE DEPRESSIONS OBSOLETE?

At the end of this long analysis of economic fluctuations and stabilization policy, a concluding question: Are depressions obsolete? Are improved private practices plus the impressive arsenal of the government's monetary-fiscal tools sufficient to protect us against another debacle like the 1930's? Against smaller recessions?

The history of the last quarter century is encouraging. We weathered two wars, two reconversions to peace, and a wide variety of other economic shocks, without a major bust, albeit

[7] A difficult brain-teaser: What growth in the supply of liquid assets will be required to facilitate a stably growing, high-employment economy? Answer: Just enough liquid assets each year to absorb the savings made at high-employment g.n.p., less the amount that savers put directly into real investment themselves. In terms of financial asset structure, the right mix of money and other financial assets is that mix which gives people just the amounts of money and other financial assets they want to hold at the growing high-employment levels of g.n.p.

with a good deal of war-induced inflation. The post-World War II growth in real g.n.p. has been remarkably steady compared to its roller-coaster performance between World Wars I and II. And we surely know a lot more than we did about what makes business cycles tick and how to damp them down. The optimists list the following specific factors, in roughly ascending order of importance.

1. Businessmen now plan their investment on a longer-range basis. Thus, investment plans are less susceptible to short-term swings in expectations. Long-run growth is widely recognized as a dominant factor in business planning, and this factor will keep business investment plans from serious short-run collapse.

2. Consumers in America have become adjusted to a high and rising standard of living, and they will not be panicked into cutting back their spending even though business conditions weaken. If incomes slide, consumers draw on liquid assets and borrow to protect their living standards, looking forward to a resumption of better times in the near future. This fact has been demonstrated repeatedly during the postwar years when consumer expenditures have continued to increase through thick and thin.

3. Federal, state, and local government spending of about $250 billion annually provides a massive, stable component of g.n.p. Never before has there been such a huge, stable block of spending.

4. Federal tax and spending arrangements now have a large element of built-in countercyclical flexibility. Even if economists can't predict the cycle very well, with our present system tax liabilities fall rapidly if incomes drop. Hence, disposable personal income drops far less than do wages, salaries, and other income before taxes. Similarly with business profits after tax. Moreover, spending on unemployment insurance and price-support payments to farmers increase automatically if employment and prices fall. All things considered, built-in federal fiscal flexibility will automatically absorb maybe a third of the shock of any drop in national income.

5. The banking and financial system has been greatly strengthened since the crash of 1929. We need never again have the enormous credit

contraction that was the core of the 1929–33 collapse and of every other great depression. Federal insurance of bank deposits has substantially removed the danger of runs on banks. Government supervision of banking practices is closer than before. But most important, the Federal Reserve now stands ready to convert bank assets into cash reserves in case of any major banking crisis, so a general financial collapse like 1929–1933 is no longer thinkable.

6. Most important of all, we have learned how to fight depression through government monetary and fiscal policy. We now understand business slumps far better than in 1929, and we have powerful tools to check any major slump in aggregate demand. The Federal Reserve has been greatly strengthened to prevent financial panic and to see that plenty of money is available. And there is now general recognition that government deficit spending can provide buying power when private spending slumps. This was the lesson of World War II, when mass government spending rapidly bailed us out of unemployment into peak production and employment.

How convincing are these arguments? We're surely in better shape than ever before to avoid major depressions. We seem to be protected against another liquidity collapse, and we have government deficit financing to greatly lessen the likelihood of another debacle like the 1930's. But while we have cannon to wheel up against big depressions, our small artillery to fight minor fluctuations merits less confidence. The inventory cycle alone is big enough to give us some nasty bumps, and no one has much hope yet of eliminating inventory fluctuations. Best professional opinion places a good deal of weight on items 2, 3, and 4 to moderate economic swings, but surely not to eliminate little recessions, or possibly even middle-sized ones. Effective stabilization policy still faces many problems.

Yet to end on a negative note would be mistaken. Combined monetary and fiscal policy, plus other improvements in our institutional arrangements, provide a powerful arsenal against instability that should eliminate massive depressions and help substantially to smooth out smaller fluctuations.

For Analysis and Discussion

1. As a practical matter, is the present level of unemployment as low as we can expect without substantial inflation? Explain.
2. In the last three decades labor unions have become much more powerful than before. Under these circumstances, according to some economists, government assurance that total spending will be kept up to high-employment levels would be in effect a guarantee of continued inflation. Why, if at all, would this be so? Does it seem to you a serious danger? How would you go about assuring high-level employment without inflation?
3. Do the wage-price guideposts provide an equitable solution to the persistent quarrel between management and labor over income shares? Do they provide an effective means of solving the dilemma of high employment without inflation? Do they represent a dangerous intrusion of government into the private economy?
4. How would you rate the following for quick action to fight a recession: monetary policy, tax reductions, and increased government spending?
5. If you were a congressman, would you vote to delegate the power to change tax rates to the President? To the Secretary of the Treasury? To the Federal Reserve Board? To anyone? Explain. Would your answer be the same on delegating power to start previously approved public works projects?
6. You are asked to give an hour's talk before your local Kiwanis Club on the subject, "What Should We Do About Our National Debt?" Outline your talk, indicating briefly under each point how you would develop it. Bear in mind the backgrounds and opinions of the group in planning your talk.
7. The National Association of Manufacturers has stated: "A government cannot continue indefinitely to run at a deficit without creating an in-

flationary trend which will in time undermine public confidence in its obligations." Do you agree or disagree with this statement? Why? To what extent does your answer depend on your expectation of persistent stagnation or inflationary pressures?

8. Economic growth over the years ahead will mean large personal and business savings year after year. Unless savers have attractive outlets for these funds, investment will not offset the savings and depression will result. Therefore, debt (public or private) must rise steadily over the years ahead to absorb the savings that will be made. Proposals to pay off the federal debt should be viewed with alarm. Instead, we should plan to increase it steadily to support stable economic growth. Evaluate this argument, and its policy conclusion.

9. Is public debt more dangerous than private debt, or vice versa? Why?

10. Are depressions obsolete?

FIFTEEN

THE THEORY OF ECONOMIC GROWTH

Some Facts on Growth.

The Theory of Economic Growth.

Growth in Developed Economies.

Appendix: Some Special Points
on Economic Growth.

For two-thirds of the world's population—over 2 billion people—the number one economic problem is getting enough to eat and a place to sleep. By our standards, they are desperately poor. For these people, economic growth—more goods and services per capita—offers the only real hope of rising above a bare subsistence level of food and shelter.

Few people in the United States today need fear starvation. Yet even here there are millions of poor, miles of squalid slums—and few in our population of over 200 million do not continually hope for more income to spend, for the better things in life. Thus, here too economic growth is a central issue, though a far less pressing need than for the world's underdeveloped, poverty-stricken nations.

Moreover, during the 1950's most Americans became painfully aware that Russia's rate of economic growth exceeded ours by a wide margin. Happily, the margin between the two rates has narrowed in the 1960's, for comparison between the communist and free world growth rates is a critical factor in the eyes of many underdeveloped nations in determining whether they go the communist or the capitalist way. Economic growth has become a central issue in the world-wide battle for men's minds.

This chapter begins with some facts on economic growth, but it is concerned primarily with the theory of growth. Why do economies grow as fast or as slowly as they do? What are the major forces on which we must rely for a long-term rise in per capita output? Chapters 16 and 17 then use this theoretical framework to explain the growth in today's American economy; and Chapter 18 does the same for the underdeveloped economies, which contain the great bulk of the world's population.

SOME FACTS ON GROWTH

Economic Growth Defined

Economic growth means growth in the amount of goods and services produced—in total, or per capita. For some purposes, growth in total output is most important—for example, in assessing a nation's economic potential for fighting a war, its ability to provide large amounts of foreign aid, and the like. But for most purposes we are more interested in output per capita (or per family)—that is, growth in the ratio: $\frac{\text{total output}}{\text{total population}}$. For output per capita provides a rough measure of the average standard of living of individuals in the economy. You will find "economic growth" used widely in both senses, but here economic growth will mean growth in output per capita unless growth in total output is specified.

The two definitions can color the facts quite differently. If total output grows but population grows even faster, the standard of living of the typical individual is sliding down, not rising. In this country, total output has risen on the average between 3 and 4 per cent annually over the last century, while output per capita has risen only about 2–3 per cent per annum as population grew about 1 per cent per annum. In India, total output has grown too, recently, at a rate not far under ours, but population has grown as fast as output. Hence there has been little change in output per capita, and the Indian standard of living today is little, if any, higher than it was a century ago.

Economic Growth in Perspective

Look back at Table 1-1 and then ahead to Table 18-1 to get a first picture of the results of such widely varying economic growth rates over the world today. The United States stands at the top. We are far ahead of the nearest challengers—even though we are a much newer nation than many of the others shown. The success story of the American economy is written in these figures, in the spectacular results of our economic growth over a mere two or three centuries of the world's history.

Second, what about comparative growth rates for major industrialized countries over the last century? Table 15-1 tells the story. Growth rates have varied widely even among such industrialized nations. Although some rates are surprisingly close (for example, those of the United States and Sweden), don't forget the enormous difference that even a fraction of one per cent annually can make when compounded over an entire century. Beginning from a level of 100, a growth rate of 1.5 per cent per annum would give a total of 443 in 100 years; a growth rate of 2 per cent 725; and a growth rate of 3 per cent 1,922. A difference of even a half per cent in the annual growth rate can make a huge difference in comparative living standards over only a few generations.

TABLE 15-1

LONG-TERM GROWTH RATES IN OUTPUT PER CAPITA *

	Annual Percentage Increase
Japan	3.0
Sweden	2.2
United States	2.1
Russia	2.0
Canada	1.8
Denmark	1.7
France	1.6
Germany	1.6
United Kingdom	1.2
Italy	1.2

* Based on data for approximately 100 years. Exact beginning date varies slightly; for example, U.S. data begin in 1871 to avoid Civil War period. Data from D. C. Paige, "Economic Growth: The Last Hundred Years," *National Institute Economic Review*, July 1961; Simon Kuznets, "The Pattern of U.S. Economic Growth," *The Nation's Economic Objectives* (E. Edwards, ed.; Chicago: U. of Chicago Press, 1964); and United Nations.

Try matching up these rates with the present standings shown in Table 1-1. When, for example, did the United States gain its present big advantage over Japan, Sweden, and the U.S.S.R.? Does our relatively late industrialization explain much of our excellent performance over the past century compared to most European nations which had already partly industrialized by the 1860's? How about Japan, which began to industrialize very late? Tables like these explain why economic historians and economic theorists have a fascinating time explaining the facts.

One last introductory look at the facts. What about recent comparative growth rates? Although the U.S. has been a spectacular success over the long pull, are we maintaining our outstanding record?

Table 15-2 gives the answer. Since World War II we have grown faster than over the previous century. But a number of other nations have done still better, especially Japan, West Germany, and the U.S.S.R. And the order is very different from those of Tables 1-1 and 15-1.

TABLE 15-2
COMPARATIVE ANNUAL GROWTH RATES, 1950-66 *

	G.N.P. per Capita	G.N.P.
Japan	8.8	9.9
West Germany	5.9	7.0
U.S.S.R.	5.0	5.9
Italy	4.9	5.6
France	3.9	4.8
Sweden	3.3	3.9
U.S.A.	2.8	3.9
Canada	2.5	4.6
United Kingdom	2.4	2.9

* Based on United Nations and International Monetary Fund data; in real terms.

A word of warning is needed here, however. Growth figures for any short period are tricky, and the years in Table 15-2 reflect partly special circumstances growing out of World War II. Indeed, in the last few years the European nations shown in the table have been slowing down, while the U.S. has speeded up a bit. Certainly the long-term rates in Table 15-1 are of greater historical significance. But there's no getting around the fact that our growth rate has been below the leaders' since World War II.

The Difference Between Growth and Cycle Upswings

It is important to distinguish between long-run growth rates and short-run swings reflecting business-cycle fluctuations. For example, output per capita usually rises rapidly as an economy moves from depression to high employment. But this is clearly a temporary factor, and should not be extrapolated out as a long-run growth rate. Thus, most economists look upon the long-run growth rate as something to be measured only over extended periods which cover at least the years from one cycle peak to another, and preferably several cycles. Alternatively, they look at the growth in the "full-employment capacity" of the economy—that is, its growing capacity to produce at "full employment" of men and machines.

THE THEORY OF ECONOMIC GROWTH

Why have some nations grown so fast and others not at all? How do some nations push out their production-possibilities curves so much faster than others? What, in short, is the theory of economic growth? Only through answering this question can we really understand why some nations are rich and some are poor. Alas, there is no one simple theory that seems to explain everything. But there is growing consensus on some central factors in the growth process and it is on these that we shall concentrate.

Supply and Demand Factors in Economic Growth

As we shall see, the classical economists had a simple answer to questions about economic growth. The basic productive factors were land, labor, and capital. Growth in total output depended on the combined expansion of these productive factors, reflecting especially enterprise, hard work, and thrift. And the growth in output per capita depended largely on the growth in population relative to the growth in land and capital available for production. They stressed the *supply* factors—the ones that move out the nation's production-possibilities curve.

Nearly two centuries later the classical economists still look basically right. It is the "real" (supply) factors that matter most in economic growth—the accumulation of productive capital goods, the growth in the size and efficiency of the labor force, the natural resources ("land") which a nation has; and how we add on research, education, and technical advance which permit us to produce more with any given amount of capital, labor, and natural resources.

Beyond land, labor, capital and technology, many historians and economists point to other, more tenuous factors—the energy and "drive" of a nation's people, the social and economic mobility of its classes, the economic institutions it devises, its governmental and political structure and traditions. Although we set most of these forces aside for the moment, it is important not to forget them.

These "supply" factors matter most, but in a private-enterprise economy money demand matters too. Unless aggregate demand is adequate to take goods off the market, they will not long be produced. And unless prospective money demand promises reasonable returns, the new capital goods and research necessary for economic growth will not be forthcoming.

Summary: On the supply side, the problem of economic growth is to increase the productive capacity of the economy—basically through diverting resources from current consumption to investment in capital goods, research, education, and other activities that increase future productive capacity; through increasing the size and quality of the labor force; and through improving the economic and social-political organization of the society. *On the demand side*, the first problem is to be sure that there is always adequate total demand to induce high-level utilization of the productive capacity that exists; otherwise, potentially available output is wasted and the inducement to new investment is reduced. (This has been the focus of Chapters 11 to 14.) The second problem on the demand side is to channel spending from consumption into saving and investment, so that society's stock of capital goods and human resources will be built up to increase future output. Thus, on the demand side, both the level of aggregate demand $(C + I + GE)$ and the pro-

portion going into investment (private and governmental) help to control the growth rate.

Almost all economists would agree with the preceding paragraphs. But just how these forces interact, and which are more important under what circumstances, are more difficult questions. A brief look at the historical development of the theory of economic growth is a good way to start to answer them.

Adam Smith—Progress through Enterprise and Thrift

Men have long been concerned with progress, with a better life. This is not surprising, since man, for most of his history, has been hungry, often unprotected from the elements, bitterly poor by the standards we now know. How is it that in the last 200 years, mainly only in a few now-industrialized nations of the Western world, has man managed to rise rapidly from poverty to our present comfortable ways of living?

Adam Smith, in his famous *Wealth of Nations* in 1776, first saw the central rationale of an individual-self-interest, market-directed economy. Let each individual seek his own self-interest—the highest profit he can make, a job at the best wage he can command. But let there be competition in the market so that no seller dares put his price above what others charge, and no buyer can drive down the price of labor he hires because workers will go elsewhere. Then, Smith wrote, self-interest, the most powerful motivating force of all, will be harnessed by the forces of competition to produce those goods men want to buy at the lowest prices that cover their cost of production. Better than any planner or dictator could, self-interest, harnessed by competition, will produce the greatest good for all—as if directed by an invisible hand. This was the case for a self-interest, private-enterprise, market-directed economy—in dramatic contrast to the "command" economies of the lords, the kings, and the pharaohs who had ruled the world's economies through many centuries before.

But Smith was interested equally in the progress of society. Would these forces lead man to an ever-better life? His answer was "yes"—because self-interest could produce not only hard work and enterprise, but also thrift and accumulation. As man saved part of what he produced, the savings of many individuals could mean new factories, new machines, better houses. Thus, thrift and accumulation, savings from the fruits of hard labor, were the foundations of economic growth, of progress toward a better life.

To be sure, more machinery and more capital would mean a larger demand for workmen, and this in turn would lead to higher wages, until profits—the special source of, and stimulus to, accumulation—were eaten away. But Smith saw no crisis in this process. He observed that higher wages and more food would lead to more people, and thus to more workers. This in turn would tend to push wages back down, lowering the costs of businessmen as it lowered the real wages of the worker. And so profits and accumulation would again become possible, with further progress.

While Smith was crystal clear on the role of the market in organizing a self-regulating economy, he was less explicit on just where this interacting process of accumulation and population growth would take society and on how fast it would raise real wages (output per worker). And little wonder. Economists still, 200 years later, debate the answer. But Smith's was an optimistic world, of self-interest and of order. It was a world of progress for those who worked hard and saved, and for societies made up of such men. And Smith's analysis still has fundamental lessons to teach us in the world of today.

**Malthus, Ricardo, and Marx—
Strife and Diminishing Returns**

Two Englishmen, writing soon after Adam Smith, saw instead a gloomy world of conflict and strife—of workers, capitalists, and landlords climbing on each others' backs, each trying to increase his own share of the sustenance produced by society. T. R. Malthus and David Ricardo, two other great founders of modern economics, challenged the orderly world of Adam Smith with disturbing predictions which also have a modern look today, nearly two centuries later.

Malthus and the Specter of Famine. More people mean more power to produce and more output. But more people also mean more mouths to feed, more backs to clothe. In 1798, Malthus, then a young British minister, wrote his now-famous *Essay on the Principle of Population.* He gloomily predicted that population would rise far faster than the productive power associated with more people. Looking at rising birth rates, Malthus pointed out that the population could double every generation if each woman had only four surviving children, half of them girls who would produce more children in the next generation. Malthus felt that this might well give a geometrical population increase—2, 4, 8, 16, 32, 64, and so on—with a doubling each generation.

But the world's land could not possibly increase its food output at this rate over the long run, Malthus argued. Thus, unless population growth was checked by moral restraint, or by such disasters as war or disease, it must ultimately be checked by recurrent famines as the population out-ran the food supply. The British standard of living was hardly above the subsistence level for much of the population; unless steps were taken to control the growth of population, the outlook for growth in output per capita and for a better life was bleak.

Ricardo and the "Law of Diminishing Returns." David Ricardo, another famous British economist, provided a further intellectual justification for Malthus' fears. Ricardo first stated the "law of diminishing returns." Loosely, the law says that if the number of workers applied to any fixed supply of land is increased, the crops obtained from the land will increase, but sooner or later output will increase at a slower rate than the rate at which workers are added.

The implications of this "law" for the standard of living of a growing population seemed clear. Given the world's supply of tillable land, sooner or later food output per worker would fall when the point of diminishing returns was passed in the application of more and more workers to the limited supply of land. And as population grew thereafter, food output per capita (more accurately, per worker) would decline steadily.

But at the same time as diminishing returns pressed down on the food available for individual workers, it would enrich the landlords. For as more and more workers sought sustenance from the land, the price of each piece of land (in sale or in rent) would rise. Ricardo, the economic theorist par excellence, explained through the law of diminishing returns precisely how fast rents would rise and wage rates fall as more workers were applied to the increasingly scarce land.

Assume momentarily that all land and all workers are identical in productive power. Then basically the wage rate would be set by the (declining) contribution each additional worker added to total output. Rent per acre would be set in the same way by the (rising) contribution attributable to each increasingly scarce acre. In a market system, the price of land and labor would be bid up or down to just what each was "worth" through its contribution to a businessman or farmer hiring it in search of profits. Why? Because it would pay profit-seeking businessmen and farmers to pay up to the amount added by each additional worker or acre; and competition for workers and land would drive wages and rents up to those levels. Here we need not be concerned about the details. You merely need to see that, under diminishing returns, with a growing labor force the nation's total output might grow, but marginal, or additional, output per worker (and therefore the worker's real wage) would fall. At the same time output per acre (which determines the rent paid to the landowner) would rise steadily.[1]

But what of capital accumulation, the path to progress in Smith's system? Ricardo saw the importance of thrift and accumulation in man's attempt to improve his lot. But here again, Ricardo wrote, the fact of diminishing returns rears its ugly head. As more and more capital is accumulated relative to scarce land, the return on capital (interest or profits) will be squeezed down more and more. In the end it is the landlords who wax ever richer, while both workers and capitalists find their individual returns (in the form of wages and of profits) squeezed to the barest minimum.

Were Malthus and Ricardo right? If history has proved them wrong in the nations of the

Western world, where did they go astray? Have they been proved right in China and India, where starvation is an ever-present threat for a billion people? Have the rising standards of living of the Western world been temporary, and will Malthus' specter reappear with the modern population explosion? As with Smith, Malthus and Ricardo have lessons for today. Their arguments will reappear in the modern analysis of growth.

Marx and the Collapse of Capitalism. Fifty years later came Karl Marx, the gloomy prophet of the downfall of the entire capitalist system which Adam Smith had praised so highly. Like his classical predecessors, Marx was interested in the grand dynamics—the progress of society or its road to collapse. But he saw no progress. Instead, he foresaw collapse, as capitalists seized ever-larger profits while forcing the workers into the degradation and eventually to revolt which would overthrow the capitalist system.

Marx built an elaborate theoretical structure on the fallacy that labor is the source of all value. He said that any return to another productive resource, such as capital or land, is merely a misappropriation of the "surplus value" produced by labor. But we need not be concerned with the details of this argument. To Marx, capital accumulation was again at the center of things. The desire for profit leads men to accumulate capital and to wring every ounce of effort out of the workingmen who must labor for their bread. Because capitalists are powerful and rich while laborers are poor and divided, capitalists can in fact push down the real wages of their workers to the point where workers can barely subsist. The higher profits lead to more and more capital accumulation, as Smith and Ricardo had predicted before him.

But to Marx the end result of all this was quite different, though it had been hinted in the worryings of Parson Malthus. Capitalism will develop increasing crises, Marx wrote. Too much of society's income will go to the rich capitalists. Too little will be paid to the masses to permit them to buy the output of the new factories and machines. Thus capitalism will face increasingly severe crises and depressions, with resulting unemployment and chaos. Finally, the hungry workers, long

---

[1] If you don't want to accept this loose statement as intuitively right, look ahead to the Appendix to Chapter 22 where the principle is stated precisely and explained more fully.

ground under the heel of the wealthy capitalists, will rise in revolt and overthrow the capitalist system. So, wrote Marx, would come the downfall of capitalism, brought on by the very process of capital accumulation which the classical economists had praised as the foundation of economic growth.

Clearly, Marx has been wrong in the Western world. Real wages have not been ground down over the long run. Both they and profits have risen rapidly in total, and real wages per worker are vastly higher now than a hundred years ago. Interestingly, the rate of return per dollar of capital invested (loosely, the profit rate or the interest rate) has apparently not increased, though of course the total return to capital has grown enormously with the vast accumulation of capital. And apparently modern monetary-fiscal policy has brought great depressions under control.

Let us stop now and examine more rigorously some of the issues that were exposed by Smith, Malthus, Ricardo, and Marx.

The Deepening of Capital and Diminishing Returns. It is relatively easy to explain the growth in total output of an economy as capital and labor grow. The production-possibilities curve moves out. Unless unbalanced ("excessive") capital accumulation brings on the crises suggested by Malthus and Marx, an increase in any or all of the factors of production will raise total output. Thus, more workers, more capital goods, or more natural resources will increase total production. (Note that increased natural resources are a real possibility in new nations; for example, until nearly 1900 the United States had continuous access to more land through the open frontier westward.) But how to increase output *per capita* is a much more difficult problem. For more workers, given the law of diminishing returns, will produce more total output, but output per worker will fall, assuming that the stock of capital and land remain constant.

Neglect for a moment the supply of land (natural resources) as of decreasing importance in the advanced economies. Then, if the number of workers increases, at least a parallel increase in the stock of capital would appear to be the only hope for avoiding declining real wages as a result of the law of diminishing returns. If the ratio of workers to capital rises, output per additional worker will fall. The stock of capital must rise faster than population grows, if output per worker is to rise.

This is what economists call the "deepening" of capital—more capital per unit of labor. *It is this deepening of capital, the analysis of the preceding paragraphs suggests, that is the fundamental hope for progress, for economic growth.*

Let us reconsider now, more analytically, the effects of capital deepening in a simple system. To take the simplest case, assume there is no land, but merely labor and capital as productive factors. Suppose capital grows faster than the labor supply. What then happens to per capita output? The answer is given by Ricardo's law of diminishing returns. Total output will grow, but not in proportion to the growth in the capital stock. Thus, the return per unit of capital (the interest rate or profit rate) will fall as capital deepens. Here labor is the relatively fixed factor (just as was land in Ricardo's case). Thus, the wage rate (the return to labor) will be bid up as labor becomes ever more scarce relative to capital; labor replaces the "greedy landlord" of Ricardo's system. But last, note that higher wage rates and lower interest rates in the system do *not* necessarily imply a higher percentage share of the total national output for labor. This is because there are more units of capital being used. The increased number of units may more than offset the lower return per unit and thus keep the aggregate share of capital in the national output from falling absolutely, or even relatively to the share of labor.

It is important to be clear about the reasoning of the preceding paragraph. It is the foundation for much of the modern theory of growth, and for moving on now to a new factor—technological progress.

The New Look—
Technical Advance and Innovation

Why have Malthus, Ricardo, and Marx proved wrong in nearly all of the Western world, although they may be discomfortingly right for 2 billion people in the underdeveloped nations? Is the answer a simple one—that Adam Smith was basically right in his optimistic prediction of growth in private-enterprise economies, but that the underdeveloped nations have not yet heeded his advice?

Most modern economists would say that Smith deserves credit for correct analysis of some of the basic forces. But something else has been added to give the victory to Smith's optimism over Malthus' and Ricardo's gloom. This is technical advance and its handmaiden, innovation, that bring to society the fruits of new ways of doing things, new products, new approaches. *The revolution of science, technology, and education has saved us from diminishing returns!*

The basic fact is that total output has grown much faster than the combined inputs of the factors of production. Only about half the growth in total U.S. output since 1900 is explained by the growth in capital and labor inputs, disregarding land as substantially fixed in quantity. Similar patterns apparently prevail in other advanced industrial nations.

The main reason, modern economics says, is technical progress and innovation. New machines, better management methods, computers to do the work of adding machines, new fertilizers to double output of farm crops, new management techniques—these have more than offset the once-feared law of diminishing returns.

It is important to remember that technical change shows up in higher skills and better education for workers, scientists, and managers, as well as in new machines and methods. Modern computers drastically reduce business costs and make possible fantastic new scientific developments. Is the technical advance in the computers, or is it in the skills of the scientists who designed the computers and the programers who apply them to new problems? Both, is the answer. Thus technical advance is introduced through education and training (through investment in human beings) as well as through new capital goods and techniques (through investment in research and development and in new capital).

Technical progress—embodied in new machines, new methods, and better skills for workers —has made Adam Smith right. It has gone far to prove that the pessimists were wrong, mainly because they overlooked the vast power of modern technical change. Joseph Schumpeter, a famous economist writing early in this century, first stressed innovation (in productive techniques and in new products) as the mainspring of economic growth. Modern research seems to be bearing Schumpeter out.

GROWTH IN DEVELOPED ECONOMIES

A satisfactory modern theory of growth for the developed Western economies like the United States must explain at least the following facts.

1. The strong, upward movement in real wages in the face of a rapidly rising population and labor force. (In the U.S., population has tripled since 1900 while real wages have risen more than fivefold.)

2. A still more rapid increase in the capital stock, with a resultant deepening of capital, but (disregarding business-cycle fluctuations) with a roughly stable long-term interest rate, contrary to the expectation given by the law of diminishing returns. (The U.S. capital stock has risen nearly sixfold since 1900, while net national product has risen a little more.)

3. A slightly falling ratio of capital to total output for the economy in the face of the rapid deepening of capital, where the law of diminishing returns would lead us to suppose that this capital-output ratio would rise.

4. A roughly constant division of the total national product between wages and salaries on the one hand and returns to property (profits, interest, and rent) on the other—with a slight tendency in recent decades for the labor share to increase.

Supply Factors:
Capital, Labor and Technology

Modern growth theory stresses the fact that total output grows when capital and labor grow and technology improves, disregarding land as a relatively minor factor in highly developed countries.[2] In general, then, output *per capita* will

---

[2] Some economists like to summarize this relationship in a simple "production function" for the entire economy:

$$\text{Output} = a(A \cdot K \cdot L)$$

where K is the stock of capital; L is the stock of labor; and A is technical progress. Thus, output depends on the combined effect of all three. For a more complete discussion, see the Appendix to this chapter.

grow only when capital grows faster than labor or when there is technical advance, or both. When capital is deepened, unless there is technical change the law of diminishing returns will reduce the rate of return on capital and increase the real wage of labor. But with technical advance, the rate of return on capital need not fall; it may be stable or even rise while the real wage rises even more rapidly. What happens to the relative shares of capital and labor in the total national income depends on the relative rates of growth of the two, and on the technical relations between capital and labor in the productive processes of that economy.

Saving and investment (diversion of real resources from consumption to increase investment) is thus central to the growth process. For investment is required both for capital deepening and, in most instances, to incorporate technical advance. The larger the portion of its current output a society devotes to investment, the faster capital will deepen and the faster output per capita will rise. Moreover, the more of its resources it devotes to investment in research and development and to education, the faster technical progress will occur.

Demand Factors

Malthus and Marx warned of breakdowns in the growth process because aggregate demand might fall short of buying all the goods that could be produced as the stock of capital grows. Modern economists recognize that this was a valid warning, though both Malthus and Marx had flaws in their reasoning. We now recognize that aggregate demand must grow roughly apace with the productive capacity of the economy if unemployment and inflation are to be avoided. It is clear, further, that when aggregate demand does fall short and depression occurs, the ratio of investment to g.n.p. declines and therefore so does the rate of economic growth.

Equally important, decisions on money spending or saving within the total are vital to a stable growth process. This is because they largely control the division of the national output between consumption on the one hand and saving-investment on the other. For a brain-teaser on the saving-investment rate needed to just maintain stable growth in g.n.p., see the Appendix.

Growth and Fluctuations

Schumpeter stressed the intimate relationship between growth and economic fluctuations. Partly, Schumpeter argued, this was a real phenomenon. As we saw in Chapter 10, the bunching of real investment is the essence of a boom and of rapid growth. But this very process usually involves overshooting the amount of real productive capacity needed to meet consumer demands. When the overshoot becomes obvious, private investment is cut back and a recession occurs until a better balance between capacity and growing consumption is restored. Partly, Schumpeter stressed, this is a monetary phenomenon. Excessive expansion of credit helps to speed investment booms, supplementing the intended savings of the public and thus intensifying the overinvestment beyond a sustainable growth rate. On both real and monetary scores, the theory of growth and the theory of fluctuations are inseparable, Schumpeter emphasized. Even if monetary-fiscal policy could assure the continuous smooth conversion of intended saving into real investment, we might still have real investment booms (bursts of growth) that were extremely difficult to maintain without ensuing recession.

The Eclectic Consensus. Most modern economists look at the stock of capital, the stock of labor, and technical advance as a framework for analyzing growth in total output. The law of diminishing returns, partially or completely offset by technical advance and innovation, provides a powerful tool for understanding what happens to output per capita, and to the relative shares of capital and labor, in the growth process. The extent to which any growth is sustainable, rather than leading to "overinvestment" through excessive capital accumulation, depends partially on monetary-fiscal factors and partially on the bunching of real investment in the process. This general theory, or framework, helps to explain the basic facts on growth listed at the beginning of this section.

Other Factors

One last preliminary word is needed. Many economists believe that this framework is too narrow to explain the basic forces of economic growth, in either the United States or underdeveloped nations. They say that private initiative and our free-enterprise economic institutions have played a major role in explaining our rapid growth over the centuries. Our success breeds further success, since our markets are now so big that we can take full advantage of the economies of mass production, an important factor in making effective use of our resources. The "noneconomic" factors mentioned at the outset—the initiative of the people and their "drive," social and economic mobility in the system, the flexibility of economic and social institutions, religious traditions and

ethical mores, and particularly the political stability and structure of a nation—may be as important as the purely "economic" factors stressed in the preceding pages. Certainly this appears to be true for some of the so-called "underdeveloped" nations (in Chapter 18). The simple theoretical framework sketched in this chapter provides a useful guide to thinking about economic growth. But, as with other theoretical models, it is only a framework for more thorough investigation of the complex process of economic growth in any particular case.

REVIEW

Concepts To Remember

Be sure you understand the following basic concepts introduced in this chapter. They are reused repeatedly in the rest of the book.

economic growth	demand (money) factors in growth
growth vs. cycle upswings	technical advance
supply (real) factors in growth	capital deepening

For Analysis and Discussion

1. Does Adam Smith or Malthus-Ricardo provide a better explanation of economic growth over the past century in the United States? In India and the underdeveloped nations? If your answers are different, why?
2. Suppose you want to explain Japan's rapid rate of economic growth. At what factors does the theory of Chapter 15 suggest you should look?
3. "Increased aggregate demand is a first-rate answer to the depression problem, but it can't help much to speed up long term growth." Do you agree? Why or why not?
4. Suppose you want to speed up the rate of economic growth in the U. S. What does the theory of Chapter 15 suggest as the most promising measures? Would your answer be different if you measured economic growth by total g.n.p. instead of g.n.p. per capita?
5. In what sense, if any, has modern technological advance repealed Ricardo's law of diminishing returns?
6. If the rate of population growth speeds up relative to the rate of capital accumulation, what effect, if any, would you predict on the shares of labor and capital in the national income?

Appendix

SOME SPECIAL POINTS ON ECONOMIC GROWTH

Growth theory raises a host of interesting problems. This appendix is intended for students who want to look a little further into the intricacies of the subject.

A Simple Growth Model. Shortly after World II, Oxford's Sir Roy Harrod and M.I.T.'s Evsey Domar simultaneously developed a simple growth model that has since been widely used. It builds on the fact that investment (increase in the capital stock) is a prime cause of economic growth, and assumes for simplicity that the capital/output ratio is constant. Note that a constant capital/output ratio assumes away the existence of diminishing returns.

Let Y = output, K = capital stock, and designate changes in any variable by Δ. Suppose the constant capital/output ratio is β— for example, 3—so that 3 of additional capital means 1 of additional output. Suppose further that savings (S) are a constant proportion of income (Y). Let that proportion be σ. Lastly, let us assume full employment; that is, we are concerned with the growth in full-employment potential output for the economy.

Since β is fixed, we know how much Y will increase for any increase in K:

$$\Delta K = \beta \Delta Y$$

But ΔK in any year is simply net investment in that year, and we know that saving equals investment in any year. Thus:

$$\Delta K = I = S = \sigma Y$$

Now combine the equations, substituting σY for ΔK. Then:

$$\beta \Delta Y = \sigma Y, \text{ so}$$
$$\frac{\beta \Delta Y}{Y} = \sigma, \text{ or}$$
$$\frac{\Delta Y}{Y} = \frac{\sigma}{\beta}$$

Since ($\Delta Y/Y$) is the growth rate, the full-employment growth rate for the economy is given by $\frac{\sigma}{\beta}$. Thus, if β is 3 and σ is 15 per cent, the economy will grow at 5 per cent per year ($\frac{.15}{3} = .05$).

This model stresses some important relationships. But remember the simplified assumptions before you conclude it will tell you just how much saving your favorite economy needs to grow at 5 per cent annually. In the real world, we often don't know what the capital/output ratio for new capital will be, and the savings/income ratio also has a slippery way of sliding around. Moreover, we've abstracted from a lot of real-world factors, such as business savings, taxes, and the like.

How To Maintain Stable Growth. A difficult brain-teaser: Is there some rate of saving and investment out of total output that is necessary for "balanced" or "sustainable" growth, avoiding too rapid or slow an increase of capital that might lead to an "oversupply" or "undersupply" of productive capacity? If there is a constant capital-output ratio given by technology, then we can show that there is indeed such a required rate. Suppose labor grows at 1 per cent annually and technological advance at 2 per cent, so the basic capacity of the system to produce grows at 3 per cent. Suppose further that the fixed capital-output ratio is 3:1. That is, three dollars of additional capital will produce one dollar of additional output.

Then, using the oversimplified Harrod-Domar model above, we can show that the economy must save and invest just 9 per cent of its output to grow stably. Why? Begin with a total output of 100. The extra 9 units of capital (i.e., σ = 9 per cent) will produce just the 3 additional units of output that match the 3 per cent growth in potential output from more labor and technical change (β = 3). Less saving and investment would provide inadequate capital to produce the possible 3 per cent annual growth in output, given the 3:1 capital-output ratio. Larger saving and investment would pile up more capital than could be used in producing the 3 per cent growth in output. In this model, a knife-edge saving rate is required for stable economic growth. But remember that this is only one model, based on extremely limited assumptions, so the conclusion may not apply directly to the real world.

Is Technical Progress "Neutral"? Does technical progress tend to increase the share of Y going to labor or to capital, or is it "neutral" as between the two shares. Obviously, technical progress might be "labor-saving" or "capital-saving." That is, it might reduce or increase the relative amount of labor or capital needed to produce a given output. If the technical advance is labor-saving so that less labor is now needed for a given output, we might predict that the labor share of Y would fall.

In fact, we observe in the real world that the labor and capital shares of national income have been surprisingly constant (abstracting from cyclical fluctuations), with a small tendency for the labor share to rise. Can we infer that technical progress has been "neutral" in the above sense? Consider two possible explanations.

First, it is possible that in the absence of technical change the elasticity of substitution between

K and L is 1. That is, if the wage rate falls relative to the cost of capital, businessmen will hire just enough more labor to offset the lower wage rate, and just enough less capital to offset the higher price per unit. Then the relative income shares of capital and labor will remain unchanged. We can write an aggregate "production function" to show this case as follows:

$$\text{Output} = A \, (L^a \cdot K^{1-a}),$$

where A is technical progress, L is the stock of labor, and K is the stock of capital. If this is the economy's production function, constant relative shares of total output for labor and capital are shown by the co-efficients a and 1-a; a is the fraction of total output earned by labor, and 1-a is the corresponding fraction for capital. This is sometimes called a Cobb-Douglas production function, after the economists who developed it to explain the apparent stability of relative income shares. If the elasticity of substitution between capital and labor is 1, the a and 1-a will be constant shares of total output going to labor and capital, and A is "neutral" with respect to the relative shares going to labor and capital.[3]

Alternatively, it may be that without technical

---

[3] For a more complete account of the forces determining the incomes received by labor and capital see Part Four, and Mathematical Appendix IV which provides a rigorous analysis of the Cobb-Douglas production function.

change the elasticity of substitution is not one. Then if investment produces a relatively faster growth in capital (as in the U.S. economy), the interest rate might fall enough and the wage rate might rise enough so that the income share of capital would fall, that of labor would rise. Indeed, there seems little *a priori* reason to suppose the elasticity of substitution between K and L is just 1. But if so, how shall we explain the surprising relative stability of income shares? The answer, some modern economists argue, is that technical progress is not neutral, but instead it provides a built-in mechanism for keeping income shares roughly constant. If, for example, this second case occurs, businessmen will be induced by the profit motive to shift their technical change (innovations) toward the labor-saving type. They do so because labor is becoming relatively more expensive, capital relatively cheaper. Moreover, it is argued, this inducement will be roughly enough to offset any tendency for the relative shares of capital and labor to shift.

Is this induced-innovation theory of stable income shares right? Or is innovation generally "neutral" so that the observed rough stability in income shares comes from an elasticity of substitution between K and L of about 1? Answer: We don't know. This is the kind of research project on which modern economists work—both because it is intellectually challenging and because the conclusions may throw light on fundamental social issues.

SIXTEEN

ECONOMIC GROWTH
IN THE UNITED STATES

Explaining U.S. Growth to Date.

Natural Resources.

Capital Goods and Capital Accumulation.

Technical Change.

Population and the Labor Force.

Economic Organization and Social-Political Environment.

Scale of Market.

Aggregate Demand.

Conclusion.

We think of ourselves as the richest and most progressive nation in the world. We have a right to. Starting from nowhere only two centuries ago, the United States' economy has produced results that are spectacular by any standards. Our 1967 g.n.p. of nearly $800 billion was one-third of the world's total, yet we have only 6 per cent of the world's population. It was more than double that of our nearest competitor, the U.S.S.R.; and on a per capita basis it led the world by a wide margin.

Since World War II, the American economy has grown at about 4 per cent annually in total output, nearly one-third faster than over the preceding century. But many of the other advanced industrial nations have done even better.

How have we done so well over the long pull? What is the outlook for the future? This chapter tries to answer the first question. Chapter 17 looks to the future.

The U.S. Record

Figure 16-1 shows the record. Over the past century total U.S. real g.n.p. (in 1964 prices) has risen from about $18 billion to $750 billion, or nearly fortyfold. Over the same period per capita g.n.p. (also in 1964 prices) rose from about $450 to $3,700, or about eightfold. Total output has grown at a rate of 3+ per cent, and per capita output at about 2 per cent annually.

The historical record raises some intriguing problems. Table 15-1 showed our long-term growth rate compared to those of other leading industrialized countries over the past century. We come off well, but some of the rates are surprisingly close. If these facts are correct, and they

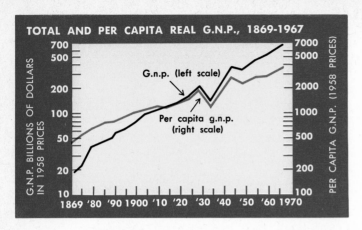

FIG. 16-1 Both total and per capita real g.n.p. have risen persistently over the past century, faltering seriously only during the 1930's. Data are plotted only at 5 year intervals to show the main growth trends. (Source: U.S. Department of Commerce.)

grew very fast during the first century of its existence, so that we had already established a substantial lead over the other nations by the middle of the nineteenth century, since which time the growth rates have not differed so widely. But many observers reject this explanation, arguing that the U.S. growth rate began to pick up with the Industrial Revolution here in the middle 1800's. Whatever the answer, don't forget one impressive fact. Only a fraction of a percentage point difference in annual growth rate can accumulate to enormous totals over a century or more.

To fill in the factual backdrop, let us take a closer look at the anatomy of U.S. economic growth since 1900. Figure 16-2 shows the trends since 1900 in the major variables in the growth process which were stressed in the theory of Chapter 15.

What can we see here? A rapid but jagged rate of growth in real g.n.p., reflecting a roughly similar rate of growth in the capital stock and a

are the estimates of the best research workers in the world today, how shall we explain the wide lead of present United States output per capita over that of other nations such as Japan and the U.S.S.R.? A plausible inference from the estimates would be that somehow the United States

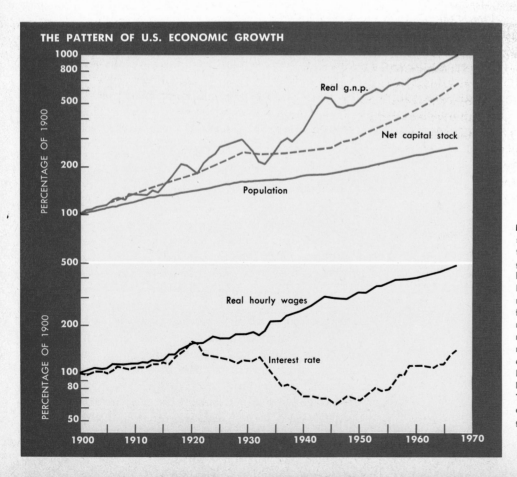

FIG. 16-2 Since 1900 the capital stock has grown much faster than the labor force, and g.n.p. has grown faster than have the combined inputs of labor and capital. Real wages and interest rates have moved about as would be expected from our theory of growth, recognizing the big role played by technological advance and other elements beyond the growth in labor and capital. (Source: Long Term Economic Growth, 1860–1965, U.S. Department of Commerce, 1966. This volume summarizes much of the available statistical data on U.S. growth.)

much slower growth in population. The theory of Chapter 15 would suggest rising real wages relative to the return on capital, and this is indeed what we see in the lower part of the chart. Further, the theory would predict that, without technical progress, the rate of return on capital would fall absolutely. But, interestingly, the return on capital, though fluctuating widely in the great depression, is roughly flat in trend. Something, presumably technical advance, has buoyed up both real wages and the return to capital, as the theory suggests. And the capital-output ratio, not shown on the chart, was also roughly flat in trend, contrary to the increase we would expect with rapid capital deepening in the absence of technical advance. Our growth theory from Chapter 15, with technical advance included, is confirmed by the evidence.

EXPLAINING U.S. GROWTH TO DATE

The Sources of Growth

What have been the main sources of economic growth in the United States? Table 16-1 gives one courageous expert's estimates of the quantitative importance of the big forces at work during this century. Although he doesn't pretend that these are more than crude approximations,

they provide an interesting introduction to the rest of this chapter.

Note the significant differences between the pre- and post-1929 periods. The increasing *quantity* of labor and capital goods dominates the pre-1929 picture. Since 1929, improvements in the *quality* of labor and capital (technical advance incorporated in both real capital and human beings) have accounted for over half of our total growth according to these estimates. And if we eliminate growth in the labor force (population) because it doesn't significantly raise output *per capita*, these improvements in quality accounted for over two-thirds of the total increase. An interesting question: How much growth in the capital stock do we need merely to permit introduction of technical advance, even though mere duplication of existing capital goods may not produce rapid growth? Don't underrate capital accumulation, even if Denison's estimates are right.

Now let us use the basic theoretical model of Chapter 15, which also lies behind Denison's table, as a framework for looking at the actual forces underlying U.S. economic growth over the past century.

NATURAL RESOURCES

Natural resources—land, minerals, power resources, and the like—are the foundation that nature gave us for economic growth. They are substantially fixed in amount; note that for that reason Table 16-1 gives them no credit for our growth since 1909. We may use part or all of them, but we cannot increase their quantity. To be sure, by using fertilizers and irrigation we can improve the crop-bearing ability of land, but this is really capital investment. Through improved technology we may use natural resources that have previously been useless; solar power may run the factories of tomorrow. But it was the fixed supply of natural resources (especially productive land) that underlay Malthus' worries. Today we have broadened the category of land to include all natural resources, but they are still fixed in supply.

Strikingly, the law of diminishing returns has never seemed to drag seriously on U.S. eco-

TABLE 16-1

SOURCES OF U.S. ECONOMIC GROWTH, 1909–1957 *

Source	Percentage of Total Growth	
	1909–29	1929–57
Total growth in national real income	100	100
Increase in labor force **	39	27
Improved education and training	13	27
Increased stock of capital goods	26	15
Improved technology	12	20
All other ***	10	11

* Edward Denison, *The Sources of Economic Growth in the United States* (Committee for Economic Development, 1962).

** Adjusted for decreasing number of working hours per year.

*** Mainly due to increased economies of large-scale production with growing total size of the market.

nomic growth, even though population has grown rapidly. When the first settlers arrived in the New World they found a wealth of fertile land, plenty of vegetation and timber, and a temperate climate. Until nearly 1900 the steady westward movement of the frontier revealed ever more bountiful resources. Thus, in effect we could increase our natural resources—by moving west. But even today our natural resources are so vast, and the ratio of people to natural resources so low here compared to most of the rest of the world, that few observers worry greatly that the law of diminishing returns on natural resources will exert a major drag on our progress.

TABLE 16-2			
U.S. ENERGY SOURCES, 1850–1965 *			
	Percentage of Total		
	1850	1900	1965
Human power	13	5	0.8
Animal power	52	22	0.5
Inanimate power (water, petroleum, etc.)	35	73	98.7
Total	100	100	100.0

* Based on estimates of J. F. Dewhurst and Associates, *America's Needs and Resources* (Twentieth Century Fund, 1955).

One reason many observers don't worry is our ingenuity in developing new ways to use the resources we have. Table 16-2 shows the revolu-

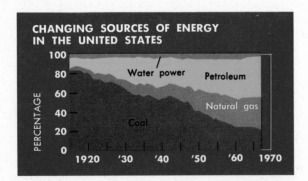

CHANGING SOURCES OF ENERGY IN THE UNITED STATES

FIG. 16-3 Petroleum and natural gas have increased steadily as major sources of energy for the modern economy. Will nuclear and solar power soon take over? (Source: National Industrial Conference Board.)

tionary replacement of human beings and animals by inanimate energy sources. Figure 16-3 shows another way the economy has adjusted to the need for new and larger power sources. The old concept of a fixed stock of land requires a new look in the light of our ever-growing abilities to use existing resources more flexibly and efficiently. Accumulation of capital goods, technical progress, and education have swamped the law of diminishing returns over a period of three centuries. They are our hope for the future.

CAPITAL GOODS AND CAPITAL ACCUMULATION

History suggests that the long-term economic growth rates of the major countries correspond roughly to the proportion of their total outputs they save and invest. When we recognize that most technical advance also requires investment (in research and development, in human beings, and as a vehicle for introducing technical changes), the need to save and invest for economic growth becomes doubly obvious.

Throughout the nineteenth century, the United States was a high-saving and high-investment economy. It paced the world in economic growth. During the present century, though we have become ever richer, the proportion of our national product devoted to investment has dropped substantially—especially during the Great Depression of the 1930's and again after the Korean War.

Figure 16-4 tells the story. Gross and net capital formation were high percentages of g.n.p. during the last century, but both have clearly trended downward during the last half century, though with an upward surge again in recent years.[1]

Despite this downward trend, year after year

[1] In principle, only net investment should contribute to the accumulation of capital and productive capacity. But in fact our measures of depreciation are rough and the replacement of depreciated capital goods often does increase our productive capacity because the new machines almost always embody technical advances. But even if we use gross investment, this rate too has fallen, and it is now well below those of the rapid growth nations.

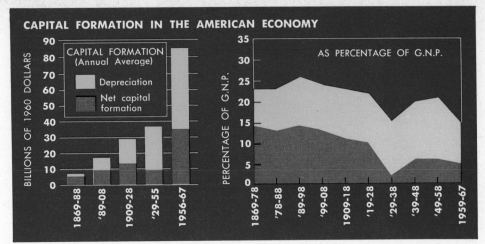

CAPITAL FORMATION IN THE AMERICAN ECONOMY

CAPITAL FORMATION (Annual Average)
- Depreciation
- Net capital formation

BILLIONS OF 1960 DOLLARS

AS PERCENTAGE OF G.N.P.

PERCENTAGE OF G.N.P.

FIG. 16-4 Gross capital formation has risen ten-fold over the past century, but recently both gross and net capital formation have been much smaller percentages of g.n.p. than in earlier decades. (Sources: S. Kuznets, *Capital in the American Economy,* Princeton Univ. Press, 1961; and Council of Economic Advisers.)

American businesses have invested huge sums. Private homes and apartment houses have been built on an unprecedented scale. U.S. private investment in capital goods and housing (excluding investment in consumers' durables like automobiles) reached the staggering total of $125 billion in 1967. Government investment in highways, public buildings, and other civilian-type goods accounted for perhaps $15–$25 billion more. This huge total was more than the entire g.n.p. of any other country in the world, except the U.S.S.R.

The result of this saving-investment process over the centuries is that America has an enormous stock of capital. Our capital goods are estimated at over $1.7 trillion (excluding stocks of goods held by consumers, such as furniture and clothing); this amounts to around $30,000 per family. Consumer durables raise the total to over $2 trillion. A century ago, the figure was only $7 billion. If we look at manufacturing plant and equipment alone, the type of capital goods that comes most readily to mind, capital per wage earner in manufacturing averaged over $22,000 in 1966, far above the figure for any other nation; and it exceeded $100,000 per worker in petroleum. Capital has deepened steadily, except in the great depression of the 1930's. Remember that our capital stock has grown sixfold since 1900, while population has only tripled.

One more word on the process of saving and capital investment in the American economy. Private saving and investment decisions have produced most of this growth. But governments and the political process have played a big role too. When we levy taxes on ourselves and use the funds to build public capital goods like highways, we accumulate capital through diverting current output from use in current consumption, much as with private saving and investment.

TECHNICAL CHANGE

Since 1900, national output has risen twice as fast as the input of labor and capital combined. Technical advance must account for a good share of the difference. Table 16-2 breaks down technical advance between improvement in the quality of capital and the quality of labor. Unfortunately, we have little direct quantitative information on technological advance. Indeed, just how to measure such advance quantitatively is a very difficult question. But whatever the precise figures, American technology over the past century speaks for itself. Look at a modern oil refinery. Or walk through an automobile assembly plant. Visit a midwestern farm, complete with automatic farm machinery and fertilizers. This is modern technology, the trademark of America, and a source of never-ending amazement to visitors from abroad.

Increased investment in research and development is one major explanation for the rate of technological advance. Figure 16-5 shows the spectacular growth of spending on research and development in the United States since World War II. R and D spending by the government and private industry has grown by more than 10 per cent annually. Since 1960, we have spent two-thirds as much on research and development as on total investment in fixed plant—perhaps a harbinger of a speeded growth rate in the future.

213

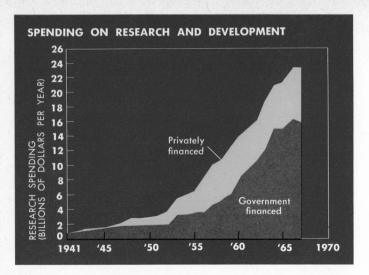

FIG. 16-5 Research is the newest major industry in the United States. It has developed largely since World War II, and is about two-thirds government financed. Most is applied and developmental, only a little basic, research. (Source: National Science Foundation.)

Certainly, U.S. growth has been substantially faster since World War II than over the preceding century.

The National Science Foundation suggests that research has a lagged effect on real output. Some observers argue that we are now seeing its accelerated impact, in computers and electronic devices, atomic and solar energy, satellites circling the earth, and modern chemistry and machinery on the farm where productivity has increased even faster than in industry.

Interestingly, most of the basic research in America has been financed by government, often through military funds. The most spectacular growth in output per man-hour—in agriculture—has come about through research financed almost entirely by the government, through universities and agricultural experiment stations which have taken the new knowledge to the farmers. Private industry has concentrated largely on developing the basic research of others into commercially profitable applications. Large digital computers, many drugs, atomic energy, missiles, and modern aircraft are notable examples of major innovations originally stimulated and financed by government research funds.

Perhaps Denison is wrong in giving so much credit to technological advance (20 per cent of our total growth since 1929), more than to capital accumulation itself. Or perhaps he has given

214

technical advance too little credit. But as best we can tell, technological advance appears to have been roughly as important as capital accumulation, and to have become increasingly important in recent decades.

POPULATION AND THE LABOR FORCE

Human beings are the most important productive resource of all. Denison allocated from 27 to 39 per cent of total U.S. output growth to increased *quantity* of labor, and another 13 to 27 per cent to improvements in its *quality*.

Figure 16-6 presents the facts on U.S. population growth rates since 1800. During the nineteenth century we were one of the world's high-growth-rate nations. Recently we have fallen far behind the underdeveloped nations, reflecting in part a gradual decline in birth rates here but primarily a dramatic extension of the life-span in the underdeveloped nations. During the first half of the 1800's our population grew at around 35 per cent per decade, about 3 per cent annually. During the depression decade of the 1930's, the rate was down to less than 8 per cent for the entire 10 years. For the 1950's it was back up only to around 20 per cent, but even that rate meant some 30 million more people over the single decade. Remember that population is the

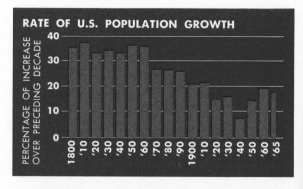

FIG. 16-6 The postwar baby boom produced a big increase in our population growth rate. But the rate was higher still a century ago. Each bar shows percentage increase over preceding decade. (Source: U.S. Bureau of the Census.)

denominator of the ratio $\dfrac{\text{output}}{\text{population}}$ that gives output per capita.[2]

The Labor Force

Population growth means more mouths to feed and more backs to clothe, but not immediately an increase in the number of workers, since babies don't work. By definition the "labor force" includes all persons of 16 or older who hold or are looking for paid jobs, or who are self-employed. The concept thus provides a rough measure of the currently available work force. In the United States, this includes most men between 16 and 65 except those who are in school, and about a third of all women.

Figure 16-7 shows what has happened to the labor force since 1900. It has grown steadily except for big bulges during the two major wars, averaging around 40 per cent of total population. Now, as the postwar babies grow up, the average annual increase is over a million persons a year, far more than the economy has ever before had to absorb.

Beyond the 75 million people in paid jobs

[2] Some experts forecast a U.S. population of a billion people by 2050, only 80 years away, when some of you may still be alive. Given the present average life span, this would require about 96 per cent of all women to marry and to have an average of three and one-third children each.

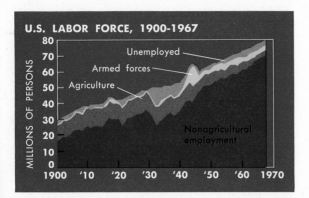

FIG. 16-7 The U.S. labor force has grown steadily, with temporary bulges during major wars. Most have taken nonagricultural jobs. Note the big unemployment pocket during the 1930's. (Source: U.S. Department of Labor.)

of all sorts, there are now some 40 million housewives plus perhaps 15 million retired persons and young people in high school and college who are quite capable of performing productive work. Indeed, the unmeasured economic contribution of the housewives who keep house and raise children, though unpaid in the market place, is probably considerably greater than that of the one-third of all women who hold paid jobs. The "labor force" is an obviously arbitrary, though useful, concept.

What determines the proportion of the population who "work"? Clearly, a lot of factors. A wealthy nation like ours can afford to keep its children in school until they are grown and thoroughly educated, in contrast with poor nations where everyone must turn to work at an early age. We have steadily increased the years of schooling before our youth enter the job market. Offsetting this drain, the proportion of women working has risen rapidly in recent decades. A century ago, few women worked at paid jobs. Once married, a girl retired sedately to her new home to keep the furniture dusted, get the meals ready on time, and raise a family. But today, over a third of all married women have paid jobs, and the 25 million women at work compose a third of the labor force. Earlier retirement age is a force pushing in the opposite direction.

Closely related is the question of the average number of the working hours per year for the labor force. A century ago, the average factory worker in the U.S. put in 75 to 80 hours a week —generally 10 hours or more a day including Sundays. Today he works only around 40 hours, and a standard 35-hour 5-day work week may not be far away. The New York electricians won a contract for a 25-hour work week in 1962.

Thus, over the decades America has faced a continual choice between work and leisure. We have chosen a steady increase in the amount of leisure, even though we may have thereby reduced somewhat the growth rate in real output. It is important to be clear that there is no obvious answer to the best balance between work and leisure for a society. Short hours and long vacations may produce fewer cars and airplanes, but leisure, though not sold in the market place, has a real value for the persons enjoying it. Remember that the g.n.p. figures place no value on the vast amount of added leisure achieved by the American people over the past century.

Investment in Human Capital

Investment in human capital—better education, training on the job, healthier workers, and the like—may have accounted for a quarter of our economic growth duing the last quarter century, and it is growing in importance.[3] No other factor has been more important for American growth since 1929, if Table 16-1 is right.

The growth of education in America has been phenomenal. In colonial days, few people received any formal education beyond elementary reading and writing. By 1880, only one in 15 persons of high school age was attending school. Today this figure has risen to 95 per cent, with 12 million students in some 25,000 high schools, and with the proportion of illiterates in the population below 3 per cent. Over 40 per cent of all high school graduates now go on to college, while only a generation ago a college education was a special privilege available only to the well-to-do.

Figure 16-8 shows the rapid growth in spending on education since 1900. During the first three decades of the century, the rate of growth in investment in human resources was more than twice that in nonhuman capital; the upward slope of the education line on the ratio chart is roughly twice that of the top line showing investment in capital goods. (Query: How long is the time lag between more education and a resulting increase in output per capita?)

Figure 16-8 indicates some other interesting facts: (1) The growth in spending on education has been much more stable than on private investment in capital goods. (2) Since World War II, the rates of growth in investment in human and nonhuman resources have been roughly comparable, unlike the 1900–1930 period. (3) The overwhelming bulk of our expenditure on education goes into elementary and secondary schools. Even with our recent big increase in college education, it still accounts for only a minor portion of our total investment in human capital.

[3] Chicago's T. W. Schultz argues that investment in education may be even more important than this. See his "Investment in Human Capital," *American Economic Review*, March, 1961.

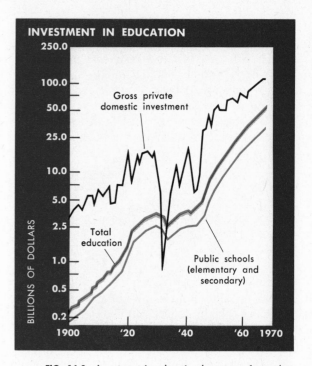

FIG. 16-8 Investment in education has grown faster than private investment in capital goods since 1900, and at a much more stable rate. (Sources: U.S. Departments of Commerce, and Health, Education and Welfare.)

The scarcest resource has become not land or coal or even skilled workers, but brainpower. The achievements of modern science—atomic power, electronics, the "wonder drugs"—are worth the muscle-power of millions of human backs, the output of untold acres of land. Will we run out of oil? If nuclear and solar energy take its place, the world may little care. Will human needs for food outrun the world's land supply? Not if the scientists' amazing accomplishments in producing new fertilizers, hybrid high-yield crops, and new types of cultivating machines continue. In the ultimate improvement of human welfare, one Einstein or Edison is worth thousands of ordinary mortals like most of us. Outstanding brainpower is beyond price.

But a major challenge in education still faces America today. Only two-thirds of the top fifth of high school graduating classes go on to college; only half of the second fifth. Although most boys and girls now finish high school, hundreds of thousands of youngsters are lost through pregraduation drop-outs every year. To repeat the theme from above, brainpower is our scarcest resource. High-grade education and training that push our ablest people to their utmost are among the cheapest and surest investments in progress, both for the individuals and for the nation. We have made great progress, but the job is far from done.

The American Entrepreneur [4]

One group in the labor force deserves a special section. One of the greatest "quality" superiorities in the United States has been the ingenuity and energy of its "entrepreneurs"—its business innovators, managers, and risk-takers. The spirit of inquiry and innovation, and the organizing and operating energy of the American entrepreneur deserve much credit for our spectacular economic progress.

Later on, Parts Three and Four of this book look intensively at the function of the entrepreneur as a central organizer of economic activity in a private-enterprise economy. Pending this detailed look, this section represents only a passing bow to his special role in economic growth. The absence of a comparable spirit of entrepreneurship goes far to explain the slower growth of many of the underdeveloped countires of Asia and Africa.

People and Productivity
in American Growth

Average hourly or annual output per worker is often called worker "productivity." Thus, total output can be viewed as the number of workers times average output per worker. But don't let the common practice of using "productivity" to mean output per man mislead you into attributing all the increased output to workers. We could equally well do a productivity calculation showing output per unit of capital, by dividing total output by the number of units of capital employed. But like it or not, "labor productivity" is in the newspapers and labor-management arguments all the time. And you can understand the complex growth process better if you recognize the widely

[4] *Enterpreneur* is a widely used economic term. An entrepreneur is an enterpriser, loosely a businessman who is prepared to undertake the production of goods or services when there appears to be a potential profit in doing so. For a more complete analysis, see Part Three.

divergent patterns of change in productivity that make up the total.

Table 16-3 points up the wide fluctuations from decade to decade. Rough data going back to 1850 suggest similar fluctuations in the nineteenth century. Annual increases vary from as high as 12 per cent (1919) to minus 8 per cent (1917), though few years show a negative figure.

TABLE 16-3

AVERAGE ANNUAL GAIN IN U.S. PRODUCTIVITY, 1909–1967 *

Period	Average Annual Gain (Percentage)
1909–1918	0.5
1919–1928	2.7
1929–1938	2.4
1939–1948	2.1
1949–1958	3.0
1959–1967	3.2

* Data from National Industrial Conference Board and *Economic Report of the President*; 1967 estimated by author. "Productivity" is output per man-hour in the private sector of the economy.

Moreover, the economy-wide figure for any year covers up wide differences among different industries. For example, since 1929 average output per man-hour has increased about 3 per cent a year. But Fig. 16-9 shows the widely differing increases in different sectors of the economy. Separate data on individual firms within industries would show an even more dramatic spread.

Figure 16-9 also suggests that occupational shifts may significantly affect the national average growth rate. The persistent shift of manpower out of agriculture, for example, has recently meant a move of workers from lower- to higher-productivity industries (though productivity is growing faster in agriculture). The recent great increase in spending on services, where productivity is low and growing slowly, has held down the average growth rate. We may note, parenthetically, that rapid output growth in Western Europe following World War II reflected massive shifts of workers from low productivity agriculture to high productivity industry. Without this shift, their total growth rates would have been little higher than ours.

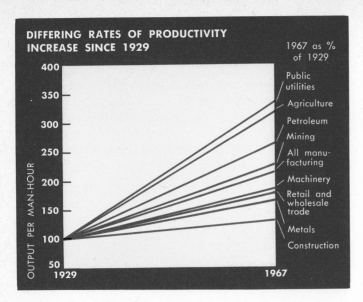

FIG. 16-9   Since 1929, output per man-hour has increased at widely differing rates in different sectors of the economy. (Sources: National Bureau of Economic Research and Council of Economic Advisers.)

ECONOMIC ORGANIZATION AND SOCIAL-POLITICAL ENVIRONMENT

How much of our economic growth is due to the individual-initiative, basically private-enterprise, free society that we prize so highly? There is no simple quantitative answer. Looking backward, it seems clear that America's economic, political, and religious atmosphere has been peculiarly favorable to individual initiative, hard work, and the pursuit of material rewards. Success in business has been a mark of distinction. The "Protestant ethic," which looks upon work as good in itself, has had an important role in establishing our mores. And the basic tradition of "each man for himself" has provided an inviting setting for individual attempts to move up the economic ladder. Experts trying to help the "underdeveloped" countries are increasingly impressed with the value of such traditions as a foundation for hard work and economic growth. (Some fascinating contrasts are pointed out in Chapter 18.)

American economic institutions have shown unusual flexibility in adjusting to the needs of the growing economy. Banking and financial institutions developed rapidly in response to the need to accumulate savings for investment in business units, and to provide the money to finance the economy's growth. Development of the

modern corporation facilitated the accumulation of capital for business ventures without undue risk for nonmanagerial investors. Risk-taking was encouraged by financial intermediaries which spread the risk, thereby making investments more attractive to private savers.

Individual freedom to work where a man wished, to set up in business when he liked, to invest his savings as he preferred, provided a setting unique in the modern world. It was a setting ideally designed to stimulate initiative, risk-taking, and personal effort. And it was coupled with unparalleled political freedom and social flexibility for the man who could win out in the open competition of the new economy.

Reflecting this climate, government was generally friendly to vigorous, open competition. Preservation of peace and order, protection of property rights, general maintenance of laissez-faire conditions, and provision of necessary government services such as education, highways, and communications, all provided a foundation for vigorous economic activity. On the regulatory side, the government has largely limited itself to checking undue restrictions on competition. Only with the long depression of the 1930's did far-reaching governmental concern with economic security begin to encroach substantially on the strong tradition of individual initiative in the market place.

How much credit should Professor Denison have given these factors back in Table 16-1? He couldn't measure them so he didn't put them in. Yet many observers feel they deserve a lot of the credit for our superior performance.

SCALE OF MARKET

Mass production is obviously more efficient than small-scale output in many industries. Steel, aluminum, automobiles, glass, and dozens of other major products must be produced on a massive scale to permit use of the expensive capital equipment and sophisticated techniques which characterize modern mass production. Long ago, Adam Smith spelled out the economies to be had from specialization and division of labor in making pins.

Thus, an economy must have large markets if it is to take advantage of the economies of mass production. The very fact that the American economy grew so fast and became so large gave it an edge for still faster growth, compared to the smaller economies of the world. Again, no one can measure exactly how important these growing markets have been in permitting us to take advantage of what economists call "economies of scale." But historians and economists agree that they have played a large role.

Table 16-1 allocates 10 per cent of our total growth this century to economies of scale. Other economists have come up with even larger estimates. Chalk up economies of scale as an obviously important factor, and one on which the United States has had a big advantage. But the figures are only the crudest of approximations.

AGGREGATE DEMAND

The preceding look at the sources of economic growth in the United States has stressed primarily the potential supply side, and properly so. For it is the "real" supply factors that basically determine how fast an economy grows. Enough aggregate demand to avoid the waste of unemployment is indeed critical. But once this condition is met, more aggregate demand will merely generate inflation.

Today we recognize that government monetary-fiscal policy can go a long way toward assuring roughly the right rate of growth in aggregate demand. Through most of our history, however, this was not true, and it is only since the 1930's that monetary-fiscal policy has been seriously mobilized to maintain a stably growing level of aggregate demand. To be sure, some attempts were made earlier to avoid monetary excesses in both expansion and contraction, but fundamentally, planned stabilizing monetary-fiscal policy is new. Thus, before the 1930's growth in the money stock and in aggregate money spending was to a considerable extent the "accidental" result of the growth in our monetary institutions and their operations in search of private profits.

Look back at Fig. 8-1 to see what has happened to the growth in the money stock and aggregate money demand since 1900. Whether the growth in the money stock has been mainly cause or effect of the growth in real output, the end result has been somewhat faster growth in money and aggregate demand than in real output, with a resulting gradual inflationary trend. Except during the long depression of the 1930's, it is not clear that deficit aggregate demand has seriously held back our rate of economic growth.

Many observers point to our repeated booms and depressions, arguing that misbehavior of aggregate demand has indeed slowed growth. One test would be the average level of unemployment of men and machines over the long pull. Here we have little reliable information beyond a quarter-century back. New figures by Wesleyan's Stanley Lebergott suggest that the decade of the 1930's was our big failure on unemployment; on the average we have had about 5 per cent of our labor force unemployed over the past century. Is this a bad, or a good, performance for a basically market-directed, individualistic economy? Views differ widely. But either way, the factors summarized back in Fig. 15-1 and Table 16-1, rather than monetary-fiscal policies, look like the critical forces in explaining U.S. economic growth over the past century.

CONCLUSION

In retrospect, does the theory of Chapter 15 do a good job of explaining U.S. economic growth? The answer appears to be, "yes." Growth in the U.S. has been a complex, shifting process, and no single, simple explanation can be satisfactory. But this basic analytical framework can go a long way in pointing up the main forces, and in keeping you from getting bogged down in details.

For Analysis and Discussion

1. Has the U.S. record on economic growth been satisfactory over the period since World War II? What criteria do you use in judging?

2. Make a list of the major factors likely to increase the labor force over the next 20 years, and those likely to decrease it. Which are likely to dominate?

3. How long should the work-week be? What seem to you the major considerations in answering this question?

4. Is Denison right (Table 16-1) in giving no weight to natural resources in explaining the causes of U.S. economic growth since 1909? Explain.

5. Most Americans feel that private initiative and our market system deserve great credit for our high standard of living compared to other nations. Suppose you meet a foreigner who disagrees. What arguments can you advance to convince him?

6. Critics of the law of diminishing returns argue that the law must be unimportant or invalid in the U.S. since the U.S. population has grown enormously over the past century while the stock of natural resources has been fixed, yet output of food per capita has risen greatly. Are the critics right?

7. "More rapid growth of population in the United States would mean a more rapid growth in our standard of living." Do you agree? Explain.

SEVENTEEN
GROWTH POLICY
IN THE UNITED STATES

Growth Targets and the Cost of Growth.

How To Grow Faster: The Supply Side.

Demand Policy for Stable Growth.

Now, a look to the future. How fast should we grow? Four per cent a year? Five per cent? As fast as we can? Most living things—trees, animals, people—grow more slowly as they mature. Is this true of economies too? If so, should we expect our past growth rate to slow down, or are we still a healthy growing youngster? The rate of growth has become a major issue of national economic policy. What, if anything, should we do to grow faster?

GROWTH TARGETS
AND THE COST OF GROWTH

The Payoff of Rapid Growth

Rapid economic growth is not merely a matter of national pride. How fast we grow will largely determine how high your standard of living is over the rest of your life. Consider Table 17-1, which shows U.S. real g.n.p. in 1975 and 2000 in case we grow at 3, 4, or 5 per cent for the rest of this century.

Put most simply, your standard of living (as measured by real g.n.p. per capita), will be twice as high by the end of the century if we can grow at 5 rather than 3 per cent per annum. Five per cent would be very high by historical standards, but it is the goal set by most West European nations in their recent planning. Even 4 per cent, about our post-World War II rate, would yield an extra trillion dollars *annually* by the year 2000, as compared to the 3 per cent that marked our performance before World War II. Even by 1975, an extra 1 per cent in annual growth can provide the average American family with an extra $1,500.

221

TABLE 17-1

U.S. REAL G.N.P.
FOR ALTERNATIVE GROWTH RATES
(In billions, at 1965 prices)

	1965	1975	2000
With 3 per cent annual growth	$680	$ 850	$1,750
With 4 per cent annual growth	680	950	2,700
With 5 per cent annual growth	680	1,050	3,500

Figure 17-1 puts these same alternative growth rates in graphical form, to provide historical perspective. The stakes in the growth game are huge! Your standard of living and your children's will be spectacularly higher if we can raise our growth rate by 1 or 2 per cent.

The Costs of Growth

But raising the growth rate isn't so simple. Growth costs something. Basically, it costs either more and harder work or reduced consumption now to permit higher investment that will raise future output. Economists often say, "There is no such thing as a free lunch," to emphasize the fundamental economic problem. Given full employment, we can have more of something only by

having less of something else. We can grow faster only by accepting less leisure and lower consumption now.

Of course, we can expand total output faster by having a larger population. But this does nothing to raise *per capita* output and the real standard of living. Indeed, a higher birth rate will decrease output per capita in the short run, because new babies eat but do not work. Even immigration doesn't help much, because it provides more workers only at the cost of more mouths to feed. Thus, only if we ourselves work harder or longer can we hope to speed growth per capita through the quantity-of-labor route.

It is to capital accumulation, to technical advance, and to investment in human beings that we must basically look for faster growth in output per capita. And these routes require more saving and investment—a cost now for a future benefit. The critical issue is how we weigh the present against the future—our work and our comforts against those of our children and our grandchildren.

Perhaps the payoff on investment in research and in education will prove to be quick and spectacular. Improved science and technology may produce more rapid growth with little further diversion of resources from current consumption. But even with great research success, most technological advance requires capital investment to put it into effect. It seems unlikely that there is an easy road to faster growth that does not require higher saving and investment. Growth has a cost. The problem is to weigh the cost against the benefits.

Your inclination may be to say, "Of course we should save more today for a better tomorrow. We should sacrifice more for the benefit of our children and grandchildren." But don't be too quick. Even with the present growth rate, the average per capita income of your children a generation hence will be more than 50 per cent higher than yours is today; that of your grandchildren two generations hence will be far more than double the present level. Given these facts, some observers don't find the case for paying the cost of faster growth very impressive. Why, they ask, should we squeeze down on consumption now to make the future even richer?

FIG. 17-1 U.S. real g.n.p. has grown since 1900 at somewhat over 3 per cent per annum. If we can raise the rate to 4 or 5 per cent, the payoff in more output will be enormous over the years ahead.

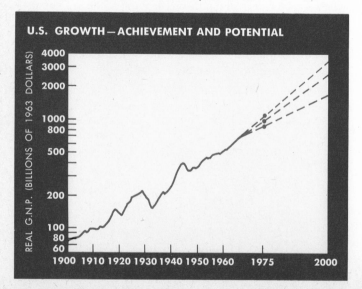

U.S. GROWTH—ACHIEVEMENT AND POTENTIAL

A Target Growth Rate?

Should we set a desired growth rate as a major goal of national policy (say 4 per cent a year in total output)? Or leave the outcome pretty much to individual and business decisions and to the forces of the market place? The staunch believer in individual choice and in the market economy will answer firmly, "The latter!" Why, he will ask, should society through government action impose on the individual its collective will as to how much present consumption he should give up so we may all live better in the future? Leave individuals free to save what they will for the future, and the market will convert these savings into investment. Growth will be as fast or as slow as free individual saving decisions make it. If people don't voluntarily save more, that's prima facie evidence they prefer not to pay the price of faster growth.

But others argue that faster economic growth should be a prime goal of national economic policy, and that collective action is required to achieve it. They contend, first, that in fact the government has no choice but to influence the growth rate. Every act of fiscal and monetary policy influences the rate of growth. Higher interest rates deter investment; lower ones encourage it. The structure of our tax system influences consumption-versus-saving decisions at every turn. There is no such thing as "neutrality" of the government with respect to the growth rate, so it is better to face up to the issue and decide rationally how fast we want to grow in making our monetary and fiscal decisions.

Second, the growthmen argue, private markets and individual decisions don't effectively mirror our collective preferences for faster growth. Most people don't appreciate the enormous importance of economic growth. Moreover, we know that our capital markets are imperfect, so that savings decisions are often not transmitted effectively into real investment. With imperfect capital markets, it is logical for the government to step in with taxes and absorb some of the savings we would otherwise have been willing to make in order to achieve widely desired social objectives—highways, slum clearance, cleaner cities, better parks, and the like. These advocates claim, in essence, that there are many social goods for which people would save if given a real choice in the market place, but which the private market place does not provide effectively.

Third, claim the growthmen, faster growth is essential to preserve our international position in the world. The vast uncommitted billions of the world's underdeveloped economies are watching the race between communism and capitalism with a close eye. We dare not lag behind.

Should we have a target growth rate as national policy? Here you will have to decide your own position. Much will depend on your attitude toward governmental intervention in general. But it should depend too on careful analysis of just how much might be accomplished through the various governmental and private measures to speed growth that are considered in the following section.

In any case, don't forget that a rise of 1 per cent in the annual growth rate (from, say, 3 to 4 per cent annually) would mean a 33⅓ per cent increase in our annual growth rate. Looked at this way, 1 per cent looms far larger. And to achieve it may not be easy. Brookings' Edward Denison, who made the estimates in Table 16-1, has mapped out a series of steps that might provide this extra 1 per cent annually over the next two decades. He finds no single step which is consistent with a basically private-enterprise economy that promises to provide as much as a quarter of 1 per cent in itself; indeed he has to suggest some two dozen separate measures to achieve the extra 1 per cent.[1]

HOW TO GROW FASTER: THE SUPPLY SIDE

Experts estimating long-run growth in the economy's full-employment production potential often use a two-stage process. First, they estimate what the labor force will be. This is not too difficult to forecast for a decade or two, because nearly all the labor force is already born and we know the age and sex distribution. When we adjust for

[1] "How to Raise the High-Employment Growth Rate by One Percentage Point," *American Economic Review*, May 1962.

a gradual reduction in the work week, for longer education, and for more women in the labor force, a figure of 1 to 1½ per cent growth per annum emerges, depending on the period concerned.

Second, the experts estimate the growth in output per man hour or man year. This estimate of "productivity" is harder, since it lumps together the effects of capital accumulation, education, and improving technology—everything except the quantity of labor. Yet, over the long pull the growth in productivity has been reasonably stable. In the century before World War II it was around 2 per cent per annum; since World War II it has been nearer 3 per cent.

Lastly, they combine these two estimates and get an estimate of growth in aggregate output. Three to four per cent a year is a common range for the U.S. economy. But with the postwar speedup in productivity and a higher labor force growth, hopes have crept up, to 4 or 4½ per cent. Remember, this is the growth in potential high-employment output. If there is substantial unemployment, actual g.n.p. will be correspondingly less.

This simple procedure gives a manageable framework for making rough estimates of total output potential for any future year. But it also should emphasize the need to look behind the two key figures, since they sum up the forces that will make the economy grow faster or slower. How can we speed economic growth for the future?

More Work

Population has been growing faster since World War II, reversing a century-long downtrend (see Fig. 16-6). After a lag, more people mean more workers, but the increase in total output doesn't mean more output per capita. If we want to raise per capita g.n.p. we need to raise the labor force participation rate (the proportion of the total population who work) or to increase the average number of working hours per year per worker.

Most of the experts expect a gradual increase in participation by women to be roughly offset by longer education for young people before they enter the labor force. The U.S. Department of Labor estimates that over the coming decade our labor force will grow at a high 1.8 per cent annually, compared to only 1.3 per cent over the preceding 15 years. But this will be partly offset by a continuing drop in the average work week. Labor Department experts estimate about an hour a week less by 1975. This estimate pulls down the effective growth in annual hours worked to about 1.5 per cent, somewhat above the expected rate of population growth of 1 to 1.25 per cent.

Ours is a free society. We believe that a housewife and her husband, not the government, should decide whether she stays home or looks for a job. How many hours a week you work is largely up to you and your employer. The government may plead and explain the facts of economic growth. But short of national emergencies like war, there is little it can do to change the long-term trends of labor-force participation and the gradually falling work week. Indeed, government's main intervention has been through extending the period of free, or cheap, education, thereby reducing the labor-force participation rate. If we want to speed economic growth through national policy, we must probably look to other approaches.

Research and Technical Advance

Modern research has produced spectacular results. Basic research in chemistry is rapidly giving us, in essence, more usable resources—fertilizers for poor soil, means of refining low-grade metallic ores, and dozens of other such improvements. Science has opened up vast new power sources for economical use—oil, then nuclear energy, perhaps solar power next. Food from seawater and power from the sun may be tomorrow's answer to the law of diminishing returns. Moreover, we have significantly speeded the translation of research into widespread use. Perhaps the most important social change of our time is the growing contrivance and management of change itself.

Figure 16-5 showed the explosion of spending on research and development since World War II. Half of all measured research in our history has occurred in the last ten years. Since research obviously has a lagged effect on actual production, perhaps we have already put a mighty force in motion—a force just beginning to show in modern "automation," computers, satellites, solar power, and the like. Output per worker has grown at 3 per cent annually, not its historical 2 per cent, since World War II. But two decades is too short a period on which to generalize. How much modern R and D has speeded long-run economic growth remains to be seen.

Figure 16-5 indicated also that much of the research and development in America has been financed by the federal government. Almost all the funds for "basic" research have come from government sources. During the early 1960's the federal government was financing about two-thirds of all R and D spending (mainly through its defense and space budgets), although nearly three-fourths of the actual work was done in industry and much of the rest in universities. Industry itself financed only about a quarter of the total, and foundations and universities the rest.

Private industry can probably be counted on to finance most developmental and applied research leading directly to salable products. There is no obvious way to increase such private spending on research and development, short of providing a governmental subsidy. One possibility is special tax treatment for R and D expenditures, although firms already can charge off most research expenses as direct costs and hence as full tax deductions. But the case for government support of *basic* research is much stronger. Truly basic research is often expensive; its results are unpredictable; and they seldom have direct commercial profitability. Even more important, if a company does make a major basic breakthrough, it is seldom able to protect its discovery for long from use by its competitors and by others. Thus, it is hard to see why many firms will spend much money on such basic research. But history records that it is the basic research breakthroughs that have provided the foundation for the great scientific and practical benefits of our times.

The economic case for government financing of *basic* research is thus strong. Such research is a classic case of "external economies." That is, the results of the investment may provide social benefits far beyond any returns which a private

company could hope to reap from its research expenditure. If U.S. Steel were to spend a large sum on basic research in metallurgy and obtain a major breakthrough on the molecular structure of some metal, this might mean a revolution in steel-making and steel use. But such secrets are very hard to keep, and soon U.S. Steel would find that it had financed mainly gains for its competitors and steel users throughout the world, without much benefit to U.S. Steel profits. So the probability is that U.S. Steel will stick to more clearly profitable applied research, and the basic research with its promising externalities may go undone.

Government support for the rapid dissemination of new knowledge and techniques also makes sense, on the same grounds of external economies. This is especially true for the outpouring of information from the government's own vast R and D spending on defense, space, and health projects. The agricultural experiment stations and extension services established at state universities throughout the nation a century ago have played a major role in speeding innovation in American agriculture. Similar aid in manufacturing, services, and other areas might produce similar results.

Saving and Capital Accumulation

How can public policy divert more of our current incomes and output to saving and investment—to the future as against the present? For the most part, this allocation is now determined by millions of rich and middle-class families and by the managers of the nation's business firms. For it is they who make most of the nation's saving and investment decisions.

It is not easy to change the decisions of so many million savers and investors. If we want the economy to save and invest more, we can change the tax structure to lessen the burden on high incomes where most of the saving is done, and place more of the burden on the poor, where it will surely reduce consumption. But at the margin, the differences in the marginal propensities to consume out of income are surprisingly small. Similarly, reduced taxes on corporate profits would raise profits and stimulate investment. Special provisions to permit corporations to charge off depreciation faster for tax purposes can raise profit rates and stimulate investment. All these measures involve conscious government action to change the balance between present and future consumption, and all are being used to varying extents.

Still more directly, the government may raise taxes and invest the money itself. Under our political process, presumably each man, rich or poor, has one vote, and society may vote this way to raise investment. Every year our governments already tax away billions of dollars to use in constructing and maintaining public capital resources—schools, highways, airports, parks, and other such investments. In addition, some new military equipment might be viewed as a temporary accumulation of national capital. In 1966, some $15–$25 billion was channeled into public capital accumulation in this way through federal, state, and local governments. Here is a direct way social action can change the saving-current consumption mix.

But direct government intervention to increase investment relative to consumption faces a basic problem. Private citizens are free to offset the government action through switching their individual consumption-saving mixes in allocating the income they have left after taxes so as to restore roughly their previous levels of consumption. Insofar as this happens, the government policy is thwarted, private saving is reduced, and the result is simply a substitution of public investment for private.

In an economy like the U.S.S.R.'s, the rate of capital accumulation is determined directly by the state. The Kremlin decrees that resources will be used to produce factories and dams rather than consumer goods. Current consumption by the masses has been held down by dictatorial planning which we would find intolerable except in case of war. Yet the Russians argue that the people basically want heavy investment to raise living standards for the future. They say that state action makes it possible for the economy to grow faster than can the vast unplanned chaos that they see in our capitalist system. Few here favor direct government control over investment, but the issues are similar in both economies. How far should we go in raising the investment rate through governmental measures?

Investment in Human Beings

Human beings are capital to a society, just as are buildings and machines. Improvement in the quality of our human capital through education and training provides a social payout through increasing future output, just as does investment in research and development. Indeed, modern research suggests that the return on investment in human capital (through formal education, retraining, and the like) may be considerably higher than the return on investment in capital goods. The interest rate on high-grade corporate bonds hovers around 4 to 5 per cent; the return on good-grade corporate stocks provided by today's stock market is even less. Yet most estimates of the *private and social* return on additional dollars invested in education run well above those figures. If this is true, both individuals and society would gain economically by spending more on education. In addition, we would get the large but unmeasurable benefits of a better-educated population for a stable social-political system. The external economies again make a strong case for government action.

If education is such a good investment, why don't private individuals make the investment themselves voluntarily? Many do. Almost everyone now gets through grade school and into high school on public funds. Most finish high school. Perhaps a third of the population goes on to at least some college work, and a much higher proportion of upper-income families send their children to college. Anyone who has done the arithmetic knows that a good education for his son is likely to be a better investment than buying the best stocks and bonds.

Nevertheless, either most of the population hasn't done the arithmetic or doesn't believe it. Two-thirds of our youngsters don't go to college, and most families and teenagers are reluctant to borrow to make this investment in human resources, even though it is clearly profitable in the long run. Moreover, our society frowns on slavery; thus there is no sure way a capitalist with spare funds can get back a big return if he wants to invest in John Jones' education, instead of in a business venture.[2]

[2] Some who resist public compulsion (which is involved in the expenditure of tax funds on more education) urge,

Improved Economic Efficiency

If we can increase the output obtained from any given capital and labor input through increased efficiency, obviously there is social gain. Two measures have been widely suggested to speed economic growth this way.

The first is to break up monopolies, because monopoly (as will be explained in Part Three) generally leads to an inefficient allocation of resources and thus to less output than could otherwise be obtained from any given input of capital and labor. The second is to improve labor markets so workers will move more promptly from declining to expanding industries and areas. This would help to lessen "frictional" and "structural" unemployment, which exist because of poor information or immobility. Better information on job openings, government help in retraining, moving allowances, government subsidies to bring new industries to unemployed workers—all have been used successfully in Europe, where unemployment since World War II has been much lower than ours. More sweepingly, some argue that we should reverse our trend toward providing greater security for workers. Minimum wage laws and social security taxes put the effective cost of hiring many marginal workers higher than their value to employers, and thus impede the normal functioning of the labor market. Still others advocate lowering unemployment benefits on the ground that people stay unemployed longer when they have such payments to tide them over.

Clearly it is to everyone's advantage to get frictional and structural unemployment down to minimum levels. Some policies to improve the efficiency of the labor market (such as better information on job openings) make sense for everyone. But the evidence of Chapter 14 suggests that strong aggregate demand may be the best tool of

all. For then employers themselves take over the job of finding workers and training them if need be, under the spur of the profit motive.

The Economic Climate—
Initiative and Enterprise

Everyone agrees that individual initiative, the spirit of enterprise, economic and social mobility, and a generally favorable economic-social-political climate deserve much credit for America's growth record over the past two centuries. But how to make them contribute more to growth in the future is less clear.

A favorable climate for private investment; open markets and active competition, with a chance for the best management and the best product to win out; social and political attitudes friendly toward individual initiative and business; and support for a vigorous profit-oriented economy—these are clearly favorable to rapid growth. But on these conditions you can find many modern viewers-with-alarm. Some claim that desire for security has replaced the traditional American aggressive individualism. Others claim that the American economy has become comfortable, affluent, rigid, and tradition-bound —less inclined to vigorous competition and less open to the newcomer and the new idea. Pressures for a shorter work week seem to some a threatening symptom of growing unwillingness to work hard and long in order to produce more goods and services. Another group sees growing government interference in economic life as a major threat.

Maybe the worriers will turn out to be right. Most observers, however, see in the American economic organization a still impressively vigorous, flexible, adaptive machine, providing an environment generally favorable to rapid economic growth. But even in a wealthy, high-saving economy like ours, rapid growth is not automatic. Hard work and incentives are still important, as the spectacular growth of West Germany and Japan since World War II illustrates. Sir Henry Clay, a noted economist, two decades ago put the problem provocatively: "The so-called capitalist system, so far from failing, has been almost too successful in the interests of its own survival; it has encouraged the great mass of our population to believe that the increase of wealth is easy and

---

instead, measures to improve borrowing arrangements for those who want an education and are willing to make an investment in it. They argue that we should provide everyone accurate information on the probable economic benefits of private investment in education. Then if people didn't choose to borrow to pay for their own education, there would remain no reason why society should provide the further education for them at public expense. But this argument overlooks the external-economies point, and brushes over the great difficulty the poor would have in borrowing to finance their children's education.

inevitable, and depends no longer on incentives and appropriate organization but on scientific research, adequate education, and public direction." [3] His warning is appropriate.

DEMAND POLICY
FOR STABLE GROWTH

Increasing our productive capacity (moving out the production possibilities frontier) is the main requisite for faster economic growth. But in a largely private-enterprise economy, the demand side matters too. For businessmen will not long produce goods they cannot sell at a profit. On the other side, excess aggregate demand will produce inflation and instability. What level of aggregate demand should monetary and fiscal policy produce so as to assure stable economic growth, avoiding both depressions and inflations?

What Aggregate Demand Is Needed
for Stable Economic Growth?

Assume that national productive capacity is growing 4 per cent annually because of population growth, capital investment, and technological advance. We want continuous high-level employment with stable prices. What aggregate demand is needed, assuming that we begin from a stable, high-employment situation?

The answer is clear. Aggregate demand should rise at about 4 per cent a year (the same rate as the expansion of productive capacity), and the division between consumption and investment spending should match the division between consumption and saving decisions (omitting government taxes and spending). More total spending than that will mean inflation. Less will mean underemployment and waste. A malallocation of spending between consumption and investment is likely to generate short-run fluctuations in the economy that may lead to serious booms or depressions.

Begin with the following simplified high-employment economy for 196X.

[3] Address at Wharton School of Finance and Commerce, University of Pennsylvania, January 10, 1947.

	In Billions
Total g.n.p.	$800
Consumption	540
Investment and saving	120
Government taxes and spending	140

We want to grow at 4 per cent yearly. What must 196X + 1 look like? To simplify, let us assume arbitrarily that government taxes and spending increase just 4 per cent. Then, clearly, private spending must also rise 4 per cent if 4 per cent more output is to be taken off the market at a stable price level. If the proportion between consumption and investment remains stable, 196X + 1 would look like this, with total spending up 4 per cent.

	In Billions
Total g.n.p.	$832
Consumption	562
Investment and saving	125
Government taxes and spending	145

It does not necessarily follow, of course, that a 4 per cent increase in investment any year will produce a 4 per cent increase in capacity the next year; the capital/output ratio is not necessarily stable. Remember that capacity depends on other factors in addition to investment. Perhaps total 196X + 2 full-employment capacity will be up only 3 per cent, perhaps 5 or 6. But whatever the percentage is, the full-employment-without-inflation level of aggregate demand rises by the same amount. And the same rule applies for following years.

In principle, there is no reason why we need to have a stable price level to achieve stable, full-employment growth. If, for example, total spending rises only 2 per cent while capacity grows by 4 per cent, full-employment output can still be achieved if the price level falls 2 per cent. Conversely, if total spending rises 6 per cent, full-employment output can be maintained with a 2 per cent increase in average prices.

As a practical matter, however, as we saw in Chapters 9 and 14, substantial economy-wide price reductions without serious disruption seem unlikely in the modern American economy. With downward inflexibility of costs and prices, inadequate total spending means unemployment of men and machines. Thus, few economists now believe that aggregate demand can safely grow less than roughly in proportion to total capacity. Holding aggregate money demand constant with a 4 per cent annual growth in capacity could mean something like 20 per cent unemployment of men and capacity in only 5 years. This is, indeed, roughly what happened between 1929 and 1939, when the latter year saw 8 million unemployed with about the same money g.n.p. as in peak-prosperity 1929.

A look ahead to 1980 will illustrate some of the magnitudes involved in such growth. Assume stable prices at 1967 levels and roughly constant proportions between consumption, saving-investment, and government taxes-spending. Then a 4 per cent growth rate gives a 1980 g.n.p of about $1.4 trillion, divided roughly like this:

	In Billions
Total g.n.p.	$1,400
Consumption	900
Investment and saving	230
Government taxes and spending	270

Will Private Decisions Provide the Right Total Spending?

Can we count on consumers to buy nearly $1 trillion of food, clothing, washing machines, automobiles, and other goods and services, only a decade hence? Perhaps more important, since investment is a driving force of economic growth, can we count on private businesses and households to spend $230 billion in 1980 on new plant, equipment, and construction? Remember that this 1980 figure implies they spent nearly as much in 1979, only a little less in 1978, and so on back down to the then-peak level of around $125 billion in the late 1960's. And after $230 billion in 1980, will they invest the $240 billion in 1981 and $250 billion in 1982 that will be needed, on our assumptions, to maintain economic growth and offset the growing savings made at g.n.p. levels above $1.4 trillion? What industries will require investment of these astronomical sums year after year to produce the goods consumers want to buy? Lastly, will we want governments to take away $270 billion in taxes and spend it for us?

If not, private spending will have to grow even further to take up the slack.

A further problem needs to be noted. Where will the money come from for stable economic growth? Will the private economy automatically produce the right amount? Looking back to Chapter 8, we can see that M and V combined must increase enough to produce a 4 per cent annual increase in money g.n.p.

Will private bank borrowing and spending decisions automatically add up to just the required growth in money and in aggregate demand? Obviously, there is no necessary reason they will. The case for conscious stabilizing monetary-fiscal policy to keep aggregate demand on target is loud and clear.

Capital and Labor Shares in Stable Growth

Even if aggregate demand grows stably, may not the investment-consumption balance get out of kilter? And a closely related question: What balance between wages and profits (as rough surrogates for consumption and investment) is required for stable, sustained growth?

Clearly, the answer depends partly on how fast we want to grow. Fast growth requires a high-profit, high-investment economy. Wages shouldn't rise too fast. High profits are a fine thing for rapid growth. We'd better be sure the unions don't get too much at bargaining time.

But if profits and investment get *too* large relative to wages and consumption spending, excess capacity will develop and the boom will collapse. Indeed, when it comes to maintaining high-level employment, union leaders hammer away at one proposition: Wages are the biggest single source of buying power in our economy. The major cause of depression and lagging growth, they say, is wages that are too low. If wages don't rise fast enough, profits will swell and income will be saved, not spent. Every bargaining time, union leaders mount a public-relations campaign that a wage boost will really be a boon to everyone through the increased spending it will generate.

Are the unions right that higher wage rates are the way to fight underemployment and overinvestment? The answer hinges on some technical considerations. With higher wage *rates*, will employers spend more or less on total wages for labor? If more, the higher wage rates at least have a chance of increasing consumption spending. But if employers spend less on labor, clearly the higher wage rates will reduce consumer spending. Either way, higher wage rates, other things equal, mean higher costs and prices than would otherwise prevail. And higher prices don't generally lead to more spending and jobs for more workers. Over the long pull, moreover, it's clear that higher wages steadily push toward the substitution of machinery for labor.

In any case, don't be trapped by the obvious fallacy that business profits represent savings withdrawn from the income stream. Many business profits flow directly into investment spending, and there is no necessary reason for classifying big profits as a deflationary force. What matters for economic health is total spending on consumption plus investment, not just consumption. Wages are purchasing power, but so are profits.

It should be clear that the investment-consumption balance issue is a thorny one. Economists have a variety of "growth models" which illustrate the relative paths of investment and consumption needed to assure stable, sustainable growth under different conditions—different propensities to consume, different capital/output ratios, different rates of technical progress, and the like. One such simple model was presented in the Appendix to Chapter 15. But nearly all these models, and historical experience, tell us that growth must be reasonably balanced if it is to be stable. Consumption and investment must be kept growing at *roughly* the same rates. If either investment or consumption gets too far out of line with the other, we're in for trouble. And although profits and wages are by no means identical with investment and consumption spending, *very roughly* the same balanced growth proposition holds for them.[4]

[4] It is interesting to note that the 1962 "wage-price guideposts" (see page 186) provide for this rough stability in wage and profit shares of the national income.

For Analysis and Discussion

1. How fast should the American economy grow over the decade ahead? What measures would you propose to achieve your desired growth rate?
2. How much of your personal income are you willing to use over the next decade to build up the economic capacity of the nation for future production? Does the government have a right to dictate to you a rate different from the one you prefer?
3. Since 1900 (see Fig. 17-1), have money-demand or real factors been more important in explaining our growth rate? If your answer is the real factors, how about the period of the 1930's?
4. Only about 3 per cent of the g.n.p. is devoted to research and development. Would it be sound policy to double this amount? Who should decide? If the amount should be doubled, who should pay for it?
5. Can you suggest ways of increasing the nation's rate of capital formation that do not impinge on the freedom of individuals and businesses to spend or save their incomes as they please?
6. By 1975 the population of the U.S. may be 220 million. Assume that the same proportion (about 40 per cent) of the population is in the labor force as in 1967; that the average propensity to consumer out of g.n.p. remains at about ⅔; that output per worker rises about 2 per cent per annum; and that the price level remains constant:
   a. What level of gross national expenditure will be required in 1975 to assure full employment? Explain.
   b. What level of private investment will be required, assuming government expenditures on goods and services remain at their 1967 level of about $175 billion?
   c. Suppose that only 35 per cent of the population is in the 1975 labor force. How would your answers to a and b change?
   d. Suppose now that the average work week is reduced from 40 to 30 hours. How would per capita real output compare with 1967, when population was about 200 million?

EIGHTEEN

GROWTH IN

THE UNDERDEVELOPED

COUNTRIES[1]

The Anatomy of Underdevelopment.

Policy for Economic Development.

United States Policy.

In the United States, economic growth is the road to raising further our already high standard of living. But for 2 billion people who live in the economically "underdeveloped" countries, economic growth is a necessity if they are to escape from the bitter poverty which has been their lot through history. Per capital g.n.p. in the United States in 1967 was about $3,900. In the underdeveloped countries it averaged less than $150.

Table 18-1 classifies the nations of the world into three groups, depending on their per capita annual g.n.p.'s in the early 1960's. "Highly developed" countries are those with per capita g.n.p.'s above $800. The "intermediate" group are countries where the figure was between $300 and $800. The underdeveloped nations are those with per capita g.n.p.'s below $300.

The figures in Table 18-1 are *very rough*. They probably substantially underestimate income levels in the poorer nations on two counts. First, incomes there may be underestimated relatively because so much home-produced food and clothing does not go through the market. Second, prices of the staples that form the standard of living of the masses there are generally very cheap compared to items bought by higher-income families; thus, conversion of, say, Indian rupee incomes into U.S. dollars at the official exchange rate which is based on prices of a wide range of commodities will tend to give a misleading picture of actual comparative living standards. But even if the per capita incomes in the poor nations were doubled to adjust for these possible underesti-

[1] Note to instructors: This chapter can equally well be combined with Chapter 42 as a closing unit on comparative economic systems.

TABLE 18-1

COUNTRIES GROUPED BY PER CAPITA G.N.P.—IN U.S. DOLLARS *

Highly Developed Countries (about 800 million people)
(Over $800 per capita)

In the Americas:		In Europe (cont.):	
United States	$3010	United Kingdom	$1700
Canada	2100	Denmark	1690
Puerto Rico	960	France	1680
		Netherlands	1570
In Oceania:		Belgium	1460
New Zealand	2100	U.S.S.R.	1250
Australia	1800	Austria	1040
		Italy	1030
In Europe:		Finland	920
Sweden	2100	Ireland	900
Switzerland	2080		
Norway	1880	In Asia:	
W. Germany	1770	Israel	1210

Intermediate Countries (about 500 million people)
($300–800 per capita)

In Africa:		In Asia:	
Union of South Africa	700	Japan	720
In the Americas:		In Europe:	
Venezuela	790	Poland	680
Argentina	610	Hungary	620
Uruguay	560	Spain	540
Panama	480	Greece	450
Chile	460	Portugal	420
Mexico	430		
Cuba	310		

Underdeveloped Countries (over 2 billion people)
(Less than $300 per capita)

All of Africa except		Middle East	about 150
Union of South Africa	about 100	India	78
All of the Americas except		Communist China **	75
countries listed above	about 175	All of Asia except	
		nations listed above	about 90
		Southeast Europe	about 250

* United Nations data for 1964, except for communist nations. Figures are gross domestic product for each nation converted to 1964 U.S. dollars at official exchange rates and divided by population. Remember the text warning that data are very rough for the underdeveloped nations, and that figures for such nations are probably substantially understated by using official exchange rates—perhaps by as much as 100 per cent. Several smaller nations omitted.

** Figures for Communist China are extremely rough.

mates, the underdeveloped nations would still appear desperately poor. For most of the world, poverty is far and away the number one economic problem.[2]

Worse, this huge gap between rich and poor nations is widening rapidly, not closing. The following table for the United States and India since 1960 tells the story. Although it shows the extremes, it suggests the spectacular rate at which the Western industrial nations are pulling away from the underdeveloped world. A 2 per cent annual increase on the U.S. base of $3,900 means a $78 increase in one year, equal to the *entire* per capita g.n.p. in India. In India, the same 2 per cent increase, if it could be achieved, would be about $1.50 per capita.

TABLE 18-2
PER CAPITA REAL G.N.P. IN THE U.S. AND INDIA *

	1960	1967
United States	$2,850	$3,900
India	75	78

* Data in 1967 U.S. dollars. Figures for India are probably understated relative to U.S., but the 1960–1967 change is roughly accurate.

Why do these vast differences in standards of living exist? Why is the gap between the rich and the poor widening even further? Why have per capita incomes not grown at all over the past century for hundreds of millions of the poorest people? The theories of economic growth presented in Chapter 15 can help us answer these questions, and most of the rest of this chapter is devoted to applying the same central theory of economic growth to the underdeveloped countries as was applied to the United States in Chapters

[2] Two good general references on the underdeveloped areas and their problems are Charles Kindleberger, *Economic Development* (New York: McGraw-Hill, 1965) and T. Morgan, G. Betz, and N. Choudhry, *Readings on Economic Development* (Belmont: Wadsworth, 1963). They and many other experts believe that the very low per capita incomes reported in Table 18-1 for Asia and Africa are indeed underestimated substantially, for the reasons indicated. But views differ. See also the footnote to Table 18-1.

16 and 17. But, as we shall see, the situations are vastly different.

Development of these economically "backward" countries has become the most explosive socio-economic problems of our times. Poverty is a source of acute discontent for hundreds of millions of people aroused by their nationalistic leaders. In China and India alone there are nearly a billion and a quarter people—two huge nations awakening to their potential power and to the fact that poverty and misery may not be the inescapable lot of the masses in the Orient. A great change is moving Asia, Africa, and Latin America, a change compounded of growing nationalism and a desire for economic progress and power.

We neglect their drive for economic development at our peril, even if we have no humanitarian interest in their plight. A revolution of rising expectations—of economic progress, individual status, and national prestige and power—is sweeping the underdeveloped nations.

Are the Underdeveloped Countries Really "Backward"?

Although economists sometimes refer to regions with low output per capita as "backward," some social scientists protest against the imposition of our standards on other societies. The warning is well taken. Some societies may prefer to devote themselves to aesthetic values and leisurely living rather than to accumulating material possessions. Perhaps they are happier than the Western industrialized states. Part of our material wealth may be pointless in the eyes of other nations. Cars that crowd the highways; elaborate subways to get us around the teeming cities we have created; work-filled days and activity-filled nights. All these raise the g.n.p., but do they really increase our happiness?

But having taken this warning to heart, remember that poverty and hunger are very real and unpleasant facts for hundreds of millions of people in other lands. The number of economies that have rejected additional material goods when given a practical choice is small indeed. It is precisely the leaders of the newly awakening "underdeveloped" countries who protest most violently against the poverty, disease, and misery that envelop the masses in their countries, and who resent most bitterly the wide gap between their poverty and the affluence of the industrialized nations. Today the drive for increased material well-being dominates economic thinking around the world.

THE ANATOMY
OF UNDERDEVELOPMENT

Poverty is the central economic fact of the underdeveloped areas. But there are many differences among them. Some are primitive; others, like India and China, boast civilizations which are far older than those of the West. Some have generous natural resources; others are bitterly poor in the endowments of nature. Some have a high ratio of population to land; others have vast open spaces. The poverty of a beggar in the streets of Calcutta is different from that of the Bushman of South Africa or the desert nomad of the Middle East. But in spite of these differences, there are some strong resemblances. And our theory from Chapter 15 can provide a useful framework for examining the problems of the underdeveloped nations.

Patterns of Economic Activity

First, a brief look at the economies of the underdeveloped nations as a backdrop for analysis of why they are poor, and of what can be done to raise their production.

Poverty and the Dominance of Low-Productivity Agriculture. In the underdeveloped countries, food is the main item of production and consumption. It has to be, for starvation hovers uncomfortably near. For the entire group of underdeveloped countries, about 70 per cent of all production is food. In the United States, the comparable figure is about 20 per cent. Although diets in most nations are adequate to preserve life, they are often inadequate to fend off disease or, even allowing for the small bodily stature of many peoples, to provide enough energy for continued hard work.

A mud or a thatched hut and a little simple clothing make up most of the rest of the consumption pattern in many underdeveloped countries. Remember that only around $50 *per year*

per capita is left to cover everything except food. Formal education, medical care, plumbing, highways, and other such services that we take for granted have little place in such standards of living. The masses in these nations save little or nothing at all. In Calcutta, a teeming city, between a quarter-and a half-million people have no home or job whatsoever and simply wander the streets. Their food often comes from garbage in the gutter. In Pakistan, child labor is paid 10 cents per day.

Outside a few modern industries in the cities, production is at the handicraft stage. Since human labor is very cheap and capital scarce, the most laborious details are often done by hand. Tractors and other mechanized farming equipment are little known, and would generally be unusable even if available, because of lack of fuel, maintenance facilities, and sufficient education to use them. Figure 18-1 shows vividly the great reliance on human and animal power in the poor nations, compared to the vast use of nonhuman energy (electrical, water, and mineral) in the developed nations. (In this and the following figures, income per capita, from Table 18-1, is always shown on the vertical axis. Here both income and energy use are plotted on ratio (logarithmic) scales to make relative comparisons easy.)

The nonagricultural population is crowded into a few large cities, where small-scale industry, services for the wealthy, and government employment provide most of the jobs available. Simple textiles, sometimes not much beyond the handicraft stage, are important in many underdeveloped economies; the cloth is used for clothing and home furnishings. In the more developed countries, modern large-scale industry (steel, chemicals, fertilizers, and the like) has begun to appear in the major cities. In a few cases, one basic industry dominates the economy—oil in the Middle East, rubber in Malaysia, copper in Chile.

Dual Economies: Limited Development of Markets. Thus, many nations are in essence "dual economies." One part is a money, market-oriented economy centered in a few large cities, with modern industry mixed with crowded slums. The other part is a subsistence-level, rural, barter-type economy of hand labor and primitive superstitions, comprising 75 per cent or so of

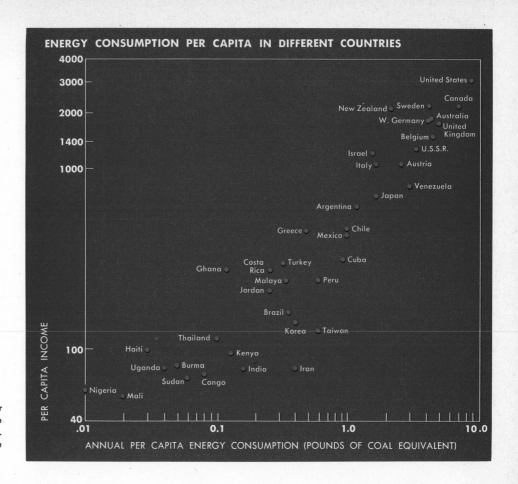

ENERGY CONSUMPTION PER CAPITA IN DIFFERENT COUNTRIES

FIG. 18-1 Energy consumption per capita is closely correlated with the degree of economic development. (Source: United Nations. Data are for 1964.)

the population, substantially isolated from the markets and industry of the cities. To go from one to the other is to go from one world to another, from the dark ages to the present.

Transportation is crude. The highways of the cities rapidly dwindle to dirt roads and to mere paths a hundred miles away. Religious and cultural barriers fragment the nation. One can scarcely call them "economies"—for economic life as we know it exists only around the cities and towns. Without roads and communication, there is little chance for a market economy to develop.

In some nations, one-product export economies have developed—coffee in Brazil, rubber in Indonesia, oil in Saudi Arabia. Much of the investment to develop these export enclaves is foreign, and resentment against foreign ownership and operation is common. Often it leads to nationalization, whether or not there is a native competence to operate the industry.

Unequal Distribution of Income. In most underdeveloped countries, income is very unequally distributed. There are often a few rich landholders, sometimes a few industrialists. The masses are dismally poor, mainly living just above subsistence level on farms or in villages. Strikingly, there is often no "middle class" of shopkeepers, professional men, and skilled workers, such as makes up a major portion of Western populations.

Weak Governments and Limited Government Services. A few underdeveloped nations have well-established democratic institutions, but they are the exception. Governments are typically unstable, revolutions are commonplace. There can be little long-range planning of basic government services such as schools, highways, and the like. Often governments are dominated by the entrenched "haves," who block social and political change which might endanger them. Tribal chieftains, religious leaders, and other guardians of the traditional culture are likely to occupy positions of great influence.

Governments, which must provide leadership for many changes in development, are usually weakly staffed, reflecting the newness of the nations and the lack of education and traditions of

235

honest civil service. Government jobs are often political perquisites, which mainly provide an accepted position for enforcing bribes and graft. All too often, confusion, red tape, and bungling characterize government "programs." There is little chance for such governments to establish and administer effective tax systems to collect the funds needed to provide schools, highways, and sanitation.

So much for a general, if discouraging, overview. Now let us look more analytically at the problem, using our theory from Chapter 15. If the theory is right, low per capita output in the underdeveloped nations should reflect a high ratio of population to natural resources and to capital; a slow rate of capital accumulation and technical advance; an uneducated, low-productivity labor force; and an economic, political, and social environment unconducive to initiative, enterprise and organized economic activity. And in fact, this is a reasonable description of most of the underdeveloped nations. Let us look now at these factors one at a time.

Natural Resources

Lack of natural resources does not explain the plight of the underdeveloped nations. Switzerland has one of the world's highest per capita incomes on virtually no natural resources; China has one of the lowest on vast natural resources. Africa is rich in natural resources. The Malthusian hypothesis suggests that per capita incomes will be lowest where the ratio of population to natural resources is highest—where people outrun the ability of the land to feed them. But this, too, is clearly too simple an explanation. The ratios of population to arable land for Switzerland, Belgium, and the Netherlands are about the same as those for Bolivia, Peru, and Egypt.

Plentiful natural resources can certainly help. The United States, Canada, and Australia all have rich resources and low ratios of population to land. Surely the vast western frontier helped to speed our early growth. Moreover, even the poor nations would be much worse off without generous resources—the copper and nitrates of Chile, the oil of the Middle East, the rubber of Sumatra. Perhaps climate, rather than natural resources in the usual sense, is critical. Most of the world's well-to-do nations lie in the

temperate zone; none of them in the tropics. But within the temperate zone there are wide variations in economic development, as there are among tropical nations. Nor does primary reliance on agriculture, for whatever reason, necessarily characterize the poor nations. Denmark and New Zealand demonstrate that agricultural countries need not be poor. The poor nations are poor not merely because they are agricultural, but because productivity in their agriculture is so low.

Shortage of Capital and Primitive Technology

The stock of capital explains much more. No underdeveloped country has a large stock of capital goods per capita; every well-to-do nation does. Modern factories, machinery and equipment, highways, hospitals—all are scarce in the underdeveloped nations. Without them, high output per capita is very difficult.

The reason is easy to see. When nations are poor, they find it hard to save. Saving in India or Tanganyika means cutting back an already pitifully low standard of living. Saving in America is easy. The underdeveloped country can divert resources from producing consumption goods to investment only through greater want and privation. Yet without capital goods it can never hope to raise the standard of living of the masses very much.

Capital investment of over $20,000 per factory worker in America was cited above. In the poorest nations, the comparable figure is only a few dollars. Gross capital formation is only 5–10 per cent of gross national product in such poor nations as Paraguay and Nigeria. In the well-to-do nations it runs 15–20 per cent, and in the very rapidly growing nations, like Japan and Austria, up to 30–40 per cent. It is easy for the rich to become richer. The poor, like the queen in *Through the Looking Glass*, must run as fast as they can merely to stay in the same place, as population grows constantly.

Closely related, most underdeveloped countries have little modern technology. Human beings and beasts do virtually all the work in agriculture. Handicraft methods dominate in small-scale industry in the towns and cities. To the illiterate native of Kenya or Yemen, Detroit's mass-production methods and Pittsburgh's steel mills have little relevance. For him the problem is to learn to use a hoe or plow.

It might seem easy for the backward nations to leap ahead by importing the readily available know-how of advanced nations. But most modern technology is expensive; without heavy capital investment it is out of the question. And much modern technology is related to large-scale production which demands mass markets that don't exist in the underdeveloped nations. Where economic development is beginning, sometimes wild contrasts exist in the dual economies. In the cities of India and Venezuela, some of the world's most modern oil refineries and chemical plants loom against the sky. Fifty miles away there is the most primitive agriculture, unchanged for a thousand years.

Overpopulation
and the Labor Force

In one fundamental sense, overpopulation is the crux of the underdeveloped economies. The population is so large that, given the natural resources and capital available, there is barely enough output per person to maintain life. And when total output increases because of improved technology or capital accumulation, population seems to increase nearly as fast, so there is little improvement in the average standard of living. This is not the picture in all the underdeveloped economies, but it is in most.

In recent years, total production has risen at substantial rates in many of the underdeveloped nations, apparently at 3–5 per cent per annum in Latin America, Africa, and southeast Asia. This is near the growth rate of total output in the industrialized countries. But per capita incomes have risen little in most underdeveloped nations because population has grown nearly as fast as output.

What are the facts about population? In most underdeveloped economies, the annual birth rate is between 30 and 50 per thousand people; in the United States and western Europe, the comparable rate has generally declined to around 15 to 25 per thousand. But in the underdeveloped economies until recently death rates typically ran from 25 to 35 per thousand, compared to 10 or below in the Western world. Malthus' specter of famine as population outruns the food supply

has always been near, aided by inadequate diet and low resistance to disease. Since it is the difference between birth and death rates that determines population growth, population growth rates in the two types of economies have until recently not been grossly different, running around 10 to 15 per thousand (1 to 1½ per cent per year).

Since World War II, this picture has changed dramatically. Western methods of disease prevention have drastically reduced the death rate in many underdeveloped countries, especially the rate of infant mortality. DDT alone has saved millions of lives through checking the spread of infectious disease. In Ceylon, the death rate was cut almost in half in three years by the virtual elimination of malaria. During the 1940–1950 decade, the death rate declined by 46 per cent in Puerto Rico, 43 per cent in Formosa, 23 per cent in Jamaica. But birth rates have dropped only slowly in most cases. The result is a population explosion in the underdeveloped nations. In Mexico, Ceylon, Venezuela, and El Salvador, population has been growing at 3 per cent per annum recently, a rate that means a doubling every 25 years. China's growth rate is nearly 2.5 per cent. Her population of over 750 million is growing by 15–20 million every year, and at the present rate will reach 1 billion before 1980.

Figure 18-2 shows this contrast dramatically. Note the high birth rates in most underdeveloped countries, and their rapid rates of population growth implied by the big spread between birth and death rates.

In many underdeveloped nations, most of the population is illiterate. New methods that involve even the simplest changes often meet barriers of superstition and inadequate understanding—for example, use of chemical fertilizers and crop rotation. In Africa, only about 25 per cent of all children between 5 and 18 go to school, about 40 per cent in Asia. In the United States, the figure is over 95 per cent.

Figure 18-3 shows the strong correlation between literacy and living standards. Plotting daily newspaper circulation per 1,000 inhabitants against per capita income gives an even more striking correlation (though here the causal chain may run strongly from income level to newspapers as well as the other way).

The absence of even qualified clerks and

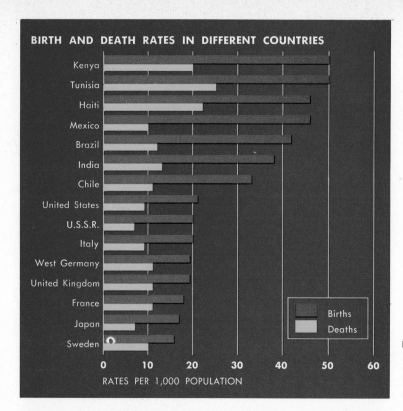

FIG. 18-2 The underdeveloped nations have the fastest-growing populations. For the whole world, the birth rate is about 34 per thousand and the death rate about 11. (Source: United Nations. Figures for 1964.)

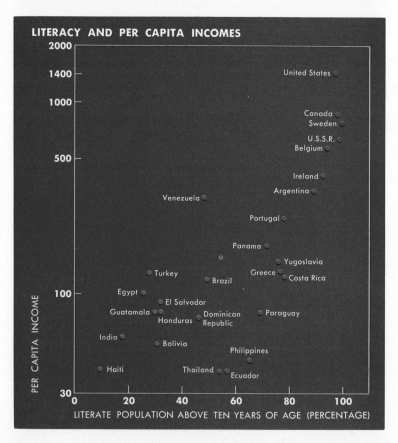

FIG. 18-3 The degree of literacy is highly correlated with the extent of economic development, as both cause and effect. (Source: UNESCO. Figures for various dates in the 1950's and 1960's.)

minor administrators poses a major problem for any commercial or business activity. The habits of honesty, reliability, and efficiency in work which we take for granted are the foundation of economic activity as we know it in the Western world. In some of the poorest nations, witch-doctors, primitive customs, even cannibalism, are still more common.

Environment and Initiative

Rapid economic growth, closely related to the industrial revolution, has occurred in the Western world where the social and economic groundwork was already well laid. Nowhere has there been rapid, continuing growth without reasonably stable government and financial and economic institutions. In all the countries of the "highly developed" group of Table 18-1 except the U.S.S.R., the profit motive and individual initiative have played a central role.

On these scores, the problems faced by the underdeveloped economies are enormous. Apathy and ignorance characterize the great mass of their populations. Except for government leaders and small educated groups, there is often little effective impetus for economic development; and all too often even the leaders appear more concerned with their own positions than with economic progress for the masses. In central Africa, the medicine man may have more influence than elected government leaders or outside experts. The head of a tribe may be held responsible for an adequate supply of rainfall as well as for selling the cocoa produced nearby. In some nations, manual labor is considered beneath the dignity of a man, certainly of an educated man, and is left entirely to women. In most of the poor nations, few of the peasants own much, if any, land. They see little reason to work harder to produce more when most of it must be given up to the absentee landlord. The tribesman in Africa has no idea of modern commercial or industrial activity, nor any interest in central government.

Thus, it is not surprising that the underdeveloped nations lack entrepreneurs—individuals with imagination and initiative to seize economic opportunities and develop them. In the traditional societies, such attitudes and activities are often frowned upon. It would seldom occur to most people in those nations to start a business, however small, or even to innovate in their day-to-day tasks of farming or handicraft work. Things have been done the same way since time immemorial.

Nor can such nations expect to surge upward without what economists call an "infrastructure" of "social overhead capital"—highways, schools, communications, hospitals, sanitation. These all require capital and planning—and their benefits to the whole economy far exceed the individual benefits that individual investors might see. Enforced saving through government tax collections is the only practical way to finance them. Thus stable, established governments, capable of collecting taxes and spending efficiently, are essential—but rare.

Absence of stable governments and well-established tax systems leads to persistent government deficits and inflation. There are vast needs. Roads, schools, fertilizer plants, irrigation projects—everything cries out to be done, and government action seems the only way. But tax systems are primitive and subsistence living standards make new taxes very difficult to impose and collect. The predictable result is government spending without corresponding tax revenues—and excess-demand inflation.

The resulting inflations are bad partly because of the inequities they wreak on the masses, who have little way to protect themselves from higher prices of essentials. Inflation thus becomes a kind of "forced saving" that substitutes for tax collections. But worse, inflation and financial instability repel foreign investors, whose capital is so desperately needed.

The Vicious Circle of Poverty

The economically underdeveloped countries vary widely. But in most the problem seems to be a vicious circle of poverty: Incomes and living standards are so low that productivity is low and saving is impossible for the mass of the population. Producing food for subsistence is the main goal. Without more saving to accumulate more capital goods, build highways, and provide education, total output per capita cannot be increased. Total output does increase as population produces more workers, and some saving by the upper-income groups and through government investing provides some additional capital goods and public services. But population grows about as fast as does total output, thus holding down living standards to present poverty levels and preventing the saving that might permit faster capital accumulations and a break-through to higher real income per capita. Even if these barriers could be overcome, the domestic market is too small to permit the economies of mass production.

Throughout the underdeveloped economies, a significant part of the farm population is "surplus," in the sense that it could be removed from the farms of the countries concerned without any reduction in *total* farm output. But to move this surplus population to productive employment seems impossible. What will keep them from starving until they become established in industrial jobs? How can uneducated people be made into effective industrial workers? Where will the industrial jobs come from—who will provide the tools for new factory workers, capital for factory equipment, and the enterprise to establish new concerns? How could the newly made industrial goods be sold either domestically or abroad without an established market and without adequate transportation and commercial facilities?

Lastly, government planning and taxation are required to enforce saving and channel investment into socially desirable channels; yet governments are weak, inefficient, unstable. Inflations and financial instability are commonplace. It seems that everywhere they turn, the underdeveloped nations face insoluble dilemmas. Their leaders may know the prescriptions of the theory of Chapter 15, but what shall they do?

POLICY FOR ECONOMIC DEVELOPMENT

How can the underdeveloped countries break out of the vicious circle of poverty and take off into self-sustaining growth? There is no simple answer. Indeed, there may be no answer at all for some of them. The main approaches suggested by the experts follow the lines of the theory suggested above.

Environment and Institutions for Economic Development

It is striking that every country except Russia in the "highly developed" group of Table 18-1 is either in Western Europe or has inherited much of Western European culture and traditions. Max Weber, a famous sociologist, in his *The Protestant Ethic and the Spirit of Capitalism* argued that the rapid economic development of Western Europe was linked intimately with what he called the "Protestant ethic"—the belief that work is good for its own sake and that the individual should be free to seek after his own welfare through work.

Weber emphasized the institutions of capitalistic society that have accompanied rapid economic development in the West: (1) private ownership and control of the means of production; (2) freedom of the market from such restrictions as guild monopolies, social-class barriers, and government price-fixing; (3) the reign of calculable law, enabling people to know in advance what rules they operate under in economic life; (4) freedom of individuals to work for wages; (5) "commercialism" of economic life through a market system of wages and prices to mobilize and allocate productive resources; and (6) speculation and risk-taking (which had been largely prevented in the preceding feudal and guild societies).

Were the Protestant ethic and the institutions of capitalism essential to the rapid economic growth of today's richest countries? The facts fit Weber's description reasonably well, but there are plenty of exceptions.

The rise of industrial Germany during the last half of the nineteenth century, for example, showed strong government encouragement of economic development within an essentially private-enterprise economy. The spectacular industrialization of Japan during the past century involved government leadership on at least a quasi-authoritarian basis. The most striking case outside the Weber pattern is modern Russia, whose rapid economic development has been accomplished through a highly centralized economic control. Communist China is perhaps the great experiment of the present generation.

Everyone agrees today that sustained rapid economic growth is extremely unlikely without a stable government, law and order. Without such stability, neither domestic nor foreign investors are willing to risk their funds. Without stable governments, the essential economic infrastructure of highways, communications, and other public utilities is unlikely to come. But revolution and instability have been common in the underdeveloped nations, especially in recent decades when the masses have increasingly challenged control by foreign nations and rich minorities. Struggles for power by competing military factions have been common. Illiterate, superstitious people find it hard to make democracy work effectively after they wrest power from rich dictators or foreign rulers. Cuba and the Dominican Republic provide vivid examples close to home. But difficult as it may be, establishment of stable government appears to be a *sine qua non* for the take-off into economic growth.

Development of individual initiative and an entrepreneurial class, plus acceptance of a market economy, is also vital. There must be individuals who take leadership in establishing enterprises, who see potential gains in taking risks, who manage to mobilize capital, who have the drive to push ahead through difficulties and to organize the work of others. There must be organizers and administrators. Acceptance of a profit motive apparently also helps, partly because profits provide a direct source of funds for further needed private investment.

Equally important, and perhaps most difficult, a spirit of greater initiative must be instilled in the masses. To be more productive, the individual must learn to want more and to work more efficiently to get it. Apathy and ignorance lead to acceptance of poverty and the status quo—to acceptance of the life of one's parents and their parents before them. No other problem seems more frustrating to the planners trying to pull economies up from poverty.

How private initiative, a market, and an entrepreneurial class develop in traditional tribal or village societies is far from clear. Sociologists, economists, and anthropologists have studied dozens of cases and find no single explanation. In some instances (e.g., Japan), an entrepreneurial class seems to develop from pressures of social and cultural change. Dissatisfied groups outside the ruling elite see trading and business as a way to rise to higher status. In other cases (e.g., Egypt), the spirit of entrepreneurship is imported through colonial rule, which later is thrown off. Increasing awareness of the outside world seems everywhere to be important. In many cases, the development of an entrepreneurial class has been a revolt against prevailing tribal or village mores, a social as well as an economic revolution.[3]

Capital Accumulation and Industrialization

As our theory would lead us to expect, substantial capital accumulation has marked every major case of rapid economic development. To rise from poverty, every nation faces the central problem of increasing saving and investment as a share of total output. Figure 18-4 shows the wide variation among countries in the ratio of gross investment to gross national product in the early 1960's. Although a few of the nations with very high savings investment ratios have relatively low per capita incomes (for example, Japan and Yugoslavia), they are now growing rapidly. The United States, with the highest per capita income, has a moderate savings-investment ratio but also a relatively slow rate of growth over recent years; we had a much higher savings ratio during the nineteenth century.

There is some evidence that it takes about $3 to $4 of new capital goods to increase current income by about $1 annually in these countries (a "capital-output ratio" of 3 or 4 to 1). With a 4 to 1 marginal capital/output ratio, an economy that saves 4 per cent of its income to accumulate capital will, other things equal, increase its national income by about 1 per cent annually. Then, if population grows at about 1 per cent annually, per capita income is just held constant. To raise its living standard the economy must either save more or slow its population growth. Any saving

[3] E. E. Hagan has spelled out an entire theory of economic growth centering around these socio-economic interactions, which also uses modern psychological analysis of personal behavior patterns in the emerging societies (*On the Theory of Social Change*; Homewood, Illinois: Dorsey Press, 1962).

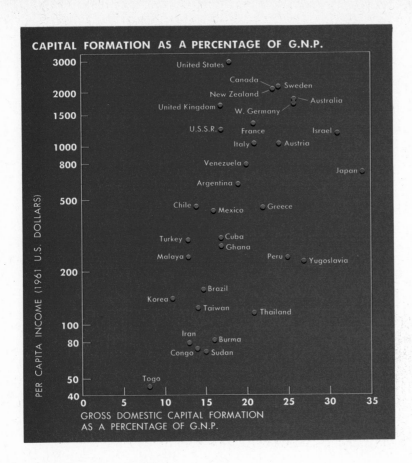

CAPITAL FORMATION AS A PERCENTAGE OF G.N.P.

PER CAPITA INCOME (1961 U.S. DOLLARS)

GROSS DOMESTIC CAPITAL FORMATION AS A PERCENTAGE OF G.N.P.

FIG. 18-4 High per capita incomes and high rates of capital formation generally go together, as interacting cause and effect. But there are exceptions; note Japan on the chart. (Source: United Nations. Data for 1964.)

rate below 4 per cent of income will mean *decreasing* per capita incomes.

This relationship between the capital output ratio and the rate of saving is illustrated by Table 18-3. If 4 per cent of total income is saved, there will be a 1.33 per cent increase in total annual output in case the capital/output ratio is 3–1, but only a 1 per cent increase with a 4–1 capital/output ratio. Similar differences exist for higher savings ratios. Obviously both higher saving ratios and lower capital/output ratios are good for economic growth. A few countries have apparently managed a capital-output ratio of 2, which has permitted them to expand output rapidly with modest saving ratios.

How can a nation be asked, or even forced, to save more when the great mass of its population is barely above subsistence level? Increasingly, the underdeveloped nations have turned to government tax and investment programs to obtain needed economic infrastructure—roads, schools, and sanitary facilities which aid development throughout the nation as a whole, even though no single investor could undertake them.

A few nations, for example India, have obtained substantial portions of their growth capital from abroad, both through private investment and through government aid. The United Nations estimates that the provision of capital by the developed to the underdeveloped nations rose from $2 billion in 1950 to $10 billion in 1965. But there again, the poor nations face a dilemma. With burgeoning national pride, they want no part of

TABLE 18-3
CAPITAL-OUTPUT AND SAVINGS RATIOS

Savings-Income Ratio	Annual Increase in Output (Percentage) with:	
	Capital-Output Ratio = 3–1	Capital-Output Ratio = 4–1
.04	1.33	1.0
.05	1.67	1.25
.10	3.33	2.5
.15	5.0	3.75

foreign control, and they distrust foreign investors who may try to exploit them and withdraw their profits once made. Thus, as badly as they need foreign capital, many of the poor nations have imposed restrictions on foreign capital, and they have hedged foreign companies around with restrictive controls reaching into day-to-day operations. A wide-armed welcome to foreign capital, aided by freedom to operate without crippling government restrictions, may seem to us an obvious answer to the capital-shortage plight of the underdeveloped nations. And the underdeveloped nations have been moving in this direction. But, much as they want more foreign capital, most have continued restrictions. The memories of exploitation under many decades of colonialism are still strong.

Technical Advance and Education

Technological advance and development of an educated, skilled labor force appear to have played a central role in the development of the Western economies. How can the poor nations achieve such technical advance?

Their problem may look easy—just borrow the technology of more advanced nations. Germany, as it developed industrially in the nineteenth century, was able to borrow productive processes developed in England. The U.S.S.R. adopted industrial methods and techniques from the West—in some cases, whole factories were reproduced. Recently India and China have imported technology heavily from both East and West. But the problems of such importation were outlined above—the necessity for heavy capital investment; the need for skilled laborers, technicians, and managers; the need for mass markets to justify many modern methods.

Think, for example, how you would go about introducing modern technology into Somalia, an emerging African nation of about 2 million people, most of them illiterate nomads. Literacy: perhaps 10 per cent. Total college graduates in the country: about 100. Per capita income: less than $50 a year. Politics: long-standing bitter rivalry among tribal groups. The problem is a far cry from the science, engineering, and management we think of in America as the solution to technological advance.

In fact, the biggest promise for technical change probably lies in agriculture rather than in industry. Primitive, low-productivity agriculture is the greatest millstone around the necks of the poor economies. Improving productivity in agriculture has led the way in nearly every case of growth—the U.S., Japan, the U.S.S.R. Here technology can be introduced in small stages, and with more modest capital costs—simple tools, fertilizers, improved irrigation.

Technological advance requires an educated labor force and willingness to accept change. Thus, mass education and development of a core of skilled technicians and teachers are goals of virtually every underdeveloped nation. Investment in education may not pay a fast return. But Figure 18-3 speaks for itself. The long-run payoff is big, in economic terms and in laying a foundation for a better life for all.

Steps toward mass education in the underdeveloped economies have been spectacular since World War II, in China and India and in many smaller nations. But schools are expensive and teachers are very scarce. Thus, educational efforts have been concentrated on the young. It will be generations before half the population in many of the underdeveloped nations is literate, much less educated to the point of being able to take on skilled jobs as we know them. Indonesia, with 110 million people, has two universities. The huge Republic of the Congo in Africa has one university, admitting a few hundred students a year. There are crying shortages of teachers in virtually every poor nation.

Population Policy

Growth theory suggests that output per capita will rise fastest when the ratio of capital to population increases. And history generally confirms this expectation. But it is precisely in the poorest countries that rates of population increases have generally been the highest. Look back at Fig. 18-3.

Governments have moved increasingly to encourage birth control and family planning. But the problem of providing effective bases for family planning among hundreds of millions of illiterate, widely scattered people is great. Religious barriers appear to be considerably less formidable than was previously believed. But in the underdeveloped economies, the family is often the economic and social unit, and parents must look to their children for support in old age. Once people in the poor nations recognize that with modern death rates they need not have seven or eight children to be reasonably sure three or four will survive, there is evidence that birth control may be more readily accepted in many of the underdeveloped areas.

Until the underdeveloped nations slow their rates of population growth, they are unlikely to escape far from Malthus' dire predictions. Even high growth rates in aggregate output cannot outdistance high rates of population growth. For many nations, Malthus' gloomy predictions still look more right than wrong. But the population experts are at last beginning to advance cautious predictions of widespread success of new birth-control approaches within the next two or three decades.

Balanced vs. Unbalanced Growth

In the underdeveloped nations and among the experts, the debate rages as to whether poor nations can grow faster by concentrating on the development of either industry or agriculture alone, or by striving to develop both sectors in balance.

Sooner or later, industrialization is necessary for full economic development. Every high-income nation in Table 18-1 has a major industrial and commercial sector. Transport and steel play prominent roles in industrialization. Adequate transport facilitates communication, permits specialization, and underlies mass production and mass markets. Steel is used in nearly every facet of modern industrial activity. Figure 18-5 shows the close correlation between miles of railroad per 10,000 people and per capita income levels. Figure 18-6 shows a similar correlation between per capita steel consumption and per capita incomes. Every

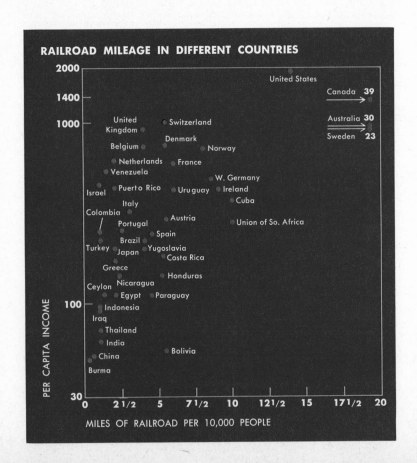

FIG. 18-5 Railroad density is also correlated with the extent of economic development, again probably as both cause and effect. (Source: United Nations. Data for late 1950's.)

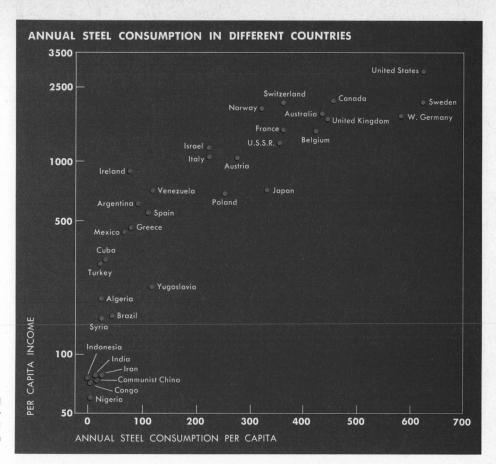

ANNUAL STEEL CONSUMPTION IN DIFFERENT COUNTRIES

FIG. 18-6 The highly developed nations use much more steel per capita than do the underdeveloped ones. (Source: United Nations. Data for 1964.)

growing nation longs for its own modern steel mill, as a symbol of national pride.

But mounting experience suggests that improving agricultural productivity is the first need if the underdeveloped nations are to break out of their vicious circle. With 70 or 80 per cent of the population in agriculture, that's where the mass of the problem is. A more efficient agriculture could produce more food for domestic use and export. More workers would be freed for gradual transfer to other jobs. In most successful cases of development, a gradual, then rapid, improvement in farm productivity has preceded industrialization. The U.S., Japan, and the U.S.S.R. are examples.

Some simple arithmetic dramatizes the importance of improving farm productivity. Suppose a nation wants to increase total output 5 per cent annually but finds it impossible to raise agricultural productivity. If the "modern," nonagricultural sector produces 20 per cent of total output, *its* productivity would have to increase 25 per cent a year in order to provide the desired over-all 5 per cent increase. Such a spectacular performance is hardly likely.

Thus, allocation of scarce capital to raising agricultural output makes sense. Improving agricultural efficiency through fertilizer, simple tools, and improved methods requires little capital compared to mass industrialization. It requires less social disruption, less transfer of people, less infrastructure, than does movement to a modern industrial sector.

But commercialization and industrialization are vital too, especially as a nation begins to rise above the poverty level. The debate over how much emphasis to place where remains unsettled. Different nations are following different policies; most are trying to develop agriculture and industry simultaneously. Perhaps 10 or 20 years hence we shall know the answer, *if* indeed there is a simple one.

Economic Planning or the Price System?

Many Americans, seeing the success of our largely private-enterprise, market-directed economy, argue that the underdeveloped nations should rely on private initiative and let the market place decide what should be produced and who should produce it. But this view has found little sympathy in the underdeveloped countries. There is too much to be done and too little evidence that individual initiative and the market place will bring the desired changes fast enough—if at all. These nations do not trust the unseen hand of Adam Smith to guide the complex process of growth, to assess the long-range importance of alternative uses of resources. They want roads, schools, fertilizers, and industrial plants now. And even in the successful developed countries, the growth process took generations under private enterprise—too slow in the eyes of nationalist leaders. Thus, government intervention on a wide scale is the active agent in underdeveloped nations. The main issue is whether it shall involve complete government control over economic life (as in Communist China) or merely government direction of broad lines of activity with wide scope left to private initiative (as in India).

Nearly everywhere it is agreed that government must provide infrastructure. Even where most of the economy stays private, basic investment priorities have become the province of the government. Nearly everywhere, foreign exchange is under government control, so that scarce foreign currencies are used for high-priority imports rather than for private luxuries.

But in recent years, the experts have increasingly turned back to the crucial importance of individual initiative, and the role of self-interest in providing that initiative. There is disenchantment with government planning to solve all the problems. Still, whether we like it or not, the American private-enterprise economy is not generally viewed as a very useful model for solving the problems of the underdeveloped countries.

Monetary-Fiscal Policy
and Economic Growth

Chapters 5 through 14 stressed aggregate demand and expansionary monetary-fiscal policy as steps to eliminate underemployment and stimulate investment. Why don't the governments of the poor nations use deficit-financed spending to set up factories and lure the surplus farm population away from disguised unemployment into useful work, thereby increasing output and improving everybody's welfare?

The answer is that the main result would probably be inflation rather than increased output. As in the U.S., speeding the long-term growth rate is basically a *real* "supply" problem, not one of inadequate demand. In the underdeveloped nations, use of monetary-fiscal policy even to eliminate underemployment promises doubtful success.

Suppose the government of Peru or Afghanistan prints money to lure workers into industry. There are no idle factories where output can be increased by calling the unemployed back to work. First the government must build the factories and provide the tools for the new workers. Where will it get the steel, machinery, skilled labor, und management? Foreigners will not ship in the essential real capital and managerial services merely for freshly printed promises to pay. Who will train the workers and managers? How will the government provide new living quarters for the families drawn into the cities? How will it get food to the cities to feed them in a largely nonmarket economy, with no regular distribution channels? Suppose all these obstacles are overcome. How long will it take before salable output begins to come out of factories manned by untrained workers, and where will the goods be sold when they are produced? Suppose the product is cloth; will there be a domestic market and distribution channels to tap the market, or will the government have to try to find markets abroad in the hectic international competition of the textile trade?

With all these obstacles to increasing real output, government spending without corresponding tax collections is likely to lead mainly to inflation as demand rises and supply does not. Rapid inflation may endanger the stability of the government. Sound government finances are the first thing outside investors look for. And the higher domestic costs and prices make it harder to sell in world markets, a major blow when foreign exchange is badly needed to finance imports.

To repeat, the problems of the underdeveloped economies are basically "real" problems. They are sectoral problems, of transferring resources into more efficient uses as well as improving their efficiency in existing uses. There is little basis for supposing that these problems can be solved by using the modern monetary and fiscal policies that seem so promising against unemployment in the Western economies. But inflation from deficit-financed government spending is one of the commonest of the poor nations' ailments. It's not hard to understand why. The pressure on the government to "do something" is enormous. Taxes are already a painful burden on the poverty-stricken masses. Maybe this time deficit-financed government spending will manage to increase real output and growth—that is the ever-present hope. But the common result is inflation and financial instability—an often inequitable form of forced saving and a major barrier to the foreign investment that is so desperately needed.

Two Important Cases:
India and China [4]

The underdeveloped areas are not just hard-to-remember small nations of Southeast Asia or Africa. One of every three living persons is Chinese or Indian. And these countries exemplify two drastically different approaches to the problem of economic development.

In many respects, India and China face similar problems. They are both vast land masses, heavily populated in many areas but with great reaches of mountains and wasteland. Both, in about 1950, had per capita incomes around $70–75 in present U.S. prices; China's was possibly lower. In both, around 80 per cent of the total population is engaged in agriculture. And both, since World War II, have undertaken vigorous planned programs of economic development.

India. In her first four "five-year plans," covering 1951 to 1971, India has chosen an essentially democratic approach. This has left freedom to private enterprise under broad government planning, while using government projects in such major areas as irrigation, transportation, and edu-

[4] John Lewis, *Quiet Crisis in India* (Washington, D.C.: Brookings Institution, 1962) and *An Economic Profile of Mainland China* (Joint Economic Committee of Congress, 1967), provide interesting overviews of the rival economies in action.

cation. Nearly half of total investment has been private. Taxes were raised only a little, and in spite of India's claim to be a "socialist" state the great bulk of her economic activity remains private. Government taxes and spending remain only about half as large a percentage of g.n.p. as in the U.S. and Western European nations. The plans pushed both industrialization and agricultural productivity—primarily the former at first, with more stress on agriculture recently. Industrial investment concentrated on both small-scale industry, such as textiles, and on larger projects such as power development, fertilizers, coal, and heavy manufacturing. The plans called for increased capital accumulation in both agriculture and industry, plus added government services.

Results of the first three plans have been mildly encouraging, but far from spectacular. Real national income rose 3 to 4 per cent per annum and population about 2½ per cent, giving perhaps a 1 per cent annual increase in per capita income —perhaps 75 cents a year. This is pitifully small, given the bitter poverty of India's masses. There was little increase in agricultural output, and it is not clear that the living standard of the Indian peasant is appreciably different from what it was a thousand years ago. The industrial improvement is more promising. Net investment rose from about 5 to over 10 per cent of net national product, and saving is apparently rising.

But the achievements were only about 75 per cent of the goals. Moreover, unemployment has risen from perhaps 10 to 20 million people in the cities, perhaps many more; no one has reliable statistics. Agriculture has been the great problem sector. And both the second and third plans would surely have foundered had not large-scale foreign aid been obtained to ease India's desperate foreign-exchange shortages as she tried to finance the imports required for food and capital investment. In the third plan, 25 per cent of the investment was scheduled to come from abroad, nearly half of it in the form of U.S. foreign aid. Figure 18-7 gives some impressions of how far India has come. But remember that this picture omits the massive problem of lagging food production. And recently, heavy military expenditures, reflecting concern over Indian relations with

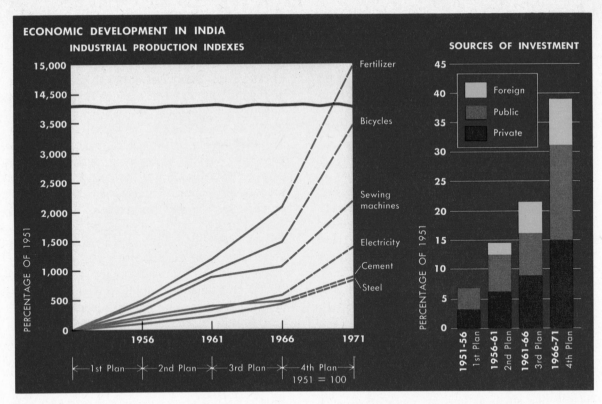

FIG. 18-7 India hopes to double her investment under the 4th Five-Year Plan, and to increase sharply the output of such products as fertilizers, steel, and consumer goods. (Source: Indian Government.)

both China and Pakistan, have cut the supply of civilian-type goods.

The government published its tentative fourth five-year plan in 1966. It calls for a 5.5 per cent annual growth in output and a large step-up in both public and private investment. The central theme is self-reliance for the Indian economy by 1975, but India hopes that foreign credits will finance about one-third of the investment called for by the fourth plan. Strikingly, this plan shifts top priority to agriculture and agricultural-support activities like irrigation and fertilizers. It also calls for a massive population-control program.

Most observers think the goals are unrealistically high. But Table 18-4 shows some of them.

The hopeful view is that India is on the verge of her take-off into self-sustaining growth. But her modest successes have been heavily dependent on foreign aid. Many Western observers, while admiring the humanistic, individualistic attitudes of India's leaders, believe she must have more firm, aggressive governmental leadership to make real progress in economic development.

248

TABLE 18-4 — INDIAN GROWTH TARGETS—THIRD AND FOURTH PLANS	Third Plan	Fourth Plan
Food grains (millions of tons)	72	120
Irrigation (millions of acres)	18	26
Fertilizers (millions of tons)	.8	3.4
Steel (millions of tons)	6	12
Cement (millions of tons)	11	20
Cotton cloth (billions of meters)	4.4	5.5
Machine tools (value-millions of rupees)	23	105

Bureaucracy, indecision, and red tape frustrate every foreign visitor who tries to help the Indians. Today India remains a restless giant, unsure of the success of her individualistic, humanistic program of mixed public-private enterprise.

China. China's first five-year plan, covering 1952–57, called for drastic increases in industrialization, collectivization of agriculture, and ruthless suppression of consumption to obtain the resources required for capital accumulation. The plan centralized economic control in the communist government. It called for rapid increases in agricultural output and mass transfer of agricultural population into industry. Voluntary private saving played only a small part; high government taxes on the masses were used to seize a far larger portion of total income for government investment than in India, and government-monopolized necessities were sold at high prices to yield large profits. The government channeled these funds into heavy investment. Hard work and long hours were forced on the Chinese people.

This was followed by a second five-year plan for 1957–62, which continued the same policies and called for an even larger increase in total output by 1962, over 10 per cent a year. This plan called for a "great leap forward" with the primary focus on heavy industry, although food targets were also up substantially. In 1958, government seizure of huge land masses and forced concentration of millions of agricultural families in huge "communes" virtually abolished individual family units and treated the peasants as hardly more than draft animals. Women were pressed into all areas of work on substantially the same basis as men, and children were placed in state nurseries. Communist dictation even of thought patterns made George Orwell's *1984* seem very real indeed.

Reliable information on China's recent economic progress is scarce. Western observers now agree that her economic advance during 1951–59 was remarkable, though short of the claims of the Chinese leaders. From a centuries-long, stagnant, poverty level, with a primitive family-type economy, per capita output apparently rose 4 or 5 per cent per annum during the decade, in spite of a huge growth in population. Industrial output appears to have risen at the spectacular rate of as much as 20 per cent per year. Net investment was pushed up to nearly 30 per cent of net national product. Food output rose substantially.

During the 1950's, on our best estimates, China's annual growth in total g.n.p. was nearly twice that of India; China's growth in industrial production was four times that of India. China's dictatorial methods, her disregard of the individual, her total reliance on central planning seemed to be winning the race by an uncomfortably wide margin.

At the end of the 1950's, something happened in China. Two years of bad weather brought massive crop failures, a heavy blow for a nation barely above the edge of starvation. The strains of the previous decade's massive conversion to industry and of the communists' ruthless abolition of traditional family values apparently forced a retreat. Industrial production fell. Since 1959 there have been no official communist figures on economic development in China, nor have Western observers been able to obtain more than scattered evidence. This evidence suggests that there was a large *reduction* in total output between 1959 and 1962, and that by the mid-1960's total g.n.p. was little higher than during the late 1950's. We know that the communists retreated substantially from their "communes" policy. Some land was returned to individual family ownership, and some degree of family life was restored. More stress was placed on food production, and industrialization plans were revised downward.

On the other hand, apparently industrial production began to rise rapidly again after 1962, and agriculture output moved up more gradually. From 1962 to 1966, total output may have grown by 5 per cent annually, industrial output at twice that rate. Then the widespread political turmoil of 1966–1967 apparently reduced total output again. Military production is a big drag on civilian industrial output. But reliable information is lacking.

What is the outcome of the race between China and India? The question is an extremely important one, for in the eyes of much of the world it is a race between democratic and communist ways, and between mixed and centrally planned approaches to economic development. During the 1950's, the results made bad reading for believers in Western democracy and private enterprise, for China was spurting ahead and India's progress was slow. China stumbled after 1959, and some Western observers thought they saw the beginning of a collapse of the Chinese economic revolution. The last few years may show that there are limits to which communist masters can push a people toward economic growth. The communists' abolition of traditional Chinese family values and individual initiative has been ruthless, and their suppression of individual choice and pressure for ever more and harder work relentless. Many Americans (and Indians) would say that Chinese economic progress, even if it does outdistance India's, is not worth its high price in terms of human values. But although the communist leaders have retreated somewhat and the Chinese economy has shown serious strains, the economic revolution is still in progress. The vitality and hard work of the Chinese people are impressive. Until the political crises of 1966–67, apparently China was again growing substantially faster than India.

India faces basic problems of human incentives, too. Can the Indian government implement its program of low consumption and capital accumulation among the people on a voluntary basis? Persuading a poverty-stricken population to hold down consumption in order to save is hard, perhaps impossible, in a democratic society; but to achieve sustained growth India must do it. India's success or failure will indicate whether social revolution and establishment of a balanced, prosperous economy are feasible without dictatorship and violence. It will determine whether democratic planning can effectively lay the foundations of the take-off into economic growth of a huge free nation.

The Future
of the Underdeveloped Nations

What is the future of the underdeveloped nations? Can they hope to "catch up" with the more developed nations?

Clearly many of the underdeveloped nations are economies in motion. But for such nations to catch up with U.S. per capita income in the foreseeable future is unbelievable. Even on the most optimistic assumptions of annual growth rates in the underdeveloped countries, the absolute gap between rich and poor nations is *widening* at a breakneck pace. A 2 per cent *annual increase* on $4,000 (roughly the present U.S. per capita figure)

is $80, about the *total* present annual per capita income in India and China. Even if the Indian-Chinese growth rates were to be double ours (say 4 per cent per capita as against 2 per cent)— a *most* unlikely situation—by the end of the century U.S. per capita income would still be nearly $8,000, Indian-Chinese about $300. Clearly the underdeveloped nations can raise their living standards greatly. Some have done so in the past two decades—Israel, Thailand, and Peru are examples. But most have made pitifully little progress, some have slipped backward. And even if success surpasses their wildest dreams, the absolute gap between the "haves" and "have nots" in our ever-smaller world seems certain to widen spectacularly over the years ahead.

UNITED STATES POLICY

Mankind is passing through the most pervasive revolution it has ever known—the revolt of two-thirds of the world's people against the poverty, misery, and degradation of their present conditions of life, and against the domination of the industrialized, wealthy, Western powers. The speed and force of this revolution are hard to perceive, sitting in the comfort of an American home or classroom. But they may well do more than any other force to determine the kind of world in which we will live a half century hence.

What should American policy be? As the world's richest nation, and the proud leader of a democratic, humanitarian tradition in today's world, what should we do to speed or slow this revolution? What interests do we have in the underdeveloped nations, many of whose names we scarcely recognize?

First, we are engaged in a contest with communism for world leadership. In a world of continued East-West tension, it is critical for us to keep many of the underdeveloped areas out of the communist orbit. If we want to maintain the prestige and attractiveness of the Western way, it is important that economic development in India and the free societies fare better than in China and the communist satellites. Whether we can buy political friendship and allegiance through help in economic development remains to be seen. This is a precarious and uncertain business. The countries that take our aid one day sometimes seem to turn on us the next, almost before the money is spent; Egypt's startling seizure of the Suez Canal in 1956 following substantial Western aid is a striking case. And we have often failed to capture the imagination and support of the people themselves; Vietnam is a painful example. But other results, for example, Mexico and India, have been more promising.

Second, our interests are economic. It would be foolish to overstress this element. Trade with the underdeveloped areas does not bulk large in the American economy. But remember that much of Latin America, one of our best customers, falls in the underdeveloped category. Except for foodstuffs and raw materials, there is relatively little direct competition in world markets between the developing economies and American exports. International exchange with such areas looks favorable for us.

Third, many Americans feel that we have a humanitarian interest in the relief of starvation, the lessening of disease and misery, and the improvement of education and living standards of the billions of people in the underdeveloped areas. There but for the grace of God go I, they say. We are very rich and they are very poor, and they need our help. Others disagree, especially when it comes time to pay the taxes to finance help to the underdeveloped nations. Here obviously is a moral issue on which you must make up your own mind.

Channels of American Aid

If we want to help, for political, economic, or humanitarian reasons, it is well first to ask the question: Can we really make any difference? The task of helping a billion people to a better life is a huge one. And the preceding pages surely show that the task is not simply one of providing a few dollars of foreign aid.

Yet we should remember some facts. The *total* income of *all* the billion people in the noncommunist underdeveloped nations in 1967 was less than $200 billion. The g.n.p. of the United States *alone* approached $800 billion. In 1967 we spent over $75 billion on military purposes. Total

arms spending in the world was perhaps $150 billion. Elimination of these war expenditures could have raised by over 50 per cent the living standard of each of the billion people.

The United States has the economic ability to help significantly. What have we done? What should we do?

Total Aid and Private Investment. First, let's take a summary look at the entire flow of government and multinational aid, plus private investment, to the underdeveloped countries. Table 18-5 summarizes this flow of funds and direct aid for 1965.

TABLE 18-5

LOANS, GRANTS, AND PRIVATE INVESTMENT IN UNDERDEVELOPED COUNTRIES, 1965 *

Source	Amount
Government loans and grants:	
From U.S.A.	$ 3.3
From other Western countries	2.6
International organizations	
(International Bank, International	
Development Association, United Nations)	1.8
Private net long-term investment	2.9
Total	$10.6

* Data from Organization for Economic Cooperation and Development. Does not include aid from China, the U.S.S.R., and other communist nations; or short-term credits and loans.

The $10.6 billion total shown in Table 18-5 has grown steadily over the past decade; it was $8 billion in 1960. The United States provides something like two-thirds of the total if we include U.S. contributions through international organizations.

Capacity of Underdeveloped Nations To Absorb Aid. Obviously the underdeveloped nations have a vast need for assistance. But, as a practical matter, how much aid in the form of foreign capital could they currently absorb effectively? The experts have come up with widely varying answers. But most estimates range between $10 and $20 billion a year. These estimates reflect the fact that development in most of the poor nations is held back by many other factors as well as capital—by lack of education, skilled workers, and managers; by unstable governments; by absence of initiative, and the like. It is clear that on these grounds some underdeveloped nations are much more "ready" to absorb foreign aid than are others, and some experts advocate concentrating aid on these nations.

1. *Government loans and gifts.* The most direct way for us to help is by government loans or gifts. Since World War II, U.S. government aid to other nations has totaled over $100 billion, first to Europe through the Marshall Plan and since then mainly to the underdeveloped nations. About two-thirds of this has been nonmilitary aid. In recent years such direct government aid has totaled around $3 to $3.5 billion annually. The biggest shares have gone to India and to Latin America.

For the most part this aid is provided through low-cost loans or direct grants, most of which must be spent on U.S. goods and services. One other big part has been direct transfers of surplus food (mainly wheat) from U.S. stocks. Such food is technically "sold" to the recipient country—for example, India. The Indian government, however, pays in rupees, which we agree to spend only for special purposes in India. The food is, thus, in large part a gift, since we are unlikely ever to use up all the rupees we accumulate. Insofar as the food is U.S. surplus, there is little real cost to us in sending our massive food grants to the underdeveloped nations.

2. *Private United States capital investment.* The large growth potential of the underdeveloped economies might seem attractive to American capital seeking investment at good rates of return. But the problems of breaking the vicious circle of poverty are apparent. Moreover, many of the underdeveloped nations distrust foreign investment as threatening foreign intervention and control. Thus they place special government regulations, special taxes, and special restrictions on withdrawal of profits on foreign investments. Moreover, many governments are unstable, and the next regime may decide to seize foreign property. Returns to foreign investors are often high, but risks are great.

Nevertheless, over the past decade private

U.S. investments in the underdeveloped nations have averaged $1 to $2 billion annually, with nearly two-thirds of the total going into Latin America. Total accumulated U.S. private investments in the underdeveloped areas by 1966 were over $20 billion, nearly all of them made during the postwar period.

Private direct investments in underdeveloped nations can hardly be considered U.S. aid, since presumably they are made as voluntary profit-seeking business ventures. However, they do represent a major source of capital for the underdeveloped nations, where capital is extremely scarce.

3. *Technical assistance.* After the postwar burst of enthusiasm for aid to the underdeveloped economies came the sobering recognition that many of the crucial problems were internal ones—ignorance and apathy among native populations, lack of real impetus for development, and unstable governments. Even billions of foreign aid might have little effect unless such factors were attacked vigorously and effectively by the underdeveloped nations themselves.

"Technical assistance" programs to help local governments and local peoples to help themselves have grown during recent years, partly because they seem to work well, partly because they are far cheaper than mass capital-investment grants. Assistance in establishing better schools, efficient local government administration, sanitation and public health projects, better farming techniques, and other such programs have generally proved successful.

U.S. and multinational technical assistance programs stress training natives to teach other natives and to take over essential jobs themselves at the earliest possible moment. In most cases, U.S. technical assistance has been provided on a matching basis, with half the cost of the joint programs being borne by local governments. Technical assistance is a bright spot in our foreign aid program.

4. *Lowering of international trade barriers and purchase of local products.* In order to grow, most underdeveloped countries must sell basic products abroad if they are to secure foreign exchange with which to finance needed imports. Many of the economies are centered around one

or two basic products—oil, rubber, nitrates, coffee, tin. Trade barriers that shut these products out of American markets strike a serious blow at the economies concerned. They raise understandable resentment among natives who hear American propaganda that we are anxious to help the developing nations. We have led the way in reducing tariff barriers and in helping to provide stable international markets for such basic commodities, but many underdeveloped nations think we should do still more.

5. *Military aid*. Presumably military aid is given mainly for military purposes. But in a country that would otherwise spend part of its national product on military activities, U.S. military aid provides direct relief to the local government budget. It thus permits local government spending to be focused on economic development.

Perspective

on United States Policy

How successful has American aid to underdeveloped countries been? If the test of success is maintenance of military alliances with America or neutrality vis-à-vis the communist bloc, the verdict is apparently favorable but still uncertain. If the test is friendliness and gratitude for American generosity, the verdict is at best mixed. Few people like to think they are objects of charity, and we probably make a great mistake to expect thankfulness in return. If the test is economic improvement and lessening of human misery abroad, the verdict is—some progress, but only a little.

To expect fast results from our foreign aid is unreasonable. Economic growth is at best a very slow process, even when the conditions are favorable. It is instructive to remember that the United States, with extremely favorable conditions for development, relied substantially on capital from abroad for nearly a century. It will, at best, be decades before substantial results become apparent from foreign aid to most of the underdeveloped nations. And even with this long lag, the results are far from certain. At most, foreign aid can only help. The real force for development must come from within the underdeveloped nations themselves.

What has our foreign aid to the underdeveloped nations really cost us? Although the total number of dollars is impressive in absolute size, it has been a tiny proportion of our total national output. Currently the aid program runs below ½ of 1 per cent of our g.n.p. Moreover, as indicated above, one big component of this aid is surplus food products. If we didn't send this food abroad, we would presumably just run up storage charges on it. Moreover, insofar as our foreign aid increases aggregate demand for American products when our economy is underemployed, such foreign aid may help increase our real g.n.p. Thus, it is by no means clear that the dollar totals reflect the real cost to the American public of providing aid to the developing nations.

Lastly, recognition of the powerful force of growing nationalism and the desire for status and respect in every underdeveloped country must be the cornerstone of successful aid, whatever our basic motives are. The battle for the friendship, or at least neutrality, of the underdeveloped areas is real and earnest. The communist bloc has proved itself highly effective in many of our propaganda and technical-aid skirmishes. As J. J. Singh, President of the India League of America, reported following a recent visit to Asia: "One of the main causes of resentment against the western powers is their arrogant assumption that the 'white fathers' know what is good for the backward Asian peoples. . . . A little friendly gesture, a little consideration, a little less of 'see what I am doing for your country,' a little respect for the aspirations and hopes of the Asian peoples will go a long way." In recognition of this attitude, some American observers, notably Senator J. W. Fulbright, have urged that all American foreign aid except technical assistance be channeled through international organizations, to remove any implication of political pressure or domination by the U.S. Those who want to use foreign aid as a political weapon or who want direct recognition understandably oppose such proposals.

Economic analysis can tell you a lot about the problem of raising living standards for the world's impoverished billions. It can give some guidance on how our help can do the most lasting good. But the problem of U.S. aid is moral and political as much as economic. It is one of the biggest issues on which this nation must take a stand over the decades ahead.

For Analysis and Discussion

1. Why don't people in many of the underdeveloped countries recognize what seems to most Americans the obvious superiority of the American economic way of life?

2. How well do the theories of Adam Smith and Malthus explain the plight of the underdeveloped nations? Has modern growth theory (from Chapter 15) added much to their analyses?

3. To develop rapidly, a nation must save and invest a substantial portion of its income. What steps would you advise the Indian government to take to increase India's saving rate when the majority of the population is on the brink of starvation?

4. A rapid increase in population is generally regarded as a major cause of poverty in underdeveloped countries like India, but is often thought to be an important cause of prosperity in the United States. Is this distinction a valid one? Explain your answer.

5. Development of an entrepreneurial class seems critical for nations trying to break out of the vicious circle of poverty. If you were a government official in Peru or the Congo, what would you do about this problem?

6. "Modern economics tells us to pump in purchasing power in order to eliminate unemployment when depression occurs in the Western world; but this approach has no relevance for the underdeveloped nations, where a shortage of real capital is the basic problem." Is this statement correct? Explain your answer.

7. The United States has spent over $70 billion annually for defense expenditures in recent years. Yet it has spent only about $2 billion annually on direct aid to the underdeveloped economies. Should we divert $10 billion annually from the military budget to an all-out effort to speed economic development and to win friends among the underdeveloped nations?

8. Will the gap between U. S. and underdeveloped nations' living standards narrow or widen over the next quarter-century?

9. Suppose the U. S. government sends you out to an underdeveloped nation to assess its development prospects over the next decade. What would be the key information you would seek for your report?

CURRENT RESEARCH

The main job of an elementary economics textbook is to stir an interest in economic problems, to present the central analytical tools of economics, and to provide some guided experience in using them to reach independent judgments on current economic developments and on public-policy measures. I hope that the preceding pages have conveyed some sense of the lively urgency of the problems with which economics deals, and some sense of the manner in which modern economics helps to solve them.

Economists spend much of their time using the tools presented here and helping to devise public policies that will make our economic system work better. But one of the further things that makes economics exciting is research—the fascination of probing for new knowledge and new insights into how the economic system works. Economics is far from a dead, stable body of theory and knowledge. It is the research of today that will make the better textbooks and the better world of tomorrow.

It is the purpose of these brief appendixes at the end of each Part to convey a brief impression of the kinds of research currently under way in economics. Some of the research cited is readily understandable by a good student at the elementary level; other parts are more difficult. But the purpose is not to provide references that all beginning students should read. Rather it is to suggest some samples of economic research that may be intriguing to students who want to look beyond the text and who want to know more about what economics is and what economists do. Pick out two or three and look at them. If they don't hit the spot, try another. The goal is to interest you and make you want to read further.

The following paragraphs report briefly a small sample of research on some major problems covered by Part Two. There is no intention to imply that they represent the best, or the most important, research under way on the problems covered. They are merely samples of research that one economist thinks might be interesting to curious students getting acquainted with economics. A major criterion in selection has been variety. A half-dozen other comparable lists could readily be provided—and, indeed, your instructor may be happy to provide one he feels is superior.[1]

Growth, Fluctuations, and Unemployment. Yale's James Tobin examines the case for faster growth as a major goal of national policy in "Economic Growth as an Objective of Government Policy" in the *American Economic Review* for May, 1964; look also at Herbert Stein's rejoinder. For perspective on growth in the long sweep of the history of the world, try Simon Kuznets' fascinating "Notes on the Pattern of U.S. Economic Growth," in *The Nation's Economic Objectives* (Univ. of Chicago Press, 1964). A quite different view of growth is given by A. D. Chandler's *Ford, G.M., and the Automobile Industry* (Harcourt, Brace & World, 1965), a case study of one major industry; and by Chap. 6 of W. Baumol's provocative little book, *Business Behavior, Value and Growth* (Macmillan, 1967). Lastly, Edward Denison's "How To Raise the High-Employment Growth Rate by One Percentage Point" (*American Economic Review*, May, 1962) presents a program that may lead you to re-examine your ideas.

On the reduction of unemployment as a national goal and some measures for dealing with it, *Prosperity and Unemployment*, R. A. and M. S. Gordon, eds. (Wiley, 1966) summarizes the views of many of America's leading economists; as does *Men*

[1] A number of the following references, in this and other appendices on current research, have been reprinted in M. Joseph, N. Seeber, and G. L. Bach, eds., *Economic Analysis and Policy*, second edition (Prentice-Hall, 1966).

Without Work, S. Lebergott, ed. (Prentice-Hall, 1964). Robert Solow's *The Nature and Sources of Unemployment in the United States* (Almquist and Wiksell, 1964) analyzes the structural vs. lack of aggregate demand controversy over the causes of unemployment. Walter Heller of the University of Minnesota, chief economic policy adviser to Presidents Kennedy and Johnson, lays out his views on the application of economic analysis to policy in *New Dimensions of Economic Policy* (Harvard Univ. Press, 1967).

If you're interested in some of the newer developments in economic forecasting and know a little mathematics, two recent pieces will give you a good introduction: "Forecasting With an Econometric Model," by Michigan's Daniel Suits (*American Economic Review*, March, 1962), and "A Short-term Forecasting Model," by Pennsylvania's I. Friend and P. Taubman (*Review of Economics and Statistics*, August, 1964). A good survey of all the modern forecasting techniques is provided by Part One of W. Butler and R. Kavesh, *How Business Economists Forecast* (Prentice-Hall, 1966).

Money and Inflation.   For an introduction to research on the role of money in growth and fluctuations, try "The Money Supply and Stable Economic Growth," by Stanford's E. S. Shaw, in *United States Monetary Policy* (The American Assembly; Columbia Univ. Press, 1958). Chicago's Milton Friedman summarizes his findings on the same problem in "The Supply of Money and Changes in Prices and Output," in *The Relation of Prices to Economic Stability and Growth*, a compendium of papers published by the Joint Economic Committee of the Congress in 1958.

This same compendium provides a broad picture of recent research relating to inflation. Sample the volume. You will find a wide range of approaches, from abstract theoretical analysis to careful empirical analysis, laced with a generous supply of advice to the Congress on what to do about inflation. The paper by Harvard's Otto Eckstein (pp. 361 ff) provides a good starting point. A broader approach, which combines economic, social, and political factors, is illustrated by G. L. Bach's *Inflation: A Study in Economics, Ethics and Politics* (Brown Univ. Press, 1958).

The Underdeveloped Economies.   There is a flood of research on the underdeveloped economies, why they are underdeveloped, and how they might grow faster. For a starter, try Albert Hirschman's *Journeys Through Progress* (Doubleday, 1963), on Latin America; or John Lewis' *Quiet Crisis in India* (Brookings, 1962). Wisconsin's R. Cameron summarizes recent experience in "Some Lessons of History for Developing Nations" (*American Economic Review*, May, 1967). At a more detailed, and more controversial, level, the Joint Economic Committee of Congress' compendium, *An Economic Profile of Mainland China* (two volumes, 1967) presents the views of a number of experts on recent developments in mainland China. See especially Volume 1.

PART THREE

MARKETS,
THE PRICE SYSTEM,
AND THE ALLOCATION
OF RESOURCES

In Part Two we were concerned mainly with macro-economics—with economic growth, fluctuations, unemployment, the price level, and the big public policy questions they raise. We paid little attention to the individual goods and services that make up g.n.p.—to how many cars and carpets are produced, to the incomes different individuals receive, to the behavior of individual businesses, and the like. Now, in Parts Three and Four we turn to micro-economics—to look at the individual units that make up our economy, at their functioning, at the prices they pay and charge, and at incomes that different individuals receive.

Imagine we are flying over America, looking down at the economy in operation. We would see millions of individual consumers spending their incomes on what they want most. We would see these purchases providing signals to businessmen on where the largest profits could be made, and businessmen responding to those signals by producing what consumers want to buy. We would see competition among sellers forcing prices down toward the lowest possible cost of producing those goods and services. We would observe that each worker generally earns the most by working where he can contribute the most to producing what consumers demand, because that is where businesses can afford to pay him the most. We would see a constantly shifting mix of goods and services being produced, as consumers change their minds as to what they want, and as businessmen try to meet these shifting consumers' demands.

For the most part, no one guides this vast, interlinked process. Workers' self-interest in trying to earn a good living, businessmen's self-interest in trying to earn large profits, consumers' self-interest in spending their incomes on what they want most—these millions of free choices are meshed together through many interlinked markets, where prices and quantities produced move up and down in response to changing demands and supplies. Viewed from above, Adam Smith wrote, it is as if a beneficent invisible hand were guiding the system so as to allocate our scarce productive resources to yield the most of what we want at the lowest possible costs.

Today's economy is far from Adam Smith's competitive ideal. And today a lot of people feel that Adam Smith was too optimistic, that any market-type economy falls short on many scores. They feel that collective (government) action is needed to make it work better, both through government regulation of the economy and through direct government provision of goods and services (such as education, highways, and national defense). We can appreciate the virtues of a private-enterprise market-type economy, and still recognize the strength of these reservations. Indeed, Part Five is devoted entirely to "The Public Sector," where the government takes over from private markets.

The following chapters take up the main actors in the American market system, beginning with the business firm, then the consumer, and then the interaction of consumer demands and business responses in different markets. Seeing the individual parts and how the individual actors behave is important. But as you go along, don't lose sight of the big picture of how the whole system fits together. For that's where we will come out at the end. And it's against that backdrop that you need to see today's issues, and to make up your mind on the policy problems we will face in the rapidly changing economy of the 1970's.

NINETEEN

BUSINESS ENTERPRISE IN THE MODERN ECONOMY

Entrepreneurs, Plants, Firms, and Industries.

The Modern Corporation.

Business Consolidations and Combinations.

Conclusion.

Appendix: The Elements of Business Accounting.

In a private-enterprise economy, the businessman is at the center of the economic process. He decides what will be produced, and how much of it. He decides how many employees to hire and how much he is willing to pay them. It is he who responds to consumer demands, and pays out most of the incomes. Within the framework of rules established by society, his decisions and policies determine most directly how effectively the private-enterprise economy functions.

In America today, government controls over business operations are numerous—so numerous that some businessmen protest that their traditional freedom is gone. Government produces some goods and services itself, in addition to its controls; and its demands in the market (for missiles, highways, schools, and many thousands of other products) give it important powers over the businesses from which it buys. Labor unions press increasingly for a share in the traditional prerogatives of management. But the businessman, harassed though he may be, remains the organizing agent at the center of our economy.

The purpose of this chapter is to provide a factual background on modern business enterprise, what it is and how it operates.

ENTREPRENEURS, PLANTS, FIRMS, AND INDUSTRIES

Business enterprises are called "firms." John Brown and his family run a farm; the farm is a firm. United States Steel is a firm, with steel mills in many cities, with iron and coal mines, with ore ships on the Great Lakes. The important characteristic of the firm is that it is owned and controlled essentially as a unit, however diverse its parts.

The function of making fundamental policy decisions in a firm is generally called "entrepreneurship." The entrepreneur decides when to establish a firm, what goods to produce, how the concern will be financed, what price policies to follow, when to expand or contract, and so on. A firm is thus a business unit under one coordinated "entrepreneurship."

In the independent corner grocery store, the proprietor is the entrepreneur. He decides whether to borrow funds to remodel his store, what prices to set on his merchandise. In bigger businesses, it is harder to pick out the entrepreneur. For example, who is the entrepreneur of American Telephone and Telegraph? The 3 million stockholders? The board of directors? The finance committee of the board? The president? Here it is impossible to pick out any person or group of persons as the entrepreneur; the functions of the entrepreneur are performed in a coordinated way by the various individuals and groups concerned.

A "plant" is a building or a group of buildings, along with other more or less fixed physical equipment, that are used together in producing something—such as a shoe-manufacturing plant or an auto-assembly plant. The Ford Motor Company is a firm with plants in Dearborn, St. Louis, Kansas City, and so forth. John Brown's farm, on the other hand, is a firm with only one plant.

An "industry" is harder to define. Usually we use the word to mean all the producers of any "commodity." Farmer Brown is part of the wheat industry if he produces wheat, part of the corn industry if he produces corn; he may be in both simultaneously. General Motors is part of many industries. The trouble comes when we try to be precise. Shall we consider a "motor-vehicles industry," or an "auto industry," or a "low-priced auto industry"? For elementary purposes, how finely we divide up commodities is not a major problem. You will seldom get in trouble if you let common sense be your guide and if you stick to the same definition of "commodity" and the associated "industry" throughout the analysis of any problem.

The Shifting Legal Organization of Firms

The legal forms of business firms have changed with the times. When small-scale business was the rule, the individual proprietorship was dominant. This is a simple arrangement in which an individual puts up the money, starts his own business, runs it himself, and has the profits and losses to himself. There are still more individual proprietorships in the United States than any other form of business organization—some 9 million in all. Of these, 3 million are in agriculture, and most of the rest are small-scale retail concerns and service enterprises, such as cleaning establishments, filling stations, doctors, lawyers, and so on.

As the need for larger capital funds increased, partnerships became popular. In these, two or more people assume joint proprietorship—usually joint provision of funds, joint management, and joint financial responsibility. This arrangement has substantial advantages over the single proprietorship, but it still falls short of providing enough capital for really large-scale business operations. And it shares one serious drawback with the single proprietorship: The partners are personally liable for all the debts of the business. Thus, in most cases, each partner is personally liable to an *unlimited* amount for the deeds of the other partners—a somewhat precarious position at best, and definitely not suited to drawing in funds from absentee investors. Partnerships are not very important in the United States today, though there are some 900,000 in existence. About half of them are in retailing; the rest are widely scattered.

THE MODERN CORPORATION

The modern corporation, conceived largely to meet the needs of large-scale business organization and to avoid the drawbacks of the other arrangements, has become the dominant form of American business enterprise. Although there are only about 1 million business corporations, they do the bulk of the nation's business, employ over 60 per cent of the workers, account for about two-thirds of the nation's privately produced income, and pay out over 50 per cent of the total national income. They do virtually all the business in public utilities, manufacturing, transportation, and finance; around half in trade and construction; but less than a quarter in services and agriculture.

The biggest modern corporations are truly Goliaths. In 1967, for example, the assets of the American Telephone and Telegraph Company (the world's largest business) exceeded $35 billion. Those of Standard Oil of New Jersey and of General Motors were $13 billion. G.M.'s 1967 sales of $20 billion were larger than the entire gross national product of most of the world's nations. In all, in 1967 there were 80 nonfinancial corporations with sales over a billion dollars.

Many financial corporations (banks and insurance companies) are as large, though most of their assets consist mainly of investments in corporate and government securities and of direct loans to businesses and individuals. In 1967, the total assets of the Prudential Life Insurance Company, the largest insurance company, approached $25 billion. Those of the Bank of America and the Chase Manhattan Bank, the two biggest banks, approached $20 billion.

Modern finance and industry are heavily concentrated in the hands of large firms, as we shall see in Chapter 27. Nevertheless, there are still many more small firms than large ones, and big business has been only gradually increasing its share of the total market in manufacturing over recent decades. And if we include government and other non-profit service industries (e.g., health and education), the share of the total national income produced by private corporations has declined slightly since hitting a peak of 55 per cent in the mid-1950's.

What Are Corporations?

A corporation is an organization that exists as a "legal-person" apart from the individuals who own and control it. A corporation may carry on business in its own name, enter into contracts, sue and be sued, own property, borrow and lend money. In general, it may as a business unit do all the things that any individual person may legally do in business.

For a long time, corporation charters specified the purpose of the corporation rather closely. Today, however, the corporation charters granted by most states are broad grants of power with only vague statements of corporate purposes that exercise little restraint over what corporations do or where they operate.

The main advantages of the corporate form of organization center around its financial arrangements. Briefly, these advantages are the following:

1. Stockholders who invest money in corporations have no liability for the debts of the corporation; at worst, they can lose their original investment. Thus, corporations can obtain funds by selling "stock" and "bonds" to many investors who merely want to earn a return on their investments without further financial involvement. These advantages are spelled out below.

2. In a corporation, management is delegated to a board of directors elected by the stockholders. The directors in turn supervise the salaried officials who actually run the business. Thus, the individual stockholder need not concern himself with the details of managing the concern unless he wishes to—quite another story from the continuous attention required in a single proprietorship or partnership. Freedom to delegate power and responsibility to expert "managers" is essential to the operation of today's mammoth business enterprises.

3. Corporate securities are readily transferable. No matter how many individual stockholders die or lose interest in the corporation, the business can go on unaffected.

Financing Corporate Enterprise— Stocks and Bonds

Corporations obtain funds by selling "corporate securities" to savers. Individual investors who buy these securities may be part-owners of the corporation, or they may simply lend money to the business. Corporate securities correspondingly fall into two broad classes: stocks, which represent ownership in the corporation; and bonds, which represent money lent to the corporation by bondholders. There are many variations within each class, and at the margin they run together. The most important differences are in: (1) the priority of the security-owner's claim on the income of the enterprise; and (2) the owner's right to vote on personnel and corporate policy, and hence his power to control the corporation.

Common stockholders are the owners of a corporation. They own the company's "stock." They have the right to elect the board of directors and hence to control the policies of the corporation. They are entitled to any income remaining after prior claims of creditors have been met. If the corporation is dissolved, they are entitled to all that remains (if anything) after everyone else has been paid. The common stockholders are the "residual claimants" to the corporation's income and property. They gain the most when income is high, and they are the first to lose when things go badly.

Profits paid out to stockholders are called "dividends." Although the profits of the business "belong" to the stockholders, often the corporation does not pay them all out, but instead re-invests part in the business. This is called "plowing back" earnings. Whether the net income is paid out or re-invested, however, it accrues to the benefit of stockholders, since re-invested earnings increase the value of the business.

Bondholders are creditors of the corporation. They own "bonds" issued by the company. When corporations want to borrow large sums for long periods, they commonly issue bonds that are sold to people or institutions with funds to invest. Bonds are promises by the corporation to repay the funds to bondholders, at some specified future date with a set rate of interest.

If you own a bond, you are merely a creditor. You ordinarily have no voting power to elect directors and control the corporation's policies. You take less risk than the stockholders, since the interest on your bonds must be paid before they get any dividends. On the other hand, you will receive only your set rate of interest no matter how big profits are. Bondholders also have a prior claim on the assets of the corporation in case of liquidation. Some bonds provide that if a corporation fails to pay interest when due, voting power is automatically given to bondholders so that they can protect their interests by having a voice in directing the policies of the business.

Preferred stockholders have a position intermediate between common stockholders and bond-holders. Preferred stock sometimes carries a vote; more often it does not. Typically, it has a set rate of dividends, say $6 per share, that must be paid before any dividends can be paid on the common stock. It also has priority over common stock in case of liquidation. But preferred stock stands behind bonds in priority of claim on income and assets.

Who Controls the Corporations?

Suppose you own 100 shares of General Electric stock. How much control do you have over how General Electric is run?

The answer is, for practical purposes, none. Not because anyone is cheating or hoodwinking you—least of all the G.E. management, which makes a continuous effort to keep stockholders informed and to get them interested in company affairs. It is because of a combination of factors. In the first place, you own only a tiny fraction of 1 per cent of the company's stock. Moreover, you don't and can't know much about the operations and internal policies of G.E., a $7 billion corporation producing thousands of products, most of them involving complex scientific processes and know-how. Besides, G.E. is paying good dividends on your 100 shares, that's what you bought them for. You haven't the slightest intention of spending a lot of money and time on an obviously fruitless trip all the way to Schenectady, New York, to try to tell the management how to run company affairs, or to throw them out for a new management.

To be sure, even if you don't go to the annual stockholders' meeting, you are entitled to send a "proxy," a person of your choice whom you designate to vote for you. Before each annual meeting, you will receive from the management a proxy form, suggesting that you designate either a management representative or someone else to vote in case you don't plan to be present. You may throw the proxy in the waste basket. If you do send it back, the chances are you'll designate the person suggested—partly because you don't know whom else to designate—thereby giving the present management the votes to re-elect themselves.

Surprisingly enough, you will be acting like the typical stockholder when you do this, even though you assume there are many other interested "big" stockholders who are keeping a sharp eye on the operating management from a stockholder viewpoint. A.T. & T. now has 3 million stockholders, no one of whom owns as much as 1 per cent of its stock. U.S. Steel has over 300,000 stockholders, Westinghouse over 175,000. On the other hand, a few well-to-do people own large blocs of stock in many well-known companies.

This wide dispersion of stock ownership, coupled with the lethargy of most stockholders, goes far to explain the substantial control over most large corporations exercised by small groups of active stockholders, and often by the operating management "insiders" who may themselves own very little stock. This divorce of active control from ownership is a major development of modern business enterprise. It is probably inevitable in the large corporation. It certainly does not provide a "democratic" government of corporation affairs in most cases, however good the intentions of the management on this score.

Of course, stockholder lethargy does not always exist. In some smaller companies, stockholders take an active interest in the conduct of the business. Even in large corporations, conflicts and sharp struggles for proxies sometimes occur, with control of the corporation at stake. But for the most part, minorities retain effective control without holding more than a small fraction of the voting stock. They are on the scene; most of the stockholders are far away and little interested.

Less than 10 per cent of the voting stock is enough to assure working control of most major corporations. Indeed, most existing managements operate with less. A 1963 study on this point covered the 200 largest nonfinancial corporations in the United States. In 85 per cent of the corporations, control was exercised by the management without material stock ownership. None of the corporations was directly controlled by a private family through ownership of over 50 per cent of the stock; and in only 12 per cent was direction exercised by a particular family or other special group of stockholders with a substantial share of the stock—say 20 to 50 per cent. Cases where the "management" (directors and officers together) hold more than 5 per cent of the company's common stock are the exception rather than the rule.

By contrast, in 1929 only 44 per cent of the top 200 companies were management-controlled, while 50 per cent were controlled by families or other special groups through substantial blocks of stock holdings. Clearly, there has been a managerial revolution in the way our major corporations are controlled.[1]

What proportion of the public owns corporation stock? By 1967 there were about 20 million individual stockholders in "publicly owned" corporations, plus probably 1 to 2 million more in "privately owned" companies whose stock was held entirely by family or private control groups. The comparable total for 1955 was only 6 or 7 million.

Thus, perhaps 15 per cent of all adults now own stock in business corporations. This is a large number, and many big companies have more stockholders than employees. But it is still a small fraction of the population. This fact, together with minority and "insider" control even in the most widely owned corporations, makes it clear that America's corporations are still largely controlled by a few people. Most of the 20 million stockholders are small owners. A large portion of all individually owned stock, as we shall see in the next section, is held by only a few thousand wealthy individuals and families.

BUSINESS CONSOLIDATIONS AND COMBINATIONS

Many of today's big corporations are the result of consolidations and mergers of separate companies. Over the past century, business combination has been a persistent, though irregular, trend. Today, the once-popular business "trusts" of the 1800's have almost vanished from the scene. But "holding companies" remain a prevalent form for organizing financial control over large aggregations of capital. And mergers and consolidations of existing firms have reached record-breaking levels.

[1] The data are from R. J. Larner, "Ownership and Control in the 200 Largest Nonfinancial Corporations," *American Economic Review*, Sept. 1966. See also R. A. Gordon, *Business Leadership in the Large Corporation* (Washington, D.C.: Brookings Institution, 1964), Chapter 2.

The Trusts

In a "trust," property is held by a trustee who has power to administer it and to dispense the income from it, as directed by the owners of the property. This scheme has often been used by people who want to have funds held safely for the benefit of their children, and for other similar purposes. The business trust was ordinarily a corporation formed to hold stocks in a number of other corporations. Owners of stock in the controlled corporations turned their securities over to the trustee corporation and received "trust certificates" on which dividends were paid. Technically, they remained owners of the stock, but their power to vote was transferred to the trustee organization which could then eliminate competition among the individual companies.

In the decade of the 1880's, the trusts grew rapidly. The most famous was the Standard Oil Company, under John D. Rockefeller. Some of the others were the whiskey, cordage, national lead, and sugar trusts.

The Holding Companies

The Sherman Antitrust Act of 1890 led to a shift away from trusts. Then the holding company became the dominant tool for concentrating control.

The holding company is similar to the trust, with one primary difference. The trust simply holds the shares of the controlled companies as trustee; it does not own them outright. The holding company buys up stock in the companies it wants to control. As the name indicates, the holding company typically owns and holds securities of other corporations; it frequently owns no land, machinery, or other such operating property itself.

Figure 19-1 illustrates how a holding company might be used to concentrate control over a vast amount of capital with a minimum of investment. Suppose there are 12 railroads, A through L. Each is capitalized at $100 million, of which half is bonds, one-fourth is nonvoting preferred stock, and one-fourth is common stock. Suppose we want to get control of these railroads, but we don't have enough money to buy control of each. The maximum total investment required to get control of railroad A is just over $12.5 million,

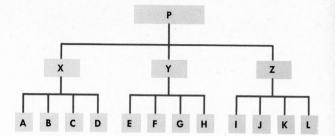

FIG. 19-1 Holding companies provide a device for holding control over a large amount of corporate assets with a relatively small investment.

which is the value of half the voting stock. We would need the same amount for each of the other railroads, if we assume that half the common is actually needed to maintain control. Actually, a smaller amount would probably do.

In this situation, we can form holding company X to buy up control of railroads A, B, C, and D. The total capital required is $50 million, since $12.5 million is needed to get control of each of the four roads. To raise this fund, suppose we sell $25 million of bonds, $12.5 million of preferred, and $12.5 million of common, in a new holding company X. Since only half the common stock is required to control company X, we need buy only $6.25 million of the common ourselves to hold control. We obtain the rest of the funds from the public. Then suppose we do the same with holding companies Y and Z to buy up control of railroads E, F, G, and H, and I, J, K, and L, respectively. We now have control of all 12 railroads, with a capital of $1.2 billion, through investing only $19 million, the amount necessary to control holding companies X, Y, and Z.

But we can go further. To control the three holding companies, about $19 million is necessary. Suppose we form another holding company, P, capitalized at $20 million, to raise these funds (as shown in the table). In forming company P, we issue $10 million of bonds, $5 million of preferred, and $5 million of common. Since only half the common is needed to control, we need put up only $2.5 million to retain control of P, with the remainder of the securities sold to the public. With this $2.5 million investment, we now have control over the entire $1.2 billion set of operating railroads. Since many stockholders fail to vote their holdings, we might be able to do the job with even less cash.

Total investment of $1.2 billion controlled by an investment of $2.5 million in the second-degree holding company, P:

Each operating company (A-L) has:

Total capitalization of	$100,000,000
Bonds	50,000,000
Preferred stock	25,000,000
Common stock (voting)	25,000,000

Each "first-degree" holding company (X, Y, Z) has:

Total capitalization of	$ 50,000,000
Bonds	25,000,000
Preferred stock	12,500,000
Common stock (voting)	12,500,000

The "second-degree" holding company (P) has:

Total capitalization of	$ 20,000,000
Bonds	10,000,000
Preferred stock	5,000,000
Common stock (voting)	5,000,000

This hypothetical example may seem fantastic. As a matter of fact, it is not. For example, in the 1930's a court found that Howard Hopson, a shrewd promoter, had managed to maintain control of the billion-dollar Associated Gas and Electric holding-company system with approximately $100,000 of voting stock. Holding companies in the public utilities and railroad fields attained almost unbelievable complexity. A diagram of the companies included in the famous billion-dollar Insull utility holding-company empire in the late 1920's would take up three or four of these pages in this size print. This was one of the most blatant cases of "insider" control and self-seeking. Small and large investors lost every cent of their investments in the Insull holding-company securities in the great crash of the early 1930's. Such abuses led to the Public Utility Holding Company Act of 1935, which ordered dissolution of all such public-utility holding-company systems.

Such familiar companies as American Tobacco, U.S. Rubber, American Can, and U.S. Steel were established as holding companies around the turn of the century. Since then, however, the holding-company approach to consoli-

dating economic control has waned outside of finance. Now direct mergers account for most intercorporate combinations. Since 1960, major corporate mergers have averaged over 1,500 annually.

Financial Control Groups in the Modern Economy

By means of large investments coupled with extensive use of financial holding companies and other minority control devices, a few very powerful financial groups have attained tremendous power over the corporate structure of the nation. Grouping the 50 largest financial corporations with the 200 largest nonfinancial, the National Resources Committee found in the late 1930's that out of total assets of $115 billion for the whole lot, the J. P. Morgan-First National Bank of New York group controlled over $30 billion, and that the Kuhn Loeb investment banking interest controlled over $10 billion, primarily railroads. Of the purely family groups, the Rockefellers controlled over $6 billion; the Mellons over $3 billion; and the DuPonts over $2.5 billion. Today the dollar amounts are much larger. By the mid-1960's it was estimated that the stock holdings alone of the DuPont, Rockefeller, and Mellon families exceeded $4 billion each. Since the extent of corporate control was undoubtedly far larger, the assets controlled by such wealthy family groups were enormous indeed, although the economy has grown so rapidly that the proportion controlled by such family blocs has declined steadily.

The upshot is that although ownership of today's big corporation is wide-spread, the holdings of most individuals are small and a large part of the total is owned by a small portion of the population. Sketchy surveys suggest that the top 1 per cent (about 550,000) of the families hold around two-thirds of all privately held stock. Although there are 20 million stockholders, most own only a few thousand dollars' worth of stock.

A big, and growing, share of all corporate stock is held by financial institutions—pension funds, bank trust departments, mutual funds, insurance companies, and the like. They probably now hold around a third of the total. To date, such financial institutions have seldom intervened directly in corporate management. But as savings pile up in such institutions, their potential power becomes enormous, far exceeding that of even the wealthiest families. Even corporations' and unions' own pension funds, amounting to billions of dollars, are now being invested in corporation stocks, posing intriguing problems of future corporate control. Who should watch over the managers of these vast accumulations of funds?

CONCLUSION

Concentration of business management in the hands of a small number of professional, salaried managers who have little direct contact with most of the owners of business is one of the major developments of twentieth-century industrial society. Coupled with this development is a concentration of financial control over the modern financial and industrial worlds by a small fraction of the population, although stock ownership is widespread among small holders.

It would be a mistake to infer from these facts that the "insiders" are using their operating control to the disadvantage of either other stockholders or consumers. On the contrary, many big business concerns are now managed both more efficiently and with a greater view to social welfare than they were under the direct control of owner-operators. If you have $5,000 invested in General Motors, it is doubtful that your interests would be better protected were Messers. James Roche and Edward Cole (the top executives of G.M.) larger stockholders than they in fact are, or if you could personally participate in the management of the business. In Messrs. Roche and Cole you are hiring a much-admired team of experts in managing a huge corporation. In general, it seems safe to assume that their goals are roughly what

yours would be (maximizing profits, for example), and that they are more expert at achieving the objectives than you would be.

Similarly, today's growing group of professional managers seems more concerned with serving the public well than was the typical captain of industry a half-century ago. Certainly the drive to "feather his nest" on a large scale is less dominant with the professional salaried manager, because he personally has so much less to gain from such behavior than did the more picturesque industrial tycoon. The earlier attitude of "the public be damned" may still exist in some companies, but it has been largely replaced by a more responsible attitude among the professional managers. Nor is there much evidence that the dominant large stockholders use these positions to exploit other stockholders or the public. Indeed, many investors prefer such companies as DuPont and Alcoa partly because they want the watchful guidance given these companies by the DuPont and Mellon families. And, whatever the abuses of big business over the years—and we shall see that there have been some—the research and mass production underlying the present spectacular American standard of living generally trace back to these same industrial giants, whose monopoly powers consumers may have grounds to fear.

There is little likelihood that the modern corporation, with its vast accumulations of capital and its professional management divorced from most stockholders, will soon disappear from the American scene. This raises a big problem for every thoughtful observer. How shall we obtain the obvious advantages offered by such huge industrial concerns while at the same time avoiding the excesses which the American public has typically feared from large concentrations of economic power? This is the problem we will come to in Chapters 27 and 28.

REVIEW

Concepts To Remember

The concepts in this chapter deal largely with institutions and legal forms. Be particularly sure that you understand the following:

entrepreneur	common stock
plant	"plowed-back" earnings

firm	preferred stock
industry	bond
individual proprietorship	trust
partnership	holding company
corporation	merger

For Analysis and Discussion

1. Suppose you are planning to set up a small shoe repair shop. Will you be better off with a single proprietorship, a partnership, or a corporation as your legal form of business? What are the main considerations involved in choosing?

2. Single proprietorships and partnerships predominate in retailing and agriculture, while corporations dominate the manufacturing industries. How do you account for these differences? How can you reconcile the above statement with the great success of such retail giants as A&P and Sears, Roebuck?

3. Public-opinion polls repeatedly indicate that the majority of the public view common stocks as a speculative and somewhat uncertain investment. How do you account for this fact, in view of the great growth in the aggregate value and earnings of American corporations over the past century?

4. If you are a stockholder in General Motors, would you prefer to have earnings paid out to you as dividends or directly re-invested by the management? Why?

5. Should individual stockholders in business concerns take a more active part in the management of the concerns involved? Why or why not?

6. (*Based on the Appendix*) Construct the profit-and-loss statement of the Amalgamated Widget Company for 1967 from the following data.

(000's omitted)

Materials used	$ 400
Net sales	2,500
Selling costs	150
Dividends on common stock	50
Provision for income taxes	180
Wages and salaries paid	400
Interest paid on bonds	20
Real estate taxes	50
Administrative costs	300
Depreciation	150
Dividends on preferred stock	10
Maintenance and repairs	200

7. (*Based on the Appendix*) A.B.C. Corporation reports the following data on its position as of Dec. 31, 1968. Construct its balance sheet. Note that the figure for surplus is missing and must be computed.

(000's omitted)

Buildings and equipment	$ 400
Inventories on hand	200
Bonds outstanding	250
Cash	200
Accounts payable	250
Common stock	400
Accounts receivable	450
Goodwill	10
Surplus	
Reserve for taxes	60
Loan from bank	180
U.S. Government bonds	50

Appendix

THE ELEMENTS OF BUSINESS ACCOUNTING

In order to understand the workings of modern business, you need to know something about the elements of business accounting. Although the details of modern accounting are complex, its fundamentals are simple. Only a knowledge of these fundamentals is essential for our purposes.

The Balance Sheet.   A balance sheet is a cross-section picture of the financial position of a firm *at some given point of time*. It is an instantaneous snapshot. A second sort of picture, discussed below, is an "income" or "profit-and-loss" statement that summarizes the firm's operations over some period of time, say a month or a year.

The balance sheet of any business rests on a fundamental equation. One side of the balance sheet shows what the business owns—its assets. Exactly corresponding to the value of these assets must be their ownership, which goes on the other side of the balance sheet. Obviously the two are always equal—the balance sheet always balances.

It is not easy to say just *who* "owns" the assets of the business. At the one extreme, the common stockholders are commonly considered the "residual owners"—that is, the ones who would get all the cash left over if the business were liquidated and its debts paid off. But this statement makes it clear that the various creditors of the business (for example,

the bank that has loaned it funds or the supplier from whom it has bought on credit) also have a claim on the assets. Such "creditors," to whom the business owes money, are at the other extreme of the claimants on the business' assets—they generally get their funds first. Bondholders, whose interest is contingent on satisfactory earnings, have a less preferred claim on the assets; preferred stockholders are still further down the list. Plainly the line between "creditors" and "owners" is indistinct. The two groups shade into one another as a continuum of claimants on the business' assets.

But fundamentally, the balance sheet reflects the basic accounting equation (or identity) that assets = liabilities + net worth; or, put the other way round, that net worth = assets − liabilities. That is, the business is worth to the stockholders what assets they would have left over if all the liabilities were paid off.

Table A is the balance sheet of a hypothetical Gadget Manufacturing Company, as of December 31, 1967. The left-hand side lists all the assets of the company—everything of value that it owns. The right-hand side lists all claims against these assets, broken down into two groups: first, its liabilities (what it owes); and second, its capital and surplus accounts (sometimes called its "net worth" or "proprietorship") on this date.

TABLE A

GADGET MANUFACTURING COMPANY

Balance Sheet, December 31, 1967

Assets			Liabilities and Proprietorship		
Current assets:			**Current liabilities:**		
Cash	$2,000,000		Accounts payable	$ 500,000	
U.S. Government securities	1,000,000		Accrued taxes	900,000	
Accounts receivable	2,000,000		Total current liabilities		$ 1,400,000
Inventories on hand	2,000,000				
Total current assets		$ 7,000,000	Bonds outstanding		3,000,000
			Capital and surplus:		
Fixed assets:			Preferred stock outstanding	$1,000,000	
Investment in affiliated company		300,000	Common stock outstanding	2,000,000	
Plant and equipment		3,000,000	Surplus	3,100,000	
Patents and goodwill		200,000	Total capital and surplus		6,100,000
Total		$10,500,000	Total		$10,500,000

Assets.   Once you see the basic equation underlying the balance sheet, most of its items are self-explanatory. For convenience, assets are often arranged beginning with the most liquid (the most readily convertible into cash) and ending with the least liquid. Those assets that are readily convertible (say within one year) are grouped together as "current assets." The others are called "fixed assets."

The last asset calls for special explanation. Two hundred thousand dollars is the value attached, for accounting purposes, to the patents and goodwill accumulated by the company. Obviously this is an estimated figure, a more or less arbitrary valuation determined by the company's officials and accountants. The item is so obviously intangible, albeit of tremendous importance for such well-established products as Coca-Cola and Lucky Strike, that it has become accepted conservative business practice to place a very low value on it.[2]

Actually, this is only the most conspicuously estimated item; others are estimated too. The current value placed on plant and equipment, as we shall see, is particularly susceptible to the vagaries of managerial and accounting judgment, because the "current value" shown is generally nothing but the original cost of the assets less an estimated amount of depreciation.[3] Current assets can be valued somewhat more precisely; but only cash is clearly and inevitably "worth" exactly the figure at which it is carried.

Liabilities and Net Worth.   The liability side seems a little more tricky at first glance. "Accounts payable" is easy—these are debts owed to suppliers. "Accrued taxes" represent tax liabilities that have been incurred but have not yet been paid. The liabilities that will come due within a year or so are grouped together to facilitate comparison with current assets. Such a comparison gives a quick picture of the short-run financial position of the company—its "current ratio."

"Capital and surplus" (net worth) consists of three items in this particular balance sheet. Part of the company's funds were obtained by sale of preferred, part by sale of common, stock. The amounts shown for each are the "par," or "face," value of the

stock outstanding. This value is presumably the amount for which the stock was originally sold, though this is not always so.[4] Surplus reflects profits of the company that have not been paid out as dividends to stockholders.

Surplus is a peculiarly misleading word. It seems to connote an extra fund of cash lying around somewhere, but such is far from the case. Surplus is nothing but a formal accounting subitem as part of the general capital and surplus (net worth) category. It could just as well be lumped in with common stock; its segregation is only a matter of accounting custom. Total "capital and surplus" is nothing but a derived figure that follows from the values placed on assets, less the company's "liabilities," which may also be partly estimated (for example, the item "reserve for contingencies" shown on some balance sheets). The fact that capital plus surplus on December 31, 1967, was $3,100,000 more than the paid-in value of the stock reflects past earnings not paid out in dividends.

There is no reason to suppose that these past profits now repose in the cash account. More likely, as part of the firm's regular operations, they have been "re-invested" or "plowed back" into inventory, plant and equipment, or some other assets. Or they may be reflected in a reduced level of the firm's liabilities. *It is essential to understand that there is no direct correspondence between individual items on the two sides of the balance sheet. Any attempt to link up individual items directly will lead to fallacious conclusions.*[5]

One other crucial warning, suggested above: The values placed on most assets, and hence on the capital and surplus group as well, are *estimated* values. *If* every one of these values is accurate, then the capital and surplus figure is accurate. But it by no means follows even then that every asset could be liquidated (sold) at the value at which it is carried on the balance sheet. Many of the items have a

---

[2] United States Steel and American Tobacco (Lucky Strike), for example, carry "goodwill and patents" at $1. Coca-Cola, on the other hand, carried goodwill, trade marks, formulae, etc., at their cost—$45 million in 1966.

[3] See the discussion of "depreciation" charges in the following section.

[4] In the 1800's, it was common practice to set a fictiously high value on the capital stock. Part of this stock was issued to original founders who provided not money but goods or services that were overvalued. The term "stock-watering" in reference to this practice came from the then-common practice of inducing cattle to drink as much water as possible just before being marketed in order to increase their weight temporarily. Although supervisory control now exercised by the U.S. Government Securities and Exchange Commission has made such watering very difficult for stocks "listed" on the major exchanges, it still can be done with unlisted stocks.

[5] The common argument that higher wages should be paid out of surpluses is an example of such an inadequate understanding of the elements of accounting.

TABLE B

GADGET MANUFACTURING COMPANY

Income Statement for Year Ended December 31, 1968

Net sales		$10,000,000
Manufacturing and selling costs:		
Materials	$2,000,000	
Labor cost	3,000,000	
Depreciation	500,000	
Maintenance and repairs	400,000	
Administrative and selling costs	1,400,000	
Taxes (other than income taxes)	600,000	7,900,000
Net profit from operations		2,100,000
Other income—interest and dividends		150,000
Less interest charges—on own bonds outstanding		50,000
Net income before federal income taxes		2,200,000
Provision for federal income taxes		1,100,000
Net income (or profit)		$ 1,100,000
Allocation of net income:		
Dividends on preferred stock		$ 100,000
Dividends on common stock		400,000
Increase in surplus		600,000

"going value" only as part of the operating concern. If the concern were to close down, it would be very doubtful whether many of the assets could be sold for their stated values (for example, semifinished gadgets in the inventory item). Going concerns are seldom completely liquidated even when they "go broke." Instead, they are often reorganized with the injection of new capital, or transferred to some other going concern, in order to maintain as much as possible of their going value.

The Income (Profit-and-Loss) Statement. The income, or profit-and-loss, statement is the accountant's summary view of a firm's operation over some time period, say a year.

Table B shows a hypothetical income statement for the Gadget Manufacturing Company during the year ending December 31, 1968, the year following the balance sheet shown in Table A. This is a straightforward account of the gross income received during the year and what was done with it. The first part of the statement summarizes the income from [6] and expenses of operations; then separate items are included for other income and

[6] The "net sales" item corresponds to the revenue from sales shown by the "demand curves" in the following chapters.

expenses; then federal income tax liability is deducted, which gives net profit after taxes for 1968.

The last part of the statement shows how the corporation allocates this profit. Only $500,000 is paid out as dividends. The other $600,000 is reinvested in the company. Capital and surplus (net worth) will now be $600,000 higher than if all the profits had been distributed to the stockholders. Common stockholders—the corporation's "owners" —may thus be as well off one way as the other. In one case, they get cash dividends; in the other, the value of their investment accumulates. Such plowing-back of earnings has long been commonplace in American industry, and many industrial giants such as Eastman Kodak and Ford have grown almost entirely through re-investment of earnings.

One warning about the profit-and-loss statement: The income and costs shown are not necessarily *cash* receipts and outlays; the profits are not necessarily *cash* profits. This distinction between cash transactions and accounting records is illustrated by the "materials" item. The materials used may have been purchased long before and already have been in inventory at the year's beginning. Or materials purchased during the year might have been double the $2,000,000 shown, if the firm had chosen to build up its inventories during the year. The $2,-

000,000 materials cost is the accounting figure for materials *used*, not for materials *bought* during the year.

The same point is well illustrated by the cost item "depreciation." Every engineer and accountant knows that plant and equipment depreciate. If a truck bought in 1968 is expected to last five years, after each year it has one year less life. At the end of five years it has only scrap value if the original estimates were accurate. The concern will not have to buy another truck until 1973, but if it does not figure the using up of the truck as a current expense it is obviously understating its costs and overstating its profits in the intervening years. If no current depreciation is charged, in 1973 the entire cost of the new truck would have to be charged against 1973 income. Hence, accountants "charge" depreciation annually, even though no cash outlay is involved. Thus, one-fifth of the value of the truck might be charged off as a current cost each year, or some more complicated depreciation formula might be used. There need be no cash expenditure that matches the depreciation shown.

Since cost and income items are accounting entries rather than cash transactions, obviously there is no necessary cash accumulation at the year's end equal to net profit earned during the year. The firm's cash may be higher or lower, depending on what has seemed to the managers the best use of available funds. Managers need only be sure they have cash on hand to meet their obligations, one of which is dividends when dividends are to be paid. In fact, dividends may be paid in years when no profits have been made. A. T. and T., for example, paid its regular cash dividend of $9 per year straight through the depression of the 1930's, even though annual profits fell well below $9. Capital and surplus, of course, declined by the excess of dividend payments over net profits.

Relation Between Income Statement and Balance Sheet. These observations tell us a good deal about the relation between the income statement and the balance sheet. Suppose now we draw up a balance sheet for the Gadget Company at the end of 1968—another spot picture, linked to the earlier one by our income statement.

During the year, assets have been continually used up in the production of current output; sales or other sources of funds have continually rebuilt the firm's assets. Since a net profit of $1,100,000 after taxes was made during 1968, total capital and surplus (net worth) was up by this amount before payment of dividends. As emphasized above, the increase in assets over the year may have come in cash, inventories, accounts receivable, or any other item—or there may have been a decrease in liabilities. All we know from the income statement is that, on balance, assets less liabilities are up $1,100,000.

This $1,100,000 is reduced to $600,000 by the payment of dividends. On the asset side the reduction is in the cash item when cash is paid out; in the capital and surplus accounts it is in the surplus item, which would have shown a steady increase through the year if monthly balance sheets had been made. This leaves the surplus account up $600,000 over December 31, 1967. Together, the income statement and balance sheets provide an over-all accounting of the firm's financial operations and status for the period.

TABLE C

GADGET MANUFACTURING COMPANY

Balance Sheet, December 31, 1968

Assets			Liabilities and Proprietorship		
Current assets:			Current liabilities:		
Cash	$2,100,000		Accounts payable	$ 400,000	
U.S. government securities	1,200,000		Accrued taxes	800,000	
Accounts receivable	2,600,000		Total current liabilities		$ 1,200,000
Inventories on hand	2,000,000				
Total current assets		$ 7,900,000	Bonds outstanding		3,000,000
			Capital and surplus:		
Fixed assets:			Preferred stock	$1,000,000	
Investment in affiliated company		300,000	Common stock	2,000,000	
Plant and equipment		2,500,000	Surplus	3,700,000	
Patents and goodwill		200,000	Total proprietorship		6,700,000
Total		$10,900,000	Total		$10,900,000

There is one other tricky spot. On the income statement, $500,000 depreciation was charged as a cost. This means that "plant and equipment" will be carried at only $2,500,000 in the December 31, 1968, balance sheet, $500,000 less than before. Actually, many firms would show the entire calculation on the balance sheet, thus:

Plant and equipment
Original cost $8,000,000
Less reserve for depreciation 5,500,000

Net plant and equipment $2,500,000

Here the $5,500,000 is the total amount of depreciation charged against the original cost of the company's existing plant and equipment to date; $500,000 of it was charged in 1968. The "reserve for depreciation" is carried as a deduction item on the asset side of the statement. It is crucial to remember, however, that the reserve is *not* a cash fund set aside and available for expenditure. It is merely the summation of depreciation costs charged against assets in making profit-and-loss calculations to date. Neither is it necessarily re-invested in plant and equipment. Whether and how it is ultimately re-invested will depend largely on the profit expectations of the concern's officials.

Throughout this Appendix, we have been primarily concerned with the mechanics of business accounting. Stop now and look for a moment at what this all means economically. During 1968, the Gadget Manufacturing Company had a good year. It made $1.1 million of profits on its total net worth (capital and surplus) of $6.1 million at the beginning of the year. This is around a 17 per cent return on net investment, even after paying taxes. Before taxes, the return was more than twice as high. If you compare this rate of return with that of many leading American corporations, you will find that it looks very good.

How did this good year show up for the common stockholders? They collected $400,000 of dividends on $5.7 million stated net worth to the common stockholders. This would be a return of 7 per cent on money invested in the stock at that price, a very high rate. We can safely assume that the price of the stock has been bid up in the market by investors to reflect this high rate of return. Although market prices of common stock fluctuate widely, depending on many circumstances, an effective dividend yield of 4 or 5 per cent on good small companies would have been reasonable in 1968; this would imply a market price for the company's shares totaling $8 million to $10 million, on which the $400,000 dividends would amount to a 4 to 5 per cent return. The price *per share* would depend on the number of shares into which the company's capital stock had been divided. Suppose there were 200,000 shares (giving an original-issue, or "par," value of $10 per share). At current market prices we might expect these shares to be selling for perhaps $40 to $50 apiece ($8 million or $10 million total value divided by the 200,000 shares).

The stockholders also gained from the $600,000 of profits plowed back into the business, which show up on the December 31, 1968, balance sheet as $600,000 additional surplus in the "Capital and Surplus" section. It means that the company now has either that many more dollars' worth of assets, or that much less debt, or some combination of both. This condition should make it a more profitable company in the future, with larger total profit figures in the years ahead. And generally this fact would be reflected in a correspondingly high value for the company's stock on the market.

REVIEW

Concepts To Remember

This Appendix has introduced several important new concepts. You will meet many of the following terms not only throughout the course but in the newspaper as well:

balance sheet	profit-and-loss statement
assets	income statement
liabilities	dividends
proprietorship	depreciation
capital	reinvested earnings
surplus	net worth

TWENTY

THE CONSUMER
AND
MARKET DEMAND [1]

Individual Demand.

Equilibrium of the Consumer.

Market Demand—Signals to Producers.

Elasticity of Demand.

In our economic system the businessman is in business to make profits—maybe not exclusively, but surely as one of his major objectives. By and large, he can make profits only by producing goods and services that people want to buy—autos, radios, dry cleaning services, movies, lamp shades, and thousands of others. If there is no consumer who is willing and able to "lay cash on the barrelhead," the businessman is pretty much out of luck. Maybe the government will temporarily come to his rescue with a subsidy, or maybe he can keep going by using up his own invested capital. But over the long pull, it is the customer who is willing and able to buy who directs production in a private-enterprise economy.

He directs it by the way he spends his money —the way he allocates his income among different goods and services. If consumers want yellow electric refrigerators, the chances are good that yellow electric refrigerators will be produced. If consumers want Bibles engraved on the heads of pins, it will not be long before some enterprising individual is turning out Bibles on pinheads.

Consumer demand is the mainspring of economic activity. But never forget—it is the consumer with money to spend who counts! Many of us would like to have a Cadillac, and T-bone steak for dinner. But unless we have the money and are willing to spend it on these objects, our desires have little significance for General Motors or the corner meat market.

Thus, your "vote" on what gets produced in a private-enterprise economy is largely determined

[1] Note to instructors: This chapter has a Mathematical Appendix at the end of the book, for those who want to assign it.

by your income, unless you have acccumulated funds to supplement your income. The mill hand has a lot less influence than the rich man, even though the former may be a virtuous, hardworking father of five needy children and the latter a ne'er-do-well who has inherited his money through no effort of his own. This is not to imply that virtue resides in poor rather than rich souls, but merely to emphasize that the private-enterprise economy responds to what people have to spend, not to who they are.

Figure 20-1 shows who had the buying power in 1966. It emphasizes again the huge buying power of the "middle class" in America. Nearly two-thirds of all families fell in the $5,000–$15,000 income group in 1966, and the average income of this group is steadily moving up.

But Figure 20-1 points up the extremes too. Ten million families, one family out of five, had an income below $3,500. These families received only 5 per cent of total personal income—far less than their proportionate say over what gets produced for the market. At the other extreme, about 1 million families (2 per cent of the total) received incomes over $22,000 and about 10 per cent of all income, giving them a huge leverage over what the system produces.

The consumer is a powerful, and sometimes capricious, monarch. Table 20-1 shows what he spends on some major categories in the American economy. He still spends the biggest chunk of his income on food, housing, and clothing. But the proportion spent on food and clothing has dropped sharply since 1929. Spending on services (medicine, transportation, recreation, and the like) has grown rapidly as we have become richer and able to devote more of our incomes to non-essentials.

TABLE 20-1
PERCENTAGE BREAKDOWN OF CONSUMER'S DOLLAR

Spending Category	1929	1966
Food and drink	28	23
Housing	14	15
Clothing	12	9
Household furnishings	6	7
Medical services	4	8
Recreation	3	6
Autos and parts	3	7

You may have heard of "the economic man" —a mythical individual who carefully calculates just what he should buy before he spends each dollar, comparing the satisfactions obtainable from every conceivable expenditure before he parts with his cash. Most of us don't operate this way, and everyone knows it. A lot of our spending is based on habit, some on impulse, and so on.

Still, most of us face a real problem of how to allocate our incomes among far more goods and services than we are able to pay for. Perhaps the Aga Khan buys everything he wants without concern for what it costs. But most of us have to calculate how to divide up our incomes among the things we want to buy. You may devote most of your income to nourishing foods, college tuition, and durable clothes; I may spend most of mine on books, phonograph records, and airplane trips; our neighbor may prefer a dissolute life of wine, women, and song. Probably none of us is the human calculating machine envisaged in "the economic man," though the less money we have the greater is the pressure to act in a careful, calculating way.

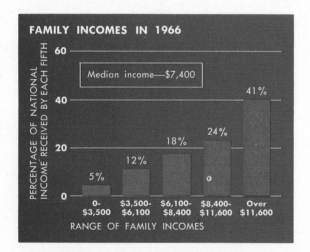

FIG. 20-1 In 1966, three-fifths of all families fell in the $3,500–$11,600 income range and they received 54 per cent of the national income. But the one-fifth receiving over $11,600 had a big chunk of total consumer spending power. (Source: U.S. Bureau of the Census.)

The economist does not pass judgment on which pattern of expenditure is the proper one. Nor does he pretend to tell you how you should spend your income to lead a happier, healthier, more learned, or other kind of life. What he does do is assume that normally you spend your money on the things you want most. Thus, if you spent a dollar on the movies this afternoon, he takes that as evidence that you preferred going to the movies over going to a prize fight at the same admission or over buying a new dollar necktie. If you stop and think about it, any other assumption leads to very strange results, as long as we assume freedom of individual action in spending incomes.[2]

These rather obvious observations become important later on when we try to evaluate how well the economic system works, since one of the main tests we will apply is: How well does the system respond to consumer wants? Unless we can assume that consumers' expenditures generally reflect what they want most, we will be at a loss for any measure of how well the system does in fact allocate its scarce productive resources to satisfying consumer wants.

INDIVIDUAL DEMAND

Since consumer demand basically directs a private-enterprise system, it is important to define "demand" accurately at the outset. *"Demand" is the schedule of amounts of any product that buyers will purchase at different prices during some stated time period.* This definition takes some explaining, since it obviously isn't quite what the word means in everyday conversation.

What is your demand for sirloin steak? A little thought will tell you that this is a meaningless question until you ask, "At what price and over how long a time?" You'll surely buy more at

[2] Some economists have worried about special difficulties in this connection. For example, suppose you buy a suit on the installment plan, and then decide you don't like the color. Is your payment of the ten-dollar installment due next month a fair measure of your preference then for the suit over other ten-dollar purchases? In this case, at the time of expenditure you don't have real freedom to allocate your income; the difficulty is avoided if you view the entire expenditure as being made at the time you buy the suit.

50 cents than at $1.00 a pound; and obviously you'll buy more in a year than in a week. Recognizing this need to specify prices and a time period, we might construct a hypothetical "schedule" of amounts you would buy at different prices during some particular time interval, say a week, as in Table 20-2. The table shows how much steak

TABLE 20-2

INDIVIDUAL DEMAND FOR SIRLOIN STEAK

Price per Pound	Pounds Bought per Week
$1.20	0
1.00	1
.80	2
.60	2
.50	3
.40	4

you will buy during the week at each price shown, *assuming that other things (especially your income and the prices of other commodities) remain unchanged.*

When we speak of your "demand" for steak, we mean this entire schedule of amounts that you would buy at various prices, other things equal. It is meaningless to say that your demand is one or three pounds a week. By "demand" we mean instead your entire state of mind as to how many pounds you would buy at different prices, other things remaining unchanged. In principle, we might list every possible price from zero to infinity. Table 20-2 pictures your demand only over the price range shown.

This state of mind (your demand) can be shown graphically, as in Fig. 20-2. If we plot price on the vertical axis and pounds bought on the horizontal axis and connect the points, we can read off the resulting curve how many pounds you will buy during the week at any price shown, continuing the assumption of other things equal. Thus, at $1.20 you will buy no steak, at $1.00 you will buy one pound, and so on down the curve, just as the schedule above shows. If you haven't had much experience with graphs, it may be useful to practice plotting and reading off a number of such points.

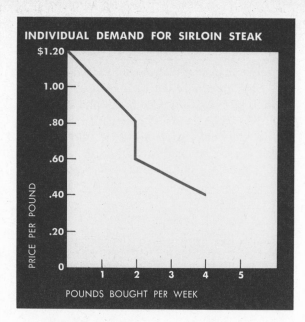

INDIVIDUAL DEMAND FOR SIRLOIN STEAK

FIG. 20-2 The demand curve shows how many pounds of steak this individual will buy in a week at different prices. He will buy more at lower than at higher prices.

Whether we use the schedule or plot the points graphically is a matter of convenience. They show the same thing. In making the graph, we merely join the plotted points. Since we knew only the points shown in the schedule, the readings from the curve between the points are only approximations. Only if the plotted points were very close together (say at one-cent intervals) would the curve properly be a continuous line, with the reading at every point meaningful and accurate. But most demand curves are shown as continuous lines because they are easier to work with that way and for our purposes are ordinarily good enough approximations between the points specifically plotted. And when we add together the demands of many people later, the bumps and corners in the curves are eliminated, so we tend to have smooth, continuous curves.

But watch out for one tricky point, whether you use schedules or graphs! Going back to your demand for steak, suppose the price is $1.00 and you are buying one pound per week. Now the local grocer lowers the price to 80 cents and you step up your weekly purchases to two pounds. *This is not a change in demand.* Your demand (your state of mind toward steak) has not changed. You have merely moved to a different point on your demand schedule, or curve, as a result of the lower price, as the original demand

276

schedule or curve says you would do. This increased purchase at a lower price is merely a reflection of the downward slope of your demand curve.

**Why Demand Curves
Slope Downward**

It seems obvious that you will buy more of anything at a low price than at a high one. Thus, on the kind of graph we have drawn, the demand curve will slope down, from northwest to southeast. Why? First, at a lower price for anything you can *afford* to buy more of it *out of any given income.* Second, at a lower price you are likely to *want* to buy more of it because it becomes relatively more attractive compared with other things you might spend your money on, *given unchanged prices of other things.* You will want to substitute sirloin for hamburger as their prices converge. And at low enough prices you may find new uses for sirloin—for example, feeding sirloin instead of dog biscuits to your dog. Thus, for both reasons, the quantity bought typically increases as the price falls.[3]

Looked at another way, the downward-sloping demand curve says that you will be willing to pay a high price for a little steak each week, but the more steak you have the less you're willing to pay per additional pound to increase your weekly consumption still further. Many economists have associated this tendency with the decreasing satisfaction, or "utility," you get from each additional pound of steak you add to your weekly diet. We call it *the law of diminishing marginal utility. The additional, or marginal, utility (or satisfaction) you obtain per unit falls as you get more units within the stated time period.* Marginal utility is the want-satisfaction obtained from having one

[3] Three exceptions should be mentioned: (1) "Prestige goods," such as mink coats or exotic perfume, may be bought largely because their price is high. A decline in price might lead some persons to buy less as the goods come down into a price range open to the less wealthy. (2) Some goods, called "inferior," are bought by poor people simply because they are cheap and useful. Potatoes in Ireland are the classic example. If the price of the food staple, potatoes, goes up, the Irish peasants may have to buy even more potatoes, which are still the cheapest food, because they have even less left than before to buy other more expensive foods. (3) When price drops, people may buy less because they expect the price to decline still further. This is a dynamic effect that depends not on whether price is high or low but on the way it is changing.

additional unit of some commodity per unit of time. Try applying the law to yourself—for oranges, movies, houses.

Changes in Demand

Remember that your "demand" for steak is your entire set of intentions about buying steak. These depend on how much income you have, how you evaluate steak compared with other things, and on the relative prices of the alternatives you are considering. Now suppose that you get tired of steak and develop a taste for seafood. You will now buy less steak than before at each of the prices shown. *This change in attitude is a change in demand. Your demand for steak has decreased.*

A change in demand is illustrated easily by using demand curves. Begin with the curve in Fig. 20-2. Your *lower* demand for steak would be reflected in a new demand curve, to the left of, or below, the old curve. You will now buy only one pound of steak per week at 60 cents, and none at any higher price; only two pounds at 50 cents; and so on. This new, *lower* demand curve is shown in Fig. 20-3 as curve *BB;* the original demand curve is *AA.* If something increases your

demand for steak, say a fatter paycheck to finance such delicacies, the new, *higher* demand might be indicated by *CC. A change in demand is shown by a move to another demand curve.*

Why would your demand for beefsteak, or Buicks, or neckties change? There are three major reasons. *First, your tastes may change.* You simply decide you don't like beefsteak, or that now you prefer Buicks to other cars. *Second, your income may change.* As a beginning office clerk, you may have to be satisfied with a secondhand Ford. With a doubled paycheck you may be in the Pontiac class. *Third, changes in the availability and prices of other commodities may change your demand.* If pork prices soar, your demand for steak may rise because you'll buy more steak than before now that pork costs more. Note that such changes in demand reflect changes in "other things" (your income and prices of other goods) which were previously being held unchanged.

It is important to distinguish between movements along the same demand curve and shifts in the curve itself. Many economic fallacies are perpetrated through slippery use of the concept of "demand." Try checking your own grasp with these questions: (1) Production of sheep rises, prices fall, and consumers buy more mutton. Is there an increase in the demand for mutton? (Hint: does the demand curve itself shift, or do customers merely buy more mutton on the same demand curve at lower prices?) (2) Chrysler comes out with a new, more powerful engine and Buick sales decline. Is there a drop in the demand for Buicks? (3) Philco raises the price of its TV sets and sales drop off. Is there a drop in demand? (4) Congress puts a new tax on movie admissions and movie attendance drops. Is there a drop in demand? [4]

EQUILIBRIUM OF THE CONSUMER

If we assume that consumers (households) generally try to maximize the utility (or satisfaction) they get by spending their incomes, two important propositions follow.

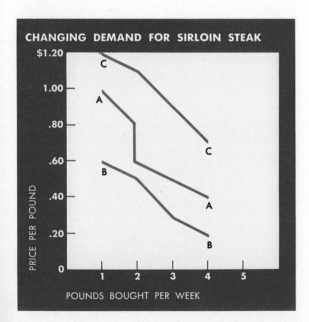

FIG. 20-3 Curve CC shows an increase in demand from AA. Curve BB shows a decrease. How much steak would each demander buy at $1 per pound?

[4] Answers: To (1), no; (2), yes; (3), no; (4), no.

1. *First, each consumer will change the pattern of goods and services he buys whenever he can get more utility by spending an extra dollar on item A rather than on item B. He will maximize his total utility when he allocates his income so that the marginal utility he receives from the last dollar spent on each item he buys is identical. When he so allocates his income, the consumer is "in equilibrium," in the sense that he is maximizing the satisfaction he can obtain by spending his income. He has no incentive to change to another spending pattern.*

This is only common sense. If the consumer can get a larger marginal utility by spending a dollar on A than B, obviously he will spend it on A. Whenever the marginal utility of the last dollar spent on different commodities is unequal, he can increase his total utility by switching from the lower to the higher marginal utility commodities. If, to simplify, we assume that the price of every commodity is the same, he will so allocate his income as to obtain the same marginal utility from every commodity he buys. We could write this in equation form as follows: $MU_x = MU_y = MU_z$, etc., where x, y, and z are the commodities bought.

If the prices of different commodities vary, as they do in actual life, the consumer in equilibrium would not expect to get the same marginal utility from each commodity, but only from the last dollar spent on each commodity. It would be nonsense to think of so allocating your income as to obtain the same marginal utility from a movie and an automobile. But if we divide the marginal utility from each by the price of each, then we have made them comparable. Then we can state our central proposition again: For the consumer to be in equilibrium, the marginal utility of the last dollar spent on each commodity must be equal. In equation form, the equilibrium condition is, therefore:

$$\frac{MU_x}{P_x} = \frac{MU_y}{P_y} = \frac{MU_z}{P_z}, \text{ etc.,}$$

where P is the price of each commodity.[5]

[5] Wouldn't this lead the consumer to allocate all his income to x instead of y or z, if x has the highest marginal utility? No, because of the law of diminishing marginal utility. Remember that the marginal utility obtained from

We can extend this reasoning to other uses of households' incomes. Clearly each household has another alternative—we may save part of our disposable income rather than spending it. To be in equilibrium, we must so allocate our incomes between saving and spending that the marginal utility obtained from a dollar saved is equal to that obtained from a dollar spent on each item we buy. Equating marginal utilities works for all uses of the dollars we have to spend or save.

2. *When consumers spend their incomes this way, their demand curves for different products accurately reflect the relative marginal utilities they think they will obtain from different products they might buy.* If A spends a dollar for a necktie rather than for a movie ticket, we can safely assume he prefers the tie to the movie. His preferences are reflected in his demand curves for the two products, and his demands will reflect to producers the relative values he places on neckties and movies.

This is an extremely important point, since in our system we rely largely on consumer demand to give signals to producers on what should be produced and in what quantities. If the system is to perform efficiently, it should allocate resources in accordance with these consumer demands. This test will be applied to different types of markets and economies in later chapters.

Some Applications

Consider three simple applications of this reasoning that consumers will always tend to move toward an equilibrium condition. First, suppose that all consumers are in equilibrium, as described above. Now consumers' tastes change and they desire more beefsteak relative to pork chops. At existing prices, consumers are now out of equilibrium, and they will switch their purchases from pork chops to steak. This increase in consumer demand for steak will both push up the price of steak and signal farmers to produce more beef, while the reverse action occurs for pork. A

an additional unit of each commodity will tend to decline as the consumer gets more of it in any time period. Thus, spending more dollars on any commodity will produce diminishing marginal utility for that commodity, and will generally keep the consumer from switching all his expenditures to any one commodity.

new consumer equilibrium will be reached when, at the new prices for beef and pork, the marginal utilities obtainable from a dollar spent on each are again equal.

A second application: Begin again with consumers in equilibrium, and now assume that a disastrous drought in Latin America drastically reduces the world's coffee supply. This will raise the price of coffee relative to the price of tea and other drinks. At the new price ratios, consumers will be out of equilibrium and will switch from buying coffee to buying more tea, until at the new relative prices the marginal utilities obtained from spending a dollar on each are roughly the same. Changes in relative prices have signaled changes in the relative costs of supplying coffee and tea, and consumers have changed their purchases of the two to re-establish a situation in which they maximize the utility obtainable from the incomes they have to spend.

A third application: When a consumer is in equilibrium he is usually receiving a "consumer surplus" on the commodities he buys. Figure 20-4 shows a typical downward-sloping consumer demand curve, say for bananas. The market price is 10 cents per banana, and this consumer buys five

per week. But his demand curve shows he would have been willing to pay 20 cents for the first banana, 17 cents for the second, and so on. He gets a "consumer's surplus" of utility on each of the first four bananas, since he has to pay only 10 cents for each. The shaded area provides a measure of this consumer's surplus, if in fact the demand curve accurately reflects the marginal utility of each additional banana to this consumer. (Thought teaser: How much consumer's surplus do you get on each gallon of water you drink? On each cubic foot of air you breathe?)

MARKET DEMAND— SIGNALS TO PRODUCERS

Millions of consumers, each allocating his income so as to provide the greatest satisfaction to himself, provide the basic signals to producers telling what they want produced. The local department store isn't much concerned with your personal demand for shirts. But it is very much concerned with the aggregate market demand for shirts in its market territory. *Aggregate, or market, demand is the sum of all the individual demands in the market under consideration. Such market demand provides the main signal to producers as to what they should supply to meet consumers' wants, and thereby to maximize their own profits.*

Consider the market demand for sugar at the crossroads store of an isolated village with only three families. The demand schedules of the three families, and the total demand, might look something like Table 20-3. The market demand schedule for sugar, as seen by the crossroads grocer, is the sum of the individual demands of his customers. It could be plotted on a graph just like the individual demands schedule. The total-expenditures column shows the grocer's total weekly sales of sugar at different prices. (For the moment, disregard the right-hand column.)

Note that if these individuals' demand schedules can be taken as indicators of the marginal utility consumers attach to an additional dollar's worth of sugar at different prices, then the market demand schedule is an effective signal to producers of the relative importance attached by these consumers to getting more pounds of sugar

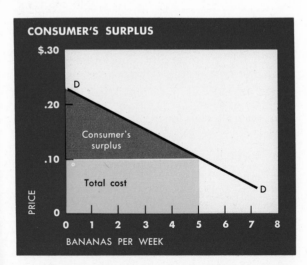

FIG. 20-4 The consumer pays only 50 cents (yellow rectangle) for his 5 bananas, but his demand curve shows he would have been willing to pay more than 10 cents for each of the first 4. Thus the red triangle measures how much more he would have been willing to pay to get the total utility provided by 5 bananas, and hence measures the "consumer's surplus" he obtains free.

TABLE 20-3

CROSSROADS DEMAND FOR SUGAR

Price per Pound	Purchases per Week by:				Expenditures	Demand
	A	B	C	All Three		
20¢	3 lb	1 lb	2 lb	6 lb	$1.20	
15¢	4 lb	2 lb	4 lb	10 lb	1.50	Elastic
10¢	6 lb	3 lb	6 lb	15 lb	1.50	Unitary
5¢	6 lb	4 lb	7 lb	17 lb	.85	Inelastic

at different prices (given their incomes and the prices of other products). And similar demand schedules exist for other products. All these demand schedules together represent the total set of signals from consumers to producers about how much consumers want of each product at each price.

The market system is an impressive device for channeling to producers the preferences of millions of different consumers. But remember that its effectiveness rests on the presumption that the demand curves do truly represent consumer preferences. Sometimes they don't, as we shall see later. If, for example, advertising should convince John Jones to buy (demand) something he hadn't previously wanted, does Jones' new demand curve truly reflect his wants? Critics of modern advertising say "no"; consumers are led to buy things they neither really want nor need. Defenders say that if a consumer spends his money without compulsion, that's the best measure we have of what he really wants, however the wants were originally established. More on this issue in Chapter 26; here the important thing is to see the critical role of market demands as signals to producers under our system, and the importance therefore that they be true signals.

ELASTICITY OF DEMAND [6]

The preceding sections say the most important things about individual and market de-

[6] Mathematical Appendix III at the end of the book provides a precise mathematical statement of demand elasticity, which may be helpful to students who think readily in mathematical terms. Ordinarily, the Appendix will be most useful *after* you have read the remainder of the chapter.

mands as signals from consumers to producers. But demands for individual products vary widely, and it is useful to be able to describe some of these differences precisely in analyzing how the economic system does respond to changing consumer demands.

Salt provides an interesting example. Suppose ordinary table salt sells for 10 cents a pound and you use about a pound a month. If the price goes up to 15 cents, how much less salt will you use? Probably no less at all. Unsalted beans and potatoes don't taste very good, and the fraction of a cent saved each day by not salting your food is trivial compared with the better taste of flavored cooking.

This is a case where quantity bought responds very little, or not at all, to price changes. Plotted on a graph, the demand curve for table salt at the local grocery store would be substantially vertical over the 10-to-15 cent price range. Try drawing it. We say that the demand for table salt is very "inelastic" over this price range. With a change in price, there is very little response, or stretch, in the quantity bought.

At the other extreme, take your demand for beefsteak at the local A&P if you are substantially indifferent about whether you eat beef or pork. Suppose beef has been $1.00 a pound but rises to $1.25 while other prices remain unchanged. The chances are you will cut back your steak purchases sharply and substitute pork. Here your demand for steak would be highly "elastic." In your purchases there would be a great response to the increase in the price of beef.

Loosely, "elasticity" is a measure that tells how much the amount bought will change in response to a change in price. Thus, elasticity of demand is a measure of the responsiveness of quantity bought to changes in price. (A more precise definition will be given on page 283.) Elasticity is one characteristic of *any given demand curve or schedule*. To say a given demand is elastic or inelastic is merely to describe it, just as you might describe your next-door neighbor as tall or short.[7]

For an illustration, look back at the last column of Table 20-3. A 25 per cent price cut from 20 to 15 cents a pound for sugar led to a 67 per cent increase in sales—from 6 to 10 pounds a week. Obviously the demand over this price range is quite *elastic*, since a relatively small price cut led to a relatively big increase in quantity bought. But a 50 per cent price cut from 10 to 5 cents a pound induced only a relatively small (13 per cent) increase in quantity sold. Over this 10 to 5 cent price range the crossroads demand for sugar is *inelastic*.

This example illustrates what we mean by elasticity. It also illustrates that the same demand curve may be elastic in some price ranges and inelastic in others. In most cases, it is not correct to speak of a demand curve as elastic or inelastic as a whole. You need to specify at what price or prices.

Total Revenue
and Elasticity of Demand

The concept of demand elasticity helps us to predict what effect price changes will have on total expenditure for a commodity. Look again at the last column of Table 20-3. It's obvious that the crossroads storekeeper would be foolish to cut the price of sugar from 10 cents to 5 cents. Although he would sell more sugar, his total revenue on sugar would decrease by almost 50 per cent, because the quantity bought would rise very little in comparison with the big percentage cut in price *where demand is highly inelastic*. On the other hand, a price cut from 20 to 15 cents

might make more sense, since this change *in the elastic demand range* would bring an increase in total revenue.

By now, if you're reasonably good at figures, you will have seen that one measure of elasticity is what happens to total revenue when price changes. *Specifically, if demand is inelastic, total expenditures on a commodity will change in the same direction as a change in price. If demand is elastic, total expenditures will change in the opposite direction from a change in price.* Examine the reasoning.

1. *Inelastic Demand—Total Revenue Moves in the Same Direction as Price.* When the crossroads grocer cuts his sugar price from 10 to 5 cents, he takes 50 per cent less for each pound of sugar. Yet he sells only 13 per cent more pounds. Obviously the volume increase, with such inelastic demand, is not great enough to offset the lower price per pound sold. Total revenue drops with a cut in price. Now reverse the process over the same price range. Suppose he raises the price from 5 to 10 cents. Here he will get 100 per cent more per pound and sales will drop by only 2 pounds, about 12 per cent. Clearly, total revenue will increase. It will move in the same direction as the price change, since demand is unresponsive—inelastic. The change in amount bought is not enough to offset the effect of the change in price in either direction.[8]

2. *Elastic Demand—Total Revenue Moves in the Opposite Direction from Price.* Now look at what happens when he cuts the price from 20 to 15 cents. Although he gets 25 per cent less per pound, he sells 50 per cent more pounds. Total revenue increases, since the increased sales volume more than offsets the decrease in price. Demand

[7] Strictly, we should call this concept "price elasticity of demand." There is a related concept, "income elasticity of demand," that measures the response in quantity bought to a change in income received. However, throughout this book we shall use "elasticity" to mean "price elasticity." At a more advanced level, we can also speak of "cross-elasticity" of demand. This is the percentage change in the amount of product A that will be bought in response to a given percentage change in the price of product B.

[8] Notice that the percentage change in price from 10 to 5 cents is different from that from 5 to 10 cents—50 per cent compared with 100 per cent. This is because the base with which we compare the 5-cent change varies with the direction in which we are calculating. The difference really doesn't matter for our purposes, since the effect on total revenue will always give the right answer. (If you always take the percentage change on the bigger price or quantity figure you'll get around this directional problem.) Obviously, the discrepancy between the two ways of figuring percentage change will gradually vanish as we take smaller and smaller price intervals—for example, a price change between 99 cents and $1.00. There is a more precise formula in the Mathematical Appendix.

is elastic. Reverse the process over the same price range and you will see again that total revenue moves in the opposite direction. Demand is elastic.

3. *Unit Elasticity—Total Revenue Is Unaffected by Price Changes.* The borderline case between elastic and inelastic demand we call "unit" elasticity. This occurs where an upward or downward shift of price is just offset by a proportional change in quantity bought, so that total revenue remains unchanged. The crossroads demand for sugar between 10 and 15 cents is a case in point. Total expenditure on sugar is identical at either price, since the shift in amount bought just offsets the change in price.

The Real-world Importance of Elasticity

The elasticity of demand for his product is a prime concern of every businessman, whether or not he uses that technical term. Consider two important real-world examples.

First, the farmer. Modern econometric studies show that the demand for most basic farm products is inelastic over the relevant price ranges. What does this mean if farmers all work hard, the weather cooperates, and a bumper crop rolls out? It means that the *total revenue* farmers get from selling their crops will be *lower* as a result of this bonanza, because the bigger crop can be sold only by cutting prices more than proportionately. This simple fact goes far to explain the continuing stream of government-sponsored crop-reduction plans, beginning with the New Deal AAA program, all aimed at raising total farm income. With inelastic demand, even a moderate crop restriction may induce a substantially higher price and more total revenue from crop sales.

Contrast this with the depression-period attempts of the railroads to increase their total revenues by raising passenger fares in the 1930's. Unfortunately for the railroads, the customers stayed away in droves. Either they stayed at home, or they traveled by bus or car. Demand turned out to be elastic and total revenue moved down, not up. Only when fares were *cut* did total revenue actually rise. Although this experience was also influenced by changing levels of national income, the impossibility of filling the coffers by raising price in an elastic-demand market is plain to see.

What Makes Demand Elastic or Inelastic?

Why people want what they want is beyond the realm of the economist. By and large, we take people's wants as given, leaving it up to the psychologist and others to explain this particular why. But we can say some things about circumstances where demand is likely to be elastic or inelastic. Briefly, demand is likely to be *inelastic* where (1) your outlay on the object is small, (2) your want for it is urgent, (3) good substitutes are unavailable, and (4) it is wanted jointly with some complementary item. For example, matches don't cost very much, and if you smoke a pipe or cigarettes you want them badly in case you don't have a functioning lighter. Unlighted tobacco doesn't make smoke. In general, wants are most urgent for goods and services for which no close substitutes are available. Nobody's want for Esso gasoline is likely to be terribly urgent so long as a similar grade of Gulf can be had for the same price across the street.

Conversely, demand is likely to be *elastic* where (1) the outlay involved bulks large in your total expenditures, (2) your want is not urgent, (3) close substitutes are available, (4) the commodity is durable or repairable, and (5) the commodity has multiple uses. The first three statements are reasonably obvious. You think a long time before you pay a 10 per cent higher price for a radio-phonograph, but not so long for a candy bar. You stop buying if the price of something you don't care much about goes up—say a certain brand of corn flakes. Other brands offer very similar products.

The points on durability and multiple uses may take a little more thought. Autos are durable and repairable. At any given time, you can usually drive your old car a few thousand miles more; a new set of tires plus a motor tune-up costs a lot less than a new car. This alternative is likely to increase the elasticity of your demand for new cars. Lastly, any commodity that has multiple uses (like butter) is likely to have an elastic demand, because as price falls new uses and buyers may come into the market. At $1.00 a pound butter is out of sight for any use at all by lots of families. Others can afford it on bread, but not on vegetables or for cooking. At 50 cents, the first group may start using butter on the dinner table, and the second may move butter on beans from the luxury to the everyday-use class. And so on for other uses as the price falls further.

A Quantitative Measure of Elasticity

For some purposes it is useful to be able to say just how elastic or inelastic demand is. A ready measure can be worked out from the previous reasoning. Elasticity depends on the *relative* changes in quantity and price. If the *percentage change* in quantity bought (Q) is more than the *percentage change* in price (P), total revenue moves in the opposite direction from price; demand is elastic. Thus, we can easily get a numerical value for elasticity by the formula:

$$\text{Elasticity} = \frac{\%\text{ change in } Q}{\%\text{ change in } P}$$

For example, if a cut in the price of steel ingots from $80 to $76 per ton (5 per cent) leads to an increase in sales from 100 million to 101 million tons (1 per cent), by inserting the 5 per cent and 1 per cent in the formula we get an elasticity of demand of .2. Any value less than 1 (unity) is called inelastic demand. Any value of more than 1 is called elastic demand. Unitary elasticity of demand means exactly offsetting changes in quantity and price. Go back and try out this approach on Table 20-3 to get the precise demand elasticities at different prices.[9]

Econometric estimates have been made of the elasticity of demand for many products, although many of these are very rough. Table 20-4 gives estimates for several common products (for price variations near their then prices). The section on what makes demand elastic or inelastic should help you explain the elasticities of the different products. Another study recently found the present demand elasticity for butter to be about 1.3, compared to a pre-World War II estimate of

---

[9] Since price and quantity move in opposite directions, elasticity will always be a negative figure. The minus sign is customarily dropped in using elasticity measures. Strictly, our formula needs to be applied only to very small changes in price and quantity. For a more precise statement, see the Mathematical Appendix.

about .6. Can you explain the difference? (Hint: consider possible substitutes.)

TABLE 20-4	
ESTIMATED ELASTICITIES OF DEMAND *	
Furs	2.6
Automobiles	1.5
Refrigerators	1.1
Local phone calls	1.0
Luggage	.8
Movie tickets	.4
Electric light bulbs	.3
Matches	0

* Treasury estimates presented before House Ways and Means Committee, 1960.

Elasticity in Graphical Presentations

A perfectly inelastic demand curve would obviously be vertical. The same quantity would be bought at every price. An example might be your demand for insulin over a wide price range if you needed the insulin to keep alive. Highly elastic demand would be a nearly horizontal demand curve. Very small changes in price would lead to very large changes in the quantity bought. But in between these extremes, trying to read elasticity by the slope of a plotted demand curve is dangerous business. Look, for example, at the two charts in Fig. 20-5. Both show the demand schedule seen by our old friend the crossroads grocer, but they use different horizontal and vertical scales. Exactly the same demand is shown on both.

Because the left-hand graph uses an extended horizontal scale, the demand curve is relatively flat throughout. Yet it is exactly the same demand as in the right-hand graph, and the elasticity at every point along it is identical with the corresponding points on the right-hand graph. Both curves are marked to show the elastic and inelastic areas. Again, the point emphasized is the danger in trying to generalize that flat demand curves are elastic whereas steep ones are inelastic. You have to remember that elasticity is a matter of *relative* (percentage) changes in price and quantity. Elasticity changes continuously along a

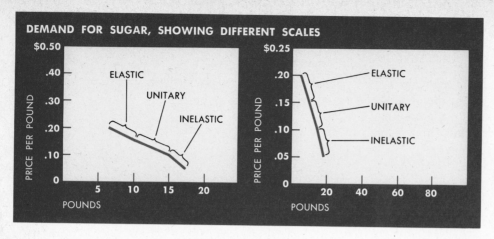

DEMAND FOR SUGAR, SHOWING DIFFERENT SCALES

FIG. 20-5 Trying to judge elasticity of demand by looking at the slope of a demand curve is tricky. These two curves show identical demands, plotted on different scales.

straight, diagonal demand curve. Check it for yourself if, as is likely, this statement seems to you intuitively wrong.[10]

Interacting Demands

If you buy a car, your demand for gasoline is pretty sure to increase. But, assuming that your total income stays unchanged, your demand for some other things (say bus rides) will drop.

The example illustrates the two main kinds of interrelationship among demands for different things: (1) complementary, or joint, and (2) sub-

[10] For mathematicians: the curve which shows unitary elasticity at all points is a rectangular hyperbola. The equation is: $xy = $ a constant.

stitutive, or competitive. When you buy the car, you take on a "complementary" demand for gasoline to run it. But now you don't need to ride the bus. Bus rides are "competitive" with cars in your demand pattern.

In the broadest sense, taking your income as given, the car must be a substitute for other expenditures lumped together. In this sense, all goods and services are competitive, or substitutive; since incomes are limited, any expenditure you make reduces your power to buy other things. But in many instances this effect is quite remote; for example, your car purchase may have little effect on your demand for potatoes. By contrast, the substitution of car rides for bus rides is very direct.

REVIEW

Concepts To Remember

This chapter has presented a string of important new analytical concepts that will be used repeatedly. Check to be sure you have them clearly in mind:

demand	elasticity of demand
individual and aggregate demand	elastic demand
the economic man	inelastic demand
marginal utility	competitive demands
total utility	complementary demands
equilibrium of consumer	unit elasticity

For Analysis and Discussion

1. Calculate roughly how big a voice people in your own family's income group have in the allocation of the economy's resources. Does it seem to you to be a fair share? (Check the income data in Table 20-1.)
2. Do you act like the mythical "economic man" in allocating your income among alternative uses so as to maximize your satisfaction from it? If your answer is "no," are you saying that you are irrational?

3. Since consumers' demand signals what is to be produced in America, it is consumers who are responsible if our economy produces "wasteful" products like elaborate chrome trim on automobiles. Do you agree or disagree?

4. How elastic is *your* demand for the following, near the present price for each?

Required textbooks	Silk shantung suits
Gasoline	Lipstick
Airplane tickets home	Ford convertibles

In each case, see if you can isolate the factors that make the elasticity what it is.

5. If the demand for wheat is inelastic, would a bumper crop raise or lower wheat farmers' total income?

6. What effect would a successful advertising campaign by the Campbell Company have on the elasticity of consumer demand for Campbell's tomato soup? Explain your answer.

7. Suppose unsold stocks of gasoline are piling up in the storage tanks of the major refineries. If you were regional sales director of one of the major companies, would you recommend a marked reduction in the filling-station price? How would you go about deciding?

TWENTY-ONE
DEMAND, SUPPLY,
AND MARKET PRICES

The Role of the Market and Market Prices.

Supply.

Demand, Supply, and Market Price.

The Economics of Price-Fixing.

Summary: Supply, Demand, and Market Equilibrium.

Chapter 2 provided a bird's-eye view of how producers respond to consumer demands in a private-enterprise, free-market economy. Now we need to examine this linkage in more detail, especially the role of the market place and market prices in connecting consumers and producers. If you thought economics was going to be about "supply and demand," this is it.

THE ROLE OF THE MARKET AND MARKET PRICES

In a loose way, it is easy to see how consumer demands get the goods and services produced that consumers want. If consumers demand more red barn paint, the immediate result is increased sales for paint stores, and these stores order more paint from wholesalers to replenish their stocks. The wholesalers in turn order more paint from the manufacturers. And the manufacturers, with joyous hearts, turn out more red barn paint, since their profits depend on producing and selling paint. The linkage may be jerky and imperfect, but each participant has an incentive to do his part—the profit incentive.

Sometimes the linkage between consumer and producer is direct. An example is the local laundry that washes your shirts. More often, consumer demand has to pass through several links before it hits the ultimate producer. An example is consumer demand for steel nails, which goes through at least the local hardware store and a wholesaler before it gets to, say, the American Steel and Wire Company, which makes nails.

But this is only part of the picture. American Steel and Wire in turn has to obtain iron ore, coal, and the other ingredients of steel, to say nothing of steel-making machinery, buildings for its operations, adding machines for its cost clerks, and stationery for its typists. Yet nails are a relatively simple commodity.

Try thinking about automobiles, or new house construction, or air travel. If you chart the branching-out relationship that starts with consumer demand, you will soon find yourself rapidly running out of sheets of paper. The complex interdependence of the modern economic system surpasses the comprehension of even the most systematic human mind. Yet consumer demands must be relayed to producers through the intricate web if the system is really to turn out what consumers want to buy.

What ties all these myriad links together is a structure of markets and market prices. The grocer knows you want sugar when you walk into his store and buy 5 or 10 pounds at the prevailing price. Similarly, there is a market that links grocers to wholesalers; one that links wholesalers and sugar-refiners; one that links sugar-refiners and sugar-growers.

In each market, price acts as the adjuster between demand and supply. When you demand more, price tends to move up. When price rises, there is an increased incentive to produce more.[1] *It is this interaction between demand, supply, and price that is the core of the self-adjusting mechanism of the private-enterprise system.*

The world is far too complex to understand if we try looking at all the details at once. Thus, it is useful to concentrate first on some very simple cases, or models, of markets. The problem of understanding the real world is, then, one of using these models to help understand the more complex markets of the real world. In many respects, markets differ widely. But they all boil down to

[1] This second statement is a more tricky proposition. Sometimes the entire response to increased consumer demand comes merely through more production at the same price. But usually, increased demand bids up the price, and this higher price helps in calling forth added supply to satisfy the increased demand. Chapters 22 to 24 provide a more thorough analysis of the relation between business costs and the goods they supply.

pretty much the same central problem of interaction between demand, supply, and price. A good understanding of the much-cited "law of supply and demand" is a powerful tool indeed for understanding how the modern economy works. We turn now to the supply side of the picture.

SUPPLY

Supply is analogous to demand. *Supply is a schedule of amounts that will be offered for sale at different prices during some time period, other factors remaining unchanged.* Supply can also be plotted on a curve with amounts on the horizontal axis and prices on the vertical one. But it differs from demand when it is plotted, since the supply curve ordinarily slopes uphill whereas the demand curve ordinarily slopes downhill. The slope of the supply curve reflects the fact that usually more units will be offered for sale at high than at low prices, in contrast to the reverse demand relationship.

Upward-sloping supply curves may seem obvious to you. The higher the price, the greater will be the profit inducement to produce and sell more. Or they may seem anything but obvious. You may think of the economies of mass production, and suspect that more units will be produced when demand increases, without any rise in price. This may, of course, be true under some circumstances, and sometimes—for example, in the automobile industry—to a significant extent.

The relation between firms' costs and the supply curves for their products is a major subject in economics. It is analyzed in detail in the following chapters. For purposes of this chapter, take it on faith that most supply curves are flat or upward-sloping, with the reasons to be examined later. And even if supply curves should turn out to be downward-sloping in some cases, the type of interaction between supply, demand, and price described in the following pages would still be generally applicable and useful.

A simple example can show how supply curves work. Suppose there are three dairy farms nearby. At various milk prices each will produce and offer different amounts for sale, as in Table

21-1. For the moment, we merely assume that each farmer will produce and offer more milk as the price rises.[2]

TABLE 21-1
SUPPLY SCHEDULE FOR MILK

Price per Quart	Number of Quarts Supplied per Week by:			
	A	B	C	All
20 cents	50	50	20	120
15 cents	40	50	20	110
10 cents	40	40	0	80
5 cents	30	35	0	65

This supply schedule can be plotted on a graph just as the demand schedule was. Again putting price on the vertical axis and quantity on the horizontal one, we get the market supply curve shown in Figure 21-1.

It is important to remember some of the same warnings on supply that apply to demand: (1) Supply is a schedule, not a single amount. Thus, more output at a higher price may be merely a movement to a new point on the supply schedule, not an increase in supply. A change in supply is a change in the schedule (a shift of the

[2] Farmer C is what some economists call a "marginal producer." He comes into the market only if the price rises to a relatively high level.

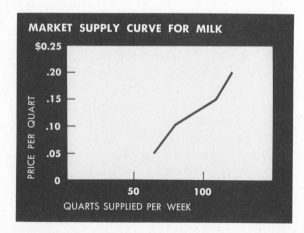

MARKET SUPPLY CURVE FOR MILK

FIG. 21-1 The supply curve shows how many quarts will be supplied each week at different prices.

curve). (2) Supply has meaning only with reference to some time period. The period should always be specified. (3) A supply schedule or curve is always drawn on the assumption of "other things equal." Just what "other things" we hold constant will vary from case to case, depending partly on the time period involved. For a one-day period, the number of cows and the amount of mechanical equipment the farmer has must be taken as constants. If we're talking about supply per year, obviously such matters become variables. This would lead you to suspect that the supply curve per year might look quite different from the supply curve per day—and it does, as we shall see presently.

Elasticity of Supply

Supply can be elastic or inelastic, just like demand. If the amount put on the market is highly responsive to price changes, the supply is elastic. If the amount offered is little affected by price variations, the supply is inelastic. Except that the amount supplied and the price ordinarily move in the same direction, whereas for demand the amount demanded and the price move in opposite directions, the two concepts are parallel.

Elasticity of supply varies with the time period involved. Take an extreme case of inelastic supply first. Suppose you have a strawberry patch and a roadside stand, but no overnight refrigeration. If you picked 20 quarts this morning, you must sell them at whatever price you can get or let them spoil (neglecting the possibilities that you may eat them fresh yourself or preserve them). Thus your supply curve *for the day* may be completely inelastic—a vertical line at 20 quarts of strawberries. By the end of the day, if you have them left you're willing to sell your 20 quarts at any price from zero up—the higher the better, of course. Figure 21-2 pictures this simple assumption, where cost of production appears to play no role.

Now take a case at the other extreme. Suppose some simple commodity like lead pencils can be reproduced almost without limit at a certain cost, say 3 cents per pencil, merely by duplicating existing manufacturing facilities, materials, and workers. Given enough time to build new facilities, almost any given number of pencils will be

FIG. 21-2 This chart shows completely inelastic supply. The same number of quarts is offered at any price shown.

produced for sale at a price of 3 cents or above. Thus, the supply curve might be completely elastic—a horizontal line, at 3 cents per pencil, as in Fig. 21-3.

This case, like that of strawberries, is oversimplified; cost per pencil may not be quite constant in the real world, and the resulting supply

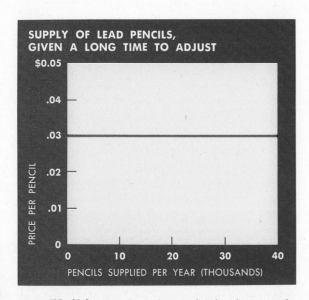

FIG. 21-3 This chart shows infinitely elastic supply. Given a long time to adjust, any number of pencils can be produced for sale at 3 cents per pencil.

curve may not be perfectly flat. But both cases serve to indicate the variations that may prevail in the supply of different kinds of commodities, depending on the time period considered. Most cases and most time periods, of course, fall somewhere between these two extremes.

DEMAND, SUPPLY, AND MARKET PRICE

You may have visited the "wheat pit" at the Board of Trade in Chicago, which is one of the world's major wheat-trading markets. Here millions of bushels of wheat are bought and sold daily by a relatively small number of men, acting largely as dealers and agents for others. Suppose the supply and demand for wheat in the pit on some particular day are as shown in Table 21-2, and that these schedules are constant for the entire day.

TABLE 21-2 SUPPLY AND DEMAND FOR WHEAT, CHICAGO, ON A GIVEN DAY		
Bushels Offered (In Millions)	Price	Bushels Demanded (In Millions)
18	$3.00	8
16	2.50	11
14	2.00	14
12	1.50	17
10	1.00	20

Suppose that the first bid on this day is $1.50 a bushel for 1000 bushels. It is readily filled, but it's clear that at this price there's going to be trouble, because buyers will demand 17 million bushels whereas sellers are willing to offer only 12 million bushels. Table 21-2 shows that lots of buyers are willing to pay more than $1.50 if they have to. And most of them soon discover they have to, because offerings are 5 million bushels short of demand at $1.50. We say there is an "excess demand" of 5 million bushels at $1.50. As buyers bid higher prices to get the wheat they want, the price will move up toward $2.00. As the price rises, those unwilling to pay the higher price will drop out and new sellers will come in, until at $2.00 the amount offered for sale just matches the amount demanded. There is no reason to suppose that the price will be bid higher this day, because everyone who is willing to pay $2.00 is getting his wheat and everyone who has wheat for sale at $2.00 sells it.

Try starting with a price of $3.00 to see whether that price could last long in this market. Where does the price stabilize?

This same analysis can be done graphically just as well. Figure 21-4 graphs these same demand and supply schedules. The curves intersect at a price of $2.00 with 14 million bushels traded. This is the only price at which the amount demanded just matches the amount supplied, and it is the price that will be reached through bargaining in the market. The reasoning is the same as with the schedules. Try any higher price, say $3.00, and you can see from Fig. 21-4 that it can't last. At $3.00, 18 million bushels will be offered but only 8 million bushels demanded; there is an "excess supply" of 10 million bushels. Competition among sellers will push the price down. At any price higher than $2.00, there is excess supply. There will be too many sellers for the buyers, and sellers will shade their prices in order to find buyers. At any lower price, buyers won't be able to get the wheat they demand and will shade up the prices they offer.

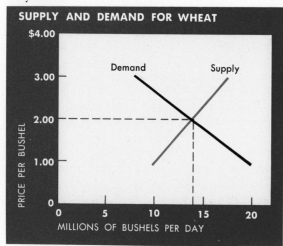

FIG. 21-4 With these supply and demand curves, the equilibrium price will be $2.00, with 14 million bushels exchanged.

Equilibrium Price and Market Equilibrium

When a price is established that just clears the market, economists call it an "equilibrium price." The amount offered just equals the amount demanded at that price. Price is in equilibrium when, with the given demand and supply curves, it stays put at that level. At any other level, price will not be in equilibrium, since there will be excess supply or excess demand, and price will move up or down toward a level that will eliminate the excess supply or excess demand.

When an equilibrium price has been reached, with given demand and supply curves, we say the market is in equilibrium. At the prevailing price, all those who want to sell are selling and all those who want to buy are buying. There is neither excess supply nor excess demand. Unless either demand or supply changes, price will remain unchanged, as will the amount bought and sold each time period.

Consumer demands and producers' responses to those demands are meshed together through market adjustments toward equilibrium. Once a market has reached equilibrium, it has impersonally and automatically:

1. Reflected the wants of all consumers willing to spend their dollars in that market, weighting each want by the number of dollars that particular consumer will spend at different prices. If each consumer's demand schedule truly reflects the marginal utilities of different amounts of the product to him, the market has given him the largest utility obtainable for his dollars.

2. Led firms to produce as much of the product as consumers will buy, taking into account the costs of producing the commodity. These costs are reflected in the supply curve; the higher costs of production are, the less will be produced at each price offered by consumers.

Only when the market is in equilibrium are the combined wants of consumers and the costs of production meshed together so as to give consumers the most that can be obtained of the commodity, given the costs of producing it. And we can be reasonably sure this equilibrium accurately reflects the preferences of all the parties concerned, buyers and sellers, because the exchanges are voluntary. If any individual saw the purchase or sale as against his best interests, he would not have bought or sold at that price.

This evaluation of the results of market equilibrium is preliminary and oversimplified. But it's a useful first approximation to keep in mind as we look in more detail at the operation of different markets through the chapters to come.

Changes in Demand and Supply

Actually, of course, demand and supply seldom stay constant for long in an active market like the wheat pit, and one price may be hardly established before demand or supply changes and price slides up or down toward a new equilibrium level. Changes like this are easy to illustrate, as in Fig. 21-5. Keeping the same supply curve as before, suppose that news of war sharply increases the demand for wheat on successive days. Common sense tells you that with constant supply and increased demand, the price will be bid up—and it is. On the second day, with increased demand D^1D^1, the price is bid up to $2.50 with 16 million bushels bought. Although the supply curve is constant, more wheat is supplied at the higher price. The result of the increased demand is *both* a higher price and more wheat traded. On the third day (demand D^2D^2) the price is still higher—up to $3.00 with eighteen million bushels bought. The demand curve slides up the fixed supply curve.

This example is useful as an exercise in analyzing the consequences of changing demand or supply curves. It is important also to point up the effective way in which market responses automatically link up demanders with suppliers, and do so in a way that generates production and sales of just the "right" amount, given the demand and supply conditions specified.

Supply and Demand:
Some Special Cases

Completely Inelastic Supply. Some extreme cases may help to clarify what is involved in market adjustments to different demand-and-supply relationships. Take first a case where the amount supplied is absolutely fixed. A favorite

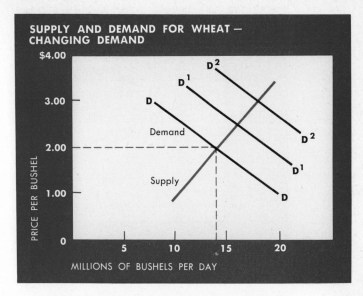

FIG. 21-5   Increases in demand to D^1D^1 and D^2D^2 cause increases in both price and quantity traded. The new equilibrium with D^2D^2 involves a price of $3.00 and 18 million bushels exchanged daily.

economists' example is that there are only four corners at State and Madison Streets in Chicago, sometimes called the busiest corner in the world. The supply curve for building space on this corner is thus completely inelastic—there's no more land available on the corner no matter how high land prices or rents may go. Suppose we graph the supply of land on this corner in square feet, and the demand (*DD*) for it on either a purchase or rental basis. The picture might look roughly like Fig. 21-6, with annual rents in equilibrium at $1,000 per square foot.

Now suppose the demand for space on the corner increases. The demand curve moves up to D^1D^1. Property-owners can now charge $1,100 per square foot. The amount of land rented is identical before and after the increase in demand. This outcome is very nice for the landowner, not so good for the consumer. But if demand falls, the full burden falls on the landowner. The price (rent) going to the supplier (landowner) is determined solely by the demand. Supply in this extreme case, and only in this case, has no active role in determining the price.

Completely Elastic Supply. Now take the other extreme—the pencil industry described before where the amount supplied could be increased at a constant cost merely by duplicating

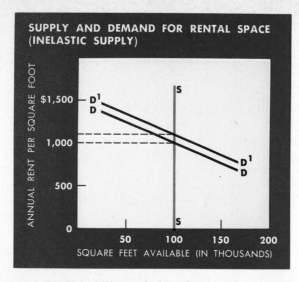

FIG. 21-6 With completely inelastic supply, increased demand means merely a higher price.

productive facilities. Given a long enough time period, the supply curve here would look perfectly flat, as in Fig. 21-7. If *DD* is the demand, the price of pencils will be 3 cents and 10,000 per day will be made and sold. Suppose now that demand increases to D^1D^1. Here the price remains unchanged while production and sales rise to 12,000 daily. And this is clearly sensible. This is a case of "constant costs." Since more pencils can be produced at the same cost per pencil, increased demand will simply call forth more pencils with-

out bidding up the price. This is the other extreme from the land-rent case above. Here consumers can be happy because rising demand brings more output without any rise in price. With the land, changing demand had no effect on the quantity sold, only on the price.

Most real-world cases lie between these two extremes—though many commodities approximate the pencil case, *given a long time period for adjustment.* If increased output can be obtained only by constructing more expensive factories, or by paying higher prices for raw materials and labor, the supply curve will slope upward. This is the case that economists call "increasing costs." If the increased output can be produced at the same cost per pencil, the long-run supply curve will be flat, as in the "constant costs" case just above.

Try working out the results of increased demand in these cases. You will see that it makes a good deal of difference to you, the consumer, which kind of product you want more of. In one case, you get more at the same price; in the other, you get more only at a higher price. (With *decreasing* costs and a *downward*-sloping supply curve, which we have temporarily ruled out, the consumer could be happier still, since then increased demand could mean more goods at a lower price.)

An Example—The Effects of Taxes. Suppose we want to analyze the probable effects of imposing an additional $1.00 tax on each fifth of whiskey distilled for sale. Assume that the long-run supply curve before the new tax is the solid curve *SS* in Fig. 21-8 (same in both halves). The left-hand diagram shows a highly elastic demand curve for whiskey, the right-hand diagram a highly inelastic one. Before the new tax the price is $5.00 per fifth, and 100,000 fifths are being sold weekly.

Now the government imposes the new tax. Consider its effects with the two different demand conditions. The tax raises the effective cost of producing whiskey by $1.00 per fifth; hence the supply curve moves to the left by $1.00 at each level of output. Less will be produced at each selling price. S^1S^1 represents the new supply curve (after tax) in both halves of the diagram. But as supply is restricted, the results are very different with the two demand curves. With highly inelas-

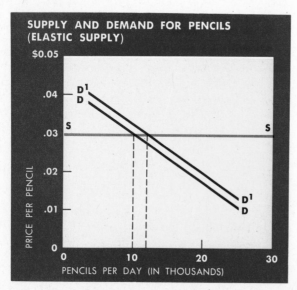

FIG. 21-7 With infinitely elastic supply, increased demand leads to more output with no increase in price.

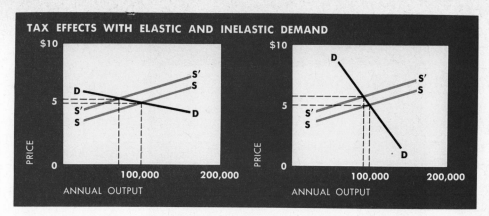

FIG. 21-8 A new tax on whiskey is largely passed on to consumers if demand is inelastic (right-hand portion), but results mainly in reduced output and purchases if demand is elastic (left-hand portion).

tic demand (right diagram), as price moves up consumers continue to buy nearly as much whiskey; the new equilibrium shows nearly as much whiskey produced and sold as before the tax, with the price to the consumer higher by nearly the full amount of the tax. With highly elastic demand (left diagram) the amount bought drops rapidly as price rises. The new after-tax equilibrium shows mainly a reduction in production and purchases, with the new price (including tax) only a little above the old $5.00 level. The main result is that consumers get less whiskey, while producers share $1 of the $5+ price with the government. Simple supply-and-demand analysis can produce highly illuminating results if we use it to examine particular markets.

"Free Goods." One last example: How is it that air, without which we should all die, is free, whereas most other things, which are much less essential, command a price? The answer is obvious once you try a demand-and-supply analysis. What is the supply of air? It is substantially unlimited at zero cost. The supply curve would rise above the zero-cost line only at some very high-quantity figure for most real-world situations. Thus, even though we might be willing, if necessary, to pay a very high price for air, it just isn't necessary. Since the air available at zero cost is practically unlimited, any demand curve would cut the supply curve at a zero cost and price.

Aside from its use as a simple supply-and-demand example, the case of air as a "free good" illustrates a very fundamental economic principle: Value depends on (1) utility, (2) scarcity, and (3) cost of production. Unless an article has utility (want-satisfying ability), no one will be willing to pay for it. Unless an article is scarce, no one needs to pay for it, however useful it is; the total

utility of air to us is very high, but its marginal utility is very low since we have so many units of air readily available, and our total "consumer surplus" on air is very large indeed. Unless an article costs something to produce, its supply will be for practical purposes infinite, and no one will need to pay for it.

THE ECONOMICS OF PRICE-FIXING

The law of supply and demand states that market price and quantity sold are determined by supply and demand under competitive conditions, such as in the wheat-market case above. But lots of times, people—labor unions, farmers, businessmen, congressmen—don't like the prices and quantities set by market demand and supply. And they want to do something about it. What then?

Price Ceilings

Most people don't like to pay high prices. When prices rise, the pressures mount on Congress and the President to hold them down. "How can I pay $1.00 a pound for butter and $125 a month rent for a poor apartment when my income is only $4,000 a year?" asks the mill hand. And he's not going to be very happy about getting an answer from the politicians in Washington that the law of supply and demand says it has to be that way. He wants something done, or he's easy picking for the other party next election.

So sometimes Congress enacts price ceilings. Suppose it slaps a price ceiling on butter below the equilibrium level. Suppose that the demand for and supply of butter are as shown in Fig. 21-9. The equilibrium price would be about $1.00 a pound. But Congress has passed a law setting a maximum price of 80 cents.

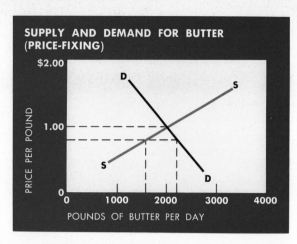

SUPPLY AND DEMAND FOR BUTTER (PRICE-FIXING)

PRICE PER POUND

$2.00

1.00

0

0   1000   2000   3000   4000

POUNDS OF BUTTER PER DAY

FIG. 21-9 When the government sets a legal maximum price below the market equilibrium price, there's trouble. More butter is demanded than is supplied at the artificially low price.

At the legal price ceiling, clearly the amounts demanded and supplied don't match. There is excess demand; people want a lot more butter than they can buy. The amount demanded daily in this local market is about 2,200 pounds; that offered is only 1,600. At the ceiling price, excess demand is 600 pounds daily.

Who gets the butter? The price system is tied down—it can't allocate the butter by equilibrating supply and demand through higher prices.

"First come, first served" may be the answer. Housewives get the children off to school early and head for the grocer's. They stand in lines in the grocery store. This solution is not calculated to make anyone very happy, least of all the grocer who fast loses his friends when there isn't enough to go around, and the working wives who can't do their shopping till evening.

In frustration, grocers may set up informal rationing systems of their own—say, only a half-pound to a customer. Or they may decide to protect their regular customers, so they put away a few cases of butter for them. This is hard on wives who shop around, and disastrous for families that move to new neighborhoods.

If enough people get unhappy enough, the government may have to step in with a formal rationing plan, whereby the customer has to have a ration ticket as well as money to buy a pound of butter. Nobody is very happy about being rationed, and everybody complains about the red

tape. Unless the government officials are both skillful and lucky, the number of ration tickets issued won't exactly match the supplies available, and a good many mixups can be counted on.

Lastly, the price system may sneak in the back door again and take over part of the equilibrating job outside the law. "Black markets" may develop. It's pretty hard for well-to-do consumers not to offer the corner grocer a little extra for an extra pound of butter. And it's pretty hard for the grocer, pinched between rising costs and fixed price ceilings, to refuse. Short of a regimented system like Hitler's Germany, it's hard to see how rigid price ceilings can be tightly enforced when excess demand is large. In World War II, such ceilings worked reasonably well in the United States, partly because of intense patriotic pressures and partly because the government gradually raised ceilings as pressures built up on various commodities. The surprising thing to most economists was not that black markets developed, but that the public's basic sense of fair play was so strong that black markets didn't blow the price-control system apart.

Whether the job is done by informal seller rationing, official government rationing, or black-market price increases, someone or something has to decide who is to get the butter when a price ceiling is imposed below the equilibrium market price. A price ceiling works no magic. It just transfers the equilibrating job to some other channel. You can't get rid of the basic supply-and-demand forces at work by passing a law.

Price Floors and Income Supports

Some people—usually sellers—worry because prices aren't high enough. Labor unions often try to set wages above free-market levels. Some business associations do the same thing with their prices. The government is a large-scale participant in the game of putting floors under prices above the free-market level; parity farm-support prices and minimum-wage legislation are two big examples.[3]

[3] This is not to say that parity price supports or minimum-wage rates are always above free-market levels. They are not. But if they weren't intended to be at least part of the time, there would be little reason for their existence.

Supply and Demand for Wheat (Price Supports). Since the 1920's, the government has been supporting farm product prices to help the farmers. Suppose the government decrees that wheat shall not sell for less than $3.00 a bushel. But suppose the free-market price would be only $2.00, as pictured in Fig. 21-10. It's clear that there is going to be a lot of unsold wheat around—excess supply at the $3.00 price is about 30 million bushels. Many buyers will pay $3.00, but a lot won't.

Suppose the government price floor is enforced and nobody undercuts the stated $3.00 price. Are wheat farmers better or worse off as a result? First, only about 80 million bushels will be bought. Another 30 million bushels are offered, and either the government will have to buy them up or strong price-cutting pressures will develop among the farmers with the unsold wheat. Second, our old friend elasticity of demand reenters. If demand is inelastic, total expenditures on wheat are larger at the higher price and total farm income is up (even though consumers get less wheat to eat). But if demand is elastic, the higher price leaves everyone worse off; then farmers get less

total income from their wheat, and consumers get less wheat.

But even if demand is inelastic over the price range involved, this simple form of government price edict won't prove very satisfactory. If you are one of the farmers with the millions of bushels of wheat that nobody bought, the higher total income of wheat farmers is small solace to you when you have no income at all. You want the government to help you, too.

So the governmental income-support program will probably take one of two basic courses. (1) The government may support the legal price through buying up the extra 30 million bushels of wheat. This would in effect move the total (private plus government) demand curve to the right, so the equilibrium price is $3.00 with 110 million bushels sold. Or (2) the government may impose some kind of restriction on wheat production (maybe through a "soil conservation" program) to reduce supply to a point where the new free-market price will approximate the legal-edict price. This policy would bring supply and demand into equilibrium at a price of $3.00 with sales of 80 million bushels, by shifting the supply curve to the left. Combinations are of course possible.

In approach (1), the government ends up buying the 30 million bushels of wheat at $3.00 a bushel—at a cost of $90 million to the taxpayers. This result is nice for the farmers but not so nice for the taxpayers. Remember, too, where the consumer stands in this plan—with less wheat and a higher price for what he buys. Moreover, unless something changes, the government will keep on piling up wheat indefinitely.

In approach (2), this situation is avoided by by having 30 million fewer bushels of wheat produced. Farmers will get more or less income, depending on the elasticity of demand. If the government merely required everybody to cut production by the required percentage, this would be the end of the matter. But actually, the government may well be expected (at least by some of the farmers) to pay those farmers who wanted to produce wheat but couldn't because of government restrictions. This was the case in the basic New Deal AAA farm programs through the 1930's, and it seems to be no less the case today. Here again the taxpayer picks up the bill for the

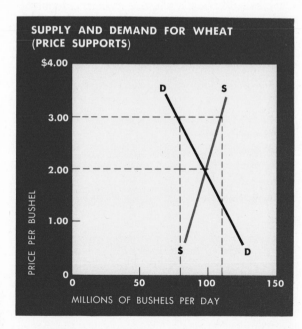

FIG. 21-10 When the government sets a minimum price higher than the market equilibrium price, there's also trouble. More is offered than customers will buy, so the government must step in to buy the surplus or to cut back production.

subsidy paid to farmers for not producing the 30 million bushels of wheat. As under approach (1), consumers pay more and get fewer bushels of wheat. The government can keep the price up—if it's willing to eliminate excess supply by buying it up or by restricting output. But laws that fix prices above or below market equilibrium levels without dealing with excess demand or supply soon face painful problems of which simple supply and demand analysis gives ample warning.

SUMMARY: SUPPLY, DEMAND, AND MARKET EQUILIBRIUM

A sure-fire way to sound like an expert in economics is to observe sagely, "You can't repeal the law of supply and demand!" This remark is especially good if the argument is running against you, or you need a devastating blast against the political party in power.

The preceding pages should help to clarify both how meaningless such a statement is until it is carefully applied to the problem at hand, and how powerful an analytical tool supply-and-demand analysis can be. The "law," or "principle,"

of supply and demand can be stated in many different ways. But however it is stated, it is nothing more than an analytical tool that can be used in thinking through economic problems. It doesn't provide ready-made answers to problems. Obviously the government and private groups can control market prices—they do it every day. But unless they recognize that they must do it ultimately through controlling either supply or demand, they're headed for some unhappy surprises.

Thus, supply-and-demand analysis provides a powerful tool in thinking through a wide range of economic problems. Market price plays a central role in compromising and meshing the multiple pressures exerted by demanders and suppliers in every market. And the concept of market equilibrium helps greatly to focus the way in which markets and market prices merge these conflicting interests toward a result that will be as nearly "optimal" for all as is feasible. This chapter provides the central tools for analyzing market forces at work. Over and over in the chapters ahead we shall be asking: What determines demand and supply in this market, how do they interact, and what is the equilibrium outcome?

REVIEW

Concepts To Remember

Recheck your understanding of the important new concepts introduced in this chapter. They are:

market price	market equilibrium
supply	excess demand
supply curve	excess supply
elasticity of supply	constant costs
equilibrium price	increasing costs

For Analysis and Discussion

1. Is it demand or supply that primarily determines price? If your answer is, "different in different cases," give an example in which you would expect each to be the dominant force.
2. Explain carefully what is meant by saying that an equilibrium price "clears the market."
3. When demand is large, we can be sure the price of the commodity will be high. True or false? Why?
4. Why are diamonds so high-priced, when they serve for the most part only as decoration?
5. Are the factors determining the price of a Picasso painting the same as those determining the price of potatoes? Explain your answer.

6. Suppose that the demand for sugar is very inelastic and a new tax is imposed on sugar. Would the tax be passed on to consumers through higher prices? Compare this with a product for which the demand is highly elastic.
7. Suppose the demand for oleomargarine increases, without any corresponding increase in the supply. What effect, if any, would this have on the demand for butter?
8. How does elasticity of demand help to explain why historically governments often imposed a salt tax when they wanted to obtain more revenue?

TWENTY-TWO

THE BUSINESS FIRM
AND ITS COSTS

Why Worry about Costs?

What Are Costs?

Cost of Production and the Rate of Output.

Unit-Cost Curves.

"Short-Run" and "Long-Run" Views of Costs.

How Big Is Optimal?

Appendix: Physical Production Relationships
Underlying Cost Curves.

In a market economy, consumer demands direct what is produced. We turn now to look in detail at the way business firms respond to consumer demands—at the supply side of the demand and supply interaction.

General Motors supplies Chevrolets. You and I buy them. Westinghouse supplies light bulbs and we buy them. In most cases where a firm manufactures a physical product, wholesalers and retailers intervene between manufacturer and consumer. In others, consumers demand services rather than goods—for instance, shirt laundering and air travel.

Obviously, there are many different kinds of suppliers. To simplify, however, in the next few chapters we shall consider manufacturing firms as suppliers and consumers as demanders, with no intermediaries. This is unrealistic, but it gives a simple first approximation to the working of the market system. And the goal here is to explain the main framework of how the economic system responds to changing consumer demands, changing cost conditions, and other such factors. You can see the main issues without getting enmeshed in the mass of detail that surrounds many markets in the real world.

WHY WORRY ABOUT COSTS?

Why worry about costs? Because a businessman's costs will largely determine how much he will produce in response to different demands. If customers will only pay $1 for a widget and the minimum cost of producing a widget is $1.25, you don't need to be an expert economist to see that not many widgets will be produced. Thus, viewed fundamentally, costs are important because they exercise a restraint on production. If there were no costs in making a product, we could get unlimited supplies whenever we wanted them. But since it does cost something to produce almost everything, we can't expect everything we want free. And how far any business will go in producing what we want will depend on how much that article costs to produce relative to what we are willing to pay for it.

Business costs are important for another reason. Looked at as wages and salaries, rent, and interest payments, business costs *are* the incomes of workers and of resource-owners. In explaining business costs, therefore, we are simultaneously explaining why most people receive the incomes they do.

This chapter considers the kinds of costs faced by business concerns. Chapter 23 then explains how these costs influence business production and pricing practices.

WHAT ARE COSTS?

Since costs are so important, they deserve careful analysis. First, how do costs look to the businessman?

Back in the profit-and-loss statement on page 270, costs were broken down into materials, labor cost, depreciation on plant and equipment, maintenance and repairs, selling and administrative costs, taxes, and interest payments on borrowed funds. Every business has its own way of classifying costs, but these main categories show up in most such statements.

Most of these costs represent direct cash outlays—wages; payments for materials; tax payments; and so on. But it is important to remember that cash outlays are by no means identical with costs.

Depreciation is an example. Depreciation is merely a bookkeeping entry estimating how much of the value of plant and equipment has been used up in producing goods during a certain time period. It is not a cash outlay at all.

Cost of materials is another illustration. This item shows the cost of materials *used* to produce goods sold during the period. It may be more or less than the cost of materials *bought* during the period. For example, a business with big materials inventories might run a whole month without buying any materials. Yet it should obviously consider as costs the value of the materials used up from inventory during the month.

These examples emphasize another point. Many important business costs are necessarily *estimated* costs. What the accountant tries to do is to get the best possible approximation of the cost of producing one ton of steel or one quart of milk. But this is a more complex problem than it sounds, both because it is hard to allocate many types of cost accurately to individual units of output, and because cost per unit in most companies varies with the scale of output and the passage of time. The problem is especially acute when a company uses the same facilities, officials, and labor to produce a variety of products. For example, how much of the president's salary should be allocated to plows, harrows, and harvesters, respectively, in the International Harvester Company?

One other reminder about costs. The modern business has losts of costs not directly related to turning out its products. For example, as a practical matter, it must give to the Community Chest and keep its plant looking reasonably attractive if it wants to be a good citizen in the community —and most companies do. It probably has to contribute to health and retirement funds for its employees, in addition to direct wages. Partly these are just examples of managerial philanthropy, but competition also drives firms to make these expenditures, just as it drives them to pay the going wages and prices for their workers and materials.

Alternative Costs

The economist is interested in these calculations. But his concern with the over-all allocation of resources in the economy leads him on to some further questions.

Thinking in "real" terms, the economist is driven by the basic fact of scarcity to the conclusion that the "real" cost of producing anything is the alternatives that are foregone. For example, the *real* cost of producing an auto is the other commodities given up that might otherwise have been produced with the same steel, glass, rubber, and labor. *The real cost is an "alternative cost" —the alternative uses of the resources that are given up when the resources are used in producing autos. Sometimes alternative cost is called "opportunity" cost.*

This fact is most obvious in a war economy, when the guns-or-butter alternative stares us in the eye. We can make more tanks, but only at the cost of giving up trucks. The real cost of the tanks is the alternative use of steel and labor foregone— trucks, refrigerators, or other civilian hard goods. The same thing is true in a peacetime economy, unless unemployed resources are available. If we use our resources for one thing, we can't use them for another.

This concept of alternative, or opportunity, cost can be put into money terms. Thus, the cost of producing one TV set is the amount of money necessary to get the factors of production needed for the set away from alternative uses. For example, as a TV manufacturer, you have to pay enough for mechanics to get them away from auto and radar plants. You have to pay enough for copper wire to bid it away from telephone companies. And so it is for every resource you use. *In economic terms, the total cost of the TV set is the amount necessary to bid all the required resources away from the strongest competing uses.*

Accounting and Economic Costs

Use of an alternative-cost concept leads economists to different cost figures from the ones that businessmen and their accountants work with. These differences arise primarily because the economist includes several items that the accountant ordinarily doesn't consider as costs when he draws up his profit-and-loss statements.

A simple example is the independent corner grocer, who has bought a store with his own funds and runs it himself. In addition to the regular business costs in the profit-and-loss statement, the economist would say:

"How about a return on your own investment and a salary for yourself? If you didn't have your money tied up in the store, you could be earning

5 per cent on it in another investment. If you weren't working in the store, you could earn $5,000 a year working for Krogers. You ought to account as costs a 5 per cent return on your investment and a $5,000 salary for yourself before you compute your profit for the year, because these reflect real alternatives that you're giving up when you stay in your business."

If the grocer does not include these costs and finds he's making a $4,000 annual profit, he may think he's doing well—but actually he's kidding himself. The $4,000 doesn't even give him the salary he could earn working for someone else, much less the return he could get by doing that and investing his money somewhere else.

A similar, though less obvious situation, is found in business corporations. Corporations pay salaries to their officers and employees, so there's no problem there. And they pay interest to their bondholders, which is considered a cost in computing profits. But what about the interest on the owners' (stockholders') investment, just as on the corner grocer's investment?

The usual accounting calculation of corporation profits omits the alternative cost of using the stockholders' capital in this firm rather than elsewhere. Profit is calculated before any payment is made to stockholders. *The economist, however, includes in the firm's costs a reasonable rate of return on stockholders' investment (measuring the alternative return that is foregone elsewhere). He therefore considers as "economic profit" only the excess income over and above this basic alternative cost, because a reasonable rate of return is part of the cost required to keep funds invested in any business.*[1]

The accountant's way of computing profits leads to some inconsistencies. Take two identical corporations, one financed by $1,000,000 of 4 per cent bonds and $1,000,000 of stock, the other by $2,000,000 of stock. Suppose each earns $100,000 after all other costs are covered. Corporation A will now show an accounting profit of only $60,-

---

[1] In economics, costs that show up in the usual accounting procedures are often called "explicit" costs, while alternative costs (like a return on stockholders' investment) which are not usually recorded in modern accounting are called "implicit" costs.

000, because the bondholders' interest takes $40,-000 of the $100,000. Corporation B, identical except for financing arrangements, shows profits of $100,000. Not the least important consequence is the difference in income tax liabilities of the two substantially identical firms, since the law permits firms to deduct bond interest as a cost in calculating profits for income tax liability, but not implicit return on stockholders' investment.

Through the rest of this book, we shall use the alternative-cost concept. Thus, costs of production will include the reasonable (or "normal") rate of return on investment necessary to keep the funds invested in any given concern rather than elsewhere. Costs will include the entrepreneur's own salary if he is self-employed. Broadly, they will include all costs required to get and keep resources in the occupation under consideration. Most costs will be the same as those used by the accountant, but the differences noted above must be kept in mind. *Especially, remember that the production-cost data and curves used here include a "normal" return on investment, if you want to avoid some dangerous pitfalls later on.*

Cash vs. Economic Profits:
A Managerial Application

A simple managerial example may help show the importance of these distinctions, as well as give you an impression of how basic economic analysis can help in day-to-day business. Suppose you're in business for yourself, doing miscellaneous repairs (carpentering, electrical wiring, and so on) at a minimum charge of $5 per call and $2 per hour additional after the first hour. Your only equipment is your family station wagon, the back end of which you have converted to carry your working tools. You are prepared to answer calls anywhere in your general area. You've spent $20 for an ad in the local paper and for a supply of mimeographed postcards mailed at random to names from the phone book.

After a month, you've collected a large amount of experience, considerable boredom waiting for the phone to ring, and $310. Have you made a profit? Should you stay in business?

The answer to the profit question hinges on what your costs have been. If you deduct the original $20 outlay, you have $290 left. Not bad for a summer month. But look again. There is clearly gas and oil for the station wagon. And wear and tear

on the same, which may be appreciable from this use. Then, aside from any materials (for which you may have charged extra), there's the question of your own time.

Suppose gas and oil allocable to this work have cost $40. And you make a rough estimate of $25 a month extra depreciation on the car. That still leaves you $225. Is that more or less than a reasonable wage for your own full time and energy for the month? Here the concept of opportunity cost provides a guide to the answer. What could you hope to make elsewhere, doing work you consider about equally interesting, difficult, and convenient? If the answer is above $225, you've made a loss, even with $250 in the bank. If it's less than $225 you've made a profit, though maybe a very small one. Central concepts from economic analysis: the distinction between cash and income, and opportunity cost. Without them you're apt to pull a real business boner.

COST OF PRODUCTION
AND THE RATE OF OUTPUT [2]

How do a business firm's costs vary with the amount it produces? Imagine a small company that produces a single product—say it assembles luxury-level hi-fi stereo sets. Suppose the company's only costs are raw materials, labor, depreciation on plant and equipment, maintenance, and return on stockholders' investment. Suppose further that, if we look at costs over the month ahead, we find that depreciation and a normal (implicit) return on stockholders' investment are "fixed" for the month—they go on whether the company operates at full capacity or part capacity, or shuts down. The other costs are "variable," depending on the company's rate of output.

Assume that the "fixed" costs amount to $1,000 per month, and that the "variable" costs vary with changes in output as in Table 22-1.

These same costs are plotted in Fig. 22-1. Cost is shown on the vertical axis, output on the horizontal one. The fixed cost totals $1,000, the

---

[2] The Appendix to this chapter, "Physical Production Relationships Underlying Cost Curves," provides the logical foundation for this cost analysis. It should be assigned here by those instructors who wish a rigorous analytical foundation for this and the following chapter, but students can grasp the central issues in the text without it.

TABLE 22-1

FIXED, VARIABLE, AND TOTAL COSTS

Output	Total Fixed Cost	Total Variable Cost	Total Cost
1	$1,000	$ 2,000	$ 3,000
2	1,000	2,500	3,500
3	1,000	3,000	4,000
4	1,000	4,000	5,000
5	1,000	5,000	6,000
6	1,000	6,600	7,600
7	1,000	10,000	11,000
8	1,000	16,000	17,000

same no matter what output is produced. On top of this, we need to put total variable cost—zero at zero output, $2,000 for one set, $2,500 for two, and so on. The total-cost curve (top line) thus shows the sum of total fixed and total variable cost at each level of output.

It is easy to see that total cost does not rise at an even rate. It doesn't cost much more in total to produce two sets than one, or three than two. But as the firm gets up to six or seven sets per month, total cost begins to rise much more rapidly. It is obviously total variable cost that begins to shoot up. The reason may be that the company was set up with a capacity of only five or six sets a month, and to exceed this capacity involves expensive readjustments in equipment, hiring more workers or overtime labor, and other such special problems. Or there may be some other explanation.

Fixed, Variable, and Total Costs per Unit

The preceding data don't show costs per set produced, and you probably think of business output in terms of cost and selling price per unit. You may already have divided the total-cost figures by the number of stereo sets produced to see what the cost per set is at different levels of output. If you haven't, it's a sensible thing to do. The result is shown in Table 22-2. These are, of course, just hypothetical figures. But their general character is important, because in some ways they are typical of all such cost data.

Fixed cost per unit will always be a steadily decreasing series, because the constant total-fixed-cost figure (here $1,000) is divided by a steadily rising volume of output. This is what is commonly known as "spreading the overhead." The drop in fixed cost per unit is very rapid at first, but as volume grows the additional cost reduction per unit steadily decreases in importance.

Variable cost per unit will generally fall at the outset, then flatten out somewhat, and then rise again as plant "capacity" is approached. To produce one set, the company has to have labor and materials of all the types needed for the set.

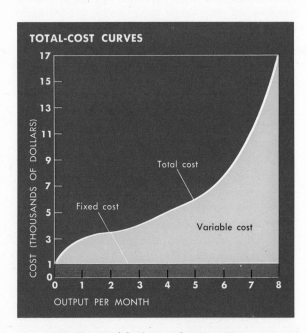

FIG. 22-1 Total fixed cost is $1,000 at all outputs. Total variable cost rises as output increases. Total cost for any output is the sum of fixed and variable costs; it rises rapidly once the "capacity" of the plant is reached.

TABLE 22-2

FIXED, VARIABLE, AND TOTAL COSTS PER UNIT

Output	Fixed Cost per Unit	Variable Cost per Unit	Total Cost per Unit
1	$1,000	$2,000	$3,000
2	500	1,250	1,750
3	333	1,000	1,333
4	250	1,000	1,250
5	200	1,000	1,200
6	167	1,100	1,267
7	143	1,430	1,573
8	125	2,000	2,125

On the labor side, it will clearly be inefficient to try to call each type of skilled labor in just long enough to work on one set. If we try to use two or three jacks-of-all-trades, we get less efficient work than by dividing the work up among experts on the various parts of the job. Similarly, it may be cheaper to buy materials in larger quantities than to buy just enough to produce one set per month. It's not efficient to produce only one or two sets a month.

At the other extreme, once the "capacity" for which the plant was planned has been reached, costs are likely to shoot up rapidly if we try to produce still more sets per month. "Capacity" is seldom an absolute limit in a plant. For example, steel plants may operate above 100 per cent of capacity; rated capacity allows for an average amount of shut-down time for maintenance and repairs, which can be postponed temporarily. But expansion of output beyond plant "capacity" often means expensive overtime work, hiring of lower-skilled workers, more spoilage under pressure of speed-up, and a variety of other such factors.

Thus, without going into details at the moment, it seems reasonable that *with any given plant* (which we have assumed) variable costs per unit will rise rapidly at some point beyond "capacity" output. Just when this point is reached depends, of course, on the individual firm. In many industries, variable costs per unit are apparently flat over wide ranges of output. In others, where small-scale operations are advantageous, increase in output beyond low levels may lead quickly to rising unit costs.

Total cost per unit is simply the sum of fixed cost per unit and variable cost per unit. Or it can be obtained by dividing total cost by the number of units produced. The decreasing fixed cost per unit will always pull down on total unit cost as output rises. At first, as long as both fixed and variable costs per unit are declining, clearly the total cost per unit is declining. But at some point total unit costs will begin to rise, often after a long flat area in which the fixed cost per unit declines slightly and the variable cost per unit is substantially constant or slightly rising. The rise in total unit cost will begin when variable cost per unit turns up more than enough to offset the downward pull of declining fixed unit costs. This point is at the sixth unit in our hi-fi plant. Total unit cost is relatively stable over the output range of three to six units, with the minimum cost per unit at an output of five sets per month.

This simple example should warn you against one common fallacy—the idea that each firm has *a* cost of production for its product. In every firm, cost of production per unit varies with output. This is certain at the extremes of very low and above-capacity output. It often also occurs over the range of normal variation in operations.

A good many firms now use what they call "standard costs" in pricing their products and in keeping control over their production processes. A "standard cost" for our hi-fi set would be an estimate by our accountant and production man of how much it should cost to produce one set at a normal, or typical, rate of output. If we think of 4 sets monthly as about normal operation, our standard-cost figure would be $1,250 per set.

Such standard-cost estimates play a useful role in modern industry. Many firms use them as a basis for setting prices, and we will meet them again in the chapters ahead. It is important, however, to remember that "standard cost" is only an *estimate* of unit cost *at some selected level of output*, not necessarily the minimum unit-cost level.

UNIT-COST CURVES

All these per unit cost data can readily be plotted on graphs as cost curves. Figure 22-2 shows the per unit cost data for our hi-fi firm. The shape of the curves corresponds, of course, to the data. Fixed cost per unit falls steadily as the constant total cost is spread over more and more units. Variable cost per unit and total cost per unit are both U-shaped, for the reasons suggested above. In most firms, the *TUC* (total-unit-cost) curve is probably flatter than in this hypothetical case. That is, there is a wider range of output over which total cost per unit is substantially constant, between the low-output inefficiencies shown at the left of the graph and the above-capacity inefficiencies at the right. (For a large, real-world plant producing many units, the cost curves would be smooth and continuous, without the corners shown in the curves for our very small firm.)

Be sure you know just what the graph means. For example, at an output of five sets next month,

FIG. 22-2 Unit-cost curves are derived by dividing the corresponding total-cost curves by total output. Here fixed unit cost slopes downward continuously as the constant total fixed cost is spread over more units of output. Other curves are U-shaped.

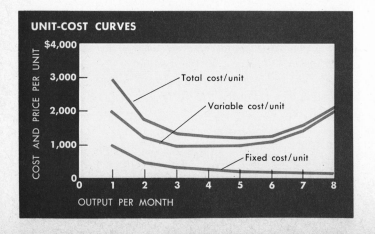

UNIT-COST CURVES

the fixed cost per set will be $200 and the variable cost per unit $1,000, for a total of $1,200. This happens to be the lowest point on the total-unit-cost curve. It is called the "least-cost combination." It is the lowest cost at which these hi-fi sets can be made, given the existing plant and the firm's other commitments for the month ahead.

"SHORT-RUN" AND "LONG-RUN" VIEWS OF COSTS

Economists speak of the "short run" and the "long run." Time is an extremely important variable in the analysis of economic problems, and this distinction is an attempt to clarify the assumptions being made about the time period involved in any case. *We mean by the "short run" any time period in which some costs (such as rent and interest on borrowed funds) are fixed and do not vary with changes in the firm's output. We mean by "long run" a time period long enough so that all costs become variable with changes in output. Thus, the distinction is an analytical one. In calendar time, the short run for one firm may be longer than a long run for another, depending on how long the cost commitments run in different cases.*

Some examples will clarify this distinction. For our firm, next month is clearly a "short run." During that month certain costs are fixed no matter how many hi-fis we produce—depreciation on the factory building, for example. Given a longer time period, the existing plant will depreciate away or it may be sold, so the capital tied up in the plant becomes available for other uses. Similarly, the manager's salary may be a fixed cost for the next month or year, but over some longer time period his contract will expire and his salary will become a variable cost. If a firm has commitments for fixed costs extending for years ahead, the "short run" for that firm will be a long time. The other extreme would be a firm with no plant of its own, no leases or salary contracts, and no other forward commitments. The commonest way to think of the "short run" is the time period over which a firm has a fixed plant and equipment to which variable agents such as labor and materials are added to achieve different output levels.

This is not a very precise way of drawing the distinction, but it conveys the general idea.

In the "long run," by contrast, *all* the firm's costs become variable. The entrepreneur can decide to build a new plant of different size if he likes. He can transfer his investment to another industry. He has complete freedom to move.

The Optimum Scale of Enterprise

The "long run" is thus a planning period, free from the short-run limitations imposed by fixed plant and other commitments. The big long-run planning problem is: What is the "optimum scale of enterprise" for the firm? How big a fixed plant, how big a labor force, how much equipment, what kind of management organization? The question involves everything related to planning the enterprise's scale of operations in the future.

Businesses seldom find themselves in a position to make all these decisions on future scale at one time. But they are continually re-evaluating their positions and planning specific long-run changes. So they may replan their over-all scale of enterprise much more frequently than would appear from a superficial glance.

Each possible scale of enterprise for any given firm can be shown as a U-shaped total-unit-cost curve associated with that scale. Clearly some scales of enterprise will be too small for reasonable efficiency. We may suspect that our stereo firm is such a producer. As the scale of enterprise becomes larger, more of the advantages of mass production and specialization of functions can be realized, bulk buying becomes possible, and skilled management can be afforded. The least-cost point on the cost curve for this larger plant will be lower than the least-cost point on the curve of a smaller enterprise. But after a certain size is reached, the firm may get too big. The least-cost point for the jumbo-sized firm may be higher than for a smaller-scale company. Why this is so, we shall consider in the next section.[3]

A set of five possible planning curves, showing expected costs for five different scales of enterprise, is given in Fig. 22-3. Actually, there could

[3] Throughout, we must assume some standard product being produced in order to keep the different scales of operation comparable.

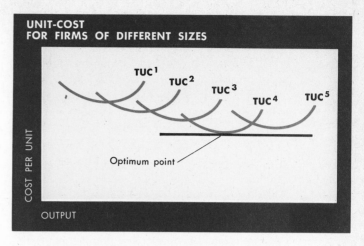

FIG. 22-3 Larger firms have lower minimum total-unit-cost points until the optimal scale of firm is reached. Then still larger firms face higher minimum TUC's.

be a much larger number of such curves, representing different scales of operation. Each *TUC* curve corresponds to a given scale of enterprise—a plant of certain size, equipment of certain sorts, and so on. The scale of enterprise giving the cost curve at the extreme left is obviously too small to be advantageous except for a very small market. In this figure, the scale corresponding to the fourth cost curve gives the lowest possible least-cost point. A firm of this size is the "optimum scale of enterprise," in the sense that it provides the possibility of the lowest cost per unit of output of any possible scale of enterprise. Note, however, that, if total market demand is small, it may still not be economical to build and operate a firm of this scale.

HOW BIG IS "OPTIMAL"?

Why are manufacturing companies typically bigger than dry-cleaning establishments? Why is retailing still mainly carried on by small-scale enterprises? Why do some firms remain small while others are huge?

These are hard questions, and the answers are complex. The primary reasons may be classed under four headings: technology, management, market opportunities, and financing channels.

Technology
and the Size of Enterprise

America is the land of mass production. American industry is admired the world over for its fabulous equipment and its technical know-how. The mass-production revolution pioneered by Henry Ford with the famous Model T has never stopped spreading. The basic advantages of today's huge steel mills, oil refineries, and auto plants boil down to four factors:

1. *Specialization and Division of Labor.* Adam Smith pointed out in 1776, in his famous *Wealth of Nations*, that specialization and division of labor in making pins would reduce the cost of pins, compared with having one man do the whole job. This principle underlies mass production. Extensive specialization and division of labor are feasible only in reasonably large firms. Such specialization pays off most where the product being turned out is complex and where many different skills and operations are involved. The auto plants of Detroit are a spectacular example of how far specialization can profitably go.

2. *Use of Elaborate, Expensive Machinery and Equipment.* No small gasoline refinery can compete effectively with the massive, automatic, multi-million-dollar refineries now used by all the major oil companies. Only a large company can afford a "cat cracker." The machinery for a modern, efficient steel-rolling mill is very expensive; only a big firm that is able to spread the cost of the equipment over a large volume of output can afford it. No small establishment could afford to use such equipment, for without large-volume output the cost per ton produced would be prohibitively high.

3. *Balancing of Processes.* In a large firm, the various stages of a productive process can be fitted together to take advantage of the optimum scale for each stage of the operation. Suppose machine A feeds machine B, but A processes 100 units per hour while B handles 150 at optimal rates. The big company can install three A machines in line with two B machines, and thus be able to use all at maximum efficiency levels. The small company, unable to use more than one machine of each type, must either keep B idle part of the time or put A on an extra-shift basis of some sort.

4. *Utilization of By-products.* The big firm can make effective use of many by-products that may be wasted in small concerns. For example, a big meat-packing firm uses cattle hoofs to make glue and other products. In a small company the number of hoofs is too small to make this recovery worthwhile.

All these technological considerations point toward large concerns as being more efficient. But economies of size don't continue indefinitely. Once a company is big enough to take full benefit of all these factors, it can realize no further cost reduction on technological grounds from growing still bigger. But there are other factors too that determine the optimal scale of enterprise.

Management and the Size of Enterprise

Someone has to manage every business firm, and good managers are scarce. Large firms can afford highly skilled managers—in purchasing, sales, production, finance, personnel. This kind of managerial specialization is quite similar in principle to the technological specialization and division of labor mentioned above. And it's a big advantage.

But there is one crucial difference. Somebody in every business has to pull the whole business together. At some point any business may get so big that managerial efficiency drops—though this point may come only after the firm is very large indeed; witness the efficiency of General Motors. The larger and more complex the firm, the more essential and yet more difficult coordination becomes. It is harder to reconcile conflicting views on policy problems. There is too much red tape, too many levels between the managers in the executive office and the workers in the factory or on the road; the structure becomes top-heavy and inflexible. Modern management emphasizes decentralization of authority and responsibility to avoid this central managerial problem. And this approach has accomplished much. But the potential diseconomies of management are a major problem for giant firms.

These possible management diseconomies may be stated in a different way—as the positive advantages of managing a small business. In the small firm, decisions can be made more easily and more quickly. There are few specialists to consult, fewer difficulties in arriving at a mutual understanding of the problems faced. This fact gives a special advantage to small firms in fields where changes must be made frequently, as in the production of style goods like women's dresses. Channels of communication are more direct between worker and management, and supervision is easier. Blind spots where wastes persist are less likely. Not least important may be the special interest, energy, and enthusiasm of men who manage their own businesses. Do these match the managerial advantages in bigness? Sometimes yes, sometimes no.

Market Opportunities and the Size of Enterprise

The size of the market may limit the size of firms. The potential market may not be big enough to permit even one firm to expand to its optimal scale. An example might be the light and power company in a small city. Often, where numerous firms compete, the share of the total market available to each places a direct limitation on the scale of enterprise. Such situations often lead to attempts by some firms to drive out competition in order to get the larger market needed to permit lower-cost production.

The big firm has obvious advantages in selling its products—large-scale advertising budgets, sales specialists, nation-wide sales organization. Similarly, big firms can often buy more cheaply through ordering large quantity lots, as well as through having more expert buyers. Often, large firms integrate vertically so that they themselves can produce many of the materials used in their own processes, whereas smaller concerns must buy their materials in the market.

All these factors may lower costs for big concerns. But it's easy to overemphasize them. The small seller retains many advantages, especially in retailing—personal contact with the customer, special services, and so on. And expected advantages of vertical integration sometimes turn sour. Many big firms have found to their dismay that they were better off going back to the market for their raw and semi-finished materials, after they had tried producing their own materials. There is no magic in producing steel for yourself if you are an auto manufacturer. The critical question is whether you can make the steel sheets cheaper than you can buy them from a steel company.

Financing Channels and the Size of Enterprise

It may be hard to get the funds necessary to start a big business. But once it is well established, it is likely to have an advantage over little businesses in getting more funds. This is partly because of its added prestige and attractiveness to investors, partly because the organized security markets are in effect accessible only to quite large firms, and partly because the costs of making large loans are less per dollar than they are for small loans.

How Big Is "Optimal"?

Thus, how big "optimal" is varies widely from industry to industry. It is clear that very large plants and firms are required in some industries to obtain peak efficiency—for example, in autos, cigarettes, petroleum, and steel. But the evidence is also clear that in many industries medium-sized, or even small, firms manage to achieve costs as low as the giants. Rates of return on invested capital do not appear to be consistently larger for huge than for medium-sized firms, though some of the giants are among the most profitable firms. An indirect test of the optimal scale of firm is provided by the size of firm that grows fastest. Here again the evidence is mixed. For the economy as a whole, the share of market obtained by the largest firms is growing, but only slowly—though nearly all firms are getting bigger as the economy grows. In only a few industries are the giants clearly increasing their dominance. In steel, for example, the share of the market held by U.S. Steel, the biggest firm, has fallen substantially over the last several decades. The empirical evidence shows clearly that there is no single, pat answer to the question, how big is optimal?

Do Businesses Operate at Optimal Scale?

If we were to look at all the firms in any particular industry, we would probably find a wide divergence in size. Why aren't all the firms the "optimal" size? There are many reasons. But a summary might look like this:

1. Optimal scale is only the lowest-cost scale of enterprise. It is not necessarily the most profitable scale. In many cases, the market simply isn't big enough to permit all firms to operate at optimal scale. In such cases, a firm may in fact operate at lower costs per unit with a small plant than it would with a large plant that was used at only partial capacity.

2. Firms may become overexpanded as part of a drive to attain dominance in their industry.

3. Some firms just want to be big. Men with dreams of industrial empire may expand beyond optimal scale in their drive for bigness and prestige. It is hard to measure this factor, but the last century of United States history has produced many cases where this motive appears to have been important.

4. Sometimes fear of government action holds firms back from profitable expansion. This is true when a firm fears that further growth may bring government action to break it up, under the Sherman Antitrust Act or other antimonopoly legislation. It is often alleged that this fear is what keeps General Motors from taking a still larger share of the automobile market.

5. Probably most important of all, errors in judgment and the inevitable slowness in adjusting to changed conditions mean that at any time most firms will not be at optimal scale. The most careful estimates in establishing a new plant are inevitably imprecise on a multitude of factors involved: new technology to be incorporated, future wage rates and prices, scale of market available, and so on. And even if the estimates could be precise, change is inescapable in economic life. Before long, new situations will arise, new technological changes will appear. Replanning optimal scale is a continuous process for the well-managed firm.

REVIEW

Concepts To Remember

This is another chapter of important concepts that will be used throughout the analysis of business-firm behavior. Be sure you understand the following:

cost	total costs
alternative cost	fixed cost per unit
opportunity cost	variable cost per unit
real costs	total cost per unit
accounting costs	least-cost combination
money costs	short run
fixed costs	long run
variable costs	optimal scale of enterprise

For Analysis and Discussion

1. If you were operating a clothing store, would there be any significant difference between your cash outlays per month and your costs per month? If so, what items would account for the difference?

2. The XYZ Company has the following costs. From this information prepare a table showing the following: fixed cost per unit, variable cost per unit, and total cost per unit. Then plot your data on a graph.

Total fixed cost per month $4,000
Total variable costs:

Units Produced	Variable Cost
10	$ 500
11	1,000
12	1,400
13	1,750
14	2,000
15	2,400

3. You are considering the possibility of setting up a pizza parlor near the campus. Make a list of all the costs you ought to have in mind in estimating whether the expected demand will produce a profit.

4. Which of the costs in question 3 would be fixed regardless of how many pizzas you sold, and which would vary from week to week with sales volume? Using this dichotomy, draw rough approximations of your fixed and variable cost curves per pizza, indicating the general shape you would expect the curves to have. From these curves, draw a rough approximation of your total cost (per pizza) curve.

5. If your total-unit curve is U-shaped (that is, if it first slopes down and then at some sales volume rises again), explain why you would expect your cost per pizza sold ever to rise as sales volume increased. What would be the primary factors determining how high your sales could run before you met rising costs per unit sold?

6. Make a list of the reasons why manufacturing concerns are typically bigger than dry-cleaning establishments. Can you reconcile your list with the observed fact that some dry-cleaning establishments are bigger than some manufacturing companies?

7. "By and large, the competitive system sees to it that every firm is near the optimal size for producing its product." Do you agree with this statement? Explain carefully why or why not.

Appendix

PHYSICAL PRODUCTION RELATIONSHIPS UNDERLYING COST CURVES [4]

This Appendix provides a brief statement of part of the "theory of production," which underlies the cost of production in a firm and provides a foundation for understanding the distribution of income to different factors of production. The purpose here is to examine rigorously the physical and technological relationships involved as the businessman combines the various factors of production in turning out his product.

The simplest case arises when one variable factor of production (say, labor) is applied to a fixed amount of some other factor (say, land). Consider the results of applying an increasing number of units of labor to a fixed plot of land, abstracting from any other factors of production, such as fertilizer and tools. Table 22-3 shows what might happen in a hypothetical case. Such a table showing the physical output obtainable from various combinations of productive factors presents what economists call a "production function."

Column 1 shows the number of laborers used. Column 2 shows the total production—say, bushels

[4] This Appendix is intended for those who want a rigorous physical-output foundation for the previous and following sections on business costs.

of wheat—obtained as more workers are added. Total product rises until at some point (12 workers with 3,300 bushels of output in this example) so many laborers are being used on this small plot of land that they get in each other's way and thereafter there is an actual *decrease* in the total output of wheat. Obviously, no intelligent farmer would ever carry production of wheat beyond this point, because by hiring more laborers he would actually decrease the total crop he obtained.

Column 3 shows the average product (bushels of wheat) per worker on the land. This average product rises at first, because total product rises faster than in proportion to the number of workers used. But the average output per worker reaches a peak (at seven workers and 2,604 bushels in this example, which gives the maximum output per worker of 372 bushels). Thereafter, even though total product continues to rise for a while, the average output per worker falls.

Column 4 shows the "marginal product" as more workers are used. This column shows the *additional*, or "marginal," output obtained by adding each extra worker. Thus, adding the first worker increases total product by 100 bushels. For the sec-

TABLE 22-3
VARIABLE OUTPUT WITH INCREASING INPUTS

Units of Input (Labor)	Total Output (Bushels)	Average Output per Unit of Labor (Bushels)	Marginal Output of Labor (Bushels)
1	100	100	100
2	350	175	250
3	702	234	352
4	1152	288	450
5	1700	340	* 548
6	2190	365	490
7	2604	* 372	414
8	2908	364	304
9	3114	346	206
10	3240	324	126
11	*3300	300	60
12	3300	275	0
13	3250	250	—50
14	3080	220	—170

* Denotes highest point for each output series.

ond worker the marginal product is 250 bushels, as total product rises from 100 to 350. Marginal product reaches its peak at five workers. After this, adding workers (up to 11) continues to increase total product, but not as rapidly as before; so the increment per additional worker falls.

These relationships can be seen readily in Figs. 22-4 and 22-5. Figure 22-4 shows total product as additional workers are hired. It rises rapidly at first as production becomes more efficient, then gradually levels off, and finally (after 12 workers and 3,300 bushels) turns down, for there are just too many workers to avoid getting in each other's way.

Figure 22-5 plots average product and marginal product from Table 22-3. Marginal product reaches its peak first and then turns down as the rate of growth of total product begins to slow. Average output per worker shows a similar inverted U, but the peak is reached with more workers, as Table 22-3 shows.

Note that the marginal-product curve cuts the average-product curve at the latter's highest point. This is necessarily true because as long as marginal product is higher than average product, each additional worker is adding more to total product than the average of all workers up to that point. As soon as the marginal worker adds less to total product than the average up to that point, the marginal-product curve will be below the average-product curve. Thus, it will always cut the average-product curve at the latter's highest point.

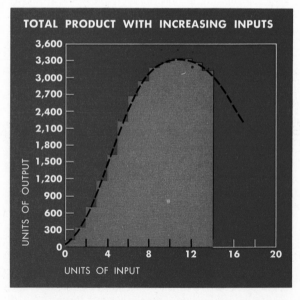

FIG. 22-4 Total output rises fast at first as variable factors are added to a fixed factor, then levels off, and eventually turns down.

The other significant point is when marginal product becomes zero. Comparing the two figures, we see that this is at 12 workers, *which is just the point where total product turns down.* This is clearly to be expected, because marginal product is merely the amount by which total product increases as additional workers are added. Thus, when adding another worker decreases total product, marginal product becomes negative.

The Law of Diminishing Returns, or Variable Proportions. The preceding paragraphs provide a statement of Ricardo's famous "law of diminishing returns." They show just what happens when additional units of one factor of production are combined with a fixed stock of some other factor or factors.

Modern economists have come to a more general statement of these relationships, which they call the "law of variable proportions." *As the proportion of one factor of production to other fixed factors increases, the average product of the increasing factor will first rise and then fall persistently; and the marginal product of the increasing factor will also first rise and then fall, cutting the average-product curve at its highest point.*

Thus, if all factors increase in proportion, there is no reason to expect Ricardo's law of diminishing returns to set in. This is a critical fact, for it says that neither an individual firm nor an economy need face diminishing returns just because it gets bigger.

Production Foundations of Cost Curves. The significance of these relationships for costs of production may be indicated briefly. Assume that the market prices of all factors of production are fixed —labor and land in our case. Then the total-fixed-cost curve (as in Fig. 22-1) is obtained directly by multiplying the fixed amount of land used (fixed factor) by its rent per acre. The total-variable-cost curve is obtained by multiplying the number of workers (variable factors) by the wage per worker.

These total costs can readily be converted to the *per unit* cost curves of Fig. 22-2 by dividing through by the number of units produced. Thus, the variable-unit-cost curve will be the inverse of the average-product-per-worker curve, since wage per worker is constant. When average product per worker is rising, variable cost per unit of output falls (we continue to assume that workers are the only variable cost involved). When average product per worker begins to fall, variable cost per unit of output begins to rise. Fixed cost per unit (rent on the land in the example above) steadily falls as more bushels are produced with the same total fixed cost for land.

The combination of the persistently declining fixed-cost-per-unit curve with the U-shaped variable-

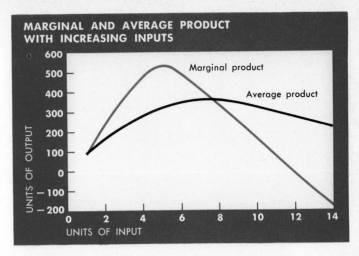

FIG. 22-5 Marginal product shoots up rapidly as total output grows fast when the first variable factors are added. It turns down as the growth in total output slows, and becomes negative when total output turns down. Check it against Fig. 22-4.

unit-cost curve gives the (flatter) U-shaped total-unit-cost curve. Thus, given the prices of the factors of production, the physical production relationships determine the shape of the fixed-cost-per-unit, the variable-cost-per-unit, and the total-cost-per-unit curves in any situation. The unit-cost curves are the inverses of the physical-production curves in Fig. 22-5.

Chapter 22 has made no use of the marginal-product curve indicated above. This curve will become the physical basis for the "marginal-cost" curve introduced in Chapter 23.

The physical productivity of varying combinations of factors of production will become of major importance again in Part 4, which considers the distribution of income. This is because what entrepreneurs are willing and able to pay in wages, rent, and so on, depends directly on the contributions different factors make to total production. In determining unit costs of production in the present chapters, we take wages, rents, and the prices of the other factors of production as given; this means that the shapes of the various cost curves depend largely on the physical-production relationships involved. In Part 4, we reverse this process and take final product prices (demand curves) as given, and then analyze entrepreneurs' demands for the various factors of production. There again, these same underlying physical production relationships will play a fundamental role in determining how many units of each factor of production it will pay enterpreneurs to hire, and how much they can afford to pay for each.

TWENTY-THREE
THE BUSINESS FIRM: COMPETITIVE OUTPUT AND PRICE IN THE SHORT RUN[1]

The Theory of the Firm.

The Competitive Firm in the Short Run.

Short-run Equilibrium of the Firm.

Short-run Cost Curves and Supply Curves.

Do Firms Try To Maximize Profits?

The Firm as a Buyer of Productive Services.

In this chapter, we examine how business firms respond to consumer demands. We will focus on firms in highly ("perfectly") competitive industries, postponing until later a look at the partially monopolized sectors of the economy.

THE THEORY OF THE FIRM

Traditionally, economists and other advocates of the private-enterprise system have pictured the business firm as, by and large, trying to maximize its profits. If we accept this position, the "theory of the firm" is a relatively simple affair.

Our "model," or "theoretical," firm wishes to maximize profits. Profits are the difference between total cost and total revenue. Hence, the firm does what it can (within the legal rules and mores of society) to maximize this difference. It tries to sell more of its own product when the price is high enough to exceed costs, and it tries to keep its costs as low as possible. That is, it tries to produce its output as efficiently as possible.

[1] *Note to instructors:* Part III of the Mathematical Appendix at the end of the text provides a concise mathematical statement (for students who know calculus) of the cost relationships of the preceding chapter and of the profit-maximizing behavior of the firm in the short run, as stated in this chapter.

Some instructors wish to concentrate on the long-run behavior of the firm and the economy, omitting the traditional marginal-cost–marginal-revenue apparatus in establishing short-run price and output. For them, the text is written so that Chapter 23 can be completely omitted. The Preface indicates which other sections of the book rest directly on this chapter and should be omitted if it is not assigned.

Whenever the firm can increase its profits by increasing its revenues or by reducing its costs, it will do so. Only when it is maximizing its profits (at least to the best of its own ability) will the manager be satisfied. Then the firm will be in "equilibrium"—in the sense that it will not change its own actions unless conditions change. Actually, external conditions (for example, consumer demand and wage rates) do change frequently, so the business firm will seldom actually reach and stay in equilibrium for long. But the firm will always be aiming at this maximum-profit position in conducting its day-to-day affairs and in its long-run planning.

We know, of course, that not all firms behave this way, and at the end of this chapter we will take a more detailed look at just how realistic this assumption is. But for the moment, assume that firms in our highly competitive industry have the single goal of profit-maximizing. What, then, can we say about how they should make their decisions?

THE COMPETITIVE FIRM
IN THE SHORT RUN

In trying to maximize its profits, the firm tries to maximize the difference between its income from sales and its costs. Since we are assuming highly competitive conditions, in which our firm represents a very small part of the market and turns out a product just like its competitors', it must take the product price as given—fixed in the market by total demand-and-supply conditions over which no one firm has any significant control. Under this assumption, our firm can't charge a higher price than the one prevailing in the market. If it does it won't sell any goods, since consumers can get all they want at the prevailing price from other sellers. This means that the firm sees the demand curve as a horizontal line at the prevailing market price. This assumption may seem to you rather extreme, and it is the limiting case of what economists call perfect competition. But it is an instructive case with which to begin. We will modify the assumption later.

Comparison of Total Costs
and Total Revenue

If the stereo hi-fi firm from Chapter 22 wants to maximize profits, it can compare its total cost with total revenue at each level of output, and thus determine the most profitable number of sets to produce. This is done in Table 23-1, *assuming that the market price is $1,800.* (Obviously the estimated total revenue will be different if the price is different, since total revenue is merely output multiplied by the price.) The table shows that the maximum profit output is six sets per month. At only one set per month, total revenue doesn't cover costs. When the plant gets up to eight sets a month, costs shoot up so fast that they exceed even the big sales income. In between, any output is profitable, but some more so than others. Profit is the largest if we produce and sell six sets.

This same comparison can be made graphically, as in Fig. 23-1. *TC* is total cost, plotted from the second column of Table 23-1. *TR* is

| **TABLE 23-1** | | | |
| **TOTAL COST, TOTAL REVENUE, AND PROFIT: PRICE = $1,800** | | | |
Output	Total Cost	Total Revenue	Profit
1	$ 3,000	$ 1,800	—$1,200
2	3,500	3,600	100
3	4,000	5,400	1,400
4	5,000	7,200	2,200
5	6,000	9,000	3,000
6	7,600	10,800	3,200
7	11,000	12,600	1,600
8	17,000	14,400	—2,600

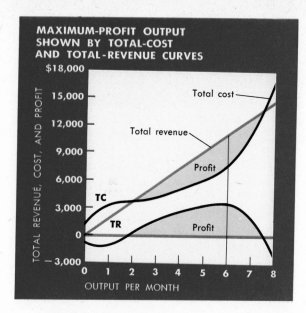

MAXIMUM-PROFIT OUTPUT SHOWN BY TOTAL-COST AND TOTAL-REVENUE CURVES

FIG. 23-1 Maximum profit is where the total-revenue curve is farthest above (in vertical distance) the total-cost curve. Potential profit range is from 2 to 7 sets per month.

total revenue, plotted from the third column. Where *TR* is above *TC*, the firm makes a profit. The profit is largest where *TR* is farthest above *TC*—here at an output of six units monthly, just as in the table. The yellow area between the two curves shows the range over which a profit is possible. The same area is shown separately at the bottom of the chart, where it is easy to see where the vertical distance (height of area) is greatest.

Marginal Analysis:

Marginal Costs

The businessman may also approach his output decision another way. First, remember that he must take the market price of $1,800 as given by the market. Now look again at his cost data. Some of the businessman's decisions are big ones—to operate or shut down, for example. Most of his decisions, however, are *marginal* ones—to take this new order at the going price or to refuse it; to cut back output 5 per cent or 10 per cent as price falls or unsold inventory piles up. In such decisions, how much *additional* cost is involved in expanding output moderately, or how much is saved by cutting output a little, becomes of special interest. The concept of "marginal cost," or "incremental cost," has been developed to help in this kind of analysis.

Marginal cost is the *addition*, or *increment*, to total cost involved in expanding output by one unit. For example, going back to the hi-fi cost data in Table 22-1, if the total cost of producing three sets per month is $4,000 and that of producing four sets $5,000, the marginal cost of expanding production from three to four units is $1,000. That's how much *extra* it costs us to get the fourth set produced.[2] This calculation is shown in Table 23-2.

TABLE 23-2		
TOTAL AND MARGINAL COSTS		
Output	Total Cost	Marginal Cost
1	$ 3,000	
2	3,500	$ 500
3	4,000	500
4	5,000	1,000
5	6,000	1,000
6	7,600	1,600
7	11,000	3,400
8	17,000	6,000

Most economic adjustments are marginal adjustments of some sort. Comparison of gains and losses "at the margin"—for example, comparison of the marginal income and marginal cost associated with increasing output from four to five sets monthly—is the core of intelligent decision-making, in economics as elsewhere. The principle is the same as when you weigh the advantages of another hour's study before an exam against the disadvantages of giving up the hour's sleep. Applications abound in every field. In building a bridge, for example, the engineer must constantly weigh the advantages of getting increased strength against the related disadvantages of incurring additional weight and expense.

---

[2] Thus marginal cost is the logical counterpart of marginal product described in the Appendix to Chapter 22. Other things equal, marginal cost will be lowest when marginal product is highest, and vice versa. As more variable productive agents are added to the fixed plant, the marginal product attributable to the variable agents first rises and then falls. At given prices of the productive agents, marginal cost will first fall and then rise correspondingly.

TABLE 23-3

HYPOTHETICAL HI-FI PRODUCER: PRICE = $1,800

Output	Fixed Cost per Unit	Variable Cost per Unit	Total Cost per Unit	Marginal Cost
1	$1,000	$2,000	$3,000	$ 500
2	500	1,250	1,750	500
3	333	1,000	1,333	1,000
4	250	1,000	1,250	1,000
5	200	1,000	1,200	1,600
6	167	1,100	1,267	3,400
7	143	1,430	1,573	6,000
8	125	2,000	2,125	

Maximizing Profits in the Short Run:
Marginal Costs and Marginal Revenue

Table 23-3 reproduces the cost data for the hi-fi firm from Chapter 22, adding a column to show the marginal cost involved in increasing output by one set at each stage. This is simply the last column of Table 23-2 above. With the market price at $1,800, how many sets per month should we produce? Try to figure it out for yourself, by comparing how much we add to costs and to income as we increase output.

The answer again is six—neither more nor less. The figures for six sets are underscored in the table. The marginal-cost column tells how much extra is added to total costs by increasing output one more unit. Now compare this with the extra income produced by each additional unit sold. Each unit we produce brings in $1,800.[3] This concept of incremental income is similar to the concept of marginal cost. *Economists call the $1,800 added to total revenue by each additional set sold the "marginal revenue." Marginal revenue is the extra revenue added by the sale of one more unit.*

So long as producing more units adds more to total revenue than to total costs, it pays to keep on increasing output. This is the same as saying that it will pay to keep on increasing output so long as marginal revenue is larger than marginal cost. At all levels of output up to and including

---

[3] Since this is a purely competitive market, we can sell all we produce at the market price, without worrying about forcing down the price by producing more.

six, producing another unit adds less than $1,800 to costs, but $1,800 to revenues. But producing the seventh unit would add an extra $3,400 to costs, and only $1,800 to revenue. Clearly we would be foolish to produce the seventh unit.

What is the total profit at six units? Total cost is about $7,600 (average unit cost of $1,267 times six sets). Total revenue is $10,800 (price of $1,800 per set times six sets). Profit is thus $3,200. This is, of course, identical to the answer obtained by comparing total costs and total revenues in Table 23-1.

The principle is: Profit will be maximized by carrying production up to the point where marginal cost equals marginal revenue (here, the price), and no further.

Ask yourself one more question, to be sure you understand. Wouldn't we be better off to produce seven units instead of six, getting the profit on the seventh, since the $1,800 price exceeds the total unit cost of $1,573 at seven units of output? The marginal-cost–marginal-revenue comparison gives the answer. The seventh set adds $3,400 to total cost and only $1,800 to total revenue. The fact that price is above total unit cost tells us that we can make *a* profit at that output level, but not that we will make our *maximum* profit at that level. Trying to pick up the profit on a seventh set would be a mistake, since it would actually involve adding more to cost than to revenue; total unit cost would be higher on all seven units if we increase output to seven. Compute the total profit at seven units and you'll see that it's only about $1,600 ($12,600 revenue less cost of about $11,000), less than at six units.

Minimizing Losses in the Short Run

With the market price at $1,800 we're in clover. But suppose consumer demand for stereo hi-fi sets nose-dives, and the market price falls to $1,100. A quick look at Table 23-3 shows that we're going to lose money at this price, no matter what we do. The lowest total cost/unit at which we can produce is $1,200, at an output of five units.

What should we do to minimize our losses? One possibility would be to shut down. This way we'd lose $1,000 a month, the amount of our fixed costs, which continue whether we operate or not. But if we operate, producing three, four, or five units, we'll be getting $1,100 per set produced and only having to spend $1,000 per set in variable (out-of-pocket) costs. This income will provide $100 per set left over to apply on our $1,000 of fixed costs, which we have to pay in any case. So we'd better operate, even though we lose money. By operating, we lose less than by shutting down altogether.

If the marginal-cost–marginal-revenue principle is a sound one, it ought to tell us now how many units to produce again this time. And it does. The answer is five. Producing every unit up to and including the fifth adds more to revenue than it does to costs. Marginal revenue for the fifth unit is $1,100; marginal cost is only $1,000. But marginal cost for the sixth set is $1,600, above marginal revenue. Our total loss at a five-set production rate figures out at $500 ($6,000 total cost less $5,500 total revenue), or only half the loss involved in shutting down completely. The principle for minimizing loss is the same as for maximizing profit: *If you operate at all, carry production up to the point where marginal costs equal marginal revenue, and no further.* Compute the loss at any other level of output, and you'll see that the rule is right.

The Decision To Shut Down
in the Short Run

Would it ever pay us to shut down in the short run? Obviously yes. If price falls below $1,000, which is the lowest variable unit cost we can manage at any output level, we'd better close

up shop. Suppose price is $900. No matter how many units we produce, our income is not even enough to cover our variable costs, much less provide anything to help cover the $1,000 of fixed costs. Suppose we produce three units. They will cost $4,000 but will bring in only $2,700, leaving a loss of $1,300 compared with only $1,000 if we just shut down. *At any price below the lowest variable-cost/unit point, we will minimize losses by shutting down altogether.* This rule doesn't contradict the marginal-cost–marginal-revenue principle for maximizing profits, since that principle tells us only what to do *if* we operate at all.

Graphical Analysis
of Short-run Behavior

This analysis can readily be put in graphical form. The cost curves in Fig. 23-2 are plotted from Table 23-3, and are the same as in Fig. 22-2 except for the addition of the marginal-cost curve. The marginal-cost curve, of course, shows the increment to total cost involved in increasing output by one unit at each stage. For example, the marginal cost involved in stepping up output from four to five units is $1,000; in going from five units to six it is $1,600.[4]

Three horizontal lines, *AA*, *BB*, and *CC*, have been added to show the market prices of $1,800, $1,100, and $900, respectively. These lines are the demand curves as seen by our firm when those are the prevailing market prices. The lines are also, of course, our marginal-revenue curves at the respective prices, since sale of one more hi-fi set adds just its price to our total revenue.

With this graph, we can readily determine the maximum-profit or minimum-loss output for any given market price. The principle is the same as before: It will pay to increase output so long as marginal revenue is above marginal cost, if we

[4] For mathematically inclined readers: Marginal cost is the first derivative of total cost (not of total cost per unit). The marginal-cost curve will always lie below the *TUC* curve when the latter is falling, and above it when the *TUC* curve is rising, cutting *TUC* at its minimum point. In nontechnical terms, this is so because the marginal cost is the increment to total cost. As long as this increment to total cost is less than the existing cost per unit, the cost per unit must be falling. As long as the increment is larger than the existing cost per unit, the cost per unit must be rising. The same reasoning holds for the relationship of the marginal-cost and variable-unit-cost curves. For more detail, see the Mathematical Appendix.

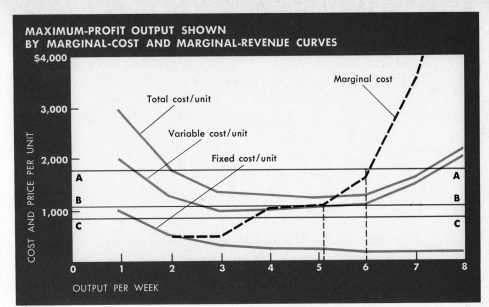

MAXIMUM-PROFIT OUTPUT SHOWN BY MARGINAL-COST AND MARGINAL-REVENUE CURVES

FIG. 23-2 Profit is maximized by carrying production up to intersection of marginal-cost and marginal-revenue curves—if you operate at all. Horizontal price lines also show marginal revenue at each price.

operate at all. We will minimize losses by shutting down completely if price falls below our lowest variable cost per unit.

Suppose the market price is $1,800 (line AA). At that price the marginal cost curve is still below marginal revenue (price) at six units, but above it at seven. We can tell by looking at the graph, therefore, that six units is the most profitable level of output. Since the $1,800 price line is above the total-unit-cost curve at this point, we can also tell that this is a profitable situation. The actual profit can be computed by multiplying the profit per unit ($533) by six units, giving the same $3,200 profit we got by tabular computation.

Similarly, with price at $1,100 (line BB), five units is the output that will minimize loss. Up to five units the marginal-cost curve is below the marginal-revenue (price) curve; at six units, it is above it.

And a quick glance at the $900 price situation will tell us to close down immediately. The $900 price line (CC) is everywhere below the variable-unit-cost curve. At $900 we can't even get enough revenue to cover variable costs, let alone accumulate anything to apply on fixed costs. If you can't cover variable costs, it is better to shut down and minimize your loss by just paying the fixed cost of $1,000.

For a quick answer to the most profitable levels of output, the graphical approach has real advantages. For computing exact profit-and-loss figures, tabular data are often more satisfactory. But the answers are the same either way.

SHORT-RUN EQUILIBRIUM OF THE FIRM

When will the business firm be in short-run equilibrium? When it is maximizing its profit or minimizes its loss, given consumer demand and given its fixed costs which it cannot alter in the short run. It will then be in short-run equilibrium when it is producing just up to the point where marginal cost is equal to marginal revenue (price). Only at that output is it maximizing its profit.

This concept of the equilibrium of the firm parallels the concept of the equilibrium of the household (or consumer) developed in Chapter 20. Both tell us the situation *toward which* an economic unit will move in trying to improve its economic position. In a real world of constant change, we would seldom expect to find firms actually in equilibrium for long. But whenever a household or firm is out of equilibrium, we can expect that economic unit to spend more or less, or produce more or less, so as to approach more closely its desired goal, be it maximum utility from spendable income for the household or maximum profit for the firm.

"Equilibrium" is thus an analytical concept. It is a position that *would be* achieved *if* the household or firm were free to adjust to the conditions specified, *and if* all other forces in the economy (the "givens") remained unchanged until the new equilibrium was reached.

Note that this chapter is only about the *short-run* equilibrium toward which the firm will move under the conditions assumed. The firm may be in short-run equilibrium when it is making a large profit, no profit at all, or even a loss, depending on its costs and the price given by the market. But, as we shall see in Chapter 24, the short-run equilibrium may not last in the long run. Long-run and short-run equilibrium may be different.

For example, if the firm's best short-run position unfortunately yields a loss (as with price B in Fig. 23-2), it is clear that the firm will go out of business in the long run to avoid incurring a continuing loss. If the firm is making a large profit (as with price A in Fig. 23-2), it is clear this will provide an incentive for new firms to move into the industry to make big profits too. If more firms do move in, we would expect the increased supply to push down the price and erode the short-run profit position of our firm. Remember: Short-run and long-run equilibrium positions may be different.

SHORT-RUN COST CURVES AND SUPPLY CURVES

If firms try to maximize profits in the short run, we can tell from a given firm's cost curves what output it will produce at any given price. The firm's marginal-cost curve will be its short-run supply curve anywhere above the minimum point on the variable-unit-cost curve. Thus, at any price below $1,000 our firm will supply zero units. At prices from $1,000 to $1,599, it will supply five units. At prices from $1,600 to $3,399, it will supply six units. And so on up the marginal-cost curve. *The short-run marginal-cost curve is the firm's short-run supply curve.*

If this is true for all firms, it is easy to get a short-run market supply curve for any industry, by adding together the short-term supply curves (or schedules) of all the individual firms. Suppose there were 1,000 identical firms in the hi-fi industry. Then the short-run industry supply schedule would look like Table 23-4. At each price the supply offered would be just 1,000 times the supply offered by our own little firm.

TABLE 23-4

SHORT-RUN INDUSTRY SUPPLY SCHEDULE

Price	Output of Typical Firm	Industry Output
Under 1,000	0	0
1,000–1,599	5	5,000
1,600–3,399	6	6,000
3,400–5,999	7	7,000
Over $6,000	8	8,000

DO FIRMS TRY TO MAXIMIZE PROFITS?

Do firms really try so logically and precisely to maximize their profits? Anyone who has spent much time around a business concern knows that this is only a rough approximation of the way businesses behave. A variety of deviations from the simple profit-maximizing model are easy to see, even in highly competitive industries.

1. The businessman who continuously adjusted his output and activities in response to every little change in affairs outside and inside the firm would have his business in a continual state of turmoil. He might also find himself overadjusting to small changes. Many businessmen follow a wait-and-see attitude; their responses are often far behind what an instantaneous-adjustment theory would presuppose.

2. Businessmen never know for sure what costs and demand in the future will be. They can only estimate, or sometimes guess—and sometimes they're wrong.

3. Cases of inefficiency in business, where better management would produce lower costs, are easy to find—at least until competition squeezes them out.

Where competition is less pressing, other deviations are likely to be added to the list, as we shall see later.

Use of a Profit-maximizing Model of the Firm

Where does this leave the model of a firm busily maximizing profits? Certainly any reasoning based on the assumption that every firm is striving exclusively to maximize profits at every moment should be suspect, and anyone who uses such reasoning as a description of reality deserves the scorn often heaped by the man in the street on "armchair economists." Yet, through all these aberrations there is impressive evidence that the desire for profits is a dominant motive in most business concerns. Perhaps some businessmen don't carefully try to maximize profits in the way we have outlined. But few consistently and knowingly adopt policies calculated to cut profits substantially below levels they could otherwise achieve.

Indeed, one of the major arguments for the competitive system is that businessmen are *forced* to act *as if* they were trying to maximize profits, whether they want to or not. Any firm that continues to operate inefficiently will be undersold in the market and will be driven either to bankruptcy or to greater efficiency. Any firm that does not respond efficiently to consumer demand will vanish from the business scene before long. Thus, even though some businessmen may not be very efficient or conscious profit-maximizers, a competitive market will force them by and large to behave the way the profit-maximizing model pictures them.

Bearing all these warnings in mind, we shall use an analytical model of business firms that act to maximize profits *as a first approximation* in our analysis of a competitive, private-enterprise economy. Remember, however, that the theory says only, *if* conditions are as they are postulated in the model, *then* the real-world results will be as described in the model. It is up to the user to see for himself in any given case how closely the real-world problem corresponds to the model he is using. Economic theory is an aid to independent thinking—not a substitute for it.[5]

THE FIRM AS A BUYER OF PRODUCTIVE SERVICES

Before ending this chapter, it is important to look at the short-run output policies of the firm from a different angle. Whenever businessmen

decide to produce 1, 10, or 1,000 units of output, they simultaneously decide to buy or hire the "inputs" of productive services needed to produce those units—labor services, raw materials, machinery, and so on.

If we liked, therefore, we could analyze the most profitable level of output in terms of units of productive inputs used, rather than in terms of units of output. For example, to simplify, assume that our plant needs only labor and raw materials, and that these are conveniently hired in units costing $100 per unit—perhaps one worker per week plus the material he uses. For each number of units of input, there will be some corresponding output of stereo sets. Thus, our cost schedules above could have been stated in terms of costs to hire varying amounts of labor-plus-materials input rather than in terms of producing one, two, three, or more sets per week as output.

Consider the problem of how many units of input to hire each month. The marginal-cost–marginal-revenue principle holds here as before. So long as adding one more unit of input adds more to revenue than to cost, it pays to increase inputs and hence output. As soon as another unit of input adds more to cost than to revenue, you'd better stop expanding, because you've come to your best profit level. The marginal-revenue–marginal-cost principle here again tells you what the maximum-profit or minimum-loss production level is.[6]

Looking at the firm's decision-making in terms of hiring labor and other productive services is particularly useful in analyzing how many workers will be hired and how wages are determined. Thus, as we shall see in Part Four, these two equivalent ways of looking at the firm's price-output decisions provide a means of integrating all of price and distribution theory.

The number of workers hired times the average wage determines the incomes received by workers. Similarly, the amount of land used times the average rent determines the incomes of landowners.

[5] For some examples of how useful the theory can be in practical business situations, see the Appendix to Chapter 27, "Some Managerial Applications."

[6] The marginal revenue from hiring an additional unit of variable input is based directly on its "marginal product," as described in the Appendix to Chapter 22, although of course the marginal product needs to be converted to dollar terms to become marginal revenue.

REVIEW

Concepts To Remember

The essence of this chapter is the way a profit-seeking firm would try to maximize profits by carrying production up to the point where marginal cost equals marginal revenue, and no further, *if* it operates at all. Check your understanding of the following concepts:

profit maximization	incremental cost
marginal cost	equilibrium of the firm
marginal revenue	unit of input of productive services

For Analysis and Discussion

1. A competitive firm will always maximize profits by producing at the lowest possible total unit cost. True or false? Explain.
2. Explain carefully why a firm will maximize its profits by carrying production up to the point where marginal cost just equals marginal revenue. If there are any exceptions to this rule, specify them.
3. You operate a roadside fruit stand. You have been selling strawberries at 50 cents a quart; they cost you 45 cents to produce. It is now mid-afternoon and raining. With customers scarce, you now estimate your demand schedule for the rest of the afternoon as follows:

Price	Quarts
50¢	20
45	30
40	50
35	60
30	75
25	80

You have 80 quarts on hand and no storage facilities to avoid spoilage before tomorrow. What price should you charge to maximize profits? Explain. What is the importance of your costs in this case?

4. You are managing the hi-fi plant shown in Fig. 23-2, and are currently producing four sets a month. You have an order for one additional set a month, but the customer will only pay $1,050 a set, less than your minimum total cost per set. Should you accept the order? Show both graphically and through arithmetical calculations why your answer is sound.

5. "A rational businessman will always disregard his fixed costs in setting his prices and current rate of output. Sunk costs are water over the dam." Do you agree with this quotation from an economics textbook? Explain fully why or why not.

6. Should businessmen be more concerned with making their companies "good citizens" in their communities or with maximizing profits? How should a manager decide how much to spend on civic causes like the Community Chest?

TWENTY-FOUR

LONG-RUN COMPETITIVE EQUILIBRIUM AND ECONOMIC EFFICIENCY

Competition and Monopoly.

Long-run Equilibrium and Equilibrium Tendencies.

Long-run Equilibrium: The Continuous Search for Profits.

General Equilibrium of a Competitive Economy.

Purely Competitive Economy—Evaluation.

Appendix: General Equilibrium and Economic Efficiency.

This is a very important chapter. After our detailed look at individual households, firms, and markets, we now need to see how all these pieces fit together in a big picture of how a highly competitive economy would work in the long run. How efficient would a highly competitive economy be in allocating the economy's scarce resources in accordance with consumers' demands?

What economics has to say about long-run competitive adjustments is more reliable than what it has to say about the short-run. In the short run, individual entrepreneurs may behave unpredictably. They may mistakenly adopt inefficient production methods. They may sell below costs. They may produce unwanted products. In most cases, entrepreneurs probably do the best they can to earn the large profits—but they may make all kinds of mistakes.

In the long run, on the other hand, in a highly competitive market we can be pretty sure about how businessmen will behave. They will act *as if* they were maximizing profits—by meeting consumer demands and by producing goods at the lowest possible costs. We know this is so, because if they don't competition will drive them out of business. And the "long run" is a period long enough for this to happen.

It was this long-run competitive pressure that led Adam Smith, in his famous *Wealth of Nations*, to speak of the "invisible hand" that leads businessmen who seek their own profits to produce the goods consumers want and to sell them at the lowest possible prices. It is the intellectual core of the support for the private-enterprise economic system today. Although a purely competitive system has never actually existed, the model has long provided a loose approximation of how a largely competitive system might work; and many observers believe that the model is a good first, rough approximation to our own system. For some, it is a "norm" of ideal behavior against which to measure actual conditions.

The main purpose of this chapter is to examine how a purely competitive system would work in terms of long-term tendencies, and to consider some of the major virtues and failings of such a system. On the basis of this examination, you can judge for yourself whether you think Adam Smith set economists off on the right track with his talk about the "invisible hand"—or whether he gave us a bad steer.

But before looking in detail at the long-run outcome of a purely competitive system, we need to be clear on two important points that have been glossed over so far. Precisely what do we mean by "pure competition" and by "long-run equilibrium"?

COMPETITION AND MONOPOLY

No business firm is free from competition. A.T. & T., for example, is often cited as a complete monopoly in the field of telephone communication in most communities. This is true in one sense, but if people get unhappy enough with telephoning they can write or telegraph. There are only six major firms that produce aluminum today. But quite aside from the competition among the six, for many uses steel, copper, and other metals are potential substitutes for aluminum. Alcoa and the other aluminum companies are acutely aware of this fact. Competition is inescapable in business.

Nevertheless, it is obvious that competition is a lot more active in some industries than it is in others. The only grocery in an isolated rural village is a good deal less exposed to competition than is the corner grocer who has Kroger and Safeway supermarkets in the next block. At the competitive extreme, far from A.T. & T., we find the individual farmer producing such standardized products as wheat, corn, and hogs. He has thou-

sands of competitors, and his product is so standardized that the buyer has no interest in who the producer is—he is interested merely in the price he has to pay. If Farmer Jones prices his No. 2 hard northern wheat one cent a bushel more than other farmers, he just won't sell any.

There is a whole spectrum of market positions between the protected monopoly position of the public utility and the extreme competition of farmers. Most of the real world lies somewhere between these two extremes, and we will look at the less competitive sectors later. Here we want to examine how the economy would function under "pure competition"—roughly the situation of the wheat farmer above, without government intervention.

Pure Competition

The essence of pure competition is that no single seller is important enough to have any appreciable influence over market price. Specifically, pure competition is characterized by:

1. Many sellers, each acting independently and each so small relative to the market as to have no appreciable effect on market price.
2. An identical product, so that the consumer is indifferent about the seller from whom he buys.[1]
3. Freedom of entry for new sellers who wish to enter the market. (This assumption is not logically necessary where 1 and 2 hold, but most economists include it in analyzing pure competition.)

The same conditions define pure competition on the buyers' side of any market.

When there are many sellers of identical products, and when no one of them *acting alone* can exert a significant influence on the market price, each producer must adjust his activities to the market price. Given his costs and the market price, he will decide how much to produce. But although he alone has no influence on market price, the *summation* of all the individual pro-

---

[1] The added assumption is also usually made that all buyers and sellers have full knowledge of prices being quoted over the entire market.

ducers' actions has a great influence on that price. If prevailing costs and market price lead each individual firm to restrict output, the summation of all the thousands of individual cutbacks will drastically reduce market supply and, other things equal, raise the price. Thus, quantity produced and sold along with market price are "automatically" determined by the impersonal mechanism of the competitive market as it responds to consumer demand.

Why Study Pure Competition?

It's clear that there aren't many purely competitive industries in the modern American economy. Even agriculture, which has long been the standard example, doesn't quite represent pure competition any more, since the government has increasingly intervened to set prices and output levels. Why study pure competition, then? There are three reasons:

1. Economics is concerned with the over-all performance of the economic system, and with the allocation of society's resources among alternative uses. To get at these problems, we must have some over-all picture of the way the various parts of the economy fit together. The purely competitive model, in which all markets are competitive, has the great virtue of providing a reasonably simple and predictable picture of the way markets signal consumer demands to producers, and the way producers respond to those demands. Many economists believe that this picture also provides at least a first approximation of the "ideal" way in which a private-enterprise system ought to work. They thus use the model as a standard of comparison to ferret out those areas of the actual economy that aren't operating as well as they ought to.

2. Pure competition, though almost nonexistent, does provide a rough approximation to the behavior of major sectors of the modern economy. Most of agriculture; broad areas of retailing, wholesaling, and service establishments; and important sectors of manufacturing where a moderate scale of plant is big enough for efficient production—all come reasonably close to the pure-competition model. To be sure, their prod-

ucts are not quite identical, and each producer has some control over the price at which he sells his product. But the pressures of competition are strong, and if he gets far out of competitive line the individual producer finds himself steadily losing out in the market.

3. We have to begin somewhere, and the basic analytical tools are pretty much the same in the competitive and partial-monopoly cases. Even where the pure-competition model is not directly applicable, the insights gained with this case will come in handy, when we look at the partial-monopoly cases.

LONG-RUN EQUILIBRIUM AND EQUILIBRIUM TENDENCIES

Long-run equilibrium is an abstract analytical concept. Here again, equilibrium is a situation that would be reached and maintained unless some external force came along to disturb it. Suppose we want to know how a purely competitive system, beginning from some equilibrium position, would respond to a change in consumer demand. Assume we can hold everything else constant—the supply of productive resources, society's technological know-how, all legal and social factors—as the consumer demand for strawberries increases. The new position to which the system would move in response solely to the changed demand would be its new long-run equilibrium position.

To be complete, we should consider all the millions of interrelated effects throughout the economic system. But once we get far from the strawberry industry, these effects are likely to be negligible. Thus, economists generally concentrate their analysis on the effects on the industry directly concerned, here the strawberry industry. This emphasis leads us to a concept of the "equilibrium of the industry" and of the firm within the industry. For some purposes we are not safe in stopping with the industry and should instead go on to study the effects on other industries, looking toward "general equilibrium" for the economy as a whole. But first let us concentrate on the conditions of equilibrium for the industry, and for firms within the industry.

The *immediate* (very short-run) adjustment to a higher strawberry demand would be a higher price for strawberries. The *short-run* adjustment would give time for existing strawberry farmers to increase their outputs if they wished, but not to vary their fixed costs. In the *long run* there would be time for new firms to move into strawberry-producing, for existing firms to vary their whole scale of operations, and for all productive factors in the economy to adjust fully to this shift in demand. Even in the long run we assume that no changes other than the new strawberry demand interfere with the full working out of the adjustment process. We hold "other things equal" analytically—even if they don't stay that way in the real world. Long-run equilibrium is the new stable position finally reached by industry, other things being held unchanged except as they may change in response to the increase in strawberry demand.

Of course, in the real world there is no way to hold "other things constant," and the real world never reaches a state of economic equilibrium. Before farmers can get thoroughly adjusted to this increase in demand for strawberries, consumers switch to raspberries. Or scientists invent a new, cheaper way of producing strawberries. Or any one of a million other things may happen. Yet this analytical device of isolating the effects of a particular event is the best way we have for getting at those effects in a real world so complex, interrelated, and ever-changing as ours is.

When we talk about long-run equilibrium, therefore, we are talking about the new situation *toward which* the industry is moving and which would ultimately be reached if no other forces interfered. Long-run analysis gives us guides to the *ultimate* effects of particular changes—for example, the ultimate effects of a new tax on cigarettes, or of improved technology in quick-freezing vegetables. Will the lower costs of improved quick-freezing be passed on to the consumer or used to swell profits? Will more or fewer workers be employed in the frozen-food industry? In agriculture? Analysis of the way a competitive system moves toward new equilibrium positions can give us strong clues to the answers to such questions in a competitive world.

LONG-RUN EQUILIBRIUM: THE CONTINUOUS SEARCH FOR PROFITS

The mainspring of the private-enterprise economy is the businessman's continuous search for profits. This does not imply that the proprietor of the local grocery spends every waking hour worrying about how to squeeze the last nickel out of his business; or that the farmer doesn't decide to go visit his friends some afternoons when he could be working. But it does imply that, by and large, the desire to earn profits is a dominant one, and business concerns adopt those policies which they think will produce the largest profits for the company.

In the short run, some costs are fixed. The businessman's search for profits is limited by this fact. He can only make the best possible adjustment to market demand by varying output from his existing plant. If he has hired a group of employees on an annual basis, he must make the best of the arrangement until the end of the year.

In the long run, however, all costs become variable. Existing plant and equipment wear out. Wage and salary contracts come up for renewal. Long-term contracts for supplies and materials expire. Long-term bonds come due for payment or refinancing. With all costs variable, the entrepreneur is completely free in making his output decisions. He can expand, contract, change the nature of his productive processes, or go out of business altogether.

Thus, in the long run, firms will move into or drop out of any purely competitive industry until expectations of profits or losses have been substantially eliminated—until it is no longer possible for anyone to better his position by moving into or out of the industry.[2] Thus, as long as the expected market price is above the expected minimum cost of producing a commodity, firms will move into the industry and present firms may expand. Output will increase, and the price will gradually be forced down to about the

---

[2] Remember that a "normal," or "going," rate of return on investment is included in the costs of each firm.

minimum-cost point. But if the expected market price is below the minimum expected cost of production, firms will drop out of the industry, output will decline, and price will gradually rise toward the minimum-cost level. *Under pure competition, with firms free to leave and enter the industry, market price cannot in the long run stay higher or lower than the minimum total cost/unit of producing the commodity. This is the long-run equilibrium price and output level toward which the industry will move.*

Three points need special emphasis here.

1. It is *expected* market prices and production costs that matter. Change is the essence of economic life. Past and present prices and costs matter only as they provide evidence to the businessman of what the future will be like.

2. Any alert businessman will tell you that it is the long pull that matters. The businesses that last and pay good dividends to their shareholders year after year are seldom out to "turn a fast buck." They are the ones that hold back new products until they have worked out all the bugs, even though short-run profits are foregone. They are the ones who say that the customer is right, even when they're burned up at his unreasonable demand on return privileges. To assert that most businesses try to maximize profits each day, or month, or even each year would be naïve indeed. But this is not to say that the continuous search for profits is not pervasive in the competitive areas of the business world.

3. In assuming pure competition, we assume that there are no artificial barriers to the free movement of resources into and out of the industry on a par with those already there. This assumption, like the others of pure competition, is seldom found true in its pure form. But, like the others, it can serve as part of the analytical model of pure competition, subject to the same warnings that apply to all other theoretical models.

Long-run Competitive Equilibrium—
The Firm and the Industry

Consumer demand provides the signals to which businessmen respond. Given some pattern of consumer demand, when will firms be in equilibrium in adjusting to those demands?

The business firm is in long-run equilibrium when there is no advantage in increasing or decreasing its output, either by varying utilization of existing plant or by changing the scale of plant. This equilibrium will be reached when (1) the firm is producing in the most efficient way available (otherwise there would be an advantage in shifting to more efficient operations), and (2) market price is equal to the least-cost point on the cost curve for that scale of enterprise. In this equilibrium position, profits have been eliminated by competition (remember that costs include a "normal" return on investment), and the firm will continue using just the same amount of all productive resources as it now uses.

The entire industry is in long-run equilibrium when each firm is in equilibrium and there is no incentive for firms either to enter or leave the industry. We can thus define long-run equilibrium either in terms of movement of firms or of movement of productive resources. In long-run equilibrium, there is no incentive for firms or for productive resources to enter or leave the industry. There is no incentive for entrepreneurs to hire more or fewer resources in the industry. Owners of productive resources (including people who sell their own labor) have no incentive to enter or leave the industry, since the returns they can earn there are about what they can earn in comparable circumstances in other industries—comparable working conditions and security for labor, comparable risk for capital investment, and so on.

Survival of the Fittest
and Pressures Toward Cost Minimization

The competitive market is an impersonal arbiter of who survives and who vanishes from the business scene. With a standard product, such as oats, the buyer is indifferent to who the producer is. He will pay the market price, and no more. Any farmer whose production cost is above the market price simply takes a loss, and in due course will vanish from the scene unless he improves his efficiency or receives a subsidy from someone. The fact that he may be a hardworking farmer with a good wife and six small children is irrelevant in the market. If his neighbor is a thoroughly unpleasant individual who throws stones at small children and refuses to contribute to the Community Chest but nonetheless produces oats at 10 cents less per bushel, his neighbor will still prosper in the market. In long-run equilibrium, only those who can produce at a cost as low as market price will survive, and this price will be no higher than the least-cost point on the cost curve of firms using the most efficient methods.

At any time, any industry includes firms of varying efficiency, with different levels of profits and losses. This is partly because of the dynamic nature of the economic world; some firms are on the way up, some on the way down. Partly it is because many industries are far from being purely competitive; the firms do not have free access to markets and technological know-how. *But if a purely competitive long-run equilibrium position were actually attained, the lowest total-unit-cost points of all firms would be the same.*

It is easy to see that in the long run inefficient firms will be eliminated by competition. But it would be unreasonable to assume that all firms become identical. Some entrepreneurs are more efficient than others. Some firms are located near good markets and pay high rents, whereas others are more distant but pay lower rents. Some firms are small, and obtain efficiency through close personal supervision; others are large, and count on mass-production methods to provide low costs. Such differences may exist in long-run equilibrium. It is not necessary that all firms be identical or have identical cost curves. It is only necessary that the method of production used by each permit it to produce at a total unit cost as low as its competitors. Persistent differences between firms are consistent with equal minimum total unit costs because there may be compensating advantages and disadvantages.

For example, suppose that one manager of a textile firm is more effective in organizing production than anyone else in the industry. Won't his firm continue to make a profit even in the long run, and won't its costs remain below the costs of other firms, since none of the others can duplicate its efficiency. The answer is "no." When the manager is hired, his firm will have to pay him a higher salary than other managers receive in order to keep him away from other firms; his salary will be bid up until it is higher than that

of a less efficient manager by roughly the differential advantage of his services. If the entrepreneur himself is the efficient manager, he must charge as a cost a salary for himself equal to what he would be able to get in alternative opportunities; this "implicit" or opportunity cost would be the compensating factor. This is true for all productive resources.

Illustration of Response
to an Increase in Demand

Suppose that the purely competitive desk-blotter industry is in long-run equilibrium and that consumer demand for blotters increases. How will the industry respond?

The immediate effect will be improved profit opportunities. (1) The price of blotters will rise. (2) Each firm will increase its output, since with a higher price it is now profitable to produce more blotters.[3] (This is a move upward along the industry short-run supply curve, before there is time for new firms to move in.) (3) As output increases, prices will fall back somewhat, but will probably stay above the original level, because in the short run output from existing firms can be increased only moderately to meet the higher demand. (4) In the new *short-run* equilibrium, price will be higher, output larger, and profits in the industry greater than before the increase in demand.

This *short-run* adjustment is pictured in Fig. 24-1. The left-hand portion shows the short-run aggregate supply of desk blotters (S^1S^1), the inital demand (D^1D^1), and the new increased demand (D^2D^2). The increased demand pulls up the price from \$.06 to \$.08, and calls forth increased production from the firms already in the industry —from 50,000 to 62,500 blotters. This increase results from the independent actions of the many purely competitive firms producing blotters.

As seen by any individual firm, the increase in demand produces a higher price, which makes it profitable to produce more blotters. In Fig. 24-1, the right-hand portion of the chart shows the posi-

[3] The exact increase in output by each firm in the short run and hence the exact slope of the short-run supply curve depend on the marginal analysis of the following footnote. This more exact information is not necessary for the general argument.

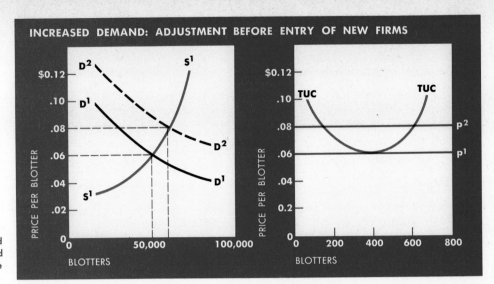

FIG. 24-1 New increased demand (D^2D^2) raises the market price and makes increased output profitable for the individual firms.

tion of a typical firm after the price increase induced by increased demand. With price at $.08, the profit picture is bright and each firm will tend to produce more.[4]

But this situation is obviously unstable. New resources will be attracted to the industry by the generous profits available. As new firms enter and

[4] The exact pattern of short-run adjustment by the typical firm in the industry can be indicated through the marginal-cost–marginal-revenue adjustment mechanism of Chapter 23. When price rises to $.08, as shown in Fig. 24-1, the new higher price will intersect the firm's marginal-cost curve at a larger output than before. This is shown in the accompanying diagram, which is simply the right-hand portion of Fig. 24-1 with the marginal-cost curve added. At the original price of $.06, the firm would produce 400 units. At $.08, the most profitable output will rise to 500 units. The firm's profit at the higher price is shown by the yellow area. As each firm increases output along its marginal-cost curve, industry output increases along the short-run industry supply curve in the left-hand portion of Fig. 24-1, which is merely the summation of all the individual-firm marginal-cost curves.

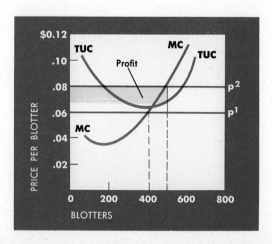

productive capacity is expanded, the industry supply curve (SS) will gradually move to the right; more will be produced as more resources move into the blotter industry.

With this expansion of output, the price of blotters will gradually fall back toward its original level. If unlimited productive resources can be attracted without having to pay more for them (that is, if new firms can enter without bidding up costs in the blotter industry), the new long-run equilibrium will be back at the original price but with more blotters being produced. This would be a case of long-run "constant costs" for the industry. If, however, the entrance of new firms raises costs for all firms, because higher payments are necessary to attract labor, materials, and other resources from other industries, we have the case of "increasing costs." Either way, as the price of the product falls back and costs rise, profits are gradually squeezed out. When the price is again equal to the anticipated lowest total unit cost of a new firm, there will be no further inducement for new firms to enter. The new long-run equilibrium will probably be at somewhat higher costs and price than originally, with a larger industry output.

These *long-run* adjustments are shown in Fig. 24-2. S^2S^2 is the new short-run aggregate supply curve after new firms have had time to come into the industry; it has shifted to the right. Under these new conditions, supply and demand are equal at a price of $.07 per blotter, with an output of 70,000 blotters in the industry as a whole. This is the new long-run industry equilibrium. It is long-run equilibrum because price is now just

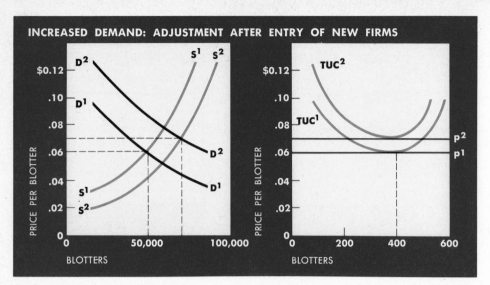

FIG. 24-2 Increased demand draws new firms into the industry and produces new equilibrium for the firms and the industry at a price of 7 cents.

equal to minimum total unit cost, so there is no longer any incentive for resources to move into or out of the industry. Note that the position of the typical firm is now changed, as shown in the right-hand part of the figure. Its cost curves have risen, because the increased production of blotters has bid up the price of labor and raw materials. On the demand side, price first rose from $.06 to $.08, and then fell back to $.07. In the new long-run equilibrium, the typical firm is again producing about the same amount as before, again at just its lowest total-unit-cost point.[5] But since there are more firms than before, the aggregate output of the industry is greater than it was initially. *In response to their increased demand, consumers are getting 20,000 more blotters, and are getting them at the lowest price that will cover costs. But they have to pay $.01 more per blotter because that much more was necessary to attract more productive resources from other uses into blotter-making.*

The adjustments following a *decrease* in demand would be the reverse. In the short run, price would fall and firms in the industry would suffer losses. After some firms had been eliminated and production reduced, price would rise back toward its original level, to a new equilib-

[5] Figure 24-2 shows the new equilibrium output of the firm identical with the old—that is, the new average-cost curve is merely raised by $.01 for each level of output. This will be the result if the costs of all factors of production rise in the same proportion. This need not, of course, be the case, and the particular type of cost increase shown is not important for the basic analysis of the industry's response to an increase in demand.

rium at the lowest point on the new total-unit-cost curve. Consumers would be getting fewer blotters, possibly at a lower price than before the decrease in demand if the smaller supply of productive resources could be obtained at lower prices.

"Constant-Cost" and "Increasing-Cost" Industries

Will unit costs rise if demand for a product increases? If an industry is very small, its chances of expanding output without bidding up productive service prices (wages, raw-material prices, and so on) may be good. Even if the industry is a large one, in the long run expanding output *may* not encounter substantially rising costs. If we assume that the total income of society is constant, then more spending on blotters will mean less spending on something else—say, books. Thus, the expanding blotter industry can get needed workers and materials from the contracting book industry. Insofar as productive resources are relatively unspecialized (for example, common labor usable in one industry as well as the other), this shift can be made easily and without bidding up wages in the blotter industry. But if the blotter industry needs specialized resources (say, skilled machinists who are not available from the contracting book industry), it will probably have to pay higher wages to lure more workers away from other industries.

Thus, the degree of specialization of resources needed, more than the size of the industry, is the critical factor determining the shape of the long-run industry supply curve, though the two factors are often closely related. Since the long run is long enough to permit retraining workers and shifting production methods, the vast majority of industries can expand output over a wide range with only negligible increases in long-run costs.

Industries that face rising costs as output expands are called "increasing-cost" industries; those that can expand without rising costs are called "constant-cost" industries. Actually, most industries are probably constant-cost industries over some range of output and increasing-cost industries thereafter, as they bulk larger and larger in the total economy. The safest general assumption for most problems is probably that of slightly increasing long-run costs, though the facts of each case should be considered individually.

When we talk about constant- and increasing-cost industries, we are talking about the shape of their long-run industry supply curves. The long-run industry supply curve is the locus of the lowest points on the individual-firm unit-cost curves as more and more firms enter the industry. Since in the constant-cost case new firms can enter without bidding up the lowest point on the unit-cost curve, the long-run industry supply curve is a horizontal line joining the lowest points of the unit-cost curves of the new firms as they enter the industry. In the increasing-cost case, as industry output is increased the lowest unit-cost point gradually rises; thus the long-run industry supply curve will slope gradually upward.

For an illustration, look back at Fig. 22-3, which shows the unit-cost curves of typical firms as industry output is increased. Beyond TCU^4, the long-run industry supply curve turns up, whereas before that point it had been decreasing.

GENERAL EQUILIBRIUM OF A COMPETITIVE ECONOMY

Now let's take an overview of the entire economy, still assuming that perfect competition prevails in all industries. Suppose the entire pattern of consumer demands for the economy is frozen, and a full "general equilibrium" adjustment to these demands has worked itself out in a purely competitive economy. What would be the main characteristics of the resulting general equilibrium?

1. *Each consumer (household) is in equilibrium.* Each household spends its income on the different goods and services it wants most. Thus, if we assume that it allocates its income so as to maximize the total utility obtained, each household buys different products until their prices are proportional to the marginal utilities they yield. Hence, consumer demand in the market place provides an accurate measure of how much satisfaction each commodity yields, and an accurate signal to producers as to how much of each commodity consumers want produced at different prices.

2. *Each business firm is in equilibrium.* Each business firm is doing everything it can to maximize its profits. To achieve this position, it carries its output up to the point where marginal cost equals price. The price is set by over-all market conditions—by consumer demand and by the prices it must pay for the resources it uses. But given these prices, each firm does the best it can to maximize profits.

3. *Each industry is in equilibrium.* The price of every commodity has been forced down by competition to the lowest point on the average unit-cost curve—that is, to the lowest total cost of production that is consistent with known technology, with the prices of productive resources used in the industry, and with the size of consumer demands. There is no longer any incentive for firms and resources to move into or out of the industry, since economic profit has been eliminated in every industry. (Remember that a normal return on investment is included in economic costs, so that accounting profits would remain in each industry in equilibrium.)

Put in other words, each businessman is producing his output in the most efficient possible way in each industry, so the minimum possible amount of society's scarce resources is being used in producing each commodity demanded by consumers. If this were not so, it would be possible for some firms to produce at a lower cost, and some firms would do so in order to obtain the profits thereby available. Only in equilibrium can we be sure that this most efficient use of resources is being achieved.

4. *Each market is in equilibrium.* In each market the amount being supplied is equal to the amount being demanded at the existing price. There is no unsatisfied demand or excess supply in any market.

5. How can we be sure that in general competitive equilibrium, the economy is (a) producing that combination of products which consumers most want, as measured by the prices they are willing to pay; and (b) using society's resources most efficiently in producing those products?

First, how much consumers buy at any price mirrors their preferences for different products. These purchases provide signals to producers.

Second, on the cost side, marginal cost in each firm provides an accurate measure of the additional cost it would take to produce one more unit of that output in responding to consumer signals. If marginal cost is below price, we know that too few resources are being used in that industry to satisfy consumer demand effectively. But if marginal cost is higher than price, too many resources are being used in the industry in response to consumer demand. In equilibrium, marginal cost is just equal to price, and price just covers the full cost of producing each product.

Put broadly, therefore, the combination of each consumer spending so as to maximize his own utility plus each businessman trying to maximize his own profits plus the force of competition in all markets has:

(a) forced each businessman to behave in the most "efficient" way if he is to remain in business;

(b) led businessmen in total to produce just as much of each product as consumers want to buy at a price which just covers the cost necessary to attract the resources needed to produce that amount; and

(c) obtained the maximum total output of wanted products from society's scarce productive resources.

6. We can now add another important proposition. The income received by each factor of production (laborers, capitalists, and the like) is the largest possible, given the productive powers of each. Assume that all workers and other resource owners (landowners and capitalists) work where the total monetary and "psychic" rewards are the highest. In other words, assume that each person does what he thinks is best for him.

Competition among businessmen for factors of production will bid up the return (wage, rent, etc.) on each to roughly the contribution it makes to the total revenue for the firm, and no higher. This is the "marginal product" of the worker or other productive resource.[6] Whenever the price of any productive service (say, the wage of a particular grade of labor) is lower than its marginal product, businessmen can increase their profits by hiring more of that factor, and this competition will bid the wage up. Whenever the price of a productive service is higher than its marginal product, businessmen will cut back on hiring that factor, and its price will fall until it just equals its marginal product. Moreover, each productive factor will have its highest marginal product (that is, it will add the most to the total output of wanted goods) when it is in the industry where its contribution is greatest—where its efficiency is highest in producing wanted products. Thus, each productive factor will earn the most when it is in that industry where it can contribute most to satisfying consumer demands as reflected in the market.

7. Last, in general equilibrium the rate of capital accumulation (investment) will reflect the public's preference for the future relative to the present, as shown by the proportion of income saved rather than spent on current consumption. When the public saves, it indicates that it prefers to forego current consumption in order to obtain future benefits, given prevailing interest rates on savings and other motives for saving. Conversion of these savings to investment reflects a judgment by profit-seeking investors (businessmen) that future consumer demands will yield returns that more than cover the interest rates required to obtain savers' funds. Interest

---

[6] Remember that marginal product is the addition to total output made by using one more unit of labor or capital.

rates (the "price" of savings) will move up or down toward equilibrium in this market, as in others (though the adjustment process may be a complex one, as noted in Part Two). In equilibrium, the economy's rate of capital accumulation would thus reflect the combined preferences of the public (supplying savings) and business (estimating future returns from investing). Again, the result depends on compromise through the market of the millions of self-seeking decisions of individual units that make up our economy.

In such a general equilibrium situation, could we say that consumers first demand certain goods and services, then businessmen respond to those demands, then competition forces their prices down to minimum costs, then wages and rents are set, then incomes are paid out to workers, landowners, and capitalists? Obviously the answer is "no." All these steps—millions of them each day—are being carried out simultaneously in the economy. The prices of all final goods and all factors of production are being set and adjusted continuously and simultaneously. Each depends on all the others.[7]

"The Invisible Hand"

Such is the case for pure competition. Everyone looks out for his own interests. The result is an organization of society's scarce resources that looks amazingly as if it had been guided by some invisible hand for the welfare of society as a whole. Each individual, as consumer, laborer, or businessman, maximizes his own advantage. No individual consumer or resource owner has any appreciable influence over what gets produced and how much of it, but in the mass they determine the allocation of society's resources among all possible alternative uses. Individual incomes, out-

[7] A more rigorous statement of these general equilibrium conditions is presented in the Appendix to this chapter. Some economists describe general equilibrium conditions in mathematical terms. Since general equilibrium involves considering a vast number of demands, costs, markets, prices, and productive factors simultaneously, we can view the system as a large set of simultaneous equations, and investigate the effects of different changes mathematically. Leon Walras, a French economist, was one of the first, a century ago, to use mathematics in analyzing economic problems and apparently the first to state the essential general equilibrium conditions for such a competitive economy.

puts, and prices are simultaneously determined. And at the center of the process, trying to buy cheap and sell dear, is the entrepreneur, continually searching for profits and thereby (perhaps unwittingly) providing the organizing service that merges and compromises all these millions of different interests.

PURELY COMPETITIVE ECONOMY— EVALUATION

The case for a purely competitive economy is an impressive one. If we want to avoid authoritarian control over what gets produced, where we work, and how we invest our savings, the purely competitive private-enterprise system offers a nonpolitical, individualistic way of making the millions of interrelated compromises required among the different interests involved.

Can we do better than Adam Smith's "invisible hand," the profit motive in competitive markets? Still assuming that pure competition might actually be attained for the entire economy and still putting aside the problem of business fluctuations, how, if at all, might such a purely competitive economic system fall short? Modern economists suggest several ways, which we can group under three main headings.

Equity and the Distribution of Income

Many observers believe that the distribution of income (wages, interest, profits, and the like) produced by a purely competitive economy would be inequitable. In a purely competitive economy, every man's income would rest on the economic contribution made by his own services or those of his property. Every man's power to direct the allocation of resources would thus depend on his marginal contribution to the economy's total output of wanted goods.

This is so because in a purely competitive economy there would be "consumers' sovereignty" over what gets produced. It would be a "one dollar, one vote" system—not a "one person, one vote" system such as we have in our political affairs. In the dollar-vote system the high-income man has lots of votes. When incomes are unequal, luxury hotels may be produced while millions are underfed and ill-clothed, all quite consistently with consumers' sovereignty.

In a purely competitive economy, moreover, there are many reasons why the incomes earned by some people would be much larger than by others. Some individuals inherit large fortunes, from which they obtain large incomes in the form of interest and profits from the funds invested. Some people have higher intellectual abilities than others, which tend to produce larger incomes for them. Some people are born into higher-income families, which means they tend to get better education and broader opportunities to develop earning power. Some people work harder and longer than others.

Some people argue that such an income distribution, based on "economic contribution," would be an eminently just and efficient arrangement. It would provide both incentives and equity for all. Whether you agree, you can decide for yourself. Lots of people don't. We will consider the problem in detail in Part Four.

Public Wants and the "Public Sector"

There is a wide range of public, or collective, wants which most people feel cannot be satisfactorily provided through the market place. National defense is the clearest example. We agree that this is essential, and through the political process legislate taxes (compulsory payments) to see that resources are used to build missiles and to train soldiers. It would be quite impractical to leave it up to each individual to buy in the market place the amount and kind of national defense he wanted. So it is with police protection, highways, education, and a variety of other public services which we agree are essential and which cannot as a practical matter be adequately provided through relying on individual purchases in the market. What we do directly through government action, we often call the "public sector" of the economy. This now totals over $250 billion annually.

Just how far we should go in using compulsory taxes to "buy" such public services is a highly debatable issue. Even with schools, we leave part of the job to private choice and the market place, with private schools and tuition at state universities. When we come to other areas, like public health services and slum clearance, the issue gets even hotter. We will take a detailed look at how big the public sector should be in Part Five, on "The Public Sector."

Problems in Making Competitive Markets Work Effectively

1. *Imperfect information, immobility, and consumer control.* For a purely competitive system to work well, consumers must be well informed about the goods and services available at different prices, and resource owners must be well informed about employment opportunities that are open to them. Farm workers in Montana may know nothing of a shortage of laborers in Detroit's auto assembly plants. Secretaries in Chicago may not know about better jobs in St. Louis.

If the Montana farm worker knows about the auto jobs in Detroit and decides to stay in Montana, even at lower pay, his decision is perfectly consistent with "ideal" resource allocation under pure competition. The competitive system acts to reflect people's preferences among types of work as well as among consumption goods. But if the farmer stays in Montana because he just doesn't know about a better job in Detroit that he would have preferred, the situation is different. Then imperfect knowledge has blocked complete competitive adjustment of resources to consumer demands. The farmer is worse off as an individual. And too many of society's resources are being allocated to producing wheat in Montana, too few to producing cars in Detroit.

The same malallocation results if resources are immobile, even though information is freely available. If our farmer has a big family and no savings, he may be quite unable to take the better Detroit job, no matter how badly he wants it. The cost of getting from Montana to Michigan, of supporting his family between jobs, and of going through a retraining period may make the change utterly impractical. Yet both the farmer and society would be better off if he could somehow get over the hump into the new industrial job.

Both imperfect information and imperfect mobility are widespread in the modern economy, especially among the lower-income groups. Both block the economy from carrying out the wishes of consumers and resource owners.

Another problem is perhaps even more serious, if we temporarily drop the assumption of a perfectly competitive economy. In the modern world, sellers influence, and sometimes even determine, what consumers want. Modern advertising and selling methods not only provide information on products but also mold consumer wants. Some people say, therefore, that the basic assumption of free consumer choice is increasingly violated. More about this in Chapter 26.

2. *The problem of minimum size for efficient production.* Pure competition requires that no one seller be large enough to have appreciable influence over market price. If he gets very big, there is a danger that he may react to increased consumer demand by putting up price and trying to shut out new competitors, rather than by expanding output.

This requirement means that there have to be lots of firms in every industry. We cannot, then, reasonably hope to have pure competition in many of the big mass-production industries. Take the flat-glass industry, for example. Eight or ten huge furnaces and glass-making tanks, together with appropriate modern rolling equipment, can apparently furnish all the flat glass the economy can use at peak production levels for the foreseeable future. Transportation costs are high for glass, so actually not more than half of these plants are in active competition in any one part of the country. Older methods of making flat glass are still usable, but only at substantially higher costs than the modern methods. Insisting on many firms would mean high production costs, and hence high prices, in such cases.

Even in small concerns, there is sometimes a conflict between competition and productive efficiency. For example, in a small town one large A&P supermarket may be able to sell at a lower price than would be forthcoming if the market were divided among four local competing grocers.

Where there are important economies of large-scale production that are unobtainable with a large number of firms, the public faces a difficult choice. We can insist on competition, but this will mean higher production costs than a

smaller number of large firms would involve. Or we can tolerate some degree of monopoly, but lose some of the pressures of competition obtainable with large numbers of producers. This dilemma poses a major issue of public policy, which is considered in detail in Chapter 28.

3. *Resource allocation when social costs differ from private costs.* To get the proper allocation of resources among different products, the price of each product to the consumer should cover the total cost of producing it. In some cases, there are hidden costs that are not paid by the producer and hence do not enter into the commodity's price but nevertheless are borne involuntarily by the rest of society. In such cases, price is lower than it should be and output is larger than is socially justifiable.

A common example is the smoke and dirt produced by many industrial plants. Smoke and dirt represent real costs to residents of the vicinity —through higher cleaning and painting bills, through impaired health, and through lessened contact with sunshine and fresh air. Yet these real costs don't enter into the firm's accounting costs of producing its product. The added cost to society of the plant's dirt isn't included in the manufacturer's price to his consumer. These are "social costs" not included in the manufacturer's "private" costs, and a market price that covers only the latter won't be high enough to cover the former.

The converse may also occur, where society gets special benefits from a producer for which it does not pay in the price of his products. An example is soil-conservation practices in agriculture. Suppose you own farm land along a stream, and you carefully plant and terrace your property to prevent erosion. This costs money. Everyone downstream from you benefits from your outlays through the decreased likelihood of floods. Yet you have no way of collecting from them in the revenues you receive from the sale of your product.

Where "private" and "social" costs and revenues diverge, a market system fails to produce an "ideal" pattern of resource allocation. Many economists believe that in such cases we should take collective (government) action to bring results nearer to the competitive ideal.

REVIEW

Concepts To Remember   Be sure you have a firm grasp of the new analytical concepts introduced in this chapter:

pure competition	constant-cost industry
long-run equilibrium	increasing-cost industry
equilibrium of the firm	long-run supply curves
equilibrium of the industry	social costs
general equilibrium	private costs
equilibrium tendencies	general economic efficiency

For Analysis and Discussion

1. Explain briefly but concisely how the self-interests of individuals and businesses interact to produce a widely beneficial outcome under competitive market conditions.
2. "Under pure competition, the consumer is king. Prices of what he wants to buy can never stay for long above the minimum cost of producing any article." Is this quotation sound?
3. Under a purely competitive system, what incentive, if any, would remain for businessmen to do an efficient job, since competition would eliminate profits?
4. Pure competition, strictly speaking, does not prevail in any part of the economy. Then why study it?
5. "A purely competitive economic system would be ideal." Do you agree? Why or why not?
6. Suppose a tax of 1 cent per blotter has been included in the costs of all blotter producers. Now the tax is removed. Beginning from the situation in Fig. 24-1, with price P^1P^1 and demand D^1D^1, trace through the adjustment to a new equilibrium.
7. Show how under long-run competitive equilibrium each household and business firm would be in its optimal (preferred) position so that it could not gain by a different pattern of behavior.
8. "Most people would agree that a dollar means more to a poor man than to a rich man. Since this is so, an economic system that merely reacts to the number of dollars spent is a grossly unfair system in the way it allocates resources." Do you agree or disagree? Why? If you agree, how should we modify the system to get around the problem?
9. Suppose you are part-owner of a steel company. The city asks you to install expensive smoke-control equipment to eliminate an alleged smoke nuisance caused by the mill. The cost will be $5 million, and most of your competitors in other cities have no such smoke eliminators. Would you agree? If you were a citizen in the community, would you favor a city ordinance requiring the mill to install the smoke eliminator?
10. How effectively would Adam Smith's invisible hand work for the general good under perfect competition? Explain your answer. What steps would be required to make the system work optimally?

Appendix

GENERAL EQUILIBRIUM
AND ECONOMIC EFFICIENCY

A purely competitive system of the sort described above would provide the most efficient possible allocation of resources in the sense described in the text of the chapter. More precisely, we can show that such a purely competitive system would allocate resources most efficiently, in the sense that no possible reallocation would increase the welfare of anyone in the system without harming someone else. This condition, which economists call "Pareto optimality" (after the famous French economist who first stated it precisely), seems to some observers a weak claim for an optimal system. But it is a major claim indeed, if you stop to think about it. For if Pareto optimality does not prevail, we could make someone better off without harming anyone else, thus unambiguously increasing the public's total utility. *Any system which does not provide Pareto optimality is producing a socially inefficient allocation of resources that holds total utility for the economy below what it could otherwise be.*

It is possible to demonstrate precisely that Pareto optimality will prevail under competitive general equilibrium (that is, no one can be made better off without injuring someone else); while under other market arrangements (e.g., with some degree of monopoly) it is generally possible to increase the welfare of someone without injuring anyone else. For simplicity, consider only two goods, x and y, although the argument can be generalized to many goods.

Assume that competitive general equilibrium prevails. We know then (from Chapter 20) that when a consumer is in equilibrium, maximizing his utility, he spends his income so that the marginal utility obtained from the last dollar spent on x is the same as that obtained from the last dollar spent on y. Alternatively, we can say that the marginal utilities of the two products must be proportional to their prices. In equation form:

$$(1) \quad \frac{MU_x}{MU_y} = \frac{P_x}{P_y}$$

We also know (from Chapters 23 and 24) that in long-run competitive equilibrium, each producer in each industry maximizes profits by producing up to the point where marginal cost equals price. Thus:

(2a) $P_x = MC_x$ (for industry x)
(2b) $P_y = MC_y$ (for industry y)

Combining equations (1) and (2), we can then write:

$$(3) \quad \frac{MU_x}{MU_y} = \frac{P_x}{P_y} = \frac{MC_x}{MC_y}$$

Equations (1), (2), and (3) state the conditions under which, with the competitive prices P_x and P_y, every consumer and business firm is in the best position it can achieve. No one can increase his utility or profits by changing his behavior. Equation (3) also emphasizes that prices provide the basic equilibrating link between consumers (expressing their preferences through expenditures) and businesses (maximizing their profits by hiring resources up to the point where marginal cost equals price).

Now, consider any situation where perfect competition does not prevail—for example, where a monopolist is restricting output and raising price to enlarge profits so that he holds his selling price above marginal cost. (We will demonstrate rigorously in the next chapter why he will do so in order to maximize his profits, once he is free from competitive pressure.) Suppose, for example, that monopoly prevails in industry y, so marginal cost in y is less than price. Then equation 2b will not hold, and hence neither will equation (3). Suppose, for example, that $\frac{MU_x}{MU_y} = 2$ but that $\frac{MC_x}{MC_y} = 3$ because marginal cost is below price in industry y while MC equals price in industry x. This means that in terms of costs, producers could make three additional units of y by giving up one of x. By so shifting resources to produce one less x and three more y we can make consumers better off, by giving them more than the two units of y they view as equivalent to one unit of x in their utility functions. Similarly, for any other condition than the (competitive) one specified in equation (3), it will be possible to make someone better off without injuring anyone else. When equation (3) is satisfied, Pareto optimality will prevail. Competitive equilibrium provides Pareto optimality, and monopolistic equilibrium does not except in some unlikely hypothetical cases which need not concern us here. Thus, economists presume that a monopolistic situation which holds marginal cost below price will generally lead to a less efficient allocation of resources than would a competitive system.

TWENTY-FIVE

MONOPOLY

The Bases of Monopoly.

Pure Monopoly.

Pure Monopoly—Evaluation.

Monopoly is something like sin. Everybody says he's against it, but a lot of people aren't very clear just what it is they're against. Like sin, monopoly has to be defined before one can talk much sense about it, or decide what, if anything, ought to be done about it.

The Spectrum
from Competition to Monopoly

Monopoly is generally defined as a market in which there is only one seller—as the Greek derivation of the word suggests. But this is deceptively simple. There is no commodity that doesn't have some substitutes, more or less close, and we have no sharp criterion of how close the substitute can be before we no longer have a monopoly. The Aluminum Company of America, up to World War II, was often called a monopoly in this sense: There was no other American producer of basic aluminum. But steel, wood, copper, and other materials are possible substitutes for aluminum, if the price of aluminum gets too high. Thus, Alcoa had a monopoly in producing aluminum, but certainly not in producing metals. Or consider General Motors. It has a monopoly in producing Chevrolets, but there is Ford next door producing close substitutes. In one sense, every producer who isn't in a purely competitive market has a monopoly in selling his own product. But the closer the substitutes produced by others, the less his "monopoly" matters as a practical matter.

Pure Monopoly

In spite of these problems, economists have defined a situation they call "pure" monopoly. Consider the local power company in a small town, as an example. It is the only producer of electricity in the town, and the substitution of candles, oil lamps, or gas lighting by consumers who rebel at high prices is not a very serious likelihood. (The big-city public utility is likely to be more exposed to potential competition, since industrial users of electricity do have less remote substitutes.) Clearly, Alcoa wasn't in as strong a position as is a public-utility company, but both fit reasonably well into the pure-monopoly classification, which is characterized by:

1. Only one seller of the good or service.
2. Rivalry from producers of substitutes so remote as to be insignificant.

Under these circumstances, the pure monopolist can set the market price himself, and customers don't have close substitutes to turn to. But even he has to face up to the realities of elasticity of demand. He can put his price where he wishes. But unless demand is perfectly inelastic, the higher he puts his price the less he can sell. Partly, the elasticity of demand for any product reflects the presence of potential substitutes, and there is no monopoly so pure that it can escape completely the possibility of partial substitutes. Thus, completely pure monopoly is never quite found in the real world, and "pure monopoly" shades imperceptibly into "monopolistic competition," just as "pure competition" shades into lesser degrees of competition.[1]

Monopolistic Competition and Oligopoly

There is a spectrum from pure competition to pure monopoly. *Where there are a good many sellers of only slightly differentiated products, but not enough to make the market perfectly competitive, we call the situation "monopolistic competition."* There may be a dozen or a hundred sellers of substantially identical products. But the products vary somewhat. For example, breakfast-

food manufacturers don't make just breakfast food. They make Wheaties, Cheerios, and all the rest. Even corn flakes aren't just corn flakes; Post and Kellogg put them in different-colored boxes under different names, and to the buyer they are at least somewhat differentiated. Or stores may provide different services with the same product— say, free delivery. The degree of "product differentiation" gets to be more substantial for, say, television sets. Philco, RCA and Sylvania may all show the same picture on the same-sized tube when turned to Channel 4, but neither the makers nor the customers believe the sets are the same.

Where there are only a few competing producers so each producer must take into account what each other producer does, we call the situation "oligopoly," which means few sellers. In the auto industry, with only a few big producers, obviously General Motors, Chrysler, and Ford have to pay a lot of attention to each other's policies in setting prices, even though their products are all somewhat differentiated. Firms in oligopolistic industries may compete actively, or they may get together ("collude") formally or informally to agree on prices and on sharing the market.

Most of the American economic system lies in between pure competition and pure monopoly. Each industry seems to be a little different. Yet we need to classify this huge "in-between" area into some major groups if we are to make any headway in analyzing how it operates. In looking at the world of monopolistic competition and oligopoly, economists often emphasize the following four questions:

1. *How many producers are there of any given commodity?* The larger the number, the more likely competition is to be active.
2. *How close are the substitutes for the commodity?* The closer the substitutes are, the less real monopoly power any firm can exercise without losing customers.
3. *Do the producers involved compete on prices, or through nonprice channels such as quality and advertising?* In some cases producers may not compete at all—they may agree to maintain fixed shares of a market at some agreed price. But in the vast majority of cases firms do compete in some way—on price, on quality of product and

[1] The analogy to pure monopoly on the buyer's side is sometimes called "pure monopsony," which means one buyer. This case might prevail where there is only one buyer for labor services—say the mill in an isolated mill town. But like pure monopoly, pure monopsony is hard to find. For instance, workers are free to move to another town if the monopsonist exploits his position too much.

services, through advertising, or in some other way.

4. *How easy is it for new firms to get into the industry, or into producing close substitutes for the industry's product?* A monopoly that can be invaded by anybody on short notice isn't much of a monopoly.

If we use these questions, we can immediately see some important subclasses under monopolistic competition and oligopoly. For example, the monopolistic-competition group is usefully subdivided into cases where competition is primarily on prices, and those where it primarily takes the form of nonprice and advertising competition. Oligopolies seem to fall into three groups depending on whether they collude on prices and output (in which case they are often called "cartels"), follow a "leader" on price-setting, or compete actively.

We come out with a division like this:

I. *Pure competition*—many sellers of an identical product (wheat).
II. *Monopolistic competition*—a substantial number of sellers of closely substitutable products.
   a. Price competition (vegetables in local grocery stores).
   b. Nonprice competition and "demand creation" (beer, men's suits).
III. *Oligopoly*—a few sellers of closely substitutable products.[2]
   a. Competition—on prices and through nonprice competition and demand creation (television, automobiles).
   b. Collaboration.
     1. Formal collusion on prices and on output—"cartels" (nickel, internationally).
     2. Price leadership or informal price stabilization (steel, gasoline).
IV. *Pure monopoly*—one seller of a product without close substitutes (local water company).

The examples are intended merely to provide some concrete impressions to go with the

[2] Where there are only two sellers, another Greek word, "duopoly," is used. This is a special case of oligopoly.

analytical categories. Few real-world cases fit neatly and exclusively into any one of the intermediate categories. For example, there is some demand creation, and quality competition as well as price competition, in groceries (case IIa); and there is surely price as well as nonprice competition in both beer and men's suits (case IIb). The main purpose of the classification is to give us a rough framework to organize analysis of the various types of market behavior. Where industries are hybrids, we may need to use two or more of the analytical models in thinking about them.

Data on particular industries and industry groups are given in the following chapters. Broadly, we can say that nearly all the "service" industries (retail trade, legal services, banking, etc.) fall in the monopolistic competition category, as do a good many manufacturing firms. Much of manufacturing (probably over half) falls under the oligopoly head. Only public utilities provide reasonable examples of "pure monopoly."

THE BASES OF MONOPOLY

The basic test of an effective monopoly is its power to exclude competitors from the market. If a firm can keep out potential competitors, it can raise prices with relative impunity. The nearer the substitutes that competitors can put on the market, the weaker is the firm's monopoly position. The ideal monopoly (from the monopolist's viewpoint) would cover an absolutely essential product with no effective substitutes.

Government Action as a Basis for Monopoly

The strongest monopolies are the public utilities. An exclusive government franchise is about as airtight protection as any monopoly can hope for. This arrangement is found in most localities for water, electricity, gas, and telephone companies. Even where multiple companies are permitted by law, the market territory is usually divided up by law or regulatory commission. Having granted this enviable monopoly position, however, governments invariably regulate the prices the monopoly can charge. Often they maintain supervision over the company's whole operations, to protect the public's interest. Otherwise, the stockholders of the local water or gas company would be in a happy position indeed.

Governments intervene in other ways to provide partial bases for monopolies. The farm-aid programs of the past three decades have supported prices and induced farmers to behave like a cartel in restricting output. Local building codes, which specify particular types of construction and particular materials, are manifestly intended to protect the public against unsafe construction and poor work, but in fact provide a widespread basis for monopolistic practices by building suppliers and building-trade unions. The entire federal patent system, discussed below, protects the monopoly position of the inventor. Federal legislation establishes the right of workers to combine in unions that in essence act as monopolies in selling their labor to employers.

Patents and Research

The patent law gives to the inventor exclusive control over his invention for 17 years. If a patent gives effective control over production of some commodity, direct competition is almost impossible. Despite some recent limitations on their use as a basis for extending monopoly positions, patents can still provide a powerful basis for monopoly powers. For example, the United Shoe Machinery Corporation for years held exclusive control over the shoemaking machinery field through its patents.

Key patents underlie the industrial position of many major American concerns. Research has become part of the American industrial scene, and the "blue chips" of American industry come automatically to mind when we think of technological advance—General Electric, DuPont, Standard Oil. These firms maintain their leading positions in oligopolistic industries in no small part by being first with the best in research. Over the past 20 years almost two-thirds of all patents have gone to corporations. General Electric alone, for example, received about 13,000; A.T. & T. about 10,000.

Research is an expensive and cumulative process. It's hard for the little firm to compete, quite aside from the patent laws. For example, DuPont's research laboratories alone would swal-low up most of the business firms in the United States, and their stable of top-notch industrial scientists is the hopeless envy of all except a few leading rivals.

Control of Raw Materials

If you can get exclusive control over the raw materials needed to make your product, you're sitting pretty—at least until someone figures out a substitute material. A few major firms have managed to get such exclusive control. Two examples described in the late 1930's by the Temporary National Economic Committee are apparently still effective.[3]

The International Nickel Company of Canada, Ltd., owns more than nine-tenths of the world's known reserve of nickel. The company produced more than 92 per cent of the world's output of nickel in 1929.

Molybdenum is an element which finds its principal employment either in competition or in combinations with other alloying metals, in the production of steels of exceptional toughness and strength. In Bartlett Mountain in Colorado, the Climax Molybdenum Company owns 95 per cent of the world's known store of commercially workable deposits of this metal.

Financial Resources and the Capital Market

The money needed to set up an efficient firm in many industries today is tens and even hundreds of millions of dollars. Not very many people have this much money, and it's hard to borrow ten million dollars unless you're already a very well-established person or firm, no matter how engaging a picture you paint of your prospects.

In a "perfect" capital market, funds would be available whenever the prospective borrower was willing and able to pay the going rate of interest on loans of comparable risk. In fact, however, it is hard for newcomers to raise funds in the market. Lenders are skeptical of unknown faces. Capital is rationed out to "desirable" borrowers rather than "sold" on the basis of borrowers' willingness to pay the quoted interest rates. Moreover, borrowing is especially expensive for small, new borrowers, even when they can get the funds.

[3] *Competition and Monopoly in American Industry,* TNEC Monograph No. 21, p. 79.

The fact that large sums are often needed to set up new firms gives an important protection to established monopolists. The imperfection of the capital market, which often makes it especially hard for the newcomer and small producer to get funds, increases this protection.

Advertising

Advertising by itself would have a hard time establishing or even maintaining a monopoly on any product. But the entrenched positions of names like Cadillac and RCA-Victor in the mind of the American consumer are a cause of dismay to prospective competitors. Modern advertising has become increasingly "institutionalized." That is, ads aim primarily at building up the company's name and prestige, rather than at selling a particular product. Large-scale prestige advertising costs big money, and only big and successful companies can afford it. The large company, which is often at least a partial monopolist, may find advertising a potent weapon for maintaining and extending its dominant position. Business outlays on advertising are huge. They totaled $15 billion in 1967.

Unfair Competition

Running the little fellow out of business by unfair price-cutting is one of the charges commonly brought against big business. If A&P prices groceries very low, it is accused of a devious intent to run the independents out and then to boost its own prices when competition is gone. And you don't have to look very far back into history to find plenty of cases where big business behaved this way. Such discriminatory price-cutting, aimed to eliminate competition, often put price below cost. Often prices were cut only in areas where competition existed; high prices in other areas were used to keep profits up while competitors were being forced to the wall. The old Standard Oil Company provided some spectacular cases of such behavior—and with great success. But the practice was widespread during the late nineteenth and early twentieth centuries.

Such unfair price competition is now illegal. But the line between legitimate price-cutting and unfair price-cutting merely to eliminate competition is hard to draw in many cases. The more

efficient producer always tends to eliminate the inefficient—unless, as is said to be the case in some modern industries, the dominant firm is already so big that it voluntarily chooses to encourage other firms in order to lessen the chance of antitrust prosecution by the government.

Large-scale Production and Decreasing Costs

Low-cost mass production is the pride of American industry. In many industries (steel, electrical equipment, automobiles, chemicals, and so on), maximum efficiency can be obtained only by large firms, each producing a substantial share of the total amount that can be sold on the market. In local areas, taking advantage of the economies of large-scale production may mean one or a few monopolistic firms—for example, the one grocery store a small town can reasonably support.

In extreme cases, the total market is not big enough to permit even one firm to operate at the optimal scale of output. Until a firm reaches this optimal scale, it is operating in its range of "decreasing costs." That is, by increasing output it can cut its cost per unit produced. This is described in common terminology as the "economies of large-scale production." In such cases, the pressures toward monopoly are great.

Figure 25-1 represents such an industry. The

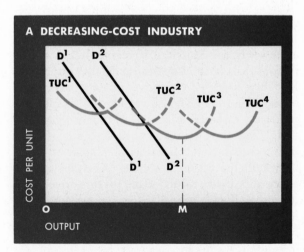

FIG. 25-1 This industry has decreasing unit costs up to output M. For any demand short of that amount, competition is unlikely to work effectively.

TUC curves are simply total-unit-cost curves for different scales of enterprise for a firm in the industry, say a local gas company. Scale TUC^3 is the most efficient scale in this case; its least-cost point is the lowest of any possible scale of enterprise. Each cost curve is drawn in a heavy line through the range in which it is lower than any other. The heavy scalloped line is therefore a curve that indicates the total unit cost at which each output can be produced as the size of the firm increases. This will be a decreasing-cost industry if demand is small relative to the scale of enterprise TUC^3—for example, if demand is D^1D^1 or D^2D^2. It is a "decreasing-cost" industry because the economics of scale of enterprise within the single firm have not yet been fully exploited at any output less than OM, the least-cost point on TUC^3.

Under what conditions will our gas company remain a one-firm monopoly? Suppose demand is D^1D^1, and it sets a price well above average cost to produce a juicy profit. If it has no government-guaranteed monopoly, these large profits are likely to attract a competitor into the market. But in this market, with demand D^1D^1 it is obviously impossible for two or more firms to cover costs if they compete actively. Demand for gas in the area isn't big enough to support even one of them at optimum scale. If they get into a price war as each tries to get a bigger share of the market to permit lower unit costs of production, the likely result is bankruptcy for the weaker, with the stronger taking over the whole market again.

In such circumstances, instead of competing aggressively, the two firms may enter into a formal agreement or unspoken understanding to maintain price and to restrict output. This arrangement is obviously wasteful of resources. Each firm is producing gas at a higher cost per cubic foot than if one firm alone were to produce the same total output. But under this market-sharing arrangement both companies may be able to make profits, and profits are likely to be the first concern of the managers. *The social advantage of limiting the industry to one firm is obvious; this is the basis for most exclusive public-utility franchises.*

How widespread decreasing-cost industries really are in the economy is a moot issue. Some claim that many firms could be more efficient if

they were to expand further and take over more of the market. It is common gossip, for example, that General Motors could undersell the entire auto industry and eliminate all the other firms if it were not held back by possible antitrust action. But even if this rumor was true, in most industries the market appears to be adequate to support more than one firm of optimum size. Whether the market is big enough to support enough firms to guarantee effective competition is another question—a more difficult one that we will consider in detail a little later.

PURE MONOPOLY [4]

Where we draw the line between pure monopoly and monopolistic competition is arbitrary, since it depends on how close the available substitutes are. In the American economy, except in the public utilities, we seldom find only one firm, no available substitutes for the commodity produced, and no possibility that other firms may invade the market. Yet looking at such an extreme case is useful, because it shows up clearly some of the attributes of monopoly. It gives some insight into what the world might be like if pure monopolies were tolerated without regulation. It suggests rules for controlling public utilities. And it may be a quite realistic description of the short-run position in which firms temporarily find themselves because of special advantages of location, development of new products ahead of competitors, or other such circumstances.

Imagine a single electric-power company in an isolated community, free to charge whatever rates it pleases. Suppose you are the owner-manager of this hypothetical concern. Waiving the fear that the local government will begin to regulate your rates, how would you go about maximizing your profits?

Costs

First, you'd want to know your costs. Your engineers and accountants will probably have estimates at hand, or can produce some for you.

---

[4] The remainder of this chapter rests directly on the marginal-cost–marginal-revenue analysis of Chapter 23.

TABLE 25-1

HOMETOWN ELECTRIC COMPANY—COST SCHEDULE*

| Kilowatts (1) | Total Cost (2) | Average Cost per Kilowatt (3) | Marginal Cost | |
			Per 100,000 Kilowatts (4)	Per Kilowatt (5)
1,000,000	$50,000	5.0¢		
1,100,000	52,800	4.8	$2,800	2.8¢
1,200,000	55,200	4.6	2,400	2.4
1,300,000	57,200	4.4	2,000	2.0
1,400,000	60,200	4.3	3,000	3.0
1,500,000	64,500	4.3	4,300	4.3
1,600,000	70,400	4.4	5,900	5.9

* Unit-cost data are rounded to the nearest tenth of a cent.

Recognizing that these estimates are probably pretty rough, suppose the cost schedule looks like the one in Table 25-1. To simplify matters, the table shows only the estimates for producing at rates from 1,000,000 to 1,600,000 kilowatt-hours, in intervals of 100,000 kilowatt-hours. (To simplify the language, we will use merely the word kilowatts hereafter, for kilowatt-hours.)[5]

The table is self-explanatory. Columns 1 and 2 are the basic total-cost estimates. Column 3, which is simply 2 divided by 1, converts total cost to cost per unit. Column 4, marginal cost per 100,000 kilowatts, shows the additional cost involved in producing an extra 100,000 kilowatts. For example, it costs an extra $2,800 to raise production from 1,000,000 to 1,100,000 kilowatts weekly. Column 5 converts this marginal cost per 100,000 kilowatts to marginal cost per kilowatt.

Sales Revenue

All this cost information doesn't do you any good unless you know something about the demand for electricity. So you have your market-research people get you the best estimates they can on the prices at which you can sell these various amounts. To simplify matters again, assume that you sell at the same price to everyone (not discriminating between residential and commercial users). Table 25-2 shows estimated de-

mand over the same output range as Table 25-1.

This table is the counterpart of the cost table. Column 2 shows the prices at which different amounts of electricity can be sold. Column 3 shows the total revenue obtained by selling at those prices. Column 4 shows the extra revenue obtained by selling an additional 100,000 kilowatts —for example, $3,600 extra obtained by boosting sales from 1,000,000 to 1,100,000 kilowatts. And Column 5 converts this marginal revenue to a per kilowatt basis, by dividing the marginal revenue per 100,000 kilowatts by 100,000.

There is one special point in this table that merits attention. Under pure competition, price and marginal revenue to the seller are identical. If the farmer sells an extra bushel of wheat at $2 a bushel, he adds $2 to his total revenue. *But for the monopolist, marginal revenue is always less than price, assuming he sells his product at the same price to everybody. This is because he must lower his price to sell more units, and he must lower it not just on the marginal unit but on all units sold.*

For example, you can sell 1,500,000 kilowatts at 6.1¢ per kilowatt. To increase sales to 1,600,000 you must reduce the price to 5.7¢ on all 1,600,000 kilowatts. Thus, your marginal revenue is your income from selling the extra 100,000 kilowatts (100,000 times 5.7¢ = $5,700) minus the .4 of a cent loss on each of the other 1,500,000 kilowatts (1,500,000 times .4¢ = $6,000). In this case, then, marginal revenue on the 100,000 kilowatts is ac-

[5] Electricity producers often face demands that fluctuate widely through the day and seasonally. For simplicity, we neglect this problem here.

TABLE 25-2

HOMETOWN ELECTRIC COMPANY—CUSTOMER DEMAND SCHEDULE

Kilowatts (1)	Price (2)	Total Revenue (3)	Marginal Revenue Per 100,000 Kilowatt (4)	Per Kilowatt (5)
1,000,000	8.0¢	$80,000	$3,600	3.6¢
1,100,000	7.6	83,600	3,400	3.4
1,200,000	7.25	87,000	2,700	2.7
1,300,000	6.9	89,700	1,300	1.3
1,400,000	6.5	91,000	500	.5
1,500,000	6.1	91,500	—300	—.3
1,600,000	5.7	91,200		

tually negative. Your total revenue will be $300 less if you cut price to 5.7¢ in order to increase sales to 1,600,000 units, even though you sell an extra 100,000 kilowatts at 5.7¢ each. All along the demand schedule, marginal revenue is less than price, for the same reason, though only when price is cut below 6.1¢ is marginal revenue actually negative.[6]

This relationship between price and marginal revenue is fundamental for every seller who is not in a perfectly competitive market. Whenever he faces a downward-sloping demand curve, to sell more he must cut price both for the extra units he hopes to sell and on the units he could otherwise sell at a higher price. His gain from cutting price is never as big as it appears that it might be at first glance.

Maximizing
Monopoly Profits

The monopolist can set his price where he pleases, and sell what the market will take at that price. Or he can decide how many units to produce, and sell them at the price which consumers will pay. But, given the market demand schedule, he cannot set both the price and the number of units he will sell. The market will determine one or the other for him.

[6] Marginal revenue is always zero when elasticity of demand is unity, positive when demand is elastic, and negative when demand is inelastic. Why? From this proposition it obviously follows that no perceptive monopolist will ever increase his output into the range where demand is inelastic.

How could you maximize your profits, if you were the manager?

One answer is simple. You compare estimated total cost and estimated total revenue at each different level of output. When you find the level that gives the biggest total profit (revenue minus cost), that's it. You plan to produce that many units and sell them at the price indicated.

This calculation is shown in Table 25-3, whose first four columns reproduce the cost and revenue figures from the preceding tables. It's plain that profit is largest if you produce 1,300,000 kilowatts weekly and sell them at a price of 6.9¢ per kilowatt, which gives a profit of $32,500. Expected profit is lower for any other level shown—though there is the possibility that some level within the 100,000-kilowatt intervals on either side of 1,300,-000 might be better.

Another way of calculating your maximum-profit position is by comparing marginal costs and marginal revenues. This comparison is made in the two right-hand columns. As long as the marginal revenue from adding an additional unit of output is greater than the marginal cost of producing the unit, obviously profit is increased by producing the extra unit. This gain is clear when you increase output from 1,000,000 to 1,100,000 units, on up to 1,200,000 units, and then to 1,300,000 units. But if you try 1,400,000 units, the marginal cost is 3¢ per unit and the marginal revenue only 1.3¢. This is a profit-reducing move, since it adds more to cost than to revenue—even though total profit would still be substantial at 1,400,000. The marginal approach gives

TABLE 25-3

HOMETOWN ELECTRIC COMPANY—PROFIT CALCULATIONS

Kilowatts	Price	Total Cost	Total Revenue	Total Profit	Marginal Unit Cost	Marginal Unit Revenue
1,000,000	8.0¢	$50,000	$80,000	$30,000		
1,100,000	7.6	52,800	83,600	30,800	2.8¢	3.6¢
1,200,000	7.25	55,200	87,000	31,800	2.4	3.4
1,300,000	6.9	57,200	89,700	* 32,500	2.0	2.7
1,400,000	6.5	60,200	91,000	30,800	3.0	1.3
1,500,000	6.1	64,500	91,500	27,000	4.3	.5
1,600,000	5.7	70,400	91,200	20,800	5.9	—.3

* Maximum total profit.

us the same answer as the total-cost--total-revenue comparison. The two are simply alternative ways of getting the same profit-maximizing answer. Still a third way of getting the same answer would be by comparing marginal cost and marginal revenue per 100,000 units, instead of on a per unit basis.

Which way is better? Take your pick. They give the same result.

Graphical Analysis
of Profit Maximization

If you think best in terms of graphs, you may ask your staff to present the cost and revenue data to you graphically. This is easy. Figure 25-2 plots the relevant per unit data for calculating your maximum-profit position graphically. *DD* is the estimated market-demand curve. *MR* is the associated marginal-revenue curve per unit, which shows the increase in your total revenue associated with each additional unit sold.[7] *TUC* is the estimated total-unit-cost curve for your lowest-cost scale of enterprise. And *MC* is the associated marginal-unit-cost curve, showing at each point the addition to your total costs involved in increasing output one unit. The solid part of each curve represents the data from Table 25-3; the dotted lines extend the curves hypothetically beyond the range of data we have.

Be sure you know how to read the various curves. Reading from the graph, for example, at 1,200,000 units output the total cost per unit is about 4.6¢. According to the demand curve, this output can be sold at a price of about 7.25¢ per kilowatt. Obviously this is a profitable level of output—the demand curve is above the total-unit-cost curve. Now look at the marginal curves. The marginal-cost curve shows that to increase output by one kilowatt—to 1,200,001 kilowatts—would involve an addition to total cost of about 2.4¢. This additional unit would add about 3.4¢ to total revenue, according to the marginal-revenue curve. Thus, we can readily see from the graph: (1) that an output of 1,200,000 kilowatts is profitable, and

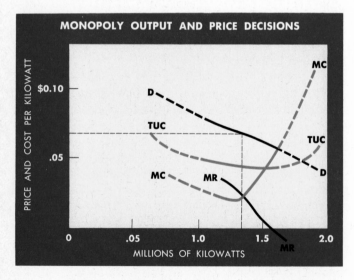

FIG. 25-2 The monopolist maximizes profit by equating marginal cost and marginal revenue—here at an output of about 1.32 million kilowatts to be sold at a price just under 7 cents.

[7] As was explained above, the marginal-revenue curve is always below its demand curve, and slopes downward more steeply.

(2) that a larger output would be still more profitable, since at the 1,200,000-kilowatt level marginal cost is still below marginal revenue.

Going on, you can easily determine the maximum-profit position. It will be the output where marginal cost just equals marginal revenue. This is a little above 1,300,000 kilowatts, which you could sell at a price of about 6.8¢, reading off the demand curve at that output. If you want to compute your total profit from this graph, you can. You find your profit per unit by first taking the distance between the selling price and your total unit cost, and then multiplying this profit per unit by the total number of units sold. This would give a profit of about $33,000 at the best level—roughly 2.5¢ per kilowatt on 1,320,000 kilowatts.

Note that this is a slightly higher profit than the maximum shown by Table 25-3. The graph, which gives you data for *all* levels of output rather than just one estimate each 100,000 kilowatts, tells you to produce an extra 20,000 kilowatts beyond the prescription of the table. The price for the larger output will only be 6.8¢, but the cost per kilowatt stays at about 4.3¢, and your total profit is about $500 larger than at 1,300,000 kilowatts.

This conclusion is suggestive: *If in fact your cost data are smooth and continuous between the original cost estimates at 100,000-kilowatt intervals, and if the demand curve is also smooth and continuous between your original market-research estimates, then you'd be money out to base your calculations solely on the few intervals at which you have estimates in the original tables above.* The continuous curves on the graph give you a quick guide to the maximum-profit level of output and prices. Whether you use the graph or not, you clearly need to make calculations covering outputs within the 100,000-kilowatt intervals used in the tables. The graph is only a short cut to these finer calculations.

PURE MONOPOLY—EVALUATION

This look at the consequences of unregulated pure monopoly, protected against entry of competitive enterprises, illustrates the extreme case of monopoly's impact on the economy.

Resource Allocation

Monopoly leads to an inefficient allocation of resources from the consumer's point of view. If the monopolist restricts output and raises price to maximize his profits, he will be holding price above marginal cost. But Chapter 24 told us that $mc = $ price is the condition for achieving the most efficient allocation of productive resources to satisfy consumers' demands. Thus, too few resources are hired into the monopolized industry. Consumers get fewer resources devoted to producing the monopolized product than would be optimal to meet their demand for it, relative to other products. *This is the basic economic criticism of monopoly.*

Conversely, too many resources are used in other sectors of the economy. Resources shut out from the monopolized industry seek employment elsewhere. In restricting his output, the monopolist is failing to bid resources away from competitive industries, even though the marginal contribution of the resources to satisfying consumer wants would be greater in the monopoly than in the competitive sector of the economy.[8]

Income Distribution

Monopoly tends toward inequality of income. Monopoly profits swell the incomes of businessmen and stockholders in monopoly concerns at the expense of the rest of society. Monopoly restriction on output cuts the demand for labor and reduces average wages and prices of other productive services. But the basic evil of monopoly is the malallocation of resources explained above, not the special profits made by the monopolist. To see this point, suppose the government taxed away, through a lump-sum tax, all special monopoly profits and returned the sum to the public through public services. The monopolist would have extracted no monopoly profit from the public. But the misallocation of resources would remain as a burden on the public; too few resources

---

[8] The difficulty in making a precise comparison with competive price and output in such a case should be clear. Since the market is unlikely to be large enough to support a large number of producers, each with a least-cost point as low as the large monopolist's, we cannot demonstrate rigorously that monopoly price is higher than competitive price would be.

would be used in producing the monopolized product, too many in producing other products, as measured by what consumers want.

Efficiency and Progress

Pure competition forces each firm to be efficient or perish. If new production techniques are developed, the laggard who fails to keep up with the leaders soon loses out in the market. Under monopoly, these pressures are weak. It does not necessarily follow that monopolies are inefficient or uninterested in progress. It only follows that they are relatively free from competitive pressures.

Many observers feel that the absence of strong competitive pressures does often lead to inefficiency and lessened interest in meeting consumer needs. Rightly or wrongly, they cite the public utilities—railways, electric power, gas companies, and so forth—as slow to adopt new ideas and techniques, slow to respond to new consumer needs. Some argue that monopolists have intentionally retarded the development and introduction of new products that might increase the obsolescence rate of their existing equipment. And even though monopoly profits don't appear excessive, this fact may reflect inefficiently high costs, protected from the pressures of competition. On the other side, A.T. & T. has large monopoly power in the telephone industry, yet it has provided a high rate of technological advance. The evidence is mixed. But the prod of competition is a powerful incentive to innovation and efficiency.

Either way, remember one earlier qualification: If the market is so small that only a few firms can be supported at efficient scales of operation, insistence on many firms would lead to higher-cost production and probably to oscillating instability through periodic price wars. Limited markets may seldom justify pure monopoly. But they often mean that the conditions of pure competition cannot be met. Most of the world lies somewhere between the two extremes.

REVIEW

Concepts To Remember

Most of the major concepts used in this chapter were introduced in earlier chapters. But there are a few important new ones:

pure (simple) monopoly   oligopoly
monopolistic competition   decreasing-cost industry

For Analysis and Discussion

1. Why have the American people traditionally distrusted both monopolies and big business? Is there any significant economic distinction between the two? How about I.B.M. and A. & P.?
2. The post office and your local water company are examples of substantially pure monopolies. How would you go about deciding whether they are doing an efficient job of serving the consumer at reasonable prices? Do you have a better way of evaluating the performance of such big partial monopolies as General Motors and Alcoa?
3. A noted economist has argued that without government support, there would be little serious monopoly in America today. He cites public utilities, government support of unions, government-sponsored cartelization in agriculture, and "fair-trade" laws to hold up prices in retailing. How sound is this argument? Can you cite counter-examples?
4. Why do economists say that the basic *economic* criticism of monopolies is that they hold price above marginal cost?
5. How strong a factor in building up and maintaining a monopoly position would you expect advertising could be? Can you cite examples on which your belief rests?
6. If a monopoly is not making excessive (i.e., above-normal) profits, it is doing no serious harm to the public. True or false? Explain.

TWENTY-SIX

MONOPOLISTIC COMPETITION

Do Partial Monopolists Maximize Profits?

Prices and Output
under Monopolistic Competition.

Quality Competition
and Competitive Demand Creation.

Measures of Market Performance.

Almost nobody has a pure monopoly. But lots of firms have partial monopolies. The corner druggist has a partial monopoly in his neighborhood. He can charge several cents more for a quart for ice cream than the big dairy stores downtown. And he can get it—because he is so conveniently located for people in the neighborhood.

Coca-Cola has a partial monopoly. No one else can make a drink exactly like Coca-Cola without infringing the law, and for years "a Coke" has been the habitual mid-morning and mid-afternoon drink of millions. But Pepsi-Cola, Royal Cola, and a good many others look and taste enough like Coca-Cola to have made Coca-Cola's share of the soft-drink market decline appreciably in the last two decades. The Coca-Cola people will tell you they're in a highly competitive field.

Bayer Aspirin has a partial monopoly. For years Bayer's held a substantial monopoly in the retail sale of aspirin, based largely on effective advertising that identified Bayer Aspirin with aspirin, even though all commercial aspirin is chemically identical. But here too other companies are after the customer's dollar and have steadily whittled away at the impression that only Bayer's is really aspirin.

A large part of the American economy is in the range between competition and monopoly—partly protected from competitors by trade names, location, tradition, quality of product, but far from perfectly protected; exposed to new competitors, but much less exposed than the wheat farmer. This is the area of "monopolistic competition." In it, each firm's product is "differentiated" from its competitors', but not enough to forestall active competition—on prices, selling costs, quality, or all three. As was indicated above, monopolistic competition does not include those cases where there are only a few firms in an industry; this few-firms case is called "oligopoly."[1]

How much of the economy is in the "monopolistic competition" category? The lines are hazy, but a fair, though very crude, answer would be, one-half the private sector. This would include nearly all of wholesale and retail trade, finance, real estate, and personal services (legal, medical, and the like); a substantial sector of manufacturing (e.g., textiles, apparel, lumber, and printing); and most of construction and of trucking. By contrast, a large part of manufacturing (autos, steel, heavy electrical equipment, glass, and tobacco products) is oligopolistic; railroads, airlines, and all public utilities are regulated by government; and agriculture is a special case of nondifferentiated products with prices substantially influenced by government policies. It's a complex world, but "monopolistically competitive" describes a big part of it.

Before going on to examine monopolistic competition in this chapter and oligopoly in the next, we need to ask an important question that applies to both.

DO PARTIAL MONOPOLISTS MAXIMIZE PROFITS?

Do these partial monopolists, operating with various degrees of protection from market competition under monopolistic competition and oligopoly, produce efficiently and maximize their profits? Maybe businessmen in highly competitive industries don't try to maximize profits. But if they don't make a fairly good stab at it, competition will remove them from the scene in due time. With the monopolist and partial monopolist, we can't count so fully on competition to exert this pressure. We need to know more about the firm's motives and patterns of behavior if we are to understand how the partially monopolized sectors of the economy work.

[1] Remember that "industry" is usually defined loosely to include all firms producing reasonably close substitutes, such as the aspirin industry, the ice-cream industry, and the steel industry.

If you asked most businessmen whether they try to maximize profits, they would probably tell you, "Yes, but. . . ." The "but" might refer to lots of things, but especially to the fact that few businessmen like to say that they exploit their position by charging the last penny the traffic will bear. Playing for the long pull makes sense to many managers. It may be good business to forego higher profits today in the interest of long-run earnings.

But do partial monopolists generally maximize even long-run profits? Back in Chapter 24, four reasons were listed why even under pure competition many firms may not be maximizing profits at any given time. These apply equally here:

1. It takes time to adjust to change.
2. Businessmen never know what costs and demand in the future will be. They can only estimate, and often they're wrong.
3. Sometimes managers just aren't very efficient. They don't do a very good job of either minimizing costs or increasing revenues.
4. Firms sometimes can't get funds to undertake potentially profitable investments that require substantial cash outlays. The capital market is more open to large than to small firms.

Beyond these four reasons, there are some others that apply especially to firms holding partial monopolies, where the pressure of competition may be weaker:

5. Unusually large profits may be an invitation to new competitors, lured by the hope of winning some away. This danger may lead the monopolistic competitor to think twice before reaching for more profits that may invite more competition.
6. Unusually large profits may bring special scrutiny from the government's antitrust officials, who may suspect illegal behavior as the basis for the profits, especially if the firm has only a few major competitors.
7. Historians point to many firms that have grown big as the result of the promoters' and managers' desire for bigness as such, in spite of the dubious profitability of such behavior. They focus

on total sales and share of market, rather than on profits *per se*. Many observers rate growth as being today the dominant single objective of large corporate management (though it is important to recognize that the growth may also be highly profitable).

8. Some managements engage in "business statesmanship." They concentrate on improving the community where they exist, or on promoting better international understanding, or on advancing industrial relations. "Business statesmanship" and concern for the "social responsibilities" of management have become very stylish in recent years. These things cost money and don't necessarily increase sales. Management generally answers that these policies help long-run profits, and that such costs have become an essential part of doing business on the modern scene.

9. Lastly, some observers stress that the modern hired manager (as distinct from the owner-operator) often has important objectives in addition to profits—the desire to get along well with others in the company; the desire to avoid ulcer-producing arguments with the union; perhaps most important, the desire to avoid looking foolish by being wrong when he takes risks. Management has more freedom to follow these other motives if it is sheltered from vigorous competition.

The fact is that nobody knows just how hard firms outside highly competitive areas try to maximize profits or how well they succeed. Clearly, there are wide differences from firm to firm and industry to industry. In the following pages, we will assume that by and large the drive of quasi-monopolies for profits is a major factor in their behavior—as it appears to be. Actual or potential competition is seldom far away. But in using profit-maximizing models, don't forget all the other motives management may have and all the slips that may occur between wish and achievement in maximizing profits.

In many ways, reason 2 above poses the toughest problems for the businessman. Maximum-profit estimates are no better than the demand and cost estimates on which they rest. Estimating the future is never easy, and it's the future that matters. Businesses spend millions of dollars keeping track of their costs in great detail and trying to get accurate forecasts of what costs and demand will be at different levels of output. Big corporations have thousands of employees in their cost- and sales-estimating departments. Yet many businesses lose more potential profit through inability to forecast their cost and demand situations accurately than through failure to act effectively on the basis of the costs and demands they estimate.

Business decisions have to be made on the basis of inadequate information and hunches more often than most people realize. When he has to guess at both future costs and revenues, no executive can calculate exactly what his optimum price and output positions are going to be. Yet he has to make these decisions, day in and day out. What does he do? Many managers look for some reasonable guiding rule to avoid the necessity of starting from scratch in solving each price problem. The practices of "standard costing" and "cost-plus pricing" have come into widespread use to meet this need.

"Standard Costing"

Cost per unit of output varies at different output levels, and you're never sure just what your output is going to be very far in the future. Yet you can't be jiggling your price up and down all the time, and usually you have to quote advance prices to customers. So a lot of businessmen ask their accountants and engineers to estimate as closely as possible the total cost of one unit of output at something reasonably near capacity operations. This estimate they call the "standard cost." It is the cost figure used in many of the firm's calculations for price-setting, even though output may vary markedly from day to day or from month to month.

"Standard costing" may not be very precise, and many economists have explained that it may lead the firm to make less profit than it could, in principle, make by calculating all costs anew for each individual transaction. But standard costing is a way of getting the day's business done. It's a rule-of-thumb short cut, albeit an imperfect one. Without such rules of thumb, the complexity of modern big business operations might lead to utter confusion and organizational breakdown rather than to a more perfect approach to profit maximization.

"Cost-Plus Pricing"

Using standard costs as a basis, many firms engage in "cost-plus," or "full-cost," or "mark-up," pricing. They price their product by taking their standard-cost estimate and adding on some allowance or mark-up—5, 10, 20, or 50 per cent—to provide a reasonable profit.[2] They are likely to use this same "full cost" to quote prices on all orders, regardless of substantial variations in the actual cost of filling the orders. This approach leads to reasonable simplicity in business operations, but it should be easy to see how it may also lead to less than maximum profits on individual orders.

Actually, businessmen are often better economists than this would suggest. When standard-cost pricing gets them too far out of line with the results they would get through using an analysis based on a more direct cost calculation, they often modify, or give up entirely, their standard-cost pricing. In booming markets where standard-cost pricing clearly undershoots what the market will bear, larger mark-ups or upward revision of quoted standard costs often result. In a serious depression when competition is sharp, pricing well below "full cost" becomes common.

"Break-Even Charts"

Some firms use another simplifying approach, "break-even charts" or "break-even analysis." In its simplest form, this technique compares total revenue at some constant market price with total cost for different levels of output. Total revenue will rise by a constant amount, say $5 for each unit sold if the price is $5. But total cost will rise at a different rate. The total cost (remember, *not* total cost *per unit*) is composed of two parts. Fixed cost is the same at any level of output—say $100 per week for rent and managerial salary. Variable cost in many firms seems to be about constant per unit of output over a considerable range—say $3 per unit for wages and materials. In

such a case, total cost at any output is $100 plus $3 times the number of units produced.

Figure 26-1 is a simple break-even chart. Line *TR* shows total revenue, growing at $5 per unit sold. Line *TC* shows total cost, beginning at $100 for zero output and rising $3 per unit thereafter. The "break-even point" is at an output of 50 units. The yellow colored areas show that a loss will occur at any output less than 50, and a profit at any higher output. The profit or loss is the vertical distance between the total-cost and total-revenue curves at any given output.

Using this chart, the businessman can see quickly about what he would make or lose at any output, given his costs and the market price of $5. Using different prices with resulting different *TR* lines on the chart, he can compare how well off he would be at different prices he might charge. The chart is one tool to help decide the best price to set.

Return on Investment

Increasingly in recent years, big corporations appear to have used some "target" return on capital investment as a rough guide to pricing policy (and to capital investment in new ventures as well). DuPont and General Motors have for years

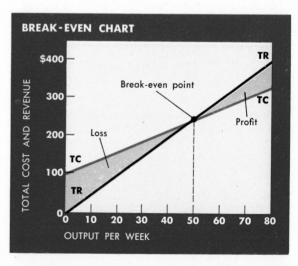

FIG. 26-1 With price at $5, *TR* is the total-revenue curve. Comparing this with the total-cost curve (*TC*), the break-even point is 50 units per week. The firm makes a profit at any higher output.

---

[2] Often the standard-cost estimate covers only manufacturing costs. In such cases, the mark-up percentage must cover all nonmanufacturing costs, as well as an allowance for profits.

followed this policy. G.M., for example, shoots for 20 per cent on invested capital after taxes. This, of course, doesn't give any automatic guide to setting prices, but it does throw out some guidelines to the men who do the price-setting. The company doesn't expect to get that return each year, through good times and bad. It takes the long view, and expects to do better than the target some years, and worse in others. Thus, current pricing and plans for expansion are all wrapped up in the same general process, in which the test of effective performance is whether it meets this profit-rate standard.

Why does G.M. choose 20 per cent as the target rate? U.S. Steel is reported to use 8 per cent after taxes, a very different figure. Alcoa is reported to use 20 per cent before taxes; General Electric 20 per cent after taxes. Maybe you'll say that, in effect, each is out to maximize profits, and their target rates are merely about the peak they think they can earn. Certainly we need to know more about how the targets are set to evaluate their impact on pricing. But for better or worse, lots of big businesses use this approach as one major guide in pricing and investment planning generally.[3]

PRICES AND OUTPUT
UNDER MONOPOLISTIC COMPETITION

The Bases
for Product Differentiation

The essence of monopolistic competition is that each firm's product is a little different from those of its competitors, but not very different. Each producer tries to differentiate his product and increase the demand for it. To the extent he succeeds, he can get away with charging a little more for his product. He has set himself apart in a partially protected position.

Sometimes product differentiation involves actual physical differentiation. For example,

[3] There is a large literature on business pricing practices. For a more detailed, interesting, easy-to-read account of some current big business pricing policies, see A. D. H. Kaplan, Joel Dirlam, and R. F. Lanzillotti, *Pricing in Big Business* (Washington: The Brookings Institution, 1958).

Schlitz beer tastes different from Pabst; a Frigidaire is different from a G.E. refrigerator. But often the differentiation hinges on the things that go along with the product—convenience of the corner grocery's location, thick carpets on the floor of the best dress shops, well-groomed waitresses in some restaurants, easy credit terms at some stores. Sometimes the differentiation is largely illusory—it exists in the mind of the customer but not in fact. Most smokers can't tell one standard cigarette brand from another when they are blindfolded. If you can really tell the difference between the various high-test gasolines in your car on the road, you're better than most of the experts. Often when you think you're getting special easy-credit terms you're paying just what is normal in the trade.

Some bases for product differentiation are more fundamental and longer-lasting than others. But whatever the reason, whenever one seller is differentiated from others in the customer's mind, that seller is able to charge a price higher than his competitors without losing all his market. His demand curve slopes downward; it is not horizontal as under perfect competition.

Short-run Output and Prices

Given his costs, the monopolistic competitor's problem is to set his price so as to maximize his profits. He has some freedom to raise price above what his competitors charge for similar products, but if he goes too far his share of the market will drop sharply. The more successful he is in differentiating his product, the less elastic his demand curve will be. With an inelastic demand curve, he can boost his price without a corresponding drop in sales. But it's hard to convince customers that no substitute will do.

The firm's optimal price-output decision in the short run is hard to specify under these conditions. It will generally try to maximize the difference between total revenue and total costs by producing efficiently and by stimulating demand for its own product. But just what the demand curve for any one firm's product looks like is hard to estimate. For it depends *both* on what this firm does through advertising to change consumer demand *and* on what competitors do that also affects the demand for our firm's product. The demand curve we face will depend on consumers' total demand for the whole group of slightly differentiated products, and on our firm's share of the total. Palmolive can increase and steepen the consumer demand curve for its soap either by getting customers away from Lux, Sweetheart, and the rest, or by somehow increasing total consumer demand for toilet soap. If Palmolive succeeds in convincing people they should wash their faces oftener, this may increase the demand for other soaps as well as for Palmolive. The trick is to be sure you get the big share of the benefit if you go in for this kind of advertising. Conversely, increased advertising by Lux may leave Palmolive with a lower, flatter demand curve, even though Palmolive soap is just as good as before. And if Palmolive advertises or steals Lux's customers in any other way, retaliation is almost certain. *Thus, it should be clear that under monopolistic competition and oligopoly, the level and elasticity of any firm's demand curve depend both on what it does and on what the other firms in the industry do as well. It is not possible to draw a stable, unambiguous demand curve for the individual firm's product.*[4]

Just how much any monopolistic competitor will spend on demand creation, trying to raise his demand curve and make it more inelastic to increase his profits, is hard to tell. Presumably he will increase his expenditures on advertising and other demand-creating activities as long as he esti-

---

[4] *Given* the firm's cost and demand curves, the technical conditions for maximizing profit in the short run are identical with those for the monopolist described in detail in the last half of Chapter 25. Thus, in the adjoining figure, to maximize profits the firm will set price and output where marginal cost equals marginal revenue. This gives output O to be sold at price P as the optimal position. But when we say *given* the demand curve, we are assuming away a big piece of the problem, as is explained in the text.

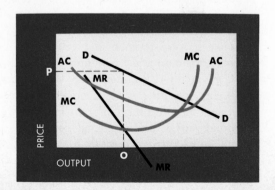

mates that the results will add more to his income than to his costs. But under monopolistic competition, partial protection from the pressures of competition, coupled with uncertainty about what competitors will do, makes short-run output and price behavior very hard to predict. Thus, even more than under pure competition, we are on much safer ground when we look at long-run adjustments, and should have little confidence in our ability to predict short-run behavior.

Long-run Adjustments under Monopolistic Competition

In the long run, new firms enter industries and old firms leave. The search for profits goes on, with productive resources freely transferable throughout the economy. Monopolistic competition is like pure competition in that new firms can enter the industry. It is different in that new firms cannot exactly duplicate the product of existing firms. A new drugstore across the street from an established one might provide very close substitutes. But a new women's wear store that sets up in competition with Saks Fifth Avenue will have a tougher time. For one thing, drugs, candy, and ice cream are relatively standardized as compared with women's clothes. For another, few drugstores have the prestige and location of Saks.

But even though newcomers face problems, high profits in any monopolistically competitive field will draw new competitors. As more firms enter and old ones expand, the total market is divided up more ways. The demand curve for each established firm is moved downward (to the left). Profits per firm are reduced by this sharing of the market. Gradually, as more firms enter, profits tend to be eliminated, just as under pure competition. A new (unstable) equilibrium with economic profits eliminated may be achieved.

This sounds just like pure competition. But it is different in two important respects. First, in this temporary equilibrium, under monopolistic competition each firm is restricting output a little to take advantage of its product differentiation. In each firm, marginal cost is less than price, since the demand curve is tangent to the cost curve to the left of the minimum point. Each firm is producing inefficiently; it is operating below its optimal capacity and producing at a cost above the least-cost point on its optimal cost curve. As a result, the equilibrium market price is higher than it would be under pure competition where price would be forced down to the least-cost point on the cost curve for the firm; and resources are wasted through the excess capacity in each firm. From a social point of view, too little of the product is being produced and sold, since price is being held above marginal cost.

This result is illustrated in Fig. 26-2. Suppose that case A pictures a typical firm in a monopolistically competitive area. The firm is making a good profit. Since its demand curve is well above its total-unit-cost curve over a substantial range, the manager can make some profit even if he isn't very alert in choosing the best short-run price and output. The demand curve is downward-sloping, because this product is differentiated from its competitors.

What will happen? Competition will pick up. As new firms enter the market, the demand curve for each old firm moves downward as its share of the market falls. Eventually, the demand curve for a typical firm will be pushed down far enough to be just tangent to the cost curve. All profit has been eliminated, and there is no further apparent incentive for new firms and new resources to enter the industry. Neither is there any incentive for existing firms to leave, unless some especially attractive opportunity opens up elsewhere in the economy. This is case C in Fig. 26-2.

But, as was indicated above, here each firm is operating to the left of the minimum point on its cost curve. Price is higher than marginal cost. As long as the demand curve for each firm is downward-sloping (as it must be when each firm is big enough and different enough to have an independent influence on price), it must become tangent to the cost curve to the left of the minimum point. In economic terms, each firm will end up restricting its output below the competitive level to try to take advantage of its differentiated position—but market competition from new firms will tend to wipe out any special profits it might have hoped for.

Look now at B in Fig. 26-2. Here existing firms are making losses. As firms gradually drop out of the industry, the demand for the products of each remaining firm gradually rises. It continues to rise until a no-loss situation has been reached, when there is no further incentive for resources to move out of the industry. This, again is case C.

The similarity of these results to those under pure competition stems primarily from the free entry of firms into the industry. Incentives to maximize efficiency and to develop products to meet consumer needs are strong. The only important difference evident so far is the somewhat higher price to the consumer under monopolistic competition. But this difference is unlikely to be very important if the competing products are close substitutes.

Equilibrium Unstable under Competitive Demand Creation

But this is not the end of the story; the equilibrium is almost surely unstable. If you were running a grocery store and were in position C in Fig. 26-2, what would you do? Maybe you'd just sit, but probably you'd try to figure a way to get more business. You might try improving your service to customers. Or putting in air con-

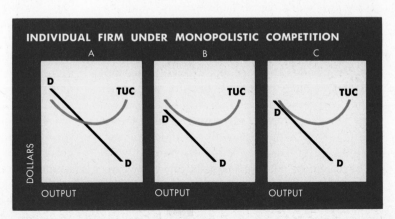

FIG. 26-2 Figure shows firm making money on left, losing money in middle, and in no-profit temporary equilibrium on right.

INDIVIDUAL FIRM UNDER MONOPOLISTIC COMPETITION

ditioning. Or advertising more vigorously. All these attempts would cost you money. They might bring you more customers—that is, they might raise your demand curve—probably by drawing customers away from competitors. And they would upset the equilibrium situation shown in C. Such attempts to increase demand for products are apparent everywhere, keeping equilibrium (with the demand curve tangent to the cost curve) from being achieved or maintained.

Imagine a monopolistically competitive milk industry in a good-sized city, with 15 milk companies of about equal size and no advertising. Company A begins an advertising campaign. It gets more customers by luring a few away from each competitor. A's costs are now higher, but its profits are up because of increased volume.

It doesn't take a business genius to predict the reaction of the other companies. After spending a few well-chosen words on the manager of Company A, they will get busy on their own advertising campaigns, designed to get their customers back and (hopefully) to lure new customers into the fold. If every company just matched A's advertising, we might think of a new equilibrium situation, with each producer having back just his original customers, but with every company's cost higher by the amount of the advertising and with price correspondingly higher to the consumer or company profits correspondingly lower.

But having tasted success, A is unlikely to sit quietly at the restored higher-price equilibrium. Nor are B, C, D, and all the others. Each will be busy contriving a new and better advertising campaign—at least to protect his sales against the selling campaigns he strongly expects from his rivals. If another round of advertising expenditures starts, or trading stamps with each gallon of milk are introduced, the result is likely to be similar. Everybody's costs go up. Nobody ends up with many more customers, or with any more profits. And consumers end up with higher prices. Now they're buying advertising and trading stamps along with their milk—without having anything to say about whether they really want to buy them or not. And nobody can tell where the whole process will stop.

Even in the happy event that the advertising

campaign increases total spending on milk, a similar problem remains. Where do these additional funds for milk come from? Maybe the milk advertising stimulates total spending and raises the level of total spending and g.n.p., but this seems unlikely on the basis of our look at the determinants of national income and employment in Part Two. If total spending is unchanged, more spending on milk must mean less spending on something else. Producers in these other industries will fight back to regain sales. This will cause another reshuffling of demand, with still other industries (possibly including milk) losing customers to the newest advertisers.

Over-all, it is difficult for anyone to gain more than temporarily from large advertising outlays in an enconomy in which counter-advertising is general. The over-all effect of advertising, on which we spent $15 billion in 1967, is to devote these productive resources (men, ink, billboards, and so forth) to producing advertising rather than to producing other goods and services.

Selling Costs and Production Costs

It is important to distinguish between "selling costs" and "production costs." The costs discussed in previous chapters were production costs, incurred to make products that meet expected consumer demands. By contrast, the selling costs discussed above are costs incurred in trying to increase the demand for a product. Production costs include costs of manufacture, transportation, financing, storage, and all other activities that are required to produce the commodity and to get it to the consumer. Selling costs include all forms of advertising and demand-creating activities—newspaper, television, magazine, and direct-mail advertising, window displays, salesmen, prize contests, and so on.

When all costs are production costs, the demand seen by any firm is not changed by the firm's own activities. But with selling costs, the seller can increase the demand for his product by spending more money—he can shift the demand curve for his own product. Whenever he tries, he is almost certain to cut the demand for his competitors' products, and you can guess what his competitors do then. They retaliate.

QUALITY COMPETITION
AND COMPETITIVE DEMAND CREATION

Every housewife knows about quality competition. She knows which stores have the freshest vegetables, and where there are enough clerks to provide quick service. When you buy a suit, you go to a store you know will stand behind it if something goes wrong. These are examples of quality competition, just as much as the more obvious cases of using better materials and better workmanship in the physical construction of products.

Alert businessmen are very much interested in knowing what quality consumers want. They spend thousands of dollars on market research to find out whether consumers want softer seats in autos, cellophane around fresh vegetables, more carbonation in ginger ale. A shrewd businessman will improve the quality of his product whenever he believes customers want the improvement enough to pay for the extra cost— and a little bit more. He will put chromium trim on automobiles, foam-rubber cushions on sofas, or fancier packages around candy if he thinks these steps will get him additional customers enough or let him charge enough higher prices to increase his profits. He will reduce product quality—for example, by putting his store on a cash-and-carry basis—whenever he believes that most customers would prefer to pay less and go without delivery service. But he will do more. He will spend money to induce present and potential customers to want the particular qualities he provides in his product.

Some observers believe that quality competition is the pervasive form of competition in modern America, and that price competition is of secondary importance. There is much evidence to support this point of view. Filling stations long ago learned that a clean rest room is more important to a touring family than a half-cent off the price of gas. The first air-conditioned movie had an enormous quality advantage. Now they're all air-conditioned.

Such is often the case in quality competition. Once one firm pioneers, others feel they must follow—or risk losing their customers as a consequence of holding out. The result is higher "quality" all around, and higher prices to cover the higher costs involved in providing it. Then every manager starts scratching his head to figure out a new improvement that will give him at least a temporary jump on the field again.

Quality competition is a perfectly valid type of competition, just as much as price competition. Sometimes people don't want the extra "quality" built into new products. But they have the option of not buying. And with active competition, there's always a competitor ready to provide a cheaper, lower "quality" product—witness the success of discount stores and of compact cars.

Annual Model Changes—
Another Example

Each year the major auto manufacturers come out with new models, announced with great fanfare. In perhaps two years out of three there are no changes of significance for the performance or comfort given by the automobile. The roof line is lowered, the dashboard modified, the horsepower upped a little. The upshot is that last year's models are now out of date, and those of two years ago are quite passé—or at least so the auto companies hope. "Planned obsolescence" is the phrase many observers use. Your old car may be good for 50,000 miles more, but the auto manufacturers are spending hundreds of millions of dollars on new models each year to convince you that you really have an old car, inferior to the shiny new models.

There is no doubt that today's autos will do many things their predecessors would not—go faster, ride smoother, eat more gas. Most people believe that each year's model is really better than last year's. But the cost of annual model changes is large—hundreds of millions of dollars for new tools and dies each year that must be charged off in the price of cars that year, since new ones will be required next year. One study, which should be recognized as very rough, put the total cost of annual autos model changes to American consumers at $35 billion between 1949 and 1961.

Annual model changes are another example of competitive selling costs. Every auto company admits it could sell cars a lot cheaper if it didn't face the enormous cost of annual model changes. And it's not clear that total car sales are much larger because of the changes, though they probably are stimulated to some extent. But no major company (except Volkswagen and a few other foreign makers) feels safe in coming out each year without new models. The situation is much like that in competitive advertising, but with real quality changes mixed in.

Does Advertising Increase Total Demand?

Many people argue that advertising increases total demand, thereby helping to provide more jobs and making possible the advantages of large-scale production. Certainly advertising and other selling costs may increase the demand for individual products. But the illustrations above should warn against easy transfer of this reasoning to aggregate demand for the economy as a whole. When everyone advertises, a main effect is likely to be the neutralization described above. If advertising increases aggregate demand, it must increase consumers' collective propensity to consume out of disposable income. It *may* do so— for example, when the auto industry comes out with major style changes and massive sales campaigns to push them. But most economists are skeptical that advertising raises the aggregate propensity to consume much. They believe the evidence points mainly to the factors listed back in Chapter 7, with the major impact of advertising on sales of particular products and brands. Note that even if advertising induces people to buy more cars this year, we need to be sure this is a net addition to total spending and not merely a transfer from other goods or services.

Should We Give Up Competitive Advertising?

If advertising and many other selling costs are so largely neutralized by counteradvertising and counterselling costs, why don't competitors simply call the whole thing off? One big reason is that each hopes to stay ahead in the race and none dares to drop out. There is usually an advantage in leading, and always a danger in curtailing. And it is very difficult to measure the results of selling costs, particularly those aimed at "goodwill" and "repeat customers." Once a firm has customers firmly tied to its product, it can afford to cut back on its advertising outlays for this purpose. But a good customer is far easier to keep than to get back once he's been lost. All this uncertainty leads to reluctance to experiment with reduced selling costs.

MEASURES OF MARKET PERFORMANCE

Monopolistic competition characterizes a large sector of the economy. In summary, what can we say about the market performance of this sector?

Allocation of Resources

Under monopolistic competition every seller has a little bit of monopoly, little though it may be if his product is only slightly differentiated. Thus, given the downward sloping demand curve he faces, it pays him to set price higher than marginal cost. Price will tend to be forced by competition to become tangent to the cost curve to the left of the minimum-cost point, and too little of the product will be produced to satisfy consumer demand most efficiently. But if competition is active and products are only slightly differentiated, each firm's demand curve will be almost horizontal and this malallocation of resources may be negligible.

The Use of Resources in Demand Creation

More important is the large allocation of productive resources to demand creation. In 1967, advertising expenditures alone totalled $15 billion. In a full-employment economy, we must choose between alternative uses of resources. For our advertising dollar (paid in the price of the product) we get information on products, TV movies and sport events, billboards, the Metropolitan Opera, and a wide variety of other services, the worth of which might be disputed vigorously. Advertising expenditures make possible 10-cent daily papers, and a 35-cent *Life* magazine; $15 billion spent on advertising provides many useful services and some not so useful. The amount spent on demand creation has soared astronomically. In 1940, total expenditures on advertising were less than $2 billion.

Is this demand creation wasteful? From the standpoint of resource allocation, the real question is: Are the services provided by advertising the services we want? No firm answer is possible. Fifteen billion dollars would buy a lot of other things—schools, highways, houses, medical research. We can only say firmly that by financing these services through advertising, little effective choice is left to the consumer as to what services he buys. The cigarette smoker buys TV westerns even though he never looks at a TV screen. Still, almost everybody buys many advertised products and enjoys some of the fruits of advertising and demand creation. Perhaps, aside from cases of misleading advertising, everything pretty much evens out and consumers get just about the information and "entertainment" they would have bought anyway with their advertising dollars. But you may have your doubts.

Advertising and Consumer Information

One important benefit from advertising is the information it makes available. To spend their money efficiently in satisfying their wants, consumers must be well informed about the products available. The better informed consumers are, the better they are able to force producers to cater to their wants by spending on those products that best meet their needs. Advertising that informs consumers about new products is also useful. In a rapidly changing economy, this is an especially valuable service. Just how many resources should be devoted to making consumers better informed is a difficult question. The price mechanism doesn't provide a measuring stick by which consumers can automatically make the decision on this use of resources, since consumers don't have a chance to buy the information separately.

But much modern advertising makes little contribution to consumer information. Many advertisers are more concerned with attracting consumers away from competitors than in providing information on which consumers can make more intelligent choices. Watch a TV set through an evening and record all the information you get that is of value in helping you decide among the products advertised. Read a copy of one of the big-selling magazines. Try the morning newspaper.

You will see ads of all sorts. Magazine and TV advertising is increasingly institutionalized—aimed at building up general goodwill and the prestige of the product. For specifically useful information, newspaper advertising is likely to come out best, largely because it is more local in nature and concentrates more on specific products, descriptions, and prices. Judge for yourself.

Lastly, advertising not only provides information. It also does much to mold the social customs and values of modern society. The movie-star glamour that graces myriads of magazine ads each month has a real impact on teen-agers and housewives alike. Few people can look day after day at advertisements for new automobiles, refrigerators, and fine clothes without gradually coming to believe that every American (or at least he himself) should have these products. Some observers worry lest all this create social dissatisfaction and neuroses, since, alas, not everybody has the money to buy all the shiny new things he sees advertised, or a complexion to match the movie stars'.

Selling Costs as a Basis for Monopoly

Product differentiation, whether based on real differences or illusions, helps provide increased opportunities for profit by setting apart the seller's product. It lets each firm boost its price somewhat. Sometimes the result may approach pure monopoly; the classic case of Bayer Aspirin, which kept dominant control of the market even when competitors sharply undercut its price on pharmaceutically identical aspirin, was mentioned above. Although advertising is seldom so successful, cases of very strong consumer attachment to trade names are commonplace. Aggressive advertising serves both to keep alive these consumer attachments and to discourage new firms from competition. It can play some role in developing and protecting seller monopolies.

Quality Competition and Price Competition

For some products, quality competition has largely replaced price competition. Improvements in quality are of real benefit to consumers, and quality competition can be just as beneficial as price competition.

Some, however, view the shift toward quality competition with alarm because they feel that such competition often produces "improvements" more illusory than real. Are the annual model changes in autos worth the huge sums they cost? Why should the consumer be forced to pay for two or three fancy "crisper trays" in a new refrigerator when he could buy a less elegant storage dish himself at a third the cost? Why should you have to pay for a fancy cut-glass bottle each time you want to buy some perfume? Indeed, many producers have pushed for "Fair Trade Laws" to forbid retailers to use price competition.

Behind these criticisms there lies a real danger—that lively price competition may be lessened, and that higher "qualities" may become so standardized that the buyer who prefers a lower-quality product at a lower price will be unable to buy it. But competition continually pushes sellers to give consumers what they want. Witness the success of compact cars as a reaction to the behemoths of the late 1950's. You can either go to a cash-and-carry supermarket, or order from a grocery that delivers. Ideally, for freedom of consumer choice, quality differentials should be available separately and charged for only when taken. To carry this principle to the extreme could lead to a chaos of products and prices, but to disregard it entirely would equally lead to serious restriction on free consumer choice and on consumer direction of resource allocation.[5]

[5] Note to instructors: Some of the examples in "Some Managerial Applications" at the end of Chapter 28 are equally usable here.

REVIEW

Concepts To Remember

Be sure you have the following new analytical concepts firmly in hand:

standard costs	quality competition
cost-plus pricing	demand creation
break-even point	selling costs
product differentiation	unstable equilibrium

For Analysis and Discussion

1. Is the absence of unreasonable profits in an industry satisfactory evidence that monopolistic competition is not injuring consumers of the product concerned? Explain your answer to a noneconomist.

2. "As long as there is relatively free entry to an industry, I can't get worried about the dangers of monopoly in that industry." Do you agree with this implication that society need only be concerned with protecting free entry into industries, so far as the monopoly problem is concerned?

3. The aggregate-output model of Chapter 6 suggests that advertising can increase total consumption expenditure only by raising the aggregate propensity to consume. Is this a fair way to state the problem? If so, does it throw any light on the likely success of national advertising in expanding total markets and employment?

4. It is alleged that quality competition is increasingly replacing price competition in the American economy. From your own observation, is this a valid observation? Insofar as it is valid, is this development advantageous or disadvantageous for the consumer?

5. As a consumer, would you like to see aggressive price competition among sellers of all the products you buy? Do you think that under such competition you would get the same breadth of display, return privileges, and charge-account arrangements now provided by major department stores?

6. Do you get your money's worth out of the advertising expenditures for which you indirectly pay?

TWENTY-SEVEN

OLIGOPOLY, COLLUSION, AND THE MIXED ECONOMY

The Foundations of Oligopoly.

Oligopoly Prices, Output, and Profits.

Oligopoly in the American Economy.

Research, Development, and Innovation.

Appendix: Some Managerial Applications.

Three companies—General Motors, Ford, and Chrysler—make nearly all the automobiles produced in the United States. The top four companies account for over 90 per cent of all flat glass and electric light bulbs produced. Over 75 per cent of the total business in the industry is done by the top four producers in cigarettes, linoleum, and rubber tires. In dozens of major industries, from half to three-fourths of the total business is done by fewer than ten firms. These are the oligopolies—industries where a few firms dominate the industry, though there may be many small firms that generally follow the leaders, or take what is left over. Figure 27-1 summarizes the degree of market domination by leading four firms in a number of major industries.

These examples are all on a national scale. The number of oligopolists in local markets is far larger. Building materials (such as cement and bricks), for example, are produced by hundreds of different firms scattered all over the country. But in any one local market, production is usually concentrated in one or a few firms. The two or three druggists in a small town are oligopolists so far as drugs are concerned—though possibly not on ice cream and soft drinks (where groceries and others compete). Other examples are commonplace. The more important transportation costs are and the harder it is for customers to shop around, the more likely local oligopolies are to be found.

Economists consider "concentration ratios" (the percentage of total sales in a market or industry concentrated in the largest four, or sometimes eight, firms) an important indication of likely market performance. But it is important to

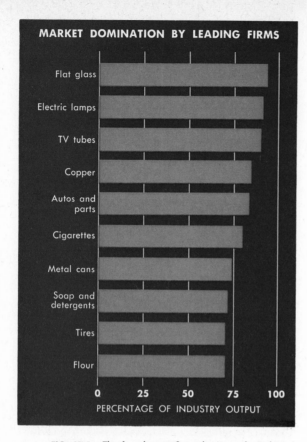

MARKET DOMINATION BY LEADING FIRMS

Industry	
Flat glass	
Electric lamps	
TV tubes	
Copper	
Autos and parts	
Cigarettes	
Metal cans	
Soap and detergents	
Tires	
Flour	

PERCENTAGE OF INDUSTRY OUTPUT

FIG. 27-1 The four largest firms dominate the industry's output in leading American industries. (Source: Federal Trade Commission; data are for 1963.)

recognize that this is only one rough measure of the degree of monopoly power held by the leading firms. Probable price-output behavior may be quite different, for example, in two industries with the same concentration ratio of 80 per cent, if in one case the biggest firm has 60 per cent of the market while in the other it has only 25. Similarly, the total number of firms in the industry outside the leaders may make a difference. The soap and match industries have similar concentration ratios, with the additional industry characteristics shown below. Which would you say is more concentrated?

	Soap	Matches
Total number of firms	267	14
Percentage of total industry sales by:		
Largest 4 firms	85	74
Largest 8 firms	89	93
Largest 20 firms	95	100

In general, economists suspect that monopoly-like results are more likely in highly-concentrated than in less-concentrated industries.

But this measure provides only a rough first presumption.

THE FOUNDATIONS OF OLIGOPOLY

At bottom, most oligopolies rest on one or both of two factors: (1) the necessity of large-scale production (relative to the size of the market) for low-cost output, and (2) barriers against the entry of new firms into the industry.

If total market demand will support only a few firms of optimum size, clearly the competitive struggle will tend to make a few big firms the winners. This situation rests fundamentally on the economies of large-scale production. In each of the industries in Fig. 27-1 large-scale production is essential to obtain low unit costs.

How do these big firms maintain their positions, once attained? As we shall see presently, aggressive price competition is unlikely. Instead, the oligopolist tries to increase his market share and his profits by improving his product, by demand-creating activities, and by setting up barriers against the intrusion of new competitors. In many oligopolies, patents, established marketing organization, or control over raw materials may be of key importance in keeping out newcomers. The bases for oligopoly power are similar to those for other monopolies indicated in Chapter 25.

Dominant firms in an oligopoly are seldom completely safe from potential competition. It is the rare oligopoly that escapes for long the pressures of competition from new firms and new products. Even patents, large size, and technological dominance provide only partial insulation. For example, General Electric long held most of the basic patents in the electric light-bulb industry. It licensed these patents to small firms on condition that total production be controlled, and to Westinghouse under fewer restrictions. G.E. and Westinghouse dominated production and prices, and the market was, for all practical purposes, shared between them in stable proportions and without aggressive price competition. Finally, G.E.'s control was weakened by expiration of the 17-year period on some patents and by threatened antitrust action. Sylvania Electric, a small but alert firm, decided to brave the uncertainties of competition. It started with certain free patents, stressed efficient technology and aggressive selling, and by the end of World War II had become a third major firm in the industry, though still far smaller than G.E. and Westinghouse.

OLIGOPOLY PRICES, OUTPUT, AND PROFITS

Analytically, the crucial thing about an oligopoly is the small number of sellers, which makes it imperative for each to weigh carefully the reactions of the others to his own price, production, and sales policies. The result is a strong pressure to collude to avoid price competition or to avoid it without formal collusion.

Absence of Aggressive Price Competition

Suppose that you are the manager of a local brick works, and that you have two competitors in the area. You are making a reasonable profit, and so are your competitors. Each of you sets the price at which he sells—an "administered" price. Each of you knows he could make a larger profit if he could manage to increase his share of the market, because each of you is operating below capacity. Will you cut your price to get customers away from your competition?

Maybe you will. But you'd better think twice before you try it. Your competitors will almost surely retaliate by meeting your price cut. Maybe they'll undercut you if you stir them up by disturbing the stability of the market. Your price advantage can't last more than a day or two before they know about it, and you can't get very rich in that length of time. Heaven only knows just what will happen if you start a local price war, but three things looks reasonably sure: All three of you will end up with lower prices; none of you will have lured many customers away from the others; and everybody's profits will have taken a beating. In the end, you might just glower at each other in the local Rotary Club meetings, but probably you'd get together and agree to put prices back to some reasonable level near where you started.

This is only a small-scale, hypothetical example. But the questions are the same ones that the presidents of huge corporations ask when they consider cutting prices in oligopolistic markets, in steel, automobiles, plate glass. With only a few firms in the industry, the forces toward letting well enough alone are strong. Most oligopolists hesitate to cut prices except to meet a price cut by another firm. Price reductions are likely to come only under severe pressures—seriously weakened over-all market demand, for example. When firms do cut, they usually do so in the expectation that their cut will be met by rivals. Thus, the cut is made with the intention of moving the whole industry price scale to a lower level, in the hope of stimulating over-all demand for the industry's product. In many cases, one major firm in an oligopolistic industry ordinarily acts as a "price leader," both upward and downward, in this way, although there may be no formal agreement.

It is not certain that oligopolistic price will be higher than competitive price would be in the same industry. But when facing a downward-sloping demand curve, there is a strong incentive for oligopolists to set price above the minimum average unit cost and above marginal cost. Oligopolists may price on a standard-cost mark-up system; they may shoot for a "satisfactory" return on capital investment; they may just follow customary price leaders. But active competition is what forces price down toward the minimum point on the unit-cost curve. In the absence of active price competition, the likelihood seems strong that oligopoly price will be at least somewhat higher. If the industry has recently gone through a couple of price wars in which everyone has temporarily lost his shirt, there will be an especially strong tendency for everyone to let price alone at a level high enough to provide a "reasonable" profit. Price policy may also be affected by public opinion, and by the federal antitrust authorities lurking in the background.

Such a "live and let live" policy makes sense to most producers—and to many others as well. It leaves room for each firm to try quality and advertising competition to increase its share of the market. It leaves room for some price shading and juggling when times are hard or when one firm is losing out badly in the market. But aggressive price competition will probably blow the situation wide open.

Oligopoly Theory:
The Kinked Demand Curve

Economic theory helps present the price problem that faces the oligopolist. Go back to the brickworks case above. The current price is 20 cents a brick, and you are selling 10,000 bricks per week. As you sit in your office, you try to imagine what your demand curve looks like, as a basis for deciding whether to change your price. Chances are you will come out with something like Fig. 27-2, a "kinked" demand curve—assuming that all bricks are substantially alike.

It says that if you raise your price and the others don't follow, your sales will fall off sharply because your customers will desert you; your demand curve looks highly elastic if you raise price above 20 cents. On the other hand, if you cut the price, you can be almost sure your rivals will follow to avoid losing customers to you. Thus, a lower price may increase sales a little, since the market will take some more bricks at a lower price; but there's little reason to suppose you'll get a bigger share of the market away from your competitors. Your demand curve looks very inelastic if you cut price below 20 cents. This situation obviously puts a high premium on keeping the

price where it is, just as the common sense reasoning above suggested.

Note now the critical assumptions. The first is that if you *raise* price, your rivals *will not* follow. It is this assumption that underlies the highly elastic curve to the left of the "corner" *P*. If, by contrast, you are a price "leader" and your rivals will follow your increase, the *DP* section of the curve will be much less elastic and will probably just extend directly on up from *D'P*, as in the dashed line. This is because you won't lose a share of the market to the others; the only loss in sales volume comes from the market as a whole, because fewer bricks will be bought at the higher price.

The second crucial assumption is that if you *cut* price, the others *will* also cut. If they do not, then *D'P* of your demand curve will probably be highly elastic, as your rivals' customers switch to you. Then the "corner" in the demand curve would again vanish and your *D'P* will just be an extension of *DP*. This would be a wonderful situation for you, but it is not very likely unless you can hide your price cuts from your rivals. And that's hard in an oligopoly.

In summary, then, the kinked demand curve exists because you assume a *different* reaction from your competitors when you raise than when you lower your price. If you are the recognized price leader, there will be no kink, and you are merely moving price up or down along the demand curve for the whole industry. If you are so little that nobody reacts to your price changes, there is also no kink—but this case is really a violation of the oligopoly situation, since the essence of oligopoly is the existence of so few competitors that each must be concerned with the others' reactions. Lastly, your freedom to move price without immediately risking rivals' reactions is larger the more differentiated your product is.[1]

[1] Where the demand curve is kinked, the corresponding marginal-revenue curve has a break, or discontinuity. The graph on page 363 shows the demand and marginal-revenue curves from Fig. 27-2. Note that given this marginal-revenue curve, a marginal-cost curve (MC) could move up or down considerably without logically leading the firm to change its price. This fact may further explain the observed oligopoly tendency toward price stability, even when costs change substantially. (The lower half of the MR curve need not be negative, though of course it will be if *D'P* shows inelastic demand.)

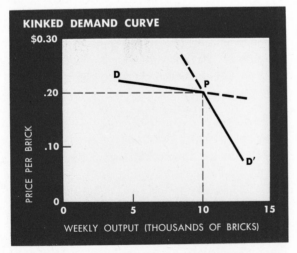

FIG. 27-2 Kinked demand curve suggests that you will lose total revenue if you either raise or lower price. Demand is elastic above 20 cents, inelastic below it.

Oligopoly and "Game Theory"

Economic theory has no clear-cut answer as to where price will be set under oligopoly, although the kinked demand curve analysis above gives some insight into likely behavior. Another approach is through "game theory." This likens competing oligopolists to participants in a game—a contest for market share and profits. In an oligopoly of, say, five leading firms, there are many possibilities of partial collusion and different forms of competition. If you change your price, will all the others react together? May they "gang up" on you? If you have been the "price leader," will they follow your lead again this time? What devices are there for implicit collusion to avoid price competition when open collusion is illegal and each of you wants a bigger share of the market? How shall you play the game to avoid having newcomers break into your profitable circle of five?

"Game theory" explores systematically the outcomes of different strategies and coalitions, depending on different assumptions about the reactions of competitors. This approach suggests the outcome of different policies, but the combinations and permutations of different assumptions mount rapidly, and the theory becomes very complex—too complex for inclusion here. Thus, unfortunately, game theory gives no clear predictions of what profit-seeking oligopolists will do, although it helps to suggest some likely limiting cases. The best we can do at the elementary level

is the broad predictions outlined in the two preceding sections.

Price-fixing and Market-sharing Arrangements (Cartels)

The line between not competing aggressively and agreeing to stabilize price is nebulous. In the brick-works example above, there was no open collusion on prices, though the result was much the same as if there had been. But before the antitrust authorities appeared on the scene, major firms got together and agreed formally to fix prices at profitable levels. Nowadays, this practice is strictly illegal. But analyzing a formal price-fixing and market-sharing cartel agreement can suggest the consequences of today's informal cartel-like price stabilization arrangements. And formal cartels are a dominant form of market organization in many European countries.

Cartels with Free Entry—a Simple Model. Assume a hypothetical furnace industry, in which there are only 10 firms. We want to analyze the long-run results caused by the establishment of a cartel in the industry, in which the 10 firms agree to "stabilize" prices and to share the market equally.

In effect, the firms will act like one pure monopoly in setting price and then divide up the business, if they act to maximize profits. Assume that the competitive price for furnaces of a particular type would be $400, the lowest point on the total-unit-cost curve of each producer. At $400, consumers would buy 30,000 furnaces monthly. But by restricting output, the 10 firms can make substantial profits. So they agree to raise the price to $500, at which level 20,000 furnaces can be sold monthly, this price being estimated as the one that will maximize total profits for the group as a whole. Then each firm sells only 2,000 furnaces monthly, but at the higher price it reaps a profit of, say, $75 per furnace (the difference between the $500 price and the $425 total unit cost at the 2,000 output level).[2]

Price is now higher than the competitive

---

[2] Logically, the cartel as a whole would maximize its profits by estimating its costs and revenues, and then setting price and output where marginal cost equals marginal revenue. For the procedure, see Fig. 25-2 and Table 25-3 in Chapter 25 on "Monopoly."

level; output is lower; employment of labor and raw materials is lower; and production is less "efficient." Each firm is operating to the left of its minimum total-unit-cost output, and for the industry as a whole, price is too high and too few resources are used. By agreeing to eliminate price competition, the furnace-makers gain; if they can keep new competitors out, they're sitting pretty. Consumers take a beating. Too few resources are allocated to making furnaces; price is well above marginal cost.

But suppose new firms can't be kept out. Oligopoly profits lure them in. The entry of new firms will divide up the same total sales among more and more firms. With 10 firms, each producer could sell 2,000 furnaces monthly; with 12 firms, individual monthly sales can be only 1,667 (assuming each firm gets the same share of the market). Thus, profits are eliminated as new firms enter, not by price reduction but by reducing output in each firm to a less and less efficient level. New firms will continue to enter, cutting down the market available to each, until finally the cost per unit has risen to equal the cartel price of $500 at an output of 1,333 for each of, say, 15 firms.

This situation is illustrated in Fig. 27-3, which shows the total-unit-cost curve of a typical producer. As was indicated above, the original cartel members agree to stabilize the price at $500, which permits each producer to sell 2,000

furnaces monthly, and to make about $75 per furnace. But as more firms enter, building similar plants, the sales allotted to each producer fall lower and lower, until with 15 producers each can sell only 1,333 furnaces monthly. At this output the average cost per furnace has risen to $500, the cartel price, because each producer's plant is used so far below the optimum level of output. Profits have been eliminated.

Now look at the results. Consumers are just as badly off as under the original 10-firm cartel, since price is still up at $500 and output is still restricted to 20,000 furnaces. And with the entry of more firms the profits of the oligopolists have been eliminated. Thus the producers are no better off than under competition, consumers suffer all the results of monopoly, and society bears the loss of extensive "overinvestment" in the industry since far more productive facilities have been built than are required. *Such a cartel arrangement with free entry, it might thus be argued, is not a halfway point between competition and monopoly, but rather an arrangement that combines the worst characteristics of each and the benefits of neither.*

Obviously, this "equilibrium" would be highly unstable. Each producer sees a big potential gain from cutting his price, and he has little inducement to remain in the agreement since profits have been eliminated. Thus, formal cartels without effective restrictions on entry seldom last long. Those with strong restrictions are more durable.

This example overstates the evils of cartels by failing to recognize the likelihood of quality competition. Cartels seldom fix market shares rigidly. Thus, producers, seeing their profits vanishing, would probably try hard to attract customers through quality improvements and other nonprice competition. These efforts would benefit at least some consumers, and might be a substantial offset to the cartel's price rigidity—though they would also raise costs.

Importance of Restrictions on Entry

The preceding section points up the importance of restrictions on entry of new firms in determining the price-output performance of an

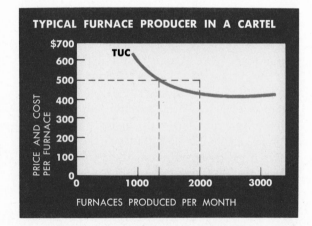

FIG. 27-3 At the cartel price of $500, firm first makes $75 profit per furnace. As more firms enter, each firm's market share and profit diminish.

oligopolistic industry. If the furnace producers above had had some effective way of keeping new firms out of the industry, their original cartel would have worked out very nicely for them in terms of continuing profits—though there would always be the danger that one firm would become dissatisfied and cut prices to increase its share of market and profits. But once outsiders are free to enter, the end of the collusive price-fixing plan is sure to come. As more and more firms enter, profits are eroded for everyone, and the incentive to fight back becomes almost irresistible.

Thus, oligopolists, like other partial monopolists, try hard to insulate themselves against new competitors, by product differentiation, by patents, by developing secret productive know-how, by bringing out new products that are hard to reproduce. And in many cases they are helped by the basic technology of the industry. As was indicated above, oligopolies tend to develop where large-scale investment and production are required for efficient output, and it's hard for newcomers to break into such industries. Look ahead to Table 28-1 to get an impression of the big investments required to compete effectively in a variety of modern American industries, and to the text there for a classification of industries by relative ease of entry.[3]

Recent research suggests that barriers to entry are effective ways of protecting above-average profits, at least temporarily. Table 27-1 classifies major oligopolistic industries by the apparent barriers they have against new entrants, and shows the average rate of return on owners' investment in each for 1950–1960. Those with the highest entry barriers generally showed the highest profit rates, though the experts disagree over the effectiveness of barriers in some industries.

OLIGOPOLY
IN THE AMERICAN ECONOMY

Collusion among firms to keep profits at profitable levels has been common since the earliest records we have of market-type economies.

[3] For a more detailed account, see Joe Bain, *Barriers to New Competition* (Cambridge: Harvard University Press, 1956).

TABLE 27-1

RATE OF RETURN ON OWNERS' INVESTMENT IN OLIGOPOLIES, 1950-1960 *

Very High Barriers to Entry:	Average Profit Rate (Percentage)	
Automobiles	15.5	
Cigarettes	11.6	
Ethical drugs	17.9	
Flat glass	18.8	
Liquor	9.0	
Nickel	18.9	
Sulphur	21.6	
Class average		16.4
Substantial Barriers to Entry:		
Aluminum reduction	10.2	
Petroleum refining	12.2	
Steel	10.8	
Soap	13.3	
Copper	11.5	
Shoe machinery	7.4	
Class average		11.3
Moderate-to-Low Barriers to Entry:		
Glass containers	13.3	
Shoes	9.6	
Rayon	8.5	
Meat packing	5.3	
Flour	8.6	
Beer	10.9	
Bituminous coal	8.8	
Class average		9.9

* Data from H. M. Mann, "Seller Concentration, Barriers to Entry, and Rates of Return in Thirty Industries," *Review of Economics and Statistics*, August, 1966. Table 27-1 shows only part of Professor Mann's entire list of industries. He also found that profit rates vary directly with the share of market held by the eight largest producers in thirty major oligopolistic industries.

In the American economy, the "pools" of the nineteenth century were formal cartel arrangements in which all the output of the industry was pooled together, then priced and sold as if the industry were essentially one monopoly. The profits were divided among the members. Economic historians have compiled a long list of pools and "trusts"—in steel rails, lumber, whiskey, brass, iron pipe, envelopes, window glass, petroleum products, wallpaper, and many others. Most of these pools temporarily prospered, then disintegrated with price wars as more and more competitors tried to invade the industry.

In 1890, the Sherman Antitrust Act made price-fixing agreements illegal. "Price stabilization," with more informal sorts of market-sharing, gradually supplanted the formal pools and "trusts." The prosperous decade of the 1920's saw informal price stabilization entrenched as sound business policy. The New Deal policies of the 1930's encouraged cartel-type arrangements in agriculture, coal, and in industry generally through the National Industrial Recovery Act. The search for ways to avoid disruptive price competition has been persistent.

Price Wars and Price Stabilization
in High-fixed-cost Industries

High-fixed-cost industries have played a major role in the history of American oligopoly. Consider the case of the railroads between New York and Chicago before railway rates were regulated by the federal government. There were four main routes. Each had an enormous fixed investment in right-of-way, stations, rolling stock, and so forth. Variable costs associated with adding a few more cars to any given train, or even adding whole trains, were inconsequential compared with the fixed costs. The TUC curve for each (for ton-miles of freight or for passengers) was downward-sloping far beyond the traffic level any one of them could realize. Hence, marginal costs were low and the incentive was great to cut prices in order to get more of the available traffic.

Under these circumstances, the New York Central could boost its profits spectacularly if it could get traffic away from the Pennsylvania. Since shippers of heavy products are sensitive to freight costs, the conclusion was easy—by cutting its prices, the Central could lure business away from its three competitors. But exactly the same thing was true for each of the others. It was not surprising, therefore, that cut-throat competition was the rule rather than the exception.[4]

You might suppose that after about the third price war the railroads would get together and agree on a market-sharing price-stabilization

---

[4] Throughout, the railroads kept up their short-haul rates to shippers who were served by only one of the four roads and who therefore had no alternatives. In many cases, it cost more to ship freight a few hundred miles between intermediate points than to ship the same freight all the way from Chicago to New York.

policy. And they did periodically. But the lure of profits was great, and those were the days of the swaggering industrial tycoon. It was not until the government stepped in with the Interstate Commerce Commission to regulate rates that the price wars were ended and price discrimination against short-haul shippers was eliminated.

The steel industry today is a comparable example of a high-fixed-cost industry. The cost of a modern steel mill has to be spread over an enormous tonnage to keep cost per ton down to a reasonable figure. Steel demand is highly sensitive to business fluctuations, and only in good times do the steel companies run near capacity. Thus, much of the time each company can increase its profits markedly by increasing volume, since its TUC curve is downward-sloping and marginal cost is low until reasonably high-level operation is reached. The pressure to shade prices is great.

Long ago, the leaders of the major steel firms recognized the problems involved. Price stabilization, with U.S. Steel acting as a "leader" in setting prices on basic products, has been the rule since the early part of the century. Over half a century, basic steel has avoided aggressive price competition much of the time—first by formal agreements, then by the famous "Gary dinners" (at which steel leaders apparently came to price agreements at sumptuous stag dinners given by Judge Gary, president of the leading steel company), and recently by more informal, tacit, "go-along" attitudes, facilitated by the American Iron and Steel Institute, the industry's trade association.

But the difficulties of avoiding aggressive price competition in a high-fixed-cost industry like steel have repeatedly led to undercover price-cutting and periodically to open price wars. In the depression of the 1930's, for example, the quoted base prices on steel became little more than a beginning point for bargaining with major consumers as to how much the price would be shaded or what other special concessions would be made. The published prices confronting the little fellow might be firm and unyielding, but in effect steel had two price systems—the published prices and the actual bargains arrived at with big buyers. Even in good times, list prices are actual prices only for small, irregular buyers in many industries. Price stabilization as a business policy by no means eliminates all price competition, though it keeps it within restricted bounds as long as the "orderly market" holds.

Electrical Equipment and Cigarettes: Two Contrasting Examples

Heavy electrical equipment and cigarettes are both oligopolies, with concentration ratios exceeding 80 per cent for the top four firms. In 1961, leading executives of General Electric, Westinghouse, and other major manufacturers of large generators, turbines, and circuit breakers were found guilty of price-fixing and market-sharing agreements over the preceding decade, carried out in secret meetings in hotels and motels around the country. Such equipment is sold on sealed bids, and the firms agreed in advance which was to get each bid and at what price. Periodically the cartel broke down under pressure of falling demand and profits in recessions, and resultant large excess capacity in the industry; the most spectacular case was the famous industry "white sale" of the middle 1950's when violent price competition broke out. But each time, the market-sharing arrangements were re-established, until the court's findings in 1961 shocked the nation and, apparently, the top management of some of the companies involved.[5]

By contrast, apparently the leading firms in the cigarette industry, with a similar concentration ratio, have scrupulously avoided direct collusion on prices for many years. Yet severe price competition has seldom developed. Observers agree that price leadership generally prevails, with competition concentrated mainly on advertising and other forms of demand creation.[6]

Why have market practices developed so differently in these two industries with similar concentration ratios? The answer is highly complex, but a few simple observations can suggest insights into the workings of oligopoly in the modern economy. Many observers point to the following explanatory variables as important.

1. *Nature of demand.* In heavy electrical equipment, demand varies markedly with the business cycle. Thus, firms are under severe profit pressure in recessions, with heavy investments in idle fixed plant and equipment. Growth in cigarette demand, by contrast, has been more stable, avoiding the severe price and excess-capacity problems which periodically plagued the electrical industry. Moreover, many consider the demand for cigarettes to be inelastic, so price-cutting for the industry as a whole would provide no gain, and individual firms are loath to risk leading the whole industry price structure down by cutting their own prices. The demand for heavy electrical equipment looks more elastic; thus, the individual producer may be more ready to risk inducing an industry-wide price cut if this should be the result of his individual price cut, unless he is bound tightly by collusive agreements. In both cases the demand as seen by one producer is surely elastic if he could cut price without retaliation, but retaliation is almost certain as a practical matter.

2. *Cost structure.* Both industries require a large investment in fixed plant and equipment for efficient production, but this investment is larger relative to the market for electrical equipment than for cigarettes. Thus, excess capacity posed an especially serious problem for electrical producers when demand slackened; marginal costs were low relative to market prices when demand was slack, and the pressures to cut price to increase share of market were great.

3. *Nature of product and difficulties of effective collusion.* Big turbines and generators are built to order. Cigarettes are highly standardized, with the price per pack visible to everyone. Thus, in the cigarette industry, each firm can quickly check up on every competitor's prices; communication on prices is easy and substantially instantaneous. Cuts are readily observable if anyone breaks the stabilization pattern. Informal avoidance of price competition is thus easy, and no one risks getting undercut without his knowing about it promptly. But in electrical equipment, without a formal agreement among the producers there is no way to check up on how competitors are pricing until the contract is finally let. There is no effective way to manage market-sharing and price stabilization without formal collusion. The prac-

---

[5] For a vivid account, see "The Incredible Electrical Conspiracy," *Fortune*, April and May, 1961.

[6] For a fuller description of the industry, see R. B. Tennant, *The American Cigarette Industry* (New Haven: Yale University Press, 1950).

tical problems of making informal (tacit) price and market collusion work are enormous for a nonstandard, special-order product like heavy electrical machinery, easier for standardized products.

4. *Number and size of firms.* The top-four concentration ratios are similar in both industries. But for practical purposes, during the 1950's only the top three producers could compete for the big orders in heavy generators, circuit breakers, and turbines, while there were numerous smaller cigarette producers beyond the big four. Thus, formal collusion was easier to arrange in heavy electrical equipment than in cigarettes; but in lighter electrical equipment there were more producers and effective formal collusion was correspondingly more difficult to arrange and maintain. Secret, illegal meetings and communications are difficult at best. As the number of parties goes up, the difficulties and dangers mount geometrically.

5. *Ease of entry.* Where entry cannot be restricted, collusive oligopoly agreements seldom last. Thus, in spite of the large market concentration in the top three producers, entry of new competitors on lighter types of equipment continued to plague the electrical conspirators. Demands of smaller newcomers for market shares continually posed crises over which requests should be granted, and how to keep the newcomers from breaking the prices needed to maintain profits. As a practical matter, even without formal collusion the cigarette industry appears to have been more successful in discouraging new entrants, though new brands have been repeatedly introduced by existing firms. (Interestingly, with the establishment of completely noncollusive pricing in the heavy electrical industry following the court decision of 1961, all firms except the big two appear to have withdrawn from major sectors of the market rather than risk open competition on such large special-order items.)

This has been an extremely sketchy analysis of the special factors at work in the electrical and cigarette oligopolies. If you want to really understand them, read the more thorough references noted. But the purpose here has been merely to provide some "feel" for how the analytical framework above can be used to study in more detail the enormously varied real-world cases of oligopoly which surround us. Oligopoly is the most unstable of all market structures and the hardest for which to predict output and price.

RESEARCH, DEVELOPMENT, AND INNOVATION

Oligopoly gets dubious marks on the criterion of efficiency in the allocation of resources. But there is another kind of efficiency as well—efficiency in using resources to promote economic progress. How does oligopoly score on that test?

The general presumption of static economic theory is against monopoly in all its forms on this score as well. The pressure of competition is the greatest prod to progress, Adam Smith and his successors tell us. The more protected from competition any businessman is, the less likely he is to work hard at producing new and better products.

But there is another side to the issue. Progress in the modern economy depends heavily on research and development spending. And only big firms have the resources to afford large R and D expenditures. Thus, as a practical matter, only with oligopolistic market structures are we likely to get the heavy R and D spending on which modern industrial progress depends.

What are the facts on this controversy? Out of $17 billion of industrial R and D expenditures in 1967, less than 5 per cent was in industries dominated by small firms—e.g., textiles and construction. Conversely, the great bulk of R and D is done by big firms, and by the same token in oligopolistic industries—e.g., aerospace, chemicals, and electrical equipment. (As was indicated in Part Two, much of this research is ultimately financed by government funds.) Only in agriculture among the industries approaching pure competition is there large R and D spending, and this is financed almost entirely by government and conducted largely in the universities.

But the picture is more complex. Among the larger firms that do have research and development organizations, the middle-sized ones spend as large a fraction of their sales dollars on research as do the huge ones. Although modern industrial research is heavily concentrated in oligopolistic industries, increasing firm size above a certain size doesn't seem to increase the relative stress on research.

Whose research contributes the most to innovation and economic progress? Do the big firms make the advances that really count, or do the important innovations come from little and medium-sized firms? The question is hard to answer, for we have few clear measures of success. Researchers have looked especially at three measures—patents received, important innovations achieved, and the rate of increase in productivity.

Jacob Schmookler of the University of Minnesota has found that a few giants dominate the total number of patents awarded (Bell Labs, G.E., and DuPont), but that in general big firms receive patents only in proportion to their larger expenditures on research. If anything, the middle-sized firms appear to have done a shade better in relation to their research spending, except for the few research giants.

A more important, but more difficult, measure is the number of important innovations actually produced by different-sized companies. Here Penn's Edwin Mansfield has studied three major industries intensively. He finds that in petroleum refining and coal mining, the larger firms have produced a larger proportion of the important innovations than their share in industry sales. But in steel, the reverse was true. He speculates on the basis of his evidence that large, but not giant-sized, companies are the most promising sources of major innovations—though this statement must be recognized as only a very tentative judgment.

Which industries show the highest rates of growth in productivity? Broadly speaking, those with the highest growth rates tend to be the oligopolies—chemicals, aerospace, and communications. Productivity has grown more slowly in industries dominated by small firms—the services, construction and textiles. Agriculture is a strong counter-example, with a very high growth rate in productivity. But there the research is almost entirely financed by the government, done in the state universities, and disseminated through state agricultural extension services.

Can we say anything about the influence of entry barriers on the rate of innovation? As was indicated above, profits on invested capital tend to be higher where barriers to entry are high, which might suggest that oligopolists have been progressive in reducing costs. However, numerous cases can be cited where well-protected oligopolists have failed to introduce major innovations until the way has been charted by outsiders, often big firms in other industries. Examples are the early introduction of radio outside G.E. and Bell Telephone, the dominant communication firms; and the development of jet engines outside the established aircraft engine manufacturers. But there are numerous counter-examples, some involving the same firms. Pending more conclusive research, we are left with only a general theoretical presumption that pressures to innovate will be strongest where firms are not protected against the threat of new entrants.

What is the conclusion on oligopoly and economic progress? Clearly firms of substantial size are needed in most industries to undertake substantial R and D activities, *if* we expect the research to be done by private firms.[7] The evidence suggests that on this score some degree of oligopoly is probably preferable to either monopoly or many small firms. But just how big firms should be for optimal progress remains a very unsettled issue.

[7] Some observers suggest introduction of government-financed research and dissemination for the business section, to parallel the arrangements that have worked so well in the small-firm argicultural sector.

REVIEW

Concepts To Remember

This chapter re-uses most of the analytical concepts introduced throughout Part Three. Beyond these, be sure you understand the following new ones:

administered prices	price leadership
cartel	price stabilization
concentration ratio	kinked demand curve

For Analysis and Discussion

1. Suppose you were manager of one of the furnace firms originally forming the cartel described in Chapter 27. What policies would you follow to promote your own best interests as additional new firms entered the industry?

2. "Competition is likely to be more vigorous among the few leading firms in an industry than among the many small concerns, who often are relatively inefficient." Do you agree or disagree? Can you cite any examples to support your position?

3. What are the main forces that determine whether there will be few or many firms in any given industry.

4. "The big oligopolies like General Motors, General Electric, Swift, and Alcoa have been primarily responsible for making better goods available to consumers. Breaking them up into smaller units to obtain more active price competition would be disastrous." Do you agree or disagree? Support your position against a critic.

5. It is sometimes argued that cartels are worse for the public than would be an outright monopoly of the industry by a single firm, since the cartel charges the high monopolistic price anyhow and also wastes resources through excess capacity. Evaluate this argument. If it seems sound, would you propose that cartels be converted into pure monopolies in the industries concerned?

6. In many of the major oligopolistic industries, entry is difficult for new firms because of both the technical know-how and the large financial investment required for effective competition. Can you suggest desirable ways to overcome these difficulties?

7. Suppose that you are president of the largest firm in an industry where the great bulk of the business is done by the five largest firms. As the industry leader, your firm ordinarily initiates any price changes in the industry.
   a. How would you go about deciding what price to charge for your product?
   b. Is there a conflict or community between your interests and those of the other four firms in the industry?
   c. Would consumers be better off, by and large, if there were active price competition rather than price leadership in the industry?

Appendix

SOME MANAGERIAL APPLICATIONS

This is primarily a book of economics for the citizen. Its main goal is to examine how the economic system works and how we might make it work better. But it's easy to show, too, how these same economic concepts and principles can help the businessman make better decisions for himself and the stockholders.[8]

[8] For more detailed analyses of the use of economic analysis in managerial decision making, see M. Spencer and L. Siegelman, *Managerial Economics* (Homewood, Ill.: Irwin, 1963); and M. Colberg, W. Bradford and R. Alt, *Business Economics* (Homewood, Ill.: Irwin, 1965).

Elasticity of Demand and Product Pricing. Demand is often elastic. And when it is, a price policy that doesn't recognize this fact can mean disaster. But a price policy founded on full knowledge of demand elasticity can make life pleasant for the stockholders, and unpleasant for competitors.

The phonograph record industry is a classic case. For decades classical records were high-priced luxury items, aimed at a small market. In 1938, Columbia reduced the price per record (on the old shellac 78-rpm records) from $2 to $1. The response was overwhelming. Total expenditure on classical records, to the amazement of almost everybody else, rose drastically. Demand turned out to be highly elastic, and the competition was left behind.

About the same time, the railroads, desperate for revenue, *raised* their fares. The result was equally impressive. The customers switched to cars and buses, or just stayed home in droves; total revenue dropped as the railroads learned about elastic demand the hard way.

Of course, individual product demand is sometimes inelastic. But over and over again, businessmen have underestimated the gain to be had from reducing prices and expanding markets where elastic demand prevails. Economists sometimes describe this as "elasticity pessimism." Mass markets based on low costs and low prices have been the foundation of the growing American economy.

New-Product Decisions—Marginal Cost vs. Average Cost.

Suppose you manage a filling station. You have handled only gasoline, oil, and a few miscellaneous supplies like auto polish, windshield wiper blades, and so on. The local wholesaler approaches you to put in a small line of batteries and tires. He argues there will be very little extra expense since you're not pressed for space, and that you have a small but ready-made market in your regular customers who don't want to go to the inconvenience of shopping around for these items.

You've had a course in economics and you know about costs. So you calculate carefully what the marginal (extra) cost of putting in these lines would be compared to the likely increase in revenue. The answer looks good. The only marginal cost you can see is the money tied up in keeping an inventory on hand, and it looks as if you might sell $200 to $300 a month worth of tires and batteries. At a markup over wholesale that will keep the final price roughly competitive with other retailers, this should yield an extra $50 to $75 a month even after allowing for interest cost on the money tied up in inventory. On the other hand, if you allocate against the tires and batteries their proportionate share of other costs (space, your time and that of the help, taxes, electricity, and so on), the line would probably show a small loss. Should you put in the tires and batteries?

The answer clearly hinges on whether you use marginal or average costs, assuming your estimates are reasonable. Adding the line will pretty clearly increase revenue more than cost for the enterprise as a whole, unless you've overlooked some new costs associated with the tires and batteries. Following the principles of Chapter 23, you'll increase your total profit by expanding, even though comparing the "total" cost of the batteries and tires against their selling prices they wouldn't appear to provide a profit. If it's total profit that matters to you, the comparison based on marginal cost will point the best answer.

But this is a rule to be used with care. It depends on careful analysis of costs, to be sure of what is truly marginal and what is not. Suppose you add the tires and they seem a great success, selling more than you'd expected and taking up more and more space and time. You have to add a new man and expand your building. Where do you allocate the cost—to the gasoline, the tires, where? You can look at any one part of your output first, and then the other looks marginal.

Many businessmen use the above kind of marginal (or incremental) analysis in adding products, but only when the addition is small relative to their total activity, and understandably so. But when any product line becomes relatively large, they expect it over the long pull to carry its regular share of the "overhead," or the "burden," as indirect costs of running the business are sometimes called. In principle, comparing marginal cost with marginal revenue always gives the right answer in deciding whether or not to take on a new product or to expand output. The trick lies in applying the principle carefully, and being sure which costs are really marginal.

Sunk Costs and Operating Decisions.

Try another case—similar but different. You manufacture men's suits. Your costs fall roughly into two groups—those variable with the level of output (mainly labor and materials), and those fixed for a considerable period without reference to the level of output (rent, management salaries, and so on). You know that for the range of output in which you usually operate, you must add about 30 per cent to your variable costs to get a price that permits you to break even; you normally price by adding 40 per cent to variable costs, with the prices of individual suits varying largely with differences in cloth and the amount of hand labor.

This season, demand has been slow and you are operating well under your normal rate. It has been a bad year, and you probably will not even break even. You have a chance to make a thousand suits on a special order from a wholesaler who is not a regular customer. However, he will only pay a price that would cover variable costs plus 20 per cent. Should you take the order?

Your fixed costs are "sunk." That is, they go on and must be paid, at least for the short run, whether you operate or not. Since they are sunk, economic analysis says they should have no effect on your decision to accept or reject the order, if your goal is to maximize profits or minimize loss in the short run. By taking the order you will cover all your variable costs and will have the 20 per cent addition to apply on your fixed costs. You may not make a profit on your total operations, but your loss will be smaller than without the order, as was explained back in Chapter 23.

The logic is right. But many businessmen would think a long time before taking the order. They worry about the long run, and properly so. Suppose you cut the price on this order and your regular customers hear about it. Might this break your whole price line, with dire results for profits over the longer run? Or might it lead your competitors to cut their prices? If the answer is "yes," looking only at the particular gain from taking this order would be wearing blinders to the long-run result. In the short run you may minimize losses by taking orders at less than total cost, but both economic analysis and managerial common sense say that in the long run your price has to cover all costs or you'll end up in bankruptcy.

The Nature of Costs: Depreciation.   You operate a fleet of taxicabs. With the hard use the cabs receive you estimate that after three years they will have depreciated to the point where it is no longer economical to operate them. At that time you anticipate you will be able to sell or trade them for about 10 per cent of the original cost of $3,000 each. Thus, you account as a cost an annual depreciation charge of 30 per cent ($300) each per cab, in addition to regular operating and maintenance costs.

At the end of three years you have fully depreciated the cabs, except for the small turn-in value. Yet they seem to be still in reasonably good condition. Should you turn them in on new cabs, using the accumulated depreciation reserve to finance the new cabs, or continue to use the old ones?

The forward-looking nature of economics, and the principle above that "sunk costs are sunk," suggest the answer. The fact that you estimated a three-year life and have now accumulated a 90 per cent depreciation reserve does not give you an answer to when you should replace these particular cabs. Don't be overimpressed by the bookkeeping. The optimal choice depends on analyzing the cost and performance of new cabs against the cost and performance of continued use of the old cabs. If the total profit by continuing to use the old cabs exceeds the profit with new cabs,[9] then keep the old ones. If not, buy new ones. The crucial point is the importance of the forward-looking decision, not the fact that three years is the end of your estimated depreciation period. If you made a mistake in estimating the cabs' useful life, it may pay you to replace long before the cabs are fully depreciated or to wait until long after. Depreciation charges represent only an estimate of the proper cost to be currently charged for the use of durable assets, not a determinant of when assets should be replaced.[10]

[9] Remembering possible consumer preferences for new models and all such relevant considerations, and recognizing that the money can temporarily be used another way if it is not used to buy new cabs.

[10] For a precise analysis of how to decide the best time to replace durable plant and equipment, a more advanced text is needed. See, for example, E. L. Grant and W. Ireson, *Principles of Engineering Economy* (New York: Ronald Press, 1960), Chapters 10 and 16.

TWENTY-EIGHT

GOVERNMENT
AND BUSINESS

Is Monopoly Growing?

Bigness, Monopoly, and Public Opinion.

The Law and Competition.

Where to from Here?

Business and Government in the New Capitalism.

Why should government intervene at all in business affairs? Adam Smith had one answer: Because the benefits of enlightened self-seeking can be obtained only if *competition* channels these efforts to the common good. Seldom do merchants gather together, he wrote, that their talk does not turn to means of getting higher prices for their produce. Without competition among sellers, more consumer spending may mean higher profits and not more products. It is the job of the government, representing all the people, to see to it that competition prevails.

Everyone agrees, moreover, that in an individualistic society there have to be some rules of fair play in economic life, just as in personal behavior. Without common consent to eliminate fraud, to respect property ownership, and to honor contractual promises, business dealings would be carried on under a great handicap. By general agreement, it is the job of government to establish and enforce these basic rules to enable men to deal effectively together; just as it is the government's job to establish and enforce laws against murder, theft, and arson to enable men to live securely together. Among Adam Smith's nineteenth-century followers, "laissez faire" never meant that the government should do nothing, but rather that it should leave economic affairs alone *within* a framework of basic moral and governmental rules of the game.

There is wide agreement on these two basic governmental functions in relation to business affairs—to insist on competitive behavior and to establish the basic rules of the game. But what do they mean in practice? Does enforcing competition mean enforcing *pure* competition as we have defined it? Obviously not, for this would leave almost the whole economy outside the pale. Does it mean breaking up General Motors, G.E., and U.S. Steel? Maybe, but if it does we'd better think such a violent step through carefully before we take it. Does it mean refusing to let present firms get any bigger through mergers?

The economic analysis of the preceding chapters provides a presumptive indictment against monopoly. Monopoly generally mal-allocates resources; it raises prices and restricts output in the monopolized industry. But most of the real world falls in between the areas of pure competition and pure monopoly, and the results suggested by the theoretical models in these in-between cases are less clear than at the two extremes. Don't forget the basic requirements for active price competition, including a market big enough to support many firms each operating near its "least-cost" point.

Economic theory gives no clear answer to just how much competition is enough, just how big is too big. Expert economists who have spent years studying the problem of "workable competition" come up with a reasonable consensus on some broad outlines of public policy against excessive monopoly, but they admit frankly they are perplexed about how to handle some of the in-between situations.

IS MONOPOLY GROWING?

Is monopoly growing? Are big firms dominating more markets? The answer is mixed. In manufacturing, the share of total assets and total output produced by the biggest firms has increased substantially since World War II. Table 28-1 tells the story.

TABLE 28-1

CONCENTRATION IN MANUFACTURING *

| | Share of Total Assets in: | |
	1950	1965
5 largest firms	9.6%	11.8%
20 largest firms	20.7	24.6
100 largest firms	38.6	45.4
200 largest firms	46.7	55.4

* Data from Federal Trade Commission.

As measured by "value added," the big firms don't bulk quite as large, but the picture is similar. Between 1947 and 1963, the share of the 100 largest firms rose from 23 to 33 per cent in manufacturing. On the other hand, the top is a slippery pinnacle. Table 28-2 shows the 10 largest industrial firms in 1909, and what had happened to them by 1960. Only two were still in the top 10, and five had vanished completely from the list of the 100 largest firms.

TABLE 28-2

TEN LARGEST INDUSTRIAL FIRMS, 1909-1960 *

| Rank | | |
1909	1960	
1	3	U. S. Steel Corporation
2	1	Standard Oil Company of New Jersey
3	42	American Tobacco Company
4	**	International Mercantile Marine Company
5	28	Anaconda Company
6	22	International Harvester Company
7	**	Central Leather Company
8	**	Pullman Company
9	**	Armour Company
10	**	American Sugar Company

* Data from A. D. H. Kaplan, *Big Enterprise in a Competitive System* (Washington, D.C., Brookings, 1964). Rankings based on total assets.
** No longer in top 100 firms.

In the rest of the economy, any trend toward concentration is less clear. In the rapidly growing services area, markets are generally divided among many relatively small sellers. Construction continues to be dominated by relatively small firms. There are still millions of farmers, though the market share of big commercial farms has been rising steadily. One striking development has been the explosive growth of the nongovernment but nonprofit sector, especially in the service areas—hospitals and Blue Cross, private education, research institutes, and the like. The share of the national income produced by private, profit-seeking corporations apparently reached a peak of 55 per cent in the mid-1950's. By 1965 it was back down to 53 per cent, its level of 20 years earlier.

The problem of economic concentration, once we eliminate the public utilities, appears to be centered in the manufacturing sector—though by no means entirely so. Against this factual backdrop, let us now turn to the intermixed problems of economic bigness and monopoly.

BIGNESS, MONOPOLY, AND PUBLIC OPINION

In 1966, the General Electric Company had assets of $5 billion, and reported profits before taxes of $700 million on sales of $7 billion. It had nearly 300,000 employees. Although no exact figures are available, G.E. apparently accounted for nearly half the total sales in the country of heavy electrical machinery, light bulbs, and other major categories of electrical equipment. It was rivaled only by Westinghouse, another giant, with assets of about $2 billion and sales and profits about a third the size of G.E.'s. Big companies like Allis Chalmers in heavy equipment and Sylvania in bulbs and lighter equipment absorbed another sizable chunk of the market, but they were far short of the two leaders in over-all size and market power.

Is G.E. a monopoly? Should it be broken up into several smaller concerns in the public interest?

Now consider Jones' Grocery Store, at the crossroads corner of an isolated village in northern Minnesota—population 150. Jones' total sales in 1966 were about $12,000, on which he realized a return after paying all costs (except his own salary) of about $3,000, as near as he could figure it. Jones had one employee—himself. His service was so-so. There is no other grocery store within 35 miles.

Is Jones' Grocery Store a monopoly? Should it be broken up into several smaller concerns in the public interest?

No reasonable person would answer that Jones' roadside store ought to be broken up by antimonopoly policy in order to provide more competition in the village. This would be nonsense. The market can't support one respectable grocery, let alone two or three. Yet Jones' monopoly power over the customers in that village may far exceed G.E.'s power over its customers. If Jones takes advantage of Widow Smith down the street and slips in a bad potato with every peck, she's pretty much out of luck. She can say

what she will about Jones—and it may be plenty —but that's about all she can do about it. Let G.E. treat one of its customers that way, and Westinghouse will get a phone call the next day from the outraged purchasing agent.

How about G.E.? If you think the Antitrust Division ought to look into G.E., why? Because G.E. clearly has a dominant position in the industry, with around half the market for many of its major products? Or because G.E. just seems to you too big—because you feel that no one business ought to control so much wealth, with the far-reaching economic and political power that goes with it?

It may be that you can't get very excited about G.E. one way or the other, if you're like a lot of other Americans today. G.E. is indeed a huge business, and you may sympathize with the workers when they strike for higher pay. But you know that G.E. has long been a pioneer in research and development of new and better products for consumers. It makes lots of money, but it turns out high-quality, reliable products, and you have at least a sneaking suspicion that it got that big by being better than its competitors. You know, too, that for every G.E. product you buy, you can find competing ones from Westinghouse and a bevy of other companies, depending on the item. That talk about heavy electrical machinery sounds pretty technical, and you're not much interested in 10,000-horsepower turbines anyway. G.E. is certainly an oligopolist, but it seems to be doing a pretty good job of serving the American consumer—and of providing a lot of well-paid, stable jobs to American workers in the process.

If you stop to think about these two cases, you'll see that two different issues are involved. One is the question of how strong a monopoly does the seller hold? This is largely an issue of the size of the seller *relative* to the market in which he sells. The second is the question of *absolute size*, which bears no necessary relationship to the degree of monopoly the firm possesses. Jones' Grocery has a pretty effective monopoly in its market, according to the economist's definition, but it's a tiny concern in absolute size. G.E. clearly holds some monopoly powers too—it's an oligopolist—but its monopoly power in its markets is less than that of Jones' Grocery. The striking difference is G.E.'s absolute size and economic power. The company affects immediately millions of consumers and hundreds of thousands of employees and stockholders by its economic actions. Its managers exert enormous power—the power of $5 billion—over the lives of 300,000 workers, over the communities in which they live, and over the consumers who buy electrical products. Never forget that our analytical monopoly and quasi-monopoly models refer to the firm's positions *relative to its market*. The issue of absolute size and power in the economy is a related but different and broader one.

These chapters are devoted primarily to helping you do your own straight thinking on the *economic* aspects of monopoly and quasi-monopoly. But it's important to recognize that public opinion—that potent force in controlling government action—often isn't very precise and logical. It often doesn't separate out the issues very sharply. If we could tap the thinking (partly subconscious) of the mythical man on the street about "monopoly," we might get something like this:

1. Is more competition practical? Would breaking up the big companies really give the consumer better products at lower prices? The cheapest products seem to come out of the mass-production industries with big firms.

2. How many firms does it really take to insure reasonable competition? Certainly not the infinitely large number required by the economist's "pure competition." Maybe only three or four big producers with several little ones nipping at their heels.

3. Some of those corporation presidents certainly do get big salaries.

4. Can you really trust anybody with the power that goes with a billion dollars? Big business has taken it out on the worker and the public lots of times in the past. They'd probably do it again if they could get away with it.

5. The little fellow deserves a break. We ought to help him a little against the giants.

6. The "blue chips" of American industry are the ones that have produced most of the good products that underlie our high standard of living—automobiles, nylon, refrigerators, and so on. Still . . . there are those stories about how they hold products off the market—razor blades that

would last two years, storage batteries that would never wear out.

7. They say that the big corporations dictate a lot of what goes into the laws made by Congress and the state legislatures. All that money surely gives them a way to buy votes that the little man can't afford.

8. Oh well, maybe with unions as strong as they are now, big business and the unions are about in balance.

This picture may not be accurate, but it does suggest the complex mixture of objectives, reasoning, and hearsay that makes up current American public opinion on "big business" and "monopoly." For the economist, big business and monopoly are far from synonymous. But the man in the street may not distinguish between them very sharply.

Elmo Roper and Lou Harris, the public opinion pollsters, have repeatedly sampled the man-in-the-street's feelings about big business. Briefly, their conclusions are: (1) Americans on the whole believe that big business is good for the economy, and that on balance it does a good job of turning out good-quality products. (2) The American public doesn't quite trust big business, and feels that we need a government that keeps an eagle eye on the big businessman to see that he doesn't abuse his enormous potential power over workers, the public, and smaller competitors.

Let us turn now to a brief look at how the law has developed over the last century in the United States, both to support competition and to restrict it. Then we'll take a concluding evaluative look at the broad problem of public policy vis-à-vis competition, market structure, and market performance. Can we make the market system serve us better?

THE LAW AND COMPETITION

The law is what is written down in the statute books, and more. It is what the courts say it is, what the long rows of past court decisions suggest, altered as the judge thinks proper in any particular case. It is what the Justice Department thinks it is; most law is enforced without ever coming near a court room. It is what the

President and his advisers think it is, through the way they instruct the government's law-enforcement branches. Above all, it is what the people will obey and support. In our democratic system, no law that does not command widespread public support can long be enforced. Sometimes the law is changed when it loses support, but equally often its enforcement varies to mirror the tenor of the times.

This description is especially accurate in the field of government-business relations. Here much of the law is in the mass of court decisions, and in the practices and policies of the government's administrative agencies. Both reflect (with lags) what the public wants—often more accurately than we realize. Our antitrust laws seldom change by formal congressional action. But in fact they alter constantly—with changing congressional appropriations for enforcement, changing antitrust personnel, changing judicial attitudes—often to the frustration of businessmen, who protest that no man can tell when he is violating the law until he sees whether the government takes him to court and the judge finds him guilty.

The Common Law

Until 1890, there was no federal legislation that declared monopoly illegal. Nor did the states have any antimonopoly laws of consequence. Under the common (unwritten) law inherited from England, contracts to restrain trade unreasonably or to raise prices were unenforceable. But the common law did not hold monopoly practices to be criminal, nor did it even provide for damages to those harmed by the restraint of trade. The contracts were merely unenforceable. Thus, the common law provided little protection to the consumer or to the little competitor who got squeezed out by combinations in restraint of trade. Some judges held extreme and vicious forms of competition to be illegal, as an extension of the law against fraud and misrepresentation, but these decisions were of little general import.

Legislation

The last half of the nineteenth century saw the development of the great trusts. Standard Oil, American Sugar, American Tobacco, and dozens of others amassed huge empires that held almost complete monopolies over the products con-

cerned. Standard Oil at its peak controlled over 90 per cent of the country's oil-refining capacity, and the bulk of the pipelines. American Sugar controlled 98 per cent of the country's sugar-refining capacity. American Tobacco had virtually complete control of tobacco manufacturing.

Moreover, the means used to build up these monopolies aroused widespread ire and fear. Standard Oil, for example, relentlessly drove small competitors to the wall by cut-throat competition, then bought them up cheap, and raised prices. Competitors who resisted found themselves up against ruthless force. Standard, with its vast resources, cut local prices to one-half of cost and made up the losses in noncompetitive areas. It bought up pipelines and refused transportation to competitors. Through its vast power, it forced railroads to give it rebates of 25 to 50 per cent, not only on its own shipments but *on the shipments of its competitors*. When competing pipelines tried to gain a foothold, Standard bought up the refineries they served and refused to take oil from the pipelines.

The Sherman and Interstate Commerce Acts. With half a hundred trust giants on the American scene, popular resentment was reflected in two major acts—the Interstate Commerce Commission Act (1887) and the Sherman Antitrust Act (1890). The Interstate Commerce Act established federal control over railroad rates and services for the first time, eliminating the cut-throat competition and rate discrimination that had long characterized this industry. The Sherman Antitrust Act was aimed at industrial monopoly. It declared illegal every contract or combination in restraint of interstate trade—to protect both small competitors and consumers.

These two pioneer acts are worth considering briefly, both because they still form the cornerstones of our federal policy on regulating monopolies and because they demonstrate two major alternative approaches to the problem.

The Interstate Commerce Act takes the alternative of strict, comprehensive government regulation of an industry that cannot operate satisfactorily on a competitive basis. By the late 1800's, it was abundantly clear that regulation of interstate railway rates and service through market competition was impracticable. At most, only two or three roads serviced most communities, and in many areas one railway had a complete monopoly. Even where two or more roads competed, as between Chicago and New York, competition was unsatisfactory because railroads are almost invariably decreasing-cost concerns and price competition leads to price wars that drive rates far below total average cost. Most markets were simply not big enough to support two or more railway systems, each operating near its minimum-cost levels.

Under such circumstances, there was little point in trying to enforce competition. Instead, the I.C.C. Act made the railroads public utilities, under the regulation of a new government body, the Interstate Commerce Commission. General operating responsibility is left with the management elected by the private stockholders, but prices and output (that is, rates, and amount and quality of service) must be approved by the I.C.C. as in keeping with the public interest. Under this approach, the railroads are guaranteed monopoly positions, but how they use their monopoly powers is carefully regulated.[1]

The Sherman Act was aimed at the other part of the economy, where competition could reasonably be expected to do a good job of regulating prices, output, and quality for the public good. Here the approach was exactly the opposite of that in the I.C.C. legislation. In order to enforce active competition, the Sherman Act outlawed restraints of trade and attempts to monopolize, as follows:

Section 1. Every contract, combination in the form of a trust or otherwise, or conspiracy, in restraint of trade or commerce among the several states, or with foreign nations, is hereby declared to be illegal. . . .

Section 2. Every person who shall monopolize, or attempt to monopolize, or combine or conspire with any other person or persons to monopolize any part of the trade or commerce among the several states, or with foreign nations, shall be deemed guilty of a misdemeanor. . . .

[1] With modern truck, bus, and airline competition, many economists now suggest that the day has come to try freer competition again, on the argument that competition provides more stimulus to efficiency and good service than does government regulation.

This was broad and sweeping language. Inevitably, a wide range of questions arose over the years as to just what was actually outlawed. What is covered by "restraint of trade," by "monopolize, or attempt to monopolize"? Another complex set of questions arose over just what activities were included under "interstate" commerce, since the federal government's power to regulate covers only commerce between states.

As with all such legislation, such questions have been answered primarily through a long series of court rulings interpreting the law. We will look at some of these rulings in the following section. But first it is important to recognize the basic problem of regulatory policy that the Sherman Act illustrates. No legislation regulating the complex modern economy can hope to specify in detail every case and situation that is to be covered. Instead, Congress must do its best to state its intentions clearly, leaving to government administrative officials, to regulatory commissions, and ultimately to the courts the job of applying the law to individual cases. The substance of regulatory law is often developed more in its interpretive application over the years than through the original legislation.

The Clayton and Federal Trade Commission Acts. One of the biggest problems in making the Sherman Act effective was the difficulty everyone had in defining just what it was that was illegal. Thus, in 1914 two new acts were passed —the Clayton Act and the Federal Trade Commission Act—to clarify this situation by specifically prohibiting certain practices, regardless of the group or individual engaging in them, and by setting up new enforcement procedures.

The Clayton Act listed specifically as illegal (1) discriminatory price-cutting; (2) tying contracts, which require buyers to purchase other items as a condition of getting one item; (3) acquisition of stock in competing companies to obtain monopoly powers; and (4) interlocking directorates in competing corporations. But each of these was prohibited only "where the effect may be to substantially lessen competition or tend to create a monopoly. . . ." Thus, the Clayton Act cleared the picture by defining some illegal acts. But it still left open the basic problem of interpretation for the courts in many individual cases.

The Federal Trade Commission Act created a commission to act as a watchdog against unfair competitive practices aimed at creating monopoly or injuring competitors. The Commission was given power to hold hearings and to issue "cease and desist" orders that require offending firms to discontinue illegal practices. When the first major appeal from a Commission ruling reached the Supreme Court in 1919, however, the Court held that it is for the courts, not for the F.T.C., to make the ultimate decisions in interpreting the law.

The effect of this ruling was to reduce sharply the F.T.C.'s powers. Major actions have reverted back to the courts, since everyone recognizes that an unfavorable F.T.C. decision can be appealed to the courts. The F.T.C. does, however, play an important role in policing cases of seller misrepresentation (for instance, artificial silk as silk, domestic lace as Irish lace), and in arranging voluntary agreements among business competitors on fair trade practices. For some interesting reading, go through one of the F.T.C. annual reports listing the cases of misrepresentation throughout the economy that have received cease and desist orders. These actions are taken to protect competitors against the unfair practice of misrepresentation, but they of course also serve to protect the consumer.

New Deal Legislation of the 1930's. Not all legislation has been designed to encourage competition. In the Great Depression of the 1930's, the New Deal was mainly concerned with recovery, greater economic security, and helping the little fellow. Ending the depression seemed to call for measures to halt falling prices and cut-throat competition for shrinking markets. The National Recovery Act (N.R.A.) led businessmen to band together in formal cartels, aimed at raising prices. In agriculture, the A.A.A. had a similar purpose—to raise farm prices and incomes by government-sponsored cartel-like agreements to restrict production. The Bituminous Coal Act did the same thing for soft coal. In labor markets, the Wagner Act threw the full force of the government behind workers' right to unionize and

bargain collectively, thus lessening the cut-throat price competition among workers for scarce jobs. These major legislative moves to raise prices and limit competition dominated moves to enforce competition under the Sherman and Clayton Acts, though popular and government antagonism to "big business" was strong during the 1930's. Both N.R.A. and A.A.A. were later declared unconstitutional, but the powerful competition-restricting effects of the agricultural and labor programs have become central parts of our governmental policy on market structure and performance.

This desire to help the small competitor and avoid "destructive" competition was reflected in two new pieces of legislation on market structure and behavior in the mid-1930's. The Robinson-Patman Act of 1936 strengthened the prohibition against price discrimination which might act to the benefit of such large buyers as chain stores and permit them to undersell small retailers. In 1937, the Miller-Tydings Act guaranteed protection from Sherman Act prosecution to manufacturers and retailers who participated in "fair-trading" arrangements, whereby the manufacturer specifies that no retailer may sell his product below a specified price. Too much competition was feared more than too little, reflecting the widespread fear of unemployment and depression. Legislation sought to protect competitors from competition—especially small firms—rather than to encourage competition.

The Celler Anti-Merger Act of 1950. After World War II, many corporations found that acquiring other companies outright was a profitable path of expansion as the economy grew. Such mergers were sometimes prompted by market-expansion goals, sometimes by special tax considerations, sometimes by the desire for diversification, sometimes by other considerations. In the first postwar decade, some 2,000 substantial corporate mergers occurred in manufacturing and mining alone. The merger movement reflected again the adaptability of American businessmen in finding ways to achieve their aims.

Such extension of market power through merger was not limited by earlier antitrust legislation, but in 1950 the Celler Anti-Merger Act was passed forbidding the acquisition of, or merger with, other companies where the effect "may be substantially to lessen competition, or tend to create a monopoly."

The Anti-Merger Act showed again the response of the law to hold business within the broad antitrust goals of our time. And the first major court test under the new law showed its potency. Bethlehem Steel and Youngstown Sheet and Tube, the second- and sixth-largest steel producers, announced plans to merge, and were brought to court in 1958 by the Justice Department. The court held that the proposed merger was prohibited. Subsequent cases have held that large companies may not merge with even very small ones in the same business; that mergers are illegal if they reduce competition between broadly competing products (e.g., glass and metal containers); and that mergers may be illegal if they threaten to reduce even *potential* competition. Moreover, the court has applied the potential-elimination-of-competition test to market areas as small as a single state or community, not merely to large areas or the whole country. Under these cases, any merger of competing firms above small size appears to be of doubtful legality, though each case is judged on its own circumstances. Nevertheless, nearly 2,000 corporate mergers were reported in 1966 alone, some 200 of them involving a firm of $100 million assets or more.

The Law in Operation

The law is what its administrators and the courts make it. And its administrators and the courts by and large make it what the public wants, often very roughly and with a considerable lag, but fairly effectively none the less.

Nowhere has this been truer than in antitrust legislation. The Sherman Act states only a broad intent. What degree of monopoly and what restraint of trade does the act really forbid? No one knows for sure, and probably most of the congressmen who voted for it had only a hazy idea themselves.

The first big enforcement campaign under the Sherman Act was President Teddy Roosevelt's, conducted with a total staff of seven lawyers and four stenographers. With this tiny staff, but with the big stick of aroused public opinion, the government tackled and broke a series of trusts.

Finally, in 1911, the Supreme Court required both Standard Oil and American Tobacco, two of the biggest trusts, to divest themselves of a large share of their holdings and to desist from numerous specific unfair competitive practices. But there, too, for the first time, the Court enunciated the now-famous "rule of reason." Only trusts that "unreasonably" restrained trade were illegal. In a series of earlier cases, the Court had given a broad interpretation to the interstate commerce clause, permitting federal regulation to apply to all firms which had any direct dealing across state lines or (later) in products or materials crossing state lines; this interpretation brought most big businesses within the purview of federal antitrust legislation.

By 1920, the attitude toward big business had altered, with the checking of the flagrant abuses of the 1800's. In the U.S. Steel Case of 1920, the Supreme Court refused to dissolve the company. It held specifically that neither mere bigness nor unexerted monopoly power was illegal as such; that actual unreasonable restraint of trade must be proved under the Sherman Act. The tenor of the 1920's was one of prosperity and "leave well enough alone." The total budget allocated the Antitrust Division averaged only $250,000 annually for the decade. Big business was popular during the twenties.

With the strong antibusiness sweep of the New Deal, the last major change in the application and interpretation of the antitrust laws began in the late 1930's. Under Thurman Arnold, Antitrust began an aggressive drive in the late 1930's against several of the industrial giants. Antitrust's budget was upped to $1 million (to police the entire economy). Its investigations in the construction field disclosed eyeopeners that aroused the public, and actions were begun against labor, agricultural, and professional groups as well as against business. The government dissolved a glass-container monopoly based on patents in the Hartford Empire Case in 1944 with a decision that greatly weakened the use of patents to support monopoly practices. In the Alcoa Case of 1945, it obtained a strongly worded ruling that market dominance itself, even though not actively used to restrain competition, is illegal. It outlawed "basing-point pricing" (under which a few leaders set industry-wide prices f.o.b. at selected factory "basing points") in the Cement Case of 1948. Application of federal legislation through the interstate commerce clause was steadily broadened.

The Eisenhower, Kennedy, and Johnson administrations have continued active prosecution under the antitrust legislation. Appropriations to both the Federal Trade Commission and the Antitrust Division of the Department of Justice have been further increased. DuPont's ownership of approximately one-fourth of General Motors' common stock was condemned. The Anti-Merger Act has become a powerful barrier to business growth through acquisition of competitiors.

But the government does not win all the cases it brings. For example, in 1956 it lost a major battle against DuPont. It argued that DuPont had monopolized the manufacture of cellophane. But the Supreme Court held that competition should be construed to include reasonably close substitutes as well as the product itself. DuPont produced almost 75 per cent of all cellophane, but cellophane constituted less than 20 per cent of all "flexible packaging material" sales. Thus, the majority declared DuPont's position legal, even though it was a monopolist in cellophane, because it held only a relatively small part of the total "flexible packaging material" market —in spite of a strong minority protest that this interpretation would emasculate the entire Sherman Act prohibition against monopoly.

Nor should you assume that all economists, understanding the theoretical presumption against monopoly, agree that the antitrust laws act in the public interest. Some economists, for example, argue that the court's strong interpretation of the Anti-Merger Act can give topsy-turvy results. To prevent mergers among relatively small firms may hinder useful, cost-saving combinations more than it protects consumers. And many economists fear that recent anti-merger decisions have reached this point—for example in the 1966 Von's Groceries case which forbade a merger between two Los Angeles grocery chains, which together held less than 8 per cent of the Los Angeles market. They fear that the result will be to protect inefficient competitors, not competition.

Where does antitrust law stand now, as a

practical matter? First, all price fixing agreements are per se illegal. Second, oligopolies where a few firms dominate the market are probably legal so long as no leading firm tries to expand its market share by merger or by aggressive competition that endangers small firms. Third, growth through merger in the same industry is virtually forbidden, except among very small firms—although growth through reinvestment of a firm's own funds is permissible. Fourth, a wide variety of practices (price discrimination, tying clauses in contracts, and the like) are illegal when they may tend to create a monopoly or significantly reduce competition. Fifth, retail price fixing under "fair trade" agreements is legal in many states, but fair-trading is of limited importance because retail competition has generally broken out in spite of the price floors set by manufacturers. A total picture of antitrust today would need a much longer list, with many more details and qualifications. This is intended merely to provide a rough, broad picture.

Why has Antitrust again become a potent force since the 1930's? First, the budget given it by Congress is now larger than before ($7 million for the Antitrust Division and $11 million for the F.T.C. in 1967); Antitrust now has some 300 lawyers to police the entire economy. This, however, is still a tiny sum compared with the vast resources of the billion-dollar corporations it has to police. More fundamental has been the changing temper of the times. The New Deal and public sentiment during the 1930's were frankly critical of big business. Antitrust was only one phase of a broad program of criticism, legislation, and administrative controls. Since then, public support for business has greatly strengthened, and the picture reported by the Roper and Harris surveys above is probably roughly accurate. But though the public admires and wants big business, it also wants the government watching closely to be sure that big business doesn't abuse its powers. Antitrust is one of the main tools the government has. And the Supreme Court has generally supported the government's accusations in recent years.

One last point on the law in action. The main impact of the antitrust law is preventive, not punitive. Since 1890, only about 1,000 suits have been brought under the Sherman Act. Of these, the government has won about 600 and lost about 200, with the rest still in the courts. Total fines paid by defendants over the half-century were only a few million dollars—very little compared to the billions of dollars of assets in the companies concerned. But in 1961 the business world was rocked by the federal court decision which sent top executives of G.E., Westinghouse, and smaller competitiors to jail for conspiring to fix prices on electrical equipment. If this marks the beginning of a new trend in antitrust enforcement, the bite of the law may be strong indeed. Some observers feel this is an improper penalty—that the guilty party is the corporation itself, not the individual managers who may be doing just what they think is expected of them in trying to make larger profits. Others argue that to free the individual of legal responsibility is to take the only really effective bite out of the law.

Most observers agree that Antitrust has been a surprisingly powerful force in the American business scene since 1890. No business likes to be called criminal. It does not like to have its affairs dragged into open court, even though it thinks it may win out in the end. Besides, most businessmen are law-abiding citizens who are reluctant to break the law—though the G.E.-Westinghouse Case raised widespread doubts on this point. American businessmen talk the strongest case for competition you can find anywhere. The difficulty comes in defining what everyone means by competition, and what interpretation of the law is the right one.

But although Antitrust has been an ever-present danger to monopolists, Congress and the state legislatures have eaten away at the Sherman Act's prohibition against price-fixing agreements in some areas, especially agriculture, labor, and retailing. The Robinson-Patman and Miller-Tydings Acts specifically limited price competition and made price floors set by manufacturers legal for their own products. Some observers feel that the loss to consumers through such legalized price-fixing may outweigh all the gains provided by the Antitrust Division. But one strong ally for the consumer has stubbornly reappeared—the profit

motive. Many retailers object to price-maintenance policies and cut prices surreptitiously or openly in defiance of manufacturers' rules. "Discount houses" are a major manifestation of this revolt. By the 1960's, most leading manufacturers had given up fair-trading because it was so hard to keep retailers from cutting prices in order to sell more goods.

WHERE TO FROM HERE?

Where to from here? Should we be fighting back toward a highly competitive system like the one envisaged in the economist's pure-competition model, even though we recognize we'll never get to that "ideal"? Or should we be satisfied with the mixed economy, perhaps not getting all the theoretically possible benefits of strong price competition but getting a lot of other benefits that come with big, stable business concerns? How shall we assure that business performance is efficient and in the public interest?

Nobody thinks the modern American economy can look like the economist's perfectly competitive model. It never has, even back in the pre-Civil War days, and it certainly doesn't now. We're in for a mixed economy of some sort. Where does this leave antitrust?

Economic theory presents a clear presumption against monopoly on grounds of inefficient allocation of resources. On grounds of economic progress, the presumption is less clear; many very small firms would produce little R and D spending and dynamic progress in many industries. Lastly, there is the issue of sheer bigness and economic power, related to but different from monopoly power. Let us consider antitrust policy on each issue in turn.

Antitrust
and Economic Efficiency

Would stronger antitrust action really produce a more "efficient" economy, in the sense of giving consumers the largest possible amount of what they want at the lowest feasible prices? More firms create a general presumption of more active competition. But no magic number of firms is needed to assure effective competition. Sometimes (for example, in the auto industry) there is aggressive competition with only two or three big firms. But most observers agree that more firms generally increase the likelihood of strong price and quality competition.

If more firms are generally good for competition, we need to face the issue of whether this condition is consistent with having firms big enough to be efficient, low-cost producers. Clearly, business has to be big for efficiency in many industries. But it's also true that business can get too big from the cost standpoint. Various studies have indicated that in many industries middle-sized to large companies have lower costs than gigantic ones. But not always.

Table 28-3 summarizes a widely quoted research study on the problem of optimum (least-cost) size of plant and firm in a sample of manufacturing industries. It reflects the wide diversity just mentioned. Column 1 shows the percentage of

national industry capacity contained in one *plant* of optimum size; the range indicates the variation in the best available estimates. Column 2 provides the same information for a *firm* of optimum size. Where the firm figure is larger than the plant figure, there are additional economies from combining a number of optimal-size plants in one firm. Column 3 shows the wide variation in the amount of capital needed to set up a new plant of about the optimum size in each industry, presumably some measure of what it would take a newcomer to enter the industry. Lastly, column 4 shows the percentage share of the national market actually held about 1950 by the average of the four largest firms in each industry. This figure is obtained by dividing the total share of the four largest firms by four. The percentage so obtained is thus smaller than the actual share of the largest firm in the industry. For example, General Motors' share of the auto market approached 50 per cent in comparison with the 23 per cent average

TABLE 28-3
ESTIMATED SIZE OF OPTIMAL PLANTS AND FIRMS IN MANUFACTURING INDUSTRIES *

Industry	Percentage of National Industry Capacity in One Plant of Optimal Size	Percentage of National Industry Capacity in One Firm of Optimal Size	Capital Required for One Efficient Plant (In Millions)	Percentage Share of National Market Held by Average of First 4 Firms
Shoes	.14 to .5	.5 to 2.5	$.5 to 2	7
Canned fruits and vegetables	.25 to .5	.25 to .5	2.5 to 3	7
Metal containers	.5 to 3	No estimate	5 to 20	20
Cement	.8 to 1	2 to 10	20 to 25	7
Steel	1 to 2.5	2 to 5	265 to 665	11
Distilled liquor	1.25 to 1.75	No estimate	30 to 42	19
Petroleum refining	1.75	1.75	193 (without transport)	9
Gypsum products	2.5 to 3	27 to 33	5 to 6	21
Tires and tubes	3	No estimate	25 to 30	19
Cigarettes	5 to 6	15 to 20	125 to 150	23
Autos	5 to 10	5 to 10	250 to 500	23
Tractors	10 to 15	10 to 15	125	17
Typewriters	10 to 30	10 to 30	No estimate	20

* From J. S. Bain, "Economies of Scale, Concentration, and Entry," *American Economic Review*, March 1954, pp. 30, 36. Data as of about 1950, when prices were substantially lower than now.

for the four largest firms. Similarly U.S. Steel had about 30 per cent of the market compared to the average of only 11 per cent for the four top firms.

The estimates of Table 28-3 suggest that the actual share of market held by many of the biggest firms is far above that needed to obtain lowest-cost production. In this sample, for example, this statement is true for shoes, canned fruits and vegetables, petroleum refining, steel, and autos. It is probably true also for metal containers, distilled liquor, and tires and tubes. Even in such industries as typewriters and cement, the market share of the biggest firm (as distinct from the average of the four biggest) is well above the minimum optimal size. Moreover, many of these firms have regional, though not national, monopoly positions; an example is cement, where transport costs are very high relative to the value of the product.

This general finding is confirmed by George Stigler of the University of Chicago and T. R. Saving of Michigan State, using a different research technique. They postulate that by and large the most efficient sizes of plant and firm will win out in the competitive race. During the postwar period, medium-sized plants (relative to their total markets) have survived most effectively in most industries. This test therefore suggests that in most industries plants small enough to permit effective competition can produce efficiently.[2]

But the other side of the picture is impressive too. In several industries the cost of an efficient plant is so high that there is no point pretending that competition can be readily open to new producers; note the figures for cigarettes, petroleum refining, tractors, autos, and steel. But there a number of industries where the minimum cost of entry is so small that entry for potential competitors should be fairly easy; note the cases of canned fruits and vegetables, and of gypsum products.

Professor Bain has summed up the over-all difficulty new firms might have in trying to

enter a sample of the nation's major industries, taking into account size of firm needed for efficiency, capital requirements, established product names, and other relevant factors. These ratings must obviously be extremely rough, but nevertheless here they are: [3]

Very Difficult	Moderately Difficult	Relatively Easy
automobiles	petroleum refining	canned goods
cigarettes	men's shoes	cement
copper	steel	flour
farm machinery		gypsum products
liquor		meat packing
soap		metal containers
tractors		rayon
typewriters		tires and tubes

Many economists are highly critical of the Robinson-Patman and Miller-Tydings Acts, another branch of our antitrust legislation. Both acts were designed primarily to protect small competitors against large ones, and they often do so even when the large competitors are more efficient in satisfying consumer needs. They tend to protect small *competitors*, not *competition*. Many small, conservative druggists liked "fair trading" fine. But why shouldn't a competitor be free to sell Colgate toothpaste for 59 cents instead of 69 if he thinks he can make a profit by doing so? Some manufacturers and retailers argue that people lose confidence in their products if price-cutting like this goes on. They argue that the established stores have to know where they stand if they're to stock manufacturers' items, and that the price-cutters are just scabs who fail to carry their own weight in the selling process. But from the economist's and the consumer's point of view, it's not clear why price-cutting isn't just what competition is supposed to produce, so long as it isn't used as a device for driving out competitors by temporarily selling below cost just to gain a monopoly position.

[2] See, for example, T. R. Saving, "Estimation of Optimum Size of Plant by the Survivor Technique," *Quarterly Journal of Economics*, November, 1961.

[3] From J. S. Bain, *Barriers to New Competition* (Cambridge: Harvard University Press, 1956). Using a similar list of industries, H. M. Mann has found that rates of return on invested capital are significantly higher in difficult-to-enter industries, as is predicted by our theory. See "Seller Concentration, Barriers to Entry, and Rates of Return," *Review of Economics and Statistics*, August, 1966.

Antitrust and Economic Progress

The other big question about monopoly and partial monopoly is what they do to the rate of economic progress—whether they contribute to, or impede, a dynamically growing economy. The issues and some of the facts were presented in the concluding section of Chapter 27, and there is no need to repeat them here. Broadly speaking, those industries with the highest growth rates tend to be oligopolies—big firms with large R and D expenditures. Most research and development spending is done by large and medium-sized firms. Productivity has grown more slowly in industries dominated by small firms (except agriculture, with its government financing and distribution of research). But the picture is far from uniform; there are numerous exceptions, and industries protected against entry by new competitors clearly have the power to suppress innovations that might otherwise have been forced by competition.

What is the implication for antitrust? Not clear. It seems certain that we can generally not expect much R and D spending from tiny firms in industries that approach perfect competition, however aggressively they may compete for the consumer's favor. If we want R and D in such industries, the pattern of government financing and dissemination of results in agriculture may be the best way. But remember that firms far short of giant size can spend heavily on research and obtain results that compete with the giants' in many industries. Even on the score of economic progress, few industries require such large firms for efficient R and D that they cannot support numerous sellers and effective price competition.

Bigness and the Concentration of Economic Power

Can antitrust do anything about the problem of the sheer power of bigness? This is the most basic question of all for some people. Political power, economic power, power over other people's lives, just the power that goes with a billion dollars—these are the things that worry many people most about big business.

The power of big business seems especially alarming to some observers because in many firms "inside management" has a substantially free hand in exercising its vast power. While the stockholders theoretically direct the management, as a practical matter few stockholders know much about the details of management or have any interest in interfering in it. To whom is big management really responsible in the exercise of its economic power?

A. A. Berle, a long-time observer of the business corporation, has pointed up this problem. Only 500 corporations control two-thirds of the entire American nonfarm economy, he writes, and within each of those 500 a relatively small group holds the ultimate decision-making power. "Since the United States carries on not quite half of the manufacturing production of the entire world today, these 500 groupings—each with its own little dominating pyramid within it—represent a concentration of power over economies which makes the medieval feudal system look like a Sunday School party. In sheer economic power this has gone far beyond anything we have yet seen." [4]

J. K. Galbraith, in his best-selling *The New Industrial State*, has argued even more—that big business planning and parallel government planning are replacing market competition in modern America. He updates Berle's data on the massive role of the few hundred largest corporations, and points to a growing tendency of self-perpetuating management in the big oligopolies toward long-range planning for efficiency, for avoidance of vigorous price competition, and for stabler relations with organized labor. Solid, prosperous growth is the keynote, without undue, disruptive, old-style competition. With these policies, the big quietly grow bigger and more powerful. In essence, government protects and approves this secure, stable world for the giants, unless they abuse the mores unduly or openly try to aggrandize their positions by acquiring or squeezing out smaller firms. Antitrust acts mainly to prevent open collusion and mergers among the smaller competitors which, as a practical matter, are prob-

[4] *Economic Power and the Free Society* (New York: Fund for the Republic, 1958), p. 14.

ably their only way of challenging the concentrated power of the giants.

Galbraith's solution? Not to break up the giants, for that would waste the economic benefits of modern technology which underlie the success of big firms. Rather he says that the answer is increasing government participation to provide the good life—more and better public services in the modern affluent society. Parks, modern housing, better education, state-supported symphonies and drama—through a bigger public sector we can improve the quality of modern life, not merely the quantity of g.n.p.

Most economists believe that Berle and Galbraith have badly overdrawn their case. Competition in most markets is far too pervasive to permit the comfortable life for the giants which Galbraith paints, except in a few industries. In the nonmanufacturing sectors of the economy, big firms are far less dominant, and manufacturing accounts for only about a third of the economy. The turnover in firms at the top is too fast to support Galbraith's picture of comfortable security. Most data suggest that we don't need firms as big as the real giants for economic efficiency, and that antitrust might reasonably be asked to tackle the job of breaking up some of the conglomerate giants into independent subparts. Table 28-3 above provides some of the relevant evidence. Nor is it clear that the real giants are needed to produce the amount of research and development needed for economic progress.

Yet Galbraith has touched a sensitive nerve. Many Americans are uneasy about the concentration of economic power in the big corporations, even though their achievements and their well-paid top managers are widely admired. Still, there is little evidence of public support for a radical extension of antitrust to break up the blue chips of American industry just because they are so big, when there is no open abuse of market power to reduce competition or fence out new competitors.

The Dilemma
of Modern Antitrust Policy

The dilemma of antitrust policy in the mixed economy can be summarized in two brief statements. The first is that of Henry C. Simons, one of the outstanding advocates of free-enter-

prise economics in the United States.[5] "Reasonable" monopoly, said Simons, is a contradiction in terms. There can be no such thing. Wide dispersion of political and economic power is the only foundation on which a democratic, free-enterprise system can long exist. The role of government is clear: (1) to maintain active competition within a general framework of free-enterprise rules of the game which disperse economic power; and (2) to own and operate directly those few industries where competition cannot be made to function effectively. Specifically, said Simons, this implies:

1. Forbidding any manufacturing or merchandising corporation to own stock in any other such corporation, and elimination of interlocking directorates except between unrelated industries.

2. An upper limit on the asset size of all corporations, far below the size of the present giants. Writing in the 1930's, he suggested $100 million in assets as a presumptive upper limit for all firms. We may need big plants for productive efficiency, but we certainly don't need gigantic corporations controlling many similar plants.

3. Provision that no firm may be big enough to dominate its industry, the F.T.C. to determine this size limit in each industry. Moreover, we must recognize that cartels among a few large firms, however informal and "respectable," are probably the most wasteful of all monopoly arrangements, and strictly forbid them.

This may strike you as a completely impractical program, which only an ivory-tower college professor could take seriously. But think about it a little. Many thoughtful observers of the American scene consider Simons the outstanding intellectual spokesman of our time for a free, private-enterprise economy.

The other statement is that of the Pittsburgh Plate Glass Company in its answer to the government lawyers in the trial brought against it and other leading glass manufacturers for al-

[5] See especially "A Positive Program for Laissez Faire," and "A Political Credo," in his *Economic Policy for a Free Society* (Chicago: University of Chicago Press, 1948).

leged violations of the antitrust laws during the late 1940's.

We certainly are a big company, said the corporation's lawyer to the judge, and we can understand why the government wanted to investigate us. It's their job to see that the competitive system stays competitive, and we believe in competition just as strongly as they do. All we want to do is to tell you something about the flat-glass industry. Then he went on to demonstrate that today six huge, efficient glass-melting tanks and rolling lines can produce all the flat glass used in the United States. Pittsburgh Plate had three of these big plants, one to serve each part of the country, since transportation is a big cost on finished glass. He didn't deny that Pittsburgh Plate Glass might be called an oligopoly. He just pointed to modern technology in relation to the market, huge as it is in the United States today, and led the judge to wonder what was to be gained by going back to smaller-scale, less efficient productive processes.

How did the case come out? It never went to a decision. After the company's presentation, the judge instructed the lawyers for both sides to go work out a consent decree for him to sign, making it clear that he was in no mood to find for the government and order dissolution of Pittsburgh Plate.[6]

Which road is better? The one taken by Pittsburgh Plate Glass, or the one taken by Simons? Most economists would say somewhere in between, and that the best market structure will be different in different industries, depending on technology, the size of the market, and other factors. Indeed, it seems clear that few major sectors of the public really want an economy of rampant competition—neither farmers, labor, businessmen, nor consumers. Most people appear to be interested, not in a perpetual competitive struggle, but in a steady job at good pay, good profits, good quality products, and predictable, stable times economically.

In conclusion, test out your own views on

[6] This is a much oversimplified version of the controversy, but it illustrates the essential issue on this major part of the case. The company agreed to alter several of its marketing practices, which were claimed to restrain competition.

the best role for antitrust over the years ahead by judging this proposal. Recently *Fortune* magazine urged a major revolution in our antitrust laws and philosophy, as follows: [7]

"Congress should amend the antitrust statutes to make it clear that the national policy is to foster competition by punishing restraints of trade, including conspiracies to fix prices, limit production, allocate markets, and suppress innovation; but that it is not the national policy to prefer any particular size, shape, or number of firms to any other size, shape or number; and that mergers—horizontal, vertical, or conglomerate—are entirely legal unless they spring from a manifest attempt to restrain trade."

Would this be a good antitrust policy?

BUSINESS AND GOVERNMENT IN THE NEW CAPITALISM

Antitrust action is the most conspicuous government regulation of business. But governments have a much wider range of impact on business in the modern American scene. The Federal Trade Commission regulates the kind of advertising business may do. The Securities and Exchange Commission regulates its practices in issuing securities. The Federal Reserve controls the terms on which it can borrow money from the banks. Federal law sets the minimum wage it must pay its workers, and prescribes that it must deal with them in unions when they choose. Through its income tax, government takes half of all business profits, and in effect prescribes what kinds of accounting procedures must be followed. On the vast amount of government contracts issued to business (over $70 billion in 1967), it sets elaborate standards of performance; specifies that business cannot discriminate amongst employees on the basis of race, creed, or color; and often reserves the right to renegotiate prices downward retroactively if business profits appear to be excessive by government standards.

When labor disputes produce long strikes that disrupt the economy, government often calls business and labor together and brings pressure

[7] Max Ways, "Antitrust in an Era of Radical Change," *Fortune*, March, 1966.

for settlement on terms that businessmen consider unfair. In 1962, President Kennedy brought the full force of the government and public opinion to force U.S. Steel to rescind price increases which, he thought, endangered the nation's anti-inflation program. If the business is an airline, it is regulated in detail by the Civil Aeronautics Authority and the Civil Aeronautics Board as to where it can fly, how much it can charge, the kinds of equipment it can use, and the safety standards it must meet. At the local level, government tells business what land can be used for, and how much taxes it must pay to help support schools and roads. Beyond all this, government constantly hovers in the background, ready to impose new restrictions or bring new pressures to bear if a considerable portion of the public becomes seriously dissatisfied with what business is doing.

Some businessmen bitterly resent this government interference with the freedom of managers to manage as they please. They argue that it has sapped the essential force of private-enterprise "capitalism." But others believe that it reflects a gradual change in the role of business toward greater responsibility to the general public —a change that has modified the nature of "capitalism" but has not fundamentally altered the basic forces of the profit motive, self-interest, and private ownership of property. The old automobile has had its face lifted; horsepower has been stepped up and gas consumption along with it;

a governor and safety padding are compulsory; the carburetor has been adjusted; power steering has become standard equipment. Sometimes the machine works better as a result of this tinkering, sometimes worse. But on the whole it is now a better automobile. And above all, the gasoline that makes it go is still the same—self-interest and the profit motive. Writers sometimes speak of "the new capitalism." Government in business is a big element in the new capitalism, but private capital and management still take the major risks, make the major economic decisions, and reap the major gains or losses those decisions produce.

There is by no means complete agreement whether this analogy is a fair one, whether the essential driving force of the traditional American private-enterprise system is as strong as, or stronger than, before. Some look toward growing cooperation between big business and the state to solve our pressing social and economic problems—urban renewal, integration of minority groups, air pollution, aid to underdeveloped nations. Perhaps imaginative, new, mixed government-business ventures are the path to the future. To make an intelligent judgment on the performance of our system, you need to look at more aspects of the record, and to compare ours with other kinds of economic systems. But it may be helpful to try a tentative summing up for yourself now. How well does our system do, as it is organized today?

For Analysis and Discussion

1. How, if at all, does the problem of business monopoly affect you personally?
2. Do you think the problem of bigness as such is more important than the problem of monopoly?
3. What are the main characteristics of an industry that determine whether a large or small number of firms is most beneficial to the public interest?
4. Many businessmen argue that vigorous government prosecution under the antitrust laws is a sign of government antagonism toward business and profits. Is this a proper criticism? If you think not, how would you explain his error to such a businessman?
5. Critics of big business corporations often argue that most huge modern corporations could be broken up into several competing units without loss of productive efficiency, because most of these corporations control many separate plants, each of which could just as well operate as a separate, competitive business. Does this argument seem to you a sound one? If so, how should we go about implementing the proposal?
6. Would you favor direct government conduct or support of all basic research, with the results freely available to all? List the advantages and disadvantages.

7. Trucks, buses, and airlines now are at least as important as railroads in freight and passenger transporation in most areas. Has the time come to abolish the Interstate Commerce Commission and turn the transportation field back to open competition, which is often claimed to provide the most effective prods to efficiency and progress?

8. Would you favor tripling the congressional appropriation to the Department of Justice for antitrust enforcement?

CURRENT RESEARCH

As with the Appendix to Part Two, the purpose here is to suggest a sample of recent research in economics that may be of interest to students who want to know more of what economists do, and especially of the excitement that goes with research—the probing for new knowledge and new understanding. Here again the items listed are merely a sample, selected to show some of the many types of research under way on the problems covered by Part Three. They are not necessarily the best, nor even a cross-section, of current research in the area. They are chosen because I hope some of them may be intriguing to you, and make you want to look further. They vary widely in approach, substance, and difficulty.

Industry and Market Studies. You can find a research study on just about every major industry. Two interesting recent ones are Merton Peck's *Competition in the Aluminum Industry, 1945–1958* (Harvard Univ. Press, 1961), and M. A. Adelman's *A & P: A Study in Price-Cost Behavior and Public Policy* (Harvard Univ. Press, 1959). For a very different industry (music, the theatre, and ballet), see W. Baumol and W. Bowen, *Performing Arts—The Economic Dilemna* (20th Century Fund, 1966). Broader coverage is given by *Pricing in Big Business: A Case Approach*, by A. D. Kaplan, J. Dirlam, and R. Lanzilotti (Brookings, 1958); and Kaplan's *Big Enterprise in a Competitive System* (Brookings, 1964) provides a further readable overview.

The most controversial and lively study of modern business is J. K. Galbraith's *The New Industrial State* (Houghton-Mifflin, 1967), a best seller almost from its publication. For an equally lively antidote, see the review of Galbraith's book in *Fortune*, July, 1967 (pages 90 ff.).

Government Antitrust Policy. A sample of leading economists' analyses of some of the central problems of antitrust policy is provided by *Perspec-*

tives on Antitrust Policy, A. Phillips, ed. (Princeton Univ. Press, 1965). Carl Kaysen's and D. Turner's *Antitrust Policy: An Economic and Legal Analysis* (Harvard Univ. Press, 1959) illustrates the intricate interrelationships between economic and legal issues. A provocative proposal is advanced by Max Ways in "Antitrust in an Era of Radical Change" (*Fortune*, March, 1966). For a broader look at the issues involved, try Edward Mason's "Introduction" to his *The Corporation in Modern Society* (Harvard Univ. Press, 1959); Jacob Viner's "The U.S. as a 'Welfare State'" in *The Nation's Economic Objectives*, E. Edwards, ed. (Univ. of Chicago Press, 1964); or Chapter 8 of Milton Friedman's *Capitalism and Freedom* (Univ. of Chicago Press, 1962).

Economic Theory and Human Behavior. You can always start a lively dispute in economics by asking how well generally accepted economic theory corresponds to actual human behavior. One persistent question is how closely consumer spending actually mirrors consumers' free choices, and how well the market responds, therefore, to consumers' desires. See the symposium on "The Doctrine of Consumer Sovereignty," especially the paper by Tibor Scitovsky, in the *American Economic Review* for May, 1962. Then look at "The Costs of Automobile Model Changes Since 1949," by F. Fisher, Z. Griliches, and C. Kaysen, in the *Journal of Political Economy* for April, 1962. On the behavior of businessmen, see R. A. Gordon's classic *Business Leadership in the Large Corporation* (Univ. of California Press, 1966). Princeton's W. Baumol in *Business Behavior, Value and Growth* (Macmillan, 1967) (Chapters 4 and 6) challenges the profit-maximizing hypothesis of most economic analysis. Wisconsin's James Earley comes to the defense of marginalism in "Marginal Policies of 'Excellently Managed' Companies" (*American Economic Review*, March, 1956).

PART FOUR

THE DISTRIBUTION
OF INCOME

TWENTY-NINE

HOW INCOME IS DISTRIBUTED: THE PRICING OF PRODUCTIVE SERVICES

Who Gets the National Income?

The Theory of Income Distribution.

The Integration of Price and Distribution Theory.

Appendix: Production Theory, Price Theory, and Distribution Theory.

One of the hottest issues in economics has long been the distribution of the national income —between wages and profits, rich and poor, the farmer and the industrial worker, the "haves" and the "have-nots." Governments have risen and fallen on the struggle for income shares. The revolutionary doctrines of Karl Marx centered around the "exploitation of the worker" by the "rich and greedy capitalist." In a different setting, this same struggle over income shares is the issue when the United Steelworkers fight the steel companies for wage increases. It is the issue behind the race riots in the cities—and when Congress votes government support for "parity prices" on farm products. Over the centuries, history tells a recurrent story of the "have-nots" fighting for more and the "haves" struggling to protect and increase their share.

Thoughtful observers of the private-enterprise economy point out that we're all in the same boat. If everybody pulls together—labor, capital, management—total output will grow and all can have more. No one who understands the basic interdependence inherent in the modern economy would deny this. There is an enormous community of interest in making the private-enterprise economy work effectively.

But part and parcel of that community of interest is a basic conflict that is rooted deep in our ethics and traditions of self-interest and competition. This is the struggle of each individual to get more for himself and his family. It is the struggle over who gets how much of the economic pie—at the level of the individual worker, his union, and his boss, and at the level of national policy. However rich or poor the nation is, we're all interested in our own shares—relative and absolute. Nothing is gained by refusing to face this fact.

Individual self-interest is at the core of the American economic tradition. We look with favor on the man who works hard, earns a good income, and provides well for himself and his family. Self-earned wealth brings widespread esteem. The man who can't earn a good living is viewed with a touch of contempt, or with sympathy if there is an obvious reason beyond his own control. The "Protestant ethic" of work and reward is strong.

Yet Americans have agreed on limits to the financial success that should be permitted. Federal income tax rates in 1968 reached 50 per cent on income above about $50,000, and a peak rate of 70 per cent on income in excess of $200,000. Some government programs are expressly aimed at reducing income inequality—for example aid to the poor. We want the incentives and productivity of an individualistic, income-motivated economy. But we apparently don't want the extremes of inequality in income and power that are the consequence of all-out adherence to individual self-interest. And we face some tough problems in compromising these desires for maximum incentive and limited inequality.

The first half of this chapter summarizes briefly some of the major facts about the distribution of income. The second half then outlines the theory which helps to explain why different people get the incomes they do; the theory turns out to be essentially an application of the same supply-and-demand analysis that was developed in Part Three. Then the following chapters apply this theory to explaining wages and salaries, rents, interest, and, last but by no means least, the same profits that were the focus of much of Part Three.

WHO GETS
THE NATIONAL INCOME?

The Income Revolution

American incomes today are higher than ever before. Our standard of living is the highest in the world. Some economists have dubbed modern America "the affluent society."

Look at Fig. 29-1 for some of the facts. Since World War II, the real national income has more than doubled—from about $275 billion to $580 billion between 1947 and 1966, in 1966 prices. In 1947, median family income was about $4,100 in 1966 dollars; in 1966 it was $7,400.[1] In 1947, nearly one-third of all families had incomes under $3,000, while by 1966 this portion had fallen to 16 per cent. In 1947 nearly two-thirds of all families received less than $5,000, and only 11 per cent over $10,000. By 1966, 25 per cent of all families received over $10,000.

The extremes are striking in the 1966 data. Eight per cent of all families received less than $2,000, and together received less than 2 per cent of the national income. And at the other extreme, 9 per cent of all families received over $15,000, and together received about 25 per cent of the entire national income. But the most striking fact is the rise of the huge middle-income class. Sixty-three per cent of all families received between $5,000 and $15,000.

Figure 29-2 suggests an interesting question about this distribution of incomes in America. The regular, bell-shaped curve shows what statisticians call a "normal" distribution. Intelligence, physical traits, and a wide variety of other phenomena seem to approximate closely this type of normal distribution, when large numbers are considered. More people are at the mid-point of the curve than at any other level, and those above and below the average shade off about equally either way.

We might assume that general ability is something like normally distributed in the total population. But incomes received, shown by the solid line, are "skewed." That is, there are many poor and relatively low-income individuals. These account for the big hump in the curve toward the lower-income end of the scale. There are a few very rich, who give the curve a long "tail" out to the right. Questions: Are incomes less "normally" distributed than human abilities? If so, why? Do differing economic opportunities for rich and poor explain the continuing skewedness of the income curve? Is it because some people work

[1] The median is the figure that divides the total number of families in half. Thus, in 1966 half of all families received over $7,400, half less.

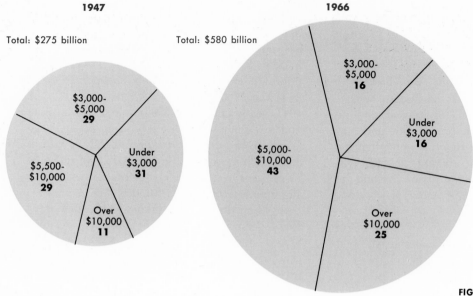

1947

Total: $275 billion

$3,000-
$5,000
29

$5,500-
$10,000
29

Under
$3,000
31

Over
$10,000
11

1966

Total: $580 billion

$3,000-
$5,000
16

Under
$3,000
16

$5,000-
$10,000
43

Over
$10,000
25

FIG. 29-1 Total real income has doubled in the last two decades. More than two-thirds now goes to families receiving over $5,000, compared to only 40 per cent in 1947. (Source: U.S. Department of Commerce.)

harder than others? Because some do more useful work than others? Why?

One last historical observation: Are the very rich—the millionaires—being squeezed out by high income- and inheritance-tax rates? Apparently not. By 1966 there were apparently some 50,000 millionaires in the nation, compared to only a few hundred in the 1920's, and in 1966 about 700 people had annual incomes exceeding $1 million. But the share of total wealth held by the top ½ of 1 per cent of all families was estimated at just under 30 per cent in 1966, compared to 36 per cent in 1929.

Occupational and Educational Differences

What jobs provide the best incomes? Table 29-1 provides part of the answer. It shows median incomes for a sample of occupations, as reported by the Census Bureau for 1966.

The table speaks for itself, but there are some surprises. The median figures for managers and proprietors don't look like the huge salaries you've heard about for corporation presidents. *Answer*: there are very few huge salaries. Nor does the figure for self-employed proprietors look as if many people in business for themselves get rich quick. On the average they do better than most workers, not as well as doctors, lawyers, engineers, and such professionals. At the bottom of the list, it's clear that farmers and unskilled la-

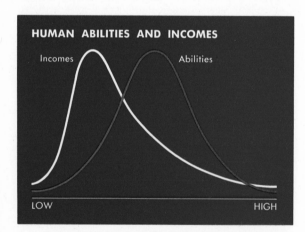

HUMAN ABILITIES AND INCOMES

Incomes

Abilities

LOW

HIGH

FIG. 29-2 Ability and most other human characteristics seem to be "normally" distributed through the population, as shown by the regular bell-shaped curve. Incomes are much more unequally distributed. Why?

TABLE 29-1

MEDIAN INCOMES OF FULL-TIME WORKERS IN DIFFERENT OCCUPATIONS IN 1966 *

Professional and technical (lawyers, doctors, engineers, etc.):	
Self-employed	$12,400
Salaried	10,200
Managers and proprietors (except farm):	
Self-employed	8,100
Salaried	10,900
Salesmen	8,900
Craftsmen, foremen, etc.	8,300
Clerical and related workers	7,700
Operatives and related workers	7,200
Service workers (except household)	6,200
Business and industrial laborers	5,600
Farmers	4,300
Farm laborers	3,200
Private household workers	2,600
Average for all workers (excluding unemployed, part-time, and armed services)	7,900

* Preliminary data from U.S. Census Bureau.

TABLE 29-2

ESTIMATED LIFETIME EARNINGS IN DIFFERENT OCCUPATIONS *

Doctors	$717,000
Lawyers	621,000
Managers and proprietors (nonfarm)	593,000
Dentists	589,000
Economists	413,000
Aeronautical engineers	395,000
Accountants	313,000
High school teachers	261,000
Electricians	251,000
Plumbers	236,000
TV mechanics	183,000
Clergymen	175,000

* From Herman Miller, *Rich Man, Poor Man* (New York: Thomas Crowell, 1964). In 1962 prices.

borers in all occupations don't do very well income-wise.

Table 29-2 presents a more detailed breakdown for a sample of occupations. The figures are *estimates* of lifetime (age 18-64) earnings in 1962 dollars, based on Census Bureau data. Note the high correlation between the amount of education and probable lifetime earnings, even when the long years of no-income schooling for professionals are figured in. The education figures show up directly, apart from the occupational break. In 1966, for example, the median income for all heads of families with eighth grade education or less was about $4,900. That for family heads with college degrees was about $10,300, and the figure rises steadily with the number of years of schooling.

Regional income differences reflect these occupational and educational facts. The high incomes are concentrated in the urban areas, where high-income occupations are centered. Incomes are generally low in the south, especially in the rural areas. Per capita incomes in the Deep South are still around the New York levels of a half-century ago. But the South is pulling up. New England, the traditional high-income area, is slipping relatively. And the West Coast is rising rapidly.

The average income of working women is about half that for working men. Women generally get less pay than do men for similar jobs. But more than that, the difference reflects the heavy concentration of women in low-pay jobs—especially clerical and service work, and unskilled labor. More women are now showing up in higher-paid occupations—the professions, skilled labor, and middle management. But most peak-income doors are still closed to them.

Older workers are another special group whose incomes are generally below average. For the highly skilled occupations—management, law, medicine—a man's earning power rises steadily until he reaches 50 or 60. But for the commonplace jobs this is not true. Workers past 40 find it hard to get new jobs, and often must move down the income ladder if they have to find another job. Unskilled laborers find the best-paying jobs in their 20's, or at the latest in their 30's.

Lastly, Negroes and other minority groups generally have low incomes. The median income for white families in 1966 was about $7,400, that for non-whites about $4,200. Negroes consistently seem to earn only about 50 to 60 per cent as much as do whites. Less than 15 per cent of all

Negro families have incomes as high as the national median. Available data for other minority groups are inadequate to justify national estimates, but evidence points clearly to the poverty of Mexican, Puerto Rican, Asiatic, and other unassimilated groups in the United States. Look at the slums of a big city. The issue of discrimination has rocked the nation in the last few years, and measures to decrease discrimination against these groups have made headway, especially in periods of high employment and labor shortages. But the Negro or "foreigner" is still generally the last to be taken on and the first to be laid off; and most of the best-paying jobs still are, for practical purposes, closed to these minority groups. Many of these income differentials go back to differences in educational opportunities.

Wages and Profits—
Functional Shares

The American economy today doesn't look much like Karl Marx's picture of capitalism in its death throes, with the workers poised to seize ownership of the means of production. American labor and management exchange some violent words, and strikes are sometimes long and bitter. But the evidence is overwhelming that American workers want a basically capitalistic, free-enterprise system. In the showdown, management and labor get together; production goes on with the worker's rights pretty well looked out for and the capitalist's control over his investment substantially maintained. When the workers go to the polls, they vote Republican or Democratic, not Communist.

But within this framework, labor and management wrestle constantly over the division of the consumer's dollar between wages and profits. In the big-union industries, this argument comes to a boil every two or three years, when the union's wage contract comes up for renewal. In nonunionized industries, the struggle is less sharply focused, and wages appear to follow the unionized leaders, such as in automobiles, steel, and coal.

Figure 29-3 gives an over-all picture of the outcome of this wage-profit bargaining over the last four decades. The left-hand part of the figure plots the actual dollar shares of national income that go to wages and salaries, corporate profits, unincorporated business incomes (a mixture of salaries and profits), rents, and interest, all before payment of income taxes. The right-hand portion shows the percentage shares that go to these various groups.

The first lesson comes from the left-hand

FIG. 29-3 Everyone's income has grown since 1929, but wages and salaries by far the biggest amount. They have also gradually increased their share of the total. Profits vanished in the great depression but have soared since then. (Source: U.S. Department of Commerce.)

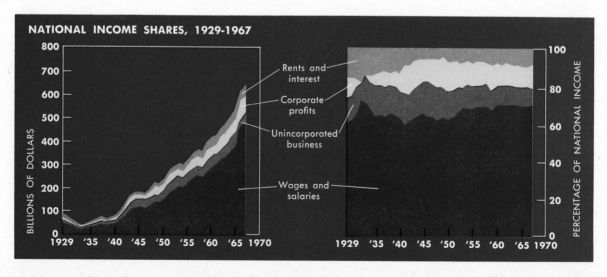

chart. Everybody's income has grown rapidly, but in a serious depression everyone takes a beating. We're very much all in the same boat. The second lesson, from the right-hand chart, is the general stability in the major income shares except in big business fluctuations. The wage and salary share has persistently hovered in the 60–70 per cent range, although it has shown a slight long-term upward trend. In the late 1920's it was around 60 per cent of the total. By the 1960's, another prosperous period, it was nearer 70 per cent. Actually, the wage increase came mainly in two quite different periods—during the depression of the 1930's when profits vanished, and during the later 1950's when wages rose faster than profits despite generally good times. Partly, the rising wage share reflects the steady population shift from farms to urban jobs.

A rather different picture of the outcome of the labor-capital struggle for income shares is given by the bottom half of Fig. 16-2, back on page 210. If we compare the return *per unit* of labor and capital used in the economy since 1900, real wages per hour are nearly five times as high as in 1900, while the long-term interest rate (a crude measure of the return per dollar of capital invested in the economy) is about the same as it was then. Looked at this way, it appears that virtually all the fruits of increased output have gone to labor and virtually none to capital.

How are these different ways of looking at the same world to be reconciled? The answer is back in Chapters 15 and 16 on economic growth. The total capital stock has grown much faster than the labor force. (1) Thus, the law of diminishing returns has acted to diminish the return per unit of capital relative to that per unit of labor. (2) But steadily improving technology has helped increase total output far faster than the combined inputs of labor and capital, so diminishing returns have not reduced the return per unit of capital, merely kept it from rising with technological advance. (3) The relatively stable total shares of labor and capital in the total g.n.p. thus reflect the rapid growth in income per unit of labor, and a correspondingly faster growth in the capital stock than in the labor force, with the two factors just about offsetting each other to

keep the labor and capital shares in g.n.p. roughly unchanged. The data are shown back in Fig. 16-2.

THE THEORY OF INCOME DISTRIBUTION

Why do people receive the incomes they do —some large, some small; some stable, some insecure? The answer is complex, as with most other important issues in economics, and there is still much debate among economists on the finer points. But the core of the answer was laid out back in Chapter 24. In competitive markets, the prices of productive services (e.g., wages) are set through supply and demand so as to roughly equal the marginal productivity of the productive resource (e.g., labor). Whenever the price of, say, labor is below its marginal product (what one more worker would add to the firm's saleable output), businessmen can increase their profits by hiring more labor. Competition among businesses for workers will bid up the wage rate toward the marginal productivity of that type of labor. Conversely, if the wage rate is more than labor's marginal product, it will pay businessmen to hire fewer workers, and the wage rate will fall. Only when the wage rate just equals labor's marginal product will business firms and the labor market be in equilibrium.

"Distribution theory," explaining why different productive resources earn the incomes they do, is thus merely price theory from Part Three, viewed from a different angle. Here we focus on the pricing of productive services, like labor; there we focused on the pricing of final products, like autos. But obviously, when the businessman decides to produce 10,000 autos this week, he is *ipso facto* deciding to hire the labor and rent or buy the machines needed to do the job. In distribution theory, we consider the decision in terms of how many workers and machines the businessman will demand. When we compare this demand with the supply of labor or machines offered, we can determine the price set for productive services through the same supply and demand mechanism as in Part Three. Obviously, the degree of competition or monopoly in the market will affect the outcome.

The remainder of this chapter lays out a supply and demand framework for explaining the incomes received by owners of productive resources—labor, land, capital. The following chapters then apply this central theory to explain wages, rents, and profits in a variety of real-world circumstances.

Incomes Are Payments
for Productive Services

Most incomes are received as payments for productive services. Wages and salaries are payments for labor services. Rents are payments for services of land and buildings. Interest is payment for the use of money, but more fundamentally for the real productive services which the money will buy. Economic profits are the residual for businessmen and risk-takers that's left over after all the other income payments are made out of business's receipts—and they're also the incentive to entrepreneurs that makes the private-enterprise system go.

Thus, most incomes are based directly on the prices received for productive services. Like others, these prices are determined by supply and demand. The following paragraphs map out a simple supply-and-demand model for analyzing productive service markets.

The Supply Side

First, we need a supply curve, or schedule. Look at the supply of some given type of labor in your community as an example. The supply of such labor this month may be highly inelastic—fixed by the number of workers there and by their strong preference to work about 40 hours a week. Or the supply may be elastic, if comparable workers can readily be drawn in from neighboring areas. Or overtime work may be feasible. Or maybe unskilled workers can be easily upgraded. Another source of elasticity may be school children and retired old people, if the job is relatively unskilled. All these things together produce a labor supply curve for the market for the time period under study, probably an upward-sloping supply curve indicating that more labor hours will be supplied at higher than at lower wage rates.

The Demand Side [2]

Next, we need a demand curve. The demand for productive services is primarily a *derived demand*. The local drugstore hires clerks because customers want clerks to wait on them—not because the druggist wants clerks in the same way he wants shirts, bread, and the other consumer goods he buys. Businesses' demands for productive services thus reflect ultimate consumer demands. If consumers want lots of Coke and ice cream, the demand for drugstore clerks will be strong. But if the customers stay away, the druggist doesn't need many clerks.

How many workers will a firm demand at any given wage rate? *If it is out to maximize profits, it will hire additional workers as long as each additional worker adds more to the firm's income than he adds to its costs. If the wage the firm has to pay for another worker is more than what that worker adds to income, to hire him would lower the firm's profits. Workers' contributions to the firms' profits will be maximized, therefore, when workers are hired just up to the point where the additional income equals the additional cost for the last worker taken on—no more workers and no fewer.*

The additional income obtained by hiring one additional worker and selling the output he adds is called the "marginal revenue product" (or sometimes the "marginal value product," and sometimes simply "marginal product"). Additional *physical* output ("marginal physical product") is what the worker adds to total output. But from management's point of view it is the increase in sales dollars that matters most; hence, it is the marginal *revenue* product in which we are most interested. It is the marginal revenue product that the businessman compares with the additional cost incurred by hiring another worker in deciding how many workers to hire to maximize his profits. To summarize, the marginal revenue product of any type of productive service sets the

[2] The Appendix to Chapter 22, "Physical Production Relationships Underlying Cost Curves," provides a rigorous logical foundation for this section. If you studied that Appendix it may be useful to review it before proceeding. The "marginal product" of that Appendix is identical with the "marginal *physical* product" of this chapter.

upper limit that a business will ordinarily pay for that service; and businesses will have an incentive to hire more productive services as long as the wage paid to each is less than its marginal productivity.[3]

Remember the process by which firms maximized profits through equating marginal cost and marginal revenue back in Chapter 23. It should be clear that the firm's decision on how much labor to hire at any wage so as to maximize profits is precisely the same process. The only difference is that here the marginal-cost–marginal-revenue comparison is made in terms of additional workers hired, whereas in Chapter 23 it was in terms of additional units of output produced. The logic of increasing output (hiring more resources) as long as the marginal cost involved is less than the marginal revenue obtained, is identical in both cases; and the equilibrium level of output (of resources hired) will obviously be the same either way the firm analyzes the decision. Looking at the number of productive resources hired is looking at the output decision from the reverse side, so to speak.[4]

It is important to note that, generally, the demand curve for any productive resource will be downward sloping. It will pay to hire fewer workers at a high than at a low wage.[5]

[3] The existence of monopoly raises some special problems, which will be considered in the next chapter.

[4] Although the above statements indicate only how much of one single resource it will pay the business to hire, this approach can readily be generalized to cover all productive resources the firm hires. It will pay to hire more of *each* resource as long as the additional cost involved is less than the revenue added (in technical terms, as long as its marginal cost is less than its marginal revenue productivity). In equilibrium, therefore, each resource will be hired up to the point where its marginal cost just equals its marginal revenue product, which is the same as saying that marginal cost equals marginal revenue for the firm as a whole, the profit-maximizing condition stated in Chapter 23. (For a more complete statement, see the Appendix to this chapter.)

[5] This seems obvious. But to demonstrate it rigorously, we need to invoke the law of diminishing returns again. The firm's demand for workers rests directly on the workers' marginal revenue productivity. If more workers are hired, their marginal value product will fall as the ratio of workers to other factors of production rises. This is *both* because marginal physical product declines *and* because the price of the final output will drop as more units are put on the market with unchanged market demand. The same is true for land, machinery, or any other productive service.

The Interaction of Supply and Demand

We now have the broad outlines of the market for productive services. We have a supply curve and a demand curve for each type of productive service in each market area, local or national. Deriving the supply curve of labor in our local area is, as we saw above, easy in principle though complex in practice. On the demand side, the marginal *physical* productivity of any type of labor in any job will be determined by its background and skills, by the equipment it has to work with, and by how many workers there are in relation to the machinery and other capital equipment available. The marginal *revenue* productivity will be determined by adding on consumer demand for the ultimate product. Marginal revenue productivity will fall as more labor is hired, other things equal; that is, the demand curve for each productive service will slope downward. As long as the wage is lower than labor's marginal revenue productivity, business will compete for labor. *This competition will bid wages up to about the level of labor's marginal productivity, and no higher. And so the wage will be set.*

Figure 29-4 pictures a simple supply-and-demand market equilibrium for one type of labor in a local market this week. The supply curve is

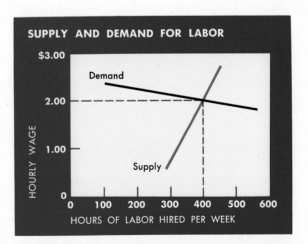

FIG. 29-4   Wages, like other prices, are determined by the interaction of supply and demand forces. Here the equilibrium wage is $2.00 an hour, with employers hiring 400 hours per week.

inelastic; in one week not many more labor hours will be supplied at moderately higher wage rates. The demand curve slopes down for the reasons suggested above. A wage of $2 per hour just clears the market, at 400 hours of labor per week demanded and supplied. At a higher wage more would be supplied but less demanded; at a lower wage, the reverse.

The following chapters use the basic analytical framework just suggested to look briefly at wages and the other major income shares. In a sense, the next chapter on wages and salaries is a case study, indicating the kind of analysis needed to explain the price of any productive service.

THE INTEGRATION OF PRICE AND DISTRIBUTION THEORY

The preceding section emphasized that price theory and distribution theory (Parts Three and Four of this book) are substantially the same. They both look at the pricing process and at the allocation of resources in response to consumer demands. But price theory focuses on consumer demand for final products, as businessmen strive to maximize profits by meeting those demands. Distribution theory looks at the same process, but focuses on its implications for the incomes received by owners of productive resources (labor, land and capital). It is very important to see this close integration between price and distribution theory in understanding how a private-enterprise, market economy works.

To see how the integrated system fits together, *go back and reread the section "General Equilibrium of a Competitive Economy" on pages 329–331 in Chaper 24. They are the core of this chapter as well.* The pricing of productive services is part and parcel of the general equilibrium pricing process. The costs paid out by business firms *are* the incomes received by the factors of production. Thus, the profit-maximizing decisions of businessmen simultaneously provide the goods most desired by consumers at the lowest feasible prices *and* provide to resource owners the largest incomes that are consistent with their abilities and willingness to contribute to producing what consumers want. The whole system relies on each individual (worker, capitalist, consumer, businessman) to look out for his own self-interest; it relies on competition in all markets to see that the end result is in the best interest of all. Adam Smith's invisible hand of self-interest and competition is a powerful mechanism for the compromise of millions of conflicting individual goals. We are ready now to go on and investigate some important real-world cases, beginning with wages and salaries.[6]

[6] Mathematically inclined readers are referred to Mathematical Appendix IV at the end of the book, where the preceding theory of income distribution (factor pricing) is stated rigorously and some of its interconnections with the macro explanations of relative income shares are explored.

REVIEW

Concepts To Remember

Check your understanding of the following new concepts introduced in this chapter. You ought to be able to relate them directly back to Part Three, especially to the various cost and demand concepts there.

derived demand

marginal physical product

marginal revenue product

marginal value product

distribution theory

For Analysis and Discussion

1. The two biggest shares of the national income are wages and profits. Are the basic interests of wage-earners and of their employers competitive or complementary?
2. Explain carefully how incomes are distributed in a highly competitive, market-type economy.

3. Are most people's incomes a good measure of what they are worth?
4. Would a distribution of income based purely on marginal productivity give everyone about what he is worth? Explain.
5. Would the equalization of incomes in the United States, as is proposed by some socialists, solve the problem of poverty? Use the figures on national income (in Chapter 4) and those on income distribution in this chapter, insofar as you think they are relevant, to support your answer.
6. According to Table 29-1, farmers and unskilled laborers have made substantially lower incomes than have the other groups shown. If this is so, why do people continue to become farmers and unskilled laborers?
7. "The distribution of incomes to factors of production is no problem to one who has studied the behavior of business firms. In determining what prices to charge and what output to produce, the firm simultaneously determines how many workers to hire and what wages to pay out, what rents and interest charges to incur, and so on for the other income shares." Can you show how your analysis of Part Three just preceding, has in effect explained the distribution of incomes?

Appendix

PRODUCTION THEORY, PRICE THEORY, AND DISTRIBUTION THEORY

This Appendix provides (for those who studied Chapter 23) a more rigorous statement of what economists call the theory of production and the way in which it underlies price theory and distribution theory.

The Theory of Production. The theory of production is concerned with the physical relationship between the factors of production used (input) and the product produced (output). The central principle is the law of diminishing returns, or of variable proportions. This law states (Appendix to Chapter 22) that as the proportion of one input to other inputs rises, the additional units of output per unit of that input may rise at first, but will sooner or later begin to fall, and fall persistently thereafter (other things, such as technology, being unchanged).[7]

Since the law of diminishing returns applies to each productive factor as more of it is used relative to others, it constitutes a powerful analytical tool for deciding the optimal proportions among factors of production if we want to obtain the most efficient, or least-cost, production of any commodity. As more of each factor is added relative to the others, its marginal physical product will decline. To obtain the

minimum cost of production for any given output, we should add more of each productive factor until the last (marginal) dollar spent on each provides the same addition to total output—that is, the same marginal physical product. This is so because under any other condition more physical product could be obtained for the same cost by switching a dollar from a lesser contributing factor of production to a higher contributing factor. Thus, in equilibrium:

$$\frac{\text{Marginal physical product of A}}{\text{Price of A}} =$$
$$\frac{\text{Marginal physical product of B}}{\text{Price of B}}, \text{etc.}$$

Another (equivalent) way of saying the same thing is that in the least-cost condition the marginal physical products of the factors of production must be proportional to their prices. That is:

$$\frac{\text{Marginal physical product of A}}{\text{Marginal physical product of B}} = \frac{\text{Price of A}}{\text{Price of B}}, \text{etc.}$$

This proposition implicitly underlies the discussion of the unit-cost curves back in Chapters 22 and 23. The U-shape of the firm's cost curve derives in part from the physical relationships described by the law of variable proportions. Most important, assuming the prices of factors of production to be given, the minimum-cost point on the firm's unit-cost curve can be achieved only when the factors of production are used in the proportions indicated above.

---

[7] A more complete analysis of these relationships may be found in most economic theory textbooks. See, for example, M. J. Bowman and G. L. Bach, *Economic Analysis and Public Policy* (Englewood Cliffs, N.J.: Prentice-Hall, 1949), Chapters 18 and 19.

This theory of production also provides the answer to how a change in the price of any factor will affect its use. If the price of one resource (say, labor) falls, its use will be increased until its marginal physical product falls to the same proportion with other marginal physical products as the new proportion among the factor prices concerned. In other words, more labor will be hired until the marginal dollar spent on labor again produces the same marginal product as when spent on any other factor of production. Hiring more labor becomes desirable even though this reduces labor's marginal physical product under the law of diminishing returns.

Maximum-Profit Positions in Price Theory and Distribution Theory. The statement of the least-cost conditions above does not necessarily specify the maximum-profit position of the firm. It only specifies the conditions for obtaining the least-cost production for any given production level. The condition for maximum-profit (or minimum-loss) production is to increase production as long as marginal cost is less than marginal revenue (up to $mc = mr$). This is identical with the proposition that maximum profit (or minimum loss) will be obtained by adding units of each factor of production as long as its marginal cost (price, under competitive conditions) is less than its marginal *revenue* product. Each proposition follows because as long as spending another dollar on costs adds more to total revenue than it does to total cost, total profit must be increased. The statement in terms of individual factors of production merely specifies in more detail the *mix* of productive factors that must be used in arriving at the maximum-profit position. The $mc = mr$ proposition of earlier chapters is silent on the optimal factor combination; it implicitly takes the optimal combination for granted. We can now add the proposition that for maximum profit the marginal cost of each factor used must be equal to its marginal revenue product and that the marginal costs of all the factors used must be proportional to their marginal revenue products:

$$\frac{\text{Marginal cost of factor A}}{\text{Marginal cost of factor B}} = \frac{\text{Marginal revenue productivity of A}}{\text{Marginal revenue productivity of B}}.$$

Or, to put it another way, that

$$\frac{\text{Marginal cost of A}}{\text{Marginal revenue productivity of A}} = \frac{\text{Marginal cost of B}}{\text{Marginal revenue productivity of B}}.$$

THIRTY

WAGES AND SALARIES: APPLYING THE THEORY

Wages in Competitive Markets.

Does Demand Reqlly Depend
on Marginal Revenue Productivity?

Supply, Demand, and Purely Competitive Wages.

Wage Determination in Monopolized Industries.

Wage Determination under Employer Monopsony.

Wage Determination under Bilateral Monopoly.

Wage and Salary Differentials.

Wages and Technological Advance.

Wages and salaries account for over two-thirds of the total national income, and for all of most people's incomes. By the same token, wages and salaries constitute around two-thirds of total business costs. So it is not surprising that people, ever since they began to write about economics, have been spinning out theories to explain why wages are what they are.

Economists' theories mirror the times in which they live, and over the last two centuries we have passed through at least three different widely-accepted theories of wage determination. Today, we do not yet have a fully satisfactory theory of wages. Yet most economists agree that the simple marginal-productivity, supply-and-demand theory stated in the last half of Chapter 29 is a fruitful way to understand why individual wages are what they are. This chapter is primarily an application of that theory to explain why different people get the wages and salaries they do.

Some Dubious Theories

But first let us turn briefly to two theories of wages that attained widespread acceptance during the last century, and that still have considerable influence in day-to-day thinking, even though economists consider them largely fallacious.

The Subsistence Theory. Chapter 15 outlined Malthus' subsistence theory of wages, sometimes also called the "Iron Law of Wages" because of the inescapable hard fate it predicted. In essence, Malthus said that population will always tend to outrun the means of subsistence. Thus, the growing supply of labor will tend always to force wages down toward the subsistence level.

Wages cannot permanently stay below the subsistence level, for obvious reasons. But they will not for long stay above it in the absence of artificial means to limit the rate of population growth. Karl Marx accepted much of the theory and predicted the downfall of capitalism, as workers become increasingly unwilling to accept their menial existence while capitalists appropriate the "surplus value" created by the workers whose wages fall increasingly short of the total value they create.

But history has shown an escape from this bitter prospect. In most Western industralized nations, technological advance and capital accumulation have saved us from Malthus and Marx. In fact, real wages have risen rapidly and (except for cyclical fluctuations) steadily over the past century. Moreover, in the nations with the highest living standards, birth rates have fallen below the rates in less advanced countries.

But we must not write off Malthus too fast. Even with modern technology and capital accumulation in the West, for well over half the world's population in the underdeveloped nations, Malthus' predictions on wages look perilously close to being right. Total output has grown in most nations, but for over half the world's population little faster than the number of mouths to feed, and starvation looms on the horizon each bad crop year.

The Lump-of-Labor Theory. Another widely held, but almost completely fallacious, theory is that there is some fixed amount of work to be done in the short run, so more people seeking work will merely bid wages down and steal jobs from those already at work. This theory, often unarticulated, lies behind widespread opposition to letting new workers into the labor market— foreigners, women, new apprentices, etc. It lies behind union restrictions on entry to many occupations. Most importantly, it lies behind widespread resistance to "automation"—to the introduction of machines which appear to replace human beings.

What is the fallacy in this lump-of-labor theory? The answer should be clear from Parts Two and Three. With proper policies to regulate aggregate demand, total money demand can always be expanded to match growing potential output. There can always be enough demand to provide jobs for as many workers as enter the labor market. At the level of the individual industry, the demand for labor is a function of the marginal productivity of that labor. Labor willing to work at a wage at or below its marginal productivity can always be employed profitably. The total amount of labor which will be hired is thus a function of both ultimate demand and the price (wage) of the labor. There is no fixed amount of work to be divided up that is independent of the number of workers seeking jobs and of the wage at which they will work.

But to point out the fallacy in lump-of-labor thinking is not to provide a satisfactory explanation of what does set wages. We need a theory that will encompass the cases where Malthus appears to be right, those where "automation" occurs, and those where new workers enter the labor market. In short, we need a more general theory of wages.

WAGES IN COMPETITIVE MARKETS

What will your income be the year after you graduate? Five years later? Will you be a salesman, an accountant, an engineer, a secretary? Would the factors governing the answer be different for a factory worker?

Basically, your salary will be set by the forces of supply and demand in the market you enter— for beginning engineers, accountants, or secretaries, wherever you go to work. And the forces of competition on the demand side of the market will bid that salary up to roughly your marginal productivity—to roughly what you are "worth" economically to the firms hiring beginners like you. They won't pay you more, and if there is active competition in hiring, you need not take less. This is what the modern theory of wage determination says, and you can see that it will serve equally well to explain the wages received under a wide variety of conditions in any market economy.

Figure 30-1 shows the close correspondence between average output per man hour and real wages in the American economy since 1900. *Although this doesn't show the path of marginal productivity, it does suggest a basic fact: it is rising productivity that has made possible the steadily rising wages of American workers. Even though there are many more workers seeking jobs now than in 1900, their average productivity is so much higher that businesses demand the larger number, and at higher wages as well.*

But before we look at the application of our theory in more detail, two preliminary warnings. First, there are nearly 80 million people in the American labor force, and in some respects, every one of them is unique. No two people are exactly alike. Thus, it is meaningless to talk of "labor" and "wages" as if they were homogeneous. We need to look separately at many different types of labor, at people with different capacities, different education and training, different attitudes, living in different places. On the other hand, unless we lump individuals into different types of labor in different market areas, we're left with the job of looking separately at 80 million individuals. So we do group workers together where they are similar and in the same area. We can talk meaningfully of different types of labor in different areas, even though no two individuals in any type are identical and even though people are continually shifting from one type and location to another.

Second, in this chapter, we shall be looking at the determinants of individual wages, or wages of particular groups of workers, in contrast to the macro issues of wage-profit shares in the national income and the relationship of wage levels to total g.n.p. *Thus, this is a chapter mainly at the micro level. It takes the levels of aggregate spending and aggregate demand for labor as given, determined by the forces described back in Part 2. Later on, we shall drop this simplifying assumption.*

Begin with a relatively simple case. What determines the wage received by Willie Welder, a hypothetical laborer who works for the Acme Plumbing Company, a small plumbing-fixtures manufacturer. There is no welders' union in the area. Willie's abilities are substantially undifferentiated from those of many other welders. There are many businesses and construction contractors in the area who hire welders. And there are many

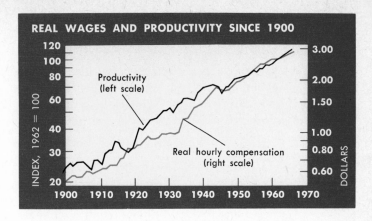

FIG. 30-1 Rising productivity has made possible the steadily rising real wages of American workers. (Source: Council of Economic Advisers.)

plumbing-supplies manufacturers in the United States who compete actively with each other in the product market. So there is active competition at three levels—among welders for jobs, among businesses for the services of welders, and among businesses for the consumer's sales dollar.

What determines Willies' wage? His boss sets the wage he pays, so we might ask him. He'd probably have a simple answer. Willie gets the going hourly rate for welders—say, $3 an hour. Acme Plumbing doesn't haggle over wage rates with each man it hires. It pays the going rate.

Something beyond Acme determines the "going rate" for welders in the area. By now, the answer "supply and demand" ought to come easily to you as the framework for looking at this price.

The Supply Side

What determines the supply of welders in the area? In any real-world case we could write a book on the subject, but the essential points would probably boil down to these:

Number of Welders in the Area. Welding is a skilled trade. There are only so many people in the area who qualify as skilled welders at any given time.

Availability of Additional Welders. The existing group of welders might be expanded either by training new welders or by bringing in men from other areas. If a small increase in the wage rate draws welders into the area and draws new recruits into the three-month training programs required to pick up the minimal skills, the supply of welders will be elastic. But if welders are immobile and the field doesn't look attractive, the supply will be inelastic. The elasticity of supply will thus depend on the desirability of the job and labor's mobility into it.

Hours of Work per Welder. For the most part, welders either put in the work-week stated by their employer or they don't get the job. But there is some flexibility in the number of hours worked per week.

Elasticity of Supply Dependent on Time Period. On any given day, the supply of welders in our area is pretty much fixed. But given six months, training new welders becomes a practical possibility. In most cases, supply becomes increasingly elastic as a longer time period is considered. But in the professions and management, many years rather than a few months are required for big increases in supply. A doctor goes through about 10 years of college, medical school, and internship before he's ready to go out on his own.

The Demand Side

The demand for welders' services is a derived demand, derived from the ultimate consumer demand for the plumbing fixtures Acme produces. Acme (and other businesses) will demand more welders whenever they have unfulfilled demand for their product at profitable prices. More precisely, Acme will demand more welders as long as the wage is below welders' marginal revenue productivity to it. Other firms will do likewise. By aggregating the demands of all firms, we could draw a demand curve for welders' services at any time. Since welders' productivity may be different in different firms, some firms' demand will drop off rapidly as the wage rate rises; others' will drop off only slowly.

If the marginal revenue productivity of welders underlies employers' demand for welders, we need to look at the underlying determinants of marginal revenue productivity. Remember, m.r.p. is compounded of marginal physical productivity and a product price factor, though they may be hard to separate in some cases—for example, in engineering and selling.

Marginal Physical Productivity. Willie the welder's marginal physical product is the addi-

tional physical product Acme Plumbing turns out by having Willie on the job, compared with the output without him, all other productive factors being identical in both cases. This marginal physical product depends on Willie's own mental and physical abilities, training, morale, and so on. It also depends, probably even more, on the other productive agents with which he works. With an old-style welding torch and poor working conditions, Willie will have a low marginal physical product. If he is well equipped and works on a well-designed, balanced production line, his marginal physical product will be higher.[1]

Marginal Revenue Productivity. The production manager is interested mainly in how many sinks get turned out in a day. But the president and the stockholders are more interested in the profit figures—in dollars and cents rather than in numbers of sinks and faucets. For top-management purposes, physical productivity figures have to be converted into *sales-dollar terms.*

Willie's marginal revenue productivity is the additional sales dollars brought in by employing him. If his marginal physical product is one sink per day, and the wholesale price of sinks is $30, then Willie's marginal revenue productivity at Acme Plumbing, with the existing number of welders, is $30. Marginal revenue productivity is found by multiplying the marginal physical product by marginal revenue (price under pure competition). Consumer demand for the ultimate product is just as important as the worker's physical output in determining his value to the business.

The marginal revenue productivity of welders will eventually decrease as more welders

---

[1] A worker's marginal physical product depends on the *proportion* of workers to other productive agents, as well as on the quality of the machinery and tools he works with. For example, if welding is one operation on a metal-sink production line, the addition of the first welder to that line means a big increase in the firm's output. Addition of a second and third welder may skyrocket output further, until the line is roughly balanced between welders and other workmen. Beyond this point, adding more welders may increase output somewhat by speeding up the line or by having a spare welder around to spell anyone who takes a coffee break, but the additional (marginal) product is much lower than it was when the first few welders were added. This is the law of diminishing returns again. It means that adding more workers in any plant will sooner or later mean a declining marginal physical product for those workers, assuming the size of the plant and the combination of other productive agents remain unchanged.

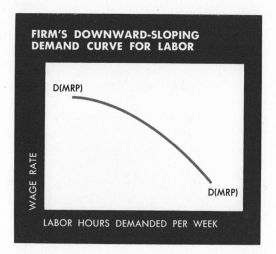

FIRM'S DOWNWARD-SLOPING DEMAND CURVE FOR LABOR

D(MRP)

WAGE RATE

D(MRP)

LABOR HOURS DEMANDED PER WEEK

FIG. 30-2 The competitive firm's demand curve for labor is downward-sloping. The demand curve is labor's marginal revenue product in the firm, since it will pay to hire more workers as long as marginal revenue product is more than the wage.

only a few employees, the boss may have a good idea of how much his daily output will go up if he puts on an extra man. And he knows the price of sinks. This was the kind of situation economists had in mind when they developed the marginal-productivity approach to explaining the demand for labor.

But what about the marginal revenue productivity of a welder like Willie in U.S. Steel? U.S. Steel has nearly 300,000 employees scattered over the United States, with hundreds of welders among them. Welders work on jobs many steps removed from the ultimate steel products sold to the company's customers. For example, one welder may do repair work on the company's railway cars that shuttle materials around the mills. What is his marginal productivity?

Obviously, no one knows. It would be impossible to isolate the effect on the ultimate production of cold-rolled steel sheets of laying off that one welder. And there are millions of workers in American industry who present similar problems in estimating marginal productivity.

Still, somehow U.S. Steel has to decide how many welders it will hire. Company officials might tell you it's simple. They hire enough welders to get the steel produced for which they have orders. But this answer, which is probably quite correct, drives us back to the question of the price at which U.S. Steel will book orders. Clearly, this decision depends in large part on the costs estimated by the steel people for producing steel sheets. Somehow all these interrelated variables have to be put together, and somehow the hiring officials down at the plant level have to decide when it will pay to hire another welder.

Where does all this leave us? First, it's clear that no very precise estimate of marginal physical productivity is possible in many cases. Second, hard as the estimating job is, businessmen have to make some such calculation (consciously or subconsciously) in their hiring decisions if they are intelligently trying to maximize profits. Third, in many cases several types of labor must be hired as a group to operate as a production unit. You either have the people it takes to run a modern assembly line, or you just shut the line down. In this common type of situation, it is very difficult to separate out the marginal physical product of each kind of laborer.

are put to work producing sinks, for two reasons. First, the law of diminishing returns will bring decreasing marginal physical productivity as the ratio of welders to other factors of production increases (see footnote 1). Second, as more sinks are produced by this and competing firms, their price will fall, consumer demand remaining unchanged—although Acme alone is too small to influence market price. Thus, the demand curve for workers will generally be downward-sloping, as in Fig. 30-2. Starting from any equilibrium position, firms will hire more labor only as wage rates fall, given an unchanged demand for sinks. In effect, the marginal-revenue-product curve for welders in the firm is that firm's demand curve for welders.[2]

DOES DEMAND REALLY DEPEND ON MARGINAL REVENUE PRODUCTIVITY?

How can businessmen ever estimate anything so complex as a worker's marginal revenue productivity?

In a little firm like Acme Plumbing, with

[2] Note that if firms are prepared to increase the amount of other resources with which welders work (for example, the scale of plant), the effect of diminishing physical productivity can be avoided. But the declining-price effect will nevertheless pull down marginal value productivity.

Out of all this emerges a rough notion that businessmen are willing to pay workers only what they are "worth," sometimes viewing workers as individuals but often as groups required for an integrated operation. What workers are worth *logically* boils down to a notion of marginal revenue productivity. Although this figure can't be estimated precisely in most cases, many businesses use their cost-accounting systems to get working ideas of when it pays to take new orders and hire more workers. Big concerns typically break down the cost of producing different commodities into a good deal of detail. Behind these money-cost data are time-and-motion studies of how much labor time should turn out how much product. Using these studies, the businessman can get a rough estimate of the "productivity" of workers of different types.

SUPPLY, DEMAND, AND PURELY COMPETITIVE WAGES

In a competitive market, price (here, the wage rate) is determined by the interaction of supply and demand. Willie will get a wage about equal to the marginal revenue productivity of welders like himself. The market will see to it.

To demonstrate rigorously that this will result, assume (1) that welders are all substantially identical, (2) that employment conditions are similar at different plants in the area, and (3) that information on wages at different plants is circulated freely. Then all plants will have to pay

about the same wage to get welders, just as there tends to be a single price for any identical commodity within any given market area.

Suppose that the going wage for welders is $24 a day. However, Acme Plumbing and some other plants figure that welders are worth to them up to around $30 per eight-hour day. In technical language, they estimate that the marginal revenue productivity of such labor is more than $24 in their plants. What will happen? Those firms will try to hire more welders. When they do, (1) the wage rate will be bid up, and (2) the value (marginal revenue productivity) of welders in these plants will fall as more labor is added because of the law of diminishing returns and possibly a lower price for sinks. Each firm will bid for additional welders as long as the rising wage is lower than what it can afford to pay additional men. At some rate between $24 and $30 a new equilibrium wage will be established, with market supply and demand in balance at that new wage.

The left-hand portion of Fig. 30-3 shows this equilibrium for the whole labor market; this is a summation of all the firms demanding welders. The right-hand portion shows that Acme hires 10 welders when the daily wage is set by the market at $27; remember that Acme simply pays the going wage rate to get the welders it needs.

In this equilibrium situation, we would expect to find the following:

1. The wage rate is equal to welders' marginal revenue productivity in the plants where they are hired.

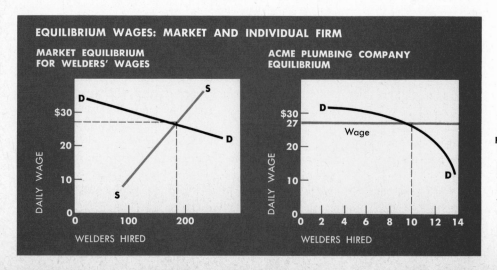

FIG. 30-3 Welders' wages are set in the market, much like other prices (left portion). At a market wage of $27, Acme maximizes profits by hiring 10 welders, at which point their wage equals their marginal revenue productivity to Acme (right portion).

2. Welders' wages are identical at all plants in the area.

3. Each firm is hiring as many welders as it "can afford" at that wage, because each firm continues to hire welders as long as the wage is lower than welders' marginal revenue productivity to it.

4. All welders in the area who are seeking work at that wage are employed. If any were still looking for work at that wage or less, the market wage rate would be bid down, since employers could hire unemployed workers at less than they were paying employed welders.

Thus, the competitive market tends to establish a wage or salary for each class of labor equal to its marginal productivity, when all workers looking for jobs at that wage or less are employed. Each worker is earning what his type of labor is "worth," as measured by its marginal contribution to producing the goods and services consumers want to buy. But remember: Each individual's marginal revenue productivity, and hence his wage, depends on a lot of forces completely outside his own control. Any change in consumer demand (because a depression comes along or because competing companies turn out a better sink) will change Willie's dollar contribution to Acme's sales revenue. And any change in technology or in Acme's production set-up can have the same result. The market pays each person about what he is "worth," but what he is worth to employers depends on a lot of forces over which he has no control.

Now try applying the same analysis to the original question. What will *your* starting salary be when you graduate? Five years later?

WAGE DETERMINATION
IN MONOPOLIZED INDUSTRIES

What difference does it make if the plumbing-supplies industry is monopolized by one or a few major producers? Continue the assumptions that each firm does the best it can to maximize profits, and that firms in this and other industries compete actively for welders.

As under competition, each firm will continue to hire more welders as long as the wage is lower than welders' estimated marginal worth to the concern. But the total number of welders hired in this industry will be lower than under competition, because the monopolist restricts output to get higher prices and higher profits.

Thus, fewer welders will have jobs in plumbing manufacture. If welders could work only there, clearly wages would be forced down by their competition for the reduced number of jobs. But welders forced out of plumbing can look for jobs elsewhere. Since we assume that welders are mobile, those forced out of plumbing will compete for jobs elsewhere, forcing down welders' wages there. Welders' wages will again be identical everywhere in the new equilibrium, but at a lower level than without the monopoly. *By restricting output below the competitive "ideal," the monopolist forces an inefficient allocation of labor, and this produces a lower wage for welders than under competition, both in the plumbing-supplies industry and elsewhere. Too few workers are employed in making plumbing supplies, too many in the rest of the economy.*[3]

To test your understanding of this reasoning, suppose now a union comes in and forces welders' wages back up to the competitive level everywhere in the economy. What will be the effect on the number of workers hired?[4]

WAGE DETERMINATION
UNDER EMPLOYER MONOPSONY

Now assume a different situation, where there is no competition among employers for labor. An example might be an isolated company mining town, where there is no significant alternative to working in the mine. The mine operator has a substantially complete "monopsony"—that

[3] The argument can be stated rigorously, as follows. Since the monopolist always faces a downward-sloping demand curve, marginal revenue is always less than price. The marginal revenue product obtained by hiring more labor is therefore always less than marginal physical product times the product price; instead, it is marginal physical product times marginal revenue. Since the marginal-revenue-product curve is the firm's demand-for-labor curve, the firm's demand for labor under monopoly will always be less than in a comparable competitive case.

[4] Answer: Some welders will be unemployed. More details in Chapter 31.

is, a monopoly in hiring workers. There is no reason to suppose that he will pay a wage as high as the workers' marginal revenue productivity to him. If the workers are immobile, he may "exploit" them—that is, he may pay them a wage below their marginal revenue productivity to him. He may be able to offer a very low wage and still get all the labor he needs.

Even here the employer doesn't have a completely free hand. If his wages get too far below rates elsewhere, workers may move away to other areas where they can earn more. Thus, the monopsonist pays what wages he has to in order to keep his workers from leaving, or to lure others if he needs more help. But when he is forced to go outside his monopsony area, competition with other employers is likely to eliminate his ability to exploit the workers.

To hear workers tell it, monopsony is a common case; the worker needs a union to protect himself against such exploitation. According to employers this is a rare case. The evidence suggests a mixed world. But everywhere the strength of monopsony positions tends to diminish as job-information channels improve, and as workers have more time and money to move to new jobs. These factors make it easier for workers to move and thereby to force employers to pay competitive wages.

A look ahead to implications for union behavior: Where monopsony exists, a union can clearly do a job for the workers. By banding together, the employees may be able to bargain their wages up to their full marginal revenue productivity without reducing employment. As long as the wage is less than the value of additional workers to the operator, even at the higher union wage, it will pay him to keep on hiring all the workers he was previously getting at a lower rate. The union may recoup for the workers the "exploitation" that had previously swollen the operator's profits.

WAGE DETERMINATION UNDER BILATERAL MONOPOLY

The next model is one that comes close to real-world conditions in some of the big-union–big-business areas of today. "Bilateral monopoly"

is the case where employers with substantial monopsony power bargain with unions with substantial monopoly power in selling labor. A simple case would be the mining-town example above after the workers formed a union to represent them as exclusive bargaining agent. A more realistic example, though not a "pure" case of bilateral monopoly, is wage bargaining in the steel industry, where the United Steelworkers represent most of the workers and the major firms in the industry in effect act together in bargaining for new contracts.

There are many other cases that might be called bilateral oligopoly, or bilateral oligopsony-monopoly. The auto industry, for example, has only four major firms, and they undoubtedly consider one another's positions as they bargain; but they do not bargain jointly as do the major steel firms.

Under bilateral monopoly or bilateral oligopoly the wage outcome is logically uncertain. The employer will be unwilling to pay more than the labor's marginal revenue productivity without cutting back the number employed; he will pay less if he can get the labor he needs at a lower wage, and without a union he can exploit the workers to some extent in this way. The union, with a monopoly in the sale of its members' services, pushes up wages as far as it can. If the wage is pushed above labor's marginal value product at the present employment level, fewer men will be hired. But the exact wage level is indeterminate between this marginal-value-product ceiling and a wage floor above which the employer could (without a union) get all the labor he needs. The outcome will depend on the relative bargaining strength of union and employer, on how badly the employer wants to avoid a strike, on the size of the union's strike fund.

A new union where the employer has "exploited" his workers can thus force up the wage rate without causing less employment. Just how far an employer may be able to hold the wage below the marginal productivity level—conversely, how high the union can force the wage toward that level—is a question to which economic theory has no answer. To a considerable extent labor is immobile. Workers do not move readily from one job or location to another. Thus, a major employer or group of employers can probably keep most of its labor supply at whatever wage rate is bargained, unless the wage is substantially below wages in alternative industries. But the union provides a strong force countering employer monopsony. Bargaining power holds the key to the outcome, within a fairly wide band.[5]

WAGE AND SALARY DIFFERENTIALS

Now turn to another application of the marginal productivity theory—the explanation of wage and salary differentials. The huge salaries of movie stars, corporation presidents, and home-run hitters are always fascinating. Why should anyone get $100,000 a year when most of us have to be content with a small fraction of that? And especially, why should they get it when their work by and large looks so pleasant compared with ditch-digging or pounding a typewriter, which pay only a couple of dollars an hour? We shall see that marginal productivity again provides the biggest part of the answer.

Even within the range of occupations which seem reasonably likely for most of us, the differentials are big. Look again at Table 29-2. In lifetime earnings, the expectations of a doctor in 1962 were $717,000, of a lawyer $621,000, of an engineer $395,000, of a high school teacher $261,000, of a plumber $236,000.

Supply and Demand Again

The most fundamental things about wage and salary differentials can be seen by using the same supply-and-demand, marginal-productivity model again. Give your theory a workout.

Salaries are extremely high where the supply is tiny and the demand is large. Wages are low where there are lots of workers relative to the demand. How "hard," how unpleasant, how tedious, the job is—such considerations aren't very important except as they influence either the supply or the demand side of the picture.

Why does Willie Mays collect an astro-

nomical salary just for playing baseball on warm summer afternoons? Mainly because he is better at hitting, catching, and throwing baseballs than almost anybody else; and we Americans lay our dollars on the line with enthusiasm to see good baseball players.[6] How can a surgeon get away with charging hundreds of dollars an hour? He gets away with it because his skills are very scarce, and the demand for them is very strong. His marginal productivity is very high. In contrast, it's easy to be a delivery boy or a retail clerk, and lots of people try these jobs. Their marginal productivity is low.

The biggest factor accounting for wage differentials thus lies in the ability of the individual to do something that few others can do—something that is demanded by consumers with money to pay for it. There are big differences in the capabilities of different people. Some of these differences we can't do much about. Joe Louis' split-second timing was largely born, not made, in spite of all the years of training that went into it. Psychologists tell us that our basic intelligence apparently changes little over the years, no matter how hard we study. But our capabilities also depend on education, hard work, and other things that are controllable. One reason that top-notch corporation lawyers are so scarce and their marginal productivity so high is that not many people have both the combination of brains and personality *and* the drive to put in the 25 years of hard work in college, law school and practice that it takes to make a fine corporation lawyer. The competition is tough for the top jobs, and most of them aren't won by fellows who work eight-hour days with Saturdays and Sundays off.

But ability and hard work aren't the whole story. Some occupations are hard to get into. You

[5] A new analytical approach from mathematics—"game theory"—presents some interesting insights into alternative outcomes under different types of bargaining strategies.

[6] Anomalously, Mickey Mantle may have been more susceptible to wage exploitation than most common laborers. This is because there could have been little active competition for his services to force the New York Yankees to pay him more; almost no one else had a big enough ball park in a city large enough to push Mantle's salary up to what he was probably "worth" to the Yankees in marginal revenue productivity (marginal cash drawing power). Moreover, under organized baseball's "reserve clause," other clubs couldn't hire Mantle away anyhow; they would have had to "buy" him from the Yankees. But Mantle obviously had a monopoly in selling his own services. Thus, the situation was one of bilateral monopoly.

can't become a lawyer or a surgeon unless you've got the money to get through law or medical school, however smart and ambitious you may be. The only way to become a senior airline pilot is to move up through a long period of training and experience. Becoming a plumber is almost impossible unless you meet the union's requirements in many areas, and the union may not want an increase in the number of plumbers. Many occupations are still substantially closed to Negroes, though the doors are gradually opening. Women are in effect excluded from many high-pay occupations.

Consider another example. When a new area develops and needs new workers, we would expect wages to be unusually high for a while. People are unlikely to give up other jobs and move across the country to take a fling in a new area unless the monetary incentive is clear. And this checks out. Wages in the Southwest are generally higher than in slower-growing sections. Most rapidly-growing areas tend to bid up wages, because labor is relatively scarce.[7]

Chapter 29 stressed the growing importance of education as a door to high-income occupations. Nine of the ten best-paid occupations on the 1960 Census list were professional or managerial, averaging over 16 years of schooling. Salary studies consistently show the dollars-and-cents value of education. Roughly speaking, every year of additional school above eighth grade seems to be worth an extra $400 to $500 a year earning power over one's entire life span. Over a working life span, this means that college may be worth over $100,000, a nice return on investment by any standards. (There is some trickery in these figures, of course, since we know that those who go on to college are generally more able and would presumably earn above average even without the extra schooling. But even making a rough allowance to eliminate that factor, higher education pays well on the average.)

Unions have some influence on wage differentials. Especially where the situation approxi-

mates employer monopsony, it is clear that unions may improve the position of workers compared to nonunion shops. But just how much difference unions really make is a subject of much dispute, to be postponed till the next chapter.

A supply-and-demand model would predict that some particularly dirty, disagreeable, dangerous jobs will command high pay because these factors restrict the supply of labor for the jobs—not because the dirt, danger, or unpleasantness themselves justify higher wages. Extra-hazard pay often goes with dangerous jobs; sandhogs, for example, make good money, but not many people line up for the job of drilling tunnels underwater. Conversely, people like white-collar jobs. The low wages paid to clerks in banks and other pleasant working places attest to the appeal of such jobs in increasing the supply even though wages are lower than elsewhere for comparable workers.

But the striking fact is that the cleanest, most attractive, most pleasant jobs are generally the ones with the *highest* pay—unless you classify responsibility as a disadvantage. Just about everybody would agree that the corporation president has a nicer job than the ditch-digger, that the lawyer leads a nicer life than the coal miner. Then why don't more people become corporation presidents and lawyers, so that the salaries there and in ditch-digging will move toward equality? Answering the question should give you some insight into the complex set of factors limiting the supply of certain kinds of abilities in our society, relative to the demand for those abilities. At the end, ask yourself one more question: Do existing income differentials (for movie stars, surgeons, corporation presidents, schoolteachers, dope-peddlers, factory workers, farm laborers) reward most highly those who make the greatest contribution to human welfare?

WAGES AND TECHNOLOGICAL ADVANCE

Technological advance is a dominant characteristic of the American economy, perhaps the single most important foundation of our rising standard of living. New methods, new machines, new products are the lifeblood of a dynamic, grow-

[7] Per capita income in California in 1966 was about $3,400, in Missouri about $2,800, in Michigan about $3,200, in Vermont about $2,600, in South Carolina about $2,000, and in Mississippi about $1,800, the lowest in the nation. Can you explain these differences on the new-area hypothesis? If not, how can they be explained?

ing economy. Without the Linotype we'd still be setting type by hand, and books and newspapers would still be for the elite few. Without the electric light bulb, we'd still be lighting our houses with candles, oil, and gas.

But recently "automation" (as technological advance is sometimes called when new automatic machines replace men) has been blamed for widespread unemployment. Big electronic computers replace hundreds of clerks in processing checks and keeping records in banks and businesses. Modern chemical plants are almost fully automated. On a humbler level, spray guns and rollers get work done a lot faster than the old fashioned paint brush. Everywhere new factories produce more goods with fewer workers.

It is not surprising that many workers worry that automation may throw them out of a job. Actually, for the economy as a whole this worry is largely unfounded. But let us put the automation-unemployment issue aside for Chapter 41, and concentrate here on the relation between technological advance and wages.

Technological progress increases output per unit of input—output per worker or output per unit of capital, whichever way you wish to divide up total output. It would appear to raise the marginal revenue productivity of both labor and capital. Thus, we might expect it to raise both wages and the rate of return on capital—and so it generally will, other things equal. But how much of the gain goes to each under what circumstances is a more complex question, and there *may* be cases where either labor or capital income is actually reduced by a particular technological innovation.

But the over-all impact on wages is clear. Look back at Fig. 30-1, which shows the steady growth of output per man-hour and of wages in the American economy. Moreover, the growth in total output has been much greater than the total input of labor and capital combined, as was shown by Fig. 16-2. While the total incomes of both capital and labor have risen greatly over the past century, the return per unit of labor (the real wage rate) has gone up much more than the return per unit of capital (the interest rate), as the bottom half of Fig. 16-2 shows dramatically. In the aggregate, labor has apparently been the great gainer from technological advance as measured this way. Measured as in Fig. 29-3, the percentage shares of the total national income going to labor and capital have been relatively stable, because the quantity of capital has grown much faster than the quantity of labor.

Against this factual backdrop, let us examine the impact of automation on wages in a particular industry and occupation. Look back at Willie, the welder. Suppose a new machine is invented that stamps out metal sinks, largely eliminating the need for welding. Let us trace through the results, assuming that all markets are perfectly competitive and all prices flexible both upward and downward.

1. Sink producers will adopt the new method if it's cheaper per sink produced than the old one was, and competition will force sink prices down to the lower cost level.

2. Many welders will lose their jobs in plumbing-supply companies. Willie will be out of a job, at least temporarily. Welders' wages will fall as they compete for jobs elsewhere.

3. Employment will increase in plants that manufacture the new machine, in industries producing raw materials and parts, and in plumbing-supply companies that need men to install, service, and operate the new machines. This increased demand will tend to offset the downward pressure on welders' wages.

4. At the lower price of sinks, more sinks will be produced and sold, and consumers will be better off. More goods in total can be produced, since some welders are freed from plumbing supplies to help produce other products.

In all of this, what has happened to the wages of different labor groups and to the wage share in the national income? Note that this question now involves a return to macro-economic issues, as well as the micro analysis we have just been using.

First, welders' wages drop. Some welders are thrown out of work, as the marginal value product of welders is reduced. They look for other jobs. If they stay unemployed, average wages of all welders are clearly down. Even if they get jobs as welders elsewhere, welders' wage rates and total wage incomes will tend to be pulled down as more welders seek jobs there.

Second, the demand for other types of labor rises—for workers to make the new machines and to service and operate them. Wages will rise in those other industries and occupations.

Third, if we assume constant total expenditures in the economy, welders thrown out of jobs will get work elsewhere or at different jobs in the sink industry, as consumers switch their expenditure patterns. Consumers will spend more on other products if they spend less on sinks, and more jobs will be available in other industries. This pleasant conclusion, however, depends on two critical assumptions: that workers are mobile in moving to new jobs, and that individual wages are flexible so that the workers can be absorbed elsewhere. Thus, it skips lightly over the big interim problems of retraining and readjustment facing individual workers. Still, as a practical matter, probably the biggest help in assuring jobs and incomes elsewhere in the face of "automation" is government assurance that aggregate demand will remain strong.

Fourth, what happens to the total wage share in the national income will depend largely on the elasticity of demand for the product concerned and on the ratio of labor to capital used in the innovating industry, relative to the rest of the economy. This gets pretty complicated. But since labor clearly benefits along with all of us in its role as consumer, in the real world it's reasonably clear that labor's *real* income is raised by technological advance, whatever happens to its *relative* share of the national income—though this is not necessarily so, according to our theory. The gradually rising share of wages and salaries in the national income over many years of rapid technological advance suggests that labor and non-labor incomes both share the benefits of technological progress, and that if anything, the labor portion has grown a little. There's no doubt that, thus far at least, wage-earners have benefited greatly from technological advance—or from automation, if you prefer that name.

For Analysis and Discussion

1. Suppose you want to maximize your lifetime income. What factors should you take into account in selecting your occupation and in timing your entry into it?

2. "Labor is just another commodity, and wages are its price. All we need to explain wages is a basic understanding of supply and demand." Do you agree with this quotation from an economics textbook? Explain.

3. One theory holds that wages are merely the result of bargaining between workers and employers, and that the only important determinant of the outcome is the relative bargaining power of the two parties. Is this theory a good one? If not, what is the matter with it?

4. Malthus argued that population would tend to outrun the world's food supply, and that wages would tend to be forced back down toward a bare subsistence level.
    a. Is this an acceptable theory of wages?
    b. How would you differentiate between its usefulness in explaining wages in America and in India?

5. To what extent are the "bargaining" and "subsistence" wage theories indicated above consistent with a supply-and-demand approach to the problem?

6. Is inequality of economic opportunity a major factor in the present unequal distribution of personal incomes in the United States? If it is important, what, if anything, should be done to reduce such inequality of opportunity?

7. Suppose you are a member of the United Auto Workers union. Would you favor a union policy opposing the introduction of automatic, labor-saving machinery? Explain your reasoning.

8. Average wages are higher in the North than in the South. Would you expect this differential to persist or vanish? Why?

THIRTY-ONE

UNIONS, COLLECTIVE BARGAINING, AND PUBLIC POLICY

History of American Unionism.

Union Wage Policy.

Collective Bargaining and Labor-Management Relations.

Government and Labor.

Should the Government Get Out?

Appendix: The Economics of Minimum-Wage Laws.

Labor unions loom large on the current American scene. On the economic front, they exercise great pressures on wages, hours, and working conditions. They are behind the worker in his differences with the foreman, the day-to-day arguments that seldom reach the public's eye. Politically, their voice is heard in the selection of candidates, and their votes are felt in elections—usually on the Democratic side. Their lobbyists are among the most effective in Washington and the state capitals, and it is a secure congressman indeed who can afford to disregard what organized labor thinks. Socially, the union has become part of the lives of millions of workers. Here they have a unity of interest and background with fellow members that they find in few other associations.

Important as unions are, it is also easy to overrate their importance. Unions do indeed influence wages and hours. But supply and demand still set a confining framework for labor-management negotiations. Although the combined A.F.L.-C.I.O. loosely joins many unions, the member groups are still separate unions, often disputing among themselves. Less than one-third of all workers are unionized, and union membership has grown little, if at all, in recent years although the labor force has expanded steadily. Throughout agriculture, the services, and clerical and professional areas, unions have little hold. Politically, the divisions within organized labor weaken the power it can exercise, and since World War II, labor has gone down to defeat on some of its most bitterly fought issues—notably the passage of the Taft-Hartley Act.

To understand organized labor's position, we must remember history. With the present powers of big unions, it may be hard for you to realize that only 40 years ago unions were hanging on by the skin of their teeth, with an active membership of only 3 million workers and little or no recognition in the great mass-production industries of the country; union leaders were tarred and feathered, heads were broken. But many union members and their leaders know it well. And that memory colors union behavior today.

HISTORY OF AMERICAN UNIONISM [1]

The foundations of labor unionism in America lay in the skilled crafts during the early 1800's. In scattered localities, craftsmen banded together, in spite of public antagonism, bitter employer resistance, and susceptibility to prosecution as criminal conspirators. Their goals were direct—to cut the working day from 12 to 10 hours, to obtain more tolerable working conditions, and to seek higher wages. But it was not until the 1870's that the first loose nationwide labor association appeared. This was the Knights of Labor, founded as a secret society (to avoid employer's reprisals against members). When the Knights foundered on dissension a decade later, the American Federation of Labor collected the stronger, skilled-craft elements and became the first effective national union organization. Under the leadership from 1886 to 1924 of Samuel Gompers, a remarkable figure in American labor history, the Federation became a significant force, with an outspoken philosophy of "practical" unionism. Gompers reflected well the spirit of the times in organized labor—"Get more, now." Only this pragmatic, typically American attitude began to win a little grudging acceptance for unionism from employers and the public at large.

But it was Franklin Roosevelt and the New Deal that gave unions their place in modern industrial society. Depression was everywhere—massive unemployment, low wages, low purchasing power. Higher wages and higher prices to promote recovery were cornerstones of the New

[1] For a good account, see U.S. Labor Department, *Brief History of the American Labor Department* (Washington, D.C.: U.S. Government Printing Office, 1964).

Deal. The National Industrial Recovery Act for the first time gave workers the right to organize and bargain collectively with employers. Union organizers went to work and membership picked up fast, although N.I.R.A. was soon declared unconstitutional. The Wagner Act of 1935, passed soon thereafter, became the foundation of modern union powers; it spelled out workers' rights vis-à-vis employers, put teeth in the unions' powers to bargain collectively, and forbade prevalent employer anti-union practices. Unions were guaranteed recognition if they won a majority vote among the workers.

The labor history of the middle 1930's was stormy and violent. The newly-formed C.I.O., with the fiery John L. Lewis as its first president, opened big organization drives—violent, spectacular, and successful. Open defiance of management rather than workers' traditional subservience was the tone. The famous sit-down strikes, when the unions seized possession of the major auto plants, rocked the companies and the public. But in the bloodshed and bitterness that ensued, the unions won recognition time after time—with the open support of the Roosevelt administration and local Democratic government officials. The Who's Who of American industry fell to C.I.O. organizing drives one by one—U.S. and Bethlehem Steel, General Motors, General Electric, Goodyear, and so on down the list. By 1940, union membership had more than doubled, to about 10 million. By 1945 it was nearly 15 million, about one-third of the nonagricultural labor force.

Public sympathy during the 1930's was by and large prolabor, though many friends were lost by the violent sit-down strikes. But strong union wage demands during World War II, interunion jurisdictional quarrels and strikes, and open defiance of the federal government by a few leaders convinced the bulk of the public that organized labor's power had gone too far. In 1947 Congress passed the Taft-Hartley Act, restricting the powers of unions and restoring some rights that employers had lost during the preceding decade. And the years since World War II have seen a definite leveling-off of union power, with widespread public disapproval of gangsterism, jurisdictional disputes, and intraunion squabbles which made the headlines intermittently.

Figure 31-1 shows the picture. Union membership (excluding Canada) rose above 17 million in the mid-1950's, but has declined since then. Unions have made slow headway with white-collar workers and employees of the rapidly growing service industries. The bottom half of the chart shows the union problem more strongly. Union membership as a percentage of total *nonagricultural* labor force hit a peak of 33 per cent in 1963, and has declined since to a 1967 level of around 26 per cent. Union membership as a percentage of the total civilian labor force (shown in Fig. 31-1) is of course still lower.

In 1955, the "merger" of the A.F.L. and the C.I.O. into one loose organization (the A.F.L.-C.I.O.) marked a major step toward a united labor movement. But interunion rivalries have kept the new organization from acting as an effective unit, economically or politically. Jurisdictional disputes have been a persistent source of quarrels, and the member unions have been unwilling to give enough power to the combined organization to make it effective. The house of labor, though it is nearly 16-million-workers strong, shows bad cracks in its walls, and many observers believe they are getting wider.

Moreover, the unions face a new problem. The average union member has a good job, and often a little house in the suburbs. He is one of the big middle-income class, well above the insecurity and poverty which threatened during the 1930's. He wants more pay, longer vacations, better fringe benefits. But the old class solidarity which once united workers against the capitalist employers is gone. There is an increasing gap between the goals of young union members and the militancy which motivated the now-aging leaders. Some describe the modern scene as "mail-order unionism." The members turn over their dues and want higher wages and other benefits delivered by union officials in exchange. Otherwise, many younger members feel little sense of belonging to the union as an organization. New paths for the American union movement may lie ahead.

UNION WAGE POLICY

From one point of view, a union is merely a monopoly that sells the labor services of its members. Neglecting for the moment all the other things that unions do, how effective is a union in raising wages under different circumstances? And how does the public come out in the bargain?

The analytical models of the last chapter

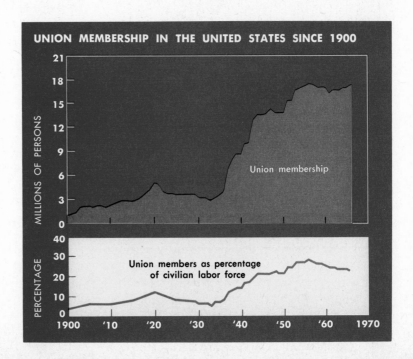

FIG. 31-1 The big growth period for unions was during the 1930's and 1940's. Since then, union membership has gradually declined as a percentage of the civilian labor force. (Sources: National Bureau of Economic Research and U.S. Department of Labor.)

give us a simple framework for examining the problem. Let us first assume that the union is a completely effective organization in controlling its workers. It speaks for them all, and it need not worry about defections from the ranks. Assume also for the moment that aggregate spending in the economy is constant, unaffected by the behavior of individual unions and employers.

Competition

First, consider the case where employers are highly competitive with one another both in selling products and in hiring workers. For example, suppose we look at unorganized retail clerks or restaurant waiters in an area where there are lots of stores and restaurants so substantially perfect competition prevails. Here, in the long run, all economic profits will tend to be eliminated. Price will be forced down to about the minimum average cost at which each product can be produced. From the labor side, wages will be roughly equal to the marginal revenue productivity of each class of labor hired.

Suppose now that a union comes in and organizes all clerks and waiters in the area. It demands a wage increase and gets it. This raises costs, and forces up prices. At the higher prices, consumers will buy fewer restaurant meals and other retail products (with total income and spending assumed constant). With less output there are fewer jobs for clerks and waiters as a result of the higher wages. This is the classic case in which union wage demands lead to fewer jobs for union members. In a highly competitive industry, there isn't much unions can do to push up wages without reducing employment in the long run (unless aggregate spending is somehow increased). The workers who keep their jobs have higher incomes, but those laid off bear the brunt. And it becomes harder for new job-seekers to find work in the industry.

Monopoly and Partial Monopoly

Second, consider the case where there is monopoly or monopolistic competition in selling products, but still active competition among firms for workers. Suppose, for example, there are only a dozen or so restaurants or stores in the area, or at the extreme only one. Can the new union now force the stores to pay higher wages without reducing the number of jobs? Our theory

tells us, probably not. If the firms are maximizing profits before the union, they will be hiring workers up to the point where the wage equals the workers' marginal revenue product. If the union raises wages, it will, logically, pay employers to cut back on the number of workers hired and to raise price; the new maximum-profit output will be smaller than before. Again, logically, the union can obtain higher wages only at the cost of less employment.

But partial monopolists—especially oligopolists—often aren't maximizing profits in the precise sense above. Oligopoly is the world of live-and-let-live, of price leadership, of partially protected markets. Under these conditions, the effect of a wage increase on prices and employment is far harder to predict. Theory gives no clear-cut presumptive answer. Since prices are set by the leader on the basis of many tenuous variables, it is hard to tell when a wage increase will lead to a change in product price—and if it does, how much. If firms have a protected profit position, this special profit provides a melon over which the union and management can bargain, and higher wages need have no effect on either product price or output and employment. In oligopolies where firms behave as if they faced kinked demand curves, the union *may* have a considerable range over which it can force up wages without inducing higher prices and reduced employment, as was indicated on page 410. But this is unlikely. Wherever the union makes substantially the same bargain for all major firms in the industry, it will be obvious to all that costs have risen and all firms are likely to expect an increase by the price leader. Where this is true, the union thus faces much the same likely result on employment and prices as with a single monopoly firm; its ability to obtain higher wages without losing jobs is very limited.

Monopsony
and Bilateral Oligopoly

Consider now a different case, where workers are being "exploited" through a wage less than their marginal revenue productivity. For example, imagine an isolated mining town where there are few jobs outside the mines. The one mining company doesn't have to pay workers their full marginal product to get all the labor it wants. Now a union organizes the workers and demands a higher wage. What is the result?

Here the union can push the wage up without decreasing employment, assuming the entrepreneur is motivated solely by a desire to maximize profits.[2] But here we get into a pure power struggle. The employer is making a special profit by exploiting the workers and theoretically the union can grab this sum back for the workers. But the employer isn't going to be enthusiastic about turning his profits over to the workers. He'll fight to keep wages down. Where this struggle comes out is indeterminate so far as economic theory is concerned. To guess who will win, look at the relative bargaining power of employer and union. How big is the union strike fund? How adept are both parties around the bargaining table? How badly does the employer want to get his customers' orders out on time?

Union Wages and Capital Substitution

The short-run effect of union wage pressures on the number of jobs in an industry is often hard to predict accurately. But a longer range effect is highly predictable. Higher labor costs will lead businessmen to invest in labor-saving machinery more rapidly than they would with lower wages. It will pay to shift to coal-mining machinery to replace miners as hourly wages rise, to install mechanical dishwashers in restaurants, to replace farm laborers by automatic vegetable pickers. Higher union wages speeding "automation" clearly change the capital-labor ratio in the industries affected. But as was noted at the end of Chapter 30, remember that this need not mean unemployment for the economy as a whole. Don't fall into the trap of the fallacy of composition.

Do Unions Really Raise Wages?

This may sound like a silly question. Everyone has read of many cases where union demands for higher wages have finally been granted by

employers. But such instances don't really answer the question. Maybe supply and demand would have produced the same raises in the market without any union. Don't forget the fallacy of *post hoc, propter hoc.*

Although any union man and most employers will tell you that of course unions raise wages, the dispassionate objective evidence is less clear. One careful study estimates that unions raised wages of their members by about 25 per cent relative to nonunion workers in 1933 at the bottom of the depression (reflecting temporary union resistance to wage cuts), by about 5 per cent in the inflationary boom of the late 1940's when all wages were bid up rapidly, and by 10–15 per cent during the 1950's.[3] Other studies generally confirm this modest, varying upward effect of unions on members' wages. The effect is greatest when market demand is weak. In prosperous periods of strong demand, market forces pull up nonunion wages about as fast as, or even faster than, those of union members.

Note a commonly cited but unconvincing bit of evidence, that union wages are by and large higher than nonunion ones. But many unionized industries have been high-wage industries anyhow, even before they were unionized—big companies with lots of skilled workmen. One other interesting piece of evidence is that labor's share in the national income has increased somewhat since the 1920's, before the big modern union increase. But the shift is not enough to provide clear evidence that unions have raised the aggregate wage share.

Fringe Benefits

Increasingly, unions have coupled their wage demands with pressures for "fringe benefits"—paid vacations, pensions, health insurance, and a dozen other such benefits. All these cost the companies money. They all have to come out of somebody's pocketbook. In this sense, they all are, in effect, wage increases, though the worker takes his pay in special forms rather than directly.

Two issues are at stake here. First, should the workers get more pay, and what will be the impact of the higher costs in any given situation?

---

[2] In fact, the union theoretically might *increase* employment by eliminating exploitation. Without the union, the employer bargains wages down and gets as many workers as possible at his low wage. With a union, he must pay the going wage and he can get as many workers as he wants at that wage. Thus he hires workers up to the point where the wage equals their marginal revenue productivity; there is no longer any incentive to restrict output and employment to get the advantage of low wages.

[3] H. G. Lewis, *Unionism and Relative Wages in the United States* (Chicago: University of Chicago Press, 1963), p. 193.

Second, should the higher pay be in the form of fringe benefits? For example, should workers be allowed (or forced) to take part of their pay in health and old-age benefits? A lot of people think so, and both union contracts and the federal social security system require employers to pay part of total wages in this form. But make up your own mind. The benefits may look very different to young and old workers. One rough estimate is that fringe benefits now account for over 15 per cent of the national wage bill; this would be around $40 to $50 billion annually. In manufacturing industries, fringe benefits in 1967 exceeded 60 cents per hour on an average hourly wage of about $2.80.

COLLECTIVE BARGAINING AND LABOR-MANAGEMENT RELATIONS

The big wage negotiations and strikes always make the headlines and news broadcasts. But the great bulk of union-management collective bargaining and negotiation goes on unheralded behind the scenes. After a union contract is signed, the day-to-day relations of the foreman and his workers take over. Wage rates have to be set for individual jobs; broad contract wage provisions must be translated into elaborate wage structures in large firms. Decisions must be made as to which jobs are on a flat hourly pay basis and which "on incentive" where the pay depends on the number of units turned out. In the latter case, standard base rates must be established for "normal" output, above which bonuses are paid. Times and rates need to be established for new work. Arrangements have to be agreed on for handling the introduction of new machinery and new methods. Wrangles between foremen and individual workers have to be adjudicated. A thousand and one problems arise in a big plant that involve disputes between labor and management.

In these disputes, the union steward is the worker's first line of protection and negotiation, just as the foreman is management's. Good feeling and cooperation between foremen and stewards can do more for effective union-management relations than almost any amount of fine top-level policy-making. Bad relations between stew-ards and foremen can block any good intentions at top levels. Down in the plant is where the work gets done and where most of the disputes arise, except for the major wage and hour negotiations at contract-expiration dates.

Some union-management agreements provide elaborate machinery for handling worker-management disputes that can't be settled by the foreman and the worker. These often culminate in calling on an impartial arbitrator, paid jointly by union and management, whose decision is final on disputed issues under the contract. Other contracts set up other procedures. There is no point in trying to describe the vast variety of them. The main point is that they try to set up a body of rules under which workers and management can minimize friction and disagreement. The contract is something like the rules of law under which we operate our democratic system. This procedure has gone far toward creating stability and order in employee-management relations in thousands of industrial plants. But in industrial as in political democracy, the rules alone can't make the system work. They only provide a framework within which men of reasonable goodwill, with a reasonable agreement on common objectives, can live and work peaceably together.[4]

Union and Management Motivation in Bargaining

You don't need a course in economics to tell you the main reason why unions fight for higher wages. The members want more pay! But some other things aren't so easy to explain.

[4] One source of controversy between unions and management is the "union shop" and "right-to-work" laws. Under a union shop agreement, everyone who works in the firm covered must join the union. The union's big argument for this arrangement is that if workers get all the benefits of union activities (higher wages, better working conditions, etc.), they should have to pay dues and bear their share of the union costs. Otherwise they get a "free ride," which makes no more sense than permitting a citizen to benefit from government but decide for himself that he won't pay taxes.

The counterargument says that union shops take away the individual worker's right to work without joining a union, and that this abrogates an important individual freedom. Make up your own mind. The union shop is legal under federal law but prohibited in a number of southern and western states which have enacted state "right-to-work" laws. Such right-to-work laws are fought bitterly by the unions.

The thing that seems to amaze people most is that unions will strike for an extra few cents an hour pay, when third-grade arithmetic will show that it would take months or even years at the extra rate to make up for the pay lost in a long strike. Why are the union leaders willing to keep the men out, at an apparent direct dollars-and-cents loss? The same question can be asked the other way around, too. The company's loss during the strike may cost more than years of paying the extra few cents to the workers. Why doesn't the company give in, and save everybody money?

Try putting yourself in the worker's shoes. What would you think? You'd think: "That so-and-so who runs the company! He gets a big salary and has everything. His plushy stockholders are getting big dividends. Yet we have to scrape along on pay that just keeps the wolf away from the door. He won't even give us a couple of cents extra when he could save himself profits by doing it instead of trying to break this strike. We'll fight it out and lick him yet!"

Now turn around and see how you'd feel as the employer. You see the generous wages your company is already paying. You see the workers stubbornly holding out for unreasonable demands, even when the strike is obviously costing them more than they can hope to get out of it. You may see the union leaders as self-seeking hypocrites, out to protect their own jobs. The whole business is just one more step in the union's attempt to dictate to management and to encroach on management prerogatives. Would you give in if you were the employer?

Now put yourself in the union president's shoes. You're probably sincerely out to do the best you can for your membership. You know that your best bet in the long run lies in getting along with management. But you also know that there's never enough money to go around, and that you're going to have to push hard to get the wages your members are (in your eyes) honestly entitled to. You know a strike is costly to everybody, but you know too that a threat often repeated but never carried out loses its force. And you don't quite trust the employer and his personnel men, even though by and large they're pretty decent people. You suspect that down underneath that surface friendliness they'd be de-

lighted to see the unions go, and to return to the old pre-union days when the employer told the workers to do what he said—or else!

You know some more things too. You know that unless you produce for your members, you're likely to be just an ex-president. If other unions have been getting 10 cents an hour plus fringe benefits, you've got to get about that much too, or you're going to have some disgruntled members. You know that your chance of rising in the union ranks, say to a position in the international, depends in part on your success in getting more than other unions do. You know that too much peace with the employer, even though it pays off handsomely in dollars and cents for your members, is going to be interpreted by some members as "selling out." As you sit across the bargaining table from management, with tempers frayed by a long strike, would you give in?

The issues at stake in a labor negotiation are seldom simple. Human motives are strong and complex. The quarrel that the public sees in the newspapers is often only part of the real issue. The fine speeches made by both sides—about the need for wage increases to prevent depression, or the need to maintain a progressive free-enterprise system through large capital expenditures out of earnings—sound good on the news broadcasts but often have little to do with settling the dispute at the bargaining table. To look at the issue in terms of a simple dollars-and-cents comparison is naive. There are few more complex jobs of compromise and good human relations than labor-management negotiations. The issues are real, and no purpose is served by pretending that nothing but common interest is involved. Unfortunately, there is seldom a clear, objective right-or-wrong answer.

The Changing Role of Strikes

Collective bargaining is a process of challenge and response. It includes innumerable variations as individual companies and unions shape it to fit their needs. For the most part it settles the disputes between employers and unions. But sometimes they can't, or won't, reach agreement. Tempers fray. Bitterness grows. Finally the union goes out on strike.

Strikes are rare events. With over 150,000 collective bargaining contracts in force, strikes over the last five years have caused a loss of less

TABLE 31-1			
TIME LOST IN STRIKES, 1935–1966 *			
Period	Number of Strikes (Annual Average)	Workers Involved (Annual Average) (In Thousands)	Percentage of Working Time Lost
1935–39	2,862	1,130	0.27
1940–44	3,754	1,386	.16
1945–50	4,210	2,940	.61
1951–55	4,540	2,510	.31
1956–60	3,602	1,620	.29
1961	3,210	1,466	.15
1962	3,612	1,230	.16
1963	3,362	941	.13
1964	3,655	1,640	.18
1965	3,963	1,550	.16
1966	4,010	1,740	.17

* Data from U.S. Department of Labor.

than ¼ of 1 per cent of the total working time involved. Table 31-1 shows the record since 1935. Time lost exceeded ¾ of 1 per cent in only one year—1947.

Moreover, most of today's strikes are orderly and nonviolent, in sharp contrast to the bitter, bloody battles of 30 years ago. Strikes now arise largely over renewal of contracts, and most often involve wage and work rule arguments, far less explosive issues than the life-or-death organizing conflicts of the 1930's. Arbitration is now largely used to settle disputes that arise during the life of the contract. International officers generally try to help avoid or settle "wildcat" strikes, in which local unions strike in contravention of contract arrangements. But bitter, violent strikes have not disappeared, especially in the South, where employer resistance to union organizing moves remains militant in some areas.

Thus, conflict resolution between labor and management has been moved increasingly to an orderly, peaceful procedural basis. But conflicts do persist, and the strike remains organized labor's weapon of last resort to enforce its views. Sometimes big strikes are enormously disruptive—for example, a long steel or public utility strike. But many labor observers feel that an occasional strike in most industries does no great harm and indeed may be a useful incident in the continuing bargaining relationship between labor and management. A strike is a device for letting off steam, for reasserting bargaining powers. It is not necessarily a symbol of the failure of collective bargaining. Thus, few labor experts favor laws to outlaw strikes, except possibly strikes that clearly threaten the public interest. For to outlaw strikes would not resolve conflicts but merely force them into other channels. As confidence grows in other dispute-solving techniques, it seems likely that resort to strikes will lessen still further. The main immediate goal is to moderate conflict and contain it in orderly channels, looking toward a heightened sense of management and labor responsibility upon which ultimate peaceful working relationships must rest.

Union Power and Union Policies

Even though violence and strikes have decreased sharply, unions still loom large on the industrial scene. Settlement of differences by negotiation has taken over much of the traditional role of the market place as the governor of economic activity. The greatly increased power of organized labor means that labor-management disputes are now more a test of strength between equals—sometimes equals of prodigious strength. When Walter Reuther sits down to bargain for the United Auto Workers, he speaks for a million men. Not millions, but billions, of dollars are at stake in these bargains; not only wages, but also the pensions of tomorrow's retired families, workers' sickness insurance, their working hours, the vacations they take. In every election, the support of organized labor is eagerly sought. Labor lobbies in Washington and the state capitals are powerful and well organized. A nationwide Teamsters strike could bring the economy to a grinding halt in a matter of days. Few other unions outside the public utilities have this power. But many can gravely disrupt economic activity and bring massive inconvenience through long strikes.

Great power is wielded by labor unions and their leaders. Is this power excessive? Many businessmen say "yes"; they stress that there are no antitrust laws to limit union power. Most laborers say "no." Whether labor power has been unduly encouraged and should be restrained by government action is one of the big politico-economic issues of our day.

The Union and Its Members

But to the union man in the mill, none of these matters is the most important thing about unions. E. Wight Bakke, a sympathetic observer of the American labor movement, two decades ago summarized his years of experience by listing five main things that workers look for in their unions—the things that explain why they join unions, why they pay their dues, and why they go on the picket line against the corporation that employs them.[5]

1. The union gives the working man a chance to be part of the group, to gain the respect of his fellow workers, to "be somebody" in an industrial world where the worker is a mere cog in an impersonal industrial plant. Everyone seeks the society and respect of his fellows, consciously or subconsciously. The union man is part of an organization that can stand up and talk back to the boss—not just to the foreman, but to the head office in New York or Pittsburgh. The desire to belong to the group, to be accepted, to be important, is one of the most fundamental in most men's lives.

2. The union promises progress toward eco-

[5] "Why Workers Join Unions," in *Unions, Management, and the Public* (New York: Harcourt, Brace, and World, 1948), pp. 41–49.

nomic security—not the security of the $50,000-a-year vice president, but a steady job and reasonable wages, enough to pay the bills and have a little left over for old age and a rainy day. Workers beef about the big salaries of their company presidents, but the evidence is strong that it's the status of the fellow just a rung or two up the ladder that matters most. Their idea of economic comforts and economic security may be based on what the foreman has, but top management is another economic world.

3. The union promises the working man an increased measure of independence and control over his own affairs. As an individual the worker is powerless before the vast economic, political, and social forces of modern society. The union gives him a channel to get at the employer, the huge impersonal corporation. As a union member he becomes increasingly aware that "something can be done" about depressions and inflation, about working conditions and hours, about the way congressmen vote and Presidents behave. Actually, membership in a big union may leave him as an individual little more direct control over his working and nonworking life than before the union. But the "feel" is often as important as the "fact," and if he has to be controlled he'd rather it would be by the union which is made up of "his people" and over which he has at least some control.

4. Workers want to understand the forces which control their lives. Nearly everyone is uneasy when he is subject to forces he doesn't understand. The corporation, the private enterprise system, balance sheets and profit-and-loss statements—the working man knows that all these are somehow important, but he understands little of what they mean or how they work. The union he can trust to explain what is going on; management he doesn't quite trust. American unions have gone only a little way in developing a folklore of the economic system for workers. Unions abroad have gone further.

5. Lastly, every man looks for self-respect. He needs to be satisfied with what he is doing, to be "doing right" by his own standards. Equally, he needs to feel that other people "treat him right." Justice is hard to define, but no man who

feels he is being treated unjustly is a happy, satisfied person. "They ought to treat you like a human being, you know." . . . "I'm as good as they are, any day." The worker's standards for self-respect and justice may be very different from yours, but they are important to him. For many, the union helps achieve this self-respect.

To describe unions as merely a mechanism through which workers bargain collectively for higher wages and shorter hours, Bakke argued, is to miss much of the flavor of unionism in America. Individual dignity and the feeling of belonging may be as important to millions of workers as higher wages and better working conditions. Unionism today is a far-reaching social and psychological institution, as well as a powerful economic and political mechanism. The rise in the status and security of the American working man over the past quarter-century is hard to understand without having personally lived through the pre-New Deal days and the New Deal struggles of the 1930's. Much of this improvement has been due to unions. But much has also been due to the changing sympathies of the American public, and to management's own initiative in doing a better, more broadly conceived job than was true in most firms a generation ago.

Unionism versus no unions is no longer the central issue in America. Most workers who want unions have them. The issue today for most Americans is how the power of unions and their leaders can be channeled effectively toward the public good. And the spectacular rise in income and security for the typical union member are signficantly changing what workers themselves want from their unions. Bakke's picture points up important truths. But the role of unions is clearly undergoing change in the American economy of today.

GOVERNMENT AND LABOR

Economically, the continuous jockeying between labor and management centers around wages and profits—the distribution of the national income. But this is only part of what is at stake. The struggle is for power, status, and security, too. Should the government encourage or discourage labor unions? Should it intervene when wages push up against its inflation-control efforts?

Major Legislation

Even before the New Deal, the tide of public opinion had begun to swing away from such complete employer dominance. But the Norris-La Guardia Act of 1932 was the first major prolabor legislation. Employers had long been able to get court injunctions against labor groups to prohibit just about anything—for example, striking or picketing. Once the injunction was obtained, labor was the wrong-doer in the eyes of the law. Norris-La Guardia outlawed the injunction in federal courts as an employer weapon against a wide variety of union activities—strikes, joining a union, peaceful picketing, or giving financial aid to unions. The intent of the law was clear. It was to give unions support in achieving a more equal bargaining status with employers, and to eliminate one of the most powerful and misused employer weapons.

The New Deal, a year later, was frankly and aggressively prolabor. The National Industrial Recovery Act stated the legal right of the workers to organize and bargain collectively. But the N.I.R.A. was short-lived; it was declared unconstitutional in 1935. Congress wasted no time in replacing its labor provisions.

The Wagner Act. The National Labor Relations Act (the "Wagner Act"), passed in 1935, is the cornerstone of modern prolabor legislation. The Act:

1. Affirmed the legal right of employees to organize and bargain collectively, free from employer interference or coercion.
2. Required employers to bargain with unions of the workers' own free choosing.
3. Specifically prohibited a list of "unfair" employer practices.
4. Set up the National Labor Relations Board to provide a mechanism through which workers could gain recognition for unions of their own choosing, and to act as a quasi-court to protect workers against unfair labor practices. (The N.L.R.B. does not act directly to mediate or settle labor-management disputes.) Employer

intimidation, anti-union discrimination in hiring and firing, company attempts to influence union elections, and a variety of other practices were soon outlawed as unfair practices as N.L.R.B. and court decisions interpreted the new law.

By the early 1940's, the bitterest union organizing struggles were over, and industrial unionism in the mass-production industries was firmly entrenched. In the courts, labor also fared better. The Supreme Court, reflecting the changing temper of the times and the presence of sev₁ eral Roosevelt-appointed judges, in the Apex and Hutcheson cases (1940 and 1941) reversed a long line of judicial precedent and granted unions virtual immunity from the Sherman Act, though in the Allen Bradley Case of 1945 an exception was made where they conspired with employers to fix prices or divide markets.

Public policy toward labor under the Wagner Act thus represents a 180 degree turn from public policy toward business combinations under the Sherman Act. The Wagner Act encourages workers to combine in unions in order to raise the prices at which they sell their labor, precisely the practice forbidden to business sellers by the Sherman Act. Should public policy face one way in labor markets and the other in commodity markets? Now is a good time to stop and ask yourself.

Fair Labor Standards Act of 1938. The Wagner Act was aimed at strengthening organized labor's power to deal with employers. The Federal Fair Labor Standards Act of 1938 established minimum wages, maximum basic hours, and other fair labor standards for all labor in interstate commerce.

The core of F.L.S.A. was its mandatory-minimum-wage and maximum-basic-hours provisions. No covered employer could pay less than 25 cents an hour. A basic work week of 40 hours was established; employees could be worked longer, but overtime work required a higher pay rate. Other fair labor standards were spelled out, notably the first federal prohibition of child labor. F.L.S.A. has been periodically amended since 1938, both to widen the coverage and to raise the minimum wage ($1.60 in 1968).

The Taft-Hartley Act. Many called the Wagner Act labor's Magna Carta. All through the 1930's and in World War II, labor rode high. But the pendulum had swung too far. More and more middle-of-the-roaders began to feel that labor had overstepped its bounds; first in the sit-down strikes of the 1930's; then in the spreading jurisdictional disputes and strikes that the public and employers seemed powerless to halt; in its persistent wage demands during the World War II fight against inflation; and lastly, in its outright defiance of the federal government itself in disputes of critical importance to the national economy. The Taft-Hartley Act was passed, over President Truman's veto, in 1947, as an attempt to redress the balance of power between management and labor. Taft-Hartley defined unfair labor practices of unions to parallel those of employers. It clarified the powers of employers to speak against unions, so long as their pronouncement contained no threats or intimidations; and it prohibited the closed shop. It contained provisions to protect the individual worker against the union; unions may not coerce workers to join, disclosure of union financial affairs is required, and nonpayment of dues is the only ground on which a union can force discharge of a worker under union-shop contract. It permitted states to prohibit union-shop contracts. Last, it empowered the President under conditions of national emergency to petition a federal court for an injunction against any strike or lock-out for an 80-day cooling-off period, and required a secret union ballot on the latest company offer before the end of that period.

The Landrum-Griffin Act. By 1959, labor racketeering had become a national scandal, and Congress passed the Landrum-Griffin Act, again over the violent objections of union leaders. Nearly everyone agreed that the law was unnecessary to regulate many American unions, which are open and law-abiding organizations. But nonetheless, there was no resisting the public pressure generated by Congressional committee disclosures of labor malpractices. Landrum-Griffin included a new "bill of rights" for individual union members, requirements for more detailed financial reporting by unions of all transactions with officials and members, a provision tightening restrictions on secondary boycotts and organizational picket-ing, a requirement for secret-ballot elections and limitations for the term of office of labor officials between elections, and a prohibition against any person who has been convicted of a felony or who has been a member of the Communist Party serv-ing as a union official for at least five years after conviction.[6]

Mediation, Conciliation, and Arbitration

Often a skillful third party can soothe hot tempers and help get labor and management to-gether when they are negotiating a contract or settling a grievance. The federal government and most state governments provide "mediators"and "conciliators" who serve as impartial go-betweens in trying to get disputes settled without resort to strikes. Sometimes these men enter at the re-quest of labor and management; sometimes they are sent by public officials who want to be sure that work stoppages are avoided. Their work is generally unheralded and unspectacular, but it is successful in a great number of cases. To watch a skilled mediator at work is an intriguing experi-ence. He has no power to force his views on either party. He must bring them together by winning their confidence, isolating the issues at stake, and somehow making each see the reasonableness of the other's position—as well as reminding both frequently of the public's interest in avoiding work stoppages.

Although governments frequently send in a mediator or conciliator, they have no general authority to act as "arbitrator" with power to prescribe settlement terms in labor disputes (ex-cept in the case of the railways). Nevertheless, as chief executive, the President has frequently stepped into disputes that vitally affect the na-tional welfare, has appointed "fact-finding boards," and in effect has brought into play the full pressure of public opinion behind the settle-ment recommended. At the local level, governors and mayors often follow similar procedures.

[6] For a fuller account of the changing legal foundations of unions and collective bargaining, see L. G. Reynolds, *Labor Economics and Labor Relations* (Englewood Cliffs, N.J.: Prentice-Hall, 1964), Chapter 5.

The Government as Watchdog

Congress has long been quick to investigate labor-management affairs. Labor racketeering and the wage-price spiral have been favorite subjects. Some investigations have been sober and careful. Others have focused mainly on the headlines. But either variety exerts a strong pressure on both labor and management to be prepared to defend in public the actions they take.

The McClellan Committee of the late 1950's, for example, played a major role in ex-posing gangsterism, bribery, and hoodlumism in the affairs and practices of some unions. Labor leader after labor leader was placed on the public stand to testify about alleged conversion of union funds to personal use, blackmail, payoffs for union protection, violence, and even arson and murder. Shocking numbers of such officials retreated be-hind the Fifth Amendment of the Constitution, refusing to answer questions on grounds their answers might tend to incriminate them in criminal actions. Although most of the labor movement is undoubtedly far from the practices exposed by the McClellan Committee, such com-mittee action points up for the public, for Con-gress, and for the unions themselves problems properly of national concern.

The Government as Wage-setter

Suppose a nation-wide steel strike is in progress. The union, pointing to rising living costs, high profits, increasing productivity, and a sweeping variety of other considerations, argues that 20 cents an hour more in pay and fringe benefits is the lowest raise it will even consider. Management in the steel industry's Big Six say they won't offer a penny more than 10 cents. They say that profits are down, that capacity is up enormously and foreign competition is mur-derous, that steel wages have risen faster than prices, and that steel workers are already among the best-paid workers in the nation. After long months of bickering back and forth with no progress, the union calls a strike. The strike has gone on now for two long months, and the steel shortage is shutting down not only civilian pro-duction but also arms production and construction of missile and other military facilities. If you were President, what would you do?

You might say, let the strike go on. It's none of the government's business. But with the economy grinding to a halt and critical defense needs, you probably wouldn't.

You might invoke the national-emergency provision of the Taft-Hartley Act. This probably would get the union back to work and would give you 80 days to bring all the pressure you could on both sides to settle their differences. You'd get your top assistants on the job, and focus as much public pressure as you could on the negotiators. If you felt strongly that right was mainly on one side or the other, you might tell the American people so and build up pressure on the other side to capitulate. But your position is especially tough if you're also worried about inflation, so you don't want to see a settlement that leads the companies to raise steel prices.

The power of the federal government is great, and chances are that this kind of pressure would bring some kind of settlement, hopefully noninflationary. No private business or union wants to fight the government. The odds are stacked in favor of the President. But . . . suppose this time neither the companies nor the union will give in. So the workers go out on strike again at the end of 80 days, more bitter than ever. What then?

Then is the tough time. By now tempers are really frayed. Labor and management have been over the issues *ad nauseam*. Each has been provoked into saying a lot of things better left unsaid. Everybody's dirty linen has been thoroughly aired before 200 million Americans.

You might decide to seize the steel industry and ask the workers to stay on the job. But this means seizing a vast, privately owned industry, against all the traditions of American freedom and probably against the Constitution. Or you might order the workers to stay on the job, in the interests of the public welfare. But you know perfectly well you can't make men make steel, either under the law or any other way, if they just won't go back to work and do it.

Well, what would *you* do?

This is an extreme example. But it drama-

tizes a problem that has arisen repeatedly in the last quarter-century. Consider the government's continuing attempt to check wage-price inflation since the Korean War. The Eisenhower, Kennedy, and Johnson administrations repeatedly exhorted management and labor to reach noninflationary settlements and hold down prices. To keep the pressure on for such settlements, monetary and fiscal policy were run as tight as was consistent with trying to avoid unemployment and stimulate more rapid growth. By the 1960's, the combination of pressures seemed to be working fairly well, but with some inflationary drift in consumer prices and the persistent danger of faster wage increases and more inflation. President Kennedy's vigorous use of presidential pressure and public opinion to roll back announced steel price increases in 1962 raised violent objections among businesses, as have presidential pressures against inflationary wage increases from union members. Presidents Kennedy and Johnson increasingly used the "wage-price guideposts" to mobilize public opinion against inflationary wage settlements and price policies.

Should the President push the guideposts now as a constraint on both labor and management? Should President Kennedy have intervened against steel price increases in 1962? Lots of people worry over the vast governmental power that can be brought to bear against unions and companies. But others say that the government has no alternative. No President, they say, could responsibly let the national interest—inflation control at home and a sound dollar abroad—be overridden by the wage and profit claims of one union or one industry, even such an important one as steel. Often unions do what they please in spite of presidential pressure, for example in the Longshoremen's crippling strikes for pay increases far above the guideposts. Should the President be given more power to deal with such cases?

Improving Labor Markets

Fiscal and monetary policies have the primary governmental responsibility for helping to assure employment opportunities for those able, willing, and seeking to work. History shows that strong aggregate demand for labor works well in bringing unemployed workers and empty jobs together; that businessmen with unfilled orders show admirable efficiency in finding and training the workers they need. But increasingly the nation has felt that government should act to improve further the efficiency of labor markets in matching workers and jobs over time, space, and occupations.

The main federal step in this direction is the U.S. Employment Service, which operates cooperatively with the states through some 1,900 local employment offices to channel information on jobs openings from employers to potential workers. The Manpower Development and Training Acts since 1962 have provided funds to train unskilled workers for job vacancies, to retrain workers thrown out of jobs, and to otherwise improve the linkage between job vacancies and workers who need aid to find and fit the jobs. Counseling for young entrants into the labor force and special aid for disadvantaged groups were provided by special antipoverty and underdeveloped-area programs.

Compared to the Wagner Act and the big shift of government labor policies outlined above, the impact of specific government measures to improve the efficiency of labor markets has thus far been small. It has been especially inadequate for the unemployed masses in the big-city slums. We have done little compared to most Western European nations, which manage much lower unemployment rates than ours. Improved job information, counseling, technical training, and labor mobility could help significantly to improve the efficiency of the economy, to facilitate adjustment to change, and to lower the margin of unemployment that is consistent with noninflationary growth in aggregate demand. Clearly, we must rely increasingly on steps to improve job markets as aggregate demand policies succeed in holding general unemployment to low levels.

SHOULD THE GOVERNMENT GET OUT?

Ours is an economy of power groups. The unions and their leaders have great power. So do employers. Wage-setting has moved from the competitive market place to the industry-wide bargaining table in many leading industries. The wage bargains set in steel, autos, electrical equipment, and coal go far to set the pattern for the rest of the economy. How can the government stand aside and see its arms program jeopardized, its anti-inflation program split open, the operation of the whole economy periled by disputes in these industries. Less than 1 per cent of the nation's labor force is employed in trucking. Yet that 1 per cent could probably bring the economy almost to a dead stop in a few weeks. An even smaller number belong to the United Mine Workers. Yet a three-month strike by the UMW through the winter months would not only shut down steel, public utilities, and other major industries, but would leave millions of homes cold and uninhabitable throughout the country. A mere handful of men can shut down the railroads and through them much of the economy, if they choose to strike.

But if it is drawn in, what can government really do? Many observers think that government intervention, especially when it becomes habitual, does more harm than good. They argue that when both sides know the government will eventually step in to settle the issue, there is little chance of settling the dispute beforehand. This is particularly true, they say, in inflationary periods when both labor and management know they will ultimately get much of what they want by putting on enough pressure, and the main question is how much prices will be pushed up for the consumer. One side or the other will nearly always feel it can get a better bargain by waiting to get government involved in the settlement. Thus excessive government intervention in bargaining may hide the need for management and labor themselves to accept basic responsibility in a free society. Private decisions within a framework of legal rules of the game is the basic philosophy on which the American system rests.

The American economy has come a long way from the highly competitive, individualistic, free-market system described by the classical economists. The leaders of big business and big labor now set wages and prices by bargaining, compromise, and discretion, albeit substantially constrained by the forces of the market. Perhaps this concentrated power is incompatible with a smoothly functioning, free-enterprise economic system and a truly democratic political system. But concentrated economic power is here, like it or not. The problem is somehow to develop a framework within which economic power is responsibly channeled to the public good. The hard fact is that we cannot order huge groups of work- ers around in a democratic society. Wage-setting must be by consensus when two powerful groups face each other across the bargaining table. And it must be by political as well as economic con- sensus, once the government steps into the scene as a major participant in the process of wage- setting.

For Analysis and Discussion

1. Over the past decade union membership has declined slightly as the demand for labor has grown mainly outside the traditionally unionized areas. What is the outlook for union power over the decade ahead?
2. "Unions are justified where employers would otherwise be able to ex- ploit employees, but nowhere else." Do you agree? Explain.
3. Should production employees be put on regular annual salary like those used for white-collar workers and middle management? If not, why not?
4. If you were a factory worker and union members in the plant put pres- sure on you to join the union, would you join? Would you consider such pressures an infringement of your personal freedom of choice?
5. Would it be better to give employees the extra money rather than all the fringe benefits commonly included in union contracts, so that each person could decide for himself how to spend the money?
6. Should compulsory arbitration be required by law to avoid strikes which affect the public interest? How would you define the public interest for this purpose?
7. Should the government get completely out of wage negotiations?
8. When the government intervenes in wage negotiations—for example, in steel—what criteria should it use in deciding what wage settlement to urge?
9. Would a higher minimum-wage law significantly raise (or lower) the incomes received by presently poverty-level workers? Explain.
10. The Taft-Hartley Act requires unions and management to bargain "in good faith." Suppose an employer decides to make his best offer at the outset and thereafter refuses to improve the offer. Is he bargaining in good faith?

Appendix

THE ECONOMICS OF MINIMUM-WAGE LAWS

What are the economic effects of a minimum- wage law covering all workers in interstate com- merce? This question provides an interesting chance to apply your economic analysis to an important issue of labor policy. Suppose, for example, that the minimum hourly wage under the Fair Labor Stan- dards Act is raised sharply to $2.00, in an attempt to raise the incomes of low-paid workers. For the moment, assume a constant level of total expendi- tures in the economy.

1. Assuming that the $2.00 is higher than the previous wage rate for some workers, economic theory says that the cost of hiring such workers will be raised, prices boosted, sales reduced, and employment cut. Those whose marginal productivity is less than $2.00 will lose their jobs, although workers who keep their jobs will get at least the $2.00 minimum rate. The new jobless may stay unemployed or they may go to work elsewhere in jobs not covered by the mini- mum-wage law (which applies only to firms in inter- state commerce). If they do the latter, the uncovered substandard wages are forced even lower as the labor supply there rises without any increase in demand. The net result is to injure precisely the lowest-wage, lowest-income workers whom it was designed to help,

since they are the ones with the lowest marginal productivities.[7]

2. However, if employers were "exploiting" labor before the law by paying wages below labor's marginal productivity, the minimum-wage law may simply boost wages without reducing employment. Wages get more of the consumer's dollar, profits get less. This is the situation implicitly assumed in most of the ardent arguments for minimum-wage legislation.

3. Even if there is no exploitation of labor, the law's upward pressure on wage rates may drive employers to more efficient methods, thereby absorbing the higher wages without reducing employment. This, too, is a favorite argument of minimum-wage-law advocates. How often it works this way is not clear from the evidence. A lot depends on how effective businessmen have been at running their businesses without the pressures of the minimum-wage laws.

4. Minimum-wage laws tend to redistribute incomes—from employers to labor and mainly from workers who get pushed out to those who keep their jobs at higher pay. What happens to the total labor share in the national income depends basically on the elasticity of demand for labor. If employers' aggregate demand is inelastic, the law will mean higher total wage payments. Unfortunately, we don't know what the general elasticity of demand for labor is, though we do know that higher wages induce the substitution of capital for labor over extended periods. It's much easier to estimate what the elasticity may be in particular industries at particular times. The impact of a minimum-wage law is uneven,

[7] Note that the effect here and in the following points is substantially the same as if an economywide union was enforcing the minimum wage.

operating mainly against low-productivity workers wherever they are.

5. Now drop the assumption of constant total spending in the economy. What does a minimum-wage law do to the total level of employment? In a boom period, probably not a lot. Any workers thrown out of jobs in covered industries can be absorbed in uncovered fields, even though they may have to take lower-paid jobs. In depression, this re-absorption is not so easy, and persisting unemployment may result from minimum-wage legislation. These issues are essentially the same ones that arise when wages are pushed up by union action. We have already looked at some of the results in Chapter 14.

Repeal by Inflation.   But don't stop with the theoretical analysis. Look at the real-world problem. As a practical matter, the minimum-wage law probably hasn't had much effect on the American economy. It has been repealed by inflation. By the time the act originally went into effect, minimum wages in most covered industries had already risen above the specified level. Then inflation and boom times pushed wages up faster than the gradual rise to 40 cents first specified by the law. Wages in a few industries lagged behind the minimum figures, but these were mainly industries not covered by the law—agriculture, services, local shops, and so on, not in interstate commerce. Further inflation and rising wages robbed first a new 75¢, then a $1.00, a $1.25, and a $1.40 legal minimum of much of their intended impact. Thus, there is little evidence that the law has thus far had a major effect on the wage structure for major industries. But it has clearly affected certain low-wage areas (especially in the South), scattered low-wage pockets throughout the economy, and such special low-productivity groups as uneducated workers and teenagers.

THIRTY-TWO
THE PROBLEMS
OF POVERTY
AND INSECURITY

Poverty.

Insecurity.

Economic Perspective
on Poverty and Insecurity.

Poverty is as old as man. America is rich, and by the standards of most of the world poverty has been virtually eliminated here. The visitor from India or the Congo would see nothing that even approaches the poverty that the mass of his people take for granted. Even by our own standards, today poverty affects only a minority of our people. But even in the "affluent society" of modern America there is an economic underworld of poverty, as well as a widespread fear of economic insecurity.

These two problems—poverty and insecurity—provide two excellent opportunities to apply the economic theory you have learned thus far in understanding why they exist, and in evaluating what, if anything, we can do about them. For both are case studies which illustrate the intricate intermix of macro- and micro-economics in the real world, and the close interactions among economic, social, and political processes in our society as well. This chapter is thus an exercise in applying macro- and micro-economic theory to two important public-policy problems.

POVERTY

Chapter 3 laid out one orderly approach to analyzing policy-type problems. First define the problem: Where are we now, and where do we want to go? Second, map out the main elements of the situation analytically, pointing up the main alternative policies for moving from where we are to where we want to be. Third, weigh the alternatives and decide which, all things considered, seems best.

Where are we now? What are the facts

about poverty? In 1966 the median family income in the United States was about $7,400. In that same year about seven million families had money incomes of less than $3,000; their median income was $1,800, and over one million of the families were raising four or more children on that income. About five million people living alone had incomes below $1,500. Together, these two groups included about 30 million Americans, nearly one-sixth of the population. These are the poor.

But there is much debate about how poverty should be defined, about where the borderline belongs between the poor and the reasonably well off. The use of $3,000 for a family and $1,500 for an individual living alone as income cut-off points is an obviously arbitrary choice, but one that has been widely adopted in recent years. For a family of four, this test means a per capita money income of about $750. For an individual living alone, $1,500 means barely over $25 a week for everything—food, lodging, clothing, medical care, recreation. Other estimates indicate that about 20 million Americans are poor enough to qualify for public assistance in their various states, with family incomes below about $2,300 (though less than half receive public assistance). To be more accurate, we should set different poverty levels for families of different sizes, living in cities or on farms, and the like. Use of such other standards gives somewhat different answers, but still leaves a large number of poor.

What is considered poverty changes with the times, and some people say we just define poverty so there will always be some. They argue that there's only a poverty problem in the eyes of the do-gooders. Twenty years ago, the median money income of all families was only about $4,000 (in 1966 prices), and $2,000 was often considered the poverty level. Then a third of all families would have fallen below the $3,000 poverty level which we use now. Economic growth has steadily pushed most families above the minimum levels which seemed reasonable a generation or two ago. But our aspirations have risen with our rising incomes.

Who Are the Poor?

In 1962, Michael Harrington wrote a book, *The Other America*, which touched the conscience of many Americans. The other America,

Harrington wrote, is the world of the poor in the midst of plenty—a world of desolation, of hopelessness, of bitterness and resentment, of slums, of discrimination. It is the world of Negroes and Puerto Ricans living in the great city slums; of old men and women living alone in rented rooms; of poor Southern farmers living in ramshackle huts without plumbing; of fatherless families whose mothers struggle to support their children; of failures and rejects for a dozen other reasons.

To understand poverty, Harrington argued, we must add sociology to economics. The poor, he wrote, live in a subculture of their own. Most of them feel—with apathy or resentment—that no one cares. It is a world whose inhabitants are isolated from the mainstream of American life and alienated from its values. It is a world whose occupants are literally concerned with day-to-day survival, where minor illness is a major tragedy, where fatback and cheap greens are a standard diet. Lastly, it is a world turned in on itself in its values and its habits, a world in which the poverty of the parents is visited upon the children.

Each year, many families move up from the ranks of the poor, and some families slide down below the imaginary line. But the great bulk of the poor stay poor.

To understand the problem of poverty, you must recognize that the poor differ widely. Five groups loom large.

Negroes. Although only two million of the seven million poor families are nonwhite, between 40 and 50 per cent of all Negro families are poor. Many of these families live in the rural South; over 80 per cent of Negro farmers are in the poverty group. But increasingly they have moved to the northern city slums. Those who live in the cities have incomes 50 per cent below whites with comparable education. In the city slums, two-thirds of Negro youths are drop-outs before they complete high school. The breakdown of the Negro family in the city slums is a critical part of the problem of Negro poverty.

Farmers. Over 40 per cent of all farm families are poor. Rural poverty is concentrated in the South. A substantial portion of poor Southern farmers are the Negroes mentioned above. Government aids to agriculture provide virtually no help to the poor farmers; the money goes largely to the big, well-capitalized farmers.

Old People. Old age brings poverty about as often as it brings adequate retirement. Of about eight million families in which the husband is over 65, nearly half fall in the poverty group. In addition there are nearly four million old people living alone on annual incomes of less than $1,500. Social security doesn't help much. The average benefit is only about $80 a month, or less than $1,000 a year, and only half of the nation's poor receive government benefit payments.

Fatherless Families. About half of all women left alone to provide for their children are poor. Fatherless families are common in the low-income groups, and the woman who has to earn her family's living must either leave her children alone (which she often does in the poverty groups) or find someone to look after them. She faces many lost work days and job instability. Often the family exists entirely on public assistance, especially in the city slums like Harlem. The breakdown of the family is near the core of the massive Negro problem in the city slums. Probably not one out of three Negro children in poor families now reaches 18 having lived his life with both his parents. The number of nonwhite women and children on public welfare has climbed sharply since 1950.

Others. About one-third of all poor families don't fit into any of the groups above. They live in depressed areas; they have poor motivation; they have low intelligence; most have bad education; they have chosen occupations which demand has passed by. By the test of the market they are failures, the rejects of our modern economy.

One generalization applies to all these groups. Most come from poor families and have been poor all their lives.

The above picture is substantially accurate, but statistics can be misleading. Some observers argue that using money incomes as a test overstates the magnitude of the problem. The poor Southern farmer with an annual income of $1,000 and six children eats better off the land than the arithmetic would suggest. Some poor families, especially the elderly, have accumulated assets, and draw on them to supplement their current in-

comes. Thus, their actual consumption is well above the incomes they report. In many ways, consumption would be a better measure of poverty than is current money income, and such a measure might show an appreciable number of the poor families better off than they seem. Clearly, families whose incomes drop temporarily may appear very poor by the income test, but they may maintain their consumption standards while waiting for a return to normal incomes. But with all these reservations, most of those who are poor by the income test above *are* poor by modern American standards.

Why Are They Poor?

There are many reasons why the poor are poor. In a brief analysis, we must simplify drastically. But, recognizing this warning, the theory of the preceding chapters should help you greatly in straightening out the causes of poverty.

Inadequate Aggregate Demand. When there is recession, unemployment raises the proportion of the population below the poverty line. Conversely, prosperity brings more jobs, especially for marginal members of the labor force who are last to be taken on. A major depression is a catastrophe for the poor.

But only a small fraction of the poor in prosperous 1966 were "unemployed," as measured by the unemployment statistics. Many of the poor were elderly people, past their working years; many in the slums, especially Negroes, had given up looking for work; others were not in the labor force for a variety of other reasons. Rising aggregate demand and falling unemployment help to lessen poverty, but they give jobs and higher incomes only to those who have a service to sell. The best estimates suggest that reduction of the overall unemployment rate from 4 per cent to 3 per cent would reduce the population below the poverty line by only about 1 percentage point.

But the indirect effects of a prosperous economy are more important than this figure suggests in lessening barriers against minority groups as labor markets tighten, in providing more on-the-job training for marginal workers, in providing partial employment for the elderly, and in other indirect ways.

Low Productivity. The message of Chapters 29 and 30 was that individual incomes generally depend, to a *rough* first approximation, on the marginal productivity of the individuals concerned. If this is correct, given a reasonable level of aggregate demand, poor people in the labor market are by-an-large poor because their marginal productivity is low. They are poor because they are not worth more to employers in a profit-motivated economy. Or, if they are elderly, they are poor now because they did not adequately plan ahead, *if* they had an adequate life income to provide a reasonable retirement income through savings.

This is a harsh conclusion, and, as we shall see in a moment, one that is only partially correct. But it has a strong core of truth. Over 60 per cent of all poor families are headed by an individual with less than an eighth-grade education; only about 22 per cent by individuals who completed high school. Many old people, even though seeking work, can offer only limited services in the market. Women attempting to support their children inescapably lose more time than others. Many of the poor have no skills, or obsolete ones.

Discrimination and Other Market Imperfections. A basic cause of Negro poverty is discrimination—in education, jobs, access to medical care, on nearly every score. Negro male incomes are roughly 50 per cent lower than those for whites at the same years of education, area of residence, and sex. If Negroes had received the same average pay as whites having the same education, the personal income of Negroes and of the nation would have been as much as $10–13 billion higher in 1966. Other nonwhites face the same type of discrimination, although estimates of its extent are very hard to make. Not only does discrimination exist, but in spite of recent improvement on civil rights generally, the spread between nonwhite and white incomes at comparable educational levels has not narrowed in recent years. The biggest relative improvement in the income position of nonwhites occurred during World War II, when boom-period demand for labor provided jobs for nonwhites and bid up their incomes rapidly relative to whites'. Elimination of discrimination

would leave many nonwhites in the poverty group, but it would dramatically improve their relative position.

Immobility, apathy, and ignorance of job openings are generally characteristic of the poor. Poor Southern farmers, both Negro and white, appear to be highly immobile, except for the young. In Appalachia, there has been a massive exodus of population, but again almost entirely of young people. Thus, the poor of middle age and beyond tend neither to know about alternative job opportunities nor to be willing or able to move to them if the information is available. To move is expensive and uncertain. The subculture of the poor has little contact with the formal processes of employment exchanges and the information and mobility devices available to the middle classes. Even in the cities, the poor have little contact with the job markets of the middle classes.

Absence from the Labor Force. Half of all poor families are headed by individuals who are not in the labor force. Many of these are elderly people, but many others are discouraged youths and mothers of fatherless families who have given up looking for work. Thus, the problems of poverty, family instability, and insecurity in old age are inseparably intertwined. Others are out of the labor force for a variety of reasons—because of ill health, lack of motivation, family circumstances, or simply because they have given up hope of finding a job. Unless rising aggregate demand, lessened discrimination, or improved information and mobility were to pull some of these individuals back into the labor force, no improvement in economic conditions or in the workings of the market can help alleviate their poverty.

Beyond these four economic causes, most observers add a socio-economic analysis. Poverty breeds poverty, in a vicious circle. A poor individual or family has a high probability of staying poor. The poor live largely in slums or in backward rural areas. Their children do not learn to read, to write, even to speak well. They grow up to apathy or resentment, and they go to poor schools with other poor children. They lag far behind children in middle-class schools, and their drop-out rate is high—not surprisingly, for there is little in their culture to make them care about education. When the poor are sick they stay sick longer because they have inadequate medical care. Thus they find it harder to keep jobs. Broken homes are common. Often there is little motivation or hope to rise from the vicious circle of poverty, either for the young or for adults.

Policies against Poverty

In 1964, President Johnson declared "unconditional war on poverty" as a major goal of his administration. But to lessen poverty is a complex, difficult problem. We cannot explore all the many approaches that have been suggested. But the above analysis, together with the theory of earlier chapters, should suggest some broad lines of attack.

Maintaining High Employment. Macro-economics tells us that maintaining high employment, a labor market in which demand for workers is strong, should be a powerful force for the reduction of poverty. Against poverty, as against many of our other problems, a combined attack on the macro and micro levels makes sense. To try to eradicate poverty without strong aggregate demand and general prosperity offers little hope of success.

Accelerating Economic Growth. Over the long run, faster growth in output per capita provides a fundamental approach to the erosion of poverty. Normal economic growth, like that of the postwar years, appears to reduce the proportion of poverty by about 1 per cent a year—e.g., from 17 to 16 per cent. Anything we can do to speed growth should correspondingly speed the elimination of poverty.

Improving the Productivity of the Poor. Probably the most basic reason for low incomes is the low productivity of the poor, certainly if we set aside the problem of the aged. By and large, investment in human beings increases their productivity, just as does investment in nonhuman wealth. For many reasons, society's investment in the poor falls far short of its investment in most

individuals who rise above poverty. The poor live in slums, in squalor. They receive short and poor educations. They receive little job training in schools or on the job, since they so often find no employment. They receive inadequate medical care. If we wish to raise the productivity of many of the poor, larger investment to develop their productive capacity is the first prescription that arises from standard economic analysis.

Lessening Discrimination. Especially for nonwhites, discrimination accounts for a significant part of the poverty problem, not merely through the barriers it erects to current jobs, but more fundamentally by limiting educational opportunities, destroying motivation, and generally reinforcing the vicious circle of poverty.

Improving Labor Markets. Many of the poor are effectively isolated from jobs by lack of information, immobility, and inertia, in addition to discrimination. This is especially true of the rural poor in the South. But it is also true in the slums of the great cities, where for thousands of unskilled and poorly educated teenagers and adults there is no practical channel into the jobs that are opening up elsewhere in the economy, even in the same city. To say that individuals with proper motivation would seek out the jobs that may be open elsewhere is a very partial answer for the Puerto Rican or Negro teenager in Harlem or in the backwoods of Alabama.

Better job-training programs, employment exchanges, guidance and counseling services, and the like could help those who suffer merely from inadequate information or are immobile because of financial difficulties. Better information, better education, and better training programs for both youth and adults make sense both to fight poverty and on their own merits to improve the efficiency of our economic system.

Many economists blame unions and the government itself for important job barriers. Many craft unions still have *de facto* barriers against nonwhites for apprenticeships and union membership, thus in effect blocking them from higher-paying jobs. And the federal minimum wage law of $1.60 per hour as of 1968, however admirable its purpose, surely shuts many low-productivity workers out of jobs which might be there at lower wage rates for such workers, especially poorly educated, poverty-group teenagers.

Money-Income Redistribution. Direct money grants of about $10 billion, or only about 1 per cent of g.n.p., would be sufficient to raise every poor family and individual above the $3,000 per family or $1,500 per individual poverty level indicated above. Some economists argue that this is the simplest attack on the poverty problem, and that it would have the great virtue of letting us see the full cost of the program. In addition, it would give recipients of aid freedom to spend their incomes as they wish, in contrast to other programs which force them to take aid through housing subsidies, medical assistance, and the like.

But this approach would not raise society's total real income; it would merely redistribute what we now produce without using the productive potential of many poor. Moreover, such direct cash grants to all the poor might face serious problems on the incentive front, since other individuals now earning somewhat more than the poverty level might prefer to take direct subsidies and avoid the work. Thus, the actual cost of such a subsidy approach to the poverty problem would probably be larger than the $10 billion indicated. At the extreme, if everyone now earning stopped work, the total cost would go up to about $25 billion. But it would still be a small percentage of g.n.p.

The "Negative Income Tax". Recently a somewhat startling proposal has been advanced to provide a direct income transfer (subsidy) to the poor without destroying their incentive to work and earn. This proposal is a "negative income tax" under which the government would pay out funds to individuals below some specified income level, rather than collecting taxes from them. Everyone, rich or poor, would file a tax return. But a *negative* tax rate would apply on incomes below some "poverty" level, and the government would pay the amount calculated to the citizen, rather than the reverse.

Table 32-1 shows how such a negative income tax might work. For a family of four it sets $3,000 as the poverty level below which the negative tax rate would apply, and also sets the negative rates so as to guarantee a minimum income of $1,500. (Obviously, the rate structure could be set to provide a higher or lower minimum.) Once an income of $3,000 is reached, a family would slide gradually over into a regular taxpayer status.

Note that the negative tax rate structure is carefully designed to assure that the poor family gets more total income (earned income plus subsidy) by working than by merely taking the negative tax payments. This effect is crucial to the plan; otherwise it would be a simple money subsidy which would directly undercut the poor family's incentive to earn. Some economists would change the rate structure so as to emphasize this incentive to work more, by having the subsidy decline more slowly as earned income rises. Advocates like the plan better than a simple money

TABLE 32-1
NEGATIVE INCOME TAX EXAMPLE * (Family of Four)

Earned Income	Taxable Income	Negative Tax Rate	Subsidy	Total After-Tax Income
$ 0	—$3,000	50%	$1,500	$1,500
1,000	— 2,000	37.5	750	1,750
2,000	— 1,000	25	250	2,250
3,000	0	0	0	3,000
4,000 **	+ 1,000	—14	—140	3,860

* On assumption that subsidy should provide minimum family income of half the $3,-000 poverty level. Rates could be adjusted to provide different subsidy levels.

** Neglects allowance for deductions available under U.S. tax law which would reduce tax below the $140 shown for typical family.

subsidy mainly because it would maintain poor people's incentive to work and earn.[1]

The Government as Residual Employer. Following the destructive riots of 1967, a still more dramatic proposal was advanced by some observers, that the government step in as residual employer for the poor who seek jobs but cannot find them, especially in the big city slum areas. The government might employ the jobless directly, in city cleanup work, in providing more mail deliveries, or in other jobs useful to the public. Or it might subsidize private businesses to employ the otherwise unemployables. Jobs, incomes, and a feeling of personal usefulness, these observers argued, are essential if we are to break the syndrome of poverty, especially in the nonwhite city "ghettos." Another 500,000 jobs for the currently unemployables, especially the youth, could make the difference between constructive forward movement and increasing social disintegration, riots, and blight in our central cities. The expense, they argue, while immediately large, would be small compared to the enormous social and economic costs of inaction.

The War on Poverty

What have we actually done to combat poverty? In 1964, Congress passed the Economic Opportunity Act (significantly, not called the antipoverty act) as the opening gun in the Administration's war against poverty. The first appropriation of $1 billion covered action on many fronts, especially massive aid to localities to work out their own attacks on local poverty and steps to raise productivity through education and retraining. "Headstart" to help poor youngsters get a better start on education; "Vista" to channel volunteer workers into backward areas; and the "Job Corps" and neighborhood "Youth Corps" primarily for disadvantaged teenagers have proved

[1] To avoid the anti-incentive effects of welfare payments which decrease dollar-for-dollar with family earnings, many other nations (especially in Western Europe) use "family allowances," which provide direct government grants based on the number of school-age or younger children. This also avoids the pressure on fathers which is inherent in most American state welfare program "means tests" to leave their families in order to permit the families to collect welfare payments.

popular—and also the targets of widespread criticism. By 1967, the total budget was about $1.75 billion, allocated as in Table 32-2.

TABLE 32-2

FEDERAL ANTIPOVERTY PROGRAM, 1967 *

	Millions of Dollars
Community action	914
Neighborhood youth corps	300
Job corps	228
Work experience	160
Migrant workers	37
Adult basic education	30
Rural loans	28
Vista	26
Small business loans	5
	1,728

* U.S. Office of Economic Opportunity.

Closely related to these projects, the Appalachia and the Area Redevelopment programs focused on providing aid to generally poor areas, as distinct from particular individuals in the areas. Thus, nearly $1 billion was allocated to Appalachia, although only one-third of the population of Appalachia was poor. Here the approach was to provide funds to improve the economy of the area, largely through new highways, public works, education, and the like; and the Area Redevelopment Program similarly provided special aid to distressed areas. How much would actually go to help the poor was widely debated.

By and large, the new federal government programs have shied away from direct money-income transfers to the poor, although governmental transfer payments already provide something like $10 billion of the $25 billion annual incomes of the poor, through public assistance, old age insurance, unemployment compensation, and the like. These payments largely come as part of other programs, which are mainly aimed at lessening insecurity for all in the economy. Half of the poor receive no income from them.

To its supporters the antipoverty program has been a pioneering social venture, underfinanced, undermanned, underappreciated. To its critics, the program has been a great political boondoggle, long on waste and political manipulation, short on results. A balanced view is still hard to form. Possibly both the advocates and the critics are partially right. Poverty in America is a difficult, complex problem to understand, even more so to eradicate. Seldom has a governmental program been more visible, more the object of public and congressional scrutiny. By the time you read this, there will be more evidence on which to base your own judgment.

Whatever the assessment of the government's antipoverty program, a reminder is in order. The problem of poverty is far deeper than economics. It is intimately bound up with the destructive race riots of Watts, Harlem, and Detroit; with the breakdown of the family in the great city ghettos and slums; with the social and political revolt of minority groups. Today in New York City alone, over 650,000 people are on relief —nearly one person out of ten. Between 1964 and 1967, unemployment in the city declined by 40,000, yet the number on relief rose by 170,000. Nearly two-thirds of those on relief are children, growing up in slums, in an atmosphere of defeat and despondency. Three of every four women and children on relief live in fatherless families. Welfare rules have contributed to family disintegration, since any income received by the family from work has been deducted from the welfare payments they receive; under the rules, a father in the home could cost the family its welfare aid in most states. The increasingly violent and destructive race riots of the 1960's warn us that poverty, the slums, family disintegration, and racial tensions are intimately merged in perhaps the most explosive social problem of our times.

INSECURITY

The second big problem—insecurity—is similar to, yet different from, poverty. Here again, economic theory can help to explain why the problem exists and what we might do about it. But here, too, using economic theory is only one part of the task. We must understand the present situation and how it came to be; we must clarify our objectives; and we must weigh carefully economic and noneconomic considerations in assessing the merits of alternative policies.

The Causes of Insecurity

Increasingly severe and far-reaching depressions, rapid technological change, and especially modern industrialization have over the past century brought nearly all groups face to face with the problem of economic insecurity at one time or another. The family farm, reasonably secure against hunger and physical privation, has become less and less important. With increased mobility, the tradition of family care for aged parents and relatives has been drastically weakened.

Until only a half-century ago, private charity, plus some state-local government help, was depended on to shoulder the burden of caring for persons unable to support themselves. Inability to provide for self-support was considered a social stigma, and the general attitude was, "If he can't make his own way, why should we look out for him?" Workers were expected to take jobs at their own risk; compensation for injuries on the job was almost impossible to collect. The specter of poverty in old age was an uncomfortable subject to be avoided in polite conversation. Though every county had its "poor house" and local "poor" laws existed in most communities, they were usually so ineffectual as to be only a sop to the consciences of the more fortunate.

The great depression of the 1930's brought the problem of insecurity inescapably to public and governmental attention. A quarter of the labor force was completely unemployed; probably not more than half had regular full-time jobs. There were hunger and privation across the land. Whatever people's previous attitudes about every man looking out for himself, it was clear someone had to do something; and the only someone with significant power to attack such a massive problem seemed to be the federal government. Part of the Roosevelt administration's program was "work relief" aimed at mitigating unemployment caused by the depression. The other part, reflecting President Roosevelt's desire to help the "underfed and underprivileged third," culminated in the Social Security Act of 1935, which provided a long-run program of aid for the aged and other needy groups. This Act, which is still the cornerstone of the nation's governmental social-security program, had two main facets: a nationwide program of unemployment insurance, and compulsory old-age insurance for workers and self-employed persons. In 1965, 30 years later, "Medicare" for the aged was added.

The causes of economic insecurity thus lie deep in the structure and pace of modern industrial, urban society. Governmental measures to lessen insecurity have been deeply built into our social mores. Direct expenditures of public agencies and private employers to soften the impact of insecurity now exceed $50 billion annually, nearly a tenth of the national income.

One big cause of insecurity is the risk of unemployment. Modern fiscal and monetary policy have apparently gone far to keep the economy nearer a stable growth path; the role of unemployment insurance as an "automatic" fiscal stabilizer and aid to the unemployed was examined in Chapter 13. The special problems of insecurity arising from rapid technological change ("automation") will be analyzed in Chapter 41, on "The Economics of Change." Let us focus here on the biggest dollar sector of the "social security" problem, public and private aid for the aged, including medicare. In 1967 federal payments under these programs exceeded $35 billion to nearly 30 million elder citizens. Moreover, totals of both dollars and persons affected are scheduled to skyrocket in the years ahead. Social security is very big business for the American economy.

The Economic Issues
in Old-Age Insecurity

The essence of an individualistic, private enterprise system is its willingness to let people make their own economic decisions, take their own risks, reap the benefits of good choices, and make their own mistakes. Some personal economic insecurity—the chance that individuals will make mistakes and face painful consequences—thus is of the essence of such a system. It is a central issue of public policy whether we are prepared to let people suffer the consequences of their own actions—conversely, to what extent we should prevent them from taking dangerous

chances or guarantee them against painful consequences (like starvation in old age). It is clear that the issues in old age insecurity are only partly economic; how we define the problem and assess alternative policies depend heavily on personal value judgments.

Economic analysis suggests three main reasons why the market system may produce socially unacceptably low asset and income levels for people past 65. First, some people have such low lifetime total incomes that there is no way they could allocate their incomes to provide above-poverty levels before and after retirement. Second, some people have high enough lifetime total incomes to be able to provide for above-poverty-level post-retirement incomes, but intentionally or haphazardly allocate too much of the total to pre-retirement consumption, too little to saving. Third, some markets discriminate against older workers, so that above-65 individuals find it difficult to supplement their retirement savings, even though they have productive abilities that could be sold on the market in the absence of such discrimination.

Consider the three causes separately.

Lifetime Poverty. If, for any of the reasons suggested above, an individual's or family's total lifetime income is below the poverty level, society cannot expect him to provide an adequate post-retirement income for himself. In such cases, the fundamental remedies lie in raising the lifetime productivity of such individuals, in assuring growing and open markets for their services, and in providing income transfers to raise their living standards to socially acceptable minimum levels.

Adequate Lifetime Incomes but Inadequate Private Provision for Old Age. It is the second case that raises the additional issues. Suppose John Doe has an above-poverty-level lifetime income, but chooses to live too well (save too little) before retirement, or perhaps risks his savings on bad investment choices. Shall society provide a guaranteed minimum post-retirement income, or force him (through compulsory government social security) to save for his own retirement? Can we think of ways to induce him to choose voluntarily to save the required amount? Or shall we let him suffer poverty in old age, since he's responsible for his own plight?

The answer in the U.S., and in most of the other Western industrialized nations, is mainly a combination of the first and second alternatives— a compulsory social security program for old age, supplemented by direct income grants in special cases not covered adequately by social security. You should be clear that this answer rests largely not on economic grounds *per se*, but on the social "value judgment" that society should insist that people save for their own retirement and guarantee at least a minimum income to the aged. We are unwilling to let most people risk making a mistake that might entail abject poverty after retirement—or, more likely, might require a direct income transfer from others in society to avoid post-retirement poverty and destitution.

Market Discrimination against Older Workers. Markets which are closed to potentially productive workers both waste potential output and make it difficult for the excluded workers to earn reasonable incomes. Many persons over 65 are unable or unwilling to work. But others are able and anxious, even at jobs below the levels they held before retirement. In America, we take retirement at about 65 as the normal path, and

many workers want it so. Moreover, our government social security program withholds benefits from those between 65 and 72 who continue to earn above $1,800 of income for themselves. But the cost of enforced retirement in terms of total g.n.p. lost may be appreciable, and barriers against those who want to work after 65 mark a discrimination similar to that against the other groups noted in the poverty section above. Maximum output in a market system calls for freedom of all productive resources to compete openly for employment.

The Federal Social Security Program

What have we done about the problem of old-age insecurity? Figure 32-1 summarizes governmental social security programs as of the mid-1960's. Old-Age and Survivors' Insurance (O.A.S.I.) is clearly the biggest element of the program. In 1966 there were nearly 30 million beneficiaries who received nearly $30 billion; and over 90 million people are now covered by O.A.S.I. About 95 per cent of all employees in the United States are in "covered" occupations. Medicare covers roughly the same group. Nearly 50 million workers are in occupations covered by unemployment insurance. In addition, other benefits, especially public assistance to the needy not receiving bene-

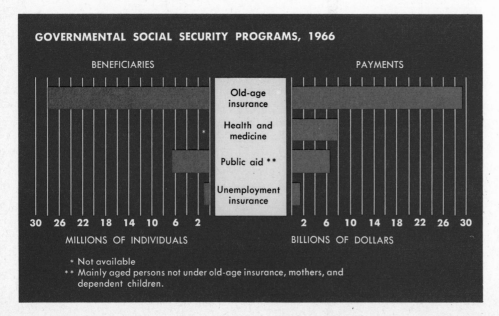

FIG. 32-1 Old-age benefits dominate the governmental social security picture, but health and other welfare benefits also run into the billions. (Source: Department of Health, Education and Welfare.)

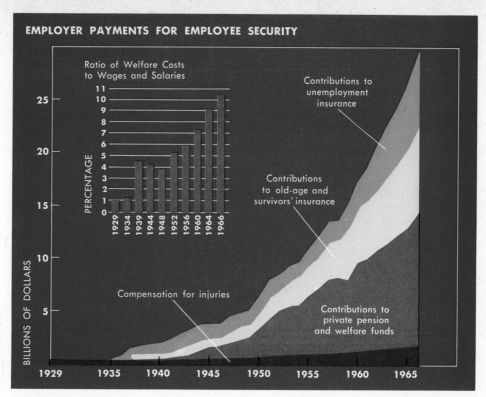

EMPLOYER PAYMENTS FOR EMPLOYEE SECURITY

Ratio of Welfare Costs to Wages and Salaries

Contributions to unemployment insurance

Contributions to old-age and survivors' insurance

Compensation for injuries

Contributions to private pension and welfare funds

FIG. 32-2 Employer payments for employee pensions and other benefits have soared. Private pension and welfare funds are now the biggest category. (Source: National Industrial Conference Board.)

fits under the other programs, reached another seven million people in 1966.

Thus, government social security now provides minimum protection against unemployment, poverty in old age, and destitution from lack of support for most of the nation's population. But the benefits under all these programs are small, and it is interesting that workers have increasingly pressed for supplementary private retirement plans. In 1929, employer contributions to employee security programs took less than 1 per cent of the total wage bill, almost entirely for executive pensions and workmen's compensation for injuries. Figure 32-2 shows what has happened to these private contributions since then. In 1966 they totaled nearly $30 billion, over 10 per cent of the entire wage bill. Of this, about one-third went into O.A.S.I. About half represented employer contributions to private employee pension and welfare funds, and this total is growing faster than O.A.S.I.

O.A.S.I. and Medicare. In 1967, about 20 million people were 65 or over, presumably out of the active labor force; another 90 million were under 20, most of them also not in the labor force. Thus, in a population of 200 million, fewer than half were between 20 and 65, the years of main contribution to the nation's output. If we allow

for housewives and others of the 20–65 group who were not looking for jobs, only about 80 million were in the labor force. Moreover, between now and 1975, this ratio of "workers" to "nonworkers" will decrease further. Viewed fundamentally, the problem of providing economic security for the aged is one of how much of the nation's real g.n.p. will we transfer to help support those past 65.

Over 70 per cent of those in the over-65 age group now receive O.A.S.I. benefits, but the average monthly aid is only about $80 since most employees still have only small benefits built up from their past tax premiums.[2] Inflation and steadily rising income levels have repeatedly led Congress to raise benefits under the program, and

[2] O.A.S.I. somewhat resembles an ordinary insurance plan. A payroll tax on the employer, matched by an equal tax on the worker (currently 4.35 per cent on each on the first $5,600 of income, and scheduled to rise gradually to 5.6 per cent on each on a wage base of $6,600 by 1987) provides the funds. The premiums must be invested in special U.S. government securities. Payments to most policy-holders begin at age 65, or at 60 on a reduced monthly-payment basis. The annuity received depends roughly on contributions made. If the insured dies before 65, his widow and dependent children receive payments. Payments begin at age 50 if a worker is disabled. Benefits, as of 1967, rose to a maximum of $135 a month for a single retired worker, and to $309 a month for a widow with two or more dependent children; but these maximum benefits apply only where the covered worker has participated in the program over a long period.

to raise payroll tax rates correspondingly to provide the needed revenue. Both benefits and tax premiums are tentatively scheduled under present legislation to continue to rise substantially through the 1970's.

The danger of large medical costs is a major source of insecurity for the aged. Old people are sick more than the young, and they stay sick longer. Many, especially those who live alone, must spend their declining years in nursing homes. Link up these observations with the very low income of many old people and it is clear that even moderate illness may mean financial disaster, given today's soaring costs of medical care. Two weeks in the hospital can easily cost, in addition to doctor bills, $500 to $1,000, perhaps a quarter to a half of the entire annual income of many aged poor couples.

In 1965, Congress added "Medicare" to the basic O.A.S.I. program, providing guaranteed minimum medical care to those over 65. The Act has three major portions. The first provides compulsory hospital and nursing insurance, up to 60 days per year with the individual paying only the first $50. These benefits are financed by matching employer-employee payroll tax contributions, added to earlier O.A.S.I. taxes. Funds go into a separate trust fund, parallel to the O.A.S.I. fund. The second section of "Medicare" provides a *voluntary* "insurance" plan to cover doctor bills, under which the government will pay most but not all of the cost of such medical insurance. The third section provides additional federal aid to states to assist them in providing medical aid for welfare cases of all ages.[3]

Economic Evaluation of O.A.S.I. Economically, O.A.S.I. represents a massive, politically-established, forced-saving plan for most of the population. Although a reserve fund of some $18 billion has been accumulated, basically O.A.S.I.

is on a pay-as-you-go basis, with current tax collections about equal to current benefit payments.

From the viewpoint of the worker, O.A.S.I. looks somewhat like a private annuity plan. But on five important points, it is significantly different.

First, participation in the federal old-age insurance program is compulsory. The worker has no voice in how he allocates his earnings as between this "insurance" and other uses; we force ourselves to save for retirement. Make up your own mind whether this compulsion is desirable; most people think it is.

Second, half the cost is financed by a payroll tax on employers. This would appear to represent a redistribution of income from businesses to workers. But more likely the tax is shifted onto the workers involved or onto consumers (see Chapter 35). Merely putting the tax on employers does not guarantee they will ultimately pay it.

Third, individual benefits under O.A.S.I. are not determined solely by that individual's contributions, as they would be under a private old-age retirement annuity. Once a person has made contributions for a certain number of years, he is entitled to the same full benefits whether he contributes all his life or only the required minimum period. Benefits are more generous in relation to contributions for low-income than for high-income earners.

Fourth, "Medicare" poses a special problem. By sharply reducing the marginal cost of medical services to the aged, Medicare may induce wasteful use of such services and thereby intensify an already serious "shortage" of doctors and medical facilities.

Fifth, looking back to the macro-economic analysis of Part Two, whether the government accumulates a surplus or runs a deficit in the O.A.S.I. program clearly may have a substantial impact on the government's total cash surplus or deficit. Currently O.A.S.I. is roughly pay-as-you-go. But under the social security amendments of 1965, O.A.S.I. tax collections will begin to exceed benefit payments in 1966 and the excess will rise steadily to a level of perhaps $5 billion annually by 1970. This is because taxes fall on future beneficiaries now, while their benefit payments begin later. If this surplus in O.A.S.I. actually is per-

---

[3] It is hard to estimate yet the annual cost of the entire Medicare program. Basic hospitalization insurance, under Section One, will probably cost over $4 billion a year. Government matching payments under the voluntary doctor-bill insurance section will probably cost around $1 billion annually. All told, payroll tax collections to finance medicare will run around $4 billion a year, so at least $1 billion dollars more will be required from the federal Treasury's general funds, in addition to Section Three payments to states.

mitted, this will represent a substantial "fiscal drag" on the private economy, other things equal.[4]

Twenty-five years ago private pension and welfare plans were almost nonexistent. Today, as Fig. 32-2 shows, their burden on employers has substantially outdistanced even the burgeoning O.A.S.I., and their lead is growing. Since World War II, unions have stressed pension plans as part of the "package" to be bargained for at each contract negotiation. By 1967, private employer contributions to employee pension and welfare funds were $14 billion annually, and were growing at a rate of over $1 billion per year. Most of these plans, unlike O.A.S.I., are fully financed by company contributions. Plans typically cover retirement pensions, death benefits, and accident, hospital, and health insurance. Figure 32-3 shows what has happened to the assets of both the public and private pension funds.

What, beyond the obvious pension benefits for the workers, is the economic significance of these burgeoning private pension plans?

First, although they have as yet paid out only relatively small benefits, the private pension plans will gradually lead to a further allocation of currently produced real income to the retired portion of the population, just as governmental old-age insurance does. They involve the same kind of burden on wage costs as does O.A.S.I. Many observers are beginning to ask: How big a cost burden can the employed sector stand without cutting incentives to increase total output?

Second, private pension plans are rapidly piling up vast reserves. These represent net withdrawals from the income stream which must be offset by new investment unless they are to be a net drag on aggregate spending. Some firms invest their pension reserves in government bonds, some in mortgages, many in common stocks. All these raise the vital macro problem (from Part Two) of

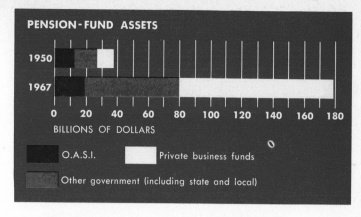

FIG. 32-3 Total assets of private and public pension funds have reached astronomical figures already, and are growing faster every year. (Source: Securities and Exchange Commission.)

assuring a continuous, stable flow of savings into real investment.

Third, the mere existence of such huge funds poses big new problems. Where should they be invested? In stocks, to protect pensions against erosion from possible inflation? In bonds, to give security of dollar income? Elsewhere? What are the implications for control of companies as more and more pension billions are poured into common stocks? Will the managers of pension funds come to wield vast power over the management of American business? With nearly $100 billion of assets already under their control, some fear that pension and private trust fund managers may become the new financial power center in our economy.[5]

Fourth, the plans may significantly reduce the flexibility and efficiency of the market economy. Few of the programs "vest" the pension benefits in individual workers as funds are set aside to provide future benefits. That is, if the worker leaves the company, he loses his accumulated pension rights. As potential pension benefits mount over the years, the incentive to stay in the same job mounts accordingly. Yet, rapid technological change and shifting demands require more mobility for a smoothly functioning economy. At the executive level, where pension plans are oldest, nonvesting pension plans are clearly a major barrier to job changes, as many companies intend them to be. For the mass of workers, the effect is

[4] J. G. Turnbull and C. A. Williams, *Economic and Social Security* (New York: Ronald Press, 1967), provides a thorough description of the American social security system. For a more thorough analysis of the impact of the present unemployment insurance program, see G. L. Bach, *Economics*, 4th edition (Prentice-Hall, Inc., Englewood Cliffs, New Jersey, 1963), pp. 700–705.

[5] For a lively discussion of the whole pension problem, see Robert Tilove's *Pension Funds and Economic Freedom* (New York: Fund for the Republic, 1959), which sees no crisis ahead. However, A. A. Berle, in *Economic Power and the Free Society*, cited in Chapter 19, finds cause for alarm.

not yet clear. Vesting benefits in individual workers (so they could take the benefits with them to other jobs) would eliminate the mobility restraint, but companies understandably fight this more expensive provision. Under present plans, substantially less than half the workers currently covered by private corporate pension plans will actually draw benefits from the plan they are now under, because they will change jobs.

ECONOMIC PERSPECTIVE ON POVERTY AND INSECURITY

Five concluding observations may help provide perspective on the problems of poverty and economic insecurity in modern America, and on our sweeping efforts to deal with these problems in recent years. As with most other big economic problems, these reflect the dynamic mix of macro- and micro-economic forces at work in today's complex world.

1. Our widespread social security and anti-poverty programs represent a major modification of our traditional individualistic philosophy of letting individuals fend for themselves, risk where they will, reap the gains, and suffer the consequences of failure. They control the use of a substantial part of the public's income, producing a large redistribution of real income from workers to persons unable or unwilling to provide an adequate income for themselves. Unless these programs increase total g.n.p., they necessarily involve such a transfer of real income. Remember the first principle of economics: With limited resources, more for one use means less for others.

This redistribution of real income is not necessarily an argument against social security and antipoverty programs. The programs themselves rest largely upon ethical and moral foundations. Their major premise is that it is the responsibility of society to care for those who for some reason are temporarily or permanently unable to care for themselves, or at least to force the improvident to save so as to be better able to care for themselves.[6]

2. A high-employment, prosperous, rapidly growing economy is the strongest single weapon against both poverty and insecurity in our economy. Over the past century, economic growth has steadily eroded poverty in America. Prosperous times wipe out the insecurity of unemployment for most workers, and permit them to build reserves against future insecurity. Only those effectively out of the labor market are not aided significantly by general prosperity. But it is also important to remember that general prosperity will not eliminate poverty; nor will it completely eliminate insecurity rising from rapid technological change, from shifting demand, and from failure to provide adequately for old age, unforeseen disability, or other such contingencies.

3. It is important to keep the goals of reducing insecurity and reducing poverty separate in your mind. Many people jump to the conclusion that our sweeping social security program in effect will take care of the poverty problem as time goes on. But this is far from true. Remember that less than half of the poor, as defined above, receive any kind of social security benefits, and only about 2 million people currently draw old-age pension benefits under organized, private-business pension programs. The federal social security program, as a practical matter, benefits the middle and lower-middle classes more than the poor. Many of the very poor do not work in covered occupations, and hence accumulate no social security benefit rights.

4. It is unclear whether the social security and antipoverty programs on balance increase or decrease current g.n.p. Unemployment insurance, which helps temporarily unemployed workers, helps to reverse recessions and clearly contributes to maintaining a stabler, high-employment economy. Other social security and antipoverty expenditures help directly to increase *future* productive power—retraining and rehabilitation, public health, child care, and educational expenditures are examples. On the other hand, as the government provides medical care, low-cost housing,

---

[6] A few years ago the American public joshed about the British "cradle-to-the-grave," or "womb-to-tomb," social security, introduced by the newly elected Labor govern-

ment. With over $50 billion annually already being set aside in America through public and private channels by the working portion of the population to take care of the voluntarily or involuntarily "idle" and "poor," now the critics say that we're there too.

better education, and minimal money incomes, the incentive to work and earn is surely diminished for some recipients. It is a basic premise of the social security and antipoverty programs that, by and large, the American people want to work and will take productive jobs when they can find them at anything like reasonable wages. But what will happen if government-guaranteed real income levels continue to move upward remains to be seen.

5. Last, the social security and antipoverty programs carry strong social and political, as well as economic, overtones. By and large, they appear likely to produce greater social stability, by lessening the likelihood of inter-income-level strife and the resentment of those who would otherwise bear the insecurity and poverty of a rapidly changing industrial society. But in recent years, the poverty issue has been strongly intertwined with the issue of civil rights. Some feel that the advocates of the Economic Opportunity Act have promised too much too fast, and have raised hopes and aspirations that will be disappointed. If so, these attempts to lessen poverty and insecurity may produce a backlash of bitter resentment and social unrest on the part of those intended as beneficiaries.

On the other side, as benefits under such programs rise, and as the middle- and upper-income groups become increasingly aware of the costs of financing such benefits for others, some predict a backlash effect here too. If society turns against the poor and the insecure after their aspirations have been raised, bitter strife may result.

For Analysis and Discussion

1. Should the government do something about the poverty problem? If so, what criteria should we use to decide who deserves help?
2. "The simplest and cheapest approach to eliminating poverty would be simply to give a tax-financed direct subsidy to each poor individual to the prescribed minimum level, perhaps through the "negative income tax" proposal. This would avoid the waste and misdirection of elaborate programs and would give each individual freedom to spend his income as he pleases." Do you agree? Why or why not?
3. List the advantages and disadvantages of a massive "Marshall Plan" to rebuild the slum areas of our major cities through government aid, as a fundamental step toward alleviating the poverty problem.
4. Would you favor government action to raise the legal minimum wage to $2 per hour as a step toward raising low incomes and eliminating poverty since lower wages generally produce poverty-level incomes? Explain.
5. What is your program to lessen or eliminate poverty in the U.S.?
6. Medicare was recently passed by Congress, providing medical assistance to the aged as part of the nation's social security arrangements. Was this a good move? If so, should it be extended downward to other age groups?
7. Why is it the responsibility of government to do anything about economic insecurity? Can't we count on individual self-interest to lead people to look out for themselves? Explain your position on these questions.
8. "A strong aggregate demand policy to assure high employment would solve the poverty and insecurity problems, and eliminate the need for the hodgepodge of government measures adopted over recent years." Do you agree?
9. How good a living can the current workers in our society afford to provide for nonworkers, like children, the aged, and unemployed? What criteria should you use in answering?

THIRTY-THREE

PROPERTY INCOMES: RENT, INTEREST, AND CAPITAL

Rent.

Interest.

Valuation of Income-Producing Property.

Appendix: Actual and Nominal Interest Rates.

Ours is a "capitalist" economy. One of its central tenets is the right of each individual to accumulate property (capital) of his own—a house, a factory, land, stocks, bonds.

Most such capital produces income for its owner—rent on land, interest on bonds, dividends on stocks. Some of the income may be consumed directly by the owner—housing services received by living in one's own house instead of renting. Indeed, every homeowner is a capitalist, just as is a bondholder or stockholder or an owner of his own farm or store. Nearly all the very rich receive most of their incomes from capital, and millions of families receive at least some income from such property.

In total, property incomes (including rent, interest, and profits) are about one-fourth of the national income, around $150 billion in 1967. What determines how big these incomes are? This chapter deals with rent and interest. It applies the same theory to the return on capital goods as we used to explain wages. Chapter 34 deals with profits alone.

RENT

In everyday usage, "rent" is the price paid for the use of land, buildings, machinery, or other durable goods. This is the way we shall use the term, except in one later section where a special meaning is given to the term "economic rent."

Rent paid for the service of property is closely analogous to wages paid for the services of workers. The same kind of demand-and-supply marginal-productivity analysis applies. There are

446

important institutional differences—we don't have a slave economy so we don't buy and sell workers the way we buy and sell land. But you should be able to transfer the general analytical framework for yourself from the wages and salaries area. This section raises only a few special points about rent.

The supply of nonhuman productive resources, like that of labor, varies widely from case to case. At one extreme, the supply of land at the corner of Madison Avenue and 42nd Street in New York City is completely inelastic—there's just so much and no more can be manufactured. At the other extreme, garden hoes, a simple productive resource, can be reproduced readily, and their supply is highly elastic. Most cases lie somewhere in between. By and large, the supply of any productive resource is likely to be reasonably elastic, given a long enough period for adjustment. Even farm land, for example, can readily be improved through the use of fertilizer, drainage, and so forth, if it pays to do so. For practical purposes, this is similar to making more land—you still have the same number of acres, but the acres have increased productivity.

The demand for the services of property depends basically on how much the service rendered is worth to the user. The same notion of marginal revenue productivity underlies the business demand for property services as for human labor. As in the case of labor services, marginal revenue productivity is often only a rough guide to thinking about the demand side of the picture—but a useful one nevertheless.

Competitive bidding by businesses tends to draw each resource into its most productive use. Each piece of land is rented to the highest bidder, and the high bidder must use the land where its marginal productivity is greatest to justify his paying the high rent. Under competition, the rent will approximate the marginal productivity of the land. Monopoly or monopsony may lead to inefficient allocation of resources, to "exploitation" of resource owners, or to unemployment of some of the resources.

An Example

Take a simple example. What will be the rent on a ten-acre site on a highway near the outskirts of a good-sized town? Look at the demand side first. One demand may be for use in truck farming. How much renters will pay for this use will depend on the fertility of the soil, the water supply, and other such factors. Another demand may be for use as small individual business properties, such as restaurants, garden-supply stores, and so on. Here the amount of traffic passing by, the convenience of the location for potential customers, and other such factors will be especially important. Still another demand might be for use by a single supermarket, with surrounding parking area. Here again, traffic flows, convenience of location for shoppers, availability of adequate parking space, and desirability of nearby neighbors might be especially important. Each potential renter would make some estimate of how much he could afford to pay in rent for the site—logically, up to its estimated marginal revenue productivity for him.

Who will get the site, and at what rent? If there is active competition among the potential renters, the rent will be bid up until only the highest bidder is left. This will be the renter who estimates the marginal revenue productivity of the site to him as being the highest. Thus, the site will be drawn into that use which promises the highest return to the renter, and through this mechanism into the use where consumers value it most highly (since the estimated high marginal revenue productivity reflects high consumer demand).

Will the rent be bid up all the way to the estimated marginal revenue productivity of the highest bidder? Not necessarily, if the value to one user is substantially higher than to others. Suppose the site is ideal for a supermarket. Then the local Kroger manager needs only bid higher than the truck farmers and small shop operators, to whom the land is potentially worth less. Kroger's may get the site at a rent below its estimated marginal value productivity as a supermarket site. On the other hand, Kroger's may not. Not if there's a local A. & P. or Safeway also in the market for sites. If there's active competition among potential renters, the rent is pretty sure to be bid up close to the land's highest estimated marginal revenue productivity. Adam Smith's invisible hand again working through self-interest and competition in the marketplace!

"Economic Rent"—

A Price-Determined Cost

Economists have one special definition of "rent" that differs from ordinary lay usage. "Economic rent" is the payment for the use of a *scarce, nonreproducible resource.* For example, the rent paid for one corner of Madison Avenue and 42nd Street in New York covers a mixture of "site value" and use of the building on the space, with all the improvements. If we could isolate the site value of a corner of Madison Avenue and 42nd Street—that is, the land itself exclusive of any of the improvements on it—we would have a resource that is scarce and completely fixed in supply; the supply is perfectly inelastic.

The rent on such nonreproducible productive agents is determined exclusively by the demand for them. The supply curve is a vertical line. If there is no demand, there is no rent; the rent rises directly as demand rises, without relation to the original costs of producing the resource. Figure 33-1 illustrates the point. Since the supply is a fixed amount, SS is a vertical line. If the demand is D^1D^1, the rent will be $20 an acre. If demand is D^2D^2, rent is only $10 an acre. If de-

mand is only D^3D^3, the land commands no rent at all.[1]

Is the "economic rent" on such a resource a cost of production? It is for the individual producer, since he has to pay the rent to the resource owner once a month. But from the viewpoint of the economy as a whole, such rents are purely price-determined (or demand-determined) costs. The economy can get exactly the same productive service from the nonreproducible scarce agent for any rent. In this sense, for the whole economy economic rent is not a cost that helps to determine the price of ultimate products.

Outside the site value of land, few cases of pure economic rent exist. But there are many with some element of economic rent. If a firm patents a new productive process, for the life of the patent the process is much like the site value of land; it cannot be reproduced (except by consent of the patent holder). Indeed, if the firm has a temporarily protected monopoly position, part of the monopoly profits may better be considered a temporary rent on the monopoly position.

INTEREST

Most of us put our savings into financial assets, instead of buying real property directly. We buy bonds, or put the money in a bank or a savings and loan association. Our property is then a financial asset—a bank account or a bond, on which we collect interest.

Why are interest rates what they are? Fundamentally, they depend on the marginal productivity of the real capital goods obtainable with the funds involved. But temporarily they may be heavily influenced by monetary policy and other special factors. The same supply and demand framework is again the right one to use in answering our question.

Interest differs from rent and wages in two major respects:

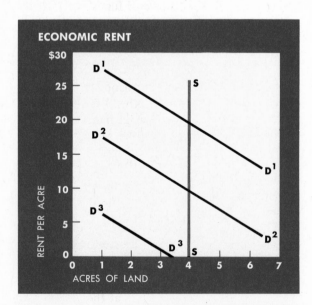

FIG. 33-1 When the supply is a fixed amount, price (rent) is determined solely by demand.

[1] Economists often use the term "quasi-rent" to describe the return on *temporarily* nonreproducible resources —for example, a patented production process. The return here is an economic rent, but one that will continue only so long as substitutes are not produced.

1. Interest is paid for the use of money, rather than directly for the use of productive resources. Money itself has no productivity. It doesn't build buildings or dig ditches. We can't explain interest directly as a payment for money's productivity. But money does give its owner purchasing power to obtain men and machines that will build buildings and dig ditches, and demand for loan funds traces back in considerable part to their power to buy or rent real productive resources.

2. Interest is stated as a *rate* of return (4 per cent) rather than as an absolute sum. To say that the interest rate is 4 per cent is merely to say that the borrower pays $4 interest per year for each $100 borrowed. The statement in percentage terms as a rate permits ready comparison between the payments of different amounts for widely differing resources. You can easily compare the return on money invested in an office building and in a turret lathe by converting both returns into a percentage on the funds invested. For example, if the office building cost $10 million and provides an annual net return of $500,000 after depreciation and other expenses, the rate is 5 per cent. If the lathe cost $1,000 and provides an annual net return of $40, the rate is 4 per cent. According to these figures, funds invested in the office building provide a better return than funds invested in turret lathes.

The Structure of Interest Rates

There are hundreds of different interest rates. In 1967, for example, the government paid about 5 per cent on bonds. Bank loans ranged from about 6 per cent for well-established business concerns to 6½ to 8 per cent on mortgage loans to buy houses, and as much as 12 per cent (1 per cent a month) on small loans to individual borrowers. Some consumer loan agencies charged up to 40 per cent per annum. You got no interest on demand deposits, but most banks paid from 3 to 4 per cent on savings deposits. The average short-term commercial loan rate at big banks in New York was about 6½ per cent, in southern and western cities about 7 per cent. Small business borrowers typically paid about 1 per cent more than large ones.

These different rates reflect differences in risk, locality, length of loan, cost of handling the loan, and a variety of other factors, as well as the "pure" interest rate that is included in each. To simplify matters, economists often talk about "the" interest rate. They mean the interest rate on a long-term, essentially riskless loan. The rate on long-term U.S. Government bonds is often considered a close approximation. At mid-1967, therefore, we might have said "the interest rate" was about 5 per cent. But don't make the mistake of assuming you could borrow money at this rate, or that most other borrowers could.

Interest as the Price of Loanable Funds

Interest is the price of money, or of loanable funds. Like any other price, it is determined by supply and demand factors in the market. But the factors determining the interest rate are complex on both the demand and supply sides. Behind the scenes, the "real" forces determining the interest rate are the supply of savings and the demand for such savings based on the marginal productivity of capital goods. On the surface, however, monetary factors can exert a big influence. For example, an easy money policy by the Fed can increase bank reserves and the supply of funds available at the banks, thus temporarily driving interest rates below the level set by the underlying real forces.

The Demand for Loanable Funds

The biggest private demand for loanable funds comes from business firms. Businesses borrow when they think they'll make money by doing so—when they expect to make a large enough return on the funds to pay back principal and interest, and have something left over for profit. Basically, they are willing to pay interest because the borrowed funds give them control over real productive resources—machinery, buildings, labor, and so on. Their demand for funds is thus based directly on the marginal value productivity of the physical productive resources themselves. It is a derived demand.

Chapter 7 looked in detail at the factors determining the "marginal efficiency of investment," analogous to the marginal revenue productivity of real productive agents. When a businessman sees an investment possibility with a marginal efficiency of investment much above the interest rate he has to pay, he will want to borrow additional funds if he doesn't have them already. Since it is the *expected* return that controls business planning, anything that affects business profit expectations will thereby affect the demand for loanable funds.

The second big private demand for loanable funds comes from individual households. In 1967, total consumer credit outstanding was nearly $100 billion, and over half of all department-store sales were made on charge accounts or installment plans. Most house purchases involve borrowing part of the price; in 1967, total mortgage debt on houses was about $240 billion, rising about $15 billion annually.

The third major demand for funds is from governments—federal, state, and local. State and local governments borrow mainly to finance long-term capital improvements—highways, schools, water works. The federal government borrows for more purposes, partly to finance capital improvements but also for other purposes like national defense. Sometimes it borrows to finance deficits intentionally generated to combat depression.

The Supply of Loanable Funds

What determines the supply of loanable funds? Your first inclination is probably to say, how much people and businesses save, and how the banking system behaves. This answer would be right, but not complete. We need also to consider other financial intermediaries as crucial links between saving and the offering of savings on the loan market. In addition, people and businesses often want to change the composition of their financial assets between money and other assets, and this shift swells or cuts the supply of loanable funds.

Personal Saving. People save for all kinds of reasons—for old age, to put children through college, to buy a house, for a "rainy day," just because they feel they ought to save. A lot of personal saving is more or less automatic. In 1966, the 10 per cent of families with the highest incomes apparently did around two-thirds of the

total net personal saving in the country. At very high income levels, people save because they have money left over after buying all the things they want. Chapter 7 looked in detail at personal consumption and saving behavior; that analysis is equally applicable here.

Business Saving. Like individuals, businesses save for a variety of reasons. Mainly, they save because it is considered sound business practice to reinvest depreciation funds and to plow back a good part of earnings each year into expansion and long-term growth, rather than pay them all out as dividends. Firms could pay out all their profits in dividends and then go into the market to borrow money for expansion purposes—but they don't. Most of their savings flow directly on into real investment within the business; only a small part comes onto the open market for loanable funds.

Saving, Cash Balances, and the Supply of Loan Funds. Savers may put their savings "in the bank." Note that this does not change either aggregate bank reserves or aggregate deposits. Thus, unless the action involves shifting funds from demand to time deposits (which have different reserve requirements), the saving will not signal bankers to expand their loans at all. Even if excess reserves are increased by the saving through a deposit shift, there is no reason to suppose the supply of loanable funds will be increased by just the amount of the new individual or business saving.

Savings may also be put into insurance, savings and loan associations, or other noncommercial banking financial intermediaries. These generally pay interest on funds. Although, unlike commercial banks, such firms can't create and destroy money directly, they can pile up or spend down their cash balances. There is no guarantee that savings flowing into these intermediaries will just match the funds being offered to borrowers by the intermediaries in any given period.

Similarly, individual and business decisions on the composition of the asset portfolios they hold may influence the supply of loan funds. When people decide to reduce the share of their assets held in the form of money, this puts the excess money into the loan market (or directly into the demand for real assets). Thus, such decisions can affect the supply of loan funds.

The Banks and the Supply of Loan Funds. Chapter 11 described the power of the commercial banking system to create and destroy money. Here is a major force on the supply side of the loan-funds market. As long as the banks have excess reserves, they can make loans without regard to what individual and business savers do. They can contract their loans with comparable independence. If they don't have excess reserves, increased private saving won't permit them to extend more loans (unless funds are shifted from demand deposits to savings deposits). The supply of loan funds in any time period is a complex matter. Fundamentally it depends on the economy's saving behavior, but as a practical matter a lot of different decisions are involved.

Determination
of the Interest Rate

Like other prices, the interest rate is determined by the interaction of supply and demand described in Chapter 21. But the loanable funds market has one special quality that needs mention. In most markets price movements are a major factor in bringing about equality between the amount demanded and the amount supplied. But in the loanable-funds market, the interest rate may have only a very slight effect on the supply of funds, and much of the equilibrating mechanism may be through other channels. For example, if the amount of loanable funds being supplied from current savings is in excess of the amount demanded, this excess intended saving may exert a strong downward push on aggregate demand. Thus, the equilibrium between the amount supplied and the amount demanded may be brought about more by changes in the level of national product than by mere fluctuations in the interest rate.[2]

[2] Advanced texts in economic theory explain that in equilibrium the interest rate must be equal to the marginal productivity of real capital (in the aggregate), must equilibrate the loanable funds market, and must equilibrate the market for money (currency and deposits) so that everyone is just willing to continue holding the existing amount of money, rather than spending it on goods and services or securities; and that it will simultaneously do all three.

Government Policy
and Interest Rates

Since the 1930's, the federal government has exerted substantial influence on interest rates. Before the New Deal, interest rates were largely set in the market by the interplay of private supply and demand, though the Federal Reserve did intervene from time to time. But after 1933, federal fiscal and monetary policy became more important on both the demand and supply sides of the money market. The government became a heavy borrower in the 1930's, and the dominant borrower in the 1940's. At the same time, the Federal Reserve pumped new reserves into the banking system to supply the funds needed by the government to finance the spending voted by Congress. The result was substantial government influence over the level of interest rates. Since World War II private forces have returned to dominance of the money markets. But, as was emphasized in Chapters 12 and 13, government monetary and fiscal policies remain powerful forces in the money market today.

Still, the basic forces determining the level of interest rates in the long run are "real" forces—fundamentally the marginal productivity of capital. In the long run, if the supply of saving is large and real capital goods accumulate rapidly relative to other factors of production, the marginal productivity of capital will decline under the law of diminishing returns and so will the price (the interest rate) that borrowers are willing to pay for it. Conversely, if capital accumulates relatively slowly, its marginal productivity is likely to rise. Technological advance will generally increase the productivity of capital and hence the demand for it. Thus, underlying the monetary (loanable funds) analysis of interest rates are the fundamental long-run forces of saving on the one hand and the demand for real capital on the other. Federal Reserve and Treasury policy can clearly influence interest rates in the short run, even for considerable periods. And if persistently easy money generates inflation, this inflation may be reflected in a "money" interest rate higher than the "real" rate, because lenders and borrowers take the inflation into account. For example, with a 3 per cent per annum inflation, a money rate of 5 per cent would mean a real rate of only 2 per cent, much lower than the market rate of 5 per cent. But the dominant, underlying forces lie in the private sector of the economy.

The Interest Rate, Resource Allocation, and Capital Accumulation

The interest rate helps potential business and individual investors allocate their funds among the millions of potential investment opportunities in the economy. When funds are allocated where the expected rate of return is highest, risk and other factors taken into account, the funds are optimally allocated from the consumer's viewpoint as well as from the investor's since the highest returns will be found where consumer demand is relatively strongest. Unless an investment promises a return high enough to pay the going rate of interest under a private-enterprise economy, it does not justify exploitation, by the test of the market. Money capital is the fluid embodiment of real productive resources. Thus, the money market, by channeling funds into those investments throughout the economy where the potential return exceeds the interest rate, provides a most valuable service, to private investors and to the society as a whole.

The interest rate plays another, more subtle, role. The going interest rate provides a rough measure of the relative advantages of current consumption and saving—of the present against the future. By saving, the individual or business can get a continuing return of, say, 4 per cent annually. If that return is enough to justify foregoing consumption now, it is advantageous to save. Without the interest rate to indicate the going return on saved funds in the economy, savers would have no standard by which to measure the relative advantages of current consumption and saving. How important this point is, hinges on how important the interest rate is in consumer and business decisions to save.

Perhaps most important, the interest rate exerts a powerful influence on the rate of economic growth in a capitalist economy like ours. A low interest rate encourages investment and faster growth. A high interest rate has the opposite effect.

VALUATION OF INCOME-PRODUCING PROPERTY

Income distribution is concerned primarily with the pricing of productive *services*, not with the prices of the productive agents themselves—land, machinery, buildings, and the stocks and bonds representing their ownership. But income-producing assets are bought and sold daily in our economy, and the interest rate plays an important part in setting the prices at which they sell.

To estimate the price of an income-producing asset, we need to know (1) its net annual return, and (2) the going rate of interest.

Valuation of Perpetual Fixed Income ("Capitalization")

Take a simple hypothetical case first. Suppose we have a mine that will produce *forever* ore worth $100 annually, net after all expenses are met. Suppose further that the going rate of interest on substantially riskless investments is 4 per cent. What will the mine be worth?

To get the answer, we simply "capitalize" $100 at 4 per cent. That is, we find that sum on which 4 per cent interest would amount to $100 annually. The arithmetic is simple. Four per cent of x (the unknown value) is $100. In equation form, this is: $.04 \cdot x = 100$. Dividing the .04 into 100, we get $2,500 as the value of the mine.

Can we be sure the mine will really sell for $2,500? No, but we can be sure it will sell for something near that. No one will be willing to pay a much higher price, since by investing $2,500 anywhere else at equal risk he can get $100 annually. On the other hand, if the mine's price is much less than $2,500, people will find it a very attractive investment and the price will be bid up toward $2,500.

Valuation of Machinery

The principle involved in valuing nonperpetual assets is the same. Consider a machine that will last 20 years and whose marginal revenue productivity (rent) per year is $60. The going rate of interest on comparable investments is 6 per cent. Using the same approach as before, we might capitalize $60 at 6 per cent, and find that $60 is 6 per cent on $1,000.

But there's a catch. The $60 annual income here only lasts for 20 years, because the machine wears out. Our problem here is: What is the present, or capitalized, value of an income stream of $60 at 6 per cent over 20 years, rather than in perpetuity? Mathematicians and industrial engineers have worked out a series of tables giving the answers for all combinations of interest rates and time periods for such problems. The answer here is $688.

The basic reasoning runs like this: At the end of the first year, we get $60. At the end of the second year we get another $60. And so on for the 20 years. Sixty dollars today is obviously worth $60, but $60 to be received, say, one year from today is clearly worth less than $60 today, since we do not have the use of it until a year hence. How much today is equivalent to $60 a year from today? If the interest rate is 6 per cent, $56.60 invested today at 6 per cent will amount to just $60 a year from now. And we can make a similar calculation to get the amount equal to $60 two years hence, and so on up to 20 years. If now we add together all these "present values" of $60 to be received at the end of each of the next 20 years, we will get how much we ought to be willing to pay now for the series of 20 annual $60 net returns anticipated from the machine. This calculation gives the $688 above, the "present worth" of the income stream promised if we buy the machine.

So you'd better not pay more than about $688 for the machine if you don't want to get stung. If you stop and think, you'll see why this amount has to be a good deal less than the $1,000 the machine would be worth if it provided the $60 annually in perpetuity. If you have to pay more than about $688, you could earn more on your money by investing it elsewhere at 6 per cent for the 20 years.

One other point is needed to complete this example. Unless this is a patented machine, others like it can be produced. If the current cost of producing such machines, for example, is only $500, you can be pretty sure that even the $688 price won't last. At a price of $688, it will pay to pro-

duce more machines like this one. As more are produced, the price will gradually fall. Not until the price falls to $500 will a new equilibrium be established. With lots more machines, the marginal revenue productivity of each will be lower, both because of the law of diminishing returns and because the product of the machine will have fallen in price so that the net annual yield per machine will no longer be $60.

To summarize: (1) At any time, the capitalized value of an income-producing asset will be based on its net yield and on the going rate of interest on investments of comparable quality. (2) In the long run, the value of any asset will tend to be equal to its cost of reproduction, although it may vary widely from this figure at any given time.

Valuation of Corporate Stocks

The same general principle holds in valuing corporate stocks and bonds, which represent claims on income earned by the issuing companies. But don't take your nest egg and rush for the stock market with this new knowledge. Corporate securities are interesting illustrations of the capitalization principle especially because they point up so many of the pitfalls. So far, we've assumed that we knew the yield of each asset, its life, and the appropriate going rate of interest. But in the real world all three of these are usually uncertain, certainly on corporate stocks. The yield on most stocks fluctuates from year to year. There is no sure way of telling what it will be for any extended period ahead. Moreover, what rate of interest should we use in capitalizing? The appropriate one is the rate that prevails on other investments of comparable risk and other characteristics. But you pick it out.

Last, and most important, the market price of stocks is determined by thousands of other people who are all guessing at the same imponderables as you are. Many of them are in the market as speculators, looking for a quick dollar on the price rise rather than for a long-pull investment. There is no reproduction cost to set a fairly stable base level that anyone can count on. The actual market price will reflect what all those people think is going to happen. So you're betting on what other people will bet on, and they in turn are betting on what you and others will bet on. The stock market is no place for neophytes. The capitalization principle can give you a rough steer and it can help you in comparing different securities. But the much-quoted statement of Bernard Baruch is relevant here:

If you are ready to give up everything else—to study the whole history and background of the market and all the principal companies whose stocks are on the board as carefully as a medical student studies anatomy. If you can do all that, and, in addition, you have the cool nerves of a great gambler, the sixth sense of a kind of clairvoyant, and the courage of a lion, you have a ghost of a chance.

The point of this section is not to warn you against investing in common stocks, but rather to emphasize the wide range of special factors at work in determining the actual market price of some types of income-producing assets. The analytical framework outlined in the simple cases above can help in most cases, but like all analytical models it gives only a framework for analyzing any particular situation in detail.

REVIEW

Concepts To Remember

This is a difficult chapter. Recheck your understanding of the following new concepts:

rent	rate of return
economic rent	capitalization
quasi-rent	"present worth" of an
interest	income stream
"the interest rate"	

For Analysis and Discussion

1. "Rent and wages are determined by substantially the same set of supply and demand forces, even though people are human and land is not." Do you agree? If not, what are the main differences?
2. "Rent is an unearned increment for any landowner, since he does not have to do any work for the rent he receives. Therefore the government should confiscate rents through special taxes." Do you agree? Why or why not?
3. "The profits made by a company on the basis of an exclusive patent are essentially rents, not profits." Do you agree or disagree?
4. List the main sources of supply of loanable funds, and of demand for such funds. Would you expect interest rates to be relatively stable or fluctuating? Check your expectation against the facts—say, in the *Federal Reserve Chart Book*.
5. Other things equal, would you expect rapid technological advance to raise or lower the long-term rate of interest? Why?
6. Assume that you have $10,000 to invest. How would you go about deciding what is a reasonable rate of interest for you to expect to receive in investing your money? What investments would you consider?
7. Suppose the Federal Reserve tightens bank reserves and raises the interest rate. Would this increase or decrease real investment, other things equal?
8. Find out the "carrying charge" on some article you are considering buying. Then calculate the interest rate you would be paying on the funds you in effect borrow from the seller. Would you be better off to go and try to borrow the money at a bank? (*See the Appendix.*)
9. Suppose you inherit an 80-acre tract of farm land. You are uncertain whether to sell it, or to retain it and rent it out. How would you go about comparing the advantages of the two courses of action?

Appendix

ACTUAL AND NOMINAL INTEREST RATES

Interest rates aren't always what they seem to be. This Appendix is intended to help you protect yourself against some common mistakes, by looking at two examples that arise frequently in everyday life.

1. Installment Charges.   Most goods you buy on installment bear a "carrying charge" to pay the seller for extending credit to you. In essence, this is an interest rate, plus something extra for the nuisance of keeping the books and maybe having to dun you for the money. If you're smart, you'll compare carefully the interest rate hidden in the carrying charge with what the money would cost you if you borrowed it directly elsewhere.

Suppose you buy a $120 rug on the installment plan, with 12 months to pay and a carrying charge of $1 a month, or $12 for the year. This looks like 10 per cent, a reasonable rate for such a loan. But look again. The actual rate is far higher. You pay a dollar each month, but the total amount you have on loan from the store goes down $10 each month. The last month you owe them only $10; yet you are still paying interest at the rate of $1 a month, or $12 per year. The actual rate on your unpaid balance during the last month is 120 per cent per annum. The average for the year is 20 per cent, twice the apparent rate, since the average loan to you is about half the purchase price of the rug.

The actual rate each month is calculated in the accompanying table.

2. Bond Yields.   Suppose you're thinking of buying a corporation bond that pays 4 per cent. It is a $1,000 face value bond, so the annual interest is $40. Its current market price is $1,100, and it is due in 10 years. Suppose your alternative is putting the money into U.S. Government Bonds, which pay 3¾ per cent. Assume that the two investments are equally safe and attractive on all other grounds. Which one should you choose?

At first glance, the corporate bond seems to win hands down. But look again. You pay $1,100 for the bond, but you'll only get back $1,000 at the end of 10 years. To get the true net yield, you need to "write off" $10 of the value of the bond each of the 10 years, so your actual net annual yield would be only $30 rather than $40. Now you can calculate the exact yield on the corporate bond. It's $30 per year on $1,100 invested. This figures out to 2.7 per cent, appreciably under 3¾ per cent. Better buy the Government bond if yield over the next 10 years is your main goal.

3. Inflation.   Inflation raises another situation where you may be tricked by the difference between actual and nominal interest rates. Suppose you have a bond which yields 3 per cent annually over the next ten years. But prices rise 2 per cent per year over the period. Thus, although the nominal rate of interest is 3 per cent, the real rate is only 1 per cent, since 2 per cent of the return has been eroded by the price inflation.

	Unpaid Balance	Interest ($1 Monthly; $12 per Year)	Interest Rate on Unpaid Balance
1st month	$120	$12	10.0%
2nd month	110	12	10.9
3rd month	100	12	12.0
4th month	90	12	13.3
5th month	80	12	15.0
6th month	70	12	17.1
7th month	60	12	20.0
8th month	50	12	24.0
9th month	40	12	30.0
10th month	30	12	40.0
11th month	20	12	60.0
12th month	10	12	120.0

THIRTY-FOUR

PROFITS

Profits on the Modern Scene.

The Two Roles of Profits.

The Theory of Profits.

Conclusion.

Ours is a private-enterprise, profit-motivated economy—not entirely but by and large. In 1967, total profits were about $100 billion, including net incomes of farmers, lawyers, doctors and the like, as well as business corporations. That's a lot of money. But was it enough to make the system function most efficiently? Or too much, as many union leaders claim?

Our look at the market system thus far has stressed two big roles for profits. They're the incentive to produce what consumers demand—the carrot that entices businessmen to perform their social function. And they're a major source of funds for the investment that makes the economy grow. Now it's time for a summary look at profits in their own right.

PROFITS ON THE MODERN SCENE

Begin by remembering how economic profits are defined. *Economic profit is the excess of income over all "economic" costs (including a normal return on investment).* Profit is thus a residual, plus or minus—what's left over after the business has met all its costs.

Potential profit indicates where society wants more resources used. Thus, the individual businessman who predicts most successfully what the consumer will want, who meets consumer demand most effectively, who handles his production most efficiently, and who buys his labor and materials most adroitly will end up with the biggest profit. The inefficient producer who fails to respond to consumers' demands is likely to end up with red ink on his books. If a seller has a partial or complete monopoly position, he may be able to maintain positive economic profits over a substantial period without innovation, real productive efficiency, or close adaptation to consumer demands. But wherever other firms are free to enter the market, competition will tend to bid prices down and costs up, eliminating economic profits. The pursuit of profits plays a central organizing role for the entire economy.

If you ask the man in the street, he probably won't be very sure just what profit does mean, but there's a good chance he'll have a mildly antagonistic attitude. Public-opinion polls suggest this attitude toward profits. And it's highly likely he will have only a vague idea about how big profits are, in total, in return per dollar of investment, or in return per dollar of business sales. So a look at the facts may be in order.

The Facts

Figure 34-1 summarizes the course of *corporate* profits since 1929.[1] In 1967 they were over $75 billion, a whopping amount. But many businessmen would protest vigorously. They'd say it's profits *after* taxes that we should look at. After taxes, profits are a lot less, only about half as much as the before-tax total. Corporate income taxes now take a much bigger share of profits than they did three decades ago. And of course inflation accounts for some of the big increases shown; prices have more than doubled over the period.

The aggregate dollar figures alone don't have much meaning. Everything in the economy has grown immensely since 1929. Have profits risen or fallen compared to other national-income shares? Are businesses making more or less profit these days per dollar of sales, or per dollar of investment? Figure 34-2 gives some of the answers.

It's clear that the profit share in the national income (based on reported corporate profits) has jumped all over the place in big business cycles. The average percentage for recent years has been a little above the 11 per cent figure for 1929. Corporate profits were actually negative in 1931–32, and hit a peak of nearly 17 per cent of the national income in the boom year of 1950.

[1] Remember that these are much larger than *economic* profits, since reported corporate profits include a normal return on stockholders' investment as well as pure profits.

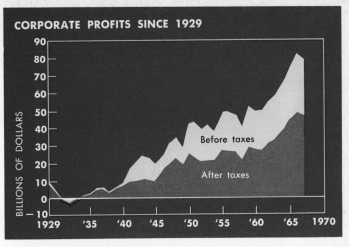

FIG. 34-1 Corporate profits, in current dollars, have risen sharply but irregularly since 1929. Corporate income taxes now take somewhat less than half the total. (Source: U.S. Department of Commerce.)

Lesson in statistics: Note how you can make the profit share look sharply rising or sharply falling, depending on which year you take as your starting point.

In spite of the high dollar-profit totals, some businessmen argue that there has been a "profit squeeze" since the mid-1950's, except for the post-1965 period. They cite especially the lower bars of Fig. 34-2. These show profits as a percentage of sales for nonfinancial corporations since 1946. There has clearly been some decline since the immediate post-World War II boom years. But again, one may ask whether this is the right basis point for a comparison. It looks different to businessmen and labor leaders when they bargain over wages.[2]

THE TWO ROLES OF PROFITS

Profits as an Incentive

The number-one function of profits is to give businessmen an incentive to produce what consumers want, when and where they want it, at the lowest feasible cost and price. This includes innovation of new products and new methods. The profit motive is at the center of a private-

[2] No official long-period series is available showing profits as a rate of return on invested capital. A private series (First National City Bank of New York) shows profits for a large sample of manufacturing corporations as 10 per cent on net worth in 1929, about zero in 1932, a peak of 14 per cent in 1948, between 9 and 13 per cent for 1960–65, and 14 per cent in 1966.

457

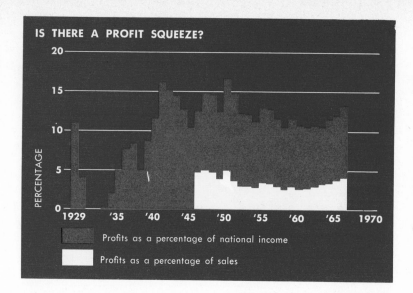

IS THERE A PROFIT SQUEEZE?

FIG. 34-2 During the last decade profits as a percentage of national income and of corporate sales have been lower than during World War II and the Korean War. Has there been a profit squeeze? (Source: U.S. Department of Commerce. Profits as a percentage of national income are *before* taxes, those as a percentage of corporate sales are *after* taxes; pre-1946 data on profit as a percentage of sales not available.)

enterprise economy, and nearly everyone in the United States agrees that it ought to stay there.

But a lot of questions are raised about just how the profit motive does, and should, work as a practical matter. For example, with professional managers (rather than owner-operators) now running most big businesses, some people ask whether profit is still the most effective incentive to innovation and efficiency. The modern corporation president gets a salary plus a bonus dependent on profits, but as president he gets only a fraction of 1 per cent of the company's total profits. What motivates him? Moreover, the job big businessmen themselves do is mainly to organize and direct production. The wage-earners and salaried employees, who do the great bulk of the company's work, have to have their carrots too if the over-all job is to be done, and company profits may not rate very high on their motivation lists.

Second, remember that it's the *expectation* of profits that must be there to make the system tick, not the achievement of profits. Over the long pull, profits are smaller than you might guess. This is a profit-*and-loss* system. Many a firm has gone broke. In prosperous times like recent decades it is easy to forget the big losses incurred across the board during past depressions.

Statistics on the rate of business failures even in prosperity are revealing. During 1966, for example, failures of incorporated businesses averaged about 1,100 per month. Total liabilities of these 1966 failures exceeded a billion dollars. Fewer than 25 per cent of the businesses established during the immediate postwar years were still operating a decade later. Yet each year new

thousands rush in, confident that they have the knack to succeed where others have failed. Big-business failures are less common than among small firms. People who have $50 million or $100 million to venture are rare, and profitability calculations on such investments are made with a great deal more care. But even here the story is far from one of unbroken success. Think of the automobile industry, with its spectacular growth over the present century. The Oakland, Stanley Steamer, Maxwell, Hupmobile, and dozens of others were once as much household words as Ford and Pontiac are today. Yet only a few decades later they are as extinct as the dodo.

But hope springs eternal in the American entrepreneur's breast. Perhaps entrepreneurs are by nature overoptimistic people. Their optimism leads to a good deal of waste in resources devoted to ventures that don't succeed. But it also helps give the American economy the dynamic vigor that has pushed the American standard of living far above its nearest competitor. It is doubtful that dynamic progress in a private-enterprise system is possible without widespread losses from bad business guesses as well as widespread profits from good ones.

**Profits as a Source
of Investment and Growth**

Profits have a second major function. Undistributed corporate profits (profits not paid out as dividends) are one important source of funds for business investment. In 1966, for example, they totalled about $27 billion, and almost all were plowed back into new plant, equipment, and other such business uses. Corporation depreciation allowances are also considered by most businessmen as sources of funds for business investments (though remember that a depreciation allowance is merely a bookkeeping charge, not actual money set aside). Since businesses seldom replace worn-out assets with identical assets, it is often hard to identify what is replacement and what net new investment. Thus, business investment is often viewed gross (including replacement), as in the gross national product accounts. In 1966, depreciation charges totalled $40 billion, so net "internal" sources for investment spending totalled $67 billion. Remember that each firm ‚has considerable discretion as to just how much depreciation to charge in any given year, so the distinction between profits and depreciation in any given year is somewhat arbitrary.

In 1966, corporations also went "to the market" for another $28 billion of capital. That is, they issued new stocks and bonds and went to the banks for that amount. Thus, it is clear that corporations in 1966 financed most of their gross investment from "internal" sources (profits and depreciation), and this has been true in most other recent years.

THE THEORY OF PROFITS

Profits in a Static Economy

In a *static* economy, without technological advance, population change, capital accumulation, and changing consumer wants, only monopoly profits would continue. Competition would gradually eliminate all other *economic* profits as resources were shifted into high-profit industries. Capitalization would bid up the prices and rents of especially productive resources until the rate of return on them was equal to that on other resources. Throughout the entire economy, economic profits would be eliminated when equilibrium was achieved except for those industries where new businesses were prevented from entering.[3] There, and there only, monopoly and oligopoly profits would continue indefinitely. In effect, monopoly and oligopoly profits then would be a kind of rent on exclusive monopoly position.

[3] Though accounting profits would, of course, continue, since they do not include a normal return on stockholders' investment as a cost.

Even in such a static economy, it's hard to say to whom, and for what, temporary profits are a return. Increasingly, the job of making profits in the modern economy falls on professional managers. The return to these men is more "wages of management" than profit, though most of them have some sort of bonus plan under which they share in profits and lose take-home pay when profits drop. Stockholders, who put up most of the capital and get the profits when there are any, are a very passive type of entrepreneur in most modern corporations. Thus, where to draw the line between profits and wages of management is a difficult question. The functions of management, entrepreneurship, and providing capital are thoroughly entangled in modern business firms.

Profits in a Dynamic Economy

But continuous, unpredictable change is the dominant characteristic of the real world. Uncertainty is everywhere. Changing demands, new products, technological advance—all these and many more confront the entrepreneur or manager every day. He must somehow "guesstimate" the future demand for his product, his future costs, future changes in technology, future behavior of his competitors. Then he must keep an eagle eye out for how the government is going to behave—on taxes, government spending, antitrust policy, labor relations, and international affairs. In the midst of all this, he needs to worry about keeping his costs below those of competitors, keeping the union at least tolerably happy, being sure that his sales organization is on its toes, and so on.

If he does all these things better than his competitors, and especially if he has a partial monopoly position to help him, he'll end up with a good profit. If he misses on many of the important decisions, the red ink will appear. The biggest job of the modern entrepreneur is to live with and make the best of uncertainty. If he doesn't thrive on this kind of life, he'd better save himself a big doctor bill for ulcers and go to work for somebody else.

Insurable Risk and Uncertainty. Many kinds of risk can be insured against. In this way, the uncertainty can be eliminated by incurring a known dollar cost. The best-known example is the risk of loss from fire or theft. Without insurance, this uncertainty would be a major problem for any business concern. But the likelihood of fire loss is reasonably predictable for a large number of buildings of any given type, even though it is unpredictable for any given building. By pooling together the moderate insurance premiums on a large number of buildings, the insurance company has enough funds to pay off the fire losses on those few buildings that do burn each year. Long experience has reduced the likelihood of such occurrences to a scientific, statistical basis. Businesses can now convert this type of uncertainty into a known cost through insurance.[4]

Professor Frank H. Knight has pointed out that insurable risks are really only another business cost to be included with other business costs, and that economic profits arise only from bona-fide cases of *uninsurable* uncertainty. Alas, the businessman can't go to his insurance agent and say: "I'm bringing out a new-style dishwasher; insure me against its being a flop." Economic profits beyond profits on monopoly positions, Knight argues, are thus analytically linked solely to a world of dynamic change and uninsurable uncertainty.

Profits and Dynamic Change. Since profits arise largely out of dynamic change and uncertainty, much of what happens to profits is outside the control of any individual manager or entrepreneur. The biggest profits arise in booms, the biggest losses in depressions. "Windfall profits" are widespread in a lusty boom; it's pretty hard for any reasonably well-situated business to avoid making good profits. In a bad depression, the best management in the world has a tough time making ends meet. The business cycle, with inflation and deflation, may well be the biggest single cause of profits and losses. The manager who can foresee business fluctuations and adjust successfully to them is worth his weight in gold.

Shifting consumer demand for individual products is a second big area of change largely outside the control of the individual businessman. Even General Motors is going to have a tough time making profits on automobiles if consumers decide to ride in helicopters instead. But the alert

entrepreneur is far from helpless. He can change his product to keep in step with the times, and through his advertising he can influence what consumers want to buy.

Changes in costs are a third big area of uncontrollable uncertainty. What happens to the price of steel is pretty much outside the control of Philco; yet steel represents one of the major costs in making Philco refrigerators. The same thing is true of most other costs. The businessman can bargain with his local union, but he isn't going to get far with a wage rate much below the rates that prevail elsewhere for similar work, any more than he can buy steel below prevailing market prices. Technological changes continually change costs.

Basically, it's the manager who does a good job of prediction under conditions of dynamic uncertainty, and who adjusts effectively to unforeseen conditions, who is likely to turn in good profits.

The Profits of Innovation. One noted economist, Joseph Schumpeter, has argued that profits boil down largely to payment for keeping a jump ahead of your competitors through innovation. The big profits come from big, successful innovations—the motor car, color TV, the diesel engine, and so on. The innovator needs both an idea and the ability to get it into operation. An invention or an idea alone makes no profits. But the utilization of that invention, if it leads to lower costs or to a successful new product, brings dollars into the coffers.

Unfortunately, no one has yet figured out a sure way of telling in advance whether a new mousetrap or a new railway car will succeed. First, there is the technological problem of developing the idea into a usable process or product. When this is licked, there is still that capricious monarch of all the surveys—the consumer. Business history tells a fascinating story of the sure things that flopped, and also of the thousand-to-one shots that have become the industrial giants of today.

Successful innovation in effect gives a temporary monopoly to the innovator, and often big profits. Like other monopoly profits, the economic profits of innovation persist only until competitors catch up and bring profits in the industry down to competitive levels. But innovations are often

---

[4] Very large firms may "self-insure." If a firm has hundreds of buildings itself, it may figure that the predictable likelihood of fire loss in any given year is less than the cost of buying commercial insurance on them.

protected by 17-year patents. And a running start on your competitor is often more important than the legal protection of patents. The firm with the know-how and experience that go with a new product or a new method is likely to have a new innovation at hand by the time competitors catch up on the last one. The continuing success of the industrial giants of today—General Motors, General Electric, Standard Oil, DuPont—rests at least as much on this kind of continuing innovation as on any other single factor.

CONCLUSION

Profits go largely to those who manage most efficiently to give consumers what they want in a world of continuous change. How big do profits have to be to give the incentives to management and entrepreneurs that we need for a dynamic, progressive, private-enterprise economy? Nobody knows. Profits are big enough when businessmen and investors act as if they are big enough. What matters are two things: that businessmen desire to innovate and to run efficient enterprises aimed at meeting consumer demands—and that profits plus other savings be big enough to support the economic growth we want.

Some people nowadays say that individual and corporation income tax rates are so high that there's no use working too hard, no use taking big risks when the government takes half of the profit and shoulders you with any loss. Others complain that labor grabs all the gains from good management and new capital investment.

But the rough stability of aggregate wage and profit shares shows that profits have grown with the economy. And there is little evidence that the dynamic impetus is gone from the American economy. There are many incentives to fine management and pioneering entrepreneurship. Pride in achievement, the social acclaim for success, traditions of sound management, the development of professional standards, the pure joy of risk-taking—all these incentives and others like them may be powerful supplements to the monetary incentive of profits. And one of the attributes of a shrewd businessman is the ability to manage affairs so as to take advantage of every possibility the law provides for minimizing taxes.

Human motivation is a very complex affair, and it varies widely from person to person. The long hours of unpaid toil that millions put in each year for causes they consider worthwhile are impressive evidence that money is far from everything. And the billions we spend each year on gambling devices we know are loaded against us provide impressive evidence of our love for risk-taking. The Irish Sweepstakes, slot machines, pari-mutuel betting on races—all are publicly announced to pay out less than the contestants put in. Yet there is always the chance that you will be a big winner. If so many of us are willing to gamble when we know that as a group we *must* lose, perhaps it is not strange that entrepreneurs continue their business risk-taking undaunted. For with business innovation there is no reason to suppose that the dice are loaded against entrepreneurs in the aggregate. Indeed, the long record of rapid growth in the economy points strongly the other way.

For Analysis and Discussion

1. What are the main functions of profits in the modern American economy?
2. "By and large, continuing profits for any firm demonstrate it is doing a good job in satisfying consumer demand." Do you agree or disagree? Explain.
3. Are current profits too big? (See Fig. 34-2 and a current issue of *Economic Indicators*.) What is the best measure of whether profits are adequate or not?
4. "So long as we let businessmen think they have a chance to make profits, it doesn't matter whether they actually make any profits or not." Is this a sound analysis of the incentive role of business profits?
5. Who actually gets the profits made by the American corporations? (Refer back to Chapter 19 for some of the relevant information.) If it is not primarily the managers, how do profits serve their presumed incentive function?

CURRENT RESEARCH

Wages, Unions, and Collective Bargaining. Sumner Slichter, one of America's famous economists, and J. Healy and R. Livernash assess the current scene in *The Impact of Collective Bargaining on Management* (Brookings, 1960). Chicago's H. G. Lewis summarizes the quantitative impact of unions on wages in "The Relative Employment Effects of Unions" (*American Economic Review*, May, 1964). A controversial analysis, *Collective Bargaining in the Steel Industry*, by Harvard's R. Livernash, looks closely at one leading industry. Solomon Barkin, one of organized labor's leading economists, analyzes some problems of the labor movement in *The Decline of the Labor Movement and What Can Be Done About It* (Center for the Study of Democratic Institutions, 1961). A lively collection of analyses is assembled in *Unions, Management, and the Public*, E. Bakke, C. Kerr and C. Anrod, eds. (Harcourt, Brace & World, 1967).

Union Attitudes and Processes. There is a vast literature describing unions and the attitudes and behavior of organized labor groups. M. Perlman's *The Machinists* (Harvard Univ. Press, 1962) is a good recent example. A collection of leading studies focused on union attitudes and behavior is assembled in *Labor and Trade Unionism*, edited by California's W. Galenson and S. Lipset. Interesting studies of grass-roots union politics and policies are presented by L. Sayles and G. Strauss, *The Local Union* (Harper and Row, 1961). See also J. Barbash's *Structure, Government, and Politics of American Unions* (Random House, 1967).

Ben Selekman's "Conservative Labor—Radical Business" (*Harvard Business Review*, March, 1962) puts a different twist on the labor-management picture.

Poverty. "Who Are the American Poor?" (*Fortune*, March, 1964), which summarizes two leading studies of poverty in the U.S.—M. Harrington's *The Other America* (Macmillan, 1962) and H. Miller's *Rich Man, Poor Man* (Crowell, 1964)—provides a good introduction. Then, for more analytical approaches to the problem, try Robert Lampman's "Approaches to the Reduction of Poverty" and T. W. Schultz's "Investing in Poor People" in the May, 1965, *American Economic Review*; and Locke Anderson's "Trickling Down: The Relationship Between Economic Growth and Poverty" (*Quarterly Journal of Economics*, November, 1964). Yale's James Tobin provides two lively, penetrating analyses in "The Case for an Income Guarantee" (*The Public Interest*, Summer, 1966), and "On Improving the Economic Status of the Negro" (*Daedalus*, Fall, 1965). More detailed studies of the Negro's economic status are provided by the University of Texas' R. Marshall's *The Negro and Organized Labor* (Wiley, 1965), and A. Batchelder's "Decline in the Relative Income of Negro Men" (*Quarterly Journal of Economics*, November, 1964).

At the other end of the income structure, R. Barlow, H. Brazer and J. Morgan of the University of Michigan have studied the richest families in *Economic Behavior of the Affluent* (Brookings, 1966).

462

THE PUBLIC SECTOR

THIRTY-FIVE

THE PUBLIC SECTOR: FUNCTIONS AND EXPENDITURES

The Four Big Functions of Government.

Government Expenditures and Revenues.

What Should the Public Sector Do?

How big should the government be? What should it do? How much should it tax and spend? The influential nineteenth-century English liberals argued that the primary function of the state was merely to set up and enforce certain "rules of the game" under which private enterprise could then be counted on to get goods efficiently produced and distributed. At the other extreme, the communists argue that all productive resources should be owned by the state, and that production and distribution should be directed in detail by the government.

The present attitude in America is in between, but much closer to the private-enterprise position. Most Americans believe strongly in capitalism and the virtues of a free, private-enterprise economy. Yet government action has grown far beyond the minimal regulatory duties prescribed by the laissez-faire advocates.

THE FOUR BIG FUNCTIONS OF GOVERNMENT

Modern government has four big economic functions. People disagree violently on how far government should go on each front, but just about everyone agrees that government needs to play all four roles.

Government as Policemen: The Rules of the Game

Even Adam Smith said that government has to act as policemen—to spell out some rules of the economic game and see that people obey them. To live effectively together in a complex economic world, we have to agree that contracts will be respected. Equally important, competition must prevail in the market place to assure the benefits of private enterprise, and only government can undertake this kind of regulation. Some would have government go further and regulate hours of work and child labor, the prices airlines can charge, the wage bargains unions and management can strike. The role of government in setting and enforcing the rules of the competitive game was a main theme of Parts Three and Four above. It's a vital role if a system like ours is to work effectively.

Government as Stabilizer:
Stably Growing Aggregate Demand

Two centuries ago Adam Smith didn't worry about booms and depressions, because they didn't exist. But with modern industrial society, economic instability became a major problem. There is no reason why aggregate spending (consumers plus businesses plus governments) will automatically just match the output potential of the system at stable prices. Clearly, no private agency can assure the needed stable growth in aggregate demand. Government has to help, through monetary and fiscal policy, if we are to avoid the massive depressions and inflations which have marred the past.

Government as Provider
of Public Services: The Public Sector

There are some things a private-enterprise, profit-motivated system doesn't provide adequately—national defense, education, highways, moon shots, police protection. Yet we want these "public goods" and "public services," and are willing collectively to pay for them through taxes. We tell the government to provide a wide variety of public services and to force us all to pay through taxes. Instead of relying on the private store to produce everything we want, we set up a public store alongside to handle things that the private store can't or won't stock under the profit incentive. The public store is the "public sector." It allocates resources to producing desired public goods which are voted through the political process, alongside the private sector where the profit motive allocates resources to meeting consumer demands expressed through the market. The public sector allocates about 20 per cent of all resources in the United States today.

Government as Income Distributor:
Transfer Payments

The fourth major economic function of government is to redistribute money income directly —by taxing some persons and making transfer payments to others. The aged, the poor, the helpless, farmers, the unemployed—all receive government transfer payments financed in considerable part by taxes on others, and these money transfers provide a corresponding shift in control over real resources. Since our tax system is "progressive" (that is, the rich pay a higher percentage of their incomes than do the poor), these transfer payments broadly shift income from the upper- to lower-income groups. Government redistribution of money income is the second big part of the public sector. It currently involves between 5 and 10 per cent of the total national income.

Part Five is about the public sector. You may think of it as a public store which allocates resources directly to producing public goods and services that are voted through the political process. This store plus direct money income transfers accounts for somewhere between 25 and 30 per cent of our total economic activity. The public sector is a big and growing part of the modern American economy.

GOVERNMENT EXPENDITURES
AND REVENUES

First, a look at the facts and at how we got where we are. In 1967, federal, state, and local governments spent nearly $250 billion, and their expenditures are rising year after year. These expenditures have been roughly matched by growing tax collections. Thus taxes, including social security taxes, are now about $1,250 annually for every man, woman, and child in the United States. Governments bought about 20 per cent of all goods and services produced in 1967. In addition, government transfer payments accounted for about 7 per cent of personal income received. One out of eight workers is on a government payroll. You may not like having government so big, or you may think it ought to be bigger, but there it is.

The Growing Role of Government

It's useful to begin with some historical perspective. Figure 35-1 shows the growth in expenditures of all governments—federal, state, and local —since 1914. The increases are phenomenal, even allowing for the price increase of about 2½-fold, which would pull the final figure down to about $100 billion in 1914 prices. What accounts for the growth?

1. One major answer is war—past, present, and future. War is fabulously expensive. Today, well over half of the annual federal budget (over $90 billion) is directly or indirectly attributable to fighting present wars, being prepared for future ones, and mopping up the obligations of past ones. This compares with total federal expenditures for *all* purposes of about $15 billion for the entire period from 1789 to 1900.

2. But expenditures for civilian goods account for two-thirds of the combined federal-state-local total—for education, highways, public welfare, and a million other things. Population has grown fast. Even if per capita government expenditures had remained constant, the doubling in population since 1914 would have meant an enormous increase in government spending.

3. We want more public goods and services today. Big cities require more government spending on sewers, streets, police, and so on, than a rural economy would. The shift from a rural to an urban economy accounts for a big share of the state-local increase. But there's a lot more than that involved. Now we want six-lane highways instead of dirt paths. Universal education and modern medical care are enormously expensive. Social security has been made a government responsibility with higher minimum standards than would have been dreamed of a century ago.

4. Partly, the increase shown simply reflects higher prices. Today's price level is the highest in our history and more than double that of 1914. Look back at Fig. 4-3 to see how important this factor is over the long pull. Adjustment to eliminate inflation would cut the growth shown by more than half.

The Public Sector Today

Look now in more detail at the public sector today. Figure 35-2 summarizes what governments spent in 1967 and the taxes they collected to pay the bills. The length of each bar shows the size of the tax or expenditure involved. Although Fig.

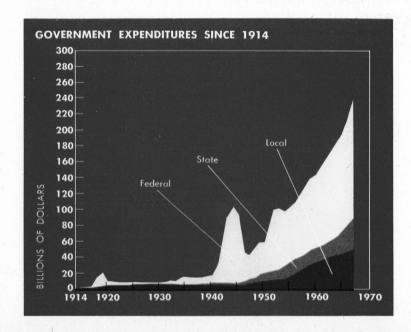

FIG. 35-1 Federal spending has shot up during wars and grown more slowly in peacetime. State and local spending has grown fast since World War II. (Source: U.S. Treasury Department. Figures are for fiscal years and include social security.)

35-2 speaks for itself, $250 billion deserves a closer look.

1. About 60 per cent of all government spending is federal, about 40 per cent state and local. But state and local governments now spend substantially more on nondefense goods and services than the federal government does. And contrary to many misconceptions about the federal bureaucracy, of the eight million people who hold government jobs (excluding military personnel), six million work for state and local governments, only about two million for the federal government. This distribution reflects the fact that the great bulk of federal spending is on goods and services (for example, missiles and aircraft) produced in private industry, and on the payment of military personnel. Large federal transfer ex-

penditures, like interest on the national debt and farm subsidies, require relatively few employees.

2. What are the major government expenditures? Spending on defense far overweighs everything else. Figure 35-3 presents the evidence. Defense, space, and spending on veterans account for 38 per cent of all government outlays (excluding self-financing social security benefits). They comprise over three-fourths of federal spending. Even with social security included, defense is over a third of all government spending. Elimination of defense spending could make over $1,500 of extra income available annually to every family in America, or could permit us to clear vast slums, build new systems of superhighways, triple our expenditures on education.

The next biggest budget items—education and streets and highways—are predominantly state

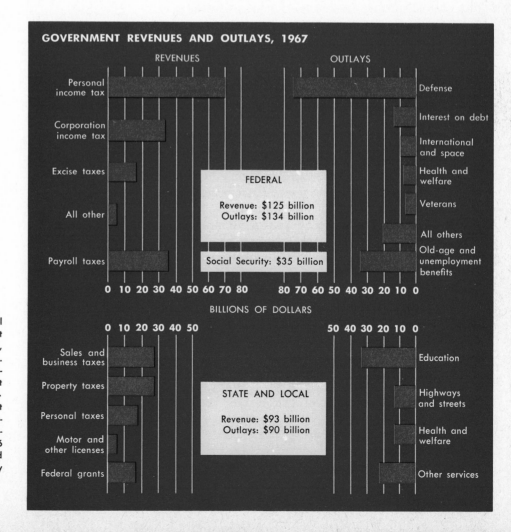

FIG. 35-2 Federal, state and local governments collected and spent about $250 billion in calendar 1967, including social security programs. Each bar shows a major tax or expenditure program. Chart does not include government-operated businesses (such as public utilities), but does overstate net government outlays by including state-local spending of federal grants totalling $16 billion. (Sources: U.S. Treasury and Commerce Departments; preliminary estimates.)

GOVERNMENT REVENUES AND OUTLAYS, 1967

REVENUES   OUTLAYS

Personal income tax   Defense
Corporation income tax   Interest on debt
Excise taxes   International and space
                                         Health and welfare
All other   Veterans

FEDERAL
Revenue: $125 billion
Outlays: $134 billion

Payroll taxes   Social Security: $35 billion   All others
                                                          Old-age and unemployment benefits

0 10 20 30 40 50 60 70 80   80 70 60 50 40 30 20 10 0

BILLIONS OF DOLLARS

0 10 20 30 40 50   50 40 30 20 10 0

Sales and business taxes   Education
Property taxes
                    STATE AND LOCAL   Highways and streets
Personal taxes   Revenue: $93 billion
                    Outlays: $90 billion Health and welfare
Motor and other licenses

Federal grants   Other services

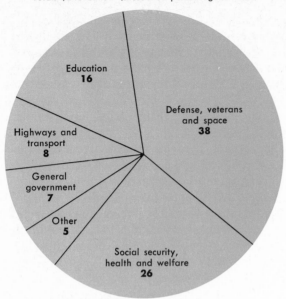

TOTAL GOVERNMENT SPENDING, 1967

Total: $243 billion (slices show percentages of total)

Education
16

Defense, veterans
and space
38

Highways and
transport
8

General
government
7

Other
5

Social security,
health and welfare
26

FIG. 35-3 Defense spending and social security-welfare payments together account for about two-thirds of all federal, state and local government spending. (Source: U.S. Treasury Department. Figures are for fiscal years and include social security.)

goods and services—for example, purchases of raw materials or trucks, hiring workers or soldiers, and the like. Transfer payments are merely monetary shifts—for example, old-age pension payments and interest on the national debt. Obviously, the immediate effect on the economy is different in the two cases; although the money transfers redistribute purchasing power, they do not *directly* reallocate, or use up, productive resources. In 1967, government real expenditures totalled about $175 billion. The other $75 billion was transfer payments.[1]

4. Figure 35-4 shows what taxes provided the revenue in 1967, combining federal, state and local governments. Ours is increasingly a personal tax system. Half of all taxes are raised that way—

[1] The distinction between "real" and "transfer" payments corresponds to that used in the g.n.p. accounts; "real" government expenditures are those on currently produced goods and services. The distinction is not, of course, the same as that between "real" and "money" g.n.p. when we are comparing g.n.p. in current prices with that in constant prices.

and local, and they have grown rapidly. Don't make the mistake of focusing all your attention on the federal government.

Social security is generally excluded from regular government budgets. Old-age and unemployment benefits are financed mainly by special taxes on the persons who receive the benefits; and receipts are placed in special trust funds, separate from regular government tax collections. But by 1967, total annual payments had reached the huge sum of $35 billion, with the payroll taxes to finance these benefits at roughly the same level. Moreover, other health and welfare programs totalled $22 billion at federal, state and local levels. Social security and health and welfare programs have been the fastest-growing nondefense part of the public sector. They have surpassed education and are second in size only to national defense.

3. It is important to recognize that there are two different types of government expenditures, "real" (or "exhaustive") expenditures on currently produced goods and services, and money "transfer payments" (or "nonexhaustive" expenditures). "Real" expenditures use up ("exhaust")

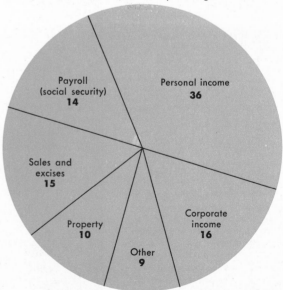

THE TAX BILL, 1967

Total: $237 billion (slices show percentages of total)

Payroll
(social security)
14

Personal income
36

Sales and
excises
15

Property
10

Other
9

Corporate
income
16

FIG. 35-4 Personal income and payroll taxes produce half the nation's tax revenue, the corporation income tax the next biggest chunk. (Source: U.S. Treasury Department. Figures are for fiscal years and include social security.)

36 per cent through personal income taxes and another 14 per cent through payroll taxes. At the federal level, these personal taxes brought in two-thirds of all revenue. Another 16 per cent came from corporate income taxes. Sales, excise, and property taxes accounted for most of the rest, mainly at state and local levels. If you feel you're taxed wherever you turn, you're right. We can't collect nearly a quarter trillion dollars to finance the services we want our governments to provide without making nearly everybody pay. Collections were about $1,200 per person on the average in 1967, though of course much of that was paid indirectly through business, sales, and property taxes.

Redistribution of Incomes through the Public Sector

The public sector allocates resources away from private to public use—to producing defense and school buildings rather than factories and private houses. It does this partly by transferring money income (which shifts purchasing power) and partly by directly reallocating resources.

We are all taxpayers and beneficiaries of government services. But we are not all affected equally. On balance, who pays what and who receives what benefits in this massive transfer? Figure 35-5 answers the question, with a *very rough* set of estimates. The very poor get a large

part of their real income indirectly through government money grants and directly from government services, but they pay taxes equal to only about 28 per cent of their income. At the other extreme, over-$15,000-income families pay about 45 per cent of their incomes in taxes, but receive benefits comprising only about 20 per cent of their real incomes. Putting taxes paid and benefits received together, it's clear that the net impact of the public sector is "progressive." That is, it tends to transfer income from the rich to the poor, to equalize incomes. Most of this effect obviously comes from the expenditure side. Percentage tax burdens are surprisingly similar at the different income levels shown; this reflects a highly progressive federal tax structure but a somewhat regressive one at state and local levels.

Figure 35-5 gives a roughly accurate picture, but don't take the precise figures too seriously. Both tax burdens and expenditure benefits are very hard to estimate accurately. On the tax side, the man who turns the money over to the government often doesn't ultimately pay the tax; he may simply pass it on to someone else. Well-known examples are the taxes on movie admissions and on cigarettes, which are noted separately in the price. To obtain the estimates in Fig. 35-5, we need to know who ultimately pays the tax, and on this score we have only rough estimates. On the expenditure side, it is even harder to estimate who

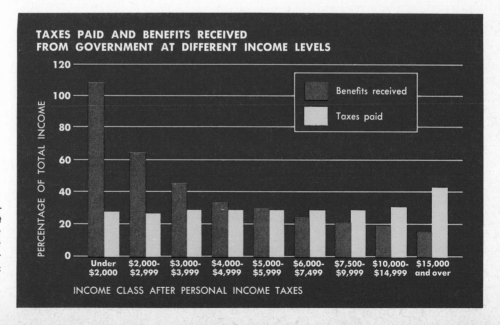

FIG. 35-5 Low-income groups receive much more from government in services and payments than they pay in taxes. The reverse is true for high-income groups. Estimates for 1965 are rough. (Source: Tax Foundation.)

gets the ultimate benefits from government spending. Old-age pensions to retired people are relatively easy. But for services like national defense, foreign aid, education, and general government, about all you can do is make an arbitrary allocation that seems not unreasonable. Thus, others have come up with estimates that disagree on the details. For example, another study shows the percentage tax burden humping in the $4,000 to 6,000 range, and sliding down in the $7,000 to 9,000 range before it rises sharply for higher incomes. But the general picture remains the same. Net real income transfers through the public sector are substantially progressive as between very low and very high incomes but apparently not through the large middle-income range of $4,000 to 10,000.

WHAT SHOULD THE PUBLIC SECTOR DO?

What should the public sector do? Who should pay the taxes, and who receive the benefits? To answer these questions meaningfully, we must ask first: What are we trying to achieve through the public sector? Until we're clear where we want to go, it's hard to say how best to get there.

Goals for the Public Sector

Chapter 3 tentatively set up five fundamental social goals as guideposts to help in evaluating how the economic system works. If these are useful in judging the entire economic system, they should be useful too in evaluating what the public sector can contribute. The goals were suggested because they seem to have widespread acceptance. But if you don't agree with them, substitute your own.

1. Progress: A rising national standard of living.
2. Freedom.
3. Security.
4. Production in accordance with consumer demands.
5. Equity in the distribution of income.

In a basically private-enterprise economy, the main job of achieving these goals has to fall on the private sector. But when should government help by stepping in with taxes and expenditures? Here we leave aside government stabilization and regulatory goals, focusing on the public sector per se.

What Should Governments Do?

In the United States we have a strong tradition of trying private enterprise first and calling on government only where private enterprise clearly would fall short. This philosophy has provided a continuous, powerful restraint on expansion of the public sector in this country. But economists often stress four major situations where there is a strong case for asking the public sector to do the job.

1. *"Essential" Collective Goods.* Some goods and services are viewed as essential and, as a practical matter, can only be provided collectively. National defense is a good example. Almost everyone agrees we need it, and there's no practical way for it to be provided through the market place.

There are two special qualities of such "collective" goods and services. First, they are collective in the sense that all citizens benefit from the service, whether or not they are willing to pay for it. Second, there is no practical way in which the benefits of the collective service can be withheld from someone who does not pay. Even though Joe Doaks pays no taxes, he benefits from national defense; there is no practicable way we can charge him for it through the market. Other examples of collective services are foreign aid, exploration of space, and police protection.

2. *External Economies.* In some cases, the benefits to society as a whole are far greater than those to any one individual who may undertake a particular activity. For example, it might not pay an individual farmer to build a dam across a river up-stream in order to obtain flood protection and irrigate his own land. Yet such a dam may return many times its original cost in benefits to thousands of farmers downstream, or even to city dwellers hundreds of miles away who need flood protection and an adequate water supply. In such cases, we say there are "external economies" from building the dam. That is, there are advantages that accrue to others beyond those to the person

making the original expenditure. In such cases, it is obviously to the combined advantage of the beneficiaries for the expenditure to be made, but there is often no practical way of getting it made except by having the government step in and do the job.

Education represents a bigger (though less sharp) example of external economies. There is a real advantage to each individual from making an expenditure on his own education. But the advantages to society as a whole may be even greater than to each individual, because we will have a more productive, stabler political economy and social system with a well-educated populace.[2]

Note that these cases of external economies and diseconomies are substantially the same as those indicated at the end of Chapter 24, where social costs and benefits differ from private costs and benefits. These are cases where the market system fails to provide an optimal allocation of resources.

3. *Large and Risky Undertakings.* Some undertakings are so large and risky that, as a practical matter, nobody except the government can be expected to take them on. The famous Tennessee Valley Authority (TVA) is a controversial example. In retrospect, the TVA has turned out to be a largely self-financing regional development project, providing valuable electricity and industrial development for a large area, whether or not one accepts the much-debated government accounting system on actual TVA costs. Yet the venture in the depressed 1930's was an extremely large and risky one that private capital was highly unlikely to undertake. A recent comparable example may be the mixed public-private financing of the international communications space satellite concern, "Comsat."

4. *Altered Patterns of Production and Consumption.* Virtually everything the public sector does alters the pattern of production and consumption. But in some cases a specific alteration is desired, either to discourage or encourage some

particular resource use, over and above the considerations just enumerated. For example, most people agree on compulsory free public education for all youngsters through some minimum age, regardless of ability or willingness to pay. Thus, we require that all children attend school and levy general taxes to pay the bills, whether or not the taxpayers have children. We build highways, and finance them by taxes.

But the highway example illustrates another point, too; sometimes the government partially levies the cost directly on the user, for example, through toll charges on toll roads and through gasoline taxes to finance highways. Thus, there need be no income redistribution. "User charges" may be very much like market prices; they may be highly appropriate in cases 2 and 3 above. They would be inappropriate where the goal is to redistribute income. For example, broad tax-financing may place the burden on people receiving little direct benefit.

Today most people agree that they want a wide range of public services. But the four guidelines above provide only a broad framework for analyzing particular cases, and there is violent disagreement on many areas (for example, medicare, urban renewal, and foreign aid). Moreover, there is a proper concern that "the test of the market," i.e., the ability of the producer to make a profit by meeting consumer demand, is absent in the public sector. Thus, when we give up the market for the public sector, we lose a major and automatic test of whether resources are being used efficiently. Nor do the four guidelines tell us *how much* the government should provide of even the agreed-on public services like police protection, education, and national defense. These issues need further exploration.

Balancing Costs and Benefits in the Public Economy

With total output fixed (as we assume here), all the government can do through the public sector is to *reallocate* resources and incomes, away from where they would go through the market economy. If the government does more, this necessarily means a transfer of resources away from private use—from taxpayers to recipients of government services. This example

---

[2] There are also external diseconomies—for example, where a steel mill spews out dirt and smoke over the surrounding neighborhood. Here the remedy usually suggested is a government regulation requiring smoke control procedures (as was indicated in Part Three). However, a special tax on the steel mill to finance cleanup benefits to the neighborhood would be another way to compensate for the external diseconomy.

reemphasizes the ever-present need to economize —to allocate our resources most effectively, here as between private and public use, to satisfy our wants.

Can "Social Welfare" Be Maximixed? In this situation, the principle of maximizing utility by equating returns at the margin suggests a rough guide to how big the public sector should be. Government expenditures should be increased up to the point where the marginal loss in giving up resources in the private sector is just equal to the marginal benefit from public expenditures. As long as the marginal gain is greater than the marginal loss, there is a net gain in over-all welfare. Unless the marginal unit of each resource yields the same economic value in all possible uses (public and private), welfare could be increased by switching the resource to a higher-yielding use.

If society were a single unity, and *if* government were the all-comprehending brain of that unity, application of this principle would be feasible. The government could then weigh satisfactions lost against those gained. But in fact there is no such all-comprehending brain. Practical application of this principle would involve comparison of the marginal satisfactions of millions of different people who might gain or lose from any proposed policy. Obviously no precise interpersonal comparison of satisfactions is possible. At best, we can make only the roughest sort of approximation. Even a very wise man would quail before the task of evaluating precisely the marginal effect of taxing and spending another $100 million on the interstate highway system. Yet, somehow we must agree on the amount we are willing to spend on this purpose. However rough its application, the marginal principle of economizing the use of scarce resources poses one of the important questions to ask in thinking about the right size for the public sector.

Cost-Benefit Analysis:
Planning-Programming-Budgeting

In recent years, economists have begun to tackle this problem empirically through "cost-benefit analysis," an approach pioneered especially under Defense Secretary Robert McNamara. Shall we spend $10 billion on a nationwide missile-shelter system? Economically, the answer involves a comparison of marginal costs and marginal benefits. First, a careful statement of objectives is required: How much protection for whom and for what is desired? What would be the savings, in terms of life, property, and ability to recover rapidly, in the event of atomic attacks of various sorts? Then a comparable set of costs for different sorts of shelter systems to provide the desired results would be calculated. If the costs far exceed the benefits, economically the civilian shelter project is a dubious one. But if the cost-benefit balance is the other way, economically the project gets a green light.

Another example is cost-benefit analysis of the big dam system to provide water from the high Sierras for the cities and fields of California. Costs of alternative dams and water distribution systems could be calculated. Benefits could be estimated—for irrigation, for industrial use, for household use in cities, for electricity generated at the dam. For a multi-billion dollar water system, the job of fully estimating the complex intermesh of costs and benefits is a complex, difficult one. But cost-benefit analysis is one of the most intriguing, fastest-growing branches of modern economics.

Another interesting example is the new U.S. supersonic transport plane given the go-ahead, mainly on government money, in 1967. The case is interesting partly because most cost-benefit analyses raised serious questions about the economic case for the SST, even weighing the long-range future benefits generously. But Congress and the Administration chose to go ahead anyhow, arguing that the international political advantages swung the balance; we just couldn't afford to let the French, British and Russians develop an effective SST far ahead of us. And they suspected that the net economic benefits will be greater than the economists calculated, in spite of sonic booms, airport problems, competition from subsonic planes, and the like.

To implement careful cost-benefit analysis of proposed governmental programs, President Johnson instructed the Budget Bureau in the mid-1960's to push the spread of "Programming-Planning-Budgeting" (P-P-B, as this approach came to be called) through the civilian agencies of the federal government. Should the Post Office automate its handling of mail? Should the Antipoverty Program spend more on retraining programs for the poor? Should the subsidy to U.S. shipbuilders be dropped, or expanded? P-P-B in principle provides an economic foundation for wiser governmental decisions on such issues. But P-P-B is still merely a lusty infant. How big a role government administrators and legislators will give it remains to be seen.

At least, this kind of marginal "cost-benefit" analysis assures that we ask the right economic questions, and it helps to avoid the nonsense often heard in public discussion of such issues. Consider these two examples: (1) The assertion is often made that we "need" more police protection, or more classrooms, or wider streets. But this gives no basis for intelligent economic judgment about whether the government should meet these "needs." To make this decision, the additional costs must be compared with the anticipated benefits. (2) Equally foolish is the common assertion that "we can afford" better schools and urban renewal; therefore we should have them. There are many things we "can afford." Their limit is set by our total productive resources. What resources should be used in the public sector, and for what, can be decided rationally only by asking how expected costs on each venture compare with expected benefits.

Consumers' Sovereignty and Citizens' Sovereignty

For the answer to what the public sector should do, we need to look beyond economics. At the most fundamental level, the issue is whether the political process or the market process does a better job of expressing people's desires on how our productive resources should be used in each case, and whose desires should have the most weight.

The allocation of resources through the private economy occurs primarily in response to consumers' money demands for goods and services. This is "consumers' sovereignty." [3] But

government services are generally made available without any market price at all. Instead, we as citizens express our preferences for roads, rockets, zoos, and so on, through voting for representatives who subscribe to our views. They in turn should vote funds to procure resources to produce the goods and services that we have indicated we want. Thus, through the public sector there is, ideally, a "citizens' sovereignty," somewhat analogous to "consumers' sovereignty" in the private economy. But there are some highly significant differences. Four, especially, deserve attention.

1. In the market place, voting for resource allocation is on a *one-dollar-one-vote* basis. In the public sector, in a democratic country, it is on a *one-person-one-vote* basis. Thus, in the private sector the rich man has many more votes than the poor man. In the public sector a democratic system attempts, though not always with complete success, to give each citizen equal voting power, regardless of whether he is rich or poor. Which way provides the better machinery for determining what to produce with our productive resources is a very fundamental question.

2. In the public sector, it is difficult for individuals to weigh specific benefits and costs, as we do daily in the private economy. In private life, Mr. X can consider carefully whether he prefers to spend $10 on football tickets, an electric razor, a new pair of shoes, or nothing at all. But when Mr. X votes to elect his representative, he votes on a whole group of economic and noneconomic issues. He has little opportunity to distinguish in detail between the things of which he approves and those of which he disapproves—he votes for one complex, ill-defined combination against another when he chooses among candidates. And once he's voted, he has to take the package of virtues and failings rolled up in his representative —and pay the taxes levied whether he thinks he gets his money's worth or not. Only when a specific decision is put up to the voters is there an exception—for example, when a special bond issue to finance a new school must be approved by the voters. And even then the individual has to accept the majority verdict. Consumer's sovereignty clearly gives him a greater power to discriminate on what he wants for his dollars.

3. The public sector thus involves a big ele-

[3] Note that the government, although it seldom does so, might follow the same policy in the public sector, selling the services it provides so as to maximize profits in response to consumer demand. Or a government enterprise, such as a public utility, may be operated to satisfy consumer demand at cost, rather than attempting to maximize profits. In these cases, allocation through the public and private sectors might not differ much.

ment of compulsion. Even with democratic processes, once the elected representatives decide we're going to put a man on the moon by 1970, you and I must pay the taxes to support the project, however foolish we may think it is. Not so in the private sector. There I'm not forced to pay for something I don't want.

Admirers of the market process stress the ability of the market to give effective representation to majority votes while adequately protecting minority interests. The market has a built-in protection for every interest. The rich man gets the most votes, but the little fellow has his say too *in proportion to the dollars he has to spend.* One dollar counts one vote, no matter how large or small the number of votes registered for any commodity. No man needs to spend a dollar on any product unless he personally decides it's worth a dollar to him. A simple, political majority-vote procedure is weaker in reflecting minority wishes, for the reasons indicated in the preceding paragraph.

In some ways, we have pragmatically adjusted our political processes to see that minority interests aren't lost. For example, at both state and national levels representatives are elected from fairly small areas, which gives local minorities a chance to be heard. In legislatures, business is largely done by committees and in informal discussions which work out compromises on important issues that can command majorities among legislators representing widely diverse interests. But this doesn't eliminate the advantage of the market on the score of reflecting "minority" voting interests.

4. The legislative and administrative processes of government favor some groups over others. Our governments are more responsive to the folks back home than we often give them credit for. But in the legislative process, pressure groups and log-rolling play an important role, sometimes a dominant one. Contrary to widespread impressions, this situation is often more true at state and local levels than in the federal government, which operates more nearly in a gold-fish bowl. The groups that are well organized receive more benefits than the rest. The "little man," the consumer, the great unorganized masses, often get the short end of the stick.

And without the test of the market there is no assurance that any public service will actually render benefits greater than its cost. Many public services, once enacted, are continued indefinitely, even though their main rationale may have vanished and their costs exceed the benefits expected by the public which voted them in years before. But here again the case can be overstated. At least in the federal government, a new budget is enacted each year, with widespread publicity about major items. The arguments aren't all on the side of either the private sector or the public sector.

The Problem of Social Balance

One last look at the central issue of consumers' versus citizens' sovereignty from another angle may be helpful. To repeat, those who say the public sector is too big have a basic assumption that individual freedom to spend incomes in the market place should guide the allocation of resources; any other allocation of resources is presumptively inferior.

Harvard's J. K. Galbraith has made a forceful counterargument in a best-selling book, *The Affluent Society.* He argues that such general distrust of the governmental process has led to a serious underallocation of resources to the public sector (leaving national defense aside). In the world's richest economy, we allocate less than 15 percent of our net national product (about $100 billion out of about $700 billion in 1967) to satisfying all nondefense collective wants through government services.

Galbraith argues that our economy is so rich we can readily afford more and better public services, that we need them badly, and that indeed the alternative is generally wasteful civilian consumption just to keep our economic machinery going. Yearly model changes on automobiles, plush night clubs, and mink coats are symbols of conspicuous consumption, meeting demands developed by pervasive advertising. Yet our public services are barely adequate. Half of our most able youths do not go to college. Our cities are marred by slums. Our streets are jammed. Our police forces and local governments are often peopled by incompetent individuals, so poorly paid as to be constant targets for graft. Few of our symphonies and art museums receive adequate public support. The scientist who invents a new gadget is greeted with public acclaim, but the politician who suggests a new public service is deemed a wastrel. All this, Galbraith argues, reflects a basic social unbalance in the affluent American economy. Somehow, we have no effective machinery to translate into reality the obvious need for greater public expenditures.

Why do we so generally assume that a dollar spent on taxes is wasted, while a dollar spent in the market provides a valuable return? Is it, as Galbraith suggests, merely that people have become so accustomed to assuming that any government spending is *prima facie* bad that they do not really examine the alternatives carefully? Some observers say that we tend to underallocate resources to the public sector because as taxpayers each of us sees the cost of public services to himself but the benefits are often so widespread and generalized that it is hard to value the benefits to oneself. This is true, for example, even of highways, which we tend to take for granted without realizing the benefits we receive from them. It is equally true of police protection, education, and the like. Foreign aid to underdeveloped nations is an even more extreme case.

Galbraith challenges, too, the widespread belief that all government activities are conducted wastefully. To be sure there is inefficiency in government, as in private business. But there are many counterexamples. The Veterans Administration now handles its millions of insurance policies with computers and only 3,000 employees instead of the 17,000 it took in 1950. Annual operating costs per policy have been cut from $9.03 to $3.88. The Department of Defense has achieved massive cost reductions under the McNamara regime and P-P-B.

Thoughtful observers recognize that economics provides no simple answer to the question of how big the public sector should be. America can clearly "afford" more public services if we want them. The test of Galbraith's position lies in whether we collectively really do want more public services badly enough to pay for them. Now that the issues are exposed, in conclusion it may be useful to look at a few special facts about public services in the American economy now, and at how we compare with other nations.

Public Services in the U.S. and in Other Countries

Figure 35-6 shows government nondefense purchases of goods and services as a percentage of total nondefense g.n.p. since 1929. Though total government spending has grown immensely, nondefense spending has grown only gradually as a share of nondefense g.n.p. Federal spending on nondefense collective services except social security has remained a very small percentage of total g.n.p. (less than 2 per cent in most years); this percentage has declined substantially since 1939. State-local spending (mainly on education, streets, and highways) is larger and has grown steadily in recent years. Put another way, in constant (1967) dollars, total government spending *per capita* on nondefense goods and services has doubled since 1929, from $170 to about $370, while real g.n.p. per capita has risen by about the same percentage, from $1,700 to about $3,900. Galbraith is clearly right in exposing the misconception that our governments are taking a vastly larger share of our dollars for such nondefense public services.

How big is the public sector (including defense expenditures) in the United States compared to other leading Western nations? Table 35-1 provides a rough summary, and includes a few less-developed nations for comparative purposes. These figures show tax collections as a percentage of gross national product in 1965, including taxes used to finance both real and transfer expenditures.

FIG. 35-6 Government spending on nondefense goods and services has risen gradually since World War II as a percentage of total nondefense g.n.p. This increase is virtually all at the state-local level. (Sources: F. Bator, *The Question of Government Spending*, Harper & Row, 1960; and U.S. Department of Commerce.)

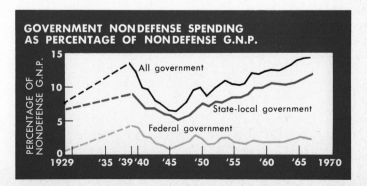

TABLE 35-1

THE PUBLIC SECTOR IN DIFFERENT NATIONS *

Country	Tax Collections as a Percentage of G.N.P.
Sweden	39
France	38
West Germany	34
United Kingdom	30
Italy	30
United States	27
Canada	27
Japan	20
Mexico	10
India	8

* Data for 1965, from Organization for Economic Cooperation and Development, except for Mexico and India.

If we look at "real" government expenditures alone, the U.S. figure was about 20 per cent of g.n.p. This compared with about 22 per cent in West Germany and the U.K., and around 20 per cent in Belgium, Sweden, and Canada. But U.S. government transfer payments (largely welfare payments) were smaller than in most West European nations—around 6 per cent of g.n.p. compared to nearly twice that ratio in West Germany and Sweden. In all the industrialized Western democracies, clearly the public sector plays a big role. In the United States, this role is smaller than in most of the leading West European nations, but much larger than in the less developed countries.

REVIEW

Concepts To Remember

Some new analytical concepts are introduced in this chapter, and important old ones are reused. Be sure you understand the following:

"the public sector"
real (or exhaustive) expenditures
transfer (or nonexhaustive) expenditures
external economies and diseconomies
consumers' sovereignty

citizens' sovereignty
balancing alternatives at the margin
maximization of "total welfare"
cost-benefit analysis

For Analysis and Discussion

1. Is government spending too big? What are your criteria for deciding?
2. Does consumers' sovereignty or citizens' sovereignty provide a better process for allocating society's productive resources?
3. If a copy is available (e.g., in *The New York Times* of about the third week of each January, or in *The Federal Budget in Brief*), read over the President's most recent budget message to Congress. What are the major increases and decreases proposed from the preceding year? Do these changes seem to you desirable? What criteria have you used, implicitly or explicitly, in making these judgments?
4. J. K. Galbraith and many others in the "liberal" wing of the Democratic Party argue that the social priorities are higher on better public services —education, slum clearance, public health, etc.—than on more consumer goods, now that America has so nearly abolished poverty. Analyze this argument.
5. Locate your family income level roughly on Fig. 35-4. Assuming that these data are roughly accurate, do you feel that your income level is being treated equitably in the government's over-all redistribution of income?
6. Give three examples of cases where probable external economies provide a basis for government provision of goods or services. (Hint: Financing of basic research is one example.)

7. Recently, much concern has been expressed that our educational facilities are inadequate in many areas, especially in some rural areas in the South. Should the federal government spend more money to improve these educational facilities, say by building new schoolhouses or making grants to raise teachers' salaries? If your answer is yes, how much would you be willing to see your taxes raised to help pay for such new expenditures?

   a. Many people believe that there is always a presumption in favor of reducing government expenditures. Do you agree? Why or why not?

   b. Why, if at all, is the above presumption more defensible than a presumption that government spending to provide public services should be increased?

8. Government is commonly alleged to be inefficient, compared with private enterprise. Using the postal system as an example, assess this argument.

THIRTY-SIX

THE PUBLIC SECTOR: TAXES

Distribution of the Tax Burden.

Good and Bad Taxes.

Tax Sharing and the "Fiscal Dividend."

Shifting and Incidence of Taxation.

A Look at the Main Taxes.

A "Model" Tax System.

Nearly everyone beefs about high taxes. But if we want public goods and services, we must get resources transferred from private to public use. If we assume full employment, taxes are the most straightforward way to get the funds needed, since they reduce private incomes which would otherwise bid for the resources. With full employment, more government spending without more taxes means increased total money spending and inflation, as more government spending bids resources away from private use. Resources are taken away from those whose incomes fall behind in the inflation.

Government spending sets the general level of taxes we need to collect. But what taxes are the best, and who should pay them? With government spending at present levels, and probably headed higher, construction of a sound and equitable tax system is of foremost importance. The multibillion-dollar federal budget may not mean much to you—the figures are too big. But the fact that you, when you leave college with an average middle-class income of perhaps $8,000, will start turning over to Uncle Sam and to local governmental units over $2,000 each year, puts the dollars and cents in more meaningful terms.

DISTRIBUTION OF THE TAX BURDEN

Who pays the taxes? Figures 36-1 and 36-2 summarize the answer on one basis—what taxes provide the revenue for federal, state, and local governments?

At the federal level, direct personal taxes (on incomes and payrolls) dominate the picture, together providing about 60 per cent of all tax revenue. The other main source is the corporation income tax. But for local governments the property tax (mainly on land and buildings) dominates, providing nearly 90 per cent of all local taxes, and nearly half of state and local taxes combined. At the state level, sales taxes are the big revenue source, accounting for half of all state taxes.

But we're at least as interested in *who* pays the taxes, as in what taxes provide the revenue. To get this information, we must estimate who *finally* pays each tax, as distinct from who turns the money over to the government. Once we make this adjustment as best we can, the combined federal-state-local tax burdens on some typical families are roughly as follows. As a background, look back at the over-all picture in Fig. 35-5.

Typical family A, with a poverty-level income of around $2,000 paid about $600 in taxes, over a quarter of its total income. Most of this $600 was "hidden" in the form of higher prices paid for taxed products, higher rents, and the like, or in the form of lower wages received. About half the total went to local governments, largely through the property tax (whether paid directly or through higher rents).

Typical family B, with a $5,000 income, paid around $1,600 in taxes. This family paid only $300 or so in federal income tax, but it was hit hard by payroll taxes and the hidden excises and property taxes that caught family A as well. In total, family B paid a lot more taxes than A, but it is striking that in percentage of income paid the two are close.

Typical family C, with an income of $15,000, paid $6,000 or so in taxes, perhaps 35–40 per cent of its income. Family C had a nice income; only one family in ten was as well off. Here the federal income tax began to bite in, though it was still only $2,500 or so. Family C also bore a small chunk of the corporation income tax, plus its share of all the same payroll, sales, and property taxes that hit A and B.

Family D, with an income of $100,000, can't be called typical, since there are so few such families. Moreover, its tax burden depended so heavily on the way in which it received its income and how adeptly it utilized tax loopholes that no

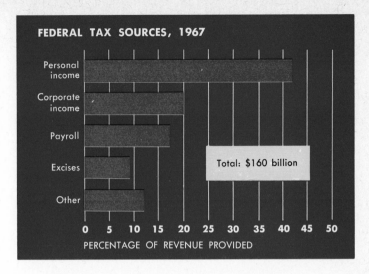

FIG. 36-1 This figure reemphasizes the dominant position of personal and corporation income taxes in financing federal government activities. (Source: U.S. Budget Bureau.)

typical tax figure is possible. Probably it paid between $35,000 and $50,000 in taxes, somewhat less than half its income. Its federal income tax would normally be nearly $40,000 if all its income came from salary, but if part of the income was received on tax-exempt securities or as "capital gains" (see below) the tax would be much smaller. D, being a substantial corporate stockholder, also may have paid heavily through the

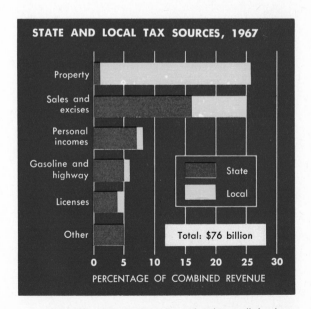

FIG. 36-2 Property taxes provide almost all local tax revenues, while sales taxes and excises provide most state funds. (Source: Preliminary estimates based on U.S. Department of Commerce data.)

479

corporation income tax. In addition, it was subject to most of the same hidden taxes as the lower-income families.

Remember that these figures tell only what "typical" families paid, not where the government's total tax revenue came from. The wealthy family pays a substantial share of its income in taxes. But for every rich family there are millions of poor and middle-income families. Thus, in 1966 about one-third of all taxes were ultimately paid by the half of all families below the $7,000-income level, even though the tax per family wasn't large; nearly another quarter by the $7,000 to $10,000 group; and the rest by the 15 million families with incomes over $10,000. Put another way, about 60 per cent of all taxes came from the under-$15,000 group. The reason was simple—that's where about two-thirds of the income was.

GOOD AND BAD TAXES

Few subjects generate as much heat in popular discussion as taxes. All too often the heat is unaccompanied by light. You can't judge intelligently what are good and what are bad taxes until you've clarified the criteria by which you're judging. Since many people don't bother, it is little wonder that they often disagree violently on what taxes should be.

The same broad social objectives we've used before can be pointed up conveniently in three questions in analyzing the tax system:

1. *Progress.* Does the tax encourage or hinder investment, employment, and economic growth? Does it encourage stable economic growth?

2. *Freedom and Individual Choice.* Does the tax hinder the allocation of resources in accordance with consumer preferences? How much does it interfere with the free choices of individuals and businesses in earning and spending?

3. *Equity.* How equitably is the tax burden distributed? Government taxing and spending significantly affect the distribution of income. Unless government tax collections exactly equal the benefits provided to each family, the issue is not *whether* the government shall redistribute income, but *how.*

Progress:
Stable Economic Growth

Economic growth depends on an intricate complex of factors, but especially on technological advance, on saving and investment, on education, and on hard work by the labor force (see Chapters 15–17). Any tax is a drain on someone's income from work or investment, and in general taxes will deter economic growth (although of course the related government expenditure may have an offsetting effect). But the government must generally levy taxes to pay for its expenditures, and one tax *structure* may be less restrictive on (more conducive to) rapid growth than another.

Theory tells us that taxes which bear on profits and other returns from investment will discourage *growth*, compared to taxes that fall on personal income and consumption. Similarly, taxes that give special advantages to expenditures on investment, research and development, and education, are an incentive to faster growth. We have learned over the past decade how to provide such incentives—the special "Investment Tax Credit" of 1962, and the more generous depreciation guidelines for plant and equipment are examples.

Tax contribution to *stability* is equally important. We want taxes which tend to keep spending growing at a reasonably stable rate, not fluctuating sharply. Individual and corporate income taxes, for example, provide such "built-in tax flexibility." When national income rises, these tax liabilities rise even more rapidly, since individual income tax rates are progressive and since corporate profits subject to tax rise sharply in business expansion. The opposite is true when national income falls. This built-in flexibility tends to damp the swings in private spending. By contrast, a tax that is insensitive to income changes (for example, the property tax or a fixed "head-tax") makes no contribution to stabilizing private spending.

Noninterference
with Free Choices

If we want free private choices to determine the allocation of resources and the distribution of income, a "good" tax system should be neutral in the sense that it does not affect these results. But a tax system as pervasive as ours cannot be truly neutral. People do take tax considerations into account in their business and personal decisions. In a few cases—for example, taxes on tobacco and liquor—we consciously discourage the use of particular products through heavy taxation. But in most cases, the distortions produced by taxes on individual commodities (excise taxes) are considered unfortunate. These distortions occur because higher taxes on particular commodities lead people to buy less of that commodity than they would otherwise buy, relative to other commodities. Or they lead people to work less in particular occupations than they would otherwise choose to do. By distorting resource use this way, a tax may thus produce a "deadweight" loss to the economy—a cost against which there is no offsetting gain. Such a cost is in excess of the resources given up by the private sector through taxation to finance public expenditures. The economy is misled into producing the wrong combination of goods, that is, into producing too few of those that are heavily taxed and into allocating resources in a nonoptimal way.

To minimize this deadweight loss while raising any given amount of revenue, we should use taxes which produce the smallest changes in private production and consumption behavior. A "head" tax (simply a lump-sum tax on each person regardless of income or expenditure) would rate high on this criterion. Since no one could avoid it, it would not affect his economic behavior much, if at all. Taxes on commodities with highly inelastic demand (for example, a salt tax) are similar, since people buy about as much of the product at the higher (taxed) price as before. Conversely, excise taxes on commodities with elastic demand are apt to be highly distorting in their effects.[1]

"Equity" in Taxation

A tax system should be equitable, as well as conducive to stable growth and nondistorting. Three tests of equity are often advanced. One is to levy taxes on the people who get the benefits. Another is to levy taxes according to ability to

---

[1] By this same criterion, to avoid distorting effects, marginal tax rates should be low relative to average rates; on this score, our progressive personal income tax rates low.

pay. The third stresses equal treatment of taxpayers equally situated. Equity means different things to different people, and economics cannot say which is right. It can only clarify the effects of different taxes so each person can judge for himself which result is most "equitable."

The "Benefit" Principle. It seems fair to a lot of people that those who benefit from government services should pay for them. No one argues that this benefit principle should be rigidly applied, but would it be a good general rule?

One obvious problem is how the principle could be applied practically. If a city is putting in a new sewer, it's easy to see who the primary beneficiaries will be and to assess the cost against these property-owners through a "special assessment." But how can the benefits derived from national defense, or the judicial system, be divided up among the citizens?

An even more fundamental question: Would we really want the benefit principle applied? Look at education, for example. Now we have free public schools for everyone. But suppose we put all education on a benefit-tax basis. Then each parent would have to pay a special school tax depending on how many children he had in school —for example, $500 per child. This policy might work out fine for the local banker and doctor. But how about the poor family on the other side of the tracks, with eight school-age children? Where would the $4,000 come from? The benefit principle applied to school taxation would mean the end of elementary and high school education for all. The well-to-do could continue sending their youngsters to school (and more cheaply than now), but millions of poor children would be priced out of the market. Government activities like poor relief would be completely ruled out by the benefit principle, since there would be little point in imposing special taxes on the poor just to return the funds to them.

Broad use of the benefit principle would thus be far more revolutionary than it sounds at first blush. It would mean in effect direct sale of government services to the user. It would preclude any redistribution of income through the public economy. Put otherwise, as soon as government deviates from strict benefit-principle taxation (that is, direct sale of all government services at cost), it is in effect redistributing income, whether we like to admit it or not. This is the meaning of the statement above that, for practical purposes, the issue is not *whether* the government will redistribute incomes, but rather *how* it will redistribute them.

The "Ability To Pay" Principle. Taxation according to ability to pay is widely favored. But how shall we measure ability to pay? Net money income received in the current year is a widely accepted criterion.

Even if we agree on net income as the best measure of ability to pay, there is still the problem of the rate at which different incomes should be taxed. Some argue that the rate should be *proportional*—that is, the same percentage of each person's income. For example, the tax rate might be 1 per cent, giving a $10 tax on $1,000; $100 on $10,000; $1,000 on $100,000. Though the rate is proportional, this procedure of course takes more dollars from high- than from low-income groups. More argue that rates should be *progressive*—that is, a higher percentage tax on high incomes than on low (for example, $5 on $1,000; $100 on $10,000; $2,000 on $100,000). This places a still heavier burden on the well-to-do. All ability-to-pay advocates argue against *regressive* taxation, in which a larger percentage of income is taken from the lower-income groups (for example, $20 on $1,000; $100 on $10,000; $500 on $100,000).

It is important to see that ability to pay as a base for taxation has no exactness or "absolute" validity. There is no objective way of deciding whether rates should be proportional or progressive, or, if progressive, how steeply progressive. The "ability" phrase is, however, convenient for working purposes, since in America we generally agree that progressive taxation of income and inheritances represents the primary application of the ability-to-pay principle. When the term is used in this book, therefore, it will mean progressively higher tax rates as net income rises, without specifying any particular rate of progression. Many writers have attempted to reach some more basic justification underlying the ability-to-pay principle, but without success. In the last analysis, the issue of how much progression is "equitable" is an ethical and moral one. It boils down largely to the question of who should get how much of the limited national income pie—a fundamental and explosive question. This issue of relative tax burden at different income levels is often called the issue of "vertical" equity.

"Equal Treatment of Those Equally Situated." A third principle of equity states that persons equally situated should be taxed equally. This is a powerful guide to tax policy, and one that is accepted by most observers. But what is "equally situated"? Are two people with the same income always equally situated? For example, is a disabled, retired man with an annual pension income of $5,000 equally situated with a healthy single man in his twenties with the same income? Are both equally situated with the $5,000-a-year laborer who has a wife and ten children to support? Does it matter where the income comes from? For example, is a factory superintendent who earns $15,000 a year equally situated with a rich young man who gets $15,000 by clipping bond coupons on a fortune left him by his father? How about a gain of $15,000 on General Motors stock which has gone up in price between your buying and selling it? Our tax laws treat the first two identically, but apply a much lower tax rate to the "capital gain" on the General Motors stock. Should they? This is the issue of "horizontal" equity.

How Much Taxation Can We Stand?

Hardly a day goes by but someone complains that we've reached the limit of our ability to pay taxes—that for the government to raise taxes further would be the last straw. Is there some definite limit to how much taxation the country can stand? Are we approaching it?

The general answer to both questions is "no." But to answer more fully, we have to ask, what is the meaning of "what we can stand?" The usual connotation is that with more taxes the system would slow its growth, people would stop working, there'd be no incentive for businessmen to invest. Faced with predictions of such a debacle, the economist asks, how will it come about, and why?

Economic analysis suggests that if more taxes are going to bring disaster, it will probably be through one or more of the following effects:

1. *Heavier taxes may reduce the incentive to work.* If the government takes too big a share of the income I earn, I may just quit working—or at least work less. Maybe there is some level of taxation at which there'd be no more incentive at all to work—but then there's always the pressing problem of how to eat. As long as something remains after taxes and most people still have much less than they want, the incentive to earn is a powerful one, even when earnings must be shared with the government. But for well-to-do people who feel less income pressure, the amount of work *may* fall off as tax rates rise. And even for middle-income people too, when it's a question of overtime work or a second job. The evidence we have isn't clear enough to settle the question. Most formal studies find little evidence that higher income taxes seriously reduce the work at any income level. But this runs contrary to many people's intuitive notions. More on this later.

2. *Heavier taxes may reduce the incentive to invest,* especially if the taxes fall heavily on profits. Again, this prediction seems intuitively reasonable, but the evidence is unclear. If taxes fall differentially on one type of investment, investors will flee from it in droves. But taxation on all investment income leaves no escape. And there's little evidence that corporations and wealthy individuals just eat more instead of investing. More likely, they complain bitterly about the low return on investment, and go on investing—*if* sales are good (which is the more fundamental stimulus to investment). But here too there is surely some deterrent marginal tax effect, and the impact of differential taxes is strong in shifting investment behavior.

3. *Heavier taxes may lead to legal tax "avoidance."* The law provides many loopholes for people who feel taxes heavily enough to hire a good tax lawyer. Congressional tax committees have repeatedly been told that almost no one, no matter how rich, needs to pay more than half his income in taxes, although the personal income tax reaches a 70 per cent peak rate. The capital-gains provision is the big loophole, but there are many others. A large amount of resources goes into legal tax avoidance. At last count, the Treasury listed about 100,000 tax counselors and tax lawyers whose business was to help on income tax returns. And the effort pays off. The legal marginal rate listed for income in excess of $200,000 was 91 per cent until 1964. Yet Treasury statistics show that only 37 per cent of all income above that level was collected in personal income taxes. What is worse, desire to avoid high tax rates often leads to distortions in investment and diversion of earning activities into special channels (like oil drilling) that permit wealthy people to avoid peak tax rates under the law.

4. *Heavier taxes may lead to illegal tax "evasion."* The case of France is often cited, where for years the government has been able to collect only a modest fraction of the taxes due because of the expense and energy required to run down the individuals who just don't pay. By and large, we Americans report and pay our taxes without being pursued. But a recent National Bureau of Economic Research estimate suggested that 5 per cent of all wages, 30 per cent of unincorporated business incomes (farmers, doctors, lawyers, and so on), 13 per cent of dividends, and no less than 63 per cent of interest on bank deposits went unreported. This would mean a total of perhaps $50 billion in a $600 billion national income. How much harder it would become to collect taxes at higher rates nobody knows. Introduction of widespread employer reporting and computerized checking of all tax returns has made tax evasion increasingly difficult for most people, and most dividend and interest income is probably now caught.

5. *Higher taxes may lead to inflation.* This seems a perverted argument, since modern fiscal policy rests on the premise that higher taxes check inflation. This argument is that if taxes get too high everyone will start raising his asking prices to offset them—unions, businessmen, lawyers, farmers, everybody. Careful thought will show that this behavior can result in continuing inflation only if the government helpfully puts in more money to support total purchasing power at the higher prices. Still, don't forget the pressures on

government to do just that, if the price of inaction or restraint is unemployment.

What do all these points add up to? Not a conclusion that we can't stand any more taxation. Clearly we can, and a lot more if we want the government services urgently enough. Our standard of living is so high we could divert far more resources to the public sector and still have the highest private consumption standard in the world. But they do point to some real dangers as the level of taxation climbs relative to the national income.

Our governments—federal, state, and local—face a tough practical political job finding new tax revenues with taxes as high as they are now. This is a major barrier to voting new government expenditures. But remember from the last chapter that our total tax take as a percentage of g.n.p. is still one of the lowest among the Western industrialized nations—around 27 per cent compared to over 30 for many European nations—out of a per capita income level far higher than theirs. One interesting difference may help explain why Americans complain so much about our taxes. Most of our federal taxes are direct and highly visible—on personal and business incomes—while in Europe more taxes are indirect and "hidden." On the whole, our tax system is probably the most "progressive" in its impact on higher incomes of any in the major industrialized nations. This combination worries those who are concerned about work and investment incentives, and pleases those who are most interested in ability-to-pay approaches to equity.

Who Must Pay?

This analysis leads to one last point, which creates some of the sharpest controversy among people who don't look at the facts. If we want a lot more tax revenue it has to come from the middle- and lower-income groups, because that's where the income is. Thomas Jefferson's ideal of "a country made a paradise by the contribution of the rich alone" won't work any more—the country's too big and there aren't enough rich. Complete confiscation of all personal incomes over $100,000 would add less than $5 billion to the total federal tax take. So if someone is going

to "stand" more taxes, it has to be the general public, not just a rich few.

Except for national defense and social welfare payments, the big increases in government spending have come at state and local levels since World War II. Educational costs have soared with the population surge and the move to the suburbs. Highway and street costs have risen nearly as fast. Rising public assistance and welfare benefits, hospitals, and general government costs have reflected widespread demands for more and better public services. Total state-local spending has risen over 600 per cent since World War II, and is currently increasing about $10 billion a year.

State and local tax revenues have risen too. Local governments rely almost entirely on property taxes; rates on land and buildings have soared and property owners have protested increasingly. Worse for the cities, as city tax rates have soared, families and businesses have fled to the suburbs. State sales taxes have been somewhat more flexible revenue sources, since taxable sales have grown with the economy. But here too rate increases have pushed total burdens to 5 per cent in many states. More and more state and local governments have faced fiscal crises.

Federal spending has soared too. But the federal individual and corporate income taxes have proved enormously productive revenue producers. Individual rates are progressive, so rising national income automatically and promptly produces more than proportional increases in tax revenues. In total, the federal tax system automatically produces a "fiscal dividend" of some $6 to $8 billion annually in increased tax revenues without any increase in tax rates, when the economy grows at its average rate.

Increasingly, the state and local governments have complained that the best revenue sources have been preempted by the federal government. And increasingly, Congress has responded with bigger direct subsidies to state and local governments—up from about $4 billion to over $15 billion annually over the past 10 years. Some have close federal controls over spending, many do not.

Figure 36-3 shows the picture. Highway and public assistance grants have been massive federal transfer programs. Education and the antipoverty program are lusty newcomers to the federal grants arena.

As the state-local tax pinch became more stringent in the early 1960's, Walter Heller of the University of Minnesota proposed that the federal government use a big part of its annual "fiscal dividend" from economic growth for direct, no-strings-tied grants to the states. This tax-sharing would, he argued, face fiscal and political realities; somehow the powerful federal revenue system must be tapped to help the foundering states without a further extension of federal power over state government activities. Nontied tax sharing to distribute the federal fiscal dividend was his answer.

On the Heller proposal controversy reigns, but federal aid to states and localities soars with each federal budget. A central issue is the degree of control over spending the federal government should retain when it turns over funds to state and local governments—for example, control over racial integration as a condition for education grants to the states.[2]

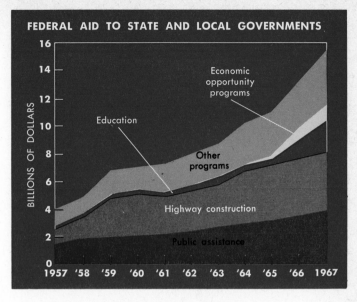

FEDERAL AID TO STATE AND LOCAL GOVERNMENTS

FIG. 36-3 Federal aid to state and local governments has soared during the last decade. (Source: U.S. Budget Bureau.)

SHIFTING AND INCIDENCE OF TAXATION

Often the person who pays over the funds to the government does not actually bear the burden of the tax. The federal tax on liquor, for example, is paid to the government by distillers. But it may be "shifted" forward to consumers through higher prices, or backward to workers through lower wages, and to owners of other resources used in the industry through lower rents or prices. The final "incidence" (or resting place) of a tax may be far from the man who turns the

money over to the government. Obviously it is this final incidence that is most important.

It is safe to assume that in most cases a taxpayer will shift a tax whenever he can. The question generally is, therefore, when *can* a tax be shifted? A tax can be shifted only when, as a result of the tax, the taxpayer is able to obtain a higher price for something he sells or to pay a lower price for something he buys. Hence a price transaction of some sort is essential if shifting is to occur.

Generally, taxes do nothing to increase demand for taxed commodities (remember that we are examining the impact of the tax alone, apart from what is done with the money collected). But taxes do often raise costs and prices. If, as a result of a tax, the price a taxpayer receives or pays is higher or lower than it otherwise would have been, the tax has been shifted to that extent.

Since tax-shifting depends on the prices charged and paid, it is largely an application of the general supply-and-demand analysis of Part Three. If an excise tax is considered a part of business costs, will these higher costs be passed on in higher prices? In a competitive market? In a monopolistic market? How about a tax on business net profits, which doesn't change business costs as usually defined? It's supply-and-demand analysis and the theory of the firm that you need to answer the questions.

[2] Note that this "fiscal dividend" is identical with the "fiscal drag" of Chapter 13. From the point of view of fiscal policy, this growing federal tax take will exert a deflationary drag if the funds are not spent. The funds, transferred to state governments which badly need them to spend, become a fiscal dividend to those governments. Obviously, they could equally well be considered a fiscal dividend available for spending by the federal government.

A warning is necessary. A rise in price following the imposition of a tax in the real world is not necessarily proof that the tax has been shifted. The price rise may have come from some other cause. (Remember the fallacy of *post hoc, propter hoc*.) Empirical verification of tax-shifting is very difficult, since it is so hard to isolate one cause and its effects in the multitude of forces simultaneously at work in economic life. Analytically, however, we can trace through the effects of any tax assuming *"other things equal"*—that is, assuming the tax to be the only new element in the situation. Such theoretical analysis is of necessity oversimplified, and the conclusions drawn are only tentative. But unless we know at least roughly the final incidence of any tax, there is little sense in talking about its place in a good tax system.

A LOOK AT THE MAIN TAXES [3]

The best way to get a good feel for how the tax system really works is to look in detail at some of the main taxes that bring in most of the revenue. The following sections do this. However, this material on individual taxes is set in smaller type to indicate that it involves a considerable level of detail. The big ideas of the chapter are contained in the preceding and concluding pages of the chapter. The look at each individual tax is essentially an application of the preceding criteria on incidence, effects, and equity. It also provides a practical exercise in applying price theory to predict who will really pay each tax when we look through to its final incidence.

Personal Income Taxes

Ours is increasingly an income tax system. Personal income taxes alone account for nearly 40 per cent of all tax revenues. They are levied by the federal government, by about two-thirds of the states, and even by a few cities, but about 95 per cent of the revenue is accounted for by the federal tax. Payroll taxes directly on wages and salaries account for another 14 per cent, and corporation income taxes for an additional 16 per cent. Altogether, the three taxes produce two thirds of total tax revenues.

The federal personal income tax applies to all money income in excess of certain deductions. (1)

[3] Note to instructors: This section on individual taxes is written to be optional, depending on instructor preferences.

A personal exemption is allowed for the taxpayer and for each dependent member of his family ($600 per person in 1968); thus, low-income families escape the tax altogether. (2) Additional deductions are permitted for expenses necessary to earning one's income (such as traveling expenses for traveling salesmen and operating expenses for farmers). (3) Deductions are also allowed for gifts to charitable and nonprofit institutions, for most other taxes paid, for interest paid, for exceptionally large medical expenses, and for certain other expenses.

The tax is progressive—large incomes are subject to higher tax rates than are small ones. In 1967, an average family of four would have paid no income tax unless its income exceeded about $3,000—$2,400 personal exemptions for four persons plus an automatic $600 deduction for gifts, interest, medical expenses, and the like. On the first $2,000 of income over these exemptions, the family was taxed 14 per cent; on the next $2,000, 16 per cent. Rapidly increasing marginal rates applied on higher incomes. The marginal rate was 50 per cent at $40,000, and it reached a maximum of 70 per cent on all income over $200,000.

It is important to note that the *effective average rate* actually paid is always less than the top applicable *marginal rate*. For example, a family receiving $22,000 in salary income would appear to face a marginal rate of 32 per cent, but its income tax bill would actually be only about 18 per cent of its income. The first $3,000–$4,000 of income would be free of tax because of exemptions. The next $2,000 would be taxed at only 14 per cent, and so on up the rate structure. Only that portion of taxable income over $20,000 (presumably none after exemptions) would be taxable at 32 per cent.

The law has several provisions that permit taxpayers to cut their actual rates further below those listed. The three most important are:

1. *Capital-gains Provision.* Capital gains (profits on assets bought and sold) on assets held over six months are taxed at only half the rate on other income, and at a maximum rate of 25 per cent. This provision encourages investment in growing industries, and it seems to many people more equitable than taxing such special gains as regular income. But by the same token it provides a major escape from peak rates for wealthy persons who invest their funds in growing firms, the stock market, or other assets where they can obtain capital gains rather than current income. Wealthy investors often thus prefer companies which plow back their earnings and thereby grow faster. The growing value of

the company's stock represents merely a capital gain, subject to tax at the reduced rate when sold to realize the gain, while dividends are currently taxed as regular income. To take advantage of this law, part of executive salaries are often paid in the form of a privilege for the executive to buy the company's stock at the present market price at a later date. If the stock goes up (as it probably will for a growing company), he can buy in later and take the profit on the stock's value as a capital gain rather than as regular income taxable at full income tax rates.

2. *Expense Accounts.* Today's corporate executive travels in luxury, holds membership in the best clubs, and has frequent health checkups, all at company expense. A star goes to London, ostensibly to advertise a new movie. Are these really necessary business expenses, or merely concealed employee income that doesn't get taxed? No one doubts the legitimacy of business expenses, and the mores of the times are that business executives entertain well and do a lot of business out of the office. But sometimes those with access to expense accounts stretch them pretty far. What worries the Treasury as much as the income that goes tax-free through plush expense accounts is the resentful feeling of millions of other taxpayers who don't have expense accounts, but who may feel it's all right to fudge a little when they think of those big fellows who seem to get away with so much.

3. *Tax-exempt State and Local Bonds.* Traditionally, interest on state and local government securities has been exempt from the federal income tax. For the rich man, this makes a whopping difference. If you are in the 66 per cent marginal tax bracket, a tax-exempt yield of 4 per cent on a local bond is equal to a yield of 12 per cent on a taxable security. This provision makes state and local bonds easier to sell, but it provides a large loophole for the well-to-do to avoid high federal income tax rates on income from their investments.

At high income levels it pays to take advantage of these legal loopholes. A good tax lawyer is worth his weight in gold if you're rich enough.

Incidence. The incidence of the personal income tax is generally on the taxpayer; the tax is hard to shift. Neither the demand for nor the supply of any good or service is likely to be much affected by the tax to permit shifting. If individuals are receiving the maximum income they can before the tax, no change will enable them to make more merely because of the tax.

The only important exceptions arise where the tax does lead people to work less, where the taxpayer's ability to get more income was not being fully exploited before imposition of the tax, or where for some reason employers are willing to pay higher wages after imposition of the tax on employees.

Effects on Growth and Stability. Present high marginal income tax rates are often said to reduce the incentive to work at upper income levels. These may be crucial levels for rapid growth; they include managers, entrepreneurs, and top scientists. Empirical studies have failed to show this deterrent effect. But people in high tax brackets generally claim that high tax rates do affect their behavior, and the evidence is not yet sufficient to brush their arguments aside. Many economists and sociologists believe that the desire to improve one's *relative* position will keep most people working hard, even when Uncle Sam gets a big chunk of the increase. Moreover, most high-income jobs are closely associated with social prestige, power, and status. At the top of the income scale, these incentives to work and advancement may rival the importance of more take-home pay.

At lower income levels, higher tax rates may cut down on overtime work, second jobs, and working wives. But here the pressures for more income are strong, and it is not clear that taxes are a major deterrent to work in most cases, so long as the earner keeps the bulk of the marginal income for himself.

A parallel argument is that peak marginal tax rates seriously deter risky investment. If you win, the government takes most of the killing; if you lose, you bear the loss. So why take the chance? This argument may deter investors from risky ventures—but remember that most such gains would be subject only to the maximum capital gains rate of 25 per cent, and substantial offsets of losses against gains are permitted in computing taxable income.

The income tax rates high as a built-in stabilizer to damp down instability. When national income soars in a boom, income tax receipts rise even faster, because a bigger proportion of people's incomes falls in the higher tax brackets. This puts a damper on the boom. Conversely, when national income slides in a recession, personal income tax receipts slide even faster, thus cushioning the recession's impact on personal disposable income.

Equity and Nondistortion. The personal income tax is widely agreed to be an equitable tax, though there is wide disagreement on the optimum rate structure. It is a progressive tax on the basis of net income received, probably the best available single indicator of ability to pay. Moreover, we can be surer than with other major taxes that the incidence will be where it is intended. Further, it probably involves less interference with free consumer, investor, and worker choices than any other major tax. Although the income tax takes a certain percentage of net income, this percentage is the same whatever the source of income,[4] and the taxpayer is left free to spend or invest his remaining income wherever he pleases without government interference. The personal income tax may stimulate leisure as against work, since it can be avoided by not working, but, as was indicated above, there is limited evidence to substantiate this effect.[5]

Corporation Income Taxes

The federal government and most states levy corporation income taxes; these yielded over $40 billion in 1967. The federal tax applies to all corporate net income, with a 48 per cent rate in 1967—except that the first $25,000 of income was taxed at only 22 per cent and over 80 per cent of the nation's million corporations make less than $25,000 annually. But the big companies, which do the great bulk of corporate business, paid the 48 per cent rate. Companies may offset losses in bad years against profits in good years to a considerable extent.

Two big issues arise in calculating a firm's "taxable income." One is "depreciation allowances."[6] How fast should companies be permitted to depreciate new plant and equipment for tax purposes? If they can accelerate depreciation, depreciation charges (allowable as business costs) will be larger and taxable profits correspondingly smaller during

the years immediately ahead. This practice permits the corporation to postpone taxes, giving it funds for current reinvestment instead. If the government wants to speed up investment, accelerated depreciation privileges on new investment appear to be an effective device.

Second, how large should "depletion" allowances (that is, a special type of depreciation allowance) be for drilling and mining companies which use up such natural resources as oil and coal. Under present law, oil companies can charge as a business cost a special depletion allowance of 27½ per cent of the gross income received from their oil wells. This special income exclusion is supported as necessary to encourage expensive exploration and drilling activities. Depletion allowances totaled about $4 billion in 1967, and succeeded in holding the average tax rate on oil company incomes down to about 20 per cent, compared to just under 48 per cent for most major companies. Critics of the provision attack it as a blatant subsidy to the oil interests. Similar, though smaller, percentage depletion allowances are provided for most other minerals.

Incidence.   The incidence of the corporation income tax is uncertain. First, assume a highly competitive economy. If a company was maximizing profits at some price-output level before the tax, this would still be the best level after the tax. The government would take some of the profits, unfortunately for the stockholders, but their profits after taxes would still be maximized at the same output and price. The new income tax might drive investment completely out of the corporate form into other kinds of investment opportunities. But for big business, incorporation is essential, and comparable investment possibilities at lower tax rates are hard to find. Or it might lead stockholders to give up investing and to consume their funds. But this too seems unlikely on any large scale. This reasoning says the tax cannot be shifted.

But the real world is one of oligopolies and partial monopolies, of imperfect information on costs and markets, of multiple motives for corporate management among which profit maximization is only one. Here the incidence of the corporate income tax is much less certain. Prices are set administratively, markets are shared, big buyers bargain with big sellers. It's not clear that firms are acting very precisely to maximize profits. If a firm does not want to disturb its position in the industry, it may be willing to absorb a modest increase in income taxes. Or the tax increase may prod the firm into breaking the

---

[4] Except for the qualifications noted above on tax loopholes and tax evasion.

[5] Death and gift taxes supplement the personal income tax. The federal government levies a progressive "estate tax" on the estate of everyone who dies with property totaling more than $60,000. Above that level, rates climb rapidly to 77 per cent on that portion of estates over $10 million, but the large exemption, plus a further special exemption of half the estate if it's given to one's husband or wife, keeps most families free from the tax. Most states have comparable taxes on the inheritance received by beneficiaries in estates, but at much lower rates, and there is a partial exemption under the federal tax for state taxes paid. The federal tax is accompanied by a gift tax to limit evasion of death taxes by giving away property before death, though there are generous exemptions for gifts spread out over several years.

[6] For a review of depreciation, look back at the Appendix to Chapter 19.

inertia of established prices and venturing a big price increase.

What has happened to post-tax corporation profits when corporation tax rates have been increased in the past? In general, profits have been squeezed, compared to lighter tax periods. This is far from convincing evidence on incidence, since many other factors influenced corporation profits in each period. But it is evidence that taxes have eaten away at profits available for stockholders and for reinvestment.

High marginal tax rates encourage current corporation expenditures, whatever the incidence of the tax itself. With a 48 per cent marginal tax rate, each dollar spent on advertising, research, or other such business purposes costs the company only 52 cents. The government in substance pays the other 48 cents. There is no way of estimating precisely the importance of this effect, but tax experts and businessmen agree that business takes a more lenient attitude on spending when the marginal tax rate is high. This was vividly demonstrated during World War II, when peak tax rates were 82 per cent and corporations could spend "18-cent dollars." But as long as the corporation keeps part of each dollar of profits, it has an incentive to hold down costs. Spending "cheap" dollars costs less than spending tax-free dollars, but it still costs potential profits.

All in all, economic analysis suggests that corporation income taxes are borne partly by stockholders and partly by consumers of corporate products. In addition, the expenditure-inducing effects of high marginal tax rates may place the cost of some business expenditures on taxpayers rather than on the consumers or stockholders.

Effects on Growth and Output.   A tax on corporate net income imposes no direct burden on costs and hence does not have the same direct deterrent effect on output and employment as do sales, excise, and payroll taxes. On the other hand, the level of business investment depends largely on profits and the expectation of profits. A tax on profits surely has some effect in slowing investment and growth. Just how much is not clear.

Most of the Western European nations and Japan have lower corporation income tax rates and more lenient depreciation policies than we do. Businessmen urge that we permit businesses (as some European nations do) to depreciate assets as fast as they wish for tax purposes, and rely more on indirect, nonbusiness taxes. Tax experts generally agree that our corporate tax rules and rates are relatively

restrictive, and that easing them should speed investment and growth. But that doesn't answer the hard question of who does pay the taxes if businesses don't.

On the score of built-in counter-cyclical flexibility, the corporation tax rates as excellent. With good times, corporation profits rise rapidly, pushing up tax liabilities and draining off funds to the government. When business declines, corporate profits drop fast, and there is a correspondingly fast reduction in corporation tax liabilities.

Effects on the Distribution of Income.   Taxes on corporate income conform fairly well to the criterion of ability to pay. The tax falls partly on corporate stockholders, and most such securities are held by the upper- and middle-income groups. But dividend income is an imperfect measure of taxpaying ability. For example, Mr. A may have an income of $5,000 annually, and own a few shares of General Motors. He loses 48 per cent (at 1967 rates) of his potential income from dividends because of corporate income taxes. The millionaire owner of General Motors stock loses the same percentage. Clearly, high-income stockholders are taxed less progressively than if all corporate income had been paid out to them for taxation as personal income, and low-income ones more so.

Under the present corporate income tax there is "double taxation" of dividends; they are taxed first as corporate profits and then as personal income to the stockholder. Critics argue that this arrangement is highly inequitable. They argue that this double taxation seizes a major share of the profits from the stockholder, and discourages precisely the type of enterprise and risk-taking that we need for economic growth and innovation. Supporters of the present arrangement retort that these are merely arguments for reducing the tax burden on the rich (the stockholders), and shoving a bigger share of total taxes back onto the poor.

Payroll Taxes

Payroll taxes are used largely to finance the federal old-age insurance program and the combined federal-state unemployment insurance plans. At $35 billion in 1967, they were second only to the personal income tax as a revenue producer.

Most payroll taxes fall in two equal parts, half levied on the employee and half on the employer. Note that payroll taxes differ significantly from personal income taxes, in that payroll taxes fall on only one type of income—wages and salaries.

Dividends, rents, interest, and all other nonpayroll income are exempted. This focus on payrolls is justified by the use of funds collected for the special benefit of the workers. Indeed, the payroll taxes to finance the federal old-age retirement program are not officially termed taxes. Instead, Old Age and Survivors' Insurance is considered an insurance plan in which payroll taxes are compulsory premiums. Second, payroll taxes are almost always at a flat rate and the federal tax applied only to the first $6,600 of income, as of 1967.

The incidence of both parts of the payroll tax (that deducted from wages and that paid by employers) is primarily on the workers covered. But the widespread imperfections in the labor market make the process of shifting uncertain and jerky. Where wages are inflexible downward, moreover, the incidence may take the form of unemployment for some workers involved. Look separately at the tax collected out of wages and that imposed on the employer.

1. The incidence of the tax deducted directly from the employee's wage is almost sure to be on the employee. There is no one to whom he can shift it backward, and there is nothing in the tax to increase the demand for labor. Powerful unions may be able to use the tax as an excuse to demand wage increases—but if they can get higher wages after the tax we have to explain why they couldn't do it before. There is little likelihood that the tax will be shifted to the employer by a withdrawal of labor to "noncovered" occupations, partly because there are few such areas and partly because workers don't want to give up the benefits of the social security program.

2. The likely incidence of the tax on the employer is also on employees. The tax increases the effective wage cost. If the firm was previously in a maximum-profit adjustment, after the tax it will be advantageous to raise selling prices or to curtail employment directly, both restricting output and substituting machinery for labor. If wages are flexible, they may move down to permit the same number of workers to be employed after the tax as before. If wage rates are inflexible, one likely effect of the tax is unemployment. Notice that this analysis holds for either competitive or monopolistic conditions where economic profits have been eliminated. When firms have a protected profit position, unions may be able to bargain wages up to offset part or all of the higher payroll taxes.

If we want workers to bear the major costs of

unemployment and old-age insurance, payroll taxes may be a good means of financing social security. They are widely supported. But don't forget that putting the tax on the employer in the present fashion, even though we *want* him to pay, doesn't necessarily mean that he *will* pay it.

Excise and Sales Taxes

Excises are taxes on particular commodities—liquor, tires, cigarettes, movie admissions. They are often collected from the manufacturer or wholesaler, so that many of them are hidden in the final price of the product, although some are by law quoted separately from the price. The bulk of federal excise tax revenue comes from gasoline, liquor, and tobacco taxes, all "visible" to consumers. Many states and localities have comparable taxes, ranging all the way up to general sales taxes which levy a flat percentage of the sales price on all items sold at retail. Sales and excise taxes produced $38 billion in 1967.

Incidence. Most people assume that excise taxes will be passed on to the consumer, and much of the time they're right. But not always. The answer comes directly from an application of the supply-and-demand analysis of Part Three. It depends on how competitive the industry is, on the demand for its product, and on the supply of labor and raw materials to the industry. Use the price theory from Chapters 20–27.

Competition. Suppose an excise tax is applied to playing cards. If competition is active in the industry so that economic profits tend to be eliminated, the tax will be shifted. It raises costs and does nothing to increase demand, so net losses will result until the tax is shifted. Firms may put prices up by the amount of the tax, or may reduce their costs by paying less for labor and raw materials, or a combination of both.

Simple supply-and-demand analysis helps to explain what happens. The lines SS and DD in Fig. 36-4 show the playing-card market before the tax, with 100,000 decks being produced and sold daily at $1 per deck. Now a tax of 25 cents per deck is imposed on producers. This increases their costs accordingly, and reduces the amount it will pay them to produce (supply) at any given price. The new industry supply curve is the line S'S', which is 25 cents lower (to the left) at each point. Thus, the tax leads to a reduced supply and a higher price (including tax). The after-tax equilibrium is about 75,000 decks daily at a price of about $1.15. Note that the new price is higher than the old by only 15 cents. The other 10 cents is

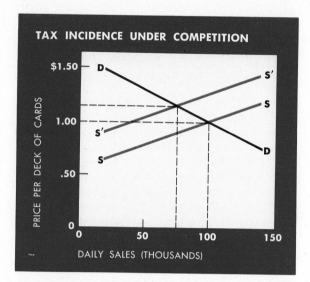

FIG. 36-4 Under competition with these supply and demand curves, new tax is partly shifted forward through a higher price and partly reduces output and consumption of cards. What would this do to the industry's demand for labor and raw materials?

shifted backward through the industry's reduced demand for labor, raw materials, and other productive resources, since fewer playing cards can be sold at the higher price after tax.

Which way will the tax be shifted? Whichever way is "easier." If demand is highly elastic, so that sales fall off rapidly as price is put up, not much of the tax will be shifted forward to consumers. If there is a strong union in the industry, so that wages are hard to push down (that is, so that the supply of productive resources is highly elastic), backward-shifting is difficult. How much of the tax goes each way depends on the relative elasticities of demand and supply in the two directions. The common presumption of forward-shifting implicitly assumes that the supply of productive resources to the taxed industry is more elastic than consumers' demand for the taxed product. Change the slopes of the demand and supply curves in Fig. 36-4, and you can see readily the importance of different elasticities.

In industries using highly specialized resources, backward-shifting is more likely than elsewhere. Suppose the playing-card industry takes the whole output of some grade of paper pulp that is not useful in any other industry. Then the supply of pulp to the card industry would be very inelastic, at least in the short run; even if the card industry offered a lower price it would still get about as much pulp, since there are few other places for the pulp to be sold. The tax would be largely shifted backward in lower pulp prices. But the more unspecialized and mobile resources are, the less they are forced to take lower payments as a result of decreased demand. And in the long run, most resources are unspecialized. Thus, in the long run a big portion of the tax is probably shifted forward to consumers.

Monopoly and Oligopoly. In monopolistic or oligopolistic markets where competition has not eliminated economic profits, the final outcome is less certain. Part of the tax may fall on profits and stay there without driving resources out of the industry. Here we are up against the uncertainty of price-making in imperfectly competitive areas. The partial monopolist may immediately add the tax to his price. Or he may absorb it rather than chance driving away his customers. Or he may use the tax as an excuse for an even larger price boost.

But through all this uncertainty, two fundamental facts stand out: (1) A large tax cannot be absorbed by monopoly profits, and will be largely shifted, as under competition. (2) A nonshifted tax eats into profits, and few businessmen like to see profits sink; they will shift the tax whenever they feel they reasonably can. Most substantial excise taxes are shifted.

Effects on Growth and Employment. The direct impact of sales and excise taxes is highly deflationary. They impose a direct burden on costs or effective purchasing power. But if we are mainly interested in rapid growth, and still must obtain some given amount of tax revenue, sales and excise taxes may nevertheless be the best bet. For they bear directly on consumption, while leaving investment untaxed.

By the same token, a general sales tax is a strong anti-inflation weapon. It hits directly at the massive consumption expenditures of the lower- and middle-income groups.

Effects on Income Distribution and Resource Allocation. A *general sales tax* is regressive. A $2,000-income family will spend almost the entire amount, except for rent payments, on taxed consumption. Assuming a forward-shifted tax of 5 per cent, it will pay a tax of $100, disregarding rent—5 per cent of total income. But a $100,000-income family will spend only part on consumption goods (say $40,000). The wealthy family is thus taxed 5 per cent on only $40,000, making a total sales tax burden of $2,000, or only 2 per cent of total income. Even though the wealthy family pays many more dollars, it pays a smaller percentage of its income.

But increasingly, major "necessities" like food and clothing have been exempted to soften this inequity. With these exemptions, plus rent, sales taxes lose most of their regression, and don't differ greatly, except at high income levels, from raising the same funds with a broad-based income tax. As a result, popular acceptance of sales taxes has risen considerably, even among "liberals" who generally favor the most progressive taxes that will raise the revenue needed.

Excise taxes discourage consumption of the taxed products. In some cases, like liquor and tobacco, the tax is specifically intended to discourage consumption. We call these "sumptuary" taxes. But it is easy to mix up economics and morals here. For example, many people think we ought to avoid taxing "necessities," but that it is all right to tax "luxuries." Taxes on "necessities" are thought to be regressive; taxes on "luxuries" progressive. These loose generalizations depend, however, on how "necessities" and "luxuries" are defined. If "necessities" are goods that everyone consumes heavily (for instance, bread), taxes on necessities are clearly regressive, since a larger proportion of income will be spent on them by low- than by high-income groups. But consider taxes on two major "luxuries"—liquor and tobacco. In fact, the demand for these products by rich and poor is relatively inelastic. The cigarette tax of about 8 cents per pack in many states often leads to lower expenditures on clothing and food, not to less smoking; many people give up what are usually called "necessities" rather than cigarettes. The same is true of liquor. Thus, liquor and tobacco taxes (on "luxuries") may be among the most regressive taxes. Elasticity of demand, rather than morals, is critical in determining who actually pays excise taxes. And any excise distorts the allocation of resources. Excises produce a relatively big "deadweight loss."

Property Taxes

Property taxes on land and buildings were, until World War II, the most important single tax source in the United States. They are also the oldest major source of tax revenue. The federal government levies no property taxes, and state governments now receive only a small sum annually from them. But local governments depend on property taxes for almost their entire income.

Administration.   How does the property tax work in practice? Most local units—cities, school districts, and the like—annually or biennially estimate the expenditures required for the coming year or two. Meanwhile, the property to be taxed has been assessed. The amount to be raised is compared with the assessed property values, and the tax rate necessary to raise the funds is determined. For example, if $1 million is to be raised and the local assessed valuation is $100 million, a tax rate of 1 per cent on assessed valuation is necessary.

Low-priced real property is widely overassessed relative to high-priced property (that is, assessment is "regressive")—partly because of "influence" with assessors and partly because most assessors have no idea of the value of expensive properties and hence depend on the figures suggested by the owners or simply follow past assessments. Thus, the actual incidence of the tax depends heavily on administrative procedures.

Incidence and "Capitalization."   There is nothing peculiarly hard about figuring out the incidence of many property taxes. Taxes on buildings will be gradually shifted if the tax drives investment out into other areas where taxes are lower, thereby reducing the supply and raising the prices of these taxed buildings. This is the same analysis as in the case of other taxes that hit only special areas or products.

An interesting point concerns the tax on land itself, as distinct from improvements on it. The first effect of the tax on land is the same as on any other investment opportunity—the net return on the property is correspondingly reduced. Thus buyers will be willing to pay less for the land after the tax has been levied. The capital value of the land is thus decreased by the imposition of the tax.

The tax is then said to have been "capitalized." Any future buyer of the land will not invest in the land unless the price is low enough to provide a net return *after real-estate taxes* equal to that obtainable on investment elsewhere. Capitalization thus puts the burden of the capitalized tax exclusively on the owner of the land at the time the tax is levied, by forcing him to pay the unshiftable tax and by forcing down the capital value of his property. Any future buyer will not bear the burden of the tax, because he anticipates the tax in the price paid for the land. Future owners buy "tax-free."

Although capitalization often does not work out so precisely, it is an important factor in connection with the real-property tax. Consider a proposal to decrease the tax on real property. Present owners have bought at lower figures because of the tax, capitalizing the burden on earlier owners. To lower the property tax now would be to give a subsidy to present owners through increasing the capital value of the land. The fact of capitalization is a strong argument against drastic reductions in long-established property tax rates.

The real-property tax is often supported on the "benefit" principle. Owners of real property receive many important special benefits, such as police and fire protection; and the larger the property holdings, the greater are the benefits received. The property tax has some virtues on the benefit criterion, and a few on ability-to-pay. But the main case for it is that it's there, and everything is pretty well adjusted to it. There is no other local tax source that looks better which could realistically replace it for local governments.

A "MODEL" TAX SYSTEM

What would a model tax system look like? What changes would you make in our tax system? As a citizen, this is one issue on which you will repeatedly get a chance to say your piece. At federal, state, and local levels, tax changes are continually being made.

It's clear that different taxes look good on different criteria. Recognizing that what is considered a "good" tax system must depend heavily on each individual's weighting of the different objectives, some economists have proposed a "model" tax system along the following lines. It would make some drastic changes in the present system, and it is presented only to stimulate you to think through your own views on what an ideal tax system would be.

This "model" tax system would have four major taxes:

1. A progressive personal income tax would account for at least two-thirds of all tax revenue. This would mean more than doubling present income tax revenues. Higher rates would reach down through the middle- and low-income groups, and the bulk of the income tax yield would necessarily come from these groups, where the income is.

This tax places the burden directly on individuals where it ultimately must rest, and it makes clear who is paying how much. The exact rate structure would depend on our collective judgments on equity, together with recognition of the importance of adequate income incentives. The tax would be supplemented by progressive death and gift taxes. To encourage incentive and economic growth and to improve equitable treatment of similarly situated people, the present punitively high peak rates of the federal tax would be lowered to about 50 per cent, but at the same time the sieve of avoidance loopholes for high-income taxpayers would be closed.

State income taxes would be added to the federal income tax, with the funds returned to the states concerned, in order to simplify tax reporting and collection procedures. Thus, the personal income tax base would be shared by federal and state governments.

2. Both to stimulate economic growth and to improve equity by switching to the personal income tax, present corporation income tax rates would be lowered substantially. The new tax would fall on all businesses, not merely corporations. At the same time, again to encourage growth, depreciation restrictions would be eased to permit faster charge-offs. But major loopholes like the present "depletion allowance" would be closed. Undistributed profits above generous reinvestment levels would be prorated out to stockholders for taxation, to avoid use of corporations as tax-avoidance devices.

3. Taxes on real property would be continued at roughly present levels, not so much because the property tax is a good tax as because it is a major revenue source for local governments to which economic life has become well adjusted, and because its removal would mean a large subsidy to present real-property owners.

4. There would be special "user charge" taxes that are clearly justifiable on the benefit principle. In this group would be: (a) special assessments; (b) highway taxes (on fuel and on vehicles), with the revenue to be spent on highways and streets; and (c) payroll taxes on the worker (not on the employer) to finance social security benefits. All three have strong claim to use as benefit levies.

Could such a tax system yield adequate revenue to pay the governments' bills? The answer is clearly "yes," since personal income tax rates could be set to produce any desired yield. Could it yield the revenue without impairing the incentive to work and earn? This is a big question raised by critics of the income tax, which in this system would supplant hidden excise and sales taxes, plus part of present corporation taxes. One way of putting the question is: Do we really want as many government services when we recognize individually what we have to pay for them? A lot of economists would replace part of the income tax with a broad sales tax, possibly excluding food and clothing to avoid serious regression, in order to lessen the possible negative incentive effects of heavier income taxes.

Taxes are going to take over a quarter of the income you earn during the rest of your life, if something like present conditions continue. Every time we tell our governments to do something more for us, we're in effect saying there'll have to be more taxes collected. Thus, getting a good tax system is one of the most important problems we face, as a nation and as individuals. So stop and ask yourself: What does *your* model tax system look like? Even more fundamentally, how big should the public sector be, and what should it do? For that is what will determine how many taxes we as a nation must ultimately pay.

REVIEW

Concepts To Remember

Public finance involves mainly the application of analytical concepts already learned in the preceding chapters. But it has some concepts and terms of its own that you need to have firmly installed in your economic tool kit:

incidence	vertical equity
shifting	horizontal equity
benefit principle	incentive effects
ability-to-pay principle	capital gain
progressive taxation	tax capitalization
regressive taxation	tax sharing
"deadweight loss"	"fiscal dividend"

For Analysis and Discussion

1. Are taxes too high? What is your criterion?
2. Can you suggest ways of minimizing the negative incentive effects of rising taxes as government expenditures grow?
3. Some tax experts argue that taxes should be highly visible (like the personal income tax) in order to make citizens keenly aware of the taxes they are paying. Others argue that indirect and hidden taxes (e.g., excise and sales taxes) are better because taxpayers don't feel the burden so strongly and are less unhappy about the costs of government services. Analyze these arguments. What are the main issues, and where do you stand on them?
4. "The government's taxing and spending policies should leave the distribution of income roughly as it would be through the private economy."

   "Every child should receive a good education at least through the grade-school level."

   Can you consistently accept both these propositions? Analyze carefully why or why not, examining specifically any apparent inconsistencies.

5. Suppose a new excise tax were imposed on the following products, at the producer's level:
    a. Steel (where there is mixed price leadership and competition, plus strong labor unions).
    b. Potatoes (where the market is highly competitive and little unionized labor is involved).
    c. Ladies' garments (where the market is highly competitive and there is a strong labor union).
    d. Refined oil and gasoline (where the market is oligopolistic and little strongly unionized labor is involved).
   Explain in each case whether you would expect the incidence of the tax to be on the consumer, labor in the industry, the producing firm, or some combination.
6. Assume a period of strong inflationary pressures as a result of government arms spending. Which of these alternatives would you consider the more equitable, and why?
    a. A general sales tax to balance the budget.
    b. Inflation.
7. Given a full-employment situation and the need for more taxes to finance more defense spending, what tax program would you propose to raise an additional $10 billion? Defend your program against likely criticism from those who would bear the major burden.
8. What is your model tax system?

CURRENT RESEARCH

Research in the area of public finance has focused heavily since the decade of the 1930's on fiscal policy to avoid depression and inflation. But in recent years, research aimed at the allocative and distributional effects of government taxes and expenditures has come back into fashion, as it becomes increasingly clear that big government spending and taxes are here to stay—at federal, state, and local levels. Since the Appendix to Part Two included research on fiscal policy, this Appendix is limited to areas covered by Chapters 35 and 36.

F. Bator's *The Question of Government Spending* (Harper and Row, 1960) is a brief, lively introduction to the major issues in how big government spending should be. U.C.L.A.'s Roland McKean adds a realistic look at the workings of the governmental process in "The Unseen Hand in Government" (*American Economic Review*, June, 1965). A comprehensive picture of modern research on federal spending is presented by *Federal Expenditure Policy for Economic Growth and Stability*, a compendium prepared for the Joint Economic Committee of Congress in 1957. Try Walter Heller's "Economics and the Applied Theory of Public Expenditures."

Cost-benefit analysis as a basis for evaluating government expenditures has been probably the fastest growing branch of economic research in recent years. Stephen Enke's "Government-Industry Development of a Commercial Supersonic Transport" in the *American Economic Review* (May, 1967) provides an accessible introduction; and the following articles on water resources and the federal antipoverty program are examples of other applications. Robert Dorfman summarizes our still-limited ability to apply cost-benefit analysis in his summary of *Measuring Benefits of Government Investments* (Brookings, 1965).

J. A. Pechman's *Federal Tax Policy* (Brookings, 1966) provides a comprehensive analytical introduction to the whole range of issues involved in determining federal tax policy. *Federal Tax Policy for Economic Growth and Stability*, a volume of papers prepared by 75 leading tax experts for the Joint Economic Committee of Congress in 1955, provides a detailed cross-section of recent research in the field of taxation. For a beginning, try R. A. Musgrave's "Incidence of the Tax Structure and Its Effects on Consumption," or Keith Butters' "Effects of Taxation on the Investment Capacities and Policies of Individuals." California's George Break looks further at the alleged deterrent effect of high personal income taxes on work, without finding much evidence of it, in "Income Taxes and Incentives to Work" (*American Economic Review*, September, 1957). H. Grubel and D. Edwards report a study of Stanford students' behavior in "Personal Income Taxes and Choice of Professions" (*Quarterly Journal of Economics*, February, 1964). George Lent, in "The Excess Profits Tax and Business Expenditures" (*National Tax Journal*, September, 1958), tries to find out just how much high marginal corporation-income-tax rates do induce free and easy spending.

On the whole taxation picture, a final reference to *Readings in the Economics of Taxation*, R. A. Musgrave and Carl Shoup, editors (Irwin, 1959), is appropriate. Though many of the articles reprinted go back several years, they were selected by editors appointed by the American Economic Association as leading recent studies on the problem. To round out the picture, a good overview is provided by D. and A. Ott, *Federal Budget Policy* (Brookings, 1965).

PART SIX

THE
INTERNATIONAL
ECONOMY

THIRTY-SEVEN

INTERNATIONAL TRADE
AND LENDING

The Balance of Trade.

The Basic Case for International Trade.

The Case for International Lending.

The Foreign Trade Multiplier and Domestic Employment.

The Balance of Payments.

International Community and Conflict of Interests.

The Great American Responsibility.

In the "one world" of today, the close inter-dependence among nations is painfully obvious. The dominating problem is war—how to assure international peace? But big economic issues fill the newspapers too. What happens if we lose more gold? Should we raise or lower our tariffs? Do low foreign wages threaten our standard of living? Is our foreign-aid program too big or too small.

Since prewar days, our sales of goods and services abroad have soared—from $4 billion in 1939 to $43 billion in 1966. Our imports from abroad have grown nearly as fast, to $38 billion in 1966. The best estimates indicate that perhaps 4 million American workers owe their jobs directly to export sales, and exports come from every state in the union. Our exports of goods and services total only about 5 per cent of the g.n.p., but to many industries foreign trade is the blood of life —we export half of our cotton crop and import over 90 per cent of the tin and nickel we use. More important, our foreign economic policies in a world of international tension are inseparable from our political and military policies. For to most of the world, foreign trade is far more urgent than it is to us. England must import most of her food or starve, and she can pay for her imports only by selling her exports abroad. And so it is with other nations; their living standards depend heavily on foreign trade.

In spite of the pressing importance of for-eign trade, governments have long followed poli-cies that restrict rather than encourage such trade —tariffs, quotas, exchange controls. *Prima facie*, the case for international division of labor and exchange is clear, as it is in domestic affairs. On the surface, there would appear to be no reason to suppose that human welfare could be improved by obstructing the processes of specialization and exchange. Why, then, have the laymen and the lawmaker so often distrusted foreign trade and favored the tariff? Why have nations so often flown in the face of apparent economic reason? Nowhere in economics is there a better opportunity to apply relatively simple economic analysis to popular fallacies.

It is well to begin by looking at what foreign trade means to the United States today—at what we export and import. Then we can analyze the basic case for international trade and lending, going on to the entire "balance of international payments" and the policy issues it raises.

THE BALANCE OF TRADE

Look first at our exports and imports of commodities. Figures 37-1 and 37-2 summarize the goods we exported and imported in 1966. The figures speak for themselves. They show the huge sales abroad by many of our basic industries, of both manufactured goods and farm products. It's

easy to see why a lot of American businessmen, workers and farmers are all for foreign trade. Figure 37-2 shows the other side of the picture—the goods we import. Some are noncompetitive with domestic production (for example, coffee and tin), but others obviously replace sales that might have been made by American producers. Thus, it's easy too to see why some businessmen and workers are opposed to foreign trade. But never forget one basic fact. Our exports (and the jobs they support) are several billion dollars bigger than our imports, $5 billion bigger in 1966.

Figure 37-3 throws more light on this comparison. It shows exports and imports of goods *and services* as a percentage of g.n.p. During the prosperous 1920's, about 7 per cent of all goods and services produced in the United States were exported. During the depression, this figure fell off to around 4 per cent, partly because of bad business conditions and partly because of growing trade barriers here and in other countries. After World War II, the ratio rose sharply, then fell back to around 5 per cent, where it has hovered since.

Don't jump to the conclusion that interna-

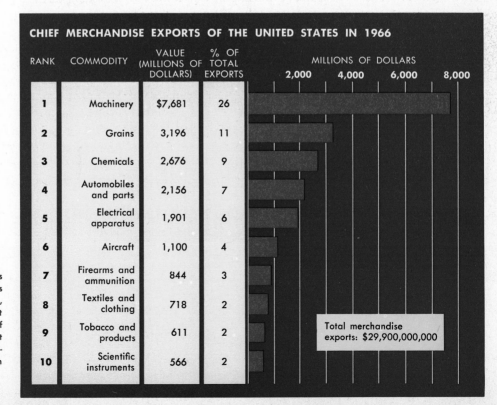

FIG. 37-1 Machinery, chemicals and other manufactured products dominate our merchandise exports, but farm products play an important role. (Source: U.S. Department of Commerce. Excludes government military aid, but includes farm products financed through U.S. foreign aid.)

CHIEF MERCHANDISE EXPORTS OF THE UNITED STATES IN 1966

RANK	COMMODITY	VALUE (MILLIONS OF DOLLARS)	% OF TOTAL EXPORTS
1	Machinery	$7,681	26
2	Grains	3,196	11
3	Chemicals	2,676	9
4	Automobiles and parts	2,156	7
5	Electrical apparatus	1,901	6
6	Aircraft	1,100	4
7	Firearms and ammunition	844	3
8	Textiles and clothing	718	2
9	Tobacco and products	611	2
10	Scientific instruments	566	2

Total merchandise exports: $29,900,000,000

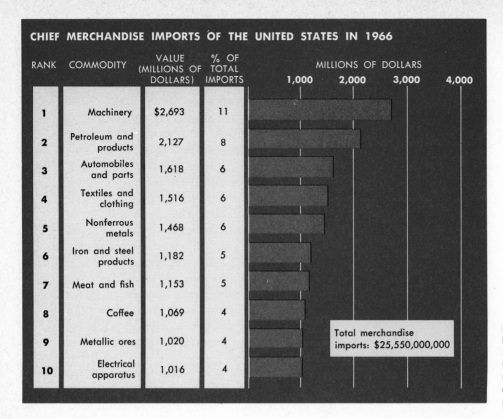

CHIEF MERCHANDISE IMPORTS OF THE UNITED STATES IN 1966

RANK	COMMODITY	VALUE (MILLIONS OF DOLLARS)	% OF TOTAL IMPORTS
1	Machinery	$2,693	11
2	Petroleum and products	2,127	8
3	Automobiles and parts	1,618	6
4	Textiles and clothing	1,516	6
5	Nonferrous metals	1,468	6
6	Iron and steel products	1,182	5
7	Meat and fish	1,153	5
8	Coffee	1,069	4
9	Metallic ores	1,020	4
10	Electrical apparatus	1,016	4

Total merchandise imports: $25,550,000,000

FIG. 37-2 Manufactured products have become our most important imports, but raw materials and foodstuffs still bulk large. Note that machinery heads both the export and import lists. (Source: U.S. Department of Commerce.)

tional trade isn't very important. Remember those huge export figures in Fig. 37-1. Similarly, many domestic industries depend heavily on foreign-produced raw materials (for example, rubber and chrome); and it is virtually impossible to get some consumption goods except from abroad (for example, tea). And to most nations abroad in a tense, uncertain world, United States demand in world markets and United States policies on foreign aid and investment are matters of vital concern.

There is still another interesting way of looking at our foreign trade picture: Who were our main customers and suppliers? Figure 37-4 gives the answer. Canada leads the list by far, and other Western Hemisphere nations combined make up to our biggest bloc of customers. But the Common Market countries of Western Europe and Japan have been coming up fast. The fact is that our foreign trade blankets the world.

The commodities we buy and sell abroad are the most visible part of our foreign trade, and the part most directly related to American jobs. But in Figs. 37-3 and 37-4, $13 billion of sales of American services abroad (shipping, banking, and similar services, plus returns on U.S. investments abroad) were added to the $30 billion of merchandise exports. To get a complete picture of the international "balance of payments," we will need also to add "capital movements" (the transfer of

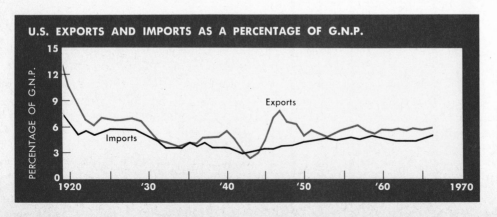

U.S. EXPORTS AND IMPORTS AS A PERCENTAGE OF G.N.P.

FIG. 37-3 U.S. exports of goods and services have consistently exceeded imports. During the last decade, both have stayed generally in the range of 4 to 6 per cent of g.n.p. (Source: U.S. Department of Commerce.)

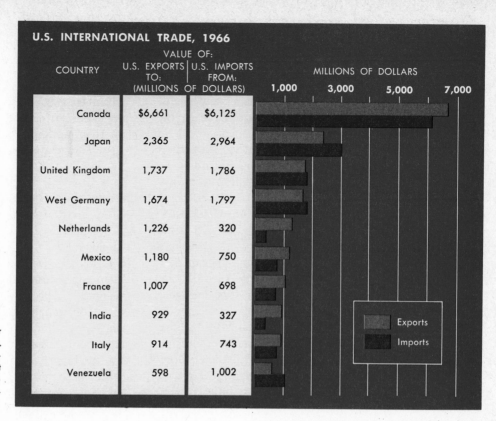

U.S. INTERNATIONAL TRADE, 1966

COUNTRY	VALUE OF: U.S. EXPORTS TO: (MILLIONS OF DOLLARS)	VALUE OF: U.S. IMPORTS FROM: (MILLIONS OF DOLLARS)
Canada	$6,661	$6,125
Japan	2,365	2,964
United Kingdom	1,737	1,786
West Germany	1,674	1,797
Netherlands	1,226	320
Mexico	1,180	750
France	1,007	698
India	929	327
Italy	914	743
Venezuela	598	1,002

FIG. 37-4 Canada is by far our best customer, followed by Japan. Altogether, Western Hemisphere nations account for over 40 per cent of our exports and Western Europe another third. (Source: U.S. Department of Commerce.)

short- and long-term monetary investments) and, lastly, gold. But first, let us consider the basic analytical case for free international trade and lending.

THE BASIC CASE
FOR INTERNATIONAL TRADE

Florida produces oranges, Iowa produces corn and hogs, Pittsburgh produces steel. Each sells its products to the others. When each specializes on what it does best, we produce more in total and all have more to consume than if each tried to be self-sufficient. In the same way, Chile sells us copper, we sell machinery to England, England sells cotton cloth to Chile. When each nation specializes on what it does best and then exchanges with others, we produce more in total and each of us ends up consuming more than if each tried to be self-sufficient.

The advantages to all in the first case—to Florida, Iowa, and Pittsburgh—are obvious. No one would question them. For each area to try to live alone, barring trade with the others, would be foolish. The advantages to nations from specialization and exchange are identical; more is produced for all to consume. The case for free inter-

national trade is that simple, and that powerful. By using our total resources most efficiently through specialization and exchange, the world can move all the way out to its combined production possibilities frontier. But it seems very hard for voters and legislators to see and remember this simple truth.

Interregional
and International Trade

Nations (like regions within a nation) vary greatly in efficiency in producing different goods, differences that persist largely because of international immobility of resources. These differences arise largely out of five considerations:

1. Over the face of the earth climatic and geographical conditions vary widely. Brazil is admirably suited for raising coffee, the lower Nile Valley for cotton production. Texas and Oklahoma are great oil-producing centers. Chile has rich nitrate deposits. Such geographical and climatic differences alone would justify worldwide specialization.

2. Human capacities vary over the globe. Some groups are large and strong, adept at physical labor. Others excel at dexterity and manual

skills. Still others stand out in enterprise and organizational ability. These differences may be due to longstanding racial characteristics, or to the political, social, and economic environment in which individuals are raised and live. Whatever the reasons, they constitute a major reason why international specialization and trade will be beneficial.

3. The accumulated supply of capital goods varies greatly from nation to nation. In some countries, centuries of accumulation have produced large supplies of fixed and mobile capital—railroads, buildings, machinery, and so forth. Examples are the U.S. and England; they specialize in industrial products. In other countries—for example, Greece and Nigeria—capital is scarce; they specialize in farming and simple production which requires little elaborate equipment. Moreover, vast differences exist between the kinds of capital accumulated in different nations.

4. The *proportions* among different types of resources vary widely from country to country. Australia has vast plains but relatively few people and capital goods. Therefore, she specializes in agricultural products that require a high proportion of natural resources to labor and capital goods. In England, land is scarce relative to human beings and capital. Therefore, she is best fitted for manufacture and industry, even though her soil may be as good as Australia's for wheat-growing.

5. In addition to these "economic" considerations, great differences exist in the political and social climate in different countries. In countries of stable government, vast industrial organizations requiring large long-period capital commitments are likely to grow up. In backward, illiterate, badly governed areas, conditions are almost prohibitory against mass-production industry. A hustling, mechanical-minded nation like the United States could hardly be expected to be satisfied again with a small-unit, predominantly rural economy, any more than we would expect the South Sea islanders to be happy or efficient automakers.

The Principle
of Comparative Advantage

Given these differences between nations, it is clear that some international trade will be advantageous. But how far each nation should specialize and how much international trade is to its advantage is not so obvious. Neglect costs of transport between nations for the moment in answering that question.

The greatest possible advantage for all from trade will be obtained if each nation devotes itself to what it can do *relatively* most cheaply. In the simple case of Iowa and Florida, where the cost advantage of each in its representative products is clear and large, Iowa should raise all the corn, Florida all the oranges. The greatest total of corn plus oranges will be obtained in that way. But such money cost comparisons don't provide much guidance when it comes to comparing costs between different nations that have different monetary units, different proportions of the factors of production, different qualities of labor, and different productive techniques. Perhaps as between coffee and factory machinery, Brazil has an "absolute" advantage in the former, the United States in the latter. But even in such an extreme case, it is hard to be precise on just why we are sure that these absolute advantages exist and what they mean. When less striking differences are considered, such as textiles in the United States and England, the difficulty of such comparisons becomes insurmountable. Monetary comparisons mean little, since different monetary units prevail in the two countries.

But fortunately, as David Ricardo demonstrated a century-and-a-half ago, the advantages of international trade don't depend on such absolute cost calculations at all. Even though one nation were more efficient than another in the production of everything, it would still be to the advantage of both to specialize and engage in international trade. Each, and both combined, would gain most when each specializes in production of those commodities where its *comparative*, or *relative*, costs of production are lowest within each country.

Let us first illustrate this "principle of comparative advantage" with a simple case involving only two countries and two commodities, the United States and France producing wheat and cloth. To simplify, let us assume that labor is the only factor of production (or that a day of labor is a shorthand measure of a bundle of land, labor, and capital used in producing things). Assume further that in the United States one man-day can produce one bushel of wheat or one yard of cloth. *Thus, in the United States we can obtain one bushel of wheat by giving up the production of one yard of cloth, and vice versa.*[1]

Assume that in France one day of labor also produces one bushel of wheat, but only a half-yard of cloth. In this sense, American labor is more productive than is French labor, but, as we shall see, this is not the critical factor. The critical factor is that in France two bushels of wheat must be given up to produce one more yard of cloth. This situation in the two countries is shown in Table 37-1.

TABLE 37-1 COMPARATIVE COSTS OF PRODUCTION, IN MAN-DAYS	In the U.S.	In France
Wheat (1 bushel)	1	1
Cloth (1 yard)	1	2

Suppose first that there is no trade between France and the U.S.; each country produces all its own wheat and cloth. Will it pay them to begin specializing and trading? The answer is "yes." In the United States, we can obtain *one* more bushel of wheat by giving up one yard of cloth. But in France they can obtain *two* more bushels of wheat by giving up one yard of cloth. *Therefore, there will be an increase in total world output if the United States uses more of her labor to produce cloth while resources in France are shifted to raising wheat. By transferring labor from cloth to wheat in France, Frenchmen produce two additional bushels of wheat for each yard of cloth they forgo; by transferring labor from wheat to cloth, the United States produces an extra yard of cloth for each bushel of wheat she forgoes. Obviously, we should shift more of our resources to producing cloth, while France should shift more of hers to wheat. Then by exchanging we can both live better.*

[1] Temporarily, assume that wheat and cloth are industries of constant costs both here and abroad. That is, unit costs of production do not increase or decrease as output in the country changes. This is sometimes called the assumption of constant returns to scale.

A simple arithmetic example may help demonstrate the point. Assume that there are 100 workers each in the United States and France. At the beginning, in each country half are producing wheat and half cloth. Total world output is 100 bushels of wheat and 75 yards of cloth, as in Table 37-2.

TABLE 37-2 WORLD OUTPUT BEFORE SPECIALIZATION
U.S.
50 workers on wheat = 50 bushels
50 workers on cloth = 50 yards
France
50 workers on wheat = 50 bushels
50 workers on cloth = 25 yards

Now suppose that we specialize completely on cloth and France specializes completely on wheat, as the principle suggests. As Table 37-3 shows, the result is 100 bushels of wheat and 100 yards of cloth, an increase of 25 yards of cloth to divide between us.

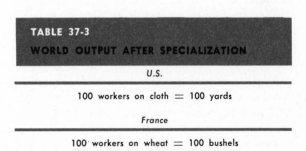

TABLE 37-3 WORLD OUTPUT AFTER SPECIALIZATION
U.S.
100 workers on cloth = 100 yards
France
100 workers on wheat = 100 bushels

It might appear from these tables that the United States has an *absolute* advantage in efficiency over France, since in France it takes two man-days to produce a yard of cloth while here it takes only one. But it is easy to show that these absolute differences are not the critical point at all. Suppose, instead, that we had begun with the assumption that French labor was the more efficient—that one man-day in France would produce two bushels of wheat or one of cloth. Total world output can be larger because of the higher productivity of French labor. But work out the new example, and you will see that it pays each country to specialize just as before, where its comparative advantage is higher, and then to exchange parts of their production.

The principle is that gain in total world output is possible from specialization and trade if the cost ratios of producing two commodities are different in different countries. This same principle would have applied in the above example had the cost ratios for producing wheat and cloth been 3:2 in the United States and 5:1 in France, or any other set of differing ratios. To repeat, absolute costs in the two countries are not relevant. It would make no difference, for example, if U.S. labor were vastly more efficient than French. Total output could be increased by further U.S. specialization on cloth, because the cost ratios differ and our *comparative* advantage is greater in producing cloth. *This is the principle of comparative advantage: total output will be maximized when each nation specializes in the lines where it has the greatest comparative advantage or the least comparative disadvantage.*[2]

From this statement we can tell also how far it is advantageous to carry specialization and trade. Gain from trade is possible until the cost ratios of producing the two commodities are the same in the United States and France. With constant costs complete specialization would occur; the cost ratios never become equal since they are fixed by the constant-cost assumption. But now, realistically, drop the assumption of constant costs. As production of cloth increases in the United States, and as production of wheat increases in France, the cost ratios will move together. In the United States, the cost of producing cloth will rise relative to that of producing wheat as more cloth is produced. In France, the cost of producing wheat will rise relative to that of pro-

ducing cloth. Finally, at some levels of output the cost ratios will become identical here and in France. Thereafter, there is no advantage in further specialization and exchange, since no further increases in total output can be obtained thereby. (Realistically, we should introduce transport costs between nations, which would correspondingly reduce the potential gains from international exchange.)

When the law of comparative advantage is generalized to many countries and thousands of products, no new principles are introduced, but the picture becomes more complex. Gain will still be maximized if each country specializes in those goods and services where its comparative advantage is greatest or its comparative disadvantage least, and if this specialization is carried to the point where the cost ratios involved are equal to those of other countries producing the same products. In any given country, production of many products will never take place, because the country's comparative disadvantage in their production is so great and because of international transportation costs. Most nations will find it advantageous to produce a variety of products.[3]

You may have noted that thus far we have said nothing about the division of the gains from international trade. For example, in the case of Table 37-3, will France or the U.S. get the extra 25 yards of cloth obtained by specialization, or will they be divided between the two nations? In most cases, the gain will be divided, with the division depending on a complex set of considerations, mainly the relative cost structures of the countries involved. In extreme cases, it is possible to demonstrate logically that all the gain would accrue to one country, but this requires some highly unlikely assumptions. In general, we are safe in assuming that each trading country will share in the benefits, but we must wait for a more advanced treatment to be able to specify just how much in each case.

[2] Note that we use this principle all the time in our domestic economic life. Suppose that in a business firm the president is also a whiz at typing, better than any of the secretaries. Should he do his own typing? Obviously not. He should specialize where his comparative advantage is greatest, in managing the firm, leaving the typing to his secretary even though she types slower than he does. Or suppose a fine surgeon is also the best driver in the community. Should he drive the hospital ambulance instead of spending all his available time in the hospital operating room?

[3] If this were an advanced treatise, we would introduce the fact that different industries in different countries may use differing ratios of labor to capital, and note that this raises interesting, intricate problems of exactly how far each country should go toward specialization in different industries. But these complications do not change the general principle of comparative advantage, and we need not become involved in them here.

The Law of Comparative Advantage, Free Trade, and the Price System

In world markets, the search for profits and the price system tend to bring about this international specialization and optimal allocation of resources in each country automatically. If we are relatively inefficient in producing coffee but very efficient in producing machine tools, American producers are going to have a tough time competing with Brazil in the world's coffee markets, but we'll beat out other machine-tool makers in the market place. Under an international free-trade system, in each country the greatest profits can be obtained by producing those commodities most desired by consumers at home and abroad. If our comparative advantage is great in producing automobiles, this fact will be reflected in high returns to resources in the automobile industry. If our comparative advantage is low in producing spices, American spice producers will be unable to pay wages high enough to bid resources away from the more efficient automobile industry, since the world prices for spices is set by relatively efficient East Indian production. Thus, under a free-price system and free trade, the resources of each nation would tend to be drawn into its most efficient industries. No one would manage or direct international trade. Each producer would simply try to maximize profits and each buyer would simply buy where the price was lowest for the commodity he wanted. The central mechanism is the same as domestically with Adam Smith's invisible hand.

Worldwide Multilateral Trade

To provide the full advantages of international specialization and exchange, trade must be multinational, or "multilateral." That is, goods and services must move freely among all nations. This eliminates the necessity that the exports and imports between any two nations must be in balance, which would severely restrict the degree of international specialization. Vis-à-vis all other countries combined, a nation's exports and imports must roughly balance (omitting "capital movements"), but with multinational trade this balance may result from a combination of export and import imbalances with different individual nations, depending on the individual-country comparative advantages involved.

This fact is illustrated by Fig. 37-5, which shows the pattern of multinational trade among major areas of the world. The United States, for example, exports more to Europe, Canada, and nontropical Latin America than it imports from them. But our imports from the tropical nations exceed our exports to them. Trace the pattern out for other areas. The data may change from year to year, but Fig. 37-5 illustrates the importance of multinational trade.

THE CASE FOR INTERNATIONAL LENDING

Society benefits when individuals and institutions save and invest, because useful capital goods and durable consumer goods are thereby accumulated. The saver gains individually from the return on his investment, and society gains from the increased efficiency of roundabout, mechanized production. Both the saver and society gain most when savings are invested where their productivity is highest.

In the domestic economy, we mainly trust the price system to allocate savings to the most desirable investments. Those who save invest their

FIG. 37-5 The yellow arrows show the directions of flow of exports where they exceed imports, while the red arrows represent the smaller amounts moving in the opposite directions. (Source: United Nations.)

THE COMPLEX PATTERN OF MULTILATERAL WORLD TRADE

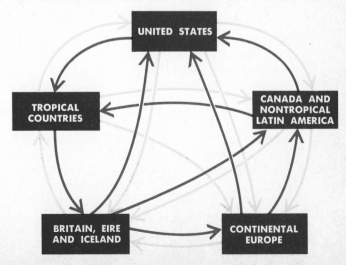

funds (either directly or through such institutions as banks) where the combination of safety, liquidity, and rate of return seems most attractive. Since the rate of return tends to be highest where investments fulfill the strongest consumer demands, savings are drawn into those industries where consumers most want output increased. Consumer choices direct the allocation of savings among investments.

Internationally, as domestically, society is generally best off if savings are allocated where their marginal productivity is greatest. International loans are "better" than domestic loans when the anticipated rate of return on them (including liquidity and risk allowance) is greater. For decades, both England and the New World gained from heavy loans by Britishers to the rapidly developing Western Hemisphere. British lenders gained by receiving good returns on their investments; U.S. borrowers gained by getting capital to combine with the plentiful natural resources of the New World. The over-all result was a faster growth in world output, divided between the U.S. and Britain. Today the United States is the big international lender, but the general result is similar. Internationally, as domestically, lending may be unwise if the loan is unsafe, or undesirably illiquid, and the risk is often greater on international investments. But here again national political boundaries do not invalidate basic economic principles: we gain as individuals and as nations from having savings invested where their marginal productivity is highest.

THE FOREIGN TRADE MULTIPLIER AND DOMESTIC EMPLOYMENT

Thus far we have been implicitly assuming that full employment prevails, and that the problem is to allocate our fully employed resources most efficiently. But in the real world of intermittent underemployment and inflation, international trade can affect the level of domestic employment and output as well.

Exports provide jobs, just as do domestic sales. Conversely, imports replace domestic jobs. Thus, the net excess of exports over imports ("net exports" in the g.n.p. accounts) is one component of aggregate demand which calls forth production

and employment. And like any other autonomous expenditure, such as private investment, it tends to have a multiplier effect on g.n.p. Thus the net export balance produces jobs in its own right and also has a further multiplier effect tending to create more jobs.

But this "foreign trade multiplier" is smaller than the regular domestic investment multiplier, because our increased exports, by increasing domestic income, will indirectly induce increased imports into the U.S. We import more when our incomes rise and these induced imports partially offset the original multiplier effect. The final foreign trade multiplier is reduced by the extent to which induced imports offset the original export balance.

This reasoning makes it easy to see why nations with unemployment especially want to increase their net export balances, by increasing exports and/or reducing imports. Either way the result will be more jobs at home. Creation of a net export surplus is a way of exporting unemployment to the nation which buys more U.S. goods or has its exports to the U.S. cut. For this reason, it is often called a "beggar-my-neighbor" policy for increasing domestic employment.

But if any nation tries to export its unemployment in a world of widespread unemployment (as in the 1930's), say by raising its tariffs to shut out imports, it's easy to predict the result. Rather than importing unemployment, other nations will retaliate by raising their tariffs too. Obviously it is not possible for all nations to increase their exports and none to increase their imports, for each export is somebody else's import. Thus the main result of import restrictions aimed at exporting unemployment is likely to be retaliation abroad, higher tariffs everywhere, and a shrinkage in the total volume of international trade with no more than transient gains to any nation. This was exactly the result in the disastrous 1930's, when snowballing trade restrictions cut world trade to a small fraction of its level during the 1920's.

THE BALANCE OF PAYMENTS

Table 37-4 summarizes the complete United States "balance of payments" in 1966, including foreign investments, government foreign aid, and gold movements, as well as exports and imports of private goods and services. Basically, the table shows what we paid to foreigners and what they paid to us. The dark shading (I) shows what they paid us, for goods, services, and interest on our investments abroad. The light shading (II, IV, V, and VI) shows what we paid them—for goods and services, in government and private aid, and in net new U.S. investments abroad, plus "errors and omissions" which were probably largely short-term capital exports. Item III is merely a memorandum item included to show where we stood on exports versus imports of goods and services alone; and VIII is another memorandum item to show where we stood on all reported payments. Since VIII shows that our payments out exceeded payments to us, we had a basic balance of payments "deficit" of $1.4 billion in 1966.

The bottom three items (IX, X and XI) show how this "deficit" was financed. Foreigners took payment partly in gold ($600 million) and partly by building up their bank deposits and short-term investments in the United States ($900 million). Disregard the special intergovernmental transactions which involve technical operations in the foreign exchange markets.

This same balance-of-payments picture is shown in T-account form, in Table 37-5. The left-hand side shows transactions involving payments *to* the United States (dark shading). The right-hand side shows transactions involving payments *from* the United States (light shading). The uncolored items—accumulation of foreign capital in the United States and gold flows—show how the $1.4 billion basic deficit was financed, as in Table 37-4.

Look at some of the individual items. We exported $5.3 billion more goods and services than we imported. But we gave foreigners $4.4 billion of unilateral aid, mainly through the govern-

---

TABLE 37-4

U.S. BALANCE OF INTERNATIONAL PAYMENTS, 1966 *

		In Billions
I. U.S. Exports:		
Merchandise	$30.0	
Services	6.8	
Income from investments abroad	6.2	
Total		$43.0 **
II. U.S. Imports:		
Merchandise	25.5	
Services and U.S. travel abroad	6.7	
Military purchases abroad	3.9	
Income on foreign investments here	1.9	
Total		37.7
III. Net balance due U.S. on goods and services		5.3
IV. U.S. government grants and net private remittances	4.4 **	
V. U.S. net capital exports	1.7	
VI. Errors and omissions	.6	
VII. Net capital outflow, plus omissions		6.7
VIII. Balance due others on all recorded transactions (payments "deficit")		1.4
IX. Accumulation of short-term foreign capital in U.S.		.9 ***
X. Special intergovernmental transactions (net)		—.1
XI. Net gold flow from U.S.		.6

 * Data from U.S. Department of Commerce. Data are rounded to nearest $100 million, so figures may not add or subtract exactly.
 ** Excludes about $1.5 billion of military aid.
 *** Sometimes considered a short-term capital inflow to U.S. See text.

TABLE 37-5

U.S. BALANCE OF PAYMENTS—T-ACCOUNT FORM, 1966 *

Payments to U.S. (In Billions)			Payments from U.S. (In Billions)		
U.S. exports:			U.S. imports:		
Merchandise	$30.0		Merchandise	$25.5	
Services	6.8		Services	6.7	
Income on investments			Military purchases abroad	3.6	
abroad	6.2		Income on foreign		
		$43.0	investments here	1.9	
Accumulation of short-term					$37.7
foreign capital in U.S.		.9	Net U.S. unilateral aid		4.4
Special intergovernmental			U.S. net capital exports		1.7
transactions		—.1	Errors and omissions		.6
Net gold flow from U.S.		.6			$44.4
		$44.4			

* See footnotes to Table 37-4.

ment's foreign-aid program but partly through private gifts; and we made $1.7 billion (net) of new private investments abroad. These big capital transfers (plus the $.6 billion of errors and omissions that are probably mainly capital exports) meant that we ended up owing foreigners $1.4 billion more in payments than they owed us, the "deficit." They might have taken all this difference in gold, and they did take $600 million. But they also chose to take $900 million in bank accounts and short-term investments in the United States.[4]

Different nations report their balance of payments data differently, and there is dispute in the U.S. over just what constitutes our balance-of-payments "deficit." The basic deficit shown in Tables 37-4 and 37-5 is often called the "liquidity" deficit, because it shows the liquid claims against us generated by our international transactions. Foreigners could take $1.4 billion in 1966 in either gold or highly liquid dollar deposits or short-term investments in the U.S. But the $.9 billion of

short-term foreign investments in the U.S. (sometimes called foreign "dollar balances") could obviously also be considered merely short-term foreign capital invested here, and hence merely an offset against U.S. investments abroad (item V). If this were done, V would be only $.8 billion, and the U.S. deficit would be only $.5 billion rather than $1.4 billion. The deficit calculated this way is often called the "official settlements" basis. It makes the U.S. deficit look smaller than the more widely used "liquidity" basis. Most other nations use the official settlements basis for calculating their official balance-of-payments positions. It pays to be sure which basis is being used, for the difference may be billions of dollars; for example, in 1964 the liquidity deficit was $3.3 billion but the official settlements deficit was only $.9 billion.[5]

The "Balance of Payments" and the "Balance of Trade"

These tables point up the importance of being clear about the difference between the "balance of payments" and the "balance of trade." The balance of payments includes all payments between the countries concerned (all of Table

[4] U.S. direct *military* aid (about $1.5 billion in 1966) is excluded completely from the tables. Such exports of military equipment (planes, missiles, and so on) might have been included in the exports figure (I) and in the balancing net-unilateral-transfers figure (IV). But such goods are not considered regular exports, and if they're not included in exports they can't be included either under unilateral grants, since to do so would throw the balance-of-payments figures out of balance.

[5] This description omits a number of other adjustments in calculating official balance-of-payments data, especially in special intergovernmental transactions, but the major items are those described in the text.

37-4). The balance of trade includes only trade in goods and services (I and II of the table).[6] Popular discussion, which generally runs in terms of the balance of trade, is often confused because of failure to consider the entire balance of payments. For example, the massive $15 billion gold inflow into this country during the 1930's, which accounts for most of our current gold stock, was due primarily to a huge flow of funds to this country for long- and short-term investment and simply for safekeeping—not to a "favorable balance of trade," as a surplus of exports over imports is popularly called. Similarly, the outflow of gold during the 1960's obviously wasn't on account of the balance of trade, since we exported some $35 billion more than we imported. Rather, it reflected governmental aid and U.S. private investment abroad. You must keep clear the distinction between the balance of payments and the balance of trade to think straight about international economic problems.

Since World War I, the United States has generally had a net export surplus—that is, exports of goods and services have consistently exceeded imports. But the total balance-of-payments picture has varied widely. During the 1920's, and 1930's, we generally accumulated gold and short-term balances abroad, because payments were due us on balance. Since about 1950, by contrast, we have run a persistent balance-of-payments deficit. Thus, foreigners have steadily accumulated gold, U.S. bank deposits and short-term investments here ("dollar balances"), as we have made large investments abroad and have annually given foreign nations a large amount of economic and military aid. Since 1950, foreigners have taken about $10 billion in gold and increased their "dollar balances" by about $20 billion. We still have about 30 per cent of the world's known monetary gold stock. But, as we shall see in Chapter 40, our persistent balance-of-payments deficit has become a serious problem in the past few years.

You have probably heard that gold is

[6] It is the difference between these two (that is, III in Table 37-4) which is the "net exports" figure shown separately in the g.n.p. accounts. When not shown separately, it is usually included as part of gross private investment.

shipped back and forth to settle differences between exports and imports in international trade. Some gold does move this way. But Tables 37-4 and 37-5 show that international imbalance in the trade accounts may equally well be settled by accumulation of short-term balances.

INTERNATIONAL COMMUNITY AND CONFLICT OF INTERESTS

Free international trade and lending are in the interest of the world as a whole. This is the big lesson to be learned.

For the most part, such free trade and lending also benefit each of the individual countries concerned, but not always. It is possible, though unlikely, that an individual nation may temporarily increase its domestic employment by shutting out competing foreign goods and increasing its export surplus. But, assuming that relatively full employment exists, some other possible conflicts of interest deserve attention here, as qualifications to the general argument.

1. *Personal Migration.* If the "economic welfare" of the world as a whole is our aim, then international migration probably should occur whenever real wages obtainable in one country are higher than in another. But for workers in high-wage countries, immigration of workers from low-wage countries might prove a major blow. Assume such an influx into the United States, and assume that the immigrants are substitutable for American workers. Work out the supply-and-demand analysis yourself. Average real wages for workers throughout the world would rise, but the influx of foreign workers would surely lower the incomes of present American workers. *Given the international distribution of resources,* the law of comparative advantage applies. But the law does not say that each nation must gain from an international shift of resources, even when the shift raises the world's average standard of living.

2. *Monopoly-type Action by One Country.* Just as a domestic monopolist can benefit himself by restricting output, so a country may be able to benefit itself by restricting trade. But the attempt

may not work. For one thing, the international monopolist must always face the potential competition of other countries. More important, any country's restrictions on imports are likely to provoke retaliatory restrictions by other countries, and then both are worse off.

The extreme cases of nations acting as monopolists are those where foreign trade is centralized under government control—Soviet Russia, for example. But to a smaller extent, other countries have also centralized their foreign-trade activities. Brazilian coffee is an example.

3. *Growth of Underdeveloped Areas.* When a rich country lends to underdeveloped areas, the lender *may* find itself worse off because of the loans. This result may occur if the new areas develop industries which compete with the lender's. More often, however, the new industries are not directly competitive. In any case, as the developing country sells abroad it can begin to buy abroad, and the law of comparative advantage ultimately applies as stated above. A major portion of United States international trade is with other highly industrialized nations. But the problem of the "underdeveloped" countries vis-à-vis the industrialized nations is a major one for the decades ahead.

4. *War.* The most important potential conflict goes beyond economics. It centers around war and preparation for war. No nation wants to be dependent on potential enemies for vital raw materials and finished goods, or to help build up the strength of potential enemies. With this major exception, however, economic and political considerations point in the same direction. Wide-ranging international trade and finance are probably the soundest bases for lasting peace.

THE GREAT AMERICAN RESPONSIBILITY

In the century before World War I, England was the world's great creditor nation and the financial center of the world. This was an era of free international trade. Trade was multilateral—based on an intricate web of exchanges in which no two countries balanced out directly with each other. The gold standard assured stable exchange rates among the world's currencies, to facilitate foreign trade. The British pound provided a standard currency and, along with gold, comprised the basic monetary reserves of most leading nations. London was the financial center of world trade and lending, the banker to the world. The system was complex, but it operated, like the free-price system, in an essentially automatic fashion—through the multitude of buying and selling activities of individuals in the many countries of the world.

The day of British leadership has passed. On the United States falls the enormous responsibility of providing leadership in the twentieth-century world economy. The dollar has become the international reserve currency of the free world, along with gold. Our task is incomparably more difficult than was Britain's in the nineteenth and early twentieth centuries. Nations no longer accept unquestioningly the "discipline" of international gold flows in regulating their domestic money supplies. "Planned" domestic economies have replaced free private enterprise in many countries. Maintenance of domestic high employment has become the first objective of most nations' economic policies. Many nations have come to look upon the United States as a continuing source of military and economic aid.

In the face of these conditions, it has been widely suggested that the United States must do four things:

1. Maintain a stable, prosperous United States economy as a foundation for international economic prosperity.

2. Maintain a strong, stable dollar internationally, as the world's major "key," or "reserve," currency.

3. Continue to lead the way toward reducing trade barriers.

4. Help to strengthen international institutions for supporting international monetary stability and for facilitating investment in underdeveloped countries.

What is America's responsibility in these matters? In today's world, few questions are more important to the American citizen. The next three chapters analyze some of the issues.

REVIEW

Concepts To Remember

International economics is essentially fundamental economics applied to international economic activity. But it has some new terms and concepts that you need if you want to be able to operate effectively on international problems:

law of comparative advantage	foreign trade multiplier
comparative costs	balance of payments surplus or deficit
balance of payments	multilateral trade
export surplus or deficit	capital movements
balance of trade	beggar-my-neighbor policies

For Analysis and Discussion

1. State the basic case for specialization, division of labor, and free exchange. Are there reasons why this case applies differently within a nation and across national boundaries?
2. Explain the difference between the balance of payments and the balance of trade. On which do the data in Figs. 37-1, 37-2, and 37-3 throw most light?
3. What industries in your area are most affected by international trade? (See Tables 37-1 and 37-2.) How important is such trade to your immediate area?
4. "Anyone who believes in free trade ought equally to believe in free international migration of labor, unrestricted by immigration barriers." Do you agree? Why or why not?
5. What is the principle of comparative advantage?
6. Why is multilateral trade more advantageous than bilateral?
7. If you were wealthy, would you invest any of your money abroad? Why or why not?
8. Why is the "foreign trade multiplier" ordinarily smaller than the domestic investment multiplier?

THIRTY-EIGHT

INTERNATIONAL
ADJUSTMENTS
AND THE BALANCE
OF PAYMENTS

Financing Foreign Transactions.

Exchange Rates.

International Economic Adjustments.

The United States—World Creditor.

Domestic and international trade are essentially similar, but in foreign trade two different currencies are involved. This chapter explains first how international transactions are financed, and then how international economic adjustments occur under different international monetary systems.

FINANCING
FOREIGN TRANSACTIONS

If you buy woolens from England, the English seller wants British pounds, not American dollars. You need to convert your dollars into pounds if you're going to buy his cloth. What do you do?

There is a continuous demand for this sort of currency conversion, and the big New York banks stand ready to sell you pounds, or almost any other foreign currency, for dollars. If you go to your local bank to buy pounds, it will simply pass the transaction along to a big bank in the foreign exchange business.

Suppose that you want to pay a Britisher £1,000 in British money for the woolen goods. You go to a bank, say the Chase Manhattan in New York, to buy 1,000 British pounds. The Chase Manhattan is a regular dealer in foreign currencies. It sells you the pounds at the going rate—say £1 for $3. You pay the Chase Manhattan Bank $3,000 and get a special check, made out to the bearer, for £1,000. This special type of check is called "foreign exchange." [1]

[1] This example is not an exactly accurate statement of how such a transaction would be executed. However, the actual procedure, though sometimes more complicated, follows the same general principle.

Then you send the check over to the British manufacturer. He takes it to his bank in London and gets his £1,000. His bank presents the check to the Chase Manhattan's London branch for payment, and the transaction is completed (except that we have omitted the small commission charged you by the Chase Manhattan on the deal). You have paid $3,000. The seller has received £1,000.

The rate at which you can buy British pounds with American dollars is called the "exchange rate." When you buy pounds with dollars, you are purchasing foreign exchange. Foreign exchange is merely a claim on some foreign currency, and the rate of exchange is the number of units of one currency it takes to purchase one unit of another currency. If the franc-dollar exchange rate is 5 to 1, for example, then it takes five francs to buy one dollar; the price of one franc is 20 cents.

Like other prices, exchange rates are determined by supply and demand. Suppose American importers need large numbers of pounds to pay British manufacturers. When they try to buy these pounds with dollars, the increased demand will force up the price of pounds, say to $4 for £1. Conversely, when Britishers want to make heavy payments here, they buy dollars. This bids up the price of dollars, and the exchange rate moves toward $2 to £1.

This situation can readily be represented by a simple supply-and-demand diagram, as in Fig. 38-1. With the solid supply and demand curves, the price of pounds is $3. If demand increases to D'D' (when American importers need more pounds to pay for their British woolens), the price of pounds goes up to $4, given the supply of pounds shown. Try for yourself showing the effect of an increased British demand for dollars to pay for movies imported from America.

There are always Americans buying British pounds with dollars, and Britishers buying dollars with pounds. This is what keeps things reasonably well in balance on both sides of the Atlantic. The demand for pounds in America comes from American importers, people planning to travel or invest in Great Britain, and people owing other debts in Great Britain. The British demand for dollars comes from comparable British sources. Thus,

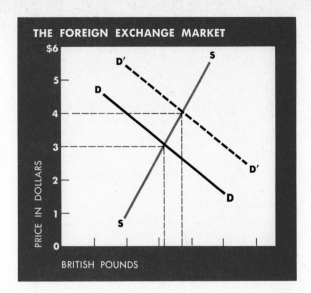

FIG. 38-1 The supply and demand for British pounds looks just like the supply and demand for a commodity.

there might be an exact offset to your payment of £1,000 to the British manufacturer—say, by a $3,000 payment to General Motors in Detroit by a British auto dealer, who bought the dollars at the Chase Manhattan's London branch. In effect, the two payments would be cancelled off against each other. Fundamentally, goods would be exchanged for goods (woolens for autos), with the help of the foreign-exchange markets.

Of course, the British auto parts dealer might not have gone to the Chase Manhattan branch in London, but instead to some other foreign-exchange dealer. This would have caused no difficulty. In both London and New York there are regular foreign-exchange markets, in which foreign exchange dealers buy and sell foreign currencies. As long as the *total* demand for pounds in New York equals the *total* demand for dollars in London, all transactions can be settled without any change in the exchange rate or any international shipment of gold. Here again the market place does the complex job more or less automatically.

EXCHANGE RATES

Freely Fluctuating Exchange Rates

Exchange rates depend on the demand for, and supply of, the currencies in question, *except* where rates are somehow fixed by government decree. In a completely "free" exchange market, exchange rates would fluctuate freely in response to varying demands for the different currencies. With fluctuating demands for currencies, substantial swings in foreign-exchange rates could be expected, especially since capital movements (for instance, shifts of funds for investment abroad) affect exchange rates as directly as do merchandise exports and imports. As long as supply and demand for the various currencies remained in balance, stable exchange rates would prevail.

Exchange Rates under the Gold Standard

For many years before World War I and again during the 1920's, most important countries were "on the gold standard." During these periods, no direct control was exercised over exchange rates by governments, but through the gold standard, exchange fluctuations were held within narrow bounds.

Under the gold standard, each monetary unit "contained" (was convertible into) a fixed number of grains of gold. For example, the prewar dollar was 23.22 grains and the prewar British pound 113 grains of fine gold. Thus, the pound had 4.86 times as much gold as the dollar, a relationship that established a par of exchange between the currencies. And remember, from Chapter 12, that domestically the money supply varied roughly in proportion to changes in each nation's gold stock.

Under these circumstances, suppose there was an increased demand for dollars which sent the price of dollars up so that one pound would buy less than $4.86 (say the exchange rate moved to 1 to 4.80). Then, instead of buying dollars and getting only $4.80 for £1, Britishers could simply convert their pounds into gold, send the gold to America, and there get $4.86 for the 113 grains of fine gold in each pound. Obviously, therefore, the exchange rate could not vary far from 4.86 to 1 or gold would be shipped instead of foreign exchange being used at all. Actually, shipping costs and interest losses in transit made it unprofitable to ship gold unless the exchange rate varied more than 3 cents either way from the 4.86 to 1 ratio. Hence, exchange rates could fluctuate within these "gold points" of 4.89 and 4.83, but no farther.

This stability of exchange rates was a great boon to international traders. They always knew just what foreign currencies would cost to make payments abroad and just what price they could get for foreign currencies received. Such stable exchanges may prevail without the gold standard, but as soon as one country is off the gold standard the *guarantee* of stable rates vanishes.

The International Gold Reserve Standard

In the Great Depression of the 1930's, every major nation went off the gold standard (see pages 168–169). Facing massive unemployment, each major Western nation chose to go its own way, refusing to be bound by international gold flows. Exchange rates fluctuated widely. Country after country imposed controls on capital outflows to conserve its scarce gold. Together with widespread tariff increases designed to stimulate domestic employment, these capital controls increasingly stifled international trade and lending, without, in retrospect, significantly helping any of the nations participating in the economic warfare.

Following World War II, everyone agreed that the folly of the 1930's must not be repeated. International cooperation, beginning with the Breton Woods Conference of 1944, reintroduced stable exchange rates among the major currencies and gradually reduced restrictions on capital outflows. Finally, in 1958 substantially free convertibility of currencies at fixed exchange rates was restored among the major nations of the "free world." Some controls over capital movements still exist, and no major nation has restored the prewar gold standard with its rigid linkage of the domestic money supply and economic conditions to international gold flows. But gold is again freely obtainable for settling international balances among central banks, and the rates of exchange among major currencies are fixed by international agreement.

This arrangement is commonly called an "international gold-reserve standard." Gold serves as an international reserve for each country, which it can use to meet its international payments. Exchange rates are fixed by international agreement and the various currencies are convertible into gold at fixed prices, as under the old gold standard. But nations do not necessarily tie their domestic monetary policies to gold flows.

INTERNATIONAL ECONOMIC ADJUSTMENTS

International trade and capital flows link together the economies of the world. It is important to understand these linkages in the modern world. For they have a major impact on most economies, and play an important role even in the United States even though foreign trade totals only about 5 per cent of our gross national product. Consider first the international adjustment process in a simple case involving only commodity trade, first under the gold standard and then under fluctuating exchanges; and finally introduce international capital movements and the entire balance of payments.

Under the Gold Standard

The full gold standard provided a more or less automatic procedure for keeping different countries "in balance" with one another. Suppose the United States begins to buy more goods and services from France without a corresponding increase in exports to France, both countries being on the gold standard. The U.S. will need an increasing number of francs to pay for its imports, and francs will become increasingly expensive in terms of dollars. But as soon as the dollar-franc rate moves to the gold point, U.S. importers will begin to ship gold rather than francs to pay for their additional imports from France.

What happens when gold moves from America to France? In America there is less gold backing for the money supply; currency and credit are contracted. In the absence of offsetting action, this movement will mean depressed prices, costs, and incomes here. In France, the reverse effect occurs. The new gold provides more bank deposits and more excess reserves. Currency and credit expand, with rising incomes, costs, and prices.

As these effects proceed, it will become harder for U.S. importers to buy from France, and easier for the French to buy here. Frenchmen have larger incomes to spend on U.S. goods, and

prices of U.S. goods are falling. Conversely, we have lower incomes to spend on French goods and French prices are rising. This combination gradually shuts off the excess of U.S. imports from France, pulling the exports and imports of the two countries back into balance. When exports and imports are restored to balance, the gold flow ceases and equilibrium has been restored in both American and French balances of payments.

But remember that gold flows tend to bring equilibrium only if they are permitted to affect prices, costs, and incomes in the countries involved.

Under Fluctuating ("Floating") Exchanges

How do international adjustments take place when exchange rates are free to fluctuate? Assume the same United States-France situation as before, with American imports overbalancing exports to France. As before, Americans will buy francs to pay for their imports, and will thereby drive up the exchange rate—that is, the cost of francs in terms of dollars. French goods become more expensive to us, and our goods become cheaper to France. French incomes rise because of their increased exports, without any such corresponding increase in America. These circumstances will gradually cut down on U.S. purchases from France, and will increase French purchases from us, until finally exports and imports between the two countries are restored to balance. As under the gold standard, there is an automatic tendency for the payments between the two countries to be brought back into equilibrium.

But the adjustment process is restricted to a smaller segment of each economy in the flexible-exchange case. The rising price of francs effectively raises the price of French exports to us, but it does so without raising French domestic prices generally in terms of dollars, as a gold inflow would have done by expanding the French money supply under the gold standard. Similarly, the falling dollar-exchange rate effectively lowers the price of U.S. exports to French buyers, but it does so without imposing deflationary pressure on the whole U.S. economy, as a gold outflow from the U.S. would have done.

All this makes a floating exchange standard

sound very attractive. But it has one very important drawback. International traders and investors would have to live in a world of uncertainty about the rates at which they convert their foreign receipts into domestic currency, and vice versa. Would you invest abroad with no assurance of what your foreign dividends would buy in terms of U.S. dollars? More on this dilemma in Chapter 40.

Under the International Gold-Reserve Standard

How do adjustments to eliminate disequilibrium occur under the international gold-reserve standard, which now prevails? The answer is not simple, and we shall mainly postpone it until Chapter 40 which deals with modern balance-of-payments problems. But the central points can be outlined here.

Suppose the same U.S.-French case, with U.S. imports exceeding exports. The deficit in the U.S. balance of payments will again lead to gold being transferred to France. But now the U.S. need not accept a deflationary contraction of her money supply, nor France an inflationary expansion of hers unless each country feels this would fit in with its domestic stabilization goals. Each nation attempts to balance its international and domestic goals.

A big country like the U.S., where gold reserves are large and international trade is a small part of g.n.p., can afford to give dominant weight to domestic goals for a long time in the face of a balance-of-payment deficit and gold outflows. Smaller countries which depend heavily on foreign trade have little option; their prices and costs must be closely in line with balance-of-payments needs or they will exhaust their limited international gold reserves and be unable to pay their bills. But either way the international adjustment process is less direct and predictable than under either the gold standard or fluctuating exchange rates. The pressures for international adjustment build up on any country which continually runs a balance-of-payments deficit, and the nation may eventually run out of reserves to pay its international bills. But it is vital to recognize that any nation may postpone adjustment to international pressures as long as its reserves hold out, in order to pursue its own domestic policies.

Capital Movements and International Adjustments

Now introduce capital movements into the picture. U.S. investment abroad involves foreign payments, just as when we buy goods abroad. If Westinghouse decides to build a plant in Holland, for example, it must have the Dutch guilders to pay its bills there. It uses dollars to buy guilders. If an individual American buys Royal Dutch Shell stock on the Dutch stock exchange, the same is true. And the effect is similar if the American government provides foreign aid to our allies or to underdeveloped countries (unless we give them goods outright). Our foreign aid provides them dollars, just as they would get dollars if they sold goods to us.

A look back at Tables 37-4 and 37-5 will show the importance of capital movements and foreign aid in the total balance of payments. Although in 1966 we had a $5.3 billion surplus of exports over imports (which means net payments due us), our net private investments abroad totaled $1.7 billion and U.S. government foreign aid totaled $4.4 billion. Thus, these capital transfers of $6.1 billion more than offset our export surplus, and, with "errors and omissions" which were probably unrecorded capital exports, we were left with a $1.4 billion "deficit" in our basic balance of payments. Other years have been different in detail, but the general picture has been the same. Exports and imports are by far the biggest parts of our total balance of payments, but capital movements also reach into the billions annually and have recently more than offset our surplus on goods and services.

Do the same adjustment mechanisms outlined above still work? The answer is "yes," but with complications. Take the 1960's. We have exported far more goods and services than we imported. But since our capital exports were so large, we nevertheless have had a big payments deficit. Under gold-standard rules, we should have lost gold and put deflationary pressure on our economy, restricting imports and encouraging exports so as to bring the balance of payments back toward equilibrium. And gold did flow out. But note that the U.S. problem was not to bring imports and exports back into balance. Rather, it was to get exports up even farther ahead of imports, to provide a payments surplus there big enough to cover the large payments deficit on capital account. The pressure of the gold outflow pushed us in the right direction—to get exports up relative to imports.

But we had over 5 per cent unemployment until mid-1965, and we were unwilling to accept a decline in U.S. incomes, prices, and costs in order to cut our imports. Letting an international-payments deficit generate a recession to close the deficit, when the economy already had unemployed men and factories, seemed like killing the patient to cure him. Moreover, it wasn't even clear that the medicine would work if used, since capital movements were such a big cause of the difficulty.

This example illustrates two basic points. First, we must always look at the entire balance of payments, not merely at the balance of trade, to understand what is going on. Second, few nations are now willing to let balance-of-payments adjustments automatically dictate the level of their domestic economies, especially when capital movements are the main disequilibrating force.

THE UNITED STATES— WORLD CREDITOR

Growing nations tend to pass through four stages of economic development. Each produces a different balance-of-payments position, and requires a different payments position for temporary balance-of-payments equilibrium.

1. *Early Borrower.* An underdeveloped country often borrows heavily abroad to obtain the capital goods it needs to develop its natural resources. For example, until about 1873 the U.S. apparently was a substantial capital importer from Europe. Imports of supplies, machinery, and consumption goods exceeded exports. In this stage, the trade balance must be "unfavorable" (imports must exceed exports) if the needed

goods and supplies are to be obtained, and this "unfavorable" balance is covered by borrowing.

2. *Mature Debtor.* After about 1873, debt repayment by the United States began to exceed new borrowing, though we were still a heavy debtor. In this stage, exports tend to exceed imports—the trade balance is "favorable." Our net export balance transferred the real goods to other nations as we paid off our debts. As in stage 1, money transfers are only the first step. It is the real transfer of goods and services that counts.

3. *Early Creditor.* Stage 3 is entered when the nation shifts over to a net creditor basis—when total investments abroad exceed foreign investments here. World War I and the 1920's thrust the United States abruptly into this stage, as we made heavy loans to our European allies. Government and private lending during and after World War II repeated the World War I experience with billions upon billions of dollars. Today, the United States is the one great creditor nation of the world. In this stage, a continued export surplus is to be expected. This surplus transfers abroad in real form the loans we make as we increase our creditor position.

4. *Mature Creditor.* In stage 4, the creditor nation's outstanding loans are so great that current income on foreign investments more than offsets the net new loans being made abroad. In this stage, the trade balance must shift to an import surplus in order to transfer to the mature creditor nation the excess of its current return on investment over new loans being made abroad. England was a mature creditor early in this century; we are moving toward that condition.

As a nation passes through these four stages, a changing trade balance is normal and essential. Whether a "favorable" balance of *trade* is in fact favorable depends basically on how well it fits in with the country's over-all balance-of-payments position. Severe disequilibrium will result if the trade balance is maintained (by tariffs or other controls) in a position unsympathetic to general balance-of-payments equilibrium requirements.

We, like other nations, must keep our balance of payments roughly in equilibrium over extended periods, though, as during the decades following World War II, it may show a substantial deficit for years if we have accumulated large reserves of gold and other currencies. Today, already the world's great creditor nation, we continue to invest huge sums abroad under the private profit incentive, and to provide billions annually in governmental foreign aid. Under these circumstances, we are still in stage 3, and one basic fact is sure: Unless we continue our heavy capital transfers abroad, we cannot hope to maintain our present huge export surplus of goods and services. Or the matter can be put the other way round: Unless we have a huge export surplus, we cannot continue to send so much capital abroad without facing a continuing payments deficit and likely depletion of our gold reserves.

What shall we do about it? That is the subject of Chapters 39 and 40.

REVIEW

Concepts To Remember

This chapter adds a few more important concepts to the list at the end of Chapter 37:

foreign exchange	gold points
exchange rate	controlled exchange rates
flexible, or "free," exchange rates	balance-of-payments equilibrium
international gold-reserve standard	

For Analysis and Discussion

1. Explain how balance-of-payments disequilibria tended to be eliminated under the gold standard, with fixed exchange rates. How would disequilibria be eliminated in a system of flexible exchange rates?
2. Using Fig. 38-1, trace through the effects of the following, beginning from the equilibrium shown by DD and SS:
   a. General Motors decides to buy a British automobile plant to get production facilities there.
   b. British students come to study in America.
   c. British citizens decide to buy General Electric stock in America at the same time as American imports from England decline.
3. Suppose that you and many others decide to travel to France next summer. Trace through carefully the effect your trip might have on dollar-franc rates, gold flows, and prices in each country under:
   a. An international gold standard.
   b. A flexible exchange rate system.
4. Domestically, free-price movements serve to equilibrate supply and demand in the markets concerned. Since foreign exchange rates are substantially frozen under the gold standard, how can the gold standard be said to be an international equilibrating system?
5. "Short-term capital movements (hot money) seeking protection from monetary and political uncertainty first in one country and then in another were the real cause of the downfall of the gold standard. No country could afford to let its monetary system be subjected to such unpredictable, violent shocks." Does this argument, based on the 1930's, apply to the United States today? Explain.

THIRTY-NINE

TARIFFS
AND FREE TRADE

The Tariff.

Intergovernmental Agreements To Expand Trade.

Current United States Trade Policy.

Adam Smith's *Wealth of Nations* in 1776 was a major attack on barriers to free international trade. The case for free trade internationally is the same as the case for free trade domestically, Smith argued. It is that specialization and division of labor with free exchange of the resulting products makes possible a higher standard of living for everyone. Tariffs or other barriers to free international trade impede such mutually advantageous specialization and exchange, and reduce living standards throughout the world, just as would barriers to free trade within a nation. In modern language, only with unfettered specialization and exchange can each nation and the world move out to be on their maximum production possibilities curves.

Yet from Smith's day to this, many have remained unconvinced. Support for tariffs to "protect the American standard of living and the high wages of American workers" is still widespread. Why, if the case for free trade is so clear, have nations retained tariffs that restrict trade?

THE TARIFF

A tariff is a tax on imports. The major goal of modern tariffs is to restrict imports—to protect domestic industry and workers from foreign competition. A secondary effect is to produce revenues for the government. But the two effects conflict—the more the tariff keeps out imports, the less revenue it raises. If the tariff is mainly for protection, it won't be much of a revenue-producer.

Figure 39-1 shows average U.S. tariff rates on dutiable imports since 1820. This shows clearly

519

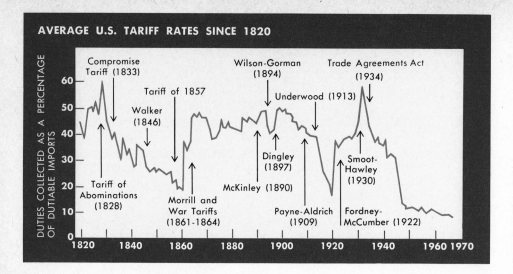

AVERAGE U.S. TARIFF RATES SINCE 1820

Compromise Tariff (1833)

Wilson-Gorman (1894)

Trade Agreements Act (1934)

Tariff of 1857

Walker (1846)

Underwood (1913)

Tariff of Abominations (1828)

Dingley (1897)

Morrill and War Tariffs (1861-1864)

McKinley (1890)

Smoot-Hawley (1930)

Payne-Aldrich (1909)

Fordney-McCumber (1922)

DUTIES COLLECTED AS A PERCENTAGE OF DUTIABLE IMPORTS

60 50 40 30 20 10 0

1820 1840 1860 1880 1900 1920 1940 1960 1970

FIG. 39-1 U.S. tariff rates have fluctuated with changing times and attitudes. Since 1934 they have been reduced sharply to the lowest levels in our history, and a further drop is due with the "Kennedy-round" reductions. (Source: U.S. Department of Commerce.)

the peaks of restrictionism and the major attempts to whittle away barriers to free international trade. From peak rates of about 60 per cent under the Tariff Act of 1833 and the Smoot-Hawley Tariff of 1930, average tariff rates on products which are covered by the tariff have been cut to below 10 per cent in the last two decades. Under the "Kennedy round" of 1967, they will be cut substantially further by 1972. These figures understate the real restrictive effect of the tariff, because some products are shut out completely by the tariff, and they don't show up in Fig. 39-1. But any way you look at it, major progress has been made in reducing U.S. tariff barriers since the early 1930's. The U.S., after a spotty history of restrictionism, has become the leader in a worldwide push toward freer trade.

The history books are full of accounts of the tariff acts battled through Congress over nearly two centuries, and of the regional and political issues underlying them. Our job is to look objectively at the economics of tariffs—to apply the economic analysis of the preceding chapters to the major arguments advanced in support of tariffs. And the central principle to use is the law of comparative advantage.

Some Partially Valid Arguments

The Infant-Industry Argument. A protective tariff may help "infant industries" until they are able to stand on their own feet. This was the most stylish argument for tariffs in the early 1800's. For example, the newly formed iron industry found it difficult to get established in the face of strong competition from British ironmakers. If foreign competition were shut out for a few years, it was

520

argued, the American iron industry could soon not only meet, but outstrip, foreign competitors.

There is some validity to the "infant industry" argument. It is hard for a new industry to establish itself in the face of vigorous competition from older competitors, even though the new industry once established may compete effectively with the old. The protective tariff on iron probably speeded the growth of an industry that would in any case have prospered.

But a tariff once on the books is hard to get off. The steel industry today, still protected a century and a half later, is a very mature infant.

The National-Self-sufficiency Argument. In a world of international tension, every nation wants to be as nearly self-sufficient as possible in the event of war. The desire for economic self-sufficiency may overbalance all other considerations, regardless of what the costs may be.

The economist cannot say whether a nation should try to become self-sufficient in the face of such considerations. But he can point out what self-sufficiency costs in terms of poor allocation of resources and a lowered standard of living, so that this factor will be weighed with others in deciding whether or not we will seek more self-sufficiency. And the cost for most nations would be great.

The Diversified-Economy Argument. When a nation is highly specialized in producing one or a few major products, its economy is highly vulnerable to variations in foreign demand. Brazil's coffee economy is an example; usually such one-product nations export a food-stuff or raw material. If foreign markets weaken, the result is domestic disaster. For such nations, greater economic diversification may be desirable, even though the new industries are comparatively inefficient. Tariffs may be used to shelter them in a diversification program. But for widely diversified countries like the United States, this argument has little relevance.

Over the last century in the United States these partially valid arguments have carried little weight in tariff controversies. Let us now turn to the arguments that have been the important ones in support of the tariff. As we shall see, they turn out to be largely fallacious.

The Favorable-Balance-of-Trade Argument

Most naive of all the tariff arguments is the desire for a "favorable balance of trade" for its own sake. It goes back to the old mercantilist desire to gain more gold and silver as national wealth. Two major fallacies are involved.

First, there is nothing generally favorable about a "favorable" balance of trade. A continued "favorable" balance means that we continually give foreigners more goods and services than they give us; we receive in exchange gold (often to be held idle at considerable storage expense) or investments abroad. Thus, it means a *reduced* standard of living for the country sending away goods and services, certainly in the short run, and indefinitely if the "favorable" balance of trade continues without willingness to accept goods from abroad. We don't eat gold. Our standard of living is made up of the goods and services we have.

Second, a favorable balance of trade is impossible as a continuing policy, if we consider only the goods and services portion of the balance of payments. Foreigners can't buy from us unless they get dollars to pay for our products. The way they get dollars is by selling us their goods and services. It is only by buying from foreigners that we can expect to sell to them.

There is no point more fundamental than this—that we can sell abroad only if we buy abroad. It is basic to understanding the fallacy in nearly every argument for protective tariffs and other trade-restriction policies. Figure 39-2 shows where other countries obtained the dollars to buy our exports from 1929 to 1967. It shows that private investments abroad and government aid helped foreigners finance their purchases from us.

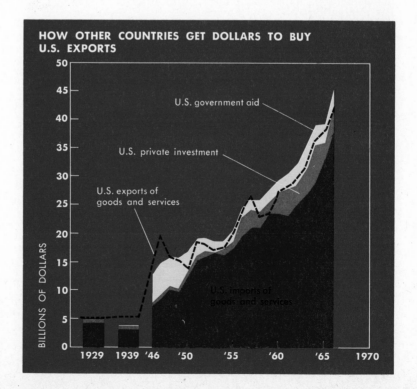

FIG. 39-2 Other countries get dollars to buy U.S. exports mainly through our payments for imports. But U.S. investments abroad and government foreign aid also provide a good many dollars. (Source: U.S. Department of Commerce. Military aid and exports excluded.)

HOW OTHER COUNTRIES GET DOLLARS TO BUY U.S. EXPORTS

U.S. government aid

U.S. private investment

U.S. exports of goods and services

U.S. imports of goods and services

BILLIONS OF DOLLARS

But our purchases of foreign goods and services have always been the big source of dollars with which foreigners bought our exports. To sell abroad we must buy abroad. We cannot shut out foreign imports and continue to export.

The Protect-Home-Industry Argument

Perhaps the most popular argument for the tariff is that we need it to protect American industry against low-cost foreign competition.

A domestic industry asking for tariff protection argues that without protection its market will be lost to foreign competitors. This will force the domestic industry out of business, throwing workers out of jobs, and decreasing our national welfare. Suppose that the industry is right; if it does not receive protection it *will* lose its market to foreign competitors. What are the effects of giving the tariff protection the industry wants?[1]

The first effect is that domestic consumers must pay more for the protected product than if it had come in free. If sugar comes in over the tariff, consumers must pay the regular price of the foreign sugar plus the tariff duty. If the tariff shuts out foreign sugar, domestic consumers must pay a higher price for domestic sugar. We know it's higher because domestic producers cannot, without a tariff, produce and sell at a price low enough to meet foreign competition. If they could, they wouldn't need the tariff.

Second, domestic sugar producers are subsidized by the tariff; they are enabled to charge higher prices than would have been possible if foreign competition had not been shut out. It's clear that domestic producers are the great gainers from a tariff on their product.

In effect, therefore, a tariff is a subsidy to domestic producers, financed by consumers through higher prices for the protected product. Moreover, the more inefficient domestic producers are, the higher tariff they need to protect them against foreign competition and the larger subsidy they receive.

Indeed, industry's argument for a tariff is

[1] Often industries seeking protective tariffs would be able to retain their markets without tariffs; tariffs enable them to raise domestic prices with lessened fear of foreign competition. Indeed, the tariff has been called "the mother of monopolies," since it helps domestic monopolies to exist without fear of foreign competition.

often for a "scientific" tariff that would just "equalize domestic and foreign costs of production." A suggestion in Congress that special taxes be levied on consumers to finance subsidies to producers, each subsidy to be based on the producer's inefficiency, would horrify everyone. Yet this is substantially the result of a "scientific" protective tariff designed to equalize foreign and domestic costs of production.

A noted economist, Frederick Bastiat, put the free-trade case against "protection" tellingly over a century ago in his satirical "Petition of the Candle-Makers." We need protection, said the candle-makers of Paris in their petition. Foreign competitors are bad enough, but it is the sun who is the most unfair competitor of all. Each day he shines and throws light over all, at no cost at all. If you only shut out the sun, pleaded the candle-makers, we can have a magnificent candle industry, giving jobs to untold numbers of workers.

Should we protect American domestic industry against cheap foreign competition today using the same arguments as Bastiat's candle-makers a century ago?

The Protect-Our-High-Wages Argument

American wages are the highest in the world. Therefore, it is argued, unless we have a protective tariff, competition from low-wage nations will push down high American wages to the level of wages abroad.

The "Petition of the Candle-Makers" should suggest a fallacy here. Would the real wages of French workers have been raised by shutting out the sun? Would the French people have been better off? As the principle of comparative advantage says, the maximum real output will come when we allocate our resources to their most efficient, not their least efficient, uses. Look at the argument in more detail.

First, why are wages now higher in the United States than in other countries? Fundamentally, because of the high productivity of American workers. Anything that raises their productivity makes it possible for them to receive higher real wages. And each worker can receive his highest possible wage when he is working in that industry where his marginal productivity is highest.

What happens when a tariff is passed to "protect" high American wages? The tariff shuts out foreign products and permits relatively inefficient American industries to grow up where otherwise they could not have existed, giving new jobs to American workers. But, as a result, American exports will fall off because foreign countries cannot buy from us unless we buy from them. (Remember Fig. 39-2.) Therefore, fewer workers are employed in the export industries. *The net result is a shift of workers from relatively efficient export industries (where they would be situated under free trade) into less efficient protected industries. As workers move to lower-marginal-productivity positions in protected industries, the wages they can receive in the new jobs are necessarily lower than they could have been before the shift. The long-run result of a protective tariff is to lower real wages, not to raise them. People earn the most when they work where they are most efficient.*[2]

To be sure you understand this point, consider an extreme example cited by proponents of a tariff to protect American wages. Suppose that Japanese labor is paid only a dollar per day and we remove all tariffs on Japanese imports. Won't

---

[2] This is not to deny that a protective tariff on a particular product may raise the real wages of workers *in that industry* by increasing the demand for labor there, so long as there are immobilities in the domestic labor market that keep other workers from moving in to take advantage of the higher labor demand provided there by protection.

American workers be forced to take much lower wages to compete?

In analyzing this case, first we need to recognize that even though Japanese daily wages are much lower, it is not necessarily true that the labor costs of Japanese producers are correspondingly lower. The Japanese worker gets lower wages, but he also produces less in a day. Therefore, the labor cost per unit of output may be as much, or more, for the Japanese producer as for the American. In the early 1960's, for example, the average hourly wage of Japanese industrial workers (without "fringe benefits") was about 25 cents, that in America was about $2.50. But suppose, for example, in the chinaware industry, that the hourly output per worker in Japan is 10 plates; then the labor cost per plate is 2.5 cents. If the hourly output per American worker is 100 plates, the labor cost per plate would be only 2.5 cents too. Wage cost per plate (per unit of output) is the one that counts.

The evidence is clear that although wages are lower everywhere else than in the United States, our unit costs are highly competitive. in many industries. Our $30 billion of annual merchandise exports is unmistakable evidence of that. Table 39-1 presents data on comparative wage-costs and output per man-hour in manufacturing for a sample of countries, data which illustrate why U.S. manufacturers do very well in world

---

TABLE 39-1

INTERNATIONAL WAGE COSTS

PER UNIT OF MANUFACTURING OUTPUT *

Country	Net Output per Man-hour	Hourly Earnings	Wage-cost per Dollar of Output
United States	$3.89	$2.68	$0.69
Canada	2.56	1.89	.74
Belgium	1.33	.74	.58
Norway	1.29	.90	.70
United Kingdom	.97	.77	.79
West Germany	.96	.70	.73
Italy	.96	.61	.64
Japan	.40	.29	.72

* Data from J. Dunlop, ed., *Automation and Technological Change* (Englewood Cliffs, N. J.: Prentice-Hall, 1962), p. 137. Figures are for 1960–61, with national currencies converted to U.S. dollars. Hourly earnings in all cases include "fringe benefits." Conversion of currencies is based on official exchange rates, and should be recognized as only a rough approximation. Since then, wage costs per dollar of output have risen only slightly in the U.S. and substantially more in most other industrialized nations.

markets in spite of paying the highest wages in the world.

The first column shows estimated net output per man-hour in manufacturing, and the second, hourly earnings in the same industries. American wages are by far the highest, but so is American output per man-hour. If you compare the wage-costs per dollar of output in the third column, you'll see that the higher American productivity roughly offsets the higher American wage costs, as compared to other nations with lower wages but also lower productivity. The estimates are very rough (see the footnote to the table), but they illustrate the basic point. It's wage cost per unit of output that counts, and on this vital score we're highly competitive on a wide range of products.[3] Look back at $5.3 billion surplus of exports over imports for 1966 in Table 37-4 for the massive evidence that we compete very effectively in world markets.

These figures show that the problem of competing with low-wage foreign labor is less dramatic than it may seem. But they don't answer the whole tariff argument, for per unit labor costs on many articles may be lower in Japan in spite of the higher output per worker here. But even then, the principle of comparative advantage shows that we would be better off as a nation without tariffs on Japanese goods.

Suppose, to continue the hypothetical example, that Japan can far undersell us on china plates, and that we remove the tariff on such plates. This move, of course, would throw workers in the American chinaware industry out of jobs. But since Japan would then be selling more to us, she could now buy more from us. She would buy from us those goods that we are able to produce most efficiently—say, machine tools. Workers thrown out of jobs in making china would gradually be drawn into the machine-tool industry. But since the United States is, by assumption, comparatively more efficient in producing machine tools than china, workers can receive higher wages making machinery. Workers in the china industry

would surely be temporarily unemployed and, if personally unadaptable, might never be re-employed. But the general public would clearly gain by obtaining cheaper china plates, and more workers would be drawn into the high-productivity industries where wages are highest. Removal of an existing tariff may ruin protected producer groups; yet in the long run average wages and the standard of living for the economy as a whole will be raised.[4]

This reasoning, however, rides easily over some tough "short-run" adjustment problems. Higher average wages for the economy don't help the 50-year-old china maker thrown out of work by the new imports. Where will he get another equally good job, or even one at all? The offsetting new jobs producing for export may not come immediately. The Japanese may temporarily accumulate dollars, or spend them elsewhere instead of here. Sooner or later, our expanded imports will mean new export markets. But with these uncertainties and delays, and the pain felt in the displaced industries, it's easy to understand why some labor opposition to tariff cuts is bitter. Nor does the higher national standard of living help those china-company stockholders whose investment is destroyed by the cheap imports. The opposition comes from investors and managers as well as from workers.

The Increased-Employment Argument

In the long run, it should by now be clear, a protective tariff neither increases nor decreases employment, but merely shifts resources from "more efficient" to "less efficient" industries. However, the *short-run* adjustments in moving toward the new long-run equilibrium may be slow and painful (as with any shift in demand). Removing an existing tariff may result in temporary unemployment, unemployment that may persist stubbornly if aggregate demand is weak.

But the protectionist argument claims more. It says that, *at least in the short run, raising* tariffs will create *more* jobs as domestic firms be-

---

[3] Note that this statement does not say that all the higher output per man-hour in America is attributable to workers, but merely that, all things considered (including more and better capital goods in America, American management, and the like), our labor costs per dollar of output are competitive with those of other nations.

[4] This argument applies strictly only if labor costs are the same proportion of total costs in the two industries concerned. In most real-world cases in the United States, this approximation is close enough to permit the above example to apply in substance.

gin selling to the customers who previously bought imported goods. And the foreign trade multiplier will amplify the creation of domestic jobs. Even though in the long run this may not increase total employment, temporarily the new tariff will raise exports relative to imports and create jobs.

But this is a short-sighted argument in most instances. Suppose America puts on a tariff to shut out foreign goods and to export our unemployment. What would you do if you were Belgium or England or France? You'd come right back with higher tariffs against American exports. And that's just what they did during the 1930's. If we can increase our exports relative to imports in a period of unemployment, this may temporarily raise employment and real g.n.p. But it's unlikely that higher tariffs will do the job, and likely that the main result will just be less trade for everybody.

Summary

From this analysis, we can draw a broad summary of the major economic effects of tariffs. *In the long run*, a protective tariff lowers real wages and the standard of living. It diverts resources from self-sustaining export industries to less efficient, protected domestic-consumption industries; and it forces consumers to pay higher prices. *In the short run*, advantages *may* be gained from imposing new tariffs to aid infant industries or to reduce unemployment. However, new tariffs will increase domestic employment only if almost inevitable retaliatory steps are not taken by other nations.[5]

Tariff-making
in the United States

If the protective tariff is open to such serious criticism, and if it benefits only particular groups at the cost of the rest of society, why did we have high protective tariffs so long? There are two chief answers.

First, public opinion on the tariff has been greatly influenced by self-seeking propaganda, and many citizens are uninformed on the nature of

international trade. Groups seeking protection have presented their case effectively in Congress and to the general public, and the appeal to nationalism against foreigners is a potent rallying cry.

Second, the benefits of freer trade are widespread—lower prices, and more jobs in export industries tomorrow. But the costs are concentrated and direct—on the businessmen and workers who lose out to cheaper foreign imports. The threatened interests are alarmed, organized, and vocal. Consumers as a whole are not organized to speak effectively. Congress passes acts covering thousands of products, and most of the actual decisions are made by small subcommittees in the House and Senate. No congressman can know about more than a comparatively small number of these thousands. But each congressman is pressed by his constituents to vote for protection for the goods that they produce. Thus, the congressman from one state will agree to vote for a tariff on shoes if his colleague from another state will vote for one on sugar. The tariff is the classic example of congressional lobbying and logrolling.

Thus, the big tariff reductions since 1930 have come through congressional delegation of tariff-cutting authority to the President. Under the Reciprocal Trade Agreements Act of 1934 and the Kennedy Trade Expansion Act of 1962, the President was authorized to bargain down U.S. tariffs in return for similar reductions by other nations. The results to date are shown in Fig. 39-1. Average U.S. tariffs will drop substantially further by 1972 under the bargains reached in the "Kennedy round" international agreements of 1967. Similar reductions have been made since the 1930's by most other major Western nations with whom we trade heavily, though many have remaining tariffs which are higher than ours.

INTERGOVERNMENTAL AGREEMENTS
TO EXPAND TRADE

The International
Trade Organization and GATT

After World War II the spirit of internationalism was strong. All the victorious nations except the U.S.S.R. moved to extend their war-

---

[5] Though as a practical matter U.S. tariff reductions are usually advocated on the presumption of reciprocal reductions by other nations, the logic of comparative advantage shows that under most circumstances even unilateral tariff reductions can benefit the country making them.

time collaboration into economic cooperation that would reverse the restrictionist wave of the 1930's. Within the framework of the United Nations, member nations pushed for an International Trade Organization, which would attempt to expand and stabilize the volume of world trade.

Prolonged debate failed to bring agreement on a charter for ITO that could command support of most of the nations concerned. Out of these discussions, however, came the General Agreement on Tariffs and Trade (GATT), now with some 40 signatory countries. GATT provides for regular discussion of means to reduce international trade restrictions among the members, and each member nation agrees to work toward freer trade practices, insofar as these practices are not in conflict with the country's national legislation. GATT today provides a ready forum for discussions and negotiations among member nations.

The European Common Market

The biggest postwar move toward international economic cooperation is the European Common Market, and a major move it is. After earlier cooperation on coal, iron, and atomic energy, in 1958 six European nations—Belgium, France, Italy, Luxembourg, the Netherlands, and West Germany—banded together in the European Economic Community, generally called the Common Market. This is a precedent-shattering agreement to eliminate all tariff and similar trade barriers against one another over a period of 12 to 17 years. Moreover, they will gradually equalize all their restrictions on trade with nations outside the six and present a common tariff to the outside world. Barriers against internal movement of capital and labor will be abolished. Other economic policies will be "harmonized." A common antitrust policy is provided to eliminate long-time restrictions on competition, though here considerable freedom is left for national differences.

Together, "the six" have a total population of 180 million, just under that of the United States and only about 20 per cent below the U.S.S.R.'s. In 1967 they accounted for over one-fourth of the world's exports, somewhat more than the United States, and their imports of $40 billion made them easily the world's largest importer. Their combined gross national product is

somewhat less than half ours, and about the same as that of the U.S.S.R.

In its first years the Common Market has been a major success. Its g.n.p. has grown at over 5 per cent per year, well above our growth rate and higher than that in most surrounding European countries. Internal tariff barriers had been cut 80 per cent by 1967, faster than the original schedule provided, and plans were under way to reach complete internal free trade in 10 years rather than the original 12. Internal trade among the member countries had grown by over 50 per cent in the first 7 years, and is still expanding rapidly. Investment in industrial facilities was high as a percentage of g.n.p., and heavy foreign investments (especially from the United States) were augmenting domestic expansion of facilities. Gold reserves by 1967 exceeded $15 billion, more than those of the United States, plus another $6 billion of dollar balances. The German mark is increasingly viewed in world financial circles as being nearly as sound as the dollar. The darkest cloud has been France's growing reluctance to push forward except on terms especially favorable to her economy.

Seven other European nations—Britain, Norway, Sweden, Denmark, Switzerland, Austria, and Portugal—in 1960 formed a parallel organization, the European Free Trade Association (EFTA). These nations for one reason or another had not joined in formation of the Common Market, mainly because they were unwilling to move as far toward economic integration as the Common Market envisioned. Britain faced an especially serious problem because of her long-standing tradition of special preferences on foreign trade to British Commonwealth nations, preferences which would have to be renounced as a condition of membership in the Common Market. EFTA, therefore, stressed elimination of internal tariff barriers among member nations almost as fast as within the Common Market. But there was no provision for a common external tariff or for the increasingly close general economic integration envisaged for the Common Market nations.

In 1963 and again in 1967, Britain applied for admission to the Common Market pact. General de Gaulle of France both times in essence vetoed the British bid, but negotiations are still in process. If, in fact, Britain and the other EFTA nations join the Common Market, the result will be a large economic free trade area indeed, with a population of over 250 million, and a g.n.p. of perhaps two-thirds ours and considerably larger than the U.S.S.R.'s. It will be by far the world's largest importer and exporter. And it could be largely self-sufficient in agriculture, raw materials, and industrial products if it should choose the path of high protection against outside products.

CURRENT UNITED STATES TRADE POLICY

The success of the Common Market, with the possibility of an even larger European free trade area and perhaps even a United States of Europe, confronted American business firms and American trade policy with a new challenge. American export markets inside the Common Market were in serious danger, since our products must pay the common external tariff while competitive products made within the Common Market pay no tariff. Intra-Common Market trade is booming and entire new patterns of trade are developing. Parisian department store counters are loaded with Italian fashions and shoes, Ger-

man leather goods and housewares, Dutch clothing and pottery. The same is true in other cities throughout the Common Market. Thanks to reduced tariffs, prices on many basic items are dramatically lower throughout the Common Market area. A revolution of consumer buying habits is under way. The comparison is widely drawn with the mass consumer market which is the foundation of the American economy.

America's response was the "Kennedy round" negotiations with some 40 nations, including the Common Market, for sweeping mutual tariff reductions. In 1967, after arduous, often acrimonious, negotiations, the results were announced. The U.S. agreed to reduce tariffs an average of 35 per cent on over 6,000 items accounting for $8 billion of imports in 1966, and widespread reciprocal reductions were obtained. Although this was less than the full 50 per cent permitted by the Kennedy Trade Expansion Act of 1962 and less than the complete tariff elimination authorized for Common Market products, it represented a sweeping further step toward complete free trade, especially on a wide variety of manufactured products. But on numerous important items, especially farm products, substantial tariff barriers remain between us and the Common Market nations.

For Analysis and Discussion

1. What is the fallacy in the "Petition of the Candle-Makers" for protection against the sun? Is the same fallacy present in other arguments for protective tariffs?

2. List the factors that explain the high wages received by American workers in the steel and chemical industries. Which, if any, would be affected, and in which direction, if American tariffs were raised on steel and chemicals?

3. Under the "Kennedy round," U.S. tariffs will be reduced sharply on a wide range of products which accounted for $8 billion of imports in 1966. Using the figures in Chapter 37, which major industries and areas are most likely to be helped and which injured? Should workers and firms presently protected by tariffs receive government subsidies for retaining and compensation for loss of markets when tariffs are reduced?

4. Are there any industries in the United States today that seem to you clearly to deserve tariff protection as "infant industries"?

5. One leading economist has argued: "Removal of tariffs is clearly desirable, but the associated transition effects would be tolerable only in times of prosperity and in the absence of monopolistic restrictions in the more efficient American industries." Can you explain this apparently paradoxical statement?

6. Can you suggest any ways whereby, in a period of depression, the United States could raise its tariffs against foreign goods so as to avoid probable retaliation?

FORTY

GOLD AND CURRENT BALANCE-OF-PAYMENTS PROBLEMS

The Downfall of the Gold Standard.

Exchange Depreciation and Exchange Controls.

The International Monetary Fund.

U.S. Foreign Lending.

The International Gold-and-Dollar Reserve Standard.

Gold and the U.S. Payments Problem.

Long-Range Reforms.

In recent years, gold losses and the deficit in our balance of payments have been front-page news. Are the predictions of impending disaster from the financial community overdone? How worried, if at all, should we be? Above all, what should we do about it?

One of the first things to recognize is that economic problems change rapidly. Two decades ago, the big international problem was the "dollar shortage" and too much of the world's gold accumulated in the United States. As this is written, it is the U.S. payments deficit and our gold losses. By the time you read this, the problem may have changed again. A brief look at history, therefore, is a useful background for understanding the problems we face today.

THE DOWNFALL OF THE GOLD STANDARD

Before 1914, the international gold standard ruled the international monetary scene. It was, in theory and to a substantial degree in practice, an "automatic" system. A balance-of-payments deficit would lead to a gold outflow, which in turn would usually reduce the nation's money stock and lower its costs, prices, and incomes, thereby cutting imports and stimulating exports so as to restore equilibrium in its balance of payments. Central banks "managed" the money supply to a limited extent, but gold was the center of a "religion" of money. It was accepted without questioning by most economists and the public alike as an ultimate repository of value. In the rapidly expanding, reasonably flexible pre-1914 world, this gold stan-

528

dard supplied an important element of international-exchange stability, and the requisite domestic price and income adjustments were generally accomplished without excessively painful consequences.

The monetary disruptions of World War I were extreme. Wild inflations occurred in several European nations, serious inflation in all. Re-establishment of the international gold standard in the 1920's was thus fraught with difficulties. What should the re-established gold values, or "contents," of the various national currencies be, in light of the preceding inflations? In other words, what should exchange rates be? In Britain, the financial center of the prewar world, the pound was finally put back "on gold" in 1925 at the prewar gold content, and the prewar dollar-pound exchange rate of $4.86 = £1 was restored. In other countries, new gold contents were prescribed for currencies in an endeavor to place them in "equilibrium" balance-of-payments positions vis-à-vis the rest of the world. The Western world went back "on gold."

But the depression of the 1930's dealt the death blow to the prewar gold standard. Losing gold in a period of growing unemployment meant even further deflationary contraction of national money supplies. First England in 1931, then most other major nations, decided this price was too high to pay. They "went off gold," devaluing their currencies relative to gold and to other currencies in order to avoid the domestic deflation implicit in adherence to the gold standard, and to encourage foreign purchases of their domestically produced products. The American dollar was devalued in 1934 to 59 per cent of its earlier gold content. Eventually every major currency was devalued, exchange and capital movement controls were established, and domestic currencies were cut loose from gold flows.

In retrospect, three major factors led to the downfall of the gold standard:

1. The great depression of the 1930's with its massive unemployment made the domestic price of financial orthodoxy too high to pay.
2. Downward cost-price rigidities aggravated the impact of price and income deflation, and thwarted the equilibrating forces previously at

work under the gold-standard system. Unions, industrial monopolies, agricultural groups—all contributed to holding up prices when incomes fell in the depression.

3. With waning faith in the gold-standard religion, and with growing political instability, capital flights to "safer" countries became common. Huge hot-money drains were more than any nation could stand. The religion of gold worked admirably so long as no infidels entered the temple to whisper misgivings. Once doubt spread, however, capital flights never envisaged in a stable, well-behaved international system spelled doom to the gold standard in a rigid, depression-conscious world.

EXCHANGE DEPRECIATION AND EXCHANGE CONTROLS

Widespread desertion of the gold standard and currency devaluations failed to bring the results expected. One country acting alone could expand its exports by depreciation. But when everyone's currency was depreciated, the actions offset one another and no one ended up with much of a gain in exports.

In retrospect, thus, the main result of the competitive depreciation race of the 1930's was disruption of international trade and investment, widespread friction and ill will, and no very important gains to any of the competitors. As with tariff increases, exchange depreciation was a "beggar-my-neighbor" attempt to shift unemployment to other nations. And it was doomed to defeat by the virtual certainty of retaliation.

As exchange depreciation failed to eliminate the unemployment that plagued the Western world, cross currents of conflict and cooperation were everywhere apparent in international economic relations. New types of exchange controls proliferated. Nations set their exchange rates at varying levels, searching for the one to maximize their gain from foreign trade. Many countries, especially Nazi Germany, "blocked" the use of foreign exchange received from their foreign sales, and rationed the foreign exchange received to control its expenditure. Every major nation introduced controls over capital exports.

THE INTERNATIONAL
MONETARY FUND

To the nations mapping peacetime reconstruction at the end of World War II, the international monetary disruption and conflict of the 1930's were bitter memories. There was little sentiment for restoring the old gold standard. But there was widespread agreement on the need for reasonable exchange stability and for reduced restrictions on international trade and capital movements.

In 1946, some 40 nations established the International Monetary Fund to help attain these goals; the total is now over 100.[1] The Fund consists of over $10 billion of gold and member-country currencies made available for stabilization activities in accordance with the Fund's charter. Each country's contribution was based on its national income; the United States put up about one-third of the total. Voting control over the Fund is roughly in proportion to contributions to its capital.

The officially stated purposes of the Fund are:

1. To promote international monetary cooperation through a permanent institution that provides the machinery for consultation and collaboration on international monetary problems.

2. To facilitate the expansion of international trade and thereby to promote and maintain high levels of employment and real income.

3. To promote exchange stability, to maintain orderly exchange arrangements among members, and to avoid competitive exchange depreciation.

4. To assist in the establishment of a multilateral system of payments on current transactions and in the elimination of exchange restrictions.

5. To provide temporary loans to members so they will have more opportunity to correct maladjustments in their balances of payments gradually without resorting to measures destructive of national and international prosperity.

[1] After participating in the planning, the Soviet-bloc countries did not join.

6. In accordance with the above, to shorten the duration and lessen the degree of disequilibrium in the international balances of payments of members.

Organization and Operations

The primary operating purpose of the Fund is to help member nations maintain exchange-rate stability, coupled with reasonable flexibility to make any long-run adjustments required. In this respect, the philosophy of the Fund differs substantially from that of the old gold standard, whose keynote was exchange stability at all costs.

The Fund is intended to help member countries meet temporary exchange deficits only—to give them time to correct balance-of-payments maladjustments without being forced to adopt depressive measures under exceptional strains. The Fund can thus lend foreign currencies to a country that is caught temporarily short of exchange. Whereas previously the only likely alternative would have been imposition of exchange controls, with the Fund's assistance such controls may be avoided. The Fund stands ready to lend to any member country up to one-fourth of its quota in any year, if the proposed use of the exchange is in keeping with the Fund's stated objectives.

If any country faces a lasting disequilibrium in its balance of payments, more fundamental steps are called for. Here the Fund tries to play a different role. First, member countries agree that they will consult through the Fund on all major international monetary problems, and that each will continuously submit to the Fund's expert staff full information on its own international monetary position. Second, any country may, if it finds its balance of payments in fundamental disequilibrium, devalue its currency by as much as 10 per cent on notification, but without official permission, of the Fund. But any greater devaluation must be approved by the Fund, which will judge on the basis of the need for such a step to restore equilibrium. This is the second aspect of the basic philosophy underlying the Fund—exchange stability, but with flexibility where required to correct fundamental disequilibria.

The Fund does not prohibit member-country controls over *capital* movements. Most participants agreed that hot-money movements may be too disruptive to tolerate, and retained their freedom to control them individually.

The Fund
in the Postwar World

On the experience thus far, the Fund appears to be a significant step toward international monetary collaboration and stabilization after the disastrous decade of the 1930's. But it can work satisfactorily only in a relatively stable world, where cases of "fundamental disequilibrium" are rare. Indeed, member countries (for example, France in the 1950's) have already defied the Fund's regulations, devaluing their own currencies when they thought it essential, without the Fund's approval. But the Fund has repeatedly helped to tide member countries over temporary balance-of-payments pressures which otherwise might have generated major international financial crises or disruptive domestic deflations. And the Fund today is the center of plans to reform the entire international liquidity system, as we shall see presently.[2]

U.S. FOREIGN LENDING

A major development of the postwar financial world has been the massive growth of U.S. lending abroad. Our large recent payments deficits

[2] Parallel to the International Monetary Fund, the same 40 countries also established the $8 billion International Bank for Reconstruction and Development. It was set up to facilitate foreign lending for post-war reconstruction and for development of underdeveloped areas. The organization and management of the Bank closely parallel those of the Fund. The Bank's operating head is from this country, in recognition of the United States' large contribution to the Bank's capital and the dominant demand for dollar loans. There are now 70 member nations.

Although the IBRD may lend out its own capital, it operates primarily through two other channels—attaching its guarantee to private loans, and borrowing funds in the various member countries to finance its loans. For example, if Peru wants a loan to develop its industries and plans to spend most of the loan in the United States, the Bank will either try to arrange a direct loan for Peru from American lenders, attaching its own guarantee to the loan, or it will float a bond issue in the American market to obtain funds for the Peruvian loan. In either case, the United States representative on the Bank's board would have to approve, since every loan must be approved by the major country in which the loan is to be raised and spent, as well as by the Bank's officers.

have been attributable entirely to our heavy private foreign investments and to government loans and foreign-aid programs, since we have continually had a large export surplus on trade and services. At the same time, U.S. investors have acquired ownership of a huge volume of assets abroad—factories, oil refineries, assembly plants. Thus, it is important to look carefully at international capital movements if we are to understand recent international economic events.

U.S. private investment abroad has burgeoned since World War II. Figure 40-1 shows the data for selected years since 1929. The three lower areas in each bar are direct American investments. The light area at the top is investment in securities, including short-term investments. Even allowing for some inflation, the rise since World War II has been phenomenal.

Figure 40-2 shows the picture in terms of annual new U.S. investment abroad and annual earnings on total American foreign investments. The bars show that our earnings each year on investments abroad just about equal our new investments abroad. Foreign investments are profitable business. As with domestic firms, a big part of new U.S. investment abroad each year consists of plowing back earnings on the investments already

FIG. 40-1 Since the 1930's, U.S. private investment abroad has soared. Oil is the biggest single industry, but investments have been widely diversified. (Source: U.S. Department of Commerce.)

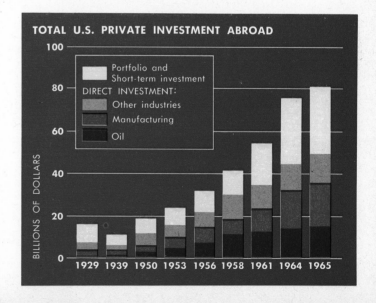

there. In recent years, this reinvestment has been about three-fourths of total new investment, and new funds from the United States only about one-fourth.

Figure 40-2 also suggests a central fact about foreign lending. To collect earnings and amortization on loans and investments abroad, either we must accept payment through importing goods and services or we must be prepared continually to reinvest the principal and earnings abroad. (Remember the early and mature creditor positions from Chapter 38.) Government and private lending abroad has been a major factor in permitting us to continue our traditional export surplus of goods and services. If we ever stop our annual net lending abroad, we will be able to collect our earnings and repayments on principal only by running a net import surplus of goods and services.

THE INTERNATIONAL
GOLD-AND-DOLLAR RESERVE STANDARD

What kind of international monetary system has evolved out of these circumstances, and what is the role of the dollar in it? To answer, we

need to review one more piece of history, the period since World War II, with particular focus on the dollar and the U.S. balance of payments.

The Post-World-War-II
"Dollar Shortage"

Western Europe, Russia, and Japan emerged from World War II tired, devastated, with their foreign assets depleted, and heavily in debt. The U.S. emerged powerful, prosperous, unbombed, and a massive international creditor. Our real g.n.p. more than doubled under the pressures of war from the depression of the late 1930's, so that we not only provided a large portion of the war materiel for our allies but simultaneously substantially raised the American standard of living in terms of consumer goods between 1940 and 1946. Until our allies used up their ability to pay, we sold war materiel and civilian supplies to them, and later provided many of them on loans and "lend-lease," rather than as gifts or our contributions to the common war.

Thus, in 1946 the reconstruction needs of Europe, Russia, and Japan were enormous. The unscathed American economy offered vast productive power to meet these needs. But foreign na-

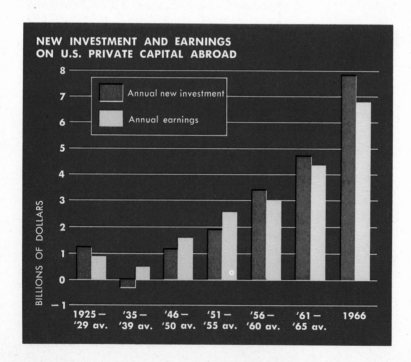

FIG. 40-2 Annual new U.S. private investment abroad has grown rapidly, but returns on such investments abroad have grown about as fast. (Source: U.S. Department of Commerce.)

tions, faced with the job of rebuilding their war-torn factories and feeding their people, had little to offer in exchange for our goods and services. Their gold and dollar reserves had been exhausted by the war, and they were already heavily in debt to us.

The resulting "dollar shortage" dominated the international scene. No nation seemed to have enough dollars to pay for the goods and services it needed from America. The Marshall Plan, under which we extended billions in reconstruction aid to allied nations, was our major answer to helping foreign nations rebuild and to alleviating this dollar shortage. Our exports of goods and services soared, financed partly by growing imports, partly by U.S. government aid, and partly by growing U.S. private investments in the rebuilding nations.

With our aid and their own effective work, Europe, Japan, and the U.S.S.R. recovered at an almost miraculous rate. Factories were rebuilt, employment was restored, prosperity was everywhere, and their economic growth rate soared to more than twice our own. With growing prosperity and profits, Europe and Japan increasingly drew American private capital for investment, and large-scale government aid continued. After about 1950, the U.S. balance of payments showed a persistent deficit. Exports of goods and services continually exceeded imports, but our private capital investment abroad plus our government aid exceeded even the growing export surpluses.

Thus, each year foreign nations received more payments from the U.S. than they made to us. With the option of taking gold or accumulating dollar balances, they mainly chose the latter through the 1950's. The dollar was better than gold. It could be freely exchanged for gold at $35 an ounce; one could earn interest on dollar balances held in New York banks or invested in short-term U.S. securities; much of what nations wanted to buy was available in the U.S. and dollars were needed to pay; and throughout the world dollars were as acceptable as gold.

Figure 40-3 shows the steady accumulation of short-term dollar balances by foreign nations during the 1950's (from about $8 billion to $20 billion), and the slow decline in the U.S. gold

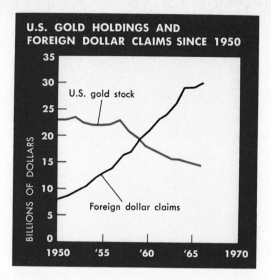

U.S. GOLD HOLDINGS AND FOREIGN DOLLAR CLAIMS SINCE 1950

FIG. 40-3 Since 1950, foreign nations have steadily built up their holdings of U.S. dollars and short term claims on dollars, but since the late 1950's have taken part of their dollar claims in gold. Do we face a gold crisis? (Source: Federal Reserve Board.)

stock as foreign nations took some payments in gold.

The U.S. Payments Deficit and the Dollar Glut

By the middle 1950's, the rehabilitation of Europe and Japan was substantially complete, and their economies were booming. The U.S. balance-of-payments deficit rose rapidly in the late 1950's to over $3 billion per year. Foreign nations, with their own international-reserve balances substantially rebuilt, continued to hold growing amounts of short-term balances in New York, but they also began to take increasing amounts of gold. Although the U.S. was still carrying the major burden of defense spending for the free world and of providing economic aid to the underdeveloped nations, increasing concern was voiced abroad over our continuing large payments deficit. International bankers and conservatives at home warned direly of dangers to the dollar and that we must "put our house in order" if we were to maintain confidence in the dollar and avoid a crisis in our international situation.

In 1960, widespread speculation that the dollar might be devalued caused a sharp run on our gold stock through withdrawal of short-term dollar balances. Over the ten years following 1957, our gold holdings declined from $23 to $13 billion, and short-term foreign dollar balances held in the United States reached $30 billion. Central banks abroad considered these dollars part of their international reserves, substantially as good as gold and convertible into gold on demand. But increasingly foreign central banks and private holders had all the dollars they wanted, and more! There was, the critics said, a dollar glut. The U.S. found itself precariously exposed to a run on gold from unwilling dollar holders.

The International Gold-and-Dollar-Reserve Standard

The international monetary system that has evolved is sometimes called the "international gold-and-dollar-reserve standard." Most nations of the Western world hold both gold and dollars as their basic international reserves, with the two freely convertible into one another. The total international reserves for the world are thus supplied by gold and by short-term dollar balances, the latter produced, in effect, by U.S. international payments deficits. The very U.S. international deficits which are so often criticized have thus been the source of about a third of the Western world's entire basic international monetary reserves since World War II. In 1967, total free-world monetary gold-holdings were about $43 billion, and total U.S. short-term dollar liabilities to foreign central banks and international monetary organizations were about $16 billion.

The United States has thus, without conscious planning, become the banker to the free world. The dollar has become the "key," or "reserve," currency of that world. It is critical to this arrangement that dollars are freely convertible into gold by official holders, even though in some nations (for example, the United States) gold is not available domestically in exchange for currency. In many nations—for example, France and Switzerland—any large holder who has dollars can convert them into gold—by first converting the dollars into (say) francs at the fixed exchange rate and then buying gold with his francs. This will, in turn, reduce the Bank of France's gold stock and build up its supply of dollars, so that the Bank of France is likely to exchange some of its increased dollars for gold from the United States. Thus, in essence, under the gold-dollar reserve system,

foreign dollar-holders can demand gold in exchange on short notice. And it is clear from Fig. 40-3 that our short-term dollar liabilities far exceed our gold holdings.

But don't jump to the conclusion that we're internationally bankrupt and the dollar of dubious value. Far from it! The dollar is backed fundamentally by the powerful U.S. economy, by far the most efficient and productive in the world. And our total foreign assets, once we add in our vast long-term investments overseas, far exceed our total liabilities, as is shown by Table 40-1.

The U.S. is in much the position of any other banker. Though our basic position is excellent, our short-term liabilities substantially exceed our reserves and other short-term assets. Widespread confidence makes such systems work well. But we are a banker without deposit insurance. Internationally there is no F.D.I.C. to insure deposits or Federal Reserve to assure liquidity to temporarily frozen assets in case a confidence crisis develops. More on this dilemma in the following sections.

GOLD AND THE U.S. PAYMENTS PROBLEM

The U.S. has had a persistent, large balance-of-payments deficit for over 15 years. Why? There is no one simple answer; on the contrary, there have been many important forces at work. A brief summary might look like this.

1. *U.S. Foreign Aid and Government Loans.* Since World War II, we have provided government direct aid and loans totaling nearly $100 billion to the rest of the world. This aid has had military, economic, and humanitarian goals, widely approved by the American people. But the net result has been a vast outflow of dollars.

2. *U.S. Inflation.* During the decade following World War II, U.S. inflation pushed up prices and costs here relative to those in countries abroad where inflations were slower. This worsened our competitive position and kept U.S. exports below what would have been possible had our costs been more competitive. But since 1957 the U.S. record on inflation has been the best of any major Western nation. Our wholesale prices, which are the

TABLE 40-1

TOTAL FOREIGN ASSETS AND LIABILITIES OF THE UNITED STATES, JAN. 1, 1967 *

	In Billions
Assets:	
Gold	$13
U.S. short-term private investments abroad	10
U.S. long-term private investments abroad	76
U.S. Government claims abroad	26
Total assets abroad plus gold	$125
Liabilities:	
Short-term balances of central banks and international organizations	19
Short-term private balances	15
Long-term foreign investments here	28
Total liabilities to foreigners	62
Excess of assets over liabilities	$63

* Preliminary data, from Department of Commerce and Federal Reserve Board.

relevant ones for most international sales, have been generally stable over the past decade, while they have risen substantially in other major nations. Nor can rising American wages be blamed for a weakened international competitive position. Labor costs per unit of output in the U.S. were also almost flat from the late 1950's through 1965, while they rose appreciably in most major competing nations.

3. *U.S. Private Investment Abroad.* In recent years, the largest single element contributing to our payments deficit has been an enormous outflow of private capital seeking profitable investment in Western Europe, the Americas, and Japan. These private investments obviously seemed economically sound to the investors, else they would not have been made. And in the long run they produce a large countervailing flow of interest and dividends. But in the short run, their net effect is to increase the size of the U.S. payments deficit.

4. *Slower Productivity Growth Here than Abroad.* Since World War II, productivity has grown at a spectacular rate in Japan, Western Europe, and apparently the U.S.S.R. Our production technology is still ahead of theirs. But starting from a postwar low their heavy new investment and rapid technological advance closed this gap rapidly, even though U.S. productivity

continued to grow at about its long-run rate. During the 1950's the higher rate of productivity growth abroad was a fundamental cause of our persistent payments deficit.

But in recent years, our productivity growth rate has speeded up while those in Western Europe and the U.S.S.R. have slowed down somewhat. If this continues, our export surplus will widen still further as American productivity resumes its long-run leadership position.

5. *Lack of Confidence in the U.S. Economy and the Dollar.* Foreign capital will not be invested in the U.S., either at long or short term, if foreigners do not have confidence in the American economy and the stability of the dollar. Over the postwar period as a whole, both the dollar and the American economy have been widely agreed to be the soundest in the world. But as our efforts to reduce our payments deficit have fallen short in recent years, criticism has been widespread. The criticism is hard to assess. Even with the talk, foreigners continue to hold large volumes of dollars, and to invest large sums here. And they are anxious to borrow American dollars.

6. *An Overvalued Dollar.* Looking at all these factors and at the continuing U.S. payments deficit, some economists argue that the U.S. dollar is "overvalued." That is, the present exchange rate between the dollar and other major currencies

make it too hard for foreigners to buy American products and too easy for us to buy foreign products and to obtain foreign currencies for investment abroad. This reasoning suggests that we could eliminate the balance-of-payments deficit by devaluing the dollar, relative to other currencies and to gold. But other economists point to our large export surplus and argue that the present exchange rates are not the basic problem; rather the basic difficulty is the underlying "real" factors above. Moreover, it's not clear that we *can* devalue the dollar relative to other major currencies. If we devalue, they might devalue too, neutralizing our move. Few economists currently advocate U.S. devaluation.

Conflict and Compromise
between Foreign and Domestic Goals

Domestically, we want a high-employment, stably-growing economy. Internationally, we want to preserve the stability of the dollar as a foundation of a stable international payments system. Often these domestic and international goals are consistent, and the policy prescription is clear. If we have an inflationary boom, which leads to a growing import surplus and international payments deficit, we should use tight money and fiscal policy to solve both problems simultaneously. Similarly, the policy need is clear if we have unemployment and a payments surplus; then we need expansionary monetary and fiscal policy. But the United States in the first half of the 1960's provided a vivid example of the policy dilemma faced when domestic and international goals conflict.

Domestically, the problem was a slack economy. The standard policy prescription was budgetary stimulus and easier money, especially since there was little evidence of inflation. Wholesale prices were stable, and the economy seemed extraordinarily well balanced except for the under-utilization of labor and industrial capacity.

But internationally our continuing large payments deficit and substantial gold outflow called, under traditional gold-standard rules, for restrictive monetary and fiscal policy. These would check the rise in American incomes and prices, and decrease our imports while expanding our exports. But the U.S. deficit position of the 1960's

didn't fit the textbook pattern. Under the traditional theory, a nation's deficit should reflect falling exports and rising imports, usually resulting from an inflationary boom at home which raises costs and prices relative to other nations. However, the U.S. export surplus in the 1960's was spectacular. U.S. costs and prices showed the least inflation of any major nation. Our businesses were competing effectively in foreign markets. The U.S. payments deficit reflected huge private investments abroad and government aid, not a deteriorating export position.

In this situation, most American economists rejected tight money and restrictive fiscal policy to reduce the international payments deficit. Although higher U.S. interest rates might have reduced the capital outflow, they would also have checked private investment at home and worsened unemployment. Moreover, higher interest rates here might simply have induced other nations to raise their interest rates correspondingly. Indeed, tighter money might have *increased* the capital outflow if it had generated recession and falling profits in the U.S., since then both American and foreign funds might have moved abroad to seek higher profits there. In fact, much of our overseas investment is in equities and direct purchase of plant and equipment, for which the profit rate, not the interest rate, is the major inducement.

Still, nearly everyone agreed that doing nothing was also unacceptable. What would you have done? Remember that unemployment involves vast economic waste at home and loss of prestige and position abroad. But remember, too, the position of the dollar as the foundation of the international-payments system, and our responsibility as leaders of the free world's economic and military struggle against totalitarianism. The life of a central banker is not easy, nor is that of his fellow economic policy-makers in the Treasury and the White House. Nor, indeed, is that of the college economics student confronted with such dilemmas.

Are Fixed Exchange Rates
and Independent National Policies Compatible?

The U.S. and the other Western nations are trying to learn how to live under a new international-payments system, one with fixed exchange rates (the core of the old gold-standard adjust-ment system) but one where each nation reserves its right to take independent monetary and fiscal action to fit its own domestic needs. It is not clear just how basic international adjustments are to be assured under this system. In the world of today, when either surplus or deficit nations find the gold-standard prescriptions out of line with their domestic needs, they insist on freedom to decide for themselves between meeting domestic and international needs. If many nations say that domestic stabilization is more important than meeting international-payments requirements, and if deficit countries have large enough reserves to permit such policies over extended periods, the international adjustment mechanism may simply cease to function.

The U.S. position is critical because of the key-currency status of the dollar, our dominant position in world markets, and our role as supplier of investment capital to much of the world. Our continuing payments deficits have produced both growing international reserves and a mounting danger, overhanging the entire world payments system. The danger is that foreign dollar-holders might lose faith in U.S. willingness to provide gold freely for dollars and might create a massive "run" on the dollar. Then we might be required either to discontinue gold payments or to take other major restrictive measures against capital outflow. The resulting shock could undermine the entire international-payments system, as did the comparable run on the British pound in 1931, which then play a role much like the dollar's now. U.S. authorities are well aware of this danger. Yet the dilemma above remains. To take restrictive monetary and fiscal action with an underem-ployed domestic economy seems to many to have costs even higher than the potential international advantages.

What is Balance-of-Payments "Equilibrium"?

Nearly everyone lectures the Administration that it must nudge the U.S. balance of payments back toward "equilibrium." But, as a practical matter, it's not so clear just what that equilibrium means.

First, there's the issue of the "liquidity" vs. the "official settlements" definition of the deficit. On the liquidity basis, our cumulative deficit since 1960 is $17 billion, on the official settlements basis only about $14 billion. The biggest question here is how we should consider foreigners' holdings of dollar balances—as just a short-term investment, or as a demand (liquid) claim against our interna-tional reserves. Most other nations include such short-term balances as regular increases in foreign investment, not as deficit items. Until recently, Americans have generally used the broader defini-tion of the deficit, which makes our international position appear worse. Since 1965, our government has published the data on both bases.[3]

Whichever definition we use, should the U.S. strive for a continuous "equilibrium" posi-tion? Most economists would reply no. As a re-serve currency country, we should expect con-tinually to run a moderate deficit, since in a growing world economy other nations will want to hold a gradually increasing volume of dollars in their international reserves. The same would be true for any other reserve currency. Remem-ber that our large cumulative deficit over the past decade has dollar-for-dollar provided international reserves for other nations, supplementing the very small increase in world monetary gold stocks (from $40 billion in 1960 to $43 billion in 1967). Without our deficits, world liquidity would surely have been inadequate to finance the swelling vol-ume of world trade, which has more than tripled from $60 billion in 1950 to nearly $200 billion in 1967.

How big a deficit should we, as a reserve currency nation, aim at to attain true equilibrium in a growing world economy? Some have sug-gested an annual U.S. deficit of $.5 to $1 billion on the liquidity basis, but there is no simple answer. The right level will vary depending on gold production flowing into monetary reserves, on the present stock of dollars in world reserves, on the desire of other nations to hold dollars, and on the growth in desired total world monetary re-serves. This is an intricate problem for the experts. But remember that some payments deficit is prob-

[3] Note that if we use the liquidity basis while other nations use an official settlements basis, we can run per-sistent deficits without their ever appearing to run offsetting surpluses.

ably the most desirable approach to a true international equilibrium position for the U.S., as a reserve currency nation—at least pending basic reform of the international monetary system.

U.S. Payments Policy

U.S. policy between 1960 and 1966 illustrates a very basic fact. Wise policy-makers, when confronted by painful dilemmas, do not necessarily choose one or the other of the unattractive alternatives, but search for other ways. So, U.S. policy has neither accepted the traditional fixed-exchange deflationary prescription for a payments deficit, nor has it ignored the deficit and concentrated on domestic policy. Instead, we have followed a multi-faceted policy aimed at making the best of both situations while avoiding the worst aspects of each traditional policy alternative.

1. First, U.S. officials have persistently and firmly stated our intention to maintain the free convertibility of the dollar into gold at the present price. Maintenance of confidence in the integrity of the dollar among foreign holders is obviously essential to the success of the entire system. Even if we were to eliminate our basic deficits tomorrow, there would still be a large overhang of dollar balances whose holders might demand gold for them at any time.

2. The Federal Reserve and the Treasury have worked cooperatively with other central banks to assure stability of their dollar balances and to get their aid in calming down fears and uncertainties abroad. A 10-nation agreement was worked out to supplement the lending facilities of the International Monetary Fund, to be sure the U.S. or other nations could borrow foreign currencies to meet any crisis situation. Other special arrangements among central banks were developed to insure against calamitous runs on the dollar, or on other currencies. (The effectiveness of these international cooperative arrangements was demonstrated in 1964 when, in the face of an impending confidence crisis, a $3 billion loan to support the British pound was arranged among the 10 on two days notice.)

3. Longer-run steps to eliminate the basic payments deficit were pushed. Government officials exhorted American businessmen and workers to hold down American costs and prices, and to push exports in every way possible. The Kennedy-Johnson wage-price guideposts were made a major part of this push to improve America's position in export markets.

4. Government spending abroad was substantially reduced, partly through cutting back military outlays in Europe and aid to underdeveloped nations. Moreover, most of our overseas aid was "tied," requiring recipients to spend the aid dollars in the U.S.

5. To lessen long-term private-capital outflows, a special "interest-equalization tax" was placed on foreign borrowing in U.S. markets in 1963, and in 1965 an extensive program of "voluntary" restraints was established, under which U.S. businesses and financial institutions would restrict their foreign investments to a modest increase over the preceding year.

6. A new monetary-fiscal policy mix was developed. Fiscal policy was given the main job of stimulating the domestic economy, mainly through the tax cuts of 1964 and 1965. Meanwhile, monetary policy nudged short-term interest rates up while holding long-term rates stable. This mix was intended to stimulate domestic employment and output through tax reduction, to avoid counteracting effects from rising long-term interest rates, and to hold volatile short-term foreign balances in this country through higher short-term interest rates.

7. Radical measures were generally rejected. Devaluation of the dollar was rejected out of hand, as being unjustified and disruptive to the entire international monetary system. Drastic reduction of government foreign aid was rejected, because the aid was considered desirable on its own merits, but by "tieing" aid its negative pressure on our international payments was essentially eliminated. Drastic deflationary measures, in line with gold-standard prescriptions, were rejected because of their unacceptable impact on domestic employment and output.

Experts disagree on whether this was the right policy mix. On the domestic front, by and large the results were good. Internationally, the payments deficit has shrunk only slowly. However you evaluate the results, it is important to see that in the complex world of national and international economic affairs, one simple policy is seldom a fully satisfactory answer. The complex, compromise set of actions indicated above is far more typical. It is not surprising that simple, monolithic answers are seldom satisfactory for handling major economic problems. We have multiple national goals and the economic world is a complex of interacting forces.

LONG-RANGE REFORMS

The international tensions of the past decade over the U.S. payments deficit, leading nations' unwillingness to subordinate domestic needs to international-payments requirements, and the precarious over-all international liquidity situation engendered by reliance on U.S. deficits to provide a major part of the growth in international reserves, have led many observers to suggest fundamental changes in international monetary arrangements. We have space to look at only three of them.

Assuring Adequate International Liquidity

A growing world economy requires a growing volume of international reserves, just as a growing domestic economy requires a growing volume of money balances to make payments and provide working balances. Remember from above that world trade has grown from $50 billion to $200 billion annually since 1950. Under the gold standard, growing international reserves (liquidity) were provided by the simple process of digging gold out of the ground. This now seems to most economists an unsatisfactory and arbitrary basis for determining the amount of international liquidity, since gold mining is a private business, where output depends on current costs and prices, just as with any other commodity. Under the present system, U.S. payments deficits provide the other main source of growth for international liquidity. This too is an arbitrary and unreliable basis on which to expand international reserves. There is no reason to believe the U.S. payments deficit will be just right to provide the needed new reserves each year. Indeed, now there is great

pressure on the U.S. to eliminate its payments deficit. This would eliminate this source of growth in international reserves.

Not only is the U.S. deficit an unreliable source of the needed growth in international liquidity. From our point of view the system puts us in the uncomfortable, though profitable, position of banker for the world—with no deposit-insurance plan. Many nations and foreign businesses and individuals hold their reserves in dollars, but they have no guarantee other than our government's word that they will be able to get their balances in gold or in foreign currencies at fixed exchange rates when they want them. Thus, foreign dollar holders are understandably more skittish and worried than are most U.S. domestic depositors about their bank accounts.

To remedy this situation, Yale's Robert Triffin has proposed, in effect, a supranational bank, which would hold the reserves of the various national central banks and would be able to create new reserves to lend to them in the event of liquidity crises, just as central banks do domestically. Perhaps equally important, the existence of such a supranational bank could, he argues, so reassure international bankers and other foreign depositors that runs on particular currencies could be substantially eliminated. The new bank could then create basic international reserves as they were needed, avoiding reliance on either gold production or deficits of individual nations to provide the needed growth in liquidity for the growing international economy.

Most economists believe that this proposal goes too far too fast, and that it would require undesirable allocation of national economic sovereignty to the proposed supranational bank. Thus, several other less radical plans have been proposed. Most of them involve expanding the powers and resources of the International Monetary Fund, plus continuous close cooperation among central banks to avoid liquidity crises. Not surprisingly, nations differ substantially on these proposals, reflecting partly their national interests and likely advantages under the various plans.

But in 1967, members of the International Monetary Fund agreed in Rio de Janeiro on an evolutionary plan to expand "drawing rights" of member nations that need extra reserves to finance growing international trade. Such drawing rights will be, in effect, new international reserves, created through the IMF. New reserves can be created only by a vote of the member nations, and both the United States and the combined Common Market nations have effective veto powers. Details remain to be worked out over the years ahead. However limited its original form, the new agreement marks a major move toward reliance on planned cooperative international action to provide needed international reserves, to supplement traditional reliance on gold and deficits of reserve currency nations.[4]

The Future Role of Gold

What is the future role of gold in the world's international monetary system? To answer, one needs a crystal ball, especially because so much of gold's present role depends on centuries-old tradition and "psychology." Perhaps much of the common man's faith in gold as the ultimate repository of value is irrational; many economists would say so. But it is real, nonetheless—though clearly to a lessening degree in the U.S. and the Western industrialized world. Given the mixture of myth and reality that surrounds gold, what can we say of its future role? The following seem probable.

1. Gold will not vanish from the center, or near-center, of world monetary arrangements. It remains the one universally acceptable means of international payments. On the other hand, nations are unlikely to return gold to a position of close control over their domestic monetary policies.

2. Gold *plus* key currencies (most likely, the dollar) or plus more new international monetary reserves (most likely, based in the International Monetary Fund) will probably constitute the international monetary reserves of most "free world" nations. Many economists nowadays predict that the *relative* role of gold will decrease; this is far

from certain. Different countries will prefer different mixes of gold and other reserves, depending on their individual trade and financial relationships.

3. What about the proposal that the U.S. simply "go off the gold standard" by eliminating our commitment to exchange gold for dollars at a fixed rate? If fear of a gold drain prevents us from taking overwise desirable domestic policies, this may appear an attractive course. But it seems unlikely in the near future, for three main reasons.

First, such a step would be highly disruptive to free-world monetary and trade arrangements. Dollars now serve as basic reserves for most of our major friends and trading partners, reflecting in considerable part our repeated commitment to provide gold for the dollars on demand. International trade and, still more, long-term investments rest on confidence in the predictable convertibility of the foreign currencies received. As the devaluation of the British pound in 1931 triggered worldwide uncertainty and runs on other major currencies, so, probably, would an announcement of our refusal to continue redeeming dollars in gold at the promised rate.

Second, going off gold would threaten, possibly destroy, the dollar's position as the free world's key reserve currency, and with it this nation's profitable position as the world's banker. If other nations were unsure about the redeemability of dollars in gold, they would be far less likely to hold excess dollars as reserves. With this uncertainty, less of the world's trade would probably be carried on in terms of dollars. How much this development might injure our international trading and banking position is hard to say. Certainly it would be a blow to our international prestige and that of the dollar as "good as gold." Unfortunately, such a step would especially penalize our friends and economic allies who have continued to hold dollars rather than asking for gold. It would help nations (like France) which have refused to cooperate in strengthening the dollar-gold international system, and, if the price of gold rose as a result, major gold producers like South Africa and the U.S.S.R. would be major beneficiaries.

Third, there seems little need to incur these costs and risks, since our present gold policy leaves

[4] A good summary of alternative proposals is presented in *International Payments Imbalances*, a report of the Joint Economic Committee of Congress (Washington, D.C.: Government Printing Office, August, 1961). Lively, conflicting statements on the issues by leading economists and government officials are presented in Joseph, Seeber, and Bach, *Economic Analysis and Policy: Background Readings for Current Issues*.

us wide flexibility for monetary policies designed to meet domestic needs. Domestic monetary policy is now tied only loosely to the state of our gold stock—although as the gold stock dwindles the tie will become even closer if we maintain our promise to buy all dollars offered at the established price of $35 an ounce.

4. Stanford's Emile Despres and other economists have recently advanced a new plan to demonetize gold gradually and shift the international system to a frankly dollar-based system. They propose that the U.S. continue selling gold for dollars as promised now, as long as we have any gold—but that we discontinue our commitment to *buy* gold. This would not hurt our friends, who could still get our gold at $35 an ounce. But it would notify the world that we no longer intend to support the price of gold and enthrone gold as the center of our monetary arrangements.

Despres predicts that with such a U.S. announcement the price of gold would *fall*, not rise, and that nations would hurry to convert their gold into dollars before its price fell further. He reasons that gold is attractive to hold mainly because its holders are guaranteed against loss by the U.S. commitment to buy all gold offered at $35 per ounce. Without our guarantee, the demand for gold would drop. It is really dollars which have the purchasing power that matters, Despres argues, and he sees no reason we should guarantee foreign gold-holders against loss. He sees the result of his proposal as a widespread shift to a dollar standard, under which we would be freed from the danger of gold-conversion runs on the dollar. And he argues that his policy would not create panic in world financial affairs, because we would not repudiate our offer to give our gold to all comers at the $35 price.

It's not likely that the Despres proposal will be accepted soon. There are many uncertainties. Would the U.S. announcement actually reduce the world demand for gold, or merely trigger a run on our gold stock and destroy confidence in the dollar? If the plan worked and dollars supplanted gold as the *de facto* reserves of the world, wouldn't the U.S. responsibility be even greater than now for adapting our domestic policies to provide international stability? But even though Despres' basic reform may not be adopted, it raises the big

issues for anyone thinking through what would be the best international monetary arrangement.

5. One last comment: It is important to recognize that the case for a fixed gold-dollar tie and that for fixed exchange rates are related, but different. We could fix our exchange rates vis-à-vis other currencies by international agreement and appropriate domestic monetary-fiscal policies, without any commitment to buy or sell gold at a set price. Adherence to a fixed price for gold imposes the discipline upon us that we must ultimately adopt domestic policies consistent with maintaining stable exchange rates and avoiding depletion of our gold reserves. Whether we want to impose that discipline is a question that underlies the entire controversy.

Fixed Exchanges, Floating Rates, or a Sliding Peg?

The present mixed international monetary system combining fixed exchange rates and national independence, provides an uncertain mechanism for bringing about international adjustments. Sooner or later, deficit nations must face up to their loss of reserves. But payments deficits may persist for long periods where (as in the U.S.) nations have large reserves. The refusal of surplus nations to permit inflationary domestic expansions (as in Western Europe over the past decade) equally blocks the effectiveness of the adjustment mechanism. Above all, if we are to live with this system we must learn to expect adjustments to come more slowly and to avoid crises because adjustments do not occur rapidly.

Many economists argue that the basic system itself must be changed to facilitate international adjustments. Academic attacks on the present system generally point toward two basic reforms: substitution of flexible for fixed exchange rates, or adoption of a "sliding peg" whereby exchange rates are adjusted gradually to fit shifting international cost-price relationships.

Flexible ("*Floating*") *Exchange Rates.* Freely fluctuating ("floating") exchange rates would automatically reflect excess demand or supply of any currency. As the price of that currency moved up or down, it would correspondingly discourage or stimulate imports into the country, and conversely for exports—thus directly pulling the country's balance of payments back into equilibrium. Moreover, the floating exchange rate would *directly* affect the prices of the nation's exports and imports. This is in contrast to the fixed exchange system, where the adjustment is brought about by an expansion or contraction of aggregate demand affecting the whole economy. With floating rates, no central bank or treasury needs to intervene to help achieve equilibrium; freely fluctuating exchange rates do the job automatically. Here again, the marketplace will do the job if we free it from restrictions.

But there is strong objection from men of affairs. Floating rates would impose major barriers to international trade and lending, because creditors would never know what their future receipts would be in terms of their own currency. Importers, lenders, and borrowers alike would face serious uncertainties on all except the shortest-term transactions. While floating rates might make over-all international adjustments easier, as a practical matter they'd kill the goose that lays the golden eggs—trade and lending itself.

Economists have an answer. Just as in the markets for wheat and copper, organized "futures" markets in different currencies would develop in which importers and exporters could buy and sell currencies for delivery at the future date needed, thus eliminating the uncertainty produced by possibly fluctuating rates. They could "hedge" against the possibility of higher or lower prices for the foreign currency involved.

But there is a counter-answer. Businessmen and bankers doubt that effective forward markets would actually develop in all major currencies, especially for long-term commitments. And both they and some economists fear that speculation on such forward markets might be destabilizing instead of stabilizing to rates themselves. With commodities the cost of production provides a central level around which prices tend to move. With foreign exchange rates there is no cost of production to serve as a stabilizing force. Instead, if the dollar weakened, speculators might lose confidence in it and all decide to sell dollars at once, driving the dollar rate far down.

Clearly, the issue of fixed versus flexible exchange rates is a complex one. It is likely to be a source of lively controversy for many years to come.

The "Sliding Peg." Facing this dilemma, many economists favor an intermediate compromise—the "sliding peg." This policy would recognize the need to keep exchange rates substantially stable as a foundation for foreign trade and lending. But it would deviate from fixed exchanges in two ways. First, it would permit exchange rates to fluctuate moderately (say by 1 to 3 per cent on each side of parity) under market pressures, so they could do part of the equilibrating job. Second, if a currency proved consistently to move above or below par vis-à-vis other currencies, the par (peg) itself could be adjusted gradually, say by 1 or 2 per cent a year. This sliding peg would be responsive to the fact that costs and prices do move differently in different nations, for example reflecting different rates of technological progress. But the changes would be gradual enough to retain most of the benefits from fixed rates.

The sliding peg doesn't solve the basic dilemma if one nation gets badly out of international equilibrium—say, because its technical progress is very slow or because it tries to live beyond its international means by importing much more than it exports. But it does offer a more flexible system than the present one, without running the risks involved in a more drastic shift to a floating rate system.

The painful fact is that no one has discovered a sure-fire system for assuring basic balance-of-payments adjustments without unwanted pressures on domestic economies. Assurance of adequate international liquidity, to avoid crises while adjustments are taking place, can help. And we must recognize that under the present system international adjustments to eliminate payments disequilibria may be very slow, compared to earlier expectations. If we want the system to work we must learn to suppress alarm and disruptive speculation merely because deficits are not eliminated overnight. But the present system seems fully satisfactory to almost no one, and there is little doubt that the search for more effective arrangements will be active over the years ahead.

For Analysis and Discussion

1. Should the United States be concerned about its continuing balance-of-payments deficit? If so, what should we do about it?
2. Do we now have enough gold for domestic and international reserve purposes? How much do we really need? Explain.
3. Should the 25 per cent gold backing requirement against Federal Reserve notes be eliminated to free all our gold for international use?
4. Given our persistent payments deficit, should we tighten credit and raise interest rates here to reduce the heavy outflow of American capital, both short and long term? In your answer consider both possible effects on domestic economic activity and possible actions by foreign nations in response.
5. How can we have a continuing balance-of-payments deficit when our exports exceed our imports by a wide margin?
6. Should we reduce our foreign-aid program and military expenditures abroad in order to protect our gold stock?
7. "Our continued balance-of-payments deficits clearly say that we are not competitive enough abroad and that restrictive monetary-fiscal policy is needed to restrain American prices and wages so we can become more competitive." Do you agree? What would be the likely consequences of such a policy?
8. Why shouldn't we simply go off the gold standard, discontinuing our purchase and sale of gold at $35 an ounce, to eliminate our gold-shortage problem?
9. What are the advantages and disadvantages of a new international liquidity plan to provide additional international reserves, as against the gold-dollar system used since World War II?

Appendix

RECENT DEVELOPMENTS VIS-A-VIS GOLD

In March, 1968, responding to a massive "run" to convert dollars and other major currencies into gold, the central banks of ten major nations agreed on a new gold policy. They jointly stated that (1) they would no longer sell gold except to one another, and that (2) they saw no need to buy further gold except from each other to serve as international monetary reserves. They noted that under a new international agreement, the International Monetary Fund would soon begin issuing Special Drawing Rights (SDR's) to supplement the existing stock of gold as an international monetary reserve. Other central banks were invited to join the agreement.

In effect, this proclamation was a major step toward the demonetization of gold internationally. Each central bank was protected as to the value of its gold holdings, since it could exchange them with other major central banks at official exchange rates

(based on $35 per ounce for gold). At the same time, the world free gold market was dissociated from the international and domestic monetary positions of the various nations. The free market price of gold might rise above $35, or even possibly fall below, depending on the supply of gold (largely from South African mines) and the demand for industrial uses and hoarding.

Whether this "two-price" system for gold will be long-lived remains to be seen. The history of "two-price" systems in economics is not bright. However, if the central banks of the ten major nations, increasingly joined by other nations, adhere firmly to the new plan, there is no reason it could not persist indefinitely, gradually moving the world to a completely "managed" reserve basis away from reliance on gold.

CURRENT RESEARCH

Research in the area of international economic affairs has snowballed since World War II. The U.S. balance-of-payments deficit and our gold position have been front-page news, and interest in the European "Common Market" has not lagged far behind. Leaving aside our problems vis-à-vis the underdeveloped areas (covered in Part Two), the following sample may provide some impression of the lively probing into international economics in recent years.

Gold and the Balance of Payments. A useful, relatively simple beginning is provided by Walter Salant's, "Does the International Monetary System Need Reform?" (Brookings, 1964), or by Henry Aubrey's *The Dollar in World Affairs* (Praeger, 1964). Then try Fritz Machlup's "The Cloakroom Rule of International Reserves," in the *Quarterly Journal of Economics*, August, 1965. Robert Roosa, an economist and former Undersecretary of the Treasury, presents his analysis in "Balance of Payments Adjustment and International Liquidity" (*Journal of Finance*, March, 1964); while Walter Salant and his colleagues use their analytical approach to peer five years into the future in *The U.S. Balance of Payments in 1968* (Brookings, 1963). Gold is the focus of M. A. Kriz' interesting *Gold: Barbarous Relic or Useful Instrument* (Princeton International Finance Section, 1967). A difficult, but fascinating, attempt to assess the relative domestic and international costs of different policies is R. A. Mundell's "Capital Mobility and Stabilization Policies under Fixed and Flexible Exchange Rates" (*Canadian Journal of Economics and Political Science*, November, 1963).

The Common Market and U.S. Trade Policies. For an overview of the economic issues raised by the new European "Common Market," try *The Common Market: Progress and Controversy*, L. Krause, ed. (Prentice-Hall, 1964). Pennsylvania's Irving Kravis presents his readable analysis in "Common Market —Lesson in Trade Expansion" (*Harvard Business Review*, March, 1962). A more advanced analysis is provided by Michigan State's M. Kreinin in "Effects of an Atlantic Free Trade Area on the American Economy" (*Southern Economic Journal*, July, 1966).

A broad picture of research on U.S. tariff policy is provided by *Foreign Trade Policy*, a compendium for the Foreign Trade Policy Subcommittee of the House Committee on Ways and Means (1958). Many of the papers are partisan pleas by industry representatives, but the papers by Piquet, Salant, and Kravis are interesting, readable, analytical research pieces. On the effects of widely differing national growth rates in productivity, try Richard Cooper's "International Aspects," in *Automation and Technical Change* (The American Assembly: Prentice-Hall, 1962). Lastly, *A New Trade Policy for the United States*, by the Committee for Economic Development (1962), though not original research, provides a good example of how economic analysis and data can be used at a nontechnical level in reaching reasoned policy conclusions.

A quite different aspect of our foreign economic relationships is pictured by T. Geiger in *The General Electric Company in Brazil* (National Planning Association, 1961), one of a series of studies of U.S. private firms that are operating in other lands.

PART SEVEN

PERSPECTIVES
ON ECONOMIC CHANGE

FORTY-ONE

THE ECONOMICS
OF CHANGE

Midway and O'Hare Airports: Chicago.

"Automation."

Disarmament.

Conclusion.

Change is evident everywhere in economic life. It is the blood of a dynamic economy. On the world front, we face a population explosion of staggering dimensions. By the year 2000 the world's population may double—another three billion people, most of them in the poverty-stricken non-Western nations that today look askance at our wealth and power. At home, a century ago 60 per cent of our jobs were in agriculture, now 6 per cent are. Massive population concentrations in urban areas are creating problems never dreamed of before. "Automation"—rapid technological advance —is revolutionizing manufacturing processes. The electronic computer has replaced thousands of clerical workers, and many believe it will soon replace lower and middle management in their decision-making functions. Patterns of consumer demand have changed dramatically over our lifetimes. Our spending on services has skyrocketed, so that today more people earn their living by producing consumer services than physical commodities. One family in five moves each year. Many of the "sure things" in business flop, a few of the longshots win. I.B.M., scarcely known 25 years ago, last year had a market value on the New York Stock Exchange approaching that of General Motors and greater than that of U.S. Steel. Fifty years ago, International Mercantile Marine was the nation's fourth largest business, U.S. Leather the seventh; who knows them today? General Motors, the largest manufacturing corporation in the world today, did not even exist.

The process of economic change presents an unrivaled opportunity to apply the economic concepts and theory developed earlier in this book. This chapter consists of three brief case studies;

then a final section summarizes some of the central elements of the way our economy adjusts to rapid economic change. The first case is a simple, though dramatic, one—the precipitous shift of virtually all airline travel into and out of Chicago from the old Midway airport on the south side to the new O'Hare airport on the north. The second is the impact of rapid nationwide technological change—some call it "automation." The third is a case where the change is government-induced—the impact of rapid disarmament should a big cutback in defense spending become feasible.

Like the earlier studies of poverty and insecurity, these cases call for an orderly job of problem-solving, using the tools of both macro and micro theory. We need to define the problem: where are we, how did we get there, and what are our objectives? We need to analyze the situation, using the theory at our command, and to lay out promising alternative policies to achieve our objectives. We need to evaluate these alternatives carefully, and decide which looks best. Here, as before, a crucial part of the job is to clarify your objectives and balance them against one another when you must accept less of one to have more of another. Particularly in looking at economic change, potential conflicts crop up everywhere among the goals of growth, economic security, and different notions of equity in the distribution of income.

MIDWAY AND O'HARE AIRPORTS: CHICAGO

Ten years ago, Midway Airport on the south side of Chicago was the world's busiest field. During rush hours planes landed and took off one a minute. Millions of passengers passed through in a year. Virtually every major airline flew into and out of the airport, and most maintained passenger service and other facilities in its sprawling buildings. Near-by were elegant motels, restaurants, hot-dog stands, filling stations, parking lots, and a multitude of other enterprises, all aimed at speeding the traveler on his way and earning a profit from him en route.

Then came the jets! Midway, barely large enough for big propeller-driven planes and squeezed on all sides by residential and business areas, was obsolete overnight. The huge new O'Hare International Airport, far out in the farmlands north of Chicago was rushed to completion. Miles of runways, acres of shining steel and glass, the most modern facilities for passengers and planes—all these made O'Hare by 1962 one of the model airports of the world, capable of handling huge planes and an enormous volume of traffic.

By 1962, a walk through Midway's sprawling terminals was a walk through a graveyard—long, dusty corridors, closed-down shops and restaurants, a few local airline counters. From being the world's busiest airport, suddenly Midway became a field used only by local feeder lines and private and freight planes. Near-by, motels permanently displayed vacancy signs. Parking lots were empty. Restaurants and hot-dog stands struggled to keep alive or closed their doors. Property values plummeted; bankruptcies soared.

The almost complete displacement of Midway by O'Hare in four short years is a classic case of economic change on a local level. With the jets, consumer demands for modern air travel simply could not be met at Midway. The federal government, as with other major airports, financed much of the basic landing facilities and equipment at O'Hare. The major airlines and a wide variety of auxiliary services, speeded by the profit motive, lost little time in shifting to O'Hare where full advantage could be taken of technological advances, and excellent service could be rendered to customers. Capital and jobs moved swiftly from Midway to O'Hare.

Since the airports are only 30 miles apart, it was relatively easy for workers to move if they chose to do so. Most of the airlines offered all Midway workers jobs at O'Hare, though for many older workers uprooting residences of many years' standing in south Chicago and making the long move out into the suburbs was difficult and uninviting. Much capital was more immobile. Owners of valuable land near the airport saw a big part of their wealth wiped out overnight. Land cannot move; when demand for it drops, its value drops accordingly. (Remember the analysis of capitalization in Chapter 33.) So it was for other relatively fixed investments at Midway—airline facilities, restaurants, shops, motels, and the like. If they could not be moved their value dropped as demand moved away. Investments in new expensive enterprises were especially hard hit. Such investors, failing to foresee the change, paid the price for their mistake in sharply reduced returns (and hence also plummeting capital values) on their buildings and facilities.

At O'Hare, just the opposite happened. New jobs opened up by the thousands. Land values around the airport soared. Motels and filling stations sprang up like mushrooms. Valuable concessions were let in the huge new terminal buildings. The airlines invested millions of dollars in facilities for passengers, freight, and equipment, all with an eye to more profits by handling more customers and cargo.

What was the end result of the move? A rapid response to shifting technology and changing consumer demand, implemented partly through government investment in the new airport itself but mainly through profit-seeking private enterprises. Vastly improved service for airline customers. Windfalls for property owners near O'Hare, and big profits for those who forsaw the change. Headaches, heartaches, and financial disaster for property owners and others left behind at Midway. Greater profits for the airlines who moved to O'Hare and invested in the new facilities.

What is the lesson of Midway and O'Hare? Many would say it is a shining example of how well our system can adjust to dramatic technological change and rising consumer demands, under the impetus of private enterprise with a little government assistance. Few argued for government aid to those left behind, or government measures to seize windfall gains from those who benefited in and around O'Hare. Because the move was local and airlines offered new jobs at O'Hare, information on new jobs and mobility to them posed relatively small problems for airline workers. Related enterprises, like the motels and restaurants, had to do the best they could. If they looked far ahead and bet right on the jets, they were among those first on the scene at O'Hare and prepared to move out of Midway as the market fell. If they didn't see ahead, they were left behind. Chicago is a big city, and Midway was a tiny part

of the area job-market. Should government—federal, state, or local—have done less or more?

"AUTOMATION"

Next consider "automation," the name some observers give to rapid technological advance that appears directly to displace workers. You see the headlines everywhere. "Electronic Computer Displaces 200 Clerks." "Fully Automated Assembly Line Installed." Ninety per cent of the nation's light bulbs are turned out by glass-blowing machines tended by 14 operators. A machine run by ten workers produces the same number of auto engine blocks turned out by 400 men ten years ago. Automation has been widely hailed as the foundation of modern industrial progress, and as widely decried as a monstrous threat to the jobs of millions of workers.

Does (will) automation cause widespread unemployment? Can the market system adjust satisfactorily to rapid technological progress? Who is helped and who is hurt?

Technological Advance, Progress, and Unemployment

Over the past century, output per man-hour in private employment has grown about 2 per cent per annum, reflecting technological advance, capital investment, improved education and skills of workers, and the variety of other factors outlined in Chapters 15 and 16.

Since World War II, this rate has stepped up to over 3 per cent. If this recent rate of 3 per cent continues (reflecting, remember, technological advance *and* other factors), over the decade ahead output must increase enough each year to provide new jobs for about two million workers no longer needed to produce the preceding year's output. That is, in 1967 the $780 billion g.n.p. was produced by 74 million civilian workers, but in 1968 the same output could be produced by only 72 million people, since on the average each worker could produce about 3 per cent more. Technological advance is vital to economic progress and our rising standard of living. Freeing two million workers each year to produce other wanted goods or to permit more leisure for all with the same output looks impressive indeed.

But technological advance is a two-edged sword. If you're a worker thrown out of a job by a new machine, you don't care much about the gross national product. You have to find another job to keep the pay checks coming in. And especially if you're middle-aged with only one skill which you've developed over a lifetime in your present job, finding another job at equal pay, or even finding another job at all, may be difficult indeed. Technological progress is a boon to society, and it may be a disaster to some individuals in that society.

Does "Automation" Cause Unemployment? Obviously automation may cause unemployment for the man thrown out of work by a new machine which does his job better or cheaper. But remember the oft-repeated warning above about the fallacy of composition. Just because Willie the welder is temporarily thrown out of work doesn't necessarily mean that there will be more unemployment in the whole economy. Indeed, both economic theory and experience give the same answer: the alarmist cries that machines will soon consign millions of men to involuntary unemployment rest more on fancy than on fact.

The historical record is clear. Over more than a century of rapid, perhaps increasingly rapid, technological progress, there is no evidence that the unemployment rate has increased. On the contrary, our economic system has shown impressive ability over the decades to provide useful jobs for not only displaced workers but for new additions to a growing labor force as well. There has consistently been some unemployment, reflecting in part lags in the adjustment to economic change. More vividly, there have been intermittent periods of mass unemployment, but these have come with recessions and weak aggregate demand, not with periods of especially rapid technological advance. On the contrary, rapid technological advance and *falling* unemployment have generally come together in business upswings, and relatively slow technological advance and rising unemployment have come together in downswings.

Economic theory explains why technological change per se is unlikely to be the cause of continuing large-scale unemployment. Part Two taught the big lesson about economy-wide unem-

ployment: Mass unemployment generally reflects a shortage of aggregate demand. And the final section of Chapter 31 showed how, if there is adequate aggregate demand, automation will lead to a redistribution of workers among industries and types of jobs, but will change the level of total employment little if at all. New machines will replace people in some jobs, but the same total stock of workers will continue to find employment through shifting to jobs where their comparative advantage is highest. But a necessary condition, remember, is that displaced workers do not insist on wages above their (possibly reduced) marginal value products.

Given market imperfections, inadequate information on job opportunities, and worker immobility, the adjustment process may be slow, and some individual workers may never be reabsorbed. But in such cases, the finger of blame should be placed where it belongs—on market imperfections and immobilities (for example, on prejudices against hiring older workers or on poor information about job openings elsewhere), not on technological advance per se. Adequate total demand assures that the total labor force can be employed, making reasonable allowance for immobilities and delays, so long as workers do not insist on wages above their marginal value products. And the micro market mechanism helps wages and prices to allocate new machines and workers into those productive channels where the comparative advantage (marginal product per dollar of cost) of each is highest. (Go back and review the underlying analysis on pp. 412–414 if the process isn't clear in your mind.)

Can We Trust the Market?

In 1962, a prestigious President's Advisory Committee on Labor-Management Policy, composed of top businessmen, labor leaders, and professional economists, reported unanimous agreement on these "fundamental points" about automation:

1. Automation and technological progress are essential to the general welfare, the economic strength, and the defense of the nation.
2. This progress can and must be achieved without the sacrifice of human values.

3. Achievements of technological progress without the sacrifice of human values requires a combination of private and governmental action, consonant with the principles of a free society.

If we accept this general position, what combination of private and governmental measures does economic analysis suggest? Can we have rapid progress, economic security, and an equitable distribution of the fruits of progress, all three? Not if we leave it entirely up to the market, the Committee said.

Aggregate Demand Policies

Stably growing aggregate demand is the first requisite for progress through technological change without unemployment. In periods of prosperity, workers displaced by technological advance find it relatively easy to move to new jobs. Indeed, then few workers are actually displaced; with growing market demand and advance planning, employers can generally shift displaced workers to other jobs in the firm as such jobs open up through normal labor turnover and retirements. New entrants into the labor force move into new job openings elsewhere. The shift in labor induced by technical progress is accomplished smoothly, with little need for older workers to move to new companies and new locations.

But note that total demand must grow enough to provide new jobs for the workers displaced by technological advance if long-run unemployment is to be avoided. If displaced workers were willing to accept lower wages in new jobs, a correspondingly smaller increase in aggregate demand would be enough to avoid unemployment. But widespread wage reductions in our economy seem unlikely, and most economists recommend growing aggregate demand to match technological advance. Wise governmental monetary and fiscal policies are the first-line defense against technological unemployment, as against other general unemployment.

Government Policies
To Improve Labor Markets

Even with adequate aggregate demand, technological progress may force difficult adjustments on displaced workers, especially older work-

ers and those heavily committed to now-obsolete skills. The market provides no guarantee that each individual worker will find a new job as good as the one he loses. But it is to everyone's advantage that he find a new job as promptly as possible where he can make his greatest contribution to total output. If the displaced worker stays unemployed because of poor information on other job openings, lack of opportunity to learn new skills, or geographical immobility, both he and society suffer. He is unemployed, and society wastes potential output.

Many economists urge greater government aid to displaced workers in finding new jobs. Most European governments do much more to provide information on job openings, to help retrain unemployed workers, and to provide funds for moving expenses than we do. These governmental activities would be very difficult for the individual to undertake efficiently on his own, but they promise to benefit society as a whole as well as the individual. Thus, there is a public good to be served, over and above the case for helping the worker as an individual.

On a longer-term basis, government can also help by providing better education and training for both youths and older workers. In a rapidly changing society, most workers will have to learn new job skills one or several times during their lives. In an individualistic society, we largely count on individuals to obtain skills for themselves after they leave school, and on employers to provide training in new skills where this will augment their profits. But this may be a haphazard process, which leaves many displaced workers without retraining. Thus, many observers ask, why should government's educational role end with young people? Wouldn't governmental responsibility for skill training over the individual's entire productive career make sense for the general welfare?

In Western Europe, nations also do more than we to bring investment to depressed areas and to unemployed workers, instead of moving displaced workers to jobs elsewhere. Italy, West Germany, France, Denmark, Belgium, and the United Kingdom all adopted legislation during the 1950's to assist local economic development. Government loans, grants, and tax concessions are used to channel new investment into areas of unemployment. In the United States, the Area Redevelopment Act of 1961 and the Appalachian Program of 1965 represent tentative moves in the same direction here. TVA in the depressed Tennessee Valley during the 1930's was a major example of this approach.

Private Employer-Employee Agreements on Automation

The President's Labor-Management Advisory Council of 1962 urged management and labor to work out their own plans jointly to permit rapid technological change while softening the impact on individual workers. Agreements covering the introduction of new methods and new machines are now common in union contracts. Many contracts provide that management must notify the union in advance when new processes and machinery are to be introduced; often, displaced workers are guaranteed any other jobs in the company before any new employees can be hired for them. Many companies provide extensive retraining for their own workers. Increasingly, technological change is managed so that it occasions few layoffs. The burden of adjustment is thrown on new entrants into the labor force, generally young people who are reasonably mobile and flexible and who may suffer less from temporary unemployment than do older workers with families.

Unions are sometimes adamantly opposed to automation which threatens their members' jobs. For example, for years the newspaper unions have delayed, or blocked completely, the introduction of highly automated devices for setting type, and have enforced their demands through effective strikes, though the new methods are far cheaper. The railway workers' brotherhoods have permitted technological advance (for example, diesel locomotives) but have fought to maintain their jobs even where the work was no longer needed. Some employers, faced by strong unions adamantly opposed to rapid technological advance, have worked out novel agreements which in effect buy union acquiesence to rapid technological change by providing generous benefit payments to displaced workers. The West Coast longshoremen are one example. They have extremely generous layoff and other benefits in exchange for their cooperation in

introducing cost-saving changes. The Kaiser Steel agreement of the early 1960's gives union members a direct share with stockholders in the gains from technical progress. Over many years, the United Mineworkers have cooperated in introducing technological change in return for high wages and generous retirement and medical aid plans. *Question:* If you were president of a steel company, would you agree to a plan like Kaiser Steel to share the benefits of automation with your workers?

How far employers find it advantageous to go in buying labor cooperation in introducing automation varies from industry to industry. Employer resentment at worker resistance to cost-saving improvements runs high. But it is clear that the mores of the times have changed. The employer's right to hire and fire is no longer absolute. The "rights" of employees to their jobs have become a moral and legal reality, increasingly built into union contracts.

In any case, private union-management agreements protect only the interests of workers in the firm or union concerned. Job security for these workers merely throws the burden of adjustment to technological progress on new workers (especially teenagers) who as yet have no jobs to protect.

The Shorter Work Week and Barriers to Automation

It is not surprising that workers worry about technological change that threatens their jobs. One major response, on both the national and individual-industry levels, has been a strong union push for a shorter work week "to create more jobs." Union leaders argue that a shorter work week, with the same weekly wage, would create jobs for displaced workers and new entrants into the labor force, and would simultaneously maintain aggregate demand for the products of those workers. Increasing union pressure has been brought on employers to cut the normal work week from 40 to 35 hours, and on the government to reduce the legal work week above which employers must pay premium overtime rates.

What does economic analysis tell us about the likely consequences of such proposals?

First, suppose that the work week in industry

is cut from 40 to 35 hours, with no change in the hourly wage rate. (Note that this is *not* the union proposal.) This plan obviously would just spread the existing amount of work among more people. Average weekly wages would fall, but the total wage bill and the output of the industry would be unchanged. The change would not significantly change either cost per unit of output or demand for the industry's product. It would "solve" the unemployment problem by taking some work and pay away from those who would otherwise work 40 hours and spreading it more widely to include those who might otherwise be unemployed.

It should be clear that the net effect is to reduce the total *potential* g.n.p. by the five hours of work given up by each worker. Real g.n.p. would be larger if everyone worked 40 hours, not 35. Perhaps, if it were impossible to provide jobs for the labor force on a 40-hour basis, it would be better to spread the work around. But if there is an unemployment problem, it would be better to raise aggregate demand to provide higher total employment at existing wage rates. Unless we really want more leisure instead of more jobs and more goods produced, this shorter-work-week approach would just accept wastage of potential productive capacity.

Second, suppose the industry work week is cut from 40 to 35 hours, but the weekly wage is kept unchanged. This is the proposal unions generally make. Here the picture is significantly different. Unless hourly output per worker increases one-eighth with reduced hours, labor costs per unit of output are raised by the change. Under competitive conditions, this will require higher prices; and the result will be reduced sales and production unless demand for the product increases. Unfortunately, there is nothing in the picture to lead to such an increase in demand for the industry's product. Even if the industry's workers receive higher total wages, they will spend most of their new incomes on the products of other industries. The predictable result, therefore, is fewer hours of work available.

Most union leaders disagree with this analysis. In many industries, they say, price need not rise. Most firms have generous profits so they can afford to pay higher wages and keep prices stable.

Then more workers would have to be taken on to continue producing the goods being sold. Or employers can increase efficiency to offset higher wage costs. But this appears to most economists to be wishful thinking. Profits are seldom large enough to absorb big wage increases per unit of output, and there is seldom enough "slack" in efficiency to permit such cost absorption either.

Third, suppose a 35-hour work week were somehow introduced for the entire economy, cutting the average work week from 40 hours. Again, unless hourly productivity was correspondingly increased by the shorter hours, wage costs per unit of output would rise and either other costs would have to be reduced, profits would be reduced, or prices would have to be increased. Since profits in the economy at large are obviously insufficient to absorb such a large wage increase and since it is unlikely that the pressure could induce such massive cuts in other costs (remember that wages account for around two-thirds of total costs for the economy), higher prices would be the likely response. If, then, monetary-fiscal policy stepped in to raise aggregate demand proportionately, the net result would be mainly inflation to match the higher wage cost per unit of output. Prices and money wages would be higher, but the total real g.n.p. would be only that producible by a 35-hour week, significantly lower than the output of a 40-hour week. Inflation and lower production would be the main results.

Alternatively, suppose the government stands firm against inflation and refuses to validate the higher prices through expansionary monetary-fiscal policy. Then the net result of the higher labor costs and higher prices would be a reduced volume of sales, less work available, and unemployment. Again, the result would be less real g.n.p. and less work because of the 35-hour work week.

The economist's answer to these problems is reasonably clear. If we voluntarily choose to reduce the work week to 35 hours because we prefer leisure over the products of the extra five hours of work, this can be a rational individual and social choice. But to accept a reduced standard of living (either with or without higher money wages) as an imagined solution to the threat of automation would be short-sighted policy indeed.

Progress, Security, and Equity

The nation benefits through greater output from technological advance. But how about the distribution of burdens and benefits? Should displaced workers and investors whose capital equipment has been made obsolete by automation bear the bulk of the cost, even if they did no wrong? Should management which introduces the innovation reap the lion's share of the benefits through higher profits? Should the gains be shared with labor in the same industry? Or should they be distributed generally to the population through lower prices as costs fall? Broadly, how high a reward do we want the system to provide for those who correctly anticipate change under uncertainty, and how far should government go to aid those injured by technological change?

In broad perspective, the macro facts are clear. Both wages and profits gain from technological progress. More advanced theories tell us this will happen under a wide range of conditions, and the facts of history back up the theories. The questions surrounding automation mainly involve its micro effects on the relative positions of different workers and industries, and *how much* of the total gain will go to profits and to wages at the macro level.[1]

A widespread policy of price reductions as costs fall with technical progress could spread the benefits widely to all users. But this would imply stable money wage rates and profits in the industry, a result neither unions nor management would like, and we have no means of enforcing such a policy. Far more likely, profits and wage rates will rise with technical advance, on the average enough to absorb the direct cost savings and to keep product prices from falling much. This approach will divide the main benefits of automation between wages and profits, with nothing going to fixed-income groups since prices do not fall. If inflationist fears are right, then wages, profits and prices will all creep upward in spite of cost-reducing technical advance.

In recent years, unions have successfully de-

manded job security for their members and costly benefits as their price for acquiescence in the introduction of technological change. Even so, many union leaders argue that we have not gone far enough to protect the innocent individual worker against technological change over which he has no control. In addition to his case as a human being and a worker, they say he will work harder and cooperate better if his interests are protected in a reasonable way. But the management counter-argument stresses that, as the costs of technological innovation are increased, the rate of innovation will be slowed, to the detriment of everyone.

It is clear we need some combination of private and governmental policies that will allay the fears of workers, employers, and the general public that automation may generate large-scale unemployment. For unless these fears are allayed, union action and resistance of individual workers will slow technological advance, often with the support of the general public. The American people want faster growth and a better life. But they have a long history of concern for the underdog. And without better understanding, this concern may well mistakenly and unintentionally check that very technological change on which our economic progress so heavily rests.[2]

DISARMAMENT

The third case of economic change is disarmament, a government-induced change if it comes. Would peace bring unemployment and economic disaster? This may seem a shocking question, but the communists argue that a major reason for our large defense program is to avoid unemployment and depression. Marxist doctrine

[1] For an excellent elementary treatment of this issue, see H. A. Simon, *The Shape of Automation* (New York: Harper and Row, 1965), Chapters 1 and 2.

[2] Why is the automation case different from Midway-O'Hare, where most people were content to let private initiative and the market work out the problems largely unaided? First, automation is nationwide, not merely local. Second, with automation there is no guarantee short of government action that aggregate demand will be maintained; whereas the Midway-O'Hare shift occurred in response to strong consumer demand in the economic sector involved so there was no danger of a shortage of the relevant demand. Third, job information and worker mobility were high in the local Midway-O'Hare shift, whereas nationwide automation raises difficult and far-reaching problems on these scores.

says that massive depression arising from shortage of consumer buying power will bring the downfall of the capitalist system, and today's communists say we dare not end the arms race because the result would be massive unemployment at home.

In 1967, defense spending was nearly $80 billion annually, 10 per cent of our g.n.p. Suppose a peaceful settlement in Vietnam or a general lessening of international tensions permitted us to cut this defense spending by $20 billion. Twenty billion dollars is about 2½ per cent of the gross national product, and it would give every family in the United States about $400 more to spend as it pleases if taxes were cut correspondingly. Or with $20 billion we could clear and rebuild vast slum areas in every major city in the United States. We could dramatically improve the quality of education from kindergarten through college. For the cost of one modern big bomber, we could build 10 modern brick schools, or a new electric power plant to serve a city of 100,000 people, or two fully-equipped modern hospitals.

But would we dare cut government spending by $20 billion to get these benefits? Here again we need to use both macro and micro theory to understand the likely results. What will be the impact on aggregate demand, and on the allocation of resources and incomes? And like the other cases we have analyzed, disarmament raises difficult questions of trade-offs among social goals, especially among progress, security, and widely held notions of equity in income distribution.[3]

Aggregate-Demand Policy

Macro theory tells us that a $20 billion cutback in government spending would reduce g.n.p. and employment, unless it were offset by some other force. Indeed, multiplier effects might lead to a drop of two or three times the $20 billion cutback. This analysis says we must have offsetting increases in other spending to avoid unemployment. It is clear that a cutback of $20 billion in defense spending would mean layoffs for the two

[3] A $20 billion cut now would be about the same percentage of g.n.p. as was the cut made immediately after the Korean War. It would be far less than the huge ($75 billion) reduction in 1945–46, after World War II.

to three million defense workers and others whose jobs directly depend on those expenditures, in addition to released military personnel—unless other spending holds up aggregate demand.

The government has three main macro alternatives if it cuts defense spending by $20 billion: (1) It can increase its spending on civilian goods and services by $20 billion, offsetting the arms reduction; (2) it can cut taxes by $20 billion; or (3) it can maintain taxes and use the hoped-for resulting budget surplus to retire the national debt. Our theory suggests that these three policies would have different results indeed.

Increase in Government Nondefense Spending. Suppose first that government spending on slum clearance, highways and education is increased by $20 billion as defense spending is cut back, and that the government announces this policy when it announces the arms cut-back. This looks like Midway-O'Hare writ large. It would maintain aggregate demand roughly unchanged. New jobs would be created in the expanding civilian-goods industries to offset those lost in the contracting arms industries, and businessmen and consumers would know this in advance.

But unlike the Midway-O'Hare case, the new jobs might be in quite different industries and localities, involving quite different skills. And investors in defense industries would be subject to disastrous losses. Possibly these "transfer" problems would result in a lot of temporary unemployment, and the next section analyzes them in detail. But if aggregate demand is kept roughly stable through the shift, there is little reason to expect continuing large-scale unemployment, tough though the transition might be (remember the automation analysis).

Keeping aggregate demand up is the biggest single safeguard against large-scale unemployment. But even continued high aggregate demand will not guarantee us against unemployment from the spending cut unless individual wage rates are reasonably flexible. Again, remember the automation analysis above. If men thrown out of work in defense industries insist on equal wages before they will accept another job, unchanged aggregate demand may leave some of them permanently unemployed. Their specialized skills have been made obsolete so their marginal products are lower when they shift to different jobs. If they refuse to take wage cuts, they stay unemployed; and the new nondefense spending that might have given them jobs instead then goes to bidding up wages of other workers whose skills are in higher demand where spending increases.

Since even unemployed workers may resist accepting lower wages, many economists suggest that major demand shifts should be accompanied by gradually rising, not merely stable, aggregate demand, in order to ease the required job transfers. This would mean an increase of more than $20 billion in government nondefense spending. But care is needed. Too big a demand increase would risk inflation.

Tax Reduction. A second alternative would be to cut taxes by $20 billion. Here the macro outcome is less obvious. If private households and businesses increase expenditures by $20 billion, the result is much as above, except that the expanding industries are those where private spending goes up, instead of highways, education, and slum clearance.

But will private spending rise by $20 billion? Probably not. Consumer spending normally rises by only a fraction of an increase in disposable income; part of the increased income is saved. Thus, spending would increase by less than the cut in individual tax liabilities. It is more difficult to predict the result of a major corporation income tax reduction. Look back at the complex determinants of investment-spending in Chapter 6 for the considerations. Perhaps business investment-spending would rise by more than the amount of a corporate tax cut, but this is unlikely. Most economists, therefore, would urge cutting tax liabilities by more than $20 billion. To raise private spending by $20 billion, a bigger tax cut or supplementary stimulative measures (e.g., easier money) would be needed. And the lag in private spending might create severe temporary problems.

Paying off the National Debt. Third, we might use the $20 billion saving on defense spending to reduce the national debt. Again, go back to macro theory to predict the consequences. Twenty billion dollars of taxes are a withdrawal

from the income stream. They exercise a deflationary impact unless they are replaced by someone's spending. Using the $20 billion tax receipts to repay $20 billion of the national debt would partially offset the withdrawal, but only partially.

First, suppose the bonds paid off are held by individuals and businesses. Repayment of this debt would return the tax money to the public, but it would also buy up from them $20 billion of government bonds. Thus, the net result of the tax collection plus debt retirement would be to reduce the net wealth (liquid assets) of the public, just as the federal borrowing had originally increased the economy's net wealth in the form of government securities. Alternatively, suppose the bonds paid off are held by banks. Then the effect of the total tax-plus-debt-retirement policy is to wipe out $20 billion of demand deposits which were created when the banks bought the bonds—although the banking system's reserves are unchanged so it has the power to re-expand its loans and deposits to the earlier level. The net effect is highly deflationary, unless bank loans are miraculously expanded without delay, leading to $20 billion more of private spending.

The World War II Experience. This analysis suggests that positive government action to keep aggregate demand up would be needed to avoid unemployment if arms spending were to be cut $20 billion. But between late 1944 and late 1946, federal war spending fell from a peak annual rate of nearly $90 billion to about $15 billion, a drop of $75 billion, or about a third of the entire g.n.p., in two years. Eight million men were demobilized from the armed forces, in addition to the cuts in defense procurement. Over the same period, federal tax receipts fell by only $3 billion, from an annual rate of $46 to $43 billion. Still, reconversion unemployment was short, and soon the economy was booming again.

How shall we reconcile this history with our analysis? Would the private market do the job again if we cut defense spending drastically today? Very unlikely, most economists answer. The post-World War II transition was a very special case. First, there was a huge pent-up demand for consumers' goods and housing after five years of war shortages. Second, the public had a huge accumulation of money and securities from government borrowing during the war, ready to pour out onto the market. Without these special circumstances, it is highly unlikely that the precipitous transition from war to peace would have occurred without at least temporary heavy unemployment.

Conclusion. A big cut in spending by any sector of the economy threatens deflation and unemployment. This is true for government, as it is for the private sector. Massive reductions like $20 billion throw the spotlight on the need for measures to offset the deflationary impact. There is no mechanism by which private spending will automatically generate the right aggregate demand to assure the gradually rising aggregate demand needed for a prosperous economy. We need positive government help to assure a stably growing economy in such a case.

The Problem
of Micro (Structural) Adjustments

Maintaining adequate aggregate demand would help smooth the adjustment to a big cut in defense spending, but it couldn't do the whole job. In our economy the main job of transferring resources in response to changing demand falls on private initiative, the profit motive, and the market place. And with the assumed $20 billion cut in defense spending, the job would be a big one.

Part of the defense spending is highly concentrated. Approximately 95 per cent of employment in aircraft and missiles, 60 per cent in shipbuilding, and 40 per cent in radio and communications equipment depend directly on defense spending. Missile and aircraft production alone in 1965 provided over 80 per cent of the manufacturing jobs in the San Diego area, 70 per cent in Wichita, 50 per cent in Seattle. About 30 per cent of all manufacturing employment in Kansas, Washington, and California depends directly on defense spending. About three-quarters of a million workers in aircraft and missiles, nearly a half-million in electrical equipment, and a quarter-million each in shipbuilding and ordnance works would be out of jobs without defense spending. All this says nothing of the jobs indirectly dependent on defense spending through production of parts and equipment and through production of goods and services these defense workers buy.

Even if civilian demand did increase $20 billion to fill the entire gap left by reduced defense spending, it's easy to see that the impact on some industries, some regions, some individual firms, and some classes of workers could be disastrous. This is Midway-O'Hare writ large, with every problem of adjustment multiplied a thousandfold. Suppose the public decides it wants more new homes and more vacation trips with its $20 billion windfall. Maybe Seattle and San Diego can turn on the advertising and pick up some of the tourist trade, but that's not going to give jobs to many of the unemployed missile workers and electronics engineers. There are going to be lots of jobs in the construction industry across the land, but most places are a long way from San Diego, Seattle, and Wichita, to mention only those three examples; and bricklaying is very different from wiring electrical relays for missile guidance systems. A lot of workers and business firms could shift readily to meet a growth in civilian demand. But to pretend there wouldn't be a major problem of structural adjustment would be blind.

Moreover, at least temporarily there might be serious shortages and price increases in civilian goods industries. In home-building, the demand for materials and skilled workers could soar. Swords do not convert easily to plowshares.[4]

A special task force of government, industrial, labor, and academic economists recently came up with the following recommendations to mitigate painful and disruptive impacts on workers, communities, and investors in defense industries in the event of major disarmament.

1. Strengthen our system of employment offices to provide faster, more accurate information on job opportunities.
2. Strengthen our unemployment insurance

[4] For an intriguing set of estimates of the possible impact of disarmament made through the use of "input-output" tables, see W. Leontief and M. Hoffenberg, "The Economic Effects of Disarmament," in the *Scientific American* for April, 1961; or a simpler version with the same title in *Disarmament and the Economy*, E. Benoit and K. Boulding, eds. (New York: Harper and Row, 1963).

program to assure a higher minimum standard of payments and duration of coverage.

3. Establish better government-aided retraining facilities.

4. Consider measures to bring new industries into hard-hit areas, rather than trying to move displaced workers out.

5. Permit defense industries to provide more generous severance allowances for laid-off workers, and charge them as costs on government contracts.

6. Encourage defense contractors to plan ahead for peacetime reconversion possibilities for their plants and workers.

These proposals have a familiar sound. They're much like the proposals to improve the flexibility and general performance of the labor market mentioned in the earlier sections on automation and poverty.

The Special Problem of Research and Development

Since the Korean War, the federal government has financed over two-thirds of all research and development spending in the American economy, and nearly all the basic research. Nearly 90 per cent of these federal R and D outlays have been under the national defense and space programs. Jet aircraft, atomic energy, electronics, computers, and a variety of other widely used civilian goods were originally developed under defense R and D contracts. Thus, an across-the-board cutback in defense spending could wipe out a big part of the nation's research and development activities, including most of our basic research on which ultimately the more applied developments rest.

In a big defense cutback, should we leave it up to the individual initiative, the profit motive, and the marketplace to reallocate the quarter million scientists and engineers now working on defense-financed research and development? Many experts argue that the national interest is at stake here in a unique way. Although we generally do not think of basic research as a part of the "public sector" of the economy, in fact it appears to be a case where external economies bulk large and hence (on the analysis of Chapter

35) where direct government financing may be socially desirable. In any event, the case of R and D in a big defense cutback illustrates the fact that the problems of adjustment to change are seldom simple, especially when the changes are large and fast. Not many people would like to see our whole basic research effort go down the drain, however enthusiastic they are about cutting government defense spending. Many economists suggest that the government should keep on financing basic research as a peacetime activity in case we drastically reduce defense spending. If so, how shall the government decide who is to work on what kind of research? If it does not, will the market expand private research to offset the government cutback? To the first question there is no easy answer. To the second, the answer is almost certainly "no."

A Final Question

With this background, a final question on disarmament. Suppose worldwide peace should break out—a happy day for mankind. U.S. defense spending is now about $80 billion annually. How would you advise the government to go about the job of converting this $80 billion peace bonus to the public good? [5]

CONCLUSION

Change is everywhere in economic life. It is the essence of a dynamic economy. Without it, our economy would stagnate. Yet every change brings problems, often painful ones for some of the participants in the economic process. When change is big and fast, the problems may envelop the whole economy.

Over the past century, rapid, flexible adaptation to change has been an outstanding mark of the American system. How to continue this dynamic performance, and to improve on it, is one of the largest challenges facing our type of economic system today. For tomorrow's changes are

[5] If you want to explore the problem further, *Defense and Disarmament*, R. E. Bolton, ed. (Englewood Cliffs, N.J.: Prentice-Hall, 1966) provides a readable set of analyses of different facets of the economics of transition to peace.

sure to be different from the ones we have learned to cope with, though we cannot know today what they will be. Abraham Lincoln wrote, a century ago: "The dogmas of the quiet past are inadequate to the stormy present. . . . We must disenthrall ourselves and then we shall save our country."

The three examples in this chapter are intended as illustrations, to stimulate you to think through analytically what an economy must do to adapt effectively to change—shifting consumer demands and social needs, technological advance, changing patterns of international economic competition, the world population explosion. If you think back, the whole book has been a steady stream of cases of economic change and how well or badly our economy adjusts to them.

Every case is different, but some central strands run through most of them. First, to under-

stand them, we need to look at both their macro and micro aspects. To focus on either alone is likely to miss a substantial part of the adjustment problem unless we are concerned with only a small segment of the total economy. Second, policies to deal with most important economic problems involve balancing off two or more social goals against one another—progress, freedom, security, and others you may rate high. Your personal values will go far in determining how big a role you believe government should take in aiding the market process to adjust to economic change. Third, don't be content with clichés and first-glance answers. Most important economic problems involve complex, interacting issues. Thus, the simple black-or-white answer is seldom the best one. The world is more often grey than pure black or white. For complex problems, complex policies often make the most sense.

For Analysis and Discussion

1. "Since society at large is the main beneficiary of rapid technological advance, we should provide reasonable government aid to workers and industries who, through no fault of their own, are displaced by such advance." Do you agree or disagree? What government aid, if any, should be provided? Who should pay?"

2. Should we place primary emphasis on assuring strong aggregate demand or on retraining and relocation of displaced workers if we are concerned about unemployment resulting from rapid automation?

3. Organized labor argues that the 35-hour work week with no reduction in pay is the best way to eliminate unemployment resulting from rapid technological advance. Businessmen reply that this would be self-defeating and would in fact cause increased unemployment, since it would raise wage costs per unit of output. Which is right? Justify your answer.

4. Is it better to move displaced workers to jobs elsewhere, or to bring capital (jobs) to workers who have lost their jobs? Explain.

5. Is the likely disruption from a rapid cutback in arms spending so serious that we should avoid such a cutback, even though world tensions ease? How fast could we afford to reduce our arms spending? What criteria would you use in deciding?

6. Since they are heavily dependent on government spending and were largely developed to meet government needs, do we owe the aircraft, missile and electronics industries (workers or stockholders) special aid in case government military spending is drastically cut back? If so, what kinds of aid? Who should pay?

7. Do external economies create a convincing case for continuing government support of research even if we cut back government arms and space spending? Explain.

8. What general rule should we follow in deciding when market forces are inadequate to handle rapid economic change satisfactorily?

FORTY-TWO

COMPARATIVE ECONOMIC SYSTEMS: U.S.A., U.S.S.R., AND THE MIXED ECONOMIES

The Comparison of Economic Systems.

How Does the Soviet Economy Work?

Comparative Economic Systems in Perspective.

Planning With Private Enterprise: The New Look?

Conclusion.

The dominant problem of the modern world is war and peace—the relentless struggle between East and West for power and position, for men's minds, for survival. In four short decades Soviet Russia has become indubitably the world's second great industrial and military power. We in the United States no longer stand as the unchallenged leader.

What is the Russian communist system, and how does it work? Will an even more extreme form of communism in mainland China dominate the communist-socialist world? Are the mixed economies of Western Europe the harbingers of the future? Who will win the respect and emulation of the world's uncommitted billion in the underdeveloped nations?

At the end of a long book devoted mainly to our largely private-enterprise system, it is well to look in detail at the great economic challenge to that system, and to think through how the two leading systems get their jobs done. For many years, capitalist observers sagely observed that national economic planning couldn't work and confidently predicted the collapse of the Soviet economy. But after 50 years of experience, it is clear that planning *has* worked in Russia. How does the U.S. economy today stack up in comparison with other systems?

THE COMPARISON OF ECONOMIC SYSTEMS

To us, ours is the normal way of life; private enterprise is the usual type of economic system. Only 40 years ago this feeling would have been

559

substantially justified for the whole Western, industrialized world. World War I was over. The postwar revolutions were done. Capitalism seemed securely re-established everywhere except in Russia, and the new communist regime there tottered precariously. Millions of Russians died of starvation; total Russian production appeared scarcely higher than it had been far back in the 1800's under the czars; internal strife split the communist nation.

Today, only four decades later, the United States stands as one of a minority of the world's nations with a basically private-enterprise, capitalist economy. Communism is the economic pattern for far more of the world's population than is the private-enterprise system we know. The U.S.S.R. and China alone account for over a billion people, one of every three human beings alive. The democratic socialism of India, too, typifies more of the world than our system does, hard as this may be for us to realize. Most of West Europe uses a mix of private and public planning that involves more government intervention than we accept. And most observers doubt that private-enterprise economics will win out over substantial governmental planning in the developing nations of Asia, Africa, and even Latin America. It is hard indeed to see other systems as the people who live in them do—to recognize that many millions do not share the ideals and values we Americans hold so dear. But this recognition is a first step toward understanding how other economic systems work.

Capitalism and Communism [1]

Communism today has heavy overtones of politics as well as economics. To look at the economic side of any "ism" alone is to miss its

[1] There are many volumes on comparative economic systems and on the "isms." Three readable ones are G. Grossman, *Economic Systems* (Englewood Cliffs, N.J.: Prentice-Hall, 1967); W. Ebenstein, *Today's Isms* (Englewood Cliffs, N.J.: Prentice-Hall, 1964), which stresses the politico-economic mix; and P. J. Wiles' *The Political Economy of Communism* (Cambridge: Harvard University Press, 1962). For comparative looks focused primarily on the American economy, try Calvin B. Hoover, *The Economy, Liberty, and the State* (New York: Twentieth Century Fund, 1959); F. A. Hayek, *The Road to Serfdom* (Chicago: University of Chicago Press, 1944); and J. A. Schumpeter, *Capitalism, Socialism and Democracy* (New York: Harper, 1942).

essence. Communism has become inseparably associated with political and economic dictatorship because we see them together in Soviet Russia and Communist China, the countries that dominate our thinking about communism today. Yet in its original form, Marxian communism or socialism was highly democratic in spirit. Karl Marx's famous *Das Kapital*, the foundation of modern communism, provided a detailed critique of capitalism, but he was conveniently vague when it came to blueprinting the communist economy to be. Still, one thing is sure. Marx wasn't looking for any political or economic dictatorship except the dictatorship of the proletariat—of the whole working class. Evolutionary socialism comes from the same roots, but it is today found in varying degrees in England, Sweden, Australia, New Zealand—all countries with the highest traditions of political democracy and protection for individual rights.

From an *economic* viewpoint, there are two big differences between capitalism and communism. *Under private-enterprise capitalism as we know it, most productive resources are privately owned, and economic activity is largely directed by prices established through the interaction of supply and demand in the market. Under communism, conversely, most productive resources are publicly owned, and economic activity is directed largely by central planning.* The two critical questions, then, are: (1) Are productive resources privately or publicly owned, and (2) is economic activity directed by individual choice and the price system or by governmental planning?

Obviously, both are matters of degree. Not all productive resources are privately owned under American capitalism—governments own land, highways, dams, buildings, and so on. Nor are all resources publicly owned in Russia. Similarly, not all economic activity is directed by the price system in the United States, nor is all economic activity centrally planned in Russia. Too, an economy can have private ownership of resources and nevertheless be centrally planned. The American economy during World War II was a partial example. Hitler's fascism in Germany was a more complete example. France and India make substantial use of central planning today.

Thus, economic systems fall along a spec-

| Private ownership | U.S.———U.K.———India————————U.S.S.R.——————China | Public ownership |
| Price-directed | U.S.———U.K.———India—U.S.S.R.——————China | Centrally planned |

trum on both these conditions, something like the arrangement shown in the diagram above. The location of the countries is only approximate, but it is intended to suggest the variation on the two scores. The American and Russian systems differ widely on both. They are thus especially worth careful comparison. But don't forget that most of the world's economies lie in between, on one or both of the spectrums shown.

Through Whose Eyes?

Through whose eyes shall we judge these widely differing systems? If your answer is, "through ours," then remember that things may look very different to the Russian, the Indian, or the Frenchman. Every nation has its own ideals, its own mores, its own history. Maybe the Russian and Egyptian economic systems look terrible to us; but if they're doing all right in the eyes of the Russians and the Egyptians, who's to say they're worse than ours? We know that our system doesn't look so good to many foreigners.

How, then, can we intelligently compare economic systems? The answer is: (1) Decide what are the main functions we expect each system to perform; (2) recognize the main standards we use to evaluate performance; (3) apply these standards systematically to each system's performance; and (4) then never forget that what looks rose-colored to us may be a dismal gray through someone else's glasses. Your views may look just as queer to the Russian as his look to you.

The Tests
of a Good Economic System

Every economic system has to do four main jobs. It must decide:

1. *What* is to be produced?
2. *How* it is to be produced?
3. *Who* is to get the goods and services produced?

4. *When*—how many of society's resources should be devoted to current consumption (the present) and how many to investment (the future)?

Every economic system gets the jobs done somehow, whether it's the U.S., the U.S.S.R., or a primitive South Sea island economy. If we want to *evaluate* the different systems, the question is, how well does each system do these jobs? And to answer rationally we need to set up criteria for judging.

At the beginning of the course, five broad socio-economic criteria were tentatively suggested:

1. Progress: Does the system provide a progressively higher standard of living—stable economic growth?
2. Freedom: Does it provide economic freedom for the individual?
3. Security: Does it provide reasonable economic security for all?
4. Individual direction: Does it produce the goods and services consumers want?
5. Equity: Does it provide an equitable distribution of income?

Substitute your own criteria if you don't like the five listed. But keep some set in mind as you read on.

The following pages are mainly an analysis of how the Soviet economy operates, and an evaluation of how well it does its job. But throughout there's a running comparison with the way the American economy accomplishes the same tasks. And at the end there's a final, comparative look at some of the in-between economies and at our own economy. A major purpose is to help you to pull together your own understanding and evaluation of the American economy which you've been studying all year.

HOW DOES
THE SOVIET ECONOMY WORK?

Objectives

The modern Soviet economy rests on the doctrines of Karl Marx. "From each according to his abilities, to each according to his needs," was Marx's foundation for the communist society. The rule of the masses, with productive resources used for the common benefit of all, remains, on paper, the foundation of the modern communist economies—of China as well as the U.S.S.R.

The goals stressed by modern communist leaders look very much like the five listed above for the American economy. While there is no one set of official goals for modern Russia, the following have been repeated many times by Soviet leaders:

1. Expansion of the productive capacity of the nation, to raise the Russian standard of living and to permit an adequate national defense against aggression.

2. Improvement in literacy and higher cultural levels.

3. Improvement in national health standards.

4. Reduction in hours and unpleasantness of work.

5. Reduction of economic insecurity.

Soviet leaders eulogize democracy and personal participation in achieving the goals of the factory, the community, and the state. Freedom of speech and assembly and all the other basic freedoms of the American Constitution are guaranteed in the Soviet Constitution—plus some others we don't include. From the words, it is hard to distinguish Soviet Russia from the Western democratic societies.

It would be foolish to accept at face value everything the Soviet leaders say about their motives. Yet it would be equally foolish to disregard their statements completely. The Soviet rulers have often been cruel, tyrannical, power-hungry men. But many Russians do believe that they are truly democratic, and that we are so only in form. And personal freedom has been substantially ex-

panded in Russia since the days of Stalin. The most favorable description of modern Russian "democracy" might be that it provides widespread participation in the discussion stage but acceptance of the decision once it has been made by the communist officials at the top.

The centralization of political power in Russia is especially significant for our economic survey, because all basic economic plans and policies are made by the controlling political group. Even after recent steps away from central control, the Soviet economy is still the most highly planned and controlled in the world, save that of Communist China. In America, we leave everyone pretty much free to use his private property and his income as he wishes within the law, and we accept the outcome as being by and large the best one for the public welfare. The Russian leaders decide what they want to happen economically, and they use a comprehensive system of plans and controls to see that it happens.

So much for Russia's stated objectives and basic approach. How do the Soviets go about solving the four big economic problems faced by every system?

(1) Deciding What To Produce
and (2) Getting It Produced [2]

In Russia, the central planners decide what is to be produced. They do this through an elaborate system of planning. After the Russian revolution of 1917–18, the communists made an almost fatal mistake. They assumed that central economic control was easy—that all they had to do was confiscate private productive resources, use a little common sense in shifting over to a communist system, tell people in general what to produce, and everything would go along nicely. It didn't! Russian total output in 1919–20 dropped back to near the 1890 level. The Russian peasants didn't see why they should produce just to have their crops taken away and given to someone else. There was virtually no modern industrial capacity in Russia. The economy was thrown into chaos by war and revolution.

[2] Two good studies of the Russian economy are H. Schwartz, *The Russian Economy Since Stalin* (Philadelphia: Lippincott, 1965); and Robert Campbell, *Soviet Economic Power* (Boston: Houghton Mifflin, 1966).

The central planners made many mistakes, but the vast complexities of a completely planned economy were gradually realized. After years of experimentation and a series of "five-year plans" for economic development since 1928, the Soviets developed this general pattern:

First, the basic policy decisions are made by the central communist authorities—what industries to develop, which to let lag, how much to allocate for consumption, how much for industrial expansion, how much for the military. Then the planners map out detailed directions for units in the economy to follow in implementing these decisions. Lastly, these plans have to be carried out by millions of Soviet officials, managers, and workers throughout Russia.

In the last decade, this process has been substantially modified in order to reduce the amount of detailed planning at the top and to place more responsibility on individual managers. This shift has reflected the growing difficulties of detailed planning in an ever-more-complex Soviet economy, and the need to provide more individual incentives to the local managers who have to carry out the broad plans made at the top. N. K. Baibakov, head of the entire Soviet planning mechanism, says their job is "to determine the correct proportions of the national economy," leaving more detailed planning to the factories and the local ministries, especially for industries not vital to Soviet defense or the national welfare.

It is still hard to tell how far this "new look" in Soviet planning will change the detailed planning process developed over the past quarter century. At the moment the process is substantially this.

Making the Plan

The broad goals for the economy are set by the Praesidium and the Central Committee of the Communist Party. Since 1928, these goals have been focused up in a series of comprehensive five-year plans, each concentrated on a few special objectives (mainly defense and industrialization) and focused on major product goals for the economy. The last formal plan ended in 1965 with serious shortfalls, and the exact goals for a 1966–70 plan have never been fully announced. In the late 1950's, Premier Khrushchev predicted repeatedly that Russia would overtake the United States economically by 1970. He said that Russian production would surpass U.S. output of cement in 1965, of steel in 1967, of oil in 1970. The Soviets met the cement goal and their economy has grown steadily. But they have fallen far short of most Khrushchev goals, especially in agriculture, and they no longer talk of overtaking the U.S. soon. Table 42-1 gives a preliminary impression of the 1970 plan for a few important products, compared to 1960 reported achievements. Over-all, the 1966–70 plan apparently calls for about a 9 per cent annual growth in output, a goal the Soviets are apparently going to miss substantially.

TABLE 42-1
SOVIET PLAN GOALS

	1960	1970	Percentage Increase
Steel (million tons)	65	145	123
Oil (million tons)	148	390	160
Cement (million tons)	46	122	168
Natural gas (billion cubic meters)	47	318	577
Electric power (billion KWH)	292	950	227
Grain (million tons)	134	229	71
Meat (million tons)	9	25	177

Within these broad objectives, the plan for each year is developed by the "Gosplan" (State Planning Commission), working with a huge Central Statistical Administration which provides data on available resources and productive capacities. Imagine their job. Suppose you had to plan only aircraft. How would you plan production of all the thousands of components that go into a single modern airplane, scheduling each to be on hand just when it was needed? Now back up and decide how you would plan the production of all the sub-components to produce the parts you need for the airplanes. By now you'll be up in the thousands of individual decisions, just for one major product. And the complexities multiply geometrically when you add other products, because of all the inter-linkages between materials, labor, and manufacturing facilities needed. It's this vast complex of decisions we leave to supply and demand in the marketplace in our private-enterprise economy. And it's these difficulties that have pushed the Soviets to simplify their planning process. How do they do it now?

First, the Soviets don't start from scratch each year. They use last year as a benchmark, which enormously simplifies the task. Second, they apparently concentrate largely on some 1,500 major commodities (industries). For each of these, they construct a "materials balance," a "labor balance," and a "geographical balance." These show the materials, labor, and other resources needed to produce the desired output throughout the economy, and the new output required to add to present inventories in order to meet the plan goals. By combining these balances for all major products, they have a reasonably complete picture of the over-all materials, labor, facilities, and regional balances for the entire economy. From this "input-output" model, they can see roughly where there are likely to be materials shortages, where labor surpluses, and so on, and can adjust accordingly.

But the Gosplan apparently focuses each year primarily on some 50 basic products and industries that are of critical importance in attaining the prime goals of the over-all plan.[3] We can safely assume, for example, that the military missile program is currently on that list. With central planning, the Russians can, and do, put first things first. We, or even the Russian people, may not agree that they're the right first things— but it's clear that planning does get resources devoted effectively to the prime planned objectives.

Once the broad outline of an annual plan is completed, it is sent to regional and industry councils throughout the economy. They check their quotas against the productive capacities in their region or industry to see whether the plan appears feasible. If they think the quotas are too high, or if they believe their tentative allocations of materials and equipment would be inadequate to meet them, they have the right to protest . . . and they do! Local plant managers often argue

---

[3] During World War II, when the U.S. industrial economy was extensively but by no means completely planned, the whole planning process hinged largely on allocation of three major materials—steel, copper, and aluminum.

that the goals are too high and that inadequate raw materials and new machinery are being allocated to meet them. The local workers may protest that they are already speeded up to the limit of their capacity. Then it's a subject for negotiation with the regional and industry-level planners, and after that between them and the national planners at the Gosplan. We know that the Soviet planning process involves lots of talk. Some observers have called it the most gigantic collective-bargaining process in history.

Finally, all this information gets reflected back up to Moscow, where the Gosplan must settle on the final plan so that everything balances out for the whole economy. The planners do the best they can, using some modern mathematical and electronic-computer techniques, and making adjustments in minor industries to accommodate the major goals.

The final stage, after the plan has been approved by top communist officials, is to send it back down to the regional and industry councils for implementation.

We know the planners make mistakes. Plans are continuously adjusted. If the small-machinery plan runs into labor shortages while that for electric light globes turns up a surplus, the planners don't wait until next year to make an adjustment. This doesn't make for a quiet life among Gosplan employees or for managers throughout the economy, and the number of adjustments has apparently snowballed in recent years as the Russian economy has grown in complexity. Complaints from below have become increasingly bitter. Industry plans are changed dozens of times a year. It is these crises that have led the pragmatic rulers in the Kremlin to fundamental changes in the planning process. Mainly these changes have involved delegating more responsibility and freedom to local managers in carrying out the broad goals handed down from above.

Carrying Out the Plan

The annual plan is a *physical* blueprint for the use of productive resources and production of intermediate and final products for the year. (Note that nothing has been said so far about money, prices, or profits.) How do the Soviets get their plans carried out? In essence, by telling people what to do and by paying them for doing it.

Managerial Incentives. Under the prevailing system, the plant manager has received a *quota*, together with detailed information on the supply of materials he will receive, the equipment he will be allocated, the labor he is to use, and so on. But it's up to him to get the final product out. His job is to meet the quota, not to question why. If he exceeds his quota, he is praised by the party and gets substantial economic rewards, including money, better housing, a car, paid vacations, and other such benefits not available except through the official reward system. These are powerful incentives in a low-consumption society. On the other hand, if his plant ends the year below quota, or if he requires more labor and materials than he's been allocated, he's done a bad job. His income goes down; his special prerequisites are taken away; in extreme cases he may be demoted or even expelled from the party, of which he is probably a member if his is an important plant.

The Soviets are thoroughly aware of the importance of good managers to the success of their plans. Managers get among the largest incomes in the economy. They receive medals and public commendation for exceeding quotas. But the communists are also harsh critics when managerial performance falls short.

How has this differed from the American scene? In many respects, not at all. In both, it's up to the manager to run the plant effectively, though the Soviet test has been real output in relation to resources allocated, while the American test is low costs and high profits. In terms of rewards, the Soviet manager can't accumulate property and live well off interest and dividends to supplement his salary and bonus. His absolute standard of living, and certainly his ability to save for his children and his future, are much lower. But *relatively* speaking, he apparently can do about as well as his American counterpart.[4]

But the Soviets have had major problems

[4] For a lively comparison of Soviet and American managers, see David Granick, *The Red Executive* (New York: Doubleday, 1960).

on managerial incentives. Since rewards have depended on meeting physical output quotas, managers try to conceal production possibilities so as to get lower quotas, to hoard materials, to avoid doing too well lest quotas be raised for next year. There is no penalty for wasteful use of materials or manpower so long as it doesn't violate the plan. Fulfilling the plan has come first, to the detriment of quality of product if need be.

"Blat" (using influence with higher-ups in industry) and "tolkachi" (special purchasing agents from plants who go around buying up scarce materials and parts outside the plan) are well-known, if technically illegal, parts of the Russian industrial scene. Russian managers have learned to make their own performances look good by hoarding labor and materials, bootlegging scarce materials outside the plan, and even fudging the basic performance reports on which they are judged. This is not utterly different from the American case, where local managers sometimes try to make their own units look good by devices that reduce rather than increase total corporate profits. Either way, it's tough to make middle managers stick to top-level plans. But in America the dollars and cents on the income statement at year-end, the percentage return on investment, and the per share earnings for the stockholders provide visible measures that probably permit more objective evaluation of management performance.

Innovation has been another special managerial problem. New ideas involve risks, and the Soviet system has lacked effective rewards for risk-taking. In the Soviet climate, doing reasonably well is more conducive to the manager's peace of mind than is taking a chance on a new idea that may flop. There's nothing like the American private-enterprise entrepreneur out to make a million (or go broke) in a gamble on a new product or new method. Maybe this means less waste under Soviet planning; it probably means less imaginative innovation except on the big problems that get the central attention of the planners. But again, many American corporations face the same problem with their managers.

Lastly, there is the problem of how much decentralization of decision-making and operating authority is optimal to make the plan work most efficiently. The parellel to the problem faced by a large American corporation, like General Motors, is striking. In America, decentralized decision-making and authority, under only broad rules from headquarters, have been widely accepted as the best way of maintaining local managerial initiative and of coupling the advantages of central planning with local, first-hand management. Strikingly, as we shall see in the "new look" section below, the big Communist change is in the same direction. But Gosplan still makes all the basic plans, and the blueprints for carrying them out for most of the economy.

Labor Incentives and Labor Unions. How do the Soviets get the workers to carry out their plans? Just as in the U.S., money is the big incentive, but it is supplemented by continuous emphasis on national pride and party loyalty for members.

The planners decide how much should be paid for each type of work, and they do it so as to get the plan carried out effectively. The biggest pay goes to scientists, artists, inventors, and managers who overproduce their quotas. About 75 per cent of all industrial workers are on "piece rates," whereby each worker gets paid according to how much he turns out. This is a much higher percentage than in the United States. Money wages thus play much the same role in pulling labor into jobs and stimulating good performance as they do in America, *except* that in Russia they are set by the planners to channel workers where the planners want them, rather than freely by market supply and demand. It is striking that money incentives—differential pay for workers turning out more output—are used more strongly than in such "capitalist" countries as the United States. And resulting pay differentials for *workers* are considerably *wider* in the U.S.S.R. than here, where union pressures have tended to lessen them. Table 42-2 shows incomes received by various Soviet groups.

How free are Soviet workers to work where they wish? Substantially free, given the immobility inevitably associated with low incomes and limited geographical fluidity—except where workers have been "recruited" for special projects or where they have received special training or education at state

TABLE 42-2 SOVIET INCOMES *	Monthly Earnings in Rubles
Leading scientist	800–1500
Senior government official	700
Opera or ballet star	500 **
Professor (science or medicine)	400–1000
Plant manager	300–1000
Engineer	100–300
Worker (skilled)	100–250
Physician	85–180
High school teacher	85–100
Worker (semi-skilled)	60–90
Worker (unskilled)	27–50

* Data for early 1960's from U.S. Department of Labor. One ruble equalled $1.11 at the official exchange rate in 1961; this exchange rate understated the real buying power of Russian incomes in our money. Figures do not include extra perquisites such as special housing, cars, and the like, or social services such as free vacations, health services, and subsidized housing for all.
** Plus outside earnings to 2000 rubles.

expense. The complaints of managers about labor turnover suggest that labor moves from job to job with considerable freedom. The main coercion used to hold workers in particular jobs is preference on desirable housing, which may be lost if the worker leaves. With a nationwide housing shortage, this is a powerful incentive.

Most Soviet workers belong to unions. But they are quite different from unions in America. Soviet unions have nothing to do with setting wages; wages are established by the central planners. The unions are worker organizations that are expected to help in implementing plans. As such they apparently have a substantial role in urging workers to meet quotas and in channeling labor from surplus to shortage occupations. They administer most worker benefits. They handle worker grievances. But they are more like workmen's clubs than like the unions we know. Make your own comparison with the role of unions in America, where there is far more union power—and far more conflict.

Checking on Performance: The Gosbank and the State Control Commission. Basic planning is done in physical terms. But the Gosplan also makes up a complete set of "value" (or financial) plans to parallel the basic physical plans. Using these financial plans, the Gosbank (state banking system) provides the money to managers needed to pay for labor and materials to carry out the production plans. For example, if the annual plan calls for 10 million pairs of shoes, the Gosbank provides shoe plant managers just enough rubles to pay for the labor, leather, and so on, allocated to the production of those shoes. It does the same for all other products. And managers must deposit their receipts in the Gosbank, except for cash payments made to workers. Except for wages and citizens' purchases of consumer goods, all transactions in Russia are made by check through the Gosbank.

The Gosbank plays two significant roles. First, it provides a financial control over managers. If they run out of money, this is a sign they are buying more than the inputs allocated to them under the physical plan. And since they can get materials and labor only by paying for them, the control is close and effective. When the manager deposits his receipts in the Gosbank, this provides an automatic check on whether he has produced the amount specified in the plan. Second, the Gosbank provides a regular banking function, transferring funds, advancing working capital, and creating a money supply for the economy.

In some respects, the Gosbank is thus like banks in the United States. It advances working capital to carry out productive processes, transfers funds, and creates money for the economy. But it is strictly government-operated, and its main goal is to help implement the physical plan. It advances new checking accounts (creates credit) when they are needed to facilitate production, and it reduces funds to industries that have been absorbing too much labor or material. (Its policies are also designed to help insure that total purchasing power is about equal to goods and services available at the desired state prices, as we shall see presently. Thus, it is a little like our Federal Reserve, but with more direct control over the supply of money.)

The other official watchdog over managers and regional officials is the State Control Commission, whose representatives function as inspectors through periodic visits and through reviewing

Gosbank checking accounts. Lastly, there are the ever-present Communist party officials, who may report lax or improper behavior to party headquarters. Often these are overlapping groups, for high officials of the planning and control agencies also often hold party office.

How does this checking on performance compare with the private-enterprise process? In America, too, the availability of funds to carry out any economic service exercises a basic control over what is done and who does it. In America, the firm gets funds continuously from selling its product; thus consumers exercise a continuous check on whether any firm is doing its job effectively. If a firm wants to expand, it must either have stored up its own profits to risk or it must go to the competitive capital markets for funds. There its project is evaluated by bankers, private investors, and other lenders against other alternative demanders of funds. If the firm's prospects look good, it will be able to borrow; if they look bad, it will have trouble raising funds. The capital market controls who can expand and who cannot.

Which process is more effective? It obviously depends on your point of view. Who should check on whom? The Soviet procedure gives a direct control to the planners through the Gosbank and the Control Commission. In America, we place most of our faith in the impersonal market, where lenders and business firms are counted on to look out for their own incomes and thereby to get our resources allocated most effectively. Here the socialists criticize the American economy vigorously. They say our capital markets are not competitive —that capital is rationed out by monopolistic lenders to big, favored borrowers in a way that makes it hard for new, smaller firms to compete effectively with the established giants. Think back to the chapters on monopoly and competition and on the American banking and credit system to decide how much weight to give this criticism.

The Recalcitrant Problem of Agriculture. Agriculture has been the communists' knottiest problem. Their early attempts to collectivize Russian agriculture, carried through by bloody force during the 1920's and 1930's, met bitter and sullen resistance. Forced to work on collective farms, farmers produced less than before and kept crops and animals for themselves rather than turning them over to Soviet authorities for export to the cities. Frustrated communist planners tried one tack, then another—but with little success in meeting expanded food goals for the rapidly growing industrial population or in freeing farm labor for industrial jobs.

In theory, a collective farm is a cooperative, democratic association of farmers who have pooled their land, tools, and labor to make a large farm, which they operate in common. Proceeds are shared in proportion to the quantity and quality of work they do. Large-scale operation produces the economies of large-scale mechanized farming, eliminating the waste and inefficiency which for centuries have characterized Russian agriculture.

It sounds fine, but not to the Russian peasants. Soviet planners found crops vanishing into farm consumption and total production declining. Bloody reprisals brought only temporary compliance and smoldering resentment. Over millions of acres and widely scattered farmers, effective control was impossible.

There are now some 100,000 collective and state farms, compared to perhaps 25 million small peasant farms four decades ago. About 5,000 of these are huge state farms of many thousand acres, operated outright as "business" firms by the Ministry of Agriculture in much the same pattern as prevails for industrial production. Some 95,000 are collective farms, ranging from a few "communes" (which involve complete sharing of property, labor, and results) to many cases where the collective farm is scarcely more than a sharing of major machinery and some exchange of labor. In most cases, part of the land is farmed collectively but each family retains a small plot for its own individual operation. These private plots make up only 5 to 10 per cent of the total land under cultivation, but they apparently produce nearly one -third of total farm output of vegetables, eggs, meat, milk and other such products which are suited to labor-intensive production and which can be sold in small lots in markets.

Payments to farmers are calculated on a complicated basis. For work on collective farms they receive largely payment in kind, but also some money income. Apparently about a third

of total output is delivered directly to the state, about a third is used on the farms for further output (seed, feed for animals, and so on), and about a third is given to the farmers themselves. A substantial portion of the latter finds its way onto the free market for food consumption in the cities. This supply is augmented by products from the millions of small family holdings, as indicated above. Private initiative is far from dead in Russian agriculture.

In any case, farm output has persistently lagged far behind the plan goals, in spite of one "reform" after another. The 1970 farm output goals in Table 42-1 are viewed by most outsiders as utterly unrealistic, and the figures for 1960 are probably overstatements. Most outsiders estimate that since 1950 Soviet farm output has grown not more than 2 or 3 per cent a year, if that much. In the mid-1960's Russia, historically a large wheat exporter, had to import large quantities of wheat for food. Food output per capita has barely held stable over the last decade.

The importance of agriculture in Russia is great. Over a third of the population lives on farms. In 1965, nearly 40 per cent of the Russian labor force was in agriculture—39 million workers, compared to 5 million in the United States. Yet U.S. total farm output substantially exceeds Russia's. U.S. farming is highly mechanized and capital-intensive; Russia's is technically backward and labor-intensive, with limited use of modern fertilizers and mechanical equipment. The Soviets badly need more efficiency on the farm, to increase output and to free labor for work in industry.

"Profits" and the New Look in Soviet Planning

In recent years, evidence has piled up that the Soviet planners have been increasingly overwhelmed by their task. As the size and complexity of an economy increase, the number of interconnections among products, labor, and materials increases exponentially. The sheer volume of work requires that it be divided among more and more offices and locations, even when modern computers are used. Mistakes and inconsistencies inevitably increase, and the number of plan modifications snowballs, wreaking havoc on the day-to-day operations of plant managers and the production process. Soviet growth slowed significantly after the late 1950's.

About 1960, a few academic economists, notably Professor Y. Liberman, began to question tentatively whether more reliance on a kind of "profit motive" for individual managers couldn't help the top planners, avoid the local wastes of physical planning, and increase total output. To the amazement of many western observers, this possibility was discussed openly during the early 1960's by intellectuals and planners alike. And in 1964 the communists announced an experiment which freed managers in the shoe and food-processing industries from planned quotas, and directed them to maximize their profits, much as in America, with their own bonuses based on the profits they make. Each manager is substantially free to set the price of his product and the wages he will pay, and to choose his own production methods. The profits themselves, above the special rewards to the successful manager, of course revert to the state.

Tales of spectacular increases in efficiency abound. In any event, increased managerial freedom, reliance on "profit" incentives, and freer prices have been rapidly extended to other non-critical areas of the economy. By 1968 apparently about one-fourth of Soviet industry was operating on this basis, and plans called for further extension to about half of total output. But the Gosplan still sets the major priorities for the system and controls in detail the areas vital to national defense, industrial expansion, and other high-priority objectives. The "new look" marks a dramatic change in Soviet economic philosophy and practice. But the U.S.S.R. is still very much a centrally planned and controlled economy.

The "new look" raises basic issues for the Soviets as they plan and operate the world's greatest "business." Whether they can manage a system half planned and half market-directed remains to be seen. Substantial widening of the experiment will inevitably involve direct conflicts with centrally planned uses of productive resources for specific national goals. It is far from clear how these conflicts will be resolved without

destroying the new managerial freedoms. Many planners strongly oppose the new moves, and there are increasing reports of top planners' intervention in the "freed" industries when such conflicts appear. Moreover, increasing reliance on the market with individual managers motivated by profits could quickly expose the Soviet economy to risks of Western-style overproduction of particular products and of unemployment. But more reliance on decentralized managerial initiative seems to the pragmatic Soviet leaders at least worth a major try. Only time will tell how far the experiment is extended and what it does to the entire structure of the Soviet economy.

(3) Deciding How Income Is To Be Distributed

Marxist doctrine says, to each according to his need. The Soviet leaders today season this liberally with, to each according to how hard he works and how much he contributes. Incomes are more equally distributed than in the United States, because in Russia income from property is very limited whereas many of the highest American incomes are from dividends, interest, and capital gains on private property. There are no millionaires in modern Russia. But money incomes derived *from work* are as unequally distributed in Russia as in America. This inequality reflects the strong use made of incentive payments to achieve the goals established by the central planners.

Table 42-2 above tells the story. Artists, scientists, professors, managers, and government officials receive the highest incomes, including special supplements in premium housing, use of government automobiles, paid vacations, and so on. As in America, common labor is at the bottom of the totem pole—except for farmers, many of whom take much of their income in kind from their farms. Within the ranks of factory workers and comparable laborers, apparently the spread between lowest and highest monthly incomes is nearly one to eight, far wider than in America.

Wage rates are adjusted up and down frequently for different occupations and industries, to help implement the over-all plan. The Soviets may be good Marxists on paper, but their behavior on wages suggests they have learned a good deal too about monetary incentives.

Government Services and Income Redistribution. Although it uses money incentives freely to stimulate production and allocate resources, the Soviet state provides widespread free social services to help the masses. Soviet authorities claim that one-third of the income of low-income groups is provided by free government services. Nearly all housing is government-owned, and rents are extremely low; on the average, Soviet citizens apparently pay only 2 to 3 per cent of their income for housing, far under the 15 to 25 per cent common in America. Russian housing is generally bad, but it's cheap. Paid vacations, government nurseries, special grants to large families, free education, and extensive health services all supplement money incomes.

But to evaluate these government services we have to ask, who pays for them? A general sales ("turnover") tax accounts for over half of all government receipts. Profits on state enterprises provide most of the rest. Direct personal taxes (mainly an income tax) take only 8 per cent of personal income. All told, government collections and expenditures somewhat comparable to our combined federal-state-local governmental taxes and expenditures apparently amount to about 35 per cent of the gross national product, though estimates vary substantially.

Since the turnover tax rate varies widely from product to product and from year to year, estimation of its incidence by income levels is extremely difficult. Increases and decreases in the tax are used to adjust the prices of individual products up and down so as to discourage or stimulate consumption. This way the planners make consumer demand match the goods produced under the plan, somewhat as free market prices provide this adjustment in the United States. This tax, therefore, substantially offsets the apparent big government supplement to low incomes.

On the other hand, the Soviets use especially low prices on some major commodities in addition to housing to subsidize low-income consumers. This means that such goods are sold below "cost." Prices are set very high on such luxuries as auto-

mobiles. Here again, pricing is used by Soviet planners to promote all the goals they consider important—stimulation or restriction of consumption, redistribution of income, and equating aggregate spendable income to aggregate supply available for purchase.

(4) Deciding Between Economic Growth and Current Consumption

In America the choice between economic growth and current consumption depends on a complex set of factors, including consumer saving, business investment decisions, private educational and research decisions, and government tax and investment behavior. In Russia, the choice is simple. It is made and implemented by the central planners. And their choice has been in favor of rapid industrialization and growth, at the expense of current consumption.

Since the early 1920's, Russia's g.n.p. has grown at about 4 per cent annually, about the same as the U.S. rate. But Soviet growth during the 1950's was spectacular—about double that rate—with a substantial slow-down since 1960. To press its postwar growth, the U.S.S.R. has allocated an extraordinarily large portion of its output to capital formation. Until recently private consumption was held below 50 per cent of g.n.p. and nonmilitary investment apparently was 20 to 25 per cent. This policy produced an average annual increase of 11 per cent in the Russian capital stock, a rate that will be very difficult to maintain. And Russia was able to borrow a large amount of technology from the West. The Russian slowdown after 1960 apparently reflected in substantial part a decline in the capital accumulation rate, as more was allocated to satisfying consumer wants. But the growth rate picked up again, at least temporarily, after 1966. Even with central planning and control rather than individual choice and the price system, Russia faces the same fundamental problem in growth as does any other economy—she must divert scarce resources from consumption to investment, improve her technology, and step up the ability and performance of her labor force. There is no other way, for either communism or capitalism. As post-Stalin liberalization has opened up the Soviet economy to Western standards and Western ideas, the pressure has intensified on communist leaders for more consumption goods.[5]

How fast the Russian economy grows depends on the decisions of the central planners, but it also depends on fundamental political forces—on how long the population will be content to see most of the increased output go into capital expansion and military products. In the American economy, the public speaks on this division continuously, through its own savings-spending behavior and through its directions to congressmen on government spending and taxes. Under the Soviet system there is little evidence that the man in the street has much voice in the decisions. Yet the Soviet leaders constantly face the need to keep the masses reasonably content if they are to stay in power. Persistent, though small, increases in consumption-goods output per capita attest to this concern.

Soviet planning for growth extends to every phase of economic life. Soviet education, in the European pattern, is deadly serious from kindergarten on. Although all youths go through elementary- and high-school-level education, only those with special capacities are sent on to what corresponds to our college-level training. For these, education is more specialized and more sharply focused on specific job training than is ours, but it is intense and thorough in those specialties, especially science, engineering, medicine, and the like. The National Science Foundation reports that Russia is currently training twice as many scientists and engineers as we are (about 125,000 a year as against our 60,000), and that her margin is apparently growing. Again, the contrast with the privately determined, free-choice ad-

vanced education system of the United States is striking.

No reliable estimates on the total Soviet expenditure on research are available, but apparently, with a national income about half ours, Russia spends at least as much as we do on basic research.

Government Monetary-Fiscal Policy and Economic Stabilization

The Soviet central planners do not program men or machines into unemployment. If there is unemployment, it is because planning has gone awry or because someone is not behaving according to plan. But there is still the problem of keeping total spending power roughly equal to goods available for purchase. If buying power gets too large, inflationary pressures will mount. If buying power is too low, prices must be cut or unsold inventories will pile up.

The Soviets manage this balance largely through the turnover tax (fiscal policy) and the Gosbank (monetary policy), the same two tools we use. In Russia, most of the burden falls on the turnover tax. If total demand is excessive and inflationary pressure exists, the turnover tax is raised all along the line, or on those products where demand seems most excessive, raising prices and siphoning off income to the government. If total demand is inadequate, turnover taxes are lowered. In a real sense, the Russians have adopted "functional finance" as the core of their stabilization and allocation mechanism.

In spite of this plan, inflation has been a persistent problem for the Soviets. The Russians are human beings too, and when there isn't enough to go around they apparently tend to plan a little more resources for all the demands than there are to parcel out. The result is a demand pressure that tends to bid up prices all along the line as shortages occur. In 1947 a drastic monetary reform confiscating most private money and government bond holdings was proclaimed to reduce excess buying power. For a while thereafter the Russians again used compulsory purchase of government bonds as an important device for soaking up excess consumer purchasing power. But as large amounts of these bonds began to

[5] Under Marxist doctrine, only labor is truly productive. Thus, interest on money or real capital plays no role in communist doctrine. Western economists properly point out that this position, if followed, will lead Soviet planners to improper decisions in allocating resources. Some methods involve a heavy use of productive resources per unit of output, others a low investment. Only by taking these differences into account can optimal decisions be made as to what capital goods should be produced. And the interest rate, as was pointed out in Chapter 33, is the price system's tool in making such comparisons among such alternatives. Interestingly, the pragmatic Soviet planners (who are smart fellows too) are now slipping the interest rate into their calculations through the back door.

come due just when inflationary pressure was mounting again in 1957, the Russians again virtually repudiated the entire national debt of 260 billion rubles. The basic pressures that make for inflation—shortage of goods relative to the purchasing power provided by incomes paid out—are the same in communist and capitalist societies.

Russia faces no serious danger of depression because of a collapse of private investment- and consumption-spending; there isn't any private investment to fluctuate. There is little doubt that the American private-enterprise market economy is more vulnerable to the economic instability and the waste of recession unemployment. And the basic fact that America is rich means that excess saving may present an unemployment problem substantially unknown to the Russian planners, who face a constant shortage of both capital and consumption goods. These are prices we pay for our individual freedom and our spectacular economic success to date. However, as the Soviets expand the "profit-motivated" sector of their economy and consumers are given a wider range of choice in retail stores, unsold inventories may pose increasing problems for the planners.[6]

COMPARATIVE ECONOMIC SYSTEMS
IN PERSPECTIVE

At the end of a long book, it may be useful briefly to compare our performance with that of Soviet Russia—not because Russia is the best standard against which to measure our performance, but because it is a comparison being made by much of the world. Most important, it should provide a last chance for you to organize your own ideas on the performance of the American system and what, if anything, you think needs to be done to improve it.

The Marxists tell everyone who will listen what's the matter with our "capitalist" society. They say we have the following big faults:

[6] A complete report on the recent performance of the Soviet economy is provided by *New Directions in the Soviet Economy*, a compendium prepared for the Joint Economic Committee of Congress (Government Printing Office, 1966), especially Parts II-A and II-B, on "Economic Performance."

1. Capitalism cannot avoid increasingly serious depressions reflecting underconsumption by the masses, and these depressions will bring about its ultimate collapse.

2. Widespread monopoly is inevitable, and the capitalist owners exploit the workers through low wages and high prices for the products they buy.

3. Private ownership of capital causes great inequality in incomes, which is unfair and helps generate massive depressions because of inadequate purchasing power by the masses.

4. Business competition is wasteful, and misdirects the economy's resources away from the socially most important uses.

Think about how you would answer these criticisms, as you pull together your own evaluation of our system.

Progress—
Stable Economic Growth

First, a summary look at the communist and American performances. Some of the communist achievements have been spectacular. From a backward, rural economy, in four decades Russia has become the world's second-greatest industrial power. During the 1950's her growth rate was extraordinary. The *increase* in Russia's steel-making capacity over the decade exceeded England's *total* capacity. Her plan calls for a 9 per cent per annum growth in output, but during the 1960's she has fallen far short of that goal. Her growth in industrial output from 1900 to 1958 was about 7 per cent, from 1958 to 1966 about 5 per cent. Table 42-3 shows how this compared with other major industrial nations, and adds other comparative data.

The facts speak for themselves. During 1950–58, the U.S.S.R. did very well compared to the capitalist economies—on g.n.p., investment, and consumption. Only West Germany outpaced her. But since 1958, most other nations have speeded up while growth in the U.S.S.R. and West Germany has slowed substantially. Japan has been the star. The U.S.S.R.'s performance has just about equalled that of the U.S.A. on the measures shown, a bit below the records of West Germany and France.

TABLE 42-3

COMPARATIVE GROWTH RATES* (Percentages per Year)

Country	Total G.N.P. 1950–58	1958–65	G.N.P./Capita 1950–58	1958–65	Investment 1950–58	1958–65	Consumption/Capita 1950–58	1958–65
West Germany	7.6	5.6	6.4	4.4	9.6	8.2	6.3	4.8
U.S.S.R.	7.1	5.1	5.2	3.3	10.8	7.0	5.0	2.4
Japan	6.1	12.0	4.8	11.0	7.7	20.0	2.3	7.5
France	4.4	5.4	3.5	4.0	5.5	6.9	3.3	3.5
U.S.A.	2.9	4.6	1.2	2.9	1.3	4.9	1.1	2.6
United Kingdom	2.4	3.9	1.9	3.1	4.4	7.0	1.6	2.4

* Data from Organization for Economic Cooperation and Development, and from *New Directions in the Soviet Economy* (op. cit.). 1965 data preliminary estimates in some cases.

Comparing U.S. and U.S.S.R. growth rates is one of the favorite statistical games of the generation. If we take the entire period since 1913, just before World War I, the Russian growth rate has been a little over 4 per cent, the American about 3.5 per cent. If we begin with 1928, the start of the first communist 5-year plan, it's about 6 per cent against our 4. But some economists argue that this is a bad comparison, since Russia is still in an early stage of growth and we are mature. They say, compare our early history with the Russian performance since 1928. If you put our 1875–1917 performance against 1928–1960 in Russia, the figures are much closer, about 5 per cent in the U.S. and 6 per cent in Russia. As with many other comparisons, you can change the picture somewhat to suit your taste by selecting the years carefully. Any way you look at it, since World War I Russia has become the industrial giant of Eurasia, surpassed in the world only by the United States.[7]

[7] The physical output comparisons for particular products in Fig. 42-1 are reasonably firm. But the aggregates (like g.n.p.), which inevitably involve summing in dollar or ruble terms before comparisons can be made, are open to wide differences of judgment. Some comparisons convert the aggregate Russian ruble totals into U.S. dollars at the official ruble-dollar exchange rate (which in 1964 was $1.11 per ruble). Others estimate that in Russia one ruble buys about as much defense output, for example, as $2.50 does in the U.S. Similar comparisons for other basic commodities vary widely. If we take an unofficial conversion rate of about $2 per ruble which is sometimes used, Russian g.n.p. is about two-thirds ours instead of about 40 per cent. Many economists now use something like an average of the two rates, which gives a Russian g.n.p. of about half ours. There's no clear answer on which is the best way to make the comparison, and it obviously makes a lot of difference in the answer you get.

But for long-run solid achievement on the economic front, the U.S. economy is far out front. Our $3,900 per capita g.n.p. in 1967 compared with only about $1,700 for the U.S.S.R. Russian per capita output is about two-thirds that in the major West European nations, and during the 1960's she has gained on them and us little if at all. Soviet achievements have been great. Yet housing, especially outside the major cities, is appallingly poor. Nearly 50 per cent of city families still live in a single room, sharing a kitchen and bath with others. Food for the masses is no more than adequate, with little variety. Consumer "hard goods" are scarce. Only the very powerful have private automobiles. In 1965, less than 10 per cent of all Russian families owned private refrigerators and washing machines, compared to over 95 per cent in the United States. Russia has 18 vacuum cleaners per thousand people, the U.S. 211. For television sets the comparable figures are 56 and 318; for sewing machines 100 and 135. Life in Russia is repeatedly described as drab. Figure 42-1 provides a comparison of recent output in the U.S. and U.S.S.R. of a range of producers' and consumers' goods in real terms, undistorted by price and currency quotations.

All in all, modern Russia is a study in contrasts. Space capsules go into orbit; accountants still use the abacus. Shiny new apartment buildings go up with antiquated elevators. Factories close down for lack of a few vital parts, but total industrial output soars impressively. Karl Marx's doctrines are everywhere, but if he gets in the way of what seems to be needed practically, he's quietly pushed aside.

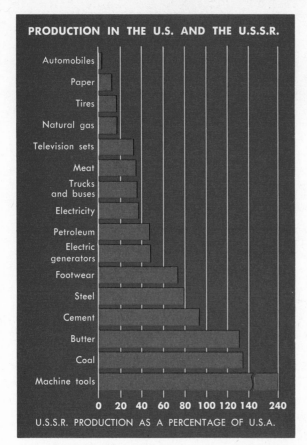

PRODUCTION IN THE U.S. AND THE U.S.S.R.

Automobiles
Paper
Tires
Natural gas
Television sets
Meat
Trucks and buses
Electricity
Petroleum
Electric generators
Footwear
Steel
Cement
Butter
Coal
Machine tools

0 20 40 60 80 100 120 140 240

U.S.S.R. PRODUCTION AS A PERCENTAGE OF U.S.A.

FIG. 42-1 U.S.S.R. production of most commodities is far below ours, but they surpass us in a few. What do you infer about Russian priorities from this partial list? (Sources: United Nations and U.S. Department of Commerce. Data for 1963; all comparisons in physical units.)

Premier Khrushchev boasted that Russia would overtake the United States by 1970, but clearly, there isn't a chance. However, if the U.S.S.R. and U.S. growth rates had continued as in the 1950's, he wouldn't have been so far off. Then Russia grew very rapidly, and we suffered from persistent slack and underemployment. Table 42-4 shows hypothetical U.S. and Soviet g.n.p. figures for 1975, 1985 and 1995 with different assumed growth rates. Unless we fall short of our historical 3 to 4 per cent growth rate, the Russians can't catch us before the 1990's unless they grow at 6 per cent or better, a very high rate. If we manage 4 per cent, the best they can reasonably hope to do is close the present gap part-way.

On the score of stability and avoidance of waste through unemployment, the American system doesn't come off as well. The Great Depression of the 1930's and even the smaller recessions

574

TABLE 42-4

HYPOTHETICAL U.S. AND U.S.S.R. GROWTH RATES*
(U.S. g.n.p. of 1965 = 100)

| | U.S., Assuming Growth Rate of: | | | U.S.S.R., Assuming Growth Rate of: | | |
	2%	3%	4%	4%	5%	6%	7%
1965—100	100	100	50	50	50	50
1975—122	134	148	74	81	90	98
1985—149	181	219	110	133	160	193
1995—181	243	324	162	216	287	380

* Table takes 1965 U.S.S.R. g.n.p. as half that of U.S. Use of other 1965 relationships changes later figures accordingly.

of 1948, 1954, 1958, and 1961 have no direct parallels in the Soviet system. Although Soviet steel capacity was less than half of ours, in our recession years of 1961 Soviet *production* of steel was nearly as high as ours because our mills were running below 60 per cent of capacity. The "new economics" says we can have stable economic growth through intelligent use of fiscal and monetary policy, and the record of the 1960's is encouraging. But our past business cycles are a weakness the communists are fond of emphasizing.

On inflation, neither communism nor capitalism can point to a clean slate. Inflation has plagued both systems through the post-war period. It is not clear that either has the problem effectively in hand. So, a nagging question: Does either capitalism or communism have a satisfactory answer to the problem of high employment without inflation?

But these problems in our economy don't change the basic picture. On the record to date, we have far outdistanced all competitors. Recessions slow us down, and we could be a lot better off without them. Another debacle like the 1930's could pull us back down to the level of the Russians. But short of that, the record of the American economy is plain for all to see. Other economies may be growing faster, but they have a long way to go to catch up.

Freedom

The American system provides almost complete freedom on where to work, where to live, how to spend your money, and other economic choices. The freedom to go into business for your-self is completely unmatched in the Soviet system. American unions are a powerful device for equal-izing the economic power of employers and em-ployees. Government taxes are heavy and to this extent economic freedom may be said to be cur-tailed—though less so than in Russia.

How much "economic freedom" the Soviet economy provides for the individual depends on what you mean by the phrase. Today, the Soviet citizen has considerable freedom to move to an-other job and apparently complete freedom to spend his income on whatever he can find to buy. But the meaning of this freedom is subject to dispute, since the government determines what goods will be available for purchase and indirectly tells him where he should work. Further, Russian unions have no voice in determining the wages at which the citizens will work.

It seems obvious to us that our individual economic freedom far surpasses that available in Russia. But the question "through whose eyes?" is relevant again. The following quotation from a speech by then-Premier Khrushchev illustrates how different things can look to someone else. He said: [8]

Indeed, there is freedom in the capitalist countries, but for whom? Of course, not for the working people, who are forced to hire themselves out to capitalists on any conditions to avoid find-ing themselves in the huge army of people who are unemployed. Neither is there freedom for the peasants, who are constantly threatened by "libera-tion" from their holdings as a result of bankruptcy. Nor is there freedom for the intelligentsia, whose creative activity is in the grip of material depen-dence on the moneybag. . . . Freedom in the cap-italist countries exists only for those who possess money and who consequently hold power.

Clearly, political and economic freedom are intimately intertwined. If in fact the Russian people completely controlled the Soviet officials who make the nation's economic plans, the com-munists could reasonably claim a high degree of individual economic freedom, exercised through voting for central economic planning rather than

[8] Speech before 21st Party Congress in Moscow, January 31, 1959.

through the marketplace. In America we freely choose to have our governments tax away part of our incomes and provide highways, schools, and the like through nonmarket channels; and there is no reason why for others to do likewise would im-ply lack of economic freedom. But without effec-tive democratic control over the central planners, the Soviet system can hardly be rated high on eco-nomic freedom.

Security

What is economic security? Is it freedom from the fear of unemployment? Freedom from the fear of arbitrary discharge? Freedom from the fear of poverty and disaster in old age or ill health? Is economic security separable from political security?

How economic security is defined will partly determine the rating of the American and Soviet systems on this score. By one test, the Soviet citizen is secure economically. The state will not let him and his family starve. He is assured of a minimum of public services and of a job if he works reasonably hard and conforms to the rules of the leaders in power. In a planned economy, workers aren't planned into unemployment. Prob-ably the Soviet leaders believe their system pro-vides more economic security than does capi-talism, where (to them) the worker lives in constant fear of discharge by the all-powerful cap-italist and of unemployment in periodic depres-sions.

Fundamentally, the greatest protection to economic security under the American system is the vast productive power it provides—the high per capita incomes that make it possible for work-ers to look out for themselves. But beyond our basic reliance on individual initiative, our govern-mental social-security system now offers pro-tection against most of the types of economic insecurity likely to strike the average individual. And private welfare and pension funds have de-veloped rapidly in recent years. Still, the capitalist system has some unwanted insecurity that will persist until we learn to substitute stable economic growth for intermittent recessions and inflations.

How much security *should* an economic sys-tem provide? Many Americans believe the system ought to deal out big rewards to those who work hard and "produce," and that those who don't produce have no right to economic security. This is the incentive that has made the American economic system a spectacular success, they argue, and to substitute guaranteed economic security would undermine the very foundation of the system. But most voters disagree, arguing that elimination of unnecessary insecurity and uncertainty will make our system work better—and even if it didn't we can now well afford the cost of reasonable economic security.

Consumer Control

Here the Soviet system rates low and ours high according to our criterion. The communist planners, not the consumers, decide what is to be produced. The "free choice" of consumers in spending their money is strictly limited—they can spend it only on goods available and at the prices set by the planners. In Moscow in 1960, ten minutes of work was required to earn enough to buy a loaf of bread; in New York five minutes was enough. For potatoes (per pound) the times were six minutes and two. But the ratios were drastically different for other products—33 minutes against seven for a quart of milk, 33 days against four for an overcoat, 25 days against one for a table radio. The central planners dictate how hard it is to get different products. And consumers have little to say about the division of resources between present and future. Don't forget, though, that in the Russian's eyes maybe a centrally planned allocation of resources makes more sense than the unplanned allocation that we get through the free-price system.

Does the American system produce the goods and services consumers want? By and large "yes," *if* we take one-dollar-one-vote as our criterion. Over three-fourths of the gross national product is allocated through the private economy, pretty much in response to consumers' dollar demands. The American system produces fewer bicycles per capita than does the Russian, twice as much sugar and cotton cloth, three times as much meat, ten times as many washing machines and refrigerators, 40 times as many autos. Look back at Fig. 42-1 for the data on a list of individual products.

The way our market system responds to consumer demands is not perfect. Varying degrees of monopoly and monopsony throughout the economy impede allocations of resources in accord with the purely competitive "ideal" of consumers' sovereignty. Introduction of new products depends on private profit incentives, with widespread failure and waste along with the successful ventures. Consumers seem to have little control over the allocation of resources to advertising and other selling costs, which are used to tell us what we ought to want. Social costs and social benefits not mirrored in prices and costs distort resource allocation. But, over-all, consumer choice is *the* powerful director of economic production in our basically price-directed, unplanned economy.

Lastly, there is the 20-odd per cent of the gross national product channelled through the public sector—presumably on a one-person-one-vote criterion rather than one-dollar-one-vote. We say this one-fifth reflects what the people want as reflected through our democratic political processes. There are obvious problems in this public sector; they were spelled out in Chapter 35. Here the economist cannot answer alone. Answer for yourself how far we should go in substituting the public sector for the market, and how our public sector compares with the Russians?

Equity

Does the Russian system provide a more equitable distribution of income than ours? By substantially eliminating incomes from property, the communists have eliminated many very high incomes of capitalist systems. Worker money-incomes, on the other hand, are more unequally distributed than in the United States, but then somewhat equalized by subsidized government services and pricing policies. This fact reflects the heavy emphasis placed on monetary work incentives by the communists.

How about American capitalism? Our incomes are unequally distributed, before and after taxes. But over the past half-century there has been some tendency toward greater equality, perhaps arising from the growth of trade unions, perhaps from government tax and expenditure policies, perhaps from other causes. The emergence of a huge, reasonably well-to-do middle class is one of the striking developments of recent American history. But how equal should incomes be, if we want to retain the incentives to work and invest which underlie our high standard of living? The question of how equal incomes should be is, ultimately, the basic one of how the g.n.p. pie should be sliced. On this ethical question, again make up your own mind. But remember the Russian experience that individual money rewards seem to be a more powerful economic incentive than the communists used to admit. And remember too the problems we will face if the wage and profit shares get badly out of line with the requirements for a continued productive, growing economy. Any income redistribution that reduces total output is hard to defend.

PLANNING WITH PRIVATE ENTERPRISE: THE NEW LOOK?

Most of the world's economies lie somewhere between America's private enterprise and Russia's communism. Some, like Yugoslavia, are near the communist end of the spectrum, but with a new twist that allows widespread individual initiative and some market guidance. Others, like the United Kingdom, are mainly private enterprise but with a number of nationalized industries. The Indian pattern with a lot of governmental planning and direct investment but with mainly private production, illustrates another "mixed" experiment, adjusted to the special needs of a developing nation.

May these new experiments in economic planning, which retain private enterprise and economic freedom, point the way to the future? Economic planning has ceased to be a dirty word to many ·conservative European businessmen. France has been one of the pioneers in this experiment. A brief look at her experience illustrates these attempts to synthesize broad planning with the market and individual initiative.

After World War II, France faced economic problems on every side—inadequate foreign-exchange reserves, intermittent unemployment, inflationary pressures, and inadequate government finances at home. Not least, she was humiliated and frustrated by her failure to play a significant role in the war against Germany. To revitalize the French economy, French government officials, in informal consultation with business and labor leaders, began to develop informal plans to encourage recovery and more stable growth for the economy. By 1960, a combined planning process had been widely accepted.

The French planning process is the outgrowth of a continuing search for means to "rationalize" economic investment and private capitalism through combined private-public planning while maintaining the right of private business to make its own decisions. Essentially, private business, labor unions, farmers, and government officials work out together a plan for stable economic growth that seems reasonable to all of them. These consultations now cover over two years for each five-year plan and normally involve some 4,000 businessmen, labor leaders, farmers, governmental officials, and academicians. Then the resulting plan is accepted as a basis for both public and private policies. But individual firms are left free to make their own decisions within this broad plan, knowing that if others go along they can count on roughly the growth and markets outlined in the plan.

Look at the 1966–70 plan. First, government economists mapped out three alternative patterns of French growth up to 1970, postulating 4, 5, and 6 per cent annual growth rates. Each one covered not only total g.n.p., but also estimates of exports and imports, consumption and investment spending, materials and labor requirements, and the like, for 28 major sectors of the economy. Second, these broad alternatives were discussed within the government and with the Economic and Social Council, an assembly of leaders of industry, labor, farmers, consumers, and other private economic groups. This Council, after much discussion, tentatively decided that a 5 per cent growth rate looked feasible, and suggested that a more detailed plan be worked out on that basis. In the third stage, this more detailed 5 per cent plan was sent out to some 25 joint public-private working committees, each of which examined the requirements and implications in detail for its sector of the economy. This involved widespread consultations with individual firms on expansion plans, labor requirements, import and export assumptions, and the like. (Remember American antitrust policy?)

In the fourth stage, all these committees reported back to Paris, where the reports were combined and reworked into a final consistent plan for the whole economy for the years 1966 through 1970, with the 5 per cent over-all growth rate. Lastly, the plan was adopted by the French cabinet and by the National Assembly as the basis for French government and private planning.

Up to this point, the plan may sound more like Moscow than Paris, except for a broader French private participation in determining the goals. But despite its official adoption, the French plan does not bind the government, business, or anybody else. Yet early evidence suggests that it is being taken most seriously as a basis for both public and private economic decisions. The Bank of France and the government ministries will hardly disregard it when their top officials were instrumental in putting it together. Private businessmen and labor leaders were similarly involved, agreeing that it was both good for France and reasonable for their sectors. Businessmen know that if the plan is adhered to, France will be prosperous and they will find markets for their own expansions called for by the plan. Moreover, most investment capital in France flows through government-controlled channels, so the government can exercise pressure if it chooses. Thus, while the plan is neither a forecast nor a binding program, it is intended to provide a widely accepted basis for combining more stable growth with private freedom. Sometimes it's called "indicative" planning. Others call the French approach "soft" planning to differentiate it from the Russian variety.

Yugoslavia illustrates another mix, over toward the communist extreme. She is especially interesting because she may present a preview of the pattern toward which Russia's "new look" is moving. Under Tito, Yugoslavia broke away from Stalinist Russia in 1948. The Yugoslavs found rigid communist planning inefficient, overcentralized, and unable to give individual workers a meaningful sense of participation in the socialist state. They gradually evolved a mixed socialist system in which (1) all major productive resources are owned by the state, (2) small farmers and enterprisers are permitted to operate independent businesses (up to five employees), (3) bigger farms and businesses are operated by the workers involved, with their own managers, (4) prices are largely determined in the marketplace, reflecting costs and consumer demands, (5) profits go mainly to provide earnings for managers and workers in each firm, (6) the state retains basic control over the economy's growth through control over investment funds and the tax and banking systems, (7) heavy state taxation obtains funds for growth-oriented investment, and (8) the growth planning process is somewhat like the French, with widespread participation but stronger state control over the final outcome.

How well have the French and Yugoslav experiments worked? On the whole, apparently well—especially the latter. Since 1950 the French economy has grown at about 5 per cent, though with repeated inflation surges as plans exceeded productive capability and with some instability. Yugoslav growth has averaged a spectacular 9 per cent, though the economy is still very poor and has also experienced persistent inflationary pressure.

Other nations have tried their own approaches to economic "rationalization" over the postwar period. Britain has moved toward a pervasive government-sponsored "incomes policy" prescribing growth rates for wages and profits in a stably growing economy, though without detailed indicative planning. Even West Germany, commonly considered far over on the private-enterprise side, does a lot of behind-the-scenes planning. During the decade ending in 1960, 56 per cent of Germany's net investment was financed by the government—directly, or indirectly through government loans and special tax privileges to industries that followed policies consistent with the plans for German growth. Japan in some ways presents the most interesting and successful experiment. Using some central planning and a public-private mix a little like France's, she has grown at a spectacular rate during the past decade, reaching 15 per cent per annum in some years. See Table 42-3 for the data.

Some observers say that these experiments are the new look for the democratic societies—planning combined with private enterprise. But others take a dimmer view. They question whether planning deserves much of the credit for the European prosperity; other forces, especially the recovery from World War II and the Common Market, may explain more of the success. West European growth has slowed substantially in the 1960's. Moreover, the critics question whether such combined public-private planning may not be an entering wedge for more governmental control over the private economy. At first the plan is voluntary. But after a while, when some private firms or unions decide not to play the roles assigned them under the plan, it may be a short step for the government to exert pressure, or even to shift the plan to a compulsory basis through legislation.

American observers raise another question: What about antitrust laws? In France, cartelization provides a long history of firms working together in the major industries. In the United States, not only is that tradition lacking but collusive price-and-output planning by competing firms is strictly illegal. Should we abrogate our antitrust laws for planning?

Lastly, informal planning sooner or later requires agreement on an "incomes policy," which specifies the shares of the growing g.n.p. that should go to labor and to profits. The unions in other nations may be a lot less agreeable than those in France, where workers are less unified than in many other nations, and even France is having serious wage problems. Dutch cooperative planning essentially blew up in the early 1960's when the unions refused to accept the wage holddowns provided in the official plans. The Kennedy-Johnson wage-price guideposts represent a tentative approach to such an incomes policy in the U.S.

Convergence
of Economic Systems?

Currently, a debate rages among economists over whether capitalist and communist economies are converging on a middle ground. No one argues that all nations will soon have identical mixed economies. It is unlikely that Russia, Yugoslavia, France, and the U.S. will soon look the same. But after a survey of European economies, Stanford's

J. E. Howell and U.C.L.A.'s Neil Jacoby advance the following two hypotheses: [9]

(1) Optimum performance by advanced economies requires a judicious and probably changing blend of central economic management and decentralized competitive market direction.
(2) There is an increasing appearance of convergence among the economic management systems of advanced countries.

Time will tell whether Howell and Jacoby are right. Do their hypotheses point the optimal path for the United States?

CONCLUSION

Since the beginning of recorded history, men have sought the perfect society. In the books that fill the libraries, many of these utopias promise peace and plenty for all. But it is a long step from dream to reality. In the real world, the utopias that look best in the writing sometimes turn sour for quite unforeseen reasons.

Over the years, some economists have worked out the details of an "ideal" democratic economy. In it, resources would be allocated in accordance with consumer market demands, individuals would be free to work and spend as they wish, state-owned capital resources would be devoted to producing what consumers want, and the proceeds from state enterprises would be distributed among the people to provide as much income equality as the public desired. This is much like the utopia of the early socialists, with state ownership of resources and operation of enterprise, with political democracy, and with economic implementation through the price system. Its advocates claim it combines the best features of private enterprise and of socialism.

But in the real world, are centralized economic control and democratic freedom in fact compatible? The Russian official blueprint looks surprisingly like this model, but in operation it looks different. Wise observers have often noted

[9] *European Economics: East and West* (New York: World Publishing Company, 1967).

that dispersion of economic and political power are usually handmaidens to each other—that centralized economic power and political democracy seldom live long together. If this is true, the attempt to "plan" and centrally control economic activity toward the goals we want may be a false dream, likely to lead to political and economic slavery rather than to organized plenty.

The economic system must be our servant, not our master, in an effective society. If the society has fundamentally democratic, individualistic ideals, most people must be at heart satisfied with the way the system works—not in detail and all the time, but by and large. Lewis Carroll, in *Alice in Wonderland*, puts his finger tellingly on the basic problem:

The Dodo suddenly called out, "The race is over!" and they all crowded round, panting, and asking, "But who has won?"

This question the Dodo could not answer without a great deal of thought, and it sat for a long time with one finger pressed upon its forehead, while the rest waited in silence. At last the Dodo said, "*Everybody* has won, and all must have prizes."

In a working, democratic society most must win, and most must have prizes. What shall the prizes be, and how can the economic system keep everyone satisfied with his reward? The American economy provides prizes in abundance, compared with all the other nations of the world. Any reasonable evaluation must count it highly successful. But to be pleased should not make us smug. The American economic system is not perfect. And it will change over the years ahead, as it adapts to both changing needs and changing objectives.

You should now be able to do a good share of your own thinking on how the American economy should steer over the years ahead. Economic analysis alone cannot give you answers to the hard problems we face. But it can help greatly to illuminate the way in a changing world.

For Analysis and Discussion

1. In the light of your study of the American economic system and alternative systems, make a careful list of the major defects, if any, you see in the American system. What, if any, reforms do you think are needed, and how feasible do you think each of your reforms is?
2. During the past half-century, the economic climate of the world has shifted markedly in the direction of central economic planning and collectivism, away from the major reliance on private-enterprise capitalism. What factors do you think have been most important in bringing about this change?
3. Recently the U.S.S.R. has apparently moved toward a limited profit motive for managers in some consumer-goods industries. If this experiment is broadened, do you think it will be compatible with basic planning for the rest of the economy? Explain your answer.
4. Since World War II, three of the nations showing the highest growth rates are Russia (a communist state), West Germany (a basically private-enterprise economy), and Yugoslavia (a modified socialist country). How do you account for this fact? Does it indicate that the two types of economic organization are equally fitted for producing continued, rapid growth? Or that other factors are the important ones in determining growth rates? Is there another explanation?
5. In Russia, wages are set by the central planners to keep total purchasing power about in line with the supply of goods to be bought. Would some variant of this plan be a good approach to our problem of avoiding creeping, wage-push inflation? If you think so, defend your answer against the likely attack of a union member.
6. Make a list of those attributes of present-day communist Russia that seem to you most objectionable. How many of these attributes are economic, how many social, how many political?
7. Do you believe the U.S. should adopt some of the informal planning approach (described in the chapter) now being used in Europe and Japan? What seem to you the main advantages and disadvantages?
8. What does your own utopia look like?

CURRENT RESEARCH

The two chapters in Part Seven raise a wide range of problems on which active research is in progress. Again, these are only a sample which will, hopefully, stir interest for more.

Adjustment to Change: Automation and Disarmament. Chapters 1 and 2 of H. A. Simon's *The Shape of Automation* (Harper and Row, 1965) provide a good introductory overview of the impact of "automation," with special emphasis on the likely role of the computer; reversing the order of the chapters may make them easier reading. C. Silberman's *Myths of Automation* (Harper and Row, 1966) brings the arguments to bear on current issues. *Automation and Technological Change*, J. Dunlop, ed. (Prentice-Hall, 1962), pulls together the work of a number of leading economists on different aspects of the problem; try especially George Taylor's analysis of automation's impact on collective bargaining.

Several recent studies illustrate different analytical approaches to the impact of disarmament, when and if it comes. In *Defense and Disarmament*, R. Bolton, ed., see especially the analysis by Washington University's M. Weidenbaum and others in Part III. "Input-Output Analysis of Disarmament Impacts" by W. Leontief and M. Hoffenberg, in *Disarmament and the Economy*, E. Benoit and K. Boulding, eds. (Harper and Row, 1963), shows how a new mathematical technique (input-output analysis) can be used to predict the impact of changes in government spending on all sectors of the economy; for a more thorough description of the technique and its results, see the *Scientific American*, April, 1961.

The U.S.S.R. and the Mixed Economies. For an introduction to the operation of the current Soviet economy, try Harry Schwartz's *The Soviet Economy Since Stalin* (Lippincott, 1965), or R. Campbell's *Soviet Economic Power* (Houghton Mifflin, 1966). *New Directions in the Soviet Economy*, a five-volume compendium by Congress' Joint Economic Committee in 1966, provides a mass of detail on recent Soviet developments. On the "new look" in Soviet planning, see G. Burck, "The Toughest Management Job in the World" (*Fortune*, July 1966); Marshall Goldman looks further ahead in "The Reluctant Consumer and Economic Fluctuations in the Soviet Union" (*Journal of Political Economy*, August, 1965), which predicts that the Soviets may soon face problems of unemployment and business fluctuations Western style. At a more advanced level, A. Bergson's *Economics of Soviet Planning* (Yale Univ. Press, 1964) provides an authoritative analysis of the entire planning process.

A readable introduction to mixed private-public planning in Europe is provided by N. Jacoby and J. E. Howell's *European Economics: East and West* (World, 1967); and by N. Chamberlain, *Private and Public Planning* (McGraw-Hill, 1966). A more advanced analysis of the planning experience in the U.S.S.R., France, India, and Yugoslavia, is provided by *National Economic Planning* (Columbia Univ. Press, 1967). A. Maddison's *Economic Growth in the West* (Twentieth Century Fund, 1964) views governmental-private policy mixes as one part of the general growth process in Western Europe, and gives most credit for success to governmental aggregate demand policies. L. A. Lecht provides a look at some implications of such approaches for the U.S. in *Goals, Priorities, and Dollars* (Free Press, 1966).

Cutting across both the Soviet and Western "mixed" economies, two studies, *The Red Executive* and *The European Executive* (Doubleday, 1959 and 1963) by Wisconsin's David Granick, draw an intriguing parallel between managerial problems and behavior in the two types of economies.

Lastly, though to us many of its articles smack more of propaganda than of research, sample the publication, *Problems of Economics*, if your library has it. This is a monthly translation into English of current papers by leading Soviet economists on all phases of Russian economics and the performance of the Soviet economy.

MATHEMATICAL
APPENDIXES [1]

I: G.N.P. Determination and the Multiplier.

II: Demand Functions and Elasticity of Demand.

III: Cost Curves and Profit Maximization.

IV: Production Functions and the Distribution of Income.

In economics, as in many other disciplines, mathematics has important uses. Mathematics provides a convenient, concise language for stating complicated ideas and relationships. It facilitates the analysis of complicated interrelationships and helps in reaching "correct" conclusions from sets of assumptions or premises. It provides a language for stating "models" or theories in a precise way that makes them testable by rigorous statistical analysis of empirical data ("econometrics").

Since an increasing number of college students know some mathematics, these brief appendixes use mathematics (through elementary calculus) to state precisely and rigorously some of the concepts and arguments developed verbally or graphically in the text. Each appendix relates directly to the chapter or section of the text indicated. If you know some mathematics and especially if you find the language of mathematics a helpful one, the following appendixes may prove a useful supplement to the verbal and graphical exposition of the same ideas in the chapters concerned.

The appendixes show, in very elementary forms, how mathematical language and mathematical reasoning can simplify and illuminate the (sometimes complex) interrelationships with which economic analysis must deal. Although a half century ago there were virtually no economists interested in applying mathematical anlysis to economic problems, today use of mathematics in economics has become commonplace; and, as the appendix to Chapter 9 indicates, "econometrics" (the use of mathematically stated models as the basis for quantitative measurement in analysis of economic variables) has become the fastest-growing branch of modern economics. The following appendixes give a small indication of how mathematics can help in stating clearly and precisely some of the important concepts and relationships in economics.[2]

---

[1] Prepared in collaboration with Professor Michael Lovell of Carnegie-Mellon University.

[2] If you find these appendixes interesting and want to investigate mathematical economics a bit further, R. G. D. Allen, *Mathematical Economics* (New York: Macmillan, 1956) provides an excellent introduction for students who know the calculus. Lawrence Klein's *Introduction to Econometrics* (Englewood Cliffs, N.J.: Prentice-Hall, 1962) is a comparable introduction to the field of econometrics, though it is designed primarily for readers who have also had a course in elementary statistics.

Appendix I (to Chapter 6)

G.N.P. DETERMINATION AND THE MULTIPLIER

Chapter 6 presents a simple algebraic model showing how, in an economy assuming no government or foreign trade, private investment and the marginal propensity to consume interact to determine the level of g.n.p. This appendix first states the model quite generally in matematical terms, and then develops more rigorously "the multiplier" and the way in which it helps explain the impact of changes in investment on g.n.p.

A. The Income-Determination Model. In Chapter 6 two consumption functions were presented. In one, consumption (C) was simply a fixed proportion of g.n.p. (Y). In the other, a somewhat more general form was used: [3]

$$C = a + bY \qquad (I.1)$$

(Of course, if $a = 0$, then this reduces to the simpler consumption function.) As in Chapter 6, since all of g.n.p. is either consumed or invested (I)

$$Y = C + I \qquad (I.2)$$

Now substitute the consumption function into this last equation in order to obtain

$$Y = a + bY + I \qquad (I.3)$$

Next, subtract bY from both sides:

$$Y - bY = (1 - b)Y = a + I \qquad (I.4)$$

Dividing both sides by the marginal propensity to save, $1 - b$, gives us

$$Y = \left(\frac{1}{1-b}\right)(a + I) \qquad (I.5)$$

as the equilibrium level of g.n.p., in which consumption is at the level prescribed by the consumption function (equation I.1) for the given level of I and the resulting level of Y. In particular, if $a = 40$, $b = .6$, and $I = 100$ (as in Chapter 6), this last equation reveals that gross national product must be 350:

$$\left(\frac{1}{1-.6}\right)(40 + 100) = 350$$

B. The Multiplier. The "multiplier" tells us what happens as a result of a rise in investment to a new

[3] You will remember from the text discussion that $0 < b < 1$.

level (I^*). Clearly g.n.p. will rise, and as people receive more income, consumption will rise as well. Let Y^* denote the new equilibrium level of income and C^* the new equilibrium level of consumption, when the increase in I has exercised its full effect.

Since these new equilibrium values, Y^* and C^*, must satisfy both equations I.1 and I.5, the same line of reasoning as before implies that

$$Y^* = \left(\frac{1}{1-b}\right)(a + I^*) \qquad (I.5^*)$$

Subtracting equation I.5 from this last expression yields

$$Y^* - Y = \left(\frac{1}{1-b}\right)(I^* - I) \qquad (I.6)$$

The expression in large parentheses, the reciprocal of the marginal propensity to save, is the multiplier. It tells us by how much the change in investment ($I^* - I$) must be multiplied in order to determine the change that it will induce in g.n.p.

C. Addition of Government Spending and Taxes. Government spending and taxes can readily be introduced into this multiplier analysis. Government spending, G, then represents purchases of one part of the current g.n.p. Consequently, we must rewrite equation I.2 to read

$$Y = C + I + G \qquad (I.7)$$

In addition, we must now recognize a distinction between gross national product and disposable income. Specifically, let T denote tax revenue, and suppose that consumption depends on disposable (after-tax) income, so that $C = a + b(Y - T)$. Then

$$Y = a + b(Y - T) + G + I \qquad (I.8)$$

Proceeding as before, we obtain

$$Y = \left(\frac{1}{1-b}\right)(a - bT + G + I)$$

as the equation explaining the equilibrium level of g.n.p. as determined by private investment, consumption behavior, government expenditure, and taxes. Note that for any given tax take, government spending and investment both have the same multiplier.

On the other hand, the effect of an increase in taxes is to change g.n.p. by a negative "tax multiplier" of $-b/(1-b)$. Thus, if government expenditure and taxes both increase by \$3 billion we would have

$$Y^* = \left(\frac{1}{1-b}\right) [a - b(T+3) + (G+3) + I] = Y + 3$$

That is, income increases by the same amount as taxes and government spending, which in Chapters 6 and 13 is called the "balanced-budget multiplier."

D. Dynamics of the Multiplier. This exercise tells us nothing about the nature of the adjustment process. Let us now consider the dynamic process by which Y rises as the result of the increase in I. This corresponds to the discussion of successive rounds of consumption-spending out of rising income in Chapter 6 on page 66. Let time be measured in discrete units, say months, and suppose that the level of consumption during the current month depends upon the income earned in the immediately preceding month. Thus

$$C_t = a + bY_t - {}_1, \qquad (I.9)$$

where the subscripts serve to indicate the time period.

Now let us suppose that the marginal propensity to consume, b, is ¾; that $a = 20$; and that initially, at time zero, investment is 67.5, $G = T = 0$, and income $Y_0 = 350$. From equation I.9 we find that, in period one, consumption will be

$$C_1 = 20 + ¾ \times 350 = 282.5$$

If investment were to remain constant at 67.5, there would be no tendency for g.n.p. to change from 350. (Check that $C_1 + I_1 = Y_1 = 350$.) This is the sense in which the economy is said to be in *equilibrium*. But suppose that instead investment increases by 10, to 77.5. Our initial equilibrium is disturbed, and the economy will gradually adjust to the disturbance. The nature of the adjustment process is suggested by the following table:

Period	$I_t - I_0$	$C_t - C_0$	$Y_t - Y_0$
1	10		10
2	10	7.5	17.5
3	10	13.1	23.1
4	10	17.3	27.3
.	.	.	.
.	.	.	.
.	.	.	.
∞	10	30	40

Each increase in income induces additional consumption in the next period, which constitutes ad-

ditional income to the seller of goods or services, and so on *ad infinitum*. Will the process stop? The total increase in income is

$$10 + 7.5 + 5.6 + 4.2 + \dots$$

But this is readily seen to be a sum of an infinite number of terms. More generally, of course, for any arbitrary marginal propensity to consume, the change in income resulting from a change in investment will be

$$\Delta I + b\Delta I + b^2\Delta I + b^3\Delta I + \dots = \Delta I(1 + b + b^2 + b^3 + \dots) \qquad (I.10)$$

The conditions under which such a sum will be finite can be determined if we recall the procedure for deriving the sum of a geometric series. Let S_n be the first n terms in such a series; i.e.

$$S_n = 1 + b + b^2 + \dots + b^n \qquad (I.11)$$

Multiplying by b gives

$$bS_n = b + b^2 + \dots + b^{n+1} \qquad (I.12)$$

Subtracting equation I.12 from I.11 yields

$$S_n - bS_n = (1 - b)S_n = 1 - b^{n+1}$$

Consequently,

$$S_n = \frac{1 - b^{n+1}}{1 - b} \qquad (I.13)$$

It is now obvious that

$$\lim_{n \to \infty} S_n = \frac{1}{1 - b} \qquad (I.14)$$

if and only if the marginal propensity to consume is less than unity. This limiting expression is, of course, the multiplier of equation I.6. If the marginal propensity to consume were greater than unity, something which is conceivable but not likely except in temporary special cases, g.n.p. would increase without bounds in response to an increase in private investment spending, at least under the simple assumptions used here.[4]

[4] Readers interested in the complexities of dynamic analysis will note that equation I.6 correctly tells us that equilibrium g.n.p. will decrease as a result of an increase in investment spending if the marginal propensity to consume is greater than unity; i.e., if, somehow, g.n.p. did decline to the level suggested by that equation it would remain there indefinitely. But if $b \geq 1$ this equilibrium is *unstable*, and with the passage of time g.n.p. will diverge further and further from its equilibrium as a result of the increased consumption induced by the augmented level of investment spending. This, however, while it is analytically interesting, is extremely unlikely, since empirical studies show that the marginal propensity to consume is less than unity except under very special circumstances.

More advanced analysis would recognize that rising g.n.p. and business sales might well induce a further rise in investment spending, and thus increase the stimulative effect of any of the above assumed increases in I or G. Such further "induced" invest-ment is often called the "accelerator" effect, and is considered more completely in Chapter 9. See especially the second appendix to that chapter for a simple mathematical model incorporating both multiplier and accelerator effects.

Appendix II (to Chapter 14)

DEMAND FUNCTIONS AND ELASTICITY OF DEMAND

The demand curve for any commodity shows how many units will be bought at each price. Looked at another way, it represents the function indicating how price responds to changes in the quantity of a commodity offered for sale, given buyer preferences and incomes, and may be denoted as $p(q)$. (This function might also be denoted by p, or by $f(q)$.) It will be assumed that this function is differentiable.

As is explained in Chapter 20, demand curves are ordinarily negatively sloped; i.e., $dp/dq < 0$. This information does not tell precisely how the total revenue obtained by the sellers will respond to changes in price and quantity sold, but simple analysis of the demand function can provide an answer to this important question.

Total revenue, denoted by $r(q)$, is simply price times quantity:

$$r(q) = p(q)q \qquad (II.1)$$

Differentiating with respect to quantity yields

$$\frac{dr}{dq} = p(q) + \frac{dp}{dq}q \qquad (II.2)$$

This derivative, which economists call *marginal revenue*, may be either positive or negative (remember, $dp/dq < 0$). Selling more at a lower price will reduce total revenue if the fall in price is not offset by the increase in the quantity of the commodity purchased; i.e., if the demand is "inelastic." (Note that this is equivalent to saying that a reduction in price will increase the number of units sold less than proportionately.)

What level of output with its resulting price would maximize *total revenue* (but not necessarily profits)? We can tell by examining the demand function with the aid of a few rules of elementary calculus. Remember that a necessary condition for a maximum is that the first derivative of revenue with respect to quantity be zero

$$\frac{dr}{dq} = p(q) + \frac{dp}{dq}q = 0 \qquad (II.3)$$

This maximum can be defined in terms of the elasticity of the demand function. Economists, following the reasoning on elasticity in Chapter 20, customarily denote elasticity more precisely as [5]

$$\eta = -\frac{dq}{dp}\cdot\frac{p}{q} \qquad (II.4)$$

Thus, when elasticity of demand is unity, revenue is maximized.

If demand is "inelastic" (i.e., $\eta < 1$), note that a reduction in the quantity of the commodity offered on the market would increase total revenue. Thus, a businessman with control over his selling price and output would be foolish to produce at a point where the demand for his commodity is inelastic, for then he could obtain more revenue by producing and selling less!

It is easy to determine graphically the elasticity of demand. Consider the demand curve q^*p^* first graph, p. 586. To find the elasticity of demand at any point a (corresponding to price p and quantity q) we note that $-dq/dp = (q^* - q)/p$; hence

$$\eta = -\frac{dq}{dp}\cdot\frac{p}{q} = \left(\frac{q^* - q}{p}\right)\frac{p}{q} = \frac{q^* - q}{q} \qquad (II.5)$$

From the last equality we see that for a linear demand curve, the elasticity of demand is simply the ratio of the excess of the quantity that could have been sold at a zero price over actual sales (i.e., $(q^* - q)$, divided by quantity sold (q)). Note that, although this demand curve has a constant slope, it is not characterized by a constant elasticity. The elasticity changes along the curve. If q^* units were sold at zero price, the elasticity of demand would be zero; for higher prices, less is sold and elasticity increases without bound as the price approaches p^*.

To determine the elasticity of demand at some point on a nonlinear demand curve, such as point a

[5] If, as for the individual seller under perfect competition, $\frac{dq}{dp} = \infty$, then we say elasticity is infinite.

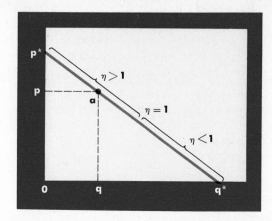

on curve DD on the second graph, draw a straight line tangent to the demand curve at that point, and from it determine the location of point q^*. Since at point a the demand curve and the tangent line have the same slope, as well as the same p and q values, they have the same elasticity at that point; hence formula II.5 again applies:

$$\eta = \frac{q^* - q}{q}$$

Is it possible for a demand curve to have constant elasticity throughout its entire length? Yes. Suppose that $q = \alpha p^{\beta}$, $\beta < 0$;

then $dq/dp = \beta \alpha p^{\beta - 1} = \beta \dfrac{q}{p}$

and $\eta = - \left(\beta \dfrac{q}{p} \right) \dfrac{p}{q} = -\beta$.

I.e., the parameter-β of the demand curve is the elasticity of demand. For example, a rectangular hyperbola has a constant elasticity $= 1$.

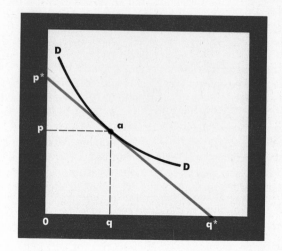

Appendix III (to Chapters 22–23)

COST CURVES AND PROFIT MAXIMIZATION

To determine what level of output will maximize profits, production costs in relation to demand considerations must be analyzed. This appendix analyzes this interrelationship mathematically.

A. Key Cost Concepts. In Chapter 22 the dependence of production costs upon the level of output was examined in detail, and a number of basic concepts were explained. Table 22-1 reported hypothetical cost figures for a firm producing a single commodity. In such cases, the *total cost function*, $c(q)$, reveals how the total costs incurred by the firm depend on the level of output; we assume that the function is differentiable. Other cost concepts discussed in the text may be expressed in terms of $c(q)$, as shown in the following list.

Fixed costs: $c(0)$
Variable costs: $c(q) - c(0)$
Total unit cost: $c(q)/q$
Variable unit cost: $[c(q) - c(0)]/q$

Fixed unit cost: $c(0)/q$
Marginal cost: $\dfrac{dc(q)}{dq}$

B. Maximizing Profits. Profit, at any level of output, $\pi(q)$, is simply the excess of total revenue over total cost; i.e.,

$$\pi(q) = r(q) - c(q) \qquad \text{(III.1)}$$

where $r(q)$ is the total revenue function discussed in Mathematical Appendix II; the three curves are plotted in Fig. 23-1 on page 314. From elementary calculus we know that if profits are maximized at some level of output $q > 0$, it is necessary that

$$\frac{\partial \pi(q)}{\partial q} = \frac{\partial r(q)}{\partial q} - \frac{\partial c(q)}{\partial q} = 0 \qquad \text{(III.2)}$$

Equation III.2 implies

$$\frac{\partial r(q)}{\partial q} = \frac{\partial c(q)}{\partial q} = 0 \qquad \text{(III.3)}$$

This states mathematically the fundamental proposition that a necessary condition for profit maximization at $q > 0$ is that marginal cost equals marginal revenue.

It is essential to note that condition III.2 does not necessarily yield a level of output, q, at which profits will be positive. In the short run, before the firm can liquidate its fixed investment, it may be worthwhile to operate at a loss rather than shut down. Remember that zero output involves fixed cost, $c(0)$, in the short run. Would a zero output minimize losses (negative profits) when there are fixed costs? Not if

$$\pi(q) = r(q) - c(q) > \pi(0) = -c(0) \quad \text{(III.4)}$$

or equivalently:

$$r(q) - [c(q) - c(0)] > 0 \qquad \text{(III.5)}$$

In other words, the firm will produce a positive output at a loss if revenue exceeds total *variable* costs. Dividing both sides of III.5 by q yields, since $r(q)/q = p$, an equivalent condition:

$$p - [c(q) - c(0)]/q > 0 \qquad \text{(III.6)}$$

This is the condition (stated on page 316) that the firm will minimize losses by shutting down altogether only if there is no positive level of output where price would exceed average variable cost.

C. Some Observations on Competitive Equilibrium. Under competitive conditions, the output of the individual firm constitutes an insignificant contribution to the total market sales of the commodity. Consequently, the price the firm receives for its output is unaffected by variation in the quantity it offers for sale; its demand curve is horizontal (i.e., $dp/dq = 0$), and from equation II.2 we have marginal revenue equal to price ($dr/dq = p$). Hence, equation III.3 implies that if firms maximize profits under competitive conditions, they produce at the point where marginal cost equals price.

This constitutes a basic proposition of economic theory which explains the general presumption of economists in favor of competition: When firms maximize profits under competitive conditions, the increment to total cost incurred in producing the last unit sold is exactly equal to the price, which is precisely as it should be. For the price reflects the consumer's evaluation of the benefits that he will obtain from the purchase of that last unit; if the benefits were less he wouldn't buy the unit, and if they were greater he would buy more units.

Chapter 24 points out that, in long-run competitive equilibrium, price is equal to the minimum point on the total-unit-cost curve. This must be the case, for a higher price would encourage new firms to enter the industry in search of profits, while a lower price would yield continued losses and induce firms to leave the industry. But if price is to be equal to the minimum point on the total-unit-cost curve, can we be sure it will also equal marginal cost, as required under competition (condition III.3, with $dr/dq = p$)? It is easy to show that the answer is, necessarily, yes. If output is at the minimum total-unit-cost level, then marginal cost will be equal to total unit cost. To establish this proposition, we note that the condition that output be at the minimum total-unit-cost level implies:

$$\frac{d\left[\dfrac{c(q)}{q}\right]}{dq} = \frac{\dfrac{dc(q)}{dq}}{q} - \frac{c(q)}{q^2} = 0$$

Multiplying through by q yields:

$$\frac{dc(q)}{dq} = \frac{c(q)}{q}$$

Thus, marginal cost is equal to average cost if output is at the firm's lowest average-unit-cost point. The marginal-cost curve cuts the average-cost curve at the latter's minimum point.

Appendix IV (to Chapters 29–30)

PRODUCTION FUNCTIONS AND THE DISTRIBUTION OF INCOME

Most firms have alternative ways to produce any given output. Thus, within limits, the services of machinery may be substituted for labor in the production of steel, or vice versa. A "production function," which states the relationship between various combinations of inputs and the resulting outputs (products), can be a helpful concept for exploring the way in which technological considerations influence the distribution of income among different factors of production (labor, capital, etc.).

A. Simple Production Functions. For simplicity, suppose that only two factors of production, labor (L) and machinery (M), are used in producing a commodity. The output (q) produced each period depends on the quantity of labor and machinery services employed. We assume that this "production function" can be described by a differentiable function of the two inputs:

$$q = f(L,M) \qquad \text{(IV.1)}$$

Such functions can be estimated empirically from business and engineering production data or derived from engineering or physical principles.

We wish to determine the optimal (i.e., highest profit) mix of labor and machinery to produce any output. We will maximize profits (π) by maximizing the excess of revenue over cost. If we assume that labor and machinery services are purchased on competitive markets at prices w and p_m, we have:

$$\pi = r(q) - wL - p_m M \qquad \text{(IV.2)}$$

or, substituting from IV.1,

$$\pi\,(L,M) = r[f(L,M)] - wL - p_m M \quad \text{(IV.3)}$$

If the optimal quantity of labor is indeed being employed, it must be impossible to increase profits by either increasing or decreasing the amount of labor used. Consequently, a necessary condition for profit maximization is that

$$\frac{\partial\pi(L,m)}{\partial L} = \frac{dr}{dq}\cdot\frac{\partial q}{\partial L} - w = 0 \qquad \text{(IV.4)}$$

Similarly, if the optimal quantity of machinery services is being employed,

$$\frac{\partial\pi(L,m)}{\partial M} = \frac{dr}{dq}\cdot\frac{\partial q}{\partial m} - p_m = 0 \qquad \text{(IV.5)}$$

As Chapters 30 and 31 indicate, economists call $\frac{\partial r}{\partial q}\cdot\frac{\partial q}{\partial L}$ the *marginal revenue product* of labor. Thus, equation IV.4 shows that to maximize profits, a firm hiring on a competitive market must hire additional workers just to the point where the marginal revenue product of labor is equal to the wage rate (pages 406 and 408).

It follows from IV.4 and IV.5 that

$$\frac{\dfrac{\partial q}{\partial m}}{p_m} = \frac{\dfrac{\partial q}{\partial L}}{w} \qquad \text{(IV.6)}$$

The economist calls $\frac{\partial q}{\partial L}$ the marginal productivity of labor; similarly, $\partial q/\partial m$ is the marginal productivity of machinery services. Equation IV.6 thus shows that under profit-maximizing equilibrium conditions in competitive markets, each factor of production is rewarded in proportion to its marginal productivity (pages 398–402).

B. The Cobb-Douglas Production Function: An Example. As an illustration, let us consider a much discussed conjecture of Professors C. W. Cobb and Paul H. Douglas (later U.S. Senator) that the total industrial output of the American economy may be described by a simple production function of the form:

$$q(L,M) = a\,L^\lambda M^{1-\lambda} \qquad \text{(IV.7)}$$

Statistical investigations have disclosed that a function of this form fits the historical data quite precisely with $\lambda = .75$. Note that this function is characterized by *constant returns to scale*; i.e., if the initial inputs are all multiplied by some scale factor $\rho > 0$, then output will also increase by ρ; more precisely:

$$q(\rho L, \rho M) = \rho q(L,M) \text{ for all } \rho \geqslant 0 \quad \text{(IV.8)}$$

What are the implications of the Cobb-Douglas analysis for the shares of labor and machinery (capital) in the national income? Not only did Cobb-Douglas find that equation IV.7 provides a reasonable explanation of how capital and labor contribute to the generation of industrial output. They also found that this function, in conjunction with equation IV.4, embodying the assumption of competition, helps to explain an important observed fact—that labor income (wages and salaries) has been a roughly stable percentage of total income over many decades.

Their explanation of the rough constancy of labor's share can be appreciated if we first observe that the marginal productivity of labor is

$$\frac{\partial q}{\partial L} = \lambda a L^{\lambda-1} M^{1-\lambda} = \lambda\frac{Q}{L} \qquad \text{(IV.9)}$$

Similarly, the marginal productivity of capital services is

$$\frac{\partial q}{\partial M} = (1-\lambda)\,aL^\lambda M^{-\lambda} = (1-\lambda)\frac{Q}{M} \quad \text{(IV.10)}$$

If output is sold on a competitive market at price p (so that $dr/dq = p$), then condition IV.4 implies

$$p\lambda\frac{Q}{L} = w \qquad \text{(IV.11)}$$

Hence,

$$\frac{Lw}{Qp} = \lambda \qquad \text{(IV.12)}$$

Now remember that Lw is labor income while Qp is the value of total output; consequently equation IV.12 implies that the ratio of labor income to total income, labor's share, is equal to the parameter λ of the Cobb-Douglas production function.

INDEX

Accelerator, 104f., 115ff.
Accounting:
  balance sheets, 268ff.
  business, 268ff.
  cost estimates, 349f.
  depreciation, 42, 269ff.
  national income accounts, 39ff.
  profit-and-loss (income) statements, 270ff.
Advantage:
  absolute, 501f.
  comparative, 502ff.
Adverse clearing balances, 140f.
Advertising:
  as a basis for monopoly, 340
  demand creation, 355f.
  evaluation, 357
AFL-CIO, 416f.
Aggregate Demand (see Demand)
Agriculture:
  in U.S.A., 4, 211ff.
  in U.S.S.R., 567f.
Alternative costs (see also Costs), 299f.
American Federation of Labor (AFL), 416ff.
Antitrust laws (see also Monopoly):
  background, 375ff.
  Celler Antimerger Act, 379f.
  Clayton Act, 378f.
  enforcement of, 380ff.
  Federal Trade Commission Act, 378f.
  impact of 381f., 387f.
  Interstate Commerce Commission Act, 377f.
  leading cases, 380ff.
  Miller-Tydings Act, 379
  research on, 462
  Robinson-Patman Act, 379
  rule of reason, 380
  Sherman Act, 264, 366, 377f.
Arbitration, 426
Assets (see also Accounting) 269
Automation (see also Technology), 412ff., 548ff.
Average cost (see Costs)

Bain, J. S., 383f.
Bakke, E. Wight, 423
Balanced-budget multiplier, 172
Balance of payments (see also International trade), 506ff., 512ff., 528ff.
Balance of trade (see also International trade), 499ff., 508f., 521f.

Balance sheet:
  banks, 136ff.
  business, 268ff.
Bank holiday, 163f.
Banks (see also Federal Reserve System and Money):
  business cycles and, 107ff.
  central, 143ff., 155ff.
  check clearance, 133ff.
  commercial, 133f.
  credit (deposit) expansion and contraction 107f., 137ff., 155ff.
  Federal Reserve, 143ff., 156ff.
  International Bank for Reconstruction and Development, 655f.
  monetary policy and, 155ff.
  reserves, 139f., 144, 155ff.
  supervision of, 145
Baruch, Bernard, 454
Bastiat, Frederick, 522
Berle, A. A., 385f.
Board of Governors of the Federal Reserve System (see Federal Reserve System)
Bonds (see Corporations, Federal Reserve System, Public debt, and Securities, corporate)
Break-even charts, 350
Budget (see Fiscal policy and Public economy)
"Built-in flexibility," 175f., 180, 480
Business cycles:
  acceleration effect, 104f., 115ff.
  analytical framework, 101ff.
  consumption behavior, 103f.
  and cost-price relationships, 105f.
  countercyclical policy (see also Economic stabilization), 184ff.
  economic growth and, 99ff., 199, 205
  fiscal policy, 171ff.
  innovation and, 106
  international aspects, 110f., 515ff.
  investment behavior, 104ff.
  money and, 86f., 107f.
  multiplier effect, 103, 115ff., 172f.
  research on, 102, 255f.
  stock market, 110
  theories of, 102f.
  turning points, 103ff., 108ff.
Business enterprise (see Firm, business)
Business forecasting (see Forecasting)
Businessmen (see Firm, business; Entrepreneur; and Profits)

Capacity (see Capital accumulation and Investment)
Capital (see also Accounting and Investment), 269ff.
Capital accumulation (see also Economic growth and Investment):
  business cycles and, 106f.
  depreciation allowances and, 43

Capital accumulation (Cont.):
  economic growth and, 200ff., 212f., 225f.
  interest rates and, 452
  in underdeveloped countries, 236f., 241ff.
  in U.S.S.R., 562ff.
Capital consumption allowances, 42f.
Capital deepening, 203, 211
Capitalism, 22f., 387f., 560ff.
Capitalization:
  in asset valuation, 452
  of property taxes, 492f.
Capital movements, international, 516f.
Capital-output ratio, 207, 211, 241ff.
Cartels, 338, 363f., 379
Cash-balances approach, 91f.
Celler Anti-Merger Act, 379f.
Central banking (see also Federal Reserve System and also Monetary policy), 143ff., 155ff.
China, 247ff., 560ff.
Circular flow of income and expenditures, 20f., 44
Clay, Sir Henry, 227f.
Clayton Act (see also Antitrust laws), 378f.
Cobb-Douglas production function, 208, 588
Collective bargaining (see also Labor unionism): 420ff., 424ff.
  research on, 462
  role of government, 424ff.
  Taft-Hartley Act, 425
  Wagner Act, 424f.
Collective goods, 332, 470
Collusion (see Antitrust laws and Price fixing)
Combinations, business (see also Antitrust laws), 263ff.
Commodity, defined, 260
Common Market, 526f.
Communism, 560ff.
Comparative advantage, principle of, 502ff.
Competition (see also Monopoly and Profits): 16ff., 321ff.
  degrees of, 322f., 336ff.
  economic efficiency and, 331ff.
  evaluation, 331ff.
  foreign, 519ff.
  income distribution and, 397ff.
  long-run equilibrium, 321ff.
  monopolistic, 337f., 347ff.
  nonprice, 355f.
  oligopoly, 337f., 359ff.
  Pareto optimality and, 335
  public policy (see also Antitrust laws) 376ff.
  pure, defined, 322f.
  quality, 355f.
  tax incidence and, 292, 486ff.
  "unfair," 340
  in determination of wages, 397f., 404ff., 408f.
Complementary products, 284
Composition, fallacy of, 34
Concentration ratios, 359f.
Conciliation, 426

Congress of Industrial Organizations (CIO), 416f.
Construction cycle (see also Business cycles), 107
Consumer credit, 150
Consumer demand:
  aggregate, 40, 228f.
  business cycles and, 103f.
  consumer sovereignty, 355ff., 473ff.
  consumption function, 63ff., 79f.
  determinants of, 76ff., 273ff.
  disposable personal income, 43, 75f.
  effects of advertising, 355ff.
  elasticity, 280ff.
  forecasting, 113f.
  patterns of, 274
  propensity to consume, 66ff.
  quality competition, 355f.
  research on, 389
  resource allocation, 323ff.
  in U.S.S.R., 562ff., 570f.
Consumers' sovereignty, 473f.
Consumer surplus, 279, 293
Consumption (see Consumer demand)
Consumption function (see also Consumer demand), 63ff., 79f.
Corporations (see also Firm, business), 260ff.
Cost-benefit analysis, 472f.
Cost of living index, 46ff.
Cost of capital, 83
Cost-plus pricing, 350
Costs: 298ff., 586f.
  accounting, 300f.
  alternative (or opportunity), 299f.
  in business cycles, 298ff.
  in business firms, 298ff.
  comparative, 502ff.
  competitive equilibrium and, 313ff.
  constant, 292, 327ff.
  decreasing, 292, 340f.
  defined, 299f.
  explicit, 300n.
  factors of production, 298ff., 309ff.
  fixed, 301ff.
  implicit, 300n.
  increasing, 292, 327ff.
  incremental, 372f.
  long-run, 304f., 321ff.
  managerial economics and, 370ff.
  marginal, 314ff.
  research on, 389
  selling, 354
  short-run, 304f., 313ff.
  social, 333
  standard, 303f., 349f.
  sunk, 371f.
  variable, 301ff.
Countercyclical policy (see Business cycles and Economic stabilization)
Credit (see also Banks, Federal Reserve System, and Money):
  business cycles and, 107f.
  consumer, 78f., 150
  creation by banks, 137ff.
  Federal Reserve control, 145ff., 155ff.
  foreign lending, 498ff.

Credit (*Cont.*):
  rationing, 157f.
Currency (*see* Money)
Current ratio, 269
Cycles (*see* Business cycles)

Das Kapital, 560
Debt (*see* Banks *and* Public debt)
Decreasing-cost industry, 340f.
Deficit spending (*see also* Fiscal policy) 171ff., 189ff.
Deflation (*see* Business cycles *and* Inflation)
Demand (*see also* Consumer demand):
  advertising and, 355f.
  aggregate, 55ff., 85ff., 157ff., 172ff., 228f., 279ff., 550
  complementary, 284
  creation, 355f.
  cross-elasticity, 281n.
  defined, 275
  derived, 104, 115ff., 398f., 406f.
  elasticity, 280ff., 585f.
  functions, 275ff., 585f.
  income elasticity, 281n.
  individual, 275ff.
  for labor, 406f.
  for loanable funds, 449f.
  market, 279ff.
  for productive services, 398ff.
  schedule, 275ff., 585f.
  supply and, 289ff.
Denison, Edward, 211, 214, 219, 233
Depletion allowance, 488
Deposits (*see* Money *and* Banks)
Depreciation, 42f., 269ff., 372, 488
Depreciation reserves, 83
Depression (*see also* Business cycles):
  analysis, 56, 99ff., 194f.
  fiscal policy, 171f., 184ff.
  monetary policy, 109, 160ff., 184ff.
  wage-price policy, 185f.
Despres, Emile, 541
Development (*see* Economic growth *and* Underdeveloped countries)
Diminishing returns, law of, 201f., 311, 406f.
Diminishing utility, 276
Disarmament, 553ff.
Disposable personal income, *defined,* 43
Distribution of income:
  analytical framework, 397ff.
  changing price levels and, 126ff.
  in a competitive economy, 331f., 397ff.
  consumer demand and, 274ff.
  educational differences and, 394ff.
  effect of minimum-wage laws, 429f.
  equity in, 393f.
  impact of taxation, 469f., 486ff.
  inflation and, 126ff.
  monopoly and, 345f.
  by occupation, 394ff.

Distribution of income (*Cont.*):
  poverty, 431ff.
  production functions and, 587f.
  social security and, 440ff.
  technological advance, 412ff., 548f.
  theory of, 397ff.
  in underdeveloped countries, 233ff.
  in U.S.S.R., 569f.
Distribution theory (*see also* Distribution of income), 397ff.
Dividends (*see also* Corporations, Profits *and* Securities, corporate), 262, 270f.
Dollar shortage, 532f.
Dollar surplus, 533f.
Dual economy, 234f.
Duopoly (*see also* Monopoly *and* Oligopoly), 338n.
Dynamic processes (*see also* Economic growth):
  in business cycles, 101ff.
  multiplier-accelerator interactions, 115ff.

Earnings (*see* Income *and* Profits)
Econometric models, 26ff., 71ff., 94n., 114
Economic analysis: 2ff., 25ff.
  fallacies, 33ff.
  methodology, 26ff.
  models and theory in 26ff., and public policy 31
  social goals and, 31f.
Economic change (*see also* Consumer demand, Economic growth, *and* Technology): 546ff.
  automation, 548ff.
  disarmament, 553ff.
  research and development, 205, 213f., 223ff., 557
Economic fluctuations (*see* Business cycles)
Economic forecasting (*see* Forecasting)
Economic freedom (*see* Freedom)
Economic goals, 31f., 185.
Economic growth (*see also* Capital accumulation *and* Technology): 7f., 19f., 48ff., 179ff., 209ff., 221ff.
  aggregate demand, 219, 228f.
  balanced vs. unbalanced, 244f.
  business cycles and, 49f., 99ff., 199, 205, 228f.
  capital accumulation and, 212f., 225f., 241ff.
  in China, 247ff.
  costs of, 222
  defined, 198
  entrepreneur's role, 205, 217
  in India, 247ff.
  inflation and, 125ff., 228f.
  international comparisons, 198f.
  investment and, 225f., 241ff.
  labor and, 204f., 215ff., 226, 243ff.
  market scale, 218f.

Economic growth (*Cont.*):
  models of, 207
  natural resources, 211f.
  noneconomic factors in, 205f., 218 240f.
  objectives, 221ff.
  population and, 214ff., 237ff.
  profits and, 239, 458f.
  research on, 255f.
  savings and, 225f., 241ff.
  sources of, 211ff.
  stability of, 99ff., 207
  tax structure and, 480, 486ff.
  technical change, 204f., 213f., 224f.
  theory of, 199ff.
  in underdeveloped countries, 231ff.
  in U.S.S.R., 570f.
  wage-price policy, 229f.
Economic insecurity (*see also* Economic security *and* Social security), 438ff.
"Economic man," 274
Economic models (*see* Economic analysis *and* Models)
Economic Opportunity Act, 437, 445
Economic planning:
  in France, 577ff.
  indicative, 578
  private enterprise and, 245f., 577ff.
  in underdeveloped countries, 245f.
  in U.S.S.R., 562ff.
Economic rent, 448
Economics, *defined,* 2
Economic security (*see also* Social security), 438ff., 553, 575f.
Economic stabilization:
  built-in flexibility, 175f, 180, 480
  economic growth and, 223ff., 228ff.
  fiscal policy, 175f., 180, 184ff.
  goals, 119ff.
  monetary policy, 157ff.
  policy guides, 223ff.
  tax structure and, 175f., 480, 486ff.
  timing, 159f., 188f.
  unemployment insurance, 175
  in U.S.S.R., 572f.
  wage-price policy, 229f.
Economic system (*see also* Price system):
  capitalism, 22f., 686ff.
  communism, 686ff.
  comparative, 685ff.
  mixed, 22, 577ff.
  private enterprise, 16ff.
Economic theory (*see* Economic analysis *and subject headings*)
Education:
  economic growth and, 216f., 238f., 243
  income levels and, 394ff.
Elasticity of demand: 280ff., 585f.
  defined, 280f., 283
  product differentiation and, 351ff.
  in tax shifting, 485f.

Elasticity of supply (*see also* Costs): 288ff.
  defined, 288
  of labor, 406
  in tax shifting, 485f.
Employment (*see also* Unemployment):
  in business cycles, 99ff.
  the effect of minimum-wage laws, 429f.
  foreign lending and, 536
  inflation and, 118ff, 185
  international trade and, 499ff., 506, 519ff.
  job security, 551f.
  minimum-wage laws, 429f.
  occupational distribution, 4f.
  union wage policy and, 417ff.
Employment Act of 1946, 185
Enterprise (*see* Firm, business)
Entrepreneur (*see also* Firm, business *and* Profits):
  defined, 217n., 260
  economic growth and, 217, 240f.
  profits and, 457f.
  in underdeveloped countries, 239ff.
Equation of exchange, 88f.
Equilibrium:
  aggregate output and employment, 62ff.
  of a competitive economy, 329ff.
  of a competitive firm, 312ff., 321ff., 325ff., 586f.
  of a competitive industry, 385ff.
  defined, 28
  under demand creation, 355f.
  demand for real balances, 92f.
  and efficiency, 335
  general, 329ff.
  long-run, 323ff.
  market price, 290f.
  under monopolistic competition, 351ff.
  underemployment, 65f.
European Economic Community (Common Market), 526f.
European Free Trade Association, 526f.
Excess reserves (*see* Banks)
Exchange depreciation, 529ff.
Exchange rates (*see also* Gold standard), 513ff., 537f.
Expectations:
  consumption and, 276n.
  investment and, 87
Exports (*see* International trade)
External economies, 225, 226n., 470f.

Factors of production (*see* Capital, Labor, *and* Production)
Fair Labor Standards Act, 425
Fair Trade Legislation (*see also* Antitrust laws), 378f.
Fallacies (*see also* Economic analysis), 33ff.
Farmers (*see* Agriculture)
Federal Deposit Insurance Corporation, 194f.

Federal Open Market Committee, 143f., 147f.
Federal Reserve System (*see also* Banks, Money, *and* Monetary policy): 143ff.
  Board of Governors, 143
  check collection, 144f.
  consumer credit controls, 150
  creation of reserves, 145ff.
  Federal Reserve notes, 144, 146f.
  gold reserves, 144, 147, 164f., 167ff., 532ff.
  history of policies, 163ff.
  member banks, 143ff.
  money supply and, 145ff., 156ff.
  "moral suasion", 149f.
  and open-market operations, 146ff.
  rediscount rates, 148
  reserve requirements, 139f., 148f.
  selective controls, 149f.
  World War II financing, 164ff.
Federal Trade Commission, 379
Final-product approach to g.n.p., 40
Financial control groups, 265f.
Financial intermediaries, 132ff., 142f.
Firm, business (*see also* Corporations, Entrepreneur, *and* Profit maximization):
  balance sheet, 268ff.
  and competitive equilibrium, 312ff., 321ff.
  concentration of control, 262f.
  costs, 298ff.
  defined, 259
  economies of scale, 292
  financing, 261f., 339f.
  income statements, 270ff.
  mergers, 263ff., 379ff.
  operation of, 259ff., 298ff.
  optimum size, 305ff., 340f., 383f.
  research on, 389
  theory of, 298ff., 312ff.
Fiscal dividend, 484f.
Fiscal policy (*see also* Taxes *and* Public debt): 68ff., 171ff.
  administrative budget, 182f.
  annually balanced budget, 179
  built-in flexibility, 175f., 180, 480
  cash budget, 183
  compensatory spending, 172
  cyclically balanced budget, 179f.
  deficit spending, 171ff.
  against depression, 171f., 184ff.
  economic growth and, 246f.
  economic stabilization and, 175ff., 184ff.
  fiscal dividend, 484f.
  fiscal drag, 178f.
  full-employment budget, 177f., 180f., 183
  functional finance, 180, 571
  guides, 181

Fiscal policy (*Cont.*):
  inflation and, 175ff., 184ff.
  monetary-fiscal policy mix, 181
  multiplier effects, 172f.
  political problems, 188f.
  public debt, 189ff.
  public investment, 174f.
  tax cuts, 175
  theory of, 172f.
  timing and lags, 188f.
  in underdeveloped countries, 246f.
  unemployment insurance, 175
  in U.S.S.R., 571f.
Fisher, Irving, 88, 90
Flow-of-funds accounts, 43n.
Forecasting, 99ff., 112ff., 188f.
Foreign exchange, 513ff.
Foreign lending, 498ff., 531f.
Foreign trade multiplier, 110f., 506
Freedom:
  economic security and, 438ff., 574ff.
  effects of tax system, 480f.
  role of government, 21f., 466, 470ff., 574ff.
  in U.S.S.R., 574f.
Free goods, 293
Free trade, 505, 519ff.
Fringe benefits, 419f.
Full employment, *defined* (*see also* Employment, Unemployment, *and* types *of* public policy), 120ff.
Full-employment budget, 177f., 180f., 183
Functional finance, 180, 571

Galbraith, J. K., 385f., 474f.
Game theory, 363, 411n.
Gary dinners, 366
General Agreement on Tariffs and Trade (GATT), 525f.
Gold standard, 155, 167ff., 514ff., 528ff.
Gompers, Samuel, 416
Gosbank, 567f.
Gosplan, 563f.
Government (*see also* Antitrust laws, Fiscal policy, *and* Public policy):
  automation and, 549ff.
  business and, 373ff.
  economic growth and, 221ff.
  economic stabilization and, 184ff.
  expanding control, 189
  expenditures and revenues, 465ff.
  functions, 464ff., 559ff.
  labor and, 424ff.
  price-fixing, 185ff., 293ff.
  public economy, 464ff.
  public services, 475f.
  research and development policy, 214, 223ff., 557
  tax policy, 478ff.
Gross national product:
  actual vs. potential, 120, 221f.
  defined, 39ff.
  deflator, 47
  economic well-being and, 50f.
  equilibrium, 62ff.

Gross national product (*Cont.*):
  history, 53f., 209ff.
  and income-expenditures approach, 40, 61ff., 87
  international trade and, 499f.
  measures of, 39f.
  monetary approach, 39, 86f.
  portfolio-balance approach, 92ff.
  public debt and, 189ff.
Growth (*see* Economic growth)
Guideposts, wage-price, 185ff.

Harrington, Michael, 432
Headstart program, 437
High-powered money, 147
Holding companies, 264f.
Human capital (*see* Labor)
Hyperinflation, 125

Imports (*see* International trade)
Income:
  circular flow of, 20f., 44
  consumption and, 79f.
  demand for money and, 91f.
  disposable personal, 43
  interest, 448ff.
  international comparisons, 232f.
  life cycle, 77
  by occupations, 394ff.
  as payments for productive services, 398f.
  permanent, 77, 175n.
  poverty, 431ff.
  profits, 457ff.
  property, 452ff.
  psychic, 51
  rent, 446ff.
  savings and, 76ff.
  statement (in accounting), 270ff.
  taxes, 486ff.
  in U.S.S.R., 566
  wages and salaries, 403ff.
Income-expenditures approach, 40, 61ff., 87, 92ff., 583ff.
Incomes policy, 185ff., 579
Income statement, 270ff.
Income taxes, 486ff.
Income velocity, 89f., 94
Index numbers, 45ff.
India, 247ff.
Indicative planning, 578
Industrialization (*see* Economic growth *and* Underdeveloped countries)
Industry:
  and competitive equilibrium, 324ff.
  constant cost, 327ff.
  decreasing cost, 340f.
  defined, 260
  entry into, 324ff.
  increasing cost, 340f.
Inelastic demand (*see* Demand)
Inelastic supply (*see* Supply)
Inferior goods, 276n.
Inflation:
  causes, 86f., 185ff., 228ff., 246f., 571f.
  costs of, 124ff.
  creeping, 125
  defined, 124
  economic growth and, 125ff., 228ff.

Inflation (*Cont.*):
  effects, 125ff.
  fiscal policy against, 175ff.
  full employment and, 58f., 65, 118ff., 185
  gold standard and, 167ff.
  hyperinflation, 125
  monetary policy against, 155ff., 184ff.
  public debt and, 191
  research on, 256
  wage-price policy, 185f., 579
Injunctions, 425
Innovation (*see* Capital accumulation, Entrepreneur, *and* Technology)
Input-output model, 556n.
Inside lag, 188
Insurance:
  old-age, 440ff.
  risk, 459f.
  unemployment, 175
Interest rates (*see also* Monetary policy):
  actual and nominal, 455
  business cycles and, 107ff.
  capital accumulation and, 452
  defined, 448f.
  demand for money and, 90f.
  determination of, 451
  implicit, 82
  investment and, 82f., 87, 156ff.
  market for loanable funds, 449ff.
  on public debt, 191f.
  structure of, 449
  valuation of property, 452ff.
  velocity of money and, 156
International Bank for Reconstruction and Development, 531n.
International gold standard (*see* Gold standard)
International lending, 498ff., 531f.
International liquidity, 539f.
International Monetary Fund, 530ff., 539f.
Inventories:
  business accounting, 268ff.
  in business cycles, 106f.
  in g.n.p. accounts, 39
Inventory cycle (*see also* Business cycles), 106f.
International trade (*see also* Exchange rates *and* Gold standard): 613ff.
  balance of payments, 506ff., 512ff., 532ff.
  balance of trade, 449ff., 508ff., 521f.
  business cycles and, 110f., 515ff.
  case for free trade, 501ff.
  comparative advantage in, 502ff.
  domestic employment and, 498, 506, 524f.
  financing of, 512ff.
  under fluctuating exchanges, 513ff.
  foreign lending, 498ff., 505ff., 531f.
  under gold standard, 167, 514ff., 532ff.
  "key" currencies, 534
  research on, 544

International trade (*Cont.*):
tariffs, 519ff.
Trade Agreements Program, 525ff.
Trade Expansion Act of 1962, 525, 527
underdeveloped countries and, 250ff., 510
U.S. as world creditor, 517f.
International Trade Organization (ITO), 525f.
Interstate Commerce Commission, 378
Investment (*see also* Capital accumulation):
acceleration effect, 104f., 115ff.
autonomous, 62ff., 68
in business cycles, 68, 104ff.
decisions in U.S.S.R., 570f.
defined, 40f.
as determinant of national income, 62ff.
determinants of, 80ff., 192f.
economic growth and, 204f., 225f., 241ff.
financial vs. real, 134f.
forecasting, 113
foreign, 505f., 531f.
function, 82f.
in human capital, 216f., 226, 243
induced, 68, 104f., 115ff.
interest rates and, 82f., 87
marginal efficiency of, 81f., 87
multiplier, 66ff.
and "plowed-back" earnings, 262, 269
price-cost relationships and, 81f.
profits and, 458f.
public, 173ff., 467ff.
savings and, 80ff., 225f., 241ff.
savings-investment channels, 132ff.
schedule, 82f.
sources of fund, 132ff., 450f.
technological progress, 82f., 203ff.
Invisible hand, 18, 258, 321f., 331
IS curve, 97f.

Job corps, 437
Job security, 551f.

Kennedy Round, 525ff.
Keynes, John Maynard, 61n., 87, 171
Kinked demand curve, 362
Knight, Frank, 460
Knights of Labor, 416f.

Labor (*see also* Labor unionism *and* Wages):
composition of labor force, 215f.
defined, 215
demand for, 406ff.
in economic growth, 204f., 215ff., 226
exploitation, 410f., 418f., 429f.
Fair Labor Standards Act, 425
government and, 424ff.

Labor (*Cont.*):
investment in human capital, 216f., 226
labor law, 424ff.
labor-management relations, 420ff., 551f.
Manpower Development and Training Acts, 428
marginal product, 406f.
minimum wage-laws, 429f.
National Labor Relations Act (Wagner Act), 416, 424f.
productivity, 217ff.
quality of, 216f., 237f.
technological change (automation) and, 412ff., 419, 548ff.
in underdeveloped countries, 237ff.
union membership, 417
in U.S.S.R., 566
wage determination, 403ff.
wage differentials, 394ff., 411f., 566
working hours, 50, 551f.
Labor Management Relations Act (Taft-Hartley Act), 415f., 425
Labor unionism:
collective bargaining, 420ff.
history, 416f., 424ff.
job security and, 551f.
Landrum-Griffin Act, 425f.
membership, 417
motives in wage bargaining, 420f.
National Labor Relations Act, 416, 424f.
New Deal and, 424f.
power, 422f.
research on, 462
responses to technological change, 419, 551f.
strikes, 421f.
Taft-Hartley Act, 415f., 425
union shop, 420n.
wage policy, 417ff.
Wagner Act, 416, 424f.
working hours, 551f.
Lags (*see* Monetary policy *and* Fiscal policy)
Laissez-faire, 21, 373
Land resources, 211f.
Landrum-Griffin Act, 425f.
Leading indicators, 114
"Leakages," 69
Lebergott, Stanley, 219
Lewis, John L., 416
Liabilities (*see also* Accounting), 269ff.
Liquid assets, 77f., 92ff., 193f.
Liquidity trap, 161
LM curve, 96ff.
Logarithmic scale, *defined*, 48f.
Long run, *defined*, 304

Macro-economics, *defined*, 258
Malthus, T. R., 201ff., 244, 403f.
Management (*see also* Entrepreneur *and* Firm, business):
of corporations, 262f.
labor-management relations, 420ff., 551f.
managerial economics, 370ff.
motives, 318f., 348ff., 420f.

Management (*Cont.*):
size of enterprise and, 306f.
in underdeveloped countries, 239
in U.S.S.R., 565f.
wages of, 411
Managerial economics, 370ff.
Manpower Development and Training Acts, 428
Marginal cost, 314ff., 402, 586ff.
Marginal efficiency of investment, 81f., 87, 104f.
Marginal equivalency conditions, 278, 329ff., 335
Marginal physical product, 309ff., 398f., 401f.
Marginal productivity (*see also* Labor *and* Productivity), 398f., 401f., 405f.
Marginal propensity to consume, 66ff., 103, 173
Marginal propensity to save, 67f.
Marginal revenue, 315ff., 342f., 402, 585f.
Marginal revenue product, 398f., 402, 406f., 588
Marginal utility, 92f., 276ff.
Margin requirements, 149
Markets (*see also* Prices, Supply, *and* Demand):
equilibrium, 290ff.
for productive services, 398
research on, 389
role of, 16ff., 286ff., 329ff., 398ff., 512ff.
in U.S.S.R., 563ff.
Market-sharing, 363f.
Market structure (*see* Competition, Monopolistic competition, Monopoly, *and* Oligopoly)
Market system (*see* Price system *and* Private enterprise)
Marshall, Alfred, 87
Marshall plan, 252, 533
Marx, Karl, 201ff., 392, 404, 560
Mediation, 426
Medicare, 439, 441f.
Mergers, 263ff., 379ff.
Micro-economics, *defined*, 258
Miller-Tydings Act, 379
Mineral resources, 211f.
Minimum-wage laws, 425, 429f.
Mixed economy, 22, 387f.
Models:
in economic analysis, 25ff., 30
simultaneous-equation, 72
single-equation, 72n.
stability properties, 584n.
Monetary policy (*see also* Federal Reserve System *and* Interest rates):
aggregate demand and, 157ff.
central-bank policy, 145ff., 155ff.
debt management, 193
employment and, 185
expansionary, 160ff.
fiscal-monetary policy mix, 181
gold standard, 155, 167ff., 514ff., 532ff.
guides, 156f., 163ff., 181ff.

Monetary policy (*Cont.*):
history, 163ff.
interest rates and, 156ff.
money supply and, 156ff.
and open-market operations, 146ff.
portfolio balancing, 92ff.
qualitative controls, 149f.
reserve requirements, 139f., 148f., 157ff.
restrictive, 157ff.
role of the Treasury, 164ff.
for stable growth, 162f., 228ff.
theory of, 155ff.
timing and lags in, 157f., 188ff.
in underdeveloped countries, 246f.
in U.S.S.R., 571f.
in World War II, 164f.
Money (*see also* Banks, Federal Reserve System, Gold standard, Monetary policy, *and* Interest rates):
aggregate demand and, 88ff., 93f.
banking system and, 133ff.
business cycles and, 86f., 107f.
cash-balances approach, 91f.
changing value of, 48
credit creation, 137ff., 141f.
currency, 135
defined, 85n., 133
demand for, 91ff.
equation of exchange, 88f.
Federal Reserve policy, 145ff., 156ff.
foreign exchange, 513ff.
gold standard, 155, 167ff., 514ff., 528ff.
history, 86f., 163ff.
in the income-expenditures model, 87
money-velocity approach, 88ff.
motives for holding, 91
near-monies, 132ff., 142f.
portfolio balancing, 92f.
price level and, 48, 86f., 185ff., 228f.
quantity theory, 82f.
real balances, 91f.
research on, 256
reserve ("key") currency, 534
supply, 135ff., 145ff., 156ff.
tight, 159
value of, 48
velocity, 88ff., 156
Money-flow accounts (*see* Flow-of-funds accounts)
Monopolistic competition, 337ff., 347ff.
evaluation, 356ff.
prices and output, 351ff.
product differentiation, 351
quality competition, 355f.
Monopoly (*see also* Antitrust laws, Monopolistic competition, Oligopoly, *and also* Mixed economy):
336ff.
advertising and, 340
bases for, 338ff., 357
bigness and, 340f., 375ff.

Monopoly (*Cont.*):
  bilateral, 410f.
  capital markets and, 339f.
  cartels, 363f.
  competition and, 322f., 412, 345f.
  decreasing costs, 340f.
  defined, 336f., 341ff.
  efficiency, 345, 346
  evaluation of, 345f.
  income-distribution effects, 345f.
  patents and, 339
  profit maximization by, 343ff., 348ff.
  public utilities, 338f.
  selling costs and, 357
  in union wage policy, 417ff.
  wage determination, 409, 417ff.
Monopsony, 409f., 418f.
"Moral suasion," 149f.
Multiplier, 25, 66ff., 94f., 103, 115ff., 583ff.
Multiplier-accelerator model, 104, 115ff.

National debt (*see* Public debt)
National income (*see also* Gross national product): 38ff.
  analytical models, 61ff., 87ff.
  defined, 42
  historical growth, 53f., 209ff.
  income-expenditures approach, 61ff., 87ff.
  international comparisons, 231ff.
  monetary approach, 87ff.
  portfolio-balancing approach, 92ff.
  shares, 42f., 396f.
National income accounts, 39, 43ff., 53f.
National Industrial Recovery Act (NIRA), 366, 416, 424
National Labor Relations Act (Wagner Act), 416 424f.
Near-monies, 132ff., 142f.
Negative income tax, 436f.
Net national product, 41f.
Net worth (*see also* Accounting), 269ff.
New Deal Legislation, 379, 416, 424f.
Neutral technical progress, 207f.
Nonprice competition, 355f.
Norris-LaGuardia Act, 424

O.A.S.I. (Old Age Survivors', and Disability insurance), 440ff.
Old-age insurance (*see* Social security)
Oligopoly (*see also* Antitrust laws *and* Monopoly): 337f., 359ff.
  administered prices, 361ff.
  bases for, 360f.
  bilateral, 418f.
  cartels, 363f.
  concentration ratios, 359f.
  defined, 337

Oligopoly (*Cont.*):
  game theory and, 363
  price leadership, 361
  prices and output, 361ff., 366f.
  price stabilization, 366f.
  research and, 368f.
  theory of, 361ff.
Open-market operations (*see* Federal Reserve System)
Opportunity cost (*see also* Costs), 299f.
Optimum size of firm, 305ff., 340f., 360f., 383f.
"Other things equal," 28
Output (*see* Production)
Outside lag, 188

Pareto optimality, 335
Partnership, 260
Par value, 269
Patents, 317, 339
Pensions, 443ff.
"Permanent income" hypothesis, 77
Personal income, *defined*, 42f.
Petition of the Candle Makers, 522
Phillips, A. W., 185
Planning (*see* Economic planning)
Plant, *defined*, 260
Pools, 365f.
Population, 214ff., 237ff., 243f.
"Portfolio balancing," 92ff.
Post hoc, propter hoc, fallacy of, 33f.
Poverty, 431ff., 462
Precautionary motive, 91
Prediction, 30, 112ff.
Present value (worth), 453
Pressure groups, 127f., 473f.
Prestige goods, 276n.
Price ceilings, 293f.
Price fixing (*see also* Antitrust laws), 293ff., 363ff.
Price floors, 294f.
Price indexes, 45ff.
Price leadership, 361
Price level (*see also* Inflation): 45ff.
  aggregate demand and, 85ff.
  in business cycles, 105f.
  price indexes and, 45ff.
  stabilization, 119ff., 155ff., 184ff.
  value of money and, 48
Prices (*see also* Competition, Demand, Markets, Price level, *and* Supply): 38ff.
  administered, 361
  basing-point pricing, 380f.
  in business cycles, 105f.
  ceilings, 293f.
  competitive, 286ff., 312ff., 321ff.
  cost-plus pricing, 350
  equilibrium, 290ff.
  floors, 294ff.
  monopolistic competition, 351ff.
  monopoly, 341ff.
  oligopoly, 361ff.
  price-fixing, business, 363, 366f.
  price wars, 366f.
  valuation of property, 452ff.
  wage-price guideposts, 185f.

Price stability (*see* Economic stabilization *and types of public policy*)
Price system (*see also* Competition, Entrepreneur, Markets, *and* Prices), 22f.
Price theory (*see* Competition, Markets, Demand, *and* Supply)
Private enterprise (*see also* Capitalism, Entrepreneur, *and* Markets), 18ff., 22f.
Producers' goods, *defined*, 40f.
Product differentiation (*see also* Monopolistic competition), 351ff.
Production (*see also* Economic growth *and* Gross national product): 38ff.
  aggregate measures, 55ff.
  costs and, 301ff., 309ff.
  decisions in business firms, 312ff., 343ff., 348ff., 361ff.
  defined, 39
  functions, 204n., 208, 301ff., 587f.
  in business cycles, 100ff.
  social security and, 444f.
  theory, 298ff., 309ff., 401f.
  in U.S.S.R., 562ff.
Production-possibilities curve, 15f., 56f., 199f.
Production-possibilities frontier, 16, 199ff.
Productivity (*see also* Automation, Capital, Investment, *and* Technology), 217f., 309ff., 405ff.
Profit-and-loss statement, 270ff.
Profit maximization:
  cartels, 363f.
  under competition, 312ff., 318f., 324ff.
  hiring of inputs, 397ff., 401f.
  mathematical representation, 586f.
  monopolistic competition, 348ff.
  oligopoly, 361ff.
  pure monopoly, 343ff.
  research on, 389
Profits (*see also* Competition; Firm, business; *and* Price system): 12ff., 456ff.
  accounting, 300f.
  in business cycles, 105f.
  defined, 300f., 456
  roles of, 457ff.
  theory of, 459ff.
  undistributed, 83
  in U.S.S.R., 568f.
Profit squeeze, 106, 457
Propensity to consume, 66ff., 103, 173
Property:
  under capitalism, 22f., 446ff., 560ff.
  income, 446ff.
  taxes, 492ff.
  valuation of, 452ff.
Proprietorship, 260
Prosperity (*see* Business cycles)

"Protestant ethic," 218, 240, 393
Proxy, 262
Public debt, 189ff.
Public economy (*see also* Fiscal policy *and* Taxes): 464ff.
  business cycles and, 171ff., 184ff.
  expenditures, 41, 68ff., 171ff., 465ff.
  goals, 470ff.
  growth in, 466ff.
  income distribution and, 465, 469f.
  public debt, 189ff.
  research on, 496
  social security, 438ff.
  taxes, 465ff., 478ff.
Public expenditures (*see* Fiscal policy *and* Public economy)
Public finance (*see* Public economy)
Public goods, 470ff.
Public policy (*see type of policy, such as* Antitrust, Fiscal, Tax)
Public revenues (*see also* Public economy *and also* Taxes), 465ff.
Public sector (*see* Government *and* Public economy)
Public utilities, 338f.
Public works (*see* Fiscal policy *and* Public expenditures)
Pump-priming, 171f.

Quantity theory of money, 87f.
Quasi-rent, 448n.

Rationing, 286ff.
Ratio scale, *defined*, 48f.
Raw materials, 211f., 339
Real balances, 91f.
Recession (*see* Business cycles)
Reciprocal trade agreements, 525
Rediscount rates (*see also* Federal Reserve System), 148
Relief (*see also* Social security), 175
Rent, 446ff.
Research (*see also* Economic growth *and* Technology, 213f., 223ff., 557
Reserve currency, 534
Reserve requirements (*see* Banks *and* Federal Reserve System)
Reserves (*see* Banks *and* Federal Reserve System)
Resource allocation (*see also* Demand, Markets, Prices *and* Supply):
  in competitive economy, 331ff.
  current vs. future (*see also* Capital accumulation *and* Investment), 19f.
  demand creation and, 356f.
  interest rates and, 452
  in international trade, 501ff.
  in mixed economy, 12ff., 577ff.
  under monopoly, 345f.

Resource allocation (*Cont.*):
through public economy, 464ff.
social security impact, 444f.
tax effects, 485f.
Resources (*see also* Economic growth *and* Resource allocation):
economic growth and, 12ff., 211f.
in international trade, 501ff.
natural, 211f., 236
Restraint of trade, 378
Revenue (*see also* Taxes), 313f.
Ricardo, David, 87, 201ff., 502
Right-to-work laws, 420n.
Risk, 459f., 471
Robinson-Patman Act, 379
Rule of reason, 380
Russia (*see* U.S.S.R.)

Salaries (*see* Wages)
Saving (*see also* Capital accumulation):
banking system and, 134
business, 83, 450
economic growth and, 205, 225f., 241ff.
function, 63ff., 76
investment and, 80ff., 225f., 241ff.
loanable funds and, 450f.
personal, 43f., 450
propensity to save, 67f.
saving-investment channels, 133ff., 449ff.
Savings, T. R., 384
Schumpeter, Joseph, 204f., 460
Securities, corporate, 261f., 269f., 453f.
Sellers (*see* Supply)
Sherman Antitrust Act, 264, 366, 377f.
Short run, *defined,* 304
Simons, Henry C., 386
Smith, Adam, 18, 87, 200ff., 218f., 258, 306, 321f., 373, 519
Smoot-Hawley Tariff, 520
Social accounts, 43n.
Socialism, 560ff.
Social security, 438ff.
Soviet Union (*see* U.S.S.R.)
Specialization, 13, 305ff., 328f., 501ff.
Speculative motive, 91
Speculation, 91, 107, 110, 149
Stabilization policies (*see* Economic stabilization)
Stagnation, 109f., 163f.
Standard of living (*see also* Economic growth, Income, *and* Production):
international comparisons, 1f., 231ff.
international trade and, 501ff.
tariffs and, 522ff.
in underdeveloped countries, 231ff.
in U.S., 3, 573ff.
in U.S.S.R., 572ff.

Stigler, George, 384
Stock, corporate (*see* Corporations *and* Securities, corporate)
Stock market, 110, 149
Strikes, 421f.
Subsidies, 522ff.
Supply (*see also* Markets *and* Production):
aggregate, 55ff.
competitive, 318ff.
curves, 318f., 329
defined, 287
demand and, 289ff.
elasticity of, 288f.
excess, 295
of labor, 398ff., 405f., 408f.
of loanable funds, 450f.
in monopolistic competition, 351ff.
in monopoly, 341ff.
in oligopoly, 361ff.
of productive services, 397ff.
schedule, 287ff.
Supply and demand, law of, 296
Surplus:
balance-of-payments, 506ff.
in business accounting, 269ff.
full-employment, 176ff.
Surplus value, 202

T-account, 137
Taft-Hartley Act, 415f., 425
Tariff (*see also* International trade), 519ff.
Taxes (*see also* Fiscal policy *and* Public economy): 465ff., 478ff., 485f.
ability-to-pay principle, 482
benefit principle, 481f.
capital gains, 486f.
corporation, 488f.
cut of 1964, 25f.
death and gift, 488n.
depletion allowance, 488
depreciation allowances, 488
distribution of burden, 478ff.
equity, 481f.
excise, 490ff.
in fiscal policy, 68f., 171ff.
incentive effects, 483
incidence, 485ff.
income redistribution, 469f., 486ff.
"model" system, 493f.
payroll, 489f.
personal income, 486ff.
progressive, 482
property, 492f.
proportional, 482
regressive, 482
research on, 496
sales, 490ff.
shifting, 485f.
social security, 489f.
special assessments, 493
state and local, 466f., 479, 492f.
Technology (*see also* Automation *and* Economic growth):

Technology (*Cont.*):
economic growth and, 12f., 203ff., 213f., 224f.
size of enterprise and, 305f.
in underdeveloped countries, 236f.
unemployment and, 412ff., 548f.
in U.S.S.R., 564ff.
wages and, 412ff.
Theory (*see* Economic analysis *and* Models)
Trade Expansion Act of 1962, 525, 527
Transactions motive, 91
Transactions velocity, 89n.
Transfer payments, 41, 465, 469f.
Triffin, Robert, 539
Trusts, 264, 380
Turning points, 103ff., 108ff.

Uncertainty, 82f., 108, 459f.
Underdeveloped countries: 231ff.
analytical framework, 234ff.
balanced vs. unbalanced growth, 244f.
capital accumulation, 236f., 241ff.
development policy, 240ff.
international comparisons, 232f.
international trade and, 252f., 510
monetary-fiscal policy, 246f.
planning vs. price system, 245f.
population, 237ff., 243f.
prospects, 250
research on, 255f.
U.S. policy towards, 250ff.
vicious circle of poverty, 239f.
Underemployment equilibrium, 65f.
Unemployment (*see also* Automation *and* Business Cycles):
costs of, 120ff.
frictional, 121, 187, 227
hidden, 122, 240
research on, 255f.
structural, 121, 186ff., 227
technological change and, 412ff., 548f.
Unemployment insurance, 175
Unions (*see* Labor unionism)
Union security, 420ff.
Union shop, 420
United States (*see also* special topics, such as Agriculture, Taxes, etc.):
economic growth, 7f., 48ff., 209ff., 221ff.
income distribution, 3f., 393ff., 431ff.
national income accounts, 40, 42ff., 52ff.
natural resources, 211f.
public sector, 5, 464ff., 478ff.
standard of living, 3, 573ff.

United States Employment Service, 428
U.S.S.R.: 560ff.
economic goals, 562
economic growth, 570f.
economic performance of, 572ff.
incentives in, 565f.
income distribution, 569f., 576f.
income in, 2ff., 566
labor unions, 566
managers, 565f.
monetary and fiscal policy, 571f.
planning, 562ff.
profits, 568f.
research on, 581
taxes, 570
Utility, diminishing, 276

Valuation of income-producing property, 452ff.
Value (*see also* Prices *and* Markets), 293
Value-added approach to g.n.p., 40
Variable proportions, law of, 311
Velocity (*see also* Money), 88ff., 156
Vista program, 437

Wage-price guideposts, 185f., 579
Wages (*see also* Labor unionism): 403ff.
collective bargaining, 420ff.
competitive, 404ff., 408f.
criteria for, 394ff., 403ff.
differentials, 394ff., 411f.
effect of labor unionism, 419
exploitation, 410f., 418f., 429f.
in inflation, 127
marginal productivity, 406ff.
minimum, 429f.
in monopolized industries, 409
and occupational differences, 394ff.
research on, 462
subsistence theory of, 403f.
tariffs, and, 522ff.
technological advance and, 412ff., 548f.
union policy, 417ff.
wage-price relationships, 105f., 185f.
Wagner Act, 416f., 424f.
Walras, L., 20n., 331n.
War financing, 164ff.
Wealth (*see* Capital accumulation)
Wealth of Nations, 18, 200, 306, 321, 519
Weber, Max, 240
Welfare economics, 471f.
Wildcat strike, 422
Working capital, 157

Youth corps, 437

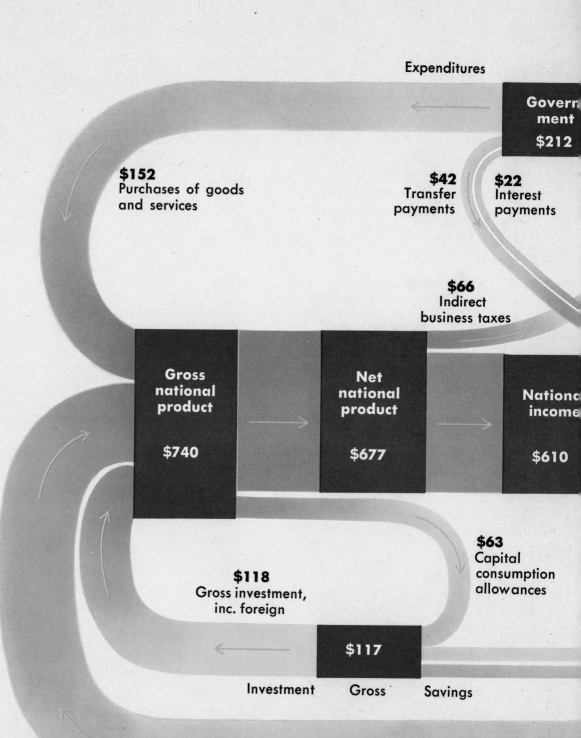

Expenditures

Government

$212

$152
Purchases of goods
and services

$42
Transfer
payments

$22
Interest
payments

$66
Indirect
business taxes

Gross
national
product

$740

Net
national
product

$677

Nationa
income

$610

$63
Capital
consumption
allowances

$118
Gross investment,
inc. foreign

$117

Investment   Gross   Savings

Consumer   outlay

$478